Strategic
Management

text and cases

fifth edition

Gregory G. Dess
University of Texas
at Dallas

G. T. Lumpkin
Syracuse University

Alan B. Eisner
Pace University

Strategic Management

text and cases

fifth edition

McGraw-Hill
Irwin

STRATEGIC MANAGEMENT: TEXT AND CASES

Published by McGraw-Hill/Irwin, a business unit of The McGraw-Hill Companies, Inc., 1221 Avenue of the Americas, New York, NY, 10020. Copyright © 2010, 2008, 2007, 2006, 2004 by The McGraw-Hill Companies, Inc. All rights reserved. No part of this publication may be reproduced or distributed in any form or by any means, or stored in a database or retrieval system, without the prior written consent of The McGraw-Hill Companies, Inc., including, but not limited to, in any network or other electronic storage or transmission, or broadcast for distance learning.

Some ancillaries, including electronic and print components, may not be available to customers outside the United States.

This book is printed on acid-free paper.

1 2 3 4 5 6 7 8 9 0 DOW/DOW 1 0 9 8 7 6 5 4 3 2 1 0

ISBN 978-0-07-131405-3
MHID 0-07-131405-9

Dedication

To my family, Margie and Taylor;
my parents, Bill and Mary Dess;
and Michael O'Brien
–Greg

To my lovely wife, Vicki,
and my students and colleagues
–Tom

To my family, Helaine,
Rachel, and Jacob
–Alan

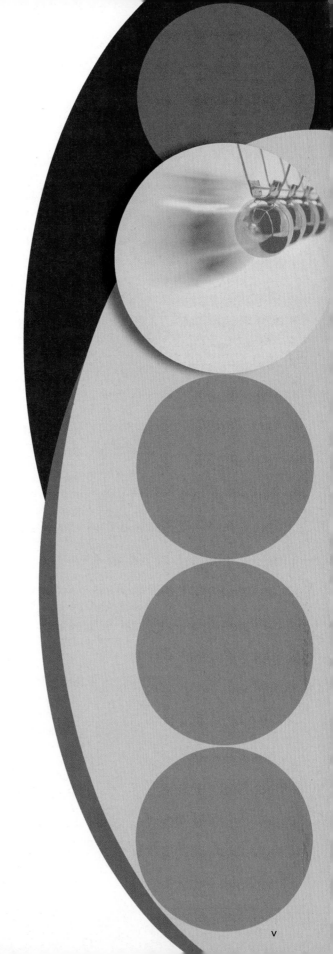

About the Authors

Gregory G. Dess is the Andrew R. Cecil Endowed Chair in Management at the University of Texas at Dallas. His primary research interests are in strategic management, organization–environment relationships, and knowledge management. He has published numerous articles on these subjects in both academic and practitioner-oriented journals. He also serves on the editorial boards of a wide range of practitioner-oriented and academic journals. In August 2000, he was inducted into the *Academy of Management Journal*'s Hall of Fame as one of its charter members. Professor Dess has conducted executive programs in the United States, Europe, Africa, Hong Kong, and Australia. During 1994 he was a Fulbright Scholar in Oporto, Portugal. In December 2009, he will receive an honorary doctorate from the University of Bern (Switzerland). He received his PhD in Business Administration from the University of Washington (Seattle) and a BIE degree from Georgia Tech.

G. T. (Tom) Lumpkin is the Chris J. Witting Chair and Professor of Entrepreneurship at Syracuse University in New York. Prior to joining the faculty at Syracuse, Tom was the Kent Hance Regents Endowed Chair and Professor of Entrepreneurship at Texas Tech University. His research interests include entrepreneurial orientation, opportunity recognition, strategy-making processes, social entrepreneurship, and innovative forms of organizing work. He has published numerous research articles in journals such as *Strategic Management Journal, Academy of Management Journal, Academy of Management Review, Journal of Business Venturing,* and *Entrepreneurship: Theory and Practice.* He is a member of the editorial review boards of *Strategic Entrepreneurship Journal, Entrepreneurship Theory & Practice,* and the *Journal of Business Venturing.* He received his PhD in management from the University of Texas at Arlington and MBA from the University of Southern California.

Alan B. Eisner is Professor of Management and Graduate Management Program Chair at the Lubin School of Business, Pace University. He received his PhD in management from the Stern School of Business, New York University. His primary research interests are in strategic management, technology management, organizational learning, and managerial decision making. He has published research articles and cases in journals such as *Advances in Strategic Management, International Journal of Electronic Commerce, International Journal of Technology Management, American Business Review, Journal of Behavioral and Applied Management,* and *Journal of the International Academy for Case Studies.* He is the Associate Editor of the Case Association's peer reviewed journal, *The CASE Journal.*

Preface

Welcome to the Fifth Edition of *Strategic Management: Text and Cases*! We're very pleased with the positive market response of our previous editions. We are also most appreciative of the extensive and constructive feedback that many strategy professionals have taken the time to give us. We are always striving to improve our work, and many of their ideas have been incorporated into the Fifth Edition as well as previous editions. We are happy to acknowledge these many contributors later in the Preface.

Let's briefly revisit a fundamental question: Why did we write the book in the first place? We would all agree that there have always been some solid strategy books in the market. However, we felt that there was a strong need for a book that students and faculty would think satisfied the three *R*'s that we always kept in mind during our work: relevant, rigorous, and readable. That is, our tagline has become: "Strong enough for the professor, but made for the student," and we have consistently received such feedback from faculty who have used our book. Perhaps Professor Stephen Vitucci (Tarleton State University) said it best:

> I want it to be rigorous but something that they can read and understand. The Dess, Lumpkin, and Eisner text I am currently using is exactly what I like and, more importantly, what my students need and like.

We were also recently contacted by Liz Welch and Sabina Nawaz, former General Manager and Senior Director, respectively, at Microsoft. They are now external consultants who conduct course offerings for Microsoft, several divisions of ITT, and other well-known firms. The author team was very gratified by their strong support of our text, which we feel verifies the "external validity" and practical relevance of our work:

> As organizational and leadership development consultants, we are always looking for great tools, case studies, and examples to better deliver core strategy concepts to our clients. Not only does DLE's *Strategic Management* provide us with that, it is almost a "one-stop shop" in this regard. The book has a comprehensive conceptual model with timely, relevant, and well-researched examples and cases. We have found it to be of conceptual as well as practical use and highly recommend it to consultants and leaders alike.

To earn such praise, we strive to use an engaging writing style free of unnecessary jargon, cover all the traditional bases, and integrate some central themes—such as globalization, technology, ethics, and entrepreneurship—throughout the book that are vital in understanding strategic management in today's global economy. We draw on short examples from business practices to bring concepts to life and provide 116 Strategy Spotlights (more detailed examples in sidebars) to drive home key points.

Unlike other strategy texts, we provide three separate chapters that address timely topics about which business students should have a solid understanding. These are the role of intellectual assets in value creation (Chapter 4), entrepreneurial strategy and competitive dynamics (Chapter 8), and fostering entrepreneurship in established organizations (Chapter 12). We also provide an excellent set of cases to help students analyze, integrate, and apply strategic management concepts.

In developing *Strategic Management: Text and Cases,* we certainly didn't forget the instructors. After all, you have a very challenging (but rewarding) job. We did our best to help you. We provide a variety of supplementary materials that should help you in class preparation and delivery. Our chapter notes, for example, do not simply summarize the material in the chapter. Rather, we always ask ourselves (consistent with the concept of strategy!): "How can we add value?" Thus, for each chapter, we provide numerous questions to pose to guide discussion, at least 12 boxed examples to supplement chapter material, and three "teaching tips" to further engage students. Also, the author team completed the entire test bank ourselves—along with the aforementioned chapter notes. That is, unlike most of our rivals, we didn't farm them out to others. We really believe that our involvement demonstrates our commitment to the entire package and helps enhance consistency and quality.

Let's now address some of the key substantive changes in the Fifth Edition. Then, we'll cover some of the major features that have been consistent throughout our editions.

What's New? Highlights of the Fifth Edition

We've endeavored to add new material to the chapters that reflects both the feedback that we have received from reviewers and the challenges and opportunities that face today's managers. This also included, of course, carefully reviewing a wide variety of books, academic journals, practitioner journals, and the business press. We've worked hard to avoid "chapter creep." That is, when we add new material, we delete others (which includes cutting redundant examples). In addition, we benefitted from the work of Rae Pinkham, a professional editor. She went over all of the chapters line-by-line to tighten our writing. The result is that we were able to update our material and add new content—and at the same time keep the chapter length about the same. We certainly appreciate her fine efforts!

Here are some of the major changes in the Fifth Edition:

- **All of the 12 opening "Learning from Mistakes" that lead off each chapter are totally new.** Unique to this text, these vignettes are all examples of what can go wrong, and they serve as an excellent vehicle for clarifying and reinforcing strategy concepts. After all, what can be learned when one simply admires perfection?
- **We have increased the number of "Strategy Spotlights" (sidebar examples) from 90 to 116.** About half of these are brand new to this edition and many of the others have been carefully updated. We were able to add more and still save some space by focusing on bringing important strategy concepts to life.
- **We have added 14 more exhibits to the text.** This, along with the two four-color pictures in each chapter (a feature that we added with the fourth edition), aids learning and improves visual appeal. To further enhance readability and impact, we work hard to write short paragraphs and provide many indented examples throughout the book.
- **"Crowdsourcing" is a new theme throughout the book.** It originated with the open-source movement, a community of developers working together to create alternatives to Microsoft's products. However, it has expanded in recent years to include many approaches in which a wide range of businesses are enlisting the masses to solve problems, suggest new products, provide feedback, and enhance demand for products and services. After introducing this theme in Chapter 1, we provide seven "Strategy Spotlights" where firms are effectively using this innovative process. For example, in Chapter 2, we discuss how Virgin Mobile USA used it for everything from designing phones to coming up with names for service plans. Chapter 3 mentions how Cookshack, a small producer of ovens for barbecue and smoked foods, used crowdsourcing to, in effect, turn its customers into its customer service department! And, in Chapter 10, we explain how Eli Lilly, the pharmaceutical giant, launched Innocentive—the first online, incentive-based scientific network for the global research and development community.
- **Our discussion of environmental sustainability has been extended throughout the text.** As noted by Daniel Esty and Andrew Winston in their award-winning book *Green to Gold*: "Environmental leaders see their businesses through an environmental lens, finding opportunities to cut costs, reduce risk, and enhance intangible value. They build deeper connections with customers, employees, and other stakeholders."[*] Given the salience of environmental sustainability in today's global

*Esty, D. C. & Winston, A. S. 2009. *Green to gold: How Smart Companies Use Environmental Sustainability to Innovate, Create Value, and Build Competitive Advantage*. Hoboken, NJ: Wiley, 14.

economy, we discuss this issue throughout the text—including eight "Strategy Spotlights." For example, in Chapter 1, we explain how Shaw Industries, an industrial flooring producer, used its recycling efforts to both reduce its costs and eliminate its need for PVC plastic—a potentially toxic substance. Chapter 4 discusses how "going green" helps attract talent, and Chapter 8 explains how "eco-entrepreneurs" have recycled milk jugs, tires, and jars to create playground equipment, garage flooring, and glass awards, respectively! To provide some balance on this topic, we also discuss how some energy companies have been accused of "greenwashing" (that is, making unsubstantiated claims about how environmentally friendly a firm's products are) in their sustainability programs.

Key content changes for the chapters include:

- **Chapter 1 introduces the concept of "crowdsourcing," which, as noted above, becomes a theme throughout the text.** This innovative approach to open sourcing has provided a wide variety of businesses with a new source for products, ideas, and many value-adding activities. We also illustrate the complexities inherent in the stakeholder concept by addressing the many conflicting demands faced by the world's largest retailer—Wal-Mart.
- **Chapter 1 provides a summary of the worldwide financial crisis that intensified in 2008 and 2009.** We address not only some of the root causes but also how it has dramatically affected many industries, such as automobiles, dining, retail, and technology.
- **Chapter 2 addresses some recent insights from Michael Porter on the effective use of the five-forces model of industry profitability.** In our previous editions, we discussed caveats in performing an industry analysis, such as how some firms have prospered in low-profit industries, the detrimental effects of exploiting buyer power, and the salient role of complementors in industry analysis. Now, we include Porter's new perspectives on the importance of understanding the structural underpinnings of profitability, such as an awareness of time horizons and the value of quantitative factors in performing an in-depth analysis.
- **Chapter 3 discusses how businesses can use blogs and social networking sites to enhance their reputation—or how such sites can erode key stakeholders' perceptions.** Comcast, for example, was badly hurt when an angry customer put a video on YouTube of a technician who fell asleep on his couch! However, on the bright side, firms like Southwest Airlines, Whole Foods, and the shoe store Zappos have effectively used social messaging services.
- **Chapter 5 extends our discussion of the industry life cycle concept by explaining why old technologies don't just fade away.** Using examples as diverse as mainframes, carburetors, and coronary bypass surgery, three approaches are suggested: retreating to more defensible ground, using the new to improve the old, and improving the price-performance trade-off.
- **Chapter 6 draws on the stakeholder concept to show how antitakeover measures may benefit stakeholders other than management.** Antitakeover defenses, such as poison pills, typically are viewed as simply measures to entrench and protect management. However, this is not always the case. We discuss how such defenses can also serve to protect employees, the community at large, and customers.
- **Chapter 7 addresses an important rationale for international expansion—taking advantage of arbitrage opportunities.** Simply put, arbitrage involves buying something where it is cheap and selling it where it commands a higher price. It can be applied to almost any factor of production and every stage of the value chain.
- **Chapter 8 (Entrepreneurial Strategy and Competitive Dynamics)** has been reconfigured to include a section on competitive dynamics that addresses the cycle

of actions and responses that are initiated when a new player enters a competitive marketplace. This is a hot issue in strategy and has important implications for competitive advantage—the core topic of our book. We address competitive dynamics for such rivals as Facebook and MySpace, as well as AMD and Intel (chip makers). The first part of the chapter draws on materials that were previously part of Chapter 13 on creating new ventures.

- **Chapter 9 extends our discussion of corporate governance in the international context.** Here, we discuss "multilatinas," which have pursued a strategy of regional and international expansion. We address some of the governance and transparency issues that Latin-owned companies need to improve upon in order to ensure access to international capital markets.

- **Chapter 11 introduces the idea of integrative thinking developed in Roger Martin's book *The Opposable Mind*.** Leaders are often faced with decision alternatives that pose difficult dilemmas. The best leaders are those who avoid thinking in terms of either-or trade-offs. Instead, they seek out creative solutions that synthesize opposing perspectives.

- **Chapter 12 draws on Christensen's work on innovation.** We distinguish between *sustaining innovations* that energize markets by, for example, extending sales and *disruptive innovations* that overturn markets by providing new approaches to meeting customer needs. In rapidly changing environments, it is vital to understand how to manage different types of innovative activity.

- **Chapter 13 updates our Appendix: Sources of Company and Industry Information.** We appreciate the contributions of Ruthie Brock and Carol Byrne in providing this comprehensive information. It is organized to cover a range of issues, such as competitive intelligence, annual report collections, company rankings, business websites, and strategic and competitive analysis. It should be invaluable in analyzing companies and industries.

- **Alan Eisner, our case author, has worked hard to further enhance our excellent case package.** These include:
  - 26 author-written cases (much more than our competition).
  - Updating our users' favorite cases (based on extensive market feedback) with new information and data to minimize instructor preparation time and maximize freshness.
  - 9 new cases and significant updates on 21 cases, including Southwest Airlines, JetBlue, General Motors, Ford, Apple, eBay, and many others.
  - Providing an excellent mix of tried-and-true classics as well as shorter favorites from Harvard.
  - A major focus on fresh and current cases about familiar firms.
  - Cases of varying lengths to best fit instructor needs.
  - Many videos to match the cases.

What Remains the Same: Key Features from Earlier Editions

Let's now briefly address some of the exciting features that remain from the earlier editions.

- **Traditional organizing framework with three other chapters on timely topics.** Crisply written chapters cover all of the strategy bases and address contemporary topics. First, the chapters are divided logically into the traditional sequence: strategy analysis, strategy formulation, and strategy implementation. Second, we include three chapters on such timely topics as intellectual capital/knowledge management, entrepreneurial strategy and competitive dynamics, and fostering corporate entrepreneurship and new ventures.

- **"Learning from Mistakes" chapter-opening cases.** To enhance student interest, we begin each chapter with a case that depicts an organization that has suffered a dramatic performance drop, or outright failure, by failing to adhere to sound strategic management concepts and principles. We believe that this feature serves to underpin the value of the concepts in the course and that it is a preferred teaching approach to merely providing examples of outstanding companies that always seem to get it right! After all, isn't it better (and more challenging) to diagnose problems than admire perfection? As Dartmouth's Sydney Finkelstein, author of *Why Smart Executives Fail,* notes: "We live in a world where success is revered, and failure is quickly pushed to the side. However, some of the greatest opportunities to learn—both for individuals and organizations—come from studying what goes wrong."* We'll see how, for example, Motorola failed to keep up with customer expectations in the Chinese mobile-phone market and saw its market share sharply erode, how Michelin's PAX "run-flat" tire failed because they didn't create a differentiation advantage that justified the premium price, and how Richard Fuld's toxic leadership played a key role in Lehman Brothers' demise. *BusinessWeek* named Fuld one of the worst managers of 2008 and claimed that he "drove his people hard and ignored warning signs, rewarding risk and greed."

- **Consistent chapter format and features to reinforce learning.** We have included several features in each chapter to add value and create an enhanced learning experience. First, each chapter begins with an overview and a set of bullets pointing to key learning objectives. Second, as previously noted, the opening case describes a situation in which a company's performance eroded because of a lack of proper application of strategy concepts. Third, at the end of each chapter there are four different types of questions/exercises that should help students assess their understanding and application of material:

  1. Summary review questions.
  2. Experiential exercises.
  3. Application questions and exercises.
  4. Ethics questions

Given the emergence of the Internet and e-commerce, each chapter contains at least one exercise that involves the use of the Internet.

- **"Reflecting on Career Implications" for each chapter.** This feature—at the end of each chapter—will help instructors drive home the immediate relevance/value of strategy concepts. It focuses on how an understanding of key concepts helps business students early in their careers.
- **Key Terms.** Approximately a dozen key terms for each chapter are identified in the margins of the pages. This addition was made in response to reviewer feedback and improves students' understanding of core strategy concepts.
- **Clear articulation and illustration of key concepts.** Key strategy concepts are introduced in a clear and concise manner and are followed by timely and interesting examples from business practice. Such concepts include value-chain analysis, the resource-based view of the firm, Porter's five-forces model, competitive advantage, boundaryless organizational designs, digital strategies, corporate governance, ethics, and entrepreneurship.
- **Extensive use of sidebars.** We include 116 sidebars (or about nine per chapter) called "Strategy Spotlights." The Strategy Spotlights not only illustrate key points but also increase the readability and excitement of new strategy concepts.

*Personal communication, June 20, 2005.

- **Integrative themes.** The text provides a solid grounding in ethics, globalization, and technology. These topics are central themes throughout the book and form the basis for many of the Strategy Spotlights.
- **Implications of concepts for small businesses.** Many of the key concepts are applied to start-up firms and smaller businesses, which is particularly important since many students have professional plans to work in such firms.
- **Not just a textbook but an entire package.** *Strategic Management* features the best chapter teaching notes available today. Rather than merely summarizing the key points in each chapter, we focus on value-added material to enhance the teaching (and learning) experience. Each chapter includes dozens of questions to spur discussion, teaching tips, in-class group exercises, and about a dozen detailed examples from business practice to provide further illustrations of key concepts.
- **Excellent set of cases.** We have selected an outstanding collection of current and classic cases for this edition, carefully including a wide variety of cases matched to key strategic concepts and organized to create maximum flexibility. We have a balance of short, concise and longer, comprehensive cases. At the same time, we maintain currency and name recognition of our cases with many new and updated classroom-tested cases. We have also updated many of the favorites from the fourth edition such as Southwest Airlines, JetBlue Airways, World Wrestling Entertainment, Ann Taylor, Apple, eBay in Asia, Nintendo, and many others to further engage students. New cases include: Jamba Juice, Geely Automotive, Lenovo, Build-A-Bear Workshop, Mattel, and Weight Watchers. We are once again pleased to include several cases from The Harvard Business School and *The Harvard Business Review,* including Crown Cork & Seal and Automation Consulting.

Student Support Materials

- **Online Learning Center (OLC).** The following resources are available to students via the publisher's OLC at www.mhhe.com/dess5e:
  - Chapter quizzes students can take to gauge their understanding of material covered in each chapter.
  - A selection of PowerPoint slides for each chapter.
  - Links to strategy simulations the Business Strategy Game & GLO-BUS. Both provide a powerful and constructive way of connecting students to the subject matter of the course with a competition among classmates on campus and around the world.

Instructor Support Materials

- **Instructor's Manual (IM).** Prepared by the textbook authors, the accompanying IM contains summary/objectives, lecture/discussion outlines, discussion questions, extra examples not included in the text, teaching tips, reflecting on career implications, experiential exercises, and more.
- **Test Bank.** Prepared by the authors, the test bank contains more than 1,000 true/false, multiple-choice, and essay questions. It has now been tagged with learning objectives as well as Bloom's Taxonomy and AACSB criteria.
  Assurance of Learning Ready. Assurance of Learning is an important element of many accreditation standards. Dess 5e is designed specifically to support your Assurance of Learning initiatives. Each chapter in the book begins with a list of numbered learning objectives that appear throughout the chapter, as well as in the end-of-chapter questions and exercises. Every test bank question is also linked to one

of these objectives, in addition to level of difficulty, topic area, Bloom's Taxonomy level, and AACSB skill area. *EZ Test,* McGraw-Hill's easy-to-use test bank software, can search the test bank by these and other categories, providing an engine for targeted Assurance of Learning analysis and assessment.

AACSB Statement. The McGraw-Hill Companies is a proud corporate member of AACSB International. Understanding the importance and value of AACSB accreditation, Dess 5e has sought to recognize the curricula guidelines detailed in the AACSB standards for business accreditation by connecting selected questions in Dess 5e and the test bank to the general knowledge and skill guidelines found in the AACSB standards. The statements contained in Dess 5e are provided only as a guide for the users of this text. The AACSB leaves content coverage and assessment within the purview of individual schools, the mission of the school, and the faculty. While Dess 5e and the teaching package make no claim of any specific AACSB qualification or evaluation, we have labeled selected questions within Dess 5e according to the six general knowledge and skills areas.

Computerized Test Bank Online. A comprehensive bank of test questions is provided within a computerized test bank powered by McGraw-Hill's flexible electronic testing program, *EZ Test Online* (www.eztestonline.com). *EZ Test Online* allows you to create paper and online tests or quizzes in this easy-to-use program! Imagine being able to create and access your test or quiz anywhere, at any time without installing the testing software. Now, with *EZ Test Online,* instructors can select questions from multiple McGraw-Hill test banks or author their own, and then either print the test for paper distribution or give it online.

Test Creation.
- Author/edit questions online using the 14 different question type templates.
- Create printed tests or deliver online to get instant scoring and feedback.
- Create questions pools to offer multiple versions online – great for practice.
- Export your tests for use in *WebCT, Blackboard, PageOut,* and Apple's *iQuiz.*
- Compatible with *EZ Test Desktop* tests you've already created.
- Sharing tests with colleagues, adjuncts, TAs is easy.

Online Test Management.
- Set availability dates and time limits for your quiz or test.
- Control how your test will be presented.
- Assign points by question or question type with drop-down menu.
- Provide immediate feedback to students or delay until all finish the test.
- Create practice tests online to enable student mastery.
- Your roster can be uploaded to enable student self-registration.

Online Scoring and Reporting.
- Automated scoring for most of *EZ Test*'s numerous question types.
- Allows manual scoring for essay and other open response questions.
- Manual rescoring and feedback is also available.
- *EZ Test*'s grade book is designed to easily export to your grade book.
- View basic statistical reports.

Support and Help.
- User's guide and built-in page-specific help.
- Flash tutorials for getting started on the support site.
- Support website: www.mhhe.com/eztest.
- Product specialist available at 1-800-331-5094.
- Online Training: http://auth.mhhe.com/mpss/workshops/.

- **PowerPoint Presentation.** Prepared by Brad Cox of Midlands Tech, it consists of more than 400 slides incorporating an outline for the chapters tied to learning objectives. Also included are multiple-choice questions that can be used as Classroom Performance System (CPS) questions as well as additional examples outside of the text to promote class discussion. Case Study PowerPoint slides are available to facilitate case study coverage.
- **Instructor's Resource CD-ROM.** All instructor supplements are available in this one-stop multimedia resource, which includes the Instructor's Manual, Test Bank, PowerPoint Presentations, and Case Study Teaching Notes.
- **Case Videos.** A set of videos related to selected cases accompanies the text to support your classroom, student lab, or for home viewing. These thought-provoking video clips are available upon adoption of this text.
- **Online Learning Center (OLC).** The instructor section of www.mhhe.com/dess5e also includes the Instructor's Manual, PowerPoint Presentations, Interactive Case Grid, and Case Study Teaching Notes as well as additional resources.
- **The Business Strategy Game and GLO-BUS Online Simulations.** Both allow teams of students to manage companies in a head-to-head contest for global market leadership. These simulations give students the immediate opportunity to experiment with various strategy options and to gain proficiency in applying the concepts and tools they have been reading about in the chapters. To find out more or to register, please visit www.mmhe.com/thompsonsims.

Additional Resources

- **McGraw-Hill/Primis Custom Publishing.** You can customize this text. McGraw-Hill/Primis Online's digital database offers you the flexibility to customize your course, including material from the largest online collection of textbooks, readings, and cases. Primis leads the way in customized eBooks with hundreds of titles available at prices that save your students over 20 percent off bookstore prices. For more information, please visit www.primisonline.com/dess or call 800-228-0634.
- *BusinessWeek* **subscription.** Students can subscribe to *BusinessWeek* for a special rate in addition to the price of the text. Students will receive a passcode card shrink-wrapped with their new text. The card directs students to a Web site where they enter the code and then gain access to *BusinessWeek's* registration page to enter their address information and set up their print and online subscription. Please ask your McGraw-Hill/Irwin representative for more information.

Acknowledgments

Strategic Management represents far more than just the joint efforts of the three co-authors. Rather, it is the product of the collaborative input of many people. Some of these individuals are academic colleagues, others are the outstanding team of professionals at McGraw-Hill/Irwin, and still others are those who are closest to us—our families. It is time to express our sincere gratitude.

First, we'd like to acknowledge the dedicated instructors who have graciously provided their insights since the inception of the text. Their input has been very helpful in both pointing out errors in the manuscript and suggesting areas that needed further development as additional topics. We sincerely believe that the incorporation of their ideas has been critical to improving the final product. These professionals and their affiliations are:

The Reviewer Hall of Fame

Moses Acquaah, *University of North Carolina–Greensboro*

Todd Alessandri, *Providence College*

Larry Alexander, *Virginia Polytechnic Institute*

Brent B. Allred, *College of William & Mary*

Allen C. Amason, *University of Georgia*

Kathy Anders, *Arizona State University*

Peter H. Antoniou, *California State University, San Marcos*

Dave Arnott, *Dallas Baptist University*

Marne L. Arthaud-Day, *Kansas State University*

Jay Azriel, *York University of Pennsylvania*

Jeffrey J. Bailey, *University of Idaho*

Bruce Barringer, *University of Central Florida*

Barbara R. Bartkus, *Old Dominion University*

Barry Bayon, *Bryant University*

Brent D. Beal, *Louisiana State University*

Joyce Beggs, *University of North Carolina–Charlotte*

Michael Behnam, *Suffolk University*

Kristen Bell DeTienne, *Brigham Young University*

Eldon Bernstein, *Lynn University*

Dusty Bodie, *Boise State University*

William Bogner, *Georgia State University*

Jon Bryan, *Bridgewater State College*

Charles M. Byles, *Virginia Commonwealth University*

Mikelle A. Calhoun, *Valparaiso University*

Thomas J. Callahan, *University of Michigan, Dearborn*

Samuel D. Cappel, *Southeastern Louisiana State University*

Gary Carini, *Baylor University*

Shawn M. Carraher, *Texas A&M University, Commerce*

Tim Carroll, *University of South Carolina*

Don Caruth, *Amberton University*

Maureen Casile, *Bowling Green State University*

Gary J. Castrogiovanni, *Florida Atlantic University*

Radha Chaganti, *Rider University*

Theresa Cho, *Rutgers University*

Bruce Clemens, *Western New England College*

Betty S. Coffey, *Appalachian State University*

Wade Coggins, *Webster University, Fort Smith Metro Campus*

Susan Cohen, *University of Pittsburgh*

George S. Cole, *Shippensburg University*

Joseph Coombs, *Texas A & M University*

Christine Cope Pence, *University of California, Riverside*

James J. Cordeiro, *SUNY Brockport*

Jeffrey Covin, *Indiana University*

Keith Credo, *Auburn University*

Deepak Datta, *University of Texas at Arlington*

James Davis, *University of Notre Dame*

David Dawley, *West Virginia University*

Helen Deresky, *State University of New York, Plattsburgh*

Rocki-Lee DeWitt, *University of Vermont*

Jay Dial, *Ohio State University*

Michael E. Dobbs, *Arkansas State University*

Jonathan Doh, *Villanova University*

Tom Douglas, *Clemson University*

Jon Down, *Oregon State University*

Alan E. Ellstrand, *University of Arkansas*

Dean S. Elmuti, *Eastern Illinois University*

Clare Engle, *Concordia University*

Tracy Ethridge, *Tri-County Technical College*

William A. Evans, *Troy State University, Dothan*

Frances H. Fabian, *University of Memphis*

Angelo Fanelli, *Warrington College of Business*

Michael Fathi, *Georgia Southwestern University*

Carolyn J. Fausnaugh, *Florida Institute of Technology*

Tamela D. Ferguson, *University of Louisiana at Lafayette*

David Flanagan, *Western Michigan University*

Isaac Fox, *University of Minnesota*

Deborah Francis, *Brevard College*

Steven A. Frankforter, *Winthrop University*

Vance Fried, *Oklahoma State University*

Naomi A. Gardberg, *CNNY Baruch College*

J. Michael Geringer, *California Polytechnic State University*

Diana L. Gilbertson, *California State University, Fresno*

Matt Gilley, *St. Mary's University*

Debora Gilliard, *Metropolitan State College of Denver*

Yezdi H. Godiwalla, *University of Wisconsin–Whitewater*

Sanjay Goel, *University of Minnesota, Duluth*

Sandy Gough, *Boise State University*

Allen Harmon, *University of Minnesota, Duluth*

Niran Harrison, *University of Oregon*

Paula Harveston, *Berry College*

Donald Hatfield, *Virginia Polytechnic Institute*

Kim Hester, *Arkansas State University*

John Hironaka, *California State University, Sacramento*

Alan Hoffman, *Bentley College*

Gordon Holbein, *University of Kentucky*

Stephen V. Horner, *Arkansas State University*

Jill Hough, *University of Tulsa*

John Humphreys, *Eastern New Mexico University*

James G. Ibe, *Morris College*

Jay J. Janney, *University of Dayton*

Lawrence Jauch, *University of Louisiana–Monroe*

Dana M. Johnson, *Michigan Technical University*

Homer Johnson, *Loyola University, Chicago*

James Katzenstein, *California State University, Dominguez Hills*

Franz Kellermanns, *Mississippi State University*

Craig Kelley, *California State University, Sacramento*

Donna Kelley, *Babson College*

Dave Ketchen, *Auburn University*

John A. Kilpatrick, *Idaho State University*

Helaine J. Korn, *Baruch College, CUNY*

Stan Kowalczyk, *San Francisco State University*

Daniel Kraska, *North Central State College*

Donald E. Kreps, *Kutztown University*

Jim Kroeger, *Cleveland State University*

Subdoh P. Kulkarni, *Howard University*

Ron Lambert, *Faulkner University*

Theresa Lant, *New York University*

Ted Legatski, *Texas Christian University*

David J. Lemak, *Washington State University–Tri-Cities*

Cynthia Lengnick-Hall, *University of Texas at San Antonio*

Donald L. Lester, *Arkansas State University*

Wanda Lester, *North Carolina A&T State University*

Benyamin Lichtenstein, *University of Massachusetts at Boston*

Jun Lin, *SUNY at New Paltz*

Zhiang (John) Lin, *University of Texas at Dallas*

Dan Lockhart, *University of Kentucky*

John Logan, *University of South Carolina*

Kevin Lowe, *University of North Carolina, Greensboro*

Doug Lyon, *Fort Lewis College*

Hao Ma, *Bryant College*

Rickey Madden, *Ph.D., Presbyterian College*

James Maddox, *Friends University*

Ravi Madhavan, *University of Pittsburgh*

Paul Mallette, *Colorado State University*

Santo D. Marabella, *Moravian College*

Catherine Maritan, *Syracuse University*

Daniel Marrone, *Farmingdale State College, SUNY*

Sarah Marsh, *Northern Illinois University*

John R. Massaua, *University of Southern Maine*

Larry McDaniel, *Alabama A&M University*

Abagail McWilliams, *University of Illinois, Chicago*

John E. Merchant, *California State University, Sacramento*

John M. Mezias, *University of Miami*

Michael Michalisin, *Southern Illinois University at Carbondale*

Doug Moesel, *University of Missouri–Columbia*

Fatma Mohamed, *Morehead State University*

Debra Moody, *University of North Carolina, Charlotte*

Gregory A. Moore, *Middle Tennessee State University*

James R. Morgan, *Dominican University and UC Berkeley Extension*

Sara A. Morris, *Old Dominion University*

Carolyn Mu, *Baylor University*

Stephen Mueller, *Northern Kentucky University*

John Mullane, *Middle Tennessee State University*

Gerry Nkombo Muuka, *Murray State University*

Anil Nair, *Old Dominion University*

V.K. Narayanan, *Drexel University*

Maria L. Nathan, *Lynchburg College*

Louise Nemanich, *Arizona State University*

Charles Newman, *University of Maryland, University College*

Stephanie Newport, *Austin Peay State University*

Bill Norton, *University of Louisville*

Yusuf A. Nur, *SUNY Brockport*

Jeffrey R. Nystrom, *University of Colorado*

d.t. ogilvie, *Rutgers University*

Floyd Ormsbee, *Clarkson University*

Karen L. Page, *University of Wyoming*

Jacquelyn W. Palmer, *University of Cincinnati*

Julie Palmer, *University of Missouri, Columbia*

Daewoo Park, *Xavier University*

Gerald Parker, *Saint Louis University*

Ralph Parrish, *University of Central Oklahoma*

Douglas K. Peterson, *Indiana State University*

Edward Petkus, *Mary Baldwin College*

Michael C. Pickett, *National University*

Peter Ping Li, *California State University, Stanislaus*

Michael W. Pitts, *Virginia Commonwealth University*

Laura Poppo, *Virginia Tech*

Steve Porth, *Saint Joseph's University*

Jodi A. Potter, *Robert Morris University*

Scott A. Quatro, *Grand Canyon University*

Nandini Rajagopalan, *University of Southern California*

Annette L. Ranft, *Florida State University*

Abdul Rasheed, *University of Texas at Arlington*

George Redmond, *Franklin University*

Kira Reed, *Syracuse University*

Clint Relyea, *Arkansas State University*

Barbara Ribbens, *Western Illinois University*

Maurice Rice, *University of Washington*

Violina P. Rindova, *University of Maryland, College Park*

Ron Rivas, *Canisius College*

David Robinson, *Indiana State University–Terre Haute*

Kenneth Robinson, *Kennesaw State University*

Simon Rodan, *San Jose State University*

Patrick R. Rogers, *North Carolina A&T State University*

John K. Ross III, *Texas State University, San Marcos*

Robert Rottman, *Kentucky State University*

Matthew R. Rutherford, *Gonzaga University*

Carol M. Sanchez, *Grand Valley State University*

William W. Sannwald, *San Diego State University*

Yolanda Sarason, *Colorado State University*

Marguerite Schneider, *New Jersey Institute of Technology*

Roger R. Schnorbus, *University of Richmond*

Terry Sebora, *University of Nebraska–Lincoln*

John Seeger, *Bentley College*

Jamal Shamsie, *Michigan State University*

Mark Shanley, *University of Illinois at Chicago*

Lois Shelton, *California State University, Northridge*

Herbert Sherman, *Long Island University*

Chris Shook, *Auburn University*

Jeremy Short, *Texas Tech University*

Mark Simon, *Oakland University, Michigan*

Rob Singh, *Morgan State University*

Bruce Skaggs, *University of Kentucky*

Wayne Smeltz, *Rider University*

Anne Smith, *University of Tennessee*

Andrew Spicer, *University of South Carolina*

James D. Spina, *University of Maryland*

John Stanbury, *George Mason University & Inter-University Institute of Macau, SAR China*

Timothy Stearns, *California State University, Fresno*

Elton Stephen, *Austin State University*

Alice Stewart, *Ohio State University*

Ram Subramanian, *Grand Valley State University*

Roy Suddaby, *University of Iowa*

Michael Sullivan, *UC Berkeley Extension*

Marta Szabo White, *Georgia State University*

Justin Tan, *York University, Canada*

Qingju Tao, *Lehigh University*

Linda Teagarden, *Virginia Tech*

Bing-Sheng Teng, *George Washington University*

Alan Theriault, *University of California–Riverside*

Tracy Thompson, *University of Washington, Tacoma*

Karen Torres, *Angelo State University*

Robert Trumble, *Virginia Commonwealth University*

K.J. Tullis, *University of Central Oklahoma*

Craig A. Turner, *Ph.D., East Tennessee State University*

Beverly Tyler, *North Carolina State University*

Rajaram Veliyath, *Kennesaw State University*

S. Stephen Vitucci, *Tarleton State University–Central Texas*

Jay A. Vora, *St. Cloud State University*

Jorge Walter, *Portland State University*

Bruce Walters, *Louisiana Tech University*

Edward Ward, *St. Cloud State University*

N. Wasilewski, *Pepperdine University*

Andrew Watson, *Northeastern University*

Larry Watts, *Stephen F. Austin University*

Paula S. Weber, *St. Cloud State University*

Kenneth E. A. Wendeln, *Indiana University*

Robert R. Wharton, *Western Kentucky University*

Laura Whitcomb, *California State University–Los Angeles*

Scott Williams, *Wright State University*

Diana Wong, *Bowling Green State University*

Beth Woodard, *Belmont University*

John E. Wroblewski, *State University of New York–Fredonia*

Anne York, *University of Nebraska, Omaha*

Michael Zhang, *Sacred Heart University*

Monica Zimmerman, *Temple University*

Second, the authors would like to thank several faculty colleagues who were particularly helpful in the review, critique, and development of the book and supplementary materials. Greg's colleagues at the University of Texas at Dallas also have been helpful and supportive. These individuals include Mike Peng, Joe Picken, Kumar Nair, John Lin, Seung-Hyun Lee, Tev Dalgic, and Jane Salk. His administrative assistant, Mary Vice, has been extremely helpful. Former MBA student Naga Damaraju, along with two doctoral students, Brian Pinkham and Erin Pleggenkuhle-Miles, have provided many useful inputs and ideas. He also appreciates the support of his dean and associate dean, Hasan Pirkul and

Varghese Jacob, respectively. Tom would like to thank Gerry Hills, Abagail McWilliams, Darold Barnum, Mike Miller, Rod Shrader, James Gillespie, Lou Coco, and other colleagues at the University of Illinois at Chicago, for their continued support. Tom also thanks Kim Boal, Keith Brigham, Will Gunderson, Joe Lee, Alejandra Marin, Todd Moss, Tyge Payne, Jeremy Short, Don Stull, Bill Wan, Abby Wang, Andy Yu, Nikki Bohannon, Bill Gardner, Emily Herrin, Beck Lopez, and Ron Mitchell at Texas Tech University for their support. Special thanks also to Jeff Stambaugh for his vital contribution to new materials prepared for the Fourth Edition. Tom also extends a special thanks to Benyamin Lichtenstein for his support and encouragement. Both Greg and Tom wish to thank a special colleague, Abdul Rasheed at the University of Texas at Arlington, who certainly has been a valued source of friendship and ideas for us for many years. He provided many valuable contributions to the Fifth Edition. Alan thanks his colleagues at Pace University and the Case Association for their support in developing these fine case selections. Special thanks go to Jamal Shamsie at Michigan State University for his support in developing the case selections for this edition. And we appreciate Doug Sanford, at University of Towson for his expertise with one of our new pedagogical features—the key terms in each chapter.

Third, we would like to thank the team at McGraw-Hill/Irwin for their outstanding support throughout the process. This begins with John Biernat, formerly Publisher, who signed us to our original contract. John was always available to provide support and valued input during the entire process. In editorial, executive editor Mike Ablassmeir, development editor Laura Griffin, and editorial coordinator Kelly Pekelder, kept things on track, responded quickly to our never-ending needs and requests, and offered insights and encouragement. Once the manuscript was completed and revised, senior project manager Harvey Yep expertly guided us through the production process. Susan Lombardi did an outstanding job in helping us with the supplementary materials. Jeremy Cheshareck, senior photo research coordinator, and freelance designer Pam Verros provided excellent design, photo, and art work. We also appreciate executive marketing manager Anke Weekes and marketing coordinator Annie Ferro for their energetic, competent, and thorough marketing efforts. Last, but certainly not least, we thank MHI's 70 plus outstanding book reps—who serve on the "front lines." Clearly, they deserve a lot of credit for our success.

Finally, we would like to thank our families. For Greg this includes his parents, William and Mary Dess, who have always been there for him. His wife, Margie, and daughter, Taylor, have been a constant source of love and companionship. Greg would also like to recognize Michael O'Brien. He was one of my first mentors—which took place in Seoul, Korea. I was attending high school there while my father served in the U.S. Air Force. Mike didn't have to lecture us on leadership and other management concepts—he led by example. He's a person with *many* friends and no enemies! Tom thanks his wife Vicki for her constant love and companionship. Tom also thanks Lee Hetherington and Thelma Lumpkin for their inspiration, as well as his mom Katy, and his sister Kitty, for a lifetime of support. Alan thanks his family—his wife Helaine and his children Rachel and Jacob—for their love and support. He also thanks his parents, Gail Eisner and the late Marvin Eisner, for their support and encouragement.

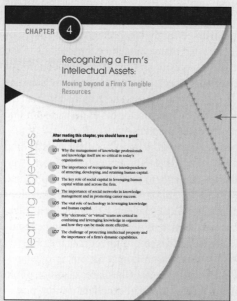

Learning Objectives

Learning Objectives now numbered LO1, LO2, LO3, etc. with corresponding icons in the margins to indicate where learning objectives are covered in the text.

Learning from Mistakes

Learning from Mistakes are examples of where things went wrong. Failures are not only interesting but also sometimes easier to learn from. And students realize strategy is not just about "right or wrong" answers, but requires critical thinking.

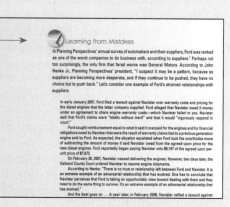

Strategy Spotlight

These boxes weave themes of ethics, globalization, and technology into every chapter of the text, providing students with a thorough grounding necessary for understanding strategic management. Select boxes incorporating crowdsourcing or environmental sustainability themes include the following icons:

Key Terms

Key Terms defined in the margins have been added to improve students' understanding of core strategy concepts.

stakeholder management A firm's strategy for recognizing and responding to the interests of all its salient stakeholders.

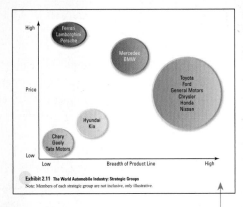

Exhibit 2.11 The World Automobile Industry: Strategic Groups
Note: Members of each strategic group are not inclusive, only illustrative.

Reflecting on Career Implications

This new section before the summary of every chapter consists of examples on how understanding of key concepts helps business students early in their careers.

Reflecting on Career Implications . . .

- *Attributes of Strategic Management:* How do your activities and actions contribute to the goals of your organization? Observe the decisions you make on the job. What are the short-term and long-term implications of your decisions and actions? Have you recently made a decision that might yield short-term profits but might negatively impact the long-term goals of the organization (e.g., cutting maintenance expenses to meet a quarterly profit target)?
- *Intended versus Emergent Strategies:* Don't be too inflexible in your career strategies; strive to take advantage of new opportunities as they arise. Many promising career opportunities may "emerge" that were not part of your intended career strategy or your specific job assignment. Take initiative by pursuing opportunities to get additional training (e.g., learn a software or a statistical package), volunteering for a short-term overseas assignment, etc.
- *Ambidexterity:* Avoid defining your role in the organization too narrowly; look for opportunities to leverage your talents and your organization's resources to create value for your organization. This often involves collaborating with people in other departments or with your organization's customers and suppliers.
- *Strategic Coherence:* Focus your efforts on the "big picture" in your organization. In doing this, you should always strive to assure that your efforts are directed toward your organization's vision, mission, and strategic objectives.

Exhibits

Both new and improved exhibits in every chapter provide visual presentations of the most complex concepts covered to support student comprehension.

Cases

Updated case lineup provides 9 new cases. The remaining have been revised to "maximize freshness" and minimize instructor preparation time. New cases for this edition include well-known companies such as Weight Watchers, Pixar, Mattel, Jamba Juice, and Keurig.

Case 22 Mattel's Misfit Toys*

Case 25 China's Geely Automotive Holdings, Ltd.: Targeting the U.S. Market

Case 30 Weight Watchers International Inc.*

Case 33 Reader's Digest: For Whom and for How Much Longer?*

support materials

Online Learning Center (OLC)

The website www.mhhe.com/dess5e follows the text chapter-by-chapter. OLC content is ancillary and supplementary germane to the textbook. As students read the book, they can go online to take self-grading quizzes, review material, or work through interactive exercises. It includes chapter quizzes, student PowerPoint slides, and links to strategy simulations The *Business Strategy Game* and GLO-BUS.

The instructor section also includes the Instructor's Manual, PowerPoint Presentations, Case Study Teaching Notes, Interactive Case Grid, Video Guide, and Case Web Links as well as all student resources.

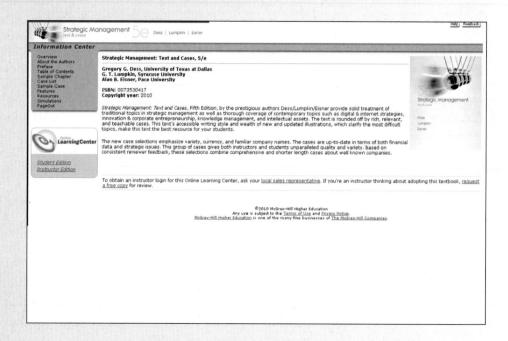

Brief Contents

Contents

part 2   Strategic Formulation

Chapter 5
Business-Level Strategy: Creating
and Sustaining Competitive
Advantages. 156

Chapter 6
Corporate-Level Strategy: Creating
Value through Diversification 194

Chapter 7
International Strategy: Creating
Value in Global Markets 232

Cases

The Strategic Management Process

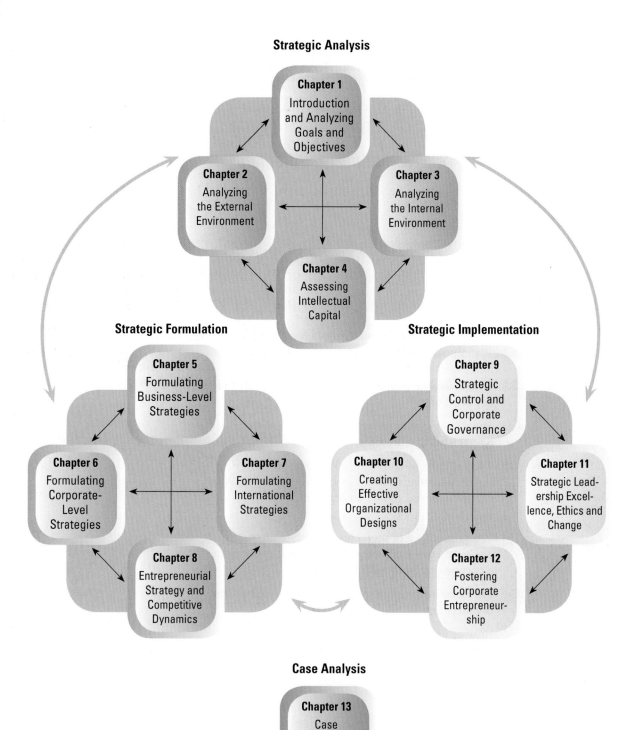

Strategic Analysis

Chapter 1
Introduction and Analyzing Goals and Objectives

Chapter 2
Analyzing the External Environment

Chapter 3
Analyzing the Internal Environment

Chapter 4
Assessing Intellectual Capital

Strategic Formulation

Chapter 5
Formulating Business-Level Strategies

Chapter 6
Formulating Corporate-Level Strategies

Chapter 7
Formulating International Strategies

Chapter 8
Entrepreneurial Strategy and Competitive Dynamics

Strategic Implementation

Chapter 9
Strategic Control and Corporate Governance

Chapter 10
Creating Effective Organizational Designs

Chapter 11
Strategic Leadership Excellence, Ethics and Change

Chapter 12
Fostering Corporate Entrepreneurship

Case Analysis

Chapter 13
Case Analysis

CHAPTER 1

Strategic Management:
Creating Competitive Advantages

>learning objectives

After reading this chapter, you should have a good understanding of:

LO1 The definition of strategic management and its four key attributes.

LO2 The strategic management process and its three interrelated and principal activities.

LO3 The vital role of corporate governance and stakeholder management as well as how "symbiosis" can be achieved among an organization's stakeholders.

LO4 The importance of social responsibility, including environmental sustainability, and how it can enhance a corporation's innovation strategy.

LO5 The need for greater empowerment throughout the organization.

LO6 How an awareness of a hierarchy of strategic goals can help an organization achieve coherence in its strategic direction.

We define strategic management as *consisting of the analyses, decisions, and actions an organization undertakes in order to create and sustain competitive advantages.* At the heart of strategic management is the question: How and why do some firms outperform others? Thus, the challenge to managers is to decide on strategies that provide advantages that can be sustained over time. There are four key attributes of strategic management. It is directed at overall organizational goals, includes multiple stakeholders, incorporates short-term as well as long-term perspectives, and recognizes trade-offs between effectiveness and efficiency. We discuss the above definition and the four key attributes in the first section.

The second section addresses the strategic management process. The three major processes are strategy analysis, strategy formulation, and strategy implementation. These three components parallel the analyses, decisions, and actions in the above definition. We discuss how each of the 12 chapters addresses these three processes and provide examples from each chapter.

The third section discusses two important and interrelated concepts: corporate governance and stakeholder management. Corporate governance addresses the issue of who "governs" the corporation and determines its direction. It consists of three primary participants: stockholders (owners), management (led by the chief executive officer), and the board of directors (elected to monitor management). Stakeholder management recognizes that the interests of various stakeholders, such as owners, customers, and employees, can often conflict and create challenging decision-making dilemmas for managers. However, we discuss how some firms have been able to achieve "symbiosis" among stakeholders wherein their interests are considered interdependent and can be achieved simultaneously. We also discuss the important role of social responsibility, including the need for corporations to incorporate environmental sustainability in their strategic actions.

The fourth section addresses factors in the business environment that have increased the level of unpredictable change for today's leaders. Such factors have also created the need for a greater strategic management perspective and reinforced the role of empowerment throughout the organization.

The final section focuses on the need for organizations to ensure consistency in their vision, mission, and strategic objectives which, collectively, form a hierarchy of goals. While visions may lack specificity, they must evoke powerful and compelling mental images. Strategic objectives are much more specific and are essential for driving toward overall goals.

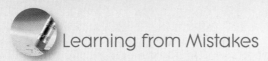
Learning from Mistakes

What makes the study of strategic management so interesting? One thing is that struggling firms can become stars, while high flyers can become earthbound very rapidly. As colorfully noted by Arthur Martinez, Sears' former chairman: "Today's peacock is tomorrow's feather duster." Consider, for example, the change in membership on the prestigious *Fortune 500* list of the largest U. S. firms:[1]

- Of the 500 companies that appeared on the first list in 1955, only 71 have a place on this list today.
- Nearly 2,000 companies have appeared on the list since its inception, and most are long gone from it. Just making the list guarantees nothing about your ability to endure.
- Some of the most powerful companies on today's list—businesses like Intel, Apple, Google, and Dell—grew from nothing to great on the strength of new technologies, bumping venerable old companies off the list.

Let's take a look at Mitch Caplan's tenure at one firm with which you may be familiar—E*Trade. Perhaps, you have used their financial services (brokerage and banking) or have watched their humorous television commercials with the "talking baby."[2] The business press glowingly wrote about how Mitch Caplan, their CEO, enacted a brilliant turnaround. After he took over in 2003, E*Trade's profits soared to $389 million in 2004—compared to an average *loss* of $75 million the previous three years. And, E*Trade was recognized by *InformationWeek* as one of the 40 top firms in the financial services industry for delivering IT solutions to solve business problems.

We'll briefly summarize how Caplan engineered E*Trade's turnaround. However, since we will be opening each chapter in *Strategic Management* with an example of "Learning from Mistakes," we will then focus on how his E*Trade career abruptly ended on a negative note. In effect, it is a "rags to riches to rags" story.

Key elements of Caplan's successful turnaround included:

- He cut costs by sharply reducing their bloated advertising budget and selling unrelated businesses, such as a national ATM network, kiosks in Target stores, a palatial New York retail branch that sold E*Trade souvenirs, and a TV business-news service. In addition, employee headcount was cut from about 5,000 to 4,000.
- Caplan changed the firm's culture and instilled more discipline. He moved the headquarters from Menlo Park, California, to New York City. In effect, he left behind the propeller beanies, rubber chickens, and geeky props that created a loose work atmosphere. In its place were jackets and ties.
- Besides cutting costs and changing the culture, Caplan also refocused the firm on its core banking operations. Here, it had a clear advantage over rivals such as Charles Schwab Corp. and Ameritrade. By offering banking products such as loans and checking accounts to its brokerage customers, he was able to build the nation's eighth-largest thrift. The new financial services became a huge profit center—accounting for 40 percent of all revenues and 48 percent of total profits. Between 2000 and 2004, E*Trade had nearly quadrupled its number of bank accounts and increased its brokerage accounts from 2.4 million to 2.9 million. And until mid-2006 E*Trade was on a tear—coming off a four-year run in which earnings rose 200 percent to $629 million. It was on track to have its best year since its founding in 1986.

So far so good. But, as we noted earlier, this story does *not* have a happy ending. While E*Trade's main business was online investing, Caplan aggressively expanded the banking operations that made and bought mortgage loans and invested in securities backed by mortgages. *[continued]*

As noted by a *Fortune* writer, "Back in 2003, the firm's banking unit began investing in mortgage-backed securities . . . a whole hodgepodge of bundled loan investments that, as it turned out, no one really understood."* In the beginning, these were great for business and by early 2007 its investments in home-equity and mortgage-based securities were worth billions. These investments threw off so much cash that they made up 58 percent of E*Trade's revenues.

However, the great ride came to a rapid halt in mid-2007. Credit markets seized up and practically overnight E*Trade watched its loan portfolio—and a significant portion of its revenues—evaporate. By November 2007, a Citigroup analyst's report suggested that the company's bad loans could push the firm into bankruptcy and E*Trade's customers withdrew $2.5 billion in assets in one day. The firm lost $1.7 billion in the last three months of 2007, and it saw over $56 billion in customer assets evaporate over a five-month period.

Mitch Caplan resigned on November, 29, 2007. At a meeting of E*Trade's board, lawyers, and bankers on that date, he said: "This company is my life. I will do what you want me to, but I think sweeping changes need to be made." One change quickly became self-evident.

It is a humiliating comedown for E*Trade and Mitch Caplan, who failed to sufficiently anticipate the impact of mortgage failures. The online broker kept moving deeper into mortgage banking and Caplan, described by the *Wall Street Journal* as "an eternally optimistic manager," often spoke of mortgages as the "bedrock asset" of America. But at one point, when E*Trade's mortgage portfolio began to rapidly deteriorate, he stated: "We honestly can't predict where this is going anymore and we just shouldn't even try to peg the bottom anymore." Perhaps that statement concisely summarizes what *really* went wrong.

In some ways E*Trade's tale is universal: Its corporate officers have seen firsthand how quickly and cruelly the market can punish any company with exposure to mortgage-backed securities—*or indeed, any business it doesn't understand.*

Today's leaders, such as those at E*Trade face a large number of complex challenges in the global marketplace. In considering how much credit (or blame) they deserve, two perspectives of leadership come immediately to mind: the "romantic" and "external control" perspectives.[3] First, let's look at the **romantic view of leadership.** Here, the implicit assumption is that the leader is the key force in determining an organization's success—or lack thereof.[4] This view dominates the popular press in business magazines such as *Fortune, BusinessWeek,* and *Forbes,* wherein the CEO is either lauded for his or her firm's success or chided for the organization's demise.[5] Consider, for example, the credit that has been bestowed on leaders such as Jack Welch, Andrew Grove, and Herb Kelleher for the tremendous accomplishments of their firms, General Electric, Intel, and Southwest Airlines, respectively.

romantic view of leadership
situations in which the leader is the key force determining the organization's success—or lack thereof.

Similarly, Apple's success in the last decade has been attributed almost entirely to Steve Jobs, its CEO.[6] Apple's string of hit products such as iMac computers, iPods, and iPhones are testament to his genius for developing innovative, user-friendly, and aesthetically pleasing products. In addition to being a perfectionist in product design, Jobs also is a master showman with a cult following. On January 14, 2009, he announced that he was taking a medical leave through June. Perhaps not surprisingly, Apple's stock immediately dropped 10 percent—wiping out approximately $8 billion in market value.

Finally, consider how David Maisel really turned around his firm's fortunes. As chairman of Marvel Studios, he convinced the board that film production "however chancy, would pay off big." And it certainly did—with the big hit *Iron Man* starring Robert Downey Jr., about an industrialist who fights terrorists and arms dealers in a red-and-yellow metal suit.

---

* Mortgage-backed securities are securities issued by lending institutions that are backed by mortgage loans. The holder of these securities receives a steady stream of cash from the repayment of principal and interest on the mortgages. Although backed by mortgage loans, the value of these securities can go down if borrowers start defaulting or if the underlying value of the real estate goes below the amount owed to lenders.

Marvel Studios: Maybe Chairman David Maisel Is the Real "Iron Man"

With 2005 revenues of only $391 million from character licensing, toy sales, and comic book publishing, Marvel needed financial heft to run with big Hollywood studios such as Sony and Warner Bros. Enter the chairman, David Maisel. In 2005, he convinced the board of directors to borrow $525 million to set up an innovative film fund to bankroll *Iron Man* and fund other film projects through 2011. To raise such a huge amount of money, Marvel pledged the future film revenues for 12 of its characters (such as Spider-Man, X-Men) as collateral for the bank loans.

To make *Iron Man,* Marvel drew down about $150 million from the film fund and is paying Paramount Pictures 10 percent of net revenues from ticket and video sales on top of its fees for marketing and distribution. The payoff: *Iron Man* could generate over $1 billion in box-office,

home-video, and other sales. (In its first three weeks of release, the film generated more than $222 million in ticket sales and by late-2008 had grossed $574 million worldwide.)

Marvel is riding high. *The Incredible Hulk,* starring Edward Norton, was released in mid-June 2008. Future films will feature *Iron Man 2, Thor,* and *Captain America.* Marvel has also signed an agreement in which Paramount will distribute Marvel's next five self-produced feature films on a worldwide basis. According to Rob Moore, Vice Chairman of Paramount Pictures: "Marvel's iconic brand, its popular characters and its proven ability to create compelling and visually spellbinding films complements Paramount's great history of filmmaking. We look forward to a long and successful run together."

Interestingly, Marvel has had a star-crossed past. It filed for bankruptcy twice in the 1990s during a period in which a speculative bubble among comic book collectors burst, sales plummeted, and lots of comic shops went out of business. But its fortunes have recently soared. During the past two years, Marvel's net profit has nearly tripled and its stock has doubled. As noted by *BusinessWeek:* "For now . . . Maisel's street cred in Hollywood is, well, super."

Sources: Siklos, R. 2008. Spoiler alert: Comic books are alive and kicking. *CNNMoney.com*, October 13: np; Rockenwagner, P. 2008. Marvel Studios enters into new worldwide distribution agreement with Paramount: Projected slate to include *Iron Man 2, Thor, Captain America* and *The Avenger. Global .factiva.com*, September 29: np; Grover, R. 2008. Iron Man spawns a marvel of a movie studio. *Businessweek.com*, April 29: np; and, Grover, R. 2008. A secret identity for Marvel. *BusinessWeek.* May 19: 34.

Many more profitable projects have followed or are in the planning stages. We address these successful initiatives in Strategy Spotlight 1.1.

On the other hand, when things don't go well, much of the failure of an organization can also, rightfully, be attributed to the leader.[7] For example, when Carly Fiorina was fired as CEO of Hewlett Packard, the firm enjoyed an immediate increase in its stock price of 7 percent—hardly a strong endorsement of her leadership! Caplan led E*Trade's foray into mortgage-backed securities. When this created enormous losses in 2008, he abruptly departed the firm.

However, this reflects only part of the picture. Consider another perspective called **external view of leadership.** Here, rather than making the implicit assumption that the leader is the most important factor in determining organizational outcomes, the focus is on external factors that may positively or negatively affect a firm's success. We don't have to look far to support this perspective. For example, E*Trade's decline can be largely attributed to external factors. The sudden decline in real estate values in 2008 sharply eroded the value of its mortgage-backed securities. This, in turn, led to huge write downs in the value of E*Trade's assets. The decline in stock prices caused far fewer people to engage in stock trades as well. The general climate of a lack of confidence in financial institutions also led to huge withdrawals from customer accounts.

external view of leadership
situations in which external forces—where the leader has limited influence—determine the organization's success.

strategy spotlight

The Financial Crisis: Its Causes and Its Effects on Industries

By early 2009, it became increasingly evident that the U.S. was entering a period of deep and prolonged recession. What seemed like years of limitless expansion had come to a screeching halt by the second half of 2008. Several banks and financial institutions had collapsed, auto companies were crying for a bailout, and the ranks of the unemployed were swelling rapidly. Despite an unprecedented $700 billion infusion into the credit markets and repeated interest rate cuts by the Federal Reserve, it was unclear if the worst was over. How did the nation get into this situation?

- Until recent years, when a bank made a mortgage loan, typically for 30 years, several safeguards were observed to make sure that the bank would be able to recover the loan. These included insisting on a substantial down payment and a thorough verification of the borrower's capacity to repay. Once a loan was made, the bank had to wait 15 or 30 years to recover the loan.

- Starting in the 1990s, banks discovered a new way to make quicker and higher profits from mortgages, called *securitization*. This involved bundling several mortgages together and selling it to an investor either at home or abroad. The investor's income came from the principal and interest payments of the mortgage loan, while the banks made their money from the fees and points collected up front. Instead of waiting 30 years, now they were getting their money back in three months, meaning that they could use the money to make fresh loans.

- Once the banks embraced securitization, the emphasis was on making more and more loans and quickly turning around and selling these mortgage-backed securities to investors. But given that there is not an infinite pool of credit-worthy borrowers who are able to make substantial down payments, banks began to relax the rules for making mortgages. Down payments went down from 20% to 10% to 5% and eventually to 0%. Then came innovations like interest-only loans (where no principal is paid), adjustable rate mortgages (where a borrower gets the benefit of a low interest rate for the first few years), and even loans in which the borrower paid only a part of the interest every month, effectively allowing the loan balance to increase every month! Some banks even began allowing "no verification" loans, wherein a borrower could state an artificially high income and qualify for a loan without any fear that the bank would verify the stated income!

- Why did banks, which are supposed to be prudent, engage in such unwise practices? And why did investors buy these mortgage-backed securities? The answer lies in their expectations about the real estate market. Given that residential real estate prices have risen steadily in the U.S. over the years, the banks felt that there was adequate collateral. Investors bought these securities because rating agencies were giving these securities high ratings. Interestingly, the very fact that anyone could qualify for a loan brought more buyers into the market, causing property prices to rise even faster, effectively causing a housing bubble.

- As more of the subprime borrowers began to default, the housing bubble eventually burst. As more foreclosed homes came into the market, property prices plummeted, and more borrowers walked away from their homes because they saw no point in paying the bank $500,000 for a house now worth only $400,000. This caused a vicious cycle of declining property values and foreclosures. The mortgage-backed securities now had insufficient collateral, forcing the banks to take massive write-offs.

- As the losses of the banks piled up, financial institutions had little money to lend, causing the credit markets to come to a standstill. Suddenly, even people with good credit ratings could not get a loan from the bank to buy a house or a car. In addition to causing real estate prices to further spiral downward, this hurt everyone who depends on credit. The auto companies saw their sales go down 30 percent to 40 percent because potential buyers could not get credit. Small businesses could not get loans from banks and were forced to lay off employees or shut down altogether. As the job losses mounted month after month, the country became mired in the worst recession since the Great Depression.

Let's see the impact the financial meltdown has had on various industries.

- The U.S. auto industry was severely negatively impacted by the financial crisis. U.S. auto sales had hit a peak of 17 million in 2005. 16.1 million cars were sold in 2007. In comparison, the 2008 sales were a dismal 13.2 million. And, according to projections by IHS Global Insight, it may go down to 10.3 million in 2009. J.D. Power Inc. estimates that at least *(continued)*

(continued) half a million customers who wanted to buy were unable to do so because of tighter credit markets in the last quarter of 2008. Such sales declines left the U.S. auto companies with no choice but to plead for bailouts from the government.

- Brinker International Inc. (parent of popular casual dining restaurants such as Chili's, On the Border, and Maggiano's Italian Grill) closed down 47 restaurants in the second half of 2008. In early January 2009, they announced that they would be closing another 35 restaurants. According to Steven Kron, restaurant analyst for Goldman Sachs, as many as 12,000 restaurants will shut down nationally before the end of the recession.

- Retail sales suffered across all segments of the retail industry. In the consumer electronics segment, Circuit City was one of the earliest victims and had to file for bankruptcy. Jewelers Tiffany and Zales experienced sales declines over 20 percent.

- Even high flyers like Micosoft and Intel found that they were not immune to the ripple effects of the financial meltdown. In January 2009 Microsoft announced they would be laying off 5,000 people, the first such layoff in the 34-year history of the company, in response to an 11 percent drop in net income in the previous quarter. Intel's sales dropped 23 percent and its net income declined a massive 90 percent in the fourth quarter of 2008, triggering layoffs of over 5,000 employees.

Sources: Spiers, E. 2008. Putting lipstick on a pig. *Fortune*, September 29: 80; Freeman, S. 2008. Auto sales fall 27% as credit tightens. *Washington Post*, October 2: D01; Robinson-Jacobs, K. 2009. Chili's parent Brinker to close 35 restaurants. *Dallas Morning News*, January 23: D3; Vance, A. 2009. Microsoft slashes jobs as sales fall. *New York Times*, January 2: np; Hamilton, A. 2008. Why Circuit City busted, while Best Buy boomed. *Time Magazine*, November 11; np; Zale drops to all-time low after CFO steps down. 2009. *Associated Press*, January 21: np; When fortune frowned: A special report on the world economy. 2008. *Economist*, October 11: 1–33; and, Blinder, A.S. 2009. Six errors on the path to financial crisis. *New York Times*, January 24: np.

The combined effects of these external factors were huge losses not just at E*Trade but at financial institutions across the country. Of course, what started as a financial industry crisis had negative effects all across the economy through massive layoffs, a sharp decline in consumer demand, and the severe erosion of profitability for firms in virtually all sectors of the economy. Strategy Spotlight 1.2 provides a more detailed look at the global financial crisis of 2008.

Before moving on, it is important to point out that successful executives are often able to navigate around the difficult circumstances that they face. At times it can be refreshing to see the optimistic position they take when they encounter seemingly insurmountable odds. Of course, that's not to say that one should be naïve or Pollyannaish. Consider, for example, how one CEO is handling trying times:[8]

Name a general economic woe, and the chances are that Charles Needham is dealing with it.

- Market turmoil has knocked 80 percent off the shares of South Africa's Metorex, the mining company that he heads.
- The plunge in global commodities is slamming prices for the copper, cobalt, and other minerals Metorex unearths across Africa. The credit crisis makes it harder to raise money.
- And fighting has again broken out in the Democratic Republic of Congo, where Metorex has a mine and several projects in development.

Such problems might send many executives to the window ledge. Yet Needham appears unruffled as he sits down at a conference table in the company's modest offices in a Johannesburg suburb. The combat in northeast Congo, he notes, is far from Metorex's mine. Commodity prices are still high, in historical terms. And Needham is confident he can raise enough capital, drawing on relationships with South African banks. "These are the kinds of things you deal with, doing business in Africa," he says.

What Is Strategic Management?

Given the many challenges and opportunities in the global marketplace, today's managers must do more than set long-term strategies and hope for the best.[9] They must go beyond what some have called "incremental management," whereby they view their job as making a series of small, minor changes to improve the efficiency of their firm's operations.[10] That is fine if your firm is competing in a very stable, simple, and unchanging industry. But there aren't many of those left. The pace of change is accelerating, and the pressure on managers to make both major and minor changes in a firm's strategic direction is increasing.

Rather than seeing their role as merely custodians of the status quo, today's leaders must be proactive, anticipate change, and continually refine and, when necessary, make dramatic changes to their strategies. The strategic management of the organization must become both a process and a way of thinking throughout the organization.

Defining Strategic Management

Strategic management consists of the analyses, decisions, and actions an organization undertakes in order to create and sustain competitive advantages. This definition captures two main elements that go to the heart of the field of strategic management.

First, the strategic management of an organization entails three ongoing processes: *analyses, decisions,* and *actions.* Strategic management is concerned with the *analysis* of strategic goals (vision, mission, and strategic objectives) along with the analysis of the internal and external environment of the organization. Next, leaders must make strategic decisions. These *decisions,* broadly speaking, address two basic questions: What industries should we compete in? How should we compete in those industries? These questions also often involve an organization's domestic and international operations. And last are the *actions* that must be taken. Decisions are of little use, of course, unless they are acted on. Firms must take the necessary actions to implement their **strategies.** This requires leaders to allocate the necessary resources and to design the organization to bring the intended strategies to reality.

Second, the essence of strategic management is the study of why some firms outperform others.[11] Thus, managers need to determine how a firm is to compete so that it can obtain advantages that are sustainable over a lengthy period of time. That means focusing on two fundamental questions:

- *How should we compete in order to create **competitive advantages** in the market-place?* Managers need to determine if the firm should position itself as the low-cost producer or develop products and services that are unique and will enable the firm to charge premium prices. Or should they do some combination of both?
- *How can we create competitive advantages in the marketplace that are unique, valu-able, and difficult for rivals to copy or substitute?* That is, managers need to make such advantages sustainable, instead of temporary.

Rivals almost always copy ideas that work. In the 1980s, American Airlines tried to establish a competitive advantage by introducing the frequent flyer program. Within weeks, all the airlines did the same thing. Overnight, frequent flyer programs became a necessary tool for competitive parity instead of a competitive advantage. The challenge, therefore, is to create competitive advantages that are sustainable.

Sustainable competitive advantage cannot be achieved through operational effective-ness alone.[12] The popular management innovations of the last two decades—total qual-ity, just-in-time, benchmarking, business process reengineering, outsourcing—are all about operational effectiveness. **Operational effectiveness** means performing similar activities better than rivals. Each of these is important, but none lead to sustainable com-petitive advantage because everyone is doing them. Strategy is all about being different.

strategic manage-ment the analyses, decisions, and actions an organiza-tion undertakes in order to create and sustain competitive advantages.

>LO1
The definition of strategic management and its four key attributes.

Strategy The ideas, decisions, and actions that enable a firm to succeed.

Competitive advantage A firm's resources and capa-bilities that enable it to overcome the competitive forces in its industry(ies).

operational effectiveness performing similar activities better than rivals.

Sustainable competitive advantage is possible only by performing different activities from rivals or performing similar activities in different ways. Companies such as Wal-Mart, Southwest Airlines, and IKEA have developed unique, internally consistent, and difficult-to-imitate activity systems that have provided them with sustained competitive advantages. A company with a good strategy must make clear choices about what it wants to accomplish. Trying to do everything that your rivals do eventually leads to mutually destructive price competition, not long-term advantage.

The Four Key Attributes of Strategic Management

Before discussing the strategic management process, let's briefly talk about four attributes of strategic management.[13] It should become clear how this course differs from other courses that you have had in functional areas, such as accounting, marketing, operations, and finance. Exhibit 1.1 provides a definition and the four attributes of strategic management.

First, strategic management is *directed toward overall organizational goals and objectives*. That is, effort must be directed at what is best for the total organization, not just a single functional area. Some authors have referred to this perspective as "organizational versus individual rationality."[14] That is, what might look "rational" or ideal for one functional area, such as operations, may not be in the best interest of the overall firm. For example, operations may decide to schedule long production runs of similar products to lower unit costs. However, the standardized output may be counter to what the marketing department needs to appeal to a demanding target market. Similarly, research and development may "overengineer" the product to develop a far superior offering, but the design may make the product so expensive that market demand is minimal. Therefore, in this course you will look at cases and strategic issues from the perspective of the organization rather than that of the functional area(s) in which you have the strongest background.

Second, strategic management *includes multiple stakeholders in decision making*.[15] **Stakeholders** are those individuals, groups, and organizations who have a "stake" in the success of the organization, including owners (shareholders in a publicly held corporation), employees, customers, suppliers, the community at large, and so on. (We'll discuss this in more detail later in this chapter.) Managers will not be successful if they focus on a single stakeholder. For example, if the overwhelming emphasis is on generating profits for the owners, employees may become alienated, customer service may suffer, and the suppliers may resent demands for pricing concessions. However, many organizations can satisfy multiple stakeholder needs simultaneously. For example, financial performance may increase because employees who are satisfied with their jobs work harder to enhance customer satisfaction—leading to higher profits.

stakeholders
individuals, groups, and organizations who have a stake in the success of the organization, including owners (shareholders in a publicly held corporation), employees, customers, suppliers, and the community at large.

Exhibit 1.1
Strategic Management Concepts

Definition: Strategic management consists of the analyses, decisions, and actions an organization undertakes in order to create and sustain competitive advantages.

Key Attributes of Strategic Management

- Directs the organization toward overall goals and objectives.
- Includes multiple stakeholders in decision making.
- Needs to incorporate short-term and long-term perspectives.
- Recognizes trade-offs between efficiency and effectiveness.

Third, strategic management *requires incorporating both short-term and long-term perspectives.*[16] Peter Senge, a leading strategic management author, has referred to this need as a "creative tension."[17] That is, managers must maintain both a vision for the future of the organization as well as a focus on its present operating needs. However, financial markets can exert significant pressures on executives to meet short-term performance targets. Studies have shown that corporate leaders often take a short-term approach to the detriment of creating long-term shareholder value. Consider the following:

> According to recent studies, only 59 percent of financial executives say they would pursue a positive net present value project if it meant missing the quarter's consensus earnings per-share estimate. Worse, 78 percent say they would sacrifice value—often a great deal of value—to smooth earnings. Similarly, managers are more likely to cut R&D to reverse an earning slide if a significant amount of the company's equity is owned by institutions with high portfolio turnover. Many companies have the same philosophy about long-term investments such as infrastructure and employee training.[18]

Fourth, strategic management *involves the recognition of trade-offs between effectiveness and efficiency.* Some authors have referred to this as the difference between "doing the right thing" (**effectiveness)** and "doing things right" (**efficiency).**[19] While managers must allocate and use resources wisely, they must still direct their efforts toward the attainment of overall organizational objectives. Managers who only focus on meeting short-term budgets and targets may fail to attain the broader goals. Consider the following amusing story told by Norman Augustine, former CEO of defense giant, Martin Marietta (now Lockheed Martin):

effectiveness
tailoring actions to the needs of an organization rather than wasting effort, or "doing the right thing."

> I am reminded of an article I once read in a British newspaper which described a problem with the local bus service between the towns of Bagnall and Greenfields. It seemed that, to the great annoyance of customers, drivers had been passing long queues of would-be passengers with a smile and a wave of the hand. This practice was, however, clarified by a bus company official who explained, "It is impossible for the drivers to keep their timetables if they must stop for passengers."[20]

efficiency
performing actions at a low cost relative to a benchmark, or "doing things right."

Clearly, the drivers who were trying to stay on schedule had ignored the overall mission. As Augustine noted, "Impeccable logic but something seems to be missing!"

Successful managers must make many trade-offs. It is central to the practice of strategic management. At times, managers must focus on the short term and efficiency; at other times the emphasis is on the long term and expanding a firm's product-market scope in order to anticipate opportunities in the competitive environment. For example, consider Kevin Sharer's perspective. He is CEO of Amgen, the giant $15 billion biotechnology firm:

> A CEO must always be switching between what I call different altitudes—tasks of different levels of abstraction and specificity. At the highest altitude you're asking the big questions: What are the company's mission and strategy? Do people understand and believe in these aims? Are decisions consistent with them? At the lowest altitude, you're looking at on-the-ground operations: Did we make that sale? What was the yield on that last lot in the factory? How many days of inventory do we have for a particular drug? And then there's everything in between: How many chemists do we need to hire this quarter? What should we pay for a small biotech company that has a promising new drug? Is our production capacity adequate to roll out a product in a new market?[21]

ambidexterity the challenge managers face of both aligning resources to take advantage of existing product markets as well as proactively exploring new opportunities.

Some authors have developed the concept of **"ambidexterity"** which refers to a manager's challenge to both align resources to take advantage of existing product markets as well as proactively explore new opportunities.[22] Strategy Spotlight 1.3 discusses ambidextrous behaviors that are required for success in today's challenging marketplace.

Ambidextrous Behaviors: Combining Alignment and Adaptability

A recent study involving 41 business units in 10 multinational companies identified four ambidextrous behaviors in individuals. Such behaviors are the essence of ambidexterity, and they illustrate how a dual capacity for alignment and adaptability can be woven into the fabric of an organization at the individual level.

They take time and are alert to opportunities beyond the confines of their own jobs. A large computer company's sales manager became aware of a need for a new software module that nobody currently offered. Instead of selling the customer something else, he worked up a business case for the new module. With management's approval, he began working full time on its development.

They are cooperative and seek out opportunities to combine their efforts with others. A marketing manager for Italy was responsible for supporting a newly acquired subsidiary. When frustrated about the limited amount of contact she had with her peers in other countries, she began discussions with them. This led to the creation of a European marketing forum which meets quarterly to discuss issues, share best practices, and collaborate on marketing plans.

They are brokers, always looking to build internal networks. When visiting the head office in St. Louis, a Canadian plant manager heard about plans for a $10 million investment for a new tape manufacturing plant. After inquiring further about the plans and returning to Canada, he contacted a regional manager in Manitoba, who he knew was looking for ways to build his business. With some generous support from the Manitoba government, the regional manager bid for, and ultimately won, the $10 million investment.

They are multitaskers who are comfortable wearing more than one hat. Although an operations manager for a major coffee and tea distributor was charged with running his plant as efficiently as possible, he took it upon himself to identify value-added services for his clients. By developing a dual role, he was able to manage operations and develop a promising electronic module that automatically reported impending problems inside a coffee vending machine. With corporate funding, he found a subcontractor to develop the software, and he then piloted the module in his own operations. It was so successful that it was eventually adopted by operations managers in several other countries.

A recent *Harvard Business Review* article provides some useful insights on how one can become a more ambidextrous leader. Consider the following questions:

- **Do you meet your numbers?**

- **Do you help others?**

- **What do you do for your peers?** Are you just their in-house competitor?

- **When you manage up, do you bring problems—or problems with possible solutions?**

- **Are you transparent?** Managers who get a reputation for spinning events gradually lose the trust of peers and superiors.

- **Are you developing a group of senior-managers who know you and are willing to back your original ideas with resources?**

Source: Birkinshaw, J. & Gibson, C. 2004. Building ambidexterity into an organization. *MIT Sloan Management Review,* 45 (4): 47–55; and, Bower, J. L. 2007. Solve the succession crisis by growing inside-out leaders. *Harvard Business Review,* 85 (11): 90–99.

>LO2
The strategic management process and its three interrelated and principal activities.

The Strategic Management Process

We've identified three ongoing processes—analyses, decisions, and actions—that are central to strategic management. In practice, these three processes—often referred to as strategy analysis, strategy formulation, and strategy implementation—are highly interdependent and do not take place one after the other in a sequential fashion in most companies.

Intended versus Realized Strategies

Henry Mintzberg, a management scholar at McGill University, argues that viewing the strategic management process as one in which analysis is followed by optimal decisions and their subsequent meticulous implementation neither describes the strategic management process accurately nor prescribes ideal practice.[23] He sees the business environment as far from predictable, thus limiting our ability for analysis. Further, decisions are seldom based on optimal rationality alone, given the political processes that occur in all organizations.[24]

Taking into consideration the limitations discussed above, Mintzberg proposed an alternative model. As depicted in Exhibit 1.2, decisions following from analysis, in this model, constitute the *intended* **strategy** of the firm. For a variety of reasons, the intended strategy rarely survives in its original form. Unforeseen environmental developments, unanticipated resource constraints, or changes in managerial preferences may result in at least some parts of the intended strategy remaining *unrealized*. On the other hand, good managers will want to take advantage of a new opportunity presented by the environment, even if it was not part of the original set of intentions. For example, consider the wind energy industry.[25]

> In October 2008, the United States Congress extended a key wind tax credit and many states have mandates requiring utilities to tap renewable energy. Such legislation, combined with falling clean energy costs and wildly cyclical prices for coal, oil, and gas, has created a surge in demand for companies such as GE Wind Energy, which makes large turbines and fan blades. Not surprisingly, such businesses have increased hiring and research and development, as well as profit and revenue forecasts.[25]

intended strategy strategy in which organizational decisions are determined only by analysis.

Thus, the final **realized strategy** of any firm is a combination of deliberate and emergent strategies.

Next, we will address each of the three key strategic management processes: strategy analysis, strategy formulation, and strategy implementation and provide a brief overview of the chapters.

Exhibit 1.3 depicts the strategic management process and indicates how it ties into the chapters in the book. Consistent with our discussion above, we use two-way arrows to convey the interactive nature of the processes.

realized strategy strategy in which organizational decisions are determined by both analysis and unforeseen environmental developments, unanticipated resource constraints, and/or changes in managerial preferences.

Strategy Analysis

Strategy analysis may be looked upon as the starting point of the strategic management process. It consists of the "advance work" that must be done in order to effectively formulate and implement strategies. Many strategies fail because managers may want to formulate

Exhibit 1.2 **Realized Strategy and Intended Strategy: Usually Not the Same**

Source: From Mintzberg, H. & Waters, J. A., "Of Strategies: Deliberate and Emergent," *Strategic Management Journal*, Vol. 6, 1985, pp. 257–272. Copyright © John Wiley & Sons Limited. Reproduced with permission.

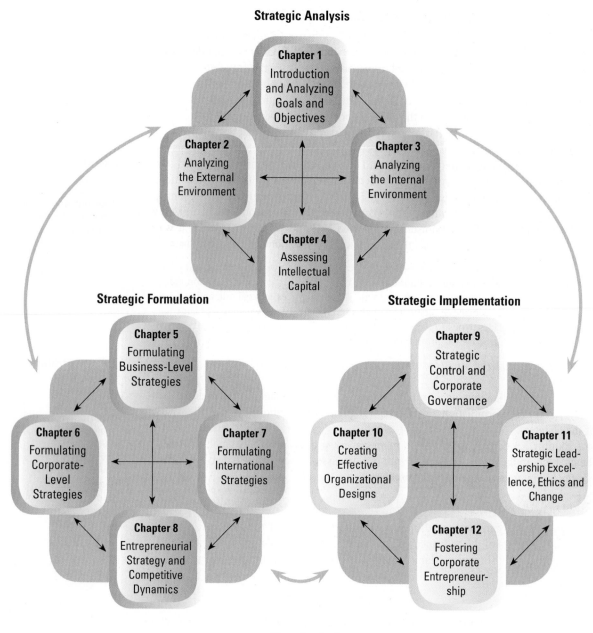

Strategic Analysis

Chapter 1
Introduction and Analyzing Goals and Objectives

Chapter 2
Analyzing the External Environment

Chapter 3
Analyzing the Internal Environment

Chapter 4
Assessing Intellectual Capital

Strategic Formulation

Chapter 5
Formulating Business-Level Strategies

Chapter 6
Formulating Corporate-Level Strategies

Chapter 7
Formulating International Strategies

Chapter 8
Entrepreneurial Strategy and Competitive Dynamics

Strategic Implementation

Chapter 9
Strategic Control and Corporate Governance

Chapter 10
Creating Effective Organizational Designs

Chapter 11
Strategic Leadership Excellence, Ethics and Change

Chapter 12
Fostering Corporate Entrepreneurship

Case Analysis

Chapter 13
Case Analysis

Exhibit 1.3 The Strategic Management Process

and implement strategies without a careful analysis of the overarching goals of the organization and without a thorough analysis of its external and internal environment.

Analyzing Organizational Goals and Objectives (Chapter 1)   A firm's vision, mission, and strategic objectives form a hierarchy of goals that range from broad statements of intent and bases for competitive advantage to specific, measurable strategic objectives.

Analyzing the External Environment of the Firm (Chapter 2)   Managers must monitor and scan the environment as well as analyze competitors. Two frameworks of the external environment are provided: (1) the general environment consists of several elements, such as demographic, technological, and economic segments, and (2) the industry environment consists of competitors and other organizations that may threaten the success of a firm's products and services.

Assessing the Internal Environment of the Firm (Chapter 3)   Analyzing the strengths and relationships among the activities that constitute a firm's value chain (e.g., operations, marketing and sales, and human resource management) can be a means of uncovering potential sources of competitive advantage for the firm.[26]

Assessing a Firm's Intellectual Assets (Chapter 4)   The knowledge worker and a firm's other intellectual assets (e.g., patents, trademarks) are becoming increasingly important as the drivers of competitive advantages and wealth creation. We also assess how well the organization creates networks and relationships as well as how technology can enhance collaboration among employees and provide a means of accumulating and storing knowledge.[27]

Strategy Formulation

A firm's strategy formulation is developed at several levels. First, business-level strategy addresses the issue of how to compete in a given business to attain competitive advantage. Second, corporate-level strategy focuses on two issues: (a) what businesses to compete in and (b) how businesses can be managed to achieve synergy; that is, they create more value by working together than if they operate as stand-alone businesses. Third, a firm must determine the best method to develop international strategies as it ventures beyond its national boundaries. Fourth, managers must formulate effective entrepreneurial initiatives.

Formulating Business-Level Strategy (Chapter 5)   The question of how firms compete and outperform their rivals and how they achieve and sustain competitive advantages goes to the heart of strategic management. Successful firms strive to develop bases for competitive advantage, which can be achieved through cost leadership and/or differentiation as well as by focusing on a narrow or industrywide market segment.[28]

Formulating Corporate-Level Strategy (Chapter 6)   Corporate-level strategy addresses a firm's portfolio (or group) of businesses. It asks (1) What business (or businesses) should we compete in? and (2) How can we manage this portfolio of businesses to create synergies among the businesses?

Formulating International Strategy (Chapter 7)   When firms enter foreign markets, they face both opportunities and pitfalls.[29] Managers must decide not only on the most appropriate entry strategy but also how they will go about attaining competitive advantages in international markets.

Entrepreneurial Strategy and Competitive Dynamics (Chapter 8)   Entrepreneurial activity aimed at new value creation is a major engine for economic growth. For entrepreneurial initiatives to succeed viable opportunities must be recognized and effective strategies must be formulated.

Strategy Implementation

Clearly, sound strategies are of no value if they are not properly implemented.[30] Strategy implementation involves ensuring proper strategic controls and organizational designs, which includes establishing effective means to coordinate and integrate activities within the firm as well as with its suppliers, customers, and alliance partners.[31] Leadership plays a central role, including ensuring that the organization is committed to excellence and ethical behavior. It also promotes learning and continuous improvement and acts entrepreneurially in creating and taking advantage of new opportunities.

Strategic Control and Corporate Governance (Chapter 9) Firms must exercise two types of strategic control. First, informational control requires that organizations continually monitor and scan the environment and respond to threats and opportunities. Second, behavioral control involves the proper balance of rewards and incentives as well as cultures and boundaries (or constraints). Further, successful firms (those that are incorporated) practice effective corporate governance.

Creating Effective Organizational Designs (Chapter 10) To succeed, firms must have organizational structures and designs that are consistent with their strategy. And, in today's rapidly changing competitive environments, firms must ensure that their organizational boundaries—those internal to the firm and external—are more flexible and permeable.[32] Often, organizations develop strategic alliances to capitalize on the capabilities of other organizations.

Creating a Learning Organization and an Ethical Organization (Chapter 11) Effective leaders set a direction, design the organization, and develop an organization that is committed to excellence and ethical behavior. In addition, given rapid and unpredictable change, leaders must create a "learning organization" to ensure that the entire organization can benefit from individual and collective talents.

Fostering Corporate Entrepreneurship (Chapter 12) With rapid and unpredictable change in the global marketplace, firms must continually improve and grow as well as find new ways to renew their organizations. Corporate entrepreneurship and innovation provide firms with new opportunities, and strategies should be formulated that enhance a firm's innovative capacity.

Chapter 13, "Analyzing Strategic Management Cases," provides guidelines and suggestions on how to evaluate cases in this course. Thus, the concepts and techniques discussed in these 12 chapters can be applied to real-world organizations.

Let's now address two concepts—corporate governance and stakeholder management—that are critical to the strategic management process.

>LO3
The vital role of corporate governance and stakeholder management as well as how "symbiosis" can be achieved among an organization's stakeholders.

The Role of Corporate Governance and Stakeholder Management

Most business enterprises that employ more than a few dozen people are organized as corporations. As you recall from your finance classes, the overall purpose of a corporation is to maximize the long-term return to the owners (shareholders). Thus, we may ask: Who is really responsible for fulfilling this purpose? Robert Monks and Neil Minow provide a useful definition of **corporate governance** as "the relationship among various participants in determining the direction and performance of corporations. The primary participants are (1) the shareholders, (2) the management (led by the chief executive officer), and (3) the board of directors."[33] This relationship is illustrated in Exhibit 1.4.

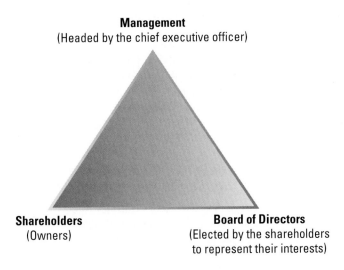

Management
(Headed by the chief executive officer)

Shareholders
(Owners)

Board of Directors
(Elected by the shareholders
to represent their interests)

Exhibit 1.4   **The Key Elements of Corporate Governance**

corporate governance the relationship among various participants in determining the direction and performance of corporations. The primary participants are (1) the share-holders, (2) the management (led by the chief executive officer), and (3) the board of directors.

The board of directors (BOD) are the elected representatives of the shareholders charged with ensuring that the interests and motives of management are aligned with those of the owners (i.e., shareholders). In many cases, the BOD is diligent in fulfilling its purpose. For example, Intel Corporation, the giant $38 billion maker of microprocessor chips, is widely recognized as an excellent example of sound governance practices. Its BOD follows guidelines to ensure that its members are independent (i.e., not members of the executive management team and do not have close personal ties to top executives) so that they can provide proper oversight, it has explicit guidelines on the selection of director candidates (to avoid "cronyism"), and it provides detailed procedures for formal evaluations of directors and the firm's top officers.[34] Such guidelines serve to ensure that management is acting in the best interests of shareholders.[35]

Recently, there has been much criticism as well as cynicism by both citizens and the business press about the poor job that management and the BODs of large corporations are doing. We only have to look at the scandals at firms such as Arthur Andersen, World-Com, Enron, Tyco, and ImClone Systems.[36] Such malfeasance has led to an erosion of the public's trust in the governance of corporations. For example, a recent Gallup poll found that 90 percent of Americans felt that people leading corporations could not be trusted to look after the interests of their employees, and only 18 percent thought that corporations looked after their shareholders. Forty-three percent, in fact, believed that senior executives were in it only for themselves. In Britain, that figure, according to another poll, was an astonishing 95 percent.[37] Perhaps worst of all, in another study, 60 percent of directors (the very people who decide how much executives should earn) felt that executives were "dramatically overpaid"![38]

It is now clear that much of the bonus pay awarded to executives on Wall Street in the past few years was richly undeserved.[39] In the three years that led up to the recent collapse of seven big financial institutions, the chief executives of those firms collected a total of $80 million in performance bonuses and raked in $210 million in severance pay and earnings from stock sales. Let's take a closer look at a few of these payouts (the amounts below represent bonus pay, severance, and gains from stock sales from 2005 to late 2008):

- Richard Fuld, Lehman Brothers ($172 million)
- Kerry Killinger, Washington Mutual ($37 million)
- Martin Sullivan, American International Group ($36 million)

- Michael Perry, Indymac, Federal Bank ($20 million)
- Kenneth Thompson, Wachovia Corporation ($14 million)

Clearly, there is a strong need for improved corporate governance, and we will address this topic in Chapter 9.[40] We focus on three important mechanisms to ensure effective corporate governance: an effective and engaged board of directors, shareholder activism, and proper managerial rewards and incentives.[41] In addition to these internal controls, a key role is played by various external control mechanisms.[42] These include the auditors, banks, analysts, an active financial press, and the threat of hostile takeovers.

Alternative Perspectives of Stakeholder Management

Stakeholder management A firm's strategy for recognizing and responding to the interests of all its salient stakeholders.

Generating long-term returns for the shareholders is the primary goal of a publicly held corporation.[43] As noted by former Chrysler vice chairman Robert Lutz, "We are here to serve the shareholder and create shareholder value. I insist that the only person who owns the company is the person who paid good money for it."[44]

Despite the primacy of generating shareholder value, managers who focus solely on the interests of the owners of the business will often make poor decisions that lead to negative, unanticipated outcomes.[45] For example, decisions such as mass layoffs to increase profits, ignoring issues related to conservation of the natural environment to save money, and exerting excessive pressure on suppliers to lower prices can certainly harm the firm in the long run. Such actions would likely lead to negative outcomes such as alienated employees, increased governmental oversight and fines, and disloyal suppliers.

Clearly, in addition to *shareholders,* there are other *stakeholders* (e.g. suppliers, customers) who must be explicitly taken into account in the strategic management process.[46] A stakeholder can be defined as an individual or group, inside or outside the company, that has a stake in and can influence an organization's performance. Each stakeholder group makes various claims on the company. Exhibit 1.5 provides a list of major stakeholder groups and the nature of their claims on the company.

Zero Sum or Symbiosis? There are two opposing ways of looking at the role of stakeholder management in the strategic management process.[47] The first one can be termed "zero sum." In this view, the role of management is to look upon the various stakeholders as competing for the organization's resources. In essence, the gain of one individual or group is the loss of another individual or group. For example, employees want higher wages (which drive down profits), suppliers want higher prices for their inputs and slower, more flexible delivery times (which drive up costs), customers want fast deliveries and higher quality (which drive up costs), the community at large wants charitable contributions (which take money from company goals), and so on. This zero-sum thinking is

Exhibit 1.5
An Organization's Key Stakeholders and the Nature of Their Claims

Stakeholder Group	Nature of Claim
Stockholders	Dividends, capital appreciation
Employees	Wages, benefits, safe working environment, job security
Suppliers	Payment on time, assurance of continued relationship
Creditors	Payment of interest, repayment of principal
Customers	Value, warranties
Government	Taxes, compliance with regulations
Communities	Good citizenship behavior such as charities, employment, not polluting the environment

rooted, in part, in the traditional conflict between workers and management, leading to the formation of unions and sometimes ending in adversarial union–management negotiations and long, bitter strikes.

Consider, for example, the many stakeholder challenges facing Wal-Mart, the world's largest retailer. We address these in Strategy Spotlight 1.4.

There will always be some conflicting demands. However, organizations can achieve mutual benefit through *stakeholder symbiosis,* which recognizes that stakeholders are dependent upon each other for their success and well-being.[48] Consider Outback Steakhouse:[49]

> Outback Steakhouse asked their employees to identify on a six-point scale how strongly they agreed or disagreed that Outback's principles and beliefs (P&Bs) were practiced in their particular restaurants. The turnover rate of the hourly employees in the group most strongly agreeing that the P&Bs were their stores' guiding ethos was half what it was in the group most strongly disagreeing. Five times as many customers in the strongly agreeing group indicated that they were likely to return. Further, at the strongly agreeing group's restaurants, revenues were 8.9 percent higher, cash flow was 27 percent higher, and pretax profit was 48 percent higher. Not surprisingly, it is now mandatory that Outback managers conduct this survey.

Crowdsourcing: Stakeholders Can Fulfill Multiple Roles Thus far, we have implicitly assumed that stakeholders' roles are fixed. That is, a stakeholder is . . . pick one: a customer, supplier, employee, competitor, and so fourth. However, in practice, that is certainly not the case. Consider Shaw Industries, a vertically integrated carpet producer (which we discuss in Chapter 6). It acquired Amoco's polypropylene fiber manufacturing facilities, which provide carpet fibers for both internal use and sale to other manufacturers. Thus, some of Shaw's competitors are also its customers. Similarly, a retailer may share space on tractor trailers that it uses to ship products to its stores. This helps to decrease everyone's logistics costs—hence rivals become customers (or collaborators). And rivals can become key allies (within the boundaries of the same firm) when a firm acquires competitors to consolidate an industry—as has been the case in a myriad of industries such as finance, defense, and funeral homes.

To show how stakeholder roles are becoming more fluid, we'd like to introduce a concept that will be a theme through the text: **crowdsourcing.**[50] When and where did the term originate? In January 2006, open sourcing was, for most businesspeople, little more than an online curiosity. At that time, Jeff Howe of *Wired* magazine started to write an article about the phenomenon. However, he soon discovered a far more important story to be told: Large—as well as small—companies in a wide variety of industries had begun farming out serious tasks to individuals and groups on the Internet. Together with his editor, Mark Robinson, they coined a new term to describe the phenomenon. In June 2006, the article appeared in which *crowdsourcing* was defined as the tapping of the "latent talent of the (online) crowd." It has become the term of choice for a process that is infiltrating many aspects of business life.

crowdsourcing
practice wherein the Internet is used to tap a broad range of individuals and groups to generate ideas and solve problems.

Clearly, *crowdsourcing* has claimed some well-known successes, particularly on the product development front: Consider:

- The Linux operating system, created as an open-source alternative to Windows and UNIX, can be downloaded free and altered to suit any user's needs. And, with all the firepower brought to bear by the online open-source community, bugs in the system get fixed in a matter of hours.
- One of Amazon's smartest moves was to invite their customers to write online reviews. The customers are neither paid nor controlled by the company, but the content that they create adds enormous value to other customers and, therefore, to Amazon.

Wal-Mart: Some Challenging Stakeholder Issues

With 2008 revenues exceeding $400 billion, Wal-Mart is the world's largest retailer. Name practically any product category, from groceries to photo processing, and there's a good chance Wal-Mart is the No. 1 player in that space. Its buyer power is immense. For example, Wal-Mart isn't just Procter & Gamble's biggest customer—Wal-Mart is bigger than P&G's next nine customers *combined*. And, as one would expect, Wal-Mart faces a lot of challenges in managing demands/expectations from various stakeholders.

● Wal-Mart, the world's largest retailer, always faces many challenging issues which affect many stakeholders.

Wal-Mart strives to ramp up growth while many stakeholders are watching nervously: employees and trade unions; shareholders, investors, and creditors; suppliers

Sources: McGregor, J. 2008. The world's most influential companies. *Business-Week*, December 22: 43–53; Camillus, J. 2008. Strategy as a wicked problem. *Harvard Business Review*, 86 (5): 100–101; Sacks, D. 2007. Working with the enemy. *Fast Company*, September: 74–81; and, Fishman, C. 2006. The Wal-Mart effect and a decent society: Who knew shopping was so important. *Academy of Management Perspectives*, 20 (3): 6–25.

and joint venture partners; the governments of the U.S. and other nations where the retailer operates; and customers. In addition, many nongovernmental organizations, particularly in countries where the retailer buys its products, are closely monitoring Wal-Mart. Wal-Mart's stakeholders have different interests, and not all of them share the firm's goals. Each group has the ability, in various degrees, to influence the firm's choices and results. Clearly, this wasn't the case when Sam Walton built his first store in Rogers, Arkansas, in 1962.

Wal-Mart's slowing growth in the U.S. has many causes: a saturated home market, its customers' limited disposable incomes, and intense competition from rivals such as Costco and Target. The company has been subjected to negative publicity because of its strong dependence on imports, criticism about the wages and benefits it offers its roughly 1.3 million employees, and charges that illegal aliens work in its stores. Such factors have generated unfavorable publicity and intensified people's opposition to Wal-Mart's opening stores in urban areas.

Compounding Wal-Mart's challenges are that some of its strengths have turned into disadvantages. For example, its large market share in some product categories makes it difficult to grow same-store sales. Its low-cost sourcing practices have rendered it vulnerable to many health, safety, and environmental concerns that surround products manufactured in China. Further, its supply chain expertise does not help in the case of fashion and organic products, and its low-price image erodes its ability to sell upscale products (which, of course, offer better profit margins). Moreover, Wal-Mart's deep roots in rural America are of little use in overseas markets.

With regard to environment sustainability, Wal-Mart is determined to use its clout for good. It's pushing to create "zero waste" stores and sell more green products, with its sales of 145 million energy-saving light bulbs already dampening U.S. electricity consumption. In October 2005, it set ambitious environmental and sustainability goals, such as cutting total packaging 5 percent by 2013 and doubling the gas mileage of its trucking fleet by 2015.

On the global front, it's forcing Chinese manufacturers to clean up their ways. In November 2008, it told big mainland suppliers that they must become 20 percent more energy-efficient within three years to stay on contract, and they must disclose more. With Wal-Mart's pressure on China, the impact could be profound. As sustainability consultant Andrew Winston argues: "Only Wal-Mart is big enough to daunt China's worst practices. Even those who blame it for other practices recognize Wal-Mart's power in going green."

Crowdsourcing: How Customers Also Became Suppliers at Intuit

Intuit, the financial software powerhouse, began operations in 1984. Its first product was Quicken, which has now been purchased by more people than all other personal finance products combined. About two decades later, Intuit decided to test the idea of customer-support forums. However, it wanted to avoid the hassles of building and managing them. Thus, it turned to LiveWorld, a specialist in creating, operating, and moderating social networks and online communities.

The Quicken forums are organized according to products and computer type—PC or Mac. Other customers quickly answer Quicken queries, typically in helpful

detail. In fact, volunteers answer 70 percent of all support questions—taking an enormous load off Quicken's customer service staff. For example, when a 10-year customer complained that some of his mutual fund data wasn't showing in a Quicken capital gains report, several other customers began a dialogue. Some wrote long, detailed explanations of the entire capital-gains process.

As one would expect, LiveWorld and its rivals charge for their services. Whether a company wants to take that route to get customers to serve themselves depends on its culture, finances, and technical savvy. However, it is an option that several companies such as America Online, Campbell Soup, Dove, and MINI Cooper, have embraced.

Source: Libert, B. & Spector, J. 2008. *We are smarter than me.* Philadelphia: Wharton School Publishing.

crowdsourcing

- Roughly five million users per month swear by Wikipedia, the free online encyclopedia created and updated by Internet volunteers to the tune of roughly two million articles and counting.

Throughout the book, we will introduce examples of *crowdsourcing* to show its relevance to key strategy concepts. For example, in Chapter 2, we'll discuss how Virgin Mobile USA has used it for everything from designing phones to coming up with names for service plans. Chapter 5 discusses Netflix, which has offered a $1 million prize to anyone who can build a system that is 10 percent better than Cinematch—its in-house system to personalize movie recommendations. And, in Chapter 10, we discuss how Eli Lilly, the pharmaceutical giant launched Innocentive, the first online, incentive-based scientific network created specifically for the global research and development community.

Strategy Spotlight 1.5 provides an example of how customers also became valued suppliers—and, in the process, help save money in its customer service operation.

Social Responsibility and Environmental Sustainability: Moving beyond the Immediate Stakeholders

Organizations cannot ignore the interests and demands of stakeholders such as citizens and society in general that are beyond its immediate constituencies—customers, owners, suppliers, and employees. That is, they must consider the needs of the broader community at large and act in a socially responsible manner.[51]

Social responsibility is the expectation that businesses or individuals will strive to improve the overall welfare of society.[52] From the perspective of a business, this means that managers must take active steps to make society better by virtue of the business being in existence.[53] Similar to norms and values, actions that constitute socially responsible behavior tend to change over time. In the 1970s affirmative action was a high priority and during the 1990s and up to the present time, the public has been concerned about environmental

social responsibility the expectation that businesses or individuals will strive to improve the overall welfare of society.

quality. Many firms have responded to this by engaging in recycling and reducing waste. And in the wake of terrorist attacks on New York City and the Pentagon, as well as the continuing threat from terrorists worldwide, a new kind of priority has arisen: the need to be vigilant concerning public safety.

Today, demands for greater corporate responsibility have accelerated.[54] These include corporate critics, social investors, activists, and, increasingly, customers who claim to assess corporate responsibility when making purchasing decisions. Such demands go well beyond product and service quality.[55] They include a focus on issues such as labor standards, environmental sustainability, financial and accounting reporting, procurement, and environmental practices.[56] At times, a firm's reputation can be tarnished by exceedingly poor judgment on the part of one of its managers.

> In 2006, Judith Regan, a publisher at HarperCollins, was set to publish a book by O. J. Simpson called *If I Did It,* detailing how he would have committed the 1995 murder of his ex-wife Nicole Brown Simpson and her friend, Ron Goldman. The book was characterized by Regan as O. J.'s "confession," and it earned the world's outrage as an "evil sweeps stunt" that will likely be remembered as a low point in American culture. Regan's boss, News Corporation Chairman Rupert Murdoch cancelled the book and the TV special that was also planned. But this was not before pre-orders for *If I Did It* cracked the Top 20 on Amazon.com. Not surprisingly, Judith Regan was fired.[57]

A key stakeholder group that appears to be particularly susceptible to corporate social responsibility (CSR) initiatives is customers.[58] Surveys indicate a strong positive relationship between CSR behaviors and consumers' reactions to a firm's products and services.[59] For example:

- Corporate Citizenship's poll conducted by Cone Communications found that "84 percent of Americans say they would be likely to switch brands to one associated with a good cause, if price and quality are similar."[60]
- Hill & Knowlton/Harris's Interactive poll reveals that "79 percent of Americans take corporate citizenship into account when deciding whether to buy a particular company's product and 37 percent consider corporate citizenship an important factor when making purchasing decisions."[61]

Such findings are consistent with a large body of research that confirms the positive influence of CSR on consumers' company evaluations and product purchase intentions across a broad range of product categories.

The Triple Bottom Line: Incorporating Financial as well as Environmental and Social Costs
Many companies are now measuring what has been called a **"triple bottom line."** This involves assessing financial, social, and environmental performance. Shell, NEC, Procter & Gamble, and others have recognized that failing to account for the environmental and social costs of doing business poses risks to the company and its community.[62]

The environmental revolution has been almost four decades in the making.[63] In the 1960s and 1970s, companies were in a state of denial regarding their firms' impact on the natural environment. However, a series of visible ecological problems created a groundswell for strict governmental regulation. In the U.S., Lake Erie was "dead," and in Japan, people died of mercury poisoning. Clearly, the effects of global warming are being felt throughout the world. Some other examples include the following:

- Ice roads are melting, so Canadian diamond miners must airlift equipment at great cost instead of trucking it in.
- More severe storms and rising seas mean oil companies must build stronger rigs, and cities must build higher seawalls.

Triple bottom line Assessment of a firm's financial, social, and environmental performance.

- The loss of permafrost and protective sea ice may force villages like Alaska's Shismaref to relocate.
- Yukon River salmon and fisheries are threatened by a surge of parasites associated with a jump in water temperature.
- Later winters have let beetles spread in British Columbia killing 22 million acres of pine forests, an area the size of Maine.
- In Mali, Africa, crops are threatened. The rainy season is now too short for rice, and the dry season is too hot for potatoes.[64]

Stuart Hart, writing in the *Harvard Business Review,* addresses the magnitude of problems and challenges associated with the natural environment:

> The challenge is to develop a *sustainable global economy:* an economy that the planet is capable of supporting indefinitely. Although we may be approaching ecological recovery in the developed world, the planet as a whole remains on an unsustainable course. Increasingly, the scourges of the late twentieth century—depleted farmland, fisheries, and forests; choking urban pollution; poverty; infectious disease; and migration—are spilling over geopolitical borders. The simple fact is this: in meeting our needs, we are destroying the ability of future generations to meet theirs ... corporations are the only organizations with the resources, the technology, the global reach, and, ultimately, the motivation to achieve sustainability.[65]

● These parabolic mirrors in a California desert focus solar energy. Solar power is a more sustainable, environmentally friendly option than nuclear power plants or coal- and oil-fired power plants.

Environmental sustainability is now a value embraced by the most competitive and successful multinational companies.[66] The McKinsey Corporation's survey of more than 400 senior executives of companies around the world found that 92 percent agreed with former Sony President Akio Morita's contention that the environmental challenge will be one of the central issues in the 21st century.[67] Virtually all executives acknowledged their firm's responsibility to control pollution, and 83 percent agreed that corporations have an environmental responsibility for their products even after they are sold.

For many successful firms, environmental values are now becoming a central part of their cultures and management processes. And, as noted earlier, environmental impacts are being audited and accounted for as the "third bottom line." According to one 2004 corporate report, "If we aren't good corporate citizens as reflected in a Triple Bottom Line that takes into account social and environmental responsibilities along with financial ones—eventually our stock price, our profits, and our entire business could suffer."[68] And, according to a KPMG study of 350 firms: "More big multinational firms are seeing the benefits of improving their environmental performance. ... Firms are saving money and boosting share performance by taking a close look at how their operations impact the environment ... Companies see that they can make money as well." Strategy Spotlight 1.6 discusses how Shaw Industries benefits financially from its environmental initiatives.

Shaw Industries: It Pays to Go Green

Shaw Industries, a Berkshire Hathaway company, produces carpet tile—industrial flooring that is installed in office buildings around the world. In 1999, Shaw was confronted by growing environmental concern over carpet waste (more than 95 percent of old carpet is ripped up and dumped in landfills) and the specter of higher raw-materials costs. Its response: embark on a major initiative to rethink its business and create what it calls "the carpet of the twenty-first century."

Carpet tile like Shaw's consists of the backing, which holds the carpet flat, and the face fiber, which creates the soft walking surface. Prior to 1995 Shaw produced a branded backing made from PVC plastic—a potentially toxic substance that is difficult to recycle. So, at substantial expense, the firm searched for a more sustainable solution.

Based on an intuitive understanding of sustainability, Shaw recognized the need for a simple palette of nontoxic materials for its product. It also made virtuous recycling a goal. Its choice of Nylon 6 face fiber, branded Eco Solution Q, and a polyolefin backing, called EcoWorx, gave Shaw materials that could be cycled from high-value application to high-value application without ever losing performance or functionality.

The company developed an integrated production system that could take carpet at the end of its useful life, separate the backing, grind it up, and put it right back into the manufacturing process. Coming out at the other end was brand-new carpet tile. The Environmental Protection Agency (EPA) recognized EcoWorx with its Presidential Green Chemistry Challenge Award in 2003. The next year, Shaw exited from PVC carpet backing not only because of environmental sustainability issues but also because 70 percent of their customers selected the new technology. As of 2008, Shaw had 500 million square feet of EcoWorx installed around the world. According to Randy Merritt, Executive Vice President of Marketing:

> EcoWorx meets customer demand for a PVC alternative product and provides a sustainable flooring solution that makes good economic, functional and environmental sense for all stakeholders.

Another key benefit was that Shaw's sustainable product platform also helped free the company from the vagaries of the raw-materials markets that plague the industry. Petroleum is the primary input for both the backing and the fiber used in most products, and when Shaw began its efforts oil was at $19 a barrel. Given that oil has typically traded at several times that figure in recent years, Shaw seems like a savvy visionary. In essence, Shaw can look to a future when the skyscrapers of the world's cities, rather than the wellheads of Saudi Arabia, will supply its raw materials!

Source: Unruh, G. C. 2008. The biosphere rules. *Harvard Business Review,* 86 (2): 111–117; www.shawgreenedge.com; and, Allmond, K. 2004. Shaw ceases production of polyvinyl chloride, replacement carpet tile backing recognized by the EPA. Shaw Industries Press Release, June 14.

environmental sustainability

The Strategic Management Perspective: An Imperative throughout the Organization

Strategic management requires managers to take an integrative view of the organization and assess how all of the functional areas and activities fit together to help an organization achieve its goals and objectives. This cannot be accomplished if only the top managers in the organization take an integrative, strategic perspective of issues facing the firm and everyone else "fends for themselves" in their independent, isolated functional areas. Instead, people throughout the organization must strive toward overall goals.

The need for such a perspective is accelerating in today's increasingly complex, interconnected, ever-changing, global economy. As noted by Peter Senge of MIT, the days when Henry Ford, Alfred Sloan, and Tom Watson (top executives at Ford, General Motors, and IBM, respectively) "learned for the organization are gone." He goes on to say:

> In an increasingly dynamic, interdependent, and unpredictable world, it is simply no longer possible for anyone to "figure it all out at the top." The old model, "the top thinks and the

local acts," must now give way to integrating thinking and acting at all levels. While the challenge is great, so is the potential payoff. "The person who figures out how to harness the collective genius of the people in his or her organization," according to former Citibank CEO Walter Wriston, "is going to blow the competition away."[69]

To develop and mobilize people and other assets, leaders are needed throughout the organization.[70] No longer can organizations be effective if the top "does the thinking" and the rest of the organization "does the work." Everyone must be involved in the strategic management process. There is a critical need for three types of leaders:

- *Local line leaders* who have significant profit-and-loss responsibility.
- *Executive leaders* who champion and guide ideas, create a learning infrastructure, and establish a domain for taking action.
- *Internal networkers* who, although they have little positional power and formal authority, generate their power through the conviction and clarity of their ideas.[71]

Sally Helgesen, author of *The Web of Inclusion: A New Architecture for Building Great Organizations,* also expressed the need for leaders throughout the organization. She asserted that many organizations "fall prey to the heroes-and-drones syndrome, exalting the value of those in powerful positions while implicitly demeaning the contributions of those who fail to achieve top rank."[72] Culture and processes in which leaders emerge at all levels, both up and down as well as across the organization, typify today's high-performing firms.[73]

Top-level executives are key in setting the tone for the empowerment of employees. Consider Richard Branson, founder of the Virgin Group, whose core businesses include retail operations, hotels, communications, and an airline. He is well known for creating a culture and an informal structure where anybody in the organization can be involved in generating and acting upon new business ideas. In an interview, he stated,

> [S]peed is something that we are better at than most companies. We don't have formal board meetings, committees, etc. If someone has an idea, they can pick up the phone and talk to me. I can vote "done, let's do it." Or, better still, they can just go ahead and do it. They know that they are not going to get a mouthful from me if they make a mistake. Rules and regulations are not our forte. Analyzing things to death is not our kind of thing. We very rarely sit back and analyze what we do.[74]

To inculcate a strategic management perspective throughout the organization, managers must often make a major effort to effect transformational change. This involves extensive communication, incentives, training, and development. For example, under the direction of Nancy Snyder, a corporate vice president, Whirlpool, the world's largest producer of household appliances, brought about a significant shift in the firm's reputation as an innovator.[75] This five-year initiative included both financial investments in capital spending as well as a series of changes in management processes, including training innovation mentors, making innovation a significant portion of leadership development programs, enrolling all salaried employees in online courses in business innovation, and providing employees with an innovation portal that allows them access to multiple innovation tools and data. We discuss Whirlpool's initiatives in more detail in Chapter 11.

We'd like to close with our favorite example of how inexperience can be a virtue. It further reinforces the benefits of having broad involvement throughout the organization in the strategic management process (see Strategy Spotlight 1.7).

Ensuring Coherence in Strategic Direction

Employees and managers throughout the organization must strive toward common goals and objectives. By specifying desired results, it becomes much easier to move forward. Otherwise, when no one knows what the firm is striving to accomplish, they have no idea of what to work toward.

>LO6
How an awareness of a hierarchy of strategic goals can help an organization achieve coherence in its strategic direction.

Strategy and the Value of Inexperience

Peter Gruber, chairman of Mandalay Entertainment, explained how his firm benefited from the creative insights of an inexperienced intern.

> Sometimes life is all about solving problems. In the movie business, at least, there seems to be one around every corner. One of the most effective lessons I've learned about tackling problems is to start by asking not "How to?" but rather "What if?" I learned that lesson from a young woman who was interning on a film I was producing. She actually saved the movie from being shelved by the studio.
>
> The movie, *Gorillas in the Mist,* had turned into a logistical nightmare. We wanted to film at an altitude of 11,000 feet, in the middle of the jungle, in Rwanda—then on the verge of a revolution—and to use more than 200 animals. Warner Brothers, the studio financing the movie, worried that we would exceed our budget. But our biggest problem was that the screenplay required the gorillas to do what we wrote—in other words, to "act." If they couldn't or wouldn't, we'd have to fall back on a formula that the studio had seen fail before: using dwarfs in gorilla suits on a soundstage.

Source: Gruber, P. 1998. My greatest lesson. *Fast Company* 15: 88, 90.

> We called an emergency meeting to solve these problems. In the middle of it, a young intern asked, "What if you let the gorillas write the story?" Everyone laughed and wondered what she was doing in the meeting with experienced filmmakers. Hours later, someone casually asked her what she had meant. She said, "What if you sent a really good cinematographer into the jungle with a ton of film to shoot the gorillas. Then you could write a story around what the gorillas did on film." It was a brilliant idea. And we did exactly what she suggested: We sent Alan Root, an Academy Award–nominated cinematographer, into the jungle for three weeks. He came back with phenomenal footage that practically wrote the story for us. We shot the film for $20 million—half of the original budget!
>
> This woman's inexperience enabled her to see opportunities where we saw only boundaries. This experience taught me three things. First, ask high-quality questions, like "What if?" Second, find people who add new perspectives and create new conversations. As experienced filmmakers, we believed that our way was the only way—and that the intern lacked the experience to have an opinion. Third, pay attention to those with new voices. If you want unlimited options for solving a problem, engage the what if before you lock onto the how to. You'll be surprised by what you discover.

hierarchy of goals organizational goals ranging from, at the top, those that are less specific yet able to evoke powerful and compelling mental images, to, at the bottom, those that are more specific and measurable.

Organizations express priorities best through stated goals and objectives that form a **hierarchy of goals,** which includes its vision, mission, and strategic objectives.[76] What visions may lack in specificity, they make up for in their ability to evoke powerful and compelling mental images. On the other hand, strategic objectives tend to be more specific and provide a more direct means of determining if the organization is moving toward broader, overall goals.[77] Visions, as one would expect, also have longer time horizons than either mission statements or strategic objectives. Exhibit 1.6 depicts the hierarchy of goals and its relationship to two attributes: general versus specific and time horizon.

Organizational Vision

vision organizational goal(s) that evoke(s) powerful and compelling mental images.

A **vision** is a goal that is "massively inspiring, overarching, and long term."[78] It represents a destination that is driven by and evokes passion. A vision may or may not succeed; it depends on whether everything else happens according to a firm's strategy. As Mark Hurd, Hewlett-Packard's CEO, humorously pointed out, "Without execution, vision is just another word for hallucination."[79]

Leaders must develop and implement a vision. In a survey of executives from 20 different countries, respondents were asked what they believed were a leader's key traits.[80]

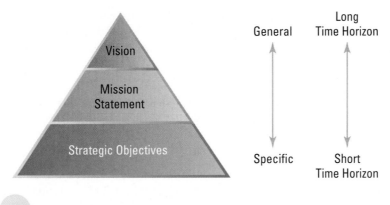

Exhibit 1.6   A Hierarchy of Goals

Ninety-eight percent responded that "a strong sense of vision" was the most important. Similarly, when asked about the critical knowledge skills, the leaders cited "strategy formulation to achieve a vision" as the most important skill. In other words, managers need to have not only a vision but also a plan to implement it. Regretfully, 90 percent reported a lack of confidence in their own skills and ability to conceive a vision. For example, T. J. Rogers, CEO of Cypress Semiconductor, an electronic chipmaker that faced some difficulties in 1992, lamented that his own shortsightedness caused the danger, "I did not have the 50,000-foot view, and got caught."[81]

One of the most famous examples of a vision is Disneyland's: "To be the happiest place on earth." Other examples are:

- "Restoring patients to full life." (Medtronic)
- "We want to satisfy all of our customers' financial needs and help them succeed financially." (Wells Fargo)
- "Our vision is to be the world's best quick service restaurant." (McDonald's)
- "To organize the world's information and make it universally accessible and useful." (Google)

Although such visions cannot be accurately measured by a specific indicator of how well they are being achieved, they do provide a fundamental statement of an organization's values, aspirations, and goals. Such visions go well beyond narrow financial objectives, of course, and strive to capture both the minds and hearts of employees.

The vision statement may also contain a slogan, diagram, or picture—whatever grabs attention.[82] The aim is to capture the essence of the more formal parts of the vision in a few words that are easily remembered, yet that evoke the spirit of the entire vision statement. In its 20-year battle with Xerox, Canon's slogan, or battle cry, was "Beat Xerox." Motorola's slogan is "Total Customer Satisfaction." Outboard Marine Corporation's slogan is "To Take the World Boating."

Clearly, vision statements are not a cure-all. Sometimes they backfire and erode a company's credibility. Visions fail for many reasons, including the following:[83]

The Walk Doesn't Match the Talk   An idealistic vision can arouse employee enthusiasm. However, that same enthusiasm can be quickly dashed if employees find that senior management's behavior is not consistent with the vision. Often, vision is a sloganeering campaign of new buzzwords and empty platitudes like "devotion to the customer," "teamwork," or "total quality" that aren't consistently backed by management's action.

Irrelevance   Visions created in a vacuum—unrelated to environmental threats or opportunities or an organization's resources and capabilities—often ignore the needs of those who are expected to buy into them. Employees reject visions that are not anchored in reality.

Not the Holy Grail   Managers often search continually for the one elusive solution that will solve their firm's problems—that is, the next "holy grail" of management. They may have tried other management fads only to find that they fell short of their expectations. However, they remain convinced that one exists. A vision simply cannot be viewed as a magic cure for an organization's illness.

Too Much Focus Leads to Missed Opportunities   The downside of too much focus is that in directing people and resources toward a grandiose vision, losses can be devastating. Consider, Samsung's ambitious venture into automobile manufacturing:

> In 1992, Kun-Hee Lee, chairman of South Korea's Samsung Group, created a bold strategy to become one of the 10 largest car makers by 2010. Seduced by the clarity of the vision, Samsung bypassed staged entry through a joint venture or initial supply contract. Instead, Samsung borrowed heavily to build a state-of-the-art research and design facility and erect a greenfield factory, complete with cutting-edge robotics. Samsung Auto suffered operating losses and crushing interest charges from the beginning. And within a few years the business was divested for a fraction of the initial investment.[84]

An Ideal Future Irreconciled with the Present   Although visions are not designed to mirror reality, they must be anchored somehow in it. People have difficulty identifying with a vision that paints a rosy picture of the future but does not account for the often hostile environment in which the firm competes or that ignores some of the firm's weaknesses.

Mission Statements

mission statement
a set of organizational goals that include both the purpose of the organization, its scope of operations, and the basis of its competitive advantage.

A company's **mission statement** differs from its vision in that it encompasses both the purpose of the company as well as the basis of competition and competitive advantage.

Exhibit 1.7 contains the vision statement and mission statement of WellPoint Health Network, a giant $61 billion managed health care organization. Note that while the vision statement is broad based, the mission statement is more specific and focused on the means by which the firm will compete.

Effective mission statements incorporate the concept of stakeholder management, suggesting that organizations must respond to multiple constituencies. Customers, employees, suppliers, and owners are the primary stakeholders, but others may also play an important role.

Exhibit 1.7
Comparing WellPoint Health Network's Vision and Mission

Vision
WellPoint *will redefine our industry:*
Through a new generation of consumer-friendly products that put individuals back in control of their future.

Mission
The WellPoint companies provide health *security* by offering a *choice* of quality branded health and related financial services *designed* to meet the *changing* expectations of individuals, families, and their sponsors throughout a *lifelong* relationship.

Source: WellPoint Health Network company records.

Mission statements also have the greatest impact when they reflect an organization's enduring, overarching strategic priorities and competitive positioning. Mission statements also can vary in length and specificity. The two mission statements below illustrate these issues.

- To produce superior financial returns for our shareholders as we serve our customers with the highest quality transportation, logistics, and e-commerce. (Federal Express)
- To be the very best in the business. Our game plan is status go . . . we are constantly looking ahead, building on our strengths, and reaching for new goals. In our quest of these goals, we look at the three stars of the Brinker logo and are reminded of the basic values that are the strength of this company . . . People, Quality and Profitability. Everything we do at Brinker must support these core values. We also look at the eight golden flames depicted in our logo, and are reminded of the fire that ignites our mission and makes up the heart and soul of this incredible company. These flames are: Customers, Food, Team, Concepts, Culture, Partners, Community, and Shareholders. As keeper of these flames, we will continue to build on our strengths and work together to be the best in the business. (Brinker International, whose restaurant chains include Chili's and On the Border)[85]

Few mission statements identify profit or any other financial indicator as the sole purpose of the firm. Indeed, many do not even mention profit or shareholder return.[86] Employees of organizations or departments are usually the mission's most important audience. For them, the mission should help to build a common understanding of purpose and commitment to nurture.

A good mission statement, by addressing each principal theme, must communicate why an organization is special and different. Two studies that linked corporate values and mission statements with financial performance found that the most successful firms mentioned values other than profits. The less successful firms focused almost entirely on profitability.[87] In essence, profit is the metaphorical equivalent of oxygen, food, and water that the body requires. They are not the point of life, but without them, there is no life.

Although vision statements tend to be quite enduring and seldom change, a firm's mission can and should change when competitive conditions dramatically change or the firm is faced with new threats or opportunities. Strategy Spotlight 1.8 provides an example of a firm, NextJet, that changed its mission in order to realize new opportunities.

Strategic Objectives

Strategic objectives are used to operationalize the mission statement.[88] That is, they help to provide guidance on how the organization can fulfill or move toward the "higher goals" in the goal hierarchy—the mission and vision. Thus, they are more specific and cover a more well-defined time frame. Setting objectives demands a yardstick to measure the fulfillment of the objectives.[89]

Exhibit 1.8 lists several firms' strategic objectives—both financial and nonfinancial. While most of them are directed toward generating greater profits and returns for the owners of the business, others are directed at customers or society at large.

For objectives to be meaningful, they need to satisfy several criteria. They must be:

- *Measurable.* There must be at least one indicator (or yardstick) that measures progress against fulfilling the objective.
- *Specific.* This provides a clear message as to what needs to be accomplished.
- *Appropriate.* It must be consistent with the organization's vision and mission.
- *Realistic.* It must be an achievable target given the organization's capabilities and opportunities in the environment. In essence, it must be challenging but doable.
- *Timely.* There must be a time frame for achieving the objective. As the economist John Maynard Keynes once said, "In the long run, we are all dead!"

NextJet's Change of Mission

The dot-com crash was only the first blow to NextJet, Inc., a Dallas-based business launched in 1999 to ship packages overnight. The bigger blow came with the September 11 terrorist attacks, when passenger airlines were forced to add security and reduce flights. One of NextJet's strengths was its nationwide network of local courier services that got packages to and from airports, all coordinated through their proprietary software that could determine the optimal routing. However, the company's business model fell apart when it could not rely on the airlines to get packages between cities quickly enough to make the added cost for same-day delivery worthwhile.

Rather than give up, NextJet reinvented the business around the idea that its most important asset was the software itself. The company's new mission received almost

Sources: Goldstein, A. 2002. NextJet is hoping that its software can deliver. *Dallas Morning News,* December 4: 1–3; Nelson, M. G. 2001. NextJet network adds wireless. *Information Week,* April 30: 34; Anonymous. 2004. Who's who in e-logistics. www.americanshipper.com, September; and Hudspeth, B., & Jones, J. 2004. Service parts and logistics: Should you in-source or outsource? *3pl line,* www.inboundlogistics.com, October.

immediate validation when its software was deployed successfully at United Parcel Service (UPS). NextJet's software provides Atlanta-based UPS with tools for setting online rates and tracking packages. While a lot of same-day business did evaporate when corporations tightened the reins on spending, some things can't wait overnight to be shipped. For example, makers of hospital equipment may need to ship critical parts within a few hours. NextJet's software can help shippers make important decisions in less than a second, finding the fastest and most economical route among air, truck, and courier operations. In addition to UPS, its customers include FedEx, Greyhound, and Menlo Worldwide.

NextJet serves a very large industry segment—Service Parts & Logistics (SPL). The annual expenditures for spare parts in the United States are estimated to be $500 billion. And managers have increased their focus on the importance of effective logistics operations, given its potential impact on a firm's income. After all, whether or not a production line is running can often depend on the quick and effective installation of relatively inexpensive spare parts.

Exhibit 1.8
Strategic Objectives

Strategic Objectives (Financial)

- Increase sales growth 6 percent to 8 percent and accelerate core net earnings growth from 13 percent to 15 percent per share in each of the next 5 years. (Procter & Gamble)
- Generate Internet-related revenue of $1.5 billion. (AutoNation)
- Increase the contribution of Banking Group earnings from investments, brokerage, and insurance from 16 percent to 25 percent. (Wells Fargo)
- Cut corporate overhead costs by $30 million per year. (Fortune Brands)

Strategic Objectives (Nonfinancial)

- We want a majority of our customers, when surveyed, to say they consider Wells Fargo the best financial institution in the community. (Wells Fargo)
- We want to operate 6,000 stores by 2010—up from 3,000 in the year 2000. (Walgreen's)
- We want to be the top-ranked supplier to our customers. (PPG)
- Reduce greenhouse gases by 10 percent (from a 1990 base) by 2010. (BP Amoco)

Sources: Company documents and annual reports.

When objectives satisfy the above criteria, there are many benefits. First, they help to channel all employees' efforts toward common goals. This helps the organization concentrate and conserve valuable resources and work collectively in a timely manner.

Second, challenging objectives can help to motivate and inspire employees to higher levels of commitment and effort. Much research has supported the notion that people work harder when they are striving toward specific goals instead of being asked simply to "do their best."

Third, as we noted earlier in the chapter, there is always the potential for different parts of an organization to pursue their own goals rather than overall company goals. Although well intentioned, these may work at cross-purposes to the organization as a whole. Meaningful objectives thus help to resolve conflicts when they arise.

Finally, proper objectives provide a yardstick for rewards and incentives. They will ensure a greater sense of equity or fairness when rewards are allocated.

In summary, an organization must take care to ensure consistency throughout in how it implements strategic objectives. Consider how Textron, a $13 billion conglomerate, ensures that its corporate goals are effectively implemented:

> At Textron, each business unit identifies "improvement priorities" that it must act upon to realize the performance outlined in the firm's overall strategic plan. Each improvement priority is translated into action items with clearly defined accountabilities, timetables, and key performance indicators (KPIs) that enable executives to tell how a unit is delivering on a priority. Improvement priorities and action items cascade to every level at the firm—from the management committee (consisting of Textron's top five executives) down to the lowest levels in each of the company's 10 business units. Says Lewis Campbell, Textron's CEO, "Everyone needs to know: 'If I have only one hour to work, here's what I'm going to focus on.' Our goal deployment process makes each individual's accountabilities and priorities clear."[90]

As indicated in this example, organizations have lower-level objectives that are more specific than strategic objectives. These are often referred to as short-term objectives—essential components of a firm's "action plan" that are critical in implementing the firm's chosen strategy. We discuss these issues in detail in Chapter 9.

Reflecting on Career Implications . . .

- *Attributes of Strategic Management:* How do your activities and actions contribute to the goals of your organization? Observe the decisions you make on the job. What are the short-term and long-term implications of your decisions and actions? Have you recently made a decision that might yield short-term profits but might negatively impact the long-term goals of the organization (e.g., cutting maintenance expenses to meet a quarterly profit target)?
- *Intended versus Emergent Strategies:* Don't be too inflexible in your career strategies; strive to take advantage of new opportunities as they arise. Many promising career opportunities may "emerge" that were not part of your intended career strategy or your specific job assignment. Take initiative by pursuing opportunities to get additional training (e.g., learn a software or a statistical package), volunteering for a short-term overseas assignment, etc.
- *Ambidexterity:* Avoid defining your role in the organization too narrowly; look for opportunities to leverage your talents and your organization's resources to create value for your organization. This often involves collaborating with people in other departments or with your organization's customers and suppliers.
- *Strategic Coherence:* Focus your efforts on the "big picture" in your organization. In doing this, you should always strive to assure that your efforts are directed toward your organization's vision, mission, and strategic objectives.

Summary

We began this introductory chapter by defining strategic management and articulating some of its key attributes. Strategic management is defined as "consisting of the analyses, decisions, and actions an organization undertakes to create and sustain competitive advantages." The issue of how and why some firms outperform others in the marketplace is central to the study of strategic management. Strategic management has four key attributes: It is directed at overall organizational goals, includes multiple stakeholders, incorporates both short-term and long-term perspectives, and incorporates trade-offs between efficiency and effectiveness.

The second section discussed the strategic management process. Here, we paralleled the above definition of strategic management and focused on three core activities in the strategic management process—strategy analysis, strategy formulation, and strategy implementation. We noted how each of these activities is highly interrelated to and interdependent on the others. We also discussed how each of the 12 chapters in this text fits into the three core activities.

Next, we introduced two important concepts—corporate governance and stakeholder management—which must be taken into account throughout the strategic management process. Governance mechanisms can be broadly divided into two groups: internal and external. Internal governance mechanisms include shareholders (owners), management (led by the chief executive officer), and the board of directors. External control is exercised by auditors, banks, analysts, and an active business press as well as the threat of takeovers. We identified five key stakeholders in all organizations: owners, customers, suppliers, employees, and society at large. Successful firms go beyond an overriding focus on satisfying solely the interests of owners. Rather, they recognize the inherent conflicts that arise among the demands of the various stakeholders as well as the need to endeavor to attain "symbiosis"—that is, interdependence and mutual benefit—among the various stakeholder groups. The emerging practice of crowdsourcing, wherein the Internet is used to generate ideas and solve problems, is leading to an evolution in stakeholder roles. Managers must also recognize the need to act in a socially responsible manner which, if done effectively, can enhance a firm's innovativeness. They also should recognize and incorporate issues related to environmental sustainability in their strategic actions.

In the fourth section, we discussed factors that have accelerated the rate of unpredictable change that managers face today. Such factors, and the combination of them, have increased the need for managers and employees throughout the organization to have a strategic management perspective and to become more empowered.

The final section addressed the need for consistency among a firm's vision, mission, and strategic objectives. Collectively, they form an organization's hierarchy of goals. Visions should evoke powerful and compelling mental images. However, they are not very specific. Strategic objectives, on the other hand, are much more specific and are vital to ensuring that the organization is striving toward fulfilling its vision and mission.

Summary Review Questions

1. How is "strategic management" defined in the text, and what are its four key attributes?
2. Briefly discuss the three key activities in the strategic management process. Why is it important for managers to recognize the interdependent nature of these activities?
3. Explain the concept of "stakeholder management." Why shouldn't managers be solely interested in stockholder management, that is, maximizing the returns for owners of the firm—its shareholders?
4. What is "corporate governance"? What are its three key elements and how can it be improved?
5. How can "symbiosis" (interdependence, mutual benefit) be achieved among a firm's stakeholders?
6. Why do firms need to have a greater strategic management perspective and empowerment in the strategic management process throughout the organization?
7. What is meant by a "hierarchy of goals"? What are the main components of it, and why must consistency be achieved among them?

Key Terms

romantic view of
   leadership,   5
external view of
   leadership,   6
strategic management,   9
strategy   9
competitive
   advantage   9
operational
   effectiveness,   9
stakeholders,   10
effectiveness,   11
efficiency,   11

ambidexterity,   11
intended strategy,   13
realized strategy,   13
corporate governance,   17
stakeholder
   management   18
crowdsourcing,   19
social responsibility,   21
triple bottom line,   22
hierarchy of goals,   26
vision,   26
mission statement,   28
strategic objectives,   29

Experiential Exercise

Using the Internet or library sources, select four organizations—two in the private sector and two in the public sector. Find their mission statements. Complete the following exhibit by identifying the stakeholders that are mentioned. Evaluate the differences between firms in the private sector and those in the public sector.

Name			
Mission Statement			
Stakeholders (✓ = mentioned)			
1. Customers			
2. Suppliers			
3. Managers/employees			
4. Community-at-large			
5. Owners			
6. Others?			
7. Others?			

Application Questions Exercises

1. Go to the Internet and look up one of these company sites: www.walmart.com, www.ge.com, or www.fordmotor.com. What are some of the key events that would represent the "romantic" perspective of leadership? What are some of the key events that depict the "external control" perspective of leadership?

2. Select a company that competes in an industry in which you are interested. What are some of the recent demands that stakeholders have placed on this company? Can you find examples of how the company is trying to develop "symbiosis" (interdependence and mutual benefit) among its stakeholders? (Use the Internet and library resources.)

3. Provide examples of companies that are actively trying to increase the amount of empowerment in the strategic management process throughout the organization. Do these companies seem to be having positive outcomes? Why? Why not?

4. Look up the vision statements and/or mission statements for a few companies. Do you feel that they are constructive and useful as a means of motivating employees and providing a strong strategic direction? Why? Why not? (*Note:* Annual reports, along with the Internet, may be good sources of information.)

Ethics Questions

1. A company focuses solely on short-term profits to provide the greatest return to the owners of the business (i.e., the shareholders in a publicly held firm). What ethical issues could this raise?

2. A firm has spent some time—with input from managers at all levels—in developing a vision statement and a mission statement. Over time, however, the behavior of some executives is contrary to these statements. Could this raise some ethical issues?

References

1. Collins, J. 2008. The secret of enduring greatness. *Fortune,* May 5: 74. It is interesting to note that a 2008 article in the *Academy of Management Perspectives* (Resnick, B. G. & Smut, T. J. From good to great. 22 [4]: 6–12) found that only 1 of the 11 companies that Collins identified as "great" in his best-selling book *Good to Great* continued to exhibit superior stock market performance according to Collins' own measure. This provides further evidence regarding the difficulty in sustaining excellence in today's global marketplace.

2. Brooker, K. 2008. The day $2 billion walked out the door. *Fortune,* April 14: 99–106; Craig, S., Zuckerman, G., & Karnitschnig, M. 2007. Why Citadel pounced on wounded E*Trade. *The Wall Street Journal,* November 30: A1, A12; Craig, S. 2007. E*Trade to get help from Citadel. *The Wall Street Journal,* November 29: A3; Craig, S. 2007. E*Trade plunges 59% on analyst's warnings; bank unit goes awry. *The Wall Street Journal,* November 13: A1; A21; Weber, J. E*Trade rises from the ashes. *BusinessWeek,* January 17: 58–59; and, Schmerken, I. 2004. Innovation in motion. *Wall Street & Technology,* October 22–26: np. We'd like to note that in Chapter 5 of our previous edition of *Strategic Management,* we—like the business press—wrote about Caplan's remarkable turnaround.

3. For a discussion of the "romantic" versus "external control" perspective, refer to Meindl, J. R. 1987. The romance of leadership and the evaluation of organizational performance. *Academy of Management Journal* 30: 92–109; and Pfeffer, J. & Salancik, G. R. 1978. *The external control of organizations: A resource dependence perspective.* New York: Harper & Row.

4. A recent perspective on the "romantic view" of leadership is provided by Mintzberg, H. 2004. Leadership and management development: An afterword. *Academy of Management Executive,* 18(3): 140–142.

5. For a discussion of the best and worst managers for 2008, read: Anonymous. 2009. The best managers. *BusinessWeeek,* January 19: 40–41; and, The worst managers. On page 42 in the same issue.

6. Burrows, P. 2009. Apple without its core? *BusinessWeek.* January 26/February 2: 31.

7. For a study on the effects of CEOs on firm performance, refer to: Kor, Y. Y. & Misangyi, V. F. 2008. *Strategic Management Journal,* 29 (11): 1357–1368.

8. Ewing, J. 2008. South Africa emerges from the shadows. *BusinessWeek.* December 15: 52–56.

9. For an interesting perspective on the need for strategists to maintain a global mind-set, refer to Begley, T. M. & Boyd, D. P. 2003. The need for a global mind-set. *MIT Sloan Management Review* 44(2): 25–32.

10. Porter, M. E. 1996. What is strategy? *Harvard Business Review* 74(6): 61–78.

11. See, for example, Barney, J. B. & Arikan, A. M. 2001. The resource-based view: Origins and implications. In Hitt, M. A., Freeman, R. E., & Harrison, J. S. (Eds.), *Handbook of strategic management:* 124–189. Malden, MA: Blackwell.

12. Porter, M. E. 1996. What is strategy? *Harvard Business Review,* 74(6): 61–78; and Hammonds, K. H. 2001. Michael Porter's big ideas. *Fast Company,* March: 55–56.

13. This section draws upon Dess, G. G. & Miller, A. 1993. *Strategic management.* New York: McGraw-Hill.

14. See, for example, Hrebiniak, L. G. & Joyce, W. F. 1986. The strategic importance of managing myopia. *Sloan Management Review,* 28(1): 5–14.

15. For an insightful discussion on how to manage diverse stakeholder groups, refer to Rondinelli, D. A. & London, T. 2003. How corporations and environmental groups cooperate: Assessing cross-sector alliances and collaborations. *Academy of Management Executive,* 17(1): 61–76.

16. Some dangers of a short-term perspective are addressed in: Van Buren, M. E. & Safferstone, T. 2009. The quick wins paradox. *Harvard Business Review,* 67(1): 54–61.

17. Senge, P. 1996. Leading learning organizations: The bold, the powerful, and the invisible. In Hesselbein, F., Goldsmith, M., & Beckhard, R. (Eds.), *The leader of the future:* 41–58. San Francisco: Jossey-Bass.

18. Samuelson, J. 2006. A critical mass for the long term. *Harvard Business Review,* 84(2): 62, 64; and, Anonymous. 2007. Power play. *The Economist,* January 20: 10–12.

19. Loeb, M. 1994. Where leaders come from. *Fortune,* September 19: 241 (quoting Warren Bennis).

20. Address by Norman R. Augustine at the Crummer Business School, Rollins College, Winter Park, FL, October 20, 1989.

21. Hemp, P. 2004. An Interview with CEO Kevin Sharer. *Harvard Business Review,* 82(7/8): 66–74.

22. New perspectives on "management models" are addressed in: Birkinshaw, J. & Goddard, J. 2009. What is your management model? *MIT Sloan Management Review,* 50 (2): 81–90.

23. Mintzberg, H. 1985. Of strategies: Deliberate and emergent. *Strategic Management Journal,* 6: 257–272.

24. Some interesting insights on decision-making processes are found in: Nutt, P. C. 2008. Investigating the success of decision making processes. *Journal of Management Studies,* 45(2): 425–455.

25. Aston, A. 2009. How to bet on cleantech. *BusinessWeek,* January 5: 70–71.

26. A study investigating the sustainability of competitive advantage is: Newbert, S. L. 2008. Value, rareness, competitive advantages, and performance: A conceptual-level empirical investigation of the resource-based view of the firm. *Strategic Management Journal,* 29(7): 745–768.

27. Good insights on mentoring are addressed in: DeLong, T. J., Gabarro, J. J., & Lees, R. J. 2008. Why mentoring matters in a hypercompetitive world. *Harvard Business Review,* 66(1): 115–121.

28. A unique perspective on differentiation strategies is: Austin, R. D. 2008. High margins and the quest for aesthetic coherence. *Harvard Business Review,* 86(1): 18–19.

29. Some insights on partnering in the global area are discussed in: MacCormack, A. & Forbath, T. 2008. *Harvard Business Review,* 66(1): 24, 26.

30. An interesting discussion of the challenges of strategy implementation is: Neilson, G. L., Martin, K. L., & Powers, E. 2008. The secrets of strategy execution. *Harvard Business Review,* 86(6): 61–70.

31. Interesting perspectives on strategy execution involving the link between strategy and operations are addressed in: Kaplan, R. S. & Norton, D.P. 2008. Mastering the management system. *Harvard Business Review,* 66(1): 62–77.

32. An innovative perspective on organizational design is found in: Garvin, D. A. & Levesque, L. C. 2008. The multiunit enterprise. *Harvard Business Review,* 86(6): 106–117.

33. Monks, R. & Minow, N. 2001. *Corporate governance* (2nd ed.). Malden, MA: Blackwell.

34. Intel Corp. 2007. *Intel corporation board of directors guidelines on significant corporate governance issues.* www.intel.com

35. Jones, T. J., Felps, W., & Bigley, G. A. 2007. Ethical theory and stakeholder-related decisions: The role of stakeholder culture. *Academy of Management Review,* 32(1): 137–155.

36. For example, see The best (& worst) managers of the year, 2003. *BusinessWeek,* January 13: 58–92; and Lavelle, M. 2003. Rogues of the year. *Time,* January 6: 33–45.

37. Handy, C. 2002. What's a business for? *Harvard Business Review,* 80(12): 49–55.

38. Anonymous, 2007. In the money. *Economist,* January 20: 3–6.

39. Hessel, E. & Woolley, S. 2008. Your money or your life. *Forbes,* October 27: 52.

40. Some interesting insights on the role of activist investors can be found in: Greenwood, R. & Schol, M. 2008. When (not) to listen to activist investors. *Harvard Business Review,* 66(1): 23–24.

41. For an interesting perspective on the changing role of boards of directors, refer to Lawler, E. & Finegold, D. 2005. Rethinking governance. *MIT Sloan Management Review,* 46(2): 67–70.

42. Benz, M. & Frey, B. S. 2007. Corporate governance: What can we learn from public governance? *Academy of Management Review,* 32(1): 92–104.

43. The salience of shareholder value is addressed in: Carrott, G. T. & Jackson, S. E. 2009. Shareholder value must top the CEO's agenda. *Harvard Business Review,* 67(1): 22–24.

44. Stakeholder symbiosis. 1998. *Fortune,* March 30: S2.

45. An excellent review of stakeholder management theory can be found in: Laplume, A. O., Sonpar, K., & Litz, R. A. 2008. Stakeholder theory: Reviewing a theory that moves us. *Journal of Management,* 34(6): 1152–1189.

46. For a definitive, recent discussion of the stakeholder concept, refer to Freeman, R. E. & McVae, J. 2001. A stakeholder approach to strategic management. In Hitt, M. A., Freeman, R. E., & Harrison, J. S. (Eds.). *Handbook of strategic management:* 189–207. Malden, MA: Blackwell.

47. For an insightful discussion on the role of business in society, refer to Handy, op. cit.

48. Stakeholder symbiosis. op. cit., p. S3.

49. Sullivan, C. T. 2005. A stake in the business. *Harvard Business Review,* 83(9): 57–67.

50. Our discussion of crowdsourcing draws on the first two books that have addressed this concept: Libert, B. & Spector, J. 2008. *We are smarter than me.* Philadelphia: Wharton Publishing; and, Howe, J. 2008. *Crowdsourcing.* New York: Crown Business. Eric von Hippel has addressed similar ideas in his earlier book (2005. *Democratizing innovation.* Cambridge, MA: MIT Press).

51. An excellent theoretical discussion on stakeholder activity is Rowley, T. J. & Moldoveanu, M. 2003. When will stakeholder groups act? An interest- and identity-based model of stakeholder group mobilization. *Academy of Management Review,* 28(2): 204–219.

52. Thomas, J. G. 2000. Macroenvironmetal forces. In Helms, M. M. (Ed.), *Encyclopedia of management.* (4th ed.): 516–520. Farmington Hills, MI: Gale Group.

53. For a strong advocacy position on the need for corporate values and social responsibility, read Hollender, J. 2004. What matters most: Corporate values and social responsibility. *California Management Review,* 46(4): 111–119.

54. Waddock, S. & Bodwell, C. 2004. Managing responsibility: What can be learned from the quality movement. *California Management Review,* 47(1): 25–37.

55. For a discussion of the role of alliances and collaboration on corporate social responsibility initiatives, refer to Pearce, J. A. II. & Doh, J. P. 2005. The high impact of collaborative social initiatives. *MIT Sloan Management Review,* 46(3): 30–40.

56. Insights on ethical behavior and performance are addressed in: Trudel, R. & Cotte, J. 2009. *MIT Sloan Management Review,* 50(2): 61–68.

57. Anonymous, 2006. If I did it. *BusinessWeek.* December 18: 108.

58. Bhattacharya, C. B. & Sen, S. 2004, Doing better at doing good: When, why, and how consumers respond to corporate social initiatives. *California Management Review,* 47(1): 9–24.

59. For some findings on the relationship between corporate social responsibility and firm performance, see: Margolis, J. D. & Elfenbein, H. A. 2008. *Harvard Business Review,* 86(1): 19–20.

60. Cone Corporate Citizenship Study, 2002, www.coneinc.com.

61. Refer to www.bsr.org.

62. An insightful discussion of the risks and opportunities associated with global warming, refer to: Lash, J. & Wellington, F. 2007. Competitive advantage on a warming planet. *Harvard Business Review*, 85(3): 94–102.

63. This section draws on Hart, S. L. 1997. Beyond greening: Strategies for a sustainable world. *Harvard Business Review*, 75(1): 66–76, and Berry, M.A. & Rondinelli, D. A. 1998. Proactive corporate environmental management: A new industrial revolution. *Academy of Management Executive*, 12(2): 38–50.

64. Carey, J. 2006. Business on a warmer planet. *BusinessWeek*, July 17: 26–29.

65. Hart, op. cit., p. 67.

66. For a creative perspective on environmental sustainability and competitive advantage as well as ethical implications, read Ehrenfeld, J. R. 2005. The roots of sustainability. *MIT Sloan Management Review*, 46(2): 23–25.

67. McKinsey & Company. 1991. *The corporate response to the environmental challenge*. Summary Report, Amsterdam: McKinsey & Company.

68. Vogel, D. J. 2005. Is there a market for virtue? The business case for corporate social responsibility. *California Management Review*, 47(4): 19–36.

69. Senge, P. M. 1990. The leader's new work: Building learning organizations. *Sloan Management Review*, 32(1): 7–23.

70. For an interesting perspective on the role of middle managers in the strategic management process, refer to Huy, Q. H. 2001. In praise of middle managers. *Harvard Business Review*, 79(8): 72–81.

71. Senge, 1996, op. cit., pp. 41–58.

72. Helgesen, S. 1996. Leading from the grass roots. In Hesselbein, F., Goldsmith, M., & Beckhard, R. (Eds.), *The leader of the future*: 19–24. San Francisco: Jossey-Bass.

73. Wetlaufer, S. 1999. Organizing for empowerment: An interview with AES's Roger Sant and Dennis Blake. *Harvard Business Review*, 77(1): 110–126.

74. Kets de Vries, M. F. R. 1998. Charisma in action: The transformational abilities of Virgin's Richard Branson and ABB's Percy Barnevik. *Organizational Dynamics*, 26(3): 7–21.

75. Hamel, G. 2006. The why, what, and how of management innovation. *Harvard Business Review*, 84(2): 72–84.

76. An insightful discussion about the role of vision, mission, and strategic objectives can be found in: Collis, D. J. & Rukstad, M. G. 2008. Can you say what your strategy is? *Harvard Business Review*, 66(4): 82–90.

77. Our discussion draws on a variety of sources. These include Lipton, M. 1996. Demystifying the development of an organizational vision. *Sloan Management Review*, 37(4): 83–92; Bart, C. K. 2000. Lasting inspiration. *CA Magazine*, May: 49–50; and Quigley, J. V. 1994.

Vision: How leaders develop it, share it, and sustain it. *Business Horizons*, September–October: 37–40.

78. Lipton, op. cit.

79. Hardy, Q. 2007. The uncarly. *Forbes*, March 12: 82–90.

80. Some interesting perspective on gender differences in organizational vision are discussed in: Ibarra, H. & Obodaru, O. 2009. Women and the vision thing. *Harvard Business Review*, 67(1): 62–70.

81. Quigley, op. cit.

82. Ibid.

83. Lipton, op. cit. Additional pitfalls are addressed in this article.

84. Sull, D. N. 2005. Strategy as active waiting. *Harvard Business Review*, 83(9): 120–130.

85. Company records.

86. Lipton, op. cit.

87. Sexton, D. A. & Van Aukun, P. M. 1985. A longitudinal study of small business strategic planning. *Journal of Small Business Management*, January: 8–15, cited in Lipton, op. cit.

88. For an insightful perspective on the use of strategic objectives, refer to Chatterjee, S. 2005. Core objectives: Clarity in designing strategy. *California Management Review*, 47(2): 33–49.

89. Ibid.

90. Mankins, M. M. & Steele, R. 2005. Turning great strategy into great performance. *Harvard Business Review*, 83(5): 66–73.

Analyzing the External Environment of the Firm

> learning objectives

After reading this chapter, you should have a good understanding of:

LO1 The importance of developing forecasts of the business environment.

LO2 Why environmental scanning, environmental monitoring, and collecting competitive intelligence are critical inputs to forecasting.

LO3 Why scenario planning is a useful technique for firms competing in industries characterized by unpredictability and change.

LO4 The impact of the general environment on a firm's strategies and performance.

LO5 How forces in the competitive environment can affect profitability, and how a firm can improve its competitive position by increasing its power vis-à-vis these forces.

LO6 How the Internet and digitally based capabilities are affecting the five competitive forces and industry profitability.

LO7 The concept of strategic groups and their strategy and performance implications.

Strategies are not and should not be developed in a vacuum. They must be responsive to the external business environment. Otherwise, your firm could become, in effect, the most efficient producer of buggy whips, leisure suits, or slide rules. To avoid such strategic mistakes, firms must become knowledgeable about the business environment. One tool for analyzing trends is forecasting. In the development of forecasts, environmental scanning and environmental monitoring are important in detecting key trends and events. Managers also must aggressively collect and disseminate competitor intelligence. The information gleaned from these three activities is invaluable in developing forecasts and scenarios to minimize present and future threats as well as to exploit opportunities. We address these issues in the first part of this chapter. We also introduce a basic tool of strategy analysis—the concept of SWOT analysis (strengths, weaknesses, opportunities, and threats).

In the second part of the chapter, we present two frameworks for analyzing the external environment—the general environment and the competitive environment. The general environment consists of six segments—demographic, sociocultural, political/legal, technological, economic, and global. Trends and events in these segments can have a dramatic impact on your firm.

The competitive environment is closer to home. It consists of five industry-related factors that can dramatically affect the average level of industry profitability. An awareness of these factors is critical in making decisions such as which industries to enter and how to improve your firm's current position within an industry. This is helpful in neutralizing competitive threats and increasing power over customers and suppliers. We also address how industry and competitive practices are being affected by the capabilities provided by Internet technologies. In the final part of this section, we place firms within an industry into strategic groups based on similarities in resources and strategies. As we will see, the concept of strategic groups has important implications for the intensity of rivalry and how the effects of a given environmental trend or event differ across groups.

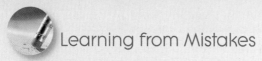

Learning from Mistakes

Until 2004, Motorola was No. 1 or No. 2 in the China mobile-phone market.[1] But in recent years, its share has plummeted from 21 percent in 2006 to about 8 percent in 2008. In contrast, Nokia's share has soared to 38 percent and Samsung has grown to 16 percent—leaving Motorola a distant third. Let's take a look at what went wrong.

In China, coming out with new models is important because big-city consumers replace their phones frequently and put a priority on models that are cool-looking and reasonably priced. According to an analyst: "They haven't come up with the next-generation product that replaces the Razr. The guys that replaced it were Nokia, Samsung, and even LG."

Unfortunately, when rivals came out with similar models, Motorola's entries were pricey multimedia phones that didn't attract consumers. And while Motorola developed a smart phone for China, the Ming, the touch screen device did little to boost Motorola's overall position.

The result: Chinese consumers have soured on the Motorola brand. Chen Xin, a 37-year-old Beijing resident who works for a local info-tech company, once bought five Motorola phones over a four-year span. But now he prefers Nokia and Sony Ericsson models, calling Motorola phones "ugly and not very easy to operate."

Such a steep decline is costly for Motorola. With 583 million cell phones in use, China is the world's largest mobile market. The Chinese bought 176 million handsets in 2007 and about 200 million in 2008. These figures compare to sales of 186 million units in the U.S. and Canada. And before its recent slide, Motorola was narrowing its overall gap with archrival Nokia.

As one would expect, Motorola's dwindling fortunes in China reflect its overall erosion in market share. For 2008's third quarter, unit sales dropped 32 percent, to 25.4 million units from a year earlier, and the company's market share dropped to 8.4 percent globally—down from 9.5 percent in the second quarter and 22.4 percent in 2006—when its Razr handset was all the rage. Motorola recently announced plans to cut about 3,000 jobs—two-thirds of them in the handset division. As one would expect, its share price has tumbled: from $21 at the end of 2006 to around $5 in early 2009.

Successful managers must recognize opportunities and threats in their firm's external environment. They must be aware of what's going on outside their company. If they focus exclusively on the efficiency of internal operations, the firm may degenerate into the world's most efficient producer of buggy whips or carbon paper. But if they miscalculate the market, opportunities will be lost—hardly an enviable position for their firm.

In *Competing for the Future,* Gary Hamel and C. K. Prahalad suggest that "every manager carries around in his or her head a set of biases, assumptions, and presuppositions about the structure of the relevant 'industry,' about how one makes money in the industry, about who the competition is and isn't, about who the customers are and aren't, and so on."[2] Environmental analysis requires you to continually question such assumptions. Peter Drucker labeled these interrelated sets of assumptions the "theory of the business."[3] The sudden reversal in Motorola's fortunes clearly illustrates that if a company does not keep pace with changes in the external environment, it becomes difficult to sustain competitive advantages and deliver strong financial results.

A firm's strategy may be good at one point in time, but it may go astray when management's frame of reference gets out of touch with the realities of the actual business situation. This results when management's assumptions, premises, or beliefs are incorrect or when internal inconsistencies among them render the overall "theory of the business" invalid. As Warren Buffett, investor extraordinaire, colorfully notes, "Beware of past performance 'proofs.' If history books were the key to riches, the Forbes 400 would consist of librarians."

In the business world, many once successful firms have fallen. Consider the high-tech company Novell, which went head-to-head with Microsoft. Novell bought market-share loser WordPerfect to compete with Microsoft Word. The result? A $1.3 billion loss when Novell sold WordPerfect to Corel. And today we may wonder who will be the next Circuit City or *Encyclopaedia Britannica.*

Creating the Environmentally Aware Organization

So how do managers become environmentally aware?[4] We will now address three important processes—scanning, monitoring, and gathering competitive intelligence—used to develop forecasts.[5] Exhibit 2.1 illustrates relationships among these important activities. We also discuss the importance of scenario planning in anticipating major future changes in the external environment and the role of SWOT analysis.[6]

The Role of Scanning, Monitoring, Competitive Intelligence, and Forecasting

Environmental Scanning   **Environmental scanning** involves surveillance of a firm's external environment to predict environmental changes and detect changes already under way.[7,8] This alerts the organization to critical trends and events before changes develop a discernible pattern and before competitors recognize them.[9] Otherwise, the firm may be forced into a reactive mode.[10]

Experts agree that spotting key trends requires a combination of knowing your business and your customer as well as keeping an eye on what's happening around you. Such a big-picture/small-picture view enables you to better identify the emerging trends that will affect your business. We suggest a few tips in Exhibit 2.2.

At times, your company may benefit from studies conducted by outside experts in a particular industry. A. T. Kearney, a large international consulting company, identified several key issues in the automobile industry, including.[11]

- *Globalization.* This is not a new trend but it has intensified, with enormous opportunities opening up in Asia, central and eastern Europe, and Latin America.[12]
- *Time to Market.* Despite recent improvements, there's still a gap between product development cycles in the United States and Europe compared to Japan. This gap may be widening as Japanese companies continue to make improvements.

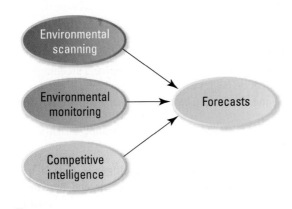

Exhibit 2.1 Inputs to Forecasting

>LO1
The importance of developing forecasts of the business environment.

>LO2
Why environmental scanning, environmental monitoring, and collecting competitive intelligence are critical inputs to forecasting.

environmental scanning surveillance of a firm's external environment to predict environmental changes and detect changes already under way.

Globalization the dual trends of a) increasing international exchange of goods, money, information, people, and ideas; and b) increasing similarity among countries of laws, rules, norms, values, and income levels.

Exhibit 2.2
**Some Suggestions on
How to Spot Hot Trends**

- **Listen.** Ask your customers questions about your products and services. Ask what they are looking for next. Find out what media they're watching and what they think of current events.

- **Pay attention.** Read trade publications related to your industry to identify key issues. Watch industries that are always on the cutting edge, such as technology, music, and fashion, in order to discover emerging trends that may affect your business.

- **Follow trends online.** Trend-hunting websites such as trendhunter.com and jwtintelligence.com offer up the trends du jour. Add them to your regular Web-surfing itinerary.

- **Go old school.** Ask your customers what they think. Organize online or in-person focus groups to find out what people are thinking. You can also launch social media groups or chat rooms to gather feedback from your audience.

Source: Moran, G. 2008. Be your own trendspotter. *Entrepreneur,* December: 17.

- *Shifting Roles and Responsibilities.* Design responsibility, purchasing, and even project management and systems engineering are shifting from original equipment manufacturers to integrators/suppliers.

Consider how disadvantaged you would be as an executive in the global automobile industry if you were unaware of such trends.

Strategy Spotlight 2.1 addresses how Virgin Mobile USA uses crowdsourcing to help it keep abreast of trends and promising opportunities.

environmental monitoring a firm's analysis of the external environment that tracks the evolution of environmental trends, sequences of events, or streams of activities.

Environmental Monitoring   **Environmental monitoring** tracks the evolution of environmental trends, sequences of events, or streams of activities. They may be trends that the firm came across by accident or ones that were brought to its attention from outside the organization. Monitoring enables firms to evaluate how dramatically environmental trends are changing the competitive landscape.

One of the authors of this text has conducted on-site interviews with executives from several industries to identify indicators that firms monitor as inputs to their strategy process. Examples of such indicators included:

- *A Motel 6 executive.* The number of rooms in the budget segment of the industry in the United States and the difference between the average daily room rate and the consumer price index (CPI).
- *A Pier 1 Imports executive.* Net disposable income (NDI), consumer confidence index, and housing starts.
- *A Johnson & Johnson medical products executive.* Percentage of gross domestic product (GDP) spent on health care, number of active hospital beds, and the size and power of purchasing agents (indicates the concentration of buyers).

Such indices are critical for managers in determining a firm's strategic direction and resource allocation.

competitive intelligence a firm's activities of collecting and interpreting data on competitors, defining and understanding the industry, and identifying competitors' strengths and weaknesses.

Competitive Intelligence   **Competitive intelligence** (CI) helps firms define and understand their industry and identify rivals' strengths and weaknesses.[13] This includes the intelligence gathering associated with collecting data on competitors and interpreting such data. Done properly, competitive intelligence helps a company avoid surprises by anticipating competitors' moves and decreasing response time.[14]

Crowdsourcing: How Virgin Mobile USA Enhances Its Environmental Awareness

Virgin Mobile USA—a joint venture of Richard Branson's Virgin Group and Sprint Nextel—relies on 2,000 carefully selected online customers, referred to as "Insiders" by Virgin, to keep it aware of trends and promising opportunities. Considered a "team of elite, young, and active customers," Virgin rewards them with free calling minutes and phone upgrades. The Insider community—a very hip focus group—provides input on everything from designing phones to coming up with names for service plans. As one executive puts it: "Ultimately, we want to put young consumers backstage, that is, in influential positions."

However, being accepted as part of the in-crowd is not the only way to be heard and earn rewards at Virgin Mobile USA. Its pay-as-you-go, no-contract service has attracted 4.6 million phone users and offers all of its mostly young "Chatty Cathys" and "Texter Thomases" the chance to earn free phone minutes merely by paying attention and providing feedback on a corporate sponsor's advertisement. Any Virgin Mobile customer who watches 30-second commercials on his or her computer screen, reads text messages on a cell phone, or fills out brand survey questionnaires can earn up to 75 minutes a month of free airtime. Called Sugar Mama, the program provides a notoriously talkative group the chance to stay one step ahead of a dead cell phone by voicing their opinions. Virgin Mobile claims that about 1,000 subscribers have signed up for the program each day since it was initiated in mid-2006. And the firm awarded around 9 million minutes. However, not everyone is a fan. According to one website post: "This may sound like a good way to get some extra minutes of air time, but the air time you earn doesn't really make it worthwhile. Why watch a 30-second commercial just for a single minute of air time? If you need the airtime that bad, you might as well throw your phone away."

Sugar Mama enables sponsoring partners to tap into the thoughts and opinions of a coveted marketing segment. And they are happy to pay for the privilege. As one corporate media executive pointed out, knowing that these young consumers don't get paid unless they watch an ad and answer questions helps assure advertisers that they are receiving honest feedback. Consider Virgin Mobile's enticing promotion directed at advertisers:

Virgin Mobile Users Are:

- First at trying new things and convincing others to do the same.
- Passionate about the brands and music they connect with.
- Not afraid to be different.
- Ambitious and career-oriented.
- Active social thought leaders

Source: Libert, B. & Spector, J. 2008. *We are smarter than me.* Philadelphia: Wharton School Publishing; www.ultramercial.com. Undated, np.; and, mobilevirgin.instantspot.com. Posted April 28, 2007.

crowdsourcing

Examples of competitive analysis are evident in daily newspapers and periodicals such as *The Wall Street Journal, BusinessWeek,* and *Fortune.* For example, banks continually track home loan, auto loan, and certificate of deposit (CD) interest rates charged by rivals. Major airlines change hundreds of fares daily in response to competitors' tactics. Car manufacturers are keenly aware of announced cuts or increases in rivals' production volume, sales, and sales incentives (e.g., rebates and low interest rates on financing). This information is used in their marketing, pricing, and production strategies.

The Internet has dramatically accelerated the speed at which firms can find competitive intelligence. Leonard Fuld, founder of the Cambridge, Massachusetts, training and consulting firm Fuld & Co., specializes in competitive intelligence.[15] His firm often profiles top company and business group managers and considers these issues: What is their background? What is their style? Are they marketers? Are they cost cutters? Fuld has found that the more articles he collects and the more biographies he downloads, the better he can develop profiles.

Ethical Guidelines on Competitive Intelligence: United Technologies

United Technologies (UT) is a $28 billion global conglomerate composed of world-leading businesses with rich histories of technological pioneering, such as Otis Elevator, Carrier Air Conditioning, and Sikorsky (helicopters). It was founded in 1853 and has an impressive history of technological accomplishments. UT built the first working helicopter, developed the first commercially available hydrogen cells, and designed complete life support systems for space shuttles. UT believes strongly in a robust code of ethics. In the last decade, they have clearly articulated their principles governing business conduct. These include an antitrust guide, an ethics guide when contracting with the U.S. government and foreign governments, a policy on accepting gifts from suppliers, and guidelines for proper usage of e-mail. One such document is the Code of Ethics Guide on Competitive Intelligence. This encourages managers and workers to ask themselves these five questions whenever they have ethical concerns.

Sources: Nelson, B. 2003. The thinker. *Forbes*, March 3: 62–64; and The Fuld war room—Survival kit 010. Code of ethics (printed 2/26/01).

1. Have I done anything that coerced somebody to share this information? Have I, for example, threatened a supplier by indicating that future business opportunities will be influenced by the receipt of information with respect to a competitor?

2. Am I in a place where I should not be? If, for example, I am a field representative with privileges to move around in a customer's facility, have I gone outside the areas permitted? Have I misled anybody in order to gain access?

3. Is the contemplated technique for gathering information evasive, such as sifting through trash or setting up an electronic "snooping" device directed at a competitor's facility from across the street?

4. Have I misled somebody in a way that the person believed sharing information with me was required or would be protected by a confidentiality agreement? Have I, for example, called and misrepresented myself as a government official who was seeking some information for some official purpose?

5. Have I done something to evade or circumvent a system intended to secure or protect information?

One of Fuld & Co.'s clients asked it to determine the size, strength, and technical capabilities of a privately held company. Initially, it was difficult to get detailed information. Then one analyst used Deja News (www.dejanews.com), now part of Google, to tap into some online discussion groups. The analyst's research determined that the company had posted 14 job openings on one Usenet group. That posting was a road map to the competitor's development strategy.

At times, a firm's aggressive efforts to gather competitive intelligence may lead to unethical or illegal behaviors.[16] Strategy Spotlight 2.2 provides an example of a company, United Technologies, that has set clear guidelines to help prevent unethical behavior.

A word of caution: Executives must be careful to avoid spending so much time and effort tracking the actions of traditional competitors that they ignore new competitors. Further, broad environmental changes and events may have a dramatic impact on a firm's viability. Peter Drucker, considered the father of modern management, wrote:

> Increasingly, a winning strategy will require information about events and conditions outside the institution: noncustomers, technologies other than those currently used by the company and its present competitors, markets not currently served, and so on.[17]

Consider the fall of the once-mighty *Encyclopaedia Britannica*.[18] Its demise was not caused by a traditional competitor in the encyclopedia industry. It was caused by new technology. CD-ROMs came out of nowhere and devastated the printed encyclopedia industry. Why? A full set of the *Encyclopaedia Britannica* sells for about $2,000, but an encyclopedia on CD-ROM, such as Microsoft *Encarta,* sells for about $50. To make matters worse, many people receive *Encarta* free with their personal computers.

Environmental Forecasting Environmental scanning, monitoring, and competitive intelligence are important inputs for analyzing the external environment. **Environmental forecasting** involves the development of plausible projections about the direction, scope, speed, and intensity of environmental change.[19] Its purpose is to predict change.[20] It asks: How long will it take a new technology to reach the marketplace? Will the present social concern about an issue result in new legislation? Are current lifestyle trends likely to continue?

Some forecasting issues are much more specific to a particular firm and the industry in which it competes. Consider how important it is for Motel 6 to predict future indicators, such as the number of rooms, in the budget segment of the industry. If its predictions are low, it will build too many units, creating a surplus of room capacity that would drive down room rates.

A danger of forecasting is that managers may view uncertainty as black and white and ignore important gray areas.[21] The problem is that underestimating uncertainty can lead to strategies that neither defend against threats nor take advantage of opportunities.

In 1977 one of the colossal underestimations in business history occurred when Kenneth H. Olsen, president of Digital Equipment Corp., announced, "There is no reason for individuals to have a computer in their home." The explosion in the personal computer market was not easy to detect in 1977, but it was clearly within the range of possibilities at the time. And, historically, there have been underestimates of the growth potential of new telecommunication services. The electric telegraph was derided by Ralph Waldo Emerson, and the telephone had its skeptics. More recently, an "infamous" McKinsey study in the early 1980s predicted fewer than 1 million cellular users in the United States by 2000. Actually, there were nearly 100 million.[22]

Obviously, poor predictions never go out of vogue. Consider some of the "gems" associated with the global financial crisis that began in 2008.[23]

- "Freddie Mac and Fannie Mae are fundamentally sound. . . . I think they are in good shape going forward."—Barney Frank (D-Mass.), House Financial Services Committee Chairman, July 14, 2008. (*Two months later, the government forced the mortgage giants into conservatorships.*)
- "Existing home sales to trend up in 2008"—Headline of a National Association of Realtors press release, December 9, 2007. (*On December 23, 2007, the group said November sales were down 11 percent from a year earlier in the worst housing slump since the Great Depression.*)
- "I think you'll see $150 a barrel [of oil] by the end of the year."—T. Boone Pickens, June 20, 2008. (*Oil was then around $135 a barrel. By late December it was around $40.*)
- "I expect there will be some failures. . . . I don't anticipate any serious problems of that sort among the large internationally active banks."—Ben Bernanke, Federal Reserve Chairman, February 28, 2008. (*In September, Washington Mutual became the largest financial institution in U.S. history to fail. Citigroup needed an even bigger rescue in November.*)
- "In today's regulatory environment, it's virtually impossible to violate rules."—Bernard Madoff, money manager, October 20, 2007. (*On December 11, 2008, Madoff was arrested for allegedly running a Ponzi scheme that may have lost investors $50 billion.*)

Scenario analysis is a more in-depth approach to forecasting. It draws on a range of disciplines and interests, among them economics, psychology, sociology, and demographics. It usually begins with a discussion of participants' thoughts on ways in which societal

environmental forecasting the development of plausible projections about the direction, scope, speed, and intensity of environmental change.

>LO3
Why scenario planning is a useful technique for firms competing in industries characterized by unpredictability and change.

scenario analysis an in-depth approach to environmental forecasting that involves experts' detailed assessments of societal trends, economics, politics, technology, or other dimensions of the external environment.

strategy spotlight

2.3

Scenario Planning at Shell Oil Company

Preparing to cope with uncertainty is one of the biggest strategic challenges faced by most businesses. There are few tools for coping with strategic uncertainty, especially over medium- to long-term horizons. One technique that has proved its usefulness is scenario planning.

Scenario planning is different from other tools for strategic planning such as trend analysis or high and low forecasts. The origins of scenario planning lie with the military, which used it to cope effectively with multiple challenges and limited resources.

In the 1960s and 1970s, Shell combined analytical tools with information to create scenarios of possible outcomes. The result of the 1973 oil embargo was a sharp increase in crude oil prices, short supplies of gasoline for consumers, and a depressed world economy. However, Shell's strategic planning, including the use of scenarios, had strongly suggested that a more unstable environment was coming, with a shift of power from oil companies to oil producers. As a result of the precautionary actions it took, Shell was in a better position than most oil companies when the 1973 embargo occurred. Shell also uses scenario planning to plan major new oil field investments because elements of risk can be identified and explored over a considerable period of time.

Sources: Martin, R. 2002. The oracles of oil. *Business 2.0*, January: 35–39; www.touchstonerenard.co.uk/Expertise/Strategy/Scenario_Planning/scenario_planning.htm; and Epstein, J. 1998. Scenario planning: An introduction. *The Futurist*, September: 50–52.

The Shell process of scenario planning involves the following stages:

1. Interviews with people both inside and outside the business, using an open-ended questioning technique to encourage full and frank answers.

2. Analysis of interviews by issue in order to build a "natural agenda" for further processing.

3. Synthesis of each agenda to draw out underlying areas of uncertainty/dispute and possible interrelationships among issues.

4. A small number of workshops to explore key issues to improve understanding and identify gaps for further research. These generate a wide range of strategy options.

5. A workshop to identify and build a small number of scenarios that may occur in the next 10 to 15 years or even later.

6. A testing of strategy options against the scenarios in order to assess robustness (i.e., whether or not a given strategy is effective under more than one scenario).

Other practitioners of scenario planning include Levi Strauss, which uses scenario planning to consider potential impacts of everything from cotton deregulation to the total disappearance of cotton from this planet. Also, a German insurance company anticipated the fall of the Berlin wall and made plans to expand in central Europe. And in 1990 when Nelson Mandela was released from a South African prison, he met with a panel that helped him create scenarios to chart out the country's future. Scenario planning helps by considering not just trends or forecasts but also how they could be upset by events and the outcomes that may result.

trends, economics, politics, and technology may affect an issue.[24] For example, consider Lego. The popular Danish toy manufacturer has a strong position in the construction toys market. But what would happen if this broadly defined market should change dramatically? After all, Lego is competing not only with producers of similar products but also on a much broader canvas for a share of children's playtime. In this market, Lego has a host of competitors, many of them computer based; still others have not yet been invented. Lego may end up with an increasing share of a narrow, shrinking market (much like IBM in the declining days of the mainframe computer). To avoid such a fate, managers must consider a wider context than their narrow, traditional markets, by laying down guidelines for at least 10 years in the future to anticipate rapid change. Strategy Spotlight 2.3 provides an example of scenario planning at Shell Oil Company.

SWOT Analysis

To understand the business environment of a particular firm, you need to analyze both the general environment and the firm's industry and competitive environment. Generally, firms compete with other firms in the same industry. An industry is composed of a set of firms that produce similar products or services, sell to similar customers, and use similar methods of production. Gathering industry information and understanding competitive dynamics among the different companies in your industry is key to successful strategic management.

One of the most basic techniques for analyzing firm and industry conditions is **SWOT analysis**. SWOT stands for strengths, weaknesses, opportunities, and threats. It provides "raw material"—a basic listing of conditions both inside and surrounding your company.

The Strengths and Weaknesses refer to the internal conditions of the firm—where your firm excels (strengths) and where it may be lacking relative to competitors (weaknesses). Opportunities and Threats are environmental conditions external to the firm. These could be factors either in the general or competitive environment. In the general environment, one might experience developments that are beneficial for most companies such as improving economic conditions, that lower borrowing costs or trends that benefit some companies and harm others. An example is the heightened concern with fitness, which is a threat to some companies (e.g., tobacco) and an opportunity to others (e.g., health clubs). Opportunities and threats are also present in the competitive environment among firms competing for the same customers.

The general idea of SWOT analysis is that a firm's strategy must:

- build on its strengths,
- remedy the weaknesses or work around them,
- take advantage of the opportunities presented by the environment, and,
- protect the firm from the threats.

Despite its apparent simplicity, the SWOT approach has been very popular. First, it forces managers to consider both internal and external factors simultaneously. Second, its emphasis on identifying opportunities and threats makes firms act proactively rather than reactively. Third, it raises awareness about the role of strategy in creating a match between the environmental conditions and the firm's internal strengths and weaknesses. Finally, its conceptual simplicity is achieved without sacrificing analytical rigor. (We will also address some of the limitations of SWOT analysis in Chapter 3.)

The General Environment

The **general environment** is composed of factors that can have dramatic effects on firm strategy.[25] Typically, a firm has little ability to predict trends and events in the general environment and even less ability to control them. When listening to CNBC, for example, you can hear many experts espouse different perspectives on what action the Federal Reserve Board may take on short-term interest rates—an action that can have huge effects on the valuation of entire economic sectors. Also, it's difficult to predict future political events such as the ongoing Middle East peace negotiations and tensions on the Korean peninsula. Dramatic innovations in information technology (e.g., the Internet) have helped keep inflation in check by lowering the cost of doing business in the United States at the beginning of the 21st century.[26]

We divide the general environment into six segments: demographic, sociocultural, political/legal, technological, economic, and global. Exhibit 2.3 provides examples of key trends and events in each of the six segments of the general environment.

SWOT analysis
a framework for analyzing a company's internal and external environment and that stands for strengths, weaknesses, opportunities, and threats.

general environment
factors external to an industry, and usually beyond a firm's control, that affect a firm's strategy.

>LO4
The impact of the general environment on a firm's strategies and performance.

Exhibit 2.3
General Environment: Key Trends and Events

Demographic

- Aging population
- Rising affluence
- Changes in ethnic composition
- Geographic distribution of population
- Greater disparities in income levels

Sociocultural

- More women in the workforce
- Increase in temporary workers
- Greater concern for fitness
- Greater concern for environment
- Postponement of family formation

Political/Legal

- Tort reform
- Americans with Disabilities Act (ADA) of 1990
- Repeal of Glass-Steagall Act in 1999 (banks may now offer brokerage services)
- Deregulation of utility and other industries
- Increases in federally mandated minimum wages
- Taxation at local, state, federal levels
- Legislation on corporate governance reforms in bookkeeping, stock options, etc. (Sarbanes-Oxley Act of 2002)

Technological

- Genetic engineering
- Emergence of Internet technology
- Computer-aided design/computer-aided manufacturing systems (CAD/CAM)
- Research in synthetic and exotic materials
- Pollution/global warming
- Miniaturization of computing technologies
- Wireless communications
- Nanotechnology

Economic

- Interest rates
- Unemployment rates
- Consumer Price Index
- Trends in GDP
- Changes in stock market valuations

Global

- Increasing global trade
- Currency exchange rates
- Emergence of the Indian and Chinese economies
- Trade agreements among regional blocs (e.g., NAFTA, EU, ASEAN)
- Creation of WTO (leading to decreasing tariffs/free trade in services)

The Demographic Segment

Demographics are the most easily understood and quantifiable elements of the general environment. They are at the root of many changes in society. Demographics include elements such as the aging population,[27] rising or declining affluence, changes in ethnic composition, geographic distribution of the population, and disparities in income level.

The impact of a demographic trend, like all segments of the general environment, varies across industries. Rising levels of affluence in many developed countries bode well for brokerage services as well as for upscale pets and supplies. However, this trend may adversely affect fast-food restaurants because people can afford to dine at higher-priced restaurants. Fast-food restaurants depend on minimum-wage employees to operate efficiently, but the competition for labor intensifies as more attractive employment opportunities become prevalent, thus threatening the employment base for restaurants. Let's look at the details of one of these trends.

The aging population in the United States and other developed countries has important implications. The U.S. Bureau of Statistics states that only 14 percent of American workers were 55 and older in 2002.[28] However, by 2012 that figure will increase to 20 percent, or one in five, of all U.S. workers. At the same time, the United States is expected to experience a significant drop in younger workers aged 25 to 44, making it increasingly important for employers to recruit and retain older workers. Similarly, the National Association of Manufacturing estimates that as baby boomers continue retiring, the United States will have 7 million more jobs than workers by 2010.

Strategy Spotlight 2.4 addresses an attractive market for financial advisors—America's 77 million baby boomers who are nearing retirement. And as we will see, not all of their motives are noble.

Demographic segment of the general environment genetic and observable characteristics of a population including the levels and growth of age, density, sex, race, ethnicity, education, geographic region, and income.

The Sociocultural Segment

Sociocultural forces influence the values, beliefs, and lifestyles of a society. Examples include a higher percentage of women in the workforce, dual-income families, increases in the number of temporary workers, greater concern for healthy diets and physical fitness, greater interest in the environment, and postponement of having children. Such forces enhance sales of products and services in many industries but depress sales in others. The increased number of women in the workforce has increased the need for business clothing merchandise but decreased the demand for baking product staples (since people would have less time to cook from scratch). This health and fitness trend has helped industries that manufacture exercise equipment and healthful foods but harmed industries that produce unhealthful foods.

Increased educational attainment by women in the workplace has led to more women in upper management positions.[29] Given such educational attainment, it is hardly surprising that companies owned by women have been one of the driving forces of the U.S. economy; these companies (now more than 9 million in number) account for 40 percent of all U.S. businesses and have generated more than $3.6 trillion in annual revenue. In addition, women have a tremendous impact on consumer spending decisions. Not surprisingly, many companies have focused their advertising and promotion efforts on female consumers. Consider, for example, Lowe's efforts to attract female shoppers:

Sociocultural segment of the general environment the values, beliefs, and lifestyles of a society.

> Lowe's has found that women prefer to do larger home-improvement projects with a man— be it a boyfriend, husband, or neighbor.[30] As a result, in addition to its "recipe card classes" (that explain various projects that take only one weekend), Lowe's offers co-ed store clinics for projects like sink installation. "Women like to feel they're given the same attention as a male customer," states Lowe's spokesperson Julie Valeant-Yenichek, who points out that most seminar attendees, whether male or female, are inexperienced.

Home Depot recently spent millions of dollars to add softer lighting and brighter signs in 300 stores. Why? It is an effort to match rival Lowe's appeal to women.

Baby Boomers' 401-k Plans: An Easy Mark?

Over the next 20 years, a record $17 trillion will move from pension funds and 401-k accounts into the hands of freshly minted retirees, according to the trade group Investment Company Institute. This reflects America's 77 million baby boomers. By 2030, nearly one in five U.S. residents is expected to be 65 and older. And looking ahead, by 2050, this group is expected to increase to 88.5 million—more than doubling the 38.7 million in 2008. What's more, the 85 and older population is expected to more than triple, from 5.4 million to 19 million between 2008 and 2050.

As one would expect, the pot of money associated with this demographic group—and the hefty asset management fees that it will generate—has financial services firms very excited. And, of course, not all of these professionals have their clients' interests at heart. Many brokers, for example, are promising early retirement, fat investment returns, and big annual cash withdrawals. Often they are succeeding in seducing investors to turn over their retirement accounts—and then putting them in high-fee and often inappropriate investments. Claims the CEO of the securities industry's private oversight group: "This is an emerging problem. The issue has intensified for the next generation of retirees—the largest we've ever seen."

Source: Der Hovanesian, M. 2008. Ruined by 401(k) predators. *BusinessWeek*, July 14 & 21: 60–66; and, Desmond, M. 2008. Cities where your nest egg goes farthest. Forbes.com. October 24: np.

Many seminars by financial advisors—both on a company's premises and off-site—can be breeding grounds for fraud. In 2007, federal and state regulators examined 110 securities firms and branch offices that offer so-called free-lunch sessions. They found most to be little more than thinly veiled sales presentations, with some suggesting unrealistic scenarios such as "How to receive a 13.3% return" and "How $100K can pay $1 million to your heirs." Under federal regulations, brokers can't guarantee specific rates of return or promise investors they'll outlive their money. The regulators' study also found that 10 percent of the seminars appeared to be downright fraudulent, prompting investigations. Below are a few examples of illegal tactics used and the associated compensation paid to injured parties:

- Regulators ordered a unit of Citigroup to pay a $3 million fine and $12.2 million to 200 ex-BellSouth employees who were told by brokers that they could earn 12 percent on their accounts.

- Four Kansas City Southern employees were awarded $2.1 million after InterSecurities brokers said that they could safely withdraw from their accounts amounts equal to their salaries.

- Thirty-two former ExxonMobil employees received $13.8 million after Securities America advisors told them they could retire at 55 and that 14 percent returns were a "no-brainer."

The Political/Legal Segment

Political/legal segment of the general environment how a society creates and exercises power, including rules, laws, and taxation policies.

Political processes and legislation influence environmental regulations with which industries must comply.[31,32] Some important elements of the political/legal arena include tort reform, the Americans with Disabilities Act (ADA) of 1990, the repeal of the Glass-Steagall Act in 1999 (banks may now offer brokerage services), deregulation of utilities and other industries, and increases in the federally mandated minimum wage.[33]

Government legislation can also have a significant impact on the governance of corporations. The U.S. Congress passed the Sarbanes-Oxley Act in 2002, which greatly increases the accountability of auditors, executives, and corporate lawyers. This act responded to the widespread perception that existing governance mechanisms failed to protect the interests of shareholders, employees, and creditors. Clearly, Sarbanes-Oxley has also created a tremendous demand for professional accounting services.

Legislation can also affect firms in the high-tech sector of the economy by expanding the number of temporary visas available for highly skilled foreign professionals.[34] For example, a bill passed by the U.S. Congress in October 2000 allowed 195,000 H-1B visas for each of the following three years—up from a cap of 115,000. However, beginning in 2006 and continuing through 2008, the annual cap on H-1B visas has shrunk to only 65,000—with an

strategy spotlight

How Microsoft "Gets Around" H-1B Visa Restrictions

In March 2008, Microsoft Chairman Bill Gates took one of his company's most problematic issues to the U.S. Senate. During his testimony, he criticized U.S. immigration policy that limits the H-1B visas issued to skilled workers from foreign countries—workers that Microsoft would urgently like to hire. Gates told the lawmakers: "It makes no sense to tell well-trained, highly skilled individuals—many of whom are educated at top universities—that the U.S. does not welcome or value them" and that the U.S. "will find it far more difficult to maintain its competitive edge over the next 50 years if it excludes those who are able

and willing to help us compete." Gates also claimed that Microsoft hires four Americans in supporting roles for every high-skilled H-1B visa holder it hires. Despite his efforts, the senators ignored his pleas and the visa policy went unchanged.

What to do? Six months later, Microsoft opened an office in Richmond, British Columbia, a suburb of Vancouver. Here, it hopes to place hundreds of workers unable to obtain visas a few miles south in the U.S. Placing workers in the same time zone will help them to collaborate—given that the facility is located just 130 miles north of Microsoft's Redmond, Washington, campus. And it is just a 2 ½ hour drive on Interstate 5 if one needs face time. It certainly doesn't hurt that Canada does not place limits on visas for skilled workers. An unusually pointed press release by Microsoft stated: "The Vancouver area is a global gateway with a diverse population, is close to Microsoft's offices in Redmond, and allows the company to recruit and retain highly skilled people affected by immigration issues in the U.S."

Sources: MacDonald, I. 2008. Finesse the visa crisis with a worker-mobility plan. *Harvard Business Review*, 86(11): 28–29; Greene, J. 2008. Case study: Microsoft's Canadian solution. *BusinessWeek*, January 28: 51; MacDonald, I. 2008. Tech firms get creative in employing foreigners. *Dallas Morning News*, November 16: 5D; and, Anonymous. 2007. Microsoft to open Canada center in response to U.S. immigration. www.workpermit.com, July 10: np.

additional 20,000 visas available for foreigners with a Master's or higher degree from a U.S. institution. Many of the visas are for professionals from India with computer and software expertise. As one would expect, this is a political "hot potato" for industry executives as well as U.S. labor and workers' right groups. The key arguments against increases in H-1B visas are that H-1B workers drive down wages and take jobs from Americans.

Strategy Spotlight 2.5 discusses one of the proactive steps that Microsoft has taken to address this issue.

The Technological Segment

Developments in technology lead to new products and services and improve how they are produced and delivered to the end user. Innovations can create entirely new industries and alter the boundaries of existing industries.[35] Technological developments and trends include genetic engineering, Internet technology, computer-aided design/computer-aided manufacturing (CAD/CAM), research in artificial and exotic materials, and, on the downside, pollution and global warming.[36] Petroleum and primary metals industries spend significantly to reduce their pollution. Engineering and consulting firms that work with polluting industries derive financial benefits from solving such problems.

Nanotechnology is becoming a very promising area of research with many potentially useful applications.[37] Nanotechnology takes place at industry's tiniest stage: one billionth of a meter. Remarkably, this is the size of 10 hydrogen atoms in a row. Matter at such a tiny scale behaves very differently. Familiar materials—from gold to carbon soot—display startling and useful new properties. Some transmit light or electricity. Others become harder than diamonds or turn into potent chemical catalysts. What's more, researchers have found that a tiny dose of nanoparticles can transform the chemistry and nature of far bigger things. Exhibit 2.4 lists a few of the potential ways in which nanotechnology could revolutionize industries.

technological segment of the general environment innovation and state of knowledge in industrial arts, engineering, applied sciences, and pure science; and their interaction with society.

Exhibit 2.4 How Nanotechnology Might Revolutionize Various Industries

- **To fight cancer,** sensors will be able to detect a single cancer cell and will help guide nanoparticles that can burn tumors from the inside out, leaving healthy cells alone.

- **To transform energy,** nano-enhanced solar panels will feed cheap electricity onto superconducting power lines made of carbon nanotubes.

- **To replace silicon,** carbon nanotubes will take over when silicon peters out, leading to far faster chips that need less power than today's chips.

- **For space travel,** podlike crawlers will carry cargo thousands of miles up a carbon-nanotube cable to a space station for billions less than rocket launches.

Source: Baker, S. & Aston, A. 2004. Universe in a grain of sand. *BusinessWeek,* October 11: 139–140.

There are downsides to technology. In addition to ethical issues in biotechnology, there are threats to our environment associated with the emission of greenhouse gases. Some firms have taken a proactive approach. BP Amoco plans to decrease its greenhouse gas emissions by giving each of its 150 business units a quota of emission permits and encouraging the units to trade them. If a unit cuts emissions and has leftover permits, it can sell them to other units that are having difficulty meeting their goals.[38]

The Economic Segment

Economic segment of the general environment characteristics of the economy including national income and monetary conditions.

The economy affects all industries, from suppliers of raw materials to manufacturers of finished goods and services, as well as all organizations in the service, wholesale, retail, government, and nonprofit sectors.[39] Key economic indicators include interest rates, unemployment rates, the Consumer Price Index, the gross domestic product, and net disposable income. Interest-rate increases have a negative impact on the residential home construction industry but a negligible (or neutral) effect on industries that produce consumer necessities such as prescription drugs or common grocery items.

Other economic indicators are associated with equity markets. Perhaps the most watched is the Dow Jones Industrial Average (DJIA), which is composed of 30 large industrial firms. When stock market indexes increase, consumers' discretionary income rises and there is often an increased demand for luxury items such as jewelry and automobiles. But when stock valuations decrease, demand for these items shrinks. Strategy Spotlight 2.6 provides some examples of how the recession that intensified throughout 2008 affected the purchase of luxury goods.

The Global Segment

Global segment of the general environment influences from foreign countries including foreign market opportunities, foreign-based competition, and expanded capital markets.

More firms are expanding their operations and market reach beyond the borders of their "home" country. Globalization provides both opportunities to access larger potential markets and a broad base of production factors such as raw materials, labor, skilled managers, and technical professionals. However, such endeavors also carry many political, social, and economic risks.[40]

Examples of key elements include currency exchange rates, increasing global trade, the economic emergence of China, trade agreements among regional blocs (e.g., North American Free Trade Agreement, European Union), and the General Agreement on Tariffs and Trade (GATT) (lowering of tariffs).[41] Increases in trade across national boundaries also provide benefits to air cargo and shipping industries but have a minimal impact on service industries such as bookkeeping and routine medical services. The emergence of China as an economic power has benefited many industries, such as construction, soft drinks, and computers. However, it has had a negative impact on the defense industry in the United States as diplomatic relations between the two nations improve.

strategy spotlight

The Recession's Impact on Luxury Goods

With financial markets in distress, extensive Wall Street layoffs, and consumer confidence sliding to its lowest point in several years, marketers of high-end goods and services—often insulated from economic slowdowns—are beginning to experience a sharp decline. Below are some examples from businesses polled by *Fortune* magazine:

- Bookings at the hotel chain, Leading Hotels of the World, declined 10 percent in 2008. With corporate clients representing 25 percent of their business, Senior Vice President Dan Neumann expects things to get worse.

- Allen Brothers, a high-end cataloger and supplier of beef to premier steakhouses such as Del Frisco's, says that restaurant customers are exchanging prime cuts for lower-grade meats.

- Fort Lauderdale–based broker Anchor Yachts says that yacht sales in the $200,000 to $800,000 range are down 50 percent. Sellers have cut prices 20 percent.

- At Pilates on Fifth in Midtown Manhattan, co-owner Katherine Corp states that many of her clients are trading down—exchanging $90 private lessons for cheaper group classes.

Sources: Helm, B. 2008. How to sell luxury to penny-pinchers. *Business-Week*, November 10: 60; and, Boyle, M. 2008. The luxury recession. *Fortune*, April 14: 30.

● Almost every industry has been adversely affected by the recession that began in 2008—including expensive yachts.

In the automobile industry, several discount players have entered the luxury game. For example, Hyundai is selling entry-level luxury in the worst possible selling environment in memory. Their strategy: depict more snooty rivals as overpriced. In its ads, Hyundai notes that its new Genesis sedan ($33,000) has the same sound system as a Rolls-Royce Phantom ($300,000-plus). Their ad says: "If you'd rather have money than a hood ornament" the Genesis may "look even better than a Rolls-Royce."

Also, consider the cost of terrorism. A recent survey indicates that for S&P 500 firms, the threat has caused direct and indirect costs of $107 billion a year. This figure includes extra spending (on insurance and redundant capacity, for instance) as well as lost revenues (from fearful consumers' decreased activity).[42]

Relationships among Elements of the General Environment

In our discussion of the general environment, we see many relationships among the various elements.[43] For example, a demographic trend in the United States, the aging of the population, has important implications for the economic segment (in terms of tax policies to provide benefits to increasing numbers of older citizens). Another example is the emergence of information technology as a means to increase the rate of productivity gains in the United States and other developed countries. Such use of IT results in lower inflation (an important element of the economic segment) and helps offset costs associated with higher labor rates.

The effects of a trend or event in the general environment vary across industries. Governmental legislation (political/legal) to permit the importation of prescription drugs from foreign countries is a very positive development for drugstores but a very negative event for U.S. drug manufacturers. Exhibit 2.5 provides other examples of how the impact of trends or events in the general environment can vary across industries.

Before moving on, let's consider the Internet. The Internet has been a leading and highly visible component of a broader technological phenomenon—the emergence of digital technology. These technologies are altering the way business is conducted and having an impact on nearly every business domain. Strategy Spotlight 2.7 addresses the impact of the Internet and digital technologies on the business environment.

Exhibit 2.5
The Impact of General Environmental Trends on Various Industries

Segment/Trends and Events	Industry	Positive	Neutral	Negative
Demographic				
Aging population	Health care	✓		
	Baby products			✓
Rising affluence	Brokerage services	✓		
	Fast foods			✓
	Upscale pets and supplies	✓		
Sociocultural				
More women in the workforce	Clothing	✓		
	Baking products (staples)			✓
Greater concern for health and fitness	Home exercise equipment	✓		
	Meat products			✓
Political/legal				
Tort reform	Legal services			✓
	Auto manufacturing	✓		
Americans with Disabilities Act (ADA)	Retail			✓
	Manufacturers of elevators, escalators, and ramps	✓		
Technological				
Genetic engineering	Pharmaceutical	✓		
	Publishing		✓	
Pollution/global warming	Engineering services	✓		
	Petroleum			✓
Economic				
Interest rate increases	Residential construction			✓
	Most common grocery products		✓	
Global				
Increasing global trade	Shipping	✓		
	Personal service		✓	
Emergence of China as an economic power	Soft drinks	✓		
	Defense			✓

strategy spotlight

The Internet and Digital Technologies: Affecting Many Environmental Segments

The Internet has dramatically changed the way business is conducted in every corner of the globe. According to digital economy visionary Don Tapscott:

> The Net is much more than just another technology development; the Net represents something qualitatively new—an unprecedented, powerful, universal communications medium. Far surpassing radio and television, this medium is digital, infinitely richer, and interactive.... Mobile computing devices, broadband access, wireless networks, and computing power embedded in everything from refrigerators to automobiles are converging into a global network that will enable people to use the Net just about anywhere and anytime.

The Internet provides a platform or staging area for the application of numerous technologies, rapid advances in knowledge, and unprecedented levels of global communication and commerce. Even technologies that don't require the Internet to function, such as wireless phones and GPS, rely on the Internet for data transfer and communications.

Growth in Internet usage has surged in recent years both among individual users as well as businesses.

Sources: Anonymous. 2005. SMBs believe in the Web. eMarketer.com, www.emarketer.com, May 16. Downes, L. & Mui, C. 1998. *Unleashing the killer app.* Boston: Harvard Business School Press. Green, H. 2003. Wi-Fi means business. *BusinessWeek*, April 28: 86–92; McGann, R. 2005. Broadband: High speed, high spend. *ClickZ Network*, www.clickz.com, January 24; Tapscott, D. 2001. Rethinking strategy in a Networked World. *Strategy and Business*, Third Quarter: 34–41; and, Yang, C. 2003. Beyond wi-fi: A new wireless age. *BusinessWeek*, December 15: 84–88.

Exhibit 2.6 illustrates (2000–2008) worldwide growth trends in Internet use. Business use of the Internet has become nearly ubiquitous throughout the economy. Major corporations all have a Web presence, and many companies use the Internet to interact with key stakeholders. For example, some companies have direct links with suppliers through online procurement systems that automatically reorder inventories and supplies. Companies such as Cisco Systems even interact with their own employees using the Internet to update employment records, such as health care information and benefits.

Small and medium-sized enterprises (SMEs) are also relying on the Internet more than ever. A recent study found that 87 percent of SMEs are receiving monthly revenue from their Web site, and 42 percent derive more than a quarter of their monthly revenue from their Internet presence. According to Joel Kocher, CEO of Interland, "We are getting to the point in most small-business categories where it will soon be safe to say that if you're not online, you're not really serious about being in business."

Despite these advances, the Internet and digital technologies still face numerous challenges. For example, international standards for digital and wireless communications are still in flux. As a result, cell phones and other devices that work in the United States are often useless in many parts of Europe and Asia. And, unlike analog systems, electronic bits of data that are zooming through space can be more easily lost, stolen, or manipulated. However, even with these problems, Internet and digital technologies will continue to be a growing global phenomenon. As Andy Grove, former chairman of Intel, stated, "The world now runs on Internet time."

Geographic Regions	Internet Users, 2000	Internet Users, 2008	%Population (Penetration)	Usage Growth, 2000–2008
Africa	4,514,400	51,065,630	5.3%	1,031%
Asia	114,304,000	578,538,257	15.3%	406%
Europe	105,096,093	384,633,765	48.1%	266%
Middle East	3,284,800	41,939,200	21.3%	1,176%
North America	108,096,800	248,241,969	73.6%	129%
Latin America/Caribbean	18,068,919	139,009,209	24.1%	669%
Oceania/Australia	7,620,480	20,204,331	59.5%	165%
World Total	360,985,492	1,463,632,361	21.9%	305%

Source: www.internetworldstats.com

Exhibit 2.6 Growth in Internet Activity

>LO5

How forces in
the competitive
environment can
affect profitability,
and how a firm
can improve its
competitive position
by increasing its
power vis-à-vis these
forces.

The Competitive Environment

Managers must consider the competitive environment (also sometimes referred to as the task or industry environment). The nature of competition in an industry, as well as the profitability of a firm, is often more directly influenced by developments in the competitive environment.

The **competitive environment** consists of many factors that are particularly relevant to a firm's strategy. These include competitors (existing or potential), customers, and suppliers. Potential competitors may include a supplier considering forward integration, such as an automobile manufacturer acquiring a rental car company, or a firm in an entirely new industry introducing a similar product that uses a more efficient technology.

Next, we will discuss key concepts and analytical techniques that managers should use to assess their competitive environments. First, we examine Michael Porter's five-forces model that illustrates how these forces can be used to explain an industry's profitability.[44] Second, we discuss how the five forces are being affected by the capabilities provided by Internet technologies. Third, we address some of the limitations, or "caveats," that managers should be familiar with when conducting industry analysis. Finally, we address the concept of strategic groups, because even within an industry it is often useful to group firms on the basis of similarities of their strategies. As we will see, competition tends to be more intense among firms *within* a strategic group than between strategic groups.

competitive environment
factors that pertain to an industry and affect a firm's strategies.

Porter's Five-Forces Model of Industry Competition

The "five-forces" model developed by Michael E. Porter has been the most commonly used analytical tool for examining the competitive environment. It describes the competitive environment in terms of five basic competitive forces.[45]

1. The threat of new entrants.
2. The bargaining power of buyers.
3. The bargaining power of suppliers.
4. The threat of substitute products and services.
5. The intensity of rivalry among competitors in an industry.

Each of these forces affects a firm's ability to compete in a given market. Together, they determine the profit potential for a particular industry. The model is shown in Exhibit 2.7. A manager should be familiar with the five-forces model for several reasons. It helps you decide whether your firm should remain in or exit an industry. It provides the rationale for increasing or decreasing resource commitments. The model helps you assess how to improve your firm's competitive position with regard to each of the five forces.[46] For example, you can use insights provided by the five-forces model to create higher entry barriers that discourage new rivals from competing with you.[47] Or you may develop strong relationships with your distribution channels. You may decide to find suppliers who satisfy the price/performance criteria needed to make your product or service a top performer.

The Threat of New Entrants   The threat of new entrants refers to the possibility that the profits of established firms in the industry may be eroded by new competitors.[48] The extent of the threat depends on existing barriers to entry and the combined reactions from existing competitors.[49] If entry barriers are high and/or the newcomer can anticipate a sharp retaliation from established competitors, the threat of entry is low. These circumstances discourage new competitors. There are six major sources of entry barriers.

Threat of new entrants the possibility that the profits of established firms in the industry may be eroded by new competitors.

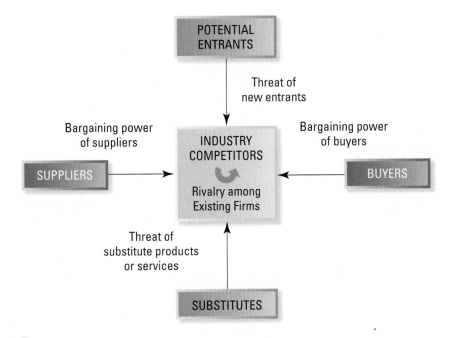

Exhibit 2.7 **Porter's Five-Forces Model of Industry Competition**

Source: Reprinted with permission of The Free Press, a division of Simon & Schuster Adult Publishing Group, from *Competitive Strategy: Techniques for Analyzing Industries and Competitors* by Michael E. Porter. Copyright © 1980, 1998 by The Free Press. All rights reserved.

Economies of Scale Economies of scale refers to spreading the costs of production over the number of units produced. The cost of a product per unit declines as the absolute volume per period increases. This deters entry by forcing the entrant to come in at a large scale and risk strong reaction from existing firms or come in at a small scale and accept a cost disadvantage. Both are undesirable options.

Product Differentiation When existing competitors have strong brand identification and customer loyalty, differentiation creates a barrier to entry by forcing entrants to spend heavily to overcome existing customer loyalties.

Capital Requirements The need to invest large financial resources to compete creates a barrier to entry, especially if the capital is required for risky or unrecoverable up-front advertising or research and development (R&D).

Switching Costs A barrier to entry is created by the existence of one-time costs that the buyer faces when switching from one supplier's product or service to another.

Access to Distribution Channels The new entrant's need to secure distribution for its product can create a barrier to entry.

Cost Disadvantages Independent of Scale Some existing competitors may have advantages that are independent of size or economies of scale. These derive from:

- Proprietary products
- Favorable access to raw materials
- Government subsidies
- Favorable government policies

In an environment where few, if any, of these entry barriers are present, the threat of new entry is high. For example, if a new firm can launch its business with a low capital investment and operate efficiently despite its small scale of operation, it is likely to be a threat. One company that failed because of low entry barriers in an industry is ProCD.[50] You probably never heard of this company. It didn't last very long. ProCD provides an example of a firm that failed because it entered an industry with very low entry barriers.

The story begins in 1986 when Nynex (a former Baby Bell company) issued the first electronic phone book, a compact disk containing all listings for the New York City area. It charged $10,000 per copy and sold the CDs to the FBI, IRS, and other large commercial and government organizations. James Bryant, the Nynex executive in charge of the project, smelled a fantastic business opportunity. He quit Nynex and set up his own firm, ProCD, with the ambitious goal of producing an electronic directory covering the entire United States.

The telephone companies, fearing an attack on their highly profitable Yellow Pages business, refused to license digital copies of their listings. Bryant was not deterred. He hired Chinese workers at $3.50 a day to type every listing from every U.S. telephone book into a database. The result contained more than 70 million phone numbers and was used to create a master disk that enabled ProCD to make hundreds of thousands of copies. Each CD sold for hundreds of dollars and cost less than a dollar each to produce.

It was a profitable business indeed! However, success was fleeting. Competitors such as Digital Directory Assistance and American Business Information quickly launched competing products with the same information. Since customers couldn't tell one product from the next, the players were forced to compete on price alone. Prices for the CD soon plummeted to a few dollars each. A high-priced, high-margin product just months earlier, the CD phone book became little more than a cheap commodity.

Bargaining power of buyers the threat that buyers may force down prices, bargain for higher quality or more services, and play competitors against each other.

The Bargaining Power of Buyers Buyers threaten an industry by forcing down prices, bargaining for higher quality or more services, and playing competitors against each other. These actions erode industry profitability.[51] The power of each large buyer group depends on attributes of the market situation and the importance of purchases from that group compared with the industry's overall business. A buyer group is powerful when:

- *It is concentrated or purchases large volumes relative to seller sales.* If a large percentage of a supplier's sales are purchased by a single buyer, the importance of the buyer's business to the supplier increases. Large-volume buyers also are powerful in industries with high fixed costs (e.g., steel manufacturing).
- *The products it purchases from the industry are standard or undifferentiated.* Confident they can always find alternative suppliers, buyers play one company against the other, as in commodity grain products.
- *The buyer faces few switching costs.* Switching costs lock the buyer to particular sellers. Conversely, the buyer's power is enhanced if the seller faces high switching costs.
- *It earns low profits.* Low profits create incentives to lower purchasing costs. On the other hand, highly profitable buyers are generally less price sensitive.
- *The buyers pose a credible threat of backward integration.* If buyers are either partially integrated or pose a credible threat of backward integration, they are typically able to secure bargaining concessions.
- *The industry's product is unimportant to the quality of the buyer's products or services.* When the quality of the buyer's products is not affected by the industry's product, the buyer is more price sensitive.

At times, a firm or set of firms in an industry may increase its buyer power by using the services of a third party. FreeMarkets Online is one such third party.[52] Pittsburgh-based FreeMarkets has developed software enabling large industrial buyers to organize online auctions for qualified suppliers of semistandard parts such as fabricated components,

Playing "Hard Ball" with Job Applicants: Buy Now, Pay Later?

Companies will likely "buy now, pay later" if they play hard ball with job applicants as the economy sours and unemployment rates rise. According to researchers at Vanderbilt University, employees who felt they were mistreated during the recruiting process feel less committed—for years. Approximately 100 MBA graduates were surveyed about how they were hired by their employers. Those who felt that they were treated unfairly were twice as likely to be looking for opportunities outside their company—even after five years!

What were some common "interactional injustices" during the hiring process? Slow responses from employers, offers that were withdrawn if not accepted immediately, and a company whose attitude is "You need us." A valuable message for businesses positioning themselves to succeed in the economic recovery: "Don't abuse the momentary power you have as an employer. It'll come back to bite you."

Source: Hof, R. D. 2008 Hired, with hard feelings. *BusinessWeek*, November 6: 15.

---

packaging materials, metal stampings, and services. By aggregating buyers, FreeMarkets increases the buyers' bargaining power. The results are impressive. In its first 48 auctions, most participating companies saved over 15 percent; some saved as much as 50 percent.

Although a firm may be tempted to take advantage of its suppliers because of high buyer power, it must be aware of the potential long-term backlash from such actions. Strategy Spotlight 2.8 discusses how newly hired employees may feel resentful and become demotivated if they believe that they were treated unfairly during the recruitment process—a time when their bargaining power may have been rather low relative to the company.

The Bargaining Power of Suppliers   Suppliers can exert bargaining power by threatening to raise prices or reduce the quality of purchased goods and services. Powerful suppliers can squeeze the profitability of firms so far that they can't recover the costs of raw material inputs.[53] The factors that make suppliers powerful tend to mirror those that make buyers powerful. A supplier group will be powerful when:

> **Bargaining power of suppliers** the threat that suppliers may raise prices or reduce the quality of purchased goods and services.

- *The supplier group is dominated by a few companies and is more concentrated (few firms dominate the industry) than the industry it sells to.* Suppliers selling to fragmented industries influence prices, quality, and terms.
- *The supplier group is not obliged to contend with substitute products for sale to the industry.* The power of even large, powerful suppliers can be checked if they compete with substitutes.
- *The industry is not an important customer of the supplier group.* When suppliers sell to several industries and a particular industry does not represent a significant fraction of its sales, suppliers are more prone to exert power.
- *The supplier's product is an important input to the buyer's business.* When such inputs are important to the success of the buyer's manufacturing process or product quality, the bargaining power of suppliers is high.
- *The supplier group's products are differentiated or it has built up switching costs for the buyer.* Differentiation or switching costs facing the buyers cut off their options to play one supplier against another.
- *The supplier group poses a credible threat of forward integration.* This provides a check against the industry's ability to improve the terms by which it purchases.

Strategy Spotlight 2.9 discusses how catfish farmers enhanced their bargaining power vis-à-vis their customers—large agribusiness firms—by forming a cooperative.

Enhancing Supplier Power: The Creation of Delta Pride Catfish

The formation of Delta Pride Catfish in 1981 is an example of the power that a group of suppliers can attain if they exercise the threat of forward integration. Catfish farmers in Mississippi had historically supplied their harvest to processing plants run by large agribusiness firms such as ConAgra and Farm Fresh. When the farmers increased their production of catfish in response to growing demand in the early 1970s, they found, much to their chagrin, that processors were holding back on their plans to increase their processing capabilities in hopes of higher retail prices for catfish.

Source: Cargile, D. 2005. Personal communication. (Vice President of Sales, Delta Pride Catfish, Inc.), February 2; Anonymous. 2003. Delta Pride Catfish names Steve Osso President and CEO. www.deltabusiness.journal.com, February; and Fritz, M. 1988. Agribusiness: Catfish story. *Forbes,* December 12: 37.

What action did the farmers take? They responded by forming a cooperative, raising $4.5 million, and constructing their own processing plant, which they supplied themselves. Within two years, ConAgra's market share had dropped from 35 percent to 11 percent, and Farm Fresh's market share fell by over 20 percent.

By the late 1980s, Delta Pride controlled over 40 percent of the 280-million-pound-per-year U.S. catfish market. It has continued to grow by including value-added products such as breaded and marinated catfish products. One such product is Country Crisp Catfish Strips, a bakeable, breaded product with country-style seasoning. By 2005, Delta Pride had more than 500 employees. Its approximately 100 shareholders are mostly catfish farmers who own more than 60,000 acres of catfish production ponds and produce more than 200 million pounds of live catfish each year.

The Threat of Substitute Products and Services All firms within an industry compete with industries producing substitute products and services.[54] Substitutes limit the potential returns of an industry by placing a ceiling on the prices that firms in that industry can profitably charge. The more attractive the price/performance ratio of substitute products, the tighter the lid on an industry's profits.

Identifying substitute products involves searching for other products or services that can perform the same function as the industry's offerings. This may lead a manager into businesses seemingly far removed from the industry. For example, the airline industry might not consider video cameras much of a threat. But as digital technology has improved and wireless and other forms of telecommunication have become more efficient, teleconferencing has become a viable substitute for business travel. That is, the rate of improvement in the price–performance relationship of the substitute product (or service) is high.

Teleconferencing can save both time and money, as IBM found out with its "Manager Jam" idea.[55] With 319,000 employees scattered around six continents, it is one of the world's largest businesses (including 32,000 managers) and can be a pretty confusing place. The shift to an increasingly mobile workplace means many managers supervise employees they rarely see face-to-face. To enhance coordination, Samuel Palmisano, IBM's new CEO, launched one of his first big initiatives: a two-year program exploring the role of the manager in the 21st century. "Manager Jam," as the project was nicknamed, was a 48-hour real-time Web event in which managers from 50 different countries swapped ideas and strategies for dealing with problems shared by all of them, regardless of geography. Some 8,100 managers logged on to the company's intranet to participate in the discussion forums.

Renewable energy resources are also a promising substitute product and are rapidly becoming more economically competitive with fossil fuels. Strategy Spotlight 2.10 addresses this critical issue.

Threat of substitute products and services the threat of limiting the potential returns of an industry by placing a ceiling on the prices that firms in that industry can profitably charge without losing too many customers to substitute products.

The Growing Viability of Renewable Resources as Substitutes for Fossil Fuels

Renewable resources currently provide just over 6 percent of total U.S. energy. However, that figure could increase rapidly in the years ahead, according to a joint report issued in September 2006 by the Worldwatch Institute and the Center for Progress, entitled "American Energy: The Renewable Path to Energy Security."

The report indicates that many of the new technologies that harness renewables are, or soon will be, economically competitive with fossil fuels. Dynamic growth rates are driving down costs and spurring rapid advances in technologies. And, since 2000, global wind energy generation has more than tripled, solar cell production has risen six-fold, production of fuel ethanol from crops has more than doubled, and biodiesel production has expanded nearly four-fold. Annual global investment in "new" renewable energy has risen almost six-fold since 1995, with cumulative investment over the period nearly $180 billion.

A November 2006 study by the RAND Corporation is consistent with the aforementioned report. It asserts that the economy of the United States would likely benefit, rather than be slowed, if the nation attained the goal of supplying 25 percent of its energy needs from renewable sources by 2025. Such developments would also reduce U.S. dependence on oil, which would mean a substantial start on capping greenhouse gas emissions, which most scientists link to global warming.

Deep Patel, founder of Los Angeles–based online clean-energy technologies retailer GoGreenSolar.com, provides some practical insights:

- *Clean energy is regional:* Think solar in sunny climates like California, geothermal in Nevada, and wind in blustery states such as Oklahoma.

- *Big corporations tend to hire established, renewable energy companies.* "But no one's paying as much attention to smaller businesses and homeowners that want to go solar. For entrepreneurs, that represents the biggest untapped market."

- *Consumers need help "taking a staged approach to going solar."* At GoGreenSolar, a "Plug N Play Solar Power Kit" starts consumers off with two solar panels that they can add to later. Patel's prediction: more such modular solutions will become available.

Sources: Anonymous. 2008. Clean Energy. *Entrepreneur*, December: 59; Clayton, M. 2006. Greener, cleaner . . . and competitive. www.csmonitor.com. December 4; and, Anonymous. 2006. Renewables becoming cost-competitive with fossil fuels in the U.S. www.worldwatch.org. September 18.

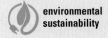

environmental sustainability

The Intensity of Rivalry among Competitors in an Industry Firms use tactics like price competition, advertising battles, product introductions, and increased customer service or warranties. Rivalry occurs when competitors sense the pressure or act on an opportunity to improve their position.[56]

Some forms of competition, such as price competition, are typically highly destabilizing and are likely to erode the average level of profitability in an industry.[57] Rivals easily match price cuts, an action that lowers profits for all firms. On the other hand, advertising battles expand overall demand or enhance the level of product differentiation for the benefit of all firms in the industry. Rivalry, of course, differs across industries. In some instances it is characterized as warlike, bitter, or cutthroat, whereas in other industries it is referred to as polite and gentlemanly. Intense rivalry is the result of several interacting factors, including the following:

- **Numerous or equally balanced competitors.** When there are many firms in an industry, the likelihood of mavericks is great. Some firms believe they can make moves without being noticed. Even when there are relatively few firms, and they are nearly equal in size and resources, instability results from fighting among companies having the resources for sustained and vigorous retaliation.

Intensity of rivalry among competitors in an industry the threat that customers will switch their business to competitors within the industry.

- *Slow industry growth.* Slow industry growth turns competition into a fight for market share, since firms seek to expand their sales.
- *High fixed or storage costs.* High fixed costs create strong pressures for all firms to increase capacity. Excess capacity often leads to escalating price cutting.
- *Lack of differentiation or switching costs.* Where the product or service is perceived as a commodity or near commodity, the buyer's choice is typically based on price and service, resulting in pressures for intense price and service competition. Lack of switching costs, described earlier, has the same effect.
- *Capacity augmented in large increments.* Where economies of scale require that capacity must be added in large increments, capacity additions can be very disruptive to the industry supply/demand balance.
- *High exit barriers.* Exit barriers are economic, strategic, and emotional factors that keep firms competing even though they may be earning low or negative returns on their investments. Some exit barriers are specialized assets, fixed costs of exit, strategic interrelationships (e.g., relationships between the business units and others within a company in terms of image, marketing, shared facilities, and so on), emotional barriers, and government and social pressures (e.g., governmental discouragement of exit out of concern for job loss).

Rivalry between firms is often based solely on price, but it can involve other factors. Take Pfizer's market position in the impotence treatment market. Pfizer was the first pharmaceutical firm to develop Viagra, a highly successful drug that treats impotence.

In several countries, the United Kingdom among them, Pfizer faced a lawsuit by Eli Lilly & Co. and Icos Corp. challenging its patent protection. These two pharmaceutical firms recently entered into a joint venture to market Cialis, a drug to compete with Viagra. The U.K. courts agreed and lifted the patent.

This opened the door for Eli Lilly and Icos to proceed with challenging Pfizer's market position. Because Cialis has fewer side effects than Viagra, the drug has the potential to rapidly decrease Pfizer's market share in the United Kingdom if physicians switch prescriptions from Viagra to Cialis. If future patent challenges are successful, Pfizer may see its sales of Viagra erode rapidly.[58] But Pfizer is hardly standing still. It recently doubled its advertising expenditures on Viagra.

Exhibit 2.8 summarizes our discussion of industry five-forces analysis. It points out how various factors such as economies of scale and capital requirements affect each "force."

How the Internet and Digital Technologies Are Affecting the Five Competitive Forces

The Internet and other digital technologies are having a significant impact on nearly every industry. These technologies have fundamentally changed the ways businesses interact with each other and with consumers. In most cases, these changes have affected industry forces in ways that have created many new strategic challenges. In this section, we will evaluate Michael Porter's five-forces model in terms of the actual use of the Internet and the new technological capabilities that it makes possible.

The Threat of New Entrants In most industries, the threat of new entrants has increased because digital and Internet-based technologies lower barriers to entry. For example, businesses that reach customers primarily through the Internet may enjoy savings on other traditional expenses such as office rent, sales-force salaries, printing, and postage. This may encourage more entrants who, because of the lower start-up expenses, see an opportunity to capture market share by offering a product or performing a service more efficiently than existing competitors. Thus, a new cyber entrant can use the savings provided by the Internet to charge lower prices and compete on price despite the incumbent's scale advantages.

Threat of New Entrants Is High When:	High	Low
Economies of scale are		X
Product differentiation is		X
Capital requirements are		X
Switching costs are		X
Incumbent's control of distribution channels is		X
Incumbent's proprietary knowledge is		X
Incumbent's access to raw materials is		X
Incumbent's access to government subsidies is		X

Power of Buyers Is High When:	High	Low
Concentration of buyers relative to suppliers is	X	
Switching costs are		X
Product differentiation of suppliers is		X
Threat of backward integration by buyers is	X	
Extent of buyer's profits is		X
Importance of the supplier's input to quality of buyer's final product is		X

Power of Suppliers Is High When:	High	Low
Concentration relative to buyer industry is	X	
Availability of substitute products is		X
Importance of customer to the supplier is		X
Differentiation of the supplier's products and services is	X	
Switching costs of the buyer are	X	
Threat of forward integration by the supplier is	X	

Threat of Substitute Products Is High When:	High	Low
The differentiation of the substitute product is	X	
Rate of improvement in price–performance relationship of substitute product is	X	

Intensity of Competitive Rivalry Is High When:	High	Low
Number of competitors is	X	
Industry growth rate is		X
Fixed costs are	X	
Storage costs are	X	
Product differentiation is		X
Switching costs are		X
Exit barriers are	X	
Strategic stakes are	X	

Exhibit 2.8 **Competitive Analysis Checklist**

Alternatively, because digital technologies often make it possible for young firms to provide services that are equivalent or superior to an incumbent, a new entrant may be able to serve a market more effectively, with more personalized services and greater attention to product details. A new firm may be able to build a reputation in its niche and charge premium prices. By so doing, it can capture part of an incumbent's business and erode profitability. Consider Voice Over Internet Protocol (VOIP), a fast growing alternative to traditional phone service, which is expected to reach 25 million U.S. households by 2012.[59] Savings of 20 to 30 percent are common for VOIP consumers. This is driving prices down and lowering telecom industry profits. More importantly it threatens the value of the phone line infrastructure that the major carriers have invested in so heavily.

Another potential benefit of Web-based business is access to distribution channels. Manufacturers or distributors that can reach potential outlets for their products more efficiently by means of the Internet may enter markets that were previously closed to them. Access is not guaranteed, however, because strong barriers to entry exist in certain industries.[60]

The Bargaining Power of Buyers The Internet and wireless technologies may increase buyer power by providing consumers with more information to make buying decisions and by lowering switching costs. But these technologies may also suppress the power of traditional buyer channels that have concentrated buying power in the hands of a few, giving buyers new ways to access sellers. To sort out these differences, let's first distinguish between two types of buyers: end users and buyer channel intermediaries.

End users are the final customers in a distribution channel. Internet sales activity that is labeled "B2C"—that is, business-to-consumer—is concerned with end users. The Internet is likely to increase the power of these buyers for several reasons. First, the Internet provides large amounts of consumer information. This gives end users the information they need to shop for quality merchandise and bargain for price concessions. The automobile industry provides an excellent example. For a small fee, agencies such as Consumers Union (publishers of *Consumer Reports*) will provide customers with detailed information about actual automobile manufacturer costs.[61] This information, available online, can be used to bid down dealers' profits. Second, an end user's switching costs are also potentially much lower because of the Internet. Switching may involve only a few clicks of the mouse to find and view a competing product or service online.

In contrast, the bargaining power of distribution channel buyers may decrease because of the Internet. *Buyer channel intermediaries* are the wholesalers, distributors, and retailers who serve as intermediaries between manufacturers and end users. In some industries, they are dominated by powerful players that control who gains access to the latest goods or the best merchandise. The Internet and wireless communications, however, make it much easier and less expensive for businesses to reach customers directly. Thus, the Internet may increase the power of incumbent firms relative to that of traditional buyer channels. Strategy Spotlight 2.11 illustrates some of the changes brought on by the Internet that have affected the industry's two types of buyers.

The Bargaining Power of Suppliers Use of the Internet and digital technologies to speed up and streamline the process of acquiring supplies is already benefiting many sectors of the economy. But the net effect of the Internet on supplier power will depend on the nature of competition in a given industry. As with buyer power, the extent to which the Internet is a benefit or a detriment also hinges on the supplier's position along the supply chain.

The role of suppliers involves providing products or services to other businesses. The term "B2B"—that is, business-to-business—often refers to businesses that supply or sell to other businesses. The effect of the Internet on the bargaining power of suppliers is a double-edged sword. On the one hand, suppliers may find it difficult to hold onto customers because buyers can do comparative shopping and price negotiations so much faster on

Buyer Power in the Book Industry: The Role of the Internet

The $25 billion book publishing industry illustrates some of the changes brought on by the Internet that have affected buying power among two types of buyers—end users and buyer channel intermediaries. Prior to the Internet, book publishers worked primarily through large distributors. These intermediaries such as Tennessee-based Ingram, one of the largest and most powerful distributors, exercised strong control over the movement of books from publishers to bookstores. This power was especially strong relative to small, independent publishers who often found it difficult to get their books into bookstores and in front of potential customers.

The Internet has significantly changed these relationships. Publishers can now negotiate distribution agreements directly with online retailers such as Amazon and Books-A-Million. Such online bookstores now account for about $4 billion in annual sales. And small publishers can use the Internet to sell directly to end users and publicize new titles, without depending on buyer channel intermediaries to handle their books. By using the Internet to appeal to niche markets, 63,000 small publishers with revenues of less than $50 million each generated $14.2 billion in sales in 2005—over half of the industry's total sales.

Future trends for the industry look favorable. The Book Industry Study Group (BISG) released figures in May 2008 which estimated that publishers' revenues in 2007 reached $37.3 billion, up 4.4 percent from 2006's total. BISG expects revenues to increase to $43.5 billion by the end of 2012. There is also good news for online book sellers: According to results from a 2008 worldwide survey by Nielsen Online, 41 percent of users had bought books online—up from 34 percent just two years earlier.

Sources: Healy, M. 2008. Book Industry Trends 2008 shows publishers' net revenues rose 4.4 percent in 2007 to reach $37.26 billion. www.bisg.org. May 31: np; Books "most popular online buy." 2008. newsvote.bbc.co.uk. January 29: np. Hoynes, M. 2002. Is it the same for book sales? BookWeb.org, www.bookweb.org, March 20; www.parapublishing.com; Teague, D. 2005. U.S. book production reaches new high of 195,000 titles in 2004; Fiction soars. Bowker.com, www.bowker.com, May 24; and Teicher, C. M. 2007. March of the small presses. *Publishers Weekly,* www.publishersweekly.com, March 26.

the Internet. This is especially damaging to supply-chain intermediaries, such as product distributors, who cannot stop suppliers from directly accessing other potential business customers. In addition, the Internet inhibits the ability of suppliers to offer highly differentiated products or unique services. Most procurement technologies can be imitated by competing suppliers, and the technologies that make it possible to design and customize new products rapidly are being used by all competitors.

On the other hand, several factors may also contribute to stronger supplier power. First, the growth of new Web-based business may create more downstream outlets for suppliers to sell to. Second, suppliers may be able to create Web-based purchasing arrangements that make purchasing easier and discourage their customers from switching. Online procurement systems directly link suppliers and customers, reducing transaction costs and paperwork.[62] Third, the use of proprietary software that links buyers to a supplier's website may create a rapid, low-cost ordering capability that discourages the buyer from seeking other sources of supply. Amazon.com, for example, created and patented One-Click purchasing technology that speeds up the ordering process for customers who enroll in the service.[63]

Finally, suppliers will have greater power to the extent that they can reach end users directly without intermediaries. Previously, suppliers often had to work through intermediaries who brought their products or services to market for a fee. But a process known as *disintermediation* is removing the organizations or business process layers responsible for intermediary steps in the value chain of many industries.[64] Just as the Internet is eliminating some business functions, it is creating an opening for new functions. These new activities are entering the value chain by a process known as *reintermediation*—the introduction of new types of intermediaries. Many of these new functions are affecting traditional supply chains. For example, delivery services are enjoying a boom because of the Internet. Many more consumers are choosing to have products delivered to their door rather than going out to pick them up.

The Threat of Substitutes   Along with traditional marketplaces, the Internet has created a new marketplace and a new channel. In general, therefore, the threat of substitutes is heightened because the Internet introduces new ways to accomplish the same tasks.

Consumers will generally choose to use a product or service until a substitute that meets the same need becomes available at a lower cost. The economies created by Internet technologies have led to the development of numerous substitutes for traditional ways of doing business. For example, a company called Conferenza is offering an alternative way to participate in conferences for people who don't want to spend the time and money to attend. Conferenza's website provides summaries of many conference events, quality ratings using an "event intelligence" score, and schedules of upcoming events.[65]

Another example of substitution is in the realm of electronic storage. With expanded desktop computing, the need to store information electronically has increased dramatically. Until recently, the trend has been to create increasingly larger desktop storage capabilities and techniques for compressing information that create storage efficiencies. But a viable substitute has recently emerged: storing information digitally on the Internet. Companies such as My Docs Online Inc. are providing Web-based storage that firms can access simply by leasing space online. Since these storage places are virtual, they can be accessed anywhere the Web can be accessed. Travelers can access important documents and files without transporting them physically from place to place. Cyberstorage is not free, but it is cheaper and more convenient than purchasing and carrying disk storage.[66]

The Intensity of Competitive Rivalry   Because the Internet creates more tools and means for competing, rivalry among competitors is likely to be more intense. Only those competitors that can use digital technologies and the Web to give themselves a distinct image, create unique product offerings, or provide "faster, smarter, cheaper" services are likely to capture greater profitability with the new technology. Such gains are hard to sustain, however, because in most cases the new technology can be imitated quickly. Thus, the Internet tends to increase rivalry by making it difficult for firms to differentiate themselves and by shifting customer attention to issues of price.

Rivalry is more intense when switching costs are low and product or service differentiation is minimized. Because the Internet makes it possible to shop around, it has "commoditized" products that might previously have been regarded as rare or unique. Since the Internet reduces the importance of location, products that previously had to be sought out in geographically distant outlets are now readily available online. This makes competitors in cyberspace seem more equally balanced, thus intensifying rivalry.

The problem is made worse for marketers by the presence of shopping robots ("bots") and infomediaries that search the Web for the best possible prices. Consumer websites like mySimon and PriceSCAN seek out all the Web locations that sell similar products and provide price comparisons.[67] Obviously, this focuses the consumer exclusively on price. Some shopping infomediaries, such as BizRate and CNET, not only search for the lowest prices on many different products but also rank the customer service quality of different sites that sell similarly priced items.[68] Such infomediary services are good for consumers because they give them the chance to compare services as well as price. For businesses, however, they increase rivalry by consolidating the marketing message that consumers use to make a purchase decision into a few key pieces of information over which the selling company has little control.

Exhibit 2.9 summarizes many of the ways the Internet is affecting industry structure. These influences will also change how companies develop and deploy strategies to generate above-average profits and sustainable competitive advantage.

Exhibit 2.9 How the Internet and Digital Technologies Influence Industry

	Benefits to Industry (+)	Disadvantages to Industry (−)
Threat of New Entrants		• Lower barriers to entry increases number of new entrants. • Many Internet-based capabilities can be easily imitated.
Bargaining Power of Buyers	• Reduces the power of buyer intermediaries in many distribution channels.	• Switching costs decrease. • Information availability online empowers end users.
Bargaining Power of Suppliers	• Online procurement methods can increase bargaining power over suppliers.	• The Internet gives suppliers access to more customers and makes it easier to reach end users. • Online procurement practices deter competition and reduce differentiating features.
Threat of Substitutes	• Internet-based increases in overall efficiency can expand industry sales.	• Internet-based capabilities create more opportunities for substitution.
Intensity of Rivalry		• Since location is less important, the number of competitors increases. • Differences among competitors are harder to perceive online. • Rivalry tends to focus on price and differentiating features are minimized.

Sources: Bodily, S. & Venkataraman, S. 2004. Not walls, windows: Capturing value in the digital age. *Journal of Business Strategy,* 25(3): 15–25; Lumpkin, G. T., Droege, S. B., & Dess, G. G. 2002. E-commerce strategies: Achieving sustainable competitive advantage and avoiding pitfalls. *Organizational Dynamics,* 30 (Spring): 1–17.

Using Industry Analysis: A Few Caveats

For industry analysis to be valuable, a company must collect and evaluate a wide variety of information. As the trend toward globalization accelerates, information on foreign markets as well as on a wider variety of competitors, suppliers, customers, substitutes, and potential new entrants becomes more critical. Industry analysis helps a firm not only to evaluate the profit potential of an industry but also consider various ways to strengthen its position vis-à-vis the five forces. However, we'd like to address a few caveats.

First, *managers must not always avoid low profit industries (or low profit segments in profitable industries).*[69] Such industries can still yield high returns for some players who pursue sound strategies. As examples, consider Paychex, a payroll-processing company, and WellPoint Health Network, a huge health care insurer:[70]

Paychex, with $2 billion in revenues, became successful by serving small businesses. Existing firms had ignored them because they assumed that such businesses could not afford the service. When Paychex's founder, Tom Golisano, failed to convince his bosses at Electronic Accounting Systems that they were missing a great opportunity, he launched the firm. It now serves nearly 600,000 clients in the United States and Germany. Paychex's after-tax-return on sales is a stunning 28 percent.

In 1986, WellPoint Health Network (when it was known as Blue Cross of California) suffered a loss of $160 million. That year, Leonard Schaeffer became CEO and challenged the conventional wisdom that individuals and small firms were money losers. (This was certainly "heresy" at the time—the firm was losing $5 million a year insuring 65,000 individuals!) However, by the early 1990s, the health insurer was leading the industry in profitability. The firm has continued to grow and outperform its rivals even during economic downturns. By 2008, its revenues and profits were $61 billion and $3.4 billion, respectively—each figure representing an *annual* increase of over 36 percent for the most recent two-year period.

Second, five-forces analysis implicitly *assumes a zero-sum game, determining how a firm can enhance its position relative to the forces.* Yet such an approach can often be short-sighted; that is, it can overlook the many potential benefits of developing constructive win–win relationships with suppliers and customers. Establishing long-term mutually beneficial relationships with suppliers improves a firm's ability to implement just-in-time (JIT) inventory systems, which let it manage inventories better and respond quickly to market demands. A recent study found that if a company exploits its powerful position against a supplier, that action may come back to haunt the company.[71] Consider, for example, General Motors' heavy-handed dealings with its suppliers:[72]

> GM has a reputation for particularly aggressive tactics. Although it is striving to crack down on the most egregious of these, it continues to rank dead last in the annual supplier satisfaction survey. "It's a brutal process," says David E. Cole, who is head of the Center for Automotive Research in Ann Arbor. "There are bodies lying by the side of the road."
>
> Suppliers point to one particularly nasty tactic: shopping their technology out the back door to see if rivals can make it cheaper. In one case, a GM purchasing manager showed a supplier's new brake design to Delphi Corporation. He was fired. However, in a recent survey, parts executives said they tend to bring hot new technology to other carmakers first. This is yet another reason GM finds it hard to compete in an intensely competitive industry.

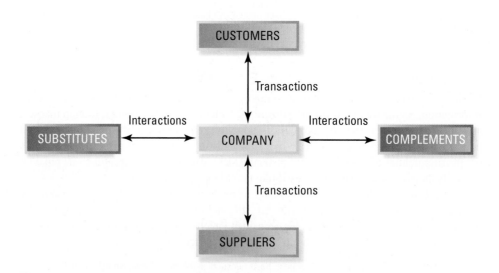

Exhibit 2.10 The Value Net

Source: Adapted and reprinted by permission of *Harvard Business Review.* Exhibit from "The Right Game: Use Game Theory to Shape Strategy," by A. Brandenburger and B. J. Nalebuff, July–August 1995. Copyright © 1995 by the Harvard Business School Publishing Corporation. All rights reserved.

Third, the five-forces analysis also has been criticized for *being essentially a static analysis.* External forces as well as strategies of individual firms are continually changing the structure of all industries. The search for a dynamic theory of strategy has led to greater use of game theory in industrial organization economics research and strategy research.

Based on game-theoretic considerations, Brandenburger and Nalebuff recently introduced the concept of the value net,[73] which in many ways is an extension of the five-forces analysis. It is illustrated in Exhibit 2.10. The value net represents all the players in the game and analyzes how their interactions affect a firm's ability to generate and appropriate value. The vertical dimension of the net includes suppliers and customers. The firm has direct transactions with them. On the horizontal dimension are substitutes and complements, players with whom a firm interacts but may not necessarily transact. The concept of complementors is perhaps the single most important contribution of value net analysis and is explained in more detail below.

Complements typically are products or services that have a potential impact on the value of a firm's own products or services. Those who produce complements are usually referred to as complementors.[74] Powerful hardware is of no value to a user unless there is software that runs on it. Similarly, new and better software is possible only if the hardware on which it can be run is available. This is equally true in the video game industry, where the sales of game consoles and video games complement each other. Nintendo's success in the early 1990s was a result of their ability to manage their relationship with their complementors. They built a security chip into the hardware and then licensed the right to develop games to outside firms. These firms paid a royalty to Nintendo for each copy of the game sold. The royalty revenue enabled Nintendo to sell game consoles at close to their cost, thereby increasing their market share, which, in turn, caused more games to be sold and more royalties to be generated.[75]

Despite efforts to create win–win scenarios, conflict among complementors is inevitable.[76] After all, it is naive to expect that even the closest of partners will do you the favor of abandoning their own interests. And even the most successful partnerships are seldom trouble free. Power is a factor that comes into play as we see in Strategy Spotlight 2.12 with the example of Apple's iPod—an enormously successful product.

We would like to close this section with some recent insights from Michael Porter, the originator of the five-forces analysis.[77] He addresses two critical issues in conducting a good industry analysis, which will yield an improved understanding of the root causes of profitability: (1) choosing the appropriate time frame and (2) a rigorous quantification of the five forces.

- *Good industry analysis looks rigorously at the structural underpinnings of profitability. A first step is to understand the time horizon.* One of the essential tasks in industry analysis is to distinguish short-term fluctuations from structural changes. A good guideline for the appropriate time horizon is the full business cycle for the particular industry. For most industries, a three- to five-year horizon is appropriate. However, for some industries with long lead times, such as mining, the appropriate horizon may be a decade or more. It is average profitability over this period, not profitability in any particular year, which should be the focus of analysis.

- *The point of industry analysis is not to declare the industry attractive or unattractive but to understand the underpinnings of competition and the root causes of profitability.* As much as possible, analysts should look at industry structure quantitatively, rather than be satisfied with lists of qualitative factors. Many elements of five forces can be quantified: the percentage of the buyer's total cost accounted for by the industry's product (to understand buyer price sensitivity); the percentage of industry sales required to fill a plant or operate a logistical network to efficient scale (to help assess barriers to entry); and the buyer's switching cost (determining the inducement an entrant or rival must offer customers).

complements
products or services that have an impact on the value of a firm's products or services.

>LO7
The concept of strategic groups and their strategy and performance implications.

Apple's iPod: Relationships with Its Complementors

In 2002, Steve Jobs began his campaign to cajole the major music companies into selling tracks to iPod users through the iTunes Music Store, an online retail site. Most industry executives, after being burned by illegal file-sharing services like Napster and Kazaa, just wanted digital music to disappear. However, Jobs's passionate vision persuaded them to climb on board. He promised to reduce the risks that they faced by offering safeguards against piracy, as well as a hip product (iPod) that would drive sales.

However, Apple had a much stronger bargaining position when its contracts with the music companies came up for renewal in April 2005. By then, iTunes had captured 80 percent of the market for legal downloads. The music companies, which were receiving between 60 and 70 cents per download, wanted more. Their reasoning: If the iTunes Music Store would only charge $1.50 or $2.00 per track, they could double or triple their revenues and profits. Since Jobs knew that he could sell more iPods if the music was cheap, he was determined to keep the price of a download at 99 cents and to maintain Apple's margins. Given iTunes' dominant position, the music companies had little choice but to relent.

Apple's foray into music has been tremendously successful. Between 2006 and 2008, iPod sales increased from $7.7 billion to $9.2 billion—a 19 percent increase. And, other music related products and services soared

Source: Hesseldahl, A. 2008. Now that we all have iPods. *BusinessWeek*, December 15: 36; Apple Computer Inc. 10-K, 2008; and, Yoffie, D. B. & Kwak, M. 2006. With friends like these: The art of managing complementors. *Harvard Business Review*, 84(9): 88–98.

from $1.9 billion to $3.3 billion over the same period—an impressive 74 percent increase. Despite tough competition, Apple still dominates the music player business with 70 percent of the U.S. market.

● A female employee sits at her desk equipped with both an iMac and an iPod. She works on a spreadsheet, uses iTunes, and listens to an iPod.

Strategic Groups within Industries

In an industry analysis, two assumptions are unassailable: (1) No two firms are totally different, and (2) no two firms are exactly the same. The issue becomes one of identifying groups of firms that are more similar to each other than firms that are not, otherwise known as **strategic groups**.[78] This is important because rivalry tends to be greater among firms that are alike. Strategic groups are clusters of firms that share similar strategies. After all, is Kmart more concerned about Nordstrom or Wal-Mart? Is Mercedes more concerned about Hyundai or BMW? The answers are straightforward.[79]

These examples are not meant to trivialize the strategic groups concept.[80] Classifying an industry into strategic groups involves judgment. If it is useful as an analytical tool, we must exercise caution in deciding what dimensions to use to map these firms. Dimensions include breadth of product and geographic scope, price/quality, degree of vertical

strategic groups
clusters of firms that share similar strategies.

integration, type of distribution (e.g., dealers, mass merchandisers, private label), and so on. Dimensions should also be selected to reflect the variety of strategic combinations in an industry. For example, if all firms in an industry have roughly the same level of product differentiation (or R&D intensity), this would not be a good dimension to select.

What value is the strategic groups concept as an analytical tool? *First, strategic groupings help a firm identify barriers to mobility that protect a group from attacks by other groups.*[81] Mobility barriers are factors that deter the movement of firms from one strategic position to another. For example, in the chainsaw industry, the major barriers protecting the high-quality/dealer-oriented group are technology, brand image, and an established network of servicing dealers.

The second value of strategic grouping is that it *helps a firm identify groups whose competitive position may be marginal or tenuous.* We may anticipate that these competitors may exit the industry or try to move into another group. In recent years in the retail department store industry, firms such as JCPenney and Sears have experienced extremely difficult times because they were stuck in the middle, neither an aggressive discount player like Wal-Mart nor a prestigious upscale player like Neiman Marcus.

Third, strategic groupings *help chart the future directions of firms' strategies.* Arrows emanating from each strategic group can represent the direction in which the group (or a firm within the group) seems to be moving. If all strategic groups are moving in a similar direction, this could indicate a high degree of future volatility and intensity of competition. In the automobile industry, for example, the competition in the minivan and sport utility segments has intensified in recent years as many firms have entered those product segments.

Fourth, strategic groups are *helpful in thinking through the implications of each industry trend for the strategic group as a whole.* Is the trend decreasing the viability of a group? If so, in what direction should the strategic group move? Is the trend increasing or decreasing entry barriers? Will the trend decrease the ability of one group to separate itself from other groups? Such analysis can help in making predictions about industry evolution. A sharp increase in interest rates, for example, tends to have less impact on providers of higher-priced goods (e.g., Porsches) than on providers of lower-priced goods (e.g., Chevrolet Cobalt) whose customer base is much more price sensitive.

Exhibit 2.11 provides a strategic grouping of the worldwide automobile industry.[82] The firms in each group are representative; not all firms are included in the mapping. We have identified four strategic groups. In the top left-hand corner are high-end luxury automakers who focus on a very narrow product market. Most of the cars produced by the members of this group cost well over $100,000. Some cost many times that amount. The 2008 Ferrari F430 costs $187,000 and the Lamborghini Gallardo $208,000[83] (in case you were wondering how to spend your employment signing bonus). Players in this market have a very exclusive clientele and face little rivalry from other strategic groups. At the other extreme, in the lower left-hand corner is a strategic group that has low-price/quality attributes and targets a narrow market. These players, Hyundai and Kia, limit competition from other strategic groups by pricing their products very low. The third group (near the middle) consists of firms high in product pricing/quality and average in their product-line breadth. The final group (at the far right) consists of firms with a broad range of products and multiple price points. These firms have entries that compete at both the lower end of the market (e.g., the Ford Focus) and the higher end (e.g., Chevrolet Corvette).

The auto market has been very dynamic and competition has intensified in recent years.[84] Many firms in different strategic groups compete in the same product markets, such as minivans and sport utility vehicles. In the late 1990s Mercedes entered the fray with its M series, and Porsche has a recent entry as well with its Cayenne, a 2004 model.

Some players are also going more upscale with their product offerings. Recently, Hyundai introduced its Genesis, starting at $33,000. This brings Hyundai into direct competition with entries from other strategic groups such as Toyota's Camry and Honda's Accord.

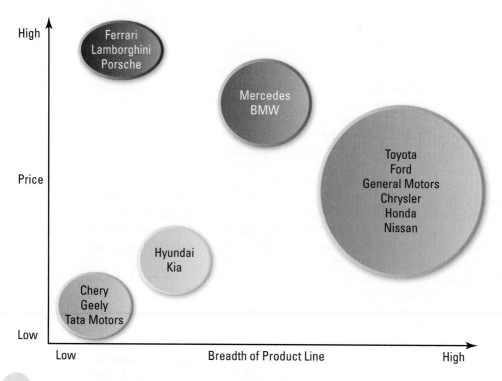

Exhibit 2.11 The World Automobile Industry: Strategic Groups

Note: Members of each strategic group are not inclusive, only illustrative.

Hyundai is offering an extensive warranty (10 years, 100,000 miles) in an effort to offset customer perceptions of their lower quality. To further intensify competition, some key automakers are providing offerings in lower-priced segments. BMW, with their 1-series, is a well-known example. Such cars, priced in the low $30,000s, compete more directly with products from broad-line manufacturers like Ford, General Motors, and Toyota.

Such models are competing in an industry that has experienced relatively flat unit sales in the first half of this decade. However, things have turned increasingly sour. U.S. automobile sales dropped to 13.2 million units in 2008—compared to 16.7 million units in 2007. Consulting firm IHS Global Insight expects 2009 U.S. sales to drop to only 10.3 million units—nearly a 40 percent decline from two years earlier.[85] Needless to say, one should expect incentive-laden offerings to appear at dealer lots for some time to come.

Our discussion would not be complete, of course, without paying some attention to recent entries in the automobile industry that will likely lead to the formation of a new strategic group—placed at the bottom left corner of the grid in Exhibit 2.11. Three firms—China's Zhejiang Geely Holding Company, China's Chery Automobile Company, and India's Tata Motors—have introduced models that bring new meaning to the term "subcompact."[86] Let's take a look at these econoboxes.

Chery's QQ model sells for between $4,000 and $7,000 in the Chinese market and sports horsepower in the range of 51 to 74. Geely's best-selling four-door sedan, the Free Cruiser, retails from $6,300 and $6,900. The firm is planning to go more upscale with the Geely KingKong ($7,500–$10,000), a four-door 1.5- to 1.8-liter sedan, and the Vision ($9,700–$15,300), a 1.8-liter four-door sedan. But, for price-points, India's Tata Motors has everyone beat. In January 2008, it unveiled the Nano with an astonishing retail price of only $2,500. It is a four-door, five-seat hatchback that gets 54 miles per gallon. But before you order one—keep in mind that it only comes with a 30 horsepower engine.

Reflecting on Career Implications . . .

- *Creating the Environmentally Aware Organization:* In your career, what are some ways in which you can engage in scanning, monitoring, and intelligence gathering for future job opportunities? Consider, for example, subscribing to your field's professional publications and becoming actively involved in relevant professional organizations.
- *SWOT Analysis:* From a career standpoint, periodically evaluate your strengths and weaknesses as well as potential opportunities and threats to your career. In addition, strive to seek input from trusted peers and superiors.
- *General Environment:* Carefully evaluate the elements of the general environment facing your firm. Identify factors (e.g., rapid technological change) that can provide promising career opportunities as well as possibilities for you to add value for your organization. In doing this, don't focus solely on "internal factors" of your organization.
- *Five-Forces Analysis:* Consider the five-forces affecting the industry within which your organization competes. If the "forces" are unfavorable, the long-term profit potential of the industry may be unattractive. And, there will likely be fewer resources available and—all other things being equal—fewer career opportunities.

Summary

Managers must analyze the external environment to minimize or eliminate threats and exploit opportunities. This involves a continuous process of environmental scanning and monitoring as well as obtaining competitive intelligence on present and potential rivals. These activities provide valuable inputs for developing forecasts. In addition, many firms use scenario planning to anticipate and respond to volatile and disruptive environmental changes.

We identified two types of environments: the general environment and the competitive environment. The six segments of the general environment are demographic, sociocultural, political/legal, technological, economic, and global. Trends and events occurring in these segments, such as the aging of the population, higher percentages of women in the workplace, governmental legislation, and increasing (or decreasing) interest rates, can have a dramatic effect on a firm. A given trend or event may have a positive impact on some industries and a negative, neutral, or no impact at all on others.

The competitive environment consists of industry-related factors and has a more direct impact than the general environment. Porter's five-forces model of industry analysis includes the threat of new entrants, buyer power, supplier power, threat of substitutes, and rivalry among competitors. The intensity of these factors determines, in large part, the average expected level of profitability in an industry. A sound awareness of such factors, both individually and in combination, is beneficial not only for deciding what industries to enter but also for assessing how a firm can improve its competitive position. We discuss how many of the changes brought about by the digital economy can be understood in the context of five-forces analysis. The limitations of five-forces analysis include its static nature and its inability to acknowledge the role of complementors. Although we addressed the general environment and competitive environment in separate sections, they are quite interdependent. A given environmental trend or event, such as changes in the ethnic composition of a population or a technological innovation, typically has a much greater impact on some industries than on others.

The concept of strategic groups is also important to the external environment of a firm. No two organizations are completely different nor are they exactly the same. The question is how to group firms in an industry on the basis of similarities in their resources and strategies. The strategic groups concept is valuable for determining mobility barriers across groups, identifying groups with marginal competitive positions, charting the future directions of firm strategies, and assessing the implications of industry trends for the strategic group as a whole.

Summary Review Questions

1. Why must managers be aware of a firm's external environment?
2. What is gathering and analyzing competitive intelligence and why is it important for firms to engage in it?
3. Discuss and describe the six elements of the external environment.
4. Select one of these elements and describe some changes relating to it in an industry that interests you.
5. Describe how the five forces can be used to determine the average expected profitability in an industry.
6. What are some of the limitations (or caveats) in using five-forces analysis?
7. Explain how the general environment and industry environment are highly related. How can such inter-relationships affect the profitability of a firm or industry?
8. Explain the concept of strategic groups. What are the performance implications?

Experiential Exercise

Select one of the following industries: personal computers, airlines, or automobiles. For this industry, evaluate the strength of each of Porter's five forces as well as complementors.

Key Terms

environmental scanning, 41
globalization 41
environmental monitoring, 42
competitive intelligence, 42
environmental forecasting, 45
scenario analysis, 45
SWOT analysis, 47
general environment, 47
demographic segment of the general environment 49
sociocultural segment of the general environment 49
political/legal segment of the general environment 50
technological segment of the general environment 51
economic segment of the general environment 52
global segment of the general environment 52
competitive environment, 56
threat of new entrants 56
bargaining power of buyers 58
bargaining power of suppliers 59
threat of substitute products and services 60
intensity of rivalry among competitors in an industry 61
complements, 69
strategic groups, 70

Industry Force	High? Medium? Low?	Why?
1. Threat of new entrants		
2. Power of buyers		
3. Power of suppliers		
4. Power of substitutes		
5. Rivalry among competitors		
6. Complementors		

Application Questions Exercises

1. Imagine yourself as the CEO of a large firm in an industry in which you are interested. Please (1) identify major trends in the general environment, (2) analyze their impact on the firm, and (3) identify major sources of information to monitor these trends. (Use Internet and library resources.)

2. Analyze movements across the strategic groups in the U.S. retail industry. How do these movements within this industry change the nature of competition?
3. What are the major trends in the general environment that have impacted the U.S. pharmaceutical industry?
4. Go to the Internet and look up www.kroger.com. What are some of the five forces driving industry competition that are affecting the profitability of this firm?

Ethics Questions

1. What are some of the legal and ethical issues involved in collecting competitor intelligence in the following situations?

    a. Hotel A sends an employee posing as a potential client to Hotel B to find out who Hotel B's major corporate customers are.

    b. A firm hires an MBA student to collect information directly from a competitor while claiming the information is for a course project.

    c. A firm advertises a nonexistent position and interviews a rival's employees with the intention of obtaining competitor information.

2. What are some of the ethical implications that arise when a firm tries to exploit its power over a supplier?

References

1. Einhorn, B. & Crockett, R. O. 2008. Motorola: Fading in China. *Business-Week*, September 8: 56; Kharif, O. & Crockett, R. O. 2008. Motorola's turnaround plans meet with skepticism. Businessweek.com, October 31: np; and, Moritz, S. 2008. Motorola delays breakup, cuts jobs. CNNMoney.com, October 30: np.

2. Hamel, G. & Prahalad, C. K. 1994. *Competing for the future.* Boston: Harvard Business School Press.

3. Drucker, P. F. 1994. Theory of the business. *Harvard Business Review,* 72: 95–104.

4. For an insightful discussion on managers' assessment of the external environment, refer to Sutcliffe, K. M. & Weber, K. 2003. The high cost of accurate knowledge. *Harvard Business Review,* 81(5): 74–86.

5. For insights on recognizing and acting on environmental opportunities, refer to: Alvarez, S. A. & Barney, J. B. 2008. Opportunities, organizations, and entrepreneurship: Theory and debate. *Strategic Entrepreneurship Journal,* 2(3): entire issue.

6. Charitou, C. D. & Markides, C. C. 2003. Responses to disruptive strategic innovation. *MIT Sloan Management Review,* 44(2): 55–64.

7. Our discussion of scanning, monitoring, competitive intelligence, and forecasting concepts draws on several sources. These include Fahey, L. & Narayanan, V. K. 1983. *Macroenvironmental analysis for strategic management.* St. Paul, MN: West; Lorange, P., Scott, F. S., & Ghoshal, S. 1986. *Strategic control.* St. Paul, MN: West;

Ansoff, H. I. 1984. *Implementing strategic management.* Englewood Cliffs, NJ: Prentice Hall; and Schreyogg, G. & Stienmann, H. 1987. Strategic control: A new perspective. *Academy of Management Review,* 12: 91–103.

8. An insightful discussion on how leaders can develop "peripheral vision" in environmental scanning is found in: Day, G. S. & Schoemaker, P. J. H. 2008. Are you a "vigilant leader"? *MIT Sloan Management Review,* 49 (3): 43–51.

9. Elenkov, D. S. 1997. Strategic uncertainty and environmental scanning: The case for institutional influences on scanning behavior. *Strategic Management Journal,* 18: 287–302.

10. For an interesting perspective on environmental scanning in emerging economies see May, R. C., Stewart, W. H., & Sweo, R. 2000. Environmental scanning behavior in a transitional economy: Evidence from Russia. *Academy of Management Journal,* 43(3): 403–27.

11. Bowles, J. 1997. Key issues for the automotive industry CEOs. *Fortune,* August 18: S3.

12. An interesting perspective on China's emergence as a global power is in: Fuller, J. 2008. The beneficent dragon. *MIT Sloan Management Review,* Spring: 88.

13. Walters, B. A. & Priem, R. L. 1999. Business strategy and CEO intelligence acquisition. *Competitive Intelligence Review,* 10(2): 15–22.

14. Prior, V. 1999. The language of competitive intelligence, Part 4. *Competitive Intelligence Review,* 10(1): 84–87.

15. Zahra, S. A. & Charples, S. S. 1993. Blind spots in competitive analysis. *Academy of Management Executive* 7(2): 7–27.

16. Wolfenson, J. 1999. The world in 1999: A battle for corporate honesty. *The Economist* 38: 13–30.

17. Drucker, P. F. 1997. The future that has already happened. *Harvard Business Review,* 75(6): 22.

18. Evans, P. B. & Wurster, T. S. 1997. Strategy and the new economics of information. *Harvard Business Review,* 75(5): 71–82.

19. Fahey & Narayanan, op. cit., p. 41.

20. Insights on how to improve predictions can be found in: Cross, R., Thomas, R. J., & Light, D. A. 2009. The prediction lover's handbook. *MIT Sloan Management Review,* 50 (2): 32–34.

21. Courtney, H., Kirkland, J., & Viguerie, P. 1997. Strategy under uncertainty. *Harvard Business Review,* 75(6): 66–79.

22. Odlyzko, A. 2003. False hopes. *Red Herring,* March: 31.

23. Coy, P. 2009. Worst predictions about 2008. *BusinessWeek,* January 12: 15–16.

24. For an interesting perspective on how Accenture practices and has developed its approach to scenario planning, refer to Ferguson, G., Mathur, S., & Shah, B. 2005. Evolving from information to insight. *MIT Sloan Management Review,* 46(2): 51–58.

25. Dean, T. J., Brown, R. L., & Bamford, C. E. 1998. Differences in large and small firm responses to environmental context: Strategic implications

from a comparative analysis of business formations. *Strategic Management Journal*, 19: 709–728.

26. Some insights on management during economic downturns are in: Colvin, G. 2009. How to manage your business in a recession. *Fortune*, January 19: 88–93.

27. Colvin, G. 1997. How to beat the boomer rush. *Fortune*, August 18: 59–63.

28. Guntner, T. 2006. Still working and loving it. *BusinessWeek*, October 16: 108; Warner, M. 2004. Home Depot goes old school. *Business 2.0*, June: 74; and, O'Brien, S. 2005. Over 50 and looking for work? www.seniorliving.about.com.

29. Challenger, J. 2000. Women's corporate rise has reduced relocations. *Lexington* (KY) *Herald-Leader*, October 29: D1.

30. Tsao, A. 2005. Retooling home improvement, Businesssweek.com, February, 14; and, Grow, B. 2004. Who wears the wallet in the family? *BusinessWeek*, August 16:10.

31. Watkins, M. D. 2003. Government games. *MIT Sloan Management Review* 44(2): 91–95.

32. A discussion of the political issues surrounding caloric content on meals is in: Orey, M. 2008. A food fight over calorie counts. *BusinessWeek*, February 11: 36.

33. For a discussion of the linkage between copyright law and innovation, read: Guterman, J. 2009. Does copyright law hinder innovation? *MIT Sloan Management Review*, 50(2): 14–15.

34. Davies, A. 2000. The welcome mat is out for nerds. *BusinessWeek*, May 21: 17; Broache, A. 2007. Annual H-1B visa cap met—already. *news.cnet.com*, April 3: np; and, Anonymous. Undated. Cap count for H-1B and H-2B workers for fiscal year 2009. www.uscis.gov: np.

35. Anonymous. Business ready for Internet revolution. 1999. *Financial Times*, May 21: 17.

36. A discussion of an alternate energy—marine energy—is the topic of: Boyle, M. 2008. Scottish power. *Fortune*. March 17: 28.

37. Baker, S. & Aston, A. 2005. The business of nanotech. *BusinessWeek*, February 14: 64–71.

38. Ginsburg, J. 2000. Letting the free market clear the air. *BusinessWeek*, November 6: 200, 204.

39. For an insightful discussion of the causes of the global financial crisis, read: Johnson, S. 2009. The global financial crisis—What really precipitated it? *MIT Sloan Management Review*. 50(2): 16–18.

40. A interesting and balanced discussion on the merits of multinationals to the U.S. economy is found in: Mandel, M. 2008. Multinationals: Are they good for America? *BusinessWeek*, March 10: 41–64.

41. Insights on risk perception across countries are addressed in: Purda, L. D. 2008. Risk perception and the financial system. *Journal of International Business Studies*, 39(7): 1178–1196.

42. Byrnes, N. 2006. The high cost of fear. *BusinessWeek*, November 6: 16.

43. Goll, I. & Rasheed, M. A. 1997. Rational decision-making and firm performance: The moderating role of environment. *Strategic Management Journal*, 18: 583–591.

44. This discussion draws heavily on Porter, M. E. 1980. *Competitive strategy:* Chapter 1. New York: Free Press.

45. Ibid.

46. Rivalry in the airline industry is discussed in: Foust, D. 2009. Which airlines will disappear in 2009? *BusinessWeek*, January 19: 46–47.

47. Fryer, B. 2001. Leading through rough times: An interview with Novell's Eric Schmidt. *Harvard Business Review*, 78(5): 117–123.

48. For a discussion on the importance of barriers to entry within industries, read Greenwald, B. & Kahn, J. 2005. *Competition demystified: A radically simplified approach to business strategy.* East Rutherford, NJ: Portfolio.

49. A discussion of how the medical industry has erected entry barriers that have resulted in lawsuits is found in: Whelan, D. 2008. Bad medicine. *BusinessWeek*, March 10: 86–98.

50. The ProCD example draws heavily upon Shapiro, C. & Varian, H. R. 2000. Versioning: The smart way to sell information. *Harvard Business Review*, 78(1): 106–114.

51. Wise, R. & Baumgarter, P. 1999. Go downstream: The new profit imperative in manufacturing. *Harvard Business Review*, 77(5): 133–141.

52. Salman, W. A. 2000. The new economy is stronger than you think. *Harvard Business Review*, 77(6): 99–106.

53. Mudambi, R. & Helper, S. 1998. The "close but adversarial" model of supplier relations in the U.S. auto industry. *Strategic Management Journal*, 19: 775–792.

54. Trends in the solar industry are discussed in: Carey, J. 2009. Solar: The sun will come out tomorrow. *BusinessWeek*, January 12: 51.

55. Tischler, L. 2002. IBM: Manager jam. *Fast Company*, October: 48.

56. An interesting analysis of self-regulation in an industry (chemical) is in: Barnett, M. L. & King, A. A. 2008. Good fences make good neighbors: A longitudinal analysis of an industry self-regulatory institution. *Academy of Management Journal*, 51(6): 1053–1078.

57. For an interesting perspective on the intensity of competition in the supermarket industry, refer to Anonymous. 2005. Warfare in the aisles. *The Economist*, April 2: 6–8.

58. Marcial, G. 2000. Giving Viagra a run for its money. *BusinessWeek*, October 23: 173.

59. McGann, R. 2005. VOIP poised to take flight? *ClickZ.com*, February 23, www.clickz.com.

60. For an interesting perspective on changing features of firm boundaries, refer to Afuah, A. 2003. Redefining firm boundaries in the face of Internet: Are firms really shrinking? *Academy of Management Review*, 28(1): 34–53.

61. www.consumerreports.org.

62. Time to rebuild. 2001. *Economist*, May 19: 55–56.

63. www.amazon.com.

64. For more on the role of the Internet as an electronic intermediary, refer to Carr, N. G. 2000. Hypermediation: Commerce as clickstream. *Harvard Business Review,* 78(1): 46–48.

65. Olofson, C. 2001. The next best thing to being there. *Fast Company,* April: 175; and www.conferenza.com.

66. Lelii, S. R. 2001. Free online storage a thing of the past *? eWEEK,* April 22.

67. www.mysimon.com; and www.pricescan.com.

68. www.cnet.com; and www.bizrate.com.

69. For insights into strategies in a low-profit industry, refer to: Hopkins, M. S. 2008. The management lessons of a beleaguered industry. *MIT Sloan Management Review,* 50(1): 25–31.

70. Foust, D. 2007. The best performers. *BusinessWeek,* March 26: 58–95; Rosenblum, D., Tomlinson, D., & Scott, L. 2003. Bottom-feeding for blockbuster businesses. *Harvard Business Review,* 81(3): 52–59; Paychex 2006 Annual Report; and, WellPoint Health Network 2005 Annual Report.

71. Kumar, N. 1996. The power of trust in manufacturer-retailer relationship. *Harvard Business Review,* 74(6): 92–110.

72. Welch, D. 2006. Renault-Nissan: Say hello to Bo. *BusinessWeek,* July 31: 56–57.

73. Brandenburger, A. & Nalebuff, B. J. 1995. The right game: Use game theory to shape strategy. *Harvard Business Review,* 73(4): 57–71.

74. For a scholarly discussion of complementary assets and their relationship to competitive advantage, refer to Stieglitz, N. & Heine, K. 2007. Innovations and the role of complementarities in a strategic theory of the firm. *Strategic Management Journal,* 28(1): 1–15.

75. A useful framework for the analysis of industry evolution has been proposed by Professor Anita McGahan of Boston University. Her analysis is based on the identification of the core activities and the core assets of an industry and the threats they face. She suggests that an industry may follow one of four possible evolutionary trajectories—radical change, creative change, intermediating change, or progressive change—based on these two types of threats of obsolescence. Refer to: McGahan, A. M. 2004. How industries change. *Harvard Business Review,* 82(10): 87–94.

76. Yoffie, D. B. & Kwak, M. 2006. With friends like these: The art of managing complementors. *Harvard Business Review,* 84(9): 88–98.

77. Porter, M. I. 2008. The five competitive forces that shape strategy. *Harvard Business Review,* 86 (1): 79–93.

78. Peteraf, M. & Shanley, M. 1997. Getting to know you: A theory of strategic group identity. *Strategic Management Journal,* 18 (Special Issue): 165–186.

79. An interesting scholarly perspective on strategic groups may be found in Dranove, D., Perteraf, M., & Shanley, M. 1998. Do strategic groups exist? An economic framework for analysis. *Strategic Management Journal,* 19(11): 1029–1044.

80. For an empirical study on strategic groups and predictors of performance, refer to Short, J. C., Ketchen, D. J., Jr., Palmer, T. B., & Hult, T. M. 2007. Firm, strategic group, and industry influences on performance. *Strategic Management Journal,* 28(2): 147–167.

81. This section draws on several sources, including Kerwin, K. R. & Haughton, K. 1997. Can Detroit make cars that baby boomers like? *BusinessWeek,* December 1: 134–148; and Taylor, A., III. 1994. The new golden age of autos. *Fortune,* April 4: 50–66.

82. Csere, C. 2001. Supercar supermarket. *Car and Driver,* January: 118–127.

83. Healey, J. R. 1999. Groomed so as not to marry. *USA Today,* August 6: B1; and, Edmunds.com.

84. For a discussion of the extent of overcapacity in the worldwide automobile industry, read: Roberts, D., Matlack, C., Busyh, J., & Rowley, I. 2009. A hundred factories too many. *BusinessWeek,* January 19: 42–43.

85. '08 ends bleakly for car makers. 2009. *Dallas Morning News,* January 6: 1D, 5D.

86. This discussion draws on: Wojdyla, B. 2008. The $2500 Tata Nano, unveiled in India. jalopnik.com, January 10: np; Roberts, D. 2008. China's Geely has global auto ambitions. businessweek.com, July 27: np; and, Fairclough, G. 2007. In China, Chery Automobile drives an industry shift. *The Wall Street Journal,* December 4: A1, A17.

Assessing the Internal Environment of the Firm

After reading this chapter, you should have a good understanding of:

LO1 The benefits and limitations of SWOT analysis in conducting an internal analysis of the firm.

LO2 The primary and support activities of a firm's value chain.

LO3 How value-chain analysis can help managers create value by investigating relationships among activities within the firm and between the firm and its customers and suppliers.

LO4 The resource-based view of the firm and the different types of tangible and intangible resources, as well as organizational capabilities.

LO5 The four criteria that a firm's resources must possess to maintain a sustainable advantage and how value created can be appropriated by employees and managers.

LO6 The usefulness of financial ratio analysis, its inherent limitations, and how to make meaningful comparisons of performance across firms.

LO7 The value of the "balanced scorecard" in recognizing how the interests of a variety of stakeholders can be interrelated.

LO8 How firms are using Internet technologies to add value and achieve unique advantages. (Appendix)

Two firms compete in the same industry and both have many strengths in a variety of functional areas: marketing, operations, logistics, and so on. However, one of these firms outperforms the other by a wide margin over a long period of time. How can this be so? This chapter endeavors to answer that question.

We begin with two sections that include frameworks for gaining key insights into a firm's internal environment: value-chain analysis and the resource-based view of the firm. In value-chain analysis, we divide a firm's activities into a series of value-creating steps. We then explore how individual activities within the firm add value, and also how *interrelationships* among activities within the firm, and between the firm and its suppliers and customers, create value.

In the resource-based view of the firm, we analyze the firm as a collection of tangible and intangible resources as well as organizational capabilities. Advantages that tend to be sustainable over time typically arise from creating *bundles* of resources and capabilities that satisfy four criteria: they are valuable, rare, difficult to imitate, and difficult to substitute. Not all of the value created by a firm will necessarily be kept (or appropriated) by the owners. We discuss the four key factors that determine how profits will be distributed between owners as well as employees and managers.

In the closing sections, we discuss how to evaluate a firm's performance and make comparisons across firms. We emphasize both the inclusion of financial resources and the interests of multiple stakeholders. Central to our discussion is the concept of the balanced scorecard, which recognizes that the interests of different stakeholders can be interrelated. We also consider how a firm's performance evolves over time and how it compares with industry norms and key competitors.

In an appendix to this chapter, we explore how Internet-based businesses and incumbent firms are using digital technologies to add value. We consider four activities—search, evaluation, problem solving, and transaction—as well as three types of content—customer feedback, expertise, and entertainment programming. Such technology-enhanced capabilities are providing new means with which firms can achieve competitive advantages.

In Planning Perspectives' annual survey of automakers and their suppliers, Ford was ranked as one of the worst companies to do business with, according to suppliers.[1] Perhaps not too surprisingly, the only firm that fared worse was General Motors. According to John Henke Jr., Planning Perspectives' president, "I suspect it may be a pattern, because as suppliers are becoming more desperate, and if they continue to be pushed, they have no choice but to push back." Let's consider one example of Ford's strained relationships with suppliers.

In early January 2007, Ford filed a lawsuit against Navistar over warranty costs and pricing for the diesel engines that the latter company supplied. Ford alleged that Navistar owed it money under an agreement to share engine warranty costs—which Navistar failed to pay. Navistar said that Ford's claims were "totally without merit" and that it would "vigorously respond in court."

Ford sought reimbursement equal to what it said it overpaid for the engines and for financial obligations owed by Navistar that were the result of warranty claims tied to a previous generation engine sold by Ford. As expected, the situation escalated when Ford took the unorthodox move of subtracting the amount of money it said Navistar owed from the agreed-upon price for the new diesel engines. Ford reportedly began paying Navistar only $6,167 of the agreed upon per-unit price of $7,673.

On February 26, 2007, Navistar ceased delivering the engines. However, two days later, the Oakland County Court ordered Navistar to resume engine shipments.

According to Henke: "There is no trust or relationship left between Ford and Navistar. It is an extreme example of an adversarial relationship that has evolved. One has to conclude that Navistar perceives that Ford is taking an opportunistic view toward dealing with them and they need to do the same thing to survive. It's an extreme example of an adversarial relationship that has evolved."

And the beat goes on . . . A year later, in February 2008, Navistar refiled a lawsuit against Ford for violating a diesel engine contract in which Ford had promised that Navistar would be Ford's primary manufacturer and supplier of V-6 and V-8 diesel engines in North America. The suit sought "at least hundreds of millions of dollars." According to the lawsuit, Ford will introduce a 4.4-liter diesel engine for production in North America by late 2009 or 2010. Ford intends to produce the engine itself for use in the F-150 pickup—and possibly other vehicles. The lawsuit claims that Ford cannot manufacture the engine without violating its contract with Navistar.

In this chapter we will place heavy emphasis on the value-chain concept. That is, we focus on the key value-creating activities (e.g., operations, marketing and sales, and procurement) that a firm must effectively manage and integrate in order to attain competitive advantages in the marketplace. However, firms must not only pay close attention to their own value-creating activities but must also maintain close and effective relationships with key organizations outside the firm boundaries such as suppliers, customers, and alliance partners. Clearly, Ford's adversarial relationship with Navistar is a good example of bad practice!

>LO1

The benefits and limitations of SWOT analysis in conducting an internal analysis of the firm.

Before moving to value-chain analysis, let's briefly revisit the benefits and limitations of SWOT analysis. As discussed in Chapter 2, a SWOT analysis consists of a careful listing of a firm's strengths, weaknesses, opportunities, and threats. While we believe SWOT analysis is very helpful as a starting point, it should not form the primary basis for evaluating a firm's internal strengths and weaknesses or the opportunities and threats in the environment. Strategy Spotlight 3.1 elaborates on the limitations of the traditional SWOT approach.

strategy spotlight

The Limitations of SWOT Analysis

SWOT analysis is a tried-and-true tool of strategic analysis. SWOT (strengths, weaknesses, opportunities, threats) analysis is used regularly in business to initially evaluate the opportunities and threats in the business environment as well as the strengths and weaknesses of a firm's internal environment. Top managers rely on SWOT to stimulate self-reflection and group discussions about how to improve their firm and position it for success.

But SWOT has its limitations. It is just a starting point for discussion. By listing the firm's attributes, managers have the raw material needed to perform more in-depth strategic analysis. However, SWOT cannot show them how to achieve a competitive advantage. They must not make SWOT analysis an end in itself, temporarily raising awareness about important issues but failing to lead to the kind of action steps necessary to enact strategic change.

Consider the ProCD example from Chapter 2, page 58. A brief SWOT analysis might include the following:

Strengths	Opportunities
First-mover advantage	Demand for electronic phone books
Low labor cost	Sudden growth in use of digital technology

Weaknesses	Threats
Inexperienced new company	Easily duplicated product
No proprietary information	Market power of incumbent firms

The combination of low production costs and an early-mover advantage in an environment where demand for CD-based phone books was growing rapidly seems to indicate that ProCD founder James Bryant had a golden opportunity. But the SWOT analysis did not reveal how to turn those strengths into a competitive advantage, nor did it highlight how rapidly the environment would change, allowing imitators to come into the market and erode his first-mover advantage. Let's look at some of the limitations of SWOT analysis.

Strengths May Not Lead to an Advantage

A firm's strengths and capabilities, no matter how unique or impressive, may not enable it to achieve a competitive advantage in the marketplace. It is akin to recruiting a concert pianist to join a gang of thugs—even though such an ability is rare and valuable, it hardly helps the organization attain its goals and objectives! Similarly, the skills of a highly creative product designer would offer little competitive advantage to a firm that produces low-cost commodity products. Indeed, the additional expense of hiring such an individual could erode the firm's cost advantages. If a firm builds its strategy on a capability that cannot, by itself, create or sustain competitive advantage, it is essentially a wasted use of resources. ProCD had several key strengths, but it did not translate them into lasting advantages in the marketplace.

SWOT's Focus on the External Environment Is Too Narrow

Strategists who rely on traditional definitions of their industry and competitive environment often focus their sights too narrowly on current customers, technologies, and competitors. Hence they fail to notice important changes on the periphery of their environment that may trigger the need to redefine industry boundaries and identify a whole new set of competitive relationships. Reconsider the example from Chapter 2 of *Encyclopaedia Britannica,* whose competitive position was severely eroded by a "nontraditional" competitor—CD-based encyclopedias (e.g., Microsoft *Encarta*) that could be used on home computers.

SWOT Gives a One-Shot View of a Moving Target

A key weakness of SWOT is that it is primarily a static assessment. It focuses too much of a firm's attention on one moment in time. Essentially, this is like studying a single frame of a motion picture. You may be able to identify the principal actors and learn something about the setting, but it doesn't tell you much about the plot. Competition among organizations is played out over time. As circumstances, capabilities, and strategies change, static analysis techniques do not reveal the dynamics of the competitive environment. Clearly, ProCD was unaware that its competitiveness was being eroded so quickly.

SWOT Overemphasizes a Single Dimension of Strategy

Sometimes firms become preoccupied with a single strength or a key feature of the product or service they are offering and ignore other factors needed for competitive success. For example, Food Lion, a large grocery retailer, paid a heavy price for its excessive emphasis on cost control. The resulting problems with labor and the negative publicity led to its eventual withdrawal from several markets.

SWOT analysis has much to offer, but only as a starting point. By itself, it rarely helps a firm develop competitive advantages that it can sustain over time.

Sources: Shapiro, C. & Varian, H. R. 2000. Versioning: The Smart Way to Sell Information. *Harvard Business Review,* 78(1): 99–106; and Picken, J. C. & Dess, G. G. 1997. *Mission Critical.* Burr Ridge, IL: Irwin Professional Publishing.

We will now turn to value-chain analysis. As you will see, it provides greater insights into analyzing a firm's competitive position than SWOT analysis does by itself.

Value-Chain Analysis

Value-chain analysis views the organization as a sequential process of value-creating activities. The approach is useful for understanding the building blocks of competitive advantage and was described in Michael Porter's seminal book *Competitive Advantage.*[2] Value is the amount that buyers are willing to pay for what a firm provides them and is measured by total revenue, a reflection of the price a firm's product commands and the quantity it can sell. A firm is profitable when the value it receives exceeds the total costs involved in creating its product or service. Creating value for buyers that exceeds the costs of production (i.e., margin) is a key concept used in analyzing a firm's competitive position.

Porter described two different categories of activities. First, five **primary activities**—inbound logistics, operations, outbound logistics, marketing and sales, and service—contribute to the physical creation of the product or service, its sale and transfer to the buyer, and its service after the sale. Second, **support activities**—procurement, technology development, human resource management, and general administration—either add value by themselves or add value through important relationships with both primary activities and other support activities. Exhibit 3.1 illustrates Porter's value chain.

To get the most out of value-chain analysis, view the concept in its broadest context, without regard to the boundaries of your own organization. That is, place your organization within a more encompassing value chain that includes your firm's suppliers, customers, and alliance partners. Thus, in addition to thoroughly understanding how value is created within the organization, be aware of how value is created for other organizations in the overall supply chain or distribution channel.[3]

Next, we'll describe and provide examples of each of the primary and support activities. Then, we'll provide examples of how companies add value by means of relationships among activities within the organization as well as activities outside the organization, such as those activities associated with customers and suppliers.[4]

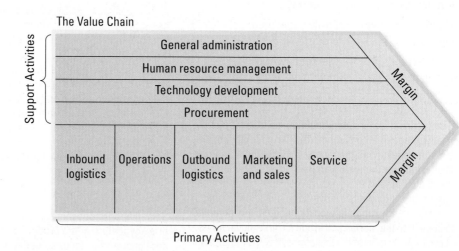

Exhibit 3.1 **The Value Chain: Primary and Support Activities**

Source: Adapted with the permission of The Free Press, a division of Simon & Schuster Adult Publishing Group, from *Competitive Advantage: Creating and Sustaining Superior Performance* by Michael E. Porter. Copyright © 1985, 1998 by Michael E. Porter. All rights reserved.

Primary Activities

Five generic categories of primary activities are involved in competing in any industry, as shown in Exhibit 3.2. Each category is divisible into a number of distinct activities that depend on the particular industry and the firm's strategy.[5]

Inbound Logistics Inbound logistics is primarily associated with receiving, storing, and distributing inputs to the product. It includes material handling, warehousing, inventory control, vehicle scheduling, and returns to suppliers.

Just-in-time (JIT) inventory systems, for example, were designed to achieve efficient inbound logistics. In essence, Toyota epitomizes JIT inventory systems, in which parts deliveries arrive at the assembly plants only hours before they are needed. JIT systems will play a vital role in fulfilling Toyota's commitment to fill a buyer's new car order in just five days.[6] This standard is in sharp contrast to most competitors that require approximately 30 days' notice to build vehicles. Toyota's standard is three times faster than even Honda Motors, considered to be the industry's most efficient in order follow-through. The five days represent the time from the company's receipt of an order to the time the car leaves the assembly plant. Actual delivery may take longer, depending on where a customer lives. How can Toyota achieve such fast turnaround?

- Its 360 key suppliers are now linked to the company by way of computer on a virtual assembly line.
- Suppliers load parts onto trucks in the order in which they will be installed.
- Parts are stacked on trucks in the same place each time to help workers unload them quickly.
- Deliveries are required to meet a rigid schedule with as many as 12 trucks a day and no more than four hours between trucks.

Exhibit 3.2
The Value Chain: Some Factors to Consider in Assessing a Firm's Primary Activities

Inbound Logistics

- Location of distribution facilities to minimize shipping times.
- Warehouse layout and designs to increase efficiency of operations for incoming materials.

Operations

- Efficient plant operations to minimize costs.
- Efficient plant layout and workflow design.
- Incorporation of appropriate process technology.

Outbound Logistics

- Effective shipping processes to provide quick delivery and minimize damages.
- Shipping of goods in large lot sizes to minimize transportation costs.

Marketing and Sales

- Innovative approaches to promotion and advertising.
- Proper identification of customer segments and needs.

Service

- Quick response to customer needs and emergencies.
- Quality of service personnel and ongoing training.

Source: Adapted from Porter, M.E. 1985. *Competitive Advantage: Creating and Sustaining Superior Performance.* New York: Free Press.

Operations Operations include all activities associated with transforming inputs into the final product form, such as machining, packaging, assembly, testing, printing, and facility operations.

Creating environmentally friendly manufacturing is one way to use operations to achieve competitive advantage. Shaw Industries (now part of Berkshire Hathaway), a world-class competitor in the floor-covering industry, is well known for its concern for the environment.[7] It has been successful in reducing the expenses associated with the disposal of dangerous chemicals and other waste products from its manufacturing operations. Its environmental endeavors have multiple payoffs. Shaw has received many awards for its recycling efforts—awards that enhance its reputation.

Outbound Logistics Outbound logistics is associated with collecting, storing, and distributing the product or service to buyers. These activities include finished goods, warehousing, material handling, delivery vehicle operation, order processing, and scheduling.

Campbell Soup uses an electronic network to facilitate its continuous-replenishment program with its most progressive retailers.[8] Each morning, retailers electronically inform Campbell of their product needs and of the level of inventories in their distribution centers. Campbell uses that information to forecast future demand and to determine which products require replenishment (based on the inventory limits previously established with each retailer). Trucks leave Campbell's shipping plant that afternoon and arrive at the retailers' distribution centers the same day. The program cuts the inventories of participating retailers from about a four- to a two-weeks' supply. Campbell Soup achieved this improvement because it slashed delivery time and because it knows the inventories of key retailers and can deploy supplies when they are most needed.

The Campbell Soup example also illustrates the win–win benefits of exemplary value-chain activities. Both the supplier (Campbell) and its buyers (retailers) come out ahead. Since the retailer makes more money on Campbell products delivered through continuous replenishment, it has an incentive to carry a broader line and give the company greater shelf space. After Campbell introduced the program, sales of its products grew twice as fast through participating retailers as through all other retailers. Not surprisingly, supermarket chains love such programs.

Marketing and Sales These activities are associated with purchases of products and services by end users and the inducements used to get them to make purchases.[9] They include advertising, promotion, sales force, quoting, channel selection, channel relations, and pricing.[10, 11]

It is not always enough to have a great product.[12] The key is to convince your channel partners that it is in their best interests not only to carry your product but also to market it in a way that is consistent with your strategy.[13] Consider Monsanto's efforts at educating distributors to improve the value proposition of its line of Saflex® windows.[14] The products had a superior attribute: The window design permitted laminators to form an exceptional type of glass by sandwiching a plastic sheet interlayer between two pieces of glass. This product is not only stronger and offers better ultraviolet protection than regular glass, but also when cracked, it adheres to the plastic sheet—an excellent safety feature for both cars and homes.

Despite these benefits, Monsanto had a hard time convincing laminators and window manufacturers to carry these products. According to Melissa Toledo, brand manager at Monsanto, "Saflex was priced at a 30 percent premium above traditional glass, and the various stages in the value chain (distributors and retailers) didn't think there would be a demand for such an expensive glass product." What did Monsanto do? It reintroduced Saflex as KeepSafe® and worked to coordinate the product's value propositions. By analyzing the experiences of all of the players in the supply chain, it was able to create marketing programs that helped each build a business aimed at selling its products. Said Toledo, "We want to know how they go about selling those types of products, what challenges they face, and what they think they need to sell our products. This helps us a lot when we try to provide them with these needs."[15]

At times, a firm's marketing initiatives may become overly aggressive and lead to actions that are both unethical and illegal.[16] For example:

- **Burdines.** This department store chain is under investigation for allegedly adding club memberships to its customers' credit cards without prior approval.
- **Fleet Mortgage.** This company has been accused of adding insurance fees for dental coverage and home insurance to its customers' mortgage loans without the customers' knowledge.
- **HCI Direct.** Eleven states have accused this direct-mail firm with charging for panty hose samples that customers did not order.
- **Juno Online Services.** The Federal Trade Commission brought charges against this Internet service provider for failing to provide customers with a telephone number to cancel service.

Strategy Spotlight 3.2 addresses a key element of marketing—marketing research. We discuss how Kraft Foods Inc. was able to reinvent their iconic cookie in the U.S. market—the Oreo—to succeed in the Chinese market.

Service   This primary activity includes all actions associated with providing service to enhance or maintain the value of the product, such as installation, repair, training, parts supply, and product adjustment.

Let's see how two retailers are providing exemplary customer service. At Sephora.com, a customer service representative taking a phone call from a repeat customer has instant access to what shade of lipstick she likes best. This will help the rep cross-sell by suggesting a matching shade of lip gloss. CEO Jim Wiggett expects such personalization to build loyalty and boost sales per customer. Nordstrom, the Seattle-based department store chain, goes even a step further. It offers a cyber-assist: A service rep can take control of a customer's Web browser and literally lead her to just the silk scarf that she is looking for. CEO Dan Nordstrom believes that such a capability will close enough additional purchases to pay for the $1 million investment in software.

Strategy Spotlight 3.3 provides an example of how a firm—Cookshack—was able to use crowdsourcing to, in effect, turn its customers into a customer service department!

Support Activities

Support activities in the value chain can be divided into four generic categories, as shown in Exhibit 3.3. Each category of the support activity is divisible into a number of distinct value activities that are specific to a particular industry. For example, technology development's discrete activities may include component design, feature design, field testing, process engineering, and technology selection. Similarly, procurement may include qualifying new suppliers, purchasing different groups of inputs, and monitoring supplier performance.

Procurement   Procurement refers to the function of purchasing inputs used in the firm's value chain, not to the purchased inputs themselves.[17] Purchased inputs include raw materials, supplies, and other consumable items as well as assets such as machinery, laboratory equipment, office equipment, and buildings.[18, 19]

Microsoft has improved its procurement process (and the quality of its suppliers) by providing formal reviews of its suppliers. One of Microsoft's divisions has extended the review process used for employees to its outside suppliers.[20] The employee services group,

Adapting Oreos to the Chinese Market

Although the Oreo has long been the top-selling cookie in the U.S. market, Kraft Foods Inc. had to reinvent it to make it sell well in the world's most populous nation. Chinese Oreo sales represent a tiny fraction of Kraft's $37.2 billion in annual revenues. However, the cookie's journey in China exemplifies the kind of entrepreneurial transformation that CEO Irene Rosenfeld is trying to spread throughout the food giant. She has been putting more power in the hands of Kraft's various business units around the world—telling employees that decisions about Kraft products should not all be made by people at the Northfield, Illinois, headquarters.

Oreos were first introduced to the U.S. market in 1912. However, it wasn't until 1996 that Kraft sold them in China. Nine years later, Shawn Warren, a 37-year-old Kraft veteran—who had spent years marketing the company's cookies and crackers around the world—arrived on the scene. He noticed that Oreo's China sales had been flat for the previous five years. The problem: Kraft kept selling the U.S. version of Oreos in China. According to Warren, Albert Einstein's definition of insanity characterized Kraft: doing the same thing over and over and expecting different results.

Mr. Warren assigned his team to a lengthy research project that yielded some interesting findings. For one thing, Kraft learned that traditional Oreos were too sweet for Chinese tastes. Also, the packages of 14 Oreos priced at 72 cents were too expensive.

The company developed 20 prototypes of reduced-sugar Oreos and tested them with Chinese consumers

Source: Jargon, J. 2008. Kraft Reformulates Oreo, Scores in China. online.wsj.com, May 1: np.

● Kraft Foods Inc. has been very successful in adapting Oreos to the Chinese market.

before arriving at a formula that tasted right. Kraft also introduced packages containing fewer Oreos for only 29 cents.

Still, Kraft realized that it needed to do more than just tweak its recipe to capture a larger share of the Chinese market. After more experimentation, it remade the Oreo in 2006—it consisted of four layers of crispy wafer filled with vanilla and chocolate cream, coated in chocolate. The firm also developed a proprietary handling process to ensure that the product could be shipped across the country, withstanding the cold climate in the north and the hot, humid weather in the south—and still be ready to melt in the mouth.

The efforts have paid off—over the past two years, Kraft has doubled its Oreo revenue in China. And, with the help of those sales, worldwide sales of Oreos topped $1 billion for the first time.

which is responsible for everything from travel to 401(k) programs to the on-site library, outsources more than 60 percent of the services it provides. Unfortunately, the employee services group was not providing them with enough feedback. This was feedback that the suppliers wanted to get and that Microsoft wanted to give.

The evaluation system that Microsoft developed helped clarify its expectations to suppliers. An executive noted: "We had one supplier—this was before the new system—that would have scored a 1.2 out of 5. After we started giving this feedback, and the supplier understood our expectations, its performance improved dramatically. Within six months, it scored a 4. If you'd asked me before we began the feedback system, I would have said that was impossible."

Crowdsourcing: How Cookshack Gets "Free" Customer Service!

For more than 40 years, Cookshack has been producing outdoor ovens for home and commercial use in a 21,000 square foot factory in Ponca City, Oklahoma. Their major claim: its machines make barbecue and smoked foods "without a lot of fuss." That's because the food is wood-cooked at low temperature under static conditions with no through movement of air (which tends to dry meat) and no need for water pans (moisture stays in the oven).

Cookshack has 25 employees and actively encourages its customers to contact the company—its toll-free number is prominently shown on every page of its website. Its forums are a key adjunct to its live customer service and are meant to provide a body of knowledge that can't be transmitted in a phone call. The forums provide assistance 24 hours a day, seven days a week, and they are clearly popular. A recent visit to the "open forum" section revealed 1,640 topics and 13,000 posts!

Hour by hour, and day by day, hundreds of online Cookshack customers sign on to its various forums to ask and answer questions about barbeque sauce (another product line), smoker and barbeque ovens, and cooking techniques for everything from sausage, turkey, and ribs—to deer, salmon, and dog bones. The last one was from "Lucy" on behalf of her dog, Carole, and received 12 responses.

Cookshack has succeeded in creating a folksy, friendly site and designing forums and archives tailored to all tastes. The end result: it has sold its customers on providing their own customer support.

Source: Libert, B. & Spector, J. 2008. *We Are Smarter Than Me*. Philadelphia: Wharton School Publishing; and forum.cookshack.com.

 **environmental sustainability**

Exhibit 3.3   The Value Chain: Some Factors to Consider in Assessing a Firm's Support Activities

General Administration

- Effective planning systems to attain overall goals and objectives.
- Excellent relationships with diverse stakeholder groups.
- Effective information technology to integrate value-creating activities.

Human Resource Management

- Effective recruiting, development, and retention mechanisms for employees.
- Quality relations with trade unions.
- Reward and incentive programs to motivate all employees.

Technology Development

- Effective R&D activities for process and product initiatives.
- Positive collaborative relationships between R&D and other departments.
- Excellent professional qualifications of personnel.

Procurement

- Procurement of raw material inputs to optimize quality and speed and to minimize the associated costs.
- Development of collaborative win-win relationships with suppliers.
- Analysis and selection of alternative sources of inputs to minimize dependence on one supplier.

Source: Adapted from Porter, M.E. 1985. *Competitive Advantage: Creating and Sustaining Superior Performance.* New York: Free Press.

Technology Development   Every value activity embodies technology.[21] The array of technologies employed in most firms is very broad, ranging from technologies used to prepare documents and transport goods to those embodied in processes and equipment or the product itself.[22] Technology development related to the product and its features supports the entire value chain, while other technology development is associated with particular primary or support activities.

The Allied Signal and Honeywell merger brought together roughly 13,000 scientists and an $870 million R&D budget that should lead to some innovative products and services in two major areas: performance materials and control systems. Some of the possible innovations include:

- *Performance materials.* The development of uniquely shaped fibers with very high absorption capability. When employed in the company's Fram oil filters, they capture 50 percent more particles than ordinary filters. This means that cars can travel further with fewer oil changes.
- *Control systems.* Working with six leading oil companies, Honeywell developed software using "self-learning" algorithms that predict when something might go wrong in an oil refinery before it actually does. Examples include a faulty gas valve or hazardous spillage.[23]

Human Resource Management   Human resource management consists of activities involved in the recruiting, hiring, training, development, and compensation of all types of personnel.[24] It supports both individual primary and support activities (e.g., hiring of engineers and scientists) and the entire value chain (e.g., negotiations with labor unions).[25]

Like all great service companies, JetBlue Airways Corporation is obsessed with hiring superior employees.[26] But they found it difficult to attract college graduates to commit to careers as flight attendants. JetBlue developed a highly innovative recruitment program for flight attendants—a one-year contract that gives them a chance to travel, meet lots of people, and then decide what else they might like to do. They also introduced the idea of training a friend and employee together so that they could share a job. With such employee-friendly initiatives, JetBlue has been very successful in attracting talent.

Jeffrey Immelt, GE's chairman, addresses the importance of effective human resource management:[27]

> Human resources has to be more than a department. GE recognized early on—50 or 60 years ago—that in a multibusiness company, the common denominators are people and culture. From an employee's first day at GE, she discovers that she's in the people-development business as much as anything else. You'll find that most good companies have the same basic HR processes that we have, but they're discrete. HR at GE is not an agenda item; it is the agenda.

Strategy Spotlight 3.4 discusses a rather unique approach to individual performance evaluations: eliminate the metrics!

General Administration   General administration consists of a number of activities, including general management, planning, finance, accounting, legal and government affairs, quality management, and information systems. Administration (unlike the other support activities) typically supports the entire value chain and not individual activities.[28]

Although general administration is sometimes viewed only as overhead, it can be a powerful source of competitive advantage. In a telephone operating company, for example, negotiating and maintaining ongoing relations with regulatory bodies can be among the most important activities for competitive advantage. Also, in some industries top management plays a vital role in dealing with important buyers.[29]

Removing Individual Metrics in Performance Evaluations

ITT China President William Taylor wanted to know why employee turnover was so high in the Shanghai sales office. The local manager knew the answer: If the sales manager gave workers an average "3" on the 1-5 performance scale, they'd stop talking to him and, in some cases, quit shortly thereafter. The manager lamented: "They're losing face in the organization. It would be great if we could do something about the scores."

Comments like that popped up around the world. For example, in southern Europe, the focus on individual performance didn't sit well with the region's more "collec-

Source: McGregor, J. 2008. Case study: To Adapt, ITT Lets Go of Unpopular Ratings. *BusinessWeek*, January 28: 46.

tive ethos," claims James Duncan, director of ITT's talent development. And in Scandinavia, where there's more of "a sense of equality between bosses and workers," says Duncan, some workers asked, "What gives you the right to rate me a 3?" That led ITT to make the radical decision to ditch performance ratings altogether.

Most employees, who still require a detailed evaluation, cheered the changes. In one of the ITT plants in Shenyang, China, the new system has helped to cut the plant's attrition rate in half. The change isn't as popular in the U.S., where some metrics-loving engineers in the defense business remain attached to the old rankings. Still, most people have come around. Says Duncan, "It's not just Asia and Europe." No matter what culture you are from, everyone "likes the fact that they're treated like an adult in this discussion."

The strong and effective leadership of top executives can also make a significant contribution to an organization's success. As we discussed in Chapter 1, chief executive officers (CEOs) such as Herb Kelleher, Andrew Grove, and Jack Welch have been credited with playing critical roles in the success of Southwest Airlines, Intel, and General Electric.

Information systems can also play a key role in increasing operating efficiencies and enhancing a firm's performance.[30] Consider Walgreen Co.'s introduction of Intercom Plus, a computer-based prescription management system. Linked by computer to both doctors' offices and third-party payment plans, the system automates telephone refills, store-to-store prescription transfers, and drug reordering. It also provides information on drug interactions and, coupled with revised workflows, frees up pharmacists from administrative tasks to devote more time to patient counseling.[31]

> **>LO3**
> How value-chain analysis can help managers create value by investigating relationships among activities within the firm and between the firm and its customers and suppliers.

Interrelationships among Value-Chain Activities within and across Organizations

We have defined each of the value-chain activities separately for clarity of presentation. Managers must not ignore, however, the importance of relationships among value-chain activities.[32] There are two levels: (1) **interrelationships** among activities within the firm and (2) relationships among activities within the firm and with other organizations (e.g., customers and suppliers) that are part of the firm's expanded value chain.[33]

With regard to the first level, recall AT&T's innovative Resource Link program wherein employees who have reached their plateau may apply for temporary positions in other parts of the organization. Clearly, this program has the potential to benefit all activities within the firm's value chain because it creates opportunities for top employees to lend their expertise to all of the organization's value-creating activities.

With regard to the second level, Campbell Soup's use of electronic networks enabled it to improve the efficiency of outbound logistics.[34] However, it also helped Campbell manage the ordering of raw materials more effectively, improve its production scheduling, and help its customers better manage their inbound logistics operations.

> **interrelationships**
> collaborative and strategic exchange relationships between value-chain activities either a) within firms or b) between firms. Strategic exchange relationships involve exchange of resources such as information, people, technology, or money that contribute to the success of the firm.

Environmental Sustainability via an Energy-Efficient Supply Chain

Given the increasing concerns about fuel prices, long-term energy availability, and climate change, many firms are paying increased attention to one of the most pervasive places where energy can be conserved: the industrial supply chain. The supply chain is the production and distribution network that encompasses the sourcing, manufacturing, transportation, commercialization, distribution, consumption, and disposal of goods.

For example, in 2006 the Carbon Trust, a United Kingdom–based research and advisory group, discovered a "perverse incentive" in the sourcing of raw potatoes for the manufacture of snack foods. Charged with studying the carbon footprint of potato chips, the Trust's researchers discovered that since prices were set by weight, farmers typically control humidification to produce moister and, hence, heavier potatoes. Even within the strictly limited specifications of moisture content set by the food manufacturers, the extra grams of water are significant. The extra cooking needed to burn them off accounted for an unexpectedly high percentage of the chips' energy consumption. In effect, production-related greenhouse gases dwarfed the emissions from transportation.

The solution, wrote the Carbon Trust, was to change the procurement contract—to provide farmers with an incentive to produce potatoes with less moisture. Thus, the manufacturers would be in a better position to take advantage of carbon trading credits and other regulations for greenhouse gas reduction. And it would serve to set a precedent for further collaboration between food producers and their agricultural suppliers.

environmental sustainability

Source: Parry, P., Martha, J., & Grenon, G. 2007. The Energy-Efficient Supply Chain. *Strategy + Business*, August 7: np.

Strategy Spotlight 3.5 discusses how attention to an energy-efficient supply chain can not only enhance environmental sustainability, but also improve production efficiency.

Applying the Value Chain to Service Organizations

The concepts of inbound logistics, operations, and outbound logistics suggest managing the raw materials that might be manufactured into finished products and delivered to customers. However, these three steps do not apply only to manufacturing. They correspond to any transformation process in which inputs are converted through a work process into outputs that add value. For example, accounting is a sort of transformation process that converts daily records of individual transactions into monthly financial reports. In this example, the transaction records are the inputs, accounting is the operation that adds value, and financial statements are the outputs.

What are the "operations," or transformation processes, of service organizations? At times, the difference between manufacturing and service is in providing a customized solution rather than mass production as is common in manufacturing. For example, a travel agent adds value by creating an itinerary that includes transportation, accommodations, and activities that are customized to your budget and travel dates. A law firm renders services that are specific to a client's needs and circumstances. In both cases, the work process (operation) involves the application of specialized knowledge based on the specifics of a situation (inputs) and the outcome that the client desires (outputs).

The application of the value chain to service organizations suggests that the value-adding process may be configured differently depending on the type of business a firm is engaged in. As the preceding discussion on support activities suggests, activities such as procurement and legal services are critical for adding value. Indeed, the activities that may only provide support to one company may be critical to the primary value-adding activity of another firm.

Exhibit 3.4 provides two models of how the value chain might look in service industries. In the retail industry, there are no manufacturing operations. A firm, such as Best

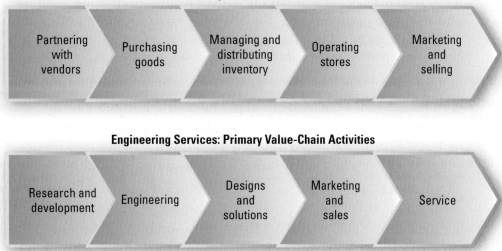

Retail: Primary Value-Chain Activities

Partnering with vendors → Purchasing goods → Managing and distributing inventory → Operating stores → Marketing and selling

Engineering Services: Primary Value-Chain Activities

Research and development → Engineering → Designs and solutions → Marketing and sales → Service

Exhibit 3.4 Some Examples of Value Chains in Service Industries

Buy, adds value by developing expertise in the procurement of finished goods and by displaying them in their stores in a way that enhances sales. Thus, the value chain makes procurement activities (i.e., partnering with vendors and purchasing goods) a primary rather than a support activity. Operations refer to the task of operating Best Buy's stores.

For an engineering services firm, research and development provides inputs, the transformation process is the engineering itself, and innovative designs and practical solutions are the outputs. Arthur D. Little, for example, is a large consulting firm with offices in 20 countries. In its technology and innovation management practice, A. D. Little strives to make the best use of the science, technology and knowledge resources available to create value for a wide range of industries and client sectors. This involves activities associated with research and development, engineering, and creating solutions as well as downstream activities such as marketing, sales, and service. How the primary and support activities of a given firm are configured and deployed will often depend on industry conditions and whether the company is service and/or manufacturing oriented.

Resource-Based View of the Firm

The **resource-based view (RBV) of the firm** combines two perspectives: (1) the internal analysis of phenomena within a company and (2) an external analysis of the industry and its competitive environment.[35] It goes beyond the traditional SWOT (strengths, weaknesses, opportunities, threats) analysis by integrating internal and external perspectives. The ability of a firm's resources to confer competitive advantage(s) cannot be determined without taking into consideration the broader competitive context. A firm's resources must be evaluated in terms of how valuable, rare, and hard they are for competitors to duplicate. Otherwise, the firm attains only competitive parity.

As noted earlier (in Strategy Spotlight 3.1), a firm's strengths and capabilities—no matter how unique or impressive—do not necessarily lead to competitive advantages in the marketplace. The criteria for whether advantages are created and whether or not they can be sustained over time will be addressed later in this section. Thus, the RBV is a very useful framework for gaining insights as to why some competitors are more profitable than

resource-based view of the firm perspective that firms' competitive advantages are due to their endowment of strategic resources that are valuable, rare, costly to imitate, and costly to substitute.

>LO4
The resource-based view of the firm and the different types of tangible and intangible resources, as well as organizational capabilities.

others. As we will see later in the book, the RBV is also helpful in developing strategies for individual businesses and diversified firms by revealing how core competencies embedded in a firm can help it exploit new product and market opportunities.

In the two sections that follow, we will discuss the three key types of resources that firms possess (summarized in Exhibit 3.5): tangible resources, intangible resources, and

Exhibit 3.5
The Resource-Based View of the Firm: Resources and Capabilities

Tangible Resources	
Financial	• Firm's cash account and cash equivalents.
	• Firm's capacity to raise equity.
	• Firm's borrowing capacity.
Physical	• Modern plant and facilities.
	• Favorable manufacturing locations.
	• State-of-the-art machinery and equipment.
Technological	• Trade secrets.
	• Innovative production processes.
	• Patents, copyrights, trademarks.
Organizational	• Effective strategic planning processes.
	• Excellent evaluation and control systems.

Intangible Resources	
Human	• Experience and capabilities of employees.
	• Trust.
	• Managerial skills.
	• Firm-specific practices and procedures.
Innovation and creativity	• Technical and scientific skills.
	• Innovation capacities.
Reputation	• Brand name.
	• Reputation with customers for quality and reliability.
	• Reputation with suppliers for fairness, non–zero-sum relationships.

Organizational Capabilities

- Firm competencies or skills the firm employs to transfer inputs to outputs.
- Capacity to combine tangible and intangible resources, using organizational processes to attain desired end.

EXAMPLES:
- Outstanding customer service.
- Excellent product development capabilities.
- Innovativeness of products and services.
- Ability to hire, motivate, and retain human capital.

Source: Adapted from Barney, J. B. 1991. Firm Resources and Sustained Competitive Advantage. *Journal of Management:* 17: 101; Grant, R. M. 1991. *Contemporary Strategy Analysis:* 100–102. Cambridge England: Blackwell Business and Hitt, M. A., Ireland, R. D., & Hoskisson, R. E. 2001. *Strategic Management: Competitiveness and Globalization* (4th ed.). Cincinnati: South-Western College Publishing.

organizational capabilities. Then we will address the conditions under which such assets and capabilities can enable a firm to attain a sustainable competitive advantage.[36]

It is important to note that resources by themselves typically do not yield a competitive advantage. Even if a basketball team recruited an all-star center, there would be little chance of victory if the other members of the team were continually outplayed by their opponents or if the coach's attitude was so negative that everyone, including the center, became unwilling to put forth their best efforts.

In a business context, a firm's excellent value-creating activities (e.g., logistics) would not be a source of competitive advantage if those activities were not integrated with other important value-creating activities such as marketing and sales. Thus, a central theme of the resource-based view of the firm is that competitive advantages are created (and sustained) through the bundling of several resources in unique combinations.[37]

Types of Firm Resources

Firm resources are all assets, capabilities, organizational processes, information, knowledge, and so forth, controlled by a firm that enable it to develop and implement value-creating strategies.

Tangible Resources   These are assets that are relatively easy to identify. They include the physical and financial assets that an organization uses to create value for its customers. Among them are financial resources (e.g., a firm's cash, accounts receivables, and its ability to borrow funds); physical resources (e.g., the company's plant, equipment, and machinery as well as its proximity to customers and suppliers); organizational resources (e.g., the company's strategic planning process and its employee development, evaluation, and reward systems); and technological resources (e.g., trade secrets, patents, and copyrights).

Many firms are finding that high-tech, computerized training has dual benefits: It develops more effective employees and reduces costs at the same time. Employees at FedEx take computer-based job competency tests every 6 to 12 months.[38] The 90-minute computer-based tests identify areas of individual weakness and provide input to a computer database of employee skills—information the firm uses in promotion decisions.

Intangible Resources   Much more difficult for competitors (and, for that matter, a firm's own managers) to account for or imitate are **intangible resources,** which are typically embedded in unique routines and practices that have evolved and accumulated over time. These include human resources (e.g., experience and capability of employees, trust, effectiveness of work teams, managerial skills), innovation resources (e.g., technical and scientific expertise, ideas), and reputation resources (e.g., brand name, reputation with suppliers for fairness and with customers for reliability and product quality). A firm's culture may also be a resource that provides competitive advantage.[39]

For example, you might not think that motorcycles, clothes, toys, and restaurants have much in common. Yet Harley-Davidson has entered all of these product and service markets by capitalizing on its strong brand image—a valuable intangible resource.[40] It has used that image to sell accessories, clothing, and toys, and it has licensed the Harley-Davidson Café in New York City to provide further exposure for its brand name and products.

Strategy Spotlight 3.6 discusses how various social networking sites have the potential to play havoc with a firm's reputation.

Organizational Capabilities   **Organizational capabilities** are not specific tangible or intangible assets, but rather the competencies or skills that a firm employs to transform inputs into outputs.[41] In short, they refer to an organization's capacity to deploy tangible and intangible resources over time and generally in combination, and to leverage those capabilities to bring about a desired end.[42] Examples of organizational capabilities are outstanding customer service, excellent product development capabilities, superb innovation processes, and flexibility in manufacturing processes.[43]

tangible resources organizational assets that are relatively easy to identify, including physical assets, financial resources, organizational resources, and technological resources.

intangible resources organizational assets that are difficult to identify and account for and are typically embedded in unique routines and practices, including human resources, innovation resources, and reputation resources.

organizational capabilities the competencies and skills that a firm employs to transform inputs into outputs.

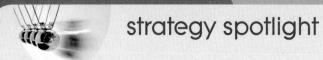

strategy spotlight

3.6

Blogs, Social Networking Sites, and Corporate Reputations: A Lethal Combination?

Customers are now connecting with and drawing power from one another. The mechanism: online social technologies such as blogs, social networking sites like MySpace, user-generated content sites like YouTube, and countless communities across the Web. They are defining their own perspective on companies and brands—a perspective that is often at odds with the image a company wants to project. This groundswell of people using technologies to get the things they need from one another, rather than from the companies, has tilted the balance of power from company to customer.

Let's look at an example: Brian Finkelstein, a law student, had trouble with the cable modem in his home. A Comcast Cable repairman arrived to fix the problem. However, when the technician had to call the home office for a key piece of information, he was put on hold for so long that he fell asleep on Finkelstein's couch. Outraged, Finkelstein made a video of the sleeping technician and posted it on YouTube. The clip became a hit—with more than a million viewings. And, to this day, it continues to undermine Comcast's efforts to improve its reputation for customer service.

Source: Bernoff, J. & Li, C. 2008. Harnessing the Power of the Oh-So-Social Web. *MIT Sloan Management Review,* 49 (3): 36–42; and, Stelter, B. 2008. Griping Online? Comcast Hears and Talks Back. nytimes.com, July 25: np.

But Comcast is working hard to improve its reputation. It has a lot of work to do—after all, the company was ranked at the bottom of the most recent American Customer Satisfaction Index, which tracks consumer opinions of more than 200 companies. And hundreds of customers have filed grievances on a site called comcastmustdie.com.

One of Comcast's initiatives to try to turn things around is headed by Frank Eliason, its digital care manager. He uses readily available online tools to monitor public comments on blogs, message boards, and social networks for any mention of Comcast. When Eliason sees a complaint, he contacts the source and tries to defuse the problem. "When you're having a two-way conversation, you really get to clear the air," says Eliason.

Comcast says the online outreach is part of a larger effort to revamp its customer service. In just five months, Eliason, whose job redefines customer service, has reached out to well over 1,000 customers online.

Comcast is not the only company trying to reach out to customers online. Using the social messaging service Twitter, Southwest Airlines answers customer questions about ticket prices and flight delays, Whole Foods Market posts details about discounts, and the chief executive of the online shoe store Zappos shares details of his life with 7,200 "followers." Many other companies also monitor online discussion groups. But given its track record, Comcast felt they needed to take the extra step: contacting customers who are discussing the company online.

Gillette's capability to combine several technologies has been one of the keys to its unparalleled success in the wet-shaving industry. Key technologies include its expertise concerning the physiology of facial hair and skin, the metallurgy of blade strength and sharpness, the dynamics of a cartridge moving across skin, and the physics of a razor blade severing the hair—highly specialized areas for which Gillette has unique capabilities. Combining these technologies has helped the company to develop innovative products such as the Excel, Sensor Excel, MACH 3, and Fusion shaving systems.[44]

Firm Resources and Sustainable Competitive Advantages

> **>LO5**
>
> The four criteria that a firm's resources must possess to maintain a sustainable advantage and how value created can be appropriated by employees and managers.

As we have mentioned, resources alone are not a basis for competitive advantages, nor are advantages sustainable over time.[45] In some cases, a resource or capability helps a firm to increase its revenues or to lower costs but the firm derives only a temporary advantage because competitors quickly imitate or substitute for it. Many e-commerce businesses in the early 2000s saw their profits seriously eroded because new (or existing) competitors easily duplicated their business model. For example, Priceline.com, expanded its offerings from enabling customers to place bids online for airline tickets to a wide variety of other products. However, it was easy for competitors (e.g., a consortium of major airlines) to duplicate Priceline's products and services. Ultimately, its market capitalization had plummeted roughly 98 percent from its all-time high.

For a resource to provide a firm with the potential for a sustainable competitive advantage, it must have four attributes.[46] First, the resource must be valuable in the sense that it exploits opportunities and/or neutralizes threats in the firm's environment. Second, it must be rare among the firm's current and potential competitors. Third, the resource must be difficult for competitors to imitate. Fourth, the resource must have no strategically equivalent substitutes. These criteria are summarized in Exhibit 3.6. We will now discuss each of these criteria. Then, we will examine how Dell's competitive advantage, which seemed secure just a few years ago, has eroded.

Is the Resource Valuable?   Organizational resources can be a source of competitive advantage only when they are valuable. Resources are valuable when they enable a firm to formulate and implement strategies that improve its efficiency or effectiveness. The SWOT framework suggests that firms improve their performance only when they exploit opportunities or neutralize (or minimize) threats.

The fact that firm attributes must be valuable in order to be considered resources (as well as potential sources of competitive advantage) reveals an important complementary relationship among environmental models (e.g., SWOT and five-forces analyses) and the resource-based model. Environmental models isolate those firm attributes that exploit opportunities and/or neutralize threats. Thus, they specify what firm attributes may be considered as resources. The resource-based model then suggests what additional characteristics these resources must possess if they are to develop a sustained competitive advantage.

Is the Resource Rare?   If competitors or potential competitors also possess the same valuable resource, it is not a source of a competitive advantage because all of these firms have the capability to exploit that resource in the same way. Common strategies based on such a resource would give no one firm an advantage. For a resource to provide competitive advantages, it must be uncommon, that is, rare relative to other competitors.

This argument can apply to bundles of valuable firm resources that are used to formulate and develop strategies. Some strategies require a mix of multiple types of resources—tangible assets, intangible assets, and organizational capabilities. If a particular bundle of firm resources is not rare, then relatively large numbers of firms will be able to conceive of and implement the strategies in question. Thus, such strategies will not be a source of competitive advantage, even if the resource in question is valuable.

Can the Resource Be Imitated Easily?   Inimitability (difficulty in imitating) is a key to value creation because it constrains competition.[47] If a resource is inimitable, then any profits generated are more likely to be sustainable.[48] Having a resource that competitors can easily copy generates only temporary value. This has important implications. Since managers

Is the resource or capability ...	Implications
Valuable?	• Neutralize threats and exploit opportunities
Rare?	• Not many firms possess
Difficult to imitate?	• Physically unique
	• Path dependency (how accumulated over time)
	• Causal ambiguity (difficult to disentangle what it is or how it could be re-created)
	• Social complexity (trust, interpersonal relationships, culture, reputation)
Difficult to substitute?	• No equivalent strategic resources or capabilities

Exhibit 3.6
Four Criteria for Assessing Sustainability of Resources and Capabilities

often fail to apply this test, they tend to base long-term strategies on resources that are imitable. IBP (Iowa Beef Processors) became the first meatpacking company in the United States to modernize by building a set of assets (automated plants located in cattle-producing states) and capabilities (low-cost "disassembly" of carcasses) that earned returns on assets of 1.3 percent in the 1970s. By the late 1980s, however, ConAgra and Cargill had imitated these resources, and IBP's profitability fell by nearly 70 percent, to 0.4 percent.

Monster.com entered the executive recruiting market by providing, in essence, a substitute for traditional bricks-and-mortar headhunting firms. Although Monster.com's resources are rare and valuable, they are subject to imitation by new rivals—other dot-com firms. Why? There are very low entry barriers for firms wanting to try their hand at recruitment. For example, many job search dot-coms have emerged in recent years, including jobsearch.com, headhunter.com, nationjob.com, and hotjobs.com. In all, there are approximately 30,000 online job boards available to job seekers. It would be most difficult for a firm to attain a sustainable advantage in this industry.

Clearly, an advantage based on inimitability won't last forever. Competitors will eventually discover a way to copy most valuable resources. However, managers can forestall them and sustain profits for a while by developing strategies around resources that have at least one of the following four characteristics.[49]

Physical Uniqueness The first source of inimitability is physical uniqueness, which by definition is inherently difficult to copy. A beautiful resort location, mineral rights, or Pfizer's pharmaceutical patents simply cannot be imitated. Many managers believe that several of their resources may fall into this category, but on close inspection, few do.

path dependency
a characteristic of resources that is developed and/or accumulated through a unique series of events.

Path Dependency A greater number of resources cannot be imitated because of what economists refer to as **path dependency.** This simply means that resources are unique and therefore scarce because of all that has happened along the path followed in their development and/or accumulation. Competitors cannot go out and buy these resources quickly and easily; they must be built up over time in ways that are difficult to accelerate.

The Gerber Products Co. brand name for baby food is an example of a resource that is potentially inimitable. Re-creating Gerber's brand loyalty would be a time-consuming process that competitors could not expedite, even with expensive marketing campaigns. Similarly, the loyalty and trust that Southwest Airlines employees feel toward their firm and its cofounder, Herb Kelleher, are resources that have been built up over a long period of time. Also, a crash R&D program generally cannot replicate a successful technology when research findings cumulate. Clearly, these path-dependent conditions build protection for the original resource. The benefits from experience and learning through trial and error cannot be duplicated overnight.

causal ambiguity
a characteristic of a firm's resources that is costly to imitate because a competitor cannot determine what the resource is and/or how it can be re-created.

Causal Ambiguity The third source of inimitability is termed **causal ambiguity.** This means that would-be competitors may be thwarted because it is impossible to disentangle the causes (or possible explanations) of either what the valuable resource is or how it can be re-created. What is the root of 3M's innovation process? You can study it and draw up a list of possible factors. But it is a complex, unfolding (or folding) process that is hard to understand and would be hard to imitate.

Often, causally ambiguous resources are organizational capabilities, involving a complex web of social interactions that may even depend on particular individuals. When Continental and United tried to mimic the successful low-cost strategy of Southwest Airlines, the planes, routes, and fast gate turnarounds were not the most difficult aspects for them to copy. Those were all rather easy to observe and, at least in principle, easy to duplicate. However, they could not replicate Southwest's culture of fun, family, frugality, and focus since no one can clearly specify exactly what that culture is or how it came to be.

social complexity
a characteristic of a firm's resources that is costly to imitate because the social engineering required is beyond the capability of competitors, including interpersonal relations among managers, organizational culture, and reputation with suppliers and customers.

Social Complexity A firm's resources may be imperfectly inimitable because they reflect a high level of **social complexity.** Such phenomena are typically beyond the ability of firms to systematically manage or influence. When competitive advantages are based on social complexity, it is difficult for other firms to imitate them.

A wide variety of firm resources may be considered socially complex. Examples include interpersonal relations among the managers in a firm, its culture, and its reputation with its suppliers and customers. In many of these cases, it is easy to specify how these socially complex resources add value to a firm. Hence, there is little or no causal ambiguity surrounding the link between them and competitive advantage. But an understanding that certain firm attributes, such as quality relations among managers, can improve a firm's efficiency does not necessarily lead to systematic efforts to imitate them. Such social engineering efforts are beyond the capabilities of most firms.

Although complex physical technology is not included in this category of sources of imperfect inimitability, the exploitation of physical technology in a firm typically involves the use of socially complex resources. That is, several firms may possess the same physical technology, but only one of them may have the social relations, culture, group norms, and so on to fully exploit the technology in implementing its strategies. If such complex social resources are not subject to imitation (and assuming they are valuable and rare and no substitutes exist), this firm may obtain a sustained competitive advantage from exploiting its physical technology more effectively than other firms.

Are Substitutes Readily Available?   The fourth requirement for a firm resource to be a source of sustainable competitive advantage is that there must be no strategically equivalent valuable resources that are themselves not rare or inimitable. Two valuable firm resources (or two bundles of resources) are strategically equivalent when each one can be exploited separately to implement the same strategies.

Substitutability may take at least two forms. First, though it may be impossible for a firm to imitate exactly another firm's resource, it may be able to substitute a similar resource that enables it to develop and implement the same strategy. Clearly, a firm seeking to imitate another firm's high-quality top management team would be unable to copy the team exactly. However, it might be able to develop its own unique management team. Though these two teams would have different ages, functional backgrounds, experience, and so on, they could be strategically equivalent and thus substitutes for one another.

Second, very different firm resources can become strategic substitutes. For example, Internet booksellers such as Amazon.com compete as substitutes for bricks-and-mortar booksellers such as B. Dalton. The result is that resources such as premier retail locations become less valuable. In a similar vein, several pharmaceutical firms have seen the value of patent protection erode in the face of new drugs that are based on different production processes and act in different ways, but can be used in similar treatment regimes. The coming years will likely see even more radical change in the pharmaceutical industry as the substitution of genetic therapies eliminates certain uses of chemotherapy.[50]

To recap this section, recall that resources and capabilities must be rare and valuable as well as difficult to imitate or substitute in order for a firm to attain competitive advantages that are sustainable over time.[51] Exhibit 3.7 illustrates the relationship among the four criteria of sustainability and shows the competitive implications.

In firms represented by the first row of Exhibit 3.7, managers are in a difficult situation. When their resources and capabilities do not meet any of the four criteria, it would be difficult to develop any type of competitive advantage, in the short or long term. The resources and capabilities they possess enable the firm neither to exploit environmental opportunities nor neutralize environmental threats. In the second and third rows, firms have resources and capabilities that are valuable as well as rare, respectively. However, in both cases the resources and capabilities are not difficult for competitors to imitate or substitute. Here, the firms could attain some level of competitive parity. They could perform on par with equally endowed rivals or attain a temporary competitive advantage. But their advantages would be easy for competitors to match. It is only in the fourth row, where all

Is a resource or capability . . .				
Valuable?	**Rare?**	**Difficult to Imitate?**	**Without Substitutes?**	**Implications for Competitiveness?**
No	No	No	No	Competitive disadvantage
Yes	No	No	No	Competitive parity
Yes	Yes	No	No	Temporary competitive advantage
Yes	Yes	Yes	Yes	Sustainable competitive advantage

Source: Adapted from Barney, J. B. 1991. Firm Resources and Sustained Competitive Advantage. *Journal of Management,* 17: 99–120.

four criteria are satisfied, that competitive advantages can be sustained over time. Next, let's look at Dell and see how its competitive advantage, which seemed to be sustainable for a rather long period of time, has eroded.

Dell's Eroding (Sustainable?) Competitive Advantage   In 1984, Michael Dell started Dell Inc. in a University of Texas dorm room with an investment of $1,000.[52] By 2006, Dell had attained annual revenues of $56 billion and a net income of $3.6 billion—making Michael Dell one of the richest people in the world. Dell achieved this meteoric growth by differentiating itself through the direct sales approach that it pioneered. Its user-configurable products met the diverse needs of its corporate and institutional customer base. Exhibit 3.8 summarizes how Dell achieved its remarkable success by integrating its tangible resources, intangible resources, and organizational capabilities.

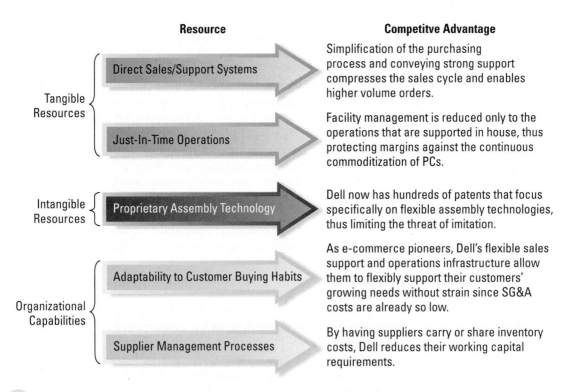

Resource	Competitve Advantage
Tangible Resources — Direct Sales/Support Systems	Simplification of the purchasing process and conveying strong support compresses the sales cycle and enables higher volume orders.
Just-In-Time Operations	Facility management is reduced only to the operations that are supported in house, thus protecting margins against the continuous commoditization of PCs.
Intangible Resources — Proprietary Assembly Technology	Dell now has hundreds of patents that focus specifically on flexible assembly technologies, thus limiting the threat of imitation.
Organizational Capabilities — Adaptability to Customer Buying Habits	As e-commerce pioneers, Dell's flexible sales support and operations infrastructure allow them to flexibly support their customers' growing needs without strain since SG&A costs are already so low.
Supplier Management Processes	By having suppliers carry or share inventory costs, Dell reduces their working capital requirements.

Exhibit 3.8   Dell's Tangible Resources, Intangible Resources, and Organizational Capabilities

Dell continued to maintain this competitive advantage by strengthening its value-chain activities and interrelationships that are critical to satisfying the largest market opportunities. It achieved this by (1) implementing e-commerce direct sales and support processes that accounted for the sophisticated buying habits of the largest markets and (2) matching its inventory management to its extensive supplier network. Dell also sustained these advantages by investing in intangible resources, such as proprietary assembly methods and packaging configurations, that helped to protect against the threat of imitation.

Dell recognized that the PC is a complex product with components sourced from several different technologies and manufacturers. Thus, in working backward from the customer's purchasing habits, Dell saw that the company could build valuable solutions by organizing its resources and capabilities around build-to-specification tastes, making both the sales and integration processes flexible, and passing on overhead expenses to its suppliers. Even as the PC industry became further commoditized, Dell was one of the few competitors that was able to retain solid margins. It accomplished this by adapting its manufacturing and assembly capabilities to match the PC market's trend toward user compatibility.

For many years, it looked as if Dell's competitive advantage over its rivals would be sustainable for a very long period of time. However, by early 2007, Dell was falling behind its rivals in market share. This led to a significant decline in its stock price—followed by a complete shake-up of the top management team. But what led to Dell's competitive decline in the first place?[53]

- Dell had become so focused on cost that it failed to pay attention to the design of the brand. Customers increasingly began to see the product as a commodity.
- Much of the growth in the PC industry today is in laptops. Customers demand a sleeker, better-designed machine instead of just the cheapest laptop. Also, they often want to see the laptop before they buy it.
- When Dell outsourced its customer service function to foreign locations, it led to a decline in customer support. This eroded Dell's brand value.
- Dell's efforts to replicate its made-to-order, no middleman strategy to other products such as printers and storage devices proved to be a failure. This is because customers saw little need for customization of these products.
- Rivals such as HP have been improving their product design and reducing their costs.[54] Thus, they now have cost parity with Dell, while enjoying a better brand image and the support of an extensive dealer network.

● Dell's competitive position in personal computers—including desktops and laptops—has eroded in recent years.

The Generation and Distribution of a Firm's Profits: Extending the Resource-Based View of the Firm

The resource-based view of the firm has been useful in determining when firms will create competitive advantages and enjoy high levels of profitability. However, it has not been developed to address how a firm's profits (often referred to as "rents" by economists) will be distributed to a firm's management and employees.[55] This becomes an important issue because firms may be successful in creating competitive advantages that can be sustainable for a period of time but much of the profits can be retained (or "appropriated") by its employees and managers instead of flowing to the owners of the firm (i.e., the stockholders).*

Consider Viewpoint DataLabs International, a Salt Lake City–based company that makes sophisticated three-dimensional models and textures for film production houses, video games, and car manufacturers. This example will help to show how employees are often able to obtain (or "appropriate") a high proportion of a firm's profits:

> Walter Noot, head of production, was having trouble keeping his highly skilled Generation X employees happy with their compensation. Each time one of them was lured away for more money, everyone would want a raise. "We were having to give out raises every six months—30 to 40 percent—then six months later they'd expect the same. It was a big struggle to keep people happy."[56]

At Viewpoint DataLabs, much of the profits are being generated by the highly skilled professionals working together. They are able to exercise their power by successfully demanding more financial compensation. In part, management has responded favorably because they are united in their demands, and their work involves a certain amount of social complexity and causal ambiguity—given the complex, coordinated efforts that their work entails.

Four factors help explain the extent to which employees and managers will be able to obtain a proportionately high level of the profits that they generate:[57]

- **Employee Bargaining Power.** If employees are vital to forming a firm's unique capability, they will earn disproportionately high wages. For example, marketing professionals may have access to valuable information that helps them to understand the intricacies of customer demands and expectations, or engineers may understand unique technical aspects of the products or services. Additionally, in some industries such as consulting, advertising, and tax preparation, clients tend to be very loyal to individual professionals employed by the firm, instead of to the firm itself. This enables them to "take the clients with them" if they leave. This enhances their bargaining power.

- **Employee Replacement Cost.** If employees' skills are idiosyncratic and rare (a source of resource-based advantages), they should have high bargaining power based on the high cost required by the firm to replace them. For example, Raymond Ozzie, the software designer who was critical in the development of Lotus Notes, was able to dictate the terms under which IBM acquired Lotus.

- **Employee Exit Costs.** This factor may tend to reduce an employee's bargaining power. An individual may face high personal costs when leaving the organization. Thus, that individual's threat of leaving may not be credible. In addition, an employee's expertise may be firm-specific and of limited value to other firms. Causal ambiguity may make it difficult for the employee to explain his or her specific contribution to a given project. Thus, a rival firm might be less likely to pay a high wage premium since it would be unsure of the employee's unique contribution.

- **Manager Bargaining Power.** Managers' power is based on how well they create resource-based advantages. They are generally charged with creating value through the process of organizing, coordinating, and leveraging employees as well as other forms of capital such as plant, equipment, and financial capital (addressed further in Chapter 4). Such activities provide managers with sources of information that may not be readily available to others. Thus, although managers may not know as much about the specific nature of customers and technologies, they are in a position to have a more thorough, integrated understanding of the total operation.

---

* Economists define rents as profits (or prices) in excess of what is required to provide a normal return.

Chapter 9 addresses the conditions under which top-level managers (such as CEOs) of large corporations have been, at times, able to obtain levels of total compensation that would appear to be significantly disproportionate to their contributions to wealth generation as well as to top executives in peer organizations. Here, corporate governance becomes a critical control mechanism. For example, William Esrey and Ronald T. LeMay (the former two top executives at Sprint Corporation) earned more than $130 million in stock options because of "cozy" relationships with members of their board of directors, who tended to approve with little debate huge compensation packages.[58]

Such diversion of profits from the owners of the business to top management is far less likely when the board members are truly independent outsiders (i.e., they do not have close ties to management). In general, given the external market for top talent, the level of compensation that executives receive is based on factors similar to the ones just discussed that determine the level of their bargaining power.[59]

Evaluating Firm Performance: Two Approaches

This section addresses two approaches to use when evaluating a firm's performance. The first is financial ratio analysis, which, generally speaking, identifies how a firm is performing according to its balance sheet, income statement, and market valuation. As we will discuss, when performing a financial ratio analysis, you must take into account the firm's performance from a historical perspective (not just at one point in time) as well as how it compares with both industry norms and key competitors.[60]

The second perspective takes a broader stakeholder view. Firms must satisfy a broad range of stakeholders, including employees, customers, and owners, to ensure their long-term viability. Central to our discussion will be a well-known approach—the balanced scorecard—that has been popularized by Robert Kaplan and David Norton.[61]

Financial Ratio Analysis

The beginning point in analyzing the financial position of a firm is to compute and analyze five different types of financial ratios:

- Short-term solvency or liquidity
- Long-term solvency measures
- Asset management (or turnover)
- Profitability
- Market value

financial ratio analysis a technique for measuring the performance of a firm according to its balance sheet, income statement, and market valuation.

Exhibit 3.9 summarizes each of these five ratios.

Appendix 1 to Chapter 13 (the Case Analysis chapter) provides detailed definitions for and discussions of each of these types of ratios as well as examples of how each is calculated. Refer to pages 486 to 494.

A meaningful ratio analysis must go beyond the calculation and interpretation of financial ratios.[62] It must include how ratios change over time as well as how they are interrelated. For example, a firm that takes on too much long-term debt to finance operations will see an immediate impact on its indicators of long-term financial leverage. The additional debt will negatively affect the firm's short-term liquidity ratio (i.e., current and quick ratios) since the firm must pay interest and principal on the additional debt each year until it is retired. Additionally, the interest expenses deducted from revenues reduce the firm's profitability.

A firm's financial position should not be analyzed in isolation. Important reference points are needed. We will address some issues that must be taken into account to make financial analysis more meaningful: historical comparisons, comparisons with industry norms, and comparisons with key competitors.

>LO6

The usefulness of financial ratio analysis, its inherent limitations, and how to make meaningful comparisons of performance across firms.

I. Short-term solvency, or liquidity, ratios

$$\text{Current ratio} = \frac{\text{Current assets}}{\text{Current liabilities}}$$

$$\text{Quick ratio} = \frac{\text{Current assets} - \text{Inventory}}{\text{Current liabilities}}$$

$$\text{Cash ratio} = \frac{\text{Cash}}{\text{Current liabilities}}$$

II. Long-term solvency, or financial leverage, ratios

$$\text{Total debt ratio} = \frac{\text{Total assets} - \text{Total equity}}{\text{Total assets}}$$

$$\text{Debt-equity ratio} = \text{Total debt/Total equity}$$

$$\text{Equity multiplier} = \text{Total assets/Total equity}$$

$$\text{Times interest earned ratio} = \frac{\text{EBIT}}{\text{Interest}}$$

$$\text{Cash coverage ratio} = \frac{\text{EBIT} + \text{Depreciation}}{\text{Interest}}$$

III. Asset utilization, or turnover, ratios

$$\text{Inventory turnover} = \frac{\text{Cost of goods sold}}{\text{Inventory}}$$

$$\text{Days' sales in inventory} = \frac{365 \text{ days}}{\text{Inventory turnover}}$$

$$\text{Receivables turnover} = \frac{\text{Sales}}{\text{Accounts receivable}}$$

$$\text{Days' sales in receivables} = \frac{365 \text{ days}}{\text{Receivables turnover}}$$

$$\text{Total asset turnover} = \frac{\text{Sales}}{\text{Total assets}}$$

$$\text{Capital intensity} = \frac{\text{Total assets}}{\text{Sales}}$$

IV. Profitability ratios

$$\text{Profit margin} = \frac{\text{Net income}}{\text{Sales}}$$

$$\text{Return on assets (ROA)} = \frac{\text{Net income}}{\text{Total assets}}$$

$$\text{Return on equity (ROE)} = \frac{\text{Net income}}{\text{Total equity}}$$

$$\text{ROE} = \frac{\text{Net income}}{\text{Sales}} \times \frac{\text{Sales}}{\text{Assets}} \times \frac{\text{Assets}}{\text{Equity}}$$

V. Market value ratios

$$\text{Price-earnings ratio} = \frac{\text{Price per share}}{\text{Earnings per share}}$$

$$\text{Market-to-book ratio} = \frac{\text{Market value per share}}{\text{Book value per share}}$$

Exhibit 3.9   A Summary of Five Types of Financial Ratios

Historical Comparisons   When you evaluate a firm's financial performance, it is very useful to compare its financial position over time. This provides a means of evaluating trends. For example, Microsoft reported revenues of $60 billion and net income of $17.7 billion in 2008. Almost all firms—except a few of the largest and most profitable companies in the world—would be very happy with such financial success. These figures reflect an annual growth in revenue and net income of 36 percent and 40 percent, respectively, for the 2004 to 2006 time period. Had Microsoft's revenues and net income in 2008 been $40 billion and $10 billion, respectively, it would still be a very large and highly profitable enterprise. However, such performance significantly damaged Microsoft's market valuation and reputation as well as the careers of many of its executives.

Exhibit 3.10 illustrates a 10-year period of return on sales (ROS) for a hypothetical company. As indicated by the dotted trend lines, the rate of growth (or decline) differs substantially over time periods.

Comparison with Industry Norms   When you are evaluating a firm's financial performance, remember also to compare it with industry norms. A firm's current ratio or profitability may appear impressive at first glance. However, it may pale when compared with industry standards or norms.

Comparing your firm with all other firms in your industry assesses relative performance. Banks often use such comparisons when evaluating a firm's creditworthiness. Exhibit 3.11

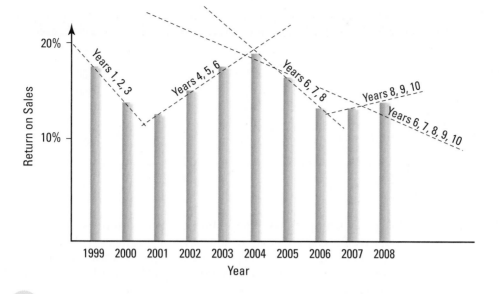

Exhibit 3.10 Historical Trends: Return on Sales (ROS) for a Hypothetical Company

includes a variety of financial ratios for three industries: semiconductors, grocery stores, and skilled-nursing facilities. Why is there such variation among the financial ratios for these three industries? There are several reasons. With regard to the collection period, grocery stores operate mostly on a cash basis, hence a very short collection period. Semiconductor manufacturers sell their output to other manufacturers (e.g., computer makers) on terms such as 2/15 net 45, which means they give a 2 percent discount on bills paid within 15 days and start charging interest after 45 days. Skilled-nursing facilities also have a longer collection period than grocery stores because they rely on payments from insurance companies.

The industry norms for return on sales also highlight differences among these industries. Grocers, with very slim margins, have a lower return on sales than either skilled-nursing facilities or semiconductor manufacturers. But how might we explain the differences between skilled-nursing facilities and semiconductor manufacturers? Health care facilities, in general, are limited in their pricing structures by Medicare/Medicaid regulations and by insurance reimbursement limits, but semiconductor producers have pricing structures determined by the market. If their products have superior performance, semiconductor manufacturers can charge premium prices.

Exhibit 3.11
How Financial Ratios
Differ across Industries

Financial Ratio	Semiconductors	Grocery Stores	Skilled-Nursing Facilities
Quick ratio (times)	1.9	0.6	1.2
Current ratio (times)	3.9	1.9	1.6
Total liabilities to net worth (%)	30.2	71.4	156.9
Collection period (days)	49.0	2.6	30.3
Assets to sales (%)	147.3	19.5	113.9
Return on sales (%)	24	1.1	2.4

Source: Dun & Bradstreet. *Industry Norms and Key Business Ratios, 2007–2008.* One Year Edition, SIC #3600–3699 (Semiconductors); SIC #5400–5499 (Grocery Stores); SIC #8000–8099 (Skilled-Nursing Facilities). New York: Dun & Bradstreet Credit Services.

Exhibit 3.12
Comparison of Procter
& Gamble's and Key
Competitors' Drug
Revenues and R&D
Expenditures

Company (or division)	Sales* ($ billions)	R&D Budget ($ billions)
P&G Drug Division	$ 0.8	$0.38
Bristol-Myers Squibb	20.2	1.80
Pfizer	27.4	4.00
Merck	32.7	2.10

Source: Berner, R. 2000. Procter & Gamble: Just Say No to Drugs. *BusinessWeek,* October 9: 128; data courtesy of Lehman Brothers and Procter & Gamble.

*Data: Lehman Brothers, Procter & Gamble Co.

Comparison with Key Competitors   Recall from Chapter 2 that firms with similar strategies are members of a strategic group in an industry. Furthermore, competition is more intense among competitors within groups than across groups. Thus, you can gain valuable insights into a firm's financial and competitive position if you make comparisons between a firm and its most direct rivals. Consider Procter & Gamble's ill-fated efforts to enter the highly profitable pharmaceutical industry. Although P&G is a giant in consumer products, its efforts over two decades produced nominal profits. In 1999 P&G spent $380 million on R&D in drugs—22 percent of its total corporate R&D budget. Its drug unit produced only 2 percent of the company's $40 billion sales. Why? While $380 million is a large sum, its key competitors dwarf P&G. Consider the drug revenues and R&D budgets of P&G compared to its main rivals as shown in Exhibit 3.12. *BusinessWeek*'s take on P&G's chances in an article entitled "Just Say No to Drugs" was this: "Don't bet on it. P&G may be a giant in detergent and toothpaste, but the consumer-products maker is simply outclassed by the competition."[63]

Integrating Financial Analysis and Stakeholder Perspectives: The Balanced Scorecard

>LO7

The value of
the "balanced
scorecard" in
recognizing how the
interests of a variety
of stakeholders can
be interrelated.

It is useful to see how a firm is performing over time in terms of several ratios. However, such traditional approaches to performance assessments can be a double-edged sword.[64] Many important transactions that managers make—investments in research and development, employee training and development, and, advertising and promotion of key brands—may greatly expand a firm's market potential and create significant long-term shareholder value. But such critical investments are not reflected positively in short-term financial reports. Financial reports typically measure expenses, not the value created. Thus, managers may be penalized for spending money in the short term to improve their firm's long-term competitive viability!

Now consider the other side of the coin. A manager may destroy the firm's future value by dissatisfying customers, depleting the firm's stock of good products coming out of R&D, or damaging the morale of valued employees. Such budget cuts, however, may lead to very good short-term financials. The manager may look good in the short run and even receive credit for improving the firm's performance. In essence, such a manager has mastered "denominator management," whereby decreasing investments makes the return on investment (ROI) ratio larger, even though the actual return remains constant or shrinks.

**balanced score-
card** a method of
evaluating a firm's
performance using
performance mea-
sures from the
customers', internal,
innovation and learn-
ing, and financial
perspectives.

The Balanced Scorecard: Description and Benefits   To provide a meaningful integration of the many issues that come into evaluating a firm's performance, Kaplan and Norton developed a **"balanced scorecard."**[65] This provides top managers with a fast but comprehensive view of the business. In a nutshell, it includes financial measures that reflect the results of actions already taken, but it complements these indicators with measures of

Exhibit 3.13
**The Balanced
Scorecard's Four
Perspectives**

- How do customers see us? (customer perspective)
- What must we excel at? (internal business perspective)
- Can we continue to improve and create value? (innovation and learning perspective)
- How do we look to shareholders? (financial perspective)

customer satisfaction, internal processes, and the organization's innovation and improvement activities—operational measures that drive future financial performance.

The balanced scorecard enables managers to consider their business from four key perspectives: customer, internal, innovation and learning, and financial. These are briefly described in Exhibit 3.13.

Customer Perspective Clearly, how a company is performing from its customers' perspective is a top priority for management. The balanced scorecard requires that managers translate their general mission statements on customer service into specific measures that reflect the factors that really matter to customers. For the balanced scorecard to work, managers must articulate goals for four key categories of customer concerns: time, quality, performance and service, and cost. For example, lead time may be measured as the time from the company's receipt of an order to the time it actually delivers the product or service to the customer.

Internal Business Perspective Customer-based measures are important. However, they must be translated into indicators of what the firm must do internally to meet customers' expectations. Excellent customer performance results from processes, decisions, and actions that occur throughout organizations in a coordinated fashion, and managers must focus on those critical internal operations that enable them to satisfy customer needs. The internal measures should reflect business processes that have the greatest impact on customer satisfaction. These include factors that affect cycle time, quality, employee skills, and productivity. Firms also must identify and measure the key resources and capabilities they need for continued success.

Innovation and Learning Perspective Given the rapid rate of markets, technologies, and global competition, the criteria for success are constantly changing. To survive and prosper, managers must make frequent changes to existing products and services as well as introduce entirely new products with expanded capabilities. A firm's ability to improve, innovate, and learn is tied directly to its value. Simply put, only by developing new products and services, creating greater value for customers, and increasing operating efficiencies can a company penetrate new markets, increase revenues and margins, and enhance shareholder value. A firm's ability to do well from an innovation and learning perspective is more dependent on its intangible than tangible assets. Three categories of intangible assets are critically important: human capital (skills, talent, and knowledge), information capital (information systems, networks), and organization capital (culture, leadership).

Financial Perspective Measures of financial performance indicate whether the company's strategy, implementation, and execution are indeed contributing to bottom-line improvement. Typical financial goals include profitability, growth, and shareholder value. Periodic financial statements remind managers that improved quality, response time, productivity, and innovative products benefit the firm only when they result in improved sales, increased market share, reduced operating expenses, or higher asset turnover.[66]

Consider how Sears, the huge retailer, found a strong causal relationship between employee attitudes, customer attitudes, and financial outcomes.[67] Through an ongoing study, Sears developed (and continues to refine) what it calls its total performance indicators, or TPI—a set of indicators for assessing their performance with customers, employees, and investors. Sears's quantitative model has shown that a 5.0 percent improvement in employee attitudes leads to a 1.3 percent improvement in customer satisfaction, which in turn drives a 0.5 percent improvement in revenue. Thus, if a single store improved its employee attitude by 5.0 percent. Sears could predict with confidence that if the revenue growth in the district as a whole were 5.0 percent, the revenue growth in this particular store would be 5.5 percent. Interestingly, Sears's managers consider such numbers as rigorous as any others that they work with every year. The company's accounting firm audits management as closely as it audits the financial statements.

A key implication is that managers do not need to look at their job as balancing stakeholder demands. They must avoid the following mind-set: "How many units in employee satisfaction do I have to give up to get some additional units of customer satisfaction or profits?" Instead, the balanced scorecard provides a win–win approach—increasing satisfaction among a wide variety of organizational stakeholders, including employees (at all levels), customers, and stockholders.

Limitations and Potential Downsides of the Balanced Scorecard   There is general agreement that there is nothing inherently wrong with the concept of the balanced scorecard.[68] The key limitation is that some executives may view it as a "quick fix" that can be easily installed. However, implementing a balanced metrics system is an evolutionary process. It is not a one-time task that can be quickly checked off as "completed." If managers do not recognize this from the beginning and fail to commit to it long term, the organization will be disappointed. Poor execution becomes the cause of such performance outcomes. And organizational scorecards must be aligned with individuals' scorecards to turn the balanced scorecards into a powerful tool for sustained performance.*

In a recent study of 50 Canadian medium-size and large organizations, the number of users expressing skepticism about scorecard performance was much greater than the number claiming positive results. However, the overwhelming perspective was that balanced scorecards can be worthwhile in clarifying an organization's strategy, and if this can be accomplished, better results will follow. A few companies stated categorically that scorecards have improved their firm's financial results. For example, one respondent claimed that "We did not meet our financial goals previously, but since implementing our balanced scorecard, we have now met our goals three years running."

On the other hand, a greater number of respondents agreed with the statement "Balanced scorecards don't really work." Some representative comments included: "It became just a number-crunching exercise by accountants after the first year," "It is just the latest management fad and is already dropping lower on management's list of priorities as all fads eventually do," and "If scorecards are supposed to be a measurement tool, why is it so hard to measure their results?" There is much work to do before scorecards can become a viable framework to measure sustained strategic performance.

Problems often occur in the balanced scorecard implementation efforts when there is an insufficient commitment to learning and the inclusion of employees' personal ambitions. Without a set of rules for employees that address continuous process improvement and the personal improvement of individual employees, there will be limited employee buy-in and insufficient cultural change. Thus, many improvements may be temporary and superficial. Often, scorecards that failed to attain alignment and improvements dissipated very quickly. And, in many cases, management's efforts to improve performance were seen

---

* Building on the concepts that are the foundation of the balanced scorecard approach, Kaplan and Norton have recently developed a useful tool called the strategy map. Strategy maps show the cause and effect links by which specific improvements in different areas lead to a desired outcome. Strategy maps also help employees see how their jobs are related to the overall objectives of the organization. They also help us understand how an organization can convert its assets—both tangible and intangible—into tangible outcomes. Refer to Kaplan, R. S. & Norton, D. P. 2000. Having Trouble with Your Strategy? Then Map It. *Harvard Business Review,* 78(10): 167–176.

Exhibit 3.14
Potential Limitations
of the Balanced
Scorecard

Most agree that the balanced scorecard concept is a useful and an appropriate management tool. However, there are many design and implementation issues that may short circuit its value, including the following:

- *Lack of a Clear Strategy.* A scorecard can be developed without the aid of a strategy. However, it then becomes a key performance indicator or stakeholder system, lacking in many of the attributes offered from a true balanced scorecard.
- *Limited or Ineffective Executive Sponsorship.* Although training and education is important, without tenacious leadership and support of a scorecard project, the effort is most likely doomed.
- *Too Much Emphasis on Financial Measures Rather than Nonfinancial Measures.* This leads to measures that do not connect to the drivers of the business and are not relevant to performance improvement.
- *Poor Data on Actual Performance.* This can negate most of the effort invested in defining performance measures because a company can't monitor actual changes in results from changes in behavior.
- *Inappropriate Links of Scorecard Measures to Compensation.* Although this can focus managerial and employee attention, exercising it too soon can produce many unintended side effects such as dysfunctional decision making by managers looking to cash in.
- *Inconsistent or Inappropriate Terminology.* Everyone must speak the same language if measurement is to be used to guide change within an organization. Translating strategy into measures becomes even more difficult if everyone cannot agree on (or understand) the same language and terminology.

Sources: Angel, R. & Rampersad, H. 2005. Do Scorecards Add Up? Camagazine.com. May: np; and Niven, P. 2002. *Balanced Scorecard Step by Step: Maximizing Performance and Maintaining Results.* New York: John Wiley & Sons.

as divisive and were viewed by employees as aimed at benefiting senior management compensation. This fostered a "what's in it for me?" attitude. Exhibit 3.14 summarizes some of the potential downsides of the balanced scorecard.

Reflecting on Career Implications . . .

- *The Value Chain:* Carefully analyze where you can add value in your firm's value chain. How might your firm's support activities (e.g., information technology, human resource practices) help you accomplish your assigned tasks more effectively?
- *The Value Chain:* Consider important relationships among activities both within your firm as well as between your firm and its suppliers, customers, and alliance partners.
- *Resource-Based View of the Firm:* Are your skills and talents rare, valuable, difficult to imitate, and have few substitutes? If so, you are in a better position to add value for your firm—and earn rewards and incentives. How can your skills and talents be enhanced to help satisfy these criteria to a greater extent? More training? Change positions within the firm? Consider career options at other organizations?
- *Balanced Scorecard:* In your decision making, strive to "balance" the four perspectives: customer, internal business, innovation and learning, and financial. Do not focus too much on short-term profits. Do your personal career goals provide opportunities to develop your skills in all four directions?

Summary

In the traditional approaches to assessing a firm's internal environment, the primary goal of managers would be to determine their firm's relative strengths and weaknesses. Such is the role of SWOT analysis, wherein managers analyze their firm's strengths and weaknesses as well as the opportunities and threats in the external environment. In this chapter, we discussed why this may be a good starting point but hardly the best approach to take in performing a sound analysis. There are many limitations to SWOT analysis, including its static perspective, its potential to overemphasize a single dimension of a firm's strategy, and the likelihood that a firm's strengths do not necessarily help the firm create value or competitive advantages.

We identified two frameworks that serve to complement SWOT analysis in assessing a firm's internal environment: value-chain analysis and the resource-based view of the firm. In conducting a value-chain analysis, first divide the firm into a series of value-creating activities. These include primary activities such as inbound logistics, operations, and service as well as support activities such as procurement and human resources management. Then analyze how each activity adds value as well as how *interrelationships* among value activities in the firm and among the firm and its customers and suppliers add value. Thus, instead of merely determining a firm's strengths and weaknesses per se, you analyze them in the overall context of the firm and its relationships with customers and suppliers—the value system.

The resource-based view of the firm considers the firm as a bundle of resources: tangible resources, intangible resources, and organizational capabilities. Competitive advantages that are sustainable over time generally arise from the creation of bundles of resources and capabilities. For advantages to be sustainable, four criteria must be satisfied: value, rarity, difficulty in imitation, and difficulty in substitution. Such an evaluation requires a sound knowledge of the competitive context in which the firm exists. The owners of a business may not capture all of the value created by the firm. The appropriation of value created by a firm between the owners and employees is determined by four factors: employee bargaining power, replacement cost, employee exit costs, and manager bargaining power.

An internal analysis of the firm would not be complete unless you evaluate its performance and make the appropriate comparisons. Determining a firm's performance requires an analysis of its financial situation as well as a review of how well it is satisfying a broad range of stakeholders, including customers, employees, and stockholders. We discussed the concept of the balanced scorecard, in which four perspectives must be addressed: customer, internal business, innovation and learning, and financial. Central to this concept is the idea that the interests of various stakeholders can be interrelated. We provide examples of how indicators of employee satisfaction lead to higher levels of customer satisfaction, which in turn lead to higher levels of financial performance. Thus, improving a firm's performance does not need to involve making trade-offs among different stakeholders. Assessing the firm's performance is also more useful if it is evaluated in terms of how it changes over time, compares with industry norms, and compares with key competitors.

In the Appendix to Chapter 3, we discuss how Internet and digital technologies have created new opportunities for firms to add value. Four value-adding activities that have been enhanced by Internet capabilities are search, evaluation, problem solving, and transaction. These four activities are supported by three different types of content that Internet businesses often use—customer feedback, expertise, and entertainment programming. Seven business models have been identified that are proving successful for use by Internet firms. These include commission, advertising, markup, production, referral, subscription, and fee-for-service–based models. Firms also are finding that combinations of these business models can contribute to greater success.

Summary Review Questions

1. SWOT analysis is a technique to analyze the internal and external environment of a firm. What are its advantages and disadvantages?

2. Briefly describe the primary and support activities in a firm's value chain.

3. How can managers create value by establishing important relationships among the value-chain activities both within their firm and between the firm and its customers and suppliers?

4. Briefly explain the four criteria for sustainability of competitive advantages.

5. Under what conditions are employees and managers able to appropriate some of the value created by their firm?

6. What are the advantages and disadvantages of conducting a financial ratio analysis of a firm?

7. Summarize the concept of the balanced scorecard. What are its main advantages?

Key Terms

Experiential Exercise

Dell Computer is a leading firm in the personal computer industry, with annual revenues of $61 billion during its 2008 fiscal year. Dell had created a very strong competitive position via its "direct model," whereby it manufactures its personal computers to detailed customer specifications. However, its advantage has been eroded recently by strong rivals such as HP.

Below we address several questions that focus on Dell's value-chain activities and interrelationships among them as well as whether they are able to attain sustainable competitive advantage(s). (We discuss Dell in this chapter on pages 98–99.)

1. Where in Dell's value chain are they creating value for their customer?

Value-Chain Activity	Yes/No	How Does Dell Create Value for the Customer?
Primary:		
Inbound logistics		
Operations		
Outbound logistics		
Marketing and sales		
Service		
Support:		
Procurement		
Technology development		
Human resource management		
General administration		

2. What are the important relationships among Dell's value-chain activities? What are the important inter-dependencies? For each activity, identify the relationships and interdependencies.

	Inbound logistics	Operations	Outbound logistics	Marketing and sales	Service	Procurement	Technology development	Human resource management	General administration
Inbound logistics	▨								
Operations		▨							
Outbound logistics			▨						
Marketing and sales				▨					
Service					▨				
Procurement						▨			
Technology development							▨		
Human resource management								▨	
General administration									▨

3. What resources, activities, and relationships enable Dell to achieve a sustainable competitive advantage?

Resource/Activity	Is It Valuable?	Is It Rare?	Are There Few Substitutes?	Is It Difficult to Make?
Inbound logistics				
Operations				
Outbound logistics				
Marketing and sales				
Service				
Procurement				
Technology development				
Human resource management				
General administration				

Application Questions Exercises

1. Using published reports, select two CEOs who have recently made public statements regarding a major change in their firm's strategy. Discuss how the successful implementation of such strategies requires changes in the firm's primary and support activities.

2. Select a firm that competes in an industry in which you are interested. Drawing upon published financial reports, complete a financial ratio analysis. Based on changes over time and a comparison with industry norms, evaluate the firm's strengths and weaknesses in terms of its financial position.

3. How might exemplary human resource practices enhance and strengthen a firm's value-chain activities?

4. Using the Internet, look up your university or college. What are some of its key value-creating activities that provide competitive advantages? Why?

Ethics Questions

1. What are some of the ethical issues that arise when a firm becomes overly zealous in advertising its products?

2. What are some of the ethical issues that may arise from a firm's procurement activities? Are you aware of any of these issues from your personal experience or businesses you are familiar with?

References

1. Wiley, R. 2008. Navistar re-files lawsuit against Ford Motor Company. reuters.com, February 28: np.; Pope, B. 2007. Ford, Navistar working toward compromise. wardsauto.com, March 8: np.; Anonymous. 2007. Navistar files another lawsuit against Ford. uk.reuters.com, np.; and, Hoffman, B. G. 2007. Ford-Navistar showdown could threaten truck production. detnews.com, February 27: np.

2. Our discussion of the value chain will draw on Porter, M. E. 1985. *Competitive advantage:* chap. 2. New York: Free Press.

3. Dyer, J. H. 1996. Specialized supplier networks as a source of competitive advantage: Evidence from the auto industry. *Strategic Management Journal,* 17: 271–291.

4. For an insightful perspective on value-chain analysis, refer to Stabell, C. B. & Fjeldstad, O. D. 1998. Configuring value for competitive advantage: On chains, shops, and networks. *Strategic Management Journal,* 19: 413–437. The authors develop concepts of value chains, value shops, and value networks to extend the value-creation logic across a broad range of industries. Their work builds on the seminal contributions of Porter, 1985, op. cit., and others who have addressed how firms create value through key interrelationships among value-creating activities.

5. Ibid.

6. Maynard, M. 1999. Toyota promises custom order in 5 days. *USA Today,* August 6: B1.

7. Shaw Industries. 1999. Annual report: 14–15.

8. Fisher, M. L. 1997. What is the right supply chain for your product? *Harvard Business Review,* 75(2): 105–116.

9. Jackson. M. 2001. Bringing a dying brand back to life. *Harvard Business Review,* 79(5): 53–61.

10. Anderson, J. C. & Nmarus, J. A. 2003. Selectively pursuing more of your customer's business. *MIT Sloan Management Review,* 44(3): 42–50.

11. Insights on advertising are addressed in: Rayport, J. F. 2008. Where is advertising? Into 'stitials. *Harvard Business Review,* 66(5): 18–20.

12. An insightful discussion of the role of identity marketing—that is, the myriad labels that people use to express who they are—in successful marketing activities is found in Reed, A., II & Bolton, L. E. 2005. The complexity of identity. *MIT Sloan Management Review,* 46(3): 18–22.

13. Insights on the usefulness of off-line ads are the focus of: Abraham, M. 2008. The off-line impact of online ads. *Harvard Business Review,* 66(4): 28.

14. Berggren, E. & Nacher, T. 2000. Why good ideas go bust. *Management Review,* February: 32–36.

15. For an insightful perspective on creating effective brand portfolios, refer to Hill, S., Ettenson, R., & Tyson, D. 2005. Achieving the ideal brand portfolio. *MIT Sloan Management Review,* 46(2): 85–90.

16. Haddad, C. & Grow, B. 2001. Wait a second—I didn't order that! *BusinessWeek,* July 16: 45.

17. For a scholarly discussion on the procurement of technology components, read Hoetker, G. 2005. How much you know versus how well I know you: Selecting a supplier for a technically innovative component. *Strategic Management Journal,* 26(1): 75–96.

18. For a discussion on criteria to use when screening suppliers for back-office functions, read Feeny, D., Lacity, M., & Willcocks, L. P. 2005. Taking the measure of outsourcing providers. *MIT Sloan Management Review,* 46(3): 41–48.

19. For a study investigating sourcing practices, refer to: Safizadeh, M. H., Field, J. M., & Ritzman, L. P. 2008. Sourcing practices and boundaries of the firm in the financial services industry. *Strategic Management Journal,* 29(1): 79–92.

20. Imperato, G. 1998. How to give good feedback. *Fast Company,* September: 144–156.

21. Bensaou, B. M. & Earl, M. 1998. The right mindset for managing information technology. *Harvard Business Review,* 96(5): 118–128.

22. A discussion of R&D in the pharmaceutical industry is in: Garnier, J-P.

2008. Rebuilding the R&D engine in big pharma. *Harvard Business Review,* 66(5): 68–76.

23. Donlon, J. P. 2000. Bonsignore's bid for the big time. *Chief Executive,* March: 28–37.

24. Ulrich, D. 1998. A new mandate for human resources. *Harvard Business Review,* 96(1): 124–134.

25. A study of human resource management in China is: Li, J., Lam, K., Sun, J. J. M., & Liu, S. X. Y. 2008. Strategic resource management, institutionalization, and employment modes: An empirical study in China. *Strategic Management Journal,* 29(3): 337–342.

26. Wood, J. 2003. Sharing jobs and working from home: The new face of the airline industry. AviationCareer.net, February 21.

27. Green, S., Hasan, F., Immelt, J. Marks, M., & Meiland, D. 2003. In search of global leaders. *Harvard Business Review,* 81(8): 38–45.

28. For insights on the role of information systems integration in fostering innovation refer to: Cash, J. I. Jr., Earl, M. J., & Morison, R. 2008. Teaming up to crack innovation and enterprise integration. *Harvard Business Review,* 66(11): 90–100.

29. For a cautionary note on the use of IT, refer to McAfee, A. 2003. When too much IT knowledge is a dangerous thing. *MIT Sloan Management Review,* 44(2): 83–90.

30. Walgreen Co. 1996. *Information technology and Walgreens: Opportunities for employment,* January; and Dess, G. G. & Picken, J. C. 1997. *Beyond productivity.* New York: AMACOM.

31. The important role in IT for a Japanese bank is addressed in: Upton, D. M. & Staats, B. R. 2008. Radically simple IT. *Harvard Business Review,* 66(3): 118–124.

32. For an interesting perspective on some of the potential downsides of close customer and supplier relationships, refer to Anderson, E. & Jap, S. D. 2005. The dark side of close relationships. *MIT Sloan Management Review,* 46(3): 75–82.

33. Day, G. S. 2003. Creating a superior customer-relating capability. *MIT Sloan Management Review,* 44(3): 77–82.

34. To gain insights on the role of electronic technologies in enhancing a firm's connections to outside suppliers and customers, refer to Lawrence, T. B., Morse, E. A., & Fowler, S. W. 2005. Managing your portfolio of connections. *MIT Sloan Management Review,* 46(2): 59–66.

35. Collis, D. J. & Montgomery, C. A. 1995. Competing on resources: Strategy in the 1990's. *Harvard Business Review,* 73(4): 119–128; and Barney, J. 1991. Firm resources and sustained competitive advantage. *Journal of Management,* 17(1): 99–120.

36. For recent critiques of the resource-based view of the firm, refer to: Sirmon, D. G., Hitt, M. A., & Ireland, R. D. 2007. Managing firm resources in dynamic environments to create value: Looking inside the black box. *Academy of Management Review,* 32(1): 273–292; and Newbert, S. L. Empirical research on the resource-based view of the firm: An assessment and suggestions for future research. *Strategic Management Journal,* 28(2): 121–146.

37. For insights into research findings on the linkage between resources and performance, refer to: Crook, T. R., Ketchen, D. J., Jr., Combs, J. G., & Todd, S. Y. 2008. Strategic resources and performance: A meta-analysis. *Strategic Management Journal,* 29(11): 1141–1154.

38. Henkoff, R. 1993. Companies that train the best. *Fortune,* March 22: 83; and Dess & Picken, *Beyond productivity,* p. 98.

39. Barney, J. B. 1986. Types of competition and the theory of strategy: Towards an integrative framework. *Academy of Management Review,* 11(4): 791–800.

40. Harley-Davidson. 1993. Annual report.

41. For a rigorous, academic treatment of the origin of capabilities, refer to Ethiraj, S. K., Kale, P., Krishnan, M. S., & Singh, J. V. 2005. Where do capabilities come from and how do they matter? A study of the software services industry. *Strategic Management Journal,* 26(1): 25–46.

42. For an academic discussion on methods associated with organizational capabilities, refer to Dutta, S., Narasimhan, O., & Rajiv, S. 2005. Conceptualizing and measuring capabilities: Methodology and empirical application. *Strategic Management Journal,* 26(3): 277–286.

43. Lorenzoni, G. & Lipparini, A. 1999. The leveraging of interfirm relationships as a distinctive organizational capability: A longitudinal study. *Strategic Management Journal,* 20: 317–338.

44. A discussion of organizational capabilities and entry timing is in: Lee, G. K. 2008. Relevance of organizational capabilities and dynamics: What to learn from entrants' product portfolios about the determinants of entry timing. *Strategic Management Journal,* 29 (12): 1257–1280.

45. A study investigating the sustainability of competitive advantage is: Newbert, S. L. 2008. Value, rareness, competitive advantages, and performance: A conceptual-level empirical investigation of the resource-based view of the firm. *Strategic Management Journal,* 29(7): 745–768.

46. Barney, J. 1991. Firm resources and sustained competitive advantage. *Journal of Management,* 17(1): 99–120.

47. Barney, 1986, op. cit. Our discussion of inimitability and substitution draws upon this source.

48. A study that investigates the performance implications of imitation is: Ethiraj, S. K. & Zhu, D. H. 2008. Performance effects of imitative entry. *Strategic Management Journal,* 29(8): 797–818.

49. Deephouse, D. L. 1999. To be different, or to be the same? It's a question (and theory) of strategic balance. *Strategic Management Journal,* 20: 147–166.

50. Yeoh, P. L. & Roth, K. 1999. An empirical analysis of sustained advantage in the U.S. pharmaceutical industry: Impact of firm resources and capabilities. *Strategic Management Journal,* 20: 637–653.

51. Robins, J. A. & Wiersema, M. F. 2000. Strategies for unstructured competitive

environments: Using scarce resources to create new markets. In Bresser, R. F., et al., (Eds.), *Winning strategies in a deconstructing world:* 201–220. New York: John Wiley.

52. For an insightful case on how Dell was able to build its seemingly sustainable competitive advantage in the marketplace, refer to "Matching Dell" by Jan W. Rivkin and Michael E. Porter, Harvard Business School Case 9-799-158 (June 6, 1999).

53. Byrnes, N. & Burrows, P. 2007. Where Dell went wrong. *BusinessWeek,* February 18: 62–63; and Smith, A. D. 2007. Dell's moves create buzz. *Dallas Morning News.* Februrary 21: D1.

54. For an insightful perspective on how HP has increased its market share and profitability in the personal computer market, refer to: Edwards, C. 2008. How HP got the wow! back. *BusinessWeek,* December 22: 60–61. HP surpassed Dell in fall 2006 to become the world's largest PC manufacturer, and it increased its market share from 14.5 percent to 18.8 percent between June 2005 and September 2008.

55. Amit, R. & Schoemaker, J. H. 1993. Strategic assets and organizational rent. *Strategic Management Journal,* 14(1): 33–46; Collis, D. J. & Montgomery, C. A. 1995. Competing on resources: Strategy in the 1990's. *Harvard Business Review,* 73(4): 118–128; Coff, R. W. 1999. When competitive advantage doesn't lead to performance: The resource-based view and stakeholder bargaining power. *Organization Science,* 10(2): 119–133; and Blyler, M. & Coff, R. W. 2003. Dynamic capabilities, social capital, and rent appropriation: Ties that split pies. *Strategic Management Journal,* 24: 677–686.

56. Munk, N. 1998. The new organization man. *Fortune,* March 16: 62–74.

57. Coff, op. cit.

58. Lavelle, L. 2003. Sprint's board needs a good sweeping, too. *Business-Week,* February 24: 40; Anonymous. 2003. Another nail in the coffin. *The Economist,* February 15: 69–70; and Byrnes, N., Dwyer, P., & McNamee, M. 2003. Hacking away at tax shelters, *BusinessWeek,* February 24: 41.

59. We have focused our discussion on how internal stakeholders (e.g., employees, managers, and top executives) may appropriate a firm's profits (or rents). For an interesting discussion of how a firm's innovations may be appropriated by external stakeholders (e.g., customers, suppliers) as well as competitors, refer to Grant, R. M. 2002. *Contemporary strategy analysis* (4th ed.): 335–340. Malden, MA: Blackwell.

60. Luehrman, T. A. 1997. What's it worth? A general manager's guide to valuation. *Harvard Business Review,* 45(3): 132–142.

61. See, for example, Kaplan, R. S. & Norton, D. P. 1992. The balanced scorecard: Measures that drive performance. *Harvard Business Review,* 69(1): 71–79.

62. Hitt, M. A., Ireland, R. D., & Stadter, G. 1982. Functional importance of company performance: Moderating effects of grand strategy and industry type. *Strategic Management Journal,* 3: 315–330.

63. Berner, R. 2000. Procter & Gamble: Just say no to drugs. *BusinessWeek,* October 9: 128.

64. Kaplan & Norton, op. cit.

65. Ibid.

66. For a discussion of the relative value of growth versus increasing margins, read Mass, N. J. 2005. The relative value of growth. *Harvard Business Review,* 83(4): 102–112.

67. Rucci, A. J., Kirn, S. P., & Quinn, R. T. 1998. The employee-customer-profit chain at Sears. *Harvard Business Review,* 76(1): 82–97.

68. Our discussion draws upon: Angel, R. & Rampersad, H. 2005. Do scorecards add up? camagazine.com. May: np.; and Niven, P. 2002. *Balanced scorecard step by step: Maximizing performance and maintaining results.* New York: John Wiley & Sons.

Appendix to Chapter 3

How the Internet and Digital Technologies Add Value

The Internet has changed the way business is conducted. By providing new ways to interact with customers and using digital technologies to streamline operations, the Internet is helping companies create new value propositions. Let's take a look at several ways these changes have added new value. Exhibit 3A.1 illustrates four related activities that are being revolutionized by the Internet—search, evaluation, problem solving, and transactions.[1]

> **>LO8**
>
> How firms are using Internet technologies to add value and achieve unique advantages. (Appendix)

Search Activities

Search refers to the process of gathering information and identifying purchase options. The Internet has enhanced both the speed of information gathering and the breadth of information that can be accessed. This enhanced search capability is one of the key reasons the Internet has lowered switching costs—by decreasing the cost of search. These efficiency gains have greatly benefited buyers.

[1] The ideas in this section draw on several sources, including Zeng, M. & Reinartz, W. 2003. Beyond Online Search: The Road to Profitability. *California Management Review,* Winter: 107–130; and Stabell, C. B. & Fjeldstad, O. D. 1998. Configuring Value for Competitive Advantage: On Chains, Shops, and Networks. *Strategic Management Journal,* 19: 413–437.

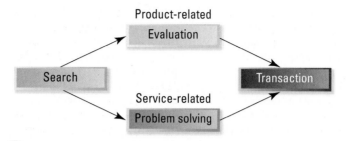

Exhibit 3A.1 Internet Activities that Add Value

Sources: Adapted from Zeng, M., & Reinartz, W. 2003. Beyond online search: The road to profitability. *California Management Review.* Winter: 107–130; and Stabell, C. B., & Fjeldstad, O. D. 1998. Configuring value for competitive advantage: On chains, shops, and networks. *Strategic Management Journal,* 19: 413–437.

search activities a way that digital technologies and the Internet have added value to firms' operations by enhancing the gathering of information and identifying purchase options.

Suppliers also have benefited. Small suppliers that had difficulty getting noticed can be found more easily, and large suppliers can publish thousands of pages of information for a fraction of the cost that hard-copy catalogs once required. Additionally, online search engines have accelerated the search process to incredible speeds. Consider the example of Google:

> Google, a search engine developed as a project by two graduate students, became the number one search service in just four years. Why? Because it is capable of incredible things. Using over 10,000 networked computers, it searches 3 billion Web pages in an average of 500 milliseconds. To do the same search manually, by thumbing through 3 billion pages at the rate of one minute per page, would take 5,707 years. This ability has made Google an essential tool for many businesses. As a result, Google has built a powerful advertising business. Mark Kini, who runs a small limousine service in Boston, spends 80 percent of his advertising budget on Google and other search engines. "It's how we survive," says Kini.[2]

Evaluation Activities

evaluation activities a way that digital technologies and the Internet have added value to firms' operations by facilitating the comparison of the costs and benefits of various options.

Evaluation refers to the process of considering alternatives and comparing the costs and benefits of various options. Online services that facilitate comparative shopping, provide product reviews, and catalog customer evaluations of performance have made the Internet a valuable resource.[3] For example, BizRate.com offers extensive product ratings that can help evaluate products. Sites such as CNET that provide comparative pricing have helped lower prices even for quality products that have traditionally maintained premium prices. Opinion-based sites such as ePinions.com and PlanetFeedback.com provide reports of consumer experiences with various vendors.

Many Internet businesses, according to digital business experts Ming Zeng and Werner Reinartz, could improve their performance by making a stronger effort to help buyers evaluate purchases.[4] Even so, only certain types of products can be evaluated online. Products such as CDs that appeal primarily to the sense of sound sell well on the Internet. But products that appeal to multiple senses are harder to evaluate online. This explains why products such as furniture and fashion have never been strong online sellers. It's one thing to look at a leather sofa, but to be able to sit on it, touch, and smell the leather online are impossible.

Problem-Solving Activities

problem-solving activities a way that digital technologies and the Internet have added value to firms' operations by identifying problems or needs and generating ideas and action plans to address those needs.

Problem solving refers to the process of identifying problems or needs and generating ideas and action plans to address those needs. Whereas evaluation is primarily product-related, problem solving is typically used in the context of services. Customers usually have unique problems that are handled one at a time. For example, online travel services such as Travelocity help customers select from many options

[2]Hardy, Q. 2003. All Eyes on Google. *Forbes,* May 26, www.forbes.com.
[3]For an interesting discussion of how successful Internet-based companies are using evaluation to add value see Weiss, L. M., Capozzi, M. M., & Prusak, L. 2004. Learning from the Internet Giants. *Sloan Management Review,* 45(4): 79–84.
[4]Zeng & Reinartz, *op.cit.*

to form a unique travel package. Furthermore, problem solving often involves providing answers immediately (compared to the creation of a new product). Firms in industries such as medicine, law, and engineering are using the Internet and digital technologies to deliver many new solutions.

Many products involve both a service and a product component; therefore, both problem solving and evaluation may be needed. Dell Computer's website is an example of a site that has combined the benefits of both. By creating a website that allows for customization of individual computers, they address the unique concerns of customers "one computer at a time." But the site also features a strong evaluative component because it allows users to compare the costs and features of various options. Shoppers can even compare their customized selection to refurbished Dell computers that are available at a substantially lower cost.

Transaction Activities

Transaction refers to the process of completing the sale, including negotiating and agreeing contractually, making payments, and taking delivery. Numerous types of Internet-enabled activities have contributed to lowering this aspect of overall transaction costs. Auctions of various sorts, from raw materials used in manufacturing to collectibles sold on eBay, facilitate the process of arriving at mutually agreed-on prices. Services such as PayPal provide a third-party intermediary that facilitates transactions between parties who never have (and probably never will) meet. Amazon.com's One-Click technology allows for very rapid purchases, and Amazon's overall superiority in managing order fulfillment has made its transactions process rapid and reliable. Amazon's success today can be attributed to a large extent to its having sold this transaction capability to other companies such as Target, Toys "R" Us and even Borders (another bookseller!).[5]

transaction activities a way that digital technologies and the Internet have added value to firms' operations by completing sales efficiently, including negotiating and agreeing contractually, making payments, and taking delivery.

Other Sources of Competitive Advantage

There are other factors that can be important sources of competitive advantage. One of the most important of these is content. The Internet makes it possible to capture vast amounts of content at a very low cost. Three types of content can improve the value proposition of a website—customer feedback, expertise, and entertainment programming.

- *Customer Feedback.* Buyers often trust what other buyers say more than a company's promises. One type of content that can enhance a website is customer testimonials. Remember the leather sofa online? The testimonials of other buyers can build confidence and add to the chances that the purchaser will buy online sight unseen. This is one way that content can be a source of competitive advantage. Being able to interact with like-minded customers by reading their experiences or hearing how they have responded to a new product offering builds a sense of belonging that is otherwise hard to create.

- *Expertise.* The Internet has emerged as a tremendously important learning tool. Fifty-one percent of users compare the Internet to a library.[6] The prime reason many users go to the Web is to gain expertise. Websites that provide new knowledge or unbiased information are highly valuable. Additionally the problem-solving function often involves educating consumers regarding options and implications of various choices. For example, LendingTree.com, the online loan company, provides a help center that includes extensive information and resources about obtaining loans, maintaining good credit, and so forth. Further, the expertise function is not limited to consumer sites. In the case of B2B businesses, websites that facilitate sharing expert knowledge help build a sense of community in industry or professional groups.

- *Entertainment Programming.* The Internet is being used by more and more people as an entertainment medium. With technologies such as streaming media, which allows the Internet to send televisionlike images and sound, computers can provide everything from breaking news to video games to online movies. A study by the Pew Internet and American Life Project indicates that among people using high-speed broadband service, TV viewing is down and online activity has increased. One reason is that the technology is interactive, which means that viewers don't just passively watch, but they use the Web to create art or play online games. Businesses have noticed this trend, of course, and are creating Web content that is not just informative but entertaining.

[5]Bayers, C. 2002. The Last Laugh. *Business 2.0,* September: 86–93.
[6]Greenspan, R. 2003. Internet Not for Everyone. *CyberAtlas,* April 16, www.cyberatlas.com.

These three types of content—customer feedback, expertise, and entertainment programming—are potential sources of competitive advantage. That is, they create advantages by making the value creation process even stronger. Or, if they are handled poorly, they diminish performance.

Business Models

business model
a method and a set of assumptions that explain how a business creates value and earns profits in a competitive environment.

The Internet provides a unique platform or staging area for business activity, which has become, in some ways, like a new marketplace. How do firms conduct business in this new arena? One way of addressing this question is by describing various Internet business models. A business model is a method and a set of assumptions that explain how a business creates value and earns profits in a competitive environment. Some of these models are quite simple and traditional even when applied in an Internet context. Others have features that are unique to the digitally networked, online environment. In this section, we discuss seven Internet business models that account for the vast majority of business conducted online.[7]

- *Commission-Based* **Models** are used by businesses that provide services for a fee. The business is usually a third-party intermediary, and the commission charged is often based on the size of the transaction. The most common type is a brokerage service, such as a stock-broker (e.g., Schwab.com), real estate broker (e.g., Remax.com), or transaction broker (e.g., PayPal.com). This category also includes auction companies such as eBay. In exchange for putting buyers and sellers together, eBay earns a commission.
- *Advertising-Based* **Models** are used by companies that provide content and/or services to visitors and sell advertising to businesses that want to reach those visitors. It is similar to the broadcast television model, in which viewers watch shows produced with advertising dollars. A key difference is that online visitors can interact with both the ads and the content. Large portals such as Yahoo.com are in this category as well as specialty portals such as iNest.com, which provides services for buyers of newly constructed homes. Epinions.com, a recommender system, is just one example of the many types of content that are often available.
- *Markup-Based* **Models** are used by businesses that add value in marketing and sales (rather than production) by acquiring products, marking up the price, and reselling them at a profit. Also known as the merchant model, it applies to both wholesalers and retailers. Amazon.com is the best-known example in this category. It also includes bricks-and-mortar companies such as Wal-Mart, which has a very successful online operation, and vendors whose products are purely digital such as Fonts.com, which sells downloadable fonts and photographs.
- *Production-Based* **Models** are used by companies that add value in the production process by converting raw materials into value-added products. Thus, it is also referred to as the manufacturing model. The Internet adds value to this model in two key ways. First, it lowers marketing costs by enabling direct contact with end users. Second, such direct contact facilitates customization and problem solving. Dell's online ordering system is supported by a state-of-the-art customized manufacturing process. Travelocity uses its rich database of travel options and customer profiles to identify, produce, and deliver unique solutions.
- *Referral-Based* **Models** are used by firms that steer customers to another company for a fee. One type is the affiliate model, in which a vendor pays an affiliate fee each time a visitor clicks through the affiliate's website and makes a purchase from the vendor. Many name-brand companies use affiliate programs. For example, WeddingChannel.com, which provides a bridal registry where wedding guests can buy gifts from companies such as Tiffany's, Macy's, or Crate & Barrel, receives a fee each time a sale is made through its website. Another referral-based example is Yesmail.com, which generates leads using e-mail marketing.
- *Subscription-Based* **Models** are used by businesses that charge a flat fee for providing either a service or proprietary content. Internet service providers are one example of this model. Companies such as America Online and Earthlink supply Internet connections for fees that are charged whether buyers use the service or not. Subscription-based models are also used by content creators such as the *Economist* or the *New York Times*. Although

[7]Afuah, A. & Tucci, C.L. 2003. *Internet Business Models and Strategies* (2nd ed). New York: McGraw-Hill; and, Timmers, P. 1999. *Electronic Commerce*. New York: Wiley.

these recognizable brands often provide free content, only a small portion is available free. The *Economist,* for example, advertises that 70 percent of its content is available only to subscribers.

- *Fee-for-Service–Based* **Models** are used by companies that provide ongoing services similar to a utility company. Unlike the commission-based model, the fee-for-service model involves a pay-as-you-go system. That is, activities are metered and companies pay only for the amount of service used. Application service providers fall in this category. For example, eProject.com provides virtual work space where people in different physical locations can collaborate online. Users essentially rent Internet space, and a host of tools that make it easy to interact, for a fee based on their usage.

Exhibit 3A.2 summarizes the key feature of each Internet business model, suggests what role content may play in the model, and addresses how the four value-adding activities—search, evaluation, problem solving, and transaction—can be sources of competitive advantage.

Exhibit 3A.2
Internet Business Models

Type	Features and Content	Sources of Competitive Advantage
Commission-Based	Charges commissions for brokerage or intermediary services. Adds value by providing expertise and/or access to a wide network of alternatives.	Search Evaluation Problem solving Transaction
Advertising-Based	Web content paid for by advertisers. Adds value by providing free or low-cost content—including customer feedback, expertise, and entertainment programming—to audiences that range from very broad (general content) to highly targeted (specialized content).	Search Evaluation
Markup-Based	Resells marked-up merchandise. Adds value through selection, through distribution efficiencies, and by leveraging brand image and reputation. May use entertainment programming to enhance sales.	Search Transaction
Production-Based	Sells manufactured goods and custom services. Adds value by increasing production efficiencies, capturing customer preferences, and improving customer service.	Search Problem solving
Referral-Based	Charges fees for referring customers. Adds value by enhancing a company's product or service offering, tracking referrals electronically, and generating demographic data. Expertise and customer feedback often included with referral information.	Search Problem solving Transaction
Subscription-Based	Charges fees for unlimited use of service or content. Adds value by leveraging strong brand name, providing high-quality information to specialized markets, or providing access to essential services. May consist entirely of entertainment programming.	Evaluation Problem solving
Fee-for-Service– Based	Charges fees for metered services. Adds value by providing service efficiencies, expertise, and practical outsourcing solutions.	Problem solving Transaction

Sources: Afuah, A. & Tucci, C. L. 2003. *Internet Business Models and Strategies* (2nd ed). New York: McGraw-Hill; Rappa, M. 2005. *Business Models on the Web,* digitalenterprise.org/models/models.html; and Timmers, P. 1999. *Electronic Commerce.* New York: Wiley.

Recognizing a Firm's Intellectual Assets:

Moving beyond a Firm's Tangible Resources

After reading this chapter, you should have a good understanding of:

LO1 Why the management of knowledge professionals and knowledge itself are so critical in today's organizations.

LO2 The importance of recognizing the interdependence of attracting, developing, and retaining human capital.

LO3 The key role of social capital in leveraging human capital within and across the firm.

LO4 The importance of social networks in knowledge management and in promoting career success.

LO5 The vital role of technology in leveraging knowledge and human capital.

LO6 Why "electronic" or "virtual" teams are critical in combining and leveraging knowledge in organizations and how they can be made more effective.

LO7 The challenge of protecting intellectual property and the importance of a firm's dynamic capabilities.

One of the most important trends that managers must consider is the significance of the knowledge worker in today's economy. Managers must both recognize the importance of top talent and provide mechanisms to leverage human capital to innovate and, in the end, develop products and services that create value.

The first section addresses the increasing role of knowledge as the primary means of wealth generation in today's economy. A company's value is not derived solely from its physical assets, such as plant, equipment, and machinery. Rather, it is based on knowledge, know-how, and intellectual assets—all embedded in people.

The second section discusses the key resource itself, human capital, which is the foundation of intellectual capital. We explore ways in which the organization can attract, develop, and retain top talent—three important, interdependent activities. With regard to attracting human capital, we address issues such as "hiring for attitude, training for skill." One of the issues regarding developing human capital is encouraging widespread involvement throughout the organization. Our discussion on retaining human capital addresses issues such as the importance of having employees identify with an organization's mission and values. We also address the value of a diverse workforce.

The attraction, development, and retention of human capital are necessary but not sufficient conditions for organizational success. In the third section we address social capital—networks of relationships among a firm's members. This is especially important where collaboration and sharing information are critical. We address why social capital can be particularly important in attracting human capital and making teams effective. We also address the vital role of social networks—both in improving knowledge management and in promoting career success.

The fourth section addresses the role of technology in leveraging human capital. Examples range from e-mail and the use of networks to facilitate collaboration among individuals to more complex forms of technologies, such as sophisticated knowledge management systems. We discuss how electronic teams can be effectively managed. We also address how technology can help to retain knowledge.

The last section discusses the differences between protection of physical property and intellectual property. We suggest that the development of dynamic capabilities may be one of the best ways that a firm can protect its intellectual property.

Consider two of the most iconoclastic artists of modern times: Vincent van Gogh and Pablo Picasso.[1] Paintings by both have fetched over $100 million. And both of them were responsible for some of the most iconic images in the art world: Van Gogh's *Self-Portrait* (the one sans the earlobe) and *Starry Night* and Picasso's *The Old Guitarist* and *Guernica*. However, there is an important difference between van Gogh and Picasso. Van Gogh died penniless. Picasso's estate was estimated at $750 million when he died in 1973. Although both were iconoclasts, it was Picasso who was the successful one—at least during his lifetime. What was the difference?

Van Gogh's primary connection to the art world was through his brother. Unfortunately, this connection did not feed directly into the money that could have turned him into a living success. In contrast, Picasso's myriad connections provided him with access to commercial riches. As noted by Gregory Berns in his new book *Iconoclast: A Neuroscientist Reveals How to Think Differently,* "Picasso's wide ranging social network, which included artists, writers, and politicians, meant that he was never more than a few people away from anyone of importance in the world."

In effect, van Gogh was a loner, and the charismatic Picasso was an active member of multiple social circles. In social networking terms, van Gogh was a solitary "node" who had few connections. Picasso, on the other hand, was a "hub" who embedded himself in a vast network that stretched across various social lines. Where Picasso smoothly navigated multiple social circles, van Gogh had to struggle just to maintain connections with even those closest to him. van Gogh inhabited an alien world; whereas, Picasso was a social magnet. And because he knew so many people, the world was at his fingertips. From his perspective, the world was smaller.

Without doubt, there were many reasons why van Gogh died penniless. His mental illness was certainly a factor (which likely contributed to his being a loner). But the broader point for corporations is the following: How do you connect talented loners to networks so that their creativity and ideas can be captured and leveraged? And how do you ensure that your talent is less like van Gogh and more like Picasso?

Managers are always looking for stellar professionals who can take their organizations to the next level. However, attracting talent is a necessary but *not* sufficient condition for success. In today's knowledge economy, it does not matter how big your stock of resources is—whether it be top talent, physical resources, or financial capital. Rather, the question becomes: How good is the organization at attracting top talent and leveraging that talent to produce a stream of products and services valued by the marketplace?

The Central Role of Knowledge in Today's Economy

>LO1

Why the management of knowledge professionals and knowledge itself are so critical in today's organizations.

Central to our discussion is an enormous change that has accelerated over the past few decades and its implications for the strategic management of organizations.[2] For most of the 20th century, managers focused on tangible resources such as land, equipment, and money as well as intangibles such as brands, image, and customer loyalty. Efforts were directed more toward the efficient allocation of labor and capital—the two traditional factors of production.

How times have changed. Today, more than 50 percent of the gross domestic product (GDP) in developed economies is knowledge-based; it is based on intellectual assets and intangible people skills.[3] In the U.S., intellectual and information processes create most of the value for firms in large service industries (e.g., software, medical care, communications, and education), which make up 76 percent of the U.S. GDP. In the manufacturing sector, intellectual activities like R&D, process design, product design, logistics, marketing, and technological innovation produce the preponderance of value added.[4] To drive home the point, Gary Hamel and C. K. Prahalad, two leading writers in strategic management state:

> The machine age was a physical world. It consisted of things. Companies made and distributed things (physical products). Management allocated things (capital budgets); management invested in things (plant and equipment).
>
> In the machine age, people were ancillary, and things were central. In the information age, things are ancillary, knowledge is central. A company's value derives not from things, but from knowledge, know-how, intellectual assets, competencies—all embedded in people.[5]

In the **knowledge economy,** wealth is increasingly created by effective management of knowledge workers instead of by the efficient control of physical and financial assets. The growing importance of knowledge, coupled with the move by labor markets to reward knowledge work, tells us that investing in a company is, in essence, buying a set of talents, capabilities, skills, and ideas—intellectual capital—not physical and financial resources.[6]

Let's provide a few examples. People don't buy Microsoft's stock because of its software factories; it doesn't own any. Rather, the value of Microsoft is bid up because it sets standards for personal-computing software, exploits the value of its name, and forges alliances with other companies. Similarly, Merck didn't become the "Most Admired" company, for seven consecutive years in *Fortune*'s annual survey, because it can manufacture pills, but because its scientists can discover medicines. P. Roy Vagelos, who was CEO of Merck, the $24 billion pharmaceutical giant, during its long run atop the "Most Admired" survey, said, "A low-value product can be made by anyone anywhere. When you have knowledge no one else has access to—that's dynamite. We guard our research even more carefully than our financial assets."[7]

To apply some numbers to our arguments, let's ask, What's a company worth?[8] Start with the "big three" financial statements: income statement, balance sheet, and statement of cash flow. If these statements tell a story that investors find useful, then a company's market value* should roughly (but not precisely, because the market looks forward and the books look backward) be the same as the value that accountants ascribe to it—the book value of the firm. However, this is not the case. A study compared the market value with the book value of 3,500 U.S. companies over a period of two decades. In 1978 the two were similar: Book value was 95 percent of market value. However, market values and book values have diverged significantly. By late 2008, the S&P industrials were—on average—trading at 2.2 times book value.[9] Robert A. Howell, an expert on the changing role of finance and accounting, muses that "The big three financial statements . . . are about as useful as an 80-year-old Los Angeles road map."

The gap between a firm's market value and book value is far greater for knowledge-intensive corporations than for firms with strategies based primarily on tangible assets.[10] Exhibit 4.1 shows the ratio of market-to-book value for some well-known companies. In firms where knowledge and the management of knowledge workers are relatively important contributors to developing products and services—and physical resources are less critical—the ratio of market-to-book value tends to be much higher. Many writers have defined **intellectual capital** as the difference between a firm's market value and book value—that is, a measure of the value of a firm's intangible assets.[11] This broad definition

knowledge economy an economy where wealth is created through the effective management of knowledge workers instead of by the efficient control of physical and financial assets.

intellectual capital the difference between the market value of the firm and the book value of the firm, including assets such as reputation, employee loyalty and commitment, customer relationships, company values, brand names, and the experience and skills of employees.

---

* The market value of a firm is equal to the value of a share of its common stock times the number of shares outstanding. The book value of a firm is primarily a measure of the value of its tangible assets. It can be calculated by the formula: total assets − total liabilities.

Exhibit 4.1
Ratio of Market Value to
Book Value for Selected
Companies

Company	Annual Sales ($ billions)	Market Value ($ billions)	Book Value ($ billions)	Ratio of Market to Book Value
Genentech	11.7	85.8	11.9	7.2
Google	16.6	101.9	22.7	4.5
Oracle	22.4	85.6	23.1	3.7
Nucor	16.6	11.8	5.1	2.3
Union Pacific (Railroad)	16.2	21.6	15.6	1.4
International Paper	21.9	4.6	8.6	.5

Note: The data on market valuations are as of January 26, 2009. All other financial data are based on the most recently available balance sheets and income statements.

human capital
the individual
capabilities,
knowledge, skills,
and experience
of a company's
employees and
managers.

includes assets such as reputation, employee loyalty and commitment, customer relationships, company values, brand names, and the experience and skills of employees.[12] Thus, simplifying, we have:

Intellectual captial = Market value of firm − Book value of the firm

How do companies create value in the knowledge-intensive economy? The general answer is to attract and leverage human capital effectively through mechanisms that create products and services of value over time.

First, **human capital** is the "*individual* capabilities, knowledge, skills, and experience of the company's employees and managers."[13] This knowledge is relevant to the task at hand, as well as the capacity to add to this reservoir of knowledge, skills, and experience through learning.[14]

social capital
the network of
friendships and
working relationships
between talented
people both inside
and outside the
organization.

Second, **social capital** is "the network of relationships that individuals have throughout the organization." Relationships are critical in sharing and leveraging knowledge and in acquiring resources.[15] Social capital can extend beyond the organizational boundaries to include relationships between the firm and its suppliers, customers, and alliance partners.[16]

Third is the concept of "knowledge," which comes in two different forms. First, there is **explicit knowledge** that is codified, documented, easily reproduced, and widely distributed, such as engineering drawings, software code, and patents.[17] The other type of knowledge is **tacit knowledge.** That is in the minds of employees and is based on their experiences and backgrounds.[18] Tacit knowledge is shared only with the consent and participation of the individual.

explicit knowledge
knowledge that
is codified,
documented,
easily reproduced,
and widely
distributed.

New knowledge is constantly created through the continual interaction of explicit and tacit knowledge. Consider, two software engineers working together on a computer code. The computer code is the explicit knowledge. By sharing ideas based on each individual's experience—that is, their tacit knowledge—they create new knowledge when they modify the code. Another important issue is the role of "socially complex processes," which include leadership, culture, and trust.[19] These processes play a central role in the creation of knowledge.[20] They represent the "glue" that holds the organization together and helps to create a working environment where individuals are more willing to share their ideas, work in teams, and, in the end, create products and services of value.[21]

tacit knowledge
knowledge that is
in the minds of
employees and
is based on their
experiences and
backgrounds.

Numerous books have been written on the subject of knowledge management and the central role that it has played in creating wealth in organizations and countries throughout the developed world.[22] Here, we focus on some of the key issues that organizations must address to compete through knowledge.

We will now turn our discussion to the central resource itself—human capital—and some guidelines on how it can be attracted/selected, developed, and retained. Tom Stewart, editor of the *Harvard Business Review,* noted that organizations must also undergo significant efforts to protect their human capital. A firm may "diversify the ownership of vital knowledge by emphasizing teamwork, guard against obsolescence by developing learning programs, and shackle key people with golden handcuffs."[23] In addition, people are less likely to leave an organization if there are effective structures to promote teamwork and information sharing, strong leadership that encourages innovation, and cultures that demand excellence and ethical behavior. Such issues are central to this chapter. Although we touch on these issues throughout this chapter, we provide more detail in later chapters. We discuss organizational controls (culture, rewards, and boundaries) in Chapter 9, organization structure and design in Chapter 10, and a variety of leadership and entrepreneurship topics in Chapters 11 and 12.

Human Capital: The Foundation of Intellectual Capital

Organizations must recruit talented people—employees at all levels with the proper sets of skills and capabilities coupled with the right values and attitudes. Such skills and attitudes must be continually developed, strengthened, and reinforced, and each employee must be motivated and her efforts focused on the organization's goals and objectives.[24]

The rise to prominence of knowledge workers as a vital source of competitive advantage is changing the balance of power in today's organization. Knowledge workers place professional development and personal enrichment (financial and otherwise) above company loyalty. Attracting, recruiting, and hiring the "best and the brightest," is a critical first step in the process of building intellectual capital. At a symposium for CEOs, Bill Gates said, "The thing that is holding Microsoft back . . . is simply how [hard] we find it to go out and recruit the kind of people we want to grow our research team."[25]

Hiring is only the first of three processes in which all successful organizations must engage to build and leverage their human capital. Firms must also *develop* employees to fulfill their full potential to maximize their joint contributions.[26] Finally, the first two processes are for naught if firms can't provide the working environment and intrinsic and extrinsic rewards to *retain* their best and brightest.[27]

These activities are highly interrelated. We would like to suggest the imagery of a three-legged stool (see Exhibit 4.2).[28] If one leg is weak or broken, the stool collapses.

> **>LO2**
> The importance of recognizing the interdependence of attracting, developing, and retaining human capital.

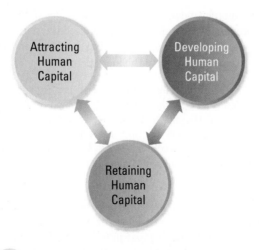

Exhibit 4.2   **Human Capital: Three Interdependent Activities**

strategy spotlight

Going "Green" Helps Attract Talent

When companies go "green," they often find that the benefits extend beyond the environment. Eco-friendly strategies can also help attract young talent and reduce costs. According to Lindsey Pollack, author of *Getting from College to Career:*

> Students are looking to work for companies that care about the environment. They are almost expecting greenness like they expect work-life balance, ethnic diversity, and globalization.

A recent poll on green employment by MonsterTRAK .com, a job website geared toward students and entry-level hires, found that 80 percent of young professionals are interested in securing a job that has a positive impact on the environment, and 92 percent would be more inclined to work for a company that is environmentally friendly. And, in another survey, 68 percent of Millennials said they would refuse to work for an employer that is not socially responsible.

In response, paper maker NewPage Corp. distributes a brochure that highlights the firm's commitment to environmental responsibility when it recruits on campuses. It showcases the company's new corporate headquarters, in Miamisburg, Ohio, that uses 28 percent to 39 percent less energy than a standard office building and is furnished with environmentally friendly materials. Says NewPage CEO Mark Sunwyn, "At the end of the day, we are competing with everyone else for the best talent, and this is a generation that is very concerned with the environment."

To meet the growing demand for students interested in working for green companies, MonsterTRAK, a unit of the giant employment firm Monster.com, launched GreenCareers. It was the first online recruitment service that focuses on green employment. EcoAmerica and the Environmental Defense Fund, two environmental nonprofits, are adding their expertise in partnership with MonsterTRAK. "EcoAmerica approached MonsterTRAK to create GreenCareers because there is an urgent need to reach and educate environmentally 'agnostic' audiences, in this case college students, about the ways they can address climate change and other serious environmental problems," claims Mark Charnock, vice president and general manager at MonsterTRAK.

Sources: Luhby, T. 2008. How to Lure Gen Y Workers? CNNMoney.com, August 17: np; Mattioli. 2007. How Going Green Draws Talent, Cut Costs. *Wall Street Journal,* November 13: B10; and, Odell, A. M. 2007. Working for the Earth: Green Companies and Green Jobs Attract Employees. www.socialfunds .com, October 9: np.

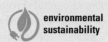

**environmental
sustainability**

To illustrate such interdependence, poor hiring impedes the effectiveness of development and retention processes. In a similar vein, ineffective retention efforts place additional burdens on hiring and development. Consider the following anecdote, provided by Jeffrey Pfeffer of the Stanford University Business School:

> Not long ago, I went to a large, fancy San Francisco law firm—where they treat their associates like dog doo and where the turnover is very high. I asked the managing partner about the turnover rate. He said, "A few years ago, it was 25 percent, and now we're up to 30 percent." I asked him how the firm had responded to that trend. He said, "We increased our recruiting." So I asked him, "What kind of doctor would you be if your patient was bleeding faster and faster, and your only response was to increase the speed of the transfusion?"[29]

Clearly, stepped-up recruiting is a poor substitute for weak retention. Although there are no simple, easy-to-apply answers, we can learn from what leading-edge firms are doing to attract, develop, and retain human capital in today's highly competitive marketplace.[30] Before moving on, Strategy Spotlight 4.1 addresses the importance of a firm's "green" or environmental sustainability strategy in attracting young talent.

Attracting Human Capital

> All we can do is bet on the people we pick. So my whole job is picking the right people.
>
> **Jack Welch,** former chairman, General Electric Company[31]

The first step in the process of building superior human capital is input control: attracting and selecting the right person. Human resource professionals often approach employee selection from a "lock and key" mentality—that is, fit a key (a job candidate) into a lock (the job). Such an approach involves a thorough analysis of the person and the job. Only then can the right decision be made as to how well the two will fit together. How can you fail, the theory goes, if you get a precise match of knowledge, ability, and skill profiles? Frequently, however, the precise matching approach places its emphasis on task-specific skills (e.g., motor skills, specific information processing capabilities, and communication skills) and puts less emphasis on the broad general knowledge and experience, social skills, values, beliefs, and attitudes of employees.

Many have questioned the precise matching approach. They argue that firms can identify top performers by focusing on key employee mind-sets, attitudes, social skills, and general orientations. If they get these elements right, the task-specific skills can be learned quickly. (This does not imply, however, that task-specific skills are unimportant; rather, it suggests that the requisite skill sets must be viewed as a necessary but not sufficient condition.) This leads us to a popular phrase today and serves as the title of the next section.

"Hire for Attitude, Train for Skill"   Organizations are increasingly emphasizing general knowledge and experience, social skills, values, beliefs, and attitudes of employees.[32] Consider Southwest Airlines' hiring practices, which focus on employee values and attitudes. Given its strong team orientation, Southwest uses an "indirect" approach. For example, the interviewing team asks a group of employees to prepare a five-minute presentation about themselves. During the presentations, interviewers observe which candidates enthusiastically support their peers and which candidates focus on polishing their own presentations while the others are presenting.[33] The former are, of course, favored.

Alan Cooper, president of Cooper Software, Inc., in Palo Alto, California, goes further. He cleverly *uses technology* to hone in on the problem-solving ability of his applicants and their attitudes before an interview even takes place. He has devised a "Bozo Filter," an online test that can be applied to any industry. Before you spend time on whether job candidates will work out satisfactorily, find out how their minds work. Cooper advised, "Hiring was a black hole. I don't talk to bozos anymore, because 90 percent of them turn away when they see our test. It's a self-administering bozo filter."[34] How does it work?

> The online test asks questions designed to see how prospective employees approach problem-solving tasks. For example, one key question asks software engineer applicants to design a table-creation software program for Microsoft Word. Candidates provide pencil sketches and a description of the new user interface. Another question used for design communicators asks them to develop a marketing strategy for a new touch-tone phone—directed at consumers in the year 1850. Candidates e-mail their answers back to the company, and the answers are circulated around the firm to solicit feedback. Only candidates with the highest marks get interviews.

Sound Recruiting Approaches and Networking   Companies that take hiring seriously must also take recruiting seriously. The number of jobs that successful knowledge-intensive companies must fill is astonishing. Ironically, many companies still have no shortage of applicants. For example, Google, ranked fourth on *Fortune*'s 2009 "100 Best Companies to Work For," still attracts 777,000 applicants a year—even though hiring has slowed.[35] The challenge becomes having the right job candidates, not the greatest number of them.

GE Medical Systems, which builds CT scanners and magnetic resonance imaging (MRI) systems, relies extensively on networking. They have found that current employees are the best source for new ones. Recently, Steven Patscot, head of staffing and leadership development, made a few simple changes to double the number of referrals. First, he simplified the process—no complex forms, no bureaucracy, and so on. Second, he increased incentives. Everyone referring a qualified candidate received a gift certificate from Sears. For referrals who were hired, the "bounty" increases to $2,000. Although this may sound like a lot of money, it is "peanuts" compared to the $15,000 to $20,000 fees that GE typically pays to headhunters for each person hired.[36] Also, when someone refers a former colleague or friend for a job, his or her credibility is on the line. Thus, employees will be careful in recommending people for employment unless they are reasonably confident that these people are good candidates. This provides a good "screen" for the firm in deciding whom to hire. Hiring the right people makes things a lot easier: fewer rules and regulations, less need for monitoring and hierarchy, and greater internalization of organizational norms and objectives.

Consider some of the approaches that companies are currently using to recruit and retain young talent. As baby boomers retire, people in this demographic group are becoming more and more important in today's workforce. We also provide some "tips" on how to get hired. We address these issues in Exhibit 4.3.

Developing Human Capital

It is not enough to hire top-level talent and expect that the skills and capabilities of those employees remain current throughout the duration of their employment. Rather, training and development must take place at all levels of the organization.[37] For example, Solectron assembles printed circuit boards and other components for its Silicon Valley clients.[38] Its employees receive an average of 95 hours of company-provided training each year. Chairman Winston Chen observed, "Technology changes so fast that we estimate 20 percent of an engineer's knowledge becomes obsolete each year. Training is an obligation we owe to our employees. If you want high growth and high quality, then training is a big part of the equation." Although the financial returns on training may be hard to calculate, most experts believe it is essential. One company that has calculated the benefit from training is Motorola. Every dollar spent on training returns $30 in productivity gains over the following three years.

In addition to training and developing human capital, firms must encourage widespread involvement, monitor and track employee development, and evaluate human capital.[39]

Encouraging Widespread Involvement   Developing human capital requires the active involvement of leaders at all levels. It won't be successful if it is viewed only as the responsibility of the human resources department. Each year at General Electric, 200 facilitators, 30 officers, 30 human resource executives, and many young managers actively participate in GE's orientation program at Crotonville, its training center outside New York City. Topics include global competition, winning on the global playing field, and personal examination of the new employee's core values vis-à-vis GE's values. As a senior manager once commented, "There is nothing like teaching Sunday school to force you to confront your own values."

Transferring Knowledge   Often in our lives, we need to either transfer our knowledge to someone else (a child, a junior colleague, a peer) or access accumulated bits of wisdom—someone else's tacit knowledge.[40] This is a vital aspect of developing human capital.[41] However, before we can even begin to plan such a transfer, we need to understand how our brains process incoming information. According to Dorothy A. Leonard of Harvard University:

> Our existing tacit knowledge determines how we assimilate new experiences. Without receptors—hooks on which to hang new information—we may not be able to perceive and process the information. It is like being sent boxes of documents but having no idea how they could or should be organized.

Here are some "best practices" that companies are using to help recruit and retain today's high-maintenance Millennials. This generation has also been termed "Generation Y" or "Echo Boom" and includes people born after 1982:

- **Don't fudge the sales pitch.** High-tech presentations and one-on-one attention may be attractive to undergrads, but the pitch had better match the experience. Today's ultraconnected students can get the lowdown on a company by spending five minutes on a social networking site.

- **Let them have a life.** Wary of their parents' 80-hour workweeks, Millennials strive for more balance, so liberal vacations are a must. They also want assurances they'll be able to use it. At KPMG, 80 percent of employees used 40 hours of paid time off in the six months through May 2006.

- **No time clocks, please.** Recent grads don't mind long hours if they can work them on their own time. Lockheed Martin and its comptroller of the currency allow employees to work nine-hour days and take every other Friday off.

- **Give them responsibility.** A chance to work on fulfilling projects and develop ones of their own is important to Millennials. Google urges entry-level employees to spend 20 percent of their time developing new ideas. PepsiCo allows promising young employees to manage small teams in six months.

- **Feedback and more feedback.** Career planning advice and frequent performance appraisals are keys to holding on to young hires. Lehman Brothers provides new hires with two mentors—a slightly older peer to help them get settled and a senior employee to give long-term guidance.

- **Giving back matters.** Today's altruistic young graduates expect to have opportunities for community service. Wells Fargo encourages its employees to teach financial literacy classes in the community. Accenture and Bain allow employees to consult for nonprofits.

Some advice on how to get hired (based on Fortune's "100 Best Companies to Work For"):

- **It helps to know someone.** Almost all of the "Best Companies" rely extensively on employee referrals. Principal Financial Group and many others get about 40 percent of new hires this way.

- **Play up volunteer work on your resume.** Companies are enthusiastic about community outreach, and they prefer to hire people who are too.

- **Unleash your inner storyteller.** By far the most popular interview style is what's known as behavioral, meaning that you will be asked to describe troublesome situations in past jobs and tell exactly how you handled them.

- **No lone rangers need apply.** By and large, team players are wanted. "I actually count the number of times a candidates says 'I' in an interview," says Adobe's recruiting director, Jeff Vijungco. "We'd rather hear 'we.'"

- **Be open to learning new things.** Showing passion is a must, and most of the "100 Best" pride themselves on creating "learning environments." Thus, talk about the skills you'd like to acquire or polish. Declaring that you're already the best at what you do is a turnoff.

Source: Fisher, A. 2008. How to Get Hired by a "Best" Company. *Fortune,* February 4: 96; and Gerdes, L. 2006. The Top 50 Employers for New College Grads. *BusinessWeek,* September 18: 64–81.

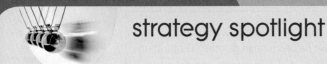
Effective Mentoring: Insights from Two Executives

Two successful executives share their insights by responding to the question: How important is finding—and being—a mentor?

Michelle Coleman Mayes, Senior Vice President and Chief Legal Officer, Allstate Corporation:

It's plural, it isn't dessert—you need more than one. I've found that the people who really get to know you well see things in you that you cannot see in yourself. And, if you think you're perfect, you probably just haven't met the right person to tell you the truth.

You need to think of an image where your hands are stretched both ways. I don't care how old you are,

you're always looking for someone when you need help, and there is always somebody that's been there before you. And you'd better pay it forward, meaning you reach back and you help somebody else.

Sheryl Sandberg, Vice President of Global Online Sales and Operations, Google Inc.

You need different kinds of mentors for different parts of your life—professional and personal. I think the best mentor-mentee relationships are based on really knowing the person in some mutual interest. So at work, the best way for me to develop people is to engage with them substantively on an issue. A better question than "Can you help me?" is "I have this problem and I'd love your views on this." Mentors aren't stamps; you can't collect them indiscriminately. You have to really develop those relationships.

Source: Hymowitz, C. 2007. View from the Top. *Wall Street Journal*, November 19: R6.

This cognitive limitation also applies to the organizational level. When GE Healthcare sets up or transfers operations, it appoints an experienced manager as the "pitcher" and a team in the receiving plant as the "catcher." These two teams work together, often over a period of years—first at the pitcher's location and then at the catcher's. To ensure a smooth transition, the pitching team needs to be sensitive to the catching team's level of experience and familiarity with GE Healthcare procedures.

Strategy Spotlight 4.2 discusses the perspective of two senior executives on how to make mentoring more effective.

Monitoring Progress and Tracking Development   Whether a firm uses on-site formal training, off-site training (e.g., universities), or on-the-job training, tracking individual progress—and sharing this knowledge with both the employee and key managers—becomes essential. Like many leading-edge firms, GlaxoSmithKline (GSK) places strong emphasis on broader experiences over longer time periods. Dan Phelan, senior vice president and director of human resources, explained, "We ideally follow a two-plus-two-plus-two formula in developing people for top management positions." This reflects the belief that GSK's best people should gain experience in two business units, two functional units (such as finance and marketing), and in two countries.

Evaluating Human Capital   In today's competitive environment, collaboration and interdependence are vital to organizational success. Individuals must share their knowledge and work constructively to achieve collective, not just individual, goals. However, traditional systems evaluate performance from a single perspective (i.e., "top down") and generally don't address the "softer" dimensions of communications and social skills, values, beliefs, and attitudes.[42]

To address the limitations of the traditional approach, many organizations use 360-degree evaluation and feedback systems.[43] Here, superiors, direct reports, colleagues,

Vision	• Has developed and communicated a clear, simple, customer-focused vision/direction for the organization.
	• Forward-thinking, stretches horizons, challenges imaginations.
	• Inspires and energizes others to commit to Vision. Captures minds. Leads by example.
	• As appropriate, updates Vision to reflect constant and accelerating change affecting the business.

Customer/Quality Focus

Integrity

Accountability/Commitment

Communication/Influence

Shared Ownership/Boundaryless

Team Builder/Empowerment

Knowledge/Expertise/Intellect

Initiative/Speed

Global Mind-Set

Source: Adapted from Slater, R. 1994. *Get Better or Get Beaten:* 152–155. Burr Ridge, IL: Irwin Professional Publishing.

Note: This evaluation system consists of 10 "characteristics"—Vision, Customer/Quality Focus, Integrity, and so on. Each of these characteristics has four "performance criteria." For illustrative purposes, the four performance criteria of "Vision" are included.

and even internal and external customers rate a person's performance.[44] Managers rate themselves to have a personal benchmark. The 360-degree feedback system complements teamwork, employee involvement, and organizational flattening. As organizations continue to push responsibility downward, traditional top-down appraisal systems become insufficient.[45] For example, a manager who previously managed the performance of 3 supervisors might now be responsible for 10 and is less likely to have the in-depth knowledge needed to appraise and develop them adequately. Exhibit 4.4 provides a portion of GE's 360-degree system.

Evaluation systems must also ensure that a manager's success does not come at the cost of compromising the organization's core values. Such behavior generally leads to only short-term wins for both the manager and the organization. The organization typically suffers long-term losses in terms of morale, turnover, productivity, and so on. Accordingly, Merck's former chairman, Ray Gilmartin, told his employees, "If someone is achieving results but not demonstrating the core values of the company, at the expense of our people, that manager does not have much of a career here."

Retaining Human Capital

It has been said that talented employees are like "frogs in a wheelbarrow."[46] They can jump out at any time! By analogy, the organization can either try to force employees to stay in the firm or try to keep them from jumping out by creating incentives.[47] In other words, today's leaders can either provide the work environment and incentives to keep productive employees and management from wanting to bail out, or they can use legal means such as employment contracts and noncompete clauses.[48] Firms must prevent the transfer of valuable and sensitive information outside the organization. Failure to do so would be the neglect of a leader's fiduciary responsibility to shareholders. However, greater efforts should be directed at the former (e.g., good work environment and incentives), but, as we all know, the latter (e.g., employment contracts and noncompete clauses) have their place.[49]

Identifying with an Organization's Mission and Values People who identify with and are more committed to the core mission and values of the organization are less likely to stray or bolt to the competition. For example, take the perspective of Steve Jobs, Apple's widely admired CEO:[50]

> When I hire somebody really senior, competence is the ante. They have to be really smart. But the real issue for me is: Are they going to fall in love with Apple? Because if they fall in love with Apple, everything else will take care of itself. They'll want to do what's best for Apple, not what's best for them, what's best for Steve, or anyone else.

"Tribal loyalty" is another key factor that links people to the organization.[51] A tribe is not the organization as a whole (unless it is very small). Rather, it is teams, communities of practice, and other groups within an organization or occupation.

Brian Hall, CEO of Values Technology in Santa Cruz, California, documented a shift in people's emotional expectations from work. From the 1950s on, a "task first" relationship— "tell me what the job is, and let's get on with it"—dominated employee attitudes. Emotions and personal life were checked at the door. In the past few years, a "relationship-first" set of values has challenged the task orientation. Hall believes that it will become dominant. Employees want to share attitudes and beliefs as well as workspace.

Challenging Work and a Stimulating Environment Arthur Schawlow, winner of the 1981 Nobel Prize in physics, was asked what made the difference between highly creative and less creative scientists. His reply: "The labor of love aspect is very important. The most successful scientists often are not the most talented.[52] But they are the ones impelled by curiosity. They've got to know what the answer is."[53] Such insights highlight the importance of intrinsic motivation: the motivation to work on something because it is exciting, satisfying, or personally challenging.[54]

One way firms keep highly mobile employees motivated and challenged is through opportunities that lower barriers to an employee's mobility within a company. For example, Shell Oil Company has created an "open sourcing" model for talent. Jobs are listed on Shell's intranet, and, with a two-month notice, employees can go to work on anything that interests them. Monsanto[55] has developed a similar approach. According to one executive:

> Because we don't have a lot of structure, people will flow toward where success and innovation are taking place. We have a free-market system where people can move, so you have an outflow of people in areas where not much progress is being made. Before, the HR function ran processes like management development and performance evaluation. Now it also facilitates this movement of people.

Exhibit 4.5 lists the best practices that leading-edge organizations are using to create a challenging and stimulating work environment to help attract and retain top young talent.

Financial and Nonfinancial Rewards and Incentives Financial rewards are a vital organizational control mechanism (as we will discuss in Chapter 9). Money—whether in the form of salary, bonus, stock options, and so forth—can mean many different things to people. It might mean security, recognition, or a sense of freedom and independence.

Paying people more is seldom the most important factor in attracting and retaining human capital.[56] Most surveys show that money is not the most important reason why people take or leave jobs, and that money, in some surveys, is not even in the top 10. Consistent with these findings, Tandem Computers (now part of Hewlett-Packard) typically doesn't tell people being recruited what their salaries would be. People who asked were told that their salaries were competitive. If they persisted along this line of questioning,

Exhibit 4.5
Creating a Challenging
and Stimulating
Workplace

Company (Industry)	Comments
Lockheed Martin (Defense)	Offers leadership programs in communications, engineering, finance, human resources, information systems, and operations.
Enterprise Rent-a-Car (Transportation)	Management training program amounts to an MBA crash course for executive wannabes. New hires get to run their own business.
Verizon Wireless (Telecommunications)	Verizon Wireless recently launched a retail training program where participants work in as many as three locations over two years.
National Instruments (Technology)	NI puts its money where its mouth is, spending over $30,000 a year to train each participant in its engineering leadership program.
L'Oreal (Consumer Goods)	Rising entry-level marketing stars are put through a fast-paced training program that lasts between 18 months and two years.
Vanguard (Financial Services)	Four extensive rotational training and development programs range from 12 to 24 months in length with three to six rotations.
Adobe Systems (Software)	A culture of openness pervades the firm: The CEO answers e-mails within 24 hours, and employee councils feed management with ideas.
Recreational Equipment (REI) (Outdoor Gear/Equipment)	Winners of challenge grants get up to $300 of gear to tackle an outdoor goal; also offers generous sabbaticals.

Source: O'Brien, J. M. 2008. The Best 100 Companies to Work For. *Fortune,* February 4: 61–94; and Gerdes, L. 2006. The Top 50 Employers for New College Grads. *BusinessWeek,* September 18: 64–81.

they would not be offered a position. Why? Tandem realized a rather simple idea: People who come for money will leave for money.

Another nonfinancial reward is accommodating working families with children. Balancing demands of family and work is a problem at some point for virtually all employees.

Strategy Spotlight 4.3 discusses some of the challenges (and solutions) with the use of flextime. With this popular employment practice, flextime allows employees greater flexibility in when and where they do their work.

Enhancing Human Capital: The Role of Diversity in the Workforce

A combination of demographic trends and accelerating globalization of business has made the management of cultural differences a critical issue.[57] Workforces, which reflect demographic changes in the overall population, will be increasingly heterogeneous along dimensions such as gender, race, ethnicity, and nationality. Demographic trends in the United States indicate a growth in Hispanic Americans from 6.9 million in 1960 to over 35 million in 2000, an expected increase to over 55 million by 2020. Similarly, the Asian-American population should grow to 20 million in 2020 from 12 million in 2000 and only 1.5 million in 1970. And the African-American population is becoming more ethnically heterogeneous. Census estimates project that by 2010 as many as 10 percent of Americans of African descent will be immigrants from Africa or the Caribbean.[58]

strategy spotlight

4.3

Solving the Challenges of Flexible Work Arrangements

A recent study by Hewitt Associates, a human resources consulting firm, found that 75 percent of companies offered some kind of flexible work arrangement. However, these policies have earned mixed results. Working remotely can leave employees feeling isolated and managers feeling they lack control. Further, flextimers often find themselves squeezed into policies that are anything but flexible. "The work–life movement has always had a heavy layer of one-size-fits-all-ism," says Stewart D. Friedman, head of the Work/Life Integration Project at the Wharton School at the University of Pennsylvania.

How are companies addressing these challenges? Let's look at two examples:

- Hewlett-Packard offers a personality test so workers can determine whether they are suited to, in effect, toiling in their pajamas. Among other things, the test assesses whether workers can handle limited supervision.

Source: Conlin, M. 2008. Out of Sight, Yes. Out of Mind, No. *Business Week,* February 18: 60; and Conlin, M. 2006. Smashing the Clock. *BusinessWeek,* December 11: 60–68.

- Studies at IBM found that if teams went more than three days without meeting, their happiness and productivity declined. Now managers are required to bring teams together at least once every three days—physically or virtually—for reasons that have nothing to do with completing an assignment.

Below are some suggested best practices or tips for making flextime programs work:

- **Measure.** Before unplugging workers, metrics are key to ensuring that productivity, engagement, and turnover improve.

- **Tailor.** Imposing new work rules rarely pays because managers and workers need to tailor schedules to their needs.

- **Trust.** Inevitably, some untethered workers will slack off. Managers need to trust, then rely on data to assess performance.

- **Educate.** Location-agnostic work is a hard concept to grasp. Thus, refresher courses are a must for managers and workers.

- **Gather.** When workers are nomads, regular gatherings, in person or by videoconference, help retain a team dynamic.

Such demographic changes have implications not only for the labor pool but also for customer bases, which are also becoming more diverse. This creates important organizational challenges and opportunities.

The effective management of diversity can enhance the social responsibility goals of an organization.[59] However, there are many other benefits as well. Six other areas where sound management of diverse workforces can improve an organization's effectiveness and competitive advantages are: (1) cost, (2) resource acquisition, (3) marketing, (4) creativity, (5) problem-solving, and (6) organizational flexibility.

- **Cost Argument.** As organizations become more diverse, firms effective in managing diversity will have a cost advantage over those that are not.
- **Resource Acquisition Argument.** Firms with excellent reputations as prospective employers for women and ethnic minorities will have an advantage in the competition for top talent. As labor pools shrink and change in composition, such advantages will become even more important.
- **Marketing Argument.** For multinational firms, the insight and cultural sensitivity that members with roots in other countries bring to marketing efforts will be very useful. A similar rationale applies to subpopulations within domestic operations.
- **Creativity Argument.** Less emphasis on conformity to norms of the past and a diversity of perspectives will improve the level of creativity.

- **Problem-Solving Argument.** Heterogeniety in decision-making and problem-solving groups typically produces better decisions because of a wider range of perspectives as well as more thorough analysis. Jim Schiro, CEO of PriceWaterhouseCoopers, explains, "When you make a genuine commitment to diversity, you bring a greater diversity of ideas, approaches, and experiences and abilities that can be applied to client problems. After all, six people with different perspectives have a better shot at solving complex problems than sixty people who all think alike."[60]
- **Organizational Flexibility Argument.** With effective programs to enhance workplace diversity, systems become less determinant, less standardized, and therefore more fluid. Such fluidity should lead to greater flexibility to react to environmental changes. Reactions should be faster and less costly.

In the past, a diversity officer ensured compliance with EEOC (Equal Employment Opportunity Commission) requirements or, at best, made minimal efforts to produce the appearance of diversity. Today organizations realize that the role of a Chief Diversity Officer (CDO) can add real value. Strategy Spotlight 4.4 discusses how the role of the CDO at MTV Networks (part of Viacom) has evolved and how its business has benefited from a diverse workforce.

● Workforces are becoming more heterogeneous along dimensions such as gender, race, ethnicity, and nationality.

The Vital Role of Social Capital

>LO3
The key role of social capital in leveraging human capital within and across the firm.

Successful firms are well aware that the attraction, development, and retention of talent *is a necessary but not sufficient condition* for creating competitive advantages.[61] In the knowledge economy, it is not the stock of human capital that is important, but the extent to which it is combined and leveraged. In a sense, developing and retaining human capital becomes less important as key players (talented professionals, in particular) take the role of "free agents" and bring with them the requisite skill in many cases. Rather, the development of social capital (that is, the friendships and working relationships among talented individuals) gains importance, because it helps tie knowledge workers to a given firm.[62] Knowledge workers often exhibit greater loyalties to their colleagues and their profession than their employing organization, which may be "an amorphous, distant, and sometimes threatening entity."[63] Thus, a firm must find ways to create "ties" among its knowledge workers.

Let's look at a hypothetical example. Two pharmaceutical firms are fortunate enough to hire Nobel Prize–winning scientists.[64] In one case, the scientist is offered a very attractive salary, outstanding facilities and equipment, and told to "go to it!" In the second case, the scientist is offered approximately the same salary, facilities, and equipment plus one additional ingredient: working in a laboratory with 10 highly skilled and enthusiastic scientists. Part of the job is to collaborate with these peers and jointly develop promising drug compounds. There is little doubt as to which scenario will lead to a higher probability of retaining the scientist. The interaction, sharing, and collaboration will create a situation in which the scientist will develop firm-specific ties and be less likely to "bolt" for a higher salary offer. Such ties are critical because knowledge-based resources tend to be more tacit in nature, as we mentioned early in this chapter. Therefore, they are much more difficult to

strategy spotlight

MTV: Benefiting from a Diverse Workforce

Managers know that heterogeneous workforces are rich seedbeds for ideas. However, companies seldom tap employees for insights and experiences specific to their cultures. Further, barriers of language, geography, and association often prevent diverse employees from collaborating on innovation efforts.

Chief Diversity Officers (CDOs) are probably more familiar with the cultural breadth and variety of their companies' talent than anyone. Consequently, they are in an excellent position to bring together different groups to produce innovation.

On October 28, 2006, MTV Networks, a unit of Viacom International Inc. announced that Billy Dexter was appointed the firm's first Executive Vice President and Chief Diversity Officer. He will lead MTV's global initiatives to foster the highest levels of diversity throughout every aspect of the business.

Source: Johansson, F . 2005. Masters of the Multicultural. *Harvard Business Review,* 83(10): 18–19; and Anonymous. 2006. MTV Networks Names Billy Dexter as Chief Diversity Officer. *PRNewswire.* October 28. np.

Judy McGrath, Chairman and CEO of MTV Networks states:

> We are completely committed to diversity and inclusion, because it's the most creative and vibrant thing we can do for our future. The audience for our content is increasingly global, diverse in thought, demographic, and lifestyle. Over the years, no other initiative has so enriched MTV Networks, or made us more relevant and successful.

How has MTV Networks benefited from their diversity?

One cross-cultural group discovered marketing opportunities in the similarities between North American country music and Latin American music, which use many of the same instruments, feature singers with similar vocal styles, and—in the U.S. Sunbelt—appeal to much the same audience. Other groups have influenced the multicultural content of Nickelodeon's children's programming. Says Tom Freston, MTV's former CEO, "Those teams are diverse by design to generate innovation. The probability that you will get a good, original, innovative idea with that type of chemistry is simply much higher."

protect against loss (i.e., the individual quitting the organization) than other types of capital, such as equipment, machinery, and land.

Another way to view this situation is in terms of the resource-based view of the firm that we discussed in Chapter 3. That is, competitive advantages tend to be harder for competitors to copy if they are based on "unique bundles" of resources.[65] So, if employees are working effectively in teams and sharing their knowledge and learning from each other, not only will they be more likely to add value to the firm, but they also will be less likely to leave the organization, because of the loyalties and social ties that they develop over time.

How Social Capital Helps Attract and Retain Talent

The importance of social ties among talented professionals creates a significant challenge (and opportunity) for organizations. In *The Wall Street Journal,* Bernard Wysocki described the increase in a type of "Pied Piper Effect," in which teams or networks of people are leaving one company for another.[66] The trend is to recruit job candidates at the crux of social relationships in organizations, particularly if they are seen as having the potential to bring with them valuable colleagues.[67] This is a process that is referred to as "hiring via personal networks." Let's look at one instance of this practice.

Gerald Eickhoff, founder of an electronic commerce company called Third Millennium Communications, tried for 15 years to hire Michael Reene. Why? Mr. Eickhoff says that he has "these Pied Piper skills." Mr. Reene was a star at Andersen Consulting in the 1980s

Alumni Programs: A Great Way to Stay in Touch

Michael Jacobson had worked in securities practices at Cooley Godward, a Palo Alto, California law firm, for a dozen years. Nobody was happy when he gave notice in 1998. Everyone felt that it would be difficult to get along without him.

However, a few months later, Cooley Godward's managers couldn't have been happier. Why? Jacobson's new job was as general counsel at a little-known online auction site called eBay! When the site needed outside counsel, Jacobsen tapped his former employer. A few months later, Cooley Godward was lead counsel for eBay's record-breaking $1.3 billion initial public offering. "It's a great relationship," says Mark Pitchford, partner and chief operating officer of the firm.

With such a "lucky break," Cooley Godward no longer leaves such matters to chance. In January 2004, it launched an alumni program to help the firm stay in touch

with its former attorneys. Such programs are not particularly new to corporate America. Firms such as McKinsey & Company, Ernst & Young, and Procter & Gamble have had them in place for years. However, as partners at Cooley Godward have found, smaller firms can also benefit from alumni initiatives. "Former employees are a resource," says John Izzo, president of Izzo Consulting, a firm based in Vancouver, Washington. The firm advises small businesses on employee training and retention issues.

Despite the potential benefits of maintaining active contact with former employees, many employers treat them as just another name in the Rolodex—or even worse, as a competitive threat. Izzo warns that this can be a big mistake. Often, he claims, former staffers can act as goodwill ambassadors for their former employers, helping to refer new talent and clients. They may even return at a later point and will require little training. And with the job market now showing signs of improvement and many employees more likely to move on, alumni programs could become very important, especially at firms that have a hard time recruiting and retaining qualified professionals.

Source: Rich, L. 2005. Don't Be a Stranger. *Inc.*, January: 32–33.

and at IBM in the 1990s. He built his businesses and kept turning down overtures from Mr. Eickhoff.

However, in early 2000, he joined Third Millennium as chief executive officer, with a salary of just $120,000 but with a 20 percent stake in the firm. Since then, he has brought in a raft of former IBM colleagues and Andersen subordinates. One protégé from his time at Andersen, Mary Goode, was brought on board as executive vice president. She promptly tapped her own network and brought along former colleagues.

Wysocki considers the Pied Piper effect one of the underappreciated factors in the war for talent today. This is because one of the myths of the New Economy is rampant individualism, wherein individuals find jobs on the Internet career sites and go to work for complete strangers. Perhaps, instead of Me Inc., the truth is closer to We Inc.[68]

Another example of social relationships causing human capital mobility is the emigration of talent from an organization to form start-up ventures. Microsoft is perhaps the best-known example of this phenomenon.[69] Professionals frequently leave Microsoft en masse to form venture capital and technology start-ups, called "Baby Bills," built around teams of software developers. For example, Ignition Corporation, of Bellevue, Washington, was formed by Brad Silverberg, a former Microsoft senior vice president. Eight former Microsoft executives, among others, founded the company.

Social relationships can provide an important mechanism for obtaining both resources and information from individuals and organizations outside the boundary of a firm.[70] Strategy Spotlight 4.5 touts the benefits of firms' alumni programs. It describes how eBay's general counsel became an excellent source of business for his prior employer.

Social Networks: Implications for Knowledge Management and Career Success

social network analysis analysis of the pattern of social interactions among individuals.

Managers face many challenges driven by such factors as rapid changes in globalization and technology. Leading a successful company is more than a one-person job. As Tom Malone recently put it in *The Future of Work,* "As managers, we need to shift our thinking from command and control to coordinate and cultivate—the best way to gain power is sometimes to give it away."[71] The move away from top-down bureaucratic control to more open, decentralized network models makes it more difficult for managers to understand how work is actually getting done, who is interacting with whom both within and outside the organization, and the consequences of these interactions for the long-term health of the organization. In short, coordination, cultivation, and collaboration are increasingly becoming the mode of work at every level.[72]

But how can this be done? **Social network analysis** depicts the pattern of interactions among individuals and helps to diagnose effective and ineffective patterns.[73] It helps identify groups or clusters of individuals that comprise the network, individuals who link the clusters, and other network members. It helps diagnose communication patterns and, consequently, communication effectiveness.[74] Such analysis of communication patterns is helpful because the configuration of group members' social ties within and outside the group affects the extent to which members connect to individuals who:

- convey needed resources,
- have the opportunity to exchange information and support,
- have the motivation to treat each other in positive ways, and,
- have the time to develop trusting relationships that might improve the groups' effectiveness.

However, such relationships don't "just happen."[75] Developing social capital requires interdependence among group members. Social capital erodes when people in the network become independent. And increased interactions between members aid in the development and maintenance of mutual obligations in a social network.[76]

Let's take a brief look at a simplified network analysis to get a grasp of the key ideas. In Exhibit 4.6, the links are used to depict informal relationships among individuals involving communication flows, personal support, and advice networks. There may be

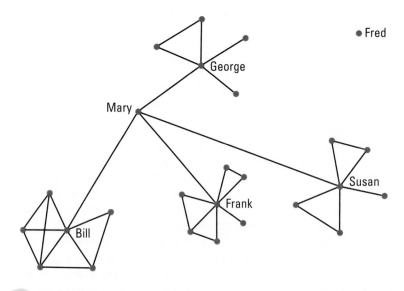

Exhibit 4.6 A Simplified Social Network

some individuals with literally no linkages, such as Fred. These individuals are typically labeled "isolates." However, most people do have some linkages with others.

To simplify, there are two primary types of mechanisms through which social capital will flow: *closure relationships* (depicted by Bill, Frank, George, and Susan) and *bridging relationships* (depicted by Mary). As we can see, in the former relationships one member is central to the communication flows in a group. In contrast, in the latter relationship, one person "bridges" or brings together groups that would have been otherwise unconnected.

Both closure and bridging relationships have important implications for the effective flow of information in organizations and for the management of knowledge. We will now briefly discuss each of these types of relationships. We will also address some of the implications that understanding social networks has for one's career success.

Closure   With **closure,** many members have relationships (or ties) with other members. As indicated in Exhibit 4.6, Bill's group would have a higher level of closure than Frank, Susan, or George's groups because more group members are connected to each other. Through closure, group members develop strong relationships with each other, high levels of trust, and greater solidarity. High levels of trust help to ensure that informal norms in the group are easily enforced and there is less "free riding." Social pressure will prevent people from withholding effort or shirking their responsibilities. In addition, people in the network are more willing to extend favors and "go the extra mile" on a colleague's behalf because they are confident that their efforts will be reciprocated by another member in their group. Another benefit of a network with closure is the high level of emotional support. This becomes particularly valuable when setbacks occur that may destroy morale or an unexpected tragedy happens that might cause the group to lose its focus. Social support helps the group to rebound from misfortune and get back on track.

But high levels of closure often come with a price. Groups that become too closed can become insular. They cut themselves off from the rest of the organization and fail to share what they are learning from people outside their group. Research shows that while managers need to encourage closure up to a point, if there is too much closure, they need to encourage people to open up their groups and infuse new ideas through bridging relationships.[77]

closure the degree to which all members of a social network have relationships (or ties) with other group members.

Bridging Relationships   The closure perspective rests on an assumption that there is a high level of similarity among group members. However, members can be quite heterogeneous with regard to their positions in either the formal or informal structures of the group or the organization. Such heterogeneity exists because of, for example, vertical boundaries (different levels in the hierarchy) and horizontal boundaries (different functional areas).

Bridging relationships, in contrast to closure, stresses the importance of ties connecting people. Employees who bridge disconnected people tend to receive timely, diverse information because of their access to a wide range of heterogeneous information flows. Such bridging relationships span a number of different types of boundaries.

The University of Chicago's Ron Burt originally coined the term **"structural holes"** to refer to the social gap between two groups. Structural holes are common in organizations. When they occur in business, managers typically refer to them as "silos" or "stovepipes." Sales and engineering are a classic example of two groups whose members traditionally interact with their peers rather than across groups.

A study that Burt conducted at Raytheon, a $21 billion U.S. electronics company and military contractor, provides further insight into the benefits of bridging.[78]

bridging relationships relationships in a social network that connect otherwise disconnected people.

structural holes social gaps between groups in a social network where there are few relationships bridging the groups.

> Burt studied several hundred managers within Raytheon's supply chain group and asked each manager to write down ideas to improve the company's supply chain management. Then he asked two Raytheon executives to rate the ideas. The conclusion: *The best suggestions consistently came from managers who discussed ideas outside their regular work group.*

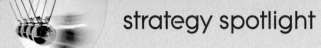

strategy spotlight

The Value (and Limitations) of Informal Friendships in Organizations

Rope courses and Outward Bound-type activities help white-collar workers develop corporate collegiality through socializing, sweating and sharing stressful situations. People go in as co-workers and come out as friends. However, wholesale congeniality can actually make teams *less* effective.

Recently, Joe Labianca (now at the University of Kentucky) and two colleagues studied 60 teams in 11 companies representing a wide variety of industries. In the most effective teams, about half of the relationships among members were close enough to be considered friendships. However, in teams where the number of friendships approached 100 percent, performance dropped dramatically. Why? Such groups suffered because they were insular, impermeable to outside influences, and unhealthily self-reliant. Members may have developed a high level of trust and commitment with each other but they were too dependent on their own members for new insights and initiatives. At times, those problems can be avoided by brainstorming or by assigning someone in the group to be a devil's advocate. But where friendships are especially close, even those techniques are unlikely to produce dramatically differing perspectives.

Sources: Labianca, J . 2004. The Ties That Bind. *Harvard Business Review,* 82(10): 19; Oh, H. Chung, M., & Labianca, G . 2004. Group Social Capital and Group Effectiveness: The Role of Informal Socializing Ties. *Academy of Management Journal,* 47(6): 860–875; and Labianca, J . 2007. Personal communication. February 28.

The friendships that benefit teams most are formed *outside the group.* Business-centered relationships with people in other parts of the company are important for transmitting simple work flow information. But even more important are relationships that extend into the social sphere—to lunches and dinners and after-work drinks. Such interactions are especially valuable sources of social capital. Team members who socialize in this way, particularly with top managers and with leaders of other teams play a key role in bridging groups and individuals who otherwise would be unconnected to their own group. This enables them to bring back to their groups strategic information, task-related advice, and political and social support.

Higher-level managers can't require employees to befriend people outside their own domains. However, they can encourage it. Team leaders should be told that developing a broad social network is part of their job. Managers should set aside funds for cross-functional social activities and create opportunities for employees to bond around common hobbies or pursuits. When composing teams, leaders should consider whom—as well as what—potential members know. And mentoring programs should aim to place company fledglings beneath the wings of veterans from other departments rather than with people they work with every day.

To sum up, there is nothing wrong with Outward Bound activities. However, instead of braving the wilderness, teams should venture into the far corners of their own organization!

Burt found that Raytheon managers were good at thinking of ideas but bad at developing them. Too often, Burt said, the managers discussed their ideas with colleagues already in their informal discussion network. Instead, he said, they should have had discussions outside their typical contacts, particularly with an informal boss, or someone with enough power to be an ally but not an actual supervisor.

Strategy Spotlight 4.6 addresses the value of informal friendships as an effective source of social capital. Interestingly, it also discusses the downside of insular, self-reliant groups.

Before we address the implications of social network theory for managers' career success, one might ask: Which is the more valuable mechanism to develop and nurture social capital—closure or bridging relationships? As with many aspects of strategic management, the answer becomes: "It all depends." So let's consider a few contingent issues.[79]

First, consider firms in competitive environments characterized by rapidly changing technologies and markets. Such firms should bridge relationships across networks because they need a wide variety of timely sources of information. Also, innovation is facilitated if there are multiple, interdisciplinary perspectives. On the other hand, firms competing in a stable environment would typically face a rather small amount of unpredictability.

Thus, the cohesive ties associated with network closure would help to ensure the timely and effective implementation of strategies.

A second contingent factor would be the type of business strategies that a firm may choose to follow (a topic that we address next in Chapter 5). Managers with social networks characterized by closure would be in a preferred position if their firm is following an overall low cost strategy.[80] Here, there is a need for control and coordination to implement strategies that are rather constrained by pressures to reduce costs. Alternatively, the uncertainties generally associated with differentiation strategies (i.e., creating products that are perceived by customers as unique and highly valued) would require a broad range of information sources and inputs. Social networks characterized by bridging relationships across groups would access the diverse informational sources needed to deal with more complex, multifaceted strategies.

A caveat: In both contingencies that we have discussed—competitive environment and business strategy—closure and bridging relationships across groups are necessary. Our purpose is to address where one type should be more dominant.

Implications for Career Success Effective social networks provide many advantages.[81] They can also play a key role in an individual's career advancement and success. From an individual's perspective, social networks deliver three unique advantages: private information, access to diverse skill sets, and power.[82] Managers see these advantages at work every day but might not consider how their networks regulate them.

Private Information We make judgments, using both public and private information. Today, public information is available from many sources, including the Internet. However, since it is so accessible, public information offers less competitive advantage than it used to.

In contrast, private information from personal contacts can offer something not found in publicly available sources, such as the release date of a new product or knowledge about what a particular interviewer looks for in candidates. Private information can give managers an edge, though it is more subjective than public information since it cannot be easily verified by independent sources, such as Dunn & Bradstreet. Consequently the value of your private information to others—and the value of others' private information to you—depends on how much trust exists in the network of relationships.

Access to Diverse Skill Sets Linus Pauling, one of only two people to win a Nobel Prize in two different areas and considered one of the towering geniuses of the 20th century, attributed his creative success not to his immense brainpower or luck but to his diverse contacts. He said, "The best way to have a good idea is to have a lot of ideas."

While expertise has become more specialized during the past 15 years, organizational, product, and marketing issues have become more interdisciplinary. This means that success is tied to the ability to transcend natural skill limitations through others. Highly diverse network relationships, therefore, can help you develop more complete, creative, and unbiased perspectives on issues. Trading information or skills with people whose experiences differ from your own, provides you with unique, exceptionally valuable resources. It is common for people in relationships to share their problems. If you know enough people, you will begin to see how the problems that another person is struggling with can be solved by the solutions being developed by others. If you can bring together problems and solutions, it will greatly benefit your career.

Power Traditionally, a manager's power was embedded in a firm's hierarchy. But, when corporate organizations became flatter, more like pancakes than pyramids, that power was repositioned in the network's brokers (people who bridged multiple networks), who could adapt to changes in the organization, develop clients, and synthesize opposing points of view. Such brokers weren't necessarily at the top of the hierarchy or experts in their fields, but they linked specialists in the firm with trustworthy and informative relationships.[83]

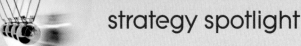

Developing Social Capital: Do Women and Men Differ?

Several years ago, Boris Groysberg conducted a study in which he warned managers about the risks associated with hiring star performers away from companies. His research investigated more than 1,000 star stock analysts, and he found that when one of them switches companies, not only does the star's performance plunge, but also the market value of the star's new company declines. In addition, the players don't tend to stay with their new firms very long—despite the generous pay packages that lured them in the first place. So everyone loses out.

However, when Groysberg further analyzed the data, he gained some new insights. One group of analysts maintained their stardom after changing employers: women. Unlike their male counterparts, female stars who switched firms performed just as well, in aggregate, as those who stayed put.

Why the gender discrepancy? There were two explanations. *First, the best female analysts appear to have built their franchises on portable, external relationships with clients and companies they covered—rather than on rela-tionships within their firms.* In contrast, male analysts built up greater firm- and team-specific human capital. That is, they invested more in internal networks and unique capabilities and resources of the firms where they worked.

Second, women took greater care when assessing a prospective employer. They evaluated their options more carefully and analyzed a wider range of factors than men did before deciding to uproot themselves from a firm where they had been successful. Female star analysts, it seems, take their work environment more seriously yet rely on it less than male stars do. And they tend to look for a firm that will allow them to keep building their successful franchise their own way.

There is a clear explanation as to why the female analysts spent more time developing their external networks. Most salespeople, traders, and investment bankers are men. And men tend to spend more time with other men. Not surprisingly, the star women in the study were generally thwarted in their efforts to integrate themselves into the existing power structure. Thus, they went to greater lengths to cultivate relationships with clients and contacts at the companies they covered. Their decision to maintain such an external focus rested on four main factors: uneasy in-house relationships, poor mentorships, neglect by colleagues, and a vulnerable position in the labor market.

Source: Groysberg, B. 2008. How Star Women Build Portable Skills. *Harvard Business Review*, 86 (2): 74–81.

Most personal networks are highly clustered; that is, an individual's friends are likely to be friends with one another as well. Most corporate networks are made up of several clusters that have few links between them. Brokers are especially powerful because they connect separate clusters, thus stimulating collaboration among otherwise independent specialists.

Before moving on, Strategy Spotlight 4.7 discusses an interesting research study. It points out how women may differ from men in how they develop their social networks.

The Potential Downside of Social Capital

We'd like to close our discussion of social capital by addressing some of its limitations. First, some firms have been adversely affected by very high levels of social capital because it may breed **"groupthink"**—a tendency not to question shared beliefs.[84] Such thinking may occur in networks with high levels of closure where there is little input from people outside of the network. In effect, too many warm and fuzzy feelings among group members prevent people from rigorously challenging each other. People are discouraged from engaging in the "creative abrasion" that Dorothy Leonard of Harvard University describes as a key source of innovation.[85] Two firms that were well known for their collegiality, strong sense of employee membership, and humane treatment—Digital Equipment (now part of Hewlett-Packard) and Polaroid—suffered greatly from market misjudgments and strategic errors. The aforementioned aspects of their culture contributed to their problems.

groupthink
a tendency in an organization for individuals not to question shared beliefs.

Second, if there are deep-rooted mindsets, there would be a tendency to develop dysfunctional human resource practices. That is, the organization (or group) would continue to hire, reward, and promote like-minded people who tend to further intensify organizational inertia and erode innovation. Such homogeneity would increase over time and decrease the effectiveness of decision-making processes.

Third, the socialization processes (orientation, training, etc.) can be expensive in terms of both financial resources and managerial commitment. Such investments can represent a significant opportunity cost that should be evaluated in terms of the intended benefits. If such expenses become excessive, profitability would be adversely affected.

Finally, individuals may use the contacts they develop to pursue their own interests and agendas that may be inconsistent with the organization's goals and objectives. Thus, they may distort or selectively use information to favor their preferred courses of action or withhold information in their own self-interest to enhance their power to the detriment of the common good. Drawing on our discussion of social networks, this is particularly true in an organization that has too many bridging relationships but not enough closure relationships. In high closure groups, it is easier to watch each other to ensure that illegal or unethical acts don't occur. By contrast, bridging relationships make it easier for a person to play one group or individual off on another, with no one being the wiser.[86] We will discuss some behavioral control mechanisms in Chapter 9 (rewards, control, boundaries) that reduce such dysfunctional behaviors and actions.[87]

Using Technology to Leverage Human Capital and Knowledge

Sharing knowledge and information throughout the organization can be a means of conserving resources, developing products and services, and creating new opportunities. In this section we will discuss how technology can be used to leverage human capital and knowledge within organizations as well as with customers and suppliers beyond their boundaries.

>LO5
The vital role of technology in leveraging knowledge and human capital.

Using Networks to Share Information

As we all know, e-mail is an effective means of communicating a wide variety of information. It is quick, easy, and almost costless. Of course, it can become a problem when employees use it extensively for personal reasons. And we all know how fast jokes or rumors can spread within and across organizations!

Below is an example of how a CEO curbed what he felt was excessive e-mail use in his firm.[88]

Scott Dockter, CEO of PBD Worldwide Fulfillment Services in Alpharetta, Georgia, launched "no e-mail Friday." Why? He suspected that overdependence on e-mail at PBD, which offers services such as call center management and distribution, was hurting productivity and, perhaps, sales. Accordingly, he instructed his 275 employees to pick up the phone or meet in person each Friday, and reduce e-mail use the rest of the time.

That was tough to digest, especially for the younger staffers. "We discovered a lot of introverts . . . who had drifted into a pattern of communicating by e-mail," says Dockter. "However, in less than four months, the simple directive resulted in quicker problem-solving, better teamwork, and, best of all, happier customers." "Our relationship with PBD is much stronger," says Cynthia Fitzpatrick of Crown Financial Ministries. "You can't get to know someone through e-mail."

E-mail can also cause embarrassment—if one is not careful. Consider the plights of Countrywide Financial Corp's embattled (and recently deposed) CEO and a potential CEO of another firm. The message certainly has a cautionary tone (Strategy Spotlight 4.8)

strategy spotlight

4.8

Email Faux Pas: How Countrywide's CEO and a "Potential CEO" Blew It

Countrywide Financial's CEO

The chairman of beleaguered Countrywide Financial Corporation raised eyebrows and tempers with his caustic reply to an e-mail plea from a man about to lose his home. "Disgusting," Angelo Mozilo wrote in his inadvertent reply to Daniel Bailey Jr., who had requested a modification in his adjustable-rate mortgage. He contended that he didn't fully understand the terms, was wrongly told he could refinance after a year, and was on the verge of losing his home of 16 years because of the steep payments. Bailey sent his e-mail to 20 Countrywide addresses. He used language from a form letter on the website LoanSafe.org, which offers advice to borrowers in trouble.

Countrywide said that such mass e-mails had flooded its inboxes and disrupted operations. Mozilo wrote: "This is unbelievable. Most of these letters now have the same wording. Obviously they are being counseled by some person or by the Internet. Disgusting." Unfortunately, Mozilo clicked "Reply" instead of "Forward"—sending his comments back to Bailey.

Bailey posted the response on a LoanSafe forum—touching off a furor on housing websites. Countrywide issued a statement saying the company and Mozilo "regret any misunderstanding caused by his inadvertent response to an e-mail by Mr. Bailey. Countrywide is actively working to help borrowers like Mr. Bailey keep their homes."

Sources: Anonymous. 2008. Countrywide CEO Mozilo Criticizes e-Mail. biz .yahoo.com, May 21: np; Angelo Mozilo, en.wikipedia.org, np; Barr, A. & Goldstein, S. 2008. Bank of America to Buy Countrywide. www.marketwatch .com, January 11: np; and Goldsmith, M . 2009. How Not to Lose the Top Job. *Harvard Business Review*, 87(1): 72–80.

Countrywide lost $1.2 billion in the third quarter of 2007 and another $222 million in the fourth quarter as the sub-prime mortgage crisis hit. And the firm's stock dropped 80 percent between February and the end of the 2007. During the same period, Mozilo received a $1.7 million salary and $20 million in performance-based stock awards and sold $121 million in stock. He was forced out of Countrywide on July 1, 2008, at which time his firm was acquired by Bank of America. As a footnote, Henry G. Cisneros, a former HUD chairman and member of the Countrywide board of directors, described Mozilo as "sick with stress—the final chapter of his life is the infamy that's been brought on him, or that he brought on himself." CNN named Mozilo as one of the "Ten Most Wanted: Culprits" of the 2008 financial collapse in the United States.

The Derailed "CEO Candidate"

Marshall Goldsmith, one of the world's best-known executive coaches, relates an example of how an executive derailed his successful career at a firm by carelessly sending a "toxic" email:

> I witnessed a series of e-mails between a potential CEO and a friend inside the company. The first e-mail to the friend provided an elaborate description of "why the current CEO is an idiot." The friend sent a reply. Several rounds of e-mails followed. Then the friend sent an e-mail containing a funny joke. The potential CEO decided that the current CEO would love this joke and forwarded it to him. You can guess what happened next. The CEO scrolled down the e-mail chain and found the "idiot" message. The heir apparent was gone in a week.

E-mail can, however, be a means for top executives to communicate information efficiently. For example, Martin Sorrell, chairman of WPP Group PLC, a $2.4 billion advertising and public relations firm, is a strong believer in the use of e-mail.[89] He e-mails all of his employees once a month to discuss how the company is doing, address specific issues, and offer his perspectives on hot issues, such as new business models for the Internet. He believes that it keeps people abreast of what he is working on.

Technology can also enable much more sophisticated forms of communication in addition to knowledge sharing. Buckman Laboratories is a $464 million specialty chemicals company based in Memphis, Tennessee, with approximately 1,450 employees in over 100 countries. Buckman has successfully used its global knowledge sharing network—known as K'Netix—to enhance its competitive advantages:[90]

Here's an example of how the network can be applied. One of Buckman's paper customers in Michigan realized that the peroxide it was adding to remove ink from old magazines was no longer working. A Buckman sales manager presented this problem to the knowledge network. Within two days, salespeople from Belgium and Finland identified a likely cause: Bacteria in the paper slurry was producing an enzyme that broke down the peroxide. The sales manager recommended a chemical to control the bacteria, solving the problem. You can imagine how positive the customer felt about Buckman. And with the company and the customer co-creating knowledge, a new level of trust and value can emerge.

Electronic Teams: Using Technology to Enhance Collaboration

Technology enables professionals to work as part of electronic, or virtual, teams to enhance the speed and effectiveness with which products are developed. For example, Microsoft has concentrated much of its development on **electronic teams** (or e-teams) that are networked together.[91] This helps to accelerate design and testing of new software modules that use the Windows-based framework as their central architecture. Microsoft is able to foster specialized technical expertise while sharing knowledge rapidly throughout the firm. This helps the firm learn how its new technologies can be applied rapidly to new business ventures such as cable television, broadcasting, travel services, and financial services.

>LO6
Why "electronic" or "virtual" teams are critical in combining and leveraging knowledge in organizations and how they can be made more effective.

What are electronic teams (or e-teams)? There are two key differences between e-teams and more traditional teams:[92]

- E-team members either work in geographically separated work places or they may work in the same space but at different times. E-teams may have members working in different spaces and time zones, as is the case with many multinational teams.
- Most of the interactions among members of e-teams occur through electronic communication channels such as fax machines and groupware tools such as e-mail, bulletin boards, chat, and videoconferencing.

electronic teams
a team of individuals that completes tasks primarily through e-mail communication.

E-teams have expanded exponentially in recent years.[93] Organizations face increasingly high levels of complex and dynamic change. E-teams are also effective in helping businesses cope with global challenges. Most e-teams perform very complex tasks and most knowledge-based teams are charged with developing new products, improving organizational processes, and satisfying challenging customer problems. For example, Eastman Kodak's e-teams design new products, Hewlett Packard's e-teams solve clients' computing problems, and Sun Microsystems' e-teams generate new business models.

Advantages　There are multiple advantages of e-teams.[94] In addition to the rather obvious use of technology to facilitate communications, the potential benefits parallel the other two major sections in this chapter—human capital and social capital.

First, e-teams are less restricted by the geographic constraints that are placed on face-to-face teams. Thus, e-teams have the potential to acquire a broader range of "human capital" or the skills and capacities that are necessary to complete complex assignments. So, e-team leaders can draw upon a greater pool of talent to address a wider range of problems since they are not constrained by geographic space. Once formed, e-teams can be more flexible in responding to unanticipated work challenges and opportunities because team members can be rotated out of projects when demands and contingencies alter the team's objectives.

Second, e-teams can be very effective in generating "social capital"—the quality of relationships and networks that leaders and team members form. Such capital is a key lubricant in work transactions and operations. Given the broader boundaries associated with e-teams, members and leaders generally have access to a wider range of social contacts than would be typically available in more traditional face-to-face teams. Such contacts are often connected to a broader scope of clients, customers, constituents, and other key stakeholders.

Challenges   However, there are challenges associated with making e-teams effective. Successful action by both traditional teams and e-teams requires that:

- Members *identify* who among them can provide the most appropriate knowledge and resources, and,
- E-team leaders and key members know how to *combine* individual contributions in the most effective manner for a coordinated and appropriate response.

Group psychologists have termed such activities "identification and combination" activities and teams that fail to perform them face a "process loss."[95] Process losses prevent teams from reaching high levels of performance because of inefficient interaction dynamics among team members. Such poor dynamics require that some collective energy, time, and effort be devoted to dealing with team inefficiencies, thus diverting the team away from its objectives. For example, if a team member fails to communicate important information at critical phases of a project, other members may waste time and energy. This can lead to conflict and resentment as well as to decreased motivation to work hard to complete tasks.

The potential for process losses tends to be more prevalent in e-teams than in traditional teams because the geographical dispersion of members increases the complexity of establishing effective interaction and exchanges. Generally, teams suffer process loss because of low cohesion, low trust among members, a lack of appropriate norms or standard operating procedures, or a lack of shared understanding among team members about their tasks. With e-teams, members are more geographically or temporally dispersed, and the team becomes more susceptible to the risk factors that can create process loss. Such problems can be exacerbated when team members have less than ideal competencies and social skills. This can erode problem-solving capabilities as well as the effective functioning of the group as a social unit.

Codifying Knowledge for Competitive Advantage

There are two different kinds of knowledge. Tacit knowledge is embedded in personal experience and shared only with the consent and participation of the individual. Explicit (or codified) knowledge, on the other hand, is knowledge that can be documented, widely distributed, and easily replicated. One of the challenges of knowledge-intensive organizations is to capture and codify the knowledge and experience that, in effect, resides in the heads of its employees. Otherwise, they will have to constantly "reinvent the wheel," which is both expensive and inefficient. Also, the "new wheel" may not necessarily be superior to the "old wheel."[96]

Once a knowledge asset (e.g., a software code or processes) is developed and paid for, it can be reused many times at very low cost, assuming that it doesn't have to be substantially modified each time. Let's take the case of a consulting company, such as Accenture (formerly Andersen Consulting).[97] Since the knowledge of its consultants has been codified and stored in electronic repositories, it can be employed in many jobs by a huge number of consultants. Additionally, since the work has a high level of standardization (i.e., there are strong similarities across the numerous client engagements), there is a rather high ratio of consultants to partners. For example, the ratio of consultants to partners is roughly 30, which is quite high. As one might expect, there must be extensive training of the newly hired consultants for such an approach to work. The recruits are trained at Accenture's Center for Professional Education, a 150-acre campus in St. Charles, Illinois. Using the center's knowledge-management repository, the consultants work through many scenarios designed to improve business processes. In effect, the information technologies enable the consultants to be "implementers, not inventors."

Access Health, a call-in medical center, also uses technology to capture and share knowledge. When someone calls the center, a registered nurse uses the company's "clinical

How 3M Retains Knowledge

As the issue of retiring employees becomes more critical at 3M, retaining employee knowledge has become a high priority. 3M applies what it calls high-tech, low-tech, and no-tech methods to a gamut of knowledge-retention measures.

"No-tech tools like storytelling work best for getting to that deep, tactical knowledge. Searchable knowledge bases are the best tools for knowledge that can be written down," according to Barry Dayton, head of 3M's knowledge-management program.

The company's searchable knowledge base, called Maven, makes the job information gleaned from 2,000 technical-service engineers across the globe accessible to all 3M employees. That's a huge business advantage in an industry where about 30 percent of U.S.-based technical-service engineers are set to retire soon, says Dayton.

Maven is a high-tech extension of a database system already in place at 3M's call centers. Historically, if call center representatives couldn't find an answer to a technical question, they'd call a technical-service

engineer. "The rep called a favorite tech engineer and that person emailed them a file or PDF," Dayton says. "With this new process, that information goes into a corporate knowledge base that the whole company can search."

Another tool in the 3M knowledge retention arsenal is storytelling—considerably less formal than Maven. How does it work? A 3M department will identify business scenarios that, though they don't crop up often, happen often enough to merit consideration. And when they do come up, they can throw a wrench into day-to-day plant operations. Examples include a switchover to a new machine or a repair to production equipment that takes it offline.

After situations are identified, Dayton's department creates groups of experts—including production, maintenance, and engineering employees who previously encountered similar situations. They sit in a conference room and have facilitators ask them questions. Software is used to map out their diagnosis of what happened and what they did as a result. "We polish that up a little bit and publish it on their plant portal so that operators, in their spare time or when something happens, can do a quick search," says Dayton.

Source: Thilmany, J . 2008. Passing on Know-How: Knowledge Retention Strategies Can Keep Employees' Workplace-Acquired Wisdom from Walking Out the Door When They Retire. *HR Magazine*, June: np.

decision architecture" to assess the caller's symptoms, rule out possible conditions, and recommend a home remedy, doctor's visit, or trip to the emergency room. The company's knowledge repository contains algorithms of the symptoms of more than 500 illnesses. According to CEO Joseph Tallman, "We are not inventing a new way to cure disease. We are taking available knowledge and inventing processes to put it to better use." The software algorithms were very expensive to develop, but the investment has been repaid many times over. The first 300 algorithms that Access Health developed have each been used an average of 8,000 times a year. Further, the company's paying customers—insurance companies and provider groups—save money because many callers would have made expensive trips to the emergency room or the doctor's office had they not been diagnosed over the phone.

The large number of baby boomers retiring over the next several years creates many key challenges for organizations. Strategy Spotlight 4.9 discusses what 3M is doing to help retain key knowledge that might otherwise be lost when boomers leave the firm.

We close this section with a series of questions managers should consider in determining (1) how effective their organization is in attracting, developing, and retaining human capital and (2) how effective they are in leveraging human capital through social capital and technology. These questions, included in Exhibit 4.7, summarize some of the key issues addressed in this chapter.

Human Capital

Recruiting "Top-Notch" Human Capital

- Does the organization assess attitude and "general makeup" instead of focusing primarily on skills and background in selecting employees at all levels?
- How important are creativity and problem-solving ability? Are they properly considered in hiring decisions?
- Do people throughout the organization engage in effective networking activities to obtain a broad pool of worthy potential employees? Is the organization creative in such endeavors?

Enhancing Human Capital through Employee Development

- Does the development and training process inculcate an "organizationwide" perspective?
- Is there widespread involvement, including top executives, in the preparation and delivery of training and development programs?
- Is the development of human capital effectively tracked and monitored?
- Are there effective programs for succession at all levels of the organization, especially at the top-most levels?
- Does the firm effectively evaluate its human capital? Is a 360-degree evaluation used? Why? Why not?
- Are mechanisms in place to assure that a manager's success does not come at the cost of compromising the organization's core values?

Retaining the Best Employees

- Are there appropriate financial rewards to motivate employees at all levels?
- Do people throughout the organization strongly identify with the organization's mission?
- Are employees provided with a stimulating and challenging work environment that fosters professional growth?
- Are valued amenities provided (e.g., flex time, child-care facilities, telecommuting) that are appropriate given the organization's mission, strategy, and how work is accomplished?
- Is the organization continually devising strategies and mechanisms to retain top performers?

Social Capital

- Are there positive personal and professional relationships among employees?
- Is the organization benefiting (or being penalized) by hiring (or by voluntary turnover) en masse?
- Does an environment of caring and encouragement rather than competition enhance team performance?
- Do the social networks within the organization have the appropriate levels of closure and bridging relationships?
- Does the organization minimize the adverse effects of excessive social capital, such as excessive costs and "groupthink"?

Technology

- Has the organization used technologies such as e-mail and networks to develop products and services?
- Does the organization effectively use technology to transfer best practices across the organization?
- Does the organization use technology to leverage human capital and knowledge both within the boundaries of the organization and among its suppliers and customers?
- Has the organization effectively used technology to codify knowledge for competitive advantage?
- Does the organization try to retain some of the knowledge of employees when they decide to leave the firm?

Source: Adapted from Dess, G. G., & Picken, J. C. 1999. *Beyond Productivity:* 63–64. New York: AMACON.

Protecting the Intellectual Assets of the Organization: Intellectual Property and Dynamic Capabilities

In today's dynamic and turbulent world, unpredictability and fast change dominate the business environment. Firms can use technology, attract human capital, or tap into research and design networks to get access to pretty much the same information as their competitors. So what would give firms a sustainable competitive advantage?[98] Protecting a firm's intellectual property requires a concerted effort on the part of the company. After all, employees become disgruntled and patents expire. The management of intellectual property (IP) involves, besides patents, contracts with confidentiality and noncompete clauses, copyrights, and the development of trademarks. Moreover, developing dynamic capabilities is the only avenue providing firms with the ability to reconfigure their knowledge and activities to achieve a sustainable competitive advantage.

>LO7
The challenge of protecting intellectual property and the importance of a firm's dynamic capabilities.

Intellectual Property Rights

Intellectual property rights are more difficult to define and protect than property rights for physical assets (e.g., plant, equipment, and land). However, if intellectual property rights are not reliably protected by the state, there will be no incentive to develop new products and services. Property rights have been enshrined in constitutions and rules of law in many countries. In the information era, though, adjustments need to be made to accommodate the new realities of knowledge. Knowledge and information are fundamentally different assets from the physical ones that property rights have been designed to protect.

The protection of intellectual rights raises unique issues, compared to physical property rights. IP is characterized by significant development costs and very low marginal costs. Indeed, it may take a substantial investment to develop a software program, an idea, or a digital music tune. Once developed, though, their reproduction and distribution cost may be almost zero, especially if the Internet is used. Effective protection of intellectual property is necessary before any investor will finance such an undertaking. Appropriation of their returns is harder to police since possession and deployment are not as readily observable. Unlike physical assets, intellectual property can be stolen by simply broadcasting it. Recall Napster and MP3 as well as the debates about counterfeit software, music CDs, and DVDs coming from developing countries such as China. Part of the problem is that using an idea does not prevent others from simultaneously using it for their own benefit, which is typically impossible with physical assets. Moreover, new ideas are frequently built on old ideas and are not easily traceable.

Strategy Spotlight 4.10 describes the many legal battles fought by a Canadian firm, Research in Motion of Waterloo, the developer of the popular BlackBerry. This example illustrates the high stakes that ride on intellectual property rights.

Countries are attempting to pass new legislation to cope with developments in new pharmaceutical compounds, stem cell research, and biotechnology. However, a firm that is faced with this challenge today cannot wait for the legislation to catch up. New technological developments, software solutions, electronic games, online services, and other products and services contribute to our economic prosperity and the creation of wealth for those entrepreneurs who have the idea first and risk bringing it to the market.

Dynamic Capabilities

Dynamic capabilities entail the capacity to build and protect a competitive advantage. This rests on knowledge, assets, competencies, and complementary assets and technologies as well as the ability to sense and seize new opportunities, generate new knowledge, and reconfigure existing assets and capabilities.[99] According to David Teece, an economist at the University of California at Berkeley, dynamic capabilities are related to the entrepreneurial side

dynamic capabilities
a firm's capacity to build and protect a competitive advantage, which rests on knowledge, assets, competencies, complementary assets, and technologies. Dynamic capabilities include the ability to sense and seize new opportunities, generate new knowledge, and reconfigure existing assets and capabilities.

Research in Motion, Maker of the BlackBerry, Loses an Intellectual Property Lawsuit

Research in Motion (RIM) is a Waterloo, Ontario–based company that is best known for developing the Black-Berry, a wireless device that integrates the functionalities of a cell phone with the ability to receive e-mail messages. During its brief history, it has become one of the fastest growing companies in North America. Founded by Mike Lazaridis, a former University of Waterloo student in 1984, Research in Motion was a competent but obscure technology firm until 1999 when the first BlackBerry was released. Through the development of integrated hardware, software, and services that support multiple wireless network standards, the BlackBerry has enabled RIM to grow from less than $50 million in sales revenue in 1999 to $6 billion by 2008. Even more impressive, by 2009 the company can boast a market capitalization in excess of $30 billion. RIM's commitment to their slogan "always on, always connected" has won them a legion of dedicated followers around the globe.

Interestingly, legal challenges have been the biggest obstacles that Research in Motion has faced in the eight years since the introduction of the first BlackBerry. In 2000, NTP, a pure patent-holding company, filed suit against RIM for violation of five of its patents and petitioned the court for an injunction on the sale and support of BlackBerry devices. The case dragged on for years, and RIM felt relatively secure that no injunction would be issued. On February 24, 2006, things dramatically changed. U.S. District Court Judge James Spencer indicated that he was inclined to grant the injunction and that his ruling was imminent. Faced with the acute risk of an unfavorable decision,

RIM settled only one week later for $612.5 million. It wound up paying a fortune for rights that were dubious at best—given that all five NTP patents had already been preliminarily invalidated by the U.S. Patent and Trademark Office and that two of them then received a final rejection.

● Research in Motion (RIM) has faced litigation over its highly successful BlackBerry.

Sources: Henkel, J. & Reitzig, M. 2008. Patent Sharks. *Harvard Business Review,* 86(6): 129–133; Hesseldahl, A. 2006. RIM's Latest Patent Problem. *BusinessWeek Online,* May 2: np; Anonymous. 2006. Settlement Reached in BlackBerry Patent Case. (The Associated Press) MSNBC.Com. March 3: np; and Wolk, M. 2006. RIM Pays Up, Taking "One for the Team." MSNBC.Com. March 3.

of the firm and are built within a firm through its environmental and technological "sensing" apparatus, its choices of organizational form, and its collective ability to strategize. Dynamic capabilities are about the ability of an organization to challenge the conventional wisdom within its industry and market, learn and innovate, adapt to the changing world, and continuously adopt new ways to serve the evolving needs of the market.[100]

Examples of dynamic capabilities include product development, strategic decision making, alliances, and acquisitions.[101] Some firms have clearly developed internal processes and routines that make them superior in such activities. For example, 3M and Apple are ahead of their competitors in product development. Cisco Systems has made numerous acquisitions over the years. They seem to have developed the capability to identify and evaluate potential acquisition candidates and seamlessly integrate them once the acquisition is completed. Other organizations can try to copy Cisco's practices. However, Cisco's combination of the resources of the acquired companies and their reconfiguration that Cisco has already achieved places them well ahead of their competitors. As markets become increasingly dynamic, traditional sources of long-term competitive advantage become less relevant. In such markets, all that a firm can strive for are a series of temporary advantages. Dynamic capabilities allow a firm to create this series of temporary advantages through new resource configurations.[102]

Reflecting on Career Implications . . .

- *Human Capital:* Does your organization effectively attract, develop, and retain talent? If not, you may have fewer career opportunities to enhance your human capital at your organization. Take advantage of your organization's human resource programs such as tuition reimbursement, mentoring, etc.
- *Human Capital:* Does your organization value diversity? What kinds of diversity seem to be encouraged (e.g., age-based or ethnicity-based)? If not, there may be limited perspectives on strategic and operational issues and a career at this organization may be less attractive to you.
- *Social Capital:* Does your organization have effective programs to build and develop social capital such that professionals develop strong "ties" to the organization? Alternatively, is social capital so strong that you see effects occur such as "groupthink"? From your perspective, how might you better leverage social capital towards pursuing other career opportunities?
- *Technology:* Does your organization provide and effectively use technology (e.g., groupware, knowledge management systems) to help you leverage your talents and expand your knowledge base?

Summary

Firms throughout the industrial world are recognizing that the knowledge worker is the key to success in the marketplace. However, we also recognize that human capital, although vital, is still only a necessary, but not a sufficient, condition for creating value. We began the first section of the chapter by addressing the importance of human capital and how it can be attracted, developed, and retained. Then we discussed the role of social capital and technology in leveraging human capital for competitive success. We pointed out that intellectual capital—the difference between a firm's market value and its book value—has increased significantly over the past few decades. This is particularly true for firms in knowledge-intensive industries, especially where there are relatively few tangible assets, such as software development.

The second section of the chapter addressed the attraction, development, and retention of human capital. We viewed these three activities as a "three-legged stool"—that is, it is difficult for firms to be successful if they ignore or are unsuccessful in any one of these activities. Among the issues we discussed in *attracting* human capital were "hiring for attitude, training for skill" and the value of using social networks to attract human capital. In particular, it is important to attract employees who can collaborate with others, given the importance of collective efforts such as teams and task forces.

With regard to *developing* human capital, we discussed the need to encourage widespread involvement throughout the organization, monitor progress and track the development of human capital, and evaluate human capital. Among the issues that are widely practiced in evaluating human capital is the 360-degree evaluation system. Employees are evaluated by their superiors, peers, direct reports, and even internal and external customers. We also addressed the value of maintaining a diverse workforce. Finally, some mechanisms for retaining human capital are employees' identification with the organization's mission and values, providing challenging work and a stimulating environment, the importance of financial and nonfinancial rewards and incentives, and providing flexibility and amenities. A key issue here is that a firm should not overemphasize financial rewards. After all, if individuals join an organization for money, they also are likely to leave for money. With money as the primary motivator, there is little chance that employees will develop firm-specific ties to keep them with the organization.

The third section of the chapter discussed the importance of social capital in leveraging human capital. Social capital refers to the network of relationships that individuals have throughout the organization as well as with customers and suppliers. Such ties can be critical in obtaining both information and resources. With regard to recruiting, for example, we saw how some firms are able to hire en masse groups of individuals who are part of social networks. Social relationships can also be very important in the effective functioning of groups. Finally, we discussed some of the potential downsides of social capital. These include the expenses that firms may bear when promoting social and working relationships among individuals as well as the potential for "groupthink," wherein individuals are reluctant to express divergent (or opposing) views on an issue because of social pressures to conform. We also introduced the concept of social networks. The relative advantages of being central in a network versus bridging multiple networks was discussed. We addressed the key role that social networks can play in both improving knowledge management and promoting career success.

The fourth section addressed the role of technology in leveraging human capital. We discussed relatively simple means of using technology, such as e-mail and networks where individuals can collaborate by way of personal computers. We provided suggestions and guidelines on how electronic teams can be effectively managed. We also addressed more sophisticated uses of technology, such as sophisticated management systems. Here knowledge can be codified and reused at very low cost, as we saw in the examples of firms in the consulting, health care, and high-technology industries.

In the last section we discussed the increasing importance of protecting a firm's intellectual property. Although traditional approaches such as patents, copyrights, and trademarks are important, the development of dynamic capabilities may be the best protection in the long run.

Summary Review Questions

1. Explain the role of knowledge in today's competitive environment.
2. Why is it important for managers to recognize the interdependence in the attraction, development, and retention of talented professionals?
3. What are some of the potential downsides for firms that engage in a "war for talent"?
4. Discuss the need for managers to use social capital in leveraging their human capital both within and across their firm.
5. Discuss the key role of technology in leveraging knowledge and human capital.

Key Terms

knowledge economy, 121	closure, 137
intellectual capital, 121	bridging
human capital, 122	relationships, 137
social capital, 122	structural holes, 137
explicit knowledge, 122	groupthink, 140
tacit knowledge, 122	electronic teams, 143
social network	dynamic
analysis, 136	capabilities, 147

Experiential Exercise

Johnson & Johnson, a leading health care firm with $64 billion in revenues, is often rated as one of *Fortune*'s "Most Admired Firms." It is also considered an excellent place to work and has generated high return to shareholders. Clearly, they value their human capital. Using the Internet and/or library resources, identify some of the actions/strategies Johnson & Johnson has taken to attract, develop, and retain human capital. What are their implications?

Activity	Actions/Strategies	Implications
Attracting human capital		
Developing human capital		
Retaining human capital		

Application Questions Exercises

1. Look up successful firms in a high-technology industry as well as two successful firms in more traditional industries such as automobile manufacturing and retailing. Compare their market values and book values. What are some implications of these differences?

2. Select a firm for which you believe its social capital—both within the firm and among its suppliers and customers—is vital to its competitive advantage. Support your arguments.

3. Choose a company with which you are familiar. What are some of the ways in which it uses technology to leverage its human capital?

4. Using the Internet, look up a company with which you are familiar. What are some of the policies and procedures that it uses to enhance the firm's human and social capital?

Ethics Questions

1. Recall an example of a firm that recently faced an ethical crisis. How do you feel the crisis and management's handling of it affected the firm's human capital and social capital?

2. Based on your experiences or what you have learned in your previous classes, are you familiar with any companies that used unethical practices to attract talented professionals? What do you feel were the short-term and long-term consequences of such practices?

References

1. Hayashi, A. M. 2008. Why Picasso out earned van Gogh. *MIT Sloan Management Review,* Fall: 11–12; and, Berns, G. 2008. *A neuroscientist reveals how to think differently.* Harvard Business Press: Boston.

2. Parts of this chapter draw upon some of the ideas and examples from Dess, G. G. & Picken, J. C. 1999. *Beyond Productivity.* New York: AMACOM.

3. An acknowledged trend: The world economic survey. 1996. *The Economist,* September 2(8): 25–28.

4. Quinn, J. B., Anderson, P., & Finkelstein, S. 1996. Leveraging intellect. *Academy of Management Executive,* 10(3): 7–27.

5. Hamel, G. & Prahalad, C. K. 1996. Competing in the new economy: Managing out of bounds. *Strategic Management Journal,* 17: 238.

6. Stewart, T. A. 1997. *Intellectual capital: The new wealth of organizations.* New York: Doubleday/Currency.

7. Leif Edvisson and Michael S. Malone have a similar, more detailed definition of *intellectual capital:* "the combined knowledge, skill, innovativeness, and ability to meet the task at hand." They consider intellectual capital to equal human capital plus structural capital. *Structural capital* is defined as "the hardware, software, databases, organization structure, patents, trademarks, and everything else of organizational capability that supports those employees' productivity—in a word, everything left at the office when the employees go home."

Edvisson, L. & Malone, M. S. 1997. *Intellectual capital: Realizing your company's true value by finding its hidden brainpower:* 10–14. New York: HarperBusiness.

8. Stewart, T. A. 2001. Accounting gets radical. *Fortune,* April 16: 184–194.

9. Adams, S. & Kichen, S. 2008. Ben Graham then and now. *Forbes,* November 10: 56.

10. An interesting discussion of Steve Jobs's impact on Apple's valuation is in: Lashinsky, A. 2009. Steve's leave—what does it really mean? *Fortune,* February 2: 96–102.

11. Thomas Stewart has suggested this formula in his book *Intellectual Capital.* He provides an insightful discussion on pages 224–225, including some of the limitations of this approach to measuring intellectual capital. We recognize, of course, that during the late 1990s and in early 2000, there were some excessive market valuations of high-technology and Internet firms. For an interesting discussion of the extraordinary market valuation of Yahoo!, an Internet company, refer to Perkins, A. B. 2001. The Internet bubble encapsulated: Yahoo! *Red Herring,* April 15: 17–18.

12. Roberts, P. W. & Dowling, G. R. 2002. Corporate reputation and sustained superior financial performance. *Strategic Management Journal,* 23(12): 1077–1095.

13. For a recent study on the relationships between human capital, learning, and sustainable competitive advantage, read Hatch, N. W. & Dyer, J. H. 2005. Human capital and learning as a source of sustainable competitive advantage. *Strategic Management Journal,* 25: 1155–1178.

14. One of the seminal contributions on knowledge management is Becker, G. S. 1993. *Human capital: A theoretical and empirical analysis with special reference to education* (3rd ed.). Chicago: University of Chicago Press.

15. For an excellent overview of the topic of social capital, read Baron, R. A. 2005. Social capital. In Hitt, M. A. & Ireland, R. D. (Eds.), *The Blackwell encyclopedia of management* (2nd ed.): 224–226. Malden, MA: Blackwell.

16. For an excellent discussion of social capital and its impact on organizational performance, refer to Nahapiet, J. & Ghoshal, S. 1998. Social capital, intellectual capital, and the organizational advantage. *Academy of Management Review,* 23: 242–266.

17. An interesting discussion of how knowledge management (patents) can enhance organizational performance can be found in Bogner, W. C. & Bansal, P. 2007. Knowledge management as the basis of sustained high performance. *Journal of Management Studies,* 44(1): 165–188.

18. Polanyi, M. 1967. *The tacit dimension.* Garden City, NY: Anchor Publishing.

19. Barney, J. B. 1991. Firm resources and sustained competitive advantage. *Journal of Management,* 17: 99–120.

20. For an interesting perspective of empirical research on how knowledge can adversely affect performance, read Haas, M. R. & Hansen, M. T. 2005. When using knowledge can hurt performance: The value of organizational capabilities in a management consulting company. *Strategic Management Journal,* 26(1): 1–24.

21. New insights on managing talent are provided in: Cappelli, P. 2008. Talent management for the twenty-first century. *Harvard Business Review,* 66(3): 74–81.

22. Some of the notable books on this topic include Edvisson & Malone, op. cit.; Stewart, op. cit.; and Nonaka, I. & Takeuchi, I. 1995. *The knowledge creating company.* New York: Oxford University Press.

23. Stewart, T. A. 2000. Taking risk to the marketplace. *Fortune,* March 6: 424.

24. Insights on the Generation X's perspective on the workplace are in: Erickson, T. J. 2008. Task, not time: Profile of a Gen Y job. *Harvard Business Review,* 86(2): 19.

25. Dutton, G. 1997. Are you technologically competent? *Management Review,* November: 54–58.

26. Some workplace implications for the aging workforce are addressed in: Strack, R., Baier, J., & Fahlander, A. 2008. Managing demographic risk. *Harvard Business Review,* 66(2): 119–128.

27. For a discussion of attracting, developing, and retaining top talent, refer to Goffee, R. & Jones, G. 2007. Leading clever people. *Harvard Business Review,* 85(3): 72–89.

28. Dess & Picken, op. cit.: 34.

29. Webber, A. M. 1998. Danger: Toxic company. *Fast Company,* November: 152–161.

30. Some interesting insights on why home-grown American talent is going abroad is found in: Saffo, P. 2009. A looming American diaspora. *Harvard Business Review,* 87(2): 27.

31. Morris, B. 1997. Key to success: People, people, people. *Fortune,* October 27: 232.

32. For insights on management development and firm performance in several countries, refer to: Mabey, C. 2008. Management development and firm performance in Germany, Norway, Spain, and the UK. *Journal of International Business Studies,* 39(8): 1327–1342.

33. Martin, J. 1998. So, you want to work for the best. . . . *Fortune,* January 12: 77.

34. Cardin, R. 1997. Make your own Bozo Filter. *Fast Company,* October–November: 56.

35. Levering, R. & Moskowitz, M. 2009. And the winners are . . . *Fortune.* February 2: 67–78.

36. Martin, op. cit.; Henkoff, R. 1993. Companies that train best. *Fortune,* March 22: 53–60.

37. An interesting perspective on developing new talent rapidly when they join an organization can be found in Rollag, K., Parise, S., & Cross, R. 2005. Getting new hires up to speed quickly. *MIT Sloan Management Review,* 46(2): 35–41.

38. Stewart, T. A. 1998. Gray flannel suit? moi? *Fortune,* March 18: 80–82.

39. An interesting perspective on how Cisco Systems develops its talent can be found in Chatman, J., O'Reilly, C., & Chang, V. 2005. Cisco Systems: Developing a human capital strategy. *California Management Review,* 47(2): 137–166.

40. This section is based on Leonard, D. A. & Swap, W. 2004. Deep smarts. *Harvard Business Review,* 82(9): 88–97.

41. Useful insights on coaching can be found in: Coutu, D. & Kauffman, C. 2009. What coaches can do for you? *Harvard Business Review,* 67(1): 91–97.

42. For an innovative perspective on the appropriateness of alternate approaches to evaluation and rewards, refer to Seijts, G. H. & Lathan, G. P. 2005. Learning versus performance goals: When should each be used? *Academy of Management Executive,* 19(1): 124–132.

43. The discussion of the 360-degree feedback system draws on the article UPS. 1997. 360-degree feedback: Coming from all sides. *Vision* (a UPS Corporation internal company publication), March: 3; Slater, R. 1994. *Get better or get beaten: Thirty-one leadership secrets from Jack Welch.* Burr Ridge, IL: Irwin; Nexon, M. 1997. General Electric: The secrets of the finest company in the world. *L'Expansion,* July 23: 18–30; and Smith, D. 1996. Bold new directions for human resources. *Merck World* (internal company publication), October: 8.

44. Interesting insights on 360-degree evaluation systems are discussed in: Barwise, P. & Meehan, Sean. 2008. So you think you're a good listener. *Harvard Business Review,* 66(4): 22–23.

45. Insights into the use of 360-degree evaluation are in: Kaplan, R. E. & Kaiser, R.B. 2009. Stop overdoing your strengths. *Harvard Business Review,* 87(2): 100–103.

46. Kets de Vries, M. F. R. 1998. Charisma in action: The transformational abilities of Virgin's Richard Branson and ABB's Percy Barnevik. *Organizational Dynamics,* Winter: 20.

47. For an interesting discussion on how organizational culture has helped Zappos become number one in *Fortune*'s 2009 survey of the best companies to work for, see: O'Brien, J. M. 2009. Zappos knows how to kick it. *Fortune,* February 2: 54–58.

48. We have only to consider the most celebrated case of industrial espionage in recent years, wherein José Ignacio Lopez was indicted in a German court for stealing sensitive product planning documents from his former employer, General Motors, and sharing them with his executive colleagues at Volkswagen. The lawsuit was dismissed by the German courts, but Lopez and his colleagues were investigated by the U.S. Justice Department. Also consider the recent litigation involving noncompete employment contracts and confidentiality clauses of *International Paper v. Louisiana-Pacific, Campbell Soup v. H. J. Heinz Co.,* and *PepsiCo v. Quaker Oats's Gatorade.* In addition to retaining valuable human resources and often their valuable network of customers, firms must also protect proprietary information and knowledge. For interesting insights, refer to Carley, W. M. 1998. CEO gets hard lesson in how not to keep his lieutenants. *The Wall Street Journal,* February 11: A1, A10; and Lenzner, R. & Shook, C. 1998. Whose Rolodex is it, anyway? *Forbes,* February 23: 100–103.

49. For an insightful discussion of retention of knowledge workers in today's economy, read Davenport, T. H. 2005. *The care and feeding of the knowledge worker.* Boston, MA: Harvard Business School Press.

50. Fisher, A. 2008. America's most admired companies. *Fortune,* March 17: 74.

51. Stewart, T. A. 2001. *The wealth of knowledge.* New York: Currency.

52. For insights on fulfilling one's potential, refer to: Kaplan, R. S. 2008. Reaching your potential. *Harvard Business Review,* 66(7/8): 45–57.

53. Amabile, T. M. 1997. Motivating creativity in organizations: On doing what you love and loving what you do. *California Management Review,* Fall: 39–58.

54. For an insightful perspective on alternate types of employee–employer relationships, read Erickson, T. J. & Gratton, L. 2007. What it means to work here. *Harvard Business Review,* 85(3): 104–112.

55. Monsanto has been part of Pharmacia since 2002. *Hoover's Handbook of Am. Bus.* 2004: 562.

56. Pfeffer, J. 2001. Fighting the war for talent is hazardous to your organization's health. *Organizational Dynamics,* 29(4): 248–259.

57. Cox, T. L. 1991. The multinational organization. *Academy of Management Executive,* 5(2): 34–47. Without doubt, a great deal has been written on the topic of creating and maintaining an effective diverse workforce. Some excellent, recent books include: Harvey, C. P. & Allard, M. J. 2005. *Understanding and managing diversity: Readings, cases, and exercises.* (3rd ed.). Upper Saddle River, NJ: Pearson Prentice-Hall; Miller, F. A. & Katz, J. H. 2002. *The inclusion breakthrough: Unleashing the real power of diversity.* San Francisco: Berrett Koehler; and Williams, M. A. 2001. *The 10 lenses: Your guide to living and working in a multicultural world.* Sterling, VA: Capital Books.

58. www.rand.org/publications/RB/RB/ 5050.

59. This section, including the six potential benefits of a diverse workforce, draws on Cox, T. H. & Blake, S. 1991. Managing cultural diversity: Implications for organizational competitiveness. *Academy of Management Executive,* 5(3): 45–56.

60. www.pwcglobal.com/us/eng/careers/ diversity/index.html.

61. This discussion draws on Dess, G. G. & Lumpkin, G. T. 2001. Emerging issues in strategy process research. In Hitt, M. A., Freeman, R. E. & Harrison, J. S. (Eds.). *Handbook of strategic management:* 3–34. Malden, MA: Blackwell.

62. Adler, P. S. & Kwon, S. W. 2002. Social capital: Prospects for a new concept. *Academy of Management Review,* 27(1): 17–40.

63. Capelli, P. 2000. A market-driven approach to retaining talent. *Harvard Business Review,* 78(1): 103–113.

64. This hypothetical example draws on Peteraf, M. 1993. The cornerstones of competitive advantage. *Strategic Management Journal,* 14: 179–191.

65. Wernerfelt, B. 1984. A resource-based view of the firm. *Strategic Management Journal,* 5: 171–180.

66. Wysocki, B., Jr. 2000. Yet another hazard of the new economy: The Pied Piper Effect. *The Wall Street Journal,* March 20: A1–A16.

67. Ideas on how managers can more effectively use their social network are addressed in: McGrath, C. & Zell, D. 2009. Profiles of trust: Who to turn to, and for what. *MIT Sloan Management Review,* 50(2): 75–80.

68. Ibid.

69. Buckman, R. C. 2000. Tech defectors from Microsoft resettle together. *The Wall Street Journal,* October: B1–B6.

70. An insightful discussion of the interorganizational aspects of social capital can be found in Dyer, J. H. & Singh, H. 1998. The relational view: Cooperative strategy and sources of interorganizational competitive advantage. *Academy of Management Review,* 23: 66–79.

71. A study of the relationship between social networks and performance in China is found in: Li, J. J., Poppo, L., & Zhou, K. Z. 2008. Do managerial ties in China always produce value? Competition, uncertainty, and domestic vs. foreign firms. *Strategic Management Journal,* 29(4): 383–400.

72. Hoppe, B. 2005. Structural holes, Part one. connectedness.blogspot.com. January 18: np.

73. There has been a tremendous amount of theory building and empirical research in recent years in the area of social network analysis. Unquestionably, two of the major contributors to this domain have been Ronald Burt and J. S. Coleman. For excellent background discussions, refer to: Burt, R. S. 1992. *Structural holes: The social structure of competition.* Cambridge, MA: Harvard University Press; Coleman, J. S. 1990. *Foundations of social theory.* Cambridge, MA: Harvard University Press; and Coleman, J. S. 1988. Social capital in the creation of human capital. *American Journal of Sociology.* 94: S95–S120. For a more recent review and integration of current thought on social network theory, consider: Burt, R. S. 2005. *Brokerage & closure: An introduction to social capital.* Oxford Press: New York.

74. Our discussion draws on the concepts developed by Burt, 1992, op. cit.; Coleman, 1990, op. cit.; Coleman, 1988, op. cit.; and Oh, H., Chung, M. & Labianca, G. 2004. Group social capital and group effectiveness: The role of informal socializing ties. *Academy of Management Journal,* 47(6): 860–875. We would like to thank Joe Labianca (University of Kentucky) for his helpful feedback and ideas in our discussion of social networks.

75. Arregle, J. L., Hitt, M. A., Sirmon, D. G., & Very, P. 2007. The development of organizational social capital: Attributes of family firms. *Journal of Management Studies,* 44(1): 73–95.

76. A novel perspective on social networks is in: Pentland, A. 2009. How social networks network best. *Harvard Business Review,* 87(2): 37.

77. Oh et al., op. cit.

78. Hoppe, op. cit.

79. The discussion of these two contingent factors draws on Dess, G. G. & Shaw, J. D. 2001. Voluntary turnover, social capital, and organizational performance. *Academy of Management Review,* 26(3): 446–456.

80. The business-level strategies of overall low cost and differentiation draws upon Michael E. Porter's classic work and will be discussed in more detail in Chapter 5. Source: Porter, M. E. 1985. *Competitive advantage.* Free Press: New York.

81. Perspectives on how to use and develop decision networks are discussed in: Cross, R., Thomas, R. J., & Light, D. A. 2009. How "who you know" affects what you decide. *MIT Sloan Management Review,* 50(2): 35–42.

82. Our discussion of the three advantages of social networks draws on Uzzi, B. & Dunlap. S. 2005. How to build your network. *Harvard Business Review,* 83(12): 53–60. For a recent, excellent review on the research exploring the relationship between social capital and managerial performance, read Moran, P. 2005. Structural vs. relational embeddedness: Social capital and managerial performance. *Strategic Management Journal,* 26(12): 1129–1151.

83. A perspective on personal influence is in: Christakis, N. A. 2009. The dynamics of personal influence. *Harvard Business Review,* 87(2): 31.

84. Prusak, L. & Cohen, D. 2001. How to invest in social capital. *Harvard Business Review,* 79(6): 86–93.

85. Leonard, D. & Straus, S. 1997. Putting your company's whole brain to work. *Harvard Business Review,* 75(4): 110–122.

86. For an excellent discussion of public (i.e., the organization) versus private (i.e., the individual manager) benefits of social capital, refer to Leana, C. R. & Van Buren, H. J. 1999. Organizational social capital and employment practices. *Academy of Management Review,* 24(3): 538–555.

87. The authors would like to thank Joe Labianca, University of Kentucky, and John Lin, University of Texas at Dallas, for their very helpful input in our discussion of social network theory and its practical implications.

88. Brady, D. 2006. *!#?@ the e-mail. Can we talk?. *BusinessWeek,* December 4: 109.

89. Taylor, W. C. 1999. Whatever happened to globalization? *Fast Company,* December: 228–236.

90. Prahalad, C. K. & Ramaswamy, V. 2004. *The future of competition: Co-creating value with customers.* Boston: Harvard Business School Press.

91. Lei, D., Slocum, J., & Pitts, R. A. 1999. Designing organizations for competitive advantage: The power of unlearning and learning. *Organizational Dynamics,* Winter: 24–38.

92. This section draws upon Zaccaro, S. J. & Bader, P. 2002. E-Leadership and the challenges of leading e-teams: Minimizing the bad and maximizing the good. *Organizational Dynamics,* 31(4): 377–387.

93. Kirkman, B. L., Rosen, B., Tesluk, P. E., & Gibson, C. B. 2004. The impact of team empowerment on virtual team performance: The moderating role of face-to-face interaction. *Academy of Management Journal,* 47(2): 175–192.

94. The discussion of the advantages and challenges associated with e-teams draws on Zacarro & Bader, op. cit.

95. For a recent study exploring the relationship between team empowerment, face-to-face interaction, and performance in virtual teams, read Kirkman, Rosen, Tesluk, & Gibson, op. cit.

96. For an innovative study on how firms share knowledge with competitors and the performance implications, read Spencer, J. W. 2003. Firms' knowledge sharing strategies in the global innovation system: Empirical evidence from the flat panel display industry. *Strategic Management Journal,* 24(3): 217–235.

97. The examples of Andersen Consulting and Access Health draw upon Hansen, M. T., Nohria, N., & Tierney, T. 1999. What's your strategy for managing knowledge? *Harvard Business Review,* 77(2): 106–118.

98. This discussion draws on Conley, J. G. 2005. Intellectual capital management, Kellogg School of Management and Schulich School of Business, York University, Toronto, KS 2003; Conley, J. G. & Szobocsan, J. 2001. Snow White shows the way. *Managing Intellectual Property,* June: 15–25; Greenspan, A. 2004. Intellectual property rights, The Federal Reserve Board, Remarks by the chairman, February 27; and Teece, D. J. 1998. Capturing value from knowledge assets, *California Management Review,* 40(3): 54–79. The authors would like to thank Professor Theo Peridis, York University, for his contribution to this section.

99. A study of the relationship between dynamic capabilities and related diversification is: Doving, E. & Gooderham, P. N. 2008. *Strategic Management Journal,* 29(8): 841–858.

100. A perspective on strategy in turbulent markets is in: Sull, D. 2009. How to thrive in turbulent markets. *Harvard Business Review,* 87 (2): 78–88.

101. Lee, G. K. 2008. Relevance of organizational capabilities and its dynamics: What to learn from entrants' product portfolios about the determinants of entry timing. *Strategic Management Journal,* 29(12): 1257–1280.

102. Eisenhardt, K. M. & Martin, J. E. 2000. Dynamic capabilities: What are they? *Strategic Management Journal,* 21: 1105–1121.

CHAPTER 5

Business-Level Strategy:

Creating and Sustaining Competitive Advantages

After reading this chapter, you should have a good understanding of:

LO1 The central role of competitive advantage in the study of strategic management.

LO2 The three generic strategies: overall cost leadership, differentiation, and focus.

LO3 How the successful attainment of generic strategies can improve a firm's relative power vis-à-vis the five forces that determine an industry's average profitability.

LO4 The pitfalls managers must avoid in striving to attain generic strategies.

LO5 How firms can effectively combine the generic strategies of overall cost leadership and differentiation.

LO6 How Internet-enabled business models are being used to improve strategic positioning.

LO7 The importance of considering the industry life cycle to determine a firm's business-level strategy and its relative emphasis on functional area strategies and value-creating activities.

LO8 The need for turnaround strategies that enable a firm to reposition its competitive position in an industry.

How firms compete with each other and how they attain and sustain competitive advantages go to the heart of strategic management. In short, the key issue becomes: Why do some firms outperform others and enjoy such advantages over time? This subject, business-level strategy, is the focus of Chapter 5.

The first part of the chapter draws on Michael Porter's framework of generic strategies. He identifies three strategies—overall cost leadership, differentiation, and focus—that firms may apply to outperform their rivals in an industry. We begin by describing each of these strategies and providing examples of firms that have successfully attained them as a means of outperforming competitors in their industry. Next, we address how these strategies help a firm develop a favorable position vis-à-vis the "five forces" (Chapter 2). We then suggest some of the pitfalls that managers must avoid if they are to successfully pursue these generic strategies and discuss the conditions under which firms may effectively combine generic strategies to outperform rivals. We close this section by addressing how competitive strategies should be revised and redeployed in light of the shifts in industry and competitive forces caused by Internet and digital strategies. Here, combination strategies are the most solid because they integrate the new capabilities with sound principles.

The second part of Chapter 5 discusses a vital consideration in the effective use of business-level strategies: industry life cycles. The four stages of the industry life cycle—introduction, growth, maturity, and decline—are indicative of an evolving management process that affects factors such as the market growth rate and the intensity of competition. Accordingly, the stages of an industry's life cycle are an important contingency that managers should take into account when making decisions concerning the optimal overall business-level strategies and the relative emphasis to place on functional capabilities and value-creating activities. At times, firms are faced with performance declines and must find ways to revitalize their competitive positions. The actions followed to do so are referred to as turnaround strategies, which may be needed at any stage of the industry life cycle. However, they occur more frequently during the maturity and decline stages.

About a half-century ago, Groupe Michelin sparked a revolution in the tire industry when it introduced the steel-belted radial.[1] In 2004, it hoped for another coup with the new PAX run-flat tire, which can keep rolling smoothly for up to 120 miles even if completely deflated by a puncture.

It was the French tire maker's biggest new product push since the radial. The appeal of a run-flat is certainly attractive to any driver who has changed a tire on the shoulder of a busy highway or wished the spare didn't take up so much room in the trunk. Michelin predicted that the PAX would one day dominate the $70 billion-a-year tire market—much as radials now do, commanding nearly 100 percent of the market in the industrialized world. Claimed Chairman Edouard Michelin: "Like the radial, the PAX system is a groundbreaking innovation." However, things didn't turn out as planned. Let's take a closer look.

On April 20, 2008, the *New York Times* carried the sad headline "Michelin Giving Up on PAX Run-Flat Tire." So much for an innovation that was supposed to revolutionize the tire industry. Clearly, this was a big bet innovation, intended to overturn the industry.

While it is easy to be an "armchair quarterback" and retrospectively criticize Michelin's innovation, there were some trouble signs early on. For example, a *BusinessWeek* article appearing about four months after PAX's introduction noted that the PAX tires didn't fit into conventionally designed vehicles. To use them, cars had to be equipped with a specially designed chassis and wheels; hence, a PAX-friendly car can't take regular tires. Thus, to get the tires replaced, a customer had to find an authorized PAX service center to repair or replace the tires. Such a lack of compatibility with preexisting infrastructure proved to be a contributor to the product's undoing. In fact, the PAX's design (with an inner ring to provide more strength) was much more difficult to repair—requiring special equipment to mount and dismount the tire. That equipment was only available at Michelin stores or Honda dealers. This led to several lawsuits, and on some websites, consumers complained about the difficulty of finding shops and equipment to work on PAX. They also cited excessive tire wear and replacement costs as high as $1,600 for a set of four tires. Perhaps not too surprisingly, about two years after PAX's introduction, it only held about 5 percent of the total market for run-flat tires.

Although Michelin enjoyed some success, such as having the PAX tires as standard equipment on the 2005–2007 Honda Odyssey Touring minivan, other firms failed to adopt. As it turned out, the PAX was not a huge advance over other run-flat technologies. And it required specialized equipment and systemic changes. Thus, it was a far cry from the promise of a tire that would revolutionize driving habits and totally change an industry.

Ultimately, the goal of all competitive strategies is to create value for the customer. Michelin was seeking to create a differentiation advantage and charge a premium price. However, customers did not perceive sufficient value in the PAX technology to cover the cost of creating the product.

Types of Competitive Advantage and Sustainability

Michael Porter presented three generic strategies that a firm can use to overcome the five forces and achieve competitive advantage.[2] Each of Porter's generic strategies has the potential to allow a firm to outperform rivals in their industry. The first, *overall cost leadership,* is based on creating a low-cost-position. Here, a firm must manage the relationships throughout the value chain and lower costs throughout the entire chain. Second, *differentiation* requires a firm to create products and/or services that are unique and valued. Here, the primary emphasis is on "nonprice" attributes for which customers will

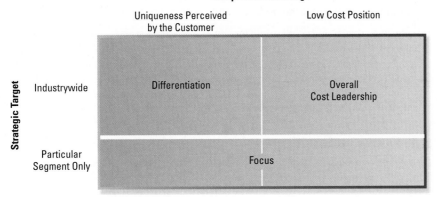

Competitive Advantage

Uniqueness Perceived by the Customer | Low Cost Position

Strategic Target

Industrywide — Differentiation | Overall Cost Leadership

Particular Segment Only — Focus

Exhibit 5.1 **Three Generic Strategies**

Source: Adapted with the permission of The Free Press, a division of Simon & Schuster Adult Publishing Group, from *Competitive Strategy: Techniques for Analyzing Industries and Competitors* by Michael E. Porter. Copyright © 1980, 1998 by The Free Press. All rights reserved.

gladly pay a premium.[3] Third, a *focus* strategy directs attention (or "focus") toward narrow product lines, buyer segments, or targeted geographic markets and they must attain advantages either through differentiation or cost leadership.[4] Whereas the overall cost leadership and differentiation strategies strive to attain advantages industrywide, focusers have a narrow target market in mind. Exhibit 5.1 illustrates these three strategies on two dimensions: competitive advantage and strategic target.

Both casual observation and research support the notion that firms that identify with one or more of the forms of competitive advantage outperform those that do not.[5] There has been a rich history of strategic management research addressing this topic. One study analyzed 1,789 strategic business units and found that businesses combining multiple forms of competitive advantage (differentiation and overall cost leadership) outperformed businesses that used only a single form. The lowest performers were those that did not identify with any type of advantage. They were classified as "stuck in the middle." Results of this study are presented in Exhibit 5.2.[6]

For an example of the dangers of being "stuck in the middle," consider Coach and Tiffany—two brands in the "affordable luxury" category.[7] Such brands target

>LO2

The three generic strategies: overall cost leadership, differentiation, and focus.

Exhibit 5.2 **Competitive Advantage and Business Performance**

	Competitive Advantage					
	Differentiation and Cost	Differentiation	Cost	Differentiation and Focus	Cost and Focus	Stuck in the Middle
Performance						
Return on investment (%)	35.5	32.9	30.2	17.0	23.7	17.8
Sales growth (%)	15.1	13.5	13.5	16.4	17.5	12.2
Gain in market share (%)	5.3	5.3	5.5	6.1	6.3	4.4
Sample size	123	160	100	141	86	105

middle-class customers for whom a $300 bag is a splurge. After sales and stock declines, they are migrating away from the middle—and going either higher or lower:

> In early 2008, Coach said that it would turn 40 of its nearly 300 stores into a more upscale format that will offer higher-end bags and concierge services. Tiffany, on the other hand, took the opposite tack. A new store opening in California will not sell any of its $148,000 diamond necklaces and instead focus on less expensive products like its $200-and-under silver jewelry. Claims Pat Conroy, head of Deloitte & Touche's consumer products sector: "Being in the middle is not a good place to be. You get assaulted from everyone."

Overall Cost Leadership

The first generic strategy is overall cost leadership. Overall cost leadership requires a tight set of interrelated tactics that include:

- Aggressive construction of efficient-scale facilities.
- Vigorous pursuit of cost reductions from experience.
- Tight cost and overhead control.
- Avoidance of marginal customer accounts.
- Cost minimization in all activities in the firm's value chain, such as R&D, service, sales force, and advertising.

Exhibit 5.3 draws on the value-chain concept (see Chapter 3) to provide examples of how a firm can attain an overall cost leadership strategy in its primary and support activities.

Key to an overall cost leadership strategy is the **experience curve**, which refers to how business "learns" to lower costs as it gains experience with production processes. With experience, unit costs of production decline as output increases in most industries. The experience curve concept is discussed in Strategy Spotlight 5.1 and Exhibit 5.4.

To generate above-average performance, a firm following an overall cost leadership position must attain **competitive parity** on the basis of differentiation relative to competitors.[8] In other words, a firm achieving parity is similar to its competitors, or "on par," with respect to differentiated products.[9] Competitive parity on the basis of differentiation permits a cost leader to translate cost advantages directly into higher profits than competitors. Thus, the cost leader earns above-average returns.[10]

The failure to attain parity on the basis of differentiation can be illustrated with an example from the automobile industry—the ill-fated Yugo. Below is an excerpt from a speech by J. W. Marriott, Jr., Chairman of the Marriott Corporation:[11]

> . . . money is a big thing. But it's not the only thing. In the 1980s, a new automobile reached North America from behind the Iron Curtain. It was called the Yugo, and its main attraction was price. About $3,000 each. But the only way they caught on was as the butt of jokes. Remember the guy who told his mechanic, "I want a gas cap for my Yugo." "OK," the mechanic replied, "that sounds like a fair trade."

Yugo was offering a lousy value proposition. The cars literally fell apart before your eyes. And the lesson was simple. Price is just one component of value. No matter how good the price, the most cost-sensitive consumer won't buy a bad product.

Next, we discuss some examples of how firms enhance cost leadership position.

While other managed care providers were having a string of weak years, WellPoint, based in Thousand Oaks, California, has had a number of banner years and recently enjoyed an annual profit growth of over 35 percent to $3.3 billion over the past three years.[12] Chairman Leonard Schaeffer credits the company's focus on innovation for both expanding revenues and cutting costs. For example, WellPoint asked the Food and Drug Administration (FDA) to make the allergy drug Claritin available over the counter. Surprisingly, this may be the first time that an insurer has approached the FDA with such a request. Schaeffer claimed, "They were kind of stunned," but the FDA agreed to consider it. It was a smart

Exhibit 5.3
Value-Chain Activities:
Examples of Overall
Cost Leadership

Support Activities

Firm Infrastructure

- Few management layers to reduce overhead costs.
- Standardized accounting practices to minimize personnel required.

Human Resource Management

- Minimize costs associated with employee turnover through effective policies.
- Effective orientation and training programs to maximize employee productivity.

Technology Development

- Effective use of automated technology to reduce scrappage rates.
- Expertise in process engineering to reduce manufacturing costs.

Procurement

- Effective policy guidelines to ensure low-cost raw materials (with acceptable quality levels).
- Shared purchasing operations with other business units.

Primary Activities

Inbound Logistics

- Effective layout of receiving dock operations.

Operations

- Effective use of quality control inspectors to minimize rework.

Outbound Logistics

- Effective utilization of delivery fleets

Marketing and Sales

- Purchase of media in large blocks.
- Sales force utilization is maximized by territory management.

Service

- Thorough service repair guidelines to minimize repeat maintenance calls.
- Use of single type of vehicle to minimize repair costs.

Source: Adapted from: Porter, M.E. 1985. *Competitive Advantage: Creating and Sustaining Superior Performance.* New York: Free Press.

move for WellPoint. If approved as an over-the-counter drug, Claritin would reduce patient visits to the doctor and eliminate the need for prescriptions—two reimbursable expenses for which WellPoint would otherwise be responsible.

Stephen Sanger, CEO of General Mills, recently came up with an idea that helped his firm cut costs.[13] To improve productivity, he sent technicians to watch pit crews during a

strategy spotlight 5.1

The Experience Curve

The experience curve, developed by the Boston Consulting Group in 1968, is a way of looking at efficiencies developed through a firm's cumulative experience. In its basic form, the experience curve relates production costs to production output. As output doubles, costs decline by 10 percent to 30 percent. For example, if it costs $1 per unit to produce 100 units, the per unit cost will decline to between 70 to 90 cents as output increases to 200 units.

What factors account for this increased efficiency? First, the success of an experience curve strategy depends on the industry life cycle for the product. Early stages of a product's life cycle are typically characterized by rapid gains in technological advances in production efficiency. Most experience curve gains come early in the product life cycle.

Second, the inherent technology of the product offers opportunities for enhancement through gained experience. High-tech products give the best opportunity for gains in production efficiencies. As technology is developed, "value engineering" of innovative production processes is implemented, driving down the per unit costs of production.

Third, a product's sensitivity to price strongly affects a firm's ability to exploit the experience curve. Cutting the price of a product with high demand elasticity—where demand increases when price decreases—rapidly creates consumer purchases of the new product. By cutting prices, a firm can increase demand for its product. The increased demand in turn increases product manufacture, thus increasing the firm's experience in the manufacturing process. So by decreasing price and increasing demand, a firm gains manufacturing experience in that particular product, which drives down per unit production costs.

Fourth, the competitive landscape factors into whether or not a firm might benefit from an experience curve strategy. If other competitors are well positioned in

Sources: Ghemawat, P. 1985. Building Strategy on the Experience Curve. *Harvard Business Review,* March–April: 143–149; Porter, M. E. 1996. *On Competition.* Boston: Harvard Business Review Press; and Oster, S. M. 1994. *Modern Competitive Analysis* (2nd ed.). New York: Oxford University Press.

the market, have strong capital resources, and are known to promote their product lines aggressively to gain market share, an experience curve strategy may lead to nothing more than a price war between two or more strong competitors. But if a company is the first to market with the product and has good financial backing, an experience curve strategy may be successful.

In an article in the *Harvard Business Review,* Pankaj Ghemawat recommended answering several questions when considering an experience curve strategy.

- Does my industry exhibit a significant experience curve?
- Have I defined the industry broadly enough to take into account interrelated experience?
- What is the precise source of cost reduction?
- Can my company keep cost reductions proprietary?
- Is demand sufficiently stable to justify using the experience curve?
- Is cumulated output doubling fast enough for the experience curve to provide much strategic leverage?
- Do the returns from an experience curve strategy warrant the risks of technological obsolescence?
- Is demand price-sensitive?
- Are there well-financed competitors who are already following an experience curve strategy or are likely to adopt one if my company does?

Michael Porter suggested, however, that the experience curve is not useful in all situations. Whether or not to base strategy on the experience curve depends on what specifically causes the decline in costs. For example, if costs drop from efficient production facilities and not necessarily from experience, the experience curve is not helpful. But as Sharon Oster pointed out in her book on competitive analysis, the experience curve can help managers analyze costs when efficient learning, rather than efficient machinery, is the source of cost savings.

NASCAR race. That experience inspired the techies to figure out how to reduce the time it takes to switch a plant line from five hours to 20 minutes. This provided an important lesson: Many interesting benchmarking examples can take place far outside of an industry. Often, process improvements involve identifying the best practices in other industries and adapting them for implementation in your own firm. After all, when firms benchmark competitors in their own industry, the end result is often copying and playing catch-up.[14]

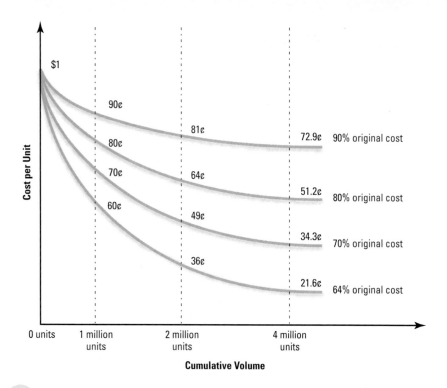

Exhibit 5.4 **Comparing Experience Curve Effects**

A business that strives for a low-cost advantage must attain an absolute cost advantage relative to its rivals.[15] This is typically accomplished by offering a no-frills product or service to a broad target market using standardization to derive the greatest benefits from economies of scale and experience. However, such a strategy may fail if a firm is unable to attain parity on important dimensions of differentiation such as quick responses to customer requests for services or design changes. Strategy Spotlight 5.2 discusses Ryanair—a firm that has developed a very unique overall cost leadership strategy. One might say that it "one upped" Southwest Airlines!

Overall Cost Leadership: Improving Competitive Position vis-à-vis the Five Forces An overall low-cost position enables a firm to achieve above-average returns despite strong competition. It protects a firm against rivalry from competitors, because lower costs allow a firm to earn returns even if its competitors eroded their profits through intense rivalry. A low-cost position also protects firms against powerful buyers. Buyers can exert power to drive down prices only to the level of the next most efficient producer. Also, a low-cost position provides more flexibility to cope with demands from powerful suppliers for input cost increases. The factors that lead to a low-cost position also provide substantial entry barriers from economies of scale and cost advantages. Finally, a low-cost position puts the firm in a favorable position with respect to substitute products introduced by new and existing competitors.

A few examples will illustrate these points. Ryanair's close attention to costs helps to protect them from buyer power and intense rivalry from competitors. Thus, they are able to drive down costs and enjoy relatively high power over their customers. By increasing productivity and lowering unit costs, General Mills (and its competitors in that industry) enjoy greater scale economies and erect higher entry barriers for others. Finally, as competitors

>LO3

How the successful attainment of generic strategies can improve a firm's relative power vis-à-vis the five forces that determine an industry's average profitability.

Ryanair: A Highly Effective Overall Cost Leadership Strategy

Michael O'Leary, CEO of Ryanair Holdings PLC, makes no apologies for his penny-pinching. Want to check luggage? You'll pay up to $9.50 per bag for the privilege. Expecting free drinks and snacks? You'll be disappointed. Even a bottle of water will cost you $3.40. And it is not just the passengers who are affected. Flight crews buy their own uniforms, and staff at Ryanair's Spartan Dublin Airport headquarters must supply their own pens. After a customer sued Ryanair for charging $34 for the use of a wheelchair, the company added a 63 cent "wheelchair levy" to every ticket!

Low-fare U.S. carriers have taken the opposite approach of Ryanair by adding perks such as leather seats, live television, and business class. "All of the low-cost carriers' costs have gotten a little out of control," says Tim Sieber, general manager of The Boyd Group, an Evergreen (Colorado) aviation consultant. Clearly Ryanair hasn't followed its industry peers.

Ryanair has been extremely successful. For 2006, its revenues were $2.1 billion—only one-seventh the size of British Airways (BA). However, its operating margins are 22.7 percent—three times as large as BA's. By 2008,

Sources: Ryanair Annual Report, 2008; Capell, K. 2006. Wal-Mart with Wings. *BusinessWeek.* November 27: 44–45; Kumar, N. 2006. Strategies to Fight Low-Cost Rivals. *Harvard Business Review,* 84(12): 104–113; and *Ryanair Annual Report,* 2006.

Ryanair's revenues had increased to $3.5 billion—a 66% increase over 2006.

What is O'Leary's secret? He thinks like a retailer and charges for every little thing. Imagine the seat as a cell phone: It comes free, or nearly free, but its owner winds up spending money on all sorts of services.

However, what O'Leary loses in seat revenue he more than makes up by turning both his planes and the Ryanair Web site into stores brimming with irresistible goodies, even as he charges for such "perks" as priority boarding and assigned seating.

Sounds outrageous? Probably so, but the strategy is clearly working. Although its average fare is $53, compared with $92 for Southwest Airlines, Ryanair's net margins are, at 18 percent—more than double the 7 percent achieved by Southwest. Says Nick van den Brul, an aviation analyst: "Ryanair is Wal-Mart with wings." As O'Leary says, "You want luxury? Go somewhere else."

A few other Ryanair practices include:

- Flight attendants sell digital cameras ($137.50) and iPocket MP3 players ($165).

- The seats don't recline, seat-back pockets have been removed to cut cleaning time and speed turn-around of the planes, there's no entertainment, and seat-back trays will soon carry ads.

- Ryanair sells more than 98 percent of its tickets online. Its Web site offers insurance, hotels, car rentals, and more—even online bingo.

such as WellPoint lower costs through means such as petitioning the FDA to make certain drugs available over the counter, they become less vulnerable to substitutes such as Internet-based competitors.

>LO4

The pitfalls managers must avoid in striving to attain generic strategies.

Potential Pitfalls of Overall Cost Leadership Strategies   Potential pitfalls of overall cost leadership strategy include:

- ***Too much focus on one or a few value-chain activities.*** Would you consider a person to be astute if he cancelled his newspaper subscription and quit eating out to save money, but then "maxed out" several credit cards, requiring him to pay hundreds of dollars a month in interest charges? Of course not. Similarly, firms need to pay attention to all activities in the value chain. Too often managers make big cuts in operating expenses, but don't question year-to-year spending on capital projects. Or managers may decide to cut selling and marketing expenses but ignore manufacturing expenses. Managers should explore *all* value-chain activities, including relationships among them, as candidates for cost reductions.

- **All rivals share a common input or raw material.** Here, firms are vulnerable to price increases in the factors of production. Since they're competing on costs, they are less able to pass on price increases, because customers can take their business to rivals who have lower prices. Consider the hardship experienced by fertilizer producers when energy prices spiked.[16] A quadrupling of prices to $10 per thousand cubic feet of natural gas forced firms to shut down nearly half of their production capacity. Why? Natural gas accounts for over 70 percent of the fertilizer's cost. According to Betty-Ann Hegge, senior vice president of Potash Corporation of Saskatchewan, Inc., North America's second largest producer, "Many companies are not even covering their cash costs at these prices."
- **The strategy is imitated too easily.** One of the common pitfalls of a cost-leadership strategy is that a firm's strategy may consist of value-creating activities that are easy to imitate.[17] Such was the case with online brokers in recent years.[18] As of early 2001, there were about 140 online brokers, hardly symbolic of an industry where imitation is extremely difficult. But according to Henry McVey, financial services analyst at Morgan Stanley, "We think you need five to ten" online brokers.

    What are some of the dynamics? First, although online brokers were geared up to handle 1.2 million trades a day, volume had shrunk to about 834,000—a 30 percent drop. Thus, competition for business intensified. Second, when the stock market is down, many investors trust their instincts less and seek professional guidance from brokerages that offer differentiated services. Eric Rajendra of A. T. Kearney, an international consulting company, claimed, "The current (online broker) model is inadequate for the pressures the industry is facing now."
- **A lack of parity on differentiation.** As noted earlier, firms striving to attain cost leadership advantages must obtain a level of parity on differentiation. Firms providing online degree programs may offer low prices. However, they may not be successful unless they can offer instruction that is perceived as comparable to traditional providers. For them, parity can be achieved on differentiation dimensions such as reputation and quality and through signaling mechanisms such as accreditation agencies.
- **Erosion of cost advantages when the pricing information available to customers increases.** This is becoming a more significant challenge as the Internet dramatically increases both the quantity and volume of information available to consumers about pricing and cost structures. Life insurance firms offering whole life insurance provide an interesting example.[19] One study found that for each 10 percent increase in consumer use of the Internet, there is a corresponding reduction in insurance prices to consumers of 3 to 5 percent. Recently, the nationwide savings (or, alternatively, reduced revenues to providers) was between $115 and $125 million annually.

Differentiation

As the name implies, a **differentiation strategy** consists of creating differences in the firm's product or service offering by creating something that is perceived *industrywide* as unique and valued by customers.[20] Differentiation can take many forms:

- Prestige or brand image (Adam's Mark hotels, BMW automobiles).[21]
- Technology (Martin guitars, Marantz stereo components, North Face camping equipment).
- Innovation (Medtronic medical equipment, Nokia cellular phones).
- Features (Cannondale mountain bikes, Honda Goldwing motorcycles).
- Customer service (Nordstrom department stores, Sears lawn equipment retailing).
- Dealer network (Lexus automobiles, Caterpillar earthmoving equipment).

Exhibit 5.5 draws on the concept of the value chain as an example of how firms may differentiate themselves in primary and support activities.

differentiation strategy
a firm's generic strategy based on creating differences in the firm's product or service offering by creating something that is perceived *industrywide* as unique and valued by customers.

Exhibit 5.5
Value-Chain
Activities: Examples of
Differentiation

Support Activities

Firm Infrastructure

- Superior MIS—To integrate value-creating activities to improve quality.
- Facilities that promote firm image.
- Widely respected CEO enhances firm reputation.

Human Resource Management

- Programs to attract talented engineers and scientists.
- Provide training and incentives to ensure a strong customer service orientation.

Technology Development

- Superior material handling and sorting technology.
- Excellent applications engineering support.

Procurement

- Purchase of high-quality components to enhance product image.
- Use of most prestigious outlets.

Primary Activities

Inbound Logistics

- Superior material handling operations to minimize damage.
- Quick transfer of inputs to manufacturing process.

Operations

- Flexibility and speed in responding to changes in manufacturing specifications.
- Low defect rates to improve quality.

Outbound Logistics

- Accurate and responsive order processing.
- Effective product replenishment to reduce customer inventory.

Marketing and Sales

- Creative and innovative advertising programs.
- Fostering of personal relationship with key customers.

Service

- Rapid response to customer service requests.
- Complete inventory of replacement parts and supplies.

Source: Adapted from Porter, M.E. 1985. *Competitive Advantage: Creating and Sustaining Superior Performance.* New York: Free Press.

Firms may differentiate themselves along several different dimensions at once.[22] For example, BMW is known for its high prestige, superior engineering, and high-quality automobiles. And, Harley-Davidson differentiates on image and dealer services.[23]

Firms achieve and sustain differentiation advantages and attain above-average performance when their price premiums exceed the extra costs incurred in being unique.[24] For example, both BMW and Harley-Davidson must increase consumer costs to offset added marketing expenses. Thus, a differentiator will always seek out ways of distinguishing itself from similar competitors to justify price premiums greater than the costs incurred by differentiating. The role of design in achieving differentiation is addressed in: Brown, T. 2008. Design thinking. *Harvard Business Review.* 86(6): 84–92. Clearly, a differentiator cannot ignore costs. After all, its premium prices would be eroded by a markedly inferior cost position. Therefore, it must attain a level of cost *parity* relative to competitors. Differentiators can do this by reducing costs in all areas that do not affect differentiation. Porsche, for example, invests heavily in engine design—an area in which its customers demand excellence—but it is less concerned and spends fewer resources in the design of the instrument panel or the arrangement of switches on the radio.[25]

Many companies successfully follow a differentiation strategy.[26] For example, FedEx's CEO and founder, Fred Smith, claims that the key to his firm's success is innovation.[27] He contends his management team didn't understand their real goal when they started the firm in 1971: "We thought that we were selling the transportation of goods; in fact, we were selling peace of mind." They now provide drivers with a handheld computer and a transmitting device so that customers can track their packages from their desktop PCs.

Lexus, a division of Toyota, provides an example of how a firm can strengthen its differentiation strategy by *achieving integration at multiple points along the value chain.*[28] Although the luxury car line was not introduced until the late 1980s, by the early 1990s the cars had already soared to the top of J. D. Power & Associates's customer satisfaction ratings.

> In the spirit of benchmarking, one of Lexus's competitors hired Custom Research Inc. (CRI), a marketing research firm, to find out why Lexus owners were so satisfied. CRI conducted a series of focus groups in which Lexus drivers eagerly offered anecdotes about the special care they experienced from their dealers. It became clear that, although Lexus was manufacturing cars with few mechanical defects, it was the extra care shown by the sales and service staff that resulted in satisfied customers. Such pampering is reflected in the feedback from one customer who claimed she never had a problem with her Lexus. However, upon further probing, she said, "Well, I suppose you could call the four times they had to replace the windshield a 'problem.' But frankly, they took care of it so well and always gave me a loaner car, so I never really considered it a problem until you mentioned it now." An insight gained in CRI's research is that perceptions of product quality (design, engineering, and manufacturing) can be strongly influenced by downstream activities in the value chain (marketing and sales, service).

Strategy Spotlight 5.3 addresses how Netflix, the successful Internet movie rental company, uses crowdsourcing to enhance its differentiation.

Differentiation: Improving Competitive Position vis-à-vis the Five Forces

Differentiation provides protection against rivalry since brand loyalty lowers customer sensitivity to price and raises customer switching costs.[29] By increasing a firm's margins, differentiation also avoids the need for a low-cost position. Higher entry barriers result because of customer loyalty and the firm's ability to provide uniqueness in its products or services.[30] Differentiation also provides higher margins that enable a firm to deal with supplier power. And it reduces buyer power, because buyers lack comparable alternatives and are therefore less price sensitive.[31] Supplier power is also decreased because there is

Crowdsourcing: How Netflix Boosts Its Differentiation

Netflix is well-known for its inviting online presentation and efficient distribution system. However, this highly successful movie-rental company prides itself on its capability to offer subscribers a compact list of films that they are likely to enjoy watching. And it must be working: Netflix sends 35,000 titles a day to its 7.5 million subscribers.

"Imagine that our Website was a brick-and-mortar store," says Netflix vice president, James Bennett. "When people walk through the door, they see DVDs rearrange themselves. The movies that might interest them fly onto the shelves, and all the rest go to the back room."

The movies, of course, don't do the rearranging— that is done by the customers themselves, with an assist from a computer program called Cinematch, which Netflix developed in 2000. Customers are invited to rate each film they watch on a 1 to 5 scale. Cinematch analyzes these ratings, searches through 80,000 titles in inventory, and determines the list of films tailored to the taste of each of the firm's subscribers. By enticing them to rate films, Netflix achieves the latest in business innovation—getting customers to serve themselves.

Netflix is not unique in their use of so-called recommenders. Consider other online retailers such as Amazon, Apple, eBay, and Overstock. All of these rely on their customers for a helping hand in predicting what products the customers will prefer—whether the product is bedding, books, CDs, or DVDs. Customer ratings are used to rank corporate service providers as well.

For all these companies, the recommender system provides more than a chance to create an extra service. It helps them to establish a stronger connection with their customers. And studies have shown that it can substantially increase online sales.

The extent of Netflix's commitment to personalized movie recommendations was made clear in 2006 when it offered a $1 million prize to anyone who could build a system that is at least 10 percent better than Cinematch. The competition is to end in 2011. Thus far, Netflix has received 169 submissions, several of which were an improvement over Cinematch. The best coders quickly managed to improve on the existing system by 5 percent. But, so far, the top contestant—a team of coders from AT&T—had still only improved on Cinematch by 8.43 percent. So close, yet so far . . .

Netflix has also developed another crowdsourcing feature called Friends. Here, subscribers see each other's list of films watched and compare the ratings they have awarded the films—in exchange for suggestions on other films to watch.

Sources: Libert, B. & Spector, J. 2008. *We Are Smarter Than Me.* Philadelphia: Wharton Publishing; and Howe, J. 2008. *Crowdsourcing.* New York: Crown Business.

crowdsourcing

a certain amount of prestige associated with being the supplier to a producer of highly differentiated products and services. Last, differentiation enhances customer loyalty, thus reducing the threat from substitutes.

Our examples illustrate these points. Lexus has enjoyed enhanced power over buyers because its top J. D. Power ranking makes buyers more willing to pay a premium price. This lessens rivalry, since buyers become less price-sensitive. The prestige associated with its brand name also lowers supplier power since margins are high. Suppliers would probably desire to be associated with prestige brands, thus lessening their incentives to drive up prices. Finally, the loyalty and "peace of mind" associated with a service provider such as FedEx makes such firms less vulnerable to rivalry or substitute products and services.

Potential Pitfalls of Differentiation Strategies   Potential pitfalls of a differentiation strategy include:

- ***Uniqueness that is not valuable.*** A differentiation strategy must provide unique bundles of products and/or services that customers value highly. It's not enough just to be "different." An example is Gibson's Dobro bass guitar. Gibson came up with a unique idea: Design and build an acoustic bass guitar with sufficient sound volume so that amplification wasn't necessary. The problem with other acoustic bass guitars was that they did not project enough volume because of the low-frequency bass notes. By adding a resonator plate on the body of the traditional acoustic bass, Gibson increased the sound volume. Gibson believed this product would serve a particular niche market—bluegrass and folk artists who played in small group "jams" with other acoustic musicians. Unfortunately, Gibson soon discovered that its targeted market was content with their existing options: an upright bass amplified with a microphone or an acoustic electric guitar. Thus, Gibson developed a unique product, but it was not perceived as valuable by its potential customers.[32]

- **Too much differentiation.** Firms may strive for quality or service that is higher than customers desire. Thus, they become vulnerable to competitors who provide an appropriate level of quality at a lower price. For example, consider the expensive Mercedes-Benz S-Class, which ranges in price between $75,000 and $125,000.[33] *Consumer Reports* described it as "sumptuous," "quiet and luxurious," and a "delight to drive." The magazine also considered it to be the least reliable sedan available in the United States. According to David Champion, who runs their testing program, the problems are electronic. "The engineers have gone a little wild," he says. "They've put every bell and whistle that they think of, and sometimes they don't have the attention to detail to make these systems work." Some features include: a computer-driven suspension that reduces body roll as the vehicle whips around a corner; cruise control that automatically slows the car down if it gets too close to another car; and seats that are adjustable 14 ways and that are ventilated by a system that uses eight fans.

- **Too high a price premium.** This pitfall is quite similar to too much differentiation. Customers may desire the product, but they are repelled by the price premium. For example, Duracell (a division of Gillette) recently charged too much for batteries.[34] The firm tried to sell consumers on its superior quality products, but the mass market wasn't convinced. Why? The price differential was simply too high. At a CVS drugstore just one block from Gillette's headquarters, a four-pack of Energizer AA batteries was on sale at $2.99 compared with a Duracell four-pack at $4.59. Duracell's market share dropped 2 percent in a recent two-year period, and its profits declined over 30 percent. Clearly, the price/performance proposition Duracell offered customers was not accepted.

- **Differentiation that is easily imitated.** As we noted in Chapter 3, resources that are easily imitated cannot lead to sustainable advantages. Similarly, firms may strive for, and even attain, a differentiation strategy that is successful for a time. However, the advantages are eroded through imitation. Consider Cereality's innovative differentiation strategy of stores which offer a wide variety of cereals and toppings for around $4.00.[35] As one would expect, once their idea proved successful, competitors entered the market because much of the initial risk had already been taken. Rivals include an Iowa City restaurant named the Cereal Cabinet, the Cereal Bowl in Miami, and Bowls: A Cereal Joint in Gainesville, Florida. Says David Roth, one of Cereality's founders: "With any good business idea, you're faced with people who see you've cracked the code and who try to cash in on it."

- **Dilution of brand identification through product-line extensions.** Firms may erode their quality brand image by adding products or services with lower prices and less quality. Although this can increase short-term revenues, it may be detrimental in the long run. Consider Gucci.[36] In the 1980s Gucci wanted to capitalize on its prestigious brand name by launching an aggressive strategy of revenue growth. It added a set of lower-priced canvas goods to its product line. It also pushed goods heavily into department stores and duty-free channels and allowed its name to appear on a host of licensed items such as watches, eyeglasses, and perfumes. In the short term, this

Overall Cost Leadership:

- Too much focus on one or a few value-chain activities.
- All rivals share a common input or raw material.
- The strategy is imitated too easily.
- A lack of parity on differentiation.
- Erosion of cost advantages when the pricing information available to customers increases.

Differentiation:

- Uniqueness that is not valuable.
- Too much differentiation.
- The price premium is too high.
- Differentiation that is easily imitated.
- Dilution of brand identification through product-line extensions.
- Perceptions of differentiation may vary between buyers and sellers.

strategy worked. Sales soared. However, the strategy carried a high price. Gucci's indiscriminate approach to expanding its products and channels tarnished its sterling brand. Sales of its high-end goods (with higher profit margins) fell, causing profits to decline.

- ***Perceptions of differentiation may vary between buyers and sellers.*** The issue here is that "beauty is in the eye of the beholder." Companies must realize that although they may perceive their products and services as differentiated, their customers may view them as commodities. Indeed, in today's marketplace, many products and services have been reduced to commodities.[37] Thus, a firm could overprice its offerings and lose margins altogether if it has to lower prices to reflect market realities.

Exhibit 5.6 summarizes the pitfalls of overall cost leadership and differentiation strategies. In addressing the pitfalls associated with these two generic strategies there is one common, underlying theme. Managers must be aware of the dangers associated with concentrating so much on one strategy that they fail to attain parity on the other.

Focus

focus strategy a firm's generic strategy based on appeal to a narrow market segment within an industry.

A **focus strategy** is based on the choice of a narrow competitive scope within an industry. A firm following this strategy selects a segment or group of segments and tailors its strategy to serve them. The essence of focus is the exploitation of a particular market niche. As you might expect, narrow focus itself (like merely "being different" as a differentiator) is simply not sufficient for above-average performance.

The focus strategy, as indicated in Exhibit 5.1, has two variants. In a cost focus, a firm strives to create a cost advantage in its target segment. In a differentiation focus, a firm seeks to differentiate in its target market. Both variants of the focus strategy rely on providing better service than broad-based competitors who are trying to serve the focuser's target segment. Cost focus exploits differences in cost behavior in some segments, while differentiation focus exploits the special needs of buyers in other segments.

Let's look at examples of two firms that have successfully implemented focus strategies. Network Appliance (NA) has developed a more cost-effective way to store and distribute computer files.[38] Its larger rival, EMC, makes mainframe-style products priced over

Paccar: 'Trucking along. . .' with a Successful Focus Strategy

Paccar, a $15 billion Bellevue, Washington–based heavy-truck maker with about 20 percent of the North American market, has chosen to focus on one group of customers: owner-operators. These are the drivers who own their trucks and contract directly with shippers or serve as subcontractors to larger trucking companies. Such operators have limited clout as truck buyers. They are also less price sensitive because of their strong emotional ties to and economic dependence on the product. They take great pride in their trucks, in which they spend most of their time.

Paccar has invested heavily to develop a variety of features with owner-operators in mind: luxurious sleeper cabins, plush leather seats, noise-insulated cabins, sleek exterior styling, and so forth. At Paccar's extensive network of dealers, prospective buyers use software to select among thousands of options to put their personal signature on their trucks. These customized trucks are built to order, not to stock, and are delivered in six to eight weeks. Paccar's trucks also have aerodynamic designs that reduce fuel consumption, and they maintain their resale value better than other trucks. Paccar's roadside assistance program and

● Paccar's Kenworth and Peterbilt brands of semi tractors have become status symbols at truck stops.

IT-supported system for distributing spare parts reduce the time a truck is out of service. All these are crucial considerations for an owner-operator. Customers pay Paccar a 10 percent premium, and its Kenworth and Peterbilt brands are considered status symbols at truck stops.

Source: Porter, M. E. 2008. The Five Competitive Forces That Shape Strategy. *Harvard Business Review*, 86(1): 78–97.

$1 million that store files and accommodate Internet traffic. NA makes devices that cost under $200,000 for particular storage jobs such as caching (temporary storage) of Internet content. Focusing on such narrow segments has certainly paid off for NA; it has posted a remarkable 20 straight quarters of revenue growth.

Bessemer Trust competes in the private banking industry.[39] A differentiation focuser, it targets families with a minimum of $5 million in assets, who desire both capital preservation and wealth accumulation. In other words, these are not people who want to put all their "eggs in a dot-com basket." Bessemer configures its activities for highly personalized service by assigning one account officer for every 14 families. Meetings are more likely to be held at a client's ranch or yacht than in Bessemer's office. Bessemer offers a wide range of customized services, such as investment management, estate administration, oversight of oil and gas investments, and accounting for race horses and aircraft. Despite the industry's most generous compensation of account officers and the highest personnel cost as a percentage of operating expenses, Bessemer's focused differentiation strategy is estimated to yield the highest return on equity in the industry.

Strategy Spotlight 5.4 discusses Paccar, a highly successful heavy-truck manufacturer that has created a successful focus strategy.

Focus: Improving Competitive Position vis-à-vis the Five Forces   Focus requires that a firm either have a low-cost position with its strategic target, high differentiation, or both. As we discussed with regard to cost and differentiation strategies, these positions provide defenses against each competitive force. Focus is also used to select niches that are least vulnerable to substitutes or where competitors are weakest.

Let's look at our examples to illustrate some of these points. First, Bessemer Trust experienced lower rivalry and greater bargaining power by providing products and services to a targeted market segment that was less price-sensitive. New rivals had difficulty attracting customers away from Bessemer based only on lower prices. Similarly, the brand image and quality that this brand evoked heightened rivals' entry barriers. Additionally, we could reasonably speculate that Bessemer Trust enjoyed some protection against substitute products and services because of their relatively high reputation, brand image, and customer loyalty. With regard to the strategy of cost focus, Network Appliances, the successful rival to EMC in the computer storage industry, was better able to absorb pricing increases from suppliers as a result of its lower cost structure, reducing supplier power.

Potential Pitfalls of Focus Strategies   Potential pitfalls of focus strategies include:

- *Erosion of cost advantages within the narrow segment.* The advantages of a cost focus strategy may be fleeting if the cost advantages are eroded over time. For example, Dell's pioneering direct selling model in the personal computer industry has been eroded by rivals such as Hewlett Packard as they gain experience with Dell's distribution method. Similarly, other firms have seen their profit margins drop as competitors enter their product segment.

- *Even product and service offerings that are highly focused are subject to competition from new entrants and from imitation.* Some firms adopting a focus strategy may enjoy temporary advantages because they select a small niche with few rivals. However, their advantages may be short-lived. A notable example is the multitude of dot-com firms that specialize in very narrow segments such as pet supplies, ethnic foods, and vintage automobile accessories. The entry barriers tend to be low, there is little buyer loyalty, and competition becomes intense. And since the marketing strategies and technologies employed by most rivals are largely nonproprietary, imitation is easy. Over time, revenues fall, profits margins are squeezed, and only the strongest players survive the shakeout.

- *Focusers can become too focused to satisfy buyer needs.* Some firms attempting to attain advantages through a focus strategy may have too narrow a product or service. Consider many retail firms. Hardware chains such as Ace and True Value are losing market share to rivals such as Lowe's and Home Depot that offer a full line of home and garden equipment and accessories. And given the enormous purchasing power of the national chains, it would be difficult for such specialty retailers to attain parity on costs.

Combination Strategies: Integrating Overall Low Cost and Differentiation

>LO5

How firms can effectively combine the generic strategies of overall cost leadership and differentiation.

Perhaps the primary benefit to firms that integrate low-cost and differentiation strategies is the difficulty for rivals to duplicate or imitate.[40] This strategy enables a firm to provide two types of value to customers: differentiated attributes (e.g., high quality, brand identification, reputation) and lower prices (because of the firm's lower costs in value-creating activities). The goal is thus to provide unique value to customers in an efficient manner.[41] Some firms are able to attain both types of advantages simultaneously. For example, superior quality can lead to lower costs because of less need for rework in manufacturing, fewer warranty claims, a reduced need for customer service personnel to resolve customer complaints, and so forth. Thus, the benefits of combining advantages can be additive, instead of merely involving trade-offs. Next, we consider three approaches to combining overall low cost and differentiation.

combination strategies firms' integrations of various strategies to provide multiple types of value to customers.

Automated and Flexible Manufacturing Systems   Given the advances in manufacturing technologies such as CAD/CAM (computer aided design and computer aided manufacturing) as well as information technologies, many firms have been able to manufacture unique products in relatively small quantities at lower costs—a concept known as **mass customization.**[42]

Let's consider Andersen Windows of Bayport, Minnesota—a $1 billion manufacturer of windows for the building industry.[43] Until about 20 years ago, Andersen was a mass producer, in small batches, of a variety of standard windows. However, to meet changing customer needs, Andersen kept adding to its product line. The result was catalogs of ever-increasing size and a bewildering set of choices for both homeowners and contractors. Over a 6-year period, the number of products tripled, price quotes took several hours, and the error rate increased. This not only damaged the company's reputation, but also added to its manufacturing expenses.

mass customization a firm's ability to manufacture unique products in small quantities at low cost.

To bring about a major change, Andersen developed an interactive computer version of its paper catalogs that it sold to distributors and retailers. Salespersons can now customize each window to meet the customer's needs, check the design for structural soundness, and provide a price quote. The system is virtually error free, customers get exactly what they want, and the time to develop the design and furnish a quotation has been cut by 75 percent. Each showroom computer is connected to the factory, and customers are assigned a code number that permits them to track the order. The manufacturing system has been developed to use some common finished parts, but it also allows considerable variation in the final products. Despite its huge investment, Andersen has been able to lower costs, enhance quality and variety, and improve its response time to customers.

Exhibit 5.7 provides other examples of how flexible production systems have enabled firms to successfully engage in mass customization for their customers:[44]

Exploiting the Profit Pool Concept for Competitive Advantage   A profit pool is defined as the total profits in an industry at all points along the industry's value chain.[45] Although the concept is relatively straightforward, the structure of the profit pool can be complex.[46] The potential pool of profits will be deeper in some segments of the value chain than in others, and the depths will vary within an individual segment. Segment profitability

---

• At Nikeid.com, customers can design an athletic or casual shoe to their specifications online, selecting almost every element of the shoe from the material of the sole to the color of the shoelace.
• Eleuria sells custom perfumes. Each product is created in response to a user profile constructed from responses to a survey about habits and preferences. Eleuria then provides a sample at modest cost to verify fit.
• Lands' End offers customized shirts and pants. Consumers specify style parameters, measurements, and fabrics through the firm's website. These settings are saved so that returning users can easily order a duplicate item.
• Cannondale permits consumers to specify the parameters that define a road bike frame, including custom colors and inscriptions. The user specifies the parameters on the firm's website and then arranges for delivery through a dealer.

Exhibit 5.7
Effective Uses of Flexible Production Systems

Source: Randall, T., Terwiesch, C. & Ulrich, K. T. 2005. Principles for User Design of Custom Products. *California Management Review,* 47 (4): 68–85.

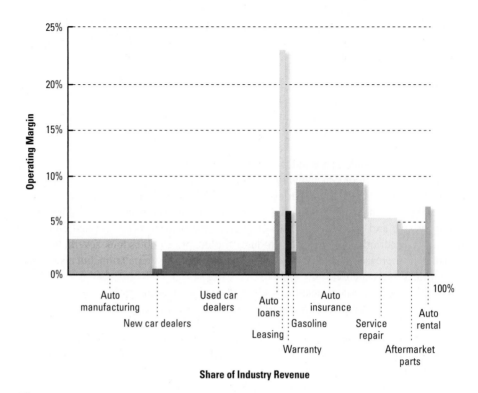

Exhibit 5.8 The U.S. Automobile Industry's Profit Pool

Source: Adapted and reprinted by permission of *Harvard Business Review,* Exhibit from "Profit Pools: A Fresh Look at Strategy," by O. Gadiesh and J. L. Gilbert, May–June 1998. Copyright © 1999 by the Harvard Business School Publishing Corporation; all rights reserved.

may vary widely by customer group, product category, geographic market, or distribution channel. Additionally, the pattern of profit concentration in an industry is very often different from the pattern of revenue generation.

Consider the automobile industry profit pool in Exhibit 5.8. Here we see little relationship between the generation of revenues and capturing of profits. While manufacturing generates most of the revenue, this value activity is far smaller profitwise than other value activities such as financing and extended warranty operations. So while a car manufacturer may be under tremendous pressure to produce cars efficiently, much of the profit (at least proportionately) can be captured in the aforementioned downstream operations. Thus, a carmaker would be ill-advised to focus solely on manufacturing and leave downstream operations to others through outsourcing.

Coordinating the "Extended" Value Chain by Way of Information Technology

Many firms have achieved success by integrating activities throughout the "extended value chain" by using information technology to link their own value chain with the value chains of their customers and suppliers. As noted in Chapter 3, this approach enables a firm to add value not only through its own value-creating activities, but also for its customers and suppliers.

Such a strategy often necessitates redefining the industry's value chain. A number of years ago, Wal-Mart took a close look at its industry's value chain and decided to reframe the competitive challenge.[47] Although its competitors were primarily focused on retailing—merchandising and promotion—Wal-Mart determined that it was not so much in the retailing industry as in the transportation logistics and communications industries.

Here, linkages in the extended value chain became central. That became Wal-Mart's chosen battleground. By redefining the rules of competition that played to its strengths, Wal-Mart has attained competitive advantages and dominates its industry.

Integrated Overall Low-Cost and Differentiation Strategies: Improving Competitive Position vis-à-vis the Five Forces Firms that successfully integrate both differentiation and cost advantages create an enviable position. For example, Wal-Mart's integration of information systems, logistics, and transportation helps it to drive down costs and provide outstanding product selection. This dominant competitive position, serves to erect high entry barriers to potential competitors that have neither the financial nor physical resources to compete head-to-head. Wal-Mart's size—over $400 billion in 2008 sales—provides the chain with enormous bargaining power over suppliers. Its low pricing and wide selection reduce the power of buyers (its customers), because there are relatively few competitors that can provide a comparable cost/value proposition. This reduces the possibility of intense head-to-head rivalry, such as protracted price wars. Finally, Wal-Mart's overall value proposition makes potential substitute products (e.g., Internet competitors) a less viable threat.

Pitfalls of Integrated Overall Cost Leadership and Differentiation Strategies The pitfalls of integrated overall cost leadership and differentiation include:

- *Firms that fail to attain both strategies may end up with neither and become "stuck in the middle."* A key issue in strategic management is the creation of competitive advantages that enable a firm to enjoy above-average returns. Some firms may become "stuck in the middle" if they try to attain both cost and differentiation advantages. An example that we are all familiar with would be the Big 3 U.S. automobile makers. They are plagued by expensive "legacy costs" associated with pension and health care obligations—a central issue in 2008 federal bailout legislation. And, they suffer from long-term customer perceptions of mediocre quality—inferior to their European and Japanese rivals. The troubling quality perceptions persist despite the fact that the Big 3 has attained approximate parity with their Japanese and European competitors in recent J. D. Power surveys.

- *Underestimating the challenges and expenses associated with coordinating value-creating activities in the extended value chain.* Integrating activities across a firm's value chain with the value chain of suppliers and customers involves a significant investment in financial and human resources. Firms must consider the expenses linked to technology investment, managerial time and commitment, and the involvement and investment required by the firm's customers and suppliers. The firm must be confident that it can generate a sufficient scale of operations and revenues to justify all associated expenses.

- *Miscalculating sources of revenue and profit pools in the firm's industry.* Firms may fail to accurately assess sources of revenue and profits in their value chain. This can occur for several reasons. For example, a manager may be biased due to his or her functional area background, work experiences, and educational background. If the manager's background is in engineering, he or she might perceive that proportionately greater revenue and margins were being created in manufacturing, product, and process design than a person whose background is in a "downstream" value-chain activity such as marketing and sales. Or politics could make managers "fudge" the numbers to favor their area of operations. This would make them responsible for a greater proportion of the firm's profits, thus improving their bargaining position.

A related problem is directing an overwhelming amount of managerial time, attention, and resources to value-creating activities that produce the greatest margins—to the detriment of other important, albeit less profitable, activities. For example, a car manufacturer may focus too much on downstream activities, such as warranty fulfillment and financing operations, to the detriment of differentiation and cost of the cars themselves.

How the Internet and Digital Technologies Are Affecting the Competitive Strategies

>LO6

How Internet-enabled business models are being used to improve strategic positioning.

Internet and digital technologies have swept across the economy and now have an impact on how nearly every company conducts its business. These changes have created new cost efficiencies and avenues for differentiation. However, the presence of these technologies is so widespread that it is questionable how any one firm can use them effectively in ways that genuinely set them apart from rivals. Thus, to stay competitive, firms must update their strategies to reflect the new possibilities and constraints that these phenomena represent. In this section, we address both the opportunities and the pitfalls that Internet and digital technologies offer to companies using overall cost leadership, differentiation, and focus strategies. We also briefly consider two major impacts that the Internet is having on business: lowering transaction costs and enabling mass customization.

Overall Cost Leadership

The Internet and digital technologies are creating new opportunities for firms to achieve low-cost advantages by enabling them to manage costs and achieve greater efficiencies. Managing costs, and even changing the cost structures of certain industries, is a key feature of the new digital economy. Most analysts agree that the Internet's ability to lower transaction costs is transforming business. Broadly speaking, *transaction costs* refer to all the various expenses associated with conducting business. It applies not just to buy/sell transactions but to the costs of interacting with every part of a firm's value chain, within and outside the firm. Think about it. Hiring new employees, meeting with customers, ordering supplies, addressing government regulations—all of these exchanges have some costs associated with them. Because business can be conducted differently on the Internet, new ways of saving money are changing the competitive landscape.

Other factors also help to lower transaction costs. The process of disintermediation (in Chapter 2) has a similar effect. Each time intermediaries are used in a transaction, additional costs are added. Removing intermediaries lowers transaction costs. The Internet reduces the costs to search for a product or service, whether it is a retail outlet (as in the case of consumers) or a trade show (as in the case of business-to-business shoppers). Not only is the need for travel eliminated but so is the need to maintain a physical address, whether it's a permanent retail location or a temporary presence at a trade show.

Exhibit 5.9 identifies several types of cost leadership strategies that are made possible by Internet and digital technologies. These cost savings are available throughout a firm's value chain, in both primary and support activities.

Exhibit 5.9

Internet-Enabled Low-Cost Leader Strategies

- Online bidding and order processing are eliminating the need for sales calls and are minimizing sales force expenses.
- Online purchase orders are making many transactions paperless, thus reducing the costs of procurement and paper.
- Direct access to progress reports and the ability for customers to periodically check work in progress is minimizing rework.
- Collaborative design efforts using Internet technologies that link designers, materials suppliers, and manufacturers are reducing the costs and speeding the process of new product development.

Potential Internet-Related Pitfalls for Low-Cost Leaders   One of the biggest threats to low-cost leaders is imitation. This problem is intensified for business done on the Internet. Most of the advantages associated with contacting customers directly, and even capabilities that are software driven (e.g., customized ordering systems or real-time access to the status of work in progress), can be duplicated quickly and without threat of infringement on proprietary information. Another pitfall relates to companies that become overly enamored with using the Internet for cost-cutting. Companies that do so may suffer if they place too much attention on one business activity and ignore others. They may jeopardize customer relations or neglect other cost centers, such as providing services or controlling turnover and recruiting expenses, which then dig into their cost advantages.

Differentiation

For many companies, Internet and digital technologies have enhanced their ability to build brand, offer quality products and services, and achieve other differentiation advantages. Among the most striking trends are new ways to interact with consumers. In particular, the Internet is creating new ways of differentiating by enabling *mass customization,* which improves the response to customer wishes. Mass customization has been growing for years as flexible manufacturing systems have made manufacturing more adaptable and electronic data interchange has made communications more direct. But the Internet has generated a giant leap forward in the amount of control customers can have in influencing the process. Such capabilities are changing the way companies develop unique product and service offerings, build their reputation, and preserve their brand image.

Methods like mass customization are changing how companies go to market and are challenging some of the tried-and-true techniques of differentiation. Traditionally, companies reached customers using high-end catalogs, the showroom floor, personal sales calls and products using prestige packaging, celebrity endorsements, and charity sponsorships. All of these avenues are still available and may still be effective, depending on a firm's competitive environment. But many customers now judge the quality and uniqueness of a product or service by their ability to be involved in its planning and design, combined with speed of delivery and reliable results. Internet and digitally based capabilities are thus changing the way differentiators make exceptional products and achieve superior service. Such improvements are being made at a reasonable cost, allowing firms to achieve parity on the basis of overall cost leadership.

Exhibit 5.10 identifies differentiation activities that are made possible by Internet and digital technologies. Opportunities to differentiate are available in all parts of a company's value chain—both primary and support activities.

Exhibit 5.10
Internet-Enabled Differentiation Strategies

- Personalized online access provides customers with their own "site within a site" in which their prior orders, status of current orders, and requests for future orders are processed directly on the supplier's website.

- Online access to real-time sales and service information is being used to empower the sales force and continually update R&D and technology development efforts.

- Internet-based knowledge management systems that link all parts of the organization are shortening response times and accelerating organization learning.

- Quick online responses to service requests and rapid feedback to customer surveys and product promotions are enhancing marketing efforts.

Potential Internet-Related Pitfalls for Differentiators   Traditional differentiation strategies such as building strong brand identity and prestige pricing have been undermined by Internet-enabled capabilities such as the ability to compare product features side-by-side or bid online for competing services. The sustainability of Internet-based gains from differentiation will deteriorate if companies offer differentiating features that customers don't want or create a sense of uniqueness that customers don't value. The result can be a failed value proposition—the value companies thought they were offering, does not translate into sales.

Focus

A focus strategy targets a narrow market segment with customized products and/or services. With focus strategies, the Internet offers new avenues in which to compete because they can access markets less expensively (low cost) and provide more services and features (differentiation). Some claim that the Internet has opened up a new world of opportunities for niche players who seek to access small markets in a highly specialized fashion.[48] Niche businesses are among the most active users of digital technologies and e-business solutions. According to the ClickZ.com division of Jupitermedia Corporation, 77 percent of small businesses agree that a website is essential for small business success. Small businesses also report that the Internet has helped them grow (58 percent), made them more profitable (51 percent), and helped reduce transaction costs (49 percent).[49] Clearly niche players and small businesses are using the Internet and digital technologies to create more viable focus strategies.

Many aspects of the Internet economy favor focus strategies because niche players and small firms have been able to extend their reach and effectively compete with larger competitors. For example, niche firms have been quicker than Fortune 1000 firms to adopt blogging as a way to create a community and gather customer feedback.[50] Effective use of blogs is an example of how focusers are using the new technology to provide the kinds of advantages that have been the hallmark of a focus strategy in the past—specialized knowledge, rapid response, and strong customer service. Thus, the Internet has provided many firms that pursue focus strategies with new tools for creating competitive advantages.

Exhibit 5.11 outlines several approaches to strategic focusing that are made possible by Internet and digital technologies. Both primary and support activities can be enhanced using the kind of singlemindedness that is characteristic of a focus strategy.

Potential Internet-Related Pitfalls for Focusers   A key danger for focusers using the Internet relates to correctly assessing the size of the online marketplace. Focusers can misread the scope and interests of their target markets. This can cause them to focus on segments that are too narrow to be profitable or to lose their uniqueness in overly broad niches, making them vulnerable to imitators or new entrants.

Exhibit 5.11
Internet-Enabled Focus Strategies

- Permission marketing techniques are focusing sales efforts on specific customers who opt to receive advertising notices.
- Niche portals that target specific groups are providing advertisers with access to viewers with specialized interests.
- Virtual organizing and online "officing" are being used to minimize firm infrastructure requirements.
- Procurement technologies that use Internet software to match buyers and sellers are highlighting specialized buyers and drawing attention to smaller suppliers.

What happens when an e-business focuser tries to overextend its niche? Efforts to appeal to a broader audience by carrying additional inventory, developing additional content, or offering additional services can cause it to lose the cost advantages associated with a limited product or service offering. Conversely, when focus strategies become too narrow, the e-business may have trouble generating enough activity to justify the expense of operating the website.

Are Combination Strategies the Key to E-Business Success?

Because of the changing dynamics presented by digital and Internet-based technologies, new strategic combinations that make the best use of the competitive strategies may hold the greatest promise.[51] Many experts agree that the net effect of the digital economy is *fewer* rather than more opportunities for sustainable advantages.[52] This means strategic thinking becomes more important.

More specifically, the Internet has provided all companies with greater tools for managing costs. So it may be that cost management and control will become more important management tools. In general, this may be good if it leads to an economy that makes more efficient use of its scarce resources. However, for individual companies, it may shave critical percentage points off profit margins and create a climate that makes it impossible to survive, much less achieve sustainable above-average profits.

Many differentiation advantages are also diminished by the Internet. The ability to comparison shop—to check product reviews and inspect different choices with a few clicks of the mouse—is depriving some companies, such as auto dealers, of the unique advantages that were the hallmark of their prior success. Differentiating is still an important strategy, of course. But how firms achieve it may change, and the best approach may be to combine differentiation with other competitive strategies.

Perhaps the greatest beneficiaries are the focusers who can use the Internet to capture a niche that previously may have been inaccessible. However, because the same factors that make it possible for a small niche player to be a contender may make that same niche attractive to a big company. That is, an incumbent firm that previously thought a niche market was not worth the effort may use Internet technologies to enter that segment for a lower cost than in the past. The larger firm can then bring its market power and resources to bear in a way that a smaller competitor cannot match.

A combination strategy challenges a company to carefully blend alternative strategic approaches and remain mindful of the impact of different decisions on the firm's value-creating processes and its extended value-chain activities. Strong leadership is needed to maintain a bird's-eye perspective on a company's overall approach and to coordinate the multiple dimensions of a combination strategy.

Strategy Spotlight 5.5 describes the efforts of Liberty Mutual, a company that used Internet and digital technologies to successfully combine both differentiation and overall low-cost advantages.

Industry Life Cycle Stages: Strategic Implications

The **industry life cycle** refers to the stages of introduction, growth, maturity, and decline that occur over the life of an industry. In considering the industry life cycle, it is useful to think in terms of broad product lines such as personal computers, photocopiers, or long-distance telephone service. Yet the industry life cycle concept can be explored from several levels, from the life cycle of an entire industry to the life cycle of a single variation or model of a specific product or service.

Why are industry life cycles important?[53] The emphasis on various generic strategies, functional areas, value-creating activities, and overall objectives varies over the course of an industry life cycle. Managers must become even more aware of their firm's strengths

industry life cycle
the stages of introduction, growth, maturity, and decline that typically occur over the life of an industry.

Liberty Mutual's Electronic Invoice System: Combining Low Cost and Differentiation Advantages

Boston-based Liberty Mutual Group is a leading global insurer and the sixth largest property and casualty insurer in the United States. Its largest line of business is personal automobile insurance. Liberty Mutual has $85.5 billion in assets and $23.5 billion in annual revenues—ranking the firm 102nd on the Fortune 500 list of the largest corporations.

In 2000, Liberty Mutual became one of the first companies to experiment with electronic invoices. It set up a pilot program with a few law firms to submit its bills through a secured website. These firms, for the most part, handle claims litigation for Liberty, defending its policyholders in lawsuits. Its success with this program convinced Liberty that it could achieve significant cost savings and also pass along differentiating features to its customers and strategic partners. Liberty now processes nearly 400,000 electronic legal-services invoices a year—70 percent of the total invoices that the firm receives.

As expected, the initial transition was quite expensive. The company invested nearly $1 million in the first four years. However, Liberty estimates that the electronic invoice program saves the company $750,000 a year in direct costs by streamlining the distribution, payment, storage, and retrieval of invoices. E-invoices enable Liberty to move from intake to payment with half the staff that it had taken to process paper invoices. The firm has also created new efficiencies by cutting costs resulting from data entry errors, late payments, and overpayments. As a relatively minor issue, Liberty saves more than $20,000 per year on postage, photocopying, archiving, and retrieval costs.

The legal invoices are organized by litigation phase or task—for example, taking a deposition or reporting a witness statement. Work is diced into tiny increments of

six minutes or less. A single invoice that covers a month of complex litigation, for example, can include well over 1,000 lines. However, by building and mining a database of law firm billing practices, Liberty is able to generate a highly granular report card about law firm activities and performance. The new knowledge generated by this system not only increases internal effectiveness but also allows Liberty to provide detailed feedback to clients and other external stakeholders.

Online invoicing has also helped speed up both processing and response time. Liberty can instantaneously see how firms deploy and bill for partners, paralegals, and other staff, how they compare with each other on rates, hours, and case outcomes; and whether, how, and how often they send duplicate invoices or charge for inappropriate services. The system also allows Liberty to instantly review all of the time billed for a particular attorney across many cases, enabling the firm to reconstruct the total time billed to Liberty during a single day. More than once they have found that attorneys have billed more than 24 hours in a day. Liberty is also able to easily expose prohibited formula billing patterns (wherein, for example, they are billed a set amount for a service instead of actual time spent). In two cases in which formula billing was used, Liberty found that there were more than $28,000 in suspected overcharges.

Liberty Mutual is in the process of developing a large database of law firms' billing practices on different types of cases. The database should eventually enable Liberty to evaluate a law firm's billing activities and compare them to the norms of all of its partner firms. With such intelligence, it will be a rather straightforward matter to rate each firm's cost effectiveness in handling certain types of cases and match firms with cases accordingly.

Liberty's decision to use electronic invoices was initially based on the potential for cost savings. But the differentiating advantages it has achieved in terms of rapid feedback, decreased response time, and a knowledge trove in databases that can be electronically mined has provided the company with a fruitful combination of Internet-based strategic advantages.

Sources: Coyle, M., & Angevine, R. 2007. Liberty Mutual Group reports fourth quarter 2006 results. February 26, www.libertymutual.com; and Smunt, T. L., & Sutcliffe, C. L., 2004. There's Gold in Them Bills. *Harvard Business Review*, 82(9): 24–25.

and weaknesses in many areas to attain competitive advantages. For example, firms depend on their research and development (R&D) activities in the introductory stage. R&D is the source of new products and features that everyone hopes will appeal to customers. Firms develop products and services to stimulate consumer demand. Later, during the maturity phase, the functions of the product have been defined, more competitors have entered the market, and competition is intense. Managers then place greater emphasis on production efficiencies and process (as opposed to the product) engineering in order to lower manufacturing costs. This helps to protect the firm's market position and to extend the product life cycle because the firm's lower costs can be passed on to consumers in the form of lower prices, and price-sensitive customers will find the product more appealing.

Exhibit 5.12 illustrates the four stages of the industry life cycle and how factors such as generic strategies, market growth rate, intensity of competition, and overall objectives change over time. Managers must strive to emphasize the key functional areas during each

>LO7
The importance of considering the industry life cycle to determine a firm's business-level strategy and its relative emphasis on functional area strategies and value-creating activities.

Stage\nFactor	Introduction	Growth	Maturity	Decline
Generic strategies	Differentiation	Differentiation	Differentiation Overall cost leadership	Overall cost leadership Focus
Market growth rate	Low	Very large	Low to moderate	Negative
Number of segments	Very few	Some	Many	Few
Intensity of competition	Low	Increasing	Very intense	Changing
Emphasis on product design	Very high	High	Low to moderate	Low
Emphasis on process design	Low	Low to moderate	High	Low
Major functional area(s) of concern	Research and development	Sales and marketing	Production	General management and finance
Overall objective	Increase market awareness	Create consumer demand	Defend market share and extend product life cycles	Consolidate, maintain, harvest, or exit

Exhibit 5.12 Stages of the Industry Life Cycle

of the four stages and to attain a level of parity in all functional areas and value-creating activities. For example, although controlling production costs may be a primary concern during the maturity stage, managers should not totally ignore other functions such as marketing and R&D. If they do, they can become so focused on lowering costs that they miss market trends or fail to incorporate important product or process designs. Thus, the firm may attain low-cost products that have limited market appeal.

It is important to point out a caveat. While the life cycle idea is analogous to a living organism (i.e., birth, growth, maturity, and death), the comparison has limitations.[54] Products and services go through many cycles of innovation and renewal. Typically, only fad products have a single life cycle. Maturity stages of an industry can be "transformed" or followed by a stage of rapid growth if consumer tastes change, technological innovations take place, or new developments occur. The cereal industry is a good example. When medical research indicated that oat consumption reduced a person's cholesterol, sales of Quaker Oats increased dramatically.[55]

Strategies in the Introduction Stage

In the **introduction stage,** products are unfamiliar to consumers.[56] Market segments are not well defined, and product features are not clearly specified. The early development of an industry typically involves low sales growth, rapid technological change, operating losses, and the need for strong sources of cash to finance operations. Since there are few players and not much growth, competition tends to be limited.

Success requires an emphasis on research and development and marketing activities to enhance awareness. The challenge becomes one of (1) developing the product and finding a way to get users to try it, and (2) generating enough exposure so the product emerges as the "standard" by which all other rivals' products are evaluated.

There's an advantage to being the "first mover" in a market.[57] It led to Coca-Cola's success in becoming the first soft-drink company to build a recognizable global brand and enabled Caterpillar to get a lock on overseas sales channels and service capabilities.

However, there can also be a benefit to being a "late mover." Target carefully considered its decision to delay its Internet strategy. Compared to its competitors Wal-Mart and Kmart, Target was definitely an industry laggard. But things certainly turned out well:[58]

> By waiting, Target gained a late mover advantage. The store was able to use competitors' mistakes as its own learning curve. This saved money, and customers didn't seem to mind the wait: When Target finally opened its website, it quickly captured market share from both Kmart and Wal-Mart Internet shoppers. Forrester Research Internet analyst Stephen Zrike commented, "There's no question, in our mind, that Target has a far better understanding of how consumers buy online."

Examples of products currently in the introductory stages of the industry life cycle include electric vehicles, solar panels, and high-definition television (HDTV).

Strategies in the Growth Stage

The **growth stage** is characterized by strong increases in sales. Such potential attracts other rivals. In the growth stage, the primary key to success is to build consumer preferences for specific brands. This requires strong brand recognition, differentiated products, and the financial resources to support a variety of value-chain activities such as marketing and sales, and research and development. Whereas marketing and sales initiatives were mainly directed at spurring *aggregate* demand—that is, demand for all such products in the introduction stage—efforts in the growth stage are directed toward stimulating *selective* demand, in which a firm's product offerings are chosen instead of a rival's.

Revenues increase at an accelerating rate because (1) new consumers are trying the product and (2) a growing proportion of satisfied consumers are making repeat purchases.[59]

In general, as a product moves through its life cycle, the proportion of repeat buyers to new purchasers increases. Conversely, new products and services often fail if there are relatively few repeat purchases. For example, Alberto-Culver introduced Mr. Culver's Sparklers, which were solid air fresheners that looked like stained glass. Although the product quickly went from the introductory to the growth stage, sales collapsed. Why? Unfortunately, there were few repeat purchasers because buyers treated them as inexpensive window decorations, left them there, and felt little need to purchase new ones. Examples of products currently in the growth stage include Internet servers and personal digital assistants (e.g., Palm Pilots).

Strategies in the Maturity Stage

In the **maturity stage** aggregate industry demand softens. As markets become saturated, there are few new adopters. It's no longer possible to "grow around" the competition, so direct competition becomes predominant.[60] With few attractive prospects, marginal competitors exit the market. At the same time, rivalry among existing rivals intensifies because of fierce price competition at the same time that expenses associated with attracting new buyers are rising. Advantages based on efficient manufacturing operations and process engineering become more important for keeping costs low as customers become more price sensitive. It also becomes more difficult for firms to differentiate their offerings, because users have a greater understanding of products and services.

An article in *Fortune* magazine that addressed the intensity of rivalry in mature markets was aptly titled "A Game of Inches." It stated, "Battling for market share in a slowing industry can be a mighty dirty business. Just ask laundry soap archrivals Unilever and Procter & Gamble."[61] These two firms have been locked in a battle for market share since 1965. Why is the competition so intense? There is not much territory to gain and industry sales were flat. An analyst noted, "People aren't getting any dirtier." Thus, the only way to win is to take market share from the competition. To increase its share, Procter & Gamble (P&G) spends $100 million a year promoting its Tide brand on television, billboards, buses, magazines, and the Internet. But Unilever isn't standing still. Armed with an $80 million budget, it launched a soap tablet product named Wisk Dual Action Tablets. For example, it delivered samples of this product to 24 million U.S. homes in Sunday newspapers, followed by a series of TV ads. P&G launched a counteroffensive with Tide Rapid Action Tablets ads showed in side-by-side comparisons of the two products dropped into beakers of water. In the promotion, P&G claimed that its product is superior because it dissolves faster than Unilever's product.

Although this is only one example, many product classes and industries, including consumer products such as beer, automobiles, and televisions, are in maturity.

Firms do not need to be "held hostage" to the life-cycle curve. By positioning or repositioning their products in unexpected ways, firms can change how customers mentally categorize them. Thus, firms are able to rescue products floundering in the maturity phase of their life cycles and return them to the growth phase.

Two positioning strategies that managers can use to affect consumers' mental shifts are **reverse positioning,** which strips away "sacred" product attributes while adding new ones, and **breakaway positioning,** which associates the product with a radically different category.[62] We discuss each of these positioning strategies below and then provide an example of each in Strategy Spotlight 5.6.

Reverse Positioning   This assumes that although customers may desire more than the baseline product, they don't necessarily want an endless list of features. Such companies make the creative decision to step off the augmentation treadmill and shed product attributes that the rest of the industry considers sacred. Then, once a product is returned to its baseline state, the stripped-down product adds one or more carefully selected attributes that

maturity stage
the third stage of the product life cycle characterized by (1) slowing demand growth, (2) saturated markets, (3) direct competition, (4) price competition, and (5) strategic emphasis on efficient operations.

reverse positioning
a break in industry tendency to continuously augment products, characteristic of the product life cycle, by offering products with fewer product attributes and lower prices.

breakaway positioning a break in industry tendency to incrementally improve products along specific dimensions, characteristic of the product life cycle, by offering products that are still in the industry but that are perceived by customers as being different.

would usually be found only in a highly augmented product. Such an unconventional combination of attributes allows the product to assume a new competitive position within the category and move backward from maturity into a growth position on the life cycle curve.

Breakaway Positioning   As noted above, with reverse positioning, a product establishes a unique position in its category but retains a clear category membership. However, with breakaway positioning, a product escapes its category by deliberately associating with a different one. Thus, managers leverage the new category's conventions to change both how products are consumed and with whom they compete. Instead of merely seeing the breakaway product as simply an alternative to others in its category, consumers perceive it as altogether different.

When a breakaway product is successful in leaving its category and joining a new one, it is able to redefine its competition. Similar to reverse positioning, this strategy permits the product to shift backward on the life-cycle curve, moving from the rather dismal maturity phase to a thriving growth opportunity.

Strategy Spotlight 5.6 provides examples of reverse and breakaway positioning.

Strategies in the Decline Stage

Although all decisions in the phases of an industry life cycle are important, they become particularly difficult in the **decline stage.** Firms must face up to the fundamental strategic choices of either exiting or staying and attempting to consolidate their position in the industry.[63]

decline stage the fourth stage of the product life cycle characterized by (1) falling sales and profits, (2) increasing price competition, and (3) industry consolidation.

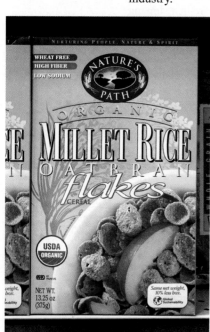

● Many consumer food products such as cereal are in the mature stage of the product life cycle. However, some organic products are enjoying high rates of growth.

The decline stage occurs when industry sales and profits begin to fall. Typically, changes in the business environment are at the root of an industry or product group entering this stage.[64] Changes in consumer tastes or a technological innovation can push a product into decline. Typewriters have entered into the decline stage because of the word processing capabilities of personal computers. Compact disks have forced cassette tapes into decline in the prerecorded music industry, and digital video disks (DVDs) are replacing compact disks. About 30 years earlier, of course, cassette tapes had led to the demise of long-playing records (LPs).

Products in the decline stage often consume a large share of management time and financial resources relative to their potential worth. Sales and profits decline. Also, competitors may start drastically cutting their prices to raise cash and remain solvent. The situation is further aggravated by the liquidation of assets, including inventory, of some of the competitors that have failed. This further intensifies price competition.

In the decline stage, a firm's strategic options become dependent on the actions of rivals. If many competitors leave the market, sales and profit opportunities increase. On the other hand, prospects are limited if all competitors remain.[65] If some competitors merge, their increased market power may erode the opportunities for the remaining players. Managers must carefully monitor the actions and intentions of competitors before deciding on a course of action.

Four basic strategies are available in the decline phase: *maintaining, harvesting, exiting,* or *consolidating.*[66]

- ***Maintaining*** refers to keeping a product going without significantly reducing marketing support, technological development, or other investments, in the hope that competitors will eventually exit the market. Many offices, for example, still use typewriters for filling out forms and other purposes that cannot be completed on a PC. In some rural

Reverse and Breakaway Positioning: How to Avoid Being Held Hostage to the Life-Cycle Curve

When firms adopt a reverse or breakaway positioning strategy, there is typically no pretense about what they are trying to accomplish. In essence, they subvert convention through unconventional promotions, prices, and attributes. That becomes a large part of their appeal—a cleverly positioned product offering. Next we discuss Commerce Bank's reverse positioning and Swatch's breakaway positioning.

Commerce Bank

While most banks offer dozens of checking and savings accounts and compete by trying to offer the highest interest rates, Commerce Bank takes a totally different approach. It pays among the lowest rates in its market. Further, it offers a very limited product line—just four checking accounts, for example. One would think that such a stingy approach would seem to scare off customers. However, Commerce Bank has been very successful. Between 1999 and 2005, it expanded from 120 to 373 branches and its total assets have soared from $5.6 billion to $39 billion.

How has it been so successful? It has stripped away all of what customers expect—lots of choices and peak interest rates and it has *reverse positioned* itself as "the most convenient bank in America." It's open seven days a week, including evenings until 8 p.m. You can get a debit card while you wait. And, when it rains, an escort with an umbrella will escort you to your car. Further, the bank offers free coffee, newspapers, and most of the branches

Sources: Moon, Y. 2005. Break Free from the Product Life Cycle. *Harvard Business Review*, 83(5): 87–94; Commerce Bancorp, Inc. www.hoovers.com; Swatch. en.wikipedia.org; and www.commercebank.com.

have free coin-counting machines that customers love (in one recent week, customers fed the machines a total of $28 million in loose change). Not too surprisingly, despite the inferior rates and few choices, new customers are flocking to the bank.

Swatch

Interestingly, the name "Swatch" is often misconstrued as a contraction of the words *Swiss watch*. However, Nicholas Hayek, Chairman, affirms that the original contraction was "Second Watch"—the new watch was introduced as a new concept of watches as casual, fun, and relatively disposable accessories. And therein lies Swatch's *breakaway positioning*.

When Swatch was launched in 1983, Swiss watches were marketed as a form of jewelry. They were serious, expensive, enduring, and discreetly promoted. Once a customer purchased one, it lasted a lifetime. Swatch changed all of that by defining its watches as playful fashion accessories which were showily promoted. They inspired impulse buying—customers would often purchase half a dozen in different designs. Their price—$40 when the brand was introduced—expanded Swatch's reach beyond its default category (watches as high-end jewelry) and moved it into the fashion accessory category, where it has different customers and competitors. Swatch was the official timekeeper of the 1996, 2000, and 2004 Summer Olympics.

Today, The Swatch Group is the largest watch company in the world. It has acquired many brands over the years including Omega, Longines, Calvin Klein, and Hamilton. Revenues have grown to $3.6 billion in 2005 and net income has increased to $500 million. And it remains on a roll. As of February 2007, its stock had soared 42 percent over the prior 52-week period.

---

areas, rotary (or dial) telephones persist because of the older technology used in central switching offices. Thus, there may still be the potential for revenues and profits.

- *Harvesting* involves obtaining as much profit as possible and requires that costs be reduced quickly. Managers should consider the firm's value-creating activities and cut associated budgets. Value-chain activities to consider are primary (e.g., operations, sales and marketing) and support (e.g., procurement, technology development). The objective is to wring out as much profit as possible.
- *Exiting the market* involves dropping the product from a firm's portfolio. Since a residual core of consumers exist, eliminating it should be carefully considered. If the firm's exit involves product markets that affect important relationships with other product markets in the corporation's overall portfolio, an exit could have

repercussions for the whole corporation. For example, it may involve the loss of valuable brand names or human capital with a broad variety of expertise in many value-creating activities such as marketing, technology, and operations.

- **Consolidation** involves one firm acquiring at a reasonable price the best of the surviving firms in an industry. This enables firms to enhance market power and acquire valuable assets. One example of a consolidation strategy took place in the defense industry in the early 1990s. As the cliché suggests, "peace broke out" at the end of the Cold War and overall U.S. defense spending levels plummeted.[67] Many companies that make up the defense industry saw more than 50 percent of their market disappear. Only one-quarter of the 120,000 companies that once supplied the Department of Defense still serve in that capacity; the others have shut down their defense business or dissolved altogether. But one key player, Lockheed Martin, became a dominant rival by pursuing an aggressive strategy of consolidation. During the 1990s, it purchased 17 independent entities, including General Dynamics' tactical aircraft and space systems divisions, GE Aerospace, Goodyear Aerospace, and Honeywell ElectroOptics. These combinations enabled Lockheed Martin to emerge as the top provider to three governmental customers: the Department of Defense, the Department of Energy, and NASA.

Examples of products currently in the decline stage of the industry life cycle include automotive spark plugs (replaced by electronic fuel ignition), videocassette recorders (replaced by digital video disk recorders), and personal computer zip drives (replaced by compact disk read-write drives). And, as we mentioned previously, compact disks are being replaced by digital video disks (DVDs).

The introduction of new technologies and associated products does not always mean that old technologies quickly fade away. Research shows that in a number of cases, old technologies actually enjoy a very profitable "last gasp."[68] Examples include mainframe computers (versus minicomputers and PCs), coronary artery bypass graft surgery (versus angioplasty), and CISC (Complex Instruction Set Computing) architecture in computer processors versus RISC (Reduced Instruction Set Computing). In each case, the advent of new technology prompted predictions of the demise of the older technology, but each of these has proved to be resilient survivors. What accounts for their continued profitability and survival?

Retreating to more defensible ground is one strategy that firms specializing in technologies threatened with rapid obsolescence have followed. For example, while angioplasty may be appropriate for relatively healthier patients with blocked arteries, sicker, higher-risk patients seem to benefit more from coronary artery bypass graft surgery. This enabled the surgeons to concentrate on the more difficult cases and improve the technology itself. The advent of television unseated the radio as the major source of entertainment from American homes. However, the radio has survived and even thrived in venues where people are also engaged in other activities, such as driving.

Using the new to improve the old is a second approach. Carburetor manufacturers have improved the fuel efficiency of their product by incorporating electronic controls that were originally developed for electronic fuel injection systems. Similarly, CISC computer chip manufacturers have adopted many features from RISC chips.

Improving the price-performance trade-off is a third approach. IBM continues to make money selling mainframes long after their obituary was written. It retooled the technology using low-cost microprocessors and cut their prices drastically. Further, it invested and updated the software, enabling them to offer clients such as banks better performance and lower costs.

Clearly, "last gasps" may not necessarily translate into longer term gains, as the experience of the integrated steel mills suggests. When the first mini-mills appeared, integrated steel mills shifted to higher margin steel, but eventually mini-mills entered even the last strongholds of the integrated steel mills.

Turnaround Strategies

A **turnaround strategy** involves reversing performance decline and reinvigorating growth toward profitability. A need for turnaround may occur at any stage in the life cycle but is more likely to occur during maturity or decline.

Most turnarounds require a firm to carefully analyze the external and internal environments.[69] The external analysis leads to identification of market segments or customer groups that may still find the product attractive.[70] Internal analysis results in actions aimed at reduced costs and higher efficiency. A firm needs to undertake a mix of both internally and externally oriented actions to effect a turnaround.[71] In effect, the cliché "you can't shrink yourself to greatness" applies.

A study of 260 mature businesses in need of a turnaround identified three strategies used by successful companies.[72]

turnaround strategy a strategy that reverses a firm's decline in performance and returns it to growth and profitability.

- *Asset and cost surgery.* Very often, mature firms tend to have assets that do not produce any returns. These include real estate, buildings, etc. Outright sales or sale and leaseback free up considerable cash and improve returns. Investment in new plants and equipment can be deferred. Firms in turnaround situations try to aggressively cut administrative expenses and inventories and speed up collection of receivables. Costs also can be reduced by outsourcing production of various inputs for which market prices may be cheaper than in-house production costs.

- *Selective product and market pruning.* Most mature or declining firms have many product lines that are losing money or are only marginally profitable. One strategy is to discontinue such product lines and focus all resources on a few core profitable areas. For example, in the early 1980s, faced with possible bankruptcy, Chrysler Corporation sold off all its nonautomotive businesses as well as all its production facilities abroad. Focus on the North American market and identification of a profitable niche—namely, minivans—were keys to their eventual successful turnaround.

- *Piecemeal productivity improvements.* There are many ways in which a firm can eliminate costs and improve productivity. Although individually these are small gains, they cumulate over a period of time to substantial gains. Improving business processes by reengineering them, benchmarking specific activities against industry leaders, encouraging employee input to identify excess costs, increasing capacity utilization, and improving employee productivity lead to a significant overall gain.

>LO8
The need for turnaround strategies that enable a firm to reposition its competitive position in an industry.

Software maker Intuit is a case of a quick but well-implemented turnaround strategy. After stagnating and stumbling during the dot-com boom, Intuit, which is known for its Quickbook and Turbotax software, hired Stephen M. Bennett, a 22-year GE veteran, in 1999. He immediately discontinued Intuit's online finance, insurance, and bill-paying operations that were losing money. Instead, he focused on software for small businesses that employ less than 250 people. He also instituted a performance-based reward system that greatly improved employee productivity. Within a few years, Intuit was once again making substantial profits and its stock was up 42 percent.[73]

Even when an industry is in overall decline, pockets of profitability remain. These are segments with customers who are relatively price insensitive. For example, the replacement demand for vacuum tubes affords its manufacturers an opportunity to earn above normal returns although the product itself is technologically obsolete. Surprisingly, within declining industries, there may still be segments that are either stable or growing. Although fountain pens ceased to be the writing instrument of choice a long time ago, the fountain pen industry has successfully reconceptualized the product as a high margin luxury item that signals accomplishment and success. In the final analysis, every business has the potential for rejuvenation. But it takes creativity, persistence, and most of all a clear strategy to translate that potential into reality.

Reflecting on Career Implications . . .

- *Types of Competitive Advantage:* Always be aware of your organization's business-level strategy. What do you do to help your firm either increase differentiation or lower costs? What are some ways that your role in the firm can help realize these outcomes?
- *Combining Sources of Competitive Advantage:* Are you engaged in activities that simultaneously help your organization increase differentiation and lower costs?
- *Industry Life Cycle:* If your firm is in the mature stage of the industry life cycle, can you think of ways to enhance your firm's level of differentiation in order to make customers less price sensitive to your organization's goods and services?
- *Industry Life Cycle:* If you sense that your career is maturing (or in the decline phase!), what actions can you take to restore career growth and momentum (e.g., training, mentoring, professional networking)? Should you actively consider professional opportunities in other industries?

Summary

How and why firms outperform each other goes to the heart of strategic management. In this chapter, we identified three generic strategies and discussed how firms are able not only to attain advantages over competitors, but also to sustain such advantages over time. Why do some advantages become long-lasting while others are quickly imitated by competitors?

The three generic strategies—overall cost leadership, differentiation, and focus—form the core of this chapter. We began by providing a brief description of each generic strategy (or competitive advantage) and furnished examples of firms that have successfully implemented these strategies. Successful generic strategies invariably enhance a firm's position vis-à-vis the five forces of that industry—a point that we stressed and illustrated with examples. However, as we pointed out, there are pitfalls to each of the generic strategies. Thus, the sustainability of a firm's advantage is always challenged because of imitation or substitution by new or existing rivals. Such competitor moves erode a firm's advantage over time.

We also discussed the viability of combining (or integrating) overall cost leadership and generic differentiation strategies. If successful, such integration can enable a firm to enjoy superior performance and improve its competitive position. However, this is challenging, and managers must be aware of the potential downside risks associated with such an initiative.

The way companies formulate and deploy strategies is changing because of the impact of the Internet and digital technologies in many industries. Further, Internet technologies are enabling the mass customization capabilities of greater numbers of competitors. Focus strategies are likely to increase in importance because the Internet provides highly targeted and lower-cost access to narrow or specialized markets. These strategies are not without their pitfalls, however, and firms need to understand the dangers as well as the potential benefits of Internet-based approaches.

The concept of the industry life cycle is a critical contingency that managers must take into account in striving to create and sustain competitive advantages. We identified the four stages of the industry life cycle—introduction, growth, maturity, and decline—and suggested how these stages can play a role in decisions that managers must make at the business level. These include overall strategies as well as the relative emphasis on functional areas and value-creating activities.

When a firm's performance severely erodes, turnaround strategies are needed to reverse its situation and enhance its competitive position. We have discussed three approaches—asset cost surgery, selective product and market pruning, and piecemeal productivity improvements.

Summary Review Questions

1. Explain why the concept of competitive advantage is central to the study of strategic management.
2. Briefly describe the three generic strategies—overall cost leadership, differentiation, and focus.
3. Explain the relationship between the three generic strategies and the five forces that determine the average profitability within an industry.
4. What are some of the ways in which a firm can attain a successful turnaround strategy?
5. Describe some of the pitfalls associated with each of the three generic strategies.
6. Can firms combine the generic strategies of overall cost leadership and differentiation? Why or why not?
7. Explain why the industry life cycle concept is an important factor in determining a firm's business-level strategy.

Key Terms

overall cost leadership, 160
experience curve, 160
competitive parity, 160
differentiation strategy, 165
focus strategy, 170
combination strategies, 173
mass customization, 173
industry life cycle, 179
introduction stage, 182
growth stage, 182
maturity stage, 183
reverse positioning, 183
breakaway positioning, 183
decline stage, 184
consolidation strategy, 186
turnaround strategy, 187

Experiential Exercise

What are some examples of primary and support activities that enable Nucor, a $23 billion steel manufacturer, to achieve a low-cost strategy? (Fill in table below.)

Application Questions Exercises

1. Go to the Internet and look up www.walmart.com. How has this firm been able to combine overall cost leadership and differentiation strategies?
2. Choose a firm with which you are familiar in your local business community. Is the firm successful in following one (or more) generic strategies? Why or why not? What do you think are some of the challenges it faces in implementing these strategies in an effective manner?
3. Think of a firm that has attained a differentiation focus or cost focus strategy. Are their advantages sustainable? Why? Why not? (*Hint:* Consider its position vis-à-vis Porter's five forces.)
4. Think of a firm that successfully achieved a combination overall cost leadership and differentiation strategy. What can be learned from this example? Are these advantages sustainable? Why? Why not? (*Hint:* Consider its competitive position vis-à-vis Porter's five forces.)

Value-Chain Activity	Yes/No	How Does Nucor Create Value for the Customer?
Primary:		
Inbound logistics		
Operations		
Outbound logistics		
Marketing and sales		
Service		
Support:		
Procurement		
Technology development		
Human resource management		
General administration		

Ethics Questions

1. Can you think of a company that suffered ethical consequences as a result of an overemphasis on a cost leadership strategy? What do you think were the financial and nonfinancial implications?

2. In the introductory stage of the product life cycle, what are some of the unethical practices that managers could engage in to enhance their firm's market position? What could be some of the long-term implications of such actions?

References

1. Jensen, C. 2008. Michelin giving up on PAX run-flat tires. nytimes.com, April 20: np; McGrath, R. 2008. Michelin PAX run-flat: A stillborn revolution. Ritamcgrath.com; Matlack, C. 2004. Michelin: New rubber hits the road. Businessweek.com, August 16: np; and Michelin says no to PAX run-flats. 2007. notchconsulting.wordpress.com, November 20: np.

2. For a recent perspective by Porter on competitive strategy, refer to Porter, M. E. 1996. What is strategy? *Harvard Business Review*, 74(6): 61–78.

3. For insights into how a start-up is using solar technology, see: Gimbel, B. 2009. Plastic power. *Fortune*, February 2: 34.

4. Useful insights on strategy in an economic downturn are in: Rhodes, D. & Stelter, D. 2009. Seize advantage in a downturn. *Harvard Business Review*, 87(2): 50–58.

5. Some useful ideas on maintaining competitive advantages can be found in Ma, H. & Karri, R. 2005. Leaders beware: Some sure ways to lose your competitive advantage. *Organizational Dynamics*, 343(1): 63–76.

6. Miller, A. & Dess, G. G. 1993. Assessing Porter's model in terms of its generalizability, accuracy, and simplicity. *Journal of Management Studies*, 30(4): 553–585.

7. Cendrowski, S. 2008. Extreme retailing. *Fortune*, March 31: 14.

8. For insights on how discounting can erode a firm's performance, read: Stibel, J. M. & Delgrosso, P. 2008. Discounts can be dangerous. *Harvard Business Review*, 66(12): 31.

9. For a scholarly discussion and analysis of the concept of competitive parity, refer to Powell, T. C.

2003. Varieties of competitive parity. *Strategic Management Journal*, 24(1): 61–86.

10. Rao, A. R., Bergen, M. E., & Davis, S. 2000. How to fight a price war. *Harvard Business Review*, 78(2): 107–120.

11. Marriot, J. W. Jr. Our competitive strength: Human capital. A speech given to the Detroit Economic Club on October 2, 2000.

12. Whalen, C. J., Pascual, A. M., Lowery, T., & Muller, J. 2001. The top 25 managers. *BusinessWeek*, January 8: 63.

13. Ibid.

14. For an interesting perspective on the need for creative strategies, refer to Hamel, G. & Prahalad, C. K. 1994. *Competing for the Future*. Boston: Harvard Business School Press.

15. Interesting insights on Wal-Mart's effective cost leadership strategy are found in: Palmeri, C. 2008. Wal-Mart is up for this downturn. *BusinessWeek*, November 6: 34.

16. Symonds, W. C., Arndt, M., Palmer, A. T., Weintraub, A., & Holmes, S. 2001. Trying to break the choke hold. *BusinessWeek*, January 22: 38–39.

17. For a perspective on the sustainability of competitive advantages, refer to Barney, J. 1995. Looking inside for competitive advantage. *Academy of Management Executive*, 9(4): 49–61.

18. Thornton, E., 2001, Why e-brokers are broker and broker. *BusinessWeek*, January 22: 94.

19. Koretz, G. 2001. E-commerce: The buyer wins. *BusinessWeek*, January 8: 30.

20. For an "ultimate" in differentiated services, consider time shares in exotic automobiles such as Lamborghinis and Bentleys. Refer to: Stead,

D. 2008. My Lamborghini—today, anyway. *BusinessWeek*, January 18:17.

21. For an interesting perspective on the value of corporate brands and how they may be leveraged, refer to Aaker, D. A. 2004, *California Management Review*, 46(3): 6–18.

22. A unique perspective on differentiation strategies is: Austin, R. D. 2008. High margins and the quest for aesthetic coherence. *Harvard Business Review*, 86(1): 18–19.

23. MacMillan, I. & McGrath, R. 1997. Discovering new points of differentiation. *Harvard Business Review*, 75(4): 133–145; Wise, R. & Baumgarter, P. 1999. Beating the clock: Corporate responses to rapid change in the PC industry. *California Management Review*, 42(1): 8–36.

24. For a discussion on quality in terms of a company's software and information systems, refer to Prahalad, C. K. & Krishnan, M. S. 1999. The new meaning of quality in the information age. *Harvard Business Review*, 77(5): 109–118.

25. Taylor, A., III. 2001. Can you believe Porsche is putting its badge on this car? *Fortune*, February 19: 168–172.

26. Ward, S., Light, L., & Goldstine, J. 1999. What high-tech managers need to know about brands. *Harvard Business Review*, 77(4): 85–95.

27. Rosenfeld, J. 2000. Unit of one. *Fast Company*, April: 98.

28. Markides, C. 1997. Strategic innovation. *Sloan Management Review*, 38(3): 9–23.

29. Bonnabeau, E., Bodick, N., & Armstrong, R. W. 2008. A more rational approach to new-product development. *Harvard Business Review*. 66(3): 96–102.

30. Insights on Google's innovation are in: Iyer, B. & Davenport, T. H. 2008. Reverse engineering Google's innovation machine. *Harvard Business Review*. 66(4): 58–68.

31. A discussion of how a firm used technology to create product differentiation is in: Mehta, S. N. 2009. Under Armor reboots. *Fortune*. February 2: 29–33. (5)

32. The authors would like to thank Scott Droege, a faculty member at Western Kentucky University, for providing this example.

33. Flint, J. 2004. Stop the nerds. *Forbes,* July 5: 80; and, Fahey, E. 2004. Overengineering 101. *Forbes,* December 13: 62.

34. Symonds, W. C. 2000. Can Gillette regain its voltage? *BusinessWeek,* October 16: 102–104.

35. Caplan, J. 2006. In a real crunch. *Inside Business,* July: A37–A38.

36. Gadiesh, O. & Gilbert, J. L. 1998. Profit pools: A fresh look at strategy. *Harvard Business Review,* 76(3): 139–158.

37. Colvin, G. 2000. Beware: You could soon be selling soybeans. *Fortune,* November 13: 80.

38. Whalen et al., op. cit.: 63.

39. Porter, M. E. 1996. What is strategy? *Harvard Business Review,* 74(6): 61–78.

40. Hall, W. K. 1980. Survival strategies in a hostile environment, *Harvard Business Review,* 58: 75–87; on the paint and allied products industry, see Dess, G. G. & Davis, P. S. 1984. Porter's (1980) generic strategies as determinants of strategic group membership and organizational performance. *Academy of Management Journal,* 27: 467–488; for the Korean electronics industry, see Kim, L. & Lim, Y. 1988. Environment, generic strategies, and performance in a rapidly developing country: A taxonomic approach. *Academy of Management Journal,* 31: 802–827; Wright, P., Hotard, D., Kroll, M., Chan, P., & Tanner, J. 1990. Performance and multiple strategies in a firm: Evidence from the apparel industry. In Dean, B. V. & Cassidy, J. C. (Eds.). *Strategic management: Methods and studies:*

93–110. Amsterdam: Elsevier-North Holland; and Wright, P., Kroll, M., Tu, H., & Helms, M. 1991. Generic strategies and business performance: An empirical study of the screw machine products industry. *British Journal of Management,* 2: 1–9.

41. Gilmore, J. H. & Pine, B. J., II. 1997. The four faces of customization. *Harvard Business Review,* 75(1): 91–101.

42. Ibid. For interesting insights on mass customization, refer to Cattani, K., Dahan, E., & Schmidt, G. 2005. Offshoring versus "spackling." *MIT Sloan Management Review,* 46(3): 6–7.

43. Goodstein, L. D. & Butz, H. E. 1998. Customer value: The linchpin of organizational change. *Organizational Dynamics,* Summer: 21–34.

44. Randall, T., Terwiesch, C., & Ulrich, K. T. 2005. Principles for user design of customized products. *California Management Review,* 47(4): 68–85.

45. Gadiesh & Gilbert, op. cit.: 139–158.

46. Insights on the profit pool concept are addressed in: Reinartz, W. & Ulaga, W. 2008. How to sell services more profitably. *Harvard Business Review,* 66(5): 90–96.

47. This example draws on Dess & Picken. 1997. op. cit.

48. Seybold, P. 2000. Niches bring riches. *Business 2.0,* June 13: 135.

49. Greenspan, R. 2004. Net drives profits to small biz. ClickZ.com, March 25, www.clickz.com. Greenspan, R. 2002. Small biz benefits from Internet tools. ClickZ.com, March 28, www.clickz.com.

50. Burns, E. 2006. Executives slow to see value of corporate blogging. ClickZ.com, May 9, www.clickz.com.

51. Empirical support for the use of combination strategies in an e-business context can be found in Kim, E., Nam, D., & Stimpert, J. L. 2004. The applicability of Porter's generic strategies in the Digital Age: Assumptions, conjectures, and suggestions. *Journal of Management,* 30(5): 569–589.

52. Porter, M. E. 2001. Strategy and the Internet. *Harvard Business Review,* 79: 63–78.

53. For an interesting perspective on the influence of the product life cycle and rate of technological change on competitive strategy, refer to Lei, D. & Slocum, J. W. Jr. 2005. Strategic and organizational requirements for competitive advantage. *Academy of Management Executive,* 19(1): 31–45.

54. Dickson, P. R. 1994. *Marketing Management:* 293. Fort Worth, TX: Dryden Press; Day, G. S. 1981. The product life cycle: Analysis and application. *Journal of Marketing Research,* 45: 60–67.

55. Bearden, W. O., Ingram, T. N., & LaForge, R. W. 1995. *Marketing principles and practices.* Burr Ridge, IL: Irwin.

56. MacMillan, I. C. 1985. Preemptive strategies. In Guth, W. D. (Ed.). *Handbook of Business Strategy:* 9-1–9-22. Boston: Warren, Gorham & Lamont; Pearce, J. A. & Robinson, R. B. 2000. *Strategic management* (7th ed.). New York: McGraw-Hill; Dickson, op. cit.: 295–296.

57. Bartlett, C. A. & Ghoshal, S. 2000. Going global: Lessons for late movers. *Harvard Business Review,* 78(2): 132–142.

58. Neuborne, E. 2000. E-tailers hit the relaunch key. *BusinessWeek,* October 17: 62.

59. Berkowitz, E. N., Kerin, R. A., & Hartley, S. W. 2000. *Marketing* (6th ed.). New York: McGraw-Hill.

60. MacMillan, op. cit.

61. Brooker, K. 2001. A game of inches. *Fortune,* February 5: 98–100.

62. Our discussion of reverse and breakaway positioning draws on Moon, Y. 2005. Break free from the product life cycle. *Harvard Business Review,* 83(5): 87–94. This article also discusses stealth positioning as a means of overcoming consumer resistance and advancing a product from the introduction to the growth phase.

63. MacMillan, op. cit

64. Berkowitz et al., op. cit.

65. Bearden et al., op. cit.

66. The discussion of these four strategies draws on MacMillan, op. cit.; Berkowitz et al., op. cit.; and Bearden et al., op. cit.

67. Augustine, N. R. 1997. Reshaping an industry: Lockheed Martin's survival story. *Harvard Business Review,* 75(3): 83–94.

68. Snow, D. C. 2008. Beware of old technologies' last gasps. *Harvard Business Review,* January: 17–18. Lohr, S. 2008. Why old technologies are still kicking. *New York Times,* March 23: np; and McGrath, R. G. 2008. Innovation and the last gaps of dying technologies. ritamcgrath.com, March 18: np.

69. A study that draws on the resource-based view of the firm to investigate successful turnaround strategies is: Morrow, J. S., Sirmon, D. G., Hitt, M. A., & Holcomb, T. R. 2007. *Strategic Management Journal,* 28(3): 271–284.

70. For a study investigating the relationship between organizational restructuring and acquisition performance, refer to: Barkema, H. G. & Schijven, M. Toward unlocking the full potential of acquisitions: The role of organizational restructuring. *Academy of Management Journal,* 51(4): 696–722.

71. For some useful ideas on effective turnarounds and handling downsizings, refer to Marks, M. S. & De Meuse, K. P. 2005. Resizing the organization: Maximizing the gain while minimizing the pain of layoffs, divestitures and closings. *Organizational Dynamics,* 34(1): 19–36.

72. Hambrick, D. C. & Schecter, S. M. 1983. Turnaround strategies for mature industrial product business units. *Academy of Management Journal,* 26(2): 231–248.

73. Mullaney, T. J. 2002. The wizard of Intuit. *BusinessWeek,* October 28: 60–63.

CHAPTER 6

Corporate-Level Strategy:

Creating Value through Diversification

After reading this chapter, you should have a good understanding of:

LO1 The reasons for the failure of many diversification efforts.

LO2 How managers can create value through diversification initiatives.

LO3 How corporations can use related diversification to achieve synergistic benefits through economies of scope and market power.

LO4 How corporations can use unrelated diversification to attain synergistic benefits through corporate restructuring, parenting, and portfolio analysis.

LO5 The various means of engaging in diversification— mergers and acquisitions, joint ventures/strategic alliances, and internal development.

LO6 Managerial behaviors that can erode the creation of value.

Corporate-level strategy addresses two related issues: (1) what businesses should a corporation compete in, and (2) how can these businesses be managed so they create "synergy"—that is, more value by working together than if they were freestanding units? As we will see, these questions present a key challenge for today's managers. Many diversification efforts fail or, in many cases, provide only marginal returns to shareholders. Thus, determining how to create value through entering new markets, introducing new products, or developing new technologies is a vital issue in strategic management.

We begin by discussing why diversification initiatives, in general, have not yielded the anticipated benefits. Then, in the next three sections of the chapter, we explore the two key alternative approaches: related and unrelated diversification. With related diversification, corporations strive to enter product markets that share some resources and capabilities with their existing business units or increase their market power. Here we suggest four means of creating value: leveraging core competencies, sharing activities, pooled negotiating power, and vertical integration. With unrelated diversification, there are few similarities in the resources and capabilities among the firm's business units, but value can be created in multiple ways. These include restructuring, corporate parenting, and portfolio analysis approaches. Whereas the synergies to be realized with related diversification come from *horizontal relationships* among the business units, the synergies from unrelated diversification are derived from *hierarchical relationships* between the corporate office and the business units.

The last two sections address (1) the various means that corporations can use to achieve diversification and (2) managerial behaviors (e.g., self-interest) that serve to erode shareholder value. We address merger and acquisitions (M&A), divestitures, joint ventures/strategic alliances, and internal development. Each of these involves the evaluation of important trade-offs. Detrimental managerial behaviors, often guided by a manager's self-interest, are "growth for growth's sake," egotism, and antitakeover tactics. Some of these behaviors raise ethical issues because managers, in some cases, are not acting in the best interests of a firm's shareholders.

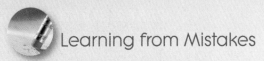

Learning from Mistakes

Normally investors will make decisions based on careful evaluation of the fundamentals underlying a company.[1] But, not always. Consider the case of SPACs, or special-purpose acquisition corporations. These are popular Wall Street vehicles whose organizers raise money to spend on yet-to-be determined targets and investors buy solely based on the pedigree of the founders. So, in a way, it is like betting on the jockey—not the horse. Let's look at a case in which, one could say, the horse came up lame.

Investors were eager to pony up $173 for Acquicor, a SPAC formed in 2005 by a group of Apple alumni: co-founder Steve Wozniak, former CEO Gil Amelio, and ex-senior executive Ellen Hancock. Unfortunately, the trio turned that cash into a highly indebted company whose market value has plummeted.

What caused their downfall was the purchase in early 2007 of a southern California chip company called Jazz Semiconductor for $253 million. The timing was terrible. Jazz sells to wireless companies, who had been in a nasty downturn. Shares of Acquicor—renamed Jazz Technologies—cratered from their IPO price of $6 to 71 cents by the end of March 2008.

The three founders had a tough decade even before this recent exploit. Amelio ended his brief reign at Apple in 1997 when Steve Jobs returned. An investment firm that he headed, AmTech, declared bankruptcy in 2003. A similar fate met Exodus Communications, the web-hosting firm that Hancock ran. As for Wozniak, long gone from Apple, a wireless company that he founded called Wheels of Zeus shut down in 2006. One *USA Today* writer humorously claimed: "This is sort of the computing equivalent of Alice Cooper, Grace Slick, and Smokey Robinson announcing they have formed a new band. Legends, yes. The outcome, less certain."

Things became rather lonely at Jazz. Hancock resigned as president in June 2007, followed by Wozniak, who had been an unpaid "chief visionary officer," in February. Amelio hung on, and in February 2008, he told investors that he had succeeded in taking Jazz "from a two-fiddle orchestra to a ten-fiddle orchestra" and that he was "laying the foundation for a much better future." Unfortunately, his optimism was not well placed. About six months later, Israel's Tower Semiconductor acquired Jazz Technologies for $40 million—a far cry from the $253 million invested about 18 months earlier!

If it is any comfort to the trio who started Acquicor, negative returns have been the norm with SPACs. According to Raj Nandiwada, a SPAC analyst: "SPACs that have completed acquisitions have fared far worse than the S&P index." He contends that such poor SPAC returns are primarily due to low-quality sponsors and overpaying for acquisitions.

>LO1

The reasons for the failure of many diversification efforts.

Acquicor's experience with acquisitions is more the rule than the exception. Research shows that the vast majority of acquisitions result in value destruction rather than value creation. Many large multinational firms have also failed to effectively integrate their acquisitions, paid too high a premium for the target's common stock, or were unable to understand how the acquired firm's assets would fit with their own lines of business.[2] And, at times, top executives may not have acted in the best interests of shareholders. That is, the motive for the acquisition may have been to enhance the executives' power and prestige rather than to improve shareholder returns. At times, the only other people who may have benefited were the shareholders of the *acquired* firms—or the investment bankers who advise the acquiring firm, because they collect huge fees upfront regardless of what happens afterward![3]

Consider, for example, Pfizer's announcement on January 26, 2009, that it was acquiring Wyeth for $68 billion in cash and stock—which represented a 15 percent premium.[4] How did the market react? In rather typical fashion, Wyeth's stock went up 2 percent; Pfizer's went down 9 percent. And, interestingly, the shares of Crucell, a Dutch biotech company, sank 10 percent after Wyeth pulled out of talks to buy it.

There have been several studies that were conducted over a variety of time periods that show how disappointing acquisitions have typically turned out. For example:

- A study evaluated the stock market reaction of 600 acquisitions over the period between 1975 and 1991. The results indicated that the acquiring firms suffered an average 4 percent drop in market value (after adjusting for market movements) in the three months following the acquisitions announcement.[5]
- In a study by Solomon Smith Barney of U.S. companies acquired since 1997 in deals for $15 billion or more, the stocks of the acquiring firms have, on average, underperformed the S&P stock index by 14 percentage points and underperformed their peer group by 4 percentage points after the deals were announced.[6]
- A study investigated 270 mergers that took place between 2000 and 2003 in multiple countries and regions. It found that after a merger, sales growth decreased by 6 percent, earnings growth dropped 9.4 percent, and market valuations declined 2.5 percent (figures are adjusted for industry trends and refer to three years pre- or postmerger).[7]

Exhibit 6.1 lists some well-known examples of failed acquisitions and mergers. Recently there have been several acquisitions—often at fire sale prices—by financial services firms during the global financial crisis in 2008. For example, Bank of America bought Merrill Lynch, Wells Fargo purchased Wachovia, and JPMorgan acquired Washington Mutual. Only time will tell how well these turn out over the next few years.

Many acquisitions ultimately result in divestiture—an admission that things didn't work out as planned. In fact, some years ago, a writer for *Fortune* magazine lamented, "Studies show that 33 percent to 50 percent of acquisitions are later divested, giving corporate marriages a divorce rate roughly comparable to that of men and women."[8]

Admittedly, we have been rather pessimistic so far.[9] Clearly, many diversification efforts have worked out very well—whether through mergers and acquisitions, strategic alliances and joint ventures, or internal development. We will discuss many success stories throughout this chapter. Next, we will discuss the primary rationales for diversification.

Exhibit 6.1
Some Well-Known M&A Blunders

Here are examples of some very expensive blunders:

- AOL paid $114 billion to acquire Time Warner in 2001. Over the next two years, AOL Time Warner lost $150 billion in market valuation.
- Conseco paid $5.8 billion to buy Green Tree, a mobile home mortgage lender, in 1998 though the company's net worth was not even $1 billion. In the next two years, Conseco lost 90 percent of its market value!
- Daimler Benz paid $36 billion to acquire Chrysler in 1998. After years of losses, it sold 80.1 percent of the unit to Cerberus Capital Management for $7.4 billion in 2007. And, as of 2009, Cerberus was trying to unload the unit.
- Quaker Oats' acquisition of the once high-flying Snapple for $1.8 billion in 1994 was followed by its divestment for $300 million three years later.
- AT&T bought computer equipment maker NCR for $7.4 billion in 1991, only to spin it off for $3.4 billion six years later.
- Sony acquired Columbia Pictures in 1989 for $4.8 billion although it had no competencies in movie production. Five years later, Sony was forced to take a $2.7 billion write-off on the acquisition.

Source: Gupta, P. 2008. Daimler May Sell Remaining Chrysler Stake. www.reuters.com, September 24: np; and Tully, S. 2006. The (Second) Worst Deal Ever. *Fortune,* October 16: 102–119.

Making Diversification Work: An Overview

Clearly, not all diversification moves, including those involving mergers and acquisitions, erode performance. For example, acquisitions in the oil industry, such as British Petroleum's purchases of Amoco and Arco, are performing well as is the Exxon-Mobil merger. In the automobile industry, the Renault-Nissan alliance, under CEO Carlos Ghosn's leadership, has led to a quadrupling of its collective market capitalization—from $20.4 billion to $84.9 billion—by the end of 2006.[10] Many leading high-tech firms such as Microsoft, Cisco Systems, and Intel have dramatically enhanced their revenues, profits, and market values through a wide variety of diversification initiatives, including acquisitions, strategic alliances, and joint ventures, as well as internal development.*

So the question becomes: Why do some diversification efforts pay off and others produce poor results? This chapter addresses two related issues: (1) What businesses should a corporation compete in? and (2) How should these businesses be managed to jointly create more value than if they were freestanding units?

Diversification initiatives—whether through mergers and acquisitions, strategic alliances and joint ventures, or internal development—must be justified by the creation of value for shareholders.[11] But this is not always the case. Acquiring firms typically pay high premiums when they acquire a target firm. For example, in 2006 Freeport-McMoran paid a 30 percent premium to acquire Phelps Dodge in order to create the largest metals and mining concern in the U.S. In contrast, you and I, as private investors, can diversify our portfolio of stocks very cheaply. With an intensely competitive online brokerage industry, we can acquire hundreds (or thousands) of shares for a transaction fee of as little as $10.00 or less—a far cry from the 30 to 40 percent (or higher) premiums that corporations typically must pay to acquire companies.

diversification
the process of firms expanding their operations by entering new businesses.

Given the seemingly high inherent downside risks and uncertainties, one might ask: Why should companies even bother with diversification initiatives? The answer, in a word, is *synergy,* derived from the Greek word *synergos,* which means "working together." This can have two different, but not mutually exclusive, meanings.

First, a firm may diversify into *related* businesses. Here, the primary potential benefits to be derived come from *horizontal relationships;* that is, businesses sharing intangible resources (e.g., core competencies such as marketing) and tangible resources (e.g., production facilities, distribution channels). Firms can also enhance their market power via pooled negotiating power and vertical integration. For example, Procter & Gamble enjoys many synergies from having businesses that share distribution resources.

Second, a corporation may diversify into *unrelated* businesses.[12] Here, the primary potential benefits are derived largely from *hierarchical relationships;* that is, value creation derived from the corporate office. Examples of the latter would include leveraging some of the support activities in the value chain that we discussed in Chapter 3, such as information systems or human resource practices. Cooper Industries has followed a successful strategy of unrelated diversification. There are few similarities in the products it makes or the industries in which it competes. However, the corporate office adds value through such activities as superb human resource practices and budgeting systems.

Please note that such benefits derived from horizontal (related diversification) and hierarchical (unrelated diversification) relationships are not mutually exclusive. Many

---

* Many high-tech firms, such as Motorola, IBM, Qualcomm, and Intel have also diversified through company-owned venture capital arms. Intel Capital, for example, has invested $4 billion in 1,000 companies over 15 years. Some 160 of those companies have been sold to other firms, while another 150 of them have been publicly listed. In 2006, Intel Capital's investments added $214 million to the parent company's net income. For an insightful discussion of how Apple might benefit from a venture capital initiative, refer to Hesseldahl, A. 2007. What to Do with Apple's Cash. *BusinessWeek,* March 19: 80.

firms that diversify into related areas benefit from information technology expertise in the corporate office. Similarly, unrelated diversifiers often benefit from the "best practices" of sister businesses even though their products, markets, and technologies may differ dramatically.

Exhibit 6.2 provides an overview of how we will address the various means by which firms create value through both related and unrelated diversification and also include a summary of some examples that we will address in this chapter.[13]

Related Diversification: Economies of Scope and Revenue Enhancement

Related diversification enables a firm to benefit from horizontal relationships across different businesses in the diversified corporation by leveraging core competencies and sharing activities (e.g., production and distribution facilities). This enables a corporation to benefit from economies of scope. **Economies of scope** refers to cost savings from leveraging core competencies or sharing related activities among businesses in the corporation. A firm can also enjoy greater revenues if two businesses attain higher levels of sales growth combined than either company could attain independently.

related diversification
a firm entering a different business in which it can benefit from leveraging core competencies, sharing activities, or building market power.

economies of scope cost savings from leveraging core competencies or sharing related activities among businesses in a corporation.

Exhibit 6.2
Creating Value through Related and Unrelated Diversification

Related Diversification: Economies of Scope

Leveraging core competencies
- 3M leverages its competencies in adhesives technologies to many industries, including automotive, construction, and telecommunications.

Sharing activities
- McKesson, a large distribution company, sells many product lines, such as pharmaceuticals and liquor, through its superwarehouses.

Related Diversification: Market Power

Pooled negotiating power
- The Times Mirror Company increases its power over customers by providing "one-stop shopping" for advertisers to reach customers through multiple media—television and newspapers—in several huge markets such as New York and Chicago.

Vertical integration
- Shaw Industries, a giant carpet manufacturer, increases its control over raw materials by producing much of its own polypropylene fiber, a key input to its manufacturing process.

Unrelated Diversification: Parenting, Restructuring, and Financial Synergies

Corporate restructuring and parenting
- The corporate office of Cooper Industries adds value to its acquired businesses by performing such activities as auditing their manufacturing operations, improving their accounting activities, and centralizing union negotiations.

Portfolio management
- Novartis, formerly Ciba-Geigy, uses portfolio management to improve many key activities, including resource allocation and reward and evaluation systems.

For example, a sporting goods store with one or several locations may acquire retail stores carrying other product lines. This enables it to leverage, or reuse, many of its key resources—favorable reputation, expert staff and management skills, efficient purchasing operations—the basis of its competitive advantage(s), over a larger number of stores.[14]

Leveraging Core Competencies

The concept of core competencies can be illustrated by the imagery of the diversified corporation as a tree.[15] The trunk and major limbs represent core products; the smaller branches are business units; and the leaves, flowers, and fruit are end products. The core competencies are represented by the root system, which provides nourishment, sustenance, and stability. Managers often misread the strength of competitors by looking only at their end products, just as we can fail to appreciate the strength of a tree by looking only at its leaves. Core competencies may also be viewed as the "glue" that binds existing businesses together or as the engine that fuels new business growth.

core competencies
a firm's strategic resources that reflect the collective learning in the organization.

Core competencies reflect the collective learning in organizations—how to coordinate diverse production skills, integrate multiple streams of technologies, and market diverse products and services. The knowledge necessary to put a radio on a chip does not in itself assure a company of the skill needed to produce a miniature radio approximately the size of a business card. To accomplish this, Casio, a giant electronic products producer, must synthesize know-how in miniaturization, microprocessor design, material science, and ultrathin precision castings. These are the same skills that it applies in its miniature card calculators, pocket TVs, and digital watches.

For a core competence to create value and provide a viable basis for synergy among the businesses in a corporation, it must meet three criteria.[16]

- ***The core competence must enhance competitive advantage(s) by creating superior customer value.*** Every value-chain activity has the potential to provide a viable basis for building on a core competence.[17] At Gillette, for example, scientists developed the Fusion and Mach 3 after the introduction of the tremendously successful Sensor System because of a thorough understanding of several phenomena that underlie shaving. These include the physiology of facial hair and skin, the metallurgy of blade strength and sharpness, the dynamics of a cartridge moving across skin, and the physics of a razor blade severing hair. Such innovations are possible only with an understanding of such phenomena and the ability to combine such technologies into innovative products. Customers are willing to pay more for such technologically differentiated products.
- ***Different businesses in the corporation must be similar in at least one important way related to the core competence.*** It is not essential that the products or services themselves be similar. Rather, at least one element in the value chain must require similar skills in creating competitive advantage if the corporation is to capitalize on its core competence. At first glance you might think that cars and houses have little in common. However, Strategy Spotlight 6.1 discusses how Toyota creates synergies in a business—manufactured homes—that has little to do with its core business—automobiles.
- ***The core competencies must be difficult for competitors to imitate or find substitutes for.*** As we discussed in Chapter 5, competitive advantages will not be sustainable if the competition can easily imitate or substitute them. Similarly, if the skills associated with a firm's core competencies are easily imitated or replicated, they are not a sound basis for sustainable advantages. Consider Sharp Corporation, a consumer electronics giant with 2008 revenues of $34 billion.[18] It has a set of specialized core competencies in optoelectronics technologies that are difficult to replicate and contribute to its competitive advantages in its core businesses.

Toyota's Diversification into Home Manufacturing

Looking for the biggest Toyota on the market? It's not the Tundra pickups and Sequoia SUVs down at your local dealer. Instead, you'll have to travel to the Toyota factory in Kasugai, a city of 300,000 about three hours west of Tokyo. There you won't see much in the way of horsepower or acceleration. But they are very roomy—as in multiple bedrooms, a living room, kitchen, bath, and patio.

At Kasugai, Toyota's houses are 85 percent completed at the plant before being transported by road and built in just six hours. To improve efficiency, Toyota borrows know-how from its fabled Toyota Production System with its principles of just-in-time delivery and *kaizen,* or continuous improvement. Using methods adopted from car production, anticorrosive paint is applied evenly to the houses' steel frames. Just as in all of Toyota's Japan automobile factories, a banner proclaiming "good thinking, good products" hangs from the roof. "We follow the Toyota way in housing," says Senta Morioka, a managing officer at Toyota.

Toyota sells about 5,000 homes a year and the operation is profitable. Toyota Homes are built from six or more

● Toyota is a world-class automobile producer. Above is a Scion, one of its popular products. Toyota has also diversified into many areas, including manufactured homes.

modules in less than 45 days. A conservative two-story home with 1,000 square feet sells for $200,000. A more expensive, custom-built 2,600 square foot home sells for about $800,000. Toyota Homes are strong and guaranteed for about 60 years—twice the average lifespan of a home in Japan. Although the unit accounts for only .5 percent of total corporate sales (or about $1.4 billion), Toyota is working hard to ramp up that number.

Source: Koerner, P. 2008. Toyota Looking to Expand Stylish Prefab Homes Unit. www.jetsongreen.com. July 3: np; and Rowley, I. 2006. Way, Way, Off-Road. *BusinessWeek,* July 17: 36–37.

Its most successful technology has been liquid crystal displays (LCDs) that are critical components in nearly all of Sharp's products. Its expertise in this technology enabled Sharp to succeed in videocassette recorders (VCRs) with its innovative LCD viewfinder and led to the creation of its Wizard, a personal electronic organizer.

Strategy Spotlight 6.2 provides Steve Jobs' insights on the importance of a firm's core competence. The Apple CEO is widely considered one of America's most respected CEOs.

Sharing Activities

As we saw above, leveraging core competencies involves transferring accumulated skills and expertise across business units in a corporation. Corporations also can achieve synergy by **sharing activities** across their business units. These include value-creating activities such as common manufacturing facilities, distribution channels, and sales forces. As we will see, sharing activities can potentially provide two primary payoffs: cost savings and revenue enhancements.

sharing activities
having activities of two or more businesses' value chains done by one of the businesses.

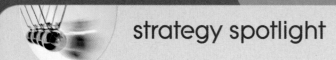

Steve Jobs Discusses Apple's Core Competence

"One of our biggest insights (years ago) was that we didn't want to get into any business where we didn't own or control the primary technology, because you'll get your head handed to you. We realized that for almost all future consumer electronics, the primary technology was

Source: Fisher, A. 2008. America's Most Admired Companies. *Fortune*, March 17: 74.

going to be software. And we were pretty good at software. We could do the operating system software. We could write applications like iTunes on the Mac or even PC. We could write the software in the device, like you might put in an iPod or an iPhone. And we could write the back-end software that runs on a cloud, like iTunes. So we could write all these different kinds of software and tweed it all together and make it work seamlessly. And you ask yourself: What other companies can do that? It's a pretty short list."

Deriving Cost Savings   Typically, this is the most common type of synergy and the easiest to estimate. Peter Shaw, head of mergers and acquisitions at the British chemical and pharmaceutical company ICI, refers to cost savings as "hard synergies" and contends that the level of certainty of their achievement is quite high. Cost savings come from many sources, including elimination of jobs, facilities, and related expenses that are no longer needed when functions are consolidated, or from economies of scale in purchasing. Cost savings are generally highest when one company acquires another from the same industry in the same country. Shaw Industries, recently acquired by Berkshire Hathaway, is the nation's largest carpet producer. Over the years, it has dominated the competition through a strategy of acquisition which has enabled Shaw, among other things, to consolidate its manufacturing operations in a few, highly efficient plants and to lower costs through higher capacity utilization.

Sharing activities inevitably involve costs that the benefits must outweigh such as the greater coordination required to manage a shared activity. Even more important is the need to compromise on the design or performance of an activity so that it can be shared. For example, a salesperson handling the products of two business units must operate in a way that is usually not what either unit would choose if it were independent. If the compromise erodes the unit's effectiveness, then sharing may reduce rather than enhance competitive advantage.

Enhancing Revenue and Differentiation   Often an acquiring firm and its target may achieve a higher level of sales growth together than either company could on its own. Shortly after Gillette acquired Duracell, it confirmed its expectation that selling Duracell batteries through Gillette's existing channels for personal care products would increase sales, particularly internationally. Gillette sold Duracell products in 25 new markets in the first year after the acquisition and substantially increased sales in established international markets. Also, a target company's distribution channel can be used to escalate the sales of the acquiring company's product. Such was the case when Gillette acquired Parker Pen. Gillette estimated that it could gain an additional $25 million in sales of its own Waterman pens by taking advantage of Parker's distribution channels.

Firms also can enhance the effectiveness of their differentiation strategies by means of sharing activities among business units. A shared order-processing system, for example, may permit new features and services that a buyer will value. Also, sharing can reduce the cost of differentiation. For instance, a shared service network may make more advanced, remote service technology economically feasible. To illustrate the potential for enhanced differentiation through sharing, consider $7 billion VF Corporation—producer of such well-known brands as Lee, Wrangler, Vanity Fair, and Jantzen.

> VF's acquisition of Nutmeg Industries and H. H. Cutler provided it with several large customers that it didn't have before, increasing its plant utilization and productivity. But more importantly, Nutmeg designs and makes licensed apparel for sports teams and organizations, while Cutler manufactures licensed brand-name children's apparel, including Walt Disney kids' wear. Such brand labeling enhances the differentiation of VF's apparel products. According to VF President Mackey McDonald, "What we're doing is looking at value-added knitwear, taking our basic fleece from Basset-Walker [one of its divisions], embellishing it through Cutler and Nutmeg, and selling it as a value-added product." Additionally, Cutler's advanced high-speed printing technologies will enable VF to be more proactive in anticipating trends in the fashion-driven fleece market. Claims McDonald, "Rather than printing first and then trying to guess what the customer wants, we can see what's happening in the marketplace and then print it up."[19]

As a cautionary note, managers must keep in mind that sharing activities among businesses in a corporation can have a negative effect on a given business's differentiation. For example, with the merger of Chrysler and Daimler-Benz, many consumers may lower their perceptions of Mercedes's quality and prestige because they felt that common production components and processes were being used across the two divisions. And Ford's Jaguar division was adversely affected as consumers came to understand that it shared many components with its sister divisions at Ford, including Lincoln. Perhaps, it is not too surprising that both Chrysler and Jaguar were divested by their parent corporations.

Strategy Spotlight 6.3 discusses how Freemantle Media leverages its hit television show *American Idol* through its core competencies and shared activities to create multiple revenue streams.

Related Diversification: Market Power

We now discuss how companies achieve related diversification through **market power.** We also address the two principal means by which firms achieve synergy through market power: *pooled negotiating power* and *vertical integration.* Managers do, however, have limits on their ability to use market power for diversification, because government regulations can sometimes restrict the ability of a business to gain very large shares of a particular market. Consider GE's attempt to acquire Honeywell:

market power firms' abilities to profit through restricting or controlling supply to a market or coordinating with other firms to reduce investment.

> When General Electric announced a $41 billion bid for Honeywell, the European Union stepped in. GE's market clout would have expanded significantly with the deal: GE would supply over one-half the parts needed to build several aircraft engines. The commission's concern, causing them to reject the acquisition, was that GE could use its increased market power to dominate the aircraft engine parts market and crowd out rivals.[20] Thus, while managers need to be aware of the strategic advantages of market power, they must at the same time be aware of regulations and legislation.

Pooled Negotiating Power

Similar businesses working together or the affiliation of a business with a strong parent can strengthen an organization's bargaining position relative to suppliers and customers and enhance its position vis-à-vis competitors. Compare, for example, the position of an independent food manufacturer with the same business within Nestlé. Being part of Nestlé provides the business with significant clout—greater bargaining power with suppliers and customers—since it is part of a firm that makes large purchases from suppliers and provides a wide variety of products. Access to the parent's deep pockets increases the business's strength, and the Nestlé unit enjoys greater protection from substitutes and new

pooled negotiating power the improvement in bargaining position relative to suppliers and customers.

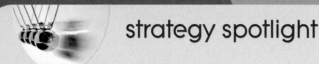

American Idol: Far More than Just a Television Show

American Idol is one of several of FremantleMedia's (FM) hit television shows. FM is a division of German media giant Bertlesmann, which has approximately $26 billion in revenues. Some of FM's other well-known television shows are The Apprentice, The Swan, and at a ripe old age of 48—The Price Is Right.

First shown in the United States in June 2002, American Idol became a tremendous overnight success. Although the show may be crass and occasionally cruel, it is undeniably brilliant. It's become the ultimate testament to a singular business achievement: FM has become extremely successful at creating truly global programming. In part, that is due to the creative minds at Fremantle. It has some of the best professionals in the business who have a talent for developing shows that appeal to huge populations with different backgrounds and circumstances.

Amazingly, FM, which created Pop Idol in Britain in 2001, is now rolling out the show in its 30th country. There's Belgium Idool, Portugal Idolos, Deutschland Sucht den SuperStar (Germany), SuperStar KZ (Kazakhstan), and of course, the largest and best-known show, American Idol, in the United States. American Idol is the primary reason that Fremantle's revenue is up 9 percent to more than $1 billion since the show was launched. According to Fremantle's CEO Tony Cohen, "Idol has become a national institution in lots of countries." To illustrate, fans cast more than 65 million votes for the American Idol finale in May, 2004—that is two-thirds as many people as voted in the 2004 U.S. presidential election.

The real key to Fremantle's success is not just adapting its television hits to other countries, but systematically leveraging its core product—television shows—to create multiple revenue streams. In essence, the "Fremantle Way" holds lessons not just for show business but for all business. It enables a company to use its core competence of making products of mass appeal and then to customize them for places with widely varying languages, cultures, and mores. It then milks the hits for every penny through tie-ins, spinoffs, innovative uses of technology, and marketing masterstrokes.

The Idol franchise has created a wide variety of new revenue streams for Fremantle's German parent, Bertelsmann. Here's how much American Idol generated in its first two years since its June 2002 launch:

- Products ($50 million). Brand extensions range from videogames and fragrances to a planned microphone-shaped soap-on-a-rope. Fremantle receives a licensing fee from manufacturers.

- TV Licensing ($75 million). For its rights fee, Fox gets to broadcast the show and, in turn, sell ads and lucrative sponsorships.

- Compact Discs (CDs) ($130 million). The most successful performers on the Idols shows have sold millions of CDs; more than one-third of the revenue goes to BMG, which, like Fremantle, is an affiliate of Bertelsmann. In fact, in a 60 Minutes interview in March 2007, Simon Cowell said that his "only interest in Idol was as a vehicle to launch records." Cowell, the show's notoriously brutal judge, works at BMG, which requires every contestant to sign a recording contract.

- Concerts ($35 million). Although artists and their management get the bulk of the take, concerts sell records and merchandise and promote the next Idol show.

In addition, Fremantle Licensing Worldwide signed Warner Brothers Publications to produce and distribute Idol audition books with CDs for the United States, Canada, United Kingdom, and Australia. The new books/CDs—Pop Idol (UK), Australian Idol, and Canadian Idol—join the American Idol book/CD.

Sources: Howe, J. 2008 Crowdsourcing. New York: Crown Business; Sloan, P. 2004. The Reality Factory. Business 2.0, August: 74–82; Cooney, J. 2004. In the News. License!, March: 48; and, Anonymous. 2005. Fox on Top in Feb; NBC Languishing at the Bottom. www.indiantelevision.com, March 2.

entrants. Not only would rivals perceive the unit as a more formidable opponent, but the unit's association with Nestlé would also provide greater visibility and improved image.

Consolidating an industry can also increase a firm's market power.[21] This is clearly an emerging trend in the multimedia industry.[22] All of these mergers and acquisitions have a common goal: to control and leverage as many news and entertainment channels as possible.

How 3M's Efforts to Increase Its Market Power Backfired

In the spring and summer of 2006, 3M found itself in court facing three class-action lawsuits launched by consumers and retailers of transparent and invisible adhesive tape (often generically known as "Scotch tape"). The suits all alleged that 3M had unlawfully bullied its way into a monopoly position in the tape market and that, as a result, consumers had been deprived of their rightful amount of choice and often paid up to 40 percent too much for their tape.

One rival that is particularly interested in these cases is LaPage's Inc. of North York, Ontario—3M's only significant competitor in the home and office adhesive tape market. LaPage's has everything to gain from court penalties against 3M's selling practices. This includes greater access to the lucrative North American market. The Canadian company started 3M's legal travails in the first place: all of the current class-action suits were initiated by LePage's.

Back in 1997, LePage's (then based in Pittsburgh) filed a complaint in the Pennsylvania District Court against 3M's practice of selling its various tape products using what was called "bundled rebates." LePage's argued that

it violated the Sherman Act, the century-old U.S. legislation that limited monopoly power. 3M's bundled rebate program offered significant rebates—sometimes in the millions of dollars—to retailers as a reward for selling targeted amounts of six product lines. LePage's claimed that such selling targets were so large that retailers could only meet them by excluding competing products—in this case LePage's tape—from store shelves. For example, LePage's argued that Kmart, which had constituted 10% of LePage's sales dropped the account when 3M started offering the discount chain $1 million in rebates in return for selling more than $15 million worth of 3M products each year. Further, LePage's offered its own conspiracy theory: 3M introduced rebates not simply to grow its sales, but to eliminate LePage's—its only significant competitor.

A jury awarded LePage's $68.5 million in damages (the amount after trebling)—almost 15 percent of the 3M Consumer and Office Business unit's operating income in 2000. The Court of Appeals for the Third Circuit rejected 3M's appeal and upheld the judgment. It concluded that rebate bundling, even if above cost, may exclude equally efficient competitors from offering product (in this case, tape). In the ruling, Judge Dolores K. Sloviter wrote that "they may foreclose portions of the market to a potential competitor who does not manufacture an equally diverse group of products and who therefore cannot make a comparable offer." Therefore, the bundled rebates were judged to be an exploitation of 3M's monopoly power.

Sources: Bush, D. & Gelb, B. D. 2005. When Marketing Practices Raise Antitrust Concerns. *MIT Sloan Management Review*, 46(4): 73–81; Campbell, C. 2006. Tale of the Tape. *Canadian Business*. April 24: 39–40; and Bergstrom, B. 2003. $68M Jury Award Upheld against 3M in Antitrust Case. *The Associated Press*: March 26.

When acquiring related businesses, a firm's potential for pooled negotiating power vis-à-vis its customers and suppliers can be very enticing. However, managers must carefully evaluate how the combined businesses may affect relationships with actual and potential customers, suppliers, and competitors. For example, when PepsiCo diversified into the fast-food industry with its acquisitions of Kentucky Fried Chicken, Taco Bell, and Pizza Hut (now part of Yum! Brands), it clearly benefited from its position over these units that served as a captive market for its soft-drink products. However, many competitors, such as McDonald's, have refused to consider PepsiCo as a supplier of its own soft-drink needs because of competition with Pepsi's divisions in the fast-food industry. Simply put, McDonald's did not want to subsidize the enemy! Thus, although acquiring related businesses can enhance a corporation's bargaining power, it must be aware of the potential for retaliation.

Strategy Spotlight 6.4 discusses how 3M's actions to increase its market power led to a lawsuit (which 3M lost) by a competitor.

Vertical Integration

vertical integration
an expansion or
extension of the firm
by integrating pre-
ceding or successive
production
processes.

Vertical integration occurs when a firm becomes its own supplier or distributor. That is, it represents an expansion or extension of the firm by integrating preceding or successive production processes.[23] The firm incorporates more processes toward the original source of raw materials (backward integration) or toward the ultimate consumer (forward integration). For example, a car manufacturer might supply its own parts or make its own engines to secure sources of supply or control its own system of dealerships to ensure retail outlets for its products. Similarly, an oil refinery might secure land leases and develop its own drilling capacity to ensure a constant supply of crude oil. Or it could expand into retail operations by owning or licensing gasoline stations to guarantee customers for its petroleum products.

Clearly, vertical integration can be a viable strategy for many firms. Strategy Spotlight 6.5 discusses Shaw Industries, a carpet manufacturer that has attained a dominant position in the industry via a strategy of vertical integration. Shaw has successfully implemented strategies of both forward and backward integration. Exhibit 6.3 depicts the stages of Shaw's vertical integration.

Benefits and Risks of Vertical Integration Vertical integration is a means for an organization to reduce its dependence on suppliers or its channels of distribution to end users. However, the benefits associated with vertical integration—backward or forward—must be carefully weighed against the risks.[24]

The *benefits* of vertical integration include (1) a secure supply of raw materials or distribution channels that cannot be "held hostage" to external markets where costs can fluctuate over time, (2) protection and control over assets and services required to produce and deliver valuable products and services, (3) access to new business opportunities and new forms of technologies, and (4) simplified procurement and administrative procedures since key activities are brought inside the firm, eliminating the need to deal with a wide variety of suppliers and distributors.

Winnebago, the leader in the market for drivable recreational vehicles with a 19.3 percent market share, illustrates some of vertical integration's benefits.[25] The word *Winnebago* means "big RV" to most Americans. And the firm has a sterling reputation for great quality. The firm's huge northern Iowa factories do everything from extruding aluminum for body parts to molding plastics for water and holding tanks to dashboards. Such vertical integration at the factory may appear to be outdated and expensive, but it guarantees excellent quality. The Recreational Vehicle Dealer Association started giving a quality award in 1996, and Winnebago has won it every year.

The *risks* of vertical integration include (1) the costs and expenses associated with increased overhead and capital expenditures to provide facilities, raw material inputs, and distribution channels inside the organization; (2) a loss of flexibility resulting from the inability to respond quickly to changes in the external environment because of the huge

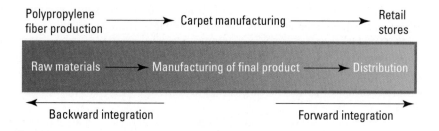

Exhibit 6.3 Simplified Stages of Vertical Integration: Shaw Industries

Vertical Integration at Shaw Industries

Shaw Industries (now part of Berkshire Hathaway) is an example of a firm that has followed a very successful strategy of vertical integration. By relentlessly pursuing both backward and forward integration, Shaw has become the dominant manufacturer of carpeting products in the United States. According to CEO Robert Shaw, "We want to be involved with as much of the process of making and selling carpets as practical. That way, we're in charge of costs." For example, Shaw acquired Amoco's polypropylene fiber manufacturing facilities in Alabama and Georgia. These new plants provide carpet fibers for internal use and for sale to other manufacturers. With this backward integration, fully one-quarter of Shaw's carpet fiber needs are now met in-house. In early 1996 Shaw began to integrate forward, acquiring seven floor-covering retailers in a move that suggested a strategy to consolidate the fragmented industry and increase its influence over retail pricing. Exhibit 6.3 provides a simplified depiction of the stages of vertical integration for Shaw Industries.

Sources: White, J. 2003. Shaw to home in on more with Georgia Tufters deal. *HFN: The Weekly Newspaper for the Home Furnishing Network,* May 5: 32; Shaw Industries. 1993, 2000. Annual reports; and Server, A. 1994. How to escape a price war. *Fortune,* June 13: 88.

investments in vertical integration activities that generally cannot be easily deployed elsewhere; (3) problems associated with unbalanced capacities or unfilled demand along the value chain; and (4) additional administrative costs associated with managing a more complex set of activities. Exhibit 6.4 summarizes the benefits and risks of vertical integration.

In making vertical integration decisions, five issues should be considered.[26]

1. *Is the company satisfied with the quality of the value that its present suppliers and distributors are providing?* If the performance of organizations in the vertical chain—both suppliers and distributors—is satisfactory, it may not, in general, be appropriate for a company to perform these activities themselves. Nike and Reebok have outsourced the manufacture of their shoes to countries such as China and Indonesia where labor costs are low. Since the strengths of these companies are typically in design and marketing, it would be advisable to continue to outsource production operations and continue to focus on where they can add the most value.

Exhibit 6.4
Benefits and Risks of Vertical Integration

Benefits
• A secure source of raw materials or distribution channels.
• Protection of and control over valuable assets.
• Access to new business opportunities.
• Simplified procurement and administrative procedures.

Risks
• Costs and expenses associated with increased overhead and capital expenditures.
• Loss of flexibility resulting from large investments.
• Problems associated with unbalanced capacities along the value chain.
• Additional administrative costs associated with managing a more complex set of activities.

2. *Are there activities in the industry value chain presently being outsourced or performed independently by others that are a viable source of future profits?* Even if a firm is outsourcing value-chain activities to companies that are doing a credible job, it may be missing out on substantial profit opportunities. To illustrate, consider the automobile industry's profit pool. As you may recall from Chapter 5, there is much more potential profit in many downstream activities (e.g., leasing, warranty, insurance, and service) than in the manufacture of automobiles. Not surprisingly, carmakers such as Toyota and Honda are undertaking forward integration strategies to become bigger players in these high-profit activities.

3. *Is there a high level of stability in the demand for the organization's products?* High demand or sales volatility are not conducive to vertical integration. With the high level of fixed costs in plant and equipment as well as operating costs that accompany endeavors toward vertical integration, widely fluctuating sales demand can either strain resources (in times of high demand) or result in unused capacity (in times of low demand). The cycles of "boom and bust" in the automobile industry are a key reason why the manufacturers have increased the amount of outsourced inputs.

4. *Does the company have the necessary competencies to execute the vertical integration strategies?* As many companies would attest, successfully executing strategies of vertical integration can be very difficult. For example, Unocal, a major petroleum refiner, which once owned retail gas stations, was slow to capture the potential grocery and merchandise side of the business that might have resulted from customer traffic to its service stations. Unocal lacked the competencies to develop a separate retail organization and culture. The company eventually sold the assets and brand.

5. *Will the vertical integration initiative have potential negative impacts on the firm's stakeholders?* Managers must carefully consider the impact that vertical integration may have on existing and future customers, suppliers, and competitors. After Lockheed Martin, a dominant defense contractor, acquired Loral Corporation, an electronics supplier, for $9.1 billion, it had an unpleasant and unanticipated surprise. Loral, as a captive supplier of Lockheed, is now viewed as a rival by many of its previous customers. Thus, before Lockheed Martin can realize any net synergies from this acquisition, it must make up for the substantial business that it has lost.

Analyzing Vertical Integration: The Transaction Cost Perspective   Another approach that has proved very useful in understanding vertical integration is the **transaction cost perspective**.[27] According to this perspective, every market transaction involves some *transaction costs*. First, a decision to purchase an input from an outside source leads to *search* costs (i.e., the cost to find where it is available, the level of quality, etc.). Second, there are costs associated with *negotiating*. Third, a *contract* needs to be written spelling out future possible contingencies. Fourth, parties in a contract have to *monitor* each other. Finally, if a party does not comply with the terms of the contract, there are *enforcement* costs. Transaction costs are thus the sum of search costs, negotiation costs, contracting costs, monitoring costs, and enforcement costs. These transaction costs can be avoided by internalizing the activity, in other words, by producing the input in-house.

A related problem with purchasing a specialized input from outside is the issue of *transaction-specific investments*. For example, when an automobile company needs an input specifically designed for a particular car model, the supplier may be unwilling to make the investments in plant and machinery necessary to produce that component

transaction cost perspective a perspective that the choice of a transaction's governance structure, such as vertical integration or market transaction, is influenced by transaction costs, including search, negotiating, contracting, monitoring, and enforcement costs, associated with each choice.

for two reasons. First, the investment may take many years to recover but there is no guarantee the automobile company will continue to buy from them after the contract expires, typically in one year. Second, once the investment is made, the supplier has no bargaining power. That is, the buyer knows that the supplier has no option but to supply at ever-lower prices because the investments were so specific that they cannot be used to produce alternative products. In such circumstances, again, vertical integration may be the only option.

Vertical integration, however, gives rise to a different set of costs. These costs are referred to as *administrative costs*. Coordinating different stages of the value chain now internalized within the firm causes administrative costs to go up. Decisions about vertical integration are, therefore, based on a comparison of transaction costs and administrative costs. If transaction costs are lower than administrative costs, it is best to resort to market transactions and avoid vertical integration. For example, McDonald's may be the world's biggest buyer of beef, but they do not raise cattle. The market for beef has low transaction costs and requires no transaction-specific investments. On the other hand, if transaction costs are higher than administrative costs, vertical integration becomes an attractive strategy. Most automobile manufacturers produce their own engines because the market for engines involves high transaction costs and transaction-specific investments.

Unrelated Diversification: Financial Synergies and Parenting

>LO4
How corporations can use unrelated diversification to attain synergistic benefits through corporate restructuring, parenting, and portfolio analysis.

With unrelated diversification, unlike related diversification, few benefits are derived from *horizontal relationships*—that is, the leveraging of core competencies or the sharing of activities across business units within a corporation. Instead, potential benefits can be gained from *vertical (or hierarchical) relationships*—the creation of synergies from the interaction of the corporate office with the individual business units. There are two main sources of such synergies. First, the corporate office can contribute to "parenting" and restructuring of (often acquired) businesses. Second, the corporate office can add value by viewing the entire corporation as a family or "portfolio" of businesses and allocating resources to optimize corporate goals of profitability, cash flow, and growth. Additionally, the corporate office enhances value by establishing appropriate human resource practices and financial controls for each of its business units.

unrelated diversification
a firm entering a different business that has little horizontal interaction with other businesses of a firm.

Corporate Parenting and Restructuring

We have discussed how firms can add value through related diversification by exploring sources of synergy *across* business units. Now, we discuss how value can be created *within* business units as a result of the expertise and support provided by the corporate office.

Parenting   The positive contributions of the corporate office are called the **"parenting advantage."**[28] Many firms have successfully diversified their holdings without strong evidence of the more traditional sources of synergy (i.e., horizontally across business units). Diversified public corporations such as BTR, Emerson Electric, and Hanson and leveraged buyout firms such as Kohlberg, Kravis, Roberts & Company, and Clayton, Dublilier & Rice are a few examples.[29] These parent companies create value through management expertise. How? They improve plans and budgets and provide especially competent central functions such as legal, financial, human resource management, procurement, and the like. They also help subsidiaries make wise choices in their own acquisitions, divestitures, and new internal development decisions. Such contributions often help business units to substantially increase their revenues and profits. Consider Texas-based Cooper Industries' acquisition of Champion International, the spark plug company, as an example of corporate parenting:[30]

parenting advantage
the positive contributions of the corporate office to a new business as a result of expertise and support provided and not as a result of substantial changes in assets, capital structure, or management.

Cooper applies a distinctive parenting approach designed to help its businesses improve their manufacturing performance. New acquisitions are "Cooperized"—Cooper audits their manufacturing operations; improves their cost accounting systems; makes their planning, budgeting, and human resource systems conform with its systems; and centralizes union negotiations. Excess cash is squeezed out through tighter controls and reinvested in productivity enhancements, which improve overall operating efficiency. As one manager observed, "When you get acquired by Cooper, one of the first things that happens is a truckload of policy manuals arrives at your door." Such active parenting has been effective in enhancing the competitive advantages of many kinds of manufacturing businesses.

restructuring the intervention of the corporate office in a new business that substantially changes the assets, capital structure, and/or management, including selling off parts of the business, changing the management, reducing payroll and unnecessary sources of expenses, changing strategies, and infusing the new business with new technologies, processes, and reward systems.

Restructuring   **Restructuring** is another means by which the corporate office can add value to a business.[31] The central idea can be captured in the real estate phrase "buy low and sell high." Here, the corporate office tries to find either poorly performing firms with unrealized potential or firms in industries on the threshold of significant, positive change. The parent intervenes, often selling off parts of the business; changing the management; reducing payroll and unnecessary sources of expenses; changing strategies; and infusing the company with new technologies, processes, reward systems, and so forth. When the restructuring is complete, the firm can either "sell high" and capture the added value or keep the business and enjoy financial and competitive benefits.[32]

Loews Corporation, a conglomerate with $18 billion in revenues competes in such industries as oil and gas, tobacco, watches, insurance, and hotels. It provides an exemplary example of how firms can successfully "buy low and sell high" as part of their corporate strategy.[33]

Energy accounts for 33 percent of Loews' $30 billion in total assets. In the 1980s it bought six oil tankers for only $5 million each during a sharp slide in oil prices. The downside was limited. After all these huge hulks could easily have been sold as scrap steel. However, that didn't have to happen. Eight years after Loews purchased the tankers, they sold them for $50 million each.

Loews was also extremely successful with its next energy play—drilling equipment. Although wildcatting for oil is very risky, selling services to wildcatters is not, especially if the assets are bought during a down cycle. Loews did just that. It purchased 10 offshore drilling rigs for $50 million in 1989 and formed Diamond Offshore Drilling. In 1995 Loews received $338 million after taking a 30 percent piece of this operation public!

For the restructuring strategy to work, the corporate management must have both the insight to detect undervalued companies (otherwise the cost of acquisition would be too high) or businesses competing in industries with a high potential for transformation.[34] Additionally, of course, they must have the requisite skills and resources to turn the businesses around, even if they may be in new and unfamiliar industries.

Restructuring can involve changes in assets, capital structure, or management.

- *Asset restructuring* involves the sale of unproductive assets, or even whole lines of businesses, that are peripheral. In some cases, it may even involve acquisitions that strengthen the core business.
- *Capital restructuring* involves changing the debt-equity mix, or the mix between different classes of debt or equity. Although the substitution of equity with debt is more common in buyout situations, occasionally the parent may provide additional equity capital.
- *Management restructuring* typically involves changes in the composition of the top management team, organizational structure, and reporting relationships. Tight financial control, rewards based strictly on meeting short- to medium-term performance goals, and reduction in the number of middle-level managers are common steps in management restructuring. In some cases, parental intervention may even result in changes in strategy as well as infusion of new technologies and processes.

Hanson, plc, a British conglomerate, made numerous such acquisitions in the United States in the 1980s, often selling these firms at significant profits after a few years of successful restructuring efforts. Hanson's acquisition and subsequent restructuring of the SCM group is a classic example of the restructuring strategy. Hanson acquired SCM, a diversified manufacturer of industrial and consumer products (including Smith-Corona typewriters, Glidden paints, and Durkee Famous Foods), for $930 million in 1986 after a bitter takeover battle. In the next few months, Hanson sold SCM's paper and pulp operations for $160 million, the chemical division for $30 million, Glidden paints for $580 million, and Durkee Famous Foods for $120 million, virtually recovering the entire original investment. In addition, Hanson also sold the SCM headquarters in New York for $36 million and reduced the headquarters staff by 250. They still retained several profitable divisions, including the titanium dioxide operations and managed them with tight financial controls that led to increased returns.[35]

Exhibit 6.5 summarizes the three primary types of restructuring activities.

Portfolio Management

During the 1970s and early 1980s, several leading consulting firms developed the concept of **portfolio management** to achieve a better understanding of the competitive position of an overall portfolio (or family) of businesses, to suggest strategic alternatives for each of the businesses, and to identify priorities for the allocation of resources. Several studies have reported widespread use of these techniques among American firms.[36]

Description and Potential Benefits The key purpose of portfolio models is to assist a firm in achieving a balanced portfolio of businesses.[37] This consists of businesses whose profitability, growth, and cash flow characteristics complements each other and adds up to a satisfactory overall corporate performance. Imbalance, for example, could be caused either by excessive cash generation with too few growth opportunities or by insufficient cash generation to fund the growth requirements in the portfolio. Monsanto, for example, used portfolio planning to restructure its portfolio, divesting low-growth commodity chemicals businesses and acquiring businesses in higher-growth industries such as biotechnology.

The Boston Consulting Group's (BCG) growth/share matrix is among the best known of these approaches.[38] In the BCG approach, each of the firm's strategic business units (SBUs) is plotted on a two-dimensional grid in which the axes are relative market share and industry growth rate. The grid is broken into four quadrants. Exhibit 6.6 depicts the BCG matrix. Following are a few clarifications:

1. Each circle represents one of the corporation's business units. The size of the circle represents the relative size of the business unit in terms of revenues.
2. Relative market share, measured by the ratio of the business unit's size to that of its largest competitor, is plotted along the horizontal axis.
3. Market share is central to the BCG matrix. This is because high relative market share leads to unit cost reduction due to experience and learning curve effects and, consequently, superior competitive position.

portfolio management a method of (a) assessing the competitive position of a portfolio of businesses within a corporation, (b) suggesting strategic alternatives for each business, and (c) to identifying priorities for the allocation of resources across the businesses.

Asset Restructuring: The sale of unproductive assets, or even whole lines of businesses, that are peripheral.

Capital Restructuring: Changing the debt-equity mix, or the mix between different classes of debt or equity.

Management Restructuring: Changes in the composition of the top management team, organization structure, and reporting relationships.

Exhibit 6.5
The Three Primary Types of Restructuring Activities

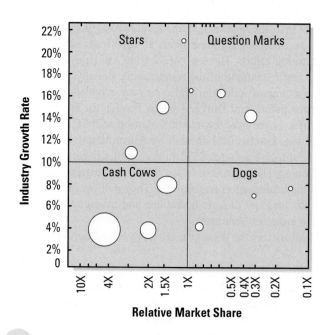

Exhibit 6.6 The Boston Consulting Group (BCG) Portfolio Matrix

Each of the four quadrants of the grid has different implications for the SBUs that fall into the category:

- **Stars** are SBUs competing in high-growth industries with relatively high market shares. These firms have long-term growth potential and should continue to receive substantial investment funding.
- **Question Marks** are SBUs competing in high-growth industries but having relatively weak market shares. Resources should be invested in them to enhance their competitive positions.
- **Cash Cows** are SBUs with high market shares in low-growth industries. These units have limited long-run potential but represent a source of current cash flows to fund investments in "stars" and "question marks."
- **Dogs** are SBUs with weak market shares in low-growth industries. Because they have weak positions and limited potential, most analysts recommend that they be divested.

In using portfolio strategy approaches, a corporation tries to create shareholder value in a number of ways.[39] First, portfolio analysis provides a snapshot of the businesses in a corporation's portfolio. Therefore, the corporation is in a better position to allocate resources among the business units according to prescribed criteria (e.g., use cash flows from the "cash cows" to fund promising "stars"). Second, the expertise and analytical resources in the corporate office provide guidance in determining what firms may be attractive (or unattractive) acquisitions. Third, the corporate office is able to provide financial resources to the business units on favorable terms that reflect the corporation's overall ability to raise funds. Fourth, the corporate office can provide high-quality review and coaching for the individual businesses. Fifth, portfolio analysis provides a basis for developing strategic goals and reward/evaluation systems for business managers. For example, managers of cash cows would have lower targets for revenue growth than managers of stars, but the former would have higher threshold levels of profit targets on proposed projects than the managers of star businesses. Compensation systems would also reflect such realities. Cash cows understandably would be rewarded more on the basis of cash that their businesses generate than would managers of star businesses. Similarly, managers of star businesses would be held to higher standards for revenue growth than managers of cash cow businesses.

To see how companies can benefit from portfolio approaches, consider Ciba-Geigy.

In 1994 Ciba-Geigy adopted portfolio planning approaches to help it manage its business units, which competed in a wide variety of industries, including chemicals, dyes, pharmaceuticals, crop protection, and animal health.[40] It placed each business unit in a category corresponding to the BCG matrix. The business unit's goals, compensation programs, personnel selection, and resource allocation were strongly associated with the category within which the business was placed. For example, business units classified as "cash cows" had much higher hurdles for obtaining financial resources (from the corporate office) for expansion than "question marks" since the latter were businesses for which Ciba-Geigy had high hopes for accelerated future growth and profitability. Additionally, the compensation of a business unit manager in a cash cow would be strongly associated with its success in generating cash to fund other businesses, whereas a manager of a question mark business would be rewarded on his or her ability to increase revenue growth and market share. The portfolio planning approaches appear to be working. In 2006, Ciba-Geigy's (now Novartis) revenues and net income stood at $26 billion and $8 billion, respectively. This represents a 22 percent increase in revenues and a most impressive 40 percent growth in net income over a two-year period.

Limitations   Despite the potential benefits of portfolio models, there are also some notable downsides. First, they compare SBUs on only two dimensions, making the implicit but erroneous assumption that (1) those are the only factors that really matter and (2) every unit can be accurately compared on that basis. Second, the approach views each SBU as a stand-alone entity, ignoring common core business practices and value-creating activities that may hold promise for synergies across business units. Third, unless care is exercised, the process becomes largely mechanical, substituting an oversimplified graphical model for the important contributions of the CEO's (and other corporate managers') experience and judgment. Fourth, the reliance on "strict rules" regarding resource allocation across SBUs can be detrimental to a firm's long-term viability. For example, according to one study, over one-half of all the businesses that should have been cash users (based on the BCG matrix) were instead cash providers.[41] Finally, while colorful and easy to comprehend, the imagery of the BCG matrix can lead to some troublesome and overly simplistic prescriptions. According to one author:

The dairying analogy is appropriate (for some cash cows), so long as we resist the urge to oversimplify it. On the farm, even the best-producing cows eventually begin to dry up. The farmer's solution to this is euphemistically called "freshening" the cow: The farmer arranges a date for the cow with a bull, she has a calf, the milk begins flowing again. Cloistering the cow—isolating her from everything but the feed trough and the milking machines—assures that she will go dry.[42]

To see what can go wrong, consider Cabot Corporation.

Cabot Corporation supplies carbon black for the rubber, electronics, and plastics industries. Following the BCG matrix, Cabot moved away from its cash cow, carbon black, and diversified into stars such as ceramics and semiconductors in a seemingly overaggressive effort to create more revenue growth for the corporation. Predictably, Cabot's return on assets declined as the firm shifted away from its core competence to unrelated areas. The portfolio model failed by pointing the company in the wrong direction in an effort to spur growth—away from their core business. Recognizing its mistake, Cabot Corporation returned to its mainstay carbon black manufacturing and divested unrelated businesses. Today the company is a leader in its field with $3.2 billion in 2008 revenues.[43]

Exhibit 6.7 summarizes the limitations of portfolio model analysis.

Exhibit 6.7
Limitations of Portfolio Models

- They are overly simplistic, consisting of only two dimensions (growth and market share).

- They view each business as separate, ignoring potential synergies across businesses.

- The process may become overly largely mechanical, minimizing the potential value of managers' judgment and experience.

- The reliance on strict rules for resource allocation across SBUs can be detrimental to a firm's long-term viability.

- The imagery (e.g., cash cows, dogs) while colorful, may lead to troublesome and overly simplistic prescriptions.

Caveat: Is Risk Reduction a Viable Goal of Diversification?

One of the purposes of diversification is to reduce the risk that is inherent in a firm's variability in revenues and profits over time. That is, if a firm enters new products or markets that are affected differently by seasonal or economic cycles, its performance over time will be more stable. For example, a firm manufacturing lawn mowers may diversify into snow blowers to even out its annual sales. Or a firm manufacturing a luxury line of household furniture may introduce a lower-priced line since affluent and lower-income customers are affected differently by economic cycles.

At first glance the above reasoning may make sense, but there are some problems with it. First, a firm's stockholders can diversify their portfolios at a much lower cost than a corporation, and they don't have to worry about integrating the acquisition into their portfolio. Second, economic cycles as well as their impact on a given industry (or firm) are difficult to predict with any degree of accuracy.

Notwithstanding the above, some firms have benefited from diversification by lowering the variability (or risk) in their performance over time. Consider Emerson Electronic.[44]

> Emerson Electronic is a $25 billion manufacturer that produces a wide variety of products, including measurement devices for heavy industry, temperature controls for heating and ventilation systems, and power tools sold at Home Depot. Recently, many analysts questioned Emerson's purchase of companies that sell power systems to the volatile telecommunications industry. Why? This industry is expected to experience, at best, minimal growth. However, CEO David Farr maintained that such assets could be acquired inexpensively because of the aggregate decline in demand in this industry. Additionally, he argued that the other business units, such as the sales of valves and regulators to the now-booming oil and natural gas companies, were able to pick up the slack. Therefore, while net profits in the electrical equipment sector (Emerson's core business) sharply decreased, Emerson's overall corporate profits increased 1.7 percent.

Risk reduction in and of itself is rarely viable as a means to create shareholder value. It must be undertaken with a view of a firm's overall diversification strategy.

>LO5

The various means of engaging in diversification— mergers and acquisitions, joint ventures/ strategic alliances, and internal development.

The Means to Achieve Diversification

We have addressed the types of diversification (e.g., related and unrelated) that a firm may undertake to achieve synergies and create value for its shareholders. Now, we address the means by which a firm can go about achieving these desired benefits.

There are three basic means. First, through acquisitions or mergers, corporations can directly acquire a firm's assets and competencies. Although the terms *mergers* and *acquisitions* are used quite interchangeably, there are some key differences. With

acquisitions, one firm buys another either through a stock purchase, cash, or the issuance of debt.[45] **Mergers,** on the other hand, entail a combination or consolidation of two firms to form a new legal entity. Mergers are relatively rare and entail a transaction among two firms on a relatively equal basis. Despite such differences, we consider both mergers and acquisitions to be quite similar in terms of their implications for a firm's corporate-level strategy.[46]

Second, corporations may agree to pool the resources of other companies with their resource base, commonly known as a joint venture or strategic alliance. Although these two forms of partnerships are similar in many ways, there is an important difference. Joint ventures involve the formation of a third-party legal entity where the two (or more) firms each contribute equity, whereas strategic alliances do not.

Third, corporations may diversify into new products, markets, and technologies through internal development. Called corporate entrepreneurship, it involves the leveraging and combining of a firm's own resources and competencies to create synergies and enhance shareholder value. We address this subject in greater length in Chapter 12.

Mergers and Acquisitions

The rate of mergers and acquisitions (M&A) had dropped off beginning in 2001. This trend was largely a result of a recession, corporate scandals, and a declining stock market. However, the situation has changed dramatically. Over the past several years, several large mergers and acquisitions were announced. These include:[47]

- Pfizer's acquisition of Wyeth for $68 billion.
- Mittal Steel's acquisition of Arcelor for $33 billion.
- BellSouth's acquisition of AT&T for $86.0 billion.
- Sprint's merger with Nextel for $39 billion.
- Boston Scientific's $27 billion acquisition of medical device maker Guidant.
- Procter & Gamble's purchase of Gillette for $54 billion.
- Kmart Holding Corp.'s acquisition of Sears, Roebuck & Co. for $11 billion.

Exhibit 6.8 illustrates the dramatic increase in worldwide M&A activity in the U.S. up until 2008, when the global recession began. Several factors help to explain the rapid rise between 2002 and 2007. First, there was the robust economy and the increasing corporate profits that had boosted stock prices and cash. For example, the S&P 500 stock index companies, including financial companies, had a record of over $2 trillion in cash and other short-term assets.

Second, the weak U.S. dollar made U.S. assets less expensive relative to other countries. That is, from the perspective of a foreign acquirer, compared to any other period in recent memory, U.S. companies were "cheap." For example, a Euro, which was worth only 80 cents in 1999, was worth $1.35 by mid-2007. This made U.S. companies a relative bargain for a European acquirer.

Third, stricter governance standards were requiring poorly performing CEOs and boards of directors to consider unsolicited offers. In essence, top executives and board members were less likely to be protected by antitakeover mechanisms such as greenmail, poison pills, and golden parachutes (discussed at the end of the chapter).

Motives and Benefits   Growth through mergers and acquisitions has played a critical role in the success of many corporations in a wide variety of high-technology and knowledge-intensive industries. Here, market and technology changes can occur very quickly and unpredictably.[48] Speed—speed to market, speed to positioning, and speed to becoming a viable company—is critical in such industries. For example, Alex Mandl, then AT&T's president, was responsible for the acquisition of McCaw Cellular. Although many industry experts felt the price was too steep, he believed that cellular technology was a

acquisitions the incorporation of one firm into another through purchase.

mergers the combining of two or more firms into one new legal entity.

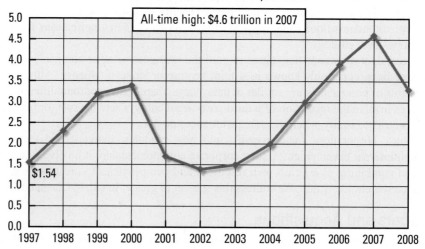

Global Value of Mergers and Acquisitions

Global mergers and acquisitions soared past their previous record and hit $4.6 trillion for the year 2007.

All-time high: $4.6 trillion in 2007

$1.54

Exhibit 6.8 Global Value of Mergers and Acquisitions

Source: Bloomberg; Dealogic; and personal communication with Meredith Leonard at Dealogic on January 27, 2009.

critical asset for the telecommunications business. Mandl claimed, "The plain fact is that acquiring is much faster than building."[49]

Mergers and acquisitions also can be a means of *obtaining valuable resources that can help an organization expand its product offerings and services.* For example, Cisco Systems, a dominant player in networking equipment, acquired more than 70 companies over a recent seven-year period.[50] This provides Cisco with access to the latest in networking equipment. Then it uses its excellent sales force to market the new technology to its corporate customers. Cisco also provides strong incentives to the staff of acquired companies to stay on. To realize the greatest value from its acquisitions, Cisco also has learned to integrate acquired companies efficiently and effectively.[51]

Mergers and acquisitions also can *provide the opportunity for firms to attain the three bases of synergy—leveraging core competencies, sharing activities, and building market power.* Consider Procter & Gamble's $57 billion acquisition of Gillette.[52] First, it helps Procter & Gamble to leverage its core competencies in marketing and product positioning in the area of grooming and personal care brands. For example, P&G has experience in repositioning brands such as Old Spice in this market (which recently passed Gillette's Right Guard brand to become No. 1 in the deodorant market). Gillette has very strong brands in razors and blades. Thus, P&G's marketing expertise enhances its market position. Second, there are opportunities to share value-creating activities. Gillette will benefit from P&G's stronger distribution network in developing countries where the potential growth rate for the industry's products remains higher than in the United States, Europe, or Japan. Consider the insight of A. F. Lafley, P&G's CEO:

> When I was in Asia in the 90s, we had already gone beyond the top 500 cities in China. Today, we're way down into the rural areas. So we add three, four, five Gillette brands, and we don't even have to add a salesperson.

Third, the addition of Gillette increases P&G's market power. In recent years, the growth of powerful global retailers such as Wal-Mart, Carrefour, and Costco has eroded much of the consumer goods industry's pricing power. A central part of P&G's recent strategy has been to focus its resources on enhancing its core brands. Today, 16 of its brands (each with revenues of over $1 billion) account for $30 billion of the firm's $51.4 billion in total revenues. Gillette, with $10.5 billion in total revenues, adds five brands which also have revenues of over $1 billion. P&G anticipates that its growing stable of "superbrands" will help it to weather the industry's tough pricing environment and enhance its power relative to large, powerful retailers such as Wal-Mart and Target.

Merger and acquisition activity also can *lead to consolidation within an industry and can force other players to merge.*[53] In the pharmaceutical industry, the patents for many top-selling drugs are expiring and M&A activity is expected to heat up.[54] For example, a few years ago SG Cowen Securities predicted that between 2000 and 2005, U.S. patents would expire on pharmaceutical products with annual domestic sales of approximately $34.6 billion. Clearly, this is an example of how the political—legal segment of the general environment (discussed in Chapter 2) can affect a corporation's strategy and performance. Although health care providers and patients are happy about the lower-cost generics that will arrive, drug firms are being pressed to make up for lost revenues. Combining top firms such as Glaxo Wellcome and SmithKline Beecham has many potential long-term benefits. They not only promise significant postmerger cost savings, but also the increased size of the combined companies brings greater research and development possibilities.

Corporations can also *enter new market segments by way of acquisitions.* Although Charles Schwab & Co. is best known for providing discount trading services for middle America, it clearly is interested in other target markets.[55] In late 2000 Schwab surprised its rivals by paying $2.7 billion to acquire (divested in 2006) U.S. Trust Corporation, a 147-year-old financial services institution that is a top estate planner for the wealthy. However, Schwab is not ignoring its core market. The firm also purchased Cybercorp Inc., a Texas brokerage company, for $488 million. That firm offers active online traders sophisticated quotes and stock-screening tools. Exhibit 6.9 summarizes the benefits of mergers and acquisitions.

Potential Limitations As noted in the previous section, mergers and acquisitions provide a firm with many potential benefits. However, at the same time, there are many potential drawbacks or limitations to such corporate activity.[56]

First, *the takeover premium that is paid for an acquisition typically is very high.* Two times out of three, the stock price of the acquiring company falls once the deal is made public. Since the acquiring firm often pays a 30 percent or higher premium for the target company, the acquirer must create synergies and scale economies that result in sales and market gains exceeding the premium price. Firms paying higher premiums set the performance hurdle even higher. For example, Household International paid an 82 percent premium to buy Beneficial, and Conseco paid an 83 percent premium to acquire Green Tree Financial. Historically, paying a high premium over the stock price has been a poor strategy.

- Obtain valuable resources that can help an organization expand its product offerings.
- Provide the opportunity for firms to attain three bases of synergy: leveraging core competencies, sharing activities, and building market power.
- Lead to consolidation within an industry and force other players to merge.
- Enter new market segments.

Exhibit 6.9
Benefits of Mergers and Acquisitions

Second, *competing firms often can imitate any advantages realized or copy synergies that result from the M&A.*[57] Thus, a firm can often see its advantages quickly erode. Unless the advantages are sustainable and difficult to copy, investors will not be willing to pay a high premium for the stock. Similarly, the time value of money must be factored into the stock price. M&A costs are paid up front. Conversely, firms pay for R&D, ongoing marketing, and capacity expansion over time. This stretches out the payments needed to gain new competencies. The M&A argument is that a large initial investment is worthwhile because it creates long-term advantages. However, stock analysts want to see immediate results from such a large cash outlay. If the acquired firm does not produce results quickly, investors often divest the stock, driving the price down.

Third, *managers' credibility and ego can sometimes get in the way of sound business decisions.* If the M&A does not perform as planned, managers who pushed for the deal find their reputation tarnished. This can lead them to protect their credibility by funneling more money, or escalating their commitment, into an inevitably doomed operation. Further, when a merger fails and a firm tries to unload the acquisition, they often must sell at a huge discount. These problems further compound the costs and erode the stock price.

Fourth, *there can be many cultural issues that may doom the intended benefits from M&A endeavors.* Consider, the insights of Joanne Lawrence, who played an important role in the merger between SmithKline and the Beecham Group.[58]

> The key to a strategic merger is to create a new culture. This was a mammoth challenge during the SmithKline Beecham merger. We were working at so many different cultural levels, it was dizzying. We had two national cultures to blend—American and British— that compounded the challenge of selling the merger in two different markets with two different shareholder bases. There were also two different business cultures: One was very strong, scientific, and academic; the other was much more commercially oriented. And then we had to consider within both companies the individual businesses, each of which has its own little culture.

Exhibit 6.10 summarizes the limitations of mergers and acquisitions.

Divestment: The Other Side of the "M&A Coin"   When firms acquire other businesses, it typically generates quite a bit of "press" in business publications such as *The Wall Street Journal, BusinessWeek,* and *Fortune.* It makes for exciting news, and one thing is for sure—large acquiring firms automatically improve their standing in the Fortune 500 rankings (since it is based solely on total revenues). However, managers must also carefully consider the strategic implications of exiting businesses.

divestment the exit of a business from a firm's portfolio.

Divestments, the exit of a business from a firm's portfolio, are quite common. One study found that large, prestigious U.S. companies divested more acquisitions than they had kept.[59] Well-known divestitures in business history include (1) Novell's purchase of WordPerfect for stock valued at $1.4 billion and later sold to Corel for $124 million, and (2) Quaker Oats' unloading of the Snapple Beverage Company to Triarc for only $300 million in 1997—three years after it had bought it for $1.8 billion!

Exhibit 6.10
Limitations of Mergers and Acquisitions

- Takeover premiums paid for acquisitions are typically very high.
- Competing firms often can imitate any advantages or copy synergies that result from the merger or acquisition.
- Managers' egos sometimes get in the way of sound business decisions.
- Cultural issues may doom the intended benefits from M&A endeavors.

Campbell Soup Divests Godiva to Focus on Its Core Business

In August 2007, Campbell Soup decided it would sell Godiva, its superpremium chocolate business— which had been a very profitable brand for them. Campbell didn't base the decision on financial considerations. Rather, Godiva was not consistent with Campbell's values, competencies, and aspirations of nutrition and simplicity. According to Doug Conant, Campbell's CEO: "Although the premium chocolate category is experiencing strong growth and Godiva is well positioned for the future, the premium chocolate business does not fit Campbell's focus on simple meals."

The firm reached an agreement to sell Godiva to Yildiz Holding (which owns the Turkish company Ulker Group) for $850 million in December 2007. By relying on its identity, rather than on financial projections, Campbell made the decision to sell the unit quickly and painlessly.

Source: Camillus, J. 2008. Strategy as a Wicked Problem. *Harvard Business Review*, 86 (5): 98–108.

● Campbell Soup divested Godiva. Even though the chocolatier had a very strong market position, Godiva did not fit Campbell's "focus on simple meals."

Divesting a business can accomplish many different objectives.* As the examples above demonstrate, it can be used to help a firm reverse an earlier acquisition that didn't work out as planned. Often, this is simply to help "cut their losses." Other objectives include: (1) enabling managers to focus their efforts more directly on the firm's core businesses,[60] (2) providing the firm with more resources to spend on more attractive alternatives; and (3) raising cash to help fund existing businesses. Strategy Spotlight 6.6 discusses why Campbell Soup divested Godiva—to concentrate on its core business.

---

* Firms can divest their businesses in a number of ways. Sell-offs, spin-offs, equity carve-outs, asset sales/dissolution, and split-ups are some such modes of divestment. In a sell-off, the divesting firm privately negotiates with a third party to divest a unit/subsidiary for cash/stock. In a spin-off, a parent company distributes shares of the unit/subsidiary being divested pro-rata to its existing shareholders and a new company is formed. Equity carve-outs are similar to spin-offs except that shares in the unit/subsidiary being divested are offered to new shareholders. Dissolution involves sale of redundant assets, not necessarily as an entire unit/subsidiary as in sell-offs but a few bits at a time. A split-up, on the other hand, is an instance of divestiture where the parent company is split into two or more new companies and the parent ceases to exist. Shares in the parent company are exchanged for shares in new companies and the exact distribution varies case by case.

Divesting can enhance a firm's competitive position only to the extent that it reduces its tangible (e.g., maintenance, investments, etc.) or intangible (e.g., opportunity costs, managerial attention) costs without sacrificing a current competitive advantage or the seeds of future advantages.[61] To be effective, divesting requires a thorough understanding of a business unit's current ability and future potential to contribute to a firm's value creation. However, since such decisions involve a great deal of uncertainty, it is very difficult to make such evaluations. In addition, because of managerial self-interests and organizational inertia, firms often delay divestments of underperforming businesses.

Successful divestment involves establishing objective criteria for determining divestment candidates.[62] Clearly, firms should not panic and sell for a song in bad times. Private equity firms and conglomerates naturally place great emphasis on value when it comes to assessing which business units to keep. In identifying which assets to sell, the management committee of $13 billion Textron, for example, applies three tests of value to the firm's diverse portfolio—which is composed of some 12 divisions and 72 strategic business units (SBUs). For Textron to retain a business unit:

- The unit's long-term fundamentals must be sound. The team gauges this by assessing the attractiveness of each SBU's market and the unit's competitive strength within that market.
- Textron must be able to grow the unit's intrinsic value by 15 percent or more annually. The team applies this screen by carefully analyzing each SBU's business plan each year and challenging its divisional management teams to assess the value-growth potential of each business objectively.
- The unit's revenues must reach a certain threshold. Textron seeks to hold a portfolio of relevant businesses, each with at least $1 billion in revenue. Businesses that are not generating $1 billion or more in sales—and are not likely to reach this watershed within the foreseeable future—are targets for divestiture.

Strategic Alliances and Joint Ventures

A **strategic alliance** is a cooperative relationship between two (or more) firms.[63] Alliances may be either informal or formal—that is, involving a written contract. **Joint ventures** represent a special case of alliances, wherein two (or more) firms contribute equity to form a new legal entity.

Strategic alliances and joint ventures are assuming an increasingly prominent role in the strategy of leading firms, both large and small.[64] Such cooperative relationships have many potential advantages.[65] Among these are entering new markets, reducing manufacturing (or other) costs in the value chain, and developing and diffusing new technologies.[66]

Entering New Markets   Often a company that has a successful product or service wants to introduce it into a new market. However, it may not have the financial resources or the requisite marketing expertise because it does not understand customer needs, know how to promote the product, or have access to the proper distribution channels.[67]

The partnerships formed between Time-Warner, Inc., and three African American–owned cable companies in New York City are examples of joint ventures created to serve a domestic market. Time-Warner built a 185,000-home cable system in the city and asked the three cable companies to operate it. Time-Warner supplied the product, and the cable companies supplied the knowledge of the community and the know-how to market the cable system. Joining with the local companies enabled Time-Warner to win the acceptance of the cable customers and to benefit from an improved image in the black community.

Crowdsourcing: Kraft's Strategic Alliance with a Bagel Maker

In 2006, Kraft Foods launched a program on its website that actively seeks out small businesses and inventors as partners for product development. "The world has gotten much smaller, and innovation is happening at small businesses," asserts Steve Goers, vice president for open innovation and investment. Entrepreneurs and inventors submit an average of 40 to 50 ideas each month through www.innovatewithkraft.com. Dozens of ideas, which may also be submitted in writing or by phone, have become new products or enhancements of existing products.

Gary Schwartzberg pitched his product, a cream-filled bagel, as an "all-in-one, portable breakfast for the on-the-go crowd." He was interested in the brand strength of Kraft's Philadelphia Cream Cheese and mailed Kraft a proposal, along with a box of Bagelers, his cream-filled bagels. Says Schwartzberg: "Bagelers are the perfect meal for busy families looking for a quick and convenient meal that tastes great. The secret is in the family recipe we have been using since 1931 coupled with our patented production technology. As we like to say, Bagelers are a whole new way to eat bagels and cream cheese."

Fortunately, Kraft had been working on something similar, in an effort to market its cream cheese in the growing portable-breakfast category. But the firm didn't have bagel-making expertise and hadn't been able to get the product just right. Schwartzberg, on the other hand, had patented a process for "encapsulating" the cream cheese in the center of the bagel without the cream cheese escaping during the baking process. After Kraft executives tasted the product, they flew to Florida to meet with Schwartzberg. They formed an internal team to evaluate the marketability of the product and looked into the production process to make sure the bagels could be produced on a national scale.

Satisfied, the two sides signed a deal in which details are unavailable because of a confidentiality agreement, which is standard practice in such situations. Schwartzberg says it is structured as a strategic alliance and he "has skin in the game." The products are now known as Bagel-Fuls, and they are available in supermarkets throughout the U.S. Branded by Kraft Foods, they are filled with Philadelphia Cream Cheese—the best-selling brand in the U.S.

Sources: Covel, S. 2008. My Brain, Your Brawn. WSJ.com, October 13: np.; and Filled Bagel Industries Announces Launch of Bagelers Cream Cheese–Filled Product. 2003. FoodserviceCentral.com, October 28: np.

crowdsourcing

Strategy Spotlight 6.7 discusses how Kraft Foods, the $37 billion consumer giant, used a strategic alliance with a small bagel producer to generate profits for both firms.

Reducing Manufacturing (or Other) Costs in the Value Chain   Strategic alliances (or joint ventures) often enable firms to pool capital, value-creating activities, or facilities in order to reduce costs. For example, Molson Companies and Carling O'Keefe Breweries in Canada formed a joint venture to merge their brewing operations. Although Molson had a modern and efficient brewery in Montreal, Carling's was outdated. However, Carling had the better facilities in Toronto. In addition, Molson's Toronto brewery was located on the waterfront and had substantial real estate value. Overall, the synergies gained by using their combined facilities more efficiently added $150 million of pretax earnings during the initial year of the venture. Economies of scale were realized and facilities were better utilized.

Developing and Diffusing New Technologies   Strategic alliances also may be used to build jointly on the technological expertise of two or more companies in order to develop products technologically beyond the capability of the companies acting independently.

STMicroelectronics (ST) is a high-tech company based in Geneva, Switzerland, that has thrived—largely due to the success of its strategic alliances.[68] The firm develops and manufactures computer chips for a variety of applications such as mobile phones, set-top boxes, smart cards, and flash memories. In 1995 it teamed up with Hewlett-Packard to develop powerful new processors for various digital applications that are now nearing completion. Another example was its strategic alliance with Nokia to develop a chip that would give Nokia's phones a longer battery life. Here, ST produced a chip that tripled standby time to 60 hours—a breakthough that gave Nokia a huge advantage in the marketplace.

The firm's CEO, Pasquale Pistorio, was among the first in the industry to form R&D alliances with other companies. Now ST's top 12 customers, including HP, Nokia, and Nortel, account for 45 percent of revenues. According to Pistorio, "Alliances are in our DNA." Such relationships help ST keep better-than-average growth rates, even in difficult times. That's because close partners are less likely to defect to other suppliers.

Potential Downsides   Despite their promise, many alliances and joint ventures fail to meet expectations for a variety of reasons.[69] First, without the proper partner, a firm should never consider undertaking an alliance, even for the best of reasons.[70] Each partner should bring the desired complementary strengths to the partnership. Ideally, the strengths contributed by the partners are unique; thus synergies created can be more easily sustained and defended over the longer term. The goal must be to develop synergies between the contributions of the partners, resulting in a win–win situation. Moreover, the partners must be compatible and willing to trust each other. Unfortunately, often little attention is given to nurturing the close working relationships and interpersonal connections that bring together the partnering organizations.

Internal Development

Firms can also diversify by means of corporate entrepreneurship and new venture development. **In today's economy, internal development is such an important means by which companies expand their businesses that we have devoted a whole chapter to it (see Chapter 12).** Sony and the Minnesota Mining & Manufacturing Co. (3M), for example, are known for their dedication to innovation, R&D, and cutting-edge technologies. For example, 3M has developed its entire corporate culture to support its ongoing policy of generating at least 25 percent of total sales from products created within the most recent four-year period. During the 1990s, 3M exceeded this goal by achieving about 30 percent of sales per year from new internally developed products.

The luxury hotel chain Ritz-Carlton has long been recognized for its exemplary service. In fact, it is the only service company ever to win two Malcolm Baldrige National Quality Awards. It has built on this capability by developing a highly successful internal venture to offer leadership development programs—both to its employees as well as to outside companies. We address this internal venture in Strategy Spotlight 6.8.

Compared to mergers and acquisitions, firms that engage in internal development capture the value created by their own innovative activities without having to "share the wealth" with alliance partners or face the difficulties associated with combining activities across the value chains of several firms or merging corporate cultures. Also, firms can often develop new products or services at a relatively lower cost and thus rely on their own resources rather than turning to external funding.

There are also potential disadvantages. It may be time consuming; thus, firms may forfeit the benefits of speed that growth through mergers or acquisitions can provide. This may be especially important among high-tech or knowledge-based organizations in fast-paced environments where being an early mover is critical. Thus, firms that choose to diversify through internal development must develop capabilities that allow them to move quickly from initial opportunity recognition to market introduction.

The Ritz-Carlton Leadership Center: A Successful Internal Venture

Companies worldwide often strive to be the "Ritz-Carlton" of their industries. Ritz-Carlton, the large luxury hotel chain, is the only service company to have won the prestigious Malcolm Baldrige National Quality Award twice—in 1992 and 1999 (one year after being acquired by Marriott). It also has placed first in guest satisfaction among luxury hotels in the most recent J.D. Power & Associates hotel survey.

Until a few years ago, being "Ritz-Carlton-like" was just a motivational simile. However, in 2000, the company launched the Ritz-Carlton Leadership Center, where it offers 12 leadership development programs for its employees and seven benchmarking seminars and workshops to outside companies. It also conducts 35 off-site presentations on such topics as "Creating a Dynamic Employee

Orientation," and "The Key to Retaining and Selecting Talented Employees." (Incidentally, Ritz-Carlton's annual turnover rate among nonmanagement employees is 25 percent—roughly half the average rate for U.S. luxury hotels.)

Within its first four years of operation, 800 different companies from such industries as health care, banking and finance, hospitality, and the automotive industries have participated in the Leadership Center's programs. And to date it has generated over $2 million in revenues. Says Diana Oreck, Vice President of RCLL: "At Ritz-Carlton we have a credo, motto, and three steps of service that are critical. You can adapt these elements to the vision of what your company culture should be."

To give a few specifics on one of the Leadership Center's programs, consider its "Legendary Service I" course. The topics that are covered include empowerment, using customer recognition to boost loyalty, and Ritz-Carlton's approach to quality. The course lasts two days and costs $2,000 per attendee. Well-known companies that have participated include Microsoft, Morgan Stanley, and Starbucks.

Sources: Jankowski, W. 2008. Ten Minutes with Diana Oreck. www.remodeling.hw.net, August 26: np; corporate.ritzcarlton.com. McDonald, D. 2004. Roll Out the Blue Carpet. *Business 2.0,* May: 53; and Johnson, G. 2003. Nine Tactics to Take Your Corporate University from Good to GREAT. *Training,* July/August: 38–41.

How Managerial Motives Can Erode Value Creation

Thus far in the chapter we have implicitly assumed that CEOs and top executives are "rational beings"; that is, they act in the best interests of shareholders to maximize long-term shareholder value. In the real world, however, they may often act in their own self-interest. We now address some managerial motives that can serve to erode, rather than enhance, value creation. These include "growth for growth's sake," excessive egotism, and the creation of a wide variety of antitake-over tactics.

Growth for Growth's Sake

There are huge incentives for executives to increase the size of their firm. And these are not consistent with increasing shareholder wealth. Top managers, including the CEO, of larger firms typically enjoy more prestige, higher rankings for their firms on the Fortune 500 list (based on revenues, *not* profits), greater incomes, more job security, and so on. There is also the excitement and associated recognition of making a major acquisition. As noted by Harvard's Michael Porter, "There's a tremendous allure to mergers and acquisitions. It's the big play, the dramatic gesture. With one stroke of the pen you can add billions to size, get a front-page story, and create excitement in markets."[71]

In recent years many high-tech firms have suffered from the negative impact of their uncontrolled growth. Consider, for example, Priceline.com's ill-fated venture into an online service to offer groceries and gasoline.[72] A myriad of problems—perhaps most

>LO6
Managerial behaviors that can erode the creation of value.

managerial motives managers acting in their own self-interest rather than in maximizing long-term shareholder value.

Cornelius Vanderbilt: Going to Great Lengths to Correct a Wrong!

Cornelius Vanderbilt's legendary ruthlessness set a bar for many titans to come. Back in 1853, the Commodore took his first vacation, an extended voyage to Europe aboard his yacht. He was in for a big surprise when he returned. Two of his associates had taken the power of attorney that he had left them and sold his interest in his steamship concern, Accessory Transit Company, to themselves.

"Gentlemen," he wrote, in a classic battle cry, "you have undertaken to cheat me. I won't sue you, for the law is too slow. I'll ruin you." He converted his yacht to a passenger ship to compete with them and added other vessels. He started a new line, appropriately named *Opposition*. Before long, he bought his way back in and regained control of the company.

Source: McGregor, J. 2007. Sweet Revenge. *BusinessWeek*, January 22: 64–70.

---

importantly, a lack of participation by manufacturers—caused the firm to lose more than $5 million a *week* prior to abandoning these ventures. Such initiatives are often little more than desperate moves by top managers to satisfy investor demands for accelerating revenues. Unfortunately, the increased revenues often fail to materialize into a corresponding hike in earnings.

At times, executives' overemphasis on growth can result in a plethora of ethical lapses, which can have disastrous outcomes for their companies. A good example (of bad practice) is Joseph Bernardino's leadership at Andersen Worldwide. Bernardino had a chance early on to take a hard line on ethics and quality in the wake of earlier scandals at clients such as Waste Management and Sunbeam. Instead, according to former executives, he put too much emphasis on revenue growth. Consequently, the firm's reputation quickly eroded when it audited and signed off on the highly flawed financial statements of such infamous firms as Enron, Global Crossing, and WorldCom. Bernardino ultimately resigned in disgrace in March 2002, and his firm was dissolved later that year.[73]

Egotism

A healthy ego helps make a leader confident, clearheaded, and able to cope with change. CEOs, by their very nature, are intensely competitive people in the office as well as on the tennis court or golf course. But, sometimes when pride is at stake, individuals will go to great lengths to win. Such behavior, of course, is not a new phenomenon. We discuss the case of Cornelius Vanderbilt, one of the original American moguls, in Strategy Spotlight 6.9.

Egos can get in the way of a "synergistic" corporate marriage. Few executives (or lower-level managers) are exempt from the potential downside of excessive egos. Consider, for example, the reflections of General Electric's former CEO Jack Welch, considered by many to be the world's most admired executive. He admitted to a regrettable decision: "My hubris got in the way in the Kidder Peabody deal. [He was referring to GE's buyout of the soon-to-be-troubled Wall Street firm.] I got wise advice from Walter Wriston and other directors who said, 'Jack, don't do this.' But I was bully enough and on a run to do it. And I got whacked right in the head."[74] In addition to poor financial results, Kidder Peabody was wracked by a widely publicized trading scandal that tarnished the reputations of both GE and Kidder Peabody. Welch ended up selling Kidder in 1994.

The business press has included many stories of how egotism and greed have infiltrated organizations. Some incidents are considered rather astonishing, such as Tyco's former (and now convicted) CEO Dennis Kozlowski's well-chronicled purchase of a $6,000 shower curtain and vodka-spewing, full-size replica of Michaelangelo's David.[75] Other well-known examples of power grabs and extraordinary consumption of compensation and perks include executives at Enron, the Rigas family who were convicted of defrauding Adelphia of roughly $1 billion, former CEO Bernie Ebbers's $408 million loan from WorldCom, and so on.

A more recent example of excess and greed was exhibited by John Thain.[76] On January 22, 2009, he was ousted as head of Merrill Lynch by Bank of America's CEO, Ken Lewis:

> Thain embarrassingly doled out $4 billion in discretionary year-end bonuses to favored employees just before Bank of America's rescue purchase of failing Merrill. The bonuses amounted to about 10 percent of Merrill's 2008 losses.
>
> Obviously, John Thain believed that he was entitled. When he took over ailing Merrill in early 2008, he began planning major cuts, but he also ordered that his office be redecorated. He spent $1.22 million of company funds to make it "livable," which, in part, included $87,000 for a rug, $87,000 for a pair of guest chairs, $68,000 for a 19th-century credenza, and (what really got the attention of the press) $35,000 for a "commode with legs."
>
> He later agreed to repay the decorating costs. However, one might still ask: What kind of person treats other people's money like this? And who needs a commode that costs as much as a new Lexus? Finally, a comment by Bob O'Brien, stock editor at Barrons.com clearly applies: "The sense of entitlement that's been engendered in this group of people has clearly not been beaten out of them by the brutal performance of the financial sector over the course of the last year."

Antitakeover Tactics

Unfriendly or hostile takeovers can occur when a company's stock becomes undervalued. A competing organization can buy the outstanding stock of a takeover candidate in sufficient quantity to become a large shareholder. Then it makes a tender offer to gain full control of the company. If the shareholders accept the offer, the hostile firm buys the target company and either fires the target firm's management team or strips them of their power. Thus, antitakeover tactics are common, including greenmail, golden parachutes, and poison pills.[77]

The first, **greenmail,** is an effort by the target firm to prevent an impending takeover. When a hostile firm buys a large block of outstanding target company stock and the target firm's management feels that a tender offer is impending, they offer to buy the stock back from the hostile company at a higher price than the unfriendly company paid for it. Although this often prevents a hostile takeover, the same price is not offered to preexisting shareholders. However, it protects the jobs of the target firm's management.

Second, a **golden parachute** is a prearranged contract with managers specifying that, in the event of a hostile takeover, the target firm's managers will be paid a significant severance package. Although top managers lose their jobs, the golden parachute provisions protect their income.

Third, **poison pills** are used by a company to give shareholders certain rights in the event of a takeover by another firm. They are also known as shareholder rights plans.

Clearly, antitakeover tactics can often raise some interesting ethical—and legal—issues. Strategy Spotlight 6.10 addresses how antitakeover measures can benefit multiple stakeholders—not just management.

greenmail a payment by a firm to a hostile party for the firm's stock at a premium, made when the firm's management feels that the hostile party is about to make a tender offer.

golden parachute a prearranged contract with managers specifying that, in the event of a hostile takeover, the target firm's managers will be paid a significant severance package.

poison pill used by a company to give shareholders certain rights in the event of takeover by another firm.

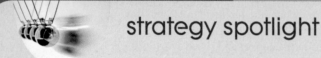

How Antitakeover Measures May Benefit Multiple Stakeholders, Not Just Management

Antitakeover defenses represent a gray area, because management can often legitimately argue that such actions are not there solely to benefit themselves. Rather, they can benefit other stakeholders, such as employees, customers, and the community.

In the late 1980s, takeovers were very popular. The Dayton Hudson Corporation (now Target) even appealed to the Minnesota legislature to pass an antitakeover bill to help Dayton Hudson in its struggle with Hafts—the former owners of Dart, a drug store chain on the East Coast. History had shown that the Dayton Hudson management in place at the time was much better able to manage Dayton Hudson in the long run. In addition to Minnesota, many states now have laws that allow firms to take the interests of all stakeholders into account when considering a takeover bid.

In the summer of 2003, Oracle launched a hostile bid for PeopleSoft. Many charged that the tactics of Oracle CEO Larry Ellison had been unfair, and many of People-

Soft's customers took its side, indicating that Oracle ownership would not be of benefit to them. PeopleSoft was concerned that Oracle was merely seeking to buy PeopleSoft for its lucrative base of application software and was not interested in supporting the company's products. Oracle, on the other hand, sued PeopleSoft in an attempt to have the latter's so-called poison pill takeover defense removed.

In December 2004, Oracle struck a deal to buy PeopleSoft—ending a bitter 18-month hostile takeover battle. Oracle's $10.3 billion acquisition valued the firm at $26.50 a share—an increase of 66 percent over its initial offer of $16 a share. Noted analyst John DiFucci: "This is a financial acquisition primarily. Oracle is buying PeopleSoft for its maintenance stream." And, worth noting, PeopleSoft executives, including CEO and company founder David Duffield, did not join Oracle during the conference call announcing the acquisition. Oracle dropped its suit against PeopleSoft in which the former charged that PeopleSoft's "poison pill" takeover defense should be dismissed.

On moral grounds, some antitakeover defenses are not undertaken to entrench and protect management, but often they are. When such defenses are used simply to keep management in power, they are wrong. However, when they are used to defend the long-term financial health of the company and to protect broader stakeholder interests, they will be morally permissible.

Sources: Bowie, N. E. & Werhane, P. H. 2005. *Management Ethics*. Malden, MA: Blackwell Publishing; and La Monica, P. R. 2004. Finally, Oracle to Buy PeopleSoft. CNNMoney.com, December 13: np.

Reflecting on Career Implications . . .

- *Corporate-Level Strategy:* Be aware of your firm's corporate-level strategy. Can you come up with an initiative that will create value both within and across business units?
- *Core Competencies:* What do you see as your core competencies? How can you leverage them both within your business unit as well as across other business units?
- *Sharing Infrastructures:* What infrastructure activities and resources (e.g., information systems, legal) are available in the corporate office that would help you add value for your business unit—or other business units?
- *Diversification:* From your career perspective, what actions can you take to diversify your employment risk (e.g., coursework at a local university, obtain professional certification such as a C.P.A., networking through professional affiliation, etc.)? For example, in periods of retrenchment, such actions will provide you with a greater number of career options.

Summary

A key challenge for today's managers is to create "synergy" when engaging in diversification activities. As we discussed in this chapter, corporate managers do not, in general, have a very good track record in creating value in such endeavors when it comes to mergers and acquisitions. Among the factors that serve to erode shareholder values are paying an excessive premium for the target firm, failing to integrate the activities of the newly acquired businesses into the corporate family, and undertaking diversification initiatives that are too easily imitated by the competition.

We addressed two major types of corporate-level strategy: related and unrelated diversification. With *related diversification* the corporation strives to enter into areas in which key resources and capabilities of the corporation can be shared or leveraged. Synergies come from horizontal relationships between business units. Cost savings and enhanced revenues can be derived from two major sources. First, economies of scope can be achieved from the leveraging of core competencies and the sharing of activities. Second, market power can be attained from greater, or pooled, negotiating power and from vertical integration.

When firms undergo *unrelated diversification* they enter product markets that are dissimilar to their present businesses. Thus, there is generally little opportunity to either leverage core competencies or share activities across business units. Here, synergies are created from vertical relationships between the corporate office and the individual business units. With unrelated diversification, the primary ways to create value are corporate restructuring and parenting, as well as the use of portfolio analysis techniques.

Corporations have three primary means of diversifying their product markets—mergers and acquisitions, joint ventures/strategic alliances, and internal development. There are key trade-offs associated with each of these. For example, mergers and acquisitions are typically the quickest means to enter new markets and provide the corporation with a high level of control over the acquired business. However, with the expensive premiums that often need to be paid to the shareholders of the target firm and the challenges associated with integrating acquisitions, they can also be quite expensive. Not surprisingly, many poorly performing acquisitions are subsequently divested. At times, however, divestitures can help firms refocus their efforts and generate resources. Strategic alliances and joint ventures between two or more firms, on the other hand, may be a means of reducing risk since they involve the sharing and combining of resources. But such joint initiatives also provide a firm with less control (than it would have with an acquisition) since governance is shared between two independent entities. Also, there is a limit to the potential upside for each partner because returns must be shared as well. Finally, with internal development, a firm is able to capture all of the value from its initiatives (as opposed to sharing it with a merger or alliance partner). However, diversification by means of internal development can be very time-consuming—a disadvantage that becomes even more important in fast-paced competitive environments.

Finally, some managerial behaviors may serve to erode shareholder returns. Among these are "growth for growth's sake," egotism, and antitakeover tactics. As we discussed, some of these issues—particularly antitakeover tactics—raise ethical considerations because the managers of the firm are not acting in the best interests of the shareholders.

Summary Review Questions

1. Discuss how managers can create value for their firm through diversification efforts.

2. What are some of the reasons that many diversification efforts fail to achieve desired outcomes?

3. How can companies benefit from related diversification? Unrelated diversification? What are some of the key concepts that can explain such success?

4. What are some of the important ways in which a firm can restructure a business?

5. Discuss some of the various means that firms can use to diversify. What are the pros and cons associated with each of these?

6. Discuss some of the actions that managers may engage in to erode shareholder value.

Key Terms

diversification 198
related
  diversification, 199
economies
  of scope, 199
core competencies, 200
sharing activities, 201
market power, 203
pooled negotiating
  power 203
vertical integration, 206

transaction cost
  perspective, 208
unrelated
  diversification 209
parenting advantage, 209
restructuring, 210
portfolio
  management, 211
acquisitions, 215
mergers, 215
divestment, 218

Application Questions Exercises

1. What were some of the largest mergers and acquisitions over the last two years? What was the rationale for these actions? Do you think they will be successful? Explain.

2. Discuss some examples from business practice in which an executive's actions appear to be in his or her self-interest rather than the corporation's well-being.

3. Discuss some of the challenges that managers must overcome in making strategic alliances successful. What are some strategic alliances with which you are familiar? Were they successful or not? Explain.

4. Use the Internet and select a company that has recently undertaken diversification into new product markets. What do you feel were some of the reasons for this diversification (e.g., leveraging core competencies, sharing infrastructures)?

Ethics Questions

1. In recent years there has been a rash of corporate downsizing and layoffs. Do you feel that such actions raise ethical considerations? Why or why not?

2. What are some of the ethical issues that arise when managers act in a manner that is counter to their firm's best interests? What are the long-term implications for both the firms and the managers themselves?

Experiential Exercise

Time Warner (formerly AOL Time Warner) is a firm that follows a strategy of related diversification. Evaluate its success (or lack thereof) with regard to how well it has: (1) built on core competencies, (2) shared infrastructures, and (3) increased market power. (Fill answers in table below.)

Rationale for Related Diversification	Successful/Unsuccessful?	Why?
1. Build on core competencies		
2. Share infrastructures		
3. Increase market power		

References

1. Lashinsky, A. 2008. A SPAC that went splat. *Fortune,* March 31: 20; 2008 pivotal year for SPAC market. 2008. www.reuters.com: np; 2008. Tower completes Jazz acquisition. www.semiconductor-today.com: np; and Maney, K. 2006. Old buddies reunite in hopes of taking the tech world by storm . . . again. www.usatoday.com, October 18: np.

2. Insights on measuring M&A performance are addressed in: Zollo, M. & Meier, D. 2008. What is M&A performance? *BusinessWeek,* 22(3): 55–77.

3. Insights on how and why firms may overpay for acquisitions are addressed in: Malhotra, D., Ku, G., & Murnighan, J. K. 2008. When winning is everything. *Harvard Business Review,* 66(5); 78–86.

4. Pfizer deal helps lift stocks. 2009. online.wsy.com, January 26: np.

5. Dr. G. William Schwert, University of Rochester study cited in Pare, T. P. 1994. The new merger boom. *Fortune.* November 28: 96.

6. Lipin, S. & Deogun, N. 2000. Big mergers of the 1990's prove disappointing to shareholders. *The Wall Street Journal.* October 30: C1.

7. Rothenbuecher, J. & Schrottke, J. 2008. To get value from a merger, grow sales. *Harvard Business Review,* 86 (5): 24–25; and Rothenbuecher, J. 2008. Personal communication, October 1.

8. Pare, T. P. 1994. The new merger boom. *Fortune,* November 28: 96.

9. A discussion of the effects of director experience and acquisition performance is in: McDonald, M. L. & Westphal, J. D. 2008. What do they know? The effects of outside director acquisition experience on firm acquisition performance. *Strategic Management Journal,* 29(11): 1155–1177.

10. Ghosn, C. 2006. Inside the alliance: The win–win nature of a unique business mode. *Address to the Detroit Economic Club,* November 16.

11. For a study that investigates several predictors of corporate diversification, read: Wiersema, M. F. & Bowen, H. P. 2008. Corporate diversification: The impact of foreign competition, industry globalization, and product diversification. *Strategic Management Journal,* 29(2): 114–132.

12. A discussion of Tyco's unrelated diversification strategy is in: Hindo, B. 2008. Solving Tyco's identity crisis. *BusinessWeek,* February 18: 62.

13. Our framework draws upon a variety of sources, including Goold, M. & Campbell, A. 1998. Desperately seeking synergy. *Harvard Business Review,* 76(5): 131–143; Porter, M. E. 1987. From advantage to corporate strategy. *Harvard Business Review,* 65(3): 43–59; and Hitt, M. A., Ireland, R. D., & Hoskisson, R. E. 2001. *Strategic management: competitiveness and globalization* (4th ed.). Cincinnati, OH: South-Western.

14. Collis, D. J. & Montgomery, C. A. 1987. *Corporate strategy: Resources and the scope of the firm.* New York: McGraw-Hill.

15. This imagery of the corporation as a tree and related discussion draws on Prahalad, C. K. & Hamel, G. 1990. The core competence of the corporation. *Harvard Business Review,* 68(3): 79–91. Parts of this section also draw on Picken, J. C. & Dess, G. G. 1997. *Mission critical:* chap. 5. Burr Ridge, IL: Irwin Professional Publishing.

16. This section draws on Prahalad & Hamel, op. cit.; and Porter, op. cit.

17. A recent study that investigates the relationship between a firm's technology resources, diversification, and performance can be found in Miller, D. J. 2004. Firms' technological resources and the performance effects of diversification. A longitudinal study. *Strategic Management Journal,* 25: 1097–1119.

18. Collis & Montgomery, op. cit.

19. Henricks, M. 1994. VF seeks global brand dominance. *Apparel Industry Magazine,* August: 21–40; VF Corporation. 1993. First quarter corporate summary report. *1993 VF Annual Report.*

20. Hill, A. & Hargreaves, D. 2001. Turbulent times for GE-Honeywell deal. *Financial Times,* February 28: 26.

21. An interesting discussion of a merger in the Russian mining industry is in: Bush, J. 2008. Welding a new metals giant. *BusinessWeek,* July 14 & 21: 56.

22. Lowry, T. 2001. Media. *BusinessWeek,* January 8: 100–101.

23. This section draws on Hrebiniak, L. G. & Joyce, W. F. 1984. *Implementing strategy.* New York: MacMillan; and Oster, S. M. 1994. *Modern competitive analysis.* New York: Oxford University Press.

24. The discussion of the benefits and costs of vertical integration draws on Hax, A. C. & Majluf, N. S. 1991. *The strategy concept and process: A pragmatic approach:* 139. Englewood Cliffs, NJ: Prentice Hall.

25. Fahey, J. 2005. Gray winds. *Forbes.* January 10: 143.

26. This discussion draws on Oster, op. cit.; and Harrigan, K. 1986. Matching vertical integration strategies to competitive conditions. *Strategic Management Journal,* 7(6): 535–556.

27. For a scholarly explanation on how transaction costs determine the boundaries of a firm, see Oliver E. Williamson's pioneering books *Markets and Hierarchies: Analysis and Antitrust Implications* (New York: Free Press, 1975) and *The Economic Institutions of Capitalism* (New York: Free Press, 1985).

28. Campbell, A., Goold, M., & Alexander, M. 1995. Corporate strategy: The quest for parenting advantage. *Harvard Business Review,* 73(2): 120–132; and Picken & Dess, op. cit.

29. Anslinger, P. A. & Copeland, T. E. 1996. Growth through acquisition: A fresh look. *Harvard Business Review,* 74(1): 126–135.

30. Campbell et al., op. cit.

31. This section draws on Porter, op. cit.; and Hambrick, D. C. 1985. Turnaround strategies. In Guth, W. D. (Ed.). *Handbook of business strategy:* 10-1–10-32. Boston: Warren, Gorham & Lamont.

32. There is an important delineation between companies that are operated for a long-term profit and those that are bought and sold for short-term gains. The latter are sometimes referred to as "holding companies" and are generally more concerned about financial issues than strategic issues.

33. Lenzner, R. 2007. High on Loews. *Forbes,* February 26: 98–102.

34. Casico. W. F. 2002. Strategies for responsible restructuring. *Academy of Management Executive,* 16(3): 80–91; and Singh, H. 1993. Challenges in researching corporate restructuring. *Journal of Management Studies,* 30(1): 147–172.

35. Cusack, M. 1987. *Hanson Trust: A review of the company and its prospects.* London: Hoare Govett.

36. Hax & Majluf, op. cit. By 1979, 45 percent of Fortune 500 companies employed some form of portfolio analysis, according to Haspelagh, P. 1982. Portfolio planning: Uses and limits. *Harvard Busines Review,* 60: 58–73. A later study conducted in 1993 found that over 40 percent of the respondents used portfolio analysis techniques, but the level of usage was expected to increase to more than 60 percent in the near future: Rigby, D. K. 1994. Managing the management tools. *Planning Review,* September–October: 20–24.

37. Goold, M. & Luchs, K. 1993. Why diversify? Four decades of management thinking. *Academy of Management Executive,* 7(3): 7–25.

38. Other approaches include the industry attractiveness–business strength matrix developed jointly by General Electric and McKinsey and Company, the life-cycle matrix developed

by Arthur D. Little, and the profitability matrix proposed by Marakon. For an extensive review, refer to Hax & Majluf, op. cit.: 182–194.

39. Porter, op. cit.: 49–52.

40. Collis, D. J. 1995. Portfolio planning at Ciba-Geigy and the Newport investment proposal. Harvard Business School Case No. 9-795-040. Novartis AG was created in 1996 by the merger of Ciba-Geigy and Sandoz.

41. Buzzell, R. D. & Gale, B. T. 1987. *The PIMS principles: Linking strategy to performance.* New York: Free Press; and Miller, A. & Dess, G. G. 1996. *Strategic management,* (2nd ed.). New York: McGraw-Hill.

42. Seeger, J. 1984. Reversing the images of BCG's growth share matrix. *Strategic Management Journal,* 5(1): 93–97.

43. Picken & Dess, op. cit.; Cabot Corporation. 2001. 10-Q filing, Securities and Exchange Commission, May 14.

44. Koudsi, S. 2001. Remedies for an economic hangover. *Fortune,* June 25: 130–139.

45. Insights on the performance of serial acquirers is found in: Laamanen, T. & Keil, T. 2008. Performance of serial acquirers: Toward an acquisition program perspective. *Strategic Management Journal,* 29(6): 663–672.

46. Some insights from Lazard's CEO on mergers and acquisitions are addressed in: Stewart, T. A. & Morse, G. 2008. Giving great advice. *Harvard Business Review,* 66(1): 106–113.

47. Coy, P., Thornton, E., Arndt, M., & Grow, B. 2005. Shake, rattle, and merge. *BusinessWeek,* January 10: 32–35; and Anonymous. 2005. Love is in the air. *Economist,* February 5: 9.

48. For an interesting study of the relationship between mergers and a firm's product-market strategies, refer to Krisnan, R. A., Joshi, S., & Krishnan, H. 2004. The influence of mergers on firms' product-mix strategies. *Strategic Management Journal,* 25: 587–611.

49. Carey, D., moderator. 2000. A CEO roundtable on making mergers succeed. *Harvard Business Review,* 78(3): 146.

50. Shinal, J. 2001. Can Mike Volpi make Cisco sizzle again? *BusinessWeek,* February 26: 102–104; Kambil, A., Eselius, E. D., & Monteiro, K. A. 2000. Fast venturing: The quick way to start Web businesses. *Sloan Management Review,* 41(4): 55–67; and Elstrom, P. 2001. Sorry, Cisco: The old answers won't work. *BusinessWeek,* April 30: 39.

51. Like many high-tech firms during the economic slump that began in mid-2000, Cisco Systems has experienced declining performance. On April 16, 2001, it announced that its revenues for the quarter closing April 30 would drop 5 percent from a year earlier—and a stunning 30 percent from the previous three months—to about $4.7 billion. Furthermore, Cisco announced that it would lay off 8,500 employees and take an enormous $2.5 billion charge to write down inventory. By late October 2002, its stock was trading at around $10, down significantly from its 52-week high of $70. Elstrom, op. cit.: 39.

52. Coy, P., Thornton, E., Arndt, M., & Grow, B. 2005, Shake, rattle, and merge. *BusinessWeek,* January 10: 32–35; and, Anonymous. 2005. The rise of the superbrands. *Economist.* February 5: 63–65; and, Sellers, P. 2005. It was a no-brainer. *Fortune,* February 21: 96–102.

53. For a discussion of the trend toward consolidation of the steel industry and how Lakshmi Mittal is becoming a dominant player, read Reed, S. & Arndt, M. 2004. The Raja of steel. *BusinessWeek,* December 20: 50–52.

54. Barrett, A. 2001. Drugs. *BusinessWeek,* January 8: 112–113.

55. Whalen, C. J., Pascual, A. M., Lowery, T., & Muller, J. 2001. The top 25 managers. *BusinessWeek,* January 8: 63.

56. This discussion draws upon Rappaport, A. & Sirower, M. L. 1999. Stock or cash? The trade-offs for buyers and sellers in mergers and acquisitions. *Harvard Business Review,* 77(6): 147–158; and Lipin, S. & Deogun, N. 2000. Big mergers of 90s prove disappointing to shareholders. *The Wall Street Journal,* October 30: C1.

57. The downside of mergers in the airline industry is found in: Gimbel, B.

2008. Why airline mergers don't fly. *Business Week,* March 17: 26.

58. Mouio, A. (Ed.). 1998. Unit of one. *Fast Company,* September: 82.

59. Porter, M. E. 1987. From competitive advantage to corporate strategy. *Harvard Business Review,* 65(3): 43.

60. The divestiture of a business which is undertaken in order to enable managers to better focus on its core business has been termed "downscoping." Refer to Hitt, M. A., Harrison, J. S., & Ireland, R. D. 2001. *Mergers and acquisitions: A guide to creating value for stakeholders.* Oxford Press: New York.

61. Sirmon, D. G., Hitt, M. A., & Ireland, R. D. 2007. Managing firm resources in dynamic environments to create value: Looking inside the black box. *Academy of Management Review,* 32(1): 273–292.

62. This discussion draws on: Mankins, M. C., Harding, D., & Weddigne, R-M. 2008. How the best divest. *Harvard Business Review,* 86 (1): 92–99.

63. A study that investigates alliance performance is: Lunnan, R. & Haugland, S. A. 2008. Predicting and measuring alliance performance: A multidimensional analysis. *Strategic Management Journal,* 29(5): 545–556.

64. For scholarly perspectives on the role of learning in creating value in strategic alliances, refer to Anard, B. N. & Khanna, T. 2000. Do firms learn to create value? *Strategic Management Journal,* 12(3): 295–317; and Vermeulen, F. & Barkema, H. P. 2001. Learning through acquisitions. *Academy of Management Journal,* 44(3): 457–476.

65. For a detailed discussion of transaction cost economics in strategic alliances, read Reuer, J. J. & Arno, A. 2007. Strategic alliance contracts: Dimensions and determinants of contractual complexity. *Strategic Management Journal,* 28(3): 313–330.

66. This section draws on Hutt, M. D., Stafford, E. R., Walker, B. A., & Reingen, P. H. 2000. Case study: Defining the strategic alliance. *Sloan Management Review,* 41(2): 51–62; and Walters, B. A., Peters, S., & Dess, G. G. 1994. Strategic alliances and joint ventures: Making them work. *Business Horizons,* 4: 5–10.

67. A study that investigates strategic alliances and networks is: Tiwana, A. 2008. Do bridging ties complement strong ties? An empirical examination of alliance ambidexterity. *Strategic Management Journal,* 29 (3): 251–272.

68. Edmondson, G. & Reinhardt, A. 2001. From niche player to Goliath. *BusinessWeek,* March 12: 94–96.

69. For an institutional theory perspective on strategic alliances, read: Dacin, M. T., Oliver, C., & Roy, J. P. 2007. The legitimacy of strategic alliances: An institutional perspective. *Strategic Management Journal,* 28(2): 169–187.

70. A study investigating factors that determine partner selection in strategic alliances is found in: Shah, R. H. & Swaminathan, V. 2008. *Strategic Management Journal,* 29(5): 471–494.

71. Porter, op. cit.: 43–59.

72. Angwin, J. S. & Wingfield, N. 2000. How Jay Walker built WebHouse on a theory that he couldn't prove. *The Wall Street Journal,* October 16: A1, A8.

73. The fallen. 2003. *BusinessWeek,* January 13: 80–82.

74. The Jack Welch example draws upon Sellers, P. 2001. Get over yourself. *Fortune,* April 30: 76–88.

75. Polek, D. 2002. The rise and fall of Dennis Kozlowski. *BusinessWeek,* December 23: 64–77.

76. John Thain and his golden commode. 2009. Editorial. Dallasnews .com, January 26: np; Task, A. 2009. Wall Street's $18.4B bonus: The sense of entitlement has not been beaten out. finance.yahoo.com, January 29: np; and Exit Thain. 2009. Newsfinancialcareers.com, January 22: np.

77. This section draws on Weston, J. F., Besley, S., & Brigham, E. F. 1996. *Essentials of managerial finance* (11th ed.): 18–20. Fort Worth, TX: Dryden Press, Harcourt Brace.

CHAPTER 7

International Strategy:

Creating Value in Global Markets

After reading this chapter, you should have a good understanding of:

LO1 The importance of international expansion as a viable diversification strategy.

LO2 The sources of national advantage; that is, why an industry in a given country is more (or less) successful than the same industry in another country.

LO3 The motivations (or benefits) and the risks associated with international expansion, including the emerging trend for greater offshoring and outsourcing activity.

LO4 The two opposing forces—cost reduction and adaptation to local markets—that firms face when entering international markets.

LO5 The advantages and disadvantages associated with each of the four basic strategies: international, global, multidomestic, and transnational.

LO6 The difference between regional companies and truly global companies.

LO7 The four basic types of entry strategies and the relative benefits and risks associated with each of them.

The global marketplace provides many opportunities for firms to increase their revenue base and their profitability. Furthermore, in today's knowledge-intensive economy, there is the potential to create advantages by leveraging firm knowledge when crossing national boundaries to do business. At the same time, however, there are pitfalls and risks that firms must avoid in order to be successful. In this chapter we will provide insights on how to be successful and create value when diversifying into global markets.

After some introductory comments on the global economy, we address the question: What explains the level of success of a given industry in a given country? To provide a framework for analysis, we draw on Michael Porter's "diamond of national advantage," in which he identified four factors that help to explain performance differences.

In the second section of the chapter, we shift our focus to the level of the firm and discuss some of the major motivations and risks associated with international expansion. Recognizing such potential benefits and risks enables managers to better assess the growth and profit potential in a given country. We also address important issues associated with a topic of growing interest in the international marketplace—offshoring and outsourcing.

Next, in the third section—the largest in this chapter—we address how firms can attain competitive advantages in the global marketplace. We discuss two opposing forces firms face when entering foreign markets: cost reduction and local adaptation. Depending on the intensity of each of these forces, they should select among four basic strategies: international, global, multidomestic, and transnational. We discuss both the strengths and limitations of each of these strategies. We also present a recent perspective which posits that even the largest multinational firms are more regional than global even today.

The final section addresses the four categories of entry strategies that firms may choose in entering foreign markets. These strategies vary along a continuum from low investment, low control (exporting) to high investment, high control (wholly owned subsidiaries and greenfield ventures). We discuss the pros and cons associated with each.

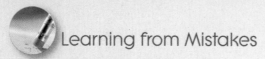 Learning from Mistakes

By 2010, Ford Motor will be introducing a new version of its highly successful small car, the Fiesta, around the world.[1] And in a decision viewed with a bit of trepidation by some executives and announced on February 14, 2008, the vehicle will have the same name in markets across Europe, Asia, South Africa, Australia, and North America. Now, no matter the market, it will be a Fiesta. But that wasn't always the case.

At Ford, as well as other car companies, the name game used to be all about adapting to local tastes. Ford's marketing teams in different countries were left alone to come up with suitable names. Sometimes that can create problems. For example, Ford ended up selling two entirely different vehicles in America and Europe that are both called Fusion. This wouldn't have been much of a problem if information wasn't so readily available online. But these days it definitely is. For example, pictures of the vehicles—one is a sedan, the other a sports-utility vehicle—get mixed up on websites, where 80 percent of car buyers begin their search. Reviews are sometimes interchanged, and consumers can easily get confused.

Finding the right name can be challenging, however. The wrong ones can convey unwanted images, or simply be hard to pronounce. Volkswagen has pushed a global naming strategy for decades and at times has come up with controversial names as a result. Consider the Bora—which is also the wind that blows north by northeast across the Adriatic Sea. After complaints from dealers that Bora sounded "boring," VW eventually renamed the car the Jetta (as in jet stream) in the U.S. More recently, the automaker came out with the Touareg, which is a nomadic African tribe in the Sahara that used to follow a certain wind pattern. A few critics have since pointed out that the tribe owned slaves and were known for their blue-dyed bodies and their talent for torture. Also, the Touareg name is odd and is something that Americans cannot spell or pronounce easily. But the slow-selling SUV is still on the market.

In this chapter we discuss how firms create value and achieve competitive advantage in the global marketplace. Multinational firms are constantly faced with the dilemma of choosing between local adaptation—in product characteristics, names, advertising, and pricing—and global integration. We discuss how firms can avoid pitfalls such as those experienced by Ford Motor and Volkswagen. In addition, we address factors that can influence a nation's success in a particular industry. In our view, this is an important context in determining how well firms might eventually do when they compete beyond their nation's boundaries.

The Global Economy: A Brief Overview

>LO1

The importance of international expansion as a viable diversification strategy.

Managers face many opportunities and risks when they diversify abroad.[2] The trade among nations has increased dramatically in recent years and it is estimated that by 2015, the trade *across* nations will exceed the trade within nations. In a variety of industries such as semiconductors, automobiles, commercial aircraft, telecommunications, computers, and consumer electronics, it is almost impossible to survive unless firms scan the world for competitors, customers, human resources, suppliers, and technology.[3]

GE's wind energy business benefits by tapping into talent around the world. The firm has built research centers in China, Germany, India, and the U.S. "We did it," says CEO Jeffrey Immelt, "to access the best brains everywhere in the world." All four centers have played a key role in GE's development of huge 92-ton turbines:[4]

- Chinese researchers in Shanghai designed the microprocessors that control the pitch of the blade.
- Mechanical engineers from India (Bangladore) devised mathematical models to maximize the efficiency of materials in the turbine.

- Power-systems experts in the U.S. (Niskayuna, New York), which has researchers from 55 countries, do the design work.
- Technicians in Munich, Germany have created a "smart" turbine that can calculate wind speeds and signal sensors in other turbines to produce maximum electricity.

The rise of **globalization**—meaning the rise of market capitalism around the world—has undeniably contributed to the economic boom in America's New Economy, where knowledge is the key source of competitive advantage and value creation.[5] It is estimated that it has brought phone service to about 300 million households in developing nations and a transfer of nearly $2 trillion from rich countries to poor countries through equity, bond investments, and commercial loans.[6]

globalization has two meanings. One is the increase in international exchange, including trade in goods and services as well as exchange of money, ideas, and information. Two is the growing similarity of laws, rules, norms, values, and ideas across countries.

There have been extremes in the effect of global capitalism on national economies and poverty levels around the world.[7] The economies of East Asia have attained rapid growth, but there has been comparatively little progress in other areas of the world. For example, income in Latin America grew by only 6 percent in the past two decades when the continent was opening up to global capitalism. Average incomes in sub-Saharan Africa and the old Eastern European bloc have actually declined. The World Bank estimates that the number of people living on $1 per day has *increased* to 1.3 billion over the past decade.

Such disparities in wealth among nations raise an important question: Why do some countries and their citizens enjoy the fruits of global capitalism while others are mired in poverty? Or why do some governments make the best use of inflows of foreign investment and know-how and others do not? There are many explanations. Among these are the need of governments to have track records of business-friendly policies to attract multinationals and local entrepreneurs to train workers, invest in modern technology, and nurture local suppliers and managers. Also, it means carefully managing the broader economic factors in an economy, such as interest rates, inflation, and unemployment, as well as a good legal system that protects property rights, strong educational systems, and a society where prosperity is widely shared.

The above policies are the type that East Asia—in locations such as Hong Kong, Taiwan, South Korea, and Singapore—has employed to evolve from the sweatshop economies of the 1960s and 1970s to industrial powers today. On the other hand, many countries have moved in the other direction. For example, in Guatemala only 52.0 percent of males complete fifth grade and an astonishing 39.8 percent of the population subsists on less than $1 per day.[8] (By comparison, the corresponding numbers for South Korea are 98 percent and less than 2 percent, respectively.)

Strategy Spotlight 7.1 provides an interesting perspective on global trade—marketing to the "bottom of the pyramid."[9] This refers to the practice of a multinational firm targeting its goods and services to the nearly 5 billion poor people in the world who inhabit developing countries. Collectively, this represents a very large market with $14 trillion in purchasing power.

Next, we will address in more detail the question of why some nations and their industries are more competitive.[10] This establishes an important context or setting for the remainder of the chapter. After we discuss why some *nations and their industries* outperform others, we will be better able to address the various strategies that *firms* can take to create competitive advantage when they expand internationally.

Factors Affecting a Nation's Competitiveness

Michael Porter of Harvard University conducted a four-year study in which he and a team of 30 researchers looked at the patterns of competitive success in 10 leading trading nations. He concluded that there are four broad attributes of nations that individually, and

strategy spotlight

Marketing to the "Bottom of the Pyramid"

Many executives wrongly believe that profitable opportunities to sell consumer goods exist only in countries where income levels are high. Even when they expand internationally, they often tend to limit their marketing to only the affluent segments within the developing countries. Such narrow conceptualizations of the market cause them to ignore the vast opportunities that exist at "the bottom of the pyramid," according to University of Michigan professor C. K. Prahalad. The *bottom of the pyramid* refers to the nearly 5 billion poor people who inhabit the developing countries. Surprisingly, they represent $14 trillion in purchasing power! And they are looking for products and services that can improve the quality of their lives such as clean energy, personal-care products, lighting, and medicines. Multinationals are missing out on growth opportunities if they ignore this vast segment of the market.

Other innovative firms have found creative ways to serve the poor and still make a profit. Grameen Bank in Bangladesh is very different from the money center banks of London or New York. Pioneers of the concept of microcredit, Grameen Bank (whose founder, Muhammad Yunus, won the 2006 Nobel Peace Prize) extends small loans— sometimes as small as $20—to thousands of struggling micro-entrepreneurs who have no collateral to offer. The value of microcredit loans has soared from $4 million to $1.3 billion between 1996 and 2006. Not only are their loan recovery rates comparable to big banks, but they are also changing the lives of thousands of people while making a profit as well. Casas Bahias, the Brazilian retailer, has built a $2.5 billion-a-year chain selling to the poor who live in the *favelas,* the illegal shanty towns. Another amazing example is Aravind Eye Care, an Indian hospital that specializes in cataract surgeries. Today, they are the largest eye care facility in the world, performing more than 200,000 surgeries per year. The secret of their volume: The surgeries cost only about $25! A comparable surgery in the West costs $3,000. And best of all, Aravind has a return on equity of more than 75 percent!

Unilever, the Anglo-Dutch maker of such brands as Dove, Lipton, and Vaseline, built a following among the world's poorest consumers by upending some of the basic rules of marketing. Instead of focusing on value for money, it shrunk packages to set a price even consumers living on $2 a day could afford. It helped people make money to buy its products. "It's not about doing good," but about tapping new markets, says Chief Executive Patrick Cescau.

The strategy was forged about 25 years ago when Indian subsidiary Hindustan Lever (HL) found its products out of reach for millions of Indians. HL came up with a strategy to lower the price while making a profit: single-use packets for everything from shampoo to laundry detergent, costing pennies a pack. A bargain? Maybe not. But it put marquee brands within reach.

It has trained rural women to sell products to their neighbors. "What Unilever does well is get inside these communities, understand their needs, and adapt its business model accordingly," notes a professor at Barcelona's IESE Business School.

No one is helped by viewing the poor as the wretched of the earth. Instead, they are the latest frontier of opportunity for those who can meet their needs. A vast market that is barely tapped, the bottom of the pyramid offers enormous opportunities.

Sources: McGregor, J. 2008. The World's Most Influential Companies. *Business-Week,* December 22: 43–53; Miller, C. C. 2006. Easy Money. *Forbes,* November 27: 134–138; Prahalad, C. K. 2004. Why Selling to the Poor Makes for Good Business. *Fortune,* 150(9): 32–33; Overholt, A. 2005. A New Path to Profit. *Fast Company,* January: 25–26; and Prahalad, C. K. 2005. *The Fortune at the Bottom of the Pyramid: Eradicating Poverty through Profits.* Philadelphia: Wharton School Publishing.

---

factor endowments (national advantage) a nation's position in factors of production.

demand conditions (national advantage) the nature of home-market demand for the industry's product or service.

as a system, constitute what is termed "the diamond of national advantage." In effect, these attributes jointly determine the playing field that each nation establishes and operates for its industries. These factors are:

- *Factor endowments.* The nation's position in factors of production, such as skilled labor or infrastructure, necessary to compete in a given industry.
- *Demand conditions.* The nature of home-market demand for the industry's product or service.
- *Related and supporting industries.* The presence or absence in the nation of supplier industries and other related industries that are internationally competitive.
- *Firm strategy, structure, and rivalry.* The conditions in the nation governing how companies are created, organized, and managed, as well as the nature of domestic rivalry.

Factor Endowments[11,12]

Classical economics suggests that factors of production such as land, labor, and capital are the building blocks that create usable consumer goods and services.[13] However, companies in advanced nations seeking competitive advantage over firms in other nations *create* many of the factors of production. For example, a country or industry dependent on scientific innovation must have a skilled human resource pool to draw upon. This resource pool is not inherited; it is created through investment in industry-specific knowledge and talent. The supporting infrastructure of a country—that is, its transportation and communication systems as well as its banking system—are also critical.

>LO2
The sources of national advantage; that is, why an industry in a given country is more (or less) successful than the same industry in another country.

Factors of production must be developed that are industry and firm specific. In addition, the pool of resources is less important than the speed and efficiency with which these resources are deployed. Thus, firm-specific knowledge and skills created within a country that are rare, valuable, difficult to imitate, and rapidly and efficiently deployed are the factors of production that ultimately lead to a nation's competitive advantage.

For example, the island nation of Japan has little land mass, making the warehouse space needed to store inventory prohibitively expensive. But by pioneering just-in-time inventory management, Japanese companies managed to create a resource from which they gained advantage over companies in other nations that spent large sums to warehouse inventory.

Demand Conditions

Demand conditions refer to the demands that consumers place on an industry for goods and services. Consumers who demand highly specific, sophisticated products and services force firms to create innovative, advanced products and services to meet the demand. This consumer pressure presents challenges to a country's industries. But in response to these challenges, improvements to existing goods and services often result, creating conditions necessary for competitive advantage over firms in other countries.

Countries with demanding consumers drive firms in that country to meet high standards, upgrade existing products and services, and create innovative products and services. The conditions of consumer demand influence how firms view a market. This, in turn, helps a nation's industries to better anticipate future global demand conditions and proactively respond to product and service requirements.

Denmark, for instance, is known for its environmental awareness. Demand from consumers for environmentally safe products has spurred Danish manufacturers to become leaders in water pollution control equipment—products it successfully exported.

Related and Supporting Industries

Related and supporting industries enable firms to manage inputs more effectively. For example, countries with a strong supplier base benefit by adding efficiency to downstream activities. A competitive supplier base helps a firm obtain inputs using cost-effective, timely methods, thus reducing manufacturing costs. Also, close working relationships with suppliers provide the potential to develop competitive advantages through joint research and development and the ongoing exchange of knowledge.

related and supporting industries (national advantage) the presence, absence, and quality in the nation of supplier industries and other related industries that supply services, support, or technology to firms in the industry value chain.

Related industries offer similar opportunities through joint efforts among firms. In addition, related industries create the probability that new companies will enter the market, increasing competition and forcing existing firms to become more competitive through efforts such as cost control, product innovation, and novel approaches to distribution. Combined, these give the home country's industries a source of competitive advantage.

In the Italian footwear industry the supporting industries enhance national competitive advantage. In Italy, shoe manufacturers are geographically located near their suppliers. The manufacturers have ongoing interactions with leather suppliers and learn about new textures, colors, and manufacturing techniques while a shoe is still in the prototype stage. The manufacturers are able to project future demand and gear their factories for new products long before companies in other nations become aware of the new styles.

Firm Strategy, Structure, and Rivalry

firm strategy, structure, and rivalry (national advantage) the conditions in the nation governing how companies are created, organized, and managed, as well as the nature of domestic rivalry.

Rivalry is particularly intense in nations with conditions of strong consumer demand, strong supplier bases, and high new entrant potential from related industries. This competitive rivalry in turn increases the efficiency with which firms develop, market, and distribute products and services within the home country. Domestic rivalry thus provides a strong impetus for firms to innovate and find new sources of competitive advantage.

This intense rivalry forces firms to look outside their national boundaries for new markets, setting up the conditions necessary for global competitiveness. Among all the points on Porter's diamond of national advantage, domestic rivalry is perhaps the strongest indicator of global competitive success. Firms that have experienced intense domestic competition are more likely to have designed strategies and structures that allow them to successfully compete in world markets.

In the U.S., for example, intense rivalry has spurred companies such as Dell Computer to find innovative ways to produce and distribute its products. This is largely a result of competition from IBM and Hewlett-Packard.

Strategy Spotlight 7.2 discusses India's software industry. It provides an integrative example of how Porter's "diamond" can help to explain the relative degree of success of an industry in a given country. Exhibit 7.1 illustrates India's "software diamond."

Concluding Comment on Factors Affecting a Nation's Competitiveness

Porter drew his conclusions based on case histories of firms in more than 100 industries. Despite the differences in strategies employed by successful global competitors, a common theme emerged: Firms that succeeded in global markets had first succeeded in intensely competitive home markets. We can conclude that competitive advantage for global firms typically grows out of relentless, continuing improvement, and innovation.[14]

International Expansion: A Company's Motivations and Risks

>LO3

The motivations (or benefits) and the risks associated with international expansion, including the emerging trend for greater offshoring and outsourcing activity.

Motivations for International Expansion

There are many motivations for a company to pursue international expansion. The most obvious one is to *increase the size of potential markets* for a firm's products and services.[15] By early 2009, the world's population exceeded 6.7 billion, with the U.S. representing less than 5 percent. Exhibit 7.2 lists the population of the U.S. compared to other major markets abroad.

Many multinational firms are intensifying their efforts to market their products and services to countries such as India and China as the ranks of their middle class have increased over the past decade. These include Procter & Gamble's success in achieving a 50 percent share in China's shampoo market as well as PepsiCo's impressive inroads in the Indian soft-drink market.[16] Let's take a brief look at China's emerging middle class:[17]

- China's middle class has finally attained a critical mass—between 35 million and 200 million people, depending on what definition is used. The larger number is preferred by Fan Gong, director of China's National Economic Research Institute, who fixes the lower boundary of "middle" as a family income of $10,000.
- The central government's emphasis on science and technology has boosted the rapid development of higher education, which is the incubator of the middle class.

India and the Diamond of National Advantage

Consider the following facts:

- SAP, the German software company, has developed new applications for notebook PCs at its 500-engineer Bangladore facility.

- General Electric plans to invest $100 million and hire 2,600 scientists to create the world's largest research and development lab in Bangalore, India.

- Microsoft plans to invest $400 million in new research partnerships in India.

Sources: Ghemawat, P. & Hout, T. 2008. Tomorrow's Global Giants. *Harvard Business Review*, 86(11): 80–88; Mathur, S. K. 2007. Indian IT Industry: A Performance Analysis and a Model for Possible Adoption. ideas.repec.org, January 1: np; Kripalani, M. 2002. Calling Bangladore: Multinationals Are Making It a Hub for High-Tech Research *BusinessWeek*, November 25: 52–54; Kapur, D. & Ramamurti, R. 2001. India's Emerging Competitive Advantage in Services. 2001. *Academy of Management Executive*, 15(2): 20–33; World Bank. *World Development Report*: 6. New York: Oxford University Press. Reuters. 2001. Oracle in India Push, Taps Software Talent. *Washington Post Online*, July 3.

- Over one-fifth of Fortune 1000 companies outsource their software requirements to firms in India.

- Indian software exports have soared from $5.9 billion in 2000 to $23.6 billion in 2005 to a predicted $60 billion by 2010.

- For the past decade, the Indian software industry has grown at a 25 percent annual rate.

- More than 800 firms in India are involved in software services as their primary activity.

- Software and information technology firms in India are projected to employ 2.3 million people by 2010.

- The information technology industry is expected to account for 7 percent of India's Gross Domestic Product (GDP) in 2010—up from only 4.8 percent in 2007.

What is causing such global interest in India's software services industry? Porter's diamond of national advantage helps clarify this question. See Exhibit 7.1.

First, *factor endowments* are conducive to the rise of India's software industry. Through investment *(continued)*

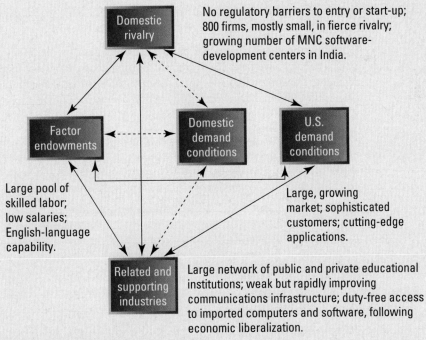

Domestic rivalry — No regulatory barriers to entry or start-up; 800 firms, mostly small, in fierce rivalry; growing number of MNC software-development centers in India.

Factor endowments — Large pool of skilled labor; low salaries; English-language capability.

U.S. demand conditions — Large, growing market; sophisticated customers; cutting-edge applications.

Related and supporting industries — Large network of public and private educational institutions; weak but rapidly improving communications infrastructure; duty-free access to imported computers and software, following economic liberalization.

Note: Dashed lines represent weaker interactions.

Exhibit 7.1 India's Diamond in Software

Source: From Kampur D. and Ramamurti R., "India's Emerging Competition Advantage in Services," *Academy of Management Executive: The Thinking Manager's Source.* Copyright © 2001 by Academy of Management. Reproduced with permission of Academy of Management via Copyright Clearance Center.

(continued) in human resource development with a focus on industry-specific knowledge, India's universities and software firms have literally created this essential factor of production. For example, India produces the second largest annual output of scientists and engineers in the world, behind only the United States. In a knowledge-intensive industry such as software, development of human resources is fundamental to both domestic and global success.

Second, *demand conditions* require that software firms stay on the cutting edge of technological innovation. India has already moved toward globalization of its software industry; consumer demand conditions in developed nations such as Germany, Denmark, parts of Southeast Asia, and the United States created the consumer demand necessary to propel India's software makers toward sophisticated software solutions.*

Third, India has the *supplier base as well as the related industries* needed to drive competitive rivalry and enhance competitiveness. In particular, information technology (IT) hardware prices declined rapidly in the 1990s.

* Although India's success cannot be explained in terms of its home market demand (according to Porter's model), the nature of the industry enables software to be transferred among different locations simultaneously by way of communications links. Thus, competitiveness of markets outside India can be enhanced without a physical presence in those markets.

Furthermore, rapid technological change in IT hardware meant that latecomers like India were not locked into older-generation technologies. Thus, both the IT hardware and software industries could "leapfrog" older technologies. In addition, relationships among knowledge workers in these IT hardware and software industries offer the social structure for ongoing knowledge exchange, promoting further enhancement of existing products. Further infrastructure improvements are occurring rapidly.

Fourth, with over 800 firms in the software services industry in India, *intense rivalry forces firms to develop competitive strategies and structures.* Although firms like TCS, Infosys, and Wipro have become large, they were quite small only five years ago. And dozens of small and midsized companies are aspiring to catch up. This intense rivalry is one of the primary factors driving Indian software firms to develop overseas distribution channels, as predicted by Porter's diamond of national advantage.

It is interesting to note that the cost advantage of Indian firms may be eroding. For example, TCS's engineers' compensation has soared 15 percent a year between 2005 and 2008, other Asian companies are trying to steal its customers, and it is working hard to better understand overseas customers. Further, IBM and Accenture are aggressively building up their Indian operations, hiring tens of thousands of sought-after Indians by paying them more, thereby lowering their costs while raising those of TCS.

- China may be viewed as a new example of economies of scale. Many American companies already have factories in China exporting goods. Now that there is a domestic market to go along with the export market, those factories can increase their output with little additional cost. That is one reason why many foreign companies' profits in China have been so strong in recent years.

Expanding a firm's global presence also automatically increases its scale of operations, providing it with a larger revenue and asset base. As we noted in Chapter 5 in discussing overall cost leadership strategies, such an increase in revenues and asset base potentially enables a firm to *attain economies of scale.* This provides multiple benefits. One advantage

Exhibit 7.2
Populations of Selected Nations and the World

Country	June 2009 (in est. millions)
China	1,337
India	1,164
United States	306
Japan	127
Germany	82
World Total	6,778

Source: www.geohive.com/global/pop_data2.php.

How Wal-Mart Profits from Arbitrage

With sales of over $400 billion and net income of $14 billion, Wal-Mart is considered one of the most successful companies in the world. In recent years, Wal-Mart has embarked upon an ambitious international expansion agenda, opening stores in countries such as Mexico, China, Japan, and England. Wal-Mart today has 3,120 stores outside the U.S. Together they account for $90 billion in sales and $4.7 billion in operating income.

Wal-Mart's above average industry profitability has been attributed to various factors, such as their superior logistics, strict control over overhead costs, and effective use of information systems. What is often lost sight of is that their "everyday low pricing" strategy cannot work successfully unless they are able to procure the thousands of items they carry in each of their stores at the lowest possible prices. This is where their expertise in arbitraging plays a critical role. In 2004, Wal-Mart bought $18 billion worth of goods directly from China. By 2006, this had grown to $26.7 billion. If one considers indirect imports through their other suppliers as well, Wal-Mart's total imports from China could be anywhere between $50 billion and $70 billion each year. At a conservative estimate, this represents cost savings of approximately $16 billion to $23 billion! Clearly, the core of Wal-Mart's international strategy is not their international store expansion strategy but their pursuit of worldwide arbitrage opportunities.

Sources: Ghemawat, P. 2007. *Redefining Global Strategy*. Boston: Harvard Business School Press; Scott, R.E. 2007. The Wal-Mart Effect. epi.org, June 26: np; and Basker, E. & Pham, V.H. 2008. Wal-Mart as Catalyst to U.S.-China Trade. ssrn.com; np.

is the spreading of fixed costs such as R&D over a larger volume of production. Examples include the sale of Boeing's commercial aircraft and Microsoft's operating systems in many foreign countries.

Taking advantage of arbitrage opportunities is a second advantage of international expansion. In its simplest form, arbitrage involves buying something from where it is cheap and selling it somewhere where it commands a higher price. A big part of Wal-Mart's success can be attributed to the company's expertise in arbitrage (see Strategy Spotlight 7.3). The possibilities for arbitrage are not necessarily confined to simple trading opportunities. It can be applied to virtually any factor of production and every stage of the value chain. For example, a firm may locate its call centers in India, its manufacturing plants in China, and its R&D in Europe, where the specific types of talented personnel may be available at the lowest possible price. In today's integrated global financial markets, a firm can borrow anywhere in the world where capital is cheap and use it to fund a project in a country where capital is expensive. Such arbitrage opportunities are even more attractive to global corporations because their larger size enables them to buy in huge volume, thus increasing their bargaining power with suppliers.

Extending the life cycle of a product that is in its maturity stage in a firm's home country but that has greater demand potential elsewhere is another benefit of international expansion. As we noted in Chapter 5, products (and industries) generally go through a four-stage life cycle of introduction, growth, maturity, and decline. In recent decades, U.S. soft-drink producers such as Coca-Cola and PepsiCo have aggressively pursued international markets to attain levels of growth that simply would not be available in the United States. Similarly, personal computer manufacturers such as Dell and Hewlett-Packard have sought out foreign markets to offset the growing saturation in the U.S. market.

Finally, *optimizing the physical location for every activity in its value chain* is another benefit. Recall from our discussions in Chapters 3 and 5 that the value chain represents the various activities in which all firms must engage to produce products and services. They include primary activities, such as inbound logistics, operations, and marketing, as well as support activities, such as procurement, R&D, and human resource management. All firms have to make

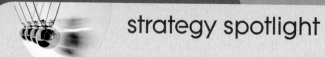

How Deere & Co. Learned from Its Indian Operations

Companies are increasingly discovering that their international operations are coming up with ideas that resonate far beyond local markets. Case in point: Deere & Co. is pursuing a new market in the U.S.—recreational farmers. And they have innovations developed at their research facility in Pune, India, to thank.

Deere, based in Moline, Illinois, opened the Pune center in 2001 as a way to enter the Indian market. The move was quite unexpected. After all, Deere is known for its heavy-duty farm equipment and big construction gear, and many of India's farmers still use oxen-pulled plows. However, Deere saw potential, and its engineers in Pune responded with four no-frills models. While they didn't include GPS or air conditioning, they were sturdy enough to handle the rigors of commercial farming.

The tractors cost between $8,400 and $11,600 in India and were so basic that Deere never considered selling them in the U.S. But then Indian tractor maker Mahin-

Sources: Mero, J. 2008. John Deere's Farm Team. *Fortune*, April 14: 119–124; and. No-Frills Indian Tractors Find Favor with US Farmers. 2008. www.thaindian .com, April 29: np.

dra & Mahindra started selling its no-frill tractors in the U.S., targeting a market that Deere had largely ignored—hobbyists as well as bargain hunters. Such buyers didn't need many advanced features. And it turned out that they coveted the same qualities as Indian farmers: affordability and maneuverability.

Deere, taking a cue from its rival, transplanted a slightly modified version (with softer seats and higher horsepower) of the Indian line of tractors. Called the 5003 model, it sold for $14,400 in the United States. And by 2008, half of the tractors Deere produces in India were making their way overseas. "These tractors are like Swiss Army knives. They get used for anything: mowing, transporting bales of hay, pushing dirt, and removing manure," claims Mike Alvin, a product manager at Deere.

Deere doesn't disclose margins for specific products. However, it certainly sees financial benefits from transplanting Indian innovations to the U.S. Raj Kalathus, the managing director of Deere's Indian division, says the 5003 tractors were born out of "frugal engineering." Because many of Deere's Indian employees witness poverty daily, they took great care to minimize costs. Such innovation isn't just global—it's good business.

critical decisions as to where each activity will take place.[18] Optimizing the location for every activity in the value chain can yield one or more of three strategic advantages: performance enhancement, cost reduction, and risk reduction. We will now discuss each of these.

Performance Enhancement   Microsoft's decision to establish a corporate research laboratory in Cambridge, England, is an example of a location decision that was guided mainly by the goal of building and sustaining world-class excellence in selected value-creating activities.[19] This strategic decision provided Microsoft with access to outstanding technical and professional talent. Location decisions can affect the quality with which any activity is performed in terms of the availability of needed talent, speed of learning, and the quality of external and internal coordination.

In Strategy Spotlight 7.4, Deere & Co., the $28 billion construction and farm equipment manufacturer, developed a new tractor at its new research facility in Pune, India, for the local market. Later, the tractor was quickly modified to create a viable alternative to a competitor's offering in the United States.

Cost Reduction   Two location decisions founded largely on cost-reduction considerations are (1) Nike's decision to source the manufacture of athletic shoes from Asian countries such as China, Vietnam, and Indonesia, and (2) the decision of many multinational companies to set up production operations just south of the U.S.–Mexico border to access lower-cost labor. These operations are called *maquiladoras*. Such location decisions can affect the cost structure in terms of local manpower and other resources, transportation and logistics, and government incentives and the local tax structure.

Performance enhancement and cost-reduction benefits parallel the business-level strategies (discussed in Chapter 5) of differentiation and overall cost leadership. They can at times be attained simultaneously. Consider our example in the previous section on the Indian software industry. When Oracle set up a development operation in that country, the company benefited both from lower labor costs and operational expenses as well as from performance enhancements realized through the hiring of superbly talented professionals.

Risk Reduction   Given the erratic swings in the exchange ratios between the U.S. dollar and the Japanese yen (in relation to each other and to other major currencies), an important basis for cost competition between Ford and Toyota has been their relative ingenuity at managing currency risks. One way for such rivals to manage currency risks has been to spread the high-cost elements of their manufacturing operations across a few select and carefully chosen locations around the world. Location decisions such as these can affect the overall risk profile of the firm with respect to currency, economic, and political risks.[20]

Potential Risks of International Expansion

When a company expands its international operations, it does so to increase its profits or revenues. As with any other investment, however, there are also potential risks.[21] To help companies assess the risk of entering foreign markets, rating systems have been developed to evaluate political, economic, as well as financial and credit risks.[22] *Euromoney* magazine publishes a semiannual "Country Risk Rating" that evaluates political, economic, and other risks that entrants potentially face.[23] Exhibit 7.3 depicts a sample of country risk ratings, published by the World Bank, from the 178 countries that *Euromoney* evaluates. Note that the lower the score, the higher the country's expected level of risk.[24]

Next we will discuss the four main types of risk: political risk, economic risk, currency risk, and management risk.

Political and Economic Risk   Generally speaking, the business climate in the United States is very favorable. However, some countries around the globe may be hazardous to the health of corporate initiatives because of **political risk**.[25] Forces such as social unrest,

political risk
potential threat to a firm's operations in a country due to ineffectiveness of the domestic political system.

Exhibit 7.3   **A Sample of International Country Risk Rankings**

Rank	Country	Total Risk Assessment	Economic Performance	Political Risk	Total of Debt Indicators	Total of Credit and Access to Finance Indicators
1	Luxembourg	99.51	25.00	24.51	20.00	30.00
2	Switzerland	98.84	23.84	25.00	20.00	30.00
3	United States	98.37	23.96	24.41	20.00	30.00
40	China	71.27	18.93	16.87	19.73	15.74
55	Poland	57.12	18.56	13.97	9.36	15.23
63	Vietnam	52.04	14.80	11.91	18.51	6.82
86	Russia	42.62	11.47	8.33	17.99	4.83
114	Albania	34.23	8.48	5.04	19.62	1.09
161	Mozambique	21.71	3.28	2.75	13.85	1.83
178	Afghanistan	3.92	0.00	3.04	0.00	0.88

Source: Adapted from worldbank.org/html/prddr/trans/so96/art7.htm.

Piracy: A Key Threat to World Trade

Counterfeiting has grown up and has become a major threat to multinational corporations. "We've seen a massive increase in the last five years, and there is a risk that it will spiral out of control," claims Anthony Simon, marketing chief of Unilever Bestfoods. "It is no longer a cottage industry."

The figures are astounding. The World Customs Organization estimates that counterfeiting accounts for about 5 percent to 7 percent of global merchandise trade—equivalent to as much as $512 billion. Seizures of fakes by United States customs jumped 46 percent last year as counterfeiters boosted exports to Western markets. Unilever Groups says that knockoffs of its shampoos, soaps, and teas are growing at a rate of 30 percent annually.

Such counterfeiting can also have health and safety implications as well. The World Health Organization says up to 10 percent of medicines worldwide are counterfeit—a deadly hazard that could be costing the pharmaceutical industry $46 billion a year. "You won't die from purchasing a pair of counterfeit blue jeans or a counterfeit golf club. You can die from taking counterfeit pharmaceutical products. And there's no doubt that people have died in China from bad medicine," says John Theirault, head of global security for American pharmaceutical giant, Pfizer. And, sadly, cases like the one in China, where fake baby formula recently killed 60 infants, have investigators stepping up enforcement at U.S. ports. Injuries from overheating counterfeit cell phone batteries purchased right on Verizon store shelves sparked a recall. According to Hal Stratton, of the Consumer Product Safety Commission, "We know of at least one apartment fire that's occurred. We know of at least one burn situation of someone's face that's occurred." And bogus car parts are a $12 billion market worldwide. "Counterfeiting has gone from a local nuisance to a global threat," says Hanns Glatz, DaimlerChrysler's point man on intellectual property.

China is the key to any solution. Given the country's economic power, its counterfeiting is turning into quite the problem itself, accounting for nearly two-thirds of all fake and pirated goods worldwide. Dan Chow, a law professor at Ohio State University who specializes in Chinese counterfeiting provides some perspective: "We have never seen a problem of this size and magnitude in world history. There's more counterfeiting going on in China now than we've ever seen anywhere. We know that 15 to 20 percent of all goods in China are counterfeit."

Source: Engardio, P. & Yang, C. 2006. The Runaway Trade Giant. *BusinessWeek.* April 24: 30–32; Letzing, J. 2007. Antipiracy Group Make's List of Worst-Offendor Nations. www.marketwatch. February 12: np. Balfour, F. 2005. Fake! *Business-Week,* February 7: 54–64; Editorial. 2005. *BusinessWeek,* February 7: 96; and Simon, B. 2004. The World's Greatest Fakes. www.cbsnews.com, August 8.

military turmoil, demonstrations, and even violent conflict and terrorism can pose serious threats.[26] Consider, for example, the ongoing tension and violence in the Middle East between Israelis and Palestinians, and the social and political unrest in Indonesia.[27] Such conditions increase the likelihood of destruction of property and disruption of operations as well as nonpayment for goods and services. Thus, countries that are viewed as high risk are less attractive for most types of business.[28]

The laws, and the enforcement of laws, associated with the protection of intellectual property rights can be a major potential **economic risk** in entering new countries.[29] Microsoft, for example, has lost billions of dollars in potential revenue through piracy of its software products in many countries, including China. Other areas of the globe, such as the former Soviet Union and some eastern European nations, have piracy problems as well.[30] Firms rich in intellectual property have encountered financial losses as imitations of their products have grown due to a lack of law enforcement of intellectual property rights.[31]

Strategy Spotlight 7.5 discusses a problem that is a severe threat to global trade—piracy. Estimates are that counterfeiting accounts for between 5 to 7 percent of global merchandise trade—the equivalent of as much as $512 billion a year. And the potential corrosive effects include health and safety, not just economic, damage.[32]

Currency Risks   Currency fluctuations can pose substantial risks. A company with operations in several countries must constantly monitor the exchange rate between its own

economic risk
potential threat to a firm's operations in a country due to economic policies and conditions, including property rights laws and enforcement of those laws.

Israel's Strong Shekel Forces Companies to Reevaluate Their Strategies

For years O.R.T. Technologies resisted moving any operations outside of Israel. However, when faced with a sharp rise in the value of the shekel, the maker of specialized software for managing gas stations froze all local hiring and decided to transfer some developmental work to Eastern Europe. Laments CEO Alex Milner: "I never thought I'd

see the day when we would have to move R&D outside of Israel, but the strong shekel has forced us to do so."

For decades, Israelis have viewed the U.S. dollar as a bedrock of financial stability. Apartment prices and salaries are often indexed to it as a hedge against inflation. However, during 2006–2007, the shekel surged 31 percent against the dollar. That also hurts the likes of software shop Flash Networks, where the bulk of the expenses are in shekels, but most sales are in U.S. dollars. Says Flash CEO Liam Galin, "We're only a month into the new year and there's already around a $1 million shortfall in our budget."

Source: Sandler, N. 2008. Israel: Attack of the Super-Shekel. *BusinessWeek,* February 25: 38.

currency and that of the host country to minimize **currency risks.** Even a small change in the exchange rate can result in a significant difference in the cost of production or net profit when doing business overseas. When the U.S. dollar appreciates against other currencies, for example, U.S. goods can be more expensive to consumers in foreign countries. At the same time, however, appreciation of the U.S. dollar can have negative implications for American companies that have branch operations overseas. The reason for this is that profits from abroad must be exchanged for dollars at a more expensive rate of exchange, reducing the amount of profit when measured in dollars. For example, consider an American firm doing business in Italy. If this firm had a 20 percent profit in euros at its Italian center of operations, this profit would be totally wiped out when converted into U.S. dollars if the euro had depreciated 20 percent against the U.S. dollar. (U.S. multinationals typically engage in sophisticated "hedging strategies" to minimize currency risk. The discussion of this is beyond the scope of this section.)

> **currency risk**
> potential threat to a firm's operations in a country due to fluctuations in the local currency's exchange rate.

It is important to note that even when government intervention is well intended, the macroeconomic effects of such action can be very negative for multinational corporations. Such was the case in 1997 when Thailand suddenly chose to devalue its currency, the baht, after months of trying to support it at an artificially high level. This, in effect, made the baht worthless compared to other currencies. And in 1998 Russia not only devalued its ruble but also elected not to honor its foreign debt obligations. Strategy Spotlight 7.6 discusses how Israel's strong currency—the shekel—forced two firms to reevaluate their strategies.

Management Risks   **Management risks** may be considered the challenges and risks that managers face when they must respond to the inevitable differences that they encounter in foreign markets. These take a variety of forms: culture, customs, language, income levels, customer preferences, distribution systems, and so on.[33] As we will note later in the chapter, even in the case of apparently standard products, some degree of local adaptation will become necessary.[34]

> **management risk**
> potential threat to a firm's operations in a country due to the problems that managers have making decisions in the context of foreign markets.

Differences in cultures across countries can also pose unique challenges for managers.[35] Cultural symbols can evoke deep feelings.[36] For example, in a series of advertisements aimed at Italian vacationers, Coca-Cola executives turned the Eiffel Tower, Empire State Building, and the Tower of Pisa into the familiar Coke bottle. So far, so good.

How a Local Custom Can Affect a Manufacturing Plant's Operations

At times, a lack of understanding and awareness of local customs can provide some frustrating and embarrassing situations. Such customs can raise issues that must be taken into account in order to make good decisions.

For example, consider the unique problem that Larry Henderson, plant manager, and John Lichthental, manager of human resources, were faced with when they were assigned by Celanese Chemical Corp. to build a new plant in Singapore. The $125 million plant was completed in July, but according to local custom, a plant should only be christened on "lucky" days. Unfortunately, the next "lucky" day was not until September 3.

Henderson and Lichthental had to convince executives at Celanese's Dallas headquarters to delay the plant opening. It wasn't easy. But after many heated telephone conversations and flaming e-mails, the president agreed to open the new plant on the "lucky" day—September 3.

Source: Harvey, M. & Buckley, M. R. 2002. Assessing the "Conventional Wisdoms" of Management for the 21st Century Organization. *Organizational Dynamics*, 30(4): 368–378.

However, when the white marble columns of the Parthenon that crowns the Acropolis in Athens were turned into Coke bottles, the Greeks became outraged. Why? Greeks refer to the Acropolis as the "holy rock," and a government official said the Parthenon is an "international symbol of excellence" and that "whoever insults the Parthenon insults international culture." Coca-Cola apologized. Below are a few examples of how culture varies across nations.[37]

- *Ecuador.* Dinners at Ecuadorian homes last for many hours. Expect drinks and appetizers around 8:00 p.m., with dinner not served until 11:00 p.m. or midnight. You will dismay your hosts if you leave as early as 1:00 a.m. A party at an Ecuadorian home will begin late and end around 4:00 a.m. or 5:00 a.m. Late guests may sometimes be served breakfast before they leave.
- *France.* Words in French and English may have the same roots but different meanings or connotations. For example, a French person might "demand" something because *demander* in French means "to ask."
- *Hong Kong.* Negotiations occur over cups of tea. Always accept an offer of tea whether you want it or not. When you are served, wait for the host to drink first.
- *Singapore.* Singaporeans associate all of the following with funerals, so do not give them as gifts: straw sandals, clocks, a stork or crane, handkerchiefs, or gifts or wrapping paper where the predominant color is white, black, or blue.

Strategy Spotlight 7.7 addresses a rather humorous example of how a local custom can affect operations at a manufacturing plant.

Global Dispersion of Value Chains: Outsourcing and Offshoring

A major recent trend has been the dispersion of the value chains of multinational corporations across different countries; that is, the various activities that constitute the value chain of a firm are now spread across several countries and continents. Such dispersion of value occurs mainly through increasing offshoring and outsourcing.

A report issued by the World Trade Organization describes the production of a particular U.S. car as follows: "30 percent of the car's value goes to Korea for assembly,

17.5 percent to Japan for components and advanced technology, 7.5 percent to Germany for design, 4 percent to Taiwan and Singapore for minor parts, 2.5 percent to U.K. for advertising and marketing services, and 1.5 percent to Ireland and Barbados for data processing. This means that only 37 percent of the production value is generated in the U.S."[38] In today's economy, we are increasingly witnessing two interrelated trends: outsourcing and offshoring.

Outsourcing occurs when a firm decides to utilize other firms to perform value-creating activities that were previously performed in-house.[39] It may be a new activity that the firm is perfectly capable of doing but chooses to have someone else perform for cost or quality reasons. Outsourcing can be to either a domestic or foreign firm.

Offshoring takes place when a firm decides to shift an activity that they were performing in a domestic location to a foreign location.[40] For example, both Microsoft and Intel now have R&D facilities in India, employing a large number of Indian scientists and engineers. Often, offshoring and outsourcing go together; that is, a firm may outsource an activity to a foreign supplier, thereby causing the work to be offshored as well.[41] Spending on offshore information technology will nearly triple between 2004 and 2010 to $60 billion, according to research firm Gartner.[42]

The recent explosion in the volume of outsourcing and offshoring is due to a variety of factors. Up until the 1960s, for most companies, the entire value chain was in one location. Further, the production took place close to where the customers were in order to keep transportation costs under control. In the case of service industries, it was generally believed that offshoring was not possible because the producer and consumer had to be present at the same place at the same time. After all, a haircut could not be performed if the barber and the client were separated!

For manufacturing industries, the rapid decline in transportation and coordination costs has enabled firms to disperse their value chains over different locations. For example, Nike's R&D takes place in the U.S., raw materials are procured from a multitude of countries, actual manufacturing takes place in China or Indonesia, advertising is produced in the U.S., and sales and service take place in practically all the countries. Each value-creating activity is performed in the location where the cost is the lowest or the quality is the best. Without finding optimal locations for each activity, Nike could not have attained its position as the world's largest shoe company.

The experience of the manufacturing sector was also repeated in the service sector by the mid-1990s. A trend that began with the outsourcing of low-level programming and data entry work to countries such as India and Ireland suddenly grew manyfold, encompassing a variety of white collar and professional activities ranging from call-centers to R&D. The cost of a long distance call from the U.S. to India has decreased from about $3 to $0.03 in the last 20 years, thereby making it possible to have call centers located in countries like India, where a combination of low labor costs and English proficiency presents an ideal mix of factor conditions.

Bangalore, India, in recent years, has emerged as a location where more and more U.S. tax returns are prepared. In India, U.S.–trained and licensed radiologists interpret chest X-rays and CT scans from U.S. hospitals for half the cost. The advantages from offshoring go beyond mere cost savings today. In many specialized occupations in science and engineering, there is a shortage of qualified professionals in developed countries, whereas countries, like India, China, and Singapore have what seems like an inexhaustible supply.[43]

For most of the 20th century, domestic companies catered to the needs of local populations. However, with the increasing homogenization of customer needs around the world and the institutionalization of free trade and investment as a global ideology (especially after the creation of the WTO), competition has become truly global. Each company has to

outsourcing using other firms to perform value-creating activities that were previously performed in-house.

offshoring shifting a value-creating activity from a domestic location to a foreign location.

Misiu Systems: Outsourcing Is Not for Everyone

When Todd Hodgen, CEO of Misiu Systems, a Bothell, Washington–based manufacturer of alarm systems, learned that he could save 65 percent of his design costs by outsourcing it to a Taiwanese firm, he was really excited. In addition to cost savings, an added bonus was that the Taiwanese engineers would be working after Misiu's engineers had gone home because of the time differences. This meant that the product development cycle could be greatly accelerated. For a start-up financed mostly with loans from friends and family, the twin advantages of cost savings and reduced cycle time were too much to resist.

After several months of discussions with the contractor and a visit to Taiwan, Hodgen signed the outsourcing agreement. However, things did not quite work out as he had expected. His feedback to the design team in Taiwan often went unheeded. The design was eventually delivered eight months late and the quality fell well short of expectations. Why? The Taiwanese engineers who were supposed to be working solely for him were also working for other clients. Business from a small firm like Misiu was not given the same priority that was given to bigger clients. Eventually Hodgen ended up terminating the agreement with the Taiwanese firm and hiring a U.S. firm to finish the project!

Source: Wahlgren, E. 2004. The Outsourcing Dilemma. *Inc.*, April: 41–43.

keep its costs low in order to survive.[44] They also must find the best suppliers and the most skilled workers as well as locate each stage of the value chain in places where factor conditions are most conducive. Thus, outsourcing and offshoring are no longer mere options to consider, but an imperative for competitive survival.

While there is a compelling logic for companies to engage in offshoring, there can be many pitfalls. Strategy Spotlight 7.8 discusses the experience of Misiu Systems, a U.S. alarm systems manufacturer that found out the hard way that offshoring is not for everyone.

Achieving Competitive Advantage in Global Markets

We now discuss the two opposing forces that firms face when they expand into global markets: cost reduction and adaptation to local markets. Then we address the four basic types of international strategies that they may pursue: international, global, multidomestic, and transnational. The selection of one of these four types of strategies is largely dependent on a firm's relative pressure to address each of the two forces.

Two Opposing Pressures: Reducing Costs and Adapting to Local Markets

> **>LO4**
>
> The two opposing forces—cost reduction and adaptation to local markets—that firms face when entering international markets.

Many years ago, the famed marketing strategist Theodore Levitt advocated strategies that favored global products and brands. He suggested that firms should standardize all of their products and services for all of their worldwide markets. Such an approach would help a firm lower its overall costs by spreading its investments over as large a market as possible. Levitt's approach rested on three key assumptions:

1. Customer needs and interests are becoming increasingly homogeneous worldwide.
2. People around the world are willing to sacrifice preferences in product features, functions, design, and the like for lower prices at high quality.
3. Substantial economies of scale in production and marketing can be achieved through supplying global markets.[45]

However, there is ample evidence to refute these assumptions.[46] Regarding the first assumption—the increasing worldwide homogeneity of customer needs and interests— consider the number of product markets, ranging from watches and handbags to soft drinks and fast foods. Companies have identified global customer segments and developed global products and brands targeted to those segments. Also, many other companies adapt lines to idiosyncratic country preferences and develop local brands targeted to local market segments. For example, Nestlé's line of pizzas marketed in the United Kingdom includes cheese with ham and pineapple topping on a French bread crust. Similarly, Coca-Cola in Japan markets Georgia (a tonic drink) as well as Classic Coke and Hi-C.

Consider the second assumption—the sacrifice of product attributes for lower prices. While there is invariably a price-sensitive segment in many product markets, there is no indication that this is increasing. In contrast, in many product and service markets—ranging from watches, personal computers, and household appliances, to banking and insurance—there is a growing interest in multiple product features, product quality, and service.

Finally, the third assumption is that significant economies of scale in production and marketing could be achieved for global products and services. Although standardization may lower manufacturing costs, such a perspective does not consider three critical and interrelated points. First, as we discussed in Chapter 5, technological developments in flexible factory automation enable economies of scale to be attained at lower levels of output and do not require production of a single standardized product. Second, the cost of production is only one component, and often not the critical one, in determining the total cost of a product. Third, a firm's strategy should not be product-driven. It should also consider other activities in the firm's value chain, such as marketing, sales, and distribution.

Based on the above, we would have a hard time arguing that it is wise to develop the same product or service for all markets throughout the world. While there are some exceptions, such as Harley-Davidson motorcycles and some of Coca-Cola's soft-drink products, managers must also strive to tailor their products to the culture of the country in which they are attempting to do business. Few would argue that "one size fits all" gener- ally applies.

The opposing pressures that managers face place conflicting demands on firms as they strive to be competitive.[47] On the one hand, competitive pressures require that firms do what they can to *lower unit costs* so that consumers will not perceive their product and service offerings as too expensive. This may lead them to consider locating manufacturing facilities where labor costs are low and developing products that are highly standardized across multiple countries.

In addition to responding to pressures to lower costs, managers also must strive to be *responsive to local pressures* in order to tailor their products to the demand of the local market in which they do business. This requires differentiating their offerings and strategies from country to country to reflect consumer tastes and preferences and mak- ing changes to reflect differences in distribution channels, human resource practices, and governmental regulations. However, since the strategies and tactics to differentiate prod- ucts and services to local markets can involve additional expenses, a firm's costs will tend to rise.

The two opposing pressures result in four different basic strategies that companies can use to compete in the global marketplace: international, global, multidomestic, and trans- national. The strategy that a firm selects depends on the degree of pressure that it is facing for cost reductions and the importance of adapting to local markets. Exhibit 7.4 shows the conditions under which each of these strategies would be most appropriate.

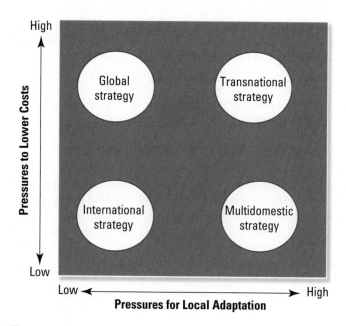

High

Pressures to Lower Costs

Low

Low ◄——————► High

Pressures for Local Adaptation

| Global strategy | Transnational strategy |
| International strategy | Multidomestic strategy |

Exhibit 7.4 Opposing Pressures and Four Strategies

It is important to note that we consider these four strategies to be "basic" or "pure"; that is, in practice, all firms will tend to have some elements of each strategy.

International Strategy

There are a small number of industries in which pressures for both local adaptation and lowering costs are rather low. An extreme example of such an industry is the "orphan" drug industry. These are medicines for diseases that are severe but affect only a small number of people. Diseases such as the Gaucher disease and Fabry disease fit into this category. Companies such as Genzyme and Oxford GlycoSciences are active in this segment of the drug industry. There is virtually no need to adapt their products to the local markets. And the pressures to reduce costs are low; even though only a few thousand patients are affected, the revenues and margins are significant, because patients are charged up to $100,000 per year. Legislation has made this industry even more attractive. The 1983 Orphan Drug Act provides various tax credits and exclusive marketing rights for any drug developed to treat a disease that afflicts fewer than 200,000 patients. Since 1983, more than 280 orphan drugs have been licensed and used to treat 14 million patients.[48]

An international strategy is based on diffusion and adaptation of the parent company's knowledge and expertise to foreign markets. Country units are allowed to make some minor adaptations to products and ideas coming from the head office, but they have far less independence and autonomy compared to multidomestic companies. The primary goal of the strategy is worldwide exploitation of the parent firm's knowledge and capabilities. All sources of core competencies are centralized.

The majority of large U.S. multinationals pursued the international strategy in the decades following World War II. These companies centralized R&D and product development but established manufacturing facilities as well as marketing organizations abroad. Companies such as McDonald's and Kellogg are examples of firms

Exhibit 7.5
Strengths and
Limitations of
International
Strategies in the
Global Marketplace

Strengths	Limitations
• Leverage and diffusion of a parent firm's knowledge and core competencies.	• Limited ability to adapt to local markets
• Lower costs because of less need to tailor products and services.	• Inability to take advantage of new ideas and innovations occurring in local markets.

following such a strategy. Although these companies do make some local adaptations, they are of a very limited nature. With increasing pressures to reduce costs due to global competition, especially from low-cost countries, opportunities to successfully employ international strategy are becoming more limited. This strategy is most suitable in situations where a firm has distinctive competencies that local companies in foreign markets lack.

Risks and Challenges   Below, are some of the risks and challenges associated with an international strategy.

- Different activities in the value chain typically have different optimal locations. That is, R&D may be optimally located in a country with an abundant supply of scientists and engineers, whereas assembly may be better conducted in a low-cost location. Nike, for example, designs its shoes in the United States, but all the manufacturing is done in countries like China or Thailand. The international strategy, with its tendency to concentrate most of its activities in one location, fails to take advantage of the benefits of an optimally distributed value chain.
- The lack of local responsiveness may result in the alienation of local customers. Worse still, the firm's inability to be receptive to new ideas and innovation from its foreign subsidiaries may lead to missed opportunities.

Exhibit 7.5 summarizes the strengths and weaknesses of international strategies in the global marketplace.

Global Strategy

global strategy a strategy based on firms' centralization and control by the corporate office, with the primary emphasis on controlling costs, and used in industries where the pressure for local adaptation is low and the pressure for lowering costs is high.

As indicated in Exhibit 7.4, a firm whose emphasis is on lowering costs tends to follow a global strategy. Competitive strategy is centralized and controlled to a large extent by the corporate office. Since the primary emphasis is on controlling costs, the corporate office strives to achieve a strong level of coordination and integration across the various businesses.[49] Firms following a global strategy strive to offer standardized products and services as well as to locate manufacturing, R&D, and marketing activities in only a few locations.[50]

A global strategy emphasizes economies of scale due to the standardization of products and services, and the centralization of operations in a few locations. As such, one advantage may be that innovations that come about through efforts of either a business unit or the corporate office can be transferred more easily to other locations. Although costs may be lower, the firm following a global strategy may, in general, have to forgo opportunities for revenue growth since it does not invest extensive resources in adapting product offerings from one market to another.

A global strategy is most appropriate when there are strong pressures for reducing costs and comparatively weak pressures for adaptation to local markets. Economies of

scale becomes an important consideration.[51] Advantages to increased volume may come from larger production plants or runs as well as from more efficient logistics and distribution networks. Worldwide volume is also especially important in supporting high levels of investment in research and development. As we would expect, many industries requiring high levels of R&D, such as pharmaceuticals, semiconductors, and jet aircraft, follow global strategies.

Another advantage of a global strategy is that it can enable a firm to create a standard level of quality throughout the world. Let's look at what Tom Siebel, chairman of Siebel Systems (now part of Oracle), the $2 billion developer of e-business application software, has to say about global standardization.

> Our customers—global companies like IBM, Zurich Financial Services, and Citicorp—expect the same high level of service and quality, and the same licensing policies, no matter where we do business with them around the world. Our human resources and legal departments help us create policies that respect local cultures and requirements worldwide, while at the same time maintaining the highest standards. We have one brand, one image, one set of corporate colors, and one set of messages, across every place on the planet. An organization needs central quality control to avoid surprises.[52]

Risks and Challenges   There are, of course, some risks associated with a global strategy.[53]

● Boeing has followed a global strategy, which requires worldwide volume to support its high level of R&D. The picture above shows Boeing 767–200 airplanes being assembled in a factory hangar.

- A firm can enjoy scale economies only by concentrating scale-sensitive resources and activities in one or few locations. Such concentration, however, becomes a "double-edged sword." For example, if a firm has only one manufacturing facility, it must export its output (e.g., components, subsystems, or finished products) to other markets, some of which may be a great distance from the operation. Thus, decisions about locating facilities must weigh the potential benefits from concentrating operations in a single location against the higher transportation and tariff costs that result from such concentration.
- The geographic concentration of any activity may also tend to isolate that activity from the targeted markets. Such isolation may be risky since it may hamper the facility's ability to quickly respond to changes in market conditions and needs.
- Concentrating an activity in a single location also makes the rest of the firm dependent on that location. Such dependency implies that, unless the location has world-class competencies, the firm's competitive position can be eroded if problems arise. A European Ford executive, reflecting on the firm's concentration of activities during a global integration program in the mid-1990s, lamented, "Now if you misjudge the market, you are wrong in 15 countries rather than only one."

Exhibit 7.6 summarizes the strengths and weaknesses of global strategies.

Exhibit 7.6
Strengths and
Limitations of Global
Strategies

Strengths	Limitations
• Strong integration across various businesses.	• Limited ability to adapt to local markets.
• Standardization leads to higher economies of scale, which lowers costs.	• Concentration of activities may increase dependence on a single facility.
• Helps create uniform standards of quality throughout the world.	• Single locations may lead to higher tariffs and transportation costs.

Multidomestic Strategy

According to Exhibit 7.4, a firm whose emphasis is on differentiating its product and service offerings to adapt to local markets follows a multidomestic strategy.[54] Decisions evolving from a multidomestic strategy tend to be decentralized to permit the firm to tailor its products and respond rapidly to changes in demand. This enables a firm to expand its market and to charge different prices in different markets. For firms following this strategy, differences in language, culture, income levels, customer preferences, and distribution systems are only a few of the many factors that must be considered. Even in the case of relatively standardized products, at least some level of local adaptation is often necessary. Consider, for example, Honda motorcycles.

> While Honda uses a common basic technology, it must develop different types of motorcycles for different regions of the world. For example, North Americans primarily use motorcycles for leisure and sports; thus aggressive looks and high horsepower are key. Southeast Asians provide a counterpoint. Here, motorcycles are a basic means of transportation. Thus, they require low cost and ease of maintenance. And, in Australia and New Zealand, shepherds use motorcycles to herd sheep. Therefore, they demand low-speed torque, rather than high speed and maintenance.[55]

In addition to the products themselves, how they are packaged must sometimes be adapted to local market conditions. Some consumers in developing countries are likely to have packaging preferences very different from Western consumers. For example, single-serve packets, or sachets, are very popular in India.[56] They permit consumers to purchase only what they need, experiment with new products, and conserve cash. Products as varied as detergents, shampoos, pickles, and cough syrup are sold in sachets in India. It is estimated that they make up 20 to 30 percent of the total sold in their categories. In China, sachets are spreading as a marketing device for such items as shampoos. This reminds us of the importance of considering all activities in a firm's value chain (discussed in Chapters 3 and 5) in determining where local adaptations may be required.

Cultural differences may also require a firm to adapt its personnel practices when it expands internationally.[57] For example, some facets of Wal-Mart stores have been easily "exported" to foreign operations, while others have required some modifications.[58] When the retailer entered the German market in 1997, it took along the company "cheer"—Give me a W! Give me an A! Give me an L! Who's Number One? The Customer!—which suited German employees. However, Wal-Mart's 10-Foot Rule, which requires employees to greet any customer within a 10-foot radius, was not so well received in Germany, where employees and shoppers alike weren't comfortable with the custom.

Strategy Spotlight 7.9 describes how U.S. multinationals have adapted to the problem of bribery in various countries while adhering to strict federal laws on corrupt practices abroad.

multidomestic strategy a strategy based on firms' differentiating their products and services to adapt to local markets, used in industries where the pressure for local adaptation is high and the pressure for lowering costs is low.

strategy spotlight

Dealing with Bribery Abroad

Most multinational firms experience difficult dilemmas when it comes to the question of adapting rules and guidelines, both formal and informal, while operating in foreign countries. A case in point is the Foreign Corrupt Practices Act of 1977, which makes it illegal for U.S. companies to bribe foreign officials to gain business or facilitate approvals and permissions. Unfortunately, in many parts of the world, bribery is a way of life, with large payoffs to government officials and politicians the norm to win government contracts. At a lower level, goods won't clear customs unless routine illegal, but well-accepted, payments, are made to officials. What is an American company to do in such situations?

Intel follows a strict rule-based definition of bribery as "a thing of value given to someone with the intent of obtaining favorable treatment from the recipient." The company strictly prohibits payments to expedite a shipment through customs if the payment did not "follow applicable rules and regulations, and if the agent gives money or payment in kind to a government official for personal benefit." Texas Instruments, on the other hand, follows a middle approach. They require employees to "exercise good judgment" in questionable circumstances "by avoiding activities that could create even the appearance that our decisions could be compromised." And Analog Devices has set up a policy manager as a consultant to overseas operations. The policy manager does not make decisions for country managers. Instead, the policy manager helps country managers think through the issues and provides information on how the corporate office has handled similar situations in the past.

Source: Begley, T. M., & Boyd, D. P. 2003. The Need for a Corporate Global Mind-Set. *MIT Sloan Management Review,* Winter: 25–32.

Risks and Challenges   As you might expect, there are some risks associated with a multidomestic strategy. Among these are the following:

- Typically, local adaptation of products and services will increase a company's cost structure. In many industries, competition is so intense that most firms can ill afford any competitive disadvantages on the dimension of cost. A key challenge of managers is to determine the trade-off between local adaptation and its cost structure. For example, cost considerations led Procter & Gamble to standardize its diaper design across all European markets. This was done despite research data indicating that Italian mothers, unlike those in other countries, preferred diapers that covered the baby's navel. Later, however, P&G recognized that this feature was critical to these mothers, so the company decided to incorporate this feature for the Italian market despite its adverse cost implications.

- At times, local adaptations, even when well intentioned, may backfire. When the American restaurant chain TGI Fridays entered the South Korean market, it purposely incorporated many local dishes, such as kimchi (hot, spicy cabbage), in its menu. This responsiveness, however, was not well received. Company analysis of the weak market acceptance indicated that Korean customers anticipated a visit to TGI Fridays as a visit to America. Thus, finding Korean dishes was inconsistent with their expectations.

- The optimal degree of local adaptation evolves over time. In many industry segments, a variety of factors, such as the influence of global media, greater international travel, and declining income disparities across countries, may lead to increasing global standardization. On the other hand, in other industry segments, especially where the product or service can be delivered over the Internet (such as music), the need for even greater customization and local adaptation may increase

Why Some Films and TV Programs Travel Well across Cultures and National Boundaries—and Others Don't

Remember *The Alamo*—not the nineteenth-century battle between Mexican forces and Texas rebels—but the 2004 movie? The film definitely met the big-budget criterion—it cost Disney nearly $100 million. It did not generate strong box office receipts in English. But what was surprising was Disney's attempt to create crossover appeal to Latinos. These efforts included a more balanced treatment of Anglos versus Mexicans, prominently featuring Tejano folk heroes in the film, and running a separate Spanish-language marketing effort. But such efforts were doomed to fail. Why? According to one authority, because the Alamo is "such an open wound among American Hispanics."

Source: Ghemawat, P. 2007. *Redefining Global Strategy*. Boston: Harvard Business School Press.

There are, however, some TV programs that successfully cross borders. Discovery Networks, which focuses on factual programs, particularly documentaries, provides an excellent example. Founder John Hendricks commented: "Nature and science documentaries are one of the few programs that can be run in almost any country because there's no cultural or political bias to these programs." Further, dubbing or subtitling requirements are minimal, especially for nature documentaries. That is not to say that no variation is required: tastes do differ. Even in documentaries, East Asians are reported to have a predilection for "bloody animal shows" and Australians for forensics. As a result, about 20 percent of Discovery's programming is local. But compared with other kinds of TV programming, these are relatively minor problems. This is why Discovery and its affiliated networks (including the Learning Channel, Travel Channel, and Animal Planet) report reaching a total of 1.4 billion subscribers worldwide.

over time. Firms must recalibrate the need for local adaptation on an ongoing basis; excessive adaptation extracts a price as surely as underadaptation.

Strategy Spotlight 7.10 discusses how some films and TV programs may cross country boundaries rather successfully, while others are less successful. Exhibit 7.7 summarizes the strengths and limitations of multidomestic strategies.

Transnational Strategy

A *transnational strategy* strives to optimize the trade-offs associated with efficiency, local adaptation, and learning.[59] It seeks efficiency not for its own sake, but as a means to achieve global competitiveness.[60] It recognizes the importance of local responsiveness but as a tool for flexibility in international operations.[61] Innovations are regarded as an outcome of a larger process of organizational learning that includes the contributions of everyone in the firm.[62] Also, a core tenet of the transnational model is that a firm's assets and capabilities are dispersed according to the most beneficial location for each activity.

transnational strategy a strategy based on firms' optimizing the trade-offs associated with efficiency, local adaptation, and learning, used in industries where the pressures for both local adaptation and lowering costs are high.

Strengths	Limitations
• Ability to adapt products and services to local market conditions.	• Decreased ability to realize cost savings through scale economies.
• Ability to detect potential opportunities for attractive niches in a given market, enhancing revenue.	• Greater difficulty in transferring knowledge across countries.
	• May lead to "overadaptation" as conditions change.

Exhibit 7.7
Strengths and Limitations of Multidomestic Strategies

Thus, managers avoid the tendency to either concentrate activities in a central location (a global strategy) or disperse them across many locations to enhance adaptation (a multidomestic strategy). Peter Brabeck, CEO of Nestlé, the giant food company, provides such a perspective.

> We believe strongly that there isn't a so-called global consumer, at least not when it comes to food and beverages. People have local tastes based on their unique cultures and traditions—a good candy bar in Brazil is not the same as a good candy bar in China. Therefore, decision making needs to be pushed down as low as possible in the organization, out close to the markets. Otherwise, how can you make good brand decisions? That said, decentralization has its limits. If you are too decentralized, you can become too complicated—you get too much complexity in your production system. The closer we come to the consumer, in branding, pricing, communication, and product adaptation, the more we decentralize. The more we are dealing with production, logistics, and supply-chain management, the more centralized decision making becomes. After all, we want to leverage Nestlé's size, not be hampered by it.[63]

The Nestlé example illustrates a common approach in determining whether or not to centralize or decentralize a value-chain activity. Typically, primary activities that are "downstream" (e.g., marketing and sales, and service), or closer to the customer, tend to require more decentralization in order to adapt to local market conditions. On the other hand, primary activities that are "upstream" (e.g., logistics and operations), or further away from the customer, tend to be centralized. This is because there is less need for adapting these activities to local markets and the firm can benefit from economies of scale. Additionally, many support activities, such as information systems and procurement, tend to be centralized in order to increase the potential for economies of scale.

A central philosophy of the transnational organization is enhanced adaptation to all competitive situations as well as flexibility by capitalizing on communication and knowledge flows throughout the organization.[64] A principal characteristic is the integration of unique contributions of all units into worldwide operations. Thus, a joint innovation by headquarters and by one of the overseas units can lead potentially to the development of relatively standardized and yet flexible products and services that are suitable for multiple markets.

Asea Brown Boveri (ABB) is a firm that successfully follows a transnational strategy. ABB, with its home bases in Sweden and Switzerland, illustrates the trend toward cross-national mergers that lead firms to consider multiple headquarters in the future. It is managed as a flexible network of units, and one of management's main functions is the facilitation of information and knowledge flows between units. ABB's subsidiaries have complete responsibility for product categories on a worldwide basis. Such a transnational strategy enables ABB to benefit from access to new markets and the opportunity to utilize and develop resources wherever they may be located.

Risks and Challenges   As with the other strategies, there are some unique risks and challenges associated with a transnational strategy.

* *The choice of a seemingly optimal location cannot guarantee that the quality and cost of factor inputs (i.e., labor, materials) will be optimal.* Managers must ensure that the relative advantage of a location is actually realized, not squandered because of weaknesses in productivity and the quality of internal operations. Ford Motor Co., for example, has benefited from having some of its manufacturing operations in Mexico. While some have argued that the benefits of lower wage rates will be partly offset by lower productivity, this does not always have to be the case. Since unemployment in Mexico is higher than in the United States, Ford can be more selective in its hiring practices for its Mexican operations. And, given the lower turnover among its Mexican employees, Ford can justify a high level of investment in training and

Strengths	Limitations
• Ability to attain economies of scale. • Ability to adapt to local markets. • Ability to locate activities in optimal locations. • Ability to increase knowledge flows and learning.	• Unique challenges in determining optimal locations of activities to ensure cost and quality. • Unique managerial challenges in fostering knowledge transfer.

Exhibit 7.8
Strengths and Limitations of Transnational Strategies

development. Thus, the net result can be not only lower wage rates but also higher productivity than in the United States.

- *Although knowledge transfer can be a key source of competitive advantage, it does not take place "automatically."* For knowledge transfer to take place from one subsidiary to another, it is important for the source of the knowledge, the target units, and the corporate headquarters to recognize the potential value of such unique know-how. Given that there can be significant geographic, linguistic, and cultural distances that typically separate subsidiaries, the potential for knowledge transfer can become very difficult to realize. Firms must create mechanisms to systematically and routinely uncover the opportunities for knowledge transfer.

Exhibit 7.8 summarizes the relative advantages and disadvantages of transnational strategies.

Global or Regional? A Second Look at Globalization

>LO6
The difference between regional companies and truly global companies.

Thus far, we have suggested four possible strategies from which a firm must choose once it has decided to compete in the global marketplace. In recent years, many writers have asserted that the process of globalization has caused national borders to become increasingly irrelevant. However, some scholars have recently questioned this perspective, and they have argued that it is unwise for companies to rush into full scale globalization.[65]

Before answering questions about the extent of firms' globalization, let's try to clarify what "globalization" means. Traditionally, a firm's globalization is measured in terms of its foreign sales as a percentage of total sales. However, this measure can be misleading. For example, consider a U.S. firm that has expanded its activities into Canada. Clearly, this initiative is qualitatively different from achieving the same sales volume in a distant country such as China. Similarly, if a Malaysian firm expands into Singapore or a German firm starts selling its products in Austria, this would represent an expansion into a geographically adjacent country. Such nearby countries would often share many common characteristics in terms of language, culture, infrastructure, and customer preferences. In other words, this is more a case of regionalization than globalization.

Extensive analysis of the distribution data of sales across different countries and regions led Alan Rugman and Alain Verbeke to conclude that there is a stronger case to be made in favor of regionalization than globalization. According to their study, a company would have to have at least 20 percent of its sales in each of the three major economic regions—North America, Europe, and Asia—to be considered a global firm. However, they found that only nine of the world's 500 largest firms met this standard! Even when they relaxed the criterion to 20 percent of sales each in at least two of the three regions, the number only increased to 25. *Thus, most companies are regional or, at best, biregional—not global—even today.* Exhibit 7.9 provides a listing of the large firms that met each of these two criteria.

In a world of instant communication, rapid transportation, and governments that are increasingly willing to open up their markets to trade and investment, why are so few

Firms with at least 20 percent sales in Asia, Europe, and North America each but with less than 50 percent sales in any one region:

IBM	Nokia	Coca-Cola
Sony	Intel	Flextronics
Philips	Canon	LVMH

Firms with at least 20 percent sales in at least two of the three regions (Asia, Europe, North America) but with less than 50 percent sales in any one region:

BP Amoco	Alstom	Michelin
Toyota	Aventis	Kodak
Nissan	Daigeo	Electrolux
Unilever	Sun Microsystems	BAE
Motorola	Bridgestone	Alcan
GlaxoSmithKline	Roche	L'Oreal
EADS	3M	Lafarge
Bayer	Skanska	
Ericsson	McDonald's	

Sources: Peng, M.W. 2006. *Global Strategy:* 387. Mason, OH: Thomson Southwestern; and Rugman, A.M., & Verbeke, A. 2004. A Perspective on Regional and Global Strategies of Multinational Enterprises. *Journal of International Business Studies,* 35: 3–18.

firms "global"? The most obvious answer is that distance still matters. After all, it is easier to do business in a neighboring country than in a far away country, all else being equal. Distance, in the final analysis, may be viewed as a concept with many dimensions, not just a measure of geographical distance. For example, both Canada and Mexico are the same distance from the U.S. However, U.S. companies find it easier to expand operations into Canada than into Mexico. Why? Canada and the U.S. share many commonalities in terms of language, culture, economic development, legal and political systems, and infrastructure development. Thus, if we view distance as having many dimensions, the U.S. and Canada are very close, whereas there is greater distance between the U.S. and Mexico. Similarly, when we look at what we might call the "true" distance between the U.S. and China, the effects of geographic distance are multiplied by distance in terms of culture, language, religion, and legal and political systems between the two countries. On the other hand, although U.S. and Australia are geographically distant, the "true" distance is somewhat less when one considers distance along the other dimensions.

Another reason for regional expansion is the rise of the trading blocs. The European Union originally started in the 1950s as a regional trading bloc. However, recently it has achieved a large degree of economic and political integration in terms of common currency and common standards that many thought infeasible, if not impossible, only 20 years ago. The resulting economic benefits have led other regions also to consider similar moves. For example, the North American Free Trade Agreement (NAFTA) has the eventual abolition of all barriers to the free movement of goods and services among Canada, the U.S., and Mexico as its goal. Other regional trading blocks include MERCOSUR (consisting of Argentina, Brazil, Paraguay, and Uruguay) and the Association of Southeast Asian Nations (ASEAN) (consisting of about a dozen Southeast Asian countries).

Regional economic integration has progressed at a faster pace than global economic integration and the trade and investment patterns of the largest companies reflect this reality. After all, regions represent the outcomes of centuries of political and cultural history that results not only in commonalities but also mutual affinity. For example, stretching from Algeria and Morocco in the West to Oman and Yemen in the East, more than 30 countries share the Arabic language and the Muslim religion, making these countries a natural regional bloc. Similarly, the countries of South and Central America share the Spanish language (except Brazil), Catholic religion, and a shared history of Spanish colonialism. No wonder firms find it easier and less risky to expand within their region than to other regions.

Entry Modes of International Expansion

>LO7
The four basic types of entry strategies and the relative benefits and risks associated with each of them.

A firm has many options available to it when it decides to expand into international markets. Given the challenges associated with such entry, many firms first start on a small scale and then increase their level of investment and risk as they gain greater experience with the overseas market in question.[66]

Exhibit 7.10 illustrates a wide variety of modes of foreign entry, including exporting, licensing, franchising, joint ventures, strategic alliances, and wholly owned subsidiaries.[67] As the exhibit indicates, the various types of entry form a continuum ranging from exporting (low investment and risk, low control) to a wholly owned subsidiary (high investment and risk, high control).[68]

There can be frustrations and setbacks as a firm evolves its international entry strategy from exporting to more expensive types, including wholly owned subsidiaries. For example, according to the CEO of a large U.S. specialty chemical company:

> In the end, we always do a better job with our own subsidiaries; sales improve, and we have greater control over the business. But we still need local distributors for entry, and we are still searching for strategies to get us through the transitions without battles over control and performance.[69]

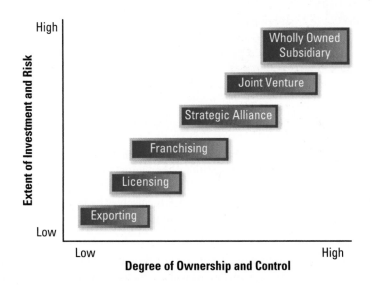

Exhibit 7.10 Entry Modes for International Expansion

Exporting

Exporting consists of producing goods in one country to sell in another.[70] This entry strategy enables a firm to invest the least amount of resources in terms of its product, its organization, and its overall corporate strategy. Many host countries dislike this entry strategy because it provides less local employment than other modes of entry.[71]

Multinationals often stumble onto a stepwise strategy for penetrating markets, beginning with the exporting of products. This often results in a series of unplanned actions to increase sales revenues. As the pattern recurs with entries into subsequent markets, this approach, named a "beachhead strategy," often becomes official policy.

Benefits Such an approach definitely has its advantages. After all, firms start from scratch in sales and distribution when they enter new markets. Because many foreign markets are nationally regulated and dominated by networks of local intermediaries, firms need to partner with local distributors to benefit from their valuable expertise and knowledge of their own markets. Multinationals, after all, recognize that they cannot master local business practices, meet regulatory requirements, hire and manage local personnel, or gain access to potential customers without some form of local partnership.

Multinationals also want to minimize their own risk. They do this by hiring local distributors and investing very little in the undertaking. In essence, the firm gives up control of strategic marketing decisions to the local partners—much more control than they would be willing to give up in their home market.

Risks and Limitations Exporting is a relatively inexpensive way to enter foreign markets. However, it can still have significant downsides. In a study of 250 instances in which multinational firms used local distributors to implement their exporting entry strategy, the results were dismal. In the vast majority of the cases, the distributors were bought (to increase control) by the multinational firm or fired. In contrast, successful distributors shared two common characteristics:

● Australia is geographically distant from the United States. However, it is much closer when other dimensions are considered, such as income levels, language, culture, and political/legal systems.

- They carried product lines that complemented, rather than competed with, the multinational's products.
- They behaved as if they were business partners with the multinationals. They shared market information with the corporations, they initiated projects with distributors in neighboring countries, and they suggested initiatives in their own or nearby markets. Additionally, these distributors took on risk themselves by investing in areas such as training, information systems, and advertising and promotion in order to increase the business of their multinational partners.

The key point is the importance of developing collaborative, win–win relationships.

To ensure more control over operations without incurring significant risks, many firms have used licensing and franchising as a mode of entry. Let's now discuss these and their relative advantages and disadvantages.

Licensing and Franchising

Licensing and franchising are both forms of contractual arrangements. **Licensing** enables a company to receive a royalty or fee in exchange for the right to use its trademark, patent, trade secret, or other valuable item of intellectual property.[72]

Franchising contracts generally include a broader range of factors in an operation and have a longer time period during which the agreement is in effect. Franchising remains a primary form of American business. According to a recent survey, more than 400 U.S. franchisers have international exposure.[73] This is greater than the combined totals of the next four largest franchiser home countries—France, the United Kingdom, Mexico, and Austria.

Benefits In international markets, an advantage of licensing is that the firm granting a license incurs little risk, since it does not have to invest any significant resources into the country itself. In turn, the licensee (the firm receiving the license) gains access to the trademark, patent, and so on, and is able to potentially create competitive advantages. In many cases, the country also benefits from the product being manufactured locally. For example, Yoplait yogurt is licensed by General Mills from Sodima, a French cooperative, for sale in the United States. The logos of college and professional athletic teams in the United States are another source of trademarks that generate significant royalty income domestically and internationally.

Franchising has the advantage of limiting the risk exposure that a firm has in overseas markets. At the same time, the firm is able to expand the revenue base of the company.

Risks and Limitations The licensor gives up control of its product and forgoes potential revenues and profits. Furthermore, the licensee may eventually become so familiar with the patent and trade secrets that it may become a competitor; that is, the licensee may make some modifications to the product and manufacture and sell it independently of the licensor without having to pay a royalty fee. This potential situation is aggravated in countries that have relatively weak laws to protect intellectual property. Additionally, if the licensee selected by the multinational firm turns out to be a poor choice, the brand name and reputation of the product may be tarnished.[74]

With franchising, the multinational firm receives only a portion of the revenues, in the form of franchise fees. Had the firm set up the operation itself (e.g., a restaurant through direct investment), it would have had the entire revenue to itself.

Companies often desire a closer collaboration with other firms in order to increase revenue, reduce costs, and enhance their learning—often through the diffusion of technology. To achieve such objectives, they enter into strategic alliances or joint ventures, two entry modes we will discuss next.

Strategic Alliances and Joint Ventures

Joint ventures and strategic alliances have recently become increasingly popular.[75] These two forms of partnership differ in that joint ventures entail the creation of a third-party legal entity, whereas strategic alliances do not. In addition, strategic alliances generally focus on initiatives that are smaller in scope than joint ventures.[76]

Benefits As we discussed in Chapter 6, these strategies have been effective in helping firms increase revenues and reduce costs as well as enhance learning and diffuse technologies. These partnerships enable firms to share the risks as well as the potential revenues and profits. Also, by gaining exposure to new sources of knowledge and technologies, such partnerships can help firms develop core competencies that can lead to competitive advantages in the marketplace.[77] Finally, entering into partnerships with host country firms can provide very useful information on local market tastes, competitive conditions, legal matters, and cultural nuances.[78]

licensing a contractual arrangement in which a company receives a royalty or fee in exchange for the right to use its trademark, patent, trade secret, or other valuable intellectual property.

franchising a contractual arrangement in which a company receives a royalty or fee in exchange for the right to use its intellectual property; it usually involves a longer time period than licensing and includes other factors, such as monitoring of operations, training, and advertising.

A Joint Venture with Partners from Three Countries

A joint venture has been formed with partners from China, India, and the United States. In December 2006, Tata Consulting Services (TCS), India's largest information technology outsourcing company, joined forces with three Chinese state-owned companies and Microsoft to form a new software development center based in Beijing, China.

The development has been hailed as one of the most striking steps forward in bilateral IT relations between India and China, which for many years have been marred by mutual suspicions. Political leaders, especially in India, have traditionally been skeptical about the export of technology skills from India to China. Why? India had concerns about assisting an economic rival.

One sign of the complexities in establishing such a partnership in China is the time that it has taken to set up TCS China: The parties had signed the initial agreement

to go ahead with the project 17 months earlier in June 2005. Under the agreement, TCS will hold 65 percent of the venture while the three Chinese partners will hold 25 percent. Microsoft will hold the remaining 10 percent. The three Chinese partners are organized under the National Development and Reform Commission, the powerful central government planning agency.

The joint venture will leverage the complementary strengths of the investing parties in technology, software development management, and talent training. Of particular value will be TCS's best processes and practices as well as its experience in handling large and industrial-scale projects. It will also benefit from the resources of the Chinese partners, which run the national software development parks.

Microsoft should also benefit. According to Jonathan Spira, chief analyst of Basex, an IT research firm: "Microsoft is a global company so it makes sense for them to invest and participate in global partnerships, especially in markets as large as China's. China is a region where Microsoft does not have anything close to resembling a foothold."

Sources: Leahy, J. 2006. Asian partnership takes off. www.ft.com, December 5: 3; Anonymous. 2005. TCS and Microsoft intend to establish joint venture with Chinese firms. Microsoft Press Release. June 30, np.; and Anonymous. 2005. Microsoft sets up JV with Tata. www.basex.com. July 1, np.

Joint ventures can often include more than two different parties. Strategy Spotlight 7.11 discusses a joint venture that involved companies from the United States, China, and India.

Risks and Limitations Managers must be aware of the risks associated with strategic alliances and joint ventures and how they can be minimized.[79] First, there needs to be a clearly defined strategy that is strongly supported by the organizations that are party to the partnership. Otherwise, the firms may work at cross-purposes and not achieve any of their goals. Second, and closely allied to the first issue, there must be a clear understanding of capabilities and resources that will be central to the partnership. Without such clarification, there will be fewer opportunities for learning and developing competencies that could lead to competitive advantages. Third, trust is a vital element. Phasing in the relationship between alliance partners permits them to get to know each other better and develop trust. Without trust, one party may take advantage of the other by, for example, withholding its fair share of resources and gaining access to privileged information through unethical (or illegal) means. Fourth, cultural issues that can potentially lead to conflict and dysfunctional behaviors need to be addressed. An organization's culture is the set of values, beliefs, and attitudes that influence the behavior and goals of its employees.[80] Thus, recognizing cultural differences as well as striving to develop elements of a "common culture" for the partnership is vital. Without a unifying culture, it will become difficult to combine and leverage resources that are increasingly important in knowledge-intensive organizations (discussed in Chapter 4).[81]

Finally, the success of a firm's alliance should not be left to chance.[82] To improve their odds of success, many companies have carefully documented alliance-management knowledge by creating guidelines and manuals to help them manage specific aspects of the entire alliance life cycle (e.g., partner selection and alliance negotiation and contracting). For example, Lotus Corp. (part of IBM) created what it calls its "35 rules of thumb" to manage each phase of an alliance from formation to termination. Hewlett-Packard developed 60 different tools and templates, which it placed in a 300-page manual for guiding decision making. The manual included such tools as a template for making the business case for an alliance, a partner evaluation form, a negotiation template outlining the roles and responsibilities of different departments, a list of the ways to measure alliance performance, and an alliance termination checklist.

When a firm desires the highest level of control, it develops wholly owned subsidiaries. Although wholly owned subsidiaries can generate the greatest returns, they also have the highest levels of investment and risk. We will now discuss them.

Wholly Owned Subsidiaries

A **wholly owned subsidiary** is a business in which a multinational company owns 100 percent of the stock. Two ways a firm can establish a wholly owned subsidiary are to (1) acquire an existing company in the home country or (2) develop a totally new operation (often referred to as a "greenfield venture").

wholly owned subsidiary a business in which a multinational company owns 100 percent of the stock.

Benefits   Establishing a wholly owned subsidiary is the most expensive and risky of the various entry modes. However, it can also yield the highest returns. In addition, it provides the multinational company with the greatest degree of control of all activities, including manufacturing, marketing, distribution, and technology development.[83]

Wholly owned subsidiaries are most appropriate where a firm already has the appropriate knowledge and capabilities that it can leverage rather easily through multiple locations. Examples range from restaurants to semiconductor manufacturers. To lower costs, for example, Intel Corporation builds semiconductor plants throughout the world—all of which use virtually the same blueprint. Knowledge can be further leveraged by hiring managers and professionals from the firm's home country, often through hiring talent from competitors.

Risks and Limitations   As noted, wholly owned subsidiaries are typically the most expensive and risky entry mode. With franchising, joint ventures, or strategic alliances, the risk is shared with the firm's partners. With wholly owned subsidiaries, the entire risk is assumed by the parent company. The risks associated with doing business in a new country (e.g., political, cultural, and legal) can be lessened by hiring local talent.

For example, Wendy's avoided committing two blunders in Germany by hiring locals to its advertising staff.[84] In one case, the firm wanted to promote its "old-fashioned" qualities. However, a literal translation would have resulted in the company promoting itself as "outdated." In another situation, Wendy's wanted to emphasize that its hamburgers could be prepared 256 ways. The problem? The German word that Wendy's wanted to use for "ways" usually meant "highways" or "roads." Although such errors may sometimes be entertaining to the public, it is certainly preferable to catch these mistakes before they confuse the consumer or embarrass the company.

We have addressed entry strategies as a progression from exporting through the creation of wholly owned subsidiaries. However, we must point out that many firms do not follow such an evolutionary approach. Instead, such firms follow rather unique entry strategies; see our discussion of Caterpillar's unconventional entry in China in Strategy Spotlight 7.12.

strategy spotlight

Caterpillar's Long March to China

Ever since it opened its doors to foreign investment a quarter century ago, China has attracted an enormous amount of foreign direct investment, currently averaging upward of $50 billion a year. However, the Chinese government has been reluctant to allow foreign companies to acquire local firms, especially in sectors that the government considers vital. For example, the attempt by Carlyle Group, a U.S. private equity firm, to buy a majority stake in Xugong Group Construction Machinery (China's leading company in this sector, with sales of $6 billion) was blocked by the Chinese government. Instead, China wants to build its own national champions in such industries.

Given this background, Caterpillar's recent acquisition of Shandong SEM Machinery, a fast-growing Chinese earth-moving-equipment manufacturer, is truly impressive. How did Caterpillar overcome China's reluctance to allow foreign companies to acquire leading Chinese companies? Investing in relationships, long-term thinking, patience, demonstrating commitment, and a creative approach to engaging the Chinese were all keys to Caterpillar's success.

Jim Owens, CEO of Caterpillar, has made numerous visits to China since he went there to negotiate a technology transfer agreement in 1983. Caterpillar started by selling designs for its equipment to several Chinese manufacturers. This not only gave Caterpillar a foothold in China in the late '80s, but it also earned them the gratitude of a nation that was embarking on one of history's biggest construction booms. During the height of the SARS crisis in 2003, Owens sent a deputy to China, thereby demonstrating Caterpillar's solidarity with China in a time of crisis. By 2005, Caterpillar was given permission to acquire a minority stake in SEM. And immediately after the Beijing Olympics of 2008, Caterpillar won the biggest prize of all: full ownership of SEM.

Currently, Caterpillar has 16 manufacturing plants in China, with sales of $2 billion. It plans to invest another $100 million in SEM to triple its output. Given China's infrastructure needs in the coming years, Caterpillar sees double-digit growth ahead for years to come. The lesson for other foreign firms on the lookout for acquisition candidates in China: Deep pockets and an open checkbook will not buy you much in China.

Source: Roberts, D. 2008. Behind Caterpillar's Big Scoop in China. *Business-Week*, December 22: 58; and www.cat.com/cda/components.

Reflecting on Career Implications . . .

- *International Strategy:* Be aware of your organization's international strategy. What percentage of the total firm activity is international? What skills are needed to enhance your company's international efforts? How can you get more involved in your organization's international strategy? For your career, what conditions in your home country might cause you to seek careers abroad?
- *Outsourcing and Offshoring:* What activities in your organization can/should be outsourced or offshored? Be aware that you are competing in the global marketplace for employment and professional advancement. Continually take inventory of your talents, skills, and competencies.
- *International Career Opportunities:* Work assignments in other countries can often provide a career boost. Be proactive in pursuing promising career opportunities in other countries. Anticipate how such opportunities will advance your short- and long-term career aspirations.
- *Management Risks:* Develop cultural sensitivity. This applies, of course, to individuals from different cultures in your home-based organization as well as in your overseas experience.

Summary

We live in a highly interconnected global community where many of the best opportunities for growth and profitability lie beyond the boundaries of a company's home country. Along with the opportunities, of course, there are many risks associated with diversification into global markets.

The first section of the chapter addressed the factors that determine a nation's competitiveness in a particular industry. The framework was developed by Professor Michael Porter of Harvard University and was based on a four-year study that explored the competitive success of 10 leading trading nations. The four factors, collectively termed the "diamond of national advantage," were factor conditions, demand characteristics, related and supporting industries, and firm strategy, structure, and rivalry.

The discussion of Porter's "diamond" helped, in essence, to set the broader context for exploring competitive advantage at the firm level. In the second section, we discussed the primary motivations and the potential risks associated with international expansion. The primary motivations included increasing the size of the potential market for the firm's products and services, achieving economies of scale, extending the life cycle of the firm's products, and optimizing the location for every activity in the value chain. On the other hand, the key risks included political and economic risks, currency risks, and management risks. Management risks are the challenges associated with responding to the inevitable differences that exist across countries such as customs, culture, language, customer preferences, and distribution systems. We also addressed some of the managerial challenges and opportunities associated with offshoring and outsourcing.

Next, we addressed how firms can go about attaining competitive advantage in global markets. We began by discussing the two opposing forces—cost reduction and adaptation to local markets—that managers must contend with when entering global markets. The relative importance of these two factors plays a major part in determining which of the four basic types of strategies to select: international, global, multidomestic, or transnational. The chapter covered the benefits and risks associated with each type of strategy. We also presented a recent perspective by Alan Rugman who argues that despite all the talk of globalization, most of the large multinationals are regional or at best biregional (in terms of geographical diversification of sales) rather than global.

The final section discussed the four types of entry strategies that managers may undertake when entering international markets. The key trade-off in each of these strategies is the level of investment or risk versus the level of control. In order of their progressively greater investment/risk and control, the strategies range from exporting to licensing and franchising, to strategic alliances and joint ventures, to wholly owned subsidiaries. The relative benefits and risks associated with each of these strategies were addressed.

Summary Review Questions

1. What are some of the advantages and disadvantages associated with a firm's expansion into international markets?

2. What are the four factors described in Porter's diamond of national advantage? How do the four factors explain why some industries in a given country are more successful than others?

3. Explain the two opposing forces—cost reduction and adaptation to local markets—that firms must deal with when they go global.

4. There are four basic strategies—international, global, multidomestic, and transnational. What are the advantages and disadvantages associated with each?

5. What is the basis of Alan Rugman's argument that most multinationals are still more regional than global? What factors inhibit firms from becoming truly global?

6. Describe the basic entry strategies that firms have available when they enter international markets. What are the relative advantages and disadvantages of each?

Key Terms

globalization, 235
factor endowments (national advantage), 236
demand conditions (national advantage), 236
related and supporting industries (national advantage), 237
firm strategy, structure, and rivalry (national advantage), 237
political risk, 243
economic risk, 244
currency risk, 245
management risk, 245
outsourcing, 247
offshoring, 247
international strategy, 250
global strategy, 251
multidomestic strategy, 253
transnational strategy, 255
exporting, 260
licensing, 261
franchising, 261
wholly owned subsidiary, 263

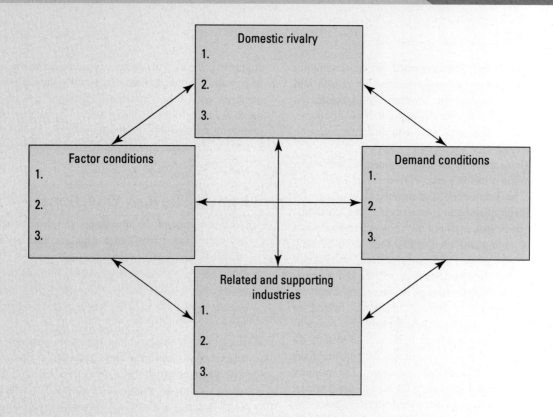

Domestic rivalry
1.
2.
3.

Factor conditions
1.
2.
3.

Demand conditions
1.
2.
3.

Related and supporting industries
1.
2.
3.

Experiential Exercise

The United States is considered a world leader in the motion picture industry. Using Porter's diamond framework for national competitiveness, explain the success of this industry.

Application Questions Exercises

1. Data on the "competitiveness of nations" can be found at www.imd.ch/wcy/ranking/. This website provides a ranking on a variety of criteria for 49 countries. How might Porter's diamond of national advantage help to explain the rankings for some of these countries for certain industries that interest you?
2. The Internet has lowered the entry barriers for smaller firms that wish to diversify into international markets. Why is this so? Provide an example.
3. Many firms fail when they enter into strategic alliances with firms that link up with companies based in other countries. What are some reasons for this failure? Provide an example.
4. Many large U.S.–based management consulting companies such as McKinsey and Company and the BCG Group have been very successful in the international marketplace. How can Porter's diamond explain their success?

Ethics Questions

1. Over the past few decades, many American firms have relocated most or all of their operations from the United States to countries such as Mexico and China that pay lower wages. What are some of the ethical issues that such actions may raise?
2. Business practices and customs vary throughout the world. What are some of the ethical issues concerning payments that must be made in a foreign country to obtain business opportunities?

References

1. Kiley, D. 2008. One world, one car, one name. *BusinessWeek*, March 24: 63; The name game Touareg? Murano? Where do they get those new car names. 2003. *Chicago Sun Times*, January 30: np; Abuelsamid, S. 2008. Geneva 2008: 2009 Ford Fiesta, a new car with Verve but an old name. autobloggreen.com, February 14: np; and Dolan, M. 2008. Ford speeds to tailor European cars for U.S. crowd: Push for smaller autos is "about our survival": Bumpers are big hurdle. *The Wall Street Journal*, September 8: B3.

2. For a recent discussion on globalization by one of international business's most respected authors, read Ohmae, K. 2005. *The next global stage: Challenges and opportunities in our borderless world*. Philadelphia: Wharton School Publishing.

3. Our discussion of globalization draws upon Engardio, P. & Belton, C. 2000. Global capitalism: Can it be made to work better? *BusinessWeek*, November 6: 72–98.

4. Sellers, P. 2005. Blowing in the wind. *Fortune*, July 25: 63.

5. An interesting and balanced discussion on the merits of multinationals to the U.S. economy is found in: Mandel, M. 2008. Multinationals: Are they good for America? *BusinessWeek*, March 10: 41–64.

6. Engardio & Belton, op. cit.

7. For insightful perspectives on strategy in emerging economies, refer to the article entitled: Strategy research in emerging economies: Challenging the conventional wisdom in the January 2005 issue of *Journal of Management Studies*, 42(1).

8. The above discussion draws on Clifford, M. L., Engardio, P., Malkin, E., Roberts, D., & Echikson, W. 2000. Up the ladder. *BusinessWeek*, November 6: 78–84.

9. A recent discussion of the "bottom of the pyramid" is: Akula, V. 2008. Business basics at the bottom of the pyramid. *Harvard Business Review*, 86(6): 53–59.

10. Some insights into how winners are evolving in emerging markets are addressed in: Ghemawat, P. & Hout, T. 2008. Tomorrow's global giants: Not the usual suspects. *Harvard Business Review*, 66(11): 80–88.

11. For another interesting discussion on a country perspective, refer to Makino, S. 1999. MITI Minister Kaora Yosano on reviving Japan's competitive advantages. *Academy of Management Executive*, 13(4): 8–28.

12. The following discussion draws heavily upon Porter, M. E. 1990. The competitive advantage of nations. *Harvard Business Review*, March–April: 73–93.

13. Landes, D. S. 1998. *The wealth and poverty of nations*. New York: W. W. Norton.

14. A recent study that investigates the relationship between international diversification and firm performance is Lu, J. W. & Beamish, P. W. 2004. International diversification and firm performance: The s-curve hypothesis. *Academy of Management Journal*, 47(4): 598–609.

15. Part of our discussion of the motivations and risks of international expansion draws upon Gregg, F. M. 1999. International strategy. In Helms, M. M. (Ed.). *Encyclopedia of management*: 434–438. Detroit: Gale Group.

16. These two examples are discussed, respectively, in Dawar, N. & Frost, T. 1999. Competing with giants: Survival strategies for local companies in emerging markets. *Harvard Business Review*, 77(2): 119–129; and Prahalad, C. K. & Lieberthal, K. 1998. The end of corporate imperialism. *Harvard Business Review*, 76(4): 68–79.

17. Meredith, R. 2004. Middle kingdom, middle class. *Forbes*, November 15: 188–192; and Anonymous. 2004. Middle class becomes rising power in China. www.Chinadaily.com. November 6.

18. This discussion draws upon Gupta, A. K. & Govindarajan, V. 2001. Converting global presence into global competitive advantage. *Academy of Management Executive*, 15(2): 45–56.

19. Stross, R. E. 1997. Mr. Gates builds his brain trust. *Fortune*, December 8: 84–98.

20. For a good summary of the benefits and risks of international expansion, refer to Bartlett, C. A. & Ghoshal, S. 1987. Managing across borders: New strategic responses. *Sloan Management Review*, 28(5): 45–53; and Brown, R. H. 1994. *Competing to win in a global economy*. Washington, DC: U.S. Department of Commerce.

21. For an interesting insight into rivalry in global markets, refer to MacMillan, I. C., van Putten, A. B., & McGrath, R. G. 2003. Global gamesmanship. *Harvard Business Review*, 81(5): 62–73.

22. It is important for firms to spread their foreign operations and outsourcing relationships with a broad, well-balanced mix of regions and countries to reduce risk and increase potential reward. For example, refer to Vestring, T., Rouse, T., & Reinert, U. 2005. Hedge your offshoring bets. *MIT Sloan Management Review*, 46(3): 27–29.

23. An interesting discussion of risks faced by Lukoil, Russia's largest oil firm is in: Gimbel, B. 2009. Russia's king of crude. *Fortune*, February 2: 88–92.

24. Some insights on how Africa has improved as a potential source of investment is in: Collier, P. & Warnholz, J-L. 2009. Now's the time to invest in Africa. *Harvard Business Review*, 87(2): 23.

25. For a discussion of some of the challenges associated with government corruption regarding entry strategies in foreign markets, read Rodriguez, P.,

Uhlenbruck, K., & Eden, L. 2005. Government corruption and entry strategies of multinationals. *Academy of Management Review,* 30(2): 383–396.

26. For a discussion of the political risks in China for United States companies, refer to Garten, J. E. 1998. Opening the doors for business in China. *Harvard Business Review,* 76(3): 167–175.

27. Shari, M. 2001. Is a holy war brewing in Indonesia? *BusinessWeek,* October 15: 62.

28. Insights on how forensic economics can be used to investigate crimes and wrongdoing are in: Fisman, R. 2009. The rise of forensic economics. *Harvard Business Review,* 87(2): 26.

29. For an interesting perspective on the relationship between diversification and the development of a nation's institutional environment, read Chakrabarti, A., Singh, K., & Mahmood, I. 2007. Diversification and performance: Evidence from East Asian firms. *Strategic Management Journal,* 28(2): 101–120.

30. A study looking into corruption and foreign direct investment is: Brouthers, L. E., Gao, Y., & McNicol, J. P. 2008. *Strategic Management Journal,* 29(6): 673–680.

31. Gikkas, N. S. 1996. International licensing of intellectual property: The promise and the peril. *Journal of Technology Law & Policy,* 1(1): 1–26.

32. Insights into bribery in the international context are addressed in: Martin, K. D., Cullen, J. B., Johnson, J. L., & Parboteeah, P. 2008. Deciding to bribe: A cross-level analysis of firm and home country influences on bribery activity. *Academy of Management Journal,* 50(6): 1401–1422.

33. For an excellent theoretical discussion of how cultural factors can affect knowledge transfer across national boundaries, refer to Bhagat, R. S., Kedia, B. L., Harveston, P. D., & Triandis, H. C. 2002. Cultural variations in the cross-border transfer of organizational knowledge: An integrative framework. *Academy of Management Review,* 27(2): 204–221.

34. An interesting discussion on how local companies compete effectively with large multinationals is in: Bhatacharya, A. K. & Michael, D. C. 2008. *Harvard Business Review,* 66(3): 84–95.

35. To gain insights on the role of national and regional cultures on knowledge management models and frameworks, read Pauleen, D. J. & Murphy, P. 2005. In praise of cultural bias. *MIT Sloan Management Review,* 46(2): 21–22.

36. Berkowitz, E. N. 2000. *Marketing* (6th ed.). New York: McGraw-Hill.

37. Morrison, T., Conaway, W., & Borden, G. 1994. *Kiss, bow, or shake hands.* Avon, MA: Adams Media; and www.executiveplanet .com/business-culture.

38. World Trade Organization. *Annual Report 1998.* Geneva: World Trade Organization.

39. Lei, D. 2005. Outsourcing. In Hitt, M. A. & Ireland, R. D. (Eds.). *The Blackwell encyclopedia of management.* Entrepreneurship: 196–199. Malden, MA: Blackwell.

40. Future trends in offshoring are addressed in: Manning, S., Massini, S., & Lewin, A. Y. 2008. A dynamic perspective on next-generation offshoring: The global sourcing of science and engineering talent. *Academy of Management Perspectives,* 22(3): 35–54.

41. An interesting perspective on the controversial issue regarding the offshoring of airplane maintenance is in: Smith, G. & Bachman, J. 2008. Flying in for a tune-up overseas. *Business Week.* April 21: 26–27.

42. Dolan, K.A. 2006. Offshoring the offshorers. *Forbes.* April 17: 74–78.

43. The discussion above draws from Colvin, J. 2004. Think your job can't be sent to India? Just watch. *Fortune,* December 13: 80; Schwartz, N. D. 2004. Down and out in white collar America. *Fortune,* June 23: 321–325; Hagel, J. 2004. Outsourcing is not just about cost cutting. *The Wall Street Journal,* March 18: A3.

44. Insightful perspectives on the outsourcing of decision making are addressed in: Davenport, T. H. & Iyer, B.

2009. Should you outsource your brain? *Harvard Business Review.* 87 (2): 38. (7)

45. Levitt, T. 1983. The globalization of markets. *Harvard Business Review,* 61(3): 92–102.

46. Our discussion of these assumptions draws upon Douglas, S. P. & Wind, Y. 1987. The myth of globalization. *Columbia Journal of World Business,* Winter: 19–29.

47. Ghoshal, S. 1987. Global strategy: An organizing framework. *Strategic Management Journal,* 8: 425–440.

48. Huber, P. 2009. Who pays for a cancer drug? *Forbes,* January 12: 72.

49. For insights on global branding, refer to Aaker, D. A. & Joachimsthaler, E. 1999. The lure of global branding. *Harvard Business Review,* 77(6): 137–146.

50. For an interesting perspective on how small firms can compete in their home markets, refer to Dawar & Frost, op. cit.: 119–129.

51. Hout, T., Porter, M. E., & Rudden, E. 1982. How global companies win out. *Harvard Business Review,* 60(5): 98–107.

52. Fryer, B. 2001. Tom Siebel of Siebel Systems: High tech the old-fashioned way. *Harvard Business Review,* 79(3): 118–130.

53. The risks that are discussed for the global, multidomestic, and transnational strategies draw upon Gupta & Govindarajan, op. cit.

54. A discussion on how McDonald's adapts its products to overseas markets is in: Gumbel, P. 2008. Big Mac's local flavor. *Fortune,* May 5: 115–121.

55. Sigiura, H. 1990. How Honda localizes its global strategy. *Sloan Management Review,* 31: 77–82.

56. Prahalad & Lieberthal, op. cit.: 68–79. Their article also discusses how firms may have to reconsider their brand management, costs of market building, product design, and approaches to capital efficiency when entering foreign markets.

57. Hofstede, G. 1980. *Culture's consequences: International differences in work-related values.* Beverly Hills, CA: Sage; Hofstede, G. 1993. Cultural

constraints in management theories. *Academy of Management Executive,* 7(1): 81–94; Kogut, B. & Singh, H. 1988. The effect of national culture on the choice of entry mode. *Journal of International Business Studies,* 19: 411–432; and Usinier, J. C. 1996. *Marketing across cultures.* London: Prentice Hall.

58. McCune, J. C. 1999. Exporting corporate culture. *Management Review,* December: 53–56.

59. Prahalad, C. K. & Doz, Y. L. 1987. *The multinational mission: Balancing local demands and global vision.* New York: Free Press.

60. For an insightful discussion on knowledge flows in multinational corporations, refer to: Yang, Q., Mudambi, R., & Meyer, K. E. 2008. Conventional and reverse knowledge flows in multinational corporations. *Journal of Management,* 34(5): 882–902.

61. Kidd, J. B. & Teramoto, Y. 1995. The learning organization: The case of Japanese RHQs in Europe. *Management international review,* 35 (Special Issue): 39–56.

62. Gupta, A. K. & Govindarajan, V. 2000. Knowledge flows within multinational corporations. *Strategic Management Journal,* 21(4): 473–496.

63. Wetlaufer, S. 2001. The business case against revolution: An interview with Nestlé's Peter Brabeck. *Harvard Business Review,* 79(2): 112–121.

64. Nobel, R. & Birkinshaw, J. 1998. Innovation in multinational corporations: Control and communication patterns in international R&D operations. *Strategic Management Journal,* 19(5): 461–478.

65. This section draws upon Ghemawat, P. 2005. Regional strategies for global leadership. *Harvard Business Review.* 84(12): 98–108; Ghemawat, P. 2006. Apocalypse now? *Harvard Business Review.* 84(12): 32; Ghemawat, P. 2001. Distance still matters: The hard reality of global expansion. *Harvard Business Review,* 79(8): 137–147; Peng, M.W. 2006. *Global strategy:* 387. Mason, OH: Thomson Southwestern; and

Rugman, A. M. & Verbeke, A. 2004. A perspective on regional and global strategies of multinational enterprises. *Journal of International Business Studies.* 35: 3–18.

66. For a rigorous analysis of performance implications of entry strategies, refer to Zahra, S. A., Ireland, R. D., & Hitt, M. A. 2000. International expansion by new venture firms: International diversity, modes of entry, technological learning, and performance. *Academy of Management Journal,* 43(6): 925–950.

67. Li, J. T. 1995. Foreign entry and survival: The effects of strategic choices on performance in international markets. *Strategic Management Journal,* 16: 333–351.

68. For a discussion of how home-country environments can affect diversification strategies, refer to Wan, W. P. & Hoskisson, R. E. 2003. Home country environments, corporate diversification strategies, and firm performance. *Academy of Management Journal,* 46(1): 27–45.

69. Arnold, D. 2000. Seven rules of international distribution. *Harvard Business Review,* 78(6): 131–137.

70. Sharma, A. 1998. Mode of entry and ex-post performance. *Strategic Management Journal,* 19(9): 879–900.

71. This section draws upon Arnold, op. cit.: 131–137; and Berkowitz, op. cit.

72. Kline, D. 2003. Strategic licensing. *MIT Sloan Management Review,* 44(3): 89–93.

73. Martin, J. 1999. Franchising in the Middle East. *Management Review.* June: 38–42.

74. Arnold, op. cit.; and Berkowitz, op. cit.

75. An in-depth case study of alliance dynamics is found in: Faems, D., Janssens, M., Madhok, A., & Van Looy, B. 2008. Toward an integrative perspective on alliance governance: Connecting contract design, trust dynamics, and contract application. *Academy of Management Journal,* 51(6): 1053–1078.

76. Knowledge transfer in international joint ventures is addressed in: Inkpen,

A. 2008. Knowledge transfer and international joint ventures. *Strategic Management Journal,* 29(4): 447–453.

77. Manufacturer–supplier relationships can be very effective in global industries such as automobile manufacturing. Refer to Kotabe, M., Martin, X., & Domoto, H. 2003. Gaining from vertical partnerships: Knowledge transfer, relationship duration, and supplier performance improvement in the U.S. and Japanese automotive industries. *Strategic Management Journal,* 24(4): 293–316.

78. For a good discussion, refer to Merchant, H. & Schendel, D. 2000. How do international joint ventures create shareholder value? *Strategic Management Journal,* 21(7): 723–738.

79. This discussion draws upon Walters, B. A., Peters, S., & Dess, G. G. 1994. Strategic alliances and joint ventures: Making them work. *Business Horizons,* 37(4): 5–11.

80. Some insights on partnering in the global area are discussed in: MacCormack, A. & Forbath, T. 2008. *Harvard Business Review,* 66(1): 24, 26.

81. For a rigorous discussion of the importance of information access in international joint ventures, refer to Reuer, J. J. & Koza, M. P. 2000. Asymmetric information and joint venture performance: Theory and evidence for domestic and international joint ventures. *Strategic Management Journal,* 21(1): 81–88.

82. Dyer, J. H., Kale, P., & Singh, H. 2001. How to make strategic alliances work. *MIT Sloan Management Review,* 42(4): 37–43.

83. For a discussion of some of the challenges in managing subsidiaries, refer to O'Donnell, S. W. 2000. Managing foreign subsidiaries: Agents of headquarters, or an independent network? *Strategic Management Journal,* 21(5): 525–548.

84. Ricks, D. 2006. *Blunders in international business* (4th ed.). Malden, MA: Blackwell Publishing.

Entrepreneurial Strategy and Competitive Dynamics

After reading this chapter, you should have a good understanding of:

LO1 The role of new ventures and small businesses in the U.S. economy.

LO2 The role of opportunities, resources, and entrepreneurs in successfully pursuing new ventures.

LO3 Three types of entry strategies—pioneering, imitative, and adaptive—commonly used to launch a new venture.

LO4 How the generic strategies of overall cost leadership, differentiation, and focus are used by new ventures and small businesses.

LO5 How competitive actions, such as the entry of new competitors into a marketplace, may launch a cycle of actions and reactions among close competitors.

LO6 The components of competitive dynamics analysis—new competitive action, threat analysis, motivation and capability to respond, types of competitive actions, and likelihood of competitive reaction.

New technologies, shifting social and demographic trends, and sudden changes in the business environment create opportunities for entrepreneurship. New ventures, which often emerge under such conditions, face unique strategic challenges if they are going to survive and grow. Young and small businesses, which are a major engine of growth in the U.S. economy because of their role in job creation and innovation, must rely on sound strategic principles to be successful.

This chapter addresses how new ventures and entrepreneurial firms can achieve competitive advantages. It also examines how entrepreneurial activity influences a firm's strategic priorities and intensifies the rivalry among an industry's close competitors.

In the first section, we discuss the role of opportunity recognition in the process of new venture creation. Three factors that are important in determining whether a value-creating opportunity should be pursued are highlighted—the nature of the opportunity, the resources available to undertake it, and the characteristics of the entrepreneur(s) pursuing it.

The second section addresses three different types of new entry strategies—pioneering, imitative, and adaptive. Then, the generic strategies (discussed in Chapter 5) as well as combination strategies are addressed in terms of how they apply to new ventures and entrepreneurial firms. Additionally, some of the pitfalls associated with each of these strategic approaches are presented.

In section three, we explain how new entrants and other competitors often set off a series of actions and reactions that affect the competitive dynamics of an industry. In determining how to react to a competitive action, firms must analyze whether they are seriously threatened by the action, how important it is for them to respond, and what resources they can muster to mount a response. They must also determine what type of action is appropriate—strategic or tactical—and whether their close competitors are likely to counterattack. Taken together, these actions often have a strong impact on the strategic choices and overall profitability of an industry.

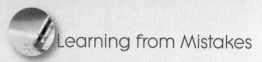

Learning from Mistakes

The success of an entrepreneurial venture—whether it is undertaken by a small start-up or a major corporation—depends on many factors. The right combination of resources, know-how, and strategic action can lead to above-average profitability and value-creating advantages. However, many things can go wrong. To see how a firm's efforts to launch an entrepreneurial new entry can turn sour, consider the example of Amp'd Mobile.

Mobile technology has turned cell phones into much more than just phones. Not only are they mini-workstations capable of handling online transactions and multiple types of communication, but they can also deliver a wide array of content—music, games, news, videos, and more. Several businesses have been launched to take advantage of these capabilities, including Amp'd Mobile, a 2003 start-up created to provide entertainment content to a unique target audience—18–25 year old males.[1]

The Amp'd business model involved supplying original programming that could be sent directly to users' handsets. The company contracted with Verizon Wireless to operate over Verizon's broadband network and turned its attention to providing edgy content—online gaming, comedy and reality shows, sports programming, and music. The company outfitted itself with an in-house studio for recording live concerts and mobile outdoor broadcasting trucks that could simulcast extreme sports events such as super-cross racing and Ultimate Fighting Championship (UFC). Amp'd also licensed content from MTV Networks and Playboy Enterprises.

The Amp'd management team, which had been successful with an earlier start-up aimed at multicultural youth, based the launch on a key assumption: 18–25 year olds were already savvy users of digital devices. By creating a service that promised "a more relevant, personal experience to the wireless lifestyle," they believed that their target audience would generate significantly more revenue per user than the typical digital phone customer. That business model helped Amp'd become a favorite among venture capitalists. It raised $360 million in equity investments and another $31 million in debt financing.

In early 2007, Amp'd reported it had well over 100,000 users paying in excess of $30 per month for content and data. Because the industry average was just $6.80 per user, its plan seemed to be working. Content alone accounted for nearly 60 percent of its revenues, compared to the average for other carriers of 25 percent. But later the same year, Amp'd Mobile filed for Chapter 11 bankruptcy protection.

What went wrong? Three things plagued this promising start-up. First, Amp'd had a serious collections problem with its 18–25-year-old target audience. According to an affidavit filed by Amp'd president Bill Stone, by May 2007 "nonpaying customers approached 80,000" out of an estimated 175,000 total customers, leading to a serious liquidity crisis. Amp'd had signed 90 percent of its customers on 18-month service contracts, but many simply stopped paying. "Youth is the least loyal [customer] in the whole wireless world," according to Alex Besen, founder of the Besen Group, a wireless industry consultancy.

Amp'd likely did not foresee its collections problem, but its other failures could well have been prevented. Amp'd executives burned through the company's $360 million of investor capital with lavish and uncontrolled spending. It hired executives from all over the U.S and flew or helicopered them to its Southern California headquarters as needed. It spent millions on marketing, including sponsoring the MTV Video Music Awards and rapper Snoop Dogg's youth football league. It was also known for cosponsoring big bashes, including pool parties at the MTV awards and the 2006 Coachella Music Festival in Palm Springs, California.

One of the biggest problems, however, had to do with the commitment and savvy of its key executives. Insiders reported that the advertising spending problem was made worse because Amp'd executives did not bargain for volume discounts but often paid full price for its ads. And operations were especially weak. Amp'd hired former T-Mobile executive Sue Swenson to bring operations depth. But because of a noncompete clause, she was unable to start *(continued)*

(continued) working for a year. Meanwhile, the operations job fell to President Stone, whose background was marketing, not operations. When customer complaints about service started mounting, Stone added customer service reps rather than investigate the reasons for the complaints.

Eventually the company ceased operations and abandoned its efforts to emerge out of bankruptcy. At the time, it had $164 million in liabilities against $46.6 million in assets. The unpaid bill to Verizon alone was $33 million.

By offering differentiated content to a gadget-loving niche audience, Amp'd Mobile seemed to have identified an attractive opportunity. But the start-up's failure shows what can go wrong when—even though a good opportunity, sufficient resources, and an experienced entrepreneurial team are brought together—that team falls short in their planning and execution efforts. Other independently run mobile virtual network operators (MVNOs), including start-ups Jitterbug and Sonopia, are thriving despite the extra cost of leasing broadband services. IT consultancy Gartner estimates that by 2014, 25 percent of U.S. subscribers will obtain services from this type of niche provider, up from less than 10 percent today. But without a clear strategy and disciplined implementation, such businesses are fighting an uphill battle. Indeed, Amp'd Mobile joins a host of players in the mobile communications space, including sports giant ESPN, who failed to operate profitable business models and were forced to shut down.

The Amp'd Mobile case illustrates how important it is for new entrepreneurial entrants—whether they are start-ups or incumbents—to think and act strategically. Even with a strong resource base and good track record, an ill-conceived strategy and strong competitive forces may prevent what seems like a good idea from taking off.

In this chapter we address entrepreneurial strategies. The previous three chapters have focused primarily on the business-level, corporate-level, and international strategies of incumbent firms. Here we ask: What about the strategies of those entering into a market or industry for the first time? Whether it's a small, young start-up such as Amp'd Mobile or an existing company seeking growth opportunities, new entrants need effective strategies.

Companies wishing to launch new ventures must also be aware that, consistent with the five forces model in Chapter 2, new entrants are a threat to existing firms in an industry. Entry into a new market arena is intensely competitive from the perspective of incumbents in that arena. Therefore, new entrants can nearly always expect a competitive response from other companies in the industry it is entering. Knowledge of the competitive dynamics that are at work in the business environment is an aspect of entrepreneurial new entry that will be addressed later in this chapter.

Before moving on, it is important to highlight the role that entrepreneurial start-ups and small business play in entrepreneurial value creation. Young and small firms are responsible for more innovations and more new job creation than any other type of business.[2] Strategy Spotlight 8.1 addresses some of the reasons why small business and entrepreneurship are viewed favorably in the United States.

> **>LO1**
> The role of new ventures and small businesses in the U.S. economy.

Recognizing Entrepreneurial Opportunities

Defined broadly, **entrepreneurship** refers to new value creation. Even though entrepreneurial activity is usually associated with start-up companies, new value can be created in many different contexts including:

- Start-up ventures
- Major corporations
- Family-owned businesses
- Non-profit organizations
- Established institutions

> **entrepreneurship**
> the creation of new value by an existing organization or new venture that involves the assumption of risk.

The Contribution of Small Businesses to the U.S. Economy

In the late 1970s, MIT professor David Birch launched a study to explore the sources of business growth. "I wasn't really looking for anything in particular," says Birch. But the findings surprised him: Small businesses create the most jobs. Since then, Birch and others have shown that it's not just big companies that power the economy. Small business and entrepreneurship have become a major component of new job creation.

Sources: Small Business Administration. 2007. *The Small Business Economy*. Washington, DC: U.S. Government Printing Office; Small Business Administration. 2006. Small Business by the Numbers. *SBA Office of Advocacy*, June, www.sba.gov/advo/; *Inc.* 2001. Small Business 2001: Where We Are Now? May 29: 18–19; Minniti, M., & Bygrave, W. D. 2004. *Global Entrepreneurship Monitor—National Entrepreneurship Assessment: United States of America 2004, Executive Report*. Kansas City, MO: Kauffman Center for Entrepreneurial Leadership; and *Fortune*. 2001. The Heroes: A Portfolio. October 4: 74.

Here are the facts:

- In the United States, there are approximately 5.6 million companies with fewer than 100 employees. Another 100,000 companies have 100 to 500 employees. In addition, approximately 17.0 million individuals are nonemployer sole proprietors.

- Small businesses create the majority of new jobs. According to recent data, small business created three-quarters of U.S. net new jobs in a recent period (2.5 million of the 3.4 million total). A small percentage of the fastest growing entrepreneurial firms (5 to 15 percent) account for a majority of the new jobs created.

- Small businesses (fewer than 500 employees) employ more than half of the private sector workforce (56 million in 2002) and account for more than 50 percent of nonfarm private gross domestic product (GDP). *(continued)*

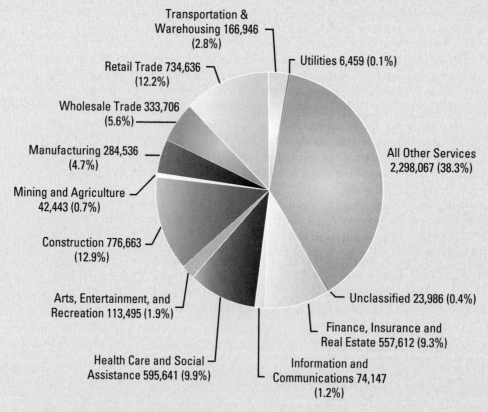

Exhibit 8.1 **All U.S. Small Companies by Industry***

*Businesses with 500 or fewer employees in 2005.

Source: Small Business Administration's Office of Advocacy, based on data provided by the U.S. Census Bureau, statistics of U.S. businesses.

(continued)

- Small firms produce 13 to 14 times more patents per employee than large patenting firms and employ 39 percent of high-tech workers (such as scientists and engineers). In addition, smaller entrepreneurial firms account for 55 percent of all innovations.
- Small businesses make up 97 percent of all U.S. exporters and accounted for 29 percent of known U.S. export value in 2001.

Exhibit 8.1 shows the number of small businesses in the United States and how they are distributed through different sectors of the economy.

There are also many types of small businesses. Exhibit 8.2 identifies three major categories that are often small and generally considered to be entrepreneurial—franchises, family businesses, and home-based businesses.

Type	Characteristics
Family Businesses	*Definition:* A family business, broadly defined, is a privately held firm in which family members have some degree of control over the strategic direction of the firm and intend for the business to remain within the family. *Scope:* According to the Family Firm Institute (FFI), family-owned businesses that meet the broad definition above comprise 80 to 90 percent of all business enterprises in the U.S., including 30 to 35 percent of the Fortune 500 companies. Further, 64 percent of the U.S. Gross Domestic Product (GDP) is generated by family-owned businesses.
Franchises	*Definition:* A franchise exists when a company that already has a successful product or service (franchisor) contracts with another business to be a dealer (franchisee) by using the franchisor's name, trademark and business system in exchange for a fee. The most common type is the Business Format Franchise in which the franchisor provides a complete plan, or format, for managing the business. *Scope:* According to the International Franchise Association (IFA), franchises were the cause of $2.31 trillion in annual output in the U.S. in 2005. There are over 900,000 franchise establishments employing more than 11 million people.
Home-Based Businesses	*Definition:* A home-based business, also referred to as SOHO (Small Office/Home Office) consists of companies with 20 or fewer employees, including the self-employed, freelancers, telecommuters, or other independent professionals working from a home-based setting. *Scope:* According to the National Association of Home-Based Businesses (NAHBB), approximately 20 million businesses are home-based. The U.S. Commerce Department estimates that more than half of all small businesses are home-based.

Sources: www.ffi.org; www.franchise.org; and www.workingsolo.com.

Exhibit 8.2 Types of Entrepreneurial Ventures

>LO2
The role of
opportunities,
resources, and
entrepreneurs
in successfully
pursuing new
ventures.

For an entrepreneurial venture to create new value, three factors must be present—an entrepreneurial opportunity, the resources to pursue the opportunity, and an entrepreneur or entrepreneurial team willing and able to undertake the opportunity.[3] The entrepreneurial strategy that an organization uses will depend on these three factors. Thus, beyond merely identifying a venture concept, the opportunity recognition process also involves organizing the key people and resources that are needed to go forward. Exhibit 8.3 depicts the three factors that are needed to successfully proceed—opportunity, resources, and entrepreneur(s). In the sections that follow, we address each of these factors.

Entrepreneurial Opportunities

The starting point for any new venture is the presence of an entrepreneurial opportunity. Where do opportunities come from? For new business start-ups, opportunities come from many sources—current or past work experiences, hobbies that grow into businesses or lead to inventions, suggestions by friends or family, or a chance event that makes an entrepreneur aware of an unmet need. For established firms, new business opportunities come from the needs of existing customers, suggestions by suppliers, or technological developments that lead to new advances.[4] For all firms, there is a major, overarching factor behind all viable opportunities that emerge in the business landscape: change. Change creates opportunities. Entrepreneurial firms make the most of changes brought about by new technology, sociocultural trends, and shifts in consumer demand.

How do changes in the external environment lead to new business creation? They spark creative new ideas and innovation. Businesspeople often have ideas for entrepreneurial ventures. However, not all such ideas are good ideas—that is, viable business opportunities. To determine which ideas are strong enough to become new ventures, entrepreneurs must go through a process of identifying, selecting, and developing potential opportunities. This is the process of **opportunity recognition.**[5]

opportunity recognition the process of discovering and evaluating changes in the business environment, such as a new technology, sociocultural trends, or shifts in consumer demand, that can be exploited.

Opportunity recognition refers to more than just the "Eureka!" feeling that people sometimes experience at the moment they identify a new idea. Although such insights are often very important, the opportunity recognition process involves two phases of activity—discovery and evaluation—that lead to viable new venture opportunities.[6]

Exhibit 8.3 **Opportunity Analysis Framework**
Sources: Based on Timmons, J. A. & Spinelli, S. 2004. *New Venture Creation* (6th ed.). New York: McGraw-Hill/Irwin; and Bygrave, W. D. 1997. The Entrepreneurial Process. In W. D. Bygrave (Ed.), *The Portable MBA in Entrepreneurship* (2nd ed.). New York: Wiley.

The discovery phase refers to the process of becoming aware of a new business concept.[7] Many entrepreneurs report that their idea for a new venture occurred to them in an instant, as a sort of "Aha!" experience—that is, they had some insight or epiphany, often based on their prior knowledge, that gave them an idea for a new business. The discovery of new opportunities is often spontaneous and unexpected. For example, Howard Schultz, CEO of Starbucks, was in Milan, Italy, when he suddenly realized that the coffee-and-conversation café model that was common in Europe would work in the U.S. as well. According to Schultz, he didn't need to do research to find out if Americans would pay $3 for a cup of coffee—he just *knew*. Starbucks was just a small business at the time but Schultz began literally shaking with excitement about growing it into a bigger business.[8] Strategy Spotlight 8.2 tells how three Internet pioneers identified their business opportunities and grew them into billion-dollar successes.

Opportunity discovery also may occur as the result of a deliberate search for new venture opportunities or creative solutions to business problems. Viable opportunities often emerge only after a concerted effort. It is very similar to a creative process, which may be unstructured and "chaotic" at first but eventually leads to a practical solution or business innovation. To stimulate the discovery of new opportunities, companies often encourage creativity, out-of-the-box thinking, and brainstorming.

Opportunity evaluation, which occurs after an opportunity has been identified, involves analyzing an opportunity to determine whether it is viable and strong enough to be developed into a full-fledged new venture. Ideas developed by new-product groups or in brainstorming sessions are tested by various methods, including talking to potential target customers and discussing operational requirements with production or logistics managers. A technique known as feasibility analysis is used to evaluate these and other critical success factors. This type of analysis often leads to the decision that a new venture project should be discontinued. If the venture concept continues to seem viable, a more formal business plan may be developed.[9]

Among the most important factors to evaluate is the market potential for the product or service. Established firms tend to operate in established markets. They have to adjust to market trends and to shifts in consumer demand, of course, but they usually have a customer base for which they are already filling a marketplace need. New ventures, in contrast, must first determine whether a market exists for the product or service they are contemplating. Thus, a critical element of opportunity recognition is assessing to what extent the opportunity is viable *in the marketplace*.

For an opportunity to be viable, it needs to have four qualities.[10]

- *Attractive.* The opportunity must be attractive in the marketplace; that is, there must be market demand for the new product or service.
- *Achievable.* The opportunity must be practical and physically possible.
- *Durable.* The opportunity must be attractive long enough for the development and deployment to be successful; that is, the window of opportunity must be open long enough for it to be worthwhile.
- *Value creating.* The opportunity must be potentially profitable; that is, the benefits must surpass the cost of development by a significant margin.

If a new business concept meets these criteria, two other factors must be considered before the opportunity is launched as a business: the resources available to undertake it, and the characteristics of the entrepreneur(s) pursuing it. In the next section, we address the issue of entrepreneurial resources; following that, we address the importance of entrepreneurial leaders and teams. But first, consider the opportunities that have been created by the recent surge in interest in environmental sustainability. Strategy Spotlight 8.3 discusses how several eco-entrepreneurs built businesses by creating products from recycled waste.

From Pioneers to Billionaires: Internet Entrepreneurs Who Recognized Winning Opportunities

When founding a business, there is always a moment when the opportunity is first recognized. The recognition may unfold in tiny steps over time or appear suddenly as an Aha! experience. When pioneering entrepreneurs act on such realizations, they change the world for the rest of us. Here are three examples of pioneers who recognized how to use the transforming technology of the Internet to create new competitive advantages and make themselves billionaires (net worth figures as of September 2008).

Pierre Omidyar, Founder of eBay.com (Net Worth: $7.7 Billion)

Most everyone has heard of eBay—it is an icon of the Internet era. The online auction model it championed made it possible for hobbyists, collectors, and seekers of highly specialized products to participate 24/7 in an enormous global "flea market." It is one of the best examples of a business that just was not possible before the Web made it so. As well-known as eBay is, its origins are a bit more murky. Legend has it that founder Pierre Omidyar launched the auction site to help his fiancée sell and find pieces for her Pez-dispenser collection. These humble beginnings, however, were contrived by a public relations manager to attract media attention. In fact, the first thing sold on eBay was a broken laser pointer for $14.83. Omidyar, incredulous, asked the winning buyer if he knew it was broken. The email reply, "I collect broken laser pointers," helped Omidyar recognize he had tapped into a gold mine of business potential. By 2008, eBay had over 15,000 employees and annual revenues of $84.6 billion.

Mark Zuckerberg, Founder of Facebook.com (Net Worth: $1.7 Billion)

It's not clear that Mark Zuckerberg knew what he was onto when he and two friends launched Facebook in a Harvard dorm room in February 2004. But they found out pretty quickly: by the end of the month, over half of Harvard's undergraduates had registered on the service. In April, the site was opened up to another 30 universities, and by June, Zuckerberg had quit Harvard and moved to Palo Alto, California, where venture capitalist Peter Thiel recognized the potential and gave him $500,000 to take

Facebook to the next level. It's been anything but level since then. Facebook took off and now has over 140 million users, making it the largest social networking website. In 2007, as investors were clamoring to get in on the action, Microsoft paid $246 million for a 1.6% stake. Facebook was still not profitable by the end of 2008, but Zuckerberg is worth a lot—at 24, he became the youngest person ever to make the Forbes billionaire list.

Marc Benioff, Founder of Salesforce.com (Net Worth: $1.2 Billion)

Managing customer relationships is important for all businesses, large and small. As information technology made it possible to automate thousands of customer accounts electronically, however, customer relationship management (CRM) systems became so complex that only very large companies could afford them. The typical corporate system included customized software, costly installations, and ongoing maintenance fees that shut out most small businesses. Benioff, who had worked for *(continued)*

● Mark Zuckerberg founded Facebook.com—and became a billionaire at the age of 24!

Sources: Farrell, A. 2008. The Web Billionaires. www.forbes.com, September 8, np.; www.ebay.com; www.facebook.com; www.salesforce.com; and www.wikipedia.com.

Entrepreneurial Resources

As Exhibit 8.3 indicates, resources are an essential component of a successful entrepreneurial launch. For start-ups, the most important resource is usually money because a new firm typically has to expend substantial sums just to start the business. However, financial resources are not the only kind of resource a new venture needs. Human capital and social capital are also important. Many firms also rely on government resources to help them thrive.[11]

Financial Resources   Hand-in-hand with the importance of markets (and marketing) to new-venture creation, entrepreneurial firms must also have financing. In fact, the level of available financing is often a strong determinant of how the business is launched and its eventual success. Cash finances are, of course, highly important. But access to capital, such as a line of credit or favorable payment terms with a supplier, can also help a new venture succeed.

The types of financial resources that may be needed depend on two factors: the stage of venture development and the scale of the venture.[12] Entrepreneurial firms that are starting from scratch—start-ups—are at the earliest stage of development. Most start-ups also begin on a relatively small scale. The funding available to young and small firms tends to be quite limited. In fact, the majority of new firms are low-budget start-ups launched with personal savings and the contributions of family and friends.[13] Among firms included in the *Entrepreneur* list of the 100 fastest-growing new businesses in a recent year, 61 percent reported that their start-up funds came from personal savings.[14]

Although bank financing, public financing, and venture capital are important sources of small business finance, these types of financial support are typically available only after a company has started to conduct business and generate sales. Even "angel" investors—private individuals who provide equity investments for seed capital during the early stages of a new venture—favor companies that already have a winning business model and dominance in a market niche.[15] According to Cal Simmons, coauthor of *Every Business Needs an Angel,* "I would much rather talk to an entrepreneur who has already put his money and his effort into proving the concept."[16] Strategy Spotlight 8.4 describes one of the newest forms of financing for young and small businesses—an Internet-based phenomenon known as peer-to-peer lending.

Once a venture has established itself as a going concern, other sources of financing become readily available. Banks, for example, are more likely to provide later-stage financing to companies with a track record of sales or other cash-generating activity. Start-ups that involve large capital investments or extensive development costs—such as manufacturing or engineering firms trying to commercialize an innovative product—may have high cash requirements soon after they are founded. Others need financing only when they are on the brink of rapid growth. To obtain such funding, entrepreneurial firms often seek venture capital.

Venture capital is a form of private equity financing through which entrepreneurs raise money by selling shares in the new venture. In contrast to angel investors, who invest their own money, venture capital companies are organized to place the funds of private investors into lucrative business opportunities. Venture capitalists nearly always have high performance expectations from the companies they invest in, but they also provide important managerial advice, and links to key contacts in an industry.[17]

Eco-Entrepreneurs: Creating New Profits from Recycled Products

The "Go Green" movement is rich with business opportunities. One of the most appealing venture ideas is making new products from recycled or waste materials. Ever wonder what happens to the cans, paper, and plastic that goes into your recycling bins? Those and other waste materials are being used to create hundreds of products by eco-entrepreneurs (or "ecopreneurs") intent on making a profit as well as contributing to a more environmentally sustainable planet. Exhibit 8.4 includes examples of several such companies.

All of the companies listed in Exhibit 8.4 are approved by the U.S. Environmental Protection Agency (EPA) to supply recycled-content products. The Resource Conservation and Recovery Act requires federal and federally funded

Sources: 2008. Virgin Atlantic Launch Worn Again Recycled Airline Seat Bags. www.terracurve.com, September 2; np.; Capell, K. 2008. The Movies and Oxygen Cost Extra. *BusinessWeek*, November 6: 15; Rechelbacher, H. 2008. *Minding Your Business: Profits That Restore the Planet*. San Rafael, CA: Earth Aware Editions; Schaper, M. 2005. *Making ecopreneurs: Developing sustainable entrepreneurship*. Surrey, UK: Ashgate Publishing; and www.epa.gov.

state and local agencies to use recycled products. To enact this law, the EPA created the Affirmative Procurement Program to designate products—everything from office supplies to roofing materials to engine coolants—made out of materials recovered from waste. Most of the suppliers of these products are entrepreneurial businesses, including minority- and women-owned businesses.

Small businesses are not the only ones launching recycling initiatives. Virgin Atlantic, a member of Virgin Group, recently donated used fabric left over from retrofitting aircraft to Worn Again, a London-based design firm that makes accessories from recycled materials. Safety belts and seat covers have been turned into handbags, carry-alls, and toiletry cases that sell from $40 to $105. According to Lysette Gauna, Virgin Atlantic's Creative Director, "Virgin Atlantic is committed to taking practical steps to make its business as sustainable as possible." The Worn Again accessories are "a fun and creative way to recycle our waste," says Gauna, "as well as giving people the chance to own a little piece of Virgin Atlantic history."

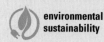

environmental sustainability

Company Name	What They Recycle	What They Make from It
BigToys Inc.	Milk jugs	Playground equipment
Future Solutions, Inc.	Blue jeans and old U.S. currency	Pencils
Rubber Flooring, Inc.	Tires	Kitchen mats and garage flooring
Weisenbach Specialty Printing & Manufacturing	Jars and old windows	Glass awards and vases

Sources: www.bigtoys.com; www.epa.gov; www.futuresolutionsinc.com; www.recycledproducts.com; and www.rubberflooringinc.com.

Exhibit 8.4   Eco-Entrepreneurs Approved by the U. S. Environmental Protection Agency

Despite the importance of venture capital to many fast-growing firms, the majority of external funding for young and small firms comes from informal sources such as family and friends. Exhibit 8.5, based on the *Global Entrepreneurship Monitor* survey of entrepreneurial firms, demonstrates this dramatic difference. A closer look reveals an interesting fact: Firms that obtain venture capital receive funding of about $2.6 million each. In contrast, companies that obtain funding from informal sources typically receive only about $10,000 each. Although relatively few companies receive venture funding, they are attractive to venture capitalists because their profit potential and impact on innovation, job growth, and wealth creation tends to be much greater. Clearly, financial resources are essential for entrepreneurial ventures.[18]

Peer-to-Peer Lending Boosts Entrepreneurs Chances

For start-up entrepreneurs, sometimes only a very small amount of money is needed to launch their ventures. Still, entrepreneurs who lack personal resources or access to funding often find it difficult to get their enterprises started. A new Internet phenomenon has recently emerged that is helping to change that: peer-to-peer lending. Also referred to as social lending, peer-to-peer (P2P) lending is seen as part of the social networking phenomenon that has been enabled by the Web 2.0 technologies that make it possible to interact directly, person to person.

Entrepreneurs who lack collateral but have viable business plans are increasingly turning to P2P solutions. For example, when Lyn Townshend, inventor of the Strock™, a sock-strap combination designed to keep pets from licking and chewing on wounded paws, won the endorsement of a veterinary hospital that is part of a 600-member chain, she needed a loan to ramp-up production. She had quit her job at IBM to start the business and had no income, so the local banks turned her down. Instead, she posted her loan request online and within a few weeks she landed a loan of $9,500 at a 12.75 percent interest rate. She used the funds to trademark her product, buy office equipment, and arrange for production at a nearby factory.

Although each P2P website uses a slightly different approach (see examples below), the basic model for P2P lending is as follows: Borrowers seeking loans post descriptions of their business concepts including the amounts they are attempting to borrow and personal information, including their credit rating. The other participants are lenders—individuals who are looking for opportunities to invest their money for a reasonable return. Lenders review various business proposals and evaluate the borrowers' backgrounds. If interested, they participate in an auctionlike process; the lenders who agree to the lowest interest rates "win" the borrower's loan. The various websites serve as the intermediaries by processing the loans and making payment arrangements. Because the loans are unsecured and the websites make no guarantees, lenders are encouraged to spread their funds around. "We tell people to buy little pieces of a lot of loans," says Ben Decio, president of GlobeFunder.com. Israel Gross, a 24-year-old Wrigley Field beer vendor and University of Chicago graduate student, says, "I have 89 loans out right now. It's small amounts to a lot of people. It's a positive way to make money."

The following Web-based enterprises offer peer-to-peer lending:

- **Lending Club**—A P2P lender that emphasizes borrower-lender interaction and community participation, it helps multiple lenders find opportunities to fund specific borrowers by issuing promissary notes that correspond to specific borrower loans.

- **Zopa**—A UK-based company that calls itself "the world's first social financing company," Zopa has positioned itself as the "anti-bank." Unlike most other P2P lenders, however, it offers CDs and savings accounts.

- **Kiva.org**—One of the first P2P lenders, it operates internationally and focuses on microlending to entrepreneurs in developing countries.

- **Fynanz**—Rather than focusing on start-ups, Fynanz is dedicated solely to student loans. Student borrowers post not only their credit ratings online but also their academic accomplishments and background.

Despite its growing popularity, Gartner bank analyst Avivah Litan is skeptical of P2P lending, in part because it is so new. Although she agrees that it is promising, Litan says, "I think it's too risky. There's no underwriting and no guarantees. It's all based on trust." But trust is part of what makes the social networking aspect of the system work. "That's when the community comes into play," says Rice University Associate Professor Paul Dholakia, an expert in online community participation. "The lenders are basically the policemen and women of the website. They have a lot of discussions. Borrowers have to spend a lot of time and effort in convincing the lenders and creating trust. . . . The community must substitute for the reputation mechanism."

Although P2P lending faces a number of challenges before it becomes a widespread practice, it is indicative of the type of opportunities that social networking has created for credit-strapped small businesses and aspiring entrepreneurs.

Sources: Bandyk, M. 2008. Is Peer-to-Peer Lending a Solution for Start-Ups? Q&A with Paul Dholakia of Rice University. www.usnews.com, July 8: np.; Benderoff, E. 2007. Financing Tool Follows Social Networking: Peer-to-Peer Lending Catching on with Investors, Borrowers. www.chicagotribune.com, October 5, np.; Lee-St. John, J. 2008. Hey, Buddy, Can You Spare $10,000? www.time.com, February 29, np.; www.fynanz.com; www.kiva.org; www.lendingclub.com; www.wikipedia.org; and www.zopa.com.

crowdsourcing

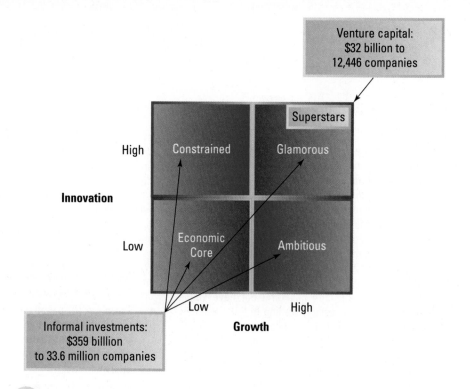

Exhibit 8.5 How Different Types of New Ventures Are Financed: Informal Investment versus Venture Capital

Source: Reynolds, P. D., Bygrave, W. D., & Autio, E. 2004. *Global Entrepreneurship Monitor: 2003 Executive Report.* Babson College, London Business School, and the Kauffman Foundation. The classification of the company system used by GEM is based on Kirchhoff, B. 1994. *Entrepreneurship and Dynamic Capitalism.* London: Praeger.

Human Capital Bankers, venture capitalists, and angel investors agree that the most important asset an entrepreneurial firm can have is strong and skilled management. According to Stephen Gaal, founding member of Walnut Venture Associates, venture investors do not invest in businesses; instead "We invest in people . . . very smart people with very high integrity." Managers need to have a strong base of experience and extensive domain knowledge, as well as an ability to make rapid decisions and change direction as shifting circumstances may require. In the case of start-ups, more is better. New ventures that are started by teams of three, four, or five entrepreneurs are more likely to succeed in the long run than are ventures launched by "lone wolf" entrepreneurs.[19]

Developing a strong team can be a challenge for early-stage entrepreneurial ventures. Cash-strapped founders may find it difficult to find and afford the kind of talent needed to make their start-ups successful. Strategy Spotlight 8.5 describes one source of human capital that not only can provide qualified executives but can also save young ventures' money.

Social Capital New ventures founded by entrepreneurs who have extensive social contacts are more likely to succeed than are ventures started without the support of a social network.[20] Even though a venture may be new, if the founders have contacts who will vouch for them, they gain exposure and build legitimacy faster.[21] This support can come from several sources: prior jobs, industry organizations, and local business groups such as the chamber of commerce. These contacts can all contribute to a growing network that provides support for the entrepreneurial firm. Janina Pawlowski,

Mommy SWAT Teams

For many entrepreneurial start-ups, experienced and professional help is often hard to find and even harder to afford. Bootstrapping founders are sometimes advised to forget about hiring the best talent and go for the available and affordable instead. But sometimes that solution just won't work—the success of a fledgling start-up may depend on having skilled decision makers involved at critical stages in the venture's development. What's an entrepreneur to do?

Enter Mommy SWAT teams, that is, "smart women with available time." Highly educated and experienced women who have elected to stay home with children can be a valuable resource. It's a win–win situation: employers get top talent at a bargain price and the women get a chance to update their skills and enjoy a professional challenge.

Consider the example of TangentWorks, a three-employee Web project-integration start-up that needed a business plan. Through informal networking, it was able to identify two highly qualified stay-at-home moms and hire them for a tenth of their former salaries. For TangentWorks, "it was like having a C-level team"—chief financial and marketing officers—"without the salaries," according to CEO Zaina Ajakie.

Bootstrappers may not be the only employers that benefit from this trend. According to Mary Naylor, CEO of VIP Desk, a customer service company that hires stay-at-home moms to provide virtual call center and concierge services, "The work-at-home industry, fueled by well-educated, hard-working stay-at-home moms, is poised to boom given the current economic trends, where companies need flexible, cost-effective employee solutions."

Sources: Shellenbarger, S. 2008. How Stay-at-Home Moms Are Filling an Executive Niche. www.wsj.com, April 30: np.; and Steiner, L. M. 2008. SWAT Moms. voices.washingtonpost.com, May 7: np.

co-founder of the online lending company E-Loan, attributes part of her success to the strong advisors she persuaded to serve on her board of directors, including Tim Koogle, former CEO of Yahoo![22]

Strategic alliances represent a type of social capital that can be especially important to young and small firms.[23] Strategy Spotlight 8.6 presents a few examples of alliances and some potential pitfalls of using alliances.[24]

Government Resources In the U.S., the federal government provides support for entrepreneurial firms in two key arenas—financing and government contracting. The Small Business Administration (SBA) has several loan guarantee programs designed to support the growth and development of entrepreneurial firms. The government itself does not typically lend money but underwrites loans made by banks to small businesses, thus reducing the risk associated with lending to firms with unproven records. The SBA also offers training, counseling, and support services through its local offices and Small Business Development Centers.[25] State and local governments also have hundreds of programs to provide funding, contracts, and other support for new ventures and small businesses.

Another key area of support is in government contracting. Programs sponsored by the SBA and other government agencies ensure that small businesses have the opportunity to bid on contracts to provide goods and services to the government. For example, several of the entrepreneurial firms identified in Strategy Spotlight 8.3 were approved by the Environmental Protection Agency to help government agencies meet federally mandated requirements to use products made from recycled materials. Although working with the government sometimes has its drawbacks in terms of issues of regulation and time-consuming decision making, programs to support small businesses and entrepreneurial activity constitute an important resource for entrepreneurial firms.

strategy spotlight

Strategic Alliances: A Key Entrepreneurial Resource

Strategic alliances provide a key avenue for growth by entrepreneurial firms. By partnering with other companies, young or small firms can expand or give the appearance of entering numerous markets and/or handling a range of operations. Here are several types of alliances that have been used to extend or strengthen entrepreneurial firms:

Technology Alliances

Tech-savvy entrepreneurial firms often benefit from forming alliances with older incumbents. The alliance allows the larger firm to enhance its technological capabilities and expands the revenue and reach of the smaller firm.

Manufacturing Alliances

The use of outsourcing and other manufacturing alliances by small firms has grown dramatically in recent years. Internet-enabled capabilities such as collaborating online

about delivery and design specifications has greatly simplified doing business, even with foreign manufacturers.

Retail Alliances

Licensing agreements allow one company to sell the products and services of another in different markets, including overseas. Specialty products—the types sometimes made by entrepreneurial firms—often seem more exotic when sold in another country.

According to the National Federation of Independent Business (NFIB), nearly two-thirds of small businesses currently hold or have held some type of alliance. Strategic alliances among entrepreneurial firms can take many different forms. Exhibit 8.6 shows the different types of partnering that small businesses and small manufacturers in the NFIB study often use.

Although such alliances often sound good, there are also potential pitfalls. Lack of oversight and control is one danger of partnering with foreign firms. Problems with product quality, timely delivery, and receiving payments can also sour an alliance relationship if it is not carefully managed. With technology alliances, there is a risk that big firms may take advantage of the technological know-how of their entrepreneurial partners. However, even with these potential problems, strategic alliances provide a good means for entrepreneurial firms to develop and grow.

Sources: Copeland, M. V. & Tilin, A. 2005. Get Someone to Build It. *Business 2.0,* 6(5): 88–90 Misner, I. 2008. Use Small Actions to Get Big Results. *Entrepreneur.* www.entrepreneur.com, December 3. Monahan, J. 2005. All Systems Grow. *Entrepreneur,* March: 78–82; Prince, C. J. 2005. Foreign Affairs. *Entrepreneur,* March: 56; and, Weaver, K. M. & Dickson, P. 2004. Strategic Alliances. In W. J. Dennis, Jr. (Ed.), *NFIB National Small Business Poll.* Washington, DC: National Federation of Independent Business.

Type of Alliance and/or Long-Term Agreement*	Small Manufacturers	Small Businesses
Licensing	20.0%	32.5%
Export/Import	14.4%	7.3%
Franchise	5.0%	5.3%
Marketing	18.0%	25.2%
Distribution	20.1%	20.5%
Production	26.5%	11.3%
Product/Services R&D	12.2%	12.6%
Process R&D	6.7%	5.3%
Purchaser/Supplier	23.5%	13.9%
Outside Contracting	23.2%	28.5%

Source: From Weaver, K. M. & Dickson, P. 2004. Strategic Alliances. In W. J. Dennis, Jr. (Ed.), *NFIB National Small Business Poll.* Washington, DC: National Federation of Independent Business. Reprinted with permission.

*Columns add to over 100 percent because firms may use multiple alliances.

Exhibit 8.6   Use of Strategic Alliances by Small Businesses and Small Manufacturers

Entrepreneurial Leadership

Whether a venture is launched by an individual entrepreneur or an entrepreneurial team, effective leadership is needed. Launching a new venture requires a special kind of leadership. It involves courage, belief in one's convictions, and the energy to work hard even in difficult circumstances. Yet these are the very challenges that motivate most business owners. Entrepreneurs put themselves to the test and get their satisfaction from acting independently, overcoming obstacles, and thriving financially. To do so, they must embody three characteristics of leadership—vision, dedication and drive, and commitment to excellence—and pass these on to all those who work with them:

- *Vision.* This may be an entrepreneur's most important asset. Entrepreneurs envision realities that do not yet exist. But without a vision, most entrepreneurs would never even get their venture off the ground. With vision, entrepreneurs are able to exercise a kind of transformational leadership that creates something new and, in some way, changes the world. Just having a vision, however, is not enough. To develop support, get financial backing, and attract employees, entrepreneurial leaders must share their vision with others.
- *Dedication and drive.* Dedication and drive are reflected in hard work. Drive involves internal motivation; dedication calls for an intellectual commitment that keeps an entrepreneur going even in the face of bad news or poor luck. They both require patience, stamina, and a willingness to work long hours. However, a business built on the heroic efforts of one person may suffer in the long run. That's why the dedicated entrepreneur's enthusiasm is also important—like a magnet, it attracts others to the business to help with the work.[26]
- *Commitment to excellence.* Excellence requires entrepreneurs to commit to knowing the customer, providing quality goods and services, paying attention to details, and continuously learning. Entrepreneurs who achieve excellence are sensitive to how these factors work together. However, entrepreneurs may flounder if they think they are the only ones who can create excellent results. The most successful, by contrast, often report that they owe their success to hiring people smarter than themselves.

In his book *Good to Great*, Jim Collins makes another important point about entrepreneurial leadership: Ventures built on the charisma of a single person may have trouble growing "from good to great" once that person leaves.[27] Thus, the leadership that is needed to build a great organization is usually exercised by a team of dedicated people working together rather than a single leader. Another aspect of this team approach is attracting team members who fit with the company's culture, goals, and work ethic. "Those people who do not share the company's core values," Collins says, "find themselves surrounded by corporate antibodies and ejected like a virus."[28] Thus, for a venture's leadership to be a valuable resource and not a liability it must be cohesive in its vision, drive and dedication, and commitment to excellence.

Once an opportunity has been recognized, and an entrepreneurial team and resources have been assembled, a new venture must craft a strategy. Prior chapters have addressed the strategies of incumbent firms. In the next section, we highlight the types of strategies and strategic considerations faced by new entrants.

Entrepreneurial Strategy

Successfully creating new ventures requires several ingredients. As indicated in Exhibit 8.2, three factors are necessary—a viable opportunity, sufficient resources, and a skilled and dedicated entrepreneur or entrepreneurial team. Once these elements are in place, the new venture needs a strategy. In this section, we consider several different strategic factors that are unique to new ventures and also how the generic strategies introduced in Chapter 5 can

entrepreneurial strategy a strategy that enables a skilled and dedicated entrepreneur, with a viable opportunity and access to sufficient resources, to successfully launch a new venture.

be applied to entrepreneurial firms. We also indicate how combination strategies might benefit entrepreneurial firms and address the potential pitfalls associated with launching new venture strategies.

To be successful, new ventures must evaluate industry conditions, the competitive environment, and market opportunities in order to position themselves strategically. However, a traditional strategic analysis may have to be altered somewhat to fit the entrepreneurial situation. For example, five-forces analysis (as discussed in Chapter 2) is typically used by established firms. It can also be applied to the analysis of new ventures to assess the impact of industry and competitive forces. But you may ask: How does a new entrant evaluate the threat of other new entrants?

First, the new entrant needs to examine barriers to entry. If the barriers are too high, the potential entrant may decide not to enter or to gather more resources before attempting to do so. Compared to an older firm with an established reputation and available resources, the barriers to entry may be insurmountable for an entrepreneurial start-up. Therefore, understanding the force of these barriers is critical in making a decision to launch.

A second factor that may be especially important to a young venture is the threat of retaliation by incumbents. In many cases, entrepreneurial ventures *are* the new entrants that pose a threat to incumbent firms. Therefore, in applying the five-forces model to new ventures, the threat of retaliation by established firms needs to be considered.

Part of any decision about what opportunity to pursue is a consideration of how a new entrant will actually enter a new market. The concept of entry strategies provides a useful means of addressing the types of choices that new ventures have.

Entry Strategies

>LO3

Three types of entry strategies— pioneering, imitative, and adaptive— commonly used to launch a new venture.

One of the most challenging aspects of launching a new venture is finding a way to begin doing business that quickly generates cash flow, builds credibility, attracts good employees, and overcomes the liability of newness. The idea of an entry strategy or "entry wedge" describes several approaches that firms may take to get a foothold in a market.[29] Several factors will affect this decision.

- Is the product/service high-tech or low-tech?
- What resources are available for the initial launch?
- What are the industry and competitive conditions?
- What is the overall market potential?
- Does the venture founder prefer to control the business or to grow it?

In some respects, any type of entry into a market for the first time may be considered entrepreneurial. But the entry strategy will vary depending on how risky and innovative the new business concept is.[30] New-entry strategies typically fall into one of three categories— pioneering new entry, imitative new entry, or adaptive new entry.

Pioneering New Entry   New entrants with a radical new product or highly innovative service may change the way business is conducted in an industry. This kind of breakthrough—creating new ways to solve old problems or meeting customers' needs in a unique new way—is referred to as a **pioneering new entry.** If the product or service is unique enough, a pioneering new entrant may actually have little direct competition. The first personal computer was a pioneering product; there had never been anything quite like it and it revolutionized computing. The first Internet browser provided a type of pioneering service. These breakthroughs created whole new industries and changed the competitive landscape. And breakthrough innovations continue to inspire pioneering entrepreneurial efforts. Strategy Spotlight 8.7 discusses SkyTower Telecommunications, an entrepreneurial venture with a pioneering solution to the problem of overcrowding on wireless transmission towers.

pioneering new entry a firm's entry into an industry with a radical new product or highly innovative service that changes the way business is conducted.

SkyTower Telecommunications' Pioneering Technology

With current technology, wireless communications systems have only three ways to get to your cell phone or computer—radio towers that are often not tall enough and are increasingly overcrowded, satellites that cost $50 to $400 million to launch, and short-range Wi-Fi transmitters. SkyTower proposes a fourth alternative: unmanned, solar-powered airplanes that look like flying wings and send out Internet, mobile phone, and high-definition TV signals.

The planes have already been successfully tested over Hawaii. They are able to fly at an altitude of 12 miles in a tight 2,000-foot-wide circle for six months at a time without landing. Designed as private communication systems for both businesses and consumers, they are able to deliver Internet service for about a third of the cost of DSL or cable.

SkyTower has already received the backing of NASA and $80 million in investment capital. Its target customers are major Internet Service Providers (ISPs). The plan is not without problems, however. For one thing, the Federal Aviation Administration (FAA) currently prohibits the launch of unpiloted planes. Even so, SkyTower's flying wing satellite is a breakthrough technology that is hoping to take wireless communications to new heights and addresses the increasing demand for cost-effective wireless systems.

Sources: Frauenfelder, M. 2002. Look! Up in the Sky! It's a Flying Cell Phone Tower! *Business 2.0*, November: 108–112; and www.avinc.com.

The pitfalls associated with a pioneering new entry are numerous. For one thing, there is a strong risk that the product or service will not be accepted by consumers. The history of entrepreneurship is littered with new ideas that never got off the launching pad. Take, for example, Smell-O-Vision, an invention designed to pump odors into movie theatres from the projection room at preestablished moments in a film. It was tried only once (for the film *Scent of a Mystery*) before it was declared a major flop. Innovative? Definitely. But hardly a good idea at the time.[31]

A pioneering new entry is disruptive to the status quo of an industry. It is likely based on a technological breakthrough such as the one proposed by SkyTower. If it is successful, other competitors will rush in to copy it. This can create issues of sustainability for an entrepreneurial firm, especially if a larger company with greater resources introduces a similar product. For a new entrant to sustain its pioneering advantage, it may be necessary to protect its intellectual property, advertise heavily to build brand recognition, form alliances with businesses that will adopt its products or services, and offer exceptional customer service.

Imitative New Entry Whereas pioneers are often inventors or tinkerers with new technology, imitators usually have a strong marketing orientation. They look for opportunities to capitalize on proven market successes. An **imitative new entry** strategy is used by entrepreneurs who see products or business concepts that have been successful in one market niche or physical locale and introduce the same basic product or service in another segment of the market.

Sometimes the key to success with an imitative strategy is to fill a market space where the need had previously been filled inadequately. Entrepreneurs are also prompted to be imitators when they realize that they have the resources or skills to do a job better than an existing competitor. This can actually be a serious problem for entrepreneurial start-ups if the imitator is an established company. Consider the example of Hugger Mugger Yoga Products, a Salt Lake City producer of yoga apparel and equipment such as yoga mats for practitioners of the ancient exercise art, with annual sales of $7.5 million in a recent year.

imitative new entry a firm's entry into an industry with products or services that capitalize on proven market successes and that usually has a strong marketing orientation.

When founder Sara Chambers started the business in the mid-1980s, there was little competition. But once yoga went mainstream and became the subject of celebrity cover stories, other competitors saw an opportunity to imitate. Then Nike and Reebok jumped into the business with their own mats, clothes, and props. Hugger Mugger was a leading provider and had enjoyed 50 percent annual growth. But even after introducing a mass market line for department stores and hiring 50 independent sales reps, its growth rate has leveled off. Then, in 2005, it sued Gaiam, Inc., another maker of yoga gear, for using Hugger Mugger's trademark on search engines to mislead customers by diverting them to the Gaiam website.[32]

● Yoga's rising popularity has increased demand for related apparel and equipment. Both small players as well as multinational giants such as Nike and Reebok have entered the market.

Recall from Chapter 3 that the quality "difficult to imitate" was viewed as one of the keys to building sustainable advantages.[33] A strategy that can be imitated, therefore, seems like a poor way to build a business. In essence, this is true. But consider the example of a franchise. Clearly, franchising is built on the idea of copying what another business has already done. If a business format is so easy to imitate, can it possibly have any competitive advantages? In the minds of many consumers of franchise products and services, the advantage is *because of* imitation. That is, consumers have confidence in franchises because they are familiar with them. "As time has gone by, the public has come to embrace franchising because they're familiar with the successful franchises and brand," claims Tony DeSio, founder of Mail Boxes Etc. "They know that, from one location to another, they can rely on product consistency." Thus, imitation is one of the central reasons why franchises are successful.

Adaptive New Entry Most new entrants use a strategy somewhere between "pure" imitation and "pure" pioneering. That is, they offer a product or service that is somewhat new and sufficiently different to create new value for customers and capture market share. Such firms are adaptive in the sense that they are aware of marketplace conditions and conceive entry strategies to capitalize on current trends.

According to business creativity coach Tom Monahan, "Every new idea is merely a spin of an old idea. [Knowing that] takes the pressure off from thinking [you] have to be totally creative. You don't. Sometimes it's one slight twist to an old idea that makes all the difference."[34] An **adaptive new entry** approach does not involve "reinventing the wheel," nor is it merely imitative either. It involves taking an existing idea and adapting it to a particular situation. Exhibit 8.7 presents examples of four young companies that successfully modified or adapted existing products to create new value.

adaptive new entry a firm's entry into an industry by offering a product or service that is somewhat new and sufficiently different to create value for customers by capitalizing on current market trends.

There are several pitfalls that might limit the success of an adaptive new entrant. First, the value proposition must be perceived as unique. Unless potential customers believe a new product or service does a superior job of meeting their needs, they will have little motivation to try it. Second, there is nothing to prevent a close competitor from mimicking the new firm's adaptation as a way to hold on to its customers. Third, once an adaptive entrant achieves initial success, the challenge is to keep the idea fresh. If the attractive features of the new business are copied, the entrepreneurial firm must find ways to adapt and improve the product or service offering.

Exhibit 8.7 Examples of Adaptive New Entrants

Company Name	Product	Adaptation	Result
Under Armour, Inc. Founded in 1995	Undershirts and other athletic gear	Used moisture-wicking fabric to create better gear for sweaty sports.	Under Armour has 1,400 employees and 2008 sales in excess of $700 million.
Mint.com Founded in 2005	Comprehensive online money management	Created software that tells users what they are spending by aggregating financial information from online bank and credit card accounts.	Mint has over 600,000 users and is tracking $50 billion in assets.
Plum Organics Founded in 2005	Organic frozen baby food	Made convenient line of frozen baby food using organic ingredients.	Added to Whole Foods product offering in 2006, Plum made $1 million in 2007.
Spanx Founded in 2000	Footless pantyhose and other undergarments for women	Combined nylon and Lycra® to create a new type of undergarment that is comfortable and eliminates panty lines.	5.4 million Spanx products have been sold since 2000.

Sources: Bryan, M. 2007. Spanx Me, Baby! www.observer.com, December 10, np.; Carey, J. 2006. Perspiration Inspiration. *BusinessWeek*, June 5: 64; Palanjian, A. 2008. A Planner Plumbs for a Niche. www.wsj.com, September 30, np.; Worrell, D. 2008. Making Mint. *Entrepreneur*, September: 55; www.mint.com; www.spanx.com; and www.underarmour.com.

Considering these choices, an entrepreneur or entrepreneurial team might ask, Which new entry strategy is best? The choice depends on many competitive, financial, and marketplace considerations. Nevertheless, research indicates that the greatest opportunities may stem from being willing to enter new markets rather than seeking growth only in existing markets. A recent study found that companies that ventured into arenas that were new to the world or new to the company earned total profits of 61 percent. In contrast, companies that made only incremental improvements, such as extending an existing product line, grew total profits by only 39 percent.[35]

These findings led W. Chan Kim and Renee Mauborgne in their new book *Blue Ocean Strategy* to conclude that companies that are willing to venture into market spaces where there is little or no competition—labeled "blue oceans"—will outperform those firms that limit growth to incremental improvements in competitively crowded industries—labeled "red oceans." Companies that identify and pursue blue ocean strategies follow somewhat different rules than those that are "bloodied" by the competitive practices in red oceans. Consider the following elements of a blue ocean strategy:

- *Create uncontested market space.* By seeking opportunities where they are not threatened by existing competitors, blue ocean firms can focus on customers rather than on competition.
- *Make the competition irrelevant.* Rather than using the competition as a benchmark, blue ocean firms cross industry boundaries to offer new and different products and services.
- *Create and capture new demand.* Rather than fighting over existing demand, blue ocean companies seek opportunities in uncharted territory.

- *Break the value/cost trade-off.* Blue ocean firms reject the idea that a trade-off between value and cost is inevitable and instead seek opportunities in areas that benefit both their cost structure and their value proposition to customers.
- *Pursue differentiation and low cost simultaneously.* By integrating the range of a firm's utility, price, and cost activities, blue ocean companies align their whole system to create sustainable strategies.

The essence of blue ocean strategy is not just to find an uncontested market, but to create one. Some blue oceans arise because new technologies create new possibilities, such as eBay's online auction business. Yet technological innovation is not a defining feature of a blue ocean strategy. Most blue oceans are created from within red oceans by companies that push beyond the existing industry boundaries. Any of the new entry strategies described earlier could be used to pursue a blue ocean strategy. Consider the example of Cirque du Soleil, which created a new market for circus entertainment by making traditional circus acts more like theatrical productions:

> By altering the industry boundaries that traditionally defined the circus concept, Cirque du Soleil created a new type of circus experience. Since the days of Ringling Bros. and Barnum & Bailey, the circus had consisted of animal acts, star performers, and Bozo-like clowns. Cirque questioned this formula and researched what audiences really wanted. It found that interest in animal acts was declining, in part because of public concerns over the treatment of circus animals. Because managing animals—and the celebrity trainers who performed with them—was costly, Cirque eliminated them.
>
> Instead, Cirque focused on three elements of the traditional circus tent event that still captivated audiences: acrobatic acts, clowns, and the tent itself. Elegant acrobatics became a central feature of its performances, and clown humor became more sophisticated and less slapstick. Cirque also preserved the image of the tent by creating exotic facades that captured the symbolic elements of the traditional tent. Finally, rather than displaying three different acts simultaneously, as in the classic three-ring circus, Cirque offers multiple productions with theatrical story lines, giving audiences a reason to go to the circus more often. Each production has a different theme and its own original musical score.
>
> Cirque's efforts to redefine the circus concept have paid off. Since 1984, Cirque's productions have been seen by over 90 million people in some 200 cities around the world.[36]

Once created, a blue ocean strategy is difficult to imitate. If customers flock to blue ocean creators, firms rapidly achieve economies of scale, learning advantages, and synergies across their organizational systems. Body Shop, for example chartered new territory by refusing to focus solely on beauty products. Traditional competitors such as Estee Lauder and L'Oreal, whose brands are based on promises of eternal youth and beauty, found it difficult to imitate this approach without repudiating their current images.

These factors suggest that blue ocean strategies provide an avenue by which firms can pursue an entrepreneurial new entry. Such strategies are not without risks, however. A new entrant must decide not only the best way to enter into business but also what type of strategic positioning will work best as the business goes forward. Those strategic choices can be informed by the guidelines suggested for the generic strategies. We turn to that subject next.

>LO4

How the generic strategies of overall cost leadership, differentiation, and focus are used by new ventures and small businesses.

Generic Strategies

Typically, a new entrant begins with a single business model that is equivalent in scope to a business-level strategy (Chapter 5). In this section we address how overall low cost, differentiation, and focus strategies can be used to achieve competitive advantages.

Overall Cost Leadership One of the ways entrepreneurial firms achieve success is by doing more with less. By holding down costs or making more efficient use of resources than larger competitors, new ventures are often able to offer lower prices and still be profitable. Thus, under the right circumstances, a low-cost leader strategy is a viable alternative for some new ventures. The way most companies achieve low-cost leadership, however, is typically different for young or small firms.

Recall from Chapter 5 that three of the features of a low-cost approach included operating at a large enough scale to spread costs over many units of production (economies of scale), making substantial capital investments in order to increase scale economies, and using knowledge gained from experience to make cost-saving improvements. These elements of a cost-leadership strategy may be unavailable to new ventures. Because new ventures are typically small, they usually don't have high economies of scale relative to competitors. Because they are usually cash strapped, they can't make large capital investments to increase their scale advantages. And because many are young, they often don't have a wealth of accumulated experience to draw on to achieve cost reductions.

Given these constraints, how can new ventures successfully deploy cost-leader strategies? Compared to large firms, new ventures often have simple organizational structures that make decision making both easier and faster. The smaller size also helps young firms change more quickly when upgrades in technology or feedback from the marketplace indicate that improvements are needed. They are also able to make decisions at the time they are founded that help them deal with the issue of controlling costs. For example, they may source materials from a supplier that provides them more cheaply or set up manufacturing facilities in another country where labor costs are especially low. Thus, new firms have several avenues for achieving low cost leadership. Strategy Spotlight 8.8 highlights the success of Vizio, Inc., a new entrant with an overall cost leadership strategy. Whatever methods young firms use to achieve a low-cost advantage, this has always been a way that entrepreneurial firms take business away from incumbents—by offering a comparable product or service at a lower price.

Differentiation Both pioneering and adaptive entry strategies involve some degree of differentiation. That is, the new entry is based on being able to offer a differentiated value proposition. In the case of pioneers, the new venture is attempting to do something strikingly different, either by using a new technology or deploying resources in a way that radically alters the way business is conducted. Often, entrepreneurs do both.

Amazon founder Jeff Bezos set out to use Internet technology to revolutionize the way books are sold. He garnered the ire of other booksellers and the attention of the public by making bold claims about being the "earth's largest bookseller." As a bookseller, Bezos was not doing anything that had not been done before. But two key differentiating features—doing it on the Internet and offering extraordinary customer service—have made Amazon a differentiated success.

There are several factors that make it more difficult for new ventures to be successful as differentiators. For one thing, the strategy is generally thought to be expensive to enact. Differentiation is often associated with strong brand identity, and establishing a brand is usually considered to be expensive because of the cost of advertising and promotion, paid endorsements, exceptional customer service, etc. Differentiation successes are sometimes built on superior innovation or use of technology. These are also factors where it may be challenging for young firms to excel relative to established competitors.

Nevertheless all of these areas—innovation, technology, customer service, distinctive branding—are also arenas where new ventures have sometimes made a name for themselves even though they must operate with limited resources and experience. To be successful, according to Garry Ridge, CEO of the WD-40 Company, "You need to have a great product, make the end user aware of it, and make it easy to buy."[37] It sounds simple, but it is a difficult challenge for new ventures with differentiation strategies.

Low-Cost Imitator Vizio, Inc., Takes Off

The popularity of flat-panel TVs has grown rapidly since they were first introduced in the late 1990s—today, 34 percent of U.S households have one. When first introduced, major manufacturers such as Samsung, Sony, and Matsushita (maker of Panasonic) made heavy investments in R&D in a competition for technological leadership. As a result, the early flat-panel TVs were expensive. Even as technological advances drove prices down, the TVs were growing larger and flatter, and they continued to command premium prices. By 2002, 50-inch plasma TVs were still selling for $8,000–$10,000. But by then, panel technology had also become somewhat commoditized. That's when William Wang, a former marketer of computer monitors, realized he could use existing technologies to create a high quality TV. Wang discovered he could keep operations lean and outsource everything from tech support to R&D, so he founded Vizio, Inc.

In January 2003, Wang pitched Costco Wholesale Corp. on a 46-inch flat-panel plasma TV for $3,800—half the price of the competition. Although Costco executives laughed when Wang said he wanted to become the next Sony, they decided to give him a chance. By March 2003, the TVs were being offered in over 300 of Costco's U.S. warehouse stores. Today, Vizio is one of Costco's largest suppliers of TVs.

Vizio's success is due not only to enlightened imitation and low-cost operations, but also to Wang's unique approach to financing growth. Although he initially mortgaged his home and borrowed from family and friends, when he needed additional funding, he targeted the manufacturing partners who were supplying him parts. In 2004, Taiwan-based contract manufacturer AmTran Technology Co. purchased an 8 percent stake in Vizio for $1 million; today, AmTran owns 23 percent of Vizio and supplies over 80 percent of its TVs. "Unlike many PC companies who try to make their money by squeezing the vendor," says Wang, "we try to work with our vendor."

Although Vizio has a long way to go to be the next Sony, it has made remarkable progress. Vizio shipped 12.4 percent of LCD TVs in North America in the last quarter of 2007. Sony's share was just 12.5 percent. Vizio expects year-end sales of $2.6 billion in 2008—not bad for a six-year-old company!

Sources: Lawton, C., Kane, Y.I., & Dean, J. 2008. U.S. Upstart Takes on TV Giants in Price War. www.wsj.com, April 15, np.; Taub, E. A. 2008. Flat-Panel TV Prices Plummet. www.nytimes.com, December 2, np.; Wilson, S. 2008. Picture It. *Entrepreneur*, July: 43; and www.wikipedia.com.

Focus   Focus strategies are often associated with small businesses because there is a natural fit between the narrow scope of the strategy and the small size of the firm. A focus strategy may include elements of differentiation and overall cost leadership, as well as combinations of these approaches. But to be successful within a market niche, the key strategic requirement is to stay focused. Here's why:

Despite all the attention given to fast-growing new industries, most start-ups enter industries that are mature.[38] In mature industries, growth in demand tends to be slow and there are often many competitors. Therefore, if a start-up wants to get a piece of the action, it often has to take business away from an existing competitor. If a start-up enters a market with a broad or aggressive strategy, it is likely to evoke retaliation from a more powerful competitor. Young firms can often succeed best by finding a market niche where they can get a foothold and make small advances that erode the position of existing competitors.[39] From this position, they can build a name for themselves and grow.

Consider, for example, the "Miniature Editions" line of books launched by Running Press, a small Philadelphia publisher. The books are palm-sized minibooks positioned at bookstore cash registers as point-of-sale impulse items costing about $4.95. Beginning with just 10 titles in 1993, Running Press grew rapidly and within 10 years had sold over 20 million copies. Even though these books represent just a tiny fraction of total sales in the $23 billion publishing industry, they have been a mainstay for Running Press.[40]

Paradise 4 Paws: A Focused Differentiator

Pampering pets is big business—a $3 billion a year industry according to the American Pet Products Manufacturing Association. So it's no surprise that niche providers of differentiated services would continue to find opportunities in this arena. One such business grew out of an entrepreneurship class at Northwestern's Kellogg School of Management. Paradise 4 Paws operates an upscale 24/7 pet hotel with a dog-bone shaped swimming pool and webcams that allow owners to view their pets remotely.

Sources: Yu, R. 2008. Fancy New Airport Hotels Are Just for Fido and Fluffy. www.usatoday.com, March 11, np.; and Zhou, J. 2008. The Lap of Luxury. *BusinessWeek*, February 4: 18.

What makes this provider of luxury accommodations for cats and dogs different? It's located at Chicago's O'Hare International Airport so that busy travelers can drop their pets off on their way out of town rather than making an extra stop at a kennel. Paradise 4 Paws, which charges $75 per night for dogs and $35 for cats, provides a 22-spot parking lot from which its customers can take a shuttle directly to the terminal. The business is also good for O'Hare, which generates nonaviation revenues from the arrangement. "Given that more people have pets, it's just a natural progression of services that airports should offer," says P4P founder Saq Nadeem. With his backers, who include Kellogg's professors, Nadeem is making plans to open 10 more P4P locations.

As the Running Press example indicates, many new ventures are very successful even though their share of the market is quite small. Giant companies such as Procter & Gamble and Ford are often described in terms of their market share—that is, their share of sales in a whole market. But many of the industries that small firms participate in have thousands of participants that are not direct competitors. For example, auto repair shops in California don't compete with those in Michigan or Georgia. These industries are considered "fragmented" because no single company is strong enough to have power over other competitors. Small firms focus on the market share only in their trade area. This may be defined as a geographical area or a small segment of a larger product group.

Combination Strategies

One of the best ways for young and small businesses to achieve success is by pursuing combination strategies. By combining the best features of low-cost, differentiation, and focus strategies, new ventures can often achieve something truly distinctive.

Entrepreneurial firms are often in a strong position to offer a combination strategy because they have the flexibility to approach situations uniquely. For example, holding down expenses can be difficult for big firms because each layer of bureaucracy adds to the cost of doing business across the boundaries of a large organization.[41]

A similar argument could be made about entrepreneurial firms that differentiate. Large firms often find it difficult to offer highly specialized products or superior customer services. Entrepreneurial firms, by contrast, can often create high-value products and services through their unique differentiating efforts. Strategy Spotlight 8.9 shows how a group of entrepreneurship students took a specialized idea and built it into a differentiated success.

For nearly all new entrants, one of the major dangers is that a large firm with more resources will copy what they are doing. Well-established incumbents that observe the success of a new entrant's product or service will copy it and use their market power to overwhelm the smaller firm. The threat may be lessened for firms that use combination strategies. Because of the flexibility of entrepreneurial firms, they can often enact combination strategies in ways that the large firms cannot copy. This makes the new entrant's strategies much more sustainable.

>LO5

How competitive actions, such as the entry of new competitors into a marketplace, may launch a cycle of actions and reactions among close competitors.

Perhaps more threatening than large competitors are close competitors, because they have similar structural features that help them adjust quickly and be flexible in decision making. Here again, a carefully crafted and executed combination strategy may be the best way for an entrepreneurial firm to thrive in a competitive environment. Nevertheless, competition among rivals is a key determinant of new venture success. To address this, we turn next to the topic of competitive dynamics.

Competitive Dynamics

New entry into markets, whether by start-ups or by incumbent firms, nearly always threatens existing competitors. This is true in part because, except in very new markets, nearly every market need is already being met, either directly or indirectly, by existing firms. As a result, the competitive actions of a new entrant are very likely to provoke a competitive response from companies that feel threatened. This, in turn, is likely to evoke a reaction to the response. As a result, a competitive dynamic—action and response—begins among the firms competing for the same customers in a given marketplace.

competitive dynamics intense rivalry, involving actions and responses, among similar competitors vying for the same customers in a marketplace.

Competitive dynamics—intense rivalry among similar competitors—has the potential to alter a company's strategy. New entrants, may be forced to change their strategies or develop new ones to survive competitive challenges by incumbent rivals. New entry is among the most common reasons why a cycle of competitive actions and reactions gets started. It might also occur because of threatening actions among existing competitors, such as aggressive cost cutting. Thus, studying competitive dynamics helps explain why strategies evolve and reveals how, why, and when to respond to the actions of close competitors. Exhibit 8.8 identifies the factors that competitors need to consider when determining how to respond to a competitive act.

>LO6

The components of competitive dynamics analysis—new competitive action, threat analysis, motivation and capability to respond, types of competitive actions, and likelihood of competitive reaction.

New Competitive Action

Entry into a market by a new competitor is a good starting point to begin describing the cycle of actions and responses characteristic of a competitive dynamic process.[42] However, new entry is only one type of competitive action. Price cutting, imitating successful products, or expanding production capacity are other examples of competitive acts that might provoke competitors to react.

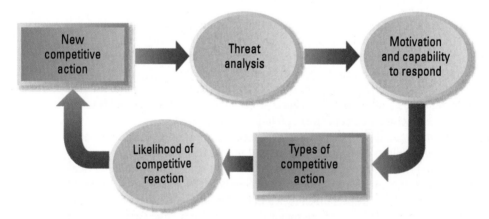

Exhibit 8.8 Model of Competitive Dynamics

Sources: Adapted from Chen, M. J. 1996. Competitor Analysis and Interfirm Rivalry: Toward a Theoretical Integration. *Academy of Management Review*, 21(1): 100–134; Ketchen, D. J., Snow, C. C., & Hoover, V. L. 2004. Research on competitive dynamics: Recent Accomplishments and Future Challenges. *Journal of Management*, 30(6): 779–804; and Smith, K. G., Ferrier, W. J., & Grimm, C. M. 2001. King of the Hill: Dethroning the Industry Leader. *Academy of Management Executive*, 15(2): 59–70.

Why do companies launch new competitive actions? There are several reasons:

- Improve market position
- Capitalize on growing demand
- Expand production capacity
- Provide an innovative new solution
- Obtain first mover advantages

Underlying all of these reasons is a desire to strengthen financial outcomes, capture some of the extraordinary profits that industry leaders enjoy, and grow the business. Some companies are also motivated to launch competitive challenges because they want to build their reputation for innovativeness or efficiency. For example, Southwest Airlines, once an upstart airline with only a few routes, has become phenomenally successful and an industry leader. For years it went virtually unchallenged. But Southwest's costs have crept up, and now start-up airlines such as JetBlue are challenging the industry leader with their own low-cost strategies.[43] This is indicative of the competitive dynamic cycle. As former Intel Chairman Andy Grove stated, "Business success contains the seeds of its own destruction. The more successful you are, the more people want a chunk of your business and then another chunk and then another until there is nothing left."[44]

When a company enters into a market for the first time, it is like an attack on existing competitors. As indicated earlier in the chapter, any of the entry strategies can be used to take competitive action. But competitive attacks come from many sources besides new entrants. Some of the most intense competition is among incumbent rivals intent on gaining strategic advantages. "Winners in business play rough and don't apologize for it," according to Boston Consulting Group authors George Stalk, Jr. and Rob Lachenauer in their book *Hardball: Are You Playing to Play or Playing to Win.*[45] Exhibit 8.9 outlines their five strategies.

The likelihood that a competitor will launch an attack depends on many factors. In the remaining sections, we discuss factors such as competitor analysis, market conditions, types of strategic actions, and the resource endowments and capabilities companies need to take competitive action.

Threat Analysis

Prior to actually observing a competitive action, companies may need to become aware of potential competitive threats. That is, companies need to have a keen sense of who their closest competitors are and the kinds of competitive actions they might be planning.[46] This may require some environmental scanning and monitoring of the sort described in Chapter 2. Awareness of the threats posed by industry rivals allows a firm to understand what type of competitive response, if any, may be necessary.

For example, Netflix founder and CEO Reed Hastings has faced numerous competitive threats since launching the online movie rental company in 1997. According to Hastings, however, not all potential threats need to be taken seriously:

> We have to recognize that now there are tens and maybe hundreds of start-ups who think that they are going to eat Netflix's lunch. The challenge for a management team is to figure out which are real threats and which aren't. . . . It's conventional to say, "only the paranoid survive" but that's not true. The paranoid die because the paranoid take all threats as serious and get very distracted.
>
> There are markets that aren't going to get very big, and then there are markets that are going to get big, but they're not directly in our path. In the first camp we have small companies like Movielink—a well-run company but not an attractive model for consumers, sort of a $4-download to watch a movie. We correctly guessed when it launched four years ago that this was not a threat and didn't react to it.

Exhibit 8.9 Five "Hardball" Strategies

Strategy	Description	Examples
Devastate rivals' profit sanctuaries	Not all business segments generate the same level of profits for a company. Through focused attacks on a rival's most profitable segments, a company can generate maximum leverage with relatively smaller-scale attacks. Recognize, however, that companies closely guard the information needed to determine just what their profit sanctuaries are.	In 2005, Wal-Mart began offering low-priced extended warranties on home electronics after learning that its rivals such as Best Buy derived most of their profits from extended warranties.
Plagiarize with pride	Just because a close competitor comes up with an idea first does not mean it cannot be successfully imitated. Second movers, in fact, can see how customers respond, make improvements, and launch a better version without all the market development costs. Successful imitation is harder than it may appear and requires the imitating firm to keep its ego in check.	Blockbuster copied the online DVD rental strategy of its rival Netflix. Not only does Blockbuster continue to struggle even after this imitation, but also Netflix sued Blockbuster for patent violations.
Deceive the competition	A good gambit sends the competition off in the wrong direction. This may cause the rivals to miss strategic shifts, spend money pursuing dead ends, or slow their responses. Any of these outcomes support the deceiving firms' competitive advantage. Companies must be sure not to cross ethical lines during these actions.	Boeing spent several years touting its plans for a new high-speed airliner. After it became clear the customer valued efficiency over speed, Boeing quietly shifted its focus. When Boeing announced its new 7e7 (now 787) Dreamliner, its competitor, Airbus Industries, was surprised and caught without an adequate response, which helped the 787 set new sales records.
Unleash massive and overwhelming force	While many hardball strategies are subtle and indirect, this one is not. This is a full-frontal attack where a firm commits significant resources to a major campaign to weaken rivals' positions in certain markets. Firms must be sure they have the mass and stamina required to win before they declare war against a rival.	Southwest Airlines took on US Airways in Baltimore and drove US Airways' market share from over 50 percent to 10 percent. Southwest recently began flying to Philadelphia and Pittsburgh as well—additional key markets for US Airways.
Raise competitors' costs	If a company has superior insight into the complex cost and profit structure of the industry, it can compete in a way that steers its rivals into relatively higher cost/lower profit arenas. This strategy uses deception to make the rivals think they are winning, when in fact they are not. Again, companies using this strategy must be confident that they understand the industry better than their rivals.	Ecolab, a company that sells cleaning supplies to businesses, encouraged a leading competitor, Diversity, to adopt a strategy to go after the low-volume, high-margin customers. What Ecolab knew that Diversity didn't is that the high servicing costs involved with this segment make the segment unprofitable—a situation Ecolab assured by bidding high enough to lose the contracts to Diversity but low enough to ensure the business lost money for Diversity.

Sources: Berner, R. 2005. Watch Out, Best Buy and Circuit City. *BusinessWeek,* November 10; Halkias, M. 2006. Blockbuster Strikes Back at Netflix Suit. *Dallas Morning News,* June 14; McCartney, S. 2007. Southwest Makes Inroads at Hubs. *The Wall Street Journal,* May 1, page D3; Stalk, G. Jr. 2006. Curveball Strategies to Fool the Competition. *Harvard Business Review,* 84(9): 114–121; and Stalk, Jr., G. & Lachenauer, R. 2004. *Hardball: Are You Playing to Play or Playing to Win?* Cambridge, MA: Harvard Business School Press. Reprinted by permission of Harvard Business School Press from G. Stalk, Jr. and R. Lachenauer. Copyright 2004 by the Harvard Business School Publishing Corporation; all rights reserved.

"The other case I brought up is markets that are going to be very large markets, but we're just not the natural leader. Advertising supported online video, whether that's at CBS.com or You Tube—great market, kind of next door to us. But we don't do advertising-supported video, we do subscription, so it would be a huge competence expansion for us. And it's not a threat to movies."

Being aware of competitors and cognizant of whatever threats they might pose is the first step in assessing the level of competitive threat. Once a new competitive action becomes apparent, companies must determine how threatening it is to their business. Competitive dynamics are likely to be most intense among companies that are competing for the same customers or who have highly similar sets of resources.[47] Two factors are used to assess whether or not companies are close competitors:

- **Market commonality**—Whether or not competitors are vying for the same customers and how many markets they share in common. For example, aircraft manufacturers Boeing and Airbus have a high degree of market commonality because they make very similar products and have many buyers in common.

- **Resource similarity**—The degree to which rivals draw on the same types of resources to compete. For example, the home pages of Google and Yahoo! may look very different, but behind the scenes, they both rely on the talent pool of high-caliber software engineers to create the cutting-edge innovations that help them compete.

When any two firms have both a high degree of market commonality and highly similar resource bases, a stronger competitive threat is present. Such a threat, however, may not lead to competitive action. On the one hand, a market rival may be hesitant to attack a company that it shares a high degree of market commonality with because it could lead to an intense battle. On the other hand, once attacked, rivals with high market commonality will be much more motivated to launch a competitive response. This is especially true in cases where the shared market is an important part of a company's overall business.

How strong a response an attacked rival can mount will be determined by their strategic resource endowments. In general, the same set of conditions holds true with regard to resource similarity. Companies that have highly similar resource bases will be hesitant to launch an initial attack but pose a serious threat if required to mount a competitive response.[48] Greater strategic resources increase a firm's capability to respond. Strategy Spotlight 8.10 addresses how the dynamics of market commonality and resource similarity have shaped the battle between chipmakers Intel and AMD and intensified their competitive rivalry.

Motivation and Capability to Respond

Once attacked, competitors are faced with deciding how to respond. Before deciding, however, they need to evaluate not only how they will respond, but also their reasons for responding and their capability to respond. Companies need to be clear about what problems a competitive response is expected to address and what types of problems it might create.[49] There are several factors to consider.

First, how serious is the impact of the competitive attack to which they are responding? For example, a large company with a strong reputation that is challenged by a small or unknown company may elect to simply keep an eye on the new competitor rather than quickly react or overreact. Part of the story of online retailer Amazon's early success is attributed to Barnes & Noble's over-reaction to Amazon's claim that it was "earth's biggest bookstore." Because Barnes & Noble was already using the phrase "world's largest bookstore," it sued Amazon, but lost. The confrontation made it to the front pages of *The Wall Street Journal* and Amazon was on its way to becoming a household name.[50]

AMD and Intel: Related Rivals

Few business battles are as intensely reported as the one between chipmakers Intel and Advanced Micro Devices (AMD). For years, Intel aggressively advertised its brand by pushing its "Intel Inside" logo to average consumers. In an effort to develop a stronger presence among consumers, AMD launched a successful initiative labeled internally, "War in the Store" to promote sales of AMD-based computers in retailers such as Best Buy. The effort prompted a retaliation by Intel that lowered the cost of chips enough to decrease PC prices $200. Meanwhile, AMD won a recent round when Dell announced it would start using AMD chips in its servers.

Why is the battle between the two companies so intense? Because they are so much alike. Both companies were founded in the late 1960s in Silicon Valley and were partners during their early history. But in 1986, Intel cancelled a key licensing agreement with AMD to manufacture microprocessors and refused to turn over technical details. AMD sued and, after years of litigation, the Supreme Court of California forced Intel to pay AMD over $1 billion in compensation for violations of the contract. The two companies have been battling ever since.

Consider how comparable the two companies are in terms of markets and resources.

Market Commonality

A key issue facing the two chipmakers is that to continue growing, they have had to enter each other's market space.

Sources: Edwards, C. 2006. AMD: Chipping Away at Intel's Lead. *Business Week*, June 12: 72–73; Edwards, C. 2006. Intel Sharpens Its Offensive Game. *Business Week*, July 31: 60. Gonsalves, A. 2007. AMD Pays the Price in Awakening Intel Goliath. *Information Week*, www.informationweek.com, April 9; Gaudin, S. 2006. AMD Cracks Top 10 Chip Ranking, Intel Sales Slump. *Information Week*, www.informationweek.com, December 5; and www.wikipedia.org.

This is a major reason why the competition has become so heated. For example, Intel dominated that high-end server business in 2003. Now AMD holds 26 percent of the U.S. server chip business and supplies a 48 percent share of the multicore processors (which feature two or more chips on one slice of silicon). To maintain its status as the number one supplier, Intel launched a new family of processors called Core 2 Duo in 2007 that combines the performance of the Pentium 4 with the energy saving features of its notebook computer processors. "We intend to energetically compete for every single microprocessor opportunity," said Intel Executive Vice President Sean M. Maloney.

Resource Similarity

Intel is the world's number one supplier of semiconductors and is expected to have five manufacturing plants by the end of 2007. Because of new manufacturing techniques at three of its plants, it can squeeze more transistors onto a chip and its processors cost less to make than AMD's. By contrast, AMD has just two manufacturing plants but it has moved aggressively to match Intel's muscle. In 2005, it paid $5.4 billion to acquire graphics chipmaker ATI Technologies and has outsourced more manufacturing to Chartered Semiconductors. One result has been that AMD, now the number two maker of processors and graphic cards, increased semiconductor sales by 90 percent in 2006.

The battle between the two companies has been costly in recent years. When Intel retaliated for AMD's rapid gains, the result was slower sales for AMD and first quarter 2006 revenues of $1.23 billion rather than the $1.55 billion analysts expected. Meanwhile, Intel was hurt when Dell decided to begin installing AMD chips in its servers after years of using Intel exclusively. "The competitive dynamics have been more intense than we expected," commented Kevin B. Rollins, Dell's former CEO.

Companies planning to respond to a competitive challenge must also understand their motivation for responding. What is the intent of the competitive response? Is it merely to blunt the attack of the competitor or is it an opportunity to enhance its competitive position? Sometimes the most a company can hope for is to minimize the damage caused by a competitive action.

A company that seeks to improve its competitive advantage may be motivated to launch an attack rather than merely respond to one. For example, Wal-Mart is known for its aggressive efforts to live up to its "everyday low prices" corporate motto. Strategy Spotlight 8.11 describes the retailer's recent assault on rivals Circuit City and Best Buy. A company must also assess its capability to respond. What strategic resources can be deployed to fend off a competitive attack? Does the company have an array of internal strengths it can draw on, or is it operating from a position of weakness?

Wal-Mart's Cutthroat Pricing Schemes

Wal-Mart has a reputation as a relentless competitor in its pursuit of an overall cost leader strategy. Most of that reputation has come from its efforts to drive down costs in its dealings with suppliers. Wal-Mart sometimes goes on the offensive with rivals as well by driving down prices.

Recently, the retail giant took on Circuit City and Best Buy whom it competes with head-on in the consumer electronics market. First Wal-Mart made big improvements in the electronics departments of 1,300 of its 3,100 U.S. stores by spiffing-up displays and adding high-end products such as Apple iPods, Toshiba laptops, and Sony liquid-crystal-display televisions. Then it delivered the two rivals a proverbial one-two punch—offering low-cost extended warranties and slashing prices on flat-panel TVs.

- **Extended warranties.** These are the multiyear protection plans that salespeople offer at the close of a sale on items such as TVs and computers. For both Circuit City and Best Buy, they are one of the most profitable segments of their business, accounting

for at least a third of their operating profits. In late 2005, Wal-Mart launched its own extended warranty program at prices nearly 50 percent lower than Best Buy and Circuit City.

- **Flat-panel TVs.** This includes both liquid crystal display and big-screen plasma models that, until the 2006 holiday season, had never sold below $1,000. Wal-Mart broke that barrier by offering a 42-inch flat-panel TV for $998. The cuts were not limited to lesser-known brands such as Viore TV. Wal-Mart also lowered the 42-inch Panasonic high-definition TV by $500 to $1,294. The response was immediate. Circuit City lowered the price on the same Panasonic TV to $1,299 and Best Buy began offering a 42-inch Westinghouse LCD for $999.

Circuit City was among the hardest hit by this cutthroat competition. After several attempts to cut costs and bolster revenues, it filed for bankruptcy in 2008 and was liquidated in 2009. Best Buy, the largest electronic retailer, did a better job of absorbing the shock. Still, its stock fell 9 percent during the first quarter of 2007. Other retailers were also hit hard by the audacious pricing that has been labeled the "Wal-Mart effect" including CompUSA, which is shuttering 126 of its 229 stores, and Tweeter's, which is closing 49 of its 153 stores and laying off 650 workers.

Sources: Boyle, M. & McConnon, A. 2008. Circuit City Files for Bankruptcy. www.businessweek.com, November 10: np. Berner, R. 2005. Watch Out, Best Buy and Circuit City. *BusinessWeek Online*, www.businessweek.com, November 10; and Gogoi, P. 2007. How Wal-Mart's TV Prices Crushed Rivals. *BusinessWeek*, www.businessweek.com, April 27.

Consider, the role of firm age and size in calculating a company's ability to respond. Most entrepreneurial new ventures start out small. The smaller size makes them more nimble compared to large firms so they can respond quickly to competitive attacks. Because they are not well-known, start-ups also have the advantage of the element of surprise in how and when they attack. Innovative uses of technology, for example, allow small firms to deploy resources in unique ways.

Because they are young, however, start-ups may not have the financial resources needed to follow through with a competitive response. In contrast, older and larger firms may have more resources and a repertoire of competitive techniques they can use in a counterattack. Large firms, however, tend to be slower to respond. Older firms tend to be predictable in their responses because they often lose touch with the competitive environment and rely on strategies and actions that have worked in the past.

Other resources may also play a role in whether a company is equipped to retaliate. For example, one avenue of counterattack may be launching product enhancements or new product/service innovations. For that approach to be successful, it requires a company to have both the intellectual capital to put forward viable innovations and the teamwork skills to prepare a new product or service and get it to market. Resources such as cross-functional teams and the social capital that makes teamwork production effective and efficient represent the type of human capital resources that enhance a company's capability to respond.

Exhibit 8.10 **Strategic and Tactical Competitive Actions**

	Actions	Examples
Strategic Actions	• Entering new markets	• Make geographical expansions • Expand into neglected markets • Target rivals' markets • Target new demographics
	• New product introductions	• Imitate rivals' products • Address gaps in quality • Leverage new technologies • Leverage brand name with related products • Protect innovation with patents
	• Changing production capacity	• Create overcapacity • Tie up raw materials sources • Tie up preferred suppliers and distributors • Stimulate demand by limiting capacity
	• Mergers/Alliances	• Acquire/partner with competitors to reduce competition • Tie up key suppliers through alliances • Obtain new technology/intellectual property • Facilitate new market entry
Tactical Actions	• Price cutting (or increases)	• Maintain low price dominance • Offer discounts and rebates • Offer incentives (e.g., frequent flyer miles) • Enhance offering to move upscale
	• Product/service enhancements	• Address gaps in service • Expand warranties • Make incremetal product improvements
	• Increased marketing efforts	• Use guerilla marketing • Conduct selective attacks • Change product packaging • Use new marketing channels
	• New distribution channels	• Access suppliers directly • Access customers directly • Develop multiple points of contact with customers • Expand Internet presence

Sources: Chen, M. J. & Hambrick, D. 1995. Speed, Stealth, and Selective Attack: How Small Firms Differ from Large Firms in Competitive Behavior. *Academy of Management Journal,* 38: 453–482; Davies, M. 1992. Sales Promotions as a Competitive Strategy. *Management Decision,* 30(7): 5–10; Ferrier, W., Smith, K., & Grimm, C. 1999. The Role of Competitive Action in Market Share Erosion and Industry Dethronement: A Study of Industry Leaders and Challengers. *Academy of Management Journal,* 42(4): 372–388; and Garda, R. A. 1991. Use Tactical Pricing to Uncover Hidden Profits. *Journal of Business Strategy,* 12(5): 17–23.

Types of Competitive Actions

Once an organization determines whether it is willing and able to launch a competitive action, it must determine what type of action is appropriate. The actions taken will be determined by both its resource capabilities and its motivation for responding. There are also marketplace considerations. What types of actions are likely to be most effective given a company's internal strengths and weaknesses as well as market conditions?

Two broadly defined types of competitive action include strategic actions and tactical actions. **Strategic actions** represent major commitments of distinctive and specific resources. Examples include launching a breakthrough innovation, building a new production facility, or merging with another company. Such actions require significant planning and resources and, once initiated, are difficult to reverse.

Tactical actions include refinements or extensions of strategies. Examples of tactical actions include cutting prices, improving gaps in service, or strengthening marketing efforts. Such actions typically draw on general resources and can be implemented quickly. Exhibit 8.10 identifies several types of strategic and tactical competitive actions.

Some competitive actions take the form of frontal assaults, that is, actions aimed directly at taking business from another company or capitalizing on industry weaknesses. This can be especially effective when firms use a low-cost strategy. The airline industry provides a good example of this head-on approach. When Southwest Airlines began its no-frills, no-meals, strategy in the late-1960s, it represented a direct assault on the major carriers of the day. In Europe, Ryanair has directly challenged the traditional carriers with an overall cost leadership strategy. Founded in 1985, Ryanair is one-seventh the size of British Airways in terms of revenues, but in 2006, due to cost-cutting measures that significantly improved operating margins, it had a higher market capitalization of $7.6 billion compared to BA's $7.3 billion.[51]

Guerilla offensives and selective attacks provide an alternative for firms with fewer resources.[52] These draw attention to products or services by creating buzz or generating enough shock value to get some free publicity. The open source software movement, which has been gaining momentum as major corporations become aware of its potential, still lacks the market power and omnipresence that software giant Microsoft enjoys.[53] Loyal users of open source software such as Linux stay connected and share software through online blogs. They also pull the occasional publicity stunt. Recently, users of Firefox, the open source browser developed by the Mozilla Corporation created a crop circle in Oregon based on the Firefox logo. The effort made the local news and garnered thousands of mentions on open source blogs and Internet news organizations.

Some companies limit their competitive response to defensive actions. Such actions rarely improve a company's competitive advantage, but a credible defensive action can lower the risk of being attacked and deter new entry. This may be especially effective during periods such as an industry shake-up, when pricing levels or future demand for a product line become highly uncertain. At such times, tactics such as lowering prices on products that are easily duplicated, buying up the available supply of goods or raw materials, or negotiating exclusive agreements with buyers and/or suppliers can insulate a company from a more serious attack.

Several of the factors discussed earlier in the chapter, such as types of entry strategies and the use of cost leadership versus differentiation strategies, can guide the decision about what types of competitive actions to take. Before launching a given strategy, however, assessing the likely response of competitors is a vital step.[54]

Likelihood of Competitive Reaction

The final step before initiating a competitive response is to evaluate what a competitor's reaction is likely to be. The logic of competitive dynamics suggests that once competitive actions are initiated, it is likely they will be met with competitive responses.[55] The last step before mounting an attack is to evaluate how competitors are likely to respond. Evaluating potential competitive reactions helps companies plan for future counterattacks. It may

strategic actions
major commitments of distinctive and specific resources to strategic initiatives.

tactical actions
refinements or extensions of strategies usually involving minor resource commitments.

also lead to a decision to hold off—that is, not to take any competitive action at all because of the possibility that a misguided or poorly planned response will generate a devastating competitive reaction.

How a competitor is likely to respond will depend on three factors: market dependence, competitor's resources, and the reputation of the firm that initiates the action (actor's reputation). The implications of each of these is described briefly in the following sections.

Market Dependence   If a company has a high concentration of its business in a particular industry, it has more at stake because it must depend on that industry's market for its sales. Single-industry businesses or those where one industry dominates are more likely to mount a competitive response. Young and small firms with a high degree of market dependence may be limited in how they respond due to resource constraints. JetBlue, itself an aggressive competitor, is unable to match some of the perks its bigger rivals can offer, such as first-class seats or international travel benefits.

Competitor's Resources   Previously, we examined the internal resource endowments that a company must evaluate when assessing its capability to respond. Here, it is the competitor's resources that need to be considered. For example, a small firm may be unable to mount a serious attack due to lack of resources. As a result, it is more likely to react to tactical actions such as incentive pricing or enhanced service offerings because they are less costly to attack than large-scale strategic actions. In contrast, a firm with financial "deep pockets" may be able to mount and sustain a costly counterattack. As a way to combat these differences in market power, young firms can strengthen their resource positions by forming strategic alliances. Yahoo!, for example, pressed hard by its young but powerful rival Google, allied itself with a group of seven newspaper chains that publish a total of 176 U.S. daily papers in a content sharing arrangement. Both Yahoo! and the newspaper chains are trying to stay ahead of Google now that it is moving aggressively beyond ads on its search pages.

Actor's Reputation   Whether a company should respond to a competitive challenge will also depend on who launched the attack against it. In previous examples, we have noted that companies such as Wal-Mart and Intel are capable of bold offenses. These competitive actors also have the ability and motivation to mount overwhelming counterattacks. Compared to relatively smaller firms with less market power, competitors are more likely to respond to competitive moves by market leaders. Another consideration is how successful prior attacks have been. For example, price-cutting by the big automakers usually has the desired result—increased sales to price-sensitive buyers—at least in the short run. Given that history, when GM offers discounts or incentives, rivals Ford and Chrysler cannot afford to ignore the challenge and quickly follow suit.

Choosing Not to React: Forbearance and Co-opetition

The above discussion suggests that there may be many circumstances in which the best reaction is no reaction at all. This is known as **forbearance**—refraining from reacting at all as well as holding back from initiating an attack. For example, none of the Japanese automakers attempted to match the employee discount pricing war that cost the big U.S. automakers heavily in terms of lower profits and lost jobs. Yet, during the same period, Honda, Toyota and Nissan enjoyed substantial sales increases over the previous year. Strategy Spotlight 8.12 highlights another recent rivalry—the one between Facebook and MySpace.

Related to forbearance is the concept of **co-opetition.** This is a term that was coined by network software company Novell's founder and former CEO Raymond Noorda to suggest that companies often benefit most from a combination of competing and cooperating.[56] Close competitors that differentiate themselves in the eyes of consumers may work together behind the scenes to achieve industrywide efficiencies.[57] For example, breweries in Sweden cooperate in recycling used bottles but still compete for customers on the basis of

forbearance a firm's choice of not reacting to a rival's new competitive action.

co-opetition a firm's strategy of both cooperating and competing with rival firms.

Facebook versus MySpace

Social networking is not just a fad anymore. It's a big business that has spawned dozens of entrepreneurial launches and captured millions of advertising dollars. Nothing illustrates this better than Rubert Murdoch's decision to pay $580 million to purchase MySpace and make it part of his News Corporation business empire (which includes Fox News and *The Wall Street Journal*). The success of MySpace, whose 2008 revenues are estimated to exceed $600 million, has attracted a host of new entrants angling to get in the social networking game. Among the most successful is Facebook, a comparable service whose number of users recently surpassed MySpace (see Exhibit 8.11).

Facebook and MySpace have a lot in common. They are both interactive, user-submitted networks of friends featuring profile pages, blogs, groups, photos, videos, and links for teenagers and adults. Both have an international following. There are also clear differences—for example, MySpace encourages users to customize their profiles, whereas Facebook allows only plain text; the entertainment-oriented MySpace is headquartered in Beverly Hills, whereas the tech-oriented Facebook is in Silicon Valley. Even so, 65 percent of Facebook users also have a MySpace account according to comScore, an Internet marketing research company. As such, the two companies are in a heated competition for the main thing that makes their business models work—advertising dollars.

Consider the actions and counter-actions the two companies have engaged in during their short histories:

- News Corp. signs a $900 million search and advertising deal with Google, enough to cover the purchase price of MySpace; Microsoft pays $246 million for a 1.6 percent stake in Facebook and assigns 400 salespeople to sell Facebook display ads.

- Facebook opens its platform to third-party developers and within a few months matches and then surpasses the features available on MySpace. A year later, MySpace opens its platform to third-party developers in an attempt to regain the edge.

- MySpace counters its entertainment-only image by opening an office in Silicon Valley with plans to hire hundreds of engineers; Facebook develops virtual gifts and interactive "engagement ads" to make the Facebook experience more entertaining.

Sources: Ante, S. E. 2008. Facebook's Land Grab in the Face of a Downturn. www.businessweek.com, November 20, np.; Kirkpatrick, D. 2007. As Facebook Takes Off, MySpace Strikes Back. www.fortune.com, September 19, np; and, Lacy, S. 2007. What MySpace-Facebook Rivalry? www.businessweek .com, October 19, np.; www.facebook.com; and www.myspace.com.

USERS VS. REVENUES

MySpace has more than twice the revenue of Facebook, but Facebook has surpassed its rival in number of users and is widening its lead

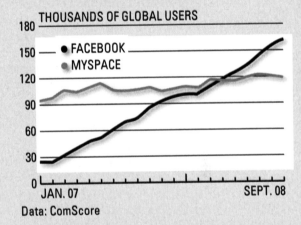

THOUSANDS OF GLOBAL USERS

● FACEBOOK
● MYSPACE

JAN. 07　　　　SEPT. 08

Data: ComScore

Exhibit 8.11 Competition between Rivals MySpace and Facebook

Source: Ante, S. E. 2008. Facebook's Land Grab in the Face of a Downturn. www.businessweek.com, November 20, np.

- Facebook creates versions of its website in multiple languages, including Xhosa, Tagalog, and French Canadian to attract niche audiences around the world; MySpace launches a music service with free streaming music as well as downloads, ringtones, and concert tickets to boost growth in customers.

The two companies currently have different strategies—Facebook is dedicated to growing the number of users, while MySpace is concentrating on increasing profits. But both are keenly aware of the high-stakes game they are playing. Although Facebook is expected to have revenues of $300 million in 2008, it is not yet showing a profit. That's not a problem in the short run, according to Peter Thiel, a Facebook investor and board member. "If we stopped growing, we could make money," says Thiel, "but it makes no sense for us to stop growing. We still think it's a land grab where we have to try to get to scale first."

In contrast, MySpace is limiting its efforts to grow users and concentrating instead on profitability. Even so, the company clearly regards Facebook's recent growth surge a threat. According to MySpace president Tom Anderson, Facebook is a formidable rival. "It's the first time I feel like we have a real competitor," says Anderson. "It's a good thing overall, because if there was any complacency within the company, now there's someone you can look at and say, 'Hey, we've got to be better.'"

taste and variety. As long as the benefits of cooperating are enjoyed by all participants in a co-opetition system, the practice can aid companies in avoiding intense and damaging competition.[58]

Despite the potential benefits of co-opetition, companies need to guard against cooperating to such a great extent that their actions are perceived as collusion, a practice that has legal ramifications in the United States. Satellite radio competitors XM and Sirius, after years of intense rivalry, faced several challenges recently related to their efforts to merge their operations.

Once a company has evaluated a competitor's likelihood of responding to a competitive challenge, it can decide what type of action is most appropriate. Competitive actions can take many forms: the entry of a start-up into a market for the first time, an attack by a lower-ranked incumbent on an industry leader, or the launch of a breakthrough innovation that disrupts the industry structure. Such actions forever change the competitive dynamics of a marketplace. Thus, the cycle of actions and reactions that occur in business every day is a vital aspect of entrepreneurial strategy that leads to continual new value creation and the ongoing advancement of economic well-being.

Reflecting on Career Implications . . .

- *Opportunity Recognition:* What ideas for new business activities are actively discussed in your work environment? Could you apply the four characteristics of an opportunity to determine whether they are viable opportunities?

- *Entrepreneurial New Entry:* Are there opportunities to launch new products or services that might add value to the organization? What are the best ways for you to bring these opportunities to the attention of key managers? Or, might this provide an opportunity for you to launch your own entrepreneurial venture?

- *Entrepreneurial Strategy:* Does your organization face competition from new ventures? If so, how are those young firms competing: Low cost? Differentiation? Focus? What could you do to help your company to address those competitive challenges?

- *Competitive Dynamics:* Is your organization "on the offense" with its close competitors or "playing defense"? What types of strategic and/or tactical actions have been taken by your close rivals recently to gain competitive advantages?

Summary

New ventures and entrepreneurial firms that capitalize on marketplace opportunities make an important contribution to the U.S. economy. They are leaders in terms of implementing new technologies and introducing innovative products and services. Yet entrepreneurial firms face unique challenges if they are going to survive and grow.

To successfully launch new ventures or implement new technologies, three factors must be present: an entrepreneurial opportunity, the resources to pursue the opportunity, and an entrepreneur or entrepreneurial team willing and able to undertake the venture. Firms must develop a strong ability to recognize viable opportunities. Opportunity recognition is a process of determining which venture ideas are, in fact, promising business opportunities.

In addition to strong opportunities, entrepreneurial firms need resources and entrepreneurial leadership to thrive. The resources that start-ups need include financial resources as well as human and social capital. Many firms also benefit from government programs that support new venture development and growth. New ventures thrive best when they are led by founders or owners who have vision, drive and dedication, and a commitment to excellence.

Once the necessary opportunities, resources, and entrepreneur skills are in place, new ventures still face numerous strategic challenges. Decisions about the strategic positioning of new entrants can benefit from conducting strategic analyses and evaluating the requirements of niche markets. Entry strategies used by new ventures take several forms, including pioneering new entry, imitative new entry, and adaptive new entry. Entrepreneurial firms can benefit from using overall low cost, differentiation, and focus strategies although each of these approaches has pitfalls that are unique to young and small firms. Entrepreneurial firms are also in a strong position to benefit from combination strategies.

The entry of a new company into a competitive arena is like a competitive attack on incumbents in that arena. Such actions often provoke a competitive response, which may, in turn, trigger a reaction to the response. As a result, a competitive dynamic—action and response—begins among close competitors. In deciding whether to attack or counterattack, companies must analyze the seriousness of the competitive threat, their ability to mount a competitive response, and the type of action—strategic or tactical—that the situation requires. At times, competitors find it is better not to respond at all or to find avenues to cooperate with, rather than challenge, close competitors.

Summary Review Questions

1. Explain how the combination of opportunities, resources, and entrepreneurs helps determine the character and strategic direction of an entrepreneurial firm.

2. What is the difference between discovery and evaluation in the process of opportunity recognition? Give an example of each.

3. Describe the three characteristics of entrepreneurial leadership: vision, dedication and drive, and commitment to excellence.

4. Briefly describe the three types of entrepreneurial entry strategies: pioneering, imitative, and adaptive.

5. Explain why entrepreneurial firms are often in a strong position to use combination strategies.

6. What does the term *competitive dynamics* mean?

7. Explain the difference between strategic actions and tactical actions and provide examples of each.

Key Terms

entrepreneurship, 273
opportunity recognition, 276
entrepreneurial strategy 285
pioneering new entry, 286
imitative new entry, 287
adaptive new entry, 288
competitive dynamics, 294
new competitive action 295
threat analysis 295
market commonality, 297
resource similarity, 297
strategic actions, 301
tactical actions, 301
forbearance 302
co-opetition 302

Applications Questions and Answers

1. E-Loan and Lending Tree are two entrepreneurial firms that offer lending services over the Internet.

Evaluate the features of these two companies and, for each company:

a. Evaluate their characteristics and assess the extent to which they are comparable in terms of market commonality and resource similarity.

Company	Market Commonality	Resource Similarity
E-Loan		
Lending Tree		

b. Based on your analysis, what strategic and/or tactical actions might these companies take to improve their competitive position? Could E-Loan and Lending Tree improve their performance more through co-opetition rather than competition? Explain your rationale.

Company	Strategic Actions	Tactical Actions
E-Loan		
Lending Tree		

2. Using the Internet, research the Small Business Administration's website (www.sba.gov). What different types of financing are available to small firms? Besides financing, what other programs are available to support the growth and development of small businesses?

3. Think of an entrepreneurial firm that has been successfully launched in the last 10 years. What kind of entry strategy did it use—pioneering, imitative, or adaptive? Since the firm's initial entry, how has it used or combined overall low-cost, differentiation and/or focus strategies?

4. Select an entrepreneurial firm you are familiar with in your local community. Research the company and discuss how it has positioned itself relative to its close competitors. Does it have a unique strategic advantage? Disadvantage? Explain.

Ethics Questions

1. Imitation strategies are based on the idea of copying another firm's idea and using it for your own purposes. Is this unethical or simply a smart business practice? Discuss the ethical implications of this practice (if any).

2. Intense competition such as price wars are an accepted practice in the United States, but cooperation between companies has legal ramifications because of antitrust laws. Should price wars that drive small businesses or new entrants out of business be illegal? What ethical considerations are raised (if any)?

References

1. The Amp'd Mobile example is based on Kharif, O. 2007. Amp'd Mobile runs out of juice. BusinessWeek.com, June 5: np; and Rosenthal, J. 2007. Mobile meltdown. *Fast Company,* September: 49–53.
2. Small Business Administration. 2004. *The small business economy* Washington, D.C.: U.S. Government Printing Office.
3. Timmons, J. A. & Spinelli, S. 2004. *New venture creation* (6th ed.). New York: McGraw-Hill/Irwin; and Bygrave, W. D. 1997. The entrepreneurial process. In W. D. Bygrave (Ed.), *The portable MBA in entrepreneurship* (2nd ed.). New York: Wiley.
4. Fromartz, S. 1998. How to get your first great idea. *Inc. Magazine,* April 1: 91–94; and, Vesper, K. H. 1990. *New venture strategies,* 2nd ed. Englewood Cliffs, NJ: Prentice-Hall.
5. For an interesting perspective on the nature of the opportunity recognition process, see Baron, R. A. 2006. Opportunity recognition as pattern recognition: How entrepreneurs 'connect the dots' to identify new business opportunities. *Academy of Management Perspectives,* February: 104–119.
6. Gaglio, C. M. 1997. Opportunity identification: Review, critique and suggested research directions. In J. A. Katz, ed. *Advances in entrepreneurship, firm emergence and growth,* vol. 3. Greenwich, CT: JAI Press: 139–202; Lumpkin, G. T., Hills, G. E., & Shrader, R. C. 2004. Opportunity recognition. In Harold L. Welsch, (Ed.), *Entrepreneurship: The Road Ahead,* pp. 73–90. London: Routledge; and, Long, W. & McMullan, W. E. 1984. Mapping the new venture opportunity identification process. *Frontiers of entrepreneurship research, 1984.*

Wellesley, MA: Babson College: 567–90.

7. For an interesting discussion of different aspects of opportunity discovery, see Shepherd, D. A. & De Tienne, D. R. 2005. Prior knowledge, potential financial reward, and opportunity identification. *Entrepreneurship theory & practice*, 29(1): 91–112; and Gaglio, C. M. 2004. The role of mental simulations and counterfactual thinking in the opportunity identification process. *Entrepreneurship theory & practice*, 28(6): 533–552.

8. Stewart, T. A. 2002. How to think with your gut. *Business 2.0*, November: 99–104.

9. For more on the opportunity recognition process, see Smith, B. R., Matthews, C. H., & Schenkel, M. T. 2009. Differences in entrepreneurial opportunities: The role of tacitness and codification in opportunity identification. *Journal of Small Business Management*, 47(1): 38–57.

10. Timmons, J. A. 1997. Opportunity recognition. In W. D. Bygrave, ed. *The portable MBA in entrepreneurship*, 2nd ed. New York: John Wiley: 26–54.

11. Social networking is also proving to be an increasingly important type of entrepreneurial resource. For an interesting discussion, see Aldrich, H. E. & Kim, P. H. 2007. Small worlds, infinite possibilities? How social networks affect entrepreneurial team formation and search. *Strategic Entrepreneurship Journal*, 1(1): 147–166.

12. Bhide, A. V. 2000. *The origin and evolution of new businesses*. New York: Oxford University Press.

13. Small Business 2001: Where are we now? 2001. *Inc. Magazine*, May 29: 18–19; and Zacharakis, A. L., Bygrave, W. D., & Shepherd, D.A. 2000. *Global entrepreneurship monitor—National entrepreneurship assessment: United States of America 2000 Executive Report*. Kansas City, MO: Kauffman Center for Entrepreneurial Leadership.

14. Cooper, S. 2003. Cash cows. *Entrepreneur*, June: 36.

15. Seglin, J. L. 1998. What angels want. *Inc. Magazine*, 20 (7): 43–44.

16. Torres, N.L. 2002. Playing an angel. *Entrepreneur*, May: 130–138.

17. For an interesting discussion of how venture capital practices vary across different sectors of the economy, see Gaba, V. & Meyer, A. D. 2008. Crossing the organizational species barrier: How venture capital practices infiltrated the information technology sector. *Academy of Management Journal*, 51(5): 391–412.

18. For more on how different forms of organizing entrepreneurial firms as well as different stages of new firm growth and development affect financing, see Cassar, G. 2004. The financing of business start-ups. *Journal of Business Venturing*, 19(2): 261–283.

19. Eisenhardt, K. M. & Schoonhoven, C. B. 1990. Organizational growth: Linking founding team, strategy, environment, and growth among U.S. semiconductor ventures, 1978–1988. *Administrative Science Quarterly*, 35: 504–529.

20. Dubini, P. & Aldrich, H. 1991. Personal and extended networks are central to the entrepreneurship process. *Journal of Business Venturing*, 6(5): 305–333.

21. For more on the role of social contacts in helping young firms build legitimacy, see Chrisman, J. J. & McMullan, W. E. 2004. Outside assistance as a knowledge resource for new venture survival. *Journal of Small Business Management*, 42(3): 229–244.

22. Vogel, C. 2000. Janina Pawlowski. *Working woman*, June: 70

23. For a recent perspective on entrepreneurship and strategic alliances, see Rothaermel, F. T. & Deeds, D. L. 2006. Alliance types, alliance experience and alliance management capability in high-technology ventures. *Journal of Business Venturing*, 21(4): 429–460; and Lu, J. W. & Beamish, P. W. 2006. Partnering strategies and performance of SMEs' international joint ventures. *Journal of Business Venturing*, 21(4): 461–486.

24. For more on the role of alliances in creating competitive advantages, see Wiklund, J. & Shepherd, D. A. 2009. The effectiveness of alliances and acquisitions: The role of resource combination activities. *Entrepreneurship Theory & Practice*, 33(1): 193–212.

25. For more information, go to the Small Business Administration website at www.sba.gov.

26. For an interesting study of the role of passion in entrepreneurial success, see Chen, X-P., Yao, X., & Kotha, S. 2009 Entrepreneur passion and preparedness in business plan presentations: A persuasion analysis of venture capitalists' funding decisions. *Academy of Management Journal*, 52 (1): 101–120.

27. Collins, J. 2001. *Good to great*. New York: HarperCollins.

28. Collins, op. cit.

29. The idea of entry wedges was discussed by Vesper, K. 1990. *New venture strategies* (2nd ed.). Englewood Cliffs, NJ: Prentice-Hall; and, Drucker, P. F. 1985. *Innovation and entrepreneurship*. New York: HarperBusiness.

30. See Dowell, G. & Swaminathan, A. 2006. Entry timing, exploration, and firm survival in the early U.S. bicycle industry. *Strategic Management Journal*, 27: 1159–1182, for a recent study of the timing of entrepreneurial new entry.

31. Maiello, M. 2002. They almost changed the world. *Forbes*, December 22: 217–220.

32. Gull, N. 2003. Just say om. *Inc. Magazine*, July: 42–44; Hugger Mugger Yoga Products sues Gaiam, Inc. in federal court for Internet trademark infringement. 2005. www.businesswire.com, March 17: np.

33. More on the role of imitation strategies is addressed in a recent article: Lieberman, M. B. & Asaba, S. 2006. Why do firms imitate each other? *Academy of Management Review*, 31(2): 366–385.

34. Williams, G. 2002. Looks like rain. *Entrepreneur*, September: 104–111.

35. Pedroza, G. M. 2002. Tech tutors. *Entrepreneur*, September: 120.

36. Kim, W. C., and Mauborgne, R. 2004. Blue ocean strategy. *Harvard Business Review*, October: 76–84; and www.cirquedusoleil.com.

37. Romanelli, E. 1989. Environments and strategies of organization start-up: Effects on early survival.

Administrative Science Quarterly, 34(3): 369–87.

38. Wallace, B. 2000. Brothers. *Philadelphia Magazine,* April: 66–75.

39. Buchanan, L. 2003. The innovation factor: A field guide to innovation. *Forbes,* April 21, www.forbes.com.

40. Kim, W. C. & Mauborgne, R. 2005. *Blue ocean strategy.* Boston: Harvard Business School Press.

41. For more on how unique organizational combinations can contribute to competitive advantages of entrepreneurial firms, see Steffens, P., Davidsson, P., & Fitzsimmons, J. Performance configurations over times: Implications for growth- and profit-oriented strategies. *Entrepreneurship Theory & Practice,* 33(1): 125–148.

42. Smith, K. G., Ferrier, W. J., & Grimm, C. M. 2001. King of the hill: Dethroning the industry leader. *Academy of Management Executive,* 15(2): 59–70.

43. Kumar, N. 2006. Strategies to fight low-cost rivals. *Harvard Business Review,* December: 104–112.

44. Grove, A. 1999. *Only the paranoid survive: How to exploit the crises points that challenge every company.* New York: Random House.

45. Stalk, Jr., G. & Lachenauer, R. 2004. *Hardball: Are you playing to play or playing to win?* Cambridge, MA: Harvard Business School Press.

46. Peteraf, M. A. & Bergen, M. A. 2003. Scanning competitive landscapes: A market-based and resource-based framework. *Strategic Management Journal,* 24: 1027–1045.

47. Chen, M. J. 1996. Competitor analysis and interfirm rivalry: Toward a theoretical integration. *Academy of Management Review,* 21(1): 100–134.

48. Chen, 1996, op.cit.

49. Chen, M. J., Su, K. H, & Tsai, W. 2007. Competitive tension: The awareness-motivation-capability perspective. *Academy of Management Journal,* 50(1): 101–118.

50. St. John, W. 1999. Barnes & Noble's Epiphany. *Wired,* www.wired.com, June.

51. Kumar 2006, op. cit.

52. Chen, M. J. & Hambrick, D. 1995. Speed, stealth, and selective attack: How small firms differ from large firms in competitive behavior. *Academy of Management Journal,* 38: 453–482.

53. Lyons, D. 2006. The cheap revolution. *Forbes,* September 18: 102–111.

54. For a discussion of how the strategic actions of Apple Computer contribute to changes in the competitive dynamics in both the cellular phone and music industries, see Burgelman, R. A. & Grove, A. S. 2008. Cross-boundary disruptors: Powerful interindustry entrepreneurial change agents. *Strategic Entrepreneurship Journal,* 1(1): 315–327,

55. Smith, K. G., Ferrier, W. J., & Ndofor, H. 2001. Competitive dynamics research: Critique and future directions. In M. A. Hitt, R. E. Freeman, & J. S. Harrison (Eds.), *The Blackwell handbook of strategic management,* pp. 315–361. Oxford, UK: Blackwell.

56. Gee, P. 2000. Co-opetition: The new market milieu. *Journal of Healthcare Management,* 45: 359–363.

57. Ketchen, D. J., Snow, C. C., & Hoover, V. L. 2004. Research on competitive dynamics: Recent accomplishments and future challenges. *Journal of Management,* 30(6): 779–804.

58. Khanna, T., Gulati, R., & Nohria, N. 2000. The economic modeling of strategy process: Clean models and dirty hands. *Strategic Management Journal,* 21: 781–790.

CHAPTER 9

Strategic Control and Corporate Governance

After reading this chapter, you should have a good understanding of:

LO1 The value of effective strategic control systems in strategy implementation.

LO2 The key difference between "traditional" and "contemporary" control systems.

LO3 The imperative for "contemporary" control systems in today's complex and rapidly changing competitive and general environments.

LO4 The benefits of having the proper balance among the three levers of behavioral control: culture; rewards and incentives; and, boundaries.

LO5 The three key participants in corporate governance: shareholders, management (led by the CEO), and the board of directors.

LO6 The role of corporate governance mechanisms in ensuring that the interests of managers are aligned with those of shareholders from both the United States and international perspectives.

Organizations must have effective strategic controls if they are to successfully implement their strategies. This includes systems that exercise both informational control and behavioral control. Controls must be consistent with the strategy that the firm is following. In addition, a firm must promote sound corporate governance to ensure that the interests of managers and shareholders are aligned.

In the first section, we address the need to have effective informational control, contrasting two approaches to informational control. The first approach, which we call "traditional," is highly sequential. Goals and objectives are set, then implemented, and after a set period of time, performance is compared to the desired standards. In contrast, the second approach, termed "contemporary," is much more interactive. Here, the internal and external environments are continually monitored, and managers determine whether the strategy itself needs to be modified. Today the contemporary approach is required, given the rapidly changing conditions in virtually all industries.

Next, we discuss behavioral control. Here the firm must strive to maintain a proper balance between culture, rewards, and boundaries. We also argue that organizations that have strong, positive cultures and reward systems can rely less on boundaries, such as rules, regulations, and procedures. When individuals in the firm internalize goals and strategies, there is less need for monitoring behavior, and efforts are focused more on important organizational goals and objectives.

The third section addresses the role of corporate governance in ensuring that managerial and shareholder interests are aligned. We provide examples of both effective and ineffective corporate governance practices. We discuss three governance mechanisms for aligning managerial and shareholder interests: a committed and involved board of directors, shareholder activism, and effective managerial rewards and incentives. Public companies are also subject to external control. We discuss several external control mechanisms, such as the market for corporate control, auditors, banks and analysts, the media, and public activists. We close with a discussion of corporate governance from an international perspective.

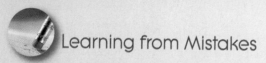 Learning from Mistakes

Customer service call centers offer companies the opportunity to communicate with customers and build a positive client relationship. However, after the merger of Sprint and Nextel in 2005, "unhappy customers defected in droves, and profits evaporated." Sprint Nextel has ranked last in customer service among wireless carriers every year since the merger in J.D. Power & Associates surveys. The downturn in business started before Daniel Hesse became CEO of Sprint in late 2007 and has yet to truly turn around.

Prior to the merger, Nextel had taken pride in the firm's strong customer service and low customer turnover rate, or churn (customers moving to another wireless carrier). On the other hand, Sprint had been very good at managing costs. The merged company adopted most of Sprint's quantitative measurement approach to control. Pressure was put on customer service representatives to shorten the amount of time it took to complete a customer call. Gayle R. Romero, who worked in Sprint Nextel call centers for six years, recalled the pressure to end calls quickly in a manager's remarks to her group: "If you don't think you can handle this, I hear McDonald's is hiring." As they feared for their jobs, employees ended calls quickly, whether or not they had really satisfied the customer inquiry. The result was a dramatic increase in customer churn, as unhappy customers moved their business elsewhere.

What went wrong? Too much behavior control can lead to too much focus on measurement of employee actions rather than measurement of outcomes and organizational goals. This leads employees to do only the things that get measured in their jobs. Employees learn to follow the rules and receive the rewards as set forth by management. Managers sometimes focus on increasing efficiency of tasks. If this comes at the expense of monitoring the effectiveness of the tasks they are measuring toward reaching organizational goals, then a perversion of incentives for employees may occur.

The problems for Sprint only increased in 2006 as the firm came under financial pressure related to losing subscribers. Customer service representatives were given sales and renewal targets and cash bonuses for increasing retention. This led to practices that drew lawsuits from customers who felt tricked into extending their subscription contracts. Some customers complained that each call to Sprint automatically increased the length of their subscription contract without their approval. By 2007, Sprint managers had even cracked down on freebies: free phones, service credits, or extra minutes that customer service representatives were allowed to give customers to keep them happy. Employee morale was so low that some workers called Sprint headquarters "Shawshank" after the Maine prison in the 1994 film *The Shawshank Redemption*. The customer base continued to shrink from 53.9 million at the beginning of 2008 to 50.5 million users by the third quarter, well behind rivals AT&T and Verizon Wireless, which had 74.9 million and 70.8 million subscribers, respectively.

New CEO Daniel Hesse changed the tune of Sprint's customer service culture and measurement systems starting in 2008. While his managers are not abandoning quantitative measurement altogether, they are focusing on measuring things that make customers happy to stay on as subscribers. Now, Sprint has eliminated the measure of the amount of time a customer call takes to complete. Instead, Sprint managers measure how frequently representatives resolve customers' problems on the first call and how long customers have to wait to have their call answered by a representative. Bob Johnson, Sprint's new chief service officer, said, "incentives and policies are now driven around improving the [customer] experience."[1]

strategic control
the process of monitoring and correcting a firm's strategy and performance.

We first explore two central aspects of **strategic control:**[2] (1) *informational control,* which is the ability to respond effectively to environmental change, and (2) *behavioral control,* which is the appropriate balance and alignment among a firm's culture, rewards, and boundaries. In the final section of this chapter, we focus on strategic control from a much broader perspective—what is referred to as *corporate governance.* Here, we direct our attention to the need for a firm's shareholders (the owners) and their elected representatives (the board of directors) to ensure that the firm's executives (the management team) strive to fulfill their fiduciary duty of maximizing long-term shareholder value.

Ensuring Informational Control: Responding Effectively to Environmental Change

We discuss two broad types of control systems: "traditional" and "contemporary." As both general and competitive environments become more unpredictable and complex, the need for contemporary systems increases.

>LO1
The value of effective strategic control systems in strategy implementation.

A Traditional Approach to Strategic Control

The **traditional** approach to **strategic control** is sequential: (1) strategies are formulated and top management sets goals, (2) strategies are implemented, and (3) performance is measured against the predetermined goal set, as illustrated in Exhibit 9.1.

Control is based on a feedback loop from performance measurement to strategy formulation. This process typically involves lengthy time lags, often tied to a firm's annual planning cycle. Such traditional control systems, termed "single-loop" learning by Harvard's Chris Argyris simply compare actual performance to a predetermined goal.[3] They are most appropriate when the environment is stable and relatively simple, goals and objectives can be measured with a high level of certainty, and there is little need for complex measures of performance. Sales quotas, operating budgets, production schedules, and similar quantitative control mechanisms are typical. The appropriateness of the business strategy or standards of performance is seldom questioned.[4]

James Brian Quinn of Dartmouth College has argued that grand designs with precise and carefully integrated plans seldom work.[5] Rather, most strategic change proceeds incrementally—one step at a time. Leaders should introduce some sense of direction, some logic in incremental steps.[6] Similarly, McGill University's Henry Mintzberg has written about leaders "crafting" a strategy.[7] Drawing on the parallel between the potter at her wheel and the strategist, Mintzberg pointed out that the potter begins work with some general idea of the artifact she wishes to create, but the details of design—even possibilities for a different design— emerge as the work progresses. For businesses facing complex and turbulent business environments, the craftsperson's method helps us deal with the uncertainty about how a design will work out in practice and allows for a creative element.

Mintzberg's argument, like Quinn's, questions the value of rigid planning and goal-setting processes. Fixed strategic goals also become dysfunctional for firms competing in highly unpredictable competitive environments. Strategies need to change frequently and opportunistically. An inflexible commitment to predetermined goals and milestones can prevent the very adaptability that is required of a good strategy.

Even organizations that have been extremely successful in the past can become complacent or fail to adapt their goals and strategies to the new conditions. An example of such a firm is American International Group (AIG), once one of the largest and most

traditional approach to strategic control a sequential method of organizational control in which (1) strategies are formulated and top management sets goals, (2) strategies are implemented, and (3) performance is measured against the predetermined goal set.

>LO2
The key difference between "traditional" and "contemporary" control systems.

Exhibit 9.1 Traditional Approach to Strategic Control

strategy spotlight

What Did American International Group Do Wrong?

We can learn some lessons from fallen stars. American International Group (AIG) was one of the largest and most sophisticated insurance firms in the world with $110 billion in annual sales and over $1 trillion in assets. This once invincible stock came crashing down from a 2008 high of $70 a share to $1.25 a share on September 16, 2008. A government funded bailout of $85 billion gave taxpayers warrants for an 80 percent stake in the company.

Problems stemmed from AIG's use of complex derivatives and swaps that transferred and insured credit risks.

Sources: Byrnes, N. 2008. Where AIG Went Wrong. *BusinessWeek*, September 29: 40–42; Chung, J., Daneshkhu, S., Felsted, A., and Guerrera, F. 2008. AIG's Complexity Blamed for Fall. *Financial Times*, October 7: 19; Loomis, C. J. & Burke, D. 2009. AIG: The Company That Came to Dinner. *Fortune*, January 19, 159(1): 70–78.

AIG's solid credit rating from its insurance business helped it "to monetize [its] crediting rating and rent it" for derivatives trades to earn large fees. AIG's problems stemmed from losses in its mortgage insurance business from defaults related to subprime lending and rapidly falling U.S. home prices.

Ratings agencies began to downgrade AIG's credit rating on September 15, 2008, triggering terms of its derivatives contracts and requiring it to put forth $14.5 billion in capital that it did not have. AIG was caught in a crisis of capital and was unable to raise money from Wall Street, so government intervention was required.

As an insurance underwriter, AIG's job was to spread risk around. However, rather than spreading risk, AIG concentrated risk, making bold bets on rising home prices and leaving its whole business exposed to catastrophic losses.

---

sophisticated insurance firms in the world with $110 billion in annual sales. AIG's stock came crashing down from an early 2008 high of $70 a share to $1.25 by the end of the year on the heels of a combination of bad bets on the direction of U.S. housing prices and margin calls on related derivative trades. AIG had failed to minimize the potential for over-concentration of risk by poor use of its information control systems. We discuss this firm in more detail in Strategy Spotlight 9.1.

A Contemporary Approach to Strategic Control

Adapting to and anticipating both internal and external environmental change is an integral part of strategic control. The relationships between strategy formulation, implementation, and control are highly interactive, as suggested by Exhibit 9.2. It also illustrates

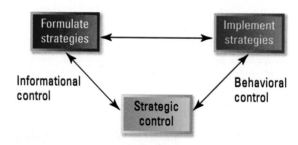

Exhibit 9.2 Contemporary Approach to Strategic Control

two different types of strategic control: informational control and behavioral control. **Informational control** is primarily concerned with whether or not the organization is "doing the right things." **Behavioral control,** on the other hand, asks if the organization is "doing things right" in the implementation of its strategy. Both the informational and behavioral components of strategic control are necessary, but not sufficient, conditions for success. What good is a well-conceived strategy that cannot be implemented? Or what use is an energetic and committed workforce if it is focused on the wrong strategic target?

John Weston is the former CEO of ADP Corporation, the largest payroll and tax-filing processor in the world. He captures the essence of contemporary control systems.

> At ADP, 39 plus 1 adds up to more than 40 plus 0. The 40-plus-0 employee is the harried worker who at 40 hours a week just tries to keep up with what's in the "in" basket. . . . Because he works with his head down, he takes zero hours to think about what he's doing, why he's doing it, and how he's doing it. . . . On the other hand, the 39-plus-1 employee takes at least 1 of those 40 hours to think about what he's doing and why he's doing it. That's why the other 39 hours are far more productive.[8]

Informational control deals with the internal environment as well as the external strategic context. It addresses the assumptions and premises that provide the foundation for an organization's strategy. Do the organization's goals and strategies still "fit" within the context of the current strategic environment? Depending on the type of business, such assumptions may relate to changes in technology, customer tastes, government regulation, and industry competition.

This involves two key issues. First, managers must scan and monitor the external environment, as we discussed in Chapter 2. Also, conditions can change in the internal environment of the firm, as we discussed in Chapter 3, requiring changes in the strategic direction of the firm. These may include, for example, the resignation of key executives or delays in the completion of major production facilities.

In the contemporary approach, information control is part of an ongoing process of organizational learning that continuously updates and challenges the assumptions that underlie the organization's strategy. In such "double-loop" learning, the organization's assumptions, premises, goals, and strategies are continuously monitored, tested, and reviewed. The benefits of continuous monitoring are evident—time lags are dramatically shortened, changes in the competitive environment are detected earlier, and the organization's ability to respond with speed and flexibility is enhanced.

Contemporary control systems must have four characteristics to be effective.[9]

1. Focus on constantly changing information that has potential strategic importance.
2. The information is important enough to demand frequent and regular attention from all levels of the organization.
3. The data and information generated are best interpreted and discussed in face-to-face meetings.
4. The control system is a key catalyst for an ongoing debate about underlying data, assumptions, and action plans.

An executive's decision to use the control system interactively—in other words, to invest the time and attention to review and evaluate new information—sends a clear signal to the organization about what is important. The dialogue and debate that emerge from such an interactive process can often lead to new strategies and innovations. Strategy Spotlight 9.2 discusses how executives at Google use an interactive control process.

informational control a method of organizational control in which a firm gathers and analyzes information from the internal and external environment in order to obtain the best fit between the organization's goals and strategies and the strategic environment.

behavioral control a method of organizational control in which a firm influences the actions of employees through culture, rewards, and boundaries.

Google's Interactive Control System

Google has tried typical hierarchical control systems typically found in large firms. However, the firm reverted to its interactive control system within weeks. All of Google's roughly 5,000 product developers work in teams of three engineers. Larger projects simply assemble several teams of three workers. Within teams, there is a rotating "über-tech leader" depending on the project. Engineers tend to work in more than one team and do not need permission to switch teams. According to Shona Brown, VP for operations, "If at all possible, we want people to commit to things rather than be assigned to things." At Google "employees don't need a lot of signoffs to try something new, but they won't get much in the way of resources until they've accumulated some positive user feedback."

Google's executives regularly review projects with project leaders and analyze data about projects. Google uses some of its own webpage ranking technology in the review of software and other business projects. Using their own employees as mini test markets, managers often solicit employee opinions and analyze usage patterns of new product features and technologies. This interactive control of corporate information allows Google to make faster decisions about its business, including:

- Compare performance of customer usage and feedback among all components of the Google business in real time.

- Quickly discover shortfalls before major problems arise.

Sources: Hamel, G. 2007. Break Free. *Fortune*, October 1, 156(7): 119–126; Iyer, B. and Davenport, T. 2008. Reverse Engineering Google's Innovation Machine. *Harvard Business Review*, April: 59–68; Pham, A. 2008. Google to End Virtual World, Lively, Launched by the Internet Giant Less Than Five Months Ago. *Los Angeles Times*, November 21: C3; and Helft, M. 2009. Google Ends Sale of Ads in Papers after 2 Years. *New York Times*, January 21: B3.

- Become aware of unexpected successes that have often led to innovations.

- Discontinue failing products and services in a timely manner to save the company money.

These manager meetings return significant rewards for Google. Innovations that have been implemented as a result of high information control include:

- Gmail, an email system that utilizes Google's core search features to help users organize and find email messages easily.

- Google News, a computer-generated news site that aggregates headlines from more than 4,500 English-language news sources worldwide, groups similar stories together, and displays them according to each reader's personalized interests.

- Google AdSense, a service that matches ads to a website's content and audience and operates on a revenue-sharing business model.

Google managers are able to quickly analyze user feedback and revenue data to discontinue projects that are not working out as originally intended. This information control allows managers to reallocate resources to more promising projects in a timely manner.

- Google Lively, a virtual world simulation, was launched and shut down after five months in 2008 after management determined that the service was not competitive.

- Google Print Ads, Google's automated method of selling ads through auctions to the newspaper industry, was terminated in early 2009 when managers analyzed the data and determined that the revenue stream was negligible compared to the costs of the program.

>LO4

The benefits of having the proper balance among the three levers of behavioral control: culture, rewards and incentives, and boundaries.

Attaining Behavioral Control: Balancing Culture, Rewards, and Boundaries

Behavioral control is focused on implementation—doing things right. Effectively implementing strategy requires manipulating three key control "levers": culture, rewards, and boundaries (see Exhibit 9.3). There are two compelling reasons for an increased emphasis on culture and rewards in a system of behavioral controls.

First, the competitive environment is increasingly complex and unpredictable, demanding both flexibility and quick response to its challenges. As firms simultaneously downsize and

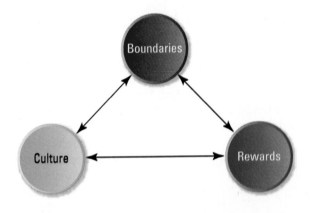

Exhibit 9.3 **Essential Elements of Behavioral Control**

face the need for increased coordination across organizational boundaries, a control system based primarily on rigid strategies, rules, and regulations is dysfunctional. The use of rewards and culture to align individual and organizational goals becomes increasingly important.

Second, the implicit long-term contract between the organization and its key employees has been eroded.[10] Today's younger managers have been conditioned to see themselves as "free agents" and view a career as a series of opportunistic challenges. As managers are advised to "specialize, market yourself, and have work, if not a job," the importance of culture and rewards in building organizational loyalty claims greater importance.

Each of the three levers—culture, rewards, and boundaries—must work in a balanced and consistent manner. Let's consider the role of each.

Building a Strong and Effective Culture

Organizational culture is a system of shared values (what is important) and beliefs (how things work) that shape a company's people, organizational structures, and control systems to produce behavioral norms (the way we do things around here).[11] How important is culture? Very. Over the years, numerous best sellers, such as *Theory Z, Corporate Cultures, In Search of Excellence,* and *Good to Great,* [12] have emphasized the powerful influence of culture on what goes on within organizations and how they perform.

Collins and Porras argued in *Built to Last* that the key factor in sustained exceptional performance is a cultlike culture.[13] You can't touch it or write it down, but it's there in every organization; its influence is pervasive; it can work for you or against you.[14] Effective leaders understand its importance and strive to shape and use it as one of their important levers of strategic control.[15]

The Role of Culture   Culture wears many different hats, each woven from the fabric of those values that sustain the organization's primary source of competitive advantage. Some examples are:

- Federal Express and Southwest Airlines focus on customer service.
- Lexus (a division of Toyota) and Hewlett-Packard emphasize product quality.
- Newell Rubbermaid and 3M place a high value on innovation.
- Nucor (steel) and Emerson Electric are concerned, above all, with operational efficiency.

Culture sets implicit boundaries—unwritten standards of acceptable behavior—in dress, ethical matters, and the way an organization conducts its business.[16] By creating a

organizational culture a system of shared values and beliefs that shape a company's people, organizational structures, and control systems to produce behavioral norms.

framework of shared values, culture encourages individual identification with the organization and its objectives. Culture acts as a means of reducing monitoring costs.[17]

Sustaining an Effective Culture   Powerful organizational cultures just don't happen overnight, and they don't remain in place without a strong commitment—both in terms of words and deeds—by leaders throughout the organization.[18] A viable and productive organizational culture can be strengthened and sustained. However, it cannot be "built" or "assembled"; instead, it must be cultivated, encouraged, and "fertilized."[19]

● 3M is well known for its innovative culture. The picture above shows Post-it Notes attached to a computer monitor.

Storytelling is one way effective cultures are maintained. Many are familiar with the story of how Art Fry's failure to develop a strong adhesive led to 3M's enormously successful Post-it Notes. Perhaps less familiar is the story of Francis G. Okie.[20] In 1922 Okie came up with the idea of selling sandpaper to men as a replacement for razor blades. The idea obviously didn't pan out, but Okie was allowed to remain at 3M. Interestingly, the technology developed by Okie led 3M to develop its first blockbuster product: a waterproof sandpaper that became a staple of the automobile industry. Such stories foster the importance of risk taking, experimentation, freedom to fail, and innovation—all vital elements of 3M's culture.

Rallies or "pep talks" by top executives also serve to reinforce a firm's culture. The late Sam Walton was known for his pep rallies at local Wal-Mart stores. Four times a year, the founders of Home Depot—former CEO Bernard Marcus and Arthur Blank—used to don orange aprons and stage Breakfast with Bernie and Arthur, a 6:30 a.m. pep rally, broadcast live over the firm's closed-circuit TV network to most of its 45,000 employees.[21]

Southwest Airlines' "Culture Committee" is a unique vehicle designed to perpetuate the company's highly successful culture. The following excerpt from an internal company publication describes its objectives:

The goal of the Committee is simple—to ensure that our unique Corporate Culture stays alive. . . . Culture Committee members represent all regions and departments across our system and they are selected based upon their exemplary display of the "Positively Outrageous Service" that won us the first-ever Triple Crown; their continual exhibition of the "Southwest Spirit" to our Customers and to their fellow workers; and their high energy level, boundless enthusiasm, unique creativity, and constant demonstration of teamwork and love for their fellow workers.[22]

Motivating with Rewards and Incentives

Reward and incentive systems represent a powerful means of influencing an organization's culture, focusing efforts on high-priority tasks, and motivating individual and collective task performance.[23] Just as culture deals with influencing beliefs, behaviors, and attitudes of people within an organization, the **reward system**—by specifying who gets rewarded and why—is an effective motivator and control mechanism.[24] Consider how John

reward system
policies that specify who gets rewarded and why.

Thompson, CEO of $11 billion software security firm Symantec, distributes financial rewards based on contribution:[25]

> When Thompson arrived at Symantec, any executive who was promoted to vice president automatically received a BMW. Senior management's bonuses were paid quarterly and were heavily skewed toward cash, not stock. Thompson says: "So if the stock didn't do well, they didn't care. We now have a stock option plan that is broad based but not universal. One of the things we recognized early on was that if we were going to grow at the rate that we were growing, we have to be more selective in who we gave options to so as not to dilute the value of our stock. And, the first thing we did was identify a range of employees who were valuable to the company but didn't need equity to come to work, and we focused their compensation around cash bonuses. Then we increased the equity we gave to the engineers and other people that were critical to our long-term success." By paying the two groups of people in a different manner, the new compensation scheme recognizes their distinctive importance.

The Potential Downside   Generally speaking, people in organizations act rationally, each motivated by their personal best interest.[26] However, the collective sum of individual behaviors of an organization's employees does not always result in what is best for the organization; individual rationality is no guarantee of organizational rationality.

As corporations grow and evolve, they often develop different business units with multiple reward systems. They may differ based on industry contexts, business situations, stage of product life cycles, and so on. Subcultures within organizations may reflect differences among functional areas, products, services, and divisions. To the extent that reward systems reinforce such behavioral norms, attitudes, and belief systems, cohesiveness is reduced; important information is hoarded rather than shared, individuals begin working at cross-purposes, and they lose sight of overall goals.

Such conflicts are commonplace in many organizations. For example, sales and marketing personnel promise unrealistically quick delivery times to bring in business, much to the dismay of operations and logistics; overengineering by R&D creates headaches for manufacturing; and so on. Conflicts also arise across divisions when divisional profits become a key compensation criterion. As ill will and anger escalate, personal relationships and performance may suffer.

Creating Effective Reward and Incentive Programs   To be effective, incentive and reward systems need to reinforce basic core values, enhance cohesion and commitment to goals and objectives, and meet with the organization's overall mission and purpose.[27]

At General Mills, to ensure a manager's interest in the overall performance of his or her unit, half of a manager's annual bonus is linked to business-unit results and half to individual performance.[28] For example, if a manager simply matches a rival manufacturer's performance, his or her salary is roughly 5 percent lower. However, if a manager's product ranks in the industry's top 10 percent in earnings growth and return on capital, the manager's total pay can rise to nearly 30 percent beyond the industry norm.

Effective reward and incentive systems share a number of common characteristics. (see Exhibit 9.4). The perception that a plan is "fair and equitable" is critically important. The firm must have the flexibility to respond to changing requirements as its direction and objectives change. In recent years many companies have begun to place more emphasis on growth. Emerson Electric has shifted its emphasis from cost cutting to growth. To ensure that changes take hold, the management compensation formula has been changed from a largely bottom-line focus to one that emphasizes growth, new products, acquisitions, and international expansion. Discussions about profits are handled separately, and a culture of risk taking is encouraged.[29]

Exhibit 9.4
Characteristics of
Effective Reward and
Evaluation Systems

- Objectives are clear, well understood, and broadly accepted.
- Rewards are clearly linked to performance and desired behaviors.
- Performance measures are clear and highly visible.
- Feedback is prompt, clear, and unambiguous.
- The compensation "system" is perceived as fair and equitable.
- The structure is flexible; it can adapt to changing circumstances.

Setting Boundaries and Constraints

In an ideal world, a strong culture and effective rewards should be sufficient to ensure that all individuals and subunits work toward the common goals and objectives of the whole organization.[30] However, this is not usually the case. Counterproductive behavior can arise because of motivated self-interest, lack of a clear understanding of goals and objectives, or outright malfeasance. **Boundaries and constraints** can serve many useful purposes for organizations, including:

boundaries and constraints
rules that specify behaviors that are acceptable and unacceptable.

- Focusing individual efforts on strategic priorities.
- Providing short-term objectives and action plans to channel efforts.
- Improving efficiency and effectiveness.
- Minimizing improper and unethical conduct.

Focusing Efforts on Strategic Priorities Boundaries and constraints play a valuable role in focusing a company's strategic priorities. A well-known example of a strategic boundary is Jack Welch's (former CEO of General Electric) demand that any business in the corporate portfolio be ranked first or second in its industry. Similarly, Eli Lilly has reduced its research efforts to five broad areas of disease, down from eight or nine a decade ago.[31] This concentration of effort and resources provides the firm with greater strategic focus and the potential for stronger competitive advantages in the remaining areas.

Norman Augustine, Lockheed Martin's former chairman, provided four criteria for selecting candidates for diversification into "closely related" businesses.[32] They must (1) be high tech, (2) be systems-oriented, (3) deal with large customers (either corporations or government) as opposed to consumers, and (4) be in growth businesses. Augustine said, "We have found that if we can meet most of those standards, then we can move into adjacent markets and grow."

Boundaries also have a place in the nonprofit sector. For example, a British relief organization uses a system to monitor strategic boundaries by maintaining a list of companies whose contributions it will neither solicit nor accept. Such boundaries are essential for maintaining legitimacy with existing and potential benefactors.

Providing Short-Term Objectives and Action Plans In Chapter 1 we discussed the importance of a firm having a vision, mission, and strategic objectives that are internally consistent and that provide strategic direction. In addition, short-term objectives and action plans provide similar benefits. That is, they represent boundaries that help to allocate resources in an optimal manner and to channel the efforts of employees at all levels throughout the organization.[33] To be effective, short-term objectives must have several attributes. They should:

- Be specific and measurable.
- Include a specific time horizon for their attainment.
- Be achievable, yet challenging enough to motivate managers who must strive to accomplish them.

Research has found that performance is enhanced when individuals are encouraged to attain specific, difficult, yet achievable, goals (as opposed to vague "do your best" goals).[34]

Short-term objectives must provide proper direction and also provide enough flexibility for the firm to keep pace with and anticipate changes in the external environment, new government regulations, a competitor introducing a substitute product, or changes in consumer taste. Unexpected events within a firm may require a firm to make important adjustments in both strategic and short-term objectives. The emergence of new industries can have a drastic effect on the demand for products and services in more traditional industries.

Action plans are critical to the implementation of chosen strategies. Unless action plans are specific, there may be little assurance that managers have thought through all of the resource requirements for implementing their strategies. In addition, unless plans are specific, managers may not understand what needs to be implemented or have a clear time frame for completion. This is essential for the scheduling of key activities that must be implemented. Finally, individual managers must be held accountable for the implementation. This helps to provide the necessary motivation and "sense of ownership" to implement action plans on a timely basis. Strategy Spotlight 9.3 illustrates how action plans fit into the mission statement and objectives of a small manufacturer of aircraft interior components. Exhibit 9.5 provides details of an action plan to fulfill one of the firm's objectives.

Improving Operational Efficiency and Effectiveness Rule-based controls are most appropriate in organizations with the following characteristics:

- Environments are stable and predictable.
- Employees are largely unskilled and interchangeable.
- Consistency in product and service is critical.
- The risk of malfeasance is extremely high (e.g., in banking or casino operations).[35]

McDonald's Corp. has extensive rules and regulations that regulate the operation of its franchises.[36] Its policy manual states, "Cooks must turn, never flip, hamburgers. If they haven't been purchased, Big Macs must be discarded in 10 minutes after being cooked and French fries in 7 minutes. Cashiers must make eye contact with and smile at every customer."

Guidelines can also be effective in setting spending limits and the range of discretion for employees and managers, such as the $2,500 limit that hotelier Ritz-Carlton uses to empower employees to placate dissatisfied customers. Regulations also can be initiated to improve the use of an employee's time at work.[37] Computer Associates restricts the use of e-mail during the hours of 10 a.m. to noon and 2 p.m. to 4 p.m. each day.[38]

Minimizing Improper and Unethical Conduct Guidelines can be useful in specifying proper relationships with a company's customers and suppliers.[39] Many companies have explicit rules regarding commercial practices, including the prohibition of any form of payment, bribe, or kickback. Cadbury Schweppes has followed a simple but effective step in controlling the use of bribes by specifying that all payments, no matter how unusual, are recorded on the company's books. Its former chairman, Sir Adrian Cadbury, contended that such a practice causes managers to pause and consider whether a payment is simply a bribe or a necessary and standard cost of doing business.[40]

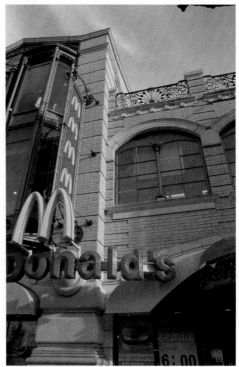

● McDonald's relies on extensive rules and regulations to maintain efficient operations at its restaurants.

Developing Meaningful Action Plans: Aircraft Interior Products, Inc.

MSA Aircraft Interior Products, Inc., is a manufacturing firm based in San Antonio, Texas, that was founded in 1983 by Mike Spraggins and Robert Plenge. The firm fulfills a small but highly profitable niche in the aviation industry with two key products. The Accordia line consists of patented, lightweight, self-contained window-shade assemblies. MSA's interior cabin shells are state-of-the-art assemblies that include window panels, side panels, headliners, and suspension system structures. MSA's products have been installed on a variety of aircraft, such as the Gulfstream series; the Cessna Citation; and Boeing's 727, 737, 757, and 707.

Much of MSA's success can be attributed to carefully articulated action plans consistent with the firm's mission and objectives. During the past five years, MSA has increased its sales at an annual rate of 15 to 18 percent. It has also succeeded in adding many prestigious companies to its customer base. Below are excerpts from MSA's mission statement and objectives as well as the action plans to achieve a 20 percent annual increase in sales.

Mission Statement

- Be recognized as an innovative and reliable supplier of quality interior products for the high-end, personalized transportation segments of the aviation, marine, and automotive industries.

- Design, develop, and manufacture interior fixtures and components that provide exceptional value to the customer through the development of innovative designs in a manner that permits decorative design flexibility while retaining the superior functionality, reliability, and maintainability of well-engineered, factory-produced products.

- Grow, be profitable, and provide a fair return, commensurate with the degree of risk, for owners and stockholders.

Objectives

1. Achieve sustained and profitable growth over the next three years:
   - 20 percent annual growth in revenues
   - 12 percent pretax profit margins
   - 18 percent return on shareholder's equity

2. Expand the company's revenues through the development and introduction of two or more new products capable of generating revenues in excess of $8 million a year by 2012.

3. Continue to aggressively expand market opportunities and applications for the Accordia line of window-shade assemblies, with the objective of sustaining or exceeding a 20 percent annual growth rate for at least the next three years.

Exhibit 9.5 details an "Action Plan" for Objective 3.

MSA's action plans are supported by detailed month-by-month budgets and strong financial incentives for its executives. Budgets are prepared by each individual department and include all revenue and cost items. Managers are motivated by their participation in a profit-sharing program, and the firm's two founders each receive a bonus equal to three percent of total sales.

Source: For purposes of confidentiality, some of the information presented in this spotlight has been disguised. We would like to thank company management and Joseph Picken, consultant, for providing us with the information used in this application.

Description	Primary Responsibility	Target Date
1. Develop and implement 2008 marketing plan, including specific plans for addressing Falcon 20 retrofit programs and expanded sales of cabin shells.	R. H. Plenge (V.P. Marketing)	December 15, 2009
2. Negotiate new supplier agreement with Gulfstream Aerospace.	M. Spraggins (President)	March 1, 2010
3. Continue and complete the development of the UltraSlim window and have a fully tested and documented design ready for production at a manufacturing cost of less than $900 per unit.	D. R. Pearson (V.P. Operations)	June 15, 2010
4. Develop a window design suitable for L-1011 and similar wide-body aircraft and have a fully tested and documented design ready for production at a manufacturing cost comparable to the current Boeing window.	D. R. Pearson (V.P. Operations)	September 15, 2010

Exhibit 9.5 Action Plan for Objective Number 3

Regulations backed up with strong sanctions can also help an organization avoid conducting business in an unethical manner. After the passing of the Sarbanes-Oxley Act (which provides for stiffer penalties for financial reporting misdeeds), many chief financial officers (CFOs) have taken steps to ensure ethical behavior in the preparation of financial statements. For example, Home Depot's CFO, Carol B. Tome, strengthened the firm's code of ethics and developed stricter guidelines. Now all 25 of her subordinates must sign personal statements that all of their financial statements are correct—just as she and her CEO, have to do now.[41]

Behavioral Control in Organizations: Situational Factors

Here, the focus is on ensuring that the behavior of individuals at all levels of an organization is directed toward achieving organizational goals and objectives. The three fundamental types of control are culture, rewards and incentives, and boundaries and constraints. An organization may pursue one or a combination of them on the basis of a variety of internal and external factors.

Not all organizations place the same emphasis on each type of control.[42] In high-technology firms engaged in basic research, members may work under high levels of autonomy. An individual's performance is generally quite difficult to measure accurately because of the long lead times involved in R&D activities. Thus, internalized norms and values become very important.

When the measurement of an individual's output or performance is quite straightforward, control depends primarily on granting or withholding rewards. Frequently, a sales manager's compensation is in the form of a commission and bonus tied directly to his or her sales volume, which is relatively easy to determine. Here, behavior is influenced more strongly by the attractiveness of the compensation than by the norms and values implicit in the organization's culture. The measurability of output precludes the need for an elaborate system of rules to control behavior.

Control in bureaucratic organizations is dependent on members following a highly formalized set of rules and regulations. Most activities are routine and the desired behavior can be specified in a detailed manner because there is generally little need for innovative or creative activity. Managing an assembly plant requires strict adherence to many rules as well as exacting sequences of assembly operations. In the public sector, the Department of Motor Vehicles in most states must follow clearly prescribed procedures when issuing or renewing driver licenses.

Exhibit 9.6 provides alternate approaches to behavioral control and some of the situational factors associated with them.

Evolving from Boundaries to Rewards and Culture

In most environments, organizations should strive to provide a system of rewards and incentives, coupled with a culture strong enough that boundaries become internalized. This reduces the need for external controls such as rules and regulations.

First, hire the right people—individuals who already identify with the organization's dominant values and have attributes consistent with them. We addressed this issue in Chapter 4; recall the "Bozo Filter" developed by Cooper Software. Microsoft's David Pritchard is well aware of the consequences of failing to hire properly.

> If I hire a bunch of bozos, it will hurt us, because it takes time to get rid of them. They start
> infiltrating the organization and then they themselves start hiring people of lower quality.
> At Microsoft, we are always looking for people who are better than we are.

Second, training plays a key role. For example, in elite military units such as the Green Berets and Navy SEALs, the training regimen so thoroughly internalizes the culture that individuals, in effect, lose their identity. The group becomes the overriding concern and focal point of their energies. At firms such as FedEx, training not only builds skills, but also plays a significant role in building a strong culture on the foundation of each organization's dominant values.

Exhibit 9.6
Organizational Control:
Alternative Approaches

Approach	Some Situational Factors
Culture: A system of unwritten rules that forms an internalized influence over behavior.	• Often found in professional organizations. • Associated with high autonomy. • Norms are the basis for behavior.
Rules: Written and explicit guidelines that provide external constraints on behavior.	• Associated with standardized output. • Tasks are generally repetitive and routine. • Little need for innovation or creative activity.
Rewards: The use of performance-based incentive systems to motivate.	• Measurement of output and performance is rather straightforward. • Most appropriate in organizations pursuing unrelated diversification strategies. • Rewards may be used to reinforce other means of control.

Third, managerial role models are vital. Andy Grove, former CEO and co-founder of Intel, didn't need (or want) a large number of bureaucratic rules to determine who is responsible for what, who is supposed to talk to whom, and who gets to fly first class (no one does). He encouraged openness by not having many of the trappings of success—he worked in a cubicle like all the other professionals. Can you imagine any new manager asking whether or not he can fly first class? Grove's personal example eliminated such a need.

Fourth, reward systems must be clearly aligned with the organizational goals and objectives. Where do you think rules and regulations are more important in controlling behavior—Home Depot, with its generous bonus and stock option plan, or Wal-Mart, which does not provide the same level of rewards and incentives?

The Role of Corporate Governance

We now address the issue of strategic control in a broader perspective, typically referred to as "corporate governance." Here we focus on the need for both shareholders (the owners of the corporation) and their elected representatives, the board of directors, to actively ensure that management fulfills its overriding purpose of increasing long-term shareholder value.[43]

Robert Monks and Nell Minow, two leading scholars in **corporate governance,** define it as "the relationship among various participants in determining the direction and performance of corporations. The primary participants are (1) the shareholders, (2) the management (led by the CEO), and (3) the board of directors."* Our discussion will center on how corporations can succeed (or fail) in aligning managerial motives with the interests of the shareholders and their elected representatives, the board of directors.[44] As you will recall from Chapter 1, we discussed the important role of boards of directors and provided some examples of effective and ineffective boards.[45]

corporate governance the relationship among various participants in determining the direction and performance of corporations. The primary participants are (1) the shareholders, (2) the management, and (3) the board of directors.

___

* Management cannot ignore the demands of other important firm stakeholders such as creditors, suppliers, customers, employees, and government regulators. At times of financial duress, powerful creditors can exert strong and legitimate pressures on managerial decisions. In general, however, the attention to stakeholders other than the owners of the corporation must be addressed in a manner that is still consistent with maximizing long-term shareholder returns. For a seminal discussion on stakeholder management, refer to Freeman, R. E. 1984. *Strategic Management: A Stakeholder Approach.* Boston: Pitman.

Good Corporate Governance and Performance: Research Evidence

Several studies found a positive relationship between the extent to which a firm practices good corporate governance and its performance outcomes. The results of two of these studies are summarized below.

Sources: Gill, A. 2001. Credit Lyonnais Securities (Asia). *Corporate Governance in Emerging Markets: Saints and Sinners*, April; and Low, C. K. 2002. *Corporate Governance: An Asia-Pacific Critique.* Hong Kong: Sweet & Maxwell Asia; Yu, L. 2008. Does Corporate Governance Matter? *MIT Sloan Management Review,* January 1: 49(2): 10; Abdullah, M., Shah, S., & Hassan, A. 2008. Impact of Corporate Governance on Financial Performance of Firms: Evidence from Pakistan. *Business Review, Cambridge,* December 1: 11(2): 282–289; Jermias, J. 2007. The Effects of Corporate Governance on the Relationship between Innovative Efforts and Performance. *European Accounting Review,* 16(4): 827–854.

1. *A strong correlation between corporate governance and price performance of large companies.* Over a recent three-year period, the average return of large capitalized firms with the best governance practices was more than five times higher than the performance of firms in the bottom corporate governance quartile.

2. *Across emerging markets.* In 10 of the 11 Asian and Latin American markets, companies in the top corporate governance quartile for their respective regions had a significantly higher (averaging 10 percentage points) return on capital employed (ROCE) than their market sample. In 12 of the emerging markets analyzed, companies in the lowest corporate governance quartile had a lower ROCE than the market average.

Good corporate governance plays an important role in the investment decisions of major institutions, and a premium is often reflected in the price of securities of companies that practice it. The corporate governance premium is larger for firms in countries with sound corporate governance practices compared to countries with weaker corporate governance standards.[46] There is a strong correlation between strong corporate governance and superior financial performance (see Strategy Spotlight 9.4).

At the same time, few topics in the business press are generating as much interest (and disdain!) as corporate governance.

Some recent notable examples of flawed corporate governance include:[47]

- Satyam Computer Services, a leading Indian outsourcing company that serves more than a third of the Fortune 500 companies, significantly inflated its earnings and assets for years. The chairman, Ramalinga Raju, resigned and admitted he had cooked the books. Mr. Raju said he had overstated cash on hand by $1 billion and inflated profits and revenues in the September 2008 quarter. Satyam shares sank 78 percent, and the benchmark Sensex index lost 7.3 percent that day (January 7, 2009).

- Former Brocade CEO Gregory Reyes was sentenced to 21 months in prison and fined $15 million for his involvement in backdating stock option grants. Mr. Reyes was the first executive to go on trial and be convicted over the improper dating of stock-option awards, which dozens of companies have acknowledged since the practice came to light (January 17, 2008).

- Hewlett-Packard admitted that outside investigators, led by Chairman Patricia Dunn, used a potentially illegal tactic in which they impersonated directors, journalists, and two employees to obtain personal phone records. Dunn resigned (September 12, 2006).

- Walter Forbes, former chairman of Cendant Corp. (now known as Avis Budget Group, Inc.), was sentenced to 12 years in prison and ordered to pay $3.3 billion in one of America's biggest accounting scandals. He oversaw a decade-long accounting scheme that overstated income. He was convicted on one count of conspiracy and two counts of false reporting (January 17, 2006).

- Board members of Nortel Networks meet with governance-minded investors to discuss possible changes to the board. This is after 10 executives and accounting officials are fired for artificially boosting the company's 2003 financial results (September 30, 2004).

Because of the many lapses in corporate governance, we can see the benefits associated with effective practices.[48] However, corporate managers may behave in their own self-interest, often to the detriment of shareholders. Next we address the implications of the separation of ownership and management in the modern corporation, and some mechanisms that can be used to ensure consistency (or alignment) between the interests of shareholders and those of the managers to minimize potential conflicts.

The Modern Corporation: The Separation of Owners (Shareholders) and Management

Some of the proposed definitions for a *corporation* include:

- "The business corporation is an instrument through which capital is assembled for the activities of producing and distributing goods and services and making investments. Accordingly, a basic premise of corporation law is that a business corporation should have as its objective the conduct of such activities with a view to enhancing the corporation's profit and the gains of the corporation's owners, that is, the shareholders." (Melvin Aron Eisenberg, *The Structure of Corporation Law*)
- "A body of persons granted a charter legally recognizing them as a separate entity having its own rights, privileges, and liabilities distinct from those of its members." (*American Heritage Dictionary*)
- "An ingenious device for obtaining individual profit without individual responsibility." (Ambrose Bierce, *The Devil's Dictionary*)[49]

All of these definitions have some validity and each one reflects a key feature of the corporate form of business organization— its ability to draw resources from a variety of groups and establish and maintain its own persona that is separate from all of them. As Henry Ford once said, "A great business is really too big to be human."

Simply put, a **corporation** is a mechanism created to allow different parties to contribute capital, expertise, and labor for the maximum benefit of each party.[50] The shareholders (investors) are able to participate in the profits of the enterprise without taking direct responsibility for the operations. The management can run the company without the responsibility of personally providing the funds. The shareholders have limited liability as well as rather limited involvement in the company's affairs. However, they reserve the right to elect directors who have the fiduciary obligation to protect their interests.

Over 70 years ago, Columbia University professors Adolf Berle and Gardiner C. Means addressed the divergence of the interests of the owners of the corporation from the professional managers who are hired to run it. They warned that widely dispersed ownership "released management from the overriding requirement that it serve stockholders." The separation of ownership from management has given rise to a set of ideas called "agency theory." Central to agency theory is the relationship between two primary players—the *principals* who are the owners of the firm (stockholders) and the *agents,* who are the people paid by principals to perform a job on their behalf (management). The stockholders elect and are represented by a board of directors that has a fiduciary responsibility to ensure that management acts in the best interests of stockholders to ensure long-term financial returns for the firm.

Agency theory is concerned with resolving two problems that can occur in agency relationships.[51] *The first is the agency problem that arises (1) when the goals of the principals and agents conflict, and (2) when it is difficult or expensive for the principal to*

corporation a mechanism created to allow different parties to contribute capital, expertise, and labor for the maximum benefit of each party.

agency theory a theory of the relationship between principals and their agents, with emphasis on two problems: (1) the conflicting goals of principals and agents, along with the difficulty of principals to monitor the agents, and (2) the different attitudes and preferences towards risk of principals and agents.

verify what the agent is actually doing. The board of directors would be unable to confirm that the managers were actually acting in the shareholders' interests because managers are "insiders" with regard to the businesses they operate and thus are better informed than the principals. Thus, managers may act "opportunistically" in pursuing their own interests—to the detriment of the corporation.[52] Managers may spend corporate funds on expensive perquisites (e.g., company jets and expensive art), devote time and resources to pet projects (initiatives in which they have a personal interest but that have limited market potential), engage in power struggles (where they may fight over resources for their own betterment and to the detriment of the firm), and negate (or sabotage) attractive merger offers because they may result in increased employment risk.[53]

The second issue is the problem of risk sharing. This arises when the principal and the agent have different attitudes and preferences toward risk. The executives in a firm may favor additional diversification initiatives because, by their very nature, they increase the size of the firm and thus the level of executive compensation.[54] At the same time, such diversification initiatives may erode shareholder value because they fail to achieve some synergies that we discussed in Chapter 6 (e.g., building on core competencies, sharing activities, or enhancing market power). Agents (executives) may have a stronger preference toward diversification than shareholders because it reduces their personal level of risk from potential loss of employment. Executives who have large holdings of stock in their firms were more likely to have diversification strategies that were more consistent with shareholder interests—increasing long-term returns.[55] At times, top-level managers engage in actions that reflect their self-interest rather than the interests of shareholders (see Strategy Spotlight 9.5).

Governance Mechanisms: Aligning the Interests of Owners and Managers

>LO6
The role of corporate governance mechanisms in ensuring that the interests of managers are aligned with those of shareholders from both the United States and international perspectives.

As noted above, a key characteristic of the modern corporation is the separation of ownership from control. To minimize the potential for managers to act in their own self-interest, or "opportunistically," the owners can implement some governance mechanisms.[56] First, there are two primary means of monitoring the behavior of managers. These include (1) a committed and involved *board of directors* that acts in the best interests of the shareholders to create long-term value and (2) *shareholder activism,* wherein the owners view themselves as share*owners* instead of share*holders* and become actively engaged in the governance of the corporation. Finally, there are managerial incentives, sometimes called "contract-based outcomes," which consist of *reward and compensation agreements.* Here the goal is to carefully craft managerial incentive packages to align the interests of management with those of the stockholders.[57]

A Committed and Involved Board of Directors
The **board of directors** acts as a fulcrum between the owners and controllers of a corporation. They are the intermediaries who provide a balance between a small group of key managers in the firm based at the corporate headquarters and a sometimes vast group of shareholders. In the United States, the law imposes on the board a strict and absolute fiduciary duty to ensure that a company is run consistent with the long-term interests of the owners—the shareholders. The reality, as we have seen, is somewhat more ambiguous.[58]

The Business Roundtable, representing the largest U.S. corporations, describes the duties of the board as follows:

1. Select, regularly evaluate, and, if necessary, replace the CEO. Determine management compensation. Review succession planning.
2. Review and, where appropriate, approve the financial objectives, major strategies, and plans of the corporation.

board of directors
a group that has a fiduciary duty to ensure that the company is run consistently with the long-term interests of the owners, or shareholders, of a corporation and that acts as an intermediary between the shareholders and management.

strategy spotlight

9.5

Crony Capitalism: Several Examples

When President George W. Bush signed the Sarbanes-Oxley Act into law on July 30, 2002, one of its goals was to prevent the kind of self-dealing and other conflicts of interest that had brought down Enron, WorldCom, Adelphia, and other corporate giants. Among other things, the Sarbanes-Oxley Act bans company loans to executives and prohibits extending the terms of existing loans.

Many companies, however, acted quickly *before* the bill was signed. For example, *one day* before the bill was signed, Crescent Real Estate Equities of Fort Worth, Texas, extended the payback deadline by 10 years on a loan of $26 million to its chief executive, John Goff. And Electronic Arts gave a $4 million loan to Warren Johnson, its chief financial officer, admitting in a filing that it was doing so a month prior to the "prohibition on loans to executive officers."

Despite legislation such as Sarbanes-Oxley and pressures from shareholders, related-party deals are quite common. According to the Corporate Library, a research group in Portland, Maine, 75 percent of 2,000 companies that were studied still engage in them. In essence, that means that companies must make embarrassing disclosures in their proxy statements about nepotism, property leased from top managers, corporate-owned apartments, and other forms of "insiderism."

Consider some examples:

- Two hundred companies have leased or bought airplanes from insiders. For example, Pilgrim's Pride of Pittsburg, Texas, a chicken processor with

$2.6 billion in annual sales has leased an airplane from its chief executive and founder Lonnie Pilgrim since 1985. Mr. Pilgrim made $656,000 in fiscal 2003 from this deal to go along with his $1.7 million in compensation. The company defends the pact as cost-efficient since its headquarters is located in a small town. Pilgrim also provides some bookkeeping services for his personal businesses, but he won't provide details.

- Micky M. Arison is chief executive of Carnival, the big cruise line. He is also chief executive and owner of the Miami Heat of the National Basketball Association. Carnival paid the Heat $675,000 in fiscal 2002 and 2003 for sponsorship and advertising as well as season tickets. Although that may be a rather small sum, given Carnival's $2.2 billion in net income for the period, we could still ask if the money would have been spent on something else if Arison didn't own the team.

- Alliance Semiconductor CEO N. Damodar Reddy has committed $20 million to Solar Ventures, a venture capital company run by his brother C. N. Reddy. Other unnamed insiders purchased undisclosed stakes in Solar. However, Alliance won't disclose whether its CEO is one of them. To date it has invested $12.5 million in Solar. Beth Young, senior research associate of the Corporate Library poses an interesting question: "Is Reddy using shareholder capital just to keep afloat his brother's fund and the insiders' investment?"

Source: MacDonald, E. 2004. Crony Capitalism. *Forbes*, June 21: 140–146.

---

3. Provide advice and counsel to top management.
4. Select and recommend to shareholders for election an appropriate slate of candidates for the board of directors; evaluate board processes and performance.
5. Review the adequacy of the systems to comply with all applicable laws/regulations.[59]

Given these principles, what makes for a good board of directors?[60] According to the Business Roundtable, the most important quality is a board of directors who are active, critical participants in determining a company's strategies.[61] That does not mean board members should micromanage or circumvent the CEO. Rather, they should provide strong oversight going beyond simply approving the CEO's plans. A board's primary responsibilities are to ensure that strategic plans undergo rigorous scrutiny, evaluate managers against high performance standards, and take control of the succession process.

Although boards in the past were often dismissed as CEO's rubber stamps, increasingly they are playing a more active role by forcing out CEOs who cannot deliver on performance.[62] According to the consulting firm Booz Allen Hamilton, the rate of CEO departures for performance reasons has more than tripled, from 1.3 percent to 4.2 percent, between 1995 and 2002.[63] In 2006, turnover among CEOs increased 30 percent over the previous year.[64] Well-known CEOs like Gerald M. Levin of AOL Time Warner and Jack M. Greenberg of McDonald's paid the price for poor financial performance by being forced to leave. Others, such as Bernard Ebbers of WorldCom, Inc., and Dennis Kozlowski of Tyco International, lost their jobs due to scandals. "Deliver or depart" is clearly the new message from the boards.

Another key component of top-ranked boards is director independence.[65] Governance experts believe that a majority of directors should be free of all ties to either the CEO or the company.[66] That means a minimum of "insiders" (past or present members of the management team) should serve on the board, and that directors and their firms should be barred from doing consulting, legal, or other work for the company.[67] Interlocking directorships—in which CEOs and other top managers serve on each other's boards—are not desirable. But perhaps the best guarantee that directors act in the best interests of shareholders is the simplest: Most good companies now insist that directors own significant stock in the company they oversee.[68]

Such guidelines are not always followed. At times, the practices of the boards of directors are the antithesis of such guidelines. Consider the Walt Disney Co. Over a five-year period, former CEO Michael Eisner pocketed an astonishing $531 million. He likely had very little resistance from his board of directors:

> Many investors view the Disney board as an anachronism. Among Disney's 16 directors is Eisner's personal attorney—who for several years was chairman of the company's compensation committee! There was also the architect who designed Eisner's Aspen home and his parents' apartment. Joining them are the principal of an elementary school once attended by his children and the president of a university to which Eisner donated $1 million. The board also includes the actor Sidney Poitier, seven current and former Disney executives, and an attorney who does business with Disney. Moreover, most of the outside directors own little or no Disney stock. "It is an egregiously bad board—a train wreck waiting to happen," warns Michael L. Useem, a management professor at the University of Pennsylvania's Wharton School.[69]

This example also shows that "outside directors" are only beneficial to strong corporate governance if they are vigilant in carrying out their responsibilities.[70] As humorously suggested by Warren Buffett, founder and chairman of Berkshire Hathaway: "The ratcheting up of compensation has been obscene. . . . There is a tendency to put cocker spaniels on compensation committees, not Doberman pinschers."[71]

Many firms do have exemplary board practices. Below we list some of the excellent practices at Intel Corp., the world's largest semiconductor chip manufacturer, with $35 billion in revenues:[72]

- *Mix of inside and outside directors.* The board believes that there should be a majority of independent directors on the board. However, the board is willing to have members of management, in addition to the CEO, as directors.
- *Board presentations and access to employees.* The board encourages management to schedule managers to be present at meetings who: (1) can provide additional insight into the items being discussed because of personal involvement in these areas, or (2) have future potential that management believes should be given exposure to the board.
- *Formal evaluation of officers.* The Compensation Committee conducts, and reviews with the outside directors, an annual evaluation to help determine the salary and executive bonus of all officers, including the chief executive officer.

Exhibit 9.7 shows how boards of directors can improve their practices.

Exhibit 9.7
Best Practice Ideas: The New Rules for Directors

Issue	Suggestion
Pay	**Know the Math**
Companies will disclose full details of CEO payouts. Activist investors are already drawing up hit lists of companies where CEO paychecks are out of line with performance.	Before okaying any financial package, directors must make sure they can explain the numbers. They need to adopt the mindset of an activist investor and ask: What's the harshest criticism someone could make about this package?
Strategy	**Make It a Priority**
Boards have been so focused on compliance that duties like strategy and leadership oversight too often get ignored. Only 59 percent of directors in a recent study rated their board favorably on setting strategy	To avoid spending too much time on compliance issues, move strategy up to the beginning of the meeting. Annual one-, two- or three-day offsite meetings on strategy alone are becoming standard for good boards.
Financials	**Put in the Time**
Although 95 percent of directors in the recent study said they were doing a good job of monitoring financials, the number of earnings restatements hit a new high in 2006, after breaking records in 2004 and 2005.	Even nonfinancial board members need to monitor the numbers and keep a close eye on cash flows. Audit committee members should prepare to spend 300 hours a year on committee responsibilities.
Crisis Management	**Dig in**
Some 120 companies are under scrutiny for options backdating, and the 100 largest companies have replaced 56 CEOs in the past five years—nearly double the terminations in the prior five years.	The increased scrutiny on boards means that a perfunctory review will not suffice if a scandal strikes. Directors can no longer afford to defer to management in a crisis. They must roll up their sleeves and move into watchdog mode.

Source: Byrnes, N. & Sassen, J. 2007. Board of Hard Knocks. *BusinessWeek.* January 22: 36–39.

Shareholder Activism   As a practical matter, there are so many owners of the largest American corporations that it makes little sense to refer to them as "owners" in the sense of individuals becoming informed and involved in corporate affairs.[73] However, even an individual shareholder has several rights, including (1) the right to sell the stock, (2) the right to vote the proxy (which includes the election of board members), (3) the right to bring suit for damages if the corporation's directors or managers fail to meet their obligations, (4) the right to certain information from the company, and (5) certain residual rights following the company's liquidation (or its filing for reorganization under bankruptcy laws), once creditors and other claimants are paid off.[74]

Collectively, shareholders have the power to direct the course of corporations.[75] This may involve acts such as being party to shareholder action suits and demanding that key issues be brought up for proxy votes at annual board meetings.[76] The power of shareholders has intensified in recent years because of the increasing influence of large institutional investors such as mutual funds (e.g., T. Rowe Price and Fidelity Investments) and retirement systems such as TIAA-CREF (for university faculty members and school administrative staff).[77] Institutional investors hold approximately 50 percent of all listed corporate stock in the United States.[78]

Shareholder activism refers to actions by large shareholders, both institutions and individuals, to protect their interests when they feel that managerial actions diverge from shareholder value maximization.

Many institutional investors are aggressive in protecting and enhancing their investments. They are shifting from traders to owners. They are assuming the role of permanent shareholders and rigorously analyzing issues of corporate governance. In the process they are reinventing systems of corporate monitoring and accountability.[79]

Consider the proactive behavior of CalPERS, the California Public Employees' Retirement System, which manages over $200 billion in assets and is the third largest pension fund in the world. Every year CalPERS reviews the performance of U.S. companies in its stock portfolio and identifies those that are among the lowest long-term relative performers and have governance structures that do not ensure full accountability to company owners. This generates a long list of companies, each of which may potentially be publicly identified as a CalPERS "Focus Company"—corporations to which CalPERS directs specific suggested governance reforms. CalPERS meets with the directors of each of these companies to discuss performance and governance issues. The CalPERS Focus List contains those companies that continue to merit public and market attention at the end of the process.

The CalPERS 2008 Focus List singled out four U.S. companies for poor financial and corporate governance.[80] Firms on the list were: *Cheesecake Factory Incorporated* of Calabasas Hills, California; *Hilb Rogal & Hobbs Company* of Glen Allen, Virginia; *Invacare Corporation* of Elyria, Ohio; *La-Z-Boy* of Monroe, Michigan; and *Standard Pacific Corporation* of Irvine, California. A few of CalPERS's concerns:

- Cheesecake Factory, an operator of upscale, full-service, casual dining restaurants, suffers from declining same-store performance and a lack of board accountability to shareholders. The board would not agree to seek shareholder approval to remove the company's 80 percent supermajority voting requirements to amend its corporate bylaws. It has performed well below its peer group for the past five years.
- La-Z-Boy, a manufacturer and marketer of upholstered furniture, has severely underperformed relative to both market indices and its peer group for the past five years. It also lacks board accountability in refusing to remove its classified or "staggered" board structure.

While appearing punitive to company management, such aggressive activism has paid significant returns for CalPERS (and other stockholders of the "Focused" companies). A Wilshire Associates study of the "CalPERS Effect" of corporate governance examined the performance of 62 targets over a five-year period: while the stock of these companies trailed the Standard & Poor's Index by 89 percent in the five-year period before CalPERS acted, the same stocks outperformed the index by 23 percent in the following five years, adding approximately $150 million annually in additional returns to the fund.

Perhaps no discussion of shareholder activism would be complete without mention of Carl Icahn, a famed activist with a personal net worth of about $13 billion:

> The bogeyman I am now chasing is the structure of American corporations, which permit managements and boards to rule arbitrarily and too often receive egregious compensation even after doing a subpar job. Yet they remain accountable to no one.[81]

Managerial Rewards and Incentives　As we discussed earlier in the chapter, incentive systems must be designed to help a company achieve its goals.[82] From the perspective of governance, one of the most critical roles of the board of directors is to create incentives that align the interests of the CEO and top executives with the interests of owners of the corporation—long-term shareholder returns.[83] Shareholders rely on CEOs to adopt policies and strategies that maximize the value of their shares.[84] A combination of three basic policies may create the right monetary incentives for CEOs to maximize the value of their companies:[85]

1. Boards can require that the CEOs become substantial owners of company stock.
2. Salaries, bonuses, and stock options can be structured so as to provide rewards for superior performance and penalties for poor performance.
3. Threat of dismissal for poor performance can be a realistic outcome.

In recent years the granting of stock options has enabled top executives of publicly held corporations to earn enormous levels of compensation. In 2007, the average CEO in the Standard & Poor's 500 stock index took home 433 times the pay of the average worker—up from 40 times the average in 1980. The counterargument, that the ratio is down from the 514 multiple in 2000, doesn't get much traction.[86] It has been estimated that there could be as many as 50 or more companies with CEO pay packages over $150 million.[87]

Many boards have awarded huge option grants despite poor executive performance, and others have made performance goals easier to reach. In 2002 nearly 200 companies swapped or repriced options—all to enrich wealthy executives who are already among the country's richest people. However, stock options can be a valuable governance mechanism to align the CEO's interests with those of the shareholders. The extraordinarily high level of compensation can, at times, be grounded in sound governance principles.[88] For example, Howard Solomon, CEO of Forest Laboratories, received total compensation of $148.5 million in 2001.[89] This represented $823,000 in salary, $400,000 in bonus, and $147.3 million in stock options that were exercised. However, shareholders also did well, receiving gains of 40 percent. The firm has enjoyed spectacular growth over the past ten years, and Solomon has been CEO since 1977. Thus, huge income is attributed largely to gains that have built up over many years. As stated by compensation committee member Dan Goldwasser, "If a CEO is delivering substantial increases in shareholder value, . . . it's only appropriate that he be rewarded for it."

However, the "pay for performance" principle doesn't always hold.[90] In addition to the granting of stock options, boards of directors are often failing to fulfill their fiduciary responsibilities to shareholders when they lower the performance targets that executives need to meet in order to receive millions of dollars. At Ford, for example, its "profit" goal for 2007 was to *lose* $4.9 billion. Ford beat the target, however, and lost *only* $3.9 billion. CEO Alan Mulally was rewarded $12 million in compensation, including a $7 million bonus for exceeding the profit goal. Ford's stock price fell 10 percent in 2007.

TIAA-CREF has provided several principles of corporate governance with regard to executive compensation (see Exhibit 9.8).[91] These include the importance of aligning the rewards of all employees—rank and file as well as executives—to the long-term performance of the corporation; general guidelines on the role of cash compensation, stock, and "fringe benefits"; and the mission of a corporation's compensation committee.[92]

external governance control mechanisms methods that ensure that managerial actions lead to shareholder value maximization and do not harm other stakeholder groups and that are outside the control of the corporate governance system.

External Governance Control Mechanisms

Thus far, we've discussed internal governance mechanisms. Internal controls, however, are not always enough to ensure good governance. The separation of ownership and control that we discussed earlier requires multiple control mechanisms, some internal and some external, to ensure that managerial actions lead to shareholder value maximization. Further, society-at-large wants some assurance that this goal is met without harming other stakeholder groups. Now we discuss several **external governance control mechanisms** that have developed in most modern economies. These include the market for corporate control, auditors, governmental regulatory bodies, banks and analysts, media, and public activists.

Stock-based compensation plans are a critical element of most compensation programs and can provide opportunities for managers whose efforts contribute to the creation of shareholder wealth. In evaluating the suitability of these plans, considerations of reasonableness, scale, linkage to performance, and fairness to shareholders and all employees also apply. TIAA-CREF, the largest pension system in the world, has set forth the following guidelines for stock-based compensation. Proper stock-based plans should:

- Allow for creation of executive wealth that is reasonable in view of the creation of shareholder wealth. Management should not prosper through stock while shareholders suffer.

- Have measurable and predictable outcomes that are directly linked to the company's performance.

- Be market oriented, within levels of comparability for similar positions in companies of similar size and business focus.

- Be straightforward and clearly described so that investors and employees can understand them.

- Be fully disclosed to the investing public and be approved by shareholders.

Source: www.tiaa-cref.org/pubs.

The Market for Corporate Control   Let us assume for a moment that internal control mechanisms in a company are failing. This means that the board is ineffective in monitoring managers and is not exercising the oversight required of them and that shareholders are passive and are not taking any actions to monitor or discipline managers. Under these circumstances managers may behave opportunistically.[93] Opportunistic behavior can take many forms. First, they can *shirk* their responsibilities. Shirking means that managers fail to exert themselves fully, as is required of them. Second, they can engage in *on the job consumption.* Examples of on the job consumption include private jets, club memberships, expensive artwork in the offices, and so on. Each of these represents consumption by managers that does not in any way increase shareholder value. Instead, they actually diminish shareholder value. Third, managers may engage in *excessive product-market diversification.*[94] As we discussed in Chapter 6, such diversification serves to reduce only the employment risk of the managers rather than the financial risk of the shareholders, who can more cheaply diversify their risk by owning a portfolio of investments. Is there any external mechanism to stop managers from shirking, consumption on the job, and excessive diversification?

The **market for corporate control** is one external mechanism that provides at least some partial solution to the problems described. If internal control mechanisms fail and the management is behaving opportunistically, the likely response of most shareholders will be to sell their stock rather than engage in activism.[95] As more stockholders vote with their feet, the value of the stock begins to decline. As the decline continues, at some point the market value of the firm becomes less than the book value. A corporate raider can take over the company for a price less than the book value of the assets of the company. The first thing that the raider may do on assuming control over the company will be to fire the underperforming management. The risk of being acquired by a hostile raider is often referred to as the **takeover constraint.** The takeover constraint deters management from engaging in opportunistic behavior.[96]

Although in theory the takeover constraint is supposed to limit managerial opportunism, in recent years its effectiveness has become diluted as a result of a number of

market for corporate control an external control mechanism in which shareholders dissatisfied with a firm's management sell their shares.

takeover constraint the risk to management of the firm being acquired by a hostile raider.

defense tactics adopted by incumbent management (see Chapter 6). Foremost among them are poison pills, greenmail, and golden parachutes. Poison pills are provisions adopted by the company to reduce its worth to the acquirer. An example would be payment of a huge one-time dividend, typically financed by debt. Greenmail involves buying back the stock from the acquirer, usually at an attractive premium. Golden parachutes are employment contracts that cause the company to pay lucrative severance packages to top managers fired as a result of a takeover, often running to several million dollars.

Auditors   Even when there are stringent disclosure requirements, there is no guarantee that the information disclosed will be accurate. Managers may deliberately disclose false information or withhold negative financial information as well as use accounting methods that distort results based on highly subjective interpretations. Therefore, all accounting statements are required to be audited and certified to be accurate by external auditors. These auditing firms are independent organizations staffed by certified professionals who verify the firm's books of accounts. Audits can unearth financial irregularities and ensure that financial reporting by the firm conforms to standard accounting practices.

Recent developments leading to the bankruptcy of firms such as Enron and World-Com and a spate of earnings restatements raise questions about the failure of the auditing firms to act as effective external control mechanisms. Why did an auditing firm like Arthur Andersen, with decades of good reputation in the auditing profession at stake, fail to raise red flags about accounting irregularities? First, auditors are appointed by the firm being audited. The desire to continue that business relationship sometimes makes them overlook financial irregularities. Second, most auditing firms also do consulting work and often have lucrative consulting contracts with the firms that they audit. Understandably, some of them tend not to ask too many difficult questions, because they fear jeopardizing the consulting business, which is often more profitable than the auditing work.

The recent restatement of earnings by Xerox is an example of the lack of independence of auditing firms. The SEC filed a lawsuit against KPMG, the world's third largest accounting firm, in January 2003 for allowing Xerox to inflate its revenues by $3 billion between 1997 and 2000. Of the $82 million that Xerox paid KPMG during those four years, only $26 million was for auditing. The rest was for consulting services. When one of the auditors objected to Xerox's practice of booking revenues for equipment leases earlier than it should have, Xerox asked KPMG to replace him. It did.[97]

Banks and Analysts   Commercial and investment banks have lent money to corporations and therefore have to ensure that the borrowing firm's finances are in order and that the loan covenants are being followed. Stock analysts conduct ongoing in-depth studies of the firms that they follow and make recommendations to their clients to buy, hold, or sell. Their rewards and reputation depend on the quality of these recommendations. Their access to information, knowledge of the industry and the firm, and the insights they gain from interactions with the management of the company enable them to alert the investing community of both positive and negative developments relating to a company.

It is generally observed that analyst recommendations are often more optimistic than warranted by facts. "Sell" recommendations tend to be exceptions rather than the norm. Many analysts failed to grasp the gravity of the problems surrounding failed companies such as Enron and Global Crossing till the very end. Part of the explanation may lie in the fact that most analysts work for firms that also have investment banking relationships with the companies they follow. Negative recommendations by analysts can displease the management, who may decide to take their investment banking business to a rival firm. Otherwise independent and competent analysts may be pressured to overlook negative information or tone down their criticism. A recent settlement between the Securities and Exchange Commission and the New York State Attorney General with 10 banks requires them to pay $1.4 billion in penalties and to fund independent research for investors.[98]

Regulatory Bodies   The extent of government regulation is often a function of the type of industry. Banks, utilities, and pharmaceuticals are subject to more regulatory oversight because of their importance to society. Public corporations are subject to more regulatory requirements than private corporations.[99]

All public corporations are required to disclose a substantial amount of financial information by bodies such as the Securities and Exchange Commission. These include quarterly and annual filings of financial performance, stock trading by insiders, and details of executive compensation packages. There are two primary reasons behind such requirements. First, markets can operate efficiently only when the investing public has faith in the market system. In the absence of disclosure requirements, the average investor suffers from a lack of reliable information and therefore may completely stay away from the capital market. This will negatively impact an economy's ability to grow. Second, disclosure of information such as insider trading protects the small investor to some extent from the negative consequences of information asymmetry. The insiders and large investors typically have more information than the small investor and can therefore use that information to buy or sell before the information becomes public knowledge.

The failure of a variety of external control mechanisms led the U.S. Congress to pass the Sarbanes-Oxley Act in 2002. This act calls for many stringent measures that would ensure better governance of U.S. corporations. Some of these measures include:[100]

- *Auditors* are barred from certain types of nonaudit work. They are not allowed to destroy records for five years. Lead partners auditing a client should be changed at least every five years.
- *CEOs* and *CFOs* must fully reveal off-balance-sheet finances and vouch for the accuracy of the information revealed.
- *Executives* must promptly reveal the sale of shares in firms they manage and are not allowed to sell when other employees cannot.
- *Corporate lawyers* must report to senior managers any violations of securities law lower down.

Strategy Spotlight 9.6 discusses some of the expenses that companies have incurred in complying with the Sarbanes-Oxley Act.

Media and Public Activists   The press is not usually recognized as an external control mechanism in the literature on corporate governance. There is no denying that in all developed capitalist economies, the financial press and media play an important indirect role in monitoring the management of public corporations. In the United States, business magazines such as *BusinessWeek* and *Fortune,* financial newspapers such as *The Wall Street Journal* and *Investors Business Daily,* as well as television networks like Financial News Network and CNBC are constantly reporting on companies. Public perceptions about a company's financial prospects and the quality of its management are greatly influenced by the media. Food Lion's reputation was sullied when ABC's *Prime Time Live* in 1992 charged the company with employee exploitation, false package dating, and unsanitary meat handling practices. Bethany McLean of *Fortune* magazine is often credited as the first to raise questions about Enron's long-term financial viability.[101]

Similarly, consumer groups and activist individuals often take a crusading role in exposing corporate malfeasance. Well-known examples include Ralph Nader and Erin Brockovich, who played important roles in bringing to light the safety issues related to GM's Corvair and environmental pollution issues concerning Pacific Gas and Electric Company, respectively. Ralph Nader has created over 30 watchdog groups including:[102]

- *Aviation Consumer Action Project.* Works to propose new rules to prevent flight delays, impose penalties for deceiving passengers about problems, and push for higher compensation for lost luggage.

Governance Reform: The Costs Add Up

In the aftermath of Enron and WorldCom and a spate of corporate scandals early in the decade, the U.S. Congress passed the Sarbanes-Oxley Act in 2002. It was an effort to restore investor confidence in the governance of corporations in general and financial reporting in particular. Three years later, a backlash seems to be developing among executives about the high compliance costs and some of the more draconian requirements.

The major source of resentment is the issue of cost. It is estimated that large corporations with revenues over $4 billion have to spend an average of $35 million a year to implement Sarbanes-Oxley. Medium-sized companies spend $3.1 million a year on average. Smaller companies find the cost of compliance particularly burdensome because they have a smaller revenue base. Some critics go to the extent of arguing that this amounts to a form of regressive taxation against small businesses. Many are even considering delisting to avoid compliance costs.

Costs are not the only problem that companies face. Meeting the requirements of Sarbanes-Oxley is very time consuming as well. For example, the law requires that financial numbers such as value of inventory and receivables are cross-checked. But it requires an army

Source: Brown, E. 2006. London Calling. *Forbes,* May 8: 51–52; and Henry, D. 2005. Death, Taxes & Sarbanes-Oxley? *BusinessWeek,* January 17: 28–31.

of additional people and significant additional costs to ensure this. Yellow Roadway Corporation, the nation's largest trucking firm, had to use 200 employees and $9 million to accomplish this in 2004. This was three percent of their total profits. And just think of the lost productivity!

Nasdaq officials say the Sarbanes-Oxley burden is heaviest on the smallest companies, and firms with less than $100 million in revenues make up half of Nasdaq's 3,000 listings. The regulatory costs average two percent of revenue at firms with revenue under $100 million, while they are only 0.1 percent for the biggest companies. Theodore Stebbins, chairman of investment banking at Canaccord Adams says, "Clearly, the low end of the Nasdaq is broken. We can no longer in good conscience recommend to our small clients that they go public on Nasdaq."

How much has Sarbanes-Oxley succeeded in improving governance and ensuring the accuracy and reliability of financial reporting? While it is too early to assess the impact, there is at least some anecdotal evidence that it is having some impact. Visteon Corp., an auto-parts supplier, reported that they uncovered problems with their accounts receivable while complying with the requirements of the act. Similarly, SunTrust Banks Inc. fired three officers after discovering errors in the calculation of loan allowances in their portfolios. Tough but fair regulations can improve governance, but the costs of compliance cannot be ignored.

- *Center for Auto Safety.* Helps consumers find plaintiff lawyers and agitate for vehicle recalls, increased highway safety standards, and lemon laws.
- *Center for Study of Responsive Law.* This is Nader's headquarters. Home of a consumer project on technology, this group sponsored seminars on Microsoft remedies and pushed for tougher Internet privacy rules. It also took on the drug industry over costs.
- *Pension Rights Center.* This center helped employees of IBM, General Electric, and other companies to organize themselves against cash-balance pension plans.

Corporate Governance: An International Perspective

The topic of corporate governance has long been dominated by agency theory and based on the explicit assumption of the separation of ownership and control.[103] The central conflicts are principal–agent conflicts between shareholders and management. However, such an underlying assumption seldom applies outside of the United States and the United Kingdom. This is particularly true in emerging economies and continental Europe. Here, there is often concentrated ownership, along with extensive family ownership and control, business group structures, and weak legal protection for minority shareholders. Serious conflicts tend to exist between two classes of principals: controlling shareholders and minority shareholders. Such conflicts can be called **principal–principal (PP) conflicts,** as opposed to *principal–agent* conflicts (see Exhibits 9.9 and 9.10).

Strong family control is one of the leading indicators of concentrated ownership. In East Asia (excluding China), approximately 57 percent of the corporations have board chairmen and CEOs from the controlling families. In continental Europe, this number is 68 percent. A very common practice is the appointment of family members as board chairman, CEOs, and other top executives. This happens because the families are controlling (not necessarily majority) shareholders. In 2003, 30-year-old James Murdoch was appointed CEO of British Sky Broadcasting (BSkyB), Europe's largest satellite broadcaster. There was very vocal resistance by minority shareholders. Why was he appointed in the first place? James's father just happened to be Rupert Murdoch, who controlled 35 percent of BSkyB and chaired the board. Clearly, this is a case of a PP conflict.

In general, three conditions must be met for PP conflicts to occur:

- A dominant owner or group of owners who have interests that are distinct from minority shareholders.
- Motivation for the controlling shareholders to exercise their dominant positions to their advantage.
- Few formal (such as legislation or regulatory bodies) or informal constraints that would discourage or prevent the controlling shareholders from exploiting their advantageous positions.

principal–principal conflicts conflicts between two classes of principals—controlling shareholders and minority shareholders—within the context of a corporate governance system.

	Principal–Agent Conflicts	Principal–Principal Conflicts
Goal Incongruence	Between shareholders and professional managers who own a relatively small portion of the firm's equity.	Between controlling shareholders and minority shareholders.
Ownership Pattern	Dispersed—5%–20% is considered "concentrated ownership."	Concentrated—Often greater than 50% of equity is controlled by controlling shareholders.
Manifestations	Strategies that benefit entrenched managers at the expense of shareholders in general (e.g., shirking, pet projects, excessive compensation, and empire building).	Strategies that benefit controlling shareholders at the expense of minority shareholders (e.g., minority shareholder expropriation, nepotism, and cronyism).
Institutional Protection of Minority Shareholders	Formal constraints (e.g., judicial reviews and courts) set an upper boundary on potential expropriation by majority shareholders. Informal norms generally adhere to shareholder wealth maximization.	Formal institutional protection is often lacking, corrupted, or un-enforced. Informal norms are typically in favor of the interests of controlling shareholders ahead of those of minority investors.

Source: Adapted from Young, M., Peng, M. W., Ahlstrom, D., & Bruton, G. 2002. Governing the Corporation in Emerging Economies: A Principal–Principal Perspective. *Academy of Management Best Papers Proceedings,* Denver.

Exhibit 9.9   Traditional Principal–Agent Conflicts versus Principal–Principal Conflicts: How They Differ along Dimensions

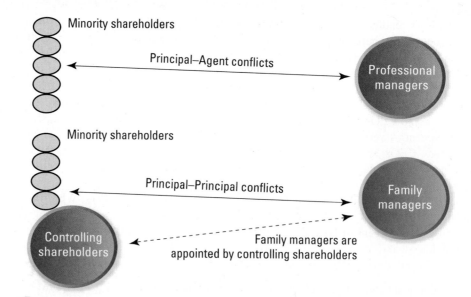

Exhibit 9.10 **Principal–Agent Conflicts and Principal–Principal Conflicts: A Diagram**

Source: Young, M. N., Peng, M. W., Ahlstrom, D., Bruton, G. D., & Jiang, 2008. Principal–Principal Conflicts in Corporate Governance. *Journal of Management Studies* 45(1):196–220; and Peng, M. V. 2006. *Global Strategy.* Cincinnati: Thomson South-Western. We are very appreciative of the helpful comments of Mike Young of Hong Kong Baptist University and Mike Peng of the University of Texas at Dallas.

expropriation of minority shareholders
activities that enrich the controlling shareholders at the expense of the minority shareholders.

The result is often that family managers, who represent (or actually are) the controlling shareholders, engage in **expropriation of minority shareholders**, which is defined as activities that enrich the controlling shareholders at the expense of minority shareholders. What is their motive? After all, controlling shareholders have incentives to maintain firm value. But controlling shareholders may take actions that decrease aggregate firm performance if their personal gains from expropriation exceed their personal losses from their firm's lowered performance.

Another ubiquitous feature of corporate life outside of the United States and United Kingdom are *business groups* such as the keiretsus of Japan and the chaebols of South Korea. This is particularly dominant in emerging economies. A **business group** is "a set of firms that, though legally independent, are bound together by a constellation of formal and informal ties and are accustomed to taking coordinated action."[104] Business groups are especially common in emerging economies, and they differ from other organizational forms in that they are communities of firms without clear boundaries.

business groups
a set of firms that, though legally independent, are bound together by a constellation of formal and informal ties and are accustomed to taking coordinated action.

Business groups have many advantages that can enhance the value of a firm. They often facilitate technology transfer or intergroup capital allocation that otherwise might be impossible because of inadequate institutional infrastructure such as excellent financial services firms. On the other hand, informal ties—such as cross-holdings, board interlocks, and coordinated actions—can often result in intragroup activities and transactions, often at very favorable terms to member firms. Expropriation can be legally done through *related transactions,* which can occur when controlling owners sell firm assets to another firm they own at below market prices or spin off the most profitable part of a public firm and merge it with another of their private firms.

Strategy Spotlight 9.7 provides examples from Latin America of effective corporate governance.

Effective and Ineffective Corporate Governance among "Multilatinas"

Latin-owned companies, such as Mexico's Cemex, Argentina's Arcor, and Brazil's Embraer, have been successful in their home markets against U.S. and European competitors. Several of these companies have become "multilatinas," pursuing a strategy of regional and international expansion. Recently, 82 percent of merger and acquisition deals in Latin America were originated by Latin companies. However, while the rise of these Latin firms is promising, it is not enough to ensure they will be competitive globally against large industrialized multinational firms. Access to international capital markets necessary for the "multilatinas" to grow has created a need for a new openness in corporate governance and transparency for these firms.

There are three components emerging-market multinational firms need to implement to succeed:

Sources: Pigorini, P., Ramos, A., & de Souza, I. 2008. Pitting Latin Multinationals against Established Giants. *Strategy+Business,* November 4: www.strategy-business.com/media/file/leading_ideas-20081104.pdf; Martinez, J., Esperanca, J., & de la Torre, J. 2005. Organizational Change among Emerging Latin American Firms: From "Multilatinas" to Multinationals. *Management Research,* 3(3): 173–188; Krauss, C. 2007. Latin American Companies Make Big U.S. Gains. *New York Times,* May 2: www.nytimes.com/2007/05/02/business/worldbusiness/02latin.html.

- **Shareholder rights.** Minority shareholders must be protected through clear and fair dividend distribution and fair valuation in the event of mergers and acquisitions.

- **Compliance.** The audit committee of the board must be empowered to evaluate the financial statements of the firm and interact with both internal and external auditors.

- **Board and management composition.** Because many multilatinas are still in the process of building effective governance systems, it is important that the board members and top managers have credible professional backgrounds and experience.

These firms need to set up the right board and manager dynamics both to improve access to capital and to implement international management. Many multilatinas were or still are family-owned firms. Boards of these firms tend to be filled with members who have a strong loyalty to the controlling family, but not necessarily exposure to global strategic initiatives and strategies. Many of these firms still use centralized information control systems. In order to grow, some firms may have to consider giving local country managers more authority to make decisions.

Reflecting on Career Implications . . .

- *Behavioral Control:* What sources of behavioral control does your organization employ? In general, too much emphasis on rules and regulations may stifle initiative and be detrimental to your career opportunities.
- *Rewards and Incentives:* Is your organization's reward structure fair and equitable? Does it effectively reward outstanding performance? If not, there may be a long-term erosion of morale which may have long-term adverse career implications for you.
- *Culture:* Consider the type of organization culture that would provide the best work environment for your career goals. How does your organization's culture deviate from this concept? Does your organization have a strong and effective culture? If so, professionals are more likely to develop strong "firm specific" ties, which further enhances collaboration.
- *Corporate Governance:* Does your organization practice effective corporate governance? Such practices will enhance a firm's culture and it will be easier to attract top talent. Operating within governance guidelines is usually a strong indicator of organizational citizenship which, in turn, should be good for your career prospects.

Summary

For firms to be successful, they must practice effective strategic control and corporate governance. Without such controls, the firm will not be able to achieve competitive advantages and outperform rivals in the marketplace.

We began the chapter with the key role of informational control. We contrasted two types of control systems: what we termed "traditional" and "contemporary" information control systems. Whereas traditional control systems may have their place in placid, simple competitive environments, there are fewer of those in today's economy. Instead, we advocated the contemporary approach wherein the internal and external environment are constantly monitored so that when surprises emerge, the firm can modify its strategies, goals, and objectives.

Behavioral controls are also a vital part of effective control systems. We argued that firms must develop the proper balance between culture, rewards and incentives, and boundaries and constraints. Where there are strong and positive cultures and rewards, employees tend to internalize the organization's strategies and objectives. This permits a firm to spend fewer resources on monitoring behavior, and assures the firm that the efforts and initiatives of employees are more consistent with the overall objectives of the organization.

In the final section of this chapter, we addressed corporate governance, which can be defined as the relationship between various participants in determining the direction and performance of the corporation. The primary participants include shareholders, management (led by the chief executive officer), and the board of directors. We reviewed studies that indicated a consistent relationship between effective corporate governance and financial performance. There are also several internal and external control mechanisms that can serve to align managerial interests and shareholder interests. The internal mechanisms include a committed and involved board of directors, shareholder activism, and effective managerial incentives and rewards. The external mechanisms include the market for corporate control, banks and analysts, regulators, the media, and public activists. We also addressed corporate governance from both a United States and an international perspective.

Summary Review Questions

1. Why are effective strategic control systems so important in today's economy?

2. What are the main advantages of "contemporary" control systems over "traditional" control systems? What are the main differences between these two systems?

3. Why is it important to have a balance between the three elements of behavioral control—culture; rewards and incentives; and, boundaries?

4. Discuss the relationship between types of organizations and their primary means of behavioral control.

5. Boundaries become less important as a firm develops a strong culture and reward system. Explain.

6. Why is it important to avoid a "one best way" mentality concerning control systems? What are the consequences of applying the same type of control system to all types of environments?

7. What is the role of effective corporate governance in improving a firm's performance? What are some of the key governance mechanisms that are used to ensure that managerial and shareholder interests are aligned?

8. Define principal–principal (PP) conflicts. What are the implications for corporate governance?

Key Terms

strategic control 312
traditional approach to strategic control, 313
informational control, 315
behavioral control, 315
organizational culture, 317
reward system 318
boundaries and constraints 320
corporate governance, 324
corporation, 326

agency theory, 326
board of directors, 327
shareholder activism, 331
external governance control mechanisms, 332
market for corporate control, 333
takeover constraint, 333
principal–principal conflicts, 337
expropriation of minority shareholders 338
business groups, 338

Experiential Exercise

McDonald's Corporation, the world's largest fast-food restaurant chain, with 2008 revenues of $24 billion, has recently been on a "roll." Its shareholder value has more than tripled between April 2003 and April 2009. Using the Internet or library sources, evaluate the quality of the corporation in terms of management, the board of directors, and shareholder activism. Are the issues you list favorable or unfavorable for sound corporate governance?

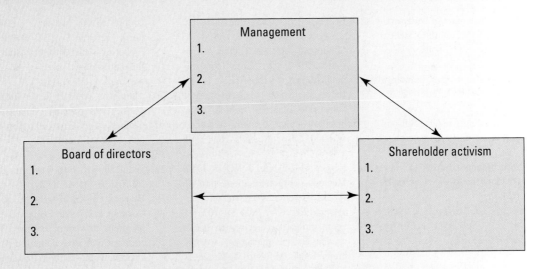

Management

1.
2.
3.

Board of directors

1.
2.
3.

Shareholder activism

1.
2.
3.

Application Questions Exercises

1. The problems of many firms may be attributed to a "traditional" control system that failed to continuously monitor the environment and make necessary changes in their strategy and objectives. What companies are you familiar with that responded appropriately (or inappropriately) to environmental change?

2. How can a strong, positive culture enhance a firm's competitive advantage? How can a weak, negative culture erode competitive advantages? Explain and provide examples.

3. Use the Internet to research a firm that has an excellent culture and/or reward and incentive system. What are this firm's main financial and nonfinancial benefits?

4. Using the Internet, go to the website of a large, publicly held corporation in which you are interested. What evidence do you see of effective (or ineffective) corporate governance?

Ethics Questions

1. Strong cultures can have powerful effects on employee behavior. How does this create inadvertent control mechanisms? That is, are strong cultures an ethical way to control behavior?

2. Rules and regulations can help reduce unethical behavior in organizations. To be effective, however, what other systems, mechanisms, and processes are necessary?

References

1. Ante, S. E. 2008. Sprint's wake-up call. *BusinessWeek,* March 3: 54–57; Holson, L. 2008. Bedeviled by the churn, Sprint tries to win back disgruntled customers. *New York Times,* July 8, Technology: http://www.nytimes.com/2008/07/08/technology/08sprint.html; and Cheng, R. & Sharma, A. 2008. Sprint squeezed as customers flee; Wireless carrier sees drop of 1.3 million subscribers; negotiates new credit agreement. *The Wall Street Journal,* November 8: B5.

2. This chapter draws upon Picken, J. C. & Dess, G. G. 1997. *Mission critical.* Burr Ridge, IL: Irwin Professional Publishing.

3. Argyris, C. 1977. Double-loop learning in organizations. *Harvard Business Review,* 55: 115–125.

4. Simons, R. 1995. Control in an age of empowerment. *Harvard Business Review,* 73: 80–88. This chapter draws on this source in the discussion of informational control.

5. Goold, M. & Quinn, J. B. 1990. The paradox of strategic controls. *Strategic Management Journal,* 11: 43–57.

6. Quinn, J. B. 1980. *Strategies for change.* Homewood, IL: Richard D. Irwin.

7. Mintzberg, H. 1987. Crafting strategy. *Harvard Business Review,* 65: 66–75.

8. Weston, J. S. 1992. Soft stuff matters. *Financial Executive,* July–August: 52–53.

9. This discussion of control systems draws upon Simons, op. cit.

10. For an interesting perspective on this issue and how a downturn in the economy can reduce the tendency toward "free agency" by managers and professionals, refer to Morris, B. 2001. White collar blues. *Fortune,* July 23: 98–110.

11. For a colorful example of behavioral control in an organization, see: Beller, P. C. 2009. Activision's unlikely hero. *Forbes.* February 2: 52–58.

12. Ouchi, W. 1981. *Theory Z.* Reading, MA: Addison-Wesley; Deal, T. E. & Kennedy, A. A. 1982. *Corporate cultures.* Reading, MA: Addison-Wesley; Peters, T. J. & Waterman, R. H. 1982. *In search of excellence.* New York: Random House; Collins, J. 2001. *Good to great.* New York: HarperCollins.

13. Collins, J. C. & Porras, J. I. 1994. *Built to last: Successful habits of visionary companies.* New York: Harper Business.

14. Lee, J. & Miller, D. 1999. People matter: Commitment to employees, strategy, and performance in Korean firms. *Strategic Management Journal,* 6: 579–594.

15. For an insightful discussion of IKEA's unique culture, see Kling, K. & Goteman, I. 2003. IKEA CEO Anders Dahlvig on international growth and IKEA's unique corporate culture and brand identity. *Academy of Management Executive,* 17(1): 31–37.

16. For a discussion of how professionals inculcate values, refer to Uhl-Bien, M. & Graen, G. B. 1998. Individual self-management: Analysis of professionals' self-managing activities in functional and cross-functional work teams. *Academy of Management Journal,* 41(3): 340–350.

17. A perspective on how antisocial behavior can erode a firm's culture can be found in Robinson, S. L. & O'Leary-Kelly, A. M. 1998. Monkey see, monkey do: The influence of work groups on the antisocial behavior of employees. *Academy of Management Journal,* 41(6): 658–672.

18. An interesting perspective on organization culture is in: Mehta, S. N. 2009. UnderArmour reboots. *Fortune,* February 2: 29–33.

19. For insights on social pressure as a means for control, refer to: Goldstein, N. J. 2009. Harnessing social pressure. *Harvard Business Review,* 87(2): 25.

20. Mitchell, R. 1989. Masters of innovation. *BusinessWeek,* April 10: 58–63.

21. Sellers, P. 1993. Companies that serve you best. *Fortune,* May 31: 88.

22. Southwest Airlines Culture Committee. 1993. *Luv Lines* (company publication), March–April: 17–18; for an interesting perspective on the "downside" of strong "cultlike" organizational cultures, refer to Arnott, D. A. 2000. *Corporate cults.* New York: AMACOM.

23. Kerr, J. & Slocum, J. W., Jr. 1987. Managing corporate culture through reward systems. *Academy of Management Executive,* 1(2): 99–107.

24. For a unique perspective on leader challenges in managing wealthy professionals, refer to Wetlaufer, S. 2000. Who wants to manage a millionaire? *Harvard Business Review,* 78(4): 53–60.

25. Neilson, G. L., Pasternack, B. A., & Van Nuys, K. E. 2005. The passive-aggressive organization. *Harvard Business Review,* 83(10): 82–95.

26. These next two subsections draw upon Dess, G. G. & Picken, J. C. 1997. *Beyond productivity.* New York: AMACOM.

27. For a discussion of the benefits of stock options as executive compensation, refer to Hall, B. J. 2000. What you need to know about stock options. *Harvard Business Review,* 78(2): 121–129.

28. Tully, S. 1993. Your paycheck gets exciting. *Fortune,* November 13: 89.

29. Zellner, W., Hof, R. D., Brandt, R., Baker, S., & Greising, D. 1995. Go-go goliaths. *BusinessWeek,* February 13: 64–70.

30. This section draws on Dess & Picken, op. cit.: chap. 5.

31. Simons, op. cit.

32. Davis, E. 1997. Interview: Norman Augustine. *Management Review,* November: 11.

33. This section draws upon Dess, G. G. & Miller, A. 1993. *Strategic management.* New York: McGraw-Hill.

34. For a good review of the goal-setting literature, refer to Locke, E. A. & Latham, G. P. 1990. *A theory of goal setting and task performance.* Englewood Cliffs, NJ: Prentice Hall.

35. For an interesting perspective on the use of rules and regulations that is counter to this industry's (software) norms, refer to Fryer, B. 2001. Tom Siebel of Siebel Systems: High tech the old fashioned way. *Harvard Business Review,* 79(3): 118–130.

36. Thompson, A. A. Jr. & Strickland, A. J., III. 1998. *Strategic management: Concepts and cases* (10th ed.): 313. New York: McGraw-Hill.

37. Ibid.

38. Teitelbaum, R. 1997. Tough guys finish first. *Fortune,* July 21: 82–84.

39. Weaver, G. R., Trevino, L. K., & Cochran, P. L. 1999. Corporate ethics programs as control systems: Influences of executive commitment and environmental factors. *Academy of Management Journal,* 42(1): 41–57.

40. Cadbury, S. A. 1987. Ethical managers make their own rules. *Harvard Business Review,* 65: 3, 69–73.

41. Weber, J. 2003. CFOs on the hot seat. *BusinessWeek,* March 17: 66–70.

42. William Ouchi has written extensively about the use of clan control (which is viewed as an alternate to bureaucratic or market control). Here, a powerful culture results in people aligning their individual interests with those of the firm. Refer to Ouchi, op. cit. This section also draws on Hall, R. H. 2002. *Organizations: Structures, processes, and outcomes* (8th ed.). Upper Saddle River, NJ: Prentice Hall.

43. Interesting insights on corporate governance are in: Kroll, M., Walters, B. A., & Wright, P. 2008. Board vigilance, director experience, and corporate outcomes. *Strategic Management Journal,* 29(4): 363–382.

44. For a brief review of some central issues in corporate governance research, see: Hambrick, D. C., Werder, A. V., & Zajac, E. J. 2008. New directions in corporate governance research. *Organization Science,* 19(3): 381–385.

45. Monks, R. & Minow, N. 2001. *Corporate governance* (2nd ed.). Malden, MA: Blackwell.

46. Pound, J. 1995. The promise of the governed corporation. *Harvard Business Review,* 73(2): 89–98.

47. Maurer, H. & Linblad, C. 2009. Scandal at Satyam. *BusinessWeek,* January 19: 8; Scheck, J. & Stecklow, S. 2008.

Brocade ex-CEO gets 21 months in prison. *The Wall Street Journal,* January 17: A3; Heinzl, M. 2004. Nortel's directors and investors discuss changes to the board. *The Wall Street Journal,* September 30: B4; Editorial. 2003. Pulling Boeing out of a tailspin. *BusinessWeek,* December 15: 136; and Zimmerman, A., Ball, D., & Veen, M. 2003. A global journal report: Supermarket giant Ahoud ousts CEO in big accounting scandal. *The Wall Street Journal,* February 25: A1; Ibid; and Maurer, H. 2006. Is this "the HP way"? *BusinessWeek,* September 25: 34.

48. Corporate governance and social networks are discussed in: McDonald, M.L., Khanna, P., & Westphal, J.D. 2008. *Academy of Management Journal.* 51(3): 453-475.

49. This discussion draws upon Monks & Minow, op. cit.

50. For an interesting perspective on the politicization of the corporation, read: Palazzo, G. & Scherer, A. G. 2008. Corporate social responsibility, democracy, and the politicization of the corporation. *Academy of Management Review,* 33(3): 773–774.

51. Eisenhardt, K. M. 1989. Agency theory: An assessment and review. *Academy of Management Review,* 14(1): 57–74. Some of the seminal contributions to agency theory include Jensen, M. & Meckling, W. 1976. Theory of the firm: Managerial behavior, agency costs, and ownership structure. *Journal of Financial Economics,* 3: 305–360; Fama, E. & Jensen, M. 1983. Separation of ownership and control. *Journal of Law and Economics,* 26: 301, 325; and Fama, E. 1980. Agency problems and the theory of the firm. *Journal of Political Economy,* 88: 288–307.

52. Managers may also engage in "shirking"—that is, reducing or withholding their efforts. See, for example, Kidwell, R. E., Jr. & Bennett, N. 1993. Employee propensity to withhold effort: A conceptual model to intersect three avenues of research. *Academy of Management Review,* 18(3): 429–456.

53. For an interesting perspective on agency and clarification of many related concepts and terms, visit the following website: www.encycogov .com.

54. The relationship between corporate ownership structure and export intensity in Chinese firms is discussed in: Filatotchev, I., Stephan, J., & Jindra, B. 2008. Ownership structure, strategic controls and export intensity of foreign-invested firms in transition economies. *Journal of International Business,* 39(7): 1133–1148.

55. Argawal, A. & Mandelker, G. 1987. Managerial incentives and corporate investment and financing decisions. *Journal of Finance,* 42: 823–837.

56. For an insightful, recent discussion of the academic research on corporate governance, and in particular the role of boards of directors, refer to Chatterjee, S. & Harrison, J. S. 2001. Corporate governance. In Hitt, M. A., Freeman, R. E., & Harrison, J. S. (Eds.). *Handbook of strategic management:* 543–563. Malden, MA: Blackwell.

57. For an interesting theoretical discussion on corporate governance in Russia, see: McCarthy, D. J. & Puffer, S. M. 2008. Interpreting the ethicality of corporate governance decisions in Russia: Utilizing integrative social contracts theory to evaluate the relevance of agency theory norms. *Academy of Management Review,* 33(1): 11–31.

58. This opening discussion draws on Monks & Minow, op. cit. 164, 169; see also Pound, op. cit.

59. Business Roundtable. 1990. *Corporate governance and American competitiveness,* March: 7.

60. The director role in acquisition performance is addressed in: Westphal, J. D. & Graebner, M. E. 2008. What do they know? The effects of outside director acquisition experience on firm acquisition performance. *Strategic Management Journal,* 29(11): 1155–1178.

61. Byrne, J. A., Grover, R., & Melcher, R. A. 1997. The best and worst boards. *BusinessWeek,* November 26: 35–47. The three key roles of boards of directors are monitoring the actions of executives, providing advice, and providing links to the external environment to provide resources. See Johnson, J. L., Daily, C. M., & Ellstrand, A. E. 1996. Boards of directors: A review and research agenda. *Academy of Management Review,* 37: 409–438.

62. The role of outside directors is discussed in: Lester, R. H., Hillman, A., Zardkoohi, A., & Cannella, A. A. Jr. 2008. Former government officials as outside directors: The role of human and social capital. *Academy of Management Journal,* 51(5): 999–1013.

63. McGeehan, P. 2003. More chief executives shown the door, study says. *New York Times,* May 12: C2.

64. Gerdes, L. 2007. Hello, goodbye. *BusinessWeek,* January 22: 16.

65. For an analysis of the effects of outside directors' compensation on acquisition decisions, refer to Deutsch, T., Keil, T., & Laamanen, T. 2007. Decision making in acquisitions: The effect of outside directors' compensation on acquisition patterns. *Journal of Management,* 33(1): 30–56.

66. Director interlocks are addressed in: Kang, E. 2008. Director interlocks and spillover effects of reputational penalties from financial reporting fraud. *Academy of Management Journal,* 51 (3): 537–556.

67. There are benefits, of course, to having some insiders on the board of directors. Inside directors would be more aware of the firm's strategies. Additionally, outsiders may rely too often on financial performance indicators because of information asymmetries. For an interesting discussion, see Baysinger, B. D. & Hoskisson, R. E. 1990. The composition of boards of directors and strategic control: Effects on corporate strategy. *Academy of Management Review,* 15: 72–87.

68. Hambrick, D. C. & Jackson, E. M. 2000. Outside directors with a stake: The linchpin in improving governance. *California Management Review,* 42(4): 108–127.

69. Ibid.

70. Disney has begun to make many changes to improve its corporate governance, such as assigning only

independent directors to important board committees, restricting directors from serving on more than three boards, and appointing a lead director who can convene the board without approval by the CEO. In recent years, the Disney Co. has shown up on some "best" board lists. In addition Eisner has recently relinquished the chairman position.

71. Talk show. 2002. *BusinessWeek,* September 30: 14.

72. Ward, R. D. 2000. *Improving corporate boards.* New York: Wiley.

73. A discussion on the shareholder approval process in executive compensation is presented in: Brandes, P., Goranova, M., & Hall, S. 2008. Navigating shareholder influence: Compensation plans and the shareholder approval process. *Academy of Management Perspectives,* 22(1): 41–57.

74. Monks and Minow, op. cit.: 93.

75. A discussion of the factors that lead to shareholder activism is found in Ryan, L. V. & Schneider, M. 2002. The antecedents of institutional investor activism. *Academy of Management Review,* 27(4): 554–573.

76. For an insightful discussion of investor activism, refer to David, P., Bloom, M., & Hillman, A. 2007. Investor activism, managerial responsiveness, and corporate social performance. *Strategic Management Journal,* 28(1): 91–100.

77. There is strong research support for the idea that the presence of large block shareholders is associated with value-maximizing decisions. For example, refer to Johnson, R. A., Hoskisson, R. E., & Hitt, M. A. 1993. Board of director involvement in restructuring: The effects of board versus managerial controls and characteristics. *Strategic Management Journal,* 14: 33–50.

78. For a discussion of institutional activism and its link to CEO compensation, refer to: Chowdhury, S. D. & Wang, E. Z. 2009. Institutional activism types and CEO compensation. *Journal of Management,* 35(1): 5–36.

79. For an interesting perspective on the impact of institutional ownership on a firm's innovation strategies, see Hoskisson, R. E., Hitt, M. A., Johnson, R. A., & Grossman, W. 2002. *Academy of Management Journal,* 45(4): 697–716.

80. www.calpers.ca.gov/index.jsp

81. Icahn, C. 2007. Icahn: On activist investors and private equity run wild. *BusinessWeek,* March 12: 21–22. For an interesting perspective on Carl Icahn's transition (?) from corporate raider to shareholder activist, read Grover, R. 2007. Just don't call him a raider. *BusinessWeek,* March 5: 68–69. The quote in the text is part of Icahn's response to the article by R. Grover.

82. For a study of the relationship between ownership and diversification, refer to Goranova, M., Alessandri, T. M., Brandes, P., & Dharwadkar, R. 2007. Managerial ownership and corporate diversification: A longitudinal view, *Strategic Management Journal,* 28(3): 211–226.

83. Jensen, M. C. & Murphy, K. J. 1990. CEO incentives—It's not how much you pay, but how. *Harvard Business Review,* 68(3): 138–149.

84. For a perspective on the relative advantages and disadvantages of "duality"—that is, one individual serving as both Chief Executive Office and Chairman of the Board, see Lorsch, J. W. & Zelleke, A. 2005. Should the CEO be the chairman? *MIT Sloan Management Review,* 46(2): 71–74.

85. A discussion of knowledge sharing is addressed in: Fey, C. F. & Furu, P. 2008. Top management incentive compensation and knowledge sharing in multinational corporations. *Strategic Management Journal,* 29(12): 1301–1324.

86. Sasseen, J. 2007. A better look at the boss's pay. *BusinessWeek,* February 26: 44–45; and Weinberg, N., Maiello, M., & Randall, D. 2008. Paying for failure. *Forbes,* May 19: 114, 116.

87. Byrnes, N. & Sasseen, J. 2007. Board of hard knocks. *BusinessWeek,* January 22: 36–39.

88. Research has found that executive compensation is more closely aligned with firm performance in companies with compensation committees and boards dominated by outside directors. See, for example, Conyon, M. J. & Peck, S. I. 1998. Board control, remuneration committees, and top management compensation. *Academy of Management Journal,* 41: 146–157.

89. Lavelle, L., Jespersen, F. F., & Arndt, M. 2002. Executive pay. *BusinessWeek,* April 15: 66–72.

90. A perspective on whether or not CEOs are overpaid is provided in: Kaplan, S. N. 2008. Are U.S. CEOs overpaid: A response to Bogle and Walsh, J. P. *Academy of Management Perspectives.* 22(3): 28–34.

91. www.tiaa-cref.org/pubs.

92. Some insights on CEO compensation—and the importance of ethics—are addressed in: Heineman, B. W. Jr. 2008. The fatal flaw in pay for performance. *Harvard Business Review.* 86(6): 31, 34.

93. Such opportunistic behavior is common in all principal-agent relationships. For a description of agency problems, especially in the context of the relationship between shareholders and managers, see Jensen, M. C. & Meckling, W. H. 1976. Theory of the firm: Managerial behavior, agency costs, and ownership structure. *Journal of Financial Economics,* 3: 305–360.

94. Hoskisson, R. E. & Turk, T. A. 1990. Corporate restructuring: Governance and control limits of the internal market. *Academy of Management Review,* 15: 459–477.

95. For an insightful perspective on the market for corporate control and how it is influenced by knowledge intensity, see Coff, R. 2003. Bidding wars over R&D-intensive firms: Knowledge, opportunism, and the market for corporate control. *Academy of Management Journal,* 46(1): 74–85.

96. Walsh, J. P. & Kosnik, R. D. 1993. Corporate raiders and their disciplinary role in the market for corporate control. *Academy of Management Journal,* 36: 671–700.

97. Gunning for KPMG. 2003. *Economist,* February 1: 63.

98. Timmons, H. 2003. Investment banks: Who will foot their bill? *BusinessWeek,* March 3: 116.

99. The role of regulatory bodies in the banking industry is addressed in: Bhide, A. 2009. Why bankers got so reckless. *BusinessWeek,* February 9: 30–31.

100. Wishy-washy: The SEC pulls its punches on corporate-governance rules. 2003. *Economist,* February 1: 60.

101. McLean, B. 2001. Is Enron overpriced? *Fortune,* March 5: 122–125.

102. Bernstein, A. 2000. Too much corporate power. *BusinessWeek,* September 11: 35–37.

103. This section draws upon Young, M. N., Peng, M. W., Ahlstrom, D., Bruton, G. D., & Jiang, Y. 2005. Principal–principal conflicts in corporate governance (un-published manuscript); and, Peng, M. W. 2006. *Globalstrategy.* Cincinnati: Thomson South-Western. We are very appreciative of the helpful comments of Mike Young of Hong Kong Baptist University and Mike Peng of the University of Texas at Dallas.

104. Khanna, T. & Rivkin, J. 2001. Estimating the performance effects of business groups in emerging markets. *Strategic Management Journal,* 22: 45–74.

Creating Effective Organizational Designs

After reading this chapter, you should have a good understanding of:

LO1 The growth patterns of major corporations and the relationship between a firm's strategy and its structure.

LO2 Each of the traditional types of organizational structure: simple, functional, divisional, and matrix.

LO3 The implications of a firm's international operations for organizational structure.

LO4 Why there is no "one best way" to design strategic reward and evaluation systems, and the important contingent roles of business- and corporate-level strategies.

LO5 The different types of boundaryless organizations—barrier-free, modular, and virtual—and their relative advantages and disadvantages.

LO6 The need for creating ambidextrous organizational designs that enable firms to explore new opportunities and effectively integrate existing operations.

To implement strategies successfully, firms must have appropriate organizational designs. These include the processes and integrating mechanisms necessary to ensure that boundaries among internal activities and external parties, such as suppliers, customers, and alliance partners, are flexible and permeable. A firm's performance will suffer if its managers don't carefully consider both of these organizational design attributes.

In the first section, we begin by discussing the growth patterns of large corporations to address the important relationships between the strategy that a firm follows and its corresponding structure. For example, as firms diversify into related product-market areas, they change their structure from functional to divisional. We then address the different types of traditional structures—simple, functional, divisional, and matrix—and their relative advantages and disadvantages. We close with a discussion of the implications of a firm's international operations for the structure of its organization.

The second section takes the perspective that there is no "one best way" to design an organization's strategic reward and evaluation system. Here we address two important contingencies: business- and corporate-level strategy. For example, when strategies require a great deal of collaboration, as well as resource and information sharing, there must be incentives and cultures that encourage and reward such initiatives.

The third section discusses the concept of the "boundaryless" organization. We do *not* argue that organizations should have no internal and external boundaries. Instead, we suggest that in rapidly changing and unpredictable environments, organizations must strive to make their internal and external boundaries both flexible and permeable. We suggest three different types of boundaryless organizations: barrier-free, modular, and virtual.

The fourth section focuses on the need for managers to recognize that they typically face two opposing challenges: (1) being proactive in taking advantage of new opportunities and (2) ensuring the effective coordination and integration of existing operations. This suggests the need for ambidextrous organizations; that is, firms that can both be efficient in how they manage existing assets and competencies and take advantage of opportunities in rapidly changing and unpredictable environments—conditions that are becoming more pronounced in today's global markets.

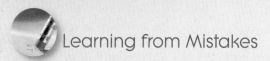
Learning from Mistakes

Carl Pope, Executive Director of the Sierra Club, claimed he was "bemused" as he rang the opening bell of the New York Stock Exchange on the Monday before Earth Day 2008 along with Donald Knauss, the CEO of Clorox. But Pope said, "Environmentalists and capitalism have an uneasy relationship, and for many of the companies listed on the Big Board, their most memorable experience with the Sierra Club came in the form of papers served for environmental lawsuits we've brought. [However,] companies are an essential part of the solution if we're going to reshape our economy along sustainable lines."

The Sierra Club has long been associated with the protection of nature. From its inception in 1892, John Muir and other supporters formed the Sierra Club "to make the mountains glad." John Muir was the club's first president, an office he held until his death in 1914. Muir's Sierra Club has gone on to help establish a series of new national parks and a National Wilderness Preservation System. However, Muir would never have imagined that this clean-living organization would partner with a chemical company in 2009.

Clorox introduced its "Green Works" line of products carrying a Sierra Club Logo. It looked like a good deal for both organizations. Clorox should have been pleased that Green Works products were selling well. The Sierra Club, in exchange for its endorsement, received large payments that could be used to help further its environmental conservation work. It seems like this partnership should have been a "clean solution" for the environment.[1]

What Went Wrong? Unfortunately, several key members of the Sierra Club were a little less than bemused with the deal Carl Pope had struck. Pope did not practice "boundaryless" organization coordination by communicating with other parts of the organization in executing the Clorox endorsement. Pope mentioned publicly that the Sierra Club's due diligence included the "toughest scrutiny" of the Clorox products being endorsed. Pope told Sierra Club leaders that "we consulted with the executive committee of the board of directors, the corporate relations committee, the toxics committee, the energy committee, and the environmental quality committee. None of these entities found fault with the Green Works as a product line."

However, others in the organization did not see the same picture of agreement painted by Mr. Pope. Jessica Frohman, the co-chair of the toxics committee, said that her panel never voted on the Clorox products. She said that, while her committee did review Environmental Protection Agency data on the products, its members did not test the products themselves. Furthermore, Frohman said that her committee members were not trained chemists and were not really in a position to guarantee anything about the products. The club's committee on corporate relations did take a vote on the Clorox endorsement deal and rejected it. However, Pope and the executive board "rejected the rejection" by the corporate relations committee and signed the Clorox agreement anyway.

Inside and outside the Sierra Club, tensions ran high and there were unhappy voices. One Clorox advisor, Adviser Makower, said of the deal the Sierra Club struck: "To be tied directly to sales and not reveal [the details], and to be endorsing the products, is, in any world, borderline unethical. ... It soils the living room for everybody." A former Sierra Club director said that the current club leaders were "destroying the club's credibility. They should all be ashamed of themselves."

While Pope and the Sierra Club have lost loyal members over this controversy, they may have found a silver lining. Millions of shoppers, many of whom had never heard of the Sierra Club, are now being introduced to the club every day as they see the club logo on their bottles of Clorox Green Works cleaning products.

One of the central concepts in this chapter is the importance of boundaryless organizations. Successful organizations create permeable boundaries among the internal activities as well as between the organization and its external customers, suppliers, and alliance partners. We introduced this idea in Chapter 3 in our discussion of the value-chain concept, which consisted of several primary (e.g., inbound logistics, marketing and sales) and support activities (e.g., procurement, human resource management). The underlying cause of the Sierra Club's problem was its inability to establish close and effective working relationships between its various committees and volunteers. Frequently, managers were seemingly more focused on the financial health of the club than on the interests of the club's members.

Today's managers are faced with two ongoing and vital activities in structuring and designing their organizations. First, they must decide on the most appropriate type of organizational structure. Second, they need to assess what mechanisms, processes, and techniques are most helpful in enhancing the permeability of both internal and external boundaries.

Traditional Forms of Organizational Structure

Organizational structure refers to the formalized patterns of interactions that link a firm's tasks, technologies, and people.[2] Structures help to ensure that resources are used effectively in accomplishing an organization's mission. Structure provides a means of balancing two conflicting forces: a need for the division of tasks into meaningful groupings and the need to integrate such groupings in order to ensure efficiency and effectiveness. Structure identifies the executive, managerial, and administrative organization of a firm and indicates responsibilities and hierarchical relationships. It also influences the flow of information as well as the context and nature of human interactions.[3]

Most organizations begin very small and either die or remain small. Those that survive and prosper embark on strategies designed to increase the overall scope of operations and enable them to enter new product-market domains. Such growth places additional pressure on executives to control and coordinate the firm's increasing size and diversity. The most appropriate type of structure depends on the nature and magnitude of growth.

Patterns of Growth of Large Corporations: Strategy-Structure Relationships

A firm's strategy and structure change as it increases in size, diversifies into new product markets, and expands its geographic scope.[4] Exhibit 10.1 illustrates common growth patterns of firms.

A new firm with a *simple structure* typically increases its sales revenue and volume of outputs over time. It may also engage in some vertical integration to secure sources of supply (backward integration) as well as channels of distribution (forward integration). The simple-structure firm then implements a *functional structure* to concentrate efforts on both increasing efficiency and enhancing its operations and products. This structure enables the firm to group its operations into either functions, departments, or geographic areas. As its initial markets mature, a firm looks beyond its present products and markets for possible expansion.

A strategy of related diversification requires a need to reorganize around product lines or geographic markets. This leads to a *divisional structure.* As the business expands in terms of sales revenues, and domestic growth opportunities become somewhat limited, a firm may seek opportunities in international markets. A firm has a wide variety of structures to choose from. These include *international division, geographic area, worldwide product division, worldwide functional,* and *worldwide matrix.* Deciding upon the most appropriate structure when a firm has international operations depends on three primary factors: the extent of international expansion, type of strategy (global, multidomestic, or transnational), and the degree of product diversity.[5]

Some firms may find it advantageous to diversify into several product lines rather than focus their efforts on strengthening distributor and supplier relationships through vertical integration. They would organize themselves according to product lines by implementing a divisional structure. Also, some firms may choose to move into unrelated product areas,

organizational structure the formalized patterns of interactions that link a firm's tasks, technologies, and people.

>LO1
The growth patterns of major corporations and the relationship between a firm's strategy and its structure.

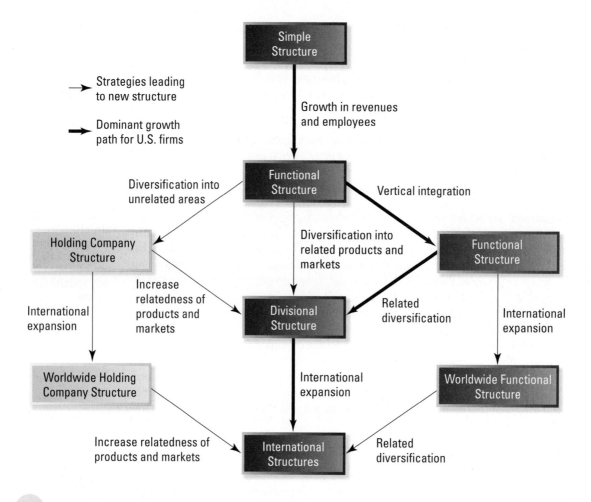

Exhibit 10.1 **Dominant Growth Patterns of Large Corporations**

Source: Adapted from J. R. Galbraith and R. K. Kazanjian. *Strategy Implementation: Structure, Systems and Process,* 2nd ed. Copyright © 1986.

typically by acquiring existing businesses. Frequently, their rationale is that acquiring assets and competencies is more economical or expedient than developing them internally. Such an unrelated, or conglomerate, strategy requires relatively little integration across businesses and sharing of resources. Thus, a *holding company structure* becomes appropriate. There are many other growth patterns, but these are the most common.*

Now we will discuss some of the most common types of organizational structures—simple, functional, divisional (including two variants: *strategic business unit* and *holding company*), and matrix and their advantages and disadvantages. We will close the section with a discussion of the structural implications when a firm expands its operations into international markets.[6]

---

* The lowering of transaction costs and globalization have led to some changes in the common historical patterns that we have discussed. Some firms are, in effect, bypassing the vertical integration stage. Instead, they focus on core competencies and outsource other value-creation activities. Also, even relatively young firms are going global early in their history because of lower communication and transportation costs. For an interesting perspective on global start-ups, see McDougall, P. P. & Oviatt, B. M. 1996. New Venture Internationalization, Strategic Change and Performance: A Follow-Up Study. *Journal of Business Venturing,* 11: 23–40; and McDougall, P. P. & Oviatt, B. M. (Eds.). 2000. The Special Research Forum on International Entrepreneurship. *Academy of Management Journal,* October: 902–1003.

Simple Structure

The **simple organizational structure** is the oldest, and most common, organizational form. Most organizations are very small and have a single or very narrow product line in which the owner-manager (or top executive) makes most of the decisions. The owner-manager controls all activities, and the staff serves as an extension of the top executive.

Advantages   The simple structure is highly informal and the coordination of tasks is accomplished by direct supervision. Decision making is highly centralized, there is little specialization of tasks, few rules and regulations, and an informal evaluation and reward system. Although the owner-manager is intimately involved in almost all phases of the business, a manager is often employed to oversee day-to-day operations.

Disadvantages   A simple structure may foster creativity and individualism since there are generally few rules and regulations. However, such "informality" may lead to problems. Employees may not clearly understand their responsibilities, which can lead to conflict and confusion. Employees may take advantage of the lack of regulations, act in their own self-interest, which can erode motivation and satisfaction and lead to the possible misuse of organizational resources. Small organizations have flat structures that limit opportunities for upward mobility. Without the potential for future advancement, recruiting and retaining talent may become very difficult.

Functional Structure

When an organization is small (15 employees or less), it is not necessary to have a variety of formal arrangements and groupings of activities. However, as firms grow, excessive demands may be placed on the owner-manager in order to obtain and process all of the information necessary to run the business. Chances are the owner will not be skilled in all specialties (e.g., accounting, engineering, production, marketing). Thus, he or she will need to hire specialists in the various functional areas. Such growth in the overall scope and complexity of the business necessitates a **functional organizational structure** wherein the major functions of the firm are grouped internally. The coordination and integration of the functional areas becomes one of the most important responsibilities of the chief executive of the firm (see Exhibit 10.2).

Functional structures are generally found in organizations in which there is a single or closely related product or service, high production volume, and some vertical integration. Initially, firms tend to expand the overall scope of their operations by penetrating existing markets, introducing similar products in additional markets, or increasing the level of vertical integration. Such expansion activities clearly increase the scope and complexity of the operations. The functional structure provides for a high level of centralization that helps to ensure integration and control over the related product-market activities or multiple primary activities (from inbound logistics to operations to marketing, sales, and service) in the value chain (addressed in Chapters 3 and 4). Strategy Spotlight 10.1 provides an example of an effective functional organization structure—Parkdale Mills.

Exhibit 10.2
Functional Organizational Structure

simple organizational structure an organizational form in which the owner-manager makes most of the decisions and controls activities, and the staff serves as an extension of the top executive.

functional organizational structure an organizational form in which the major functions of the firm, such as production, marketing, R&D, and accounting, are grouped internally.

Parkdale Mills: A Successful Functional Organizational Structure

For more than 80 years, Parkdale Mills, with approximately $1 billion in revenues, has been the industry leader in the production of cotton and cotton blend yarns. Their expertise comes by concentrating on a single product line, perfecting processes, and welcoming innovation. According to CEO Andy Warlick, "I think we've probably spent more than any

two competitors combined on new equipment and robotics. We do this because we have to compete in a global market where a lot of the competition has a lower wage structure and gets subsidies that we don't receive, so we really have to focus on consistency and cost control." Yarn making is generally considered to be a commodity business, and Parkdale is the industry's low-cost producer.

Tasks are highly standardized and authority is centralized with Duke Kimbrell, founder and chairman, and CEO Andy Warlick. The firm operates a bare-bones staff with a small staff of top executives. Kimbrell and Warlick are considered shrewd about the cotton market, technology, customer loyalty, and incentive pay.

Sources: Stewart, C. 2003. The Perfect Yarn. The Manufacturer.com, July 31; www.parkdalemills.com; Berman, P. 1987. The Fast Track Isn't Always the Best Track. *Forbes*, November 2: 60–64; and personal communication with Duke Kimbrell, March 11, 2005.

Advantages By bringing together specialists into functional departments, a firm is able to enhance its coordination and control within each of the functional areas. Decision making in the firm will be centralized at the top of the organization. This enhances the organizational-level (as opposed to functional area) perspective across the various functions in the organization. In addition, the functional structure provides for a more efficient use of managerial and technical talent since functional area expertise is pooled in a single department (e.g., marketing) instead of being spread across a variety of product-market areas. Finally, career paths and professional development in specialized areas are facilitated.

Disadvantages The differences in values and orientations among functional areas may impede communication and coordination. Edgar Schein of MIT has argued that shared assumptions, often based on similar backgrounds and experiences of members, form around functional units in an organization. This leads to what are often called "stove pipes" or "silos," in which departments view themselves as isolated, self-contained units with little need for interaction and coordination with other departments. This erodes communication because functional groups may have not only different goals but also differing meanings of words and concepts. According to Schein:

> The word "marketing" will mean product development to the engineer, studying customers through market research to the product manager, merchandising to the salesperson, and constant change in design to the manufacturing manager. When they try to work together, they will often attribute disagreements to personalities and fail to notice the deeper, shared assumptions that color how each function thinks.[7]

Such narrow functional orientations also may lead to short-term thinking based largely upon what is best for the functional area, not the entire organization. In a manufacturing firm, sales may want to offer a wide range of customized products to appeal to the firm's customers; R&D may overdesign products and components to achieve technical elegance; and manufacturing may favor no-frills products that can be produced at low cost by means of long production runs. Functional structures may overburden the top executives in the firm because conflicts have a tendency to be "pushed up" to the top of the organization since there are no managers who are responsible for the specific product lines. Functional structures make it difficult to establish uniform performance standards across the entire organization. It may be relatively easy to evaluate production managers on the basis of production volume and cost control, but establishing performance measures for engineering, R&D, and accounting become more problematic.

Divisional Structure

The **divisional organizational structure** (sometimes called the multidivisional structure or M-Form) is organized around products, projects, or markets. Each of the divisions, in turn, includes its own functional specialists who are typically organized into departments.[8] A divisional structure encompasses a set of relatively autonomous units governed by a central corporate office. The operating divisions are relatively independent and consist of products and services that are different from those of the other divisions. Operational decision making in a large business places excessive demands on the firm's top management. In order to attend to broader, longer-term organizational issues, top-level managers must delegate decision making to lower-level managers. Divisional executives play a key role: they help to determine the product-market and financial objectives for the division as well as their division's contribution to overall corporate performance.[9] The rewards are based largely on measures of financial performance such as net income and revenue. Exhibit 10.3 illustrates a divisional structure.

General Motors was among the earliest firms to adopt the divisional organizational structure.[10] In the 1920s the company formed five major product divisions (Cadillac, Buick, Oldsmobile, Pontiac, and Chevrolet) as well as several industrial divisions. Since then, many firms have discovered that as they diversified into new product-market activities, functional structures—with their emphasis on single functional departments—were unable to manage the increased complexity of the entire business.

Advantages By creating separate divisions to manage individual product markets, there is a separation of strategic and operating control. Divisional managers can focus their efforts on improving operations in the product markets for which they are responsible, and corporate officers can devote their time to overall strategic issues for the entire corporation. The focus on a division's products and markets—by the divisional executives—provides the corporation with an enhanced ability to respond quickly to important changes. Since there

divisional organizational structure an organizational form in which products, projects, or product markets are grouped internally.

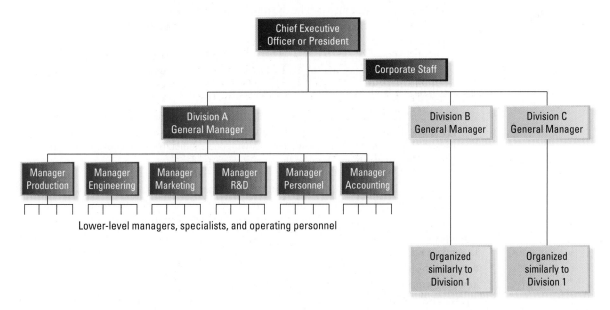

Exhibit 10.3 Divisional Organizational Structure

Brinker International Changes to a Divisional Organizational Structure

Although Brinker International had a traditional functional structure, changes in its competitive outlook forced management to take a closer look at the organizational design of the firm. The firm controls a variety of restaurant chains and bakeries, including Wildfire, Big Bowl, and Chili's.

With all these interests under one corporate roof, management of these disparate entities became difficult. The fragmented $330 billion restaurant and bakery industry caters to highly focused market niches. The original

Source: CEO interview: Ronald A. McDougall, Brinker International. 1999. *Wall Street Transcript*, January 20: 1–4.

functional design of the Brinker chain had some disadvantages as the company grew. With areas separated by function, it became hard to focus efforts on a single restaurant chain. The diverse markets served by the bakeries and restaurants began to lose their focus.

As a result, Brinker International changed to a divisional structure. This allowed the company to consolidate individuals who worked with a single restaurant or bakery chain into a separate division. Brinker referred to these as concept teams, with each concept team responsible for the operation of a single line of business. This focused effort streamlined the company's ability to concentrate on the market niche served by each of its restaurants and bakeries.

are functional departments within each division of the corporation, the problems associated with sharing resources across functional departments are minimized. Because there are multiple levels of general managers (executives responsible for integrating and coordinating all functional areas), the development of general management talent is enhanced. Strategy Spotlight 10.2 discusses the rationale behind Brinker Corporation's change in structure from functional to divisional.

Disadvantages   It can be very expensive; there can be increased costs due to the duplication of personnel, operations, and investment since each division must staff multiple functional departments. There also can be dysfunctional competition among divisions since each division tends to become concerned solely about its own operations. Divisional managers are often evaluated on common measures such as return on assets and sales growth. If goals are conflicting, there can be a sense of a "zero-sum" game that would discourage sharing ideas and resources among the divisions for the common good of the corporation. Ghoshal and Bartlett, two leading strategy scholars, note:

> As their label clearly warns, divisions divide. The divisional model fragmented companies' resources; it created vertical communication channels that insulated business units and prevented them from sharing their strengths with one another. Consequently, the whole of the corporation was often less than the sum of its parts.[11]

With many divisions providing different products and services, there is the chance that differences in image and quality may occur across divisions. One division may offer no-frills products of lower quality that may erode the brand reputation of another division that has top quality, highly differentiated offerings. Since each division is evaluated in terms of financial measures such as return on investment and revenue growth, there is often an urge to focus on short-term performance. If corporate management uses quarterly profits as the key performance indicator, divisional management may tend to put significant emphasis on "making the numbers" and minimizing activities, such as advertising, maintenance, and capital investments, which would detract from short-term performance measures.

We'll discuss two variations of the divisional form: the strategic business unit (SBU) and holding company structures.

Strategic Business Unit (SBU) Structure Highly diversified corporations such as ConAgra, a $12 billion food producer, may consist of dozens of different divisions.[12] If ConAgra were to use a purely divisional structure, it would be nearly impossible for the corporate office to plan and coordinate activities because the span of control would be too large. To attain synergies, ConAgra has put its diverse businesses into three primary SBUs: food service (restaurants), retail (grocery stores), and agricultural products.

With an **SBU structure,** divisions with similar products, markets, and/or technologies are grouped into homogeneous units to achieve some synergies. These include those discussed in Chapter 6 for related diversification, such as leveraging core competencies, sharing infrastructures, and market power. Generally the more related businesses are within a corporation, the fewer SBUs will be required. Each of the SBUs in the corporation operates as a profit center.

strategic business unit (SBU) structure an organizational form in which products, projects, or product market divisions are grouped into homogeneous units.

Advantages The SBU structure makes the task of planning and control by the corporate office more manageable. Also, with greater decentralization of authority, individual businesses can react more quickly to important changes in the environment than if all divisions had to report directly to the corporate office.

Disadvantages Since the divisions are grouped into SBUs, it may become difficult to achieve synergies across SBUs. If divisions in different SBUs have potential sources of synergy, it may become difficult for them to be realized. The additional level of management increases the number of personnel and overhead expenses, while the additional hierarchical level removes the corporate office further from the individual divisions. The corporate office may become unaware of key developments that could have a major impact on the corporation.

Holding Company Structure The **holding company structure** (sometimes referred to as a *conglomerate*) is also a variation of the divisional structure. Whereas the SBU structure is often used when similarities exist between the individual businesses (or divisions), the holding company structure is appropriate when the businesses in a corporation's portfolio do not have much in common. Thus, the potential for synergies is limited.

holding company structure an organizational form that is a variation of the divisional organizational structure in which the divisions have a high degree of autonomy both from other divisions and from corporate headquarters.

Holding company structures are most appropriate for firms with a strategy of unrelated diversification. Companies such as Hanson Trust, ITT, and the CP group of Thailand have used holding company structure to implement their unrelated diversification strategies. Since there are few similarities across the businesses, the corporate offices in these companies provide a great deal of autonomy to operating divisions and rely on financial controls and incentive programs to obtain high levels of performance from the individual businesses. Corporate staffs at these firms tend to be small because of their limited involvement in the overall operation of their various businesses.[13]

Advantages The holding company structure has the cost savings associated with fewer personnel and the lower overhead resulting from a small corporate office and fewer hierarchical levels. The autonomy of the holding company structure increases the motivational level of divisional executives and enables them to respond quickly to market opportunities and threats.

Disadvantages There is an inherent lack of control and dependence that corporate-level executives have on divisional executives. Major problems could arise if key divisional executives leave the firm, because the corporate office has very little "bench strength"— additional managerial talent ready to quickly fill key positions. If problems arise in a division, it may become very difficult to turn around individual businesses because of limited staff support in the corporate office.

Matrix Structure

One approach that tries to overcome the inadequacies inherent in the other structures is the **matrix organizational structure.** It is a combination of the functional and divisional structures. Most commonly, functional departments are combined with product groups on a project basis. For example, a product group may want to develop a new addition to its line; for this project, it obtains personnel from functional departments such as marketing, production, and engineering. These personnel work under the manager of the product group for the duration of the project, which can vary from a few weeks to an open-ended period of time. The individuals who work in a matrix organization become responsible to two managers: the project manager and the manager of their functional area. Exhibit 10.4 illustrates a matrix structure.

Some large multinational corporations rely on a matrix structure to combine product groups and geographical units. Product managers have global responsibility for the development, manufacturing, and distribution of their own line, while managers of geographical regions have responsibility for the profitability of the businesses in their regions. In the mid-1990s, Caterpillar, Inc., implemented this type of structure.

Dell Computer relies on the matrix concept, with its dual reporting responsibility, to enhance accountability as well as develop general managers. According to former CEO Kevin Rollins:[14]

> We're organized in a matrix of sales regions and product groups. Then we break each of those groups down to a pretty fine level of sub-products and sales sub-segments. Dell has more P&L managers, and smaller business units, than most companies its size. This not only increases accountability to the customer, it helps train general managers by moving them from smaller to larger businesses as their skills develop.
>
> Our matrix organization has a third level—our business councils. For example, we have a small-business sales group in each country, along with product development people who become very familiar with what small-business customers buy. In addition, we have our worldwide small-business council made up of all our small-business GMs and product managers. Everyone in these councils sees everyone else's P&L, so it provides another set of checks and balances.

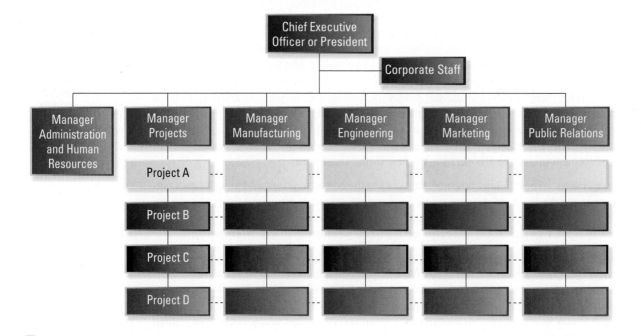

Exhibit 10.4 **Matrix Organizational Structure**

Advantages The matrix structure facilitates the use of specialized personnel, equipment, and facilities. Instead of duplicating functions, as would be the case in a divisional structure based on products, the resources are shared. Individuals with high expertise can divide their time among multiple projects. Such resource sharing and collaboration enable a firm to use resources more efficiently and to respond more quickly and effectively to changes in the competitive environment. The flexibility inherent in a matrix structure provides professionals with a broader range of responsibility. Such experience enables them to develop their skills and competencies.

Disadvantages The dual-reporting structures can result in uncertainty and lead to intense power struggles and conflict over the allocation of personnel and other resources. Working relationships become more complicated. This may result in excessive reliance on group processes and teamwork, along with a diffusion of responsibility, which in turn may erode timely decision making. Exhibit 10.5 briefly summarizes the advantages and disadvantages of the functional, divisional, and matrix organizational structures.

International Operations: Implications for Organizational Structure

>LO3
The implications of a firm's international operations for organizational structure.

Today's managers must maintain an international outlook on their firm's businesses and competitive strategies. In the global marketplace, managers must ensure consistency between their strategies (at the business, corporate, and international levels) and the structure of their organization. As firms expand into foreign markets, they generally follow a pattern of change in structure that parallels the changes in their strategies. Three major contingencies that influence the chosen structure are (1) the type of strategy that is driving a firm's foreign operations, (2) product diversity, and (3) the extent to which a firm is dependent on foreign sales.[15]

As international operations become an important part of a firm's overall operations, managers must make changes that are consistent with their firm's structure. The primary types of structures used to manage a firm's international operations are:[16]

- International division
- Geographic-area division
- Worldwide functional
- Worldwide product division
- Worldwide matrix

Multidomestic strategies are driven by political and cultural imperatives requiring managers within each country to respond to local conditions. The structures consistent with such a strategic orientation are the **international division** and **geographic-area division structures.** Here local managers are provided with a high level of autonomy to manage their operations within the constraints and demands of their geographic market. As a firm's foreign sales increase as a percentage of its total sales, it will likely change from an international division to a geographic-area division structure. And, as a firm's product and/or market diversity becomes large, it is likely to benefit from a **worldwide matrix structure.**

Global strategies are driven by economic pressures that require managers to view operations in different geographic areas to be managed for overall efficiency. The structures consistent with the efficiency perspective are the *worldwide functional* and *worldwide product division* structures. Here, division managers view the marketplace as homogeneous and devote relatively little attention to local market, political, and economic factors. The choice between these two types of structures is guided largely by the extent of product diversity. Firms with relatively low levels of product diversity may opt for a worldwide product division structure. However, if significant product–market diversity results from highly unrelated international acquisitions, a worldwide holding company structure should

international division structure an organizational form in which international operations are in a separate, autonomous division. Most domestic operations are kept in other parts of the organization.

geographic-area division structure a type of divisional organizational structure in which operations in geographical regions are grouped internally.

worldwide matrix structure a type of matrix organizational structure that has one line of authority for geographic-area divisions and another line of authority for worldwide product divisions.

Exhibit 10.5 Functional, Divisional, and Matrix Organizational Structures: Advantages and Disadvantages

Functional Structure

Advantages	Disadvantages
• Pooling of specialists enhances coordination and control.	• Differences in functional area orientation impede communication and coordination.
• Centralized decision making enhances an organizational perspective across functions.	• Tendency for specialists to develop short-term perspective and narrow functional orientation.
• Efficient use of managerial and technical talent.	• Functional area conflicts may overburden top-level decision makers.
• Facilitates career paths and professional development in specialized areas.	• Difficult to establish uniform performance standards.

Divisional Structure

Advantages	Disadvantages
• Increases strategic and operational control, permitting corporate-level executives to address strategic issues.	• Increased costs incurred through duplication of personnel, operations, and investment.
• Quick response to environmental changes.	• Dysfunctional competition among divisions may detract from overall corporate performance.
• Increases focus on products and markets.	• Difficult to maintain uniform corporate image.
• Minimizes problems associated with sharing resources across functional areas.	• Overemphasis on short-term performance.
• Facilitates development of general managers.	

Matrix Structure

Advantages	Disadvantages
• Increases market responsiveness through collaboration and synergies among professional colleagues.	• Dual-reporting relationships can result in uncertainty regarding accountability.
• Allows more efficient utilization of resources.	• Intense power struggles may lead to increased levels of conflict.
• Improves flexibility, coordination, and communication.	• Working relationships may be more complicated and human resources duplicated.
• Increases professional development through a broader range of responsibility.	• Excessive reliance on group processes and teamwork may impede timely decision making.

be implemented. Such firms have very little commonality among products, markets, or technologies, and have little need for integration.

Global Start-Ups: A New Phenomenon

International expansion occurs rather late for most corporations, typically after possibilities of domestic growth are exhausted. Increasingly, we are seeing two interrelated phenomena. First, many firms now expand internationally relatively early in their history. Second, some firms are "born global"—that is, from the very beginning, many start-ups are global in their activities. For example, Logitech Inc., a leading producer of personal computer accessories, was global from day one. Founded in 1982 by a Swiss national and two Italians, the company was headquartered both in California and Switzerland. R&D and manufacturing were also conducted in both locations and, subsequently, in Taiwan and Ireland.[17]

The success of companies such as Logitech challenges the conventional wisdom that a company must first build up assets, internal processes, and experience before venturing into faraway lands. It also raises a number of questions: What exactly is a global start-up? Under what conditions should a company start out as a global start-up? What does it take to succeed as a global start-up?

A **global start-up** has been defined as a business organization that, from inception, seeks to derive significant competitive advantage from the use of resources and the sale of outputs in multiple countries. Right from the beginning, it uses in-puts from around the world and sells its products and services to customers around the world. Geographical boundaries of nation-states are irrelevant for a global start-up.

There is no reason for every start-up to be global. Being global necessarily involves higher communication, coordination, and transportation costs. Therefore, it is important to identify the circumstances under which going global from the beginning is advantageous.[18] First, if the required human resources are globally dispersed, going global may be the best way to access those resources. For example, Italians are masters in fine leather and Europeans in ergonomics. Second, in many cases foreign financing may be easier to obtain and more suitable. Traditionally, U.S. venture capitalists have shown greater willingness to bear risk, but they have shorter time horizons in their expectations for return. If a U.S. start-up is looking for patient capital, it may be better off looking overseas. Third, the target customers in many specialized industries are located in other parts of the world. Fourth, in many industries a gradual move from domestic markets to foreign markets is no longer possible because, if a product is successful, foreign competitors may immediately imitate it. Therefore, preemptive entry into foreign markets may be the only option. Finally, because of high up-front development costs, a global market is often necessary to recover the costs. This is particularly true for start-ups from smaller nations that do not have access to large domestic markets.

Successful management of a global start-up presents many challenges. Communication and coordination across time zones and cultures are always problematic. Since most global start-ups have far less resources than well-established corporations, one key for success is to internalize few activities and outsource the rest. Managers of such firms must have considerable prior international experience so that they can successfully handle the inevitable communication problems and cultural conflicts. Another key for success is to keep the communication and coordination costs low. The only way to achieve this is by creating less costly administrative mechanisms. The boundaryless organizational designs that we discuss in the next section are particularly suitable for global start-ups because of their flexibility and low cost.

Strategy Spotlight 10.3 discusses three global start-ups.

How an Organization's Structure Can Influence Strategy Formulation

Discussions of the relationship between strategy and structure usually strongly imply that structure follows strategy. The strategy that a firm chooses (e.g., related diversification) dictates such structural elements as the division of tasks, the need for integration of activities, and authority relationships within the organization. However, an existing structure can influence strategy formulation. Once a firm's structure is in place, it is very difficult and expensive to change.[19] Executives may not be able to modify their duties and responsibilities greatly, or may not welcome the disruption associated with a transfer to a new location. There are costs associated with hiring, training, and replacing executive, managerial, and operating personnel. Strategy cannot be formulated without considering structural elements.

An organization's structure can also have an important influence on how it competes in the marketplace. It can also strongly influence a firm's strategy, day-to-day operations, and performance.[20] We discussed Brinker International's move to a divisional structure in

strategy spotlight

Global on Day One

Conventional wisdom would suggest that a firm "get it right" in its home market before venturing abroad. Once established in the home market, a firm could consider the relatively risky move of selling in other countries. However, many new firms are turning conventional wisdom on its head.

More and more start-ups are being born global for two basic reasons. One reason is defensive: to be competitive, many new businesses need to globalize some parts of their business to control costs, access customers, or tap employees from day one. While this might seem an obviously logical choice, until recently many venture capital firms required companies to build locally first, gain a track record, and then branch out. The other reason firms are born global is offensive; many entrepreneurs find that new business opportunities span multiple countries. Going after opportunities in several countries simultaneously from the start can sometimes give firms the operating scope they need to thrive.

Going global is not without significant challenges. Coping with distance in terms of physical, time zone, and cultural dimensions is perhaps a larger hurdle for smaller organizations to tackle. However, start-ups that can articulate a global purpose tend to do better than those with weaker goal orientation toward a global strategy. The following three examples are of start-ups that thought global from day one:

- In 2008, Actavis Pharmaceuticals' revenues were over $2 billion. Robert Wessman took control of this

small generic pharmaceutical maker in his native Iceland in 1999. Within weeks of taking over, he realized that to succeed in the generics market, a player had to globalize its core functions, including manufacturing and R&D. Actavis has since entered 60 countries to gain scale and develop a larger portfolio of drugs. By 2009 the company had 650 products on the market and 400 more in development.

- Baradok Pridor, 38, and Yonatan Aumann, 42, Israeli founders of ClearForest, developed an innovative software product—a program that can analyze unstructured electronic data, such as a webpage or a video clip, as if it were already in a spreadsheet or database. Instead of waiting for customers to show up, right from the beginning, they started sending their engineers to make presentations to potential clients around the world. Today, the company's customers include Dow Chemical, Thomson Financial, and the FBI! They have raised $33 million so far in three rounds of venture financing. Interestingly, the headquarters of the 83-person company is in Boston!

- HyperRoll, an Israeli company that makes software for analyzing massive databases, has raised $28 million in venture funding. Referring to the firm's hiring practices, Yossi Matias, founder of HyperRoll, says, "We build the strongest team possible, unconstrained by locality, affinity, or culture. It requires every employee to accept and support a multicultural environment." Although the firm is essentially an Israeli start-up, he even banned the use of Hebrew in the office to facilitate greater integration between the American and Israeli employees.

Sources: Isenberg, D. J. 2008. The Global Entrepreneur. *Harvard Business Review*, December: 107–111; Copeland, M. V. 2004. The Start-Up Oasis. *Business 2.0*, August: 46–48.; Brown, E. 2004. Global Start-Up. *Forbes*, November 29: 150–161.

order to organize its restaurant groups into different units to focus on market niches. This new structure should enable the firm to adapt to change more rapidly and innovate more effectively with the various restaurant brands. Brinker's management did not feel that they were as effective with their previous functional organizational structure.

> **>LO4**
>
> Why there is no "one best way" to design strategic reward and evaluation systems, and the important contingent roles of business- and corporate-level strategies.

Linking Strategic Reward and Evaluation Systems to Business-Level and Corporate-Level Strategies

The effective use of reward and evaluation systems can play a critical role in motivating managers to conform to organizational strategies, achieve performance targets, and reduce the gap between organizational and individual goals. In contrast, reward systems, if improperly designed, can lead to behaviors that either are detrimental to organizational performance or can lower morale and cause employee dissatisfaction.

As we will see in this section, there is no "one best way" to design reward and evaluation systems. Instead, it is contingent on many factors. Two of the most important factors are a firm's business-level strategy (see Chapter 5) and its corporate-level strategy (see Chapter 6).

Business-Level Strategy: Reward and Evaluation Systems

In Chapter 5 we discussed two approaches that firms may take to secure competitive advantages: overall cost leadership and differentiation.[21] As we might expect, implementing these strategies requires fundamentally different organizational arrangements, approaches to control, and reward and incentive systems.

Overall Cost Leadership   This strategy requires that product lines remain rather stable and that innovations deal mostly with production processes. Given the emphasis on efficiency, costly changes even in production processes tend to be rare. Since products are quite standardized and change rather infrequently, procedures can be developed to divide work into its basic components—those that are routine, standardized, and ideal for semiskilled and unskilled employees. As such, firms competing on the basis of cost must implement tight cost controls, frequent and comprehensive reports to monitor the costs associated with outputs, and highly structured tasks and responsibilities. Incentives tend to be based on explicit financial targets since innovation and creativity are expensive and might tend to erode competitive advantages.

Nucor a highly successful steel producer with $23 billion in revenues, competes primarily on the basis of cost and has a reward and incentive system that is largely based on financial outputs and financial measures.[22] Nucor uses four incentive compensation systems that correspond to the levels of management.

1. *Production incentive program.* Groups of 20 to 40 people are paid a weekly bonus based on either anticipated product time or tonnage produced. Each shift and production line is in a separate bonus group.
2. *Department managers.* Bonuses are based on divisional performance, primarily measured by return on assets.
3. *Employees not directly involved in production.* These include engineers, accountants, secretaries, receptionists, and others. Bonuses are based on two factors: divisional and corporate return on assets.
4. *Senior incentive programs.* Salaries are lower than comparable companies, but a significant portion of total compensation is based on return on stockholder equity. A portion of pretax earnings is placed in a pool and divided among officers as bonuses that are part cash and part stock.

The culture at Nucor reflects its reward and incentive system. Since incentive compensation can account for more than half of their paychecks, employees become nearly obsessed with productivity and apply a lot of pressure on each other. Ken Iverson, a former CEO, recalled an instance in which one employee arrived at work in sunglasses instead of safety glasses, preventing the team from doing any work. Furious, the other workers chased him around the plant with a piece of angle iron!

Differentiation   This strategy involves the development of innovative products and services that require experts who can identify the crucial elements of intricate, creative designs and marketing decisions. Highly trained professionals such as scientists and engineers are essential for devising, assessing, implementing and continually changing complex product designs. This also requires extensive collaboration and cooperation among specialists and functional managers from different areas within a firm. They must evaluate and implement a new design, constantly bearing in mind marketing, financial, production, and engineering considerations.

Given the need for cooperation and coordination in many functional areas, it becomes difficult to evaluate individuals using set quantitative criteria. It also is difficult to measure specific outcomes of such efforts and attribute outcomes to specific individuals. More behavioral measures (how effectively employees collaborate and share information) and intangible incentives and rewards become necessary to support a strong culture and to motivate employees. Consider 3M, a highly innovative company whose core value is innovation.

> Rewards are tied closely to risk-taking and innovation-oriented behavior. Managers are not penalized for product failures. Instead, those same people are encouraged to work on another project that borrows from their shared experience and insight. A culture of creativity and "thinking out of the box" is reinforced by their well-known "15 percent rule," which permits employees to set aside 15 percent of their work time to pursue personal research interests. And a familiar 3M homily, "Thou shall not kill new ideas for products," is known as the 11th commandment. It is the source of countless stories, including one that tells how L. D. DeSimone (3M's former CEO) tried five times (and failed) to kill the project that yielded the 3M blockbuster product, Thinsulate.[23]

Corporate-Level Strategy: Reward and Evaluation Systems

In Chapter 6 we discussed two broad types of diversification strategies: related and unrelated. The type of diversification strategy that a firm follows has important implications for the type of reward and evaluation systems that it should use.

Sharp Corporation, a $36 billion Japanese consumer electronics giant follows a strategy of *related* diversification.[24] Its most successful technology has been liquid crystal displays (LCDs) that are critical components in nearly all of the firm's products. With their expertise in this area, they are moving into high-end displays for cellular telephones, handheld computers, and digital computers.[25]

Given the need to leverage such technologies across multiple product lines, Sharp needs reward and evaluation systems that foster coordination and sharing. It must focus more on individuals' behavior rather than on short-term financial outcomes. Promotion is a powerful incentive, and it is generally based on seniority and subtle skills exhibited over time, such as teamwork and communication. It helps to ensure that the company's reward system will not reward short-term self-interested orientations.

Like many Japanese companies, Sharp's culture reinforces the view that the firm is a family whose members should cooperate for the greater good. With the policy of lifetime employment, turnover is low. This encourages employees to pursue what is best for the entire company. Such an outlook lessens the inevitable conflict over sharing important resources such as R&D knowledge.

In contrast to Sharp, Hanson PLC (a British conglomerate) followed a strategy of unrelated diversification for most of its history. At one time it owned as many as 150 operating companies in areas such as tobacco, footwear, building products, brewing, and food. There were limited product similarities across businesses and therefore little need for sharing of resources and knowledge across divisional boundaries. James Hanson and Gordon White, founders of the company, actually did not permit any sharing of resources between operating companies even if it was feasible!

Their reward and evaluation system placed such heavy emphasis on individual accountability that they viewed resource sharing, with its potential for mutual blaming, unacceptable. The operating managers had more than 60 percent of their compensation tied to annual financial performance of their subsidiaries. All decision making was decentralized so that subsidiary managers could be held responsible for the return on capital they employed. However, there was one area in which they had to obtain approval from the corporate office. No subsidiary manager was allowed to incur a capital expenditure greater than $3,000 without permission from the corporate office. Hanson managed to be successful with a very small corporate office because of its decentralized structure, tight financial controls, and an

Exhibit 10.6
Summary of
Relationships
between Reward and
Evaluation Systems
and Business-Level
and Corporate-Level
Strategies

Level of Strategy	Types of Strategy	Need for Interdependence	Primary Type of Reward and Evaluation System
Business-level	Overall cost leadership	Low	Financial
Business-level	Differentiation	High	Behavioral
Corporate-level	Related diversification	High	Behavioral
Corporate-level	Unrelated diversification	Low	Financial

incentive system that motivated managers to meet financial goals. Gordon White was proud of claiming that he had never visited any of the operating companies that were part of the Hanson empire.[26]

The key issue becomes the need for *in*dependence versus *inter*dependence. With cost leadership strategies and unrelated diversification, there tends to be less need for interdependence. The reward and evaluation systems focus more on the use of financial indicators because unit costs, profits, and revenues can be rather easily attributed to a given business unit or division.

In contrast, firms that follow related diversification strategies have intense needs for tight interdependencies among the functional areas and business units. Sharing of resources, including raw materials, R&D knowledge, marketing information, and so on, is critical to organizational success. It is more important to achieve synergies with value-creating activities and business units than with cost leadership or unrelated strategies. Reward and evaluation systems tend to incorporate more behavioral indicators.

Although Exhibit 10.6 suggests guidelines on how an organization should match its strategies to its evaluation and reward systems, all organizations must have combinations of both financial and behavioral rewards. Both overall cost leadership and unrelated diversification strategies require a need for collaboration and the sharing of best practices across both value-creating activities and business units. General Electric has developed many integrating mechanisms to enhance sharing "best practices" across what would appear to be rather unrelated businesses such as jet engines, appliances, and network television. For both differentiation and related diversification strategies, financial indicators such as revenue growth and profitability should not be overlooked at both the business-unit and corporate levels.

Boundaryless Organizational Designs

The term *boundaryless* may bring to mind a chaotic organizational reality in which "anything goes." This is not the case. As Jack Welch, GE's former CEO, has suggested, boundaryless does not imply that all internal and external boundaries vanish completely, but that they become more open and permeable.[27] Strategy Spotlight 10.4 discusses four types of boundaries.

We are not suggesting that **boundaryless organizational designs** replace the traditional forms of organizational structure, but they should complement them. Sharp Corp. has implemented a functional structure to attain economies of scale with its applied research and manufacturing skills. However, to bring about this key objective, Sharp has relied on several integrating mechanisms and processes:

> To prevent functional groups from becoming vertical chimneys that obstruct product development, Sharp's product managers have responsibility—but not authority—for coordinating the entire set of value-chain activities. And the company convenes enormous numbers of cross-unit and corporate committees to ensure that shared activities, including the corporate R&D unit and sales forces, are optimally configured and allocated among the different product lines. Sharp invests in such time-intensive coordination to minimize the inevitable conflicts that arise when units share important activities.[28]

>LO5
The different types of boundaryless organizations— barrier-free, modular, and virtual—and their relative advantages and disadvantages.

boundaryless organizational designs organizations in which the boundaries, including vertical, horizontal, external, and geographic boundaries, are permeable.

strategy spotlight

Boundary Types

There are primarily four types of boundaries that place limits on organizations. In today's dynamic business environment, different types of boundaries are needed to foster high degrees of interaction with outside influences and varying levels of permeability.

1. *Vertical boundaries between levels in the organization's hierarchy.* SmithKline Beecham asks employees at different hierarchical levels to brainstorm ideas for managing clinical trial data. The ideas are incorporated into action plans that significantly cut the new product approval time of its pharmaceuticals. This would not have been possible if the barriers between levels of individuals in the organization had been too high.

2. *Horizontal boundaries between functional areas.* Fidelity Investments makes the functional barriers

more porous and flexible among divisions, such as marketing, operations, and customer service, in order to offer customers a more integrated experience when conducting business with the company. Customers can take their questions to one person, reducing the chance that customers will "get the runaround" from employees who feel customer service is not their responsibility. At Fidelity, customer service is everyone's business, regardless of functional area.

3. *External boundaries between the firm and its customers, suppliers, and regulators.* GE Lighting, by working closely with retailers, functions throughout the value chain as a single operation. This allows GE to track point-of-sale purchases, giving it better control over inventory management.

4. *Geographic boundaries between locations, cultures, and markets.* The global nature of today's business environment spurred PricewaterhouseCoopers to use a global groupware system. This allows the company to instantly connect to its 26 worldwide offices.

Source: Ashkenas, R. 1997. The Organization's New Clothes. In Hesselbein, F., Goldsmith, M., and Beckhard, R. (Eds.). *The Organization of the Future:* 104–106. San Francisco: Jossey Bass.

We will discuss three approaches to making boundaries more permeable, that help to facilitate the widespread sharing of knowledge and information across both the internal and external boundaries of the organization. The *barrier-free* type involves making all organizational boundaries—internal and external—more permeable. Teams are a central building block for implementing the boundaryless organization. The *modular* and *virtual* types of organizations focus on the need to create seamless relationships with external organizations such as customers or suppliers. While the modular type emphasizes the outsourcing of noncore activities, the virtual (or network) organization focuses on alliances among independent entities formed to exploit specific market opportunities.

The Barrier-Free Organization

The "boundary" mind-set is ingrained deeply into bureaucracies. It is evidenced by such clichés as "That's not my job," "I'm here from corporate to help," or endless battles over transfer pricing. In the traditional company, boundaries are clearly delineated in the design of an organization's structure. Their basic advantage is that the roles of managers and employees are simple, clear, well-defined, and long-lived. A major shortcoming was pointed out to the authors during an interview with a high-tech executive: "Structure tends to be divisive; it leads to territorial fights."

Such structures are being replaced by fluid, ambiguous, and deliberately ill-defined tasks and roles. Just because work roles are no longer clearly defined, however, does not mean that differences in skills, authority, and talent disappear. A **barrier-free organization** enables a firm to bridge real differences in culture, function, and goals to find common ground that facilitates information sharing and other forms of cooperative behavior. Eliminating the multiple boundaries that stifle productivity and innovation can enhance the

barrier-free organization an organizational design in which firms bridge real differences in culture, function, and goals to find common ground that facilitates information sharing and other forms of cooperative behavior.

United Technologies Corporation's PureCycle: An Effective Use of the Boundaryless Concept

United Technologies Corporation is a giant manufacturing conglomerate that has been on a roll. Revenues and profits for 2006 were $48 billion and $3.7 billion, respectively, which represents an annual increase of over 15 percent over the most recent four-year period.

Like many diversified firms, UTC faced a challenge in developing synergies across business units. UTC's wide variety of products include Carrier heating and air conditioning, Hamilton Sundstrand aerospace systems and industrial products, Otis elevators and escalators, Pratt & Whitney aircraft engines, Sikorsky helicopters, UTC Fire & Security systems, and UTC Power fuel cells. Overall, UTC spends a huge amount of money on research—about 3.5 percent of total revenues.

Historically, UTC's culture placed a high value on decentralized decision making, with each unit operating almost entirely independently of the others. Such an approach may have motivational benefits and helps each unit focus their efforts. However, it leads to "silo business units" and prevents the corporation from generating innovations in the white spaces between business units.

This approach to business troubled UTC senior vice president John Cassidy and Carl Nett, director of the firm's corporate research center, UTRC. The center is staffed with nearly 500 scientists, engineers, and staff who are charged with "bringing future technologies to the point of product insertion." They both believed that tremendous potential for growth existed in the junctures between the business units. However, such collaboration was not consistent with the

history, work practices, and cultural norms at UTC. In fact, Cassidy felt that integrating expertise and talent across business units was an "unnatural act."

What did they do? In 2002, the two executives invited top technical talent from each unit to several brainstorming sessions. The goal was to bring together a diverse set of talented professionals to create and service new markets.

Early on, a potential winner emerged from the intersection of cooling, heating, and power. Engineers from Carrier, Pratt & Whitney, and UTRC recognized that using cooling and heating equipment could transform an innovative power generation concept into a revolutionary product. Called PureCycle, the product contained virtually no new components. However, it offered a breakthrough value proposition: Customers could convert waste heat to electricity at rates substantially below those of utilities. The product held great promise because U.S. industrial plants emit roughly as much waste heat as a 50-gigawatt power plant generates (enough to run most major U.S. cities). Such an innovation certainly helps to conserve natural resources.

In retrospect, engineers involved in the PureCycle project find it hard to believe that nobody had previously thought of the idea. Thierry Jomard, a former Carrier engineer who transferred to UTRC to head the effort explains, "Carrier people are trained to think in terms of using heat exchange to produce cold air—that's the output that counts: the compressor is just there to move the fluid. Pratt & Whitney engineers, on the other hand, are power people. The outcome they are about is power, and they use turbines to get it." It wasn't until they began their collaboration that anyone recognized the opportunities before them.

Sources: www.utc.com; 2005 *UTC Annual Report;* Davidson, A. 2007. Conglomerates: United Technologies. *Forbes,* January 8: 96; and Cross, R., Liedtka, J., & Weiss, L. 2005. A Practical Guide to Social Networks. *Harvard Business Review,* 83(3): 92–101.

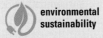

environmental sustainability

---

potential of the entire organization. Strategy Spotlight 10.5 describes how United Technologies Corporation used the boundaryless concept.

Creating Permeable Internal Boundaries For barrier-free organizations to work effectively, the level of trust and shared interests among all parts of the organization must be raised. The organization needs to develop among its employees the skill level needed to work in a more democratic organization. Barrier-free organizations also require a shift in the organization's philosophy from executive to organizational development, and from investments in high-potential individuals to investments in leveraging the talents of all individuals.

Teams can be an important aspect of barrier-free structures.[29] Jeffrey Pfeffer, author of several insightful books, including *The Human Equation,* suggests that teams have three primary advantages.[30] First, teams substitute peer-based control for hierarchical control of work activities. Employees control themselves, reducing the time and energy management needs to devote to control. Second, teams frequently develop more creative solutions to problems because they encourage the sharing of the tacit knowledge held by individuals.[31] Brainstorming, or group problem solving, involves the pooling of ideas and expertise to enhance the chances that at least one group member will think of a way to solve the problems at hand. Third, by substituting peer control for hierarchical control, teams permit the removal of layers of hierarchy and absorption of administrative tasks previously performed by specialists. This avoids the costs of having people whose sole job is to watch the people who watch other people do the work.

● Teams frequently develop more creative solutions to problems because they can share each individual's knowledge.

Effective barrier-free organizations must go beyond achieving close integration and coordination within divisions in a corporation. Research on multidivisional organizations has stressed the importance of interdivisional coordination and resource sharing.[32] This requires interdivisional task forces and committees, reward and incentive systems that emphasize interdivisional cooperation, and common training programs.

Frank Carruba (former head of Hewlett-Packard's labs) found that the difference between mediocre teams and good teams was generally varying levels of motivation and talent.[33] But what explained the difference between good teams and truly superior teams? The key difference—and this explained a 40 percent overall difference in performance—was the way members treated each other: the degree to which they believed in one another and created an atmosphere of encouragement rather than competition. Vision, talent, and motivation could carry a team only so far. What clearly stood out in the "super" teams were higher levels of authenticity and caring, which allowed the full synergy of their individual talents, motivation, and vision.

Developing Effective Relationships with External Constituencies
In barrier-free organizations, managers must also create flexible, porous organizational boundaries and establish communication flows and mutually beneficial relationships with internal (e.g., employees) and external (e.g., customers) constituencies.[34] Michael Dell, founder and CEO of Dell Computer, is a strong believer in fostering close relationships with his customers:

> We're not going to be just your PC vendor anymore. We're going to be your IT department for PCs. Boeing, for example, has 100,000 Dell PCs, and we have 30 people that live at Boeing, and if you look at the things we're doing for them or for other customers, we don't look like a supplier, we look more like Boeing's PC department. We become intimately involved in planning their PC needs and the configuration of their network.
>
> It's not that we make these decisions by ourselves. They're certainly using their own people to get the best answer for the company. But the people working on PCs together, from both Dell and Boeing, understand the needs in a very intimate way. They're right there living it and breathing it, as opposed to the typical vendor who says, "Here are your computers. See you later."[35]

Barrier-free organizations create successful relationships between both internal and external constituencies, but there is one additional constituency—competitors—with whom some organizations have benefited as they developed cooperative relationships. After years of seeing its empty trucks return from warehouses back to production facilities after deliveries, General Mills teamed up with 16 of its competitors. They formed an e-commerce business to help the firms find carriers with empty cargo trailers to piggyback freight loads to distributors near the production facilities.[36] This increases revenue for all network members and reduces fuel costs.

Risks, Challenges, and Potential Downsides   Many firms find that creating and managing a barrier-free organization can be frustrating.[37] Puritan-Bennett Corporation, a manufacturer of respiratory equipment, found that its product development time more than doubled after it adopted team management. Roger J. Dolida, director of R&D, attributed this failure to a lack of top management commitment, high turnover among team members, and infrequent meetings. Often, managers trained in rigid hierarchies find it difficult to make the transition to the more democratic, participative style that teamwork requires.

Christopher Barnes, a consultant with PricewaterhouseCoopers, previously worked as an industrial engineer for Challenger Electrical Distribution (a subsidiary of Westinghouse, now part of CBS) at a plant which produced circuit-breaker boxes. His assignment was to lead a team of workers from the plant's troubled final-assembly operation with the mission: "Make things better." That vague notion set the team up for failure. After a year of futility, the team was disbanded. In retrospect, Barnes identified several reasons for the debacle: (1) limited personal credibility—he was viewed as an "outsider"; (2) a lack of commitment to the team—everyone involved was forced to be on the team; (3) poor communications—nobody was told why the team was important; (4) limited autonomy—line managers refused to give up control over team members; and (5) misaligned incentives—the culture rewarded individual performance over team performance. Barnes's experience has implications for all types of teams, whether they are composed of managerial, professional, clerical, or production personnel.[38] The pros and cons of barrier-free structures are summarized in Exhibit 10.7.

The Modular Organization

As Charles Handy, author of *The Age of Unreason,* has noted:

> While it may be convenient to have everyone around all the time, having all of your workforce's time at your command is an extravagant way of marshaling the necessary resources. It is cheaper to keep them outside the organization . . . and to buy their services when you need them.[39]

The **modular organization** outsources nonvital functions, tapping into the knowledge and expertise of "best in class" suppliers, but retains strategic control. Outsiders

modular organization an organization in which nonvital functions are outsourced, which uses the knowledge and expertise of outside suppliers while retaining strategic control.

Exhibit 10.7
Pros and Cons of Barrier-Free Structures

Pros	Cons
• Leverages the talents of all employees.	• Difficult to overcome political and authority boundaries inside and outside the organization.
• Enhances cooperation, coordination, and information sharing among functions, divisions, SBUs, and external constituencies.	• Lacks strong leadership and common vision, which can lead to coordination problems.
• Enables a quicker response to market changes through a single-goal focus.	• Time-consuming and difficult-to-manage democratic processes.
• Can lead to coordinated win–win initiatives with key suppliers, customers, and alliance partners.	• Lacks high levels of trust, which can impede performance.

• Adidas is one of many athletic shoe companies that has outsourced most of its production to low-cost labor countries such as China and Vietnam.

may be used to manufacture parts, handle logistics, or perform accounting activities.[40] The value chain can be used to identify the key primary and support activities performed by a firm to create value: Which activities do we keep "in-house" and which activities do we outsource to suppliers?[41] The organization becomes a central hub surrounded by networks of outside suppliers and specialists and parts can be added or taken away. Both manufacturing and service units may be modular.[42]

Apparel is an industry in which the modular type has been widely adopted. Nike and Reebok, for example, concentrate on their strengths: designing and marketing high-tech, fashionable footwear. Nike has few production facilities and Reebok owns no plants. These two companies contract virtually all their footwear production to suppliers in China, Vietnam, and other countries with low-cost labor. Avoiding large investments in fixed assets helps them derive large profits on minor sales increases. Nike and Reebok can keep pace with changing tastes in the marketplace because their suppliers have become expert at rapidly retooling to produce new products.[43]

In a modular company, outsourcing the noncore functions offers three advantages.

1. A firm can decrease overall costs, stimulate new product development by hiring suppliers with superior talent to that of in-house personnel, avoid idle capacity, reduce inventories, and avoid being locked into a particular technology.
2. A company can focus scarce resources on the areas where it holds a competitive advantage. These benefits can translate into more funding for R&D hiring the best engineers, and providing continuous training for sales and service staff.
3. An organization can tap into the knowledge and expertise of its specialized supply-chain partners, adding critical skills and accelerating organizational learning.[44]

The modular type enables a company to leverage relatively small amounts of capital and a small management team to achieve seemingly unattainable strategic objectives.[45] Certain preconditions are necessary before the modular approach can be successful. First, the company must work closely with suppliers to ensure that the interests of each party are being fulfilled. Companies need to find loyal, reliable vendors who can be trusted with trade secrets. They also need assurances that suppliers will dedicate their financial, physical, and human resources to satisfy strategic objectives such as lowering costs or being first to market.

Second, the modular company must be sure that it selects the proper competencies to keep in-house. For Nike and Reebok, the core competencies are design and marketing, not shoe manufacturing; for Honda, the core competence is engine technology. An organization must avoid outsourcing components that may compromise its long-term competitive advantages.

Strategic Risks of Outsourcing   The main strategic concerns are (1) loss of critical skills or developing the wrong skills, (2) loss of cross-functional skills, and (3) loss of control over a supplier.[46]

Too much outsourcing can result in a firm "giving away" too much skill and control. Outsourcing relieves companies of the requirement to maintain skill levels needed to manufacture essential components.[47] At one time, semiconductor chips seemed like a simple

Outsourcing for Talent: How Sony Develops Video Games

The convergence of Hollywood and Silicon Valley has led to the explosive growth of the worldwide video game industry, with revenues of $66.5 billion in 2008. Recently, it has overtaken the movie industry's box office receipts. While broadcast TV audiences dwindle and movie going stagnates, gaming is emerging as the newest and perhaps strongest pillar in the media world. So it's no surprise that film studios, media giants, game makers, and Japanese electronics companies are all battling to win the "Game Wars." "This is a huge shift we're seeing, and nobody wants to be left behind," says Sony Entertainment Chairman, Michael Lynton.

Sony sells hardware with its PlayStation 3 (PS3) consoles, and it has developed its handheld PlayStation Portable (PSP) product. It also develops games, such as the popular *Gran Turismo* racing and *EverQuest* online. And it owns Sony Pictures and MGM movie studios, whose Spider-Man and James Bond franchises have been mega hit games for Activision and EA. The real payoff for Sony

comes in game software sales. While Sony and other console makers sell their hardware for a loss, they typically make $5 to $10 in royalties for every game sold on their platform. PS3 had more than 300 software titles by early 2009.

Starting in 2002 with the previous generation game console, the PS2, Sony has used outside developers to produce most of its games. It has even reached out to gamers themselves. "We didn't want outside developers to be peripheral to our business model," says Andrew House, an early PlayStation team member and executive vice president of Sony Computer Entertainment America. "We knew that the widest variety of content possible was the best way to build the largest consumer base possible." Sony has searched high and low for talent. In 1997, it launched a developer kit aimed at hobbyists. "We sent it to budding college developers who wanted to try their hands," House says. Ideas from those amateurs made their way into commercial games in Japan. Meanwhile, externally developed titles, like *Final Fantasy* and *Madden NFL Football,* helped put Sony's PS2 at the top of the heap in 2001. Sony also launched a Linux developer kit for just $199 in 2002. "It's our way of feeding the market for the future. Some of the first great games were developed by people at home in their garages," says House. "If we're not getting people involved and looking for opportunities very early on, we really are missing out."

Sources: www.sony.com, 2009; Euromonitor International, 2009, Consumer Electronics Report, Global Market Information Database; House, A. 2004. Sony. *Fast Company,* April: 65; and Grover, R., Edwards, C., Rowley, I., & Moon, I. 2005. Game Wars. *BusinessWeek,* February 28: 35–40.

technology to outsource, but they have now become a critical component of a wide variety of products. Companies that have outsourced the manufacture of these chips run the risk of losing the ability to manufacture them as the technology escalates. They become more dependent upon their suppliers.

Cross-functional skills refer to the skills acquired through the interaction of individuals in various departments within a company.[48] Such interaction assists a department in solving problems as employees interface with others across functional units. However, if a firm outsources key functional responsibilities, such as manufacturing, communication across departments can become more difficult. A firm and its employees must now integrate their activities with a new, outside supplier.

The outsourced products may give suppliers too much power over the manufacturer. Suppliers that are key to a manufacturer's success can, in essence, hold the manufacturer "hostage." Nike manages this potential problem by sending full-time "product expatriates" to work at the plants of its suppliers. Also, Nike often brings top members of supplier management and technical teams to its headquarters. This way, Nike keeps close tabs on the pulse of new developments, builds rapport and trust with suppliers, and develops long-term relationships with suppliers to prevent hostage situations.

Strategy Spotlight 10.6 discusses how Sony outsources for talent to develop games for its highly successful video game business. Exhibit 10.8 summarizes the pros and cons of modular structures.[49]

Exhibit 10.8

Pros and Cons of Modular Structures

Pros	Cons
• Directs a firm's managerial and technical talent to the most critical activities.	• Inhibits common vision through reliance on outsiders.
• Maintains full strategic control over most critical activities—core competencies.	• Diminishes future competitive advantages if critical technologies or other competencies are outsourced.
• Achieves "best in class" performance at each link in the value chain.	• Increases the difficulty of bringing back into the firm activities that now add value due to market shifts.
• Leverages core competencies by outsourcing with smaller capital commitment.	• Leads to an erosion of cross-functional skills.
• Encourages information sharing and accelerates organizational learning.	• Decreases operational control and potential loss of control over a supplier.

The Virtual Organization

In contrast to the "self-reliant" thinking that guided traditional organizational designs, the strategic challenge today has become doing more with less and looking outside the firm for opportunities and solutions to problems. The virtual organization provides a new means of leveraging resources and exploiting opportunities.[50]

virtual organization a continually evolving network of independent companies that are linked together to share skills, costs, and access to one another's markets.

The **virtual organization** can be viewed as a continually evolving network of independent companies—suppliers, customers, even competitors—linked together to share skills, costs, and access to one another's markets.[51] The members of a virtual organization, by pooling and sharing the knowledge and expertise of each of the component organizations, simultaneously "know" more and can "do" more than any one member of the group could do alone. By working closely together, each gains in the long run from individual and organizational learning.[52] The term *virtual,* meaning "being in effect but not actually so," is commonly used in the computer industry. A computer's ability to appear to have more storage capacity than it really possesses is called virtual memory. Similarly, by assembling resources from a variety of entities, a virtual organization may seem to have more capabilities than it really possesses.[53]

The virtual organization is a grouping of units from different organizations that have joined in an alliance to exploit complementary skills in pursuing common strategic objectives. A case in point is Lockheed Martin's use of specialized coalitions between and among three entities—the company, academia, and government—to enhance competitiveness. According to former CEO Norman Augustine:

> The underlying beauty of this approach is that it forces us to reach outward. No matter what your size, you have to look broadly for new ideas, new approaches, new products. Lockheed Martin used this approach in a surprising manner when it set out during the height of the Cold War to make stealth aircraft and missiles. The technical idea came from research done at the Institute of Radio Engineering in Moscow in the 1960s that was published, and publicized, quite openly in the academic media.
>
> Despite the great contrasts among government, academia and private business, we have found ways to work together that have produced very positive results, not the least of which is our ability to compete on a global scale.[54]

Virtual organizations need not be permanent and participating firms may be involved in multiple alliances. Virtual organizations may involve different firms performing complementary value activities, or different firms involved jointly in the same value activities,

How Eli Lilly Used the Collaborative Power of Internet-Based Collaboration to Foster Innovation

The e.Lilly division of pharmaceutical giant Eli Lilly was among the first to harness the collaborative power of the Internet when it launched Innocentive in 2001. Innocentive is the first online, incentive-based scientific network created specifically for the global research and development community. Innocentive's online platform enabled world-class scientists and R&D-based companies to collaborate to attain innovative solutions to complex challenges.

Innocentive offers "seeker companies" the opportunity to increase their R&D potential by posting challenges without violating their confidentiality and intellectual property interests. Seeker companies might be looking for a chemical to be used in art restoration, for example, or the efficient synthesis of butane tetracarboxylic acid. David Bradin, a patent attorney from Seattle, was recently paid

$4,000 for his tetracarboxylic acid formula. And Proctor & Gamble claims that Innocentive has increased its share of its new products originating outside the company from 20 to 35 percent.

Often individuals outside of the seeker company find the best solutions to the company's problem. By using Innocentive to post their problems, companies do not have to admit publicly that they need help, yet they get access to a much broader range of ideas than can be generated inside the firm. Within firms, even those firms hiring the best and brightest scientists and engineers, ideas are tossed around by the same few people over and over. This situation can create a narrowing of the possible solutions to a problem (i.e., groupthink can occur) rather than searching over the broadest range of ideas. Anne Goldberg, technical knowledge manager at Solvay Pharmaceuticals, said, "The benefits [of Innocentive] are mainly in the simultaneous access to a lot of different scientific backgrounds that could bring new perspectives on sometimes old problems."

Sources: Libert, B. & Spector, J. 2008. *We Are Smarter Than Me.* Wharton School Publishing, Philadelphia; Lakhani, K. & Jeppesen, L. 2007. Getting Unusual Suspects to Solve R&D Puzzles. *Harvard Business Review,* 85(5): 30–32; Caldwell, T. 2007. R&D Finds Answers in the Crowd. *Information World Review,* 236: 8.

crowdsourcing

such as production, R&D, and distribution. The percentage of activities that are jointly performed with partners may vary significantly from alliance to alliance.[55]

How does the virtual type of structure differ from the modular type? Unlike the modular type, in which the focal firm maintains full strategic control, the virtual organization is characterized by participating firms that give up part of their control and accept interdependent destinies. Participating firms pursue a collective strategy that enables them to cope with uncertainty through cooperative efforts. The benefit is that, just as virtual memory increases storage capacity, the virtual organizations enhance the capacity or competitive advantage of participating firms. Strategy Spotlight 10.7 addresses the variety of collaborative relationships in the biotechnology industry.

Each company that links up with others to create a virtual organization contributes only what it considers its core competencies. It will mix and match what it does best with the best of other firms by identifying its critical capabilities and the necessary links to other capabilities.[56]

Challenges and Risks   Such alliances often fail to meet expectations: The alliance between IBM and Microsoft soured in early 1991 when Microsoft began shipping Windows in direct competition to OS/2, which they jointly developed. The runaway success of Windows frustrated IBM's ability to set an industry standard. In retaliation, IBM entered into an alliance with Microsoft's archrival, Novell, to develop network software to compete with Microsoft's LAN Manager.

The virtual organization demands that managers build relationships with other companies, negotiate win–win deals for all parties find the right partners with compatible goals and values, and provide the right balance of freedom and control. Information systems must be designed and integrated to facilitate communication with current and potential partners.

Managers must be clear about the strategic objectives while forming alliances. Some objectives are time bound, and those alliances need to be dissolved once the objective is fulfilled. Some alliances may have relatively long-term objectives and will need to be clearly monitored and nurtured to produce mutual commitment and avoid bitter fights for control. The highly dynamic personal computer industry is characterized by multiple temporary alliances among hardware, operating systems, and software producers.[57] But alliances in the more stable automobile industry, such as those involving Nissan and Volkswagen have long-term objectives and tend to be relatively stable.

The virtual organization is a logical culmination of joint-venture strategies of the past. Shared risks, costs, and rewards are the facts of life in a virtual organization.[58] When virtual organizations are formed, they involve tremendous challenges for strategic planning. As with the modular corporation, it is essential to identify core competencies. However, for virtual structures to be successful, a strategic plan is also needed to determine the effectiveness of combining core competencies.

The strategic plan must address the diminished operational control and overwhelming need for trust and common vision among the partners. This new structure may be appropriate for firms whose strategies require merging technologies (e.g., computing and communication) or for firms exploiting shrinking product life cycles that require simultaneous entry into multiple geographical markets. It may be effective for firms that desire to be quick to the market with a new product or service. The recent profusion of alliances among airlines was primarily motivated by the need to provide seamless travel demanded by the full-fare paying business traveler. Exhibit 10.9 summarizes the advantages and disadvantages.

Boundaryless Organizations: Making Them Work

Designing an organization that simultaneously supports the requirements of an organization's strategy, is consistent with the demands of the environment, and can be effectively implemented by the people around the manager is a tall order for any manager.[59] The most effective solution is usually a combination of organizational types. That is, a firm may

Exhibit 10.9
Pros and Cons of Virtual Structures

Pros	Cons
• Enables the sharing of costs and skills.	• Harder to determine where one company ends and another begins, due to close interdependencies among players.
• Enhances access to global markets.	
• Increases market responsiveness.	
• Creates a "best of everything" organization since each partner brings core competencies to the alliance.	• Leads to potential loss of operational control among partners.
	• Results in loss of strategic control over emerging technology.
• Encourages both individual and organizational knowledge sharing and accelerates organizational learning.	• Requires new and difficult-to-acquire managerial skills.

Source: Miles, R. E., & Snow, C. C. 1986. Organizations: New Concepts for New Forms. *California Management Review*, Spring: 62–73; Miles & Snow. 1999. Causes of Failure in Network Organizations. *California Management Review*, Summer: 53–72; and Bahrami, H. 1991. The Emerging Flexible Organization: Perspectives from Silicon Valley. *California Management Review*, Summer: 33–52.

10.8

Technical Computer Graphics' Boundaryless Organization

The Technical Computer Graphics (TCG) group manufactures items such as handheld bar code readers and scanning software. The company uses 13 "alliances," or small project teams, employing a total of 200 employees. Each team is responsible for either specific customers or specific products. Alliance teams share a common infrastructure, but they can develop new business opportunities without approval from upper management. Projects often emerge from listening to what customers need.

TCG uses a "triangulation approach"—alliances that include customers, suppliers, and other alliances. Suppliers and customers who provide funding are involved at the outset of the project. The alliances recognize that attaining the initial customer funding is crucial; it stimulates them to focus on what customers have to say. With an emphasis on speed, new products come to market quickly, providing

Source: Snow, C. 1997. Twenty-First Century Organizations: Implications for a New Marketing Paradigm. *Journal of the Academy of Marketing Science,* Winter: 72–74; Allred, B., Snow, C., & Miles, R. 1996. Characteristics of Managerial Careers of the 21st Century. *Academy of Management Executive,* November: 17–27; Herzog, V. L. 2001. Trust Building on Corporate Collaborative Teams. *Project Management Journal,* March: 28–41.

the firm and its partners with tangible benefits. Sometimes another alliance acts as either the customer or the supplier and provides funding.

While each alliance is independent, it shares financial concern for other alliance teams. When a new business opportunity is discovered, an alliance draws on technical expertise from the other alliances. The purpose is not only to acquire additional knowledge, but also to share accumulated learning. There's no benefit to hoarding information: Learning gained from one software project might prove especially valuable to one under way in another alliance. This technological diffusion of information produces products that quickly reach the market.

TCG's formal structure is designed to ensure that such knowledge diffusion occurs. The company's culture is structured to encourage this as well. The TCG culture attracts both the entrepreneur and the team-oriented person at the same time. Working with multiple stakeholders through TCG's triangulation model forces employees to listen to the customers and respond quickly. Because the customer matters more than the functional title, teams lend expertise to each other in return for sharing the gains realized from supplying value to the customer.

outsource many parts of its value chain to reduce costs and increase quality, engage simultaneously in multiple alliances to take advantage of technological developments or penetrate new markets, and break down barriers within the organization to enhance flexibility. In Strategy Spotlight 10.8, we see how Technical Computer Graphics combines both barrier-free and virtual organizational forms.

When an organization faces external pressures, resource scarcity, and declining performance, it tends to become more internally focused, rather than directing its efforts toward managing and enhancing relationships with existing and potential external stakeholders. This may be the most opportune time for managers to carefully analyze their value-chain activities and evaluate the potential for adopting elements of modular, virtual, and barrier-free organizational types.

Achieving the coordination and integration necessary to maximize the potential of an organization's human capital involves much more than just creating a new structure. Techniques and processes to ensure the coordination and integration of an organization's key value-chain activities are critical. Teams are key building blocks of the new organizational forms, and teamwork requires new and flexible approaches to coordination and integration.

Managers trained in rigid hierarchies may find it difficult to make the transition to the more democratic, participative style that teamwork requires. As Douglas K. Smith, co-author of *The Wisdom of Teams,* pointed out, "A completely diverse group must agree on a goal, put the notion of individual accountability aside and figure out how to work with each other. Most of all, they must learn that if the team fails, it's everyone's fault."[60]

Within the framework of an appropriate organizational design, managers must select a mix and balance of tools and techniques to facilitate the effective coordination and integration of key activities. Some of the factors that must be considered include:

- Common culture and shared values.
- Horizontal organizational structures.
- Horizontal systems and processes.
- Communications and information technologies.
- Human resource practices.

Common Culture and Shared Values   Shared goals, mutual objectives, and a high degree of trust are essential to the success of boundaryless organizations. In the fluid and flexible environments of the new organizational architectures, common cultures, shared values, and carefully aligned incentives are often less expensive to implement and are often a more effective means of strategic control than rules, boundaries, and formal procedures.

horizontal organizational structures
organizational forms that group similar or related business units under common management control, facilitate sharing resources and infrastructures to exploit synergies among operating units and help to create a sense of common purpose.

Horizontal Organizational Structures   These structures, which group similar or related business units under common management control, facilitate sharing resources and infrastructures to exploit synergies among operating units and help to create a sense of common purpose. Consistency in training and the development of similar structures across business units facilitates job rotation and cross training and enhances understanding of common problems and opportunities. Cross-functional teams and inter-divisional committees and task groups represent important opportunities to improve understanding and foster cooperation among operating units.

Horizontal Systems and Processes   Organizational systems, policies, and procedures are the traditional mechanisms for achieving integration among functional units. Existing policies and procedures often do little more than institutionalize the barriers that exist from years of managing within the framework of the traditional model. Beginning with an understanding of basic business processes in the context of "a collection of activities that takes one or more kinds of input and creates an output that is of value to the customer," Michael Hammer and James Champy's 1993 best-selling *Reengineering the Corporation* outlined a methodology for redesigning internal systems and procedures that has been embraced by many organizations.[61] Successful reengineering lowers costs, reduces inventories and cycle times, improves quality, speeds response times, and enhances organizational flexibility. Others advocate similar benefits through the reduction of cycle times, total quality management, and the like.

Communications and Information Technologies (IT)   The effective use of IT can play an important role in bridging gaps and breaking down barriers between organizations. Electronic mail and videoconferencing can improve lateral communications across long distances and multiple time zones and circumvent many of the barriers of the traditional model. IT can be a powerful ally in the redesign and streamlining of internal business processes and in improving coordination and integration between suppliers and customers. Internet technologies have eliminated the paperwork in many buyer–supplier relationships, enabling cooperating organizations to reduce inventories, shorten delivery cycles, and reduce operating costs. IT must be viewed more as a prime component of an organization's overall strategy than simply in terms of administrative support.

Human Resource Practices   Change always involves and affects the human dimension of organizations. The attraction, development, and retention of human capital are vital to value creation. As boundaryless structures are implemented, processes are reengineered, and organizations become increasingly dependent on sophisticated ITs, the skills of workers and managers alike must be upgraded to realize the full benefits.

Creating Ambidextrous Organizational Designs

>LO6
The need for creating ambidextrous organizational designs that enable firms to explore new opportunities and effectively integrate existing operations.

In Chapter 1, we introduced the concept of "ambidexterity," which incorporates two contradictory challenges faced by today's managers.[62] First, managers must explore new opportunities and adjust to volatile markets in order to avoid complacency. They must ensure that they maintain *adaptability* and remain proactive in expanding and/or modifying their product–market scope to anticipate and satisfy market conditions. Such competencies are especially challenging when change is rapid and unpredictable.

Second, managers must also effectively exploit the value of their existing assets and competencies. They need to have *alignment,* which is a clear sense of how value is being created in the short term and how activities are integrated and properly coordinated. Firms that achieve both adaptability and alignment are considered *ambidextrous organizations*— aligned and efficient in how they manage today's business but flexible enough to changes in the environment so that they will prosper tomorrow.

Handling such opposing demands is difficult because there will always be some degree of conflict. Firms often suffer when they place too strong a priority on either adaptability or alignment. If it places too much focus on adaptability, the firm will suffer low profitability in the short term. If managers direct their efforts primarily at alignment, they will likely miss out on promising business opportunities.

Ambidextrous Organizations: Key Design Attributes

A recent study by Charles O'Reilly and Michael Tushman[63] provides some insights into how some firms were able to create successful **ambidextrous organizational designs.** They investigated companies that attempted to simultaneously pursue modest, incremental innovations as well as more dramatic, breakthrough innovations. The team investigated 35 attempts to launch breakthrough innovations undertaken by 15 business units in nine different industries. They studied the organizational designs and the processes, systems, and cultures associated with the breakthrough projects as well as their impact on the operations and performance of the traditional businesses.

ambidextrous organizational designs organization designs that attempt to simultaneously pursue modest, incremental innovations as well as more dramatic, breakthrough innovations.

Companies structured their breakthrough projects in one of four primary ways:

- Seven were carried out within existing *functional organizational structures.* The projects were completely integrated into the regular organizational and management structure.
- Nine were organized as *cross-functional teams.* The groups operated within the established organization but outside of the existing management structure.
- Four were organized as *unsupported teams.* Here, they became independent units set up outside the established organization and management hierarchy.
- Fifteen were conducted within *ambidextrous organizations.* Here, the breakthrough efforts were organized within structurally independent units, each having its own processes, structures, and cultures. However, they were integrated into the existing senior management structure.

The performance results of the 35 initiatives were tracked along two dimensions:

- Their success in creating desired innovations was measured by either the actual commercial results of the new product or the application of practical market or technical learning.
- The performance of the existing business was evaluated.

The study found that the organizational structure and management practices employed had a direct and significant impact on the performance of both the breakthrough initiative and the traditional business. The ambidextrous organizational designs were more effective than the other three designs on both dimensions: launching breakthrough products or services (i.e., adaptation) and improving the performance of the existing business (i.e., alignment).

Why Was the Ambidextrous Organization the Most Effective Structure?

The study found that there were many factors. A clear and compelling vision, consistently communicated by the company's senior management team was critical in building the ambidextrous designs. The structure enabled cross-fertilization while avoiding cross-contamination. The tight coordination and integration at the managerial levels enabled the newer units to share important resources from the traditional units such as cash, talent, and expertise. Such sharing was encouraged and facilitated by effective reward systems that emphasized overall company goals. The organizational separation ensured that the new units' distinctive processes, structures, and cultures were not overwhelmed by the forces of "business as usual." The established units were shielded from the distractions of launching new businesses, and they continued to focus all of their attention and energy on refining their operations, enhancing their products, and serving their customers.

Reflecting on Career Implications . . .

- *Strategy–Structure:* Is there an effective "fit" between your organization's strategy and its structure? If not, there may be inconsistencies in how you are evaluated which often leads to role ambiguity and confusion. A poor fit could also affect communication among departments as well as across the organization's hierarchy.
- *Matrix Structure:* If your organization employs elements of a matrix structure (e.g., dual reporting relationships), are there effective structural supporting elements (e.g., culture and rewards)? If not, there could be a high level of dysfunctional conflict among managers.
- *The "Fit" between Rewards and Incentives and "Levels of Strategy" (Business- and Corporate-Level):* What metrics are used to evaluate the performance of your work unit? Are there strictly financial measures of success or are you also rewarded for achieving competitive advantages (through effective innovation, organizational learning, or other activities that increase knowledge but may be costly in the short run)?
- *Boundaryless Organizational Designs:* Does your firm have structural mechanisms (e.g., culture, human resource practices) that facilitate sharing of information across boundaries? If so, you should be better able to enhance your human capital by leveraging your talents and competencies.

Summary

Successful organizations must ensure that they have the proper type of organizational structure. Furthermore, they must ensure that their firms incorporate the necessary integration and processes so that the internal and external boundaries of their firms are flexible and permeable. Such a need is increasingly important as the environments of firms become more complex, rapidly changing, and unpredictable.

In the first section of the chapter, we discussed the growth patterns of large corporations. Although most organizations remain small or die, some firms continue to grow in terms of revenues, vertical integration, and diversity of products and services. In addition, their geographical scope may increase to include international operations. We traced the dominant pattern of growth, which evolves from a simple structure to a functional structure as a firm grows in terms of size and increases its level of vertical integration. After a firm expands into related products and services, its structure changes from a functional to a divisional form of organization.

Finally, when the firm enters international markets, its structure again changes to accommodate the change in strategy.

We also addressed the different types of organizational structure—simple, functional, divisional (including two variations—strategic business unit and holding company), and matrix—as well as their relative advantages and disadvantages. We closed the section with a discussion of the implications for structure when a firm enters international markets. The three primary factors to take into account when determining the appropriate structure are type of international strategy, product diversity, and the extent to which a firm is dependent on foreign sales.

In the second section, we took a contingency approach to the design of reward and evaluation systems. That is, we argued that there is no one best way to design such systems; rather, it is dependent on a variety of factors. The two that we discussed are business- and corporate-level strategies. With an overall cost leadership strategy and unrelated diversification, it is appropriate to rely primarily on cultures and reward systems that emphasize the production outcomes of the organization, because it is rather easy to quantify such indicators. In contrast, differentiation strategies and related diversification require cultures and incentive systems that encourage and reward creativity initiatives as well as the cooperation among professionals in many different functional areas. Here it becomes more difficult to measure accurately each individual's contribution, and more subjective indicators become essential.

The third section of the chapter introduced the concept of the boundaryless organization. We did not suggest that the concept of the boundaryless organization replaces the traditional forms of organizational structure. Rather, it should complement them. This is necessary to cope with the increasing complexity and change in the competitive environment. We addressed three types of boundaryless organizations. The barrier-free type focuses on the need for the internal and external boundaries of a firm to be more flexible and permeable. The modular type emphasizes the strategic outsourcing of noncore activities. The virtual type centers on the strategic benefits of alliances and the forming of network organizations. We discussed both the advantages and disadvantages of each type of boundaryless organization as well as suggested some techniques and processes that are necessary to successfully implement them. These are common culture and values, horizontal organizational structures, horizontal systems and processes, communications and information technologies, and human resource practices.

The final section addresses the need for managers to develop ambidextrous organizations. In today's rapidly changing global environment, managers must be responsive and proactive in order to take advantage of new opportunities. At the same time, they must effectively integrate and coordinate existing operations. Such requirements call for organizational designs that establish project teams that are structurally independent units, with each having its own processes, structures, and cultures. But, at the same time, each unit needs to be effectively integrated into the existing management hierarchy.

Summary Review Questions

1. Why is it important for managers to carefully consider the type of organizational structure that they use to implement their strategies?

2. Briefly trace the dominant growth pattern of major corporations from simple structure to functional structure to divisional structure. Discuss the relationship between a firm's strategy and its structure.

3. What are the relative advantages and disadvantages of the types of organizational structure—simple, functional, divisional, matrix—discussed in the chapter?

4. When a firm expands its operations into foreign markets, what are the three most important factors to take into account in deciding what type of structure is most appropriate? What are the types of international structures discussed in the text and what are the relationships between strategy and structure?

5. Briefly describe the three different types of boundaryless organizations: barrier-free, modular, and virtual.

6. What are some of the key attributes of effective groups? Ineffective groups?

7. What are the advantages and disadvantages of the three types of boundaryless organizations: barrier-free, modular, and virtual?

8. When are ambidextrous organizational designs necessary? What are some of their key attributes?

Key Terms

organizational structure 349
simple organizational structure, 351
functional organizational structure, 351
divisional organizational structure, 353
strategic business unit (SBU) structure, 355

holding company structure, 355
matrix organizational structure, 356
international division structure 357
geographic-area division structure 357
worldwide matrix structure 357

Experiential Exercise

Many firms have recently moved toward a modular structure. For example, they have increasingly outsourced many of their information technology (IT) activities. Identify three such organizations. Using secondary sources, evaluate (1) the firm's rationale for IT outsourcing and (2) the implications for performance.

Firm	Rationale	Implication(s) for Performance
1.		
2.		
3.		

Application Questions Exercises

1. Select an organization that competes in an industry in which you are particularly interested. Go on the Internet and determine what type of organizational structure this organization has. In your view, is it consistent with the strategy that it has chosen to implement? Why? Why not?

2. Choose an article from *BusinessWeek, Fortune, Forbes, Fast Company,* or any other well-known publication that deals with a corporation that has undergone a significant change in its strategic direction. What are the implications for the structure of this organization?

3. Go on the Internet and look up some of the public statements or speeches of an executive in a major corporation about a significant initiative such as entering into a joint venture or launching a new product line. What do you feel are the implications for making the internal and external barriers of the firm more flexible and permeable? Does the executive discuss processes, procedures, integrating mechanisms, or cultural issues that should serve this purpose? Or are

other issues discussed that enable a firm to become more boundaryless?

4. Look up a recent article in the publications listed in question 2 above that addresses a firm's involvement in outsourcing (modular organization) or in strategic alliance or network organizations (virtual organization). Was the firm successful or unsuccessful in this endeavor? Why? Why not?

Ethics Questions

1. If a firm has a divisional structure and places extreme pressures on its divisional executives to meet short-term profitability goals (e.g., quarterly income), could this raise some ethical considerations? Why? Why not?

2. If a firm enters into a strategic alliance but does not exercise appropriate behavioral control of its employees (in terms of culture, rewards and incentives, and boundaries—as discussed in Chapter 9) that are involved in the alliance, what ethical issues could arise? What could be the potential long-term and short-term downside for the firm?

References

1. Pope, Carl. 2008. *Taking the initiative.* Sierra Club executive blog, http://sierraclub.typepad.com/carlpope/2008/04/wall-street-a-1.html; www.sierraclub.org; Kamenetz, A. 2008. Cleaning solutions. *Fast Company,* September: 121–125; and Being green and in the black. 2008. *Retailing Today,* April 28: 47(5): 10, 16.

2. This introductory discussion draws upon Hall, R. H. 2002. *Organizations: Structures, processes, and outcomes* (8th ed.). Upper Saddle River, NJ: Prentice Hall; and Duncan, R. E. 1979. What is the right organization structure? Decision-tree analysis provides the right answer. *Organizational Dynamics,* 7(3): 59–80. For an insightful discussion of strategy-structure relationships in the organization theory and strategic management literatures, refer to Keats, B. & O'Neill, H. M. 2001. Organization structure: Looking through a strategy lens. In Hitt, M. A., Freeman, R. E., & Harrison, J. S. 2001. *The Blackwell handbook of strategic management:* 520–542. Malden, MA: Blackwell.

3. An interesting discussion on the role of organizational design in strategy execution is in: Neilson, G. L., Martin, K. L., & Powers, E. 2009. The secrets to successful strategy execution. *Harvard Business Review,* 87(2): 60–70.

4. This discussion draws upon Chandler, A. D. 1962. *Strategy and structure.* Cambridge, MA: MIT Press; Galbraith J. R. & Kazanjian, R. K. 1986. *Strategy implementation: The role of structure and process.* St. Paul, MN: West Publishing; and Scott, B. R. 1971. Stages of corporate development. Intercollegiate Case Clearing House, 9-371-294, BP 998. Harvard Business School.

5. Our discussion of the different types of organizational structures draws on a variety of sources, including Galbraith & Kazanjian, op. cit.; Hrebiniak, L. G. & Joyce, W. F. 1984. *Implementing strategy.* New York: Macmillan; Distelzweig, H. 2000. Organizational structure. In Helms, M. M. (Ed.). *Encyclopedia of management:* 692–699. Farmington Hills, MI: Gale; and Dess, G. G. & Miller, A. 1993. *Strategic management.* New York: McGraw-Hill.

6. A discussion of an innovative organizational design is in: Garvin, D. A. & Levesque, L. C. 2009. The multiunit enterprise. *Harvard Business Review,* 87(2): 106–117.

7. Schein, E. H. 1996. Three cultures of management: The key to organizational learning. *Sloan Management Review,* 38(1): 9–20.

8. Insights on governance implications for multidivisional forms are in: Verbeke, A. & Kenworthy, T. P. 2008. Multidivisional vs. metanational governance. *Journal of International Business,* 39(6): 940–956.

9. For a discussion of performance implications, refer to Hoskisson, R. E. 1987. Multidivisional structure and performance: The contingency of diversification strategy. *Academy of Management Journal,* 29: 625–644.

10. For a thorough and seminal discussion of the evolution toward the divisional form of organizational structure in the United States, refer to Chandler, op. cit. A rigorous empirical study of the strategy and structure relationship is found in Rumelt, R. P. 1974. *Strategy, structure, and economic performance.* Cambridge, MA: Harvard Business School Press.

11. Ghoshal S. & Bartlett, C. A. 1995. Changing the role of management: Beyond structure to processes. *Harvard Business Review,* 73(1): 88.

12. Koppel, B. 2000. Synergy in ketchup? *Forbes,* February 7: 68–69; and Hitt, M. A., Ireland, R. D., & Hoskisson, R. E. 2001. *Strategic management: Competitiveness and globalization* (4th ed.). Cincinnati, OH: Southwestern Publishing.

13. Pitts, R. A. 1977. Strategies and structures for diversification. *Academy of Management Journal,* 20(2): 197–208.

14. Dell, M. & Rollins, K. 2005. Execution without excuses. *Harvard Business Review,* 83(3): 102–111.

15. Daniels, J. D., Pitts, R. A., & Tretter, M. J. 1984. Strategy and structure of U.S. multinationals: An exploratory study. *Academy of Management Journal,* 27(2): 292–307.

16. Habib, M. M. & Victor, B. 1991. Strategy, structure, and performance of U.S. manufacturing and service MNCs: A comparative analysis. *Strategic Management Journal,* 12(8): 589–606.

17. Our discussion of global start-ups draws from Oviatt, B. M. & McDougall, P. P. 2005. The internationalization of entrepreneurship. *Journal of International Business Studies,* 36(1): 2–8; Oviatt, B. M. & McDougall, P. P. 1994. Toward a theory of international new ventures. *Journal of International Business Studies,* 25(1): 45–64; and Oviatt, B. M. & McDougall, P. P. 1995. Global start-ups: Entrepreneurs on a worldwide stage. *Academy of Management Executive,* 9(2): 30–43.

18. Some useful guidelines for global start-ups are provided in Kuemmerle, W. 2005. The entrepreneur's path for global expansion. *MIT Sloan Management Review,* 46(2): 42–50.

19. See, for example, Miller, D. & Friesen, P. H. 1980. Momentum and revolution in organizational structure. *Administrative Science Quarterly,* 13: 65–91.

20. Many authors have argued that a firm's structure can influence its strategy and performance. These include Amburgey, T. L. & Dacin, T. 1995. As the left foot follows the right? The dynamics of strategic and structural change. *Academy of Management Journal,* 37: 1427–1452; Dawn, K. & Amburgey, T. L. 1991.

Organizational inertia and momentum: A dynamic model of strategic change. *Academy of Management Journal,* 34: 591–612; Fredrickson, J. W. 1986. The strategic decision process and organization structure. *Academy of Management Review,* 11: 280–297; Hall, D. J. & Saias, M. A. 1980. Strategy follows structure! *Strategic Management Journal,* 1: 149–164; and Burgelman, R. A. 1983. A model of the interaction of strategic behavior, corporate context, and the concept of strategy. *Academy of Management Review,* 8: 61–70.

21. This discussion of generic strategies and their relationship to organizational control draws upon Porter, M. E. 1980. *Competitive strategy.* New York: Free Press; and Miller, D. 1988. Relating Porter's business strategies to environment and structure: Analysis and performance implications. *Academy of Management Journal,* 31(2): 280–308.

22. Rodengen, J. L. 1997. *The legend of Nucor Corporation.* Fort Lauderdale, FL: Write Stuff Enterprises.

23. The 3M example draws upon *Blueprints for service quality.* 1994. New York: American Management Association; personal communication with Katerine Hagmeier, program manager, external communications, 3M Corporation, March 26, 1998; Lei, D., Slocum, J. W., & Pitts, R. A. 1999. Designing organizations for competitive advantage: The power of unlearning and learning. *Organizational Dynamics,* 27(3): 24–38; and Graham, A. B. & Pizzo, V. G. 1996. A question of balance: Case studies in strategic knowledge management. *European Management Journal,* 14(4): 338–346.

24. The Sharp Corporation and Hanson plc examples are based on Collis, D. J. & Montgomery, C. A. 1998. Creating corporate advantage. *Harvard Business Review,* 76(3): 70–83.

25. Kunii, I. 2002. Japanese companies' survival skills. *BusinessWeek,* November 18: 18.

26. White, G. 1988. How I turned $3,000 into $10 billion. *Fortune,* November 7: 80–89. After the death of the founders, the Hanson plc conglomerate was found to be too unwieldy and was broken up into several separate, publicly traded corporations. For more on its more limited current scope of operations, see www.hansonplc.com.

27. An interesting discussion on how the Internet has affected the boundaries of firms can be found in Afuah, A. 2003. Redefining firm boundaries in the face of the Internet: Are firms really shrinking? *Academy of Management Review,* 28(1): 34–53.

28. Collis & Montgomery, op. cit.

29. For a discussion of the role of coaching on developing high performance teams, refer to Kets de Vries, M. F. R. 2005. Leadership group coaching in action: The zen of creating high performance teams. *Academy of Management Executive,* 19(1): 77–89.

30. Pfeffer, J. 1998. *The human equation: Building profits by putting people first.* Cambridge, MA: Harvard Business School Press.

31. For a discussion on how functional area diversity affects performance, see Bunderson, J. S. & Sutcliffe, K. M. 2002. *Academy of Management Journal,* 45(5): 875–893.

32. See, for example, Hoskisson, R. E., Hill, C. W. L., & Kim, H. 1993. The multidivisional structure: Organizational fossil or source of value? *Journal of Management,* 19(2): 269–298.

33. Pottruck, D. A. 1997. Speech delivered by the co-CEO of Charles Schwab Co., Inc., to the Retail Leadership Meeting, San Francisco, CA, January 30; and Miller, W. 1999. Building the ultimate resource. *Management Review,* January: 42–45.

34. Public-private partnerships are addressed in: Engardio, P. 2009. State capitalism. *BusinessWeek,* February 9: 38–43.

35. Magretta, J. 1998. The power of virtual integration: An interview with Dell Computer's Michael Dell. *Harvard Business Review,* 76(2): 75.

36. Forster, J. 2001. Networking for cash. *BusinessWeek,* January 8: 129.

37. Dess, G. G., Rasheed, A. M. A., McLaughlin, K. J., & Priem, R. 1995. The new corporate architecture. *Academy of Management Executive,* 9(3): 7–20.

38. Barnes, C. 1998. A fatal case. *Fast Company,* February–March: 173.

39. Handy, C. 1989. *The age of unreason.* Boston: Harvard Business School Press; Ramstead, E. 1997. APC maker's low-tech formula: Start with the box. *The Wall Street Journal,* December 29: B1; Mussberg, W. 1997. Thin screen PCs are looking good but still fall flat. *The Wall Street Journal,* January 2: 9; Brown, E. 1997. Monorail: Low cost PCs. *Fortune,* July 7: 106–108; and Young, M. 1996. Ex-Compaq executives start new company. *Computer Reseller News,* November 11: 181.

40. An original discussion on how open-sourcing could help the Big 3 automobile companies is in: Jarvis, J. 2009. How the Google model could help Detroit. *BusinessWeek,* February 9: 32–36.

41. For a discussion of some of the downsides of outsourcing, refer to Rossetti, C. & Choi, T. Y. 2005. On the dark side of strategic sourcing: Experiences from the aerospace industry. *Academy of Management Executive,* 19(1): 46–60.

42. Tully, S. 1993. The modular corporation. *Fortune,* February 8: 196.

43. Offshoring in manufacturing firms is addressed in: Coucke, K. & Sleuwaegen, L. 2008. Offshoring as a survival strategy: Evidence from manufacturing firms in Belgium. *Journal of International Business Studies,* 39(8): 1261–1277.

44. Quinn, J. B. 1992. *Intelligent enterprise: A knowledge and service based paradigm for industry.* New York: Free Press.

45. For an insightful perspective on outsourcing and its role in developing capabilities, read Gottfredson, M., Puryear, R., & Phillips, C. 2005. Strategic sourcing: From periphery to the core. *Harvard Business Review,* 83(4): 132–139.

46. This discussion draws upon Quinn, J. B. & Hilmer, F. C. 1994. Strategic outsourcing. *Sloan Management Review,* 35(4): 43–55.

47. Insights on outsourcing and private branding can be found in: Cehn, S-F. S. 2009. A transaction cost rationale for private branding and its implications for the choice of domestic vs. offshore outsourcing. *Journal of*

International Business Strategy, 40(1): 156–175.

48. For an insightful perspective on the use of outsourcing for decision analysis, read: Davenport, T. H. & Iyer, B. 2009. Should you outsource your brain? *Harvard Business Review,* 87(2): 38.

49. See also Stuckey, J. & White, D. 1993. When and when not to vertically integrate. *Sloan Management Review,* Spring: 71–81; Harrar, G. 1993. Outsource tales. *Forbes ASAP,* June 7: 37–39, 42; and Davis, E. W. 1992. Global outsourcing: Have U.S. managers thrown the baby out with the bath water? *Business Horizons,* July–August: 58–64.

50. For a discussion of knowledge creation through alliances, refer to Inkpen, A. C. 1996. Creating knowledge through collaboration. *California Management Review,* 39(1): 123–140; and Mowery, D. C., Oxley, J. E., & Silverman, B. S. 1996. Strategic alliances and interfirm knowledge transfer. *Strategic Management Journal,* 17 (Special Issue, Winter): 77–92.

51. Doz, Y. & Hamel, G. 1998. *Alliance advantage: The art of creating value through partnering.* Boston: Harvard Business School Press.

52. DeSanctis, G., Glass, J. T., & Ensing, I. M. 2002. Organizational designs for R&D. *Academy of Management Executive,* 16(3): 55–66.

53. Barringer, B. R. & Harrison, J. S. 2000. Walking a tightrope: Creating value through interorganizational alliances. *Journal of Management,* 26: 367–403.

54. Davis, E. 1997. Interview: Norman Augustine. *Management Review,* November: 14.

55. One contemporary example of virtual organizations is R&D consortia. For an insightful discussion, refer to Sakaibara, M. 2002. Formation of R&D consortia: Industry and company effects. *Strategic Management Journal,* 23(11): 1033–1050.

56. Bartness, A. & Cerny, K. 1993. Building competitive advantage through a global network of capabilities. *California Management Review,* Winter: 78–103. For an insightful historical discussion of the usefulness of alliances in the computer industry, see Moore, J. F. 1993. Predators and prey: A new ecology of competition. *Harvard Business Review,* 71(3): 75–86.

57. See Lorange, P. & Roos, J. 1991. Why some strategic alliances succeed and others fail. *Journal of Business Strategy,* January–February: 25–30; and Slowinski, G. 1992. The human touch in strategic alliances. *Mergers and Acquisitions,* July–August: 44–47. A compelling argument for strategic alliances is provided by Ohmae, K. 1989. The global logic of strategic alliances. *Harvard Business Review,* 67(2): 143–154.

58. Some of the downsides of alliances are discussed in Das, T. K. & Teng, B. S. 2000. Instabilities of strategic alliances: An internal tensions perspective. *Organization Science,* 11: 77–106.

59. This section draws upon Dess, G. G. & Picken, J. C. 1997. *Mission critical.*

Burr Ridge, IL: Irwin Professional Publishing.

60. Katzenbach, J. R. & Smith, D. K. 1994. *The wisdom of teams: Creating the high performance organization.* New York: HarperBusiness.

61. Hammer, M. & Champy, J. 1993. *Reengineering the corporation: A manifesto for business revolution.* New York: HarperCollins.

62. This section draws on Birkinshaw, J. & Gibson, C. 2004. Building ambidexterity into an organization. *MIT Sloan Management Review,* 45(4): 47–55; and Gibson, C. B. & Birkinshaw, J. 2004. The antecedents, consequences, and mediating role of organizational ambidexterity. *Academy of Management Journal,* 47(2): 209–226. Robert Duncan is generally credited with being the first to coin the term "ambidextrous organizations" in his article entitled: Designing dual structures for innovation. In Kilmann, R. H., Pondy, L. R., & Slevin, D. (Eds.). 1976. *The management of organizations,* vol. 1: 167–188. For a seminal academic discussion of the concept of exploration and exploitation, which parallels adaptation and alignment, refer to: March, J. G. 1991. Exploration and exploitation in organizational learning. *Organization Science,* 2: 71–86.

63. This section is based on O'Reilly, C. A. & Tushman, M. L. 2004. The ambidextrous organization. *Harvard Business Review,* 82(4): 74–81.

CHAPTER 11

Strategic Leadership:

Creating a Learning Organization and an Ethical Organization

>learning objectives

After reading this chapter, you should have a good understanding of:

LO1 The three key interdependent activities in which all successful leaders must be continually engaged.

LO2 Three elements of effective leadership: integrative thinking, overcoming barriers to change, and the effective use of power.

LO3 The crucial role of emotional intelligence (EI) in successful leadership as well as its potential drawbacks.

LO4 The value of creating and maintaining a learning organization in today's global marketplace.

LO5 The leader's role in establishing an ethical organization.

LO6 The difference between integrity-based and compliance-based approaches to organizational ethics.

LO7 Several key elements that organizations must have to become an ethical organization.

To compete in the global marketplace, organizations need to have strong and effective leadership. This involves the active process of both creating and implementing proper strategies. In this chapter we address key activities in which leaders throughout the organization must be involved to be successful in creating and sustaining competitive advantages.

In the first section, we provide a brief overview of the three key leadership activities. These are (1) setting a direction, (2) designing the organization, and (3) nurturing a culture committed to excellence and ethical behavior. Each of these activities is "necessary but not sufficient"; that is, to be effective, leaders must give proper attention to each of them.

Section two addresses practices and capabilities that enable executives to be effective as leaders. To be successful in a complex business environment, leaders must perform a variety of functions and exhibit key strengths. We focus on three capabilities that effective leaders often exhibit—integrative thinking, overcoming barriers to change, and the effective use of power.

The third section discusses the vital role of emotional intelligence (EI) in effective strategic leadership. EI refers to an individual's capacity for recognizing his or her emotions and those of others. It consists of five components: self-awareness, self-regulation, motivation, empathy, and social skills. We also address potential downsides or drawbacks that may result from the ineffective use of EI.

Next we address the important role of a leader in creating a learning organization. Here, leaders must strive to harness the individual and collective talents of individuals throughout the entire organization. Creating a learning organization is particularly important in today's competitive environment, which is increasingly unpredictable, dynamic, and interdependent. The key elements of a learning organization are inspiring and motivating people with a mission or purpose, empowering employees at all levels, accumulating and sharing internal and external information, and challenging the status quo to enable creativity.

The final section discusses a leader's challenge in creating and maintaining an ethical organization. There are many benefits of having an ethical organization. It can provide financial benefits, enhance human capital, and help to ensure positive relationships with suppliers, customers, society at large, and governmental agencies. By contrast failure to operate ethically leading to an ethical crisis can be very costly for many reasons. We address four key elements of an ethical organization: role models, corporate credos and codes of conduct, reward and evaluation systems, and policies and procedures.

Learning from Mistakes

The financial crisis that struck U.S. markets in the fall of 2008 dealt a devastating blow to many companies. Few were hit as hard as Lehman Brothers, the global financial services company that went under in the largest bankruptcy in U.S. history. During a crucial period when stock markets around the world were spiraling downward because of heavy investments in overvalued assets such as subprime mortgages, Lehman was in the center of the storm. It was unable to obtain a government bailout or a buyer, either of which might have saved it from being wiped out. According to some, at least one reason Lehman could not seem to get help and failed when other troubled companies were being salvaged was due to the leadership of the man at the helm—Chairman and CEO Richard S. Fuld, Jr.[1]

Although many would agree that bad luck and bad timing contributed to Lehman's downfall, Fuld was clearly part of the problem. A 30-year veteran of the company, Fuld started as a commercial paper trader and moved through the ranks of Lehman as it expanded into a host of financial services, including investment banking, equity and fixed income sales, research and trading, investment management, and private banking. Fuld was considered a supreme trader by many and, according to a senior partner, "a very smart guy, tough as nails." He was also highly respected for providing strong leadership during some of Lehman's most difficult periods, such as the Asian debt crisis of 1998.

What went wrong? Fuld exhibited traits that may have shaped the culture of Lehman or merely reflected it. Lehman had a reputation for being aggressive; so did Fuld, who was known for his combative nature. Because he was a good trader, he was given a leadership role. But his skills as a manager of people were lacking. He had an intimidating presence and a reputation for speaking to people in monosyllables. He was also said to have an especially bad temper, one that earned him the nickname "Gorilla." Among its worst managers of 2008, *BusinessWeek* reported that Fuld "drove his people hard and ignored warning signs, rewarding risk and greed."

Fuld also seemed to lack a certain sensitivity that good leaders often display. When most Wall Street firms were reeling after the September 11th terrorist attack, Fuld seized the opportunity to grow the investment banking side of the business. For 2001, a year when a global recession and financial crisis led other chief executives to reduce their pay packages, Fuld received a $105 million compensation package, making him the fourth-highest-paid CEO in the United States. His reputation for lavish compensation became part of a reputation that stuck with and later hurt him.

Perhaps his greatest downfall was that he was unwilling or unable to recognize how serious the problems were that were plaguing Lehman and was reluctant to make changes even when he had the chance. For example, Fuld passed up an opportunity to sell 25 percent of the business to the Korean Development Bank, a move that might have provided the cash infusion Lehman needed to survive, because he thought the price was too low. He also reportedly balked at an offer to sell up to half of Lehman's shares to China's CITIC Securities because of a dispute over price. "Dick Fuld blew it," declared William Smith of New York–based Smith Asset Management. "How many opportunities did he have to sell Lehman?" According to Dartmouth professor Sydney Finkelstein, who studies the biases that cause CEOs to make bad decisions, Fuld "was unable to break out of his own experience and history by seeing the risks that Lehman had." "Nobody was more convinced [than Fuld] that Lehman was too big to fail," reported *BusinessWeek.*

Disbelief about the company's situation may have also led Fuld to act unethically. In testimony to the U.S. Congress about the financial collapse, he was questioned about making overly positive statements to analysts about Lehman's balance sheet just five days before it declared bankruptcy. Maryland Representative John Sarbanes called Fuld's statements to analysts "simply implausible," but Fuld did not admit to any wrongdoing. "Fuld went wrong in not taking seriously enough the impairment of his balance sheet. He had the typical hubris that any long-term CEO has: 'I built this thing, and it's got more value than the marketplace understands,'" said Charles Peabody, an analyst at Portales Partners, an independent research firm. Weeks after the Lehman bankruptcy, Fuld's questionable ethics made the news again when he sold his Florida mansion valued at $13.75 million to his wife for $100, a move considered by most to be an effort to prevent the home from being confiscated to pay creditors.

Fuld's failure to accept blame angered many and took its toll on his reputation. On the day Lehman declared bankruptcy, an irate employee punched Fuld in the face while he was on the treadmill at the bank's gym and knocked him out cold. Protesters gathered at the congressional hearing the day Fuld testified, to express outrage over his excessive pay and call for him to be jailed. Upon reviewing the Lehman bankruptcy filing, New York State Controller Thomas DiNapoli filed a motion in the U.S. Bankruptcy Court demanding Fuld's ouster. "Mr. Fuld's decisions drove the company toward ruin," wrote DiNapoli. "Without question, Mr. Fuld's stewardship of the company was a large factor in its demise." With that, Lehman's board of directors had little choice but to dismiss Fuld as CEO. In retrospect, regardless of who is to blame, it was Fuld's responsibility as Lehman's chairman and CEO to lead the company through the crisis. His failure to do so led to one of Wall Street's biggest failures ever.

Clearly, many of the decisions and actions of Richard Fuld were not in the best interests of the firm and its shareholders. In contrast, effective leaders play an important and often pivotal role in creating and implementing strategies.

This chapter provides insights into the role of strategic leadership in managing, adapting, and coping in the face of increased environmental complexity and uncertainty. First, we define leadership and its components. Then, we identify three elements of leadership that contribute to success—integrative thinking, overcoming barriers to change, and the effective use of power. The third section focuses on emotional intelligence, a trait that is increasingly acknowledged to be critical to successful leadership. Next, we emphasize the importance of developing a learning organization and how leaders can help their firms learn and proactively adapt in the face of accelerating change. Here, we focus on empowerment wherein employees and managers throughout an organization develop a sense of self-determination, competence, meaning, and impact that is centrally important to learning. Finally, we address the leader's role in building an ethical organization and the elements of an ethical culture that contribute to firm effectiveness.

Leadership: Three Interdependent Activities

In today's chaotic world, few would argue against the need for leadership, but how do we go about encouraging it? Is it enough to merely keep an organization afloat, or is it essential to make steady progress toward some well-defined objective? We believe custodial management is not leadership. Leadership is proactive, goal-oriented, and focused on the creation and implementation of a creative vision. **Leadership** is the process of transforming organizations from what they are to what the leader would have them become. This definition implies a lot: *dissatisfaction* with the status quo, a *vision* of what should be, and a *process* for bringing about change. An insurance company executive shared the following insight: "I lead by the Noah Principle: It's all right to know when it's going to rain, but, by God, you had better build the ark."

Doing the right thing is becoming increasingly important. Many industries are declining; the global village is becoming increasingly complex, interconnected, and unpredictable; and product and market life cycles are becoming increasingly compressed. When asked to describe the life cycle of his company's products, the CEO of a supplier of computer components replied, "Seven months from cradle to grave—and that includes three months to design the product and get it into production!" Richard D'Aveni, author of *Hypercompetition,* argued that in a world where all dimensions of competition appear to be compressed in time and heightened in complexity, *sustainable* competitive advantages are no longer possible.

leadership the process of transforming organizations from what they are to what the leader would have them become.

Despite the importance of doing the "right thing," leaders must also be concerned about "doing things right." Charan and Colvin strongly believe that execution, that is, the implementation of strategy, is also essential to success.

> Mastering execution turns out to be the odds-on best way for a CEO to keep his job. So what's the right way to think about that sexier obsession, strategy? It's vitally important—obviously. The problem is that our age's fascination feeds the mistaken belief that developing exactly the right strategy will enable a company to rocket past competitors. In reality, that's less than half the battle.[2]

Thus, leaders are change agents whose success is measured by how effectively they formulate *and* implement a strategic vision and mission.[3]

>LO1
The three key interdependent activities in which all successful leaders must be continually engaged.

Many authors contend that successful leaders must recognize three interdependent activities that must be continually reassessed for organizations to succeed. As shown in Exhibit 11.1, these are: (1) setting a direction, (2) designing the organization, and (3) nurturing a culture dedicated to excellence and ethical behavior.[4] Strategy Spotlight 11.1 describes how three successful leaders have exhibited these attributes in their organizations.

The interdependent nature of these three activities is self-evident. Consider an organization with a great mission and a superb organizational structure, but a culture that implicitly encourages shirking and unethical behavior. Or one with a sound direction and strong culture, but counterproductive teams and a "zero-sum" reward system that leads to the dysfunctional situation in which one party's gain is viewed as another party's loss, and collaboration and sharing are severely hampered. Clearly, such combinations would be ineffective.

Often, failure of today's organizations can be attributed to a lack of equal consideration of these three activities. The imagery of a three-legged stool is instructive: It will collapse if one leg is missing or broken. Let's briefly look at each of these activities.

Setting a Direction

setting a direction
a strategic leadership activity of strategy analysis and strategy formulation.

A holistic understanding of an organization's stakeholders requires an ability to scan the environment to develop a knowledge of all of the company's stakeholders and other salient environmental trends and events. Managers must integrate this knowledge into a vision of what the organization could become.[5] It necessitates the capacity to solve increasingly complex problems, become proactive in approach, and develop viable strategic options. A strategic vision provides many benefits: a clear future direction; a framework for the organization's mission and goals; and enhanced employee communication, participation, and commitment.

At times the creative process involves what the CEO of Yokogawa, GE's Japanese partner in the Medical Systems business, called "bullet train" thinking.[6] That is, if you

Exhibit 11.1 Three Interdependent Activities of Leadership

strategy spotlight

How Leaders Lead in Tough Times

As companies failed and billions of dollars of shareholder wealth was lost during the financial crisis that began in 2008, new demands were placed on company executives to exhibit strong leadership. In the face of challenges, the leaders below displayed the three aspects of leadership that are the mark of successful organizations—setting a direction, designing the organization, and nurturing a culture dedicated to excellence and ethical behavior.

Dave Yost—Setting a Clear Direction

AmerisourceBergen is a $66 billion drug distribution company headquartered in Valley Forge, Pennsylvania. Because it's in an industry that operates on razor-thin margins—just one percent on average—holding down expenses is a companywide priority. As a result, Amerisource CEO Dave Yost is a model of frugality. He answers his own phone, keeps plastic plants in the lobby to save on watering, and flies economy class. Sitting in a 1970s-style plaid chair that looks like a yard sale item, Yost says, "The leader is very important in controlling business costs." He considers the familiar adage "stick to the knitting" outdated and says instead, "We're focused on knitting faster, better, and more creatively than anyone else." Although his tactics sound extreme, there are important payoffs: Amerisource profits increased 30 percent in a recent quarter compared to 8 percent at McKesson and 13 percent at Cardinal Health, its closest rivals. Company cost cutting also provided $500 million for recent investments to improve customer service technology and upgrade operations at key distribution centers.

Chad Holliday—Designing the Organization in the Face of a Crisis

DuPont is a $32 billion Delaware-based company with 60,000 employees. Its CEO, Chad Holliday, was meeting with a major customer in Japan in 2008 when the seriousness of the emerging financial crisis first struck him. The Japanese CEO said concern over a financial contagion was making him conserve cash for fear of not being able to raise capital. Upon returning home, Holliday received more bad news: Because DuPont provides paint for more than 30 percent of U.S. cars on a just-in-time basis, the automakers share their production schedules. Faced with

collapsing auto sales, production scheduling had been temporarily halted. Based on such grim reports, Holliday reluctantly invoked the company's Corporate Crisis Management plan to identify a new set of mechanisms to integrate activities across all parts of the organization. Within hours, executive teams gathered to formulate a plan; within 10 days of creating the plan, every DuPont employee met face-to-face with a manager who explained their new responsibilities. Even though the initial response went smoothly, Holliday realized that some managers were not responding fast enough. "They were talking about things that would be implemented by January or February [2009], but there were things we needed implemented in October," explained Holliday. More meetings were held to heighten accountability and implement control systems that targeted costs, scheduled shutdowns, and revised working capital projections. Over 20,000 outside contractors were cut back, and employees whose operations were slowing were used to do the work instead. Within six weeks, Holliday's reality check led to a major redesign of DuPont's priorities and helped position it more securely for an uncertain future.

Herb Kelleher—Nurturing a Culture by Setting an Ethical Example

In Chapter 9, we discussed the executive pay dilemma: offering appealing pay packages to attract top talent versus providing over-the-top compensation for underperforming executives. For Herb Kelleher, Southwest Airlines' legendary former chairman and CEO, there is no dilemma for executives willing to do the right thing. From the start, Southwest took steps to maintain its unique culture—what Kelleher calls "this joie de vivre, this effervescence, in our company." Fairness and a willingness to share the pain during difficult times has been an important part of its corporate philosophy. When pilots were asked to freeze pay for five years, Kelleher also voluntarily took a five-year pay freeze "to honor what they had done. And I have turned down many, many millions of dollars in salary and options because it didn't set a good example." Corporate officers follow a similar practice. According to Kelleher, "Our officers have never received a salary increase that is larger on average than our noncontract employees have gotten. In other words, if they get a 3.5 percent increase, our officers get a 3.5 percent increase." Such policies have no doubt contributed to Southwest's remarkable success: As of 2008, the Dallas, Texas–based company has been profitable for 35 consecutive years and now carries more passengers per year than any other airline.

Sources: Charam, R. 2009 *Leadership in the Era of Economic Uncertainty.* New York: McGraw-Hill; McConnon, A. 2008. Lessons from a Skinflint CEO. *BusinessWeek,* October 6: 54–55; Smith, E. 2008. Herb Kelleher. *Texas Monthly,* June: 78–85; and, www.wikipedia.org.

want to increase the speed by 10 miles per hour, you look for incremental advances. However, if you want to double the speed, you've got to think "out of the box" (e.g., widen the track, change the overall suspension system). Leaders need more creative solutions than just keeping the same train with a few minor tweaks. Instead, they must come up with more revolutionary visions.

Robert Tillman, CEO of Lowe's, dramatically revitalized his firm by setting a clear and compelling direction:

> He made Lowe's into a formidable competitor to Home Depot, Inc.[7] In his six years as CEO, Tillman has transformed the $43 billion chain, based in Wilkesboro, North Carolina. Its shares have more than doubled over the past four years, while Home Depot's have fallen about 20 percent.
>
> Tillman has redirected Lowe's strategy by responding effectively to research showing that women initiate 80 percent of home projects. While Home Depot has focused on the professionals and male customers, Tillman has redesigned Lowe's stores to give them a brighter appearance, stocked them with more appliances, and focused on higher-margin goods (including everything from Laura Ashley paints to high-end bathroom fixtures). Like Wal-Mart, Lowe's has one of the best inventory systems in retailing. As a result, Lowe's profits are expected to continue to rise faster than Home Depot's.

Designing the Organization

designing the organization a strategic leadership activity of building structures, teams, systems, and organizational processes that facilitate the implementation of the leader's vision and strategies.

At times, almost all leaders have difficulty implementing their vision and strategies. Such problems may stem from a variety of sources:

- Lack of understanding of responsibility and accountability among managers.
- Reward systems that do not motivate individuals (or collectives such as groups and divisions) toward desired organizational goals.
- Inadequate or inappropriate budgeting and control systems.
- Insufficient mechanisms to integrate activities across the organization.

Successful leaders are actively involved in building structures, teams, systems, and organizational processes that facilitate the implementation of their vision and strategies. We discussed the necessity for consistency between business-level and corporate-level strategies and organizational control in Chapter 9. Without appropriately structuring organizational activities, a firm would generally be unable to attain an overall low-cost advantage by closely monitoring its costs through detailed and formalized cost and financial control procedures. With regard to corporate-level strategy, a related diversification strategy would necessitate reward systems that emphasize behavioral measures, whereas an unrelated strategy should rely more on financial (or objective) indicators of performance.

These examples illustrate the important role of leadership in creating systems and structures to achieve desired ends. As Jim Collins says about the importance of designing the organization, "Along with figuring out what the company stands for and pushing it to understand what it's really good at, building mechanisms is the CEO's role—the leader as architect."[8]

Nurturing an Excellent and Ethical Culture

excellent and ethical organizational culture an organizational culture focused on core competencies and high ethical standards.

Organizational culture can be an effective means of organizational control. Leaders play a key role in changing, developing, and sustaining an organization's culture. After he became CEO of AMD, a $6 billion microprocessor producer, Hector Ruiz dramatically improved his firm's competitive position vis-à-vis Intel—a firm six times as large. He says:[9]

> We have gotten larger and more complex. By definition that means we're going to make some mistakes. I'm much more comfortable in an environment when I know that's going to happen. That means we're learning. An aura of confidence begins to develop around people who can make mistakes and learn and go forward. At employee meetings I say, "Please, go get speeding tickets. I don't want you to get parking tickets."

Whirlpool: Becoming a Leader in Innovation

David R. Whitwam realized he had a major problem. The chairman and CEO had helped build Whirlpool into the world's number one maker of big-ticket appliances, attaining unmatched economies of scale. He had also repeatedly cut costs by hundreds of millions of dollars. However, in 1999, everything—the stock price, profit margins, market share—had been about where it was a decade earlier. At the time, housing and sales of Whirlpool appliances were booming. Despite the strong demand, prices were falling by an average of 3.4 percent a year. The underlying problem was that its machines had been reduced to commodities. The solution was straightforward: Whirlpool had to come up with exciting new products that could command premium prices.

Whitman's goal of "innovation from everyone, everywhere" required major changes in the firm's management processes and culture, which had been designed to drive operational efficiency. He appointed Nancy Snyder, a corporate vice president to be Whirlpool's first "innovation czar." She rallied her colleagues around what was to become a five-year quest to reinvent the company's management processes. Key changes included:

- Making innovation a central topic in Whirlpool's leadership development programs.

- Setting aside $45 million from the capital budget for innovation in 2000 and doubling it in 2001 for projects that met a stringent standard of innovativeness.

- Requiring every product development plan to contain a sizable component of new-to-market innovation.

Sources: Arndt, M. 2006. Creativity Overflowing. www.businessweek.com, May 8; Hamel, G. 2006. The Why, What, and How of Management Innovation. *Harvard Business Review*, 84(2): 72–87; and Salter, C. 2005. Whirlpool Finds Its Cool. *Fast Company*, June: 73.

- Training more than 600 innovation mentors charged with encouraging a culture of innovation throughout the company.

- Setting up an intranet site that offered a do-it-yourself course on innovation and listing every project in the pipeline.

- Establishing innovation as a significant component of senior management's compensation program. If they failed to meet annual revenue and pipeline targets, they could lose 30 percent of their annual bonus.

- Setting aside time in quarterly business review meetings for an in-depth discussion of each unit's innovation performance.

Whirlpool's innovation efforts are paying off. The Duet, a matching washer and dryer introduced in 2001, has become a must-have appliance that seems to be selling like iPods. At $2,000, it is the company's most expensive washer-dryer set. With its stylish lines, portholelike door, and eye-catching colors, the Duet, says Chuck Jones, Whirlpool's Design Chief, "is like a Ferrari in your laundry room." That same year, Paris's Louvre Museum displayed Whirlpool's next generation concept products. And, in 2002, the Smithsonian Institution named Whirlpool the winner of its annual National Design Award in corporate achievement.

The bottom line results of Snyder's initiatives have been impressive. Since 2001, revenues from products that fit the company's definition of innovation have soared from $10 million to $760 million by 2005, or over five percent of the firm's record $14.3 billion revenue. Whirlpool's shares as of early 2007 were around $90—nearly double what they were five years earlier. And prices were no longer eroding. Over the previous three years, the average price of Whirlpool's appliances had risen five percent annually.

In sharp contrast, leaders can also have a very detrimental effect on a firm's culture and ethics. Imagine the negative impact that Todd Berman's illegal activities have had on a firm that he cofounded—New York's private equity firm Chartwell Investments.[10] He stole more than $3.6 million from the firm and its investors. Berman pleaded guilty to fraud charges brought by the Justice Department. For 18 months he misled Chartwell's investors concerning the financial condition of one of the firm's portfolio companies by falsely claiming it needed to borrow funds to meet operating expenses. Instead, Berman transferred the money to his personal bank account, along with fees paid by portfolio companies.

Clearly, a leader's ethical behavior can make a strong impact on an organization—for good or for bad. Strategy Spotlight 11.2 provides a positive example. It discusses how Nancy Snyder was effective in instilling a culture of innovation at Whirlpool Corporation.

Managers and top executives must accept personal responsibility for developing and strengthening ethical behavior throughout the organization. They must consistently demonstrate that such behavior is central to the vision and mission of the organization. Several elements must be present and reinforced for a firm to become highly ethical, including role models, corporate credos and codes of conduct, reward and evaluation systems, and policies and procedures. Given the importance of these elements, we address them in detail in the last section of this chapter.

Elements of Effective Leadership

The demands on leaders in today's business environment require them to perform a variety of functions. The success of their organizations often depends on how they as individuals meet challenges and deliver on promises. What practices and skills are needed to get the job done effectively? In this section, we focus on three capabilities that are marks of successful leadership—integrative thinking, overcoming barriers to change, and the effective use of power. Then, in the next section, we will examine an important human trait that helps leaders be more effective—emotional intelligence.

Integrative Thinking

integrative thinking a process of reconciling opposing thoughts by generating new alternatives and creative solutions rather than rejecting one thought in favor of another.

The challenges facing today's leaders require them to confront a host of opposing forces. As the previous section indicated, maintaining consistency across a company's culture, vision, and organizational design can be difficult, especially if the three activities are out of alignment.

How does a leader make good strategic decisions in the face of multiple contingencies and diverse opportunities? A recent study by Roger L. Martin reveals that executives who have a capability known as "integrative thinking" are among the most effective leaders. In his book *The Opposable Mind,* Martin contends that people who can consider two conflicting ideas simultaneously, without dismissing one of the ideas or becoming discouraged about reconciling them, often make the best problem solvers because of their ability to creatively synthesize the opposing thoughts. In explaining the source of his title, Martin quotes F. Scott Fitzgerald, who observed, "The test of a first-rate intelligence is the ability to hold two opposing ideas in mind at the same time and still retain the ability to function. One should, for example, be able to see that things are hopeless yet be determined to make them otherwise."[11]

In contrast to conventional thinking, which tends to focus on making choices between competing ideas from a limited set of alternatives, integrative thinking is the process by which people reconcile opposing thoughts to identify creative solutions that provide them with more options and new alternatives. Exhibit 11.2 outlines the four stages of the integrative thinking and deciding process. Martin uses the admittedly simple example of deciding where to go on vacation to illustrate the stages:

- *Salience*—Take stock of what features of the decision you consider relevant and important. For example: Where will you go? What will you see? Where will you stay? What will it cost? Is it safe? Other features may be less important, but try to think of everything that may matter.
- *Causality*—Make a mental map of the causal relationships between the features, that is, how the various features are related to one another. For example, is it worth it to invite friends to share expenses? Will an exotic destination be less safe?
- *Architecture*—Use the mental map to arrange a sequence of decisions that will lead to a specific outcome. For example, will you make the hotel and flight arrangements

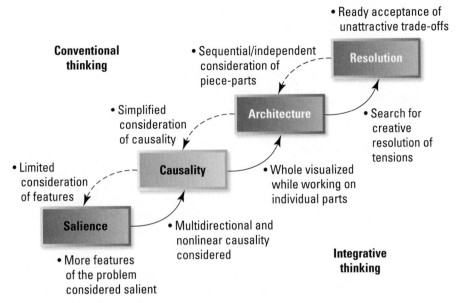

Conventional thinking

• Ready acceptance of unattractive trade-offs

Resolution

• Sequential/independent consideration of piece-parts

• Simplified consideration of causality

Architecture

• Search for creative resolution of tensions

• Limited consideration of features

Causality

• Whole visualized while working on individual parts

Salience

• Multidirectional and nonlinear causality considered

Integrative thinking

• More features of the problem considered salient

Source: Martin, R. L. 2007. *The Opposable Mind.* Boston: Harvard Business School Press.

Exhibit 11.2 Integrative Thinking: The Process of Thinking and Deciding

first, or focus on which sightseeing tours are available? No particular decision path is right or wrong, but considering multiple options simultaneously may lead to a better decision.

• ***Resolution***—Make your selection. For example, choose which destination, which flight, and so forth. You final resolution is linked to how you evaluated the first three stages; if you are dissatisfied with your choices, the dotted arrows in the diagram (Exhibit 11.2) suggest you can go back through the process and revisit your assumptions.

Applied to business, an integrative thinking approach enables decision makers to consider situations not as forced trade-offs—either decrease costs or invest more; either satisfy shareholders or please the community—but as a method for synthesizing opposing ideas into a creative solution. The key is to think in terms of "both-and" rather than "either-or." "Integrative thinking," says Martin, "shows us that there's a way to integrate the advantages of one solution without canceling out the advantages of an alternative solution."

Although Martin found that integrative thinking comes naturally to some people, he also believes it can be taught. But it may be difficult to learn, in part because it requires people to *un*learn old patterns and become aware of how they think. For executives willing to take a deep look at their habits of thought, integrative thinking can be developed into a valuable skill. Strategy Spotlight 11.3 tells how Red Hat, Inc. cofounder Bob Young made his company a market leader by using integrative thinking to resolve a major problem in the domain of open-source software.

Overcoming Barriers to Change

What are the **barriers to change** that leaders often encounter, and how can they best bring about organizational change? After all, people generally have some level of choice about how strongly they support or resist a leader's change initiatives. Why is there often so much

barriers to change characteristics of individuals and organizations that prevent a leader from transforming an organization.

>LO2
Three elements of effective leadership: integrative thinking, overcoming barriers to change, and the effective use of power.

Integrative Thinking at Red Hat, Inc.

How can a software developer make money giving away free software? That was the dilemma Red Hat founder Bob Young was facing during the early days of the open-source software movement. A Finnish developer named Linus Torvalds, using freely available UNIX software, had developed an operating system dubbed "Linux" that was being widely circulated in the freeware community. The software was intended specifically as an alternative to the pricey proprietary systems sold by Microsoft and Oracle. To use proprietary software, corporations had to pay hefty installation fees and were required to call Microsoft or Oracle engineers to fix it when anything went wrong. In Young's view it was a flawed and unsustainable business model.

But the free model was flawed as well. Although several companies had sprung up to help companies use Linux, there were few opportunities to profit from using it. As Young said, "You couldn't make any money selling [the Linux] operating system because all this stuff was free, and if you started to charge money for it, someone else would come in and price it lower. It was a commodity in the truest sense of the word." To complicate matters, hundreds of developers were part of the software community that was constantly modifying and debugging Linux—at a rate equivalent to three updates per day. As a result, systems administrators at corporations that tried to adopt the software spent so much time keeping track of updates that they didn't enjoy the savings they expected from using free software.

Young saw the appeal of both approaches but also realized a new model was needed. While contemplating

the dilemma, he realized a salient feature that others had overlooked—because most major corporations have to live with software decisions for at least ten years, they will nearly always choose to do business with the industry leader. Young realized he had to position Red Hat as the top provider of Linux software. To do that, he proposed a radical solution: provide the authoritative version of Linux and deliver it in a new way—as a download rather than on CD. He hired programmers to create a downloadable version—still free—and promised, in essence, to maintain its quality (for a fee, of course) by dealing with all the open-source programmers who were continually suggesting changes. In the process, he created a product companies could trust and then profited by establishing ongoing service relationships with customers. Red Hat's version of Linux became the de facto standard. By 2000, Linux was installed in 25 percent of server operating systems worldwide and Red Hat had captured over 50 percent of the global market for Linux systems.

By recognizing that a synthesis of two flawed business models could provide the best of both worlds, Young exhibited the traits of integrative thinking. He pinpointed the causal relationships between the salient features of the marketplace and Red Hat's path to prosperity. He then crafted an approach that integrated aspects of the two existing approaches into a new alternative. By resolving to provide a free downloadable version, Young also took responsibility for creating his own path to success. The pay-off was substantial: when Red Hat went public in 1999, Young became a billionaire on the first day of trading. And, by 2008 Red Hat had over $.5 billion in annual revenues and a market capitalization of over $3 billion.

Source: Martin, R. L. 2007. *The Opposable Mind.* Boston: Harvard Business School Press.

---

resistance? Organizations at all levels are prone to inertia and are slow to learn, adapt, and change because:

1. Many people have **vested interests in the status quo.** People tend to be risk averse and resistant to change. There is a broad stream of research on "escalation," wherein certain individuals continue to throw "good money at bad decisions" despite negative performance feedback.[12]

systemic barriers
barriers to change that stem from an organizational design that impedes the proper flow and evaluation of information.

2. There are **systemic barriers.** The design of the organization's structure, information processing, reporting relationships, and so forth impede the proper flow and evaluation of information. A bureaucratic structure with multiple layers, onerous requirements for documentation, and rigid rules and procedures will often "inoculate" the organization against change.

3. **Behavioral barriers** cause managers to look at issues from a biased or limited perspective due to their education, training, work experiences, and so forth. Consider an incident shared by David Lieberman, marketing director at GVO, an innovation consulting firm:

> A company's creative type had come up with a great idea for a new product. Nearly everybody loved it. However, it was shot down by a high-ranking manufacturing representative who exploded: "A new color? Do you have any idea of the spare-parts problem that it will create?" This was not a dimwit exasperated at having to build a few storage racks at the warehouse. He'd been hearing for years about cost cutting, lean inventories, and "focus." Lieberman's comment: "Good concepts, but not always good for innovation."

4. **Political barriers** refer to conflicts arising from power relationships. This can be the outcome of a myriad of symptoms such as vested interests, refusal to share information, conflicts over resources, conflicts between departments and divisions, and petty interpersonal differences.

5. **Personal time constraints** bring to mind the old saying about "not having enough time to drain the swamp when you are up to your neck in alligators." Gresham's law of planning states that operational decisions will drive out the time necessary for strategic thinking and reflection. This tendency is accentuated in organizations experiencing severe price competition or retrenchment wherein managers and employees are spread rather thin.

Leaders must draw on a range of personal skills as well as organizational mechanisms to move their organizations forward in the face of such barriers. Integrative thinking provides one avenue by equipping leaders with an ability to consider creative alternatives to the kind of resistance and doubt that cause many barriers. Two factors mentioned earlier—building a learning organization and ethical organization—provide the kind of climate within which a leader can advance the organization's aims and make progress toward its goals. One of the most important tools a leader has for overcoming barriers to change is their personal and organizational power. On the one hand, good leaders must be on guard not to abuse power. On the other hand, successful leadership requires the measured exercise of power. We turn to that topic next.

The Effective Use of Power

Successful leadership requires effective use of power in overcoming barriers to change.[13] As humorously noted by Mark Twain, "I'm all for progress. It's change I object to." **Power** refers to a leader's ability to get things done in a way he or she wants them to be done. It is the ability to influence other people's behavior, to persuade them to do things that they otherwise would not do, and to overcome resistance and opposition to changing direction. Effective exercise of power is essential for successful leadership.[14]

A leader derives his or her power from several sources or bases. The simplest way to understand the bases of power is by classifying them as organizational and personal, as shown in Exhibit 11.3.

Organizational bases of power refer to the power that a person wields because of holding a formal management position. These include legitimate power, reward power, coercive power, and information power. *Legitimate power* is derived from organizationally conferred decision-making authority and is exercised by virtue of a manager's position in the organization. *Reward power* depends on the ability of the leader or manager to confer rewards for positive behaviors or outcomes. *Coercive power* is the power a manager exercises over employees using fear of punishment for errors of omission or commission. *Information power* arises from a manager's access, control, and distribution of information that is not freely available to everyone in an organization.

---

behavioral barriers barriers to change associated with the tendency for managers to look at issues from a biased or limited perspective based on their prior education and experience.

political barriers barriers to change related to conflicts arising from power relationships.

power a leader's ability to get things done in a way he or she wants them to be done.

organizational bases of power a formal management position that is the basis of a leader's power.

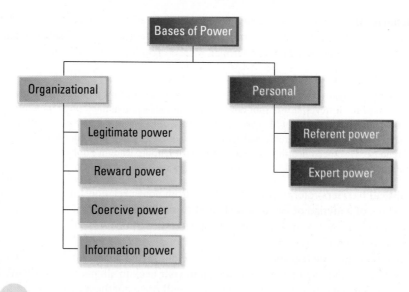

Exhibit 11.3 A Leader's Bases of Power

personal bases of power a leader's personality characteristics and behavior that are the basis of the leader's power.

A leader might also be able to influence subordinates because of his or her personality characteristics and behavior. These would be considered the **personal bases of power,** including referent power and expert power. The source of *referent power* is a subordinate's identification with the leader. A leader's personal attributes or charisma might influence subordinates and make them devoted to that leader. The source of *expert power* is the leader's expertise and knowledge in a particular field. The leader is the expert on whom subordinates depend for information that they need to do their jobs successfully.

Successful leaders use the different bases of power, and often a combination of them, as appropriate to meet the demands of a situation, such as the nature of the task, the personality characteristics of the subordinates, the urgency of the issue, and other factors. Leaders must recognize that persuasion and developing consensus are often essential, but so is pressing for action. At some point stragglers must be prodded into line.[15] Peter Georgescu, who recently retired as CEO of Young & Rubicam (an advertising and media subsidiary of the UK-based WPP Group), summarized a leader's dilemma brilliantly (and humorously), "I have knee pads and a .45. I get down and beg a lot, but I shoot people too."[16]

Strategy Spotlight 11.4 addresses some of the subtleties of power. It focuses on William Bratton, Chief of the Los Angeles Police Department, who has enjoyed a very successful career in law enforcement.

Emotional Intelligence: A Key Leadership Trait

> **>LO3**
> The crucial role of emotional intelligence (EI) in successful leadership as well as its potential drawbacks.

In the previous sections, we discussed skills and activities of strategic leadership. The focus was on "what leaders do and how they do it." Now, the issue becomes "who leaders *are,*" that is, what leadership traits are the most important. Clearly, these two issues are related, because successful leaders possess the valuable traits that enable them to perform effectively in order to create value for their organization.[17]

There has been a vast amount of literature on the successful traits of leaders.[18] These traits include integrity, maturity, energy, judgment, motivation, intelligence, expertise, and so on. For simplicity, these traits may be grouped into three broad sets of capabilities:

- Purely technical skills (like accounting or operations research).
- Cognitive abilities (like analytical reasoning or quantitative analysis).
- Emotional intelligence (like self-management and managing relationships).

William Bratton: Using Multiple Bases of Power

William Bratton, Chief of the Los Angeles Police Department has an enviable track record in turning around police departments in crime-ridden cities. First, while running the police division of Massachusetts Bay Transit Authority (MBTA) in Boston, then as police commissioner of New York in the mid-1990s, and now in Los Angeles since 2002, Chief Bratton is credited with reducing crime and improving police morale in record time. An analysis of his success at each of these organizations reveals similar patterns both in terms of the problems he faced and the many ways in which he used the different bases of power to engineer a rapid turnaround.

In Boston, New York, and Los Angeles, Chief Bratton faced similar hurdles: organizations wedded to the status quo, limited resources, demotivated staffs, and opposition from powerful vested interests. But he does not give up in the face of these seemingly insurmountable problems. He is persuasive in calls for change, capable of mobilizing the commitment of key players, silencing vocal naysayers, and building rapport with superiors and subordinates while building bridges with external constituencies.

Chief Bratton's persuasion tactics are unconventional, yet effective. When he was running the MBTA police, the Transit Authority decided to buy small squad cars, which are cheaper to buy and to run, but inadequate for the police officer's task. Instead of arguing, Bratton invited the general manager for a tour of the city. He rode with the general manager in exactly the same type of car that was ordered for ordinary officers, and drove over every pothole on the road. He moved the seats forward so that the general manager could feel how little leg room was there. And he put on his belt, cuffs, and gun so that the general manager could understand how limited the space was. After two hours in the cramped car, the general manager was ready to change the order and get more suitable cars for the officers!

Another tactic Bratton used effectively was insisting on community meetings between police officers and citizens. This went against the long-standing practice of detachment between police and community to decrease the chances of corruption. The result was that his department had a better understanding of public concerns and rearranged their priorities, which in turn led to better community relations. For internal communications, he relied mainly on professionally produced videos instead of long, boring memos.

Chief Bratton also shows a remarkable talent for building political bridges and silencing naysayers. As he was introducing his zero-tolerance policing approach that aggressively targets "quality of life" crimes such as panhandling, drunkenness, and prostitution, opposition came from the city's courts, which feared being inundated by a large number of small-crimes cases. Bratton enlisted the support of Rudolph Giuliani, the mayor of New York, who had considerable influence over the district attorneys, the courts, and the city jail. He also took the case to the *New York Times* and managed to get the issue of zero-tolerance on the front pages of the newspaper. The courts were left with no alternative but to cooperate.

To a great extent, Bratton's success can be attributed to his understanding of the subtleties of power, including persuasion, motivation, coalition building, empathy for subordinates, and a focus on goals.

Sources: Chan Kim, W. & Renee Mauborgne, R. 2003. Tipping Point Leadership. *Harvard Business Review*, 81(4): 60–69; and McCarthy, T. 2004. The Gang Buster. *Time*, January 19: 56–58.

"Emotional intelligence (EI)" has become popular in both the literature and management practice in recent years.[19] *Harvard Business Review* articles published in 1998 and 2000 by psychologist/journalist Daniel Goleman, who is most closely associated with the concept, have become *HBR*'s most highly requested reprint articles. And two of Goleman's recent books, *Emotional Intelligence* and *Working with Emotional Intelligence,* were both on the *New York Times*'s best-seller lists. Goleman defines **emotional intelligence** as the capacity for recognizing one's own emotions and those of others.[20]

Recent studies of successful managers have found that effective leaders consistently have a high level of EI.[21] Findings indicate that EI is a better predictor of life success (economic well-being, satisfaction with life, friendship, family life), including occupational attainments, than IQ. Such evidence has been extrapolated to the catchy phrase: "IQ gets you hired, but EQ (Emotional Quotient) gets you promoted." Human resource managers believe this statement to be true, even for highly technical jobs such as those of scientists and engineers.

> **emotional intelligence (EI)** an individual's capacity for recognizing his or her own emotions and those of others, including the five components of self awareness, self regulation, motivation, empathy, and social skills.

Exhibit 11.4   The Five Components of Emotional Intelligence at Work

	Definition	Hallmarks
Self-management skills:		
Self-awareness	• The ability to recognize and understand your moods, emotions, and drives, as well as their effect on others.	• Self-confidence • Realistic self-assessment • Self-deprecating sense of humor
Self-regulation	• The ability to control or redirect disruptive impulses and moods. • The propensity to suspend judgment—to think before acting.	• Trustworthiness and integrity • Comfort with ambiguity • Openness to change
Motivation	• A passion to work for reasons that go beyond money or status. • A propensity to pursue goals with energy and persistence.	• Strong drive to achieve • Optimism, even in the face of failure • Organizational commitment
Managing relationships:		
Empathy	• The ability to understand the emotional makeup of other people. • Skill in treating people according to their emotional reactions.	• Expertise in building and retaining talent • Cross-cultural sensitivity • Service to clients and customers
Social skill	• Proficiency in managing relationships and building networks. • An ability to find common ground and build rapport.	• Effectiveness in leading change • Persuasiveness • Expertise in building and leading teams

Source: Adapted and reprinted by permission of *Harvard Business Review.* Exhibit from "What Makes a Leader," by D. Goleman, January 2004. Copyright © 2004 by the Harvard Business School Publishing Corporation; all rights reserved.

This is not to say that IQ and technical skills are irrelevant, but they become "threshold capabilities." They are the necessary requirements for attaining higher-level managerial positions. EI, on the other hand, is essential for leadership success. Without it, Goleman claims, a manager can have excellent training, an incisive analytical mind, and many smart ideas but will still not be a great leader.

Exhibit 11.4 identifies the five components of EI: self-awareness, self-regulation, motivation, empathy, and social skill.

Self-Awareness

Self-awareness is the first component of EI and brings to mind that Delphic oracle who gave the advice "know thyself" thousands of years ago. Self-awareness involves a person having a deep understanding of his or her emotions, strengths, weaknesses, and drives. People with strong self-awareness are neither overly critical nor unrealistically optimistic. Instead, they are honest with themselves and others.

People generally admire and respect candor. Leaders are constantly required to make judgment calls that require a candid assessment of capabilities—their own and those of others. People who assess themselves honestly (i.e., self-aware people) are well suited to do the same for the organizations they run.[22]

Self-Regulation

Biological impulses drive our emotions. Although we cannot do away with them, we can strive to manage them. Self-regulation, which is akin to an ongoing inner conversation, frees us from being prisoners of our feelings.[23] People engaged in such conversation feel bad moods and emotional impulses just as everyone else does. However, they find ways to control them and even channel them in useful ways.

Self-regulated people are able to create an environment of trust and fairness where, political behavior and infighting are sharply reduced and productivity tends to be high. People who have mastered their emotions are better able to bring about and implement change in an organization. When a new initiative is announced, they are less likely to panic; they are able to suspend judgment, seek out information, and listen to executives explain the new program.

Motivation

Successful executives are driven to achieve beyond expectations—their own and everyone else's. Although many people are driven by external factors, such as money and prestige, those with leadership potential are driven by a deeply embedded desire to achieve for the sake of achievement.

Motivated people show a passion for the work itself, such as seeking out creative challenges, a love of learning, and taking pride in a job well done. They also have a high level of energy to do things better as well as a restlessness with the status quo. They are eager to explore new approaches to their work.

Empathy

Empathy is probably the most easily recognized component of EI. Empathy means thoughtfully considering an employee's feelings, along with other factors, in the process of making intelligent decisions. Empathy is particularly important in today's business environment for at least three reasons: the increasing use of teams, the rapid pace of globalization, and the growing need to retain talent.[24]

When leading a team, a manager is often charged with arriving at a consensus—often in the face of a high level of emotions. Empathy enables a manager to sense and understand the viewpoints of everyone around the table.

Globalization typically involves cross-cultural dialogue that can easily lead to miscues. Empathetic people are attuned to the subtleties of body language; they can hear the message beneath the words being spoken. They have a deep understanding of the existence and importance of cultural and ethnic differences.

Empathy also plays a key role in retaining talent. Human capital is particularly important to a firm in the knowledge economy when it comes to creating advantages that are sustainable. Leaders need empathy to develop and keep top talent, because when high performers leave, they take their tacit knowledge with them.

Empathetic leaders recognize that work is often demanding and employees can sometimes get worn down or stressed out. Strategy Spotlight 11.5 discusses steps some business owners are taking to create a healthy work environment and support workers' efforts to stay fit.

Social Skill

While the first three components of EI are all self-management skills, the last two—empathy and social skill—concern a person's ability to manage relationships with others. Social skill may be viewed as friendliness with a purpose: moving people in the direction you desire, whether that's agreement on a new marketing strategy or enthusiasm about a new product.

Creating a Healthy Workplace

Demanding jobs and professional challenges often make the workplace a stressful environment. And studies show that stress is a major contributor to health problems such as heart disease and musculoskeletal disorders. To counter the pressures of work, empathetic leaders have introduced wellness programs designed to make work a more pleasant and healthy experience. "With the expenditure of modest resources," says Jay Vandergriff, founder of workplace wellness provider Wellness Coaches USA, "a company can build a culture and work environment that is committed to wellness values."

Jon S. Wheeler, CEO of Virginia Beach, Virginia, real estate firm Wheeler Interests, has made corporate wellness a central part of the workplace culture. The company offers its 34 employees various perks, including midday kayaking breaks, an onsite gym, and access to a personal trainer. Rather than enforce a vacation policy, Wheeler allows his employees to take vacation time whenever they like as long as get their work done. "Employees are appreciative and supportive of the concept," says Wheeler, whose company generates over $13 million in annual revenues.

Some leaders go a step farther by providing incentives to participate in wellness programs. Scott Rosenberg, CEO of New Jersey–based Miro Consulting, a $25 million software licensing company, ran his own version of *The Biggest Loser.* After the three-month contest, members of the winning team received $500 each. John Roberson, CEO of Nashville, Tennessee–based marketing firm Advent, customizes incentives to match employees' interests. To motivate his 32 employees, he has given them everything from cowboy boots and guitar lessons to yoga classes and time off to help build orphanages in Central America.

"We define wellness more liberally than others might," says Roberson, whose sales were expected to reach $7 million in 2008. "It's about more than the physical; it's the whole person. So we encourage those things that that will help not only [employees'] physical health, but their emotional well-being, too."

Sources: Spaeder, K. E. 2008. All Well and Good. *Entrepreneur,* November: 24; Spaeder, K. E. 2008. Shape Up. *Entrepreneur,* September: 26; and, www.wikipedia.org.

Socially skilled people tend to have a wide circle of acquaintances as well as a knack for finding common ground and building rapport. They recognize that nothing gets done alone, and they have a network in place when the time for action comes.

Social skill can be viewed as the culmination of the other dimensions of EI. People will be effective at managing relationships when they can understand and control their own emotions and empathize with others' feelings. Motivation also contributes to social skill. People who are driven to achieve tend to be optimistic, even when confronted with setbacks. And when people are upbeat, their "glow" is cast upon conversations and other social encounters. They are popular, and for good reason.

Strategy Spotlight 11.6 provides John Chambers's personal reflection on how he goes about his job as CEO of Cisco Systems, the $39 billion networking giant. This empathetic leader has become one of America's most respected high-tech executives.

Emotional Intelligence: Some Potential Drawbacks and Cautionary Notes

Many great leaders have great reserves of empathy, interpersonal astuteness, awareness of their own feelings, and an awareness of their impact on others.[25] More importantly, they know how to apply these capabilities judiciously as best benefits the situation. Having some minimum level of EI will help a person be effective as a leader as long as it is channeled appropriately. However, if a person has a high level of these capabilities it may become "too much of a good thing" if he or she is allowed to drive inappropriate behaviors. Some additional potential drawbacks of EI can be gleaned by considering the flip side of its benefits.

Emotional Intelligence: Cisco Systems' CEO John Chambers's

John Chambers's recently shared his insights on how he goes about performing his responsibilities as CEO of Cisco Systems. He exemplifies many of the concepts of emotional intelligence and, in his 15 years at Cisco Systems, has become one of the most respected high-tech executives in the world. Chambers's brief essay is one of a series in *Fortune* magazine on the topic of "How I Work."

> I started with the classic communications methods when I got here 15 years ago. I'd walk around and talk to small groups and larger groups. I'd see whose car is out in the parking lot. Then e-mail became very effective, because it gave me the ability to send a message to the whole group. But I'm a voice person. I communicate with emotion that way. I like to listen to emotion too. It's a lot easier to listen to a key customer if I hear how they're describing a problem to me. I'll leave 40 or 50 voicemails a day.

> As far as how I hear from employees, I host a monthly birthday breakfast. Anybody who has a birthday in that month gets to come and quiz me for an hour and 15 minutes. No directors or VPs in the room. It's how I keep my finger on the pulse of what's working and what's not. It's brutal, but it's my most enjoyable session.

> To be informed, I like summaries. Because of my dyslexia, I do very little novel reading or that type of activity. I love quick articles. Before every meeting and every panel I study briefing binders with all the information I need: What we're doing in a presentation, who we're meeting with, backgrounds on them, etc. It's two or three pages on each topic, and that is how I like to learn.

As his essay indicates, Chambers's seems like a down-to earth guy—remarkable for the CEO and chairman of a $39 billion *Fortune* 100 company. When asked recently his counsel for making it through the difficult financial times, Chambers's said folks must, "focus on what we can influence, and not over- or underreact to things we cannot. It's a question of living in the world as it is, not the way we want it to be." That sounds like advice from someone who is emotionally balanced.

Sources: Chambers's, J. 2006. Lights! Camera! Cue From CEO! *Fortune*, August 21: 27. (Interviewed by Adam Lashinsky.) Copyright © 2006 Time, Inc. All rights reserved; McGirt, E. 2008/2009. Revolution in San Jose. *Fast Company*, December/January: 89–136; and www.wikipedia.org.

Effective Leaders Have Empathy for Others However, they also must be able to make the "tough decisions." Leaders must be able to appeal to logic and reason and acknowledge others' feelings so that people feel the decisions are correct. However, it is easy to overidentify with others or confuse empathy with sympathy. This can make it more difficult to make the tough decisions.

Effective Leaders Are Astute Judges of People A danger is that leaders may become judgmental and overly critical about the shortcomings they perceive in others. They are likely to dismiss other people's insights, making them feel undervalued.

Effective Leaders Are Passionate about What They Do, and They Show It This doesn't mean that they are always cheerleaders. Rather, they may express their passion as persistence in pursuing an objective or a relentless focus on a valued principle. However, there is a fine line between being excited about something and letting your passion close your mind to other possibilities or cause you to ignore realities that others may see.

Effective Leaders Create Personal Connections with Their People Most effective leaders take time to engage employees individually and in groups, listening to their ideas, suggestions and concerns, and responding in ways that make people feel that their ideas are respected and appreciated. However, if the leader makes too many unannounced visits, it may create a culture of fear and micromanagement. Clearly, striking a correct balance is essential.

From a moral standpoint, emotional leadership is neither good nor bad. On the one hand, emotional leaders can be altruistic, focused on the general welfare of the company and its employees, and highly principled. On the other hand, they can be manipulative, selfish, and dishonest. For example, if a person is using leadership solely to gain power, that is not leadership at all.[26] Rather, they are using their EI to grasp what people want and pander to those desires in order to gain authority and influence. After all, easy answers sell.

Next, we turn to guidelines for developing a "learning organization." In today's competitive environment, the old saying that "a chain is only as strong as the weakest link" applies more than ever before. To learn and adapt proactively, firms need "eyes, ears, and brains" throughout all parts of the organization. One person, or a small group of individuals, can no longer think and learn for the entire entity.

Developing a Learning Organization

Charles Handy, author of *The Age of Unreason* and *The Age of Paradox* and one of today's most respected business visionaries, shared an amusing story:

> The other day, a courier could not find my family's remote cottage. He called his base on his radio, and the base called us to ask directions. He was just around the corner, but his base managed to omit a vital part of the directions. So he called them again, and they called us again. Then the courier repeated the cycle a third time to ask whether we had a dangerous dog. When he eventually arrived, we asked whether it would not have been simpler and less aggravating to everyone if he had called us directly from the roadside telephone booth where he had been parked. "I can't do that," he said, "because they won't refund any money I spend." "But it's only pennies!" I exclaimed. "I know," he said, "but that only shows how little they trust us!"[27]

At first glance, it would appear that the story epitomizes the lack of empowerment and trust granted to the hapless courier: Don't ask questions, Do as you're told![28] However, implicit in this scenario is also the message that learning, information sharing, adaptation, decision making, and so on are *not* shared throughout the organization. In contrast, leading-edge organizations recognize the importance of having everyone involved in the process of actively learning and adapting. As noted by today's leading expert on learning organizations, MIT's Peter Senge, the days when Henry Ford, Alfred Sloan, and Tom Watson *"learned for the organization"* are gone.

> In an increasingly dynamic, interdependent, and unpredictable world, it is simply no longer possible for anyone to "figure it all out at the top." The old model, "the top thinks and the local acts," must now give way to integrating thinking and acting at all levels. While the challenge is great, so is the potential payoff. "The person who figures out how to harness the collective genius of the people in his or her organization," according to former Citibank CEO Walter Wriston, "is going to blow the competition away."[29]

Learning and change typically involve the ongoing questioning of an organization's status quo or method of procedure. This means that all individuals throughout the organization must be reflective. Many organizations get so caught up in carrying out their day-to-day work that they rarely, if ever, stop to think objectively about themselves and their businesses. They often fail to ask the probing questions that might lead them to call into question their basic assumptions, to refresh their strategies, or to reengineer their work processes. According to Michael Hammer and Steven Stanton, the pioneer consultants who touched off the reengineering movement:

> Reflection entails awareness of self, of competitors, of customers. It means thinking without preconception. It means questioning cherished assumptions and replacing them with new approaches. It is the only way in which a winning company can maintain its leadership position, by which a company with great assets can ensure that they continue to be well deployed.[30]

To adapt to change, foster creativity, and remain competitive, leaders must build learning organizations. Exhibit 11.5 lists the five elements of a learning organization.

Exhibit 11.5
Key Elements of a
Learning Organization

These are the five key elements of a learning organization. Each of these items should be viewed as *necessary, but not sufficient.* That is, successful learning organizations need all five elements.

1. Inspiring and motivating people with a mission or purpose.
2. Empowering employees at all levels.
3. Accumulating and sharing internal knowledge.
4. Gathering and integrating external information.
5. Challenging the status quo and enabling creativity.

Inspiring and Motivating People with a Mission or Purpose

Successful **learning organizations** create a proactive, creative approach to the unknown, actively solicit the involvement of employees at all levels, and enable all employees to use their intelligence and apply their imagination. Higher-level skills are required of everyone, not just those at the top.[31] A learning environment involves organizationwide commitment to change, an action orientation, and applicable tools and methods.[32] It must be viewed by everyone as a guiding philosophy and not simply as another change program.

A critical requirement of all learning organizations is that everyone feels and supports a compelling purpose. In the words of William O'Brien, CEO of Hanover Insurance, "Before there can be meaningful participation, people must share certain values and pictures about where we are trying to go. We discovered that people have a real need to feel that they're part of an enabling mission."[33] Such a perspective is consistent with an intensive study by Kouzes and Posner, authors of *The Leadership Challenge.*[34] They recently analyzed data from nearly one million respondents who were leaders at various levels in many organizations throughout the world. A major finding was that what leaders struggle with most is communicating an image of the future that draws others in, that is, it speaks to what others see and feel. To illustrate:

> Buddy Blanton, a principal program manager at Rockwell Collins, learned this lesson firsthand. He asked his team for feedback on his leadership, and the vast majority of it was positive. However, he got some strong advice from his team about how he could be more effective in inspiring a shared vision. "You would benefit by helping us, as a team, to understand how you go to your vision. We want to walk with you while you create the goals and vision, so we all get to the end of the vision together."[35]

Inspiring and motivating people with a mission or purpose is a necessary but not sufficient condition for developing an organization that can learn and adapt to a rapidly changing, complex, and interconnected environment.

Empowering Employees at All Levels

"The great leader is a great servant," asserted Ken Melrose, CEO of Toro Company and author of *Making the Grass Greener on Your Side.*[36] A manager's role becomes one of creating an environment where employees can achieve their potential as they help move the organization toward its goals. Instead of viewing themselves as resource controllers and power brokers, leaders must envision themselves as flexible resources willing to assume numerous roles as coaches, information providers, teachers, decision makers, facilitators, supporters, or listeners, depending on the needs of their employees.[37]

The central key to empowerment is effective leadership. Empowerment can't occur in a leadership vacuum. According to Melrose, "You best lead by serving the needs of your people. You don't do their jobs for them; you enable them to learn and progress on the job." Robert Quinn and Gretchen Spreitzer made an interesting point about two diametrically opposite perspectives on empowerment—top-down and bottom-up.[38]

learning organizations organizations that create a proactive, creative approach to the unknown, characterized by (1) inspiring and motivating people with a mission and purpose, (2) empowering employees at all levels, (3) accumulating and sharing internal knowledge, (4) gathering and integrating external information, and (5) challenging the status quo and enabling creativity.

In the top-down perspective, empowerment is about delegation and accountability—senior management has developed a clear vision and has communicated specific plans to the rest of the organization.[39] This strategy for empowerment encompasses the following:

- Start at the top.
- Clarify the organization's mission, vision, and values.
- Clearly specify the tasks, roles, and rewards for employees.
- Delegate responsibility.
- Hold people accountable for results.

By contrast, the bottom-up view looks at empowerment as concerned with risk taking, growth, and change. It involves trusting people to "do the right thing" and having a tolerance for failure. It encourages employees to act with a sense of ownership and typically "ask for forgiveness rather than permission." Here the salient elements of empowerment are:

- Start at the bottom by understanding the needs of employees.
- Teach employees self-management skills and model desired behavior.
- Build teams to encourage cooperative behavior.
- Encourage intelligent risk taking.
- Trust people to perform.

These two perspectives draw a sharp contrast in assumptions that people make about trust and control. Quinn and Spreitzer recently shared these contrasting views of empowerment with a senior management team. After an initial heavy silence, someone from the first group voiced a concern about the second group's perspective, "We can't afford loose cannons around here." A person in the second group retorted, "When was the last time you saw a cannon of any kind around here?"

Many leading-edge organizations are moving in the direction of the second perspective—recognizing the need for trust, cultural control, and expertise at all levels instead of the extensive and cumbersome rules and regulations inherent in hierarchical control.[40] Some have argued that too often organizations fall prey to the "heroes-and-drones syndrome," wherein the value of those in powerful positions is exalted and the value of those who fail to achieve top rank is diminished. Such an attitude is implicit in phrases such as "Lead, follow, or get out of the way" or, even less appealing, "Unless you're the lead horse, the view never changes." Few will ever reach the top hierarchical positions in organizations, but in the information economy, the strongest organizations are those that effectively use the talents of all the players on the team. In fact, General Electric has learned that the best method of empowering whole teams is to train them together. Strategy Spotlight 11.7 illustrates how team training can enhance organizational learning.

Accumulating and Sharing Internal Knowledge

Effective organizations must also *redistribute information, knowledge* (skills to act on the information), and *rewards*.[41] A company might give frontline employees the power to act as "customer advocates," doing whatever is necessary to satisfy customers. The company needs to disseminate information by sharing customer expectations and feedback as well as financial information. The employees must know about the goals of the business as well as how key value-creating activities in the organization are related to each other. Finally, organizations should allocate rewards on how effectively employees use information, knowledge, and power to improve customer service quality and the company's overall performance.[42]

Jack Stack is the president and CEO of Springfield ReManufacturing Corporation (SRC) in Springfield, Missouri, and author of *The Great Game of Business*. He is generally considered the pioneer of "open book" management—an innovative way to gather and disseminate internal information. Implementing this system involves three core activities.[43]

Accelerating Learning by Teaching Teams

General Electric has a long-standing tradition of using training to empower its managers to improve performance. Recently, a Leadership, Innovation, and Growth (LIG) program launched by GE in 2006 learned some important lessons: when whole teams are trained rather than individual managers, the shared learning has a more profound effect. In the past, when individual managers took the lessons learned from a program at GE's famed management development center back to their offices, they often had trouble persuading others to go along with what they had learned. By training all team members at once, LIG has accelerated the speed with which new learning is implemented as well as its long-term effectiveness. As Jon Katzenbach and Douglas Smith reported in *The Wisdom of Teams*, "by translating longer-term purposes into definable performance goals and then developing the skills needed to meet those goals, learning not only occurs in teams but endures."

The accelerated learning experience is enhanced when a few key principles are followed:

- *Reach consensus about the barriers to change and how to address them.* By having all team members together, the team can articulate both hard barriers (structural impediments, capabilities, and resource constraints) and soft barriers (team dynamics and competing priorities) that might affect proposed solutions.

- *Develop a common language.* Team members often need a new vocabulary of change—actual words that become part of the daily conversation when teams return to work. Referring to his company's new goals, GE CEO Jeffrey Immelt said the aim of the LIG program was "to embed growth into the DNA of our company." Learning a common language can help team members make the shift.

- *Create an action plan and a commitment to follow-through.* Although an initial draft is all that is typically developed in most four-day training sessions, the focused work on an actual plan forms the basis for continued effort and ongoing learning. It also builds commitment.

By making learning team-based, GE has accelerated the kinds of change processes that are needed to remain effective in a new business environment. The LIG program was developed specifically to enact Immelt's vision of a new GE—one in which expanding existing businesses and creating new ones takes priority over making acquisitions. Recognizing that such a change requires a lot of new learning, Immelt said, "A major change-management effort like this is a 10-year process. It takes a decade to build the talent, culture, and tools, and to learn from our mistakes." Clearly, creating a learning organization is a central aspect of Immelt's new plan for GE.

Sources: Katzenbach, J. R. & Smith, D. K. 2003. *The Wisdom of Teams.* New York: Collins Business; Prokesch, S. 2009. How GE Teaches Teams to Lead Change. *Harvard Business Review,* 87(1): 99–106; and www.ge.com.

First, numbers are generated daily for each of the company's employees, reflecting his or her work performance and production costs. Second, this information is aggregated once a week and shared with all of the company's people from secretaries to top management. Third, employees receive extensive training in how to use and interpret the numbers—how to understand balance sheets as well as cash flows and income statements.

In explaining why SRC embraces open book management, Stack provided an insightful counterperspective to the old adage "Information is power."

> We are building a company in which everyone tells the truth every day—not because everyone is honest but because everyone has access to the same information: operating metrics, financial data, valuation estimates. The more people understand what's really going on in their company, the more eager they are to help solve its problems. Information isn't power. It's a burden. Share information, and you share the burdens of leadership as well.

Let's take a look at Whole Foods Market, Inc., the largest natural foods grocer in the United States.[44] An important benefit of the sharing of internal information at Whole Foods becomes the active process of *internal benchmarking*. Competition is intense at Whole Foods.

Teams compete against their own goals for sales, growth, and productivity; they compete against different teams in their stores; and they compete against similar teams at different stores and regions. There is an elaborate system of peer reviews through which teams benchmark each other. The "Store Tour" is the most intense. On a periodic schedule, each Whole Foods store is toured by a group of as many as 40 visitors from another region. Lateral learning—discovering what your colleagues are doing right and carrying those practices into your organization—has become a driving force at Whole Foods.

● Whole Foods Market is well-known for sharing company information with its employees and practicing internal benchmarking.

In addition to enhancing the sharing of company information both up and down as well as across the organization, leaders also have to develop means to tap into some of the more informal sources of internal information. In a recent survey of presidents, CEOs, board members, and top executives in a variety of nonprofit organizations, respondents were asked what differentiated the successful candidates for promotion. The consensus: The executive was seen as a person who listens. According to Peter Meyer, the author of the study, "The value of listening is clear: You cannot succeed in running a company if you do not hear what your people, customers, and suppliers are telling you. . . . Listening and understanding well are key to making good decisions."[45]

Strategy Spotlight 11.8 addresses a critical aspect of obtaining information from internal sources—listening skills. General Peter Pace, former chairman of the Joint Chiefs of Staff, the highest-ranking military officer in the United States, shares his perspective on this topic.

Gathering and Integrating External Information

Recognizing opportunities, as well as threats, in the external environment is vital to a firm's success. As organizations *and* environments become more complex and evolve rapidly, it is far more critical for employees and managers to become more aware of environmental trends and events—both general and industry-specific—and more knowledgeable about their firm's competitors and customers. Next, we will discuss some ideas on how to do it.

First, the Internet has dramatically accelerated the speed with which anyone can track down useful information or locate people who might have useful information. Prior to the Net, locating someone who used to work at a company—always a good source of information—was quite a challenge. However, today people post their résumés on the Web; they participate in discussion groups and talk openly about where they work.

Marc Friedman, manager of market research at $1 billion Andrew Corporation, a fast-growing manufacturer of wireless communications products provides an example of effective Internet use.[46] One of Friedman's preferred sites to visit is Corptech's website, which provides information on 45,000 high-tech companies and more than 170,000 executives. One of his firm's product lines consisted of antennae for air-traffic control systems. He got a request to provide a country-by-country breakdown of upgrade plans for various airports. He knew nothing about air-traffic control at the time. However, he found a site on the Internet for the International Civil Aviation Organization.

Listening Skills: A Key to Obtaining Valuable Internal Information

"I don't want any yes-men around me," movie mogul Samuel Goldwyn once said. "I want them to tell me the truth, even if it costs them their jobs." We may laugh because it is often true. Organizations are usually not in the habit of rewarding people who speak uncomfortable truths—or, in the vernacular, "going against the company line." However, we need to hear from them.

According to General Peter Pace, "If you walk into a room as a senior person and innocently say, 'Here's what I'm thinking about this,' you have already skewed people's

thinking. His approach: "Start out with a question and don't voice an opinion."

Why? People can't support your position if they do not know where you stand on the issue. After all, supporting the boss is usually the politically expedient thing to do! Further, if you present subordinates with an intellectual challenge, they feel freer to offer their opinions without fear of offending somebody ranking higher in the organization. "If you are looking for answers, ask the question," suggests Pace, and "if you are looking for an honest critique, you ought to be the first person to self-critique." This is different from generals' metaphorically taking off their stars to ask for honest feedback. People know the stars will be back!

Source: Useem, M. & Useem, J. 2005. Great Escapes. *Fortune*, June 27: 98, 100.

Fortunately, it had a great deal of useful data, including several research companies working in his area of interest.

Second, company employees at all levels can use "garden variety" traditional sources to acquire external information. Much can be gleaned by reading trade and professional journals, books, and popular business magazines. Other venues for gathering external information include membership in professional or trade organizations, attendance at meetings and conventions, and networking among colleagues inside and outside of your industry. Intel's Andy Grove gathers information from people like DreamWorks SKG's Steven Spielberg and Tele-Communications Inc.'s John Malone.[47] He believes that such interaction provides insights into how to make personal computers more entertaining and better at communicating. Internally, Grove spends time with the young engineers who run Intel Architecture labs, an Oregon-based facility that Grove hopes will become the de facto R&D lab for the entire PC industry.

Third, benchmarking can be a useful means of employing external information. Here managers seek out the best examples of a particular practice as part of an ongoing effort to improve the corresponding practice in their own organization.[48] There are two primary types of benchmarking. *Competitive benchmarking* restricts the search for best practices to competitors, while *functional benchmarking* endeavors to determine best practices regardless of industry. Industry-specific standards (e.g., response times required to repair power outages in the electric utility industry) are typically best handled through competitive benchmarking, whereas more generic processes (e.g., answering 1-800 calls) lend themselves to functional benchmarking because the function is essentially the same in any industry.

Ford Motor Company used benchmarking to study Mazda's accounts payable operations.[49] Its initial goal of a 20 percent cut in its 500-employee accounts payable staff was ratcheted up to 75 percent—and met. Ford found that staff spent most of their time trying to match conflicting data in a mass of paper, including purchase orders, invoices, and receipts. Following Mazda's example, Ford created an "invoiceless system" in which invoices no longer trigger payments to suppliers. The receipt does the job.

Fourth, focus directly on customers for information. For example, William McKnight, head of 3M's Chicago sales office, required that salesmen of abrasives products talk directly to the workers in the shop to find out what they needed, instead of calling on only front-office executives.[50] This was very innovative at the time—1909! But it illustrates the need to get to the end user of a product or service. (McKnight went on to become 3M's president from 1929 to 1949 and chairman from 1949 to 1969.) More recently, James Taylor, senior vice president for global marketing at Gateway 2000, discussed the value of customer input in reducing response time, a critical success factor in the PC industry.

> We talk to 100,000 people a day—people calling to order a computer, shopping around, looking for tech support. Our website gets 1.1 million hits per day. The time it takes for an idea to enter this organization, get processed, and then go to customers for feedback is down to minutes. We've designed the company around speed and feedback.[51]

Challenging the Status Quo and Enabling Creativity

Earlier in this chapter we discussed some of the barriers that leaders face when trying to bring about change in an organization: vested interests in the status quo, systemic barriers, behavioral barriers, political barriers, and personal time constraints. For a firm to become a learning organization, it must overcome such barriers in order to foster creativity and enable it to permeate the firm. This becomes quite a challenge if the firm is entrenched in a status quo mentality.

Perhaps the best way to challenge the status quo is for the leader to forcefully create a sense of urgency. For example, when Tom Kasten was vice president of Levi Strauss, he had a direct approach to initiating change.

> You create a compelling picture of the risks of *not* changing. We let our people hear directly from customers. We videotaped interviews with customers and played excerpts. One big customer said, "We trust many of your competitors implicitly. We sample their deliveries. We open *all* Levi's deliveries." Another said, "Your lead times are the worst. If you weren't Levi's, you'd be gone." It was powerful. I wish we had done more of it.[52]

Such initiative, if sincere and credible, establishes a shared mission and the need for major transformations. It can channel energies to bring about both change and creative endeavors.

Establishing a "culture of dissent" can be another effective means of questioning the status quo and serving as a spur toward creativity. Here norms are established whereby dissenters can openly question a superior's perspective without fear of retaliation or retribution. Consider the perspective of Steven Balmer, Microsoft's CEO.

> Bill [Gates] brings to the company the idea that conflict can be a good thing. ... Bill knows it's important to avoid that gentle civility that keeps you from getting to the heart of an issue quickly. He likes it when anyone, even a junior employee, challenges him, and you know he respects you when he starts shouting back.[53]

Motorola has gone a step further and institutionalized its culture of dissent.[54] By filing a "minority report," an employee can go above his or her immediate supervisor's head and officially lodge a different point of view on a business decision. According to former CEO George Fisher, "I'd call it a healthy spirit of discontent and a freedom by and large to express your discontent around here or to disagree with whoever it is in the company, me or anybody else."

Closely related to the culture of dissent is the fostering of a culture that encourages risk taking. "If you're not making mistakes, you're not taking risks, and that means you're not going anywhere," claimed John Holt, coauthor of *Celebrate Your Mistakes*.[55] "The key is to make errors faster than the competition, so you have more chances to learn and win."

Companies that cultivate cultures of experimentation and curiosity make sure that *failure* is not, in essence, an obscene word. They encourage mistakes as a key part of their competitive advantage. This philosophy was shared by Stan Shih, CEO of Acer, a Taiwan-based computer company. If a manager at Acer took an intelligent risk and made a

ethics a system of right and wrong that assists individuals in deciding when an act is moral or immoral and/or socially desirable or not.

Exhibit 11.6   **Best Practices: Learning from Failures**

It's innovation's great paradox: Success—that is, true breakthroughs—usually comes through failure. Here are some ideas on how to help your team get comfortable with taking risks and learning from mistakes:

- **Formalize Forums for Failure**
  To keep failures and the valuable lessons they offer from getting swept under the rug, *carve out time for reflection.* GE recently began sharing lessons from failures by bringing together managers whose "Imagination Breakthrough" efforts are put on the shelf.

- **Move the Goalposts**
  Innovation requires flexibility in meeting goals, since early predictions are often little more than educated guesses. Intuit's Scott Cook even suggests that teams developing new products ignore forecasts in the early days. "For every one of our failures, we had spreadsheets that looked awesome," he says.

- **Share Personal Stories**
  If employees hear leaders discussing their own failures, *they'll feel more comfortable talking about their own.* But it's not just the CEO's job. Front-line leaders are even more important, says Harvard Business School professor Amy Edmondson. "That person needs to be inviting, curious, and the first to say: 'I made a mistake'."

- **Bring in Outsiders**
  Outsiders can *help neutralize the emotions and biases that prop up a flop.* Customers can be the most valuable. After its DNA chip failed, Corning brought pharmaceutical companies in early to test its new drug-discovery technology, Epic.

- **Prove Yourself Wrong, Not Right**
  Development teams tend to look for supporting, rather than countervailing, evidence. "You have to reframe what you're seeking in the early days," says Innosight's Scott Anthony. *"You're not really seeking proof that you have the right answer.* It's more about testing to prove yourself wrong."

- **Celebrate Smart Failures**
  Managers should design performance-management systems that reward risk taking and foster a long-term view. But they should also *celebrate failures that teach something new,* energizing people to try again and offering them closure.

Source: McGregor, J. 2006. How Failure Breeds Success. *BusinessWeek.* July 10: 42–52.

---

mistake—even a costly one—Shih wrote off the loss as tuition payment for the manager's education. Such a culture must permeate the entire organization. As a high-tech executive told us during an interview: "Every person has a freedom to fail."

Exhibit 11.6 has insights on how organizations can both embrace risk and learn from failure.

> **>LO5**
> The leader's role in establishing an ethical organization.

Creating an Ethical Organization

Ethics may be defined as a system of right and wrong.[56] Ethics assists individuals in deciding when an act is moral or immoral, socially desirable or not. The sources for an individual's ethics include religious beliefs, national and ethnic heritage, family practices, community standards, educational experiences, and friends and neighbors. Business ethics is the application of ethical standards to commercial enterprise.

Individual Ethics versus Organizational Ethics

Many leaders think of ethics as a question of personal scruples, a confidential matter between employees and their consciences. Such leaders are quick to describe any wrongdoing as an isolated incident, the work of a rogue employee. They assume the company

> **organizational ethics** the values, attitudes, and behavioral patterns that define an organization's operating culture and that determine what an organization holds as acceptable behavior.

should not bear any responsibility for individual misdeeds. In their view, ethics has nothing to do with leadership.

Ethics has everything to do with leadership. Seldom does the character flaw of a lone actor completely explain corporate misconduct. Instead, unethical business practices typically involve the tacit, if not explicit, cooperation of others and reflect the values, attitudes, and behavior patterns that define an organization's operating culture. Ethics is as much an organizational as a personal issue. Leaders who fail to provide proper leadership to institute proper systems and controls that facilitate ethical conduct share responsibility with those who conceive, execute, and knowingly benefit from corporate misdeeds.[57]

ethical orientation
the practices that firms use to promote an ethical business culture, including ethical role models, corporate credos and codes of conduct, ethically-based reward and evaluation systems, and consistently enforced ethical policies and procedures.

The **ethical orientation** of a leader is a key factor in promoting ethical behavior. Ethical leaders must take personal, ethical responsibility for their actions and decision making. Leaders who exhibit high ethical standards become role models for others and raise an organization's overall level of ethical behavior. Ethical behavior must start with the leader before the employees can be expected to perform accordingly.

There has been a growing interest in corporate ethical performance. Some reasons for this trend may be the increasing lack of confidence regarding corporate activities, the growing emphasis on quality of life issues, and a spate of recent corporate scandals. Without a strong ethical culture, the chance of ethical crises occurring is enhanced. Ethical crises can be very expensive—both in terms of financial costs and in the erosion of human capital and overall firm reputation. Merely adhering to the minimum regulatory standards may not be enough to remain competitive in a world that is becoming more socially conscious. Strategy Spotlight 11.9 highlights potential ethical problems at utility companies that are trying to capitalize on consumers' desire to participate in efforts to curb global warming.

The past several years have been characterized by numerous examples of unethical and illegal behavior by many top-level corporate executives. These include executives of firms such as Enron, Tyco, WorldCom, Inc., Adelphia, and Healthsouth Corp., who were all forced to resign and are facing (or have been convicted of) criminal charges. Perhaps the most glaring example is Bernie Madoff, whose Ponzi scheme, which unraveled in 2008, defrauded investors of $50 billion in assets they had set aside for retirement and charitable donations.

The ethical organization is characterized by a conception of ethical values and integrity as a driving force of the enterprise.[58] Ethical values shape the search for opportunities, the design of organizational systems, and the decision-making process used by individuals and groups. They provide a common frame of reference that serves as a unifying force across different functions, lines of business, and employee groups. Organizational ethics helps to define what a company is and what it stands for.

There are many potential benefits of an ethical organization, but they are often indirect. Research has found somewhat inconsistent results concerning the overall relationship between ethical performance and measures of financial performance.[59] However, positive relationships have generally been found between ethical performance and strong organizational culture, increased employee efforts, lower turnover, higher organizational commitment, and enhanced social responsibility.

The advantages of a strong ethical orientation can have a positive effect on employee commitment and motivation to excel. This is particularly important in today's knowledge-intensive organizations, where human capital is critical in creating value and competitive advantages. Positive, constructive relationships among individuals (i.e., social capital) are vital in leveraging human capital and other resources in an organization. Drawing on the concept of stakeholder management, an ethically sound organization can also strengthen its bonds among its suppliers, customers, and governmental agencies.

strategy spotlight

11.9

Green Energy: Real or Just a Marketing Ploy?

Many consumers want to "go green" and are looking for opportunities to do so. Utility companies that provide heat and electricity are one of the most obvious places to turn, because they often use fossil fuels that could be saved through energy conservation or replaced by using alternative energy sources. In fact, some consumers are willing to pay a premium to contribute to environmental sustainability efforts if paying a little more will help curb global warming. Knowing this, many power companies in the United States have developed alternative energy programs and appealed to customers to help pay for them.

Unfortunately, many of the power companies that are offering eco-friendly options are falling short on delivering on them. Some utilities have simply gotten off to a slow start or found it difficult to profitably offer alternative power. Others, however, are suspected of committing a new type of fraud—"greenwashing." This refers to companies that make unsubstantiated claims about how environmentally friendly their products or services really are. In the case of many power companies, their claims of "green power" are empty promises. Instead of actually generating additional renewable energy, most of the premiums are going for marketing costs. "They are preying on people's goodwill," says Stephen Smith, executive director of the Southern Alliance for Clean Energy, an advocacy group in Knoxville, Tennessee.

Exhibit 11.7 shows what three power companies offered and how the money was actually spent. Unfortunately, utilities that spend only a fraction of voluntary energy premiums on renewable energy are becoming more rather than less common. It will likely be up to consumers or Public Service Commissions to hold the utilities to a higher ethical standard—either by making power companies' advertising more truthful or, better still, by insisting that they deliver on their renewable energy promises. Either way, the idea of defrauding customers who are trying to "do the right thing" makes the utilities' unethical decision even more dishonorable.

Sources: Elgin, B. & Holden, D. 2008. Green Power: Buyers Beware. *BusinessWeek,* September 29: 68–70; and www.cleanenergy.org.

 **environmental sustainability**

Exhibit 11.7 How "Green" Utilities Actually Used Customer Payments

Company/Program	What Customers Were Told	What Really Happened
Duke Energy of Indiana GoGreen Power	Pay a green energy premium and a specified amount of electricity will be obtained from renewable sources.	Less than 18 percent of voluntary customer contributions in a recent year went to renewable energy development.
Alliant Energy of Iowa Second Nature ™	"Support the growth of earth-friendly 'green power' created by wind and biomass."	More than 56 percent of expenditures went to marketing and administrative costs, not green energy development.
Georgia Power Green Energy®	Paying the premium "is equivalent to planting 125 trees or not driving 2,000 miles" and will "help bring more renewable power to Georgia."	Customers pay an annual $54 premium, but green energy is actually cheaper to provide than electricity from conventional sources.

Sources: Elgin, B. & Holden, D. 2008. Green Power: Buyers Beware. *BusinessWeek,* September 29: 68–70; www.alliantenergy.com; www.duke-energy.com; and www.georgiapower.com.

>LO6

The difference between integrity-based and compliance-based approaches to organizational ethics.

Integrity-Based versus Compliance-Based Approaches to Organizational Ethics

Before discussing the key elements of an ethical organization, one must understand the links between organizational integrity and the personal integrity of an organization's members.[60] There cannot be high-integrity organizations without high-integrity individuals. However, individual integrity is rarely self-sustaining. Even good people can lose their bearings when faced with pressures, temptations, and heightened performance expectations in the absence of organizational support systems and ethical boundaries. Organizational integrity rests on a concept of purpose, responsibility, and ideals for an organization as a whole. An important responsibility of leadership is to create this ethical framework and develop the organizational capabilities to make it operational.[61]

Lynn Paine, an ethics scholar at Harvard, identifies two approaches: the compliance-based approach and the integrity-based approach. (See Exhibit 11.8 for a comparison of compliance-based and integrity-based strategies.) Faced with the prospect of litigation, several organizations reactively implement **compliance-based ethics programs.** Such programs are typically designed by a corporate counsel with the goal of preventing, detecting, and punishing legal violations. But being ethical is much more than being legal, and an integrity-based approach addresses the issue of ethics in a more comprehensive manner.

Integrity-based ethics programs combine a concern for law with an emphasis on managerial responsibility for ethical behavior. It is broader, deeper, and more demanding than a legal compliance initiative. It is broader in that it seeks to enable responsible conduct. It is deeper in that it cuts to the ethos and operating systems of an organization and its members, their core guiding values, thoughts, and actions. It is more demanding because it requires an active effort to define the responsibilities that constitute an organization's ethical compass. Most importantly, organizational ethics is seen as the responsibility of management.

A corporate counsel may play a role in designing and implementing integrity strategies, but it is managers at all levels and across all functions that are involved in the process. Once integrated into the day-to-day operations, such strategies can prevent damaging ethical lapses, while tapping into powerful human impulses for moral thought and action.

compliance-based ethics programs programs for building ethical organizations that have the goal of preventing, detecting, and punishing legal violations.

integrity-based ethics programs programs for building ethical organizations that combine a concern for law with an emphasis on managerial responsibility for ethical behavior, including (1) enabling ethical conduct; (2) examining the organization's and members' core guiding values, thoughts, and actions; and (3) defining the responsibilities and aspirations that constitute an organization's ethical compass.

Exhibit 11.8 Approaches to Ethics Management

Characteristics	Compliance-Based Approach	Integrity-Based Approach
Ethos	Conformity with externally imposed standards	Self-governance according to chosen standards
Objective	Prevent criminal misconduct	Enable responsible conduct
Leadership	Lawyer-driven	Management-driven with aid of lawyers, HR, and others
Methods	Education, reduced discretion, auditing and controls, penalties	Education, leadership, accountability, organizational systems and decision processes, auditing and controls, penalties
Behavioral Assumptions	Autonomous beings guided by material self-interest	Social beings guided by material self-interest, values, ideals, peers

Source: Reprinted by permission of *Harvard Business Review.* Exhibit from "Managing Organizational Integrity," by L. S. Paine. Copyright © 1994 by the Harvard Business School Publishing Corporation; all rights reserved.

Ethics becomes the governing ethos of an organization and not burdensome constraints. Here is an example of an organization that goes beyond mere compliance to laws in building an ethical organization:

> In teaching ethics to its employees, Texas Instruments, the $14 billion chip and electronics manufacturer, asks them to run an issue through the following steps: Is it legal? Is it consistent with the company's stated values? Will the employee feel bad doing it? What will the public think if the action is reported in the press? Does the employee think it is wrong? If the employees are not sure of the ethicality of the issue, they are encouraged to ask someone until they are clear about it. In the process, employees can approach high-level personnel and even the company's lawyers. At TI, the question of ethics goes much beyond merely being legal. It is no surprise, that this company is a benchmark for corporate ethics and has been a recipient of three ethics awards: the David C. Lincoln Award for Ethics and Excellence in Business, American Business Ethics Award, and Bentley College Center for Business Ethics Award.[62]

Compliance-based approaches are externally motivated—that is, based on the fear of punishment for doing something unlawful. On the other hand, integrity-based approaches are driven by a personal and organizational commitment to ethical behavior.

A firm must have several key elements to become a highly ethical organization:

>LO7
Several key elements that organizations must have to become an ethical organization.

- Role models.
- Corporate credos and codes of conduct.
- Reward and evaluation systems.
- Policies and procedures.

These elements are highly interrelated. Reward structures and policies will be useless if leaders are not sound role models. That is, leaders who implicitly say, "Do as I say, not as I do," will quickly have their credibility eroded and such actions will sabotage other elements that are essential to building an ethical organization.

Role Models

For good or for bad, leaders are role models in their organizations. Leaders must "walk the talk"; they must be consistent in their words and deeds. The values as well as the character of leaders become transparent to an organization's employees through their behaviors. When leaders do not believe in the ethical standards that they are trying to inspire, they will not be effective as good role models. Being an effective leader often includes taking responsibility for ethical lapses within the organization—even though the executives themselves are not directly involved. Consider the perspective of Dennis Bakke, CEO of AES, the $13 billion global electricity company based in Arlington, Virginia.

> There was a major breach (in 1992) of the AES values. Nine members of the water treatment team in Oklahoma lied to the EPA about water quality at the plant. There was no environmental damage, but they lied about the test results. A new, young chemist at the plant discovered it, told a team leader, and we then were notified. Now, you could argue that the people who lied were responsible and were accountable, but the senior management team also took responsibility by taking pay cuts. My reduction was about 30 percent.[63]

Such action enhances the loyalty and commitment of employees throughout the organization. Many would believe that it would have been much easier (and personally less expensive!) for Bakke and his management team to merely take strong punitive action against the nine individuals who were acting contrary to the behavior expected in AES's ethical culture. However, by taking responsibility for the misdeeds, the top executives—through their highly

Elements of a Corporate Code

Corporate codes are not simply useful for conveying organizational norms and policies, but they also serve to legitimize an organization in the eyes of others. In the United States, federal guidelines advise judges, when determining how to sentence a company convicted of a crime, to consider whether it had a written code and was out of compliance with its own ethical guidelines. The United Nations and countries around the world have endorsed codes as a way to promote corporate social responsibility. As such, a code provides an increasingly important corporate social contract that signals a company's willingness to act ethically.

For employees, codes of conduct serve four key purposes:

Sources: Paine, L., Deshpande, R., Margolis, J. D., & Bettcher, K. E. 2005. Up to code: Does Your Company's Conduct Meet World Class Standards? *Harvard Business Review*, 82(12): 122–126; and Stone, A. 2004. Putting Teeth in Corporate Ethics Codes. www.businessweek.com, February 19.

1. Help employees from diverse backgrounds work more effectively across cultural backgrounds.
2. Provide a reference point for decision making.
3. Help attract individuals who want to work for a business that embraces high standards.
4. Help a company to manage risk by reducing the likelihood of damaging misconduct.

With recent scandals on Wall Street, many corporations are trying to put more teeth into their codes of conduct. Nasdaq now requires that listed companies distribute a code to all employees. German software giant SAP's code informs employees that violations of the code "can result in consequences that affect employment, and could possibly lead to external investigation, civil law proceedings, or criminal charges." Clearly, codes of conduct are an important part of maintaining an ethical organization.

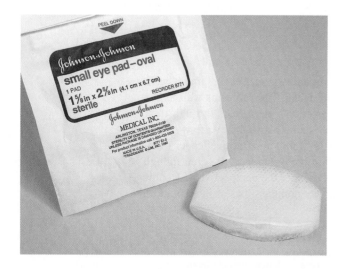

Johnson & Johnson is well known for its credo, which stresses honesty, integrity, superior products, and putting people before profits. Above is one of its many products.

visible action—made it clear that responsibility and penalties for ethical lapses go well beyond the "guilty" parties. Such courageous behavior by leaders helps to strengthen an organization's ethical environment.

Corporate Credos and Codes of Conduct

Corporate credos and codes of conduct are mechanisms that provide statements of norms and beliefs as well as guidelines for decision making. They provide employees with a clear understanding of the organization's policies and ethical position. Such guidelines also provide the basis for employees to refuse to commit unethical acts and help to make them aware of issues before they are faced with the situation. For such codes to be truly effective, organization members must be aware of them and what behavioral guidelines they contain.[64] Strategy Spotlight 11.10 identifies four key reasons why codes of conduct support organizational efforts to maintain a safe and ethical workplace.

Large corporations are not the only ones to develop and use codes of conduct. Consider the example of Wetherill Associates (WAI), a small, privately held supplier of electrical parts to the automotive market.

We believe our first responsibility is to the doctors, nurses and patients, to mothers and fathers and all others who use our products and services. In meeting their needs everything we do must be of high quality. We must constantly strive to reduce our costs in order to maintain reasonable prices. Customers' orders must be serviced promptly and accurately. Our suppliers and distributors must have an opportunity to make a fair profit.

We are responsible to our employees, the men and women who work with us throughout the world. Everyone must be considered as an individual. We must respect their dignity and recognize their merit. They must have a sense of security in their jobs. Compensation must be fair and adequate, and working conditions clean, orderly, and safe. We must be mindful of ways to help our employees fulfill their family responsibilities. Employees must feel free to make suggestions and complaints. There must be equal opportunity for employment, development, and advancement for those qualified. We must provide competent management, and their actions must be just and ethical.

We are responsible to the communities in which we live and work and to the world community as well. We must be good citizens—support good works and charities and bear our fair share of taxes. We must encourage civic improvements and better health and education. We must maintain in good order the property we are privileged to use, protecting the environment and natural resources

Our final responsibility is to our stockholders. Business must make a sound profit. We must experiment with new ideas. Research must be carried on, innovative programs developed, and mistakes paid for. New equipment must be purchased, new facilities provided, and new products launched. Reserves must be created to provide for adverse times. When we operate according to these principles, the stockholders should realize a fair return.

Source: Reprinted with permission of Johnson & Johnson Co.

Rather than a conventional code of conduct, WAI has a Quality Assurance Manual—a combination of philosophy text, conduct guide, technical manual, and company profile—that describes the company's commitment to honesty, ethical action, and integrity. WAI doesn't have a corporate ethics officer, because the company's corporate ethics officer is Marie Bothe, WAI's CEO. She sees her main function as keeping the 350-employee company on the path of ethical behavior and looking for opportunities to help the community. She delegates the "technical" aspects of the business—marketing, finance, personnel, and operations—to other members of the organization.[65]

Perhaps the best-known credo is that of Johnson & Johnson (J&J). It is reprinted in Exhibit 11.9. The credo stresses honesty, integrity, superior products, and putting people before profits. What distinguishes the J&J credo from others is the amount of energy the company's top managers devote to ensuring that employees live by its precepts:

Over a recent three-year period, Johnson & Johnson undertook a massive effort to assure that its original credo, already decades old, was still valid. More than 1,200 managers attended two-day seminars in groups of 25, with explicit instructions to challenge the credo. The president or CEO of the firm presided over each session. The company came out of the process believing that its original document was still valid. However, the questioning process continues. Such "challenge meetings" are still replicated every other year for all new managers. These efforts force J&J to question, internalize, and then implement its credo. Such investments have paid off handsomely many times—most notably in 1982, when eight people died from swallowing capsules of Tylenol, one of its flagship products, that someone had laced with cyanide. Leaders such as James Burke, who without hesitation made an across-the-board recall of the product even though it affected only a limited number of untraceable units, send a strong message throughout the firm.

Reward and Evaluation Systems

It is entirely possible for a highly ethical leader to preside over an organization that commits several unethical acts. How? A flaw in the organization's reward structure may inadvertently cause individuals to act in an inappropriate manner if rewards are seen as being distributed on the basis of outcomes rather than the means by which goals and objectives are achieved.[66]

Consider the example of Sears, Roebuck & Co.'s automotive operations. Here, unethical behavior, rooted in a faulty reward system, took place primarily at the operations level: its automobile repair facilities.[67]

> In 1992 Sears was flooded with complaints about its automotive service business. Consumers and attorneys general in more than 40 states accused the firm of misleading customers and selling them unnecessary parts and services, from brake jobs to front-end alignments.
>
> In the face of declining revenues and eroding market share, Sears's management had attempted to spur the performance of its auto centers by introducing new goals and incentives for mechanics. Automotive service advisers were given product-specific quotas for a variety of parts and repairs. Failure to meet the quotas could lead to transfers and reduced hours. Many employees spoke of "pressure, pressure, pressure" to bring in sales.
>
> Not too surprisingly, the judgment of many employees suffered. In essence, employees were left to chart their own course, given the lack of management guidance and customer ignorance. The bottom line: In settling the spate of lawsuits, Sears offered coupons to customers who had purchased certain auto services over the most recent two-year period. The total cost of the settlement, including potential customer refunds, was estimated to be $60 million. The cost in terms of damaged reputation? Difficult to assess, but certainly not trivial.

This example makes two points. First, inappropriate reward systems may cause individuals at all levels throughout an organization to commit unethical acts that they might not otherwise commit. Second, the penalties in terms of damage to reputations, human capital erosion, and financial loss—in the short run and long run—are typically much higher than any gains that could be obtained through such unethical behavior.

Many companies have developed reward and evaluation systems that evaluate whether a manager is acting in an ethical manner. For example, Raytheon, a $20 billion defense contractor, incorporates the following items in its "Leadership Assessment Instrument":[68]

- Maintains unequivocal commitment to honesty, truth, and ethics in every facet of behavior.
- Conforms with the letter and intent of company policies while working to affect any necessary policy changes.
- Actions are consistent with words; follows through on commitments; readily admits mistakes.
- Is trusted and inspires others to be trusted.

As noted by Dan Burnham, Raytheon's former CEO: "What do we look for in a leadership candidate with respect to integrity? What we're really looking for are people who have developed an inner gyroscope of ethical principles. We look for people for whom ethical thinking is part of what they do—no different from 'strategic thinking' or 'tactical thinking.'"

No More Whistleblowing Woes!

The landmark Sarbanes-Oxley Act of 2002 gives those who expose corporate misconduct strong legal protection. Henceforth, an executive who retaliates against the corporate whistleblower can be held criminally liable and imprisoned for up to 10 years. That's the same sentence a mafia don gets for threatening a witness. The Labor Department can order a company to rehire an employee without going to court. If the fired workers feel their case is moving too slowly, they can request a federal jury after six months.

Companies need to revisit their current policies, including nondisclosure pacts. They may no longer be able to enforce rules requiring employees to get permission to speak to the media or lawyers. Even layoffs should be planned in advance, lest they seem retaliatory.

Sources: www.sarbanes-oxley.com/pcaob.php/level=2&pub_id=Sarbanes-Oxley&chap_id=PCAOB11; Dwyer, P., Carney, D., Borrus, A., Woellert, L., & Palmeri, C. 2002. Year of the Whistle Blower. *BusinessWeek*, December 16: 107–109; and www.buchalter.com/FSL5CS/articles/articles204.asp.

Employees of publicly traded companies are now the most protected whistleblowers. Provisions coauthored by Senator Grassley in the Sarbanes-Oxley corporate-reform law:

- Make it unlawful to "discharge, demote, suspend or threaten, harass, or in any manner discriminate against" a whistleblower.
- Establish criminal penalties of up to 10 years in jail for executives who retaliate against whistleblowers.
- Require board audit committees to establish procedures for hearing whistleblower complaints.
- Allow the secretary of labor to order a company to rehire a terminated whistleblower with no court hearings whatsoever.
- Give a whistleblower a right to jury trial, bypassing months or years of cumbersome administrative hearings.

Policies and Procedures

Many situations that a firm faces have regular, identifiable patterns. Leaders tend to handle such routine by establishing a policy or procedure to be followed that can be applied uniformly to each occurrence. Such guidelines can be useful in specifying the proper relationships with a firm's customers and suppliers. For example, Levi Strauss has developed stringent global sourcing guidelines and Chemical Bank (part of J. P. Morgan Chase Bank) has a policy of forbidding any review that would determine if suppliers are Chemical customers when the bank awards contracts.

Carefully developed policies and procedures guide behavior so that all employees will be encouraged to behave in an ethical manner. However, they must be reinforced with effective communication, enforcement, and monitoring, as well as sound corporate governance practices. Strategy Spotlight 11.11 describes how the recently enacted Sarbanes-Oxley Act provides considerable legal protection to employees of publicly traded companies who report unethical or illegal practices.

We close our chapter on strategic leadership with a brief discussion of the Goolsby Leadership Model. It is addressed in Strategy Spotlight 11.12 and includes three dimensions: integrity, courage, and impact. The Goolsby Model synthesizes many of the ideas that we have addressed in this chapter and has important implications for career success.

The Goolsby Leadership Model: Integrity, Courage, and Impact

For many years there has been a focus in leadership research on inspirational styles that emphasize such traits as vision, charisma, and transformation. Some have criticized such approaches and have suggested that they may lead to unethical behavior. Why? They are taught to appeal to emotion rather than reason, lack checks and balances, and exploit followers to their detriment and to the benefit of the leader(s). Thus, some writers have begun to distinguish between authentic and inauthentic leaders. The Goolsby Leadership Model grows from the transformational leadership tradition and is anchored in the concept of authentic leadership.

Clearly, most would agree that a healthy leader is at the heart of a healthy organization. Consider the alternative: The unhealthy leader has drawn attention to the damaging and debilitating effects—on both individuals and organizations—that result from such behaviors as excessive narcissism and toxic micromanagement. Also, recall the unethical and illegal activities in which some leaders participate that we addressed earlier in this chapter and in our discussion on corporate governance in Chapter 9. The Goolsby Leadership Model, in contrast, sets forth a healthy, positive model based on three core concepts: integrity, courage, and impact. This model is shown in Exhibit 11.10.

Integrity

Integrity, a concept at the heart of good business practice, can be defined as consistency between word and deed as well as sound moral character. The four core questions of the Rotary Four-Way Test aim to test personal integrity.

1. Is it the truth?
2. Is it fair to all concerned?
3. Will it build goodwill and better friendships?
4. Will it be beneficial to all concerned?

In building on these questions, two key attributes of integrity in the healthy leader emerge: authenticity and emotional competence. These two attributes, in part, draw on the concept of emotional intelligence (EI) that we addressed earlier in the chapter. Authenticity includes self-awareness, transparency, positive psychological states, and personal integrity. An authentic leader possesses good self-awareness, is transparent to others while being consistent, engenders positive psychological states within himself and his followers, and is widely known for having personal integrity. The opposite of authenticity is duplicity, which is a type of Jekyll-and-Hyde personality.

The second dimension of integrity is emotional competence, which involves the integration of thought and emotion and is defined by its four dimensions: awareness of self, management of self, awareness of others, and management of others. Emotionally competent *(continued)*

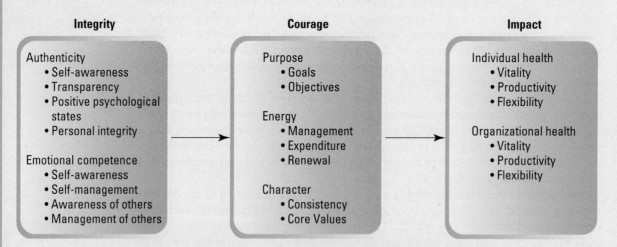

Exhibit 11.10 The Goolsby Leadership Model

Source: Quick, J. C., Macik-Frey, M., & Cooper, C. L. 2007. *Journal of Management Studies,* 44(2):195. Reprinted with permission of Wiley-Blackwell Publishing Ltd.

(continued) leaders are aware of their own feelings and emotions and aware of the feelings and emotions in other people. In addition, the emotionally competent leader is able to act in ways that appropriately manage his own emotions while accommodating the emotions of others. Emotional competence helps the healthy leader to be hopeful, positive, and compassionate in his actions and behaviors.

Courage

Courage is defined as the capacity to act, even in the presence of adversity, fear, and danger. Courage involves purpose, energy, and character. Purpose is the heart of great leadership and the heart of character. After conducting in-depth interviews with 28 senior executives, researchers recently found a wide variety of attributes and characteristics of great leaders. However, there was no variance along the dimension of purpose.

Energy and energy management are essential for healthy productivity and achievement. Consider, for example, the personal leadership track at PepsiCo's corporate leadership program in Purchase, New York. Here, consultants found that energy expenditure through full engagement is what leads to productive achievement and

Source: This Strategy Spotlight draws upon Quick, J. C., Macik-Frey, M., & Cooper, C. L. 2007. Managerial Dimensions of Organizational Health: The Healthy Leader at Work. *Journal of Management Studies*, 44(2): 189–295.

meaningful work accomplishment. PepsiCo has enjoyed an impressive 12 percent annual growth in market valuation in a recent period, twice the growth of its long-time rival Coca-Cola. Interestingly, to be most effective, the power of full engagement must be balanced with strategic disengagement through which leaders are able to achieve renewal based on the process of energy recovery.

A third dimension of courage is character, and it can be defined as who you are when no one is looking. Character is important because it leads to consistency in actions and behaviors based on core values and principles. Character is a powerful force that enables leaders to act with courage in the midst of business crises or disasters.

Impact

Strategic leadership is neither a philosophical nor contemplative activity. Great leaders have a strong impact on their followers and on the businesses they lead. Consider, for example, the impacts of such well-known leaders as Andy Grove at Intel, Richard Branson at Virgin, Inc., and Lou Gerstner at IBM. The Goolsby Leadership Model suggests that integrity and courage affect individuals and organizational health by affecting their vitality, productivity, and flexibility. When individuals and organizations function in a healthy manner, they get results and make a positive impact for a wide range of organizational stakeholders.

Reflecting on Career Implications . . .

- *Strategic Leadership:* Do managers in your firm effectively set the direction; design the organization; and, instill a culture committed to excellence and ethical behavior? If you are in a position of leadership, do you practice all of these three elements effectively?
- *Power:* What sources of power do managers in your organization use? For example, if there is an overemphasis on organizational sources of power (e.g., position power); there could be negative implications for creativity, morale and turnover among professionals. How much power do you have? What is the basis of it? How might it be used to both advance your career goals and benefit the firm?
- *Emotional Intelligence:* Do leaders of your firm have sufficient levels of EI? Alternatively, are there excessive levels of EI present that have negative implications for your organization? Is your level of EI sufficient to allow you to have effective interpersonal and judgment skills in order to enhance your career success?
- *Learning Organization:* Does your firm effectively practice all five elements of the learning organization? If one or more elements are absent, adaptability and change will be compromised. What can you do to enhance any of the elements that might be lacking?
- *Ethics:* Does your organization practice a compliance-based or integrity-based ethical culture? Integrity-based cultures can enhance your personal growth. In addition, such cultures foster greater loyalty and commitment among all employees.

Summary

Strategic leadership is vital in ensuring that strategies are formulated and implemented in an effective manner. Leaders must play a central role in performing three critical and interdependent activities: setting the direction, designing the organization, and nurturing a culture committed to excellence and ethical behavior. If leaders ignore or are ineffective at performing any one of the three, the organization will not be very successful. We also identified three elements of leadership that contribute to success—integrative thinking, overcoming barriers to change, and the effective use of power.

For leaders to effectively fulfill their activities, emotional intelligence (EI) is very important. Five elements that contribute to EI are self-awareness, self-regulation, motivation, empathy, and social skill. The first three elements pertain to self-management skills, whereas the last two are associated with a person's ability to manage relationships with others. We also addressed some of the potential drawbacks from the ineffective use of EI. These include the dysfunctional use of power as well as a tendency to become overly empathetic, which may result in unreasonably lowered performance expectations.

Leaders must also play a central role in creating a learning organization. Gone are the days when the top-level managers "think" and everyone else in the organization "does." With the rapidly changing, unpredictable, and complex competitive environments that characterize most industries, leaders must engage everyone in the ideas and energies of people throughout the organization. Great ideas can come from anywhere in the organization—from the executive suite to the factory floor. The five elements that we discussed as central to a learning organization are inspiring and motivating people with a mission or purpose, empowering people at all levels throughout the organization, accumulating and sharing internal knowledge, gathering external information, and challenging the status quo to stimulate creativity.

In the final section of the chapter, we addressed a leader's central role in instilling ethical behavior in the organization. We discussed the enormous costs that firms face when ethical crises arise—costs in terms of financial and reputational loss as well as the erosion of human capital and relationships with suppliers, customers, society at large, and governmental agencies. And, as we would expect, the benefits of having a strong ethical organization are also numerous. We contrasted compliance-based and integrity-based approaches to organizational ethics. Compliance-based approaches are largely externally motivated; that is, they are motivated by the fear of punishment for doing something that is unlawful. Integrity-based approaches, on the other hand, are driven by a personal and organizational commitment to ethical behavior. We also addressed the four key elements of an ethical organization: role models, corporate credos and codes of conduct, reward and evaluation systems, and policies and procedures.

Summary Review Questions

1. Three key activities—setting a direction, designing the organization, and nurturing a culture and ethics—are all part of what effective leaders do on a regular basis. Explain how these three activities are interrelated.

2. Define emotional intelligence (EI). What are the key elements of EI? Why is EI so important to successful strategic leadership? Address potential "downsides."

3. The knowledge a firm possesses can be a source of competitive advantage. Describe ways that a firm can continuously learn to maintain its competitive position.

4. How can the five central elements of "learning organizations" be incorporated into global companies?

5. What are the benefits to firms and their shareholders of conducting business in an ethical manner?

6. Firms that fail to behave in an ethical manner can incur high costs. What are these costs and what is their source?

7. What are the most important differences between an "integrity organization" and a "compliance organization" in a firm's approach to organizational ethics?

8. What are some of the important mechanisms for promoting ethics in a firm?

Key Terms

leadership, 385
setting a direction 386
designing the
  organization 388
excellent and ethical
  organizational
  culture 388
integrative
  thinking 390
barriers to change, 391
systemic barriers, 392
behavioral barriers, 393
political barriers, 393
power, 393

organizational bases
  of power, 393
personal bases
  of power, 394
emotional
  intelligence (EI), 395
learning organizations, 401
ethics, 406
organizational ethics 407
ethical orientation 408
compliance-based ethics
  programs, 410
integrity-based ethics
  programs, 410

Experiential Exercise

Select two well-known business leaders—one you admire and one you do not. Evaluate each of them on the five characteristics of emotional intelligence.

Emotional Intelligence Characteristics	Admired Leader	Leader Not Admired
Self-awareness		
Self-regulation		
Motivation		
Empathy		
Social skills		

Application Questions Exercises

1. Identify two CEOs whose leadership you admire. What is it about their skills, attributes, and effective use of power that causes you to admire them?

2. Founders have an important role in developing their organization's culture and values. At times, their influence persists for many years. Identify and describe two organizations in which the cultures and values established by the founder(s) continue to flourish. You may find research on the Internet helpful in answering these questions.

3. Some leaders place a great emphasis on developing superior human capital. In what ways does this help a firm to develop and sustain competitive advantages?

4. In this chapter we discussed the five elements of a "learning organization." Select a firm with which you are familiar and discuss whether or not it epitomizes some (or all) of these elements.

Ethics Questions

1. Sometimes organizations must go outside the firm to hire talent, thus bypassing employees already working for the firm. Are there conditions under which this might raise ethical considerations?

2. Ethical crises can occur in virtually any organization. Describe some of the systems, procedures, and processes that can help to prevent such crises.

References

1. The Richard Fuld example is based on Auletta, K. 1987. *Greed and glory on Wall Street: The fall of the house of Lehman.* New York: Warner Books; Becker, B. & White, B. 2008. Lehman managers portrayed as irresponsible. wwwnytimes .com, October 6; Boyle, M. 2008. Bad management: Why managers make poor decisions. www. businessweek.com, November 14; Feiden, D. 2008. Disgraced Lehman Brothers CEO Richard Fuld calling it quits. www. nydailynews.com, November 5; Goldstein, M. 2008. Lehman's Fuld goes begging. www.businessweek .com, September 10; Plumb, C. & Wilchins, D. 2008. Lehman CEO Fuld's hubris contributed to melt-down. www.reuters.com, September 14; Shin, A. 2008. Capitol grilling for Lehman CEO. www. washingtonpost.com, October 7; Worst managers of 2009. *BusinessWeek,* January 19: 42; and, www.answers.com.

2. Charan, R. & Colvin, G. 1999. Why CEOs fail. *Fortune,* June 21: 68–78.

3. Yukl, G. 2008. How leaders influence organizational effectiveness. *Leadership Quarterly,* 19(6): 708–722.

4. These three activities and our discussion draw from Kotter, J. P. 1990. What leaders really do. *Harvard Business Review,* 68(3): 103–111; Pearson, A. E. 1990. Six basics for general managers. *Harvard Business Review,* 67(4): 94–101; and Covey, S. R. 1996. Three roles of the leader in the new paradigm. In *The leader of the future:* 149–160. Hesselbein, F., Goldsmith, M., & Beckhard, R. (Eds.). San Francisco: Jossey-Bass. Some of the discussion of each of the three leadership activity concepts draws on Dess, G. G. & Miller, A. 1993. *Strategic management:* 320–325. New York: McGraw-Hill.

5. García-Morales, V. J., Lloréns-Montes, F. J., & Verdú-Jover, A. J. 2008. The effects of transformational leadership on organizational performance through knowledge and innovation. *British Journal of Management,* 19(4): 299–319.

6. Day, C., Jr. & LaBarre, P. 1994. GE: Just your average everyday $60 billion family grocery store. *Industry Week,* May 2: 13–18.

7. The best (& worst) managers of the year. 2003. *BusinessWeek,* January 13: 63.

8. Collins, J. 1997. What comes next? *Inc. Magazine.* October: 34–45.

9. Kirkpatrick, D. 2006. Use humility as a weapon. *Fortune.* October 30: 118.

10. Anonymous. 2006. Looking out for number one. *BusinessWeek,* October 30: 66.

11. Evans, R. 2007. The either/or dilemma. www.ft.com, December 19; and Martin, R. L. 2007. *The opposable mind.* Boston: Harvard Business School Press.

12. For insightful perspectives on escalation, refer to Brockner, J. 1992. The escalation of commitment to a failing course of action. *Academy of Management Review,* 17(1): 39–61; and Staw, B. M. 1976. Knee-deep in the big muddy: A study of commitment to a chosen course of action. *Organizational Behavior and Human Decision Processes,* 16: 27–44. The discussion of systemic, behavioral, and political barriers draws on Lorange, P. & Murphy, D. 1984. Considerations in implementing strategic control. *Journal of Business Strategy,* 5: 27–35. In a similar vein, Noel M. Tichy has addressed three types of resistance to change in the context of General Electric: technical resistance, political resistance, and cultural resistance. See Tichy, N. M. 1993. Revolutionalize your company. *Fortune,* December 13: 114–118. Examples draw from O'Reilly, B. 1997. The secrets of America's most admired corporations: New ideas and new products. *Fortune,* March 3: 60–64.

13. This section draws on Champoux, J. E. 2000. *Organizational behavior: Essential tenets for a new millennium.* London: South-Western; and The mature use of power in organizations. 2003. *RHR International-Executive Insights,* May 29, 12.19.168.197/execinsights/8-3.htm.

14. An insightful perspective on the role of power and politics in organizations is provided in Ciampa, K. 2005. Almost ready: How leaders move up. *Harvard Business Review,* 83(1): 46–53.

15. A discussion of the importance of persuasion in bringing about change can be found in Garvin, D. A. & Roberto, M. A. 2005. Change through persuasion. *Harvard Business Review,* 83(4): 104–113.

16. Lorsch, J. W. & Tierney, T. J. 2002. *Aligning the stars: How to succeed when professionals drive results.* Boston: Harvard Business School Press.

17. Some consider EI to be a "trait," that is, an attribute that is stable over time. However, many authors, including Daniel Goleman, have argued that it can be developed through motivation, extended practice, and feedback. For example, in D. Goleman, 1998, What makes a leader? *Harvard Business Review,* 76(5): 97, Goleman addresses this issue in a sidebar: "Can emotional intelligence be learned?"

18. For a review of this literature, see Daft, R. 1999. *Leadership: Theory and practice.* Fort Worth, TX: Dryden Press.

19. This section draws on Luthans, F. 2002. Positive organizational behavior: Developing and managing psychological strengths. *Academy of Management Executive,* 16(1): 57–72; and Goleman, D. 1998. What makes a leader? *Harvard Business Review,* 76(6): 92–105.

20. EI has its roots in the concept of "social intelligence" that was first identified by E. L. Thorndike in 1920 (Intelligence and its uses. *Harper's Magazine,* 140: 227–235). Psychologists have been uncovering other intelligences for some time now and have grouped them into such clusters as abstract intelligence (the ability to understand and manipulate verbal and mathematical symbols), concrete

intelligence (the ability to understand and manipulate objects), and social intelligence (the ability to understand and relate to people). See Ruisel, I. 1992. Social intelligence: Conception and methodological problems. *Studia Psychologica,* 34(4–5): 281–296. Refer to trochim.human.cornell.edu/gallery.

21. See, for example, Luthans, op. cit.; Mayer, J. D., Salvoney, P., & Caruso, D. 2000. Models of emotional intelligence. In Sternberg, R. J. (Ed.). *Handbook of intelligence.* Cambridge, UK: Cambridge University Press; and Cameron, K. 1999. Developing emotional intelligence at the Weatherhead School of Management. *Strategy: The Magazine of the Weatherhead School of Management,* Winter: 2–3.

22. Tate, B. 2008. A longitudinal study of the relationships among self-monitoring, authentic leadership, and perceptions of leadership. *Journal of Leadership & Organizational Studies,* 15(1): 16–29.

23. Moss, S. A., Dowling, N., & Callanan, J. 2009. Towards an integrated model of leadership and self-regulation. *Leadership Quarterly,* 20(2): 162–176.

24. An insightful perspective on leadership, which involves discovering, developing and celebrating what is unique about each individual, is found in Buckingham, M. 2005. What great managers do. *Harvard Business Review,* 83(3): 70–79.

25. This section draws upon Klemp. G. 2005. *Emotional intelligence and leadership: What really matters.* Cambria Consulting, Inc., www.cambriaconsulting.com.

26. Heifetz, R. 2004. Question authority. *Harvard Business Review,* 82(1): 37.

27. Handy, C. 1995. Trust and the virtual organization. *Harvard Business Review,* 73(3): 40–50.

28. This section draws upon Dess, G. G. & Picken, J. C. 1999. *Beyond productivity.* New York: AMACOM. The elements of the learning organization in this section are consistent with the work of Dorothy Leonard-Barton. See, for example, Leonard-Barton, D. 1992. The factory as a learning laboratory. *Sloan Management Review,* 11: 23–38.

29. Senge, P. M. 1990. The leader's new work: Building learning organizations. *Sloan Management Review,* 32(1): 7–23.

30. Hammer, M. & Stanton, S. A. 1997. The power of reflection. *Fortune,* November 24: 291–296.

31. Hannah, S. T. & Lester, P. B. 2009. A multilevel approach to building and leading learning organizations. *Leadership Quarterly,* 20(1): 34–48.

32. For some guidance on how to effectively bring about change in organizations, refer to Wall, S. J. 2005. The protean organization: Learning to love change. *Organizational Dynamics,* 34(1): 37–46.

33. Covey, S. R. 1989. *The seven habits of highly effective people: Powerful lessons in personal change.* New York: Simon & Schuster.

34. Kouzes, J. M. & Posner, B. Z. 2009. To lead, create a shared vision. *Harvard Business Review,* 87(1): 20–21.

35. Kouzes and Posner, op. cit.

36. Melrose, K. 1995. *Making the grass greener on your side: A CEO's journey to leading by servicing.* San Francisco: Barrett-Koehler.

37. Tekleab, A. G., Sims Jr., H. P., Yun, S., Tesluk, P. E., & Cox, J. 2008. Are we on the same page? Effects of self-awareness of empowering and transformational

leadership. *Journal of Leadership & Organizational Studies,* 14(3): 185–201.

38. Quinn, R. C. & Spreitzer, G. M. 1997. The road to empowerment: Seven questions every leader should consider. *Organizational Dynamics,* 25: 37–49.

39. For an interesting perspective on top-down approaches to leadership, see Pellegrini, E. K. & Scandura, T. A. 2008. Paternalistic leadership: A review and agenda for future research. *Journal of Management,* 34(3): 566–593.

40. Helgesen, S. 1996. Leading from the grass roots. In *Leader of the future:* 19–24 Hesselbein et al.

41. Bowen, D. E. & Lawler, E. E., III. 1995. Empowering service employees. *Sloan Management Review,* 37: 73–84.

42. Easterby-Smith, M. & Prieto, I. M. 2008. Dynamic capabilities and knowledge management: An integrative role for learning? *British Journal of Management,* 19(3): 235–249.

43. Stack, J. 1992. *The great game of business.* New York: Doubleday/Currency.

44. Schafer, S. 1997. Battling a labor shortage? It's all in your imagination. *Inc.,* August: 24.

45. Meyer, P. 1998. So you want the president's job . . . *Business Horizons,* January–February: 2–8.

46. Imperato, G. 1998. Competitive intelligence: Get smart! *Fast Company,* May: 268–279.

47. Novicki, C. 1998. The best brains in business. *Fast Company,* April: 125.

48. The introductory discussion of benchmarking draws on Miller, A. 1998. *Strategic management:* 142–143. New York: McGraw-Hill.

49. Port, O. & Smith, G. 1992. Beg, borrow—and benchmark. *BusinessWeek,* November 30: 74–75.

50. Main, J. 1992. How to steal the best ideas around. *Fortune,* October 19: 102–106.

51. Taylor, J. T. 1997. What happens after what comes next? *Fast Company,* December–January: 84–85.

52. Sheff, D. 1996. Levi's changes everything. *Fast Company,* June–July: 65–74.

53. Isaacson, W. 1997. In search of the real Bill Gates. *Time,* January 13: 44–57.

54. Baatz, E. B. 1993. Motorola's secret weapon. *Electronic Business,* April: 51–53.

55. Holt, J. W. 1996. *Celebrate your mistakes.* New York: McGraw-Hill.

56. This opening discussion draws upon Conley, J. H. 2000. Ethics in business. In Helms, M. M. (Ed.). *Encyclopedia of management* (4th ed.): 281–285; Farmington Hills, MI: Gale Group; Paine, L. S. 1994. Managing for organizational integrity. *Harvard Business Review,* 72(2): 106–117; and Carlson, D. S. & Perrewe, P. L. 1995. Institutionalization of organizational ethics through transformational leadership. *Journal of Business Ethics,* 14: 829–838.

57. Pinto, J., Leana, C. R., & Pil, F. K. 2008. Corrupt organizations or organizations of corrupt individuals? Two types of organization-level corruption. *Academy of Management Review,* 33(3): 685–709.

58. Soule, E. 2002. Managerial moral strategies—in search of a few good principles. *Academy of Management Review,* 27(1): 114–124.

59. Carlson & Perrewe, op. cit.

60. This discussion is based upon Paine. Managing for organizational integrity; Paine, L. S. 1997. *Cases in leadership, ethics, and organizational integrity: A Strategic approach.* Burr Ridge, IL: Irwin; and Fontrodona, J. 2002. Business ethics across the Atlantic. Business Ethics Direct, www.ethicsa.org/BED_art_fontrodone.html.

61. For more on operationalizing capabilities to sustain an ethical framework, see Largay III, J. A. & Zhang, R. 2008. Do CEOs worry about being fired when making investment decisions. *Academy of Management Perspectives,* 22(1): 60–61.

62. See www.ti.com/corp/docs/company/citizen/ethics/benchmark.shtml; and www.ti.com/corp/docs/company/citizen/ethics/quicktest.shtml.

63. Wetlaufer, S. 1999. Organizing for empowerment: An interview with AES's Roger Sant and Dennis Bakke. *Harvard Business Review,* 77(1): 110–126.

64. For an insightful, academic perspective on the impact of ethics codes on executive decision making, refer to Stevens, J. M., Steensma, H. K., Harrison, D. A., & Cochran, P. S. 2005. Symbolic or substantive document? The influence of ethics code on financial executives' decisions. *Strategic Management Journal,* 26(2): 181–195.

65. Paine. Managing for organizational integrity.

66. For a recent study on the effects of goal setting on unethical behavior, read Schweitzer, M. E., Ordonez, L., & Douma, B. 2004. Goal setting as a motivator of unethical behavior. *Academy of Management Journal,* 47(3): 422–432.

67. Paine. Managing for organizational integrity.

68. Fulmer, R. M. 2004. The challenge of ethical leadership. *Organizational Dynamics,* 33 (3): 307–317.

CHAPTER 12

Managing Innovation and Fostering Corporate Entrepreneurship

After reading this chapter, you should have a good understanding of:

LO1 The importance of implementing strategies and practices that foster innovation.

LO2 The challenges and pitfalls of managing corporate innovation processes.

LO3 How corporations use new venture teams, business incubators, and product champions to create an internal environment and culture that promote entrepreneurial development.

LO4 How corporate entrepreneurship achieves both financial goals and strategic goals.

LO5 The benefits and potential drawbacks of real options analysis in making resource deployment decisions in corporate entrepreneurship contexts.

LO6 How an entrepreneurial orientation can enhance a firm's efforts to develop promising corporate venture initiatives.

To remain competitive, established firms must continually seek out opportunities for growth and new methods for strategically renewing their performance. Changes in customer needs, new technologies, and shifts in the competitive landscape require that companies continually innovate and initiate corporate ventures in order to compete effectively. This chapter addresses how entrepreneurial activities can be an avenue for achieving competitive advantages.

In the first section, we address the importance of innovation in identifying venture opportunities and strategic renewal. Innovations can take many forms, including radical breakthroughs, incremental improvements, and disruptive innovations. Innovations often create new markets, update products or services, and help renew organizational processes. We discuss how firms can successfully manage the innovation process. Impediments and challenges to effective innovation are discussed, and examples of good innovation practices are presented.

We discuss the unique role of corporate entrepreneurship in the strategic management process in the second section. Here we highlight two types of activities corporations use to remain competitive—focused and dispersed. New venture groups and business incubators are often used to focus a firm's entrepreneurial activities. In other corporations, the entrepreneurial spirit is dispersed throughout the organization and gives rise to product champions and other autonomous strategic behaviors that organizational members engage in to foster internal corporate venturing. We also discuss the benefits and potential drawbacks of real options analysis in making decisions about which venture activities merit additional investment and which should be abandoned.

In the final section we describe how a firm's entrepreneurial orientation can contribute to its growth and renewal as well as enhance the methods and processes strategic managers use to recognize opportunities and develop initiatives for internal growth and development. The chapter also evaluates the pitfalls that firms may encounter when implementing entrepreneurial strategies.

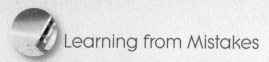 Learning from Mistakes

Companies often grow by commercializing new technologies. This is one of the most important paths to corporate entrepreneurship. But the most successful technologies are quickly imitated, and new entrants are often able to undermine the efforts of early leaders. Consider the case of Nortel Networks Corp., once a leading telecommunications industry innovator and darling of the Toronto Stock Exchange.[1]

Soon after Nortel Networks celebrated its 100-year anniversary in 1995, it became one of the leading players in the emerging digital technology revolution in the telecommunications industry. Nortel built much of the fiber optic equipment that is used today to carry data on the Internet. It pioneered the development of equipment and software that made wireless phone networks possible. It grew to be the largest employer in Ottawa, Canada, and at its peak in July 2000, Nortel's stock sold for $124.50 Canadian dollars on the Toronto Stock Exchange. When it filed for bankruptcy in January 2009, the stock closed at a market price of 12 Canadian cents.

What went wrong? What took this highly successful company from being Ottawa's "bastion of innovation" to the brink of failure? Clearly, the recent economic downturn and some bad luck contributed to its troubles. But stiff global competition, misguided innovation efforts, and a poorly managed portfolio of businesses conspired to weaken Nortel and eventually topple it. Even its tough CEO, Mike Zafirovski, brought in after leading turnaround successes at GE and Motorola, could not overcome the tidal wave of events that brought Nortel down.

An accounting scandal that led to criminal charges, though it did not occur on his watch, demanded a lot of Zafirovski's attention during his first year as CEO. It also required him to invest heavily in regaining shareholder confidence. "The stock became almost tainted merchandise," says Michel R. Sprung, president of Sprung & Co. Investment Counsel. "The investment community certainly had doubts about his ability and the board's to turn the company around."

Meanwhile, Nortel's portfolio of businesses had spread the company's efforts in a lot of directions. Some of the divisions had questionable prospects; others required that Nortel collaborate with strategic partners to be successful. Zafirovski took stock of these problems, but the speed and decisiveness with which he tried to solve them left some thinking he was not acting aggressively enough and possibly even taking the company in the wrong direction. As it grew, Nortel had extended its reach into many businesses—optical networks, wireless infrastructure, enterprise systems, and government. But it was not a leader in any of these arenas. A consensus was emerging that Nortel needed to exit some these businesses. Instead, "Nortel tried to hold on to all of its pieces," says Ronald Gruia, a telecom analyst for consulting firm Frost & Sullivan. Rather than create a manageable program of innovation and growth, Nortel seemed to be coasting.

To make matters worse, when Nortel finally did decide to exit a business, many believe it picked the wrong one. It jettisoned a promising next-generation 3G technology called UMTS because it only had a 5–6 percent market share and opted instead for a technology where it had a 22 percent share and an agreement with Verizon Wireless to keep using it. Other leading wireless providers, however, favored the more advanced UMTS, prompting analyst Gruia to declare, "Getting out of UMTS was a mistake." Zafirovski disagreed: "We looked at how do we redirect R&D spending." In hockey terms, he said Nortel "wanted to go where the puck [was being hit] rather than where the person is."

In the end, Nortel's entire enterprise became unsustainable. Although Chapter 11 bankruptcy will provide it time to reorganize, several analysts believe it is headed for liquidation. Ping Zhao, of investment research firm CreditSights gave Nortel little hope. "They were already out of favor due to their weak finances, but for any of the new projects, they are definitely out of the picture" because of the filing. "I don't think it's going to exist," commented Mark Sue, an analyst with RBC Capital Markets (a unit of the Royal Bank of Canada).

Nortel failed largely because it lost its ability to effectively manage its innovation activities. As large corporations use their early successes to expand into new areas, they often lose focus on the elements of the business that provide them with strategic advantages.

In attractive industries such as telecommunications, there are incentives for competitors to take market share through proactive and aggressive innovation efforts that often topple market leaders. When this happens, whole communities suffer. "Nortel is why Ottawa grew with new, disruptive products," says Brian Hurley, a former Nortel executive who left to found Liquid Computing. If "Nortel has to carve up its parts and sell them off, Ottawa will be a very different place. There won't be the same level of entrepreneurial activity."

In short, Nortel Networks stopped thinking and acting like an entrepreneurial firm. As a result, what had once been a leading innovator and top financial performer lost its focus and fizzled out.

Managing change is one of the most important functions performed by strategic leaders. There are two major avenues through which companies can expand or improve their business—innovation and corporate entrepreneurship. These two activities go hand-in-hand because they both have similar aims. The first is strategic renewal. Innovations help an organization stay fresh and reinvent itself as conditions in the business environment change. This is why managing innovation is such an important strategic implementation issue. The second is the pursuit of venture opportunities. Innovative breakthroughs, as well as new product concepts, evolving technologies, and shifting demand, create opportunities for corporate venturing. In this chapter we will explore these topics—how change and innovation can stimulate strategic renewal and foster corporate entrepreneurship.

>LO1
The importance of implementing strategies and practices that foster innovation.

Managing Innovation

One of the most important sources of growth opportunities is innovation. **Innovation** involves using new knowledge to transform organizational processes or create commercially viable products and services. The sources of new knowledge may include the latest technology, the results of experiments, creative insights, or competitive information. However it comes about, innovation occurs when new combinations of ideas and information bring about positive change.

The emphasis on newness is a key point. For example, for a patent application to have any chance of success, one of the most important attributes it must possess is novelty. You can't patent an idea that has been copied. This is a central idea. In fact, the root of the word *innovation* is the Latin *novus,* which means new. Innovation involves introducing or changing to something new.[2]

Among the most important sources of new ideas is new technology. Technology creates new possibilities. Technology provides the raw material that firms use to make innovative products and services. But technology is not the only source of innovations. There can be innovations in human resources, firm infrastructure, marketing, service, or in many other value-adding areas that have little to do with anything "high-tech." Strategy Spotlight 12.1 highlights a simple but effective innovation implemented by Target stores. As the Target example suggests, innovation can take many forms.

innovation the use of new knowledge to transform organizational processes or create commercially viable products and services.

Types of Innovation

Although innovations are not always high-tech, changes in technology can be an important source of change and growth. When an innovation is based on a sweeping new technology, it often has a more far-reaching impact. Sometimes even a small innovation can add

Target's Low-Tech, High-Value Design Innovation

Sometimes a simple change can make a vast improvement. That's what Target discovered when it adopted a new design for the traditional amber-colored prescription pill bottle. The new design literally flips the old bottle on its head. The base of the bottle is a large cap that uses color-coded rings to help family members distinguish between different containers. The upper part includes a flat surface that holds wider and easier-to-read labels. "They're much easier to use, and it's a lot easier to read," says Target customer Pat Howell.

Design student Deborah Adler came up with the new bottle after her grandmother Helen accidentally took her grandfather Herman's prescription. She noticed that the small lettering on the curved label of a traditional pill bottle was hard to read. Target, which commissioned a study that found that nearly 60 percent of prescription drugs are taken improperly, welcomed the design innovation. The new bottle, called the ClearRX, has won several design awards and improved Target's prescription drug sales by 14 percent—from $1.4 billion to $1.6 billion in a recent year.

Sources: Target Turns Old Pill Bottle Design on Its Head. 2005. MSNBC.com, www.msnbc.com, April 26; Finn, B. 2006. Target ClearRX Bottle. *Business 2.0*, April: 120; and www.target.com.

value and create competitive advantages. Innovation can and should occur throughout an organization—in every department and all aspects of the value chain.

One distinction that is often used when discussing innovation is between process innovation and product innovation.[3] *Product innovation* refers to efforts to create product designs and applications of technology to develop new products for end users. Recall from Chapter 5 how generic strategies were typically different depending on the stage of the industry life cycle. Product innovations tend to be more common during the earlier stages of an industry's life cycle. Product innovations are also commonly associated with a differentiation strategy. Firms that differentiate by providing customers with new products or services that offer unique features or quality enhancements often engage in product innovation.

Process innovation, by contrast, is typically associated with improving the efficiency of an organizational process, especially manufacturing systems and operations. By drawing on new technologies and an organization's accumulated experience (Chapter 5), firms can often improve materials utilization, shorten cycle time, and increase quality. Process innovations are more likely to occur in the later stages of an industry's life cycle as companies seek ways to remain viable in markets where demand has flattened out and competition is more intense. As a result, process innovations are often associated with overall cost leader strategies, because the aim of many process improvements is to lower the costs of operations.

Another way to view the impact of an innovation is in terms of its degree of innovativeness, which falls somewhere on a continuum that extends from incremental to radical.[4]

radical innovation
an innovation that fundamentally changes existing practices.

- *Radical innovations* produce fundamental changes by evoking major departures from existing practices. These breakthrough innovations usually occur because of technological change. They tend to be highly disruptive and can transform a company or even revolutionize a whole industry. They may lead to products or processes that can be patented, giving a firm a strong competitive advantage. Examples include electricity, the telephone, the transistor, desktop computers, fiber optics, artificial intelligence, and genetically engineered drugs.

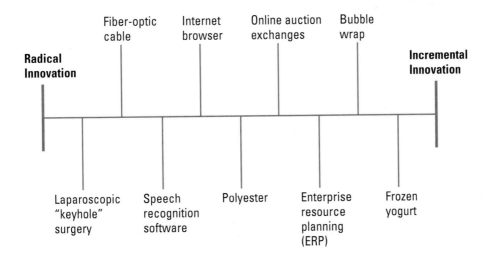

Exhibit 12.1 Continuum of Radical and Incremental Innovations

- *Incremental innovations* enhance existing practices or make small improvements in products and processes. They may represent evolutionary applications within existing paradigms of earlier, more radical innovations. Because they often sustain a company by extending or expanding its product line or manufacturing skills, incremental innovations can be a source of competitive advantage by providing new capabilities that minimize expenses or speed productivity. Examples include frozen food, sports drinks, steel-belted radial tires, electronic bookkeeping, shatterproof glass, and digital telephones.

Some innovations are highly radical; others are only slightly incremental. But most innovations fall somewhere between these two extremes (see Exhibit 12.1).

Recently, Harvard Business School Professor Clayton M. Christensen introduced another useful approach to characterize types of innovations.[5] Christensen draws a distinction between sustaining and disruptive innovations. *Sustaining innovations* are those that extend sales in an existing market, usually by enabling new products or services to be sold at higher margins. Such innovations may include either incremental or radical innovations. For example, the Internet was a breakthrough technology that transformed retail selling. But rather than disrupting the activities of catalog companies such as Lands' End and L.L. Bean, the Internet energized their existing business by extending their reach and making their operations more efficient.

By contrast, *disruptive innovations* are those that overturn markets by providing an altogether new approach to meeting customer needs. The features of a disruptive innovation make it somewhat counterintuitive. Disruptive innovations:

- Are technologically simpler and less sophisticated than currently available products or services.
- Appeal to less demanding customers who are seeking more convenient, less expensive solutions.
- Take time to take effect and only become disruptive once they have taken root in a new market or low-end part of an existing market.

Christensen cites Wal-Mart and Southwest Airlines as two disruptive examples. Wal-Mart started with a single store, Southwest with a few flights. But because they both represented major departures from existing practices and tapped into unmet needs, they steadily grew into ventures that appealed to a new category of customers and eventually overturned the status quo. "Instead of sustaining the trajectory of improvement that has been established in a market," says Christensen, a disruptive innovation "disrupts it and redefines it by bringing to the market something that is simpler."[6]

incremental innovation an innovation that enhances existing practices or makes small improvements in products and processes.

Portable Kidney Dialysis Technology: A Disruptive Innovation

In 2001, software engineer Colin Mackay got a rare auto-immune disease that destroyed his kidneys. At age 32, Mackay was faced with spending the rest of his life getting kidney dialysis. The treatment, which involves using a machine to clean the blood when normal kidney functioning has failed, is needed by over 300,000 Americans who suffer from renal failure caused by diseases such as diabetes. Patients who need the treatments check into a dialysis center for a four-hour procedure three times a week. The treatment is exhausting and between treatments, toxins build up, leading to headaches, bloating, and difficulty sleeping. One reason patients have to take treatments in a dialysis center is because the equipment is expensive and bulky—the size of a large refrigerator.

A few years later, Mackay's wife heard about a home dialysis treatment using a portable machine from NxStage Medical in Lawrence, Massachusetts. Just a few months after starting home treatments, his energy returned and the fluid build-up subsided. He was able to play soccer again with his 5- and 7-year-old children. Vanessa Evans, a 36-year-old home treatment patient who also began using the home machine used to get pounding headaches from conventional treatments in a dialysis center. "I never want to go back," declares Evans.

Sources: Christensen, C. M., Grossman, J. H., & Hwang, J. 2008. *The Innovator's Prescription.* New York: McGraw-Hill; Langreth, R. 2008. The Home Cure. *Forbes,* November, 17: 84–85; and, Templeton, D. 2008. Patients Can Learn to Do Time Consuming Dialysis at Home. www.post-gazette.com, January 9.

The NxStage machine, which is the size of a microwave and costs around $21,000, is simple to use. A key improvement over traditional models is that the filtration system uses disposable cartridges. "You slide the cartridge in, close the door, and away you go," says Mackay. Treatments can either occur more frequently for a shorter duration, or overnight while the patient sleeps. Either way, patients who have used it feel better and enjoy a healthier lifestyle.

Even so, the simple and effective home treatment is being used by only 1 percent of dialysis patients. One reason is that Medicare reimbursement rules apply only to dialysis received in dialysis centers. Some centers have bought or leased the NxStage machines so they can run home programs. Also, some doctors, including Stanford University nephrologist Glenn Chertow, have legitimate concerns whether home treatments have been sufficiently tested to claim they are as effective as treatment in dialysis centers. Such resistance has bogged down the process of making the move to a simpler, cheaper, and more convenient approach to dialysis. Yet with rising obesity rates, as many as a million people in the United States are projected to require dialysis in coming years.

In *The Innovator's Prescription,* Clayton Christensen and colleagues contend that "industry leaders have repeatedly lobbied for legislation and regulation that block disruptive approaches from being used anywhere until they are certifiably good enough to be used everywhere. This traps the industry where it began, in the world of ever higher costs. The health care industry needs to be disrupted." According to Christensen, home dialysis systems like the one produced by NxStage, are an example of the type of disruptive innovation that can begin to transform health care in the United States.

The Linux operating system provides a more recent example. When it first became available, few systems administrators used the open-source operating system even though it was free. However, problems with more expensive proprietary operating systems, such as Microsoft Windows, have made Linux increasingly popular. By 2008, the majority of Internet hosting companies and supercomputer operating systems were Linux-based. Today, in addition to being relatively more convenient to use, it is supported by a community of developers. Desktop computers preloaded with the Linux operating system have become increasingly popular.[7]

In the book *The Innovator's Prescription,* Christensen and his co-authors argue that the U.S. health care system is poised for the kind of creative disruption that is needed to stimulate badly needed improvements in health care practices. Strategy Spotlight 12.2 describes a technology that is threatening to disrupt the status quo at Medicare-supported dialysis centers—an easy to use, low-cost kidney dialysis machine that patients can use at home.[8]

Innovation is a force in both the external environment (technology, competition) and also a factor affecting a firm's internal choices (generic strategy, value-adding activities).[9] Nevertheless, innovation can be quite difficult for some firms to manage, especially those that have become comfortable with the status quo.

Challenges of Innovation

>LO2
The challenges and pitfalls of managing corporate innovation processes.

Innovation is essential to sustaining competitive advantages. Recall from Chapter 3 that one of the four elements of the Balanced Scorecard is the innovation and learning perspective. The extent and success of a company's innovation efforts are indicators of its overall performance. As management guru Peter Drucker warned, "An established company which, in an age demanding innovation, is not capable of innovation is doomed to decline and extinction."[10] In today's competitive environment, most firms have only one choice: "Innovate or die."

As with change, however, firms are often resistant to innovation. Only those companies that actively pursue innovation, even though it is often difficult and uncertain, will get a payoff from their innovation efforts. But managing innovation is challenging.[11] As former Pfizer chairman and CEO William Steere puts it: "In some ways, managing innovation is analogous to breaking in a spirited horse. You are never sure of success until you achieve your goal. In the meantime, everyone takes a few lumps."[12]

What is it that makes innovation so difficult? The uncertainty about outcomes is one factor. Companies are often reluctant to invest time and resources into activities with an unknown future. Another factor is that the innovation process involves so many choices. These choices present five dilemmas that companies must wrestle with when pursuing innovation.[13]

- *Seeds versus Weeds.* Most companies have an abundance of innovative ideas. They must decide which of these is most likely to bear fruit—the "Seeds"—and which should be cast aside—the "Weeds." This is complicated by the fact that some innovation projects require a considerable level of investment before a firm can fully evaluate whether they are worth pursuing. Firms need a mechanism with which they can choose among various innovation projects.
- *Experience versus Initiative.* Companies must decide who will lead an innovation project. Senior managers may have experience and credibility but tend to be more risk averse. Midlevel employees, who may be the innovators themselves, may have more enthusiasm because they can see firsthand how an innovation would address specific problems. Firms need to support and reward organizational members who bring new ideas to light.
- *Internal versus External Staffing.* Innovation projects need competent staffs to succeed. People drawn from inside the company may have greater social capital and know the organization's culture and routines. But this knowledge may actually inhibit them from thinking outside the box. Staffing innovation projects with external personnel requires that project managers justify the hiring and spend time recruiting, training, and relationship building. Firms need to streamline and support the process of staffing innovation efforts.
- *Building Capabilities versus Collaborating.* Innovation projects often require new sets of skills. Firms can seek help from other departments and/or partner with other companies that bring resources and experience as well as share costs of development. However, such arrangements can create dependencies and inhibit internal skills development. Further, struggles over who contributed the most or how the benefits of the project are to be allocated may arise. Firms need a mechanism for forging links with outside parties to the innovation process.

- ***Incremental versus Preemptive Launch.*** Companies must manage the timing and scale of new innovation projects. An incremental launch is less risky because it requires fewer resources and serves as a market test. But a launch that is too tentative can undermine the project's credibility. It also opens the door for a competitive response. A large-scale launch requires more resources, but it can effectively preempt a competitive response. Firms need to make funding and management arrangements that allow for projects to hit the ground running and be responsive to market feedback.

These dilemmas highlight why the innovation process can be daunting even for highly successful firms. Next, we consider four steps that firms can take to manage the innovation process.[14]

Defining the Scope of Innovation

Firms must have a means to focus their innovation efforts. By defining the "strategic envelope"—the scope of a firm's innovation efforts—firms ensure that their innovation efforts are not wasted on projects that are outside the firm's domain of interest. Strategic enveloping defines the range of acceptable projects. As Alistair Corbett, an innovation expert with the global consulting firm Bain & Company, recently said, "One man's radical innovation is another man's incremental innovation."[15] A strategic envelope creates a firm-specific view of innovation that defines how a firm can create new knowledge and learn from an innovation initiative even if the project fails. It also gives direction to a firm's innovation efforts, which helps separate seeds from weeds and builds internal capabilities.

One way to determine which projects to work on is to focus on a common technology. Then, innovation efforts across the firm can aim at developing skills and expertise in a given technical area. Another potential focus is on a market theme. Consider how DuPont responded to a growing concern for environmentally sensitive products:

> In the early 1990s, DuPont sought to use its knowledge of plastics to identify products to meet a growing market demand for biodegradable products. It conducted numerous experiments with a biodegradable polyester resin it named Biomax. By trying different applications and formulations demanded by potential customers, the company was finally able to create a product that could be produced economically and had market appeal. Recently, Biomax was certified biodegradable and compostable by the Biodegradable Products Institute, an endorsement that should further boost sales.[16]

Companies must be clear not only about the kinds of innovation they are looking for but also the expected results. Each company needs to develop a set of questions to ask itself about its innovation efforts:

- How much will the innovation initiative cost?
- How likely is it to actually become commercially viable?
- How much value will it add; that is, what will it be worth if it works?
- What will be learned if it does not pan out?

However a firm envisions its innovation goals, it needs to develop a systematic approach to evaluating its results and learning from its innovation initiatives. Viewing innovation from this perspective helps firms manage the process.[17]

Managing the Pace of Innovation

Along with clarifying the scope of an innovation by defining a strategic envelope, firms also need to regulate the pace of innovation. How long will it take for an innovation initiative to realistically come to fruition? The project time line of an incremental innovation may be 6 months to 2 years, whereas a more radical innovation is typically long term—10 years or more.[18] Radical innovations often begin with a long period of exploration in which experimentation makes strict timelines unrealistic. In contrast, firms that are innovating incrementally in order to exploit a window of opportunity may use a milestone approach that is more stringently driven by goals and deadlines. This kind of sensitivity to realistic time frames helps companies separate dilemmas temporally so they are easier to manage.

Time pacing can also be a source of competitive advantage because it helps a company manage transitions and develop an internal rhythm.[19] Time pacing does not mean the company ignores the demands of market timing; instead, companies have a sense of their own internal clock in a way that allows them to thwart competitors by controlling the innovation process.

Not all innovation lends itself to speedy development, however. Radical innovation often involves open-ended experimentation and time-consuming mistakes. The creative aspects of innovation are often difficult to time. When software maker Intuit's new CEO, Steve Bennett, began to turn around that troubled business, he required every department to implement Six Sigma, a quality control management technique that focuses on being responsive to customer needs. Everybody, that is, but the techies.

> "We're not GE, we're not a company where Jack says 'Do it,' and everyone salutes," says Bill Hensler, Intuit's vice president for process excellence. That's because software development, according to many, is more of an art than a science. At the Six Sigma Academy, president of operations Phil Samuel says even companies that have embraced Six Sigma across every other aspect of their organization usually maintain a hands-off policy when it comes to software developers. Techies, it turns out, like to go at their own pace.[20]

Some projects can't be rushed. Companies that hurry up their research efforts or go to market before they are ready can damage their ability to innovate—and their reputation. Thus, managing the pace of innovation can be an important factor in long-term success.

Staffing to Capture Value from Innovation

People are central to the processes of identifying, developing, and commercializing innovations effectively. They need broad sets of skills as well as experience—experience working with teams and experience working on successful innovation projects. To capture value from innovation activities, companies must provide strategic decision makers with staff members who make it possible.

This insight led strategy experts Rita Gunther McGrath and Thomas Keil to research the types of human resource management practices that effective firms use to capture value from their innovation efforts.[21] Four practices are especially important:

- Create innovation teams with experienced players who know what it is like to deal with uncertainty and can help new staff members learn venture management skills.
- Require that employees seeking to advance their career with the organization serve in the new venture group as part of their career climb.
- Once people have experience with the new venture group, transfer them to mainstream management positions where they can use their skills and knowledge to revitalize the company's core business.
- Separate the performance of individuals from the performance of the innovation. Otherwise, strong players may feel stigmatized if the innovation effort they worked on fails.

There are other staffing practices that may sound as if they would benefit a firm's innovation activities but may, in fact, be counterproductive:

- Creating a staff that consists only of strong players whose primary experience is related to the company's core business. This provides too few people to deal with the uncertainty of innovation projects and may cause good ideas to be dismissed because they do not appear to fit with the core business.

strategy spotlight

Staffing for Innovation Success at Air Products

When it comes to implementing its innovation efforts, Air Products and Chemicals, Inc. (APCI) recognizes the importance of staffing for achieving success. Air Products is a global manufacturer of industrial gases, chemicals, and related equipment. Headquartered in Allentown, Pennsylvania, Air Products has annual sales of $10 billion, manufacturing facilities in over 30 countries, and 22,000 employees worldwide. The company has a strong reputation for effectively embedding innovation into its culture through its unique employee engagement processes.

Ron Pierantozzi, a 30-year veteran of the company and its director of innovation and new product development, says "Innovation is about discipline.... It requires

Sources: Chesbrough, H. 2007. Why Bad Things Happen to Good Technology. *The Wall Street Journal:* April 28–29, R11; Leavitt, P. 2005. Delivering the Difference: Business Process Management at APCI. *APQC,* www.apqc.com; McGrath, R. G. & Keil, T. 2007. The value captor's process: Getting the Most out of Your New Business Ventures. *Harvard Business Review,* May: 128–136; and www.apci.com.

a different type of training, different tools and new approaches to experimentation." To enact this philosophy, Pierantozzi begins with his people. He recruits people with diverse backgrounds and a wide range of expertise including engineers, entrepreneurs, and government officials. It is made clear to those on his innovation teams that they will return to mainstream operations after four years—a fact that most consider a plus since working in the innovation unit usually provides a career boost. He also assures players that there is no stigma associated with a failed venture because experimentation is highly valued.

Innovation teams are created to manage the company's intellectual assets and determine which technologies have the most potential value. A key benefit of this approach has been to more effectively leverage its human resources to achieve innovative outcomes without increasing its R&D expenses. These efforts resulted in an innovation award from APQC (formerly known as the American Productivity and Quality Center) which recognizes companies for exemplary practices that increase productivity.

- Creating a staff that consists only of volunteers who want to work on projects they find interesting. Such players are often overzealous about new technologies or overly attached to product concepts, which can lead to poor decisions about which projects to pursue or drop.
- Creating a climate where innovation team members are considered second-class citizens. In companies where achievements are rewarded, the brightest and most ambitious players may avoid innovation projects with uncertain outcomes.

Unless an organization can align its key players into effective new venture teams, it is unlikely to create any differentiating advantages from its innovation efforts.[22] An enlightened approach to staffing a company's innovation efforts provides one of the best ways to ensure that the challenges of innovation will be effectively met. Strategy Spotlight 12.3 describes the approach Air Products and Chemicals, Inc. is using to enhance its innovation efforts.

Collaborating with Innovation Partners

It is rare for any one organization to have all the information it needs to carry an innovation from concept to commercialization. Even a company that is highly competent with its current operations usually needs new capabilities to achieve new results. Innovation partners provide the skills and insights that are needed to make innovation projects succeed.[23]

Innovation partners may come from many sources, including research universities and the federal government. Each year the federal government issues requests for proposals (RFPs) asking private companies for assistance in improving services or finding solutions to public problems. Universities are another type of innovation partner. Chip-maker Intel, for example, has benefited from underwriting substantial amounts of university research.

Rather than hand universities a blank check, Intel bargains for rights to patents that emerge from Intel-sponsored research. The university retains ownership of the patent, but Intel gets royalty-free use of it.[24]

Strategic partnering requires firms to identify their strengths and weaknesses and make choices about which capabilities to leverage, which need further development, and which are outside the firm's current or projected scope of operations.

To choose partners, firms need to ask what competencies they are looking for and what the innovation partner will contribute.[25] These might include knowledge of markets, technology expertise, or contacts with key players in an industry. Innovation partnerships also typically need to specify how the rewards of the innovation will be shared and who will own the intellectual property that is developed.[26]

Innovation efforts that involve multiple partners and the speed and ease with which partners can network and collaborate are changing the way innovation is conducted.[27] Strategy Spotlight 12.4 outlines the efforts of three major corporations that are using crowd-sourcing technologies to collaborate with customers to enhance their innovation efforts.

Successful innovation involves a companywide commitment because the results of innovation affect every part of the organization. Innovation also requires an entrepreneurial spirit and skill set to be effective. Few companies have a more exemplary reputation than W. L. Gore. Exhibit 12.2 highlights the policies that help make Gore an innovation leader. One of the most important ways that companies improve and grow is when innovation is put to the task of creating new corporate ventures.

Corporate Entrepreneurship

Corporate entrepreneurship (CE) has two primary aims: the pursuit of new venture opportunities and strategic renewal.[28] The innovation process keeps firms alert by exposing them to new technologies, making them aware of marketplace trends, and helping them evaluate new possibilities. CE uses the fruits of the innovation process to help firms build new sources of competitive advantage and renew their value propositions. Just as the innovation process helps firms to make positive improvements, corporate entrepreneurship helps firms identify opportunities and launch new ventures. Strategy Spotlight 12.5 addresses how Danish toymaker Lego effectively used entrepreneurial initiatives to strategically renew its aging business.

Corporate new venture creation was labeled "intrapreneuring" by Gifford Pinchot because it refers to building entrepreneurial businesses within existing corporations.[29] However, to engage in corporate entrepreneurship that yields above-average returns and contributes to sustainable advantages, it must be done effectively. In this section we will examine the sources of entrepreneurial activity within established firms and the methods large corporations use to stimulate entrepreneurial behavior.

In a typical corporation, what determines how entrepreneurial projects will be pursued? That depends on many factors, including:

- Corporate culture.
- Leadership.
- Structural features that guide and constrain action.
- Organizational systems that foster learning and manage rewards.

All of the factors that influence the strategy implementation process will also shape how corporations engage in internal venturing.

Other factors will also affect how entrepreneurial ventures will be pursued.

- The use of teams in strategic decision making.
- Whether the company is product or service oriented.

corporate entrepreneurship the creation of new value for a corporation, through investments that create either new sources of competitive advantage or renewal of the value proposition.

Web 2.0 Collaboration: Using Social Networking to Enhance Innovation

Throughout this text, we have shared examples of companies that are using crowdsourcing techniques to connect with customers and other stakeholders. One of the key reasons to use Web 2.0 capabilities, that is, technologies that make online collaboration and social networking possible, is to gather innovative insights from people outside the company. "The idea that the users of products are often best equipped to innovate is something many entrepreneurs know intuitively," says Max Chafkin, author of *The Customer Is the Company.* Each of the major corporations below, which are known for their innovative activities, are beginning to using crowdsourcing to enhance their entrepreneurial efforts.

Dell's IdeaStorm

One of the first social networking sites launched by a major corporation, IdeaStorm now plays an important role in driving business innovation at Dell. A key aim of the website is to help Dell learn about the latest innovations and spot business opportunities before they go mainstream. The company has implemented several of the 8,000 suggestions it has received since its launch in 2007, including offering a line of computers preloaded with Linux software. Users of the site can see the status of suggestions—"under review," "partially implemented," and so forth. Dell anticipates an even larger role for IdeaStorm in the future. Founder Michael Dell envisions it as a beginning step in "co-creation of products. . . . a company this size is not going to be about a couple of people coming with ideas. It's going to be about millions of people and harnessing the power of those ideas." Currently, Dell is considering using the IdeaStorm concept and technology to help it build a partner network consisting of IT consultants, service providers, and value-added resellers to help it reinvigorate sales and provide support in underserved markets.

General Electric's SupportCentral

GE has focused its networking efforts on internal customers. Created entirely by GE engineers, SupportCentral is a highly sophisticated enterprise collaboration system that allows GE workers to connect with one another using the network model that best suits how they work—some focused on people, others on documents, discussion groups, and so on. The searchable system offers a variety of features, such as applications, data, directories, and expert networks, designed to help workers communicate more broadly and get answers faster. Because it has replaced hundreds of separate websites and attracts 5 to 10 innovative suggestions a day, it has cut costs and saved GE "millions" according to SupportCentral manager Dr. Sukh Grewal. The system has 400,000 global users in 6,000 locations around the world, supports over 20 languages, and gets 25 million Web hits a day. Users have created 50,000 communities and over 100,000 experts are available to answer questions and manage information. According to Chief Information Officer Gary Reiner, GE has "gone out of our way to call it professional networking rather than social networking." Whatever it's called, SupportCentral is an innovation that "is becoming sort of a heartbeat of the company," Reiner admits, and is increasingly vital to GE's success.

Starbucks' MyStarbucksIdea.com

At its 2008 annual meeting, Starbucks CEO Howard Schultz stated, "We somehow evolved from a culture of entrepreneurship, creativity, and innovation to a culture of, in a way, mediocrity and bureaucracy." Schultz returned to the helm of Starbucks after an eight-year absence to help lead it out of a financial slump. He then announced a series of initiatives designed to counter that trend and renew the spirit of innovation at Starbucks. One of these was its new online community, MyStarbucksIdea.com, a website that encourages Starbucks customers to make suggestions and interact with employees. Within about four months of its launch, the site had received over 130,000 separate suggestions. One of the most frequent requests was healthier food options, and the protein-enriched Vivanno drinks launched in mid-2008 are seen as a response to that request—Starbucks' first innovative drink product since the Cinnamon Dolce Latte in 2006. Other ideas, ranging from how to have shorter lines (by, for one thing, encoding credit cards with standing orders that could be scanned as soon as a customer walks in) to suggestions for how to more aggressively participate in recycling efforts, are being seriously evaluated.

Even though these initiatives have been well-received, they are new and it is not clear what the payoff will be. For example, IdeaStorm has been criticized for being little more than an effort to make Dell look good to a small group of users rather than a serious attempt to drive innovation. Others, however, disagree, including MIT professor Eric von Hippel, an expert in innovation management. In his view, crowdsourcing approaches *(continued)*

(continued) to innovation are becoming a viable substitute for in-house R&D. "This is really the biggest

Sources: Colvin, G. 2008. Information Worth Billions. www.cnnmoney.com, July 21; Jarvis, J. 2008. One Shot of Coffee and Two Shots at Changing the Way Starbucks Is Run. www.guardian.co.uk, April 21; Kaufman, W. 2008. Crowd-sourcing Turns Business on Its Head. www.npr.com, August 20; Marks, O. 2008. GE's Enterprise Collaboration Backbone. www.zdnet.com, July 18, np.; Panettieri, J. 2008. Dell's IdeaStorm: Social Networking Driving Business Innovation. www.seekingalpha.com, April 1; Stone, B. 2008. Starbucks Plans Return to Its Roots. www.nytimes.com, March 20; and www.wikipedia.org.

paradigm shift in innovation since the Industrial Revolution," says von Hippel. "For a couple hundred years or so, manufacturers have been really imperfect at understanding people's needs. Now people get to decide what they want for themselves."

crowdsourcing

Exhibit 12.2
W. L. Gore's New Rules for Fostering Innovation

Rule	Implications
The power of small teams	Gore believes that small teams promote familiarity and autonomy. Even its manufacturing plants are capped at just 200 people. That way everyone can get to know one another on a first-name basis and work together with minimal rules. This also helps to cultivate "an environment where creativity can flourish," according to CEO Chuck Carroll.
No ranks, no titles, no bosses	Because Gore believes in maximizing individual potential, employees, dubbed "associates," decide for themselves what new commitments to take on. Associates have "sponsors," rather than bosses, and there are no standardized job descriptions or categories. Everyone is supposed to take on a unique role. Committees of co-workers evaluate each team member's contribution and decide on compensation.
Take the long view	Although impatient about the status quo, Gore exhibits great patience with the time—often years, sometimes decades—it takes to nurture and develop breakthrough products and bring them to market.
Make time for face time	Gore avoids the traditional hierarchical chain of command, opting instead for a team-based environment that fosters personal initiative. Gore also discourages memos and e-mail and promotes direct, person-to-person communication among all associates—anyone in the company can talk to anyone else.
Lead by leading	Associates are encouraged to spend about 10 percent of their time pursuing speculative new ideas. Anyone is free to champion products, as long as they have the passion and ideas to attract followers. Many of Gore's breakthroughs started with one person acting on his or her own initiative and developed as colleagues helped in their spare time.
Celebrate failure	When a project doesn't work out and the team decides to kill it, they celebrate just as they would if it had been a success—with some beer and maybe a glass of champagne. Rather than condemning failure, Gore figures that celebrating it encourages experimentation and risk taking.

Source: Deutschman, A. 2004. The Fabric of Creativity. *Fast Company,* 89: 54–62; Levering, R. & Moskowitz, M. 2006. The 100 Best Companies to Work For. *Fortune,* www.fortune.com, January; and www.gore.com.

Entrepreneurial Initiatives Help Reinvent the Lego Group

"Toy of the Century" is the lofty label given to Lego's iconic plastic bricks by *Fortune* magazine in 1999. With such impressive statistics as "seven boxes of Lego are sold every second" and "19 billion components are produced every year," the Denmark-based Lego Group would appear to be a huge success by any standards.

But 1999 was followed by a dark period for Lego, as electronic games and digital products increasingly captured children's attention. Lego took several steps to try to bolster its sinking business, including offering branded products such as books and watches and launching a Lego theme park. But for six years, the company continued to report heavy losses, including a $300 million loss in 2004. The founding family heir, CEO Kjeld Kirk Kristiansen, injected millions of his own money into the company to prevent bankruptcy and eventually resigned.

He was replaced by 35-year old Jorgen Vig Knudstrop, who made drastic changes at the company, including outsourcing manufacturing of the bricks to the Czech Republic and cutting nearly 2,000 jobs. The cost savings were matched with entrepreneurial initiatives that challenged the core of the company's business culture. It launched a series of interactive games, including a highly successful *Star Wars* computer game. But the traditional company, whose mission had always included "nurturing the child," found it difficult to depart from its image as a producer of playful, constructive toys. Referring to *Star Wars* creator George Lucas, play expert and 22-year Lego veteran Niels Sandal Jakobsen recalls, "getting the license from Lucas was nothing compared to the internal struggles over having the word *war* appear under the Lego brand." Nevertheless, Knudstrop persisted and more interactive games

were introduced, including a *Star Wars* game for the Wii and an online *Mars Mission* game.

Crowdsourcing contributed to one of Lego's digital product successes: Mindstorms, a set of programmable bricks with electronic motors, sensors, and Lego Technic pieces (such as gears, axles, and beams). Within weeks of Mindstorms' release, user groups had started reverse engineering the software to make improvements. At first, Lego threatened to sue the tinkerers, but quickly realized that might be a mistake. The company changed course, even including a "right to hack" as part of the Mindstorms software licensing agreement. The community of users expanded, and many of them now participate in the annual Lego World convention in the Netherlands. One of them showed up at a recent convention with a fully operational pinball machine made from 20,000 Lego bricks and 13 programmable microchips. And when Lego began design on the next version of Mindstorms, it took on a group of the most dedicated enthusiasts as de facto employees during the 11-month development cycle. Such innovations are indicative of the Lego Group's new entrepreneurial perspective.

The fusion of mass customization and peer production has extended beyond the Mindstorms project. Its new Lego Factory system gives customers access to a virtual warehouse where they can design their own custom Lego sets. According to Mark Hansen, director of Lego Interactive Experiences, "With Lego Factory we can expand beyond our one hundred in-house product designers to marvel at the creativity of more than three hundred thousand designers worldwide."

The entrepreneurial spirit that animates the revitalized Lego Group has paid off. Despite a downturn in toy sales worldwide, Lego reported a 32 percent increase in profits in 2008. Included in *Fast Company*'s 2009 list of the world's 50 most innovative companies, Lego has made a remarkable rebound. The reason, according to CEO Knudstrop, is because, "We're about many more things than just a set of bricks and a box. It's about everyday people getting incremental new ideas."

Sources: At 50, Lego Still Going Strong. 2008. www.abc.net.au, January 29; 2009. *Fast Company* Staff. #41 Lego. *Fast Company,* March: 93; Schwartz, N. D. 2006. One Brick at a Time. www.cnnmoney.com, June 8; Tapscott, D. & Williams, A. D. 2006. *Wikinomics.* New York: Penguin; and www.wikipedia.org.

- Whether its innovation efforts are aimed at product or process improvements.
- The extent to which it is high-tech or low-tech.

Because these factors are different in every organization, some companies may be more involved than others in identifying and developing new venture opportunities.[30] These factors will also influence the nature of the CE process.

Successful CE typically requires firms to reach beyond their current operations and markets in the pursuit of new opportunities. It is often the breakthrough opportunities that provide the greatest returns. Such strategies are not without risks, however. In the sections that follow, we will address some of the strategic choice and implementation issues that influence the success or failure of CE activities.

Two distinct approaches to corporate venturing are found among firms that pursue entrepreneurial aims. The first is *focused* corporate venturing, in which CE activities are isolated from a firm's existing operations and worked on by independent work units. The second approach is *dispersed*, in which all parts of the organization and every organization member are engaged in intrapreneurial activities.

Focused Approaches to Corporate Entrepreneurship

Firms using a focused approach typically separate the corporate venturing activity from the other ongoing operations of the firm. CE is usually the domain of autonomous work groups that pursue entrepreneurial aims independent of the rest of the firm. The advantage of this approach is that it frees entrepreneurial team members to think and act without the constraints imposed by existing organizational norms and routines. This independence is often necessary for the kind of open-minded creativity that leads to strategic breakthroughs. The disadvantage is that, because of their isolation from the corporate mainstream, the work groups that concentrate on internal ventures may fail to obtain the resources or support needed to carry an entrepreneurial project through to completion. Two forms—new venture groups (NVGs) and business incubators—are among the most common types of focused approaches.

>LO3
How corporations use new venture teams, business incubators, and product champions to create an internal environment and culture that promote entrepreneurial development.

New Venture Groups (NVGs)   Corporations often form NVGs whose goal is to identify, evaluate, and cultivate venture opportunities. These groups typically function as semi-autonomous units with little formal structure. The **new venture group** may simply be a committee that reports to the president on potential new ventures. Or it may be organized as a corporate division with its own staff and budget. The aims of the NVG may be open-ended in terms of what ventures it may consider. Alternatively, some corporations use them to promote concentrated effort on a specific problem. In both cases, they usually have a substantial amount of freedom to take risks and a supply of resources to do it with.[31]

NVGs usually have a larger mandate than a typical R&D department. Their involvement extends beyond innovation and experimentation to coordinating with other corporate divisions, identifying potential venture partners, gathering resources, and actually launching the venture.

new venture group a group of individuals, or a division within a corporation, that identifies, evaluates, and cultivates venture opportunities.

Business Incubators   The term *incubator* was originally used to describe a device in which eggs are hatched. **Business incubators** are designed to "hatch" new businesses. They are a type of corporate NVG with a somewhat more specialized purpose—to support and nurture fledgling entrepreneurial ventures until they can thrive on their own as stand-alone businesses. Corporations use incubators as a way to grow businesses identified by the NVG. Although they often receive support from many parts of the corporation, they still operate independently until they are strong enough to go it alone. Depending on the type of business, they are either integrated into an existing corporate division or continue to operate as a subsidiary of the parent firm.

Incubators typically provide some or all of the following five functions.[32]

business incubator a corporate new venture group that supports and nurtures fledgling entrepreneurial ventures until they can thrive on their own as stand-alone businesses.

- *Funding.* Includes capital investments as well as in-kind investments and loans.
- *Physical space.* Incubators in which several start-ups share space often provide fertile ground for new ideas and collaboration.

- *Business services.* Along with office space, young ventures need basic services and infrastructure; may include anything from phone systems and computer networks to public relations and personnel management.
- *Mentoring.* Senior executives and skilled technical personnel often provide coaching and experience-based advice.
- *Networking.* Contact with other parts of the firm and external resources such as suppliers, industry experts, and potential customers facilitates problem solving and knowledge sharing.

The risks associated with incubating ventures should not be overlooked. Companies have at times spent millions on new ideas with very little to show for it. Major corporations such as Lucent, British Airways, and Hewlett-Packard deactivated their incubators and scaled back new venture portfolios after experiencing major declines in value during recent financial downturns.[33]

To encourage entrepreneurship, corporations sometimes need to do more than create independent work groups or venture incubators to generate new enterprises. In some firms, the entrepreneurial spirit is spread throughout the organization.

Dispersed Approaches to Corporate Entrepreneurship

The second type of CE is dispersed. For some companies, a dedication to the principles and practices of entrepreneurship is spread throughout the organization. One advantage of this approach is that organizational members don't have to be reminded to think entrepreneurially or be willing to change. The ability to change is considered to be a core capability. This leads to a second advantage: Because of the firm's entrepreneurial reputation, stakeholders such as vendors, customers, or alliance partners can bring new ideas or venture opportunities to anyone in the organization and expect them to be well-received. Such opportunities make it possible for the firm to stay ahead of the competition. However, there are disadvantages as well. Firms that are overzealous about CE sometimes feel they must change for the sake of change, causing them to lose vital competencies or spend heavily on R&D and innovation to the detriment of the bottom line. Two related aspects of dispersed entrepreneurship include entrepreneurial cultures that have an overarching commitment to CE activities and the use of product champions in promoting entrepreneurial behaviors.

Entrepreneurial Culture   In some large corporations, the corporate culture embodies the spirit of entrepreneurship. A culture of entrepreneurship is one in which the search for venture opportunities permeates every part of the organization. The key to creating value successfully is viewing every value-chain activity as a source of competitive advantage. The effect of CE on a firm's strategic success is strongest when it animates all parts of an organization. It is found in companies where the strategic leaders and the culture together generate a strong impetus to innovate, take risks, and seek out new venture opportunities.[34]

In companies with an entrepreneurial culture, everyone in the organization is attuned to opportunities to help create new businesses. Many such firms use a top-down approach to stimulate entrepreneurial activity. The top leaders of the organization support programs and incentives that foster a climate of entrepreneurship. Many of the best ideas for new corporate ventures, however, come from the bottom up. Here's what Martin Sorrell, CEO of the WPP Group, a London-based global communication services group, says about drawing on the talents of lower-level employees:

> The people at the so-called bottom of an organization know more about what's going on than the people at the top. The people in the trenches are the ones in the best position to make critical decisions. It's up to the leaders to give those people the freedom and the resources they need.[35]

Best Buy's Spirit of Innovation

Best Buy remains the number one electronics retailer despite intense competition from competitors such as rival Wal-Mart (see Strategy Spotlight 8.11). A major key to its success is the climate of innovation that permeates the company. According to Shari Ballard, Best Buy's vice president for human resources, "If you're going to turn on an innovation engine, a lot depends on whether managers listen for the brilliance in their employees' ideas." Here are a couple of Best Buy's recent innovation successes:

- Project manager Nate Omann noticed that a high number of flat-panel TVs were being damaged during home delivery. It was making customers angry and running up replacement costs. So Nate came up with the "TV taco"—a reusable device that fits around TVs to better protect them during transit. It is expected to save the company millions of dollars.

- *Sound and Vision Magazine* awarded Best Buy the Retail Innovation Award in 2005 for its Magnolia Home Theatre store-within-a-store concept. This innovation offers the kind of services usually found only at small specialty stores—quiet demo rooms, comfortable seating, a highly knowledgeable staff, and top quality brands.

More radical than its store innovations, Best Buy is also winning kudos for innovative human resources management. It implemented a program, called ROWE for "results-only work environment," designed to dramatically increase employee autonomy by focusing on output instead of hours worked. The program has been so successful, in fact, that Best Buy formed a subsidiary named CultureRx to implement similar programs at other compa-

● Best Buy is well-known as an innovative electronics retailer.

nies. What it implements, however, is not the usual flex-time, telecommuting program. ROWE co-founders Jody Thompson and Cali Ressler consider those programs, which still focus on hours worked, to be overly bureaucratic. ROWE employees, by contrast, are required to put in only as much time as it actually takes to do their work.

Is it working? In 2006, Best Buy's procurement department increased savings by 50 percent over the previous year after it entered the ROWE program. In the online ordering division, orders processed by people not working in the office were as much as 18 percent higher than those working in the office. Across the company, voluntary turnover has decreased significantly and ROWE participants report that they feel 35 percent more productive. As a result, Workforce Management gave Best Buy and CultureRx its 2007 Optimas Award for innovation.

Sources: Anonymous. 2006. 2005 Editor's Choice Awards: Best Buy. *Sound and Vision Magazine,* www.soundandvision.mag, February; Ballard, S. 2006. Fast Talk: Best Brains, *Fast Company,* November: 66; Conlin, M. 2006. Smashing the Clock. *BusinessWeek,* www.businessweek.com, December 11; and Frauenheim, E. 2007. Best Buy & CultureRx: Optimas Award Winner for Innovation, *Workforce Management,* www.workforce.com, March 26.

An entrepreneurial culture is one in which change and renewal are on everybody's mind. Sony, 3M, Intel, and Cisco are among the corporations best known for their corporate venturing activities. Many fast-growing young corporations also attribute much of their success to an entrepreneurial culture. Best Buy's CEO Brad Anderson considers an entrepreneurial spirit to be essential for success in retailing. Strategy Spotlight 12.6 describes the kinds of activities that promote an entrepreneurial culture at Best Buy.

Product Champions   CE does not always involve making large investments in start-ups or establishing incubators to spawn new divisions. Often, innovative ideas emerge in the normal course of business and are brought forth and become part of the way of doing business. Entrepreneurial champions are often needed to take charge of internally generated ventures. **Product** (or project) **champions** are those individuals working within a corporation who bring entrepreneurial ideas forward, identify what kind of market exists for the product or service, find resources to support the venture, and promote the venture concept to upper management.[36]

product champion
an individual working within a corporation who brings entrepreneurial ideas forward, identifies what kind of market exists for the product or service, finds resources to support the venture, and promotes the venture concept to upper management.

When lower-level employees identify a product idea or novel solution, they will take it to their supervisor or someone in authority. A new idea that is generated in a technology lab may be introduced to others by its inventor. If the idea has merit, it gains support and builds momentum across the organization.[37] Even though the corporation may not be looking for new ideas or have a program for cultivating internal ventures, the independent behaviors of a few organizational members can have important strategic consequences.

No matter how an entrepreneurial idea comes to light, however, a new venture concept must pass through two critical stages or it may never get off the ground:

1. *Project definition.* An opportunity has to be justified in terms of its attractiveness in the marketplace and how well it fits with the corporation's other strategic objectives.
2. *Project impetus.* For a project to gain impetus, its strategic and economic impact must be supported by senior managers who have experience with similar projects. It then becomes an embryonic business with its own organization and budget.

For a project to advance through these stages of definition and impetus, a product champion is often needed to generate support and encouragement. Champions are especially important during the time after a new project has been defined but before it gains momentum. They form a link between the definition and impetus stages of internal development, which they do by procuring resources and stimulating interest for the product among potential customers.[38] Often, they must work quietly and alone. Consider the example of Ken Kutaragi, the Sony engineer who championed the PlayStation.

> Even though Sony had made the processor that powered the first Nintendo video games, no one at Sony in the mid-1980s saw any future in such products. "It was a kind of snobbery," Kutaragi recalled. "For Sony people, the Nintendo product would have been very embarrassing to make because it was only a toy." But Kutaragi was convinced he could make a better product. He began working secretly on a video game. Kutaragi said, "I realized that if it was visible, it would be killed." He quietly began enlisting the support of senior executives, such as the head of R&D. He made a case that Sony could use his project to develop capabilities in digital technologies that would be important in the future. It was not until 1994, after years of "underground" development and quiet building of support, that Sony introduced the PlayStation. By the year 2000, Sony had sold 55 million of them, and Kutaragi became CEO of Sony Computer Entertainment. By 2005, Kutagari was Sony's Chief Operating Officer, and was supervising efforts to launch PS3, the next generation version of the market-leading PlayStation video game console.[39]

Product champions play an important entrepreneurial role in a corporate setting by encouraging others to take a chance on promising new ideas.[40]

Measuring the Success of Corporate Entrepreneurship Activities

At this point in the discussion, it is reasonable to ask whether CE is successful. Corporate venturing, like the innovation process, usually requires a tremendous effort. Is it worth it? We consider factors that corporations need to take into consideration when evaluating the success of CE programs. We also examine techniques that companies can use to limit the expense of venturing or to cut their losses when CE initiatives appear doomed.

Comparing Strategic and Financial CE Goals   Not all corporate venturing efforts are financially rewarding. In terms of financial performance, slightly more than 50 percent of corporate venturing efforts reach profitability (measured by ROI) within six years of their launch.[41] If this were the only criterion for success, it would seem to be a rather poor return. On the one hand, these results should be expected, because CE is riskier than other investments such as expanding ongoing operations. On the other hand, corporations expect a higher return from corporate venturing projects than from normal operations. Thus, in terms of the risk–return trade-off, it seems that CE often falls short of expectations.[42]

>LO4
How corporate
entrepreneurship
achieves both
financial goals and
strategic goals.

There are several other important criteria, however, for judging the success of a corporate venture initiative. Most CE programs have strategic goals. The strategic reasons for undertaking a corporate venture include strengthening competitive position, entering into new markets, expanding capabilities by learning and acquiring new knowledge, and building the corporation's base of resources and experience. Three questions should be used to assess the effectiveness of a corporation's venturing initiatives:[43]

1. *Are the products or services offered by the venture accepted in the marketplace?* Is the venture considered to be a market success? If so, the financial returns are likely to be satisfactory. The venture may also open doors into other markets and suggest avenues for other venture projects.
2. *Are the contributions of the venture to the corporation's internal competencies and experience valuable?* Does the venture add to the worth of the firm internally? If so, strategic goals such as leveraging existing assets, building new knowledge, and enhancing firm capabilities are likely to be met.
3. *Is the venture able to sustain its basis of competitive advantage?* Does the value proposition offered by the venture insulate it from competitive attack? If so, it is likely to place the corporation in a stronger position relative to competitors and provide a base from which to build other advantages.

These criteria include both strategic and financial goals of CE. Another way to evaluate a corporate venture is in terms of the four criteria from the Balanced Scorecard (Chapter 3). In a successful venture, not only are financial and market acceptance (customer) goals met but so are the internal business and innovation and learning goals. Thus, when assessing the success of corporate venturing, it is important to look beyond simple financial returns and consider a well-rounded set of criteria.[44]

Exit Champions   Although a culture of championing venture projects is advantageous for stimulating an ongoing stream of entrepreneurial initiatives, many—in fact, most—of the ideas will not work out. At some point in the process, a majority of initiatives will be abandoned. Sometimes, however, companies wait too long to terminate a new venture and do so only after large sums of resources are used up or, worse, result in a marketplace failure. Motorola's costly global satellite telecom project known as Iridium provides a useful illustration. Even though problems with the project existed during the lengthy development process, Motorola refused to pull the plug. Only after investing $5 billion and years of effort was the project abandoned.[45]

One way to avoid these costly and discouraging defeats is to support a key role in the CE process: **exit champions.** In contrast to product champions and other entrepreneurial enthusiasts within the corporation, exit champions are willing to question the viability of a venture project.[46] By demanding hard evidence and challenging the belief system that is carrying an idea forward, exit champions hold the line on ventures that appear shaky.

Both product champions and exit champions must be willing to energetically stand up for what they believe. Both put their reputations on the line. But they also differ in important

exit champion an individual working within a corporation who is willing to question the viability of a venture project by demanding hard evidence of venture success and challenging the belief system that carries a venture forward.

ways.[47] Product champions deal in uncertainty and ambiguity. Exit champions reduce ambiguity by gathering hard data and developing a strong case for why a project should be killed. Product champions are often thought to be willing to violate procedures and operate outside normal channels. Exit champions often have to reinstate procedures and re-assert the decision-making criteria that are supposed to guide venture decisions. Whereas product champions often emerge as heroes, exit champions run the risk of losing status by opposing popular projects.

The role of exit champion may seem unappealing. But it is one that could save a corporation both financially and in terms of its reputation in the marketplace. It is especially important because one measure of the success of a firm's CE efforts is the extent to which it knows when to cut its losses and move on.

>LO5

The benefits and potential drawbacks of real options analysis in making resource deployment decisions in corporate entrepreneurship contexts.

Real Options Analysis: A Useful Tool

One way firms can minimize failure and avoid losses from pursuing faulty ideas is to apply the logic of real options. **Real options analysis** (ROA) is an investment analysis tool from the field of finance. It has been slowly, but increasingly, adopted by consultants and executives to support strategic decision making in firms. What does ROA consist of and how can it be appropriately applied to the investments required to initiate strategic decisions? To understand *real* options it is first necessary to have a basic understanding of what *options* are.

Options exist when the owner of the option has the right but not the obligation to engage in certain types of transactions. The most common are stock options. A stock option grants the holder the right to buy (call option) or sell (put option) shares of the stock at a fixed price (strike price) at some time in the future.[48] The investment to be made immediately is small, whereas the investment to be made in the future is generally larger. An option to buy a rapidly rising stock currently priced at $50 might cost as little as $.50.[49] Owners of such a stock option have limited their losses to $.50 per share, while the upside potential is unlimited. This aspect of options is attractive, because options offer the prospect of high gains with relatively small up-front investments that represent limited losses.

The phrase "real options" applies to situations where options theory and valuation techniques are applied to real assets or physical things as opposed to financial assets. Applied to entrepreneurship, real options suggest a path that companies can use to manage the uncertainty associated with launching new ventures. Some of the most common applications of real options are with property and insurance. A real estate option grants the holder the right to buy or sell a piece of property at an established price some time in the future. The actual market price of the property may rise above the established (or strike) price—or the market value may sink below the strike price. If the price of the property goes up, the owner of the option is likely to buy it. If the market value of the property drops below the strike price, the option holder is unlikely to execute the purchase. In the latter circumstance, the option holder has limited his or her loss to the cost of the option, but during the life of the option retains the right to participate in whatever the upside potential might be.

Applications of Real Options Analysis to Strategic Decisions

The concept of options can also be applied to strategic decisions where management has flexibility. Situations arise where management must decide whether to invest additional funds to grow or accelerate the activity, perhaps delay in order to learn more, shrink the scale of the activity, or even abandon it. Decisions to invest in new ventures or other

real options analysis an investment analysis tool that looks at an investment or activity as a series of sequential steps, and for each step the investor has the option of (a) investing additional funds to grow or accelerate, (b) delaying, (c) shrinking the scale of, or (d) abandoning the activity.

business activities such as R&D, motion pictures, exploration and production of oil wells, and the opening and closing of copper mines often have this flexibility.[50] Important issues to note are:

- ROA is appropriate to use when investments can be staged; a smaller investment up front can be followed by subsequent investments. Real options can be applied to an investment decision that gives the company the right, but not the obligation, to make follow-on investments.
- Strategic decision makers have "tollgates," or key points at which they can decide whether to continue, delay, or abandon the project. Executives have flexibility. There are opportunities to make other go or no-go decisions associated with each phase.
- It is expected that there will be increased knowledge about outcomes at the time of the next investment and that additional knowledge will help inform the decision makers about whether to make additional investments (i.e., whether the option is in the money or out of the money).

Many strategic decisions have the characteristic of containing a series of options. The phenomenon is called "embedded options," a series of investments in which at each stage of the investment there is a go/no–go decision. Consider the real options logic that Johnson Controls, a maker of car seats, instrument panels, and interior control systems uses to advance or eliminate entrepreneurial ideas.[51] Johnson options each new innovative idea by making a small investment in it. To decide whether to exercise an option, the idea must continue to prove itself at each stage of development. Here's how Jim Geschke, vice president and general manager of electronics integration at Johnson, describes the process:

> Think of Johnson as an innovation machine. The front end has a robust series of gates that each idea must pass through. Early on, we'll have many ideas and spend a little money on each of them. As they get more fleshed out, the ideas go through a gate where a go or no-go decision is made. A lot of ideas get filtered out, so there are far fewer items, and the spending on each goes up. . . . Several months later each idea will face another gate. If it passes, that means it's a serious idea that we are going to develop. Then the spending goes way up, and the number of ideas goes way down. By the time you reach the final gate, you need to have a credible business case in order to be accepted. At a certain point in the development process, we take our idea to customers and ask them what they think. Sometimes they say, "That's a terrible idea. Forget it." Other times they say, "That's fabulous. I want a million of them."

This process of evaluating ideas by separating winning ideas from losing ones in a way that keeps investments low has helped Johnson Controls grow its revenues to over $34 billion a year. Using real options logic to advance the development process is a key way that firms reduce uncertainty and minimize innovation-related failures.[52] Strategy Spotlight 12.7 provides an example of a pharmaceutical company that used ROA to guide its decision-making process.

Potential Pitfalls of Real Options Analysis

Despite the many benefits that can be gained from using ROA, managers must be aware of its potential limitations or pitfalls. Below we will address three major issues.[53]

Agency Theory and the Back-Solver Dilemma Let's assume that companies adopting a real-options perspective invest heavily in training and that their people understand how to effectively estimate variance—the amount of dispersion or range that is estimated for potential outcomes. Such training can help them use ROA. However, it does not solve another inherent problem: managers may have an incentive and the know-how to "game the system." Most electronic spreadsheets permit users to simply back-solve any

Using Real Options Analysis to Evaluate a Pharmaceutical Venture

Pharmaceutical companies often use real options analysis in evaluating decisions about whether to invest in new R&D ventures. Developing new pharmaceutical products requires at least four stages of investments: basic research to yield new compounds and three FDA-mandated phases of clinical trials. Generally, each phase is more expensive to undertake than the previous phase. However, as each phase unfolds, management knows more about the underlying drug and its many sources of uncertainty, including the technical difficulties it faces and external market conditions that could affect sales. With this information, management can make the decision to invest more, speed up the process, delay the start of the next phase, or even abandon the R&D project.

Consider, for example, a privately held biotechnology firm that used real options analysis to evaluate whether to invest in a veterinary pharmaceutical product. The firm had developed a unique technology for introducing the coat protein of a particular virus into animal feedstocks. Ingesting the coat protein generated an immune response, thus protecting the animal from the virus. The firm was at

Sources: Janney, J. J. & Dess, G. G. 2004. Can Real-Options Analysis Improve Decision Making? Promises and Pitfalls. *Academy of Management Executive,* 18(4): 60–75; Stockley, R. L., Jr., Curtis, S., Jafari, J., & Tibbs, K. 2003. The Options Value of an Early-Stage Biotechnology Investment. *Journal of Applied Finance,* 15(2): 44–55; and Triantis, A., et al. 2003. University of Maryland Roundtable on Real Options and Corporate Practice. *Journal of Applied Corporate Finance,* 15(2): 8–23.

the beginning of the preclinical trials stage, the first of a series of tests required by FDA regulation and conducted through the FDA subagency called the Center for Veterinary Medicine.

The company expected the stage to take 18 months and cost $2 million. Long-standing experience indicated that 95 percent of new drug investigations are abandoned during this phase. Abandonment rates in subsequent stages would decrease somewhat, but costs would rise, with a total outflow from 2002 through its anticipated launch in 2007 of at least $18.5 million. The company's best estimate of the market from 2007 through 2017 was about $85 million per year. Still, there was a possibility the product would gain as much as a 50 percent market share. In short, there was huge potential, but in the interim there was a tremendous chance of failure (i.e., high risk), significant early outflows, and delayed inflows of revenue.

A traditional net present value (NPV) analysis (which sums revenues and costs for the life of the project and then discounts them using current interest rates) yielded a negative $2 million with an 11 percent risk-adjusted discount rate. However, viewing the investment as a multistage option and incorporating management's flexibility to alter its decision at least four times between 2002 and 2007 changes the valuation markedly. That is, a real options analysis demonstrated a present value of about $22 million. The question, then, was not whether to risk $18.5 million, but whether to invest $2 million today for the opportunity to earn $22 million at a future date.

formula; that is, you can type in the answer you want and ask what values are needed in a formula to get that answer. If managers know that a certain option value must be met in order for the proposal to get approved, they can back-solve the model to find a variance estimate needed to arrive at the answer that upper management desires.

Agency problems are typically inherent in investment decisions. They may occur when the managers of a firm are separated from its owners—when managers act as "agents" rather than "principals" (owners). A manager may have something to gain by not acting in the owner's best interests, or the interests of managers and owners are not co-aligned. Agency theory suggests that as managerial and owner interests diverge, managers will follow the path of their own self-interests. Sometimes this is to secure better compensation: Managers who propose projects may believe that if their projects are approved, they stand a much better chance of getting promoted. So while managers have an incentive to propose projects that *should* be successful, they also have an incentive to propose projects that *might* be successful. And because of the subjectivity involved in formally modeling a real option, managers may have an incentive to choose variance values that increase the likelihood of approval.

Managerial Conceit: Overconfidence and the Illusion of Control   Often, poor decisions are the result of such traps as biases, blind spots, and other human frailties. Much of this literature falls under the concept of **managerial conceit.**[54]

First, managerial conceit occurs when decision makers who have made successful choices in the past come to believe that they possess superior expertise for managing uncertainty. They believe that their abilities can reduce the risks inherent in decision making to a much greater extent than they actually can. Such managers are more likely to shift away from analysis to trusting their own judgment. In the case of real options, they can simply declare that any given decision is a real option and proceed as before. If asked to formally model their decision, they are more likely to employ variance estimates that support their viewpoint.

Second, employing the real-options perspective can encourage decision makers toward a bias for action. Such a bias may lead to carelessness. Managerial conceit is as much a problem (if not more so) for small decisions as for big ones. Why? The cost to write the first stage of an option is much smaller than the cost of full commitment, and managers pay less attention to small decisions than to large ones. Because real options are designed to minimize potential losses while preserving potential gains, any problems that arise are likely to be smaller at first, causing less concern for the manager. Managerial conceit could suggest that managers will assume that those problems are the easiest to solve and control—a concern referred to as the illusion of control. Managers may fail to respond appropriately because they overlook the problem or believe that since it is small, they can easily resolve it. Thus, managers may approach each real-option decision with less care and diligence than if they had made a full commitment to a larger investment.

Managerial Conceit: Irrational Escalation of Commitment   A strength of a real options perspective is also one of its Achilles heels. Both real options and decisions involving escalation of commitment require specific environments with sequential decisions.[55] As the escalation-of-commitment literature indicates, simply separating a decision into multiple parts does not guarantee that decisions made will turn out well. This condition is potentially present whenever the exercise decision retains some uncertainty, which most still do. The decision to abandon also has strong psychological factors associated with it that affect the ability of managers to make correct exercise decisions.[56]

An option to exit requires reversing an initial decision made by someone in the organization (such as an exit champion). Organizations typically encourage managers to "own their decisions" in order to motivate them. As managers invest themselves in their decision, it proves harder for them to lose face by reversing course. For managers making the decision, it feels as if they made the wrong decision in the first place, even if it was initially a good decision. The more specific the manager's human capital becomes, the harder it is to transfer it to other organizations. Hence, there is a greater likelihood that managers will stick around and try to make an existing decision work. They are more likely to continue an existing project even if it should perhaps be ended.[57]

Despite the potential pitfalls of a real options approach, many of the strategic decisions that product champions and top managers must make are enhanced when decision makers have an entrepreneurial mind-set.

Entrepreneurial Orientation

Firms that want to engage in successful CE need to have an entrepreneurial orientation (EO).[58] EO refers to the strategy-making practices that businesses use in identifying and launching corporate ventures. It represents a frame of mind and a perspective toward entrepreneurship that is reflected in a firm's ongoing processes and corporate culture.[59]

Exhibit 12.3
Dimensions of
Entrepreneurial
Orientation

Dimension	Definition
Autonomy	Independent action by an individual or team aimed at bringing forth a business concept or vision and carrying it through to completion.
Innovativeness	A willingness to introduce novelty through experimentation and creative processes aimed at developing new products and services as well as new processes.
Proactiveness	A forward-looking perspective characteristic of a market-place leader that has the foresight to seize opportunities in anticipation of future demand.
Competitive aggressiveness	An intense effort to outperform industry rivals characterized by a combative posture or an aggressive response aimed at improving position or overcoming a threat in a competitive marketplace.
Risk taking	Making decisions and taking action without certain knowledge of probable outcomes; some undertakings may also involve making substantial resource commitments in the process of venturing forward.

Sources: Dess, G. G. & Lumpkin, G. T. 2005. The Role of Entrepreneurial Orientation in Stimulating Effective Corporate Entrepreneurship. *Academy of Management Executive,* 19(1): 147–156; Covin, J. G. & Slevin, D. P. 1991. A Conceptual Model of Entrepreneurship as Firm Behavior. *Entrepreneurship Theory & Practice,* Fall: 7–25; Lumpkin, G. T. and Dess, G. G. 1996. Clarifying the Entrepreneurial Orientation Construct and Linking It to Performance. *Academy of Management Review,* 21: 135–172; Miller, D. 1983. The Correlates of Entrepreneurship in Three Types of Firms. *Management Science,* 29: 770–791.

entrepreneurial orientation the strategy-making practices that businesses use in identifying and launching new ventures, consisting of autonomy, innovativeness, proactiveness, competitive aggressiveness, and risk taking.

An EO has five dimensions that permeate the decision-making styles and practices of the firm's members: autonomy, innovativeness, proactiveness, competitive aggressiveness, and risk taking. These factors work together to enhance a firm's entrepreneurial performance. But even those firms that are strong in only a few aspects of EO can be very successful.[60] Exhibit 12.3 summarizes the dimensions of **entrepreneurial orientation.** Below, we discuss the five dimensions of EO and how they have been used to enhance internal venture development.

Autonomy

autonomy
independent action by an individual or team aimed at bringing forth a business concept or vision and carrying it through to completion.

Autonomy refers to a willingness to act independently in order to carry forward an entrepreneurial vision or opportunity. It applies to both individuals and teams that operate outside an organization's existing norms and strategies. In the context of corporate entrepreneurship, autonomous work units are often used to leverage existing strengths in new arenas, identify opportunities that are beyond the organization's current capabilities, and encourage development of new ventures or improved business practices.[61]

The need for autonomy may apply to either dispersed or focused entrepreneurial efforts. Because of the emphasis on venture projects that are being developed outside of the normal flow of business, a focused approach suggests a working environment that is relatively autonomous. But autonomy may also be important in an organization where entrepreneurship is part of the corporate culture. Everything from the methods of group interaction to the firm's reward system must make organizational members feel as if they can think freely about venture opportunities, take time to investigate them, and act without

Exhibit 12.4 Autonomy Techniques

Autonomy		
Technique	**Description/Purpose**	**Example**
Use skunkworks to foster entrepreneurial thinking	Skunkworks are independent work units, often physically separate from corporate headquarters. They allow employees to get out from under the pressures of their daily routines to engage in creative problem solving.	Overstock.com created a skunkworks to address the problem of returned merchandise. The solution was a business within-a-business: Overstock auctions. The unit has grown by selling products returned to Overstock and offers fees 30 percent lower than eBay's auction service.
Design organizational structures that support independent action	Established companies with traditional structures often need to break out of such old forms to compete more effectively.	Deloitte Consulting, a division of Deloitte Touche Tohmatsu, found it difficult to compete against young agile firms. So it broke the firm into small autonomous units called "chip-aways" that operate with the flexibility of a start-up. In its first year, revenues were $40 million—10 percent higher than its projections.

Sources: Conlin, M. 2006. Square Feet. Oh How Square! *BusinessWeek*, www.businessweek.com, July 3; Cross, K. 2001. Bang the Drum Quickly. *Business 2.0,* May: 28–30; Sweeney, J. 2004. A Firm for All Reasons. *Consulting Magazine,* www.consultingmag.com; and Wagner, M. 2005. Out of the Skunkworks. *Internet Retailer,* January, www.internetretailer.com.

fear of condemnation. This implies a respect for the autonomy of each individual and an openness to the independent thinking that goes into championing a corporate venture idea. Thus, autonomy represents a type of empowerment (see Chapter 11) that is directed at identifying and leveraging entrepreneurial opportunities. Exhibit 12.4 identifies two techniques that organizations often use to promote autonomy.

Creating autonomous work units and encouraging independent action may have pitfalls that can jeopardize their effectiveness. Autonomous teams often lack coordination. Excessive decentralization has a strong potential to create inefficiencies, such as duplication of effort and wasting resources on projects with questionable feasibility. For example, Chris Galvin, former CEO of Motorola, scrapped the skunkworks approach the company had been using to develop new wireless phones. Fifteen teams had created 128 different phones, which led to spiraling costs and overly complex operations.[62]

For autonomous work units and independent projects to be effective, such efforts have to be measured and monitored. This requires a delicate balance: companies must have the patience and budget to tolerate the explorations of autonomous groups and the strength to cut back efforts that are not bearing fruit. It must be undertaken with a clear sense of purpose—namely, to generate new sources of competitive advantage.

Innovativeness

Innovativeness refers to a firm's efforts to find new opportunities and novel solutions. In the beginning of this chapter we discussed innovation; here the focus is on innovativeness—a firm's attitude toward innovation and willingness to innovate. It involves creativity and experimentation that result in new products, new services, or improved technological processes.[63] Innovativeness is one of the major components of an entrepreneurial strategy. As indicated at the beginning of the chapter, however, the job of managing innovativeness can be very challenging.

innovativeness
a willingness to introduce novelty through experimentation and creative processes aimed at developing new products and services as well as new processes.

Innovativeness requires that firms depart from existing technologies and practices and venture beyond the current state of the art. Inventions and new ideas need to be nurtured even when their benefits are unclear. However, in today's climate of rapid change, effectively producing, assimilating, and exploiting innovations can be an important avenue for achieving competitive advantages. Interest in global warming and other ecological concerns has led many corporations to focus their innovativeness efforts on solving environmental problems. Strategy Spotlight 12.8 describes three organizations that are using entrepreneurial thinking and innovative practices to identify socially responsible solutions.

As our earlier discussion of CE indicated, many corporations owe their success to an active program of innovation-based corporate venturing.[64] Exhibit 12.5 highlights two of the methods companies can use to enhance their competitive position through innovativeness.

Innovativeness can be a source of great progress and strong corporate growth, but there are also major pitfalls for firms that invest in innovation. Expenditures on R&D aimed at identifying new products or processes can be a waste of resources if the effort does not yield results. Another danger is related to the competitive climate. Even if a company innovates a new capability or successfully applies a technological breakthrough, another company may develop a similar innovation or find a use for it that is more profitable. Finally R&D and other innovation efforts are among the first to be cut back during an economic downturn.

Even though innovativeness is an important means of internal corporate venturing, it also involves major risks, because investments in innovations may not pay off. For strategic managers of entrepreneurial firms, successfully developing and adopting innovations can generate competitive advantages and provide a major source of growth for the firm.

Exhibit 12.5   Innovativeness Techniques

Innovativeness		
Technique	**Description/Purpose**	**Example**
Foster creativity and experimentation	Companies that support idea exploration and allow employees to express themselves creatively enhance innovation outcomes.	To tap into its reserves of innovative talent, Royal Dutch/Shell created "GameChanger" to help employees develop promising ideas. The process provides funding up to $600,000 for would-be entrepreneurs to pursue innovative projects and conduct experiments.
Invest in new technology, R&D, and continuous improvement	The latest technologies often provide sources of new competitive advantages. To extract value from a new technology, companies must invest in it.	Dell Computer Corporation's new OptiPlex manufacturing system revolutionized the traditional assembly line. Hundreds of custom-built computers can be made in an eight-hour shift using state of the art automation techniques that have increased productivity per person by 160 percent.

Sources: Breen, B. 2004. Living in Dell Time. *Fast Company,* November: 88–92: Hammonds, K. H. 2002. Size Is Not a Strategy. *Fast Company,* August: 78–83; Perman, S. 2001. Automate or Die. eCompanyNow.com, July; Dell, M. 1999. *Direct from Dell.* New York: HarperBusiness; and Watson, R. 2006. Expand Your Innovation Horizons. *Fast Company,* www.fastcompany.com, May.

Socially Responsible Corporate Entrepreneurship

One of the most important trends in U.S. business today is corporate social responsibility (CSR). Proactively oriented firms are seizing opportunities to take a leading role in issues such as the environment, product safety, and fair trade. Among the most interesting examples of this, as suggested in the Chapter 1 section on social innovation, are those firms that are taking an entrepreneurial approach to CSR. That is, they are using new technologies, environmentally friendly ventures, and entrepreneurial practices to advance their social responsibility goals. Following is a sample of three corporations that are taking a very entrepreneurial approach to corporate social responsibility.

Whirlpool Corporation—From efficiency to advocacy

Whirlpool is perhaps best known for its "white boxes"— the refrigerators, freezers, and laundry appliances that account for over 60 percent of its $13 billion in annual sales. To explore what creates customer loyalty, Whirlpool conducted a global survey of its customers. "We discovered there is a strong correlation between a company's performance in appliance markets and their social response to issues such as energy efficiency and pollution," said Steve Willis, director of Whirlpool's global environment, health, and safety programs. One result has been its innovative Duet Series of washers and dryers that significantly reduces energy consumption. Recently, Whirlpool decided to take its environmental efforts a step farther: It joined The Natural Step, an entrepreneurial organization that is advancing the movement toward environmental sustainability by advocating the development of innovative products that meet high standards of ecological sustainability.

Timberland—Green labeling its shoes

Timberland has been recognized as one of the most socially conscious companies because of its culture dedicated to environmental awareness. For example, the company sponsored the planting of a million trees and sponsored Earth Day events in countries around the world. Its "Path of Service" program allows employees to use 40 hours of paid time to volunteer for community projects. More

Sources: Asmus, P. 2005. 100 Best Corporate Citizens for 2005. *Business Ethics*, www.business-ethics.com; Asmus, P. 2003. 100 Best Corporate Citizens for 2003. *Business Ethics*, www.business-ethics.com; Baker, M. 2001. BP Anounces World's Largest Solar Project. *Business Respect*, 1: April 6; Hawken, P., Lovins, A., & Lovins, H. 2000. *Natural Capitalism*. Boston: Back Bay Books; see also www.bp.com; www.domini.com; www.hoovers.com; www.ifsia.com; and Borden, M. & Kamenetz, A. 2008. The prophet CEO. *Fast Company*, September: 126–129.

recently, the Stratham, New Hampshire, maker of footwear and apparel initiated a program to put a label on its products, similar to a food label, that tells consumers where the product was produced, how it was made, and its impact on local communities and the environment. "We thought about how closely consumers read nutritional labels on food products and thought, why doesn't this happen in our space?" says Dave Aznavorian, a senior global brand manager at Timberland. It is another move that reflects the ethics of CEO Jeff Swartz, an outspoken advocate of corporate responsibility who sees the role of Timberland as more than just manufacturing. "We are not a boot company, we are a brand," says Swartz, "and our brand is about confidently striding through life's challenges."

Green Mountain Coffee Roasters—Empowering local entrepreneurs

As the name suggests, this NASDAQ-listed corporation (GMCR) is located in the Green Mountains of Vermont. But its reach is global. As a roaster and distributor of specialty coffees, GMCR has become a leading advocate for fair trade practices and providing financial support for local coffee growers. "Our president and CEO Robert Stiller visited places where coffee is grown and was struck by the levels of poverty. He wanted to do something about it," said Rick Peyser, director of public relations. As a result, GMCR now purchases coffee beans from small farm cooperatives in Peru, Mexico, and Sumatra. It also provides micro-loans to underwrite family businesses that are trying to create more diverse agricultural economies. Back home in its Waterbury, Vermont, roasting facility, GMCR uses a 95-kilowatt cogeneration system that captures waste heat from its propane-fired generator and recycles it for both coffee roasting and space heating.

Each of these companies has recently been named one of the 100 Best Corporate Citizens by *Business Ethics* magazine. However, major corporations still have their critics. In fact, companies that claim to be making progress in advancing CSR are often the most loudly criticized. For example, British Petroleum, which has endeavored to be an oil industry leader in supporting environmentally sensitive energy development, is often attacked by environmental groups despite initiatives such as investing $48 million to develop the world's largest solar energy project. Despite such criticism, it is encouraging to note that entrepreneurial activities can help companies achieve their social responsibility goals as well as their innovation and growth goals.

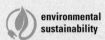

environmental sustainability

Proactiveness

Proactiveness refers to a firm's efforts to seize new opportunities. Proactive organizations monitor trends, identify the future needs of existing customers, and anticipate changes in demand or emerging problems that can lead to new venture opportunities. Proactiveness involves not only recognizing changes but also being willing to act on those insights ahead of the competition. Strategic managers who practice proactiveness have their eye on the future in a search for new possibilities for growth and development. Such a forward-looking perspective is important for companies that seek to be industry leaders. Many proactive firms seek out ways not only to be future oriented but also to change the very nature of competition in their industry.

Proactiveness puts competitors in the position of having to respond to successful initiatives. The benefit gained by firms that are the first to enter new markets, establish brand identity, implement administrative techniques, or adopt new operating technologies in an industry is called first mover advantage.[65]

First movers usually have several advantages. First, industry pioneers, especially in new industries, often capture unusually high profits because there are no competitors to drive prices down. Second, first movers that establish brand recognition are usually able to retain their image and hold on to the market share gains they earned by being first. Sometimes these benefits also accrue to other early movers in an industry, but, generally speaking,

Exhibit 12.6   **Proactiveness Techniques**

Proactiveness		
Technique	**Description/Purpose**	**Example**
Introduce new products or technological capabilities ahead of the competition.	Being a first mover provides companies with an ability to shape the playing field and shift competitive advantages in their favor.	Sony's mission states, "We should always be the pioneers with our products—out front leading the market." This philosophy has made Sony technologically strong with industry-leading products such as the PlayStation and Vaio laptop computers.
Continuously seek out new product or service offerings.	Firms that provide new resources or sources of supply can benefit from a proactive stance.	Costco seized a chance to leverage its success as a warehouse club that sells premium brands when it introduced Costco Home Stores. The home stores are usually located near its warehouse stores and its rapid inventory turnover gives it a cost advantage of 15 to 25 percent over close competitors such as Bassett Furniture and the Bombay Company.

Sources: Bryce, D. J. & Dyer, J. H. 2007. Strategies to Crack Well-Guarded Markets. *Harvard Business Review,* May: 84–92; Collins, J. C. & Porras, J. I. 1997. *Built to Last.* New York: HarperBusiness; Robinson, D. 2005. Sony Pushes Reliability in Vaio Laptops. *IT Week,* www.itweek .co.uk, October 12; and www.sony.com

first movers have an advantage that can be sustained until firms enter the maturity phase of an industry's life cycle.[66]

First movers are not always successful. The customers of companies that introduce novel products or embrace breakthrough technologies may be reluctant to commit to a new way of doing things. In his book *Crossing the Chasm,* Geoffrey A. Moore noted that most firms seek evolution, not revolution, in their operations. This makes it difficult for a first mover to sell promising new technologies.[67]

Even with these caveats, however, companies that are first movers can enhance their competitive position. Exhibit 12.6 illustrates two methods firms can use to act proactively.

Being an industry leader does not always lead to competitive advantages. Some firms that have launched pioneering new products or staked their reputation on new brands have failed to get the hoped-for payoff. Coca-Cola and PepsiCo invested $75 million to launch sodas that would capitalize on the low-carb diet trend. But with half the carbohydrates taken out, neither *C2,* Coke's entry, nor *Pepsi Edge* tasted very good. The two new brands combined never achieved more than one percent market share. PepsiCo halted production in 2005 and Coca-Cola followed suit in 2007.[68] Such missteps are indicative of the dangers of trying to proactively anticipate demand. Another danger for opportunity-seeking companies is that they will take their proactiveness efforts too far. Strategy Spotlight 12.9 discusses a pair of proactive marketing practices that may backfire with consumers.

● Coca-Cola has many successful products on supermarket shelves. C2—its low carb diet drink—isn't one of them.

Careful monitoring and scanning of the environment, as well as extensive feasibility research, are needed for a proactive strategy to lead to competitive advantages. Firms that do it well usually have substantial growth and internal development to show for it. Many of them have been able to sustain the advantages of proactiveness for years.

Competitive Aggressiveness

Competitive aggressiveness refers to a firm's efforts to outperform its industry rivals. Companies with an aggressive orientation are willing to "do battle" with competitors. They might slash prices and sacrifice profitability to gain market share or spend aggressively to obtain manufacturing capacity. As an avenue of firm development and growth, competitive aggressiveness may involve being very assertive in leveraging the results of other entrepreneurial activities such as innovativeness or proactiveness.

Competitive aggressiveness is directed toward competitors. The SWOT analysis discussed in Chapters 2 and 3 provides a useful way to distinguish between these different approaches to CE. Proactiveness, as we saw in the last section, is a response to opportunities—the O in SWOT. Competitive aggressiveness, by contrast, is a response to threats—the T in SWOT. A competitively aggressive posture is important for firms that seek to enter new markets in the face of intense rivalry.

Strategic managers can use competitive aggressiveness to combat industry trends that threaten their survival or market position. Sometimes firms need to be forceful in

competitive aggressiveness an intense effort to outperform industry rivals characterized by a combative posture or an aggressive response aimed at improving position or overcoming a threat in a competitive marketplace.

strategy spotlight

Over-the-Top Marketing Pitches: Proactiveness Gone Wild?

Research indicates that proactiveness is the EO dimension that is most likely to contribute to strong performance. Given that, can a company ever be too proactive? Definitely, according to consumers of some of the world's top brands. In the case of two popular forms of marketing—product placements and brand extensions—some well-respected name brands have taken their proactiveness beyond the limit.

Consider the hit television series *American Idol*. Viewers have started to notice how often the judges lift up their Coca-Cola cups or explain why the Apple iPhone is the perfect device for casting a vote for your favorite contestant. "I know they want to make some money," says 18-year-old Michigan viewer Caitlin Knott. "But no one wants to see Ryan Seacrest selling stuff." That sentiment

has not stopped *Idol* from rapidly increasing its placement activity: in the first 38 episodes of 2008, the show featured 4,151 product placements, according to Nielsen Media Research. That amounts to a total of 545 minutes, a 19 percent increase in screen time in one year.

The brand extensions trend is another practice that has consumers asking, "What were they thinking?" For example, famed leather-goods maker Salvatore Ferragamo recently started selling wristwatches at its Fifth Avenue store in New York City. The watches, made by Timex, will no doubt keep time just fine. But are customers going to pay $7,300, albeit for the 18-karat gold version, just because they like Ferragamo's handbags and shoes? Other luxury designers are making the same bet as Ferragamo: Prada is offering cellphones, Versace is decorating airplanes, and Giorgio Armani recently made an agreement with Samsung to produce luxury LCD televisions. The trend does not just apply to designers. Michael Stone, CEO of the Beanstalk Group, a licensing and branding unit of Omnicom Group, tells how a pizza brand recently approached him about launching a line of fashion apparel. "I thought, 'How fast can I get out of here?'" says Stone. Clearly, there is a limit to how proactively a company can extend its good name.

Sources: Binkley, C. 2007. Like Our Sunglasses? Try Our Vodka! *Wall Street Journal*, November 8: D1; Grover, R. 2008. *American Idol*'s Ads Infinitum. *BusinessWeek*, June 2: 38–39; and Rauch, A., Wiklund, J., Lumpkin, G. T., & Frese, M. 2009. Entrepreneurial Orientation and Business Performance: An Assessment of Past Research and Suggestions for the Future. *Entrepreneurship Theory and Practice*, 33(3): 49–62.

defending the competitive position that has made them an industry leader. Firms often need to be aggressive to ensure their advantage by capitalizing on new technologies or serving new market needs. Exhibit 12.7 suggests two of the ways competitively aggressive firms enhance their entrepreneurial position.

Another practice companies use to overcome the competition is to make preannouncements of new products or technologies. This type of signaling is aimed not only at potential customers but also at competitors to see how they will react or to discourage them from launching similar initiatives. Sometimes the preannouncements are made just to scare off competitors, an action that has potential ethical implications.

Competitive aggressiveness may not always lead to competitive advantages. Some companies (or their CEOs) have severely damaged their reputations by being overly aggressive. Although it continues to be a dominant player, Microsoft's highly aggressive profile makes it the subject of scorn by some businesses and individuals. Efforts to find viable replacements for the Microsoft products have helped fuel the open source software movement that threatens to erode Microsoft's leading role as a software provider.[69]

Competitive aggressiveness is a strategy that is best used in moderation. Companies that aggressively establish their competitive position and vigorously exploit opportunities

Exhibit 12.7 Competitive Aggressiveness Techniques

Competitive Aggressiveness		
Technique	**Description/Purpose**	**Example**
Enter markets with drastically lower prices.	Narrow operating margins make companies vulnerable to extended price competition.	Using open source software, California-based Zimbra, Inc. has become a leader in messaging and collaboration software. Its product costs about one-third less than its direct competitor Microsoft Exchange. Zimbra now has over 4 million users including 12,000 H&R Block tax preparers.
Find successful business models and copy them.	As long as a practice is not protected by intellectual property laws, it's probably okay to imitate it. Finding solutions to existing problems is generally quicker and cheaper than inventing them.	Best Practices, LLC is a North Carolina consulting group that seeks out best practices and then repackages and resells them. With annual revenues in excess of $8 million, Best Practices has become a leader in continuous improvement and benchmarking strategies.

Sources: Guth, R. A. 2006. Trolling the Web for Free Labor, Software Upstarts Are New Force. *The Wall Street Journal,* November 12: 1; Mochari, I. 2001. Steal This Strategy. *Inc.,* July: 62–67; www.best-in-class.com; and www.zimbra.com.

to achieve profitability may, over the long run, be better able to sustain their competitive advantages if their goal is to defeat, rather than decimate, their competitors.

Risk Taking

Risk taking refers to a firm's willingness to seize a venture opportunity even though it does not know whether the venture will be successful—to act boldly without knowing the consequences. To be successful through corporate entrepreneurship, firms usually have to take on riskier alternatives, even if it means forgoing the methods or products that have worked in the past. To obtain high financial returns, firms take such risks as assuming high levels of debt, committing large amounts of firm resources, introducing new products into new markets, and investing in unexplored technologies.

All of the approaches to internal development that we have discussed are potentially risky. Whether they are being aggressive, proactive, or innovative, firms on the path of CE must act without knowing how their actions will turn out. Before launching their strategies, corporate entrepreneurs must know their firm's appetite for risk.[70]

Three types of risk that organizations and their executives face are business risk, financial risk, and personal risk:

- *Business risk taking* involves venturing into the unknown without knowing the probability of success. This is the risk associated with entering untested markets or committing to unproven technologies.
- *Financial risk taking* requires that a company borrow heavily or commit a large portion of its resources in order to grow. In this context, risk is used to refer to the risk/return trade-off that is familiar in financial analysis.

risk taking making decisions and taking action without certain knowledge of probable outcomes. Some undertakings may also involve making substantial resource commitments in the process of venturing forward.

Exhibit 12.8   **Risk Taking Techniques**

Risk Taking		
Technique	**Description/Purpose**	**Example**
Research and assess risk factors to minimize uncertainty	Companies that "do their homework"—that is, carefully evaluate the implications of bold actions—reduce the likelihood of failure.	Graybar Electric Co. took a risk when it invested $144 million to revamp its distribution system. It consolidated 231 small centers into 16 supply warehouses and installed the latest communications network. Graybar is now considered a leader in facility redesign and its sales have increased steadily since the consolidation, topping $4 billion in sales in a recent year.
Use techniques that have worked in other domains	Risky methods that other companies have tried may provide an avenue for advancing company goals.	Autobytel.com, one of the first companies to sell cars online, decided on an approach that worked well for others—advertising during the Super Bowl. It was the first dot–com ever to do so and its $1.2 million 30-second ad paid off well by generating weeks of free publicity and favorable business press.

Sources: Anonymous. 2006. Graybar Offers Data Center Redesign Seminars. *Cabling Installation and Maintenance,* www.cim.pennnet.com, September 1; Keenan, F. & Mullaney, T. J. 2001. Clicking at Graybar. *BusinessWeek,* June 18: 132–34; Weintraub, A. 2001. Make or break for Autobytel. *BusinessWeek e.biz,* July 9: EB30-EB32; www.autobytel.com; and www.graybar.com.

- *Personal risk taking* refers to the risks that an executive assumes in taking a stand in favor of a strategic course of action. Executives who take such risks stand to influence the course of their whole company, and their decisions also can have significant implications for their careers.

Even though risk taking involves taking chances, it is not gambling. The best-run companies investigate the consequences of various opportunities and create scenarios of likely outcomes. A key to managing entrepreneurial risks is to evaluate new venture opportunities thoroughly enough to reduce the uncertainty surrounding them. Exhibit 12.8 indicates two methods companies can use to strengthen their competitive position through risk taking.

Risk taking, by its nature, involves potential dangers and pitfalls. Only carefully managed risk is likely to lead to competitive advantages. Actions that are taken without sufficient forethought, research, and planning may prove to be very costly. Therefore, strategic managers must always remain mindful of potential risks. In his book *Innovation and Entrepreneurship,* Peter Drucker argued that successful entrepreneurs are typically not risk takers. Instead, they take steps to minimize risks by carefully understanding them. That is how they avoid focusing on risk and remain focused on opportunity.[71] Risk taking is a good place to close this chapter on corporate entrepreneurship. Companies that choose to grow through internal corporate venturing must remember that entrepreneurship always involves embracing what is new and uncertain.

Reflecting on Career Implications . . .

- *Innovation:* Look around at the types of innovations being pursued by your company. Do they tend to be incremental or radical? Product-related or process-related? What new types of innovations might benefit your organization? How can you add value to such innovations?
- *Managing Innovation:* How might your organization's chances of a successful innovation increase through collaboration with innovation partners? Your ability to collaborate with individuals from other departments and firms will make you more receptive to and capable of innovation initiatives and enhance your career opportunities.
- *Corporate Entrepreneurship:* Do you consider the company you work for to be entrepreneurial? If not, what actions might you take to enhance its entrepreneurial spirit? If so, what have been the keys to its entrepreneurial success? Can these practices be repeated to achieve future successes?
- *Entrepreneurial Orientation:* Consider the five dimensions of entrepreneurial orientation. Is your organization especially strong at any of these? Especially weak? What are the career implications of your company's entrepreneurial strengths or weaknesses?

Summary

To remain competitive in today's economy, established firms must find new avenues for development and growth. This chapter has addressed how innovation and corporate entrepreneurship can be a means of internal venture creation and strategic renewal, and how an entrepreneurial orientation can help corporations enhance their competitive position.

Innovation is one of the primary means by which corporations grow and strengthen their strategic position. Innovations can take several forms, ranging from radical breakthrough innovations to incremental improvement innovations. Innovations are often used to update products and services or for improving organizational processes. Managing the innovation process is often challenging, because it involves a great deal of uncertainty and there are many choices to be made about the extent and type of innovations to pursue. By defining the scope of innovation, managing the pace of innovation, staffing to capture value from innovation, and collaborating with innovation partners, firms can more effectively manage the innovation process.

We also discussed the role of corporate entrepreneurship in venture development and strategic renewal. Corporations usually take either a focused or dispersed approach to corporate venturing. Firms with a focused approach usually separate the corporate venturing activity

from the ongoing operations of the firm in order to foster independent thinking and encourage entrepreneurial team members to think and act without the constraints imposed by the corporation. In corporations where venturing activities are dispersed, a culture of entrepreneurship permeates all parts of the company in order to induce strategic behaviors by all organizational members. In measuring the success of corporate venturing activities, both financial and strategic objectives should be considered. Real options analysis is often used to make better quality decisions in uncertain entrepreneurial situations. However, a real options approach has potential drawbacks.

Most entrepreneurial firms need to have an entrepreneurial orientation: the methods, practices, and decision-making styles that strategic managers use to act entrepreneurially. Five dimensions of entrepreneurial orientation are found in firms that pursue corporate venture strategies. Autonomy, innovativeness, proactiveness, competitive aggressiveness, and risk taking each make a unique contribution to the pursuit of new opportunities. When deployed effectively, the methods and practices of an entrepreneurial orientation can be used to engage successfully in corporate entrepreneurship and new venture creation. However, strategic managers must remain mindful of the pitfalls associated with each of these approaches.

Summary Review Questions

1. What is meant by the concept of a continuum of radical and incremental innovations?

2. What are the dilemmas that organizations face when deciding what innovation projects to pursue? What steps can organizations take to effectively manage the innovation process?

3. What is the difference between focused and dispersed approaches to corporate entrepreneurship?

4. How are business incubators used to foster internal corporate venturing?

5. What is the role of the product champion in bringing a new product or service into existence in a corporation? How can companies use product champions to enhance their venture development efforts?

6. Explain the difference between proactiveness and competitive aggressiveness in terms of achieving and sustaining competitive advantage.

7. Describe how the entrepreneurial orientation (EO) dimensions of innovativeness, proactiveness, and risk taking can be combined to create competitive advantages for entrepreneurial firms.

Key Terms

innovation, 427
radical innovation, 428
incremental innovation, 429
corporate entrepreneurship, 435
new venture group, 439
business incubator, 439
product champion, 442
exit champion, 443
real options analysis, 444
managerial conceit 447
entrepreneurial orientation, 448
autonomy, 448
innovativeness, 449
proactiveness, 452
competitive aggressiveness, 453
risk taking, 455

Experiential Exercise

Select two different major corporations from two different industries (you might use Fortune 500 companies to make your selection). Compare and contrast these organizations in terms of their entrepreneurial orientation.

Entrepreneurial Orientation	Company A	Company B
Autonomy		
Innovativeness		
Proactiveness		
Competitive Aggressiveness		
Risk Taking		

Based on Your Comparison:

1. How is the corporation's entrepreneurial orientation reflected in its strategy?

2. Which corporation would you say has the stronger entrepreneurial orientation?

3. Is the corporation with the stronger entrepreneurial orientation also stronger in terms of financial performance?

Application Questions Exercises

1. Select a firm known for its corporate entrepreneurship activities. Research the company and discuss how it has positioned itself relative to its close competitors. Does it have a unique strategic advantage? Disadvantage? Explain.

2. Explain the difference between product innovations and process innovations. Provide examples of firms

that have recently introduced each type of innovation. What are the types of innovations related to the strategies of each firm?

3. Using the Internet, select a company that is listed on the NASDAQ or New York Stock Exchange. Research the extent to which the company has an entrepreneurial culture. Does the company use product champions? Does it have a corporate venture capital fund? Do you believe its entrepreneurial efforts are sufficient to generate sustainable advantages?

4. How can an established firm use an entrepreneurial orientation to enhance its overall strategic position? Provide examples.

Ethics Questions

1. Innovation activities are often aimed at making a discovery or commercializing a technology ahead of the competition. What are some of the unethical practices that companies could engage in during the innovation process? What are the potential long-term consequences of such actions?

2. Discuss the ethical implications of using entrepreneurial policies and practices to pursue corporate social responsibility goals. Are these efforts authentic and genuine or just an attempt to attract more customers?

References

1. The Nortel Networks example is based on Austen, I. 2009. Nortel seeks bankruptcy protection. www.nytimes.com, January 15; Crockett, R. O. 2009. Nortel's road to bankruptcy. www.businessweek.com, January 15; Kerner, S. M. 2009. Nortel bankruptcy a Canadian tragedy. www.internetnews.com, January 16; *Ottawa Business Journal* Staff. 2009. Nortel news leaves tech community reeling. www.ottawabusinessjournal.com, January 15; and Silver, S. & Lublin. J. S. 2009. Nortel Networks files for Chapter 11. www.wsj.com, January 15.

2. For an interesting discussion, see Johannessen, J. A., Olsen, B., & Lumpkin, G. T. 2001. Innovation as newness: What is new, how new, and new to whom? *European Journal of Innovation Management,* 4(1): 20–31.

3. The discussion of product and process innovation is based on Roberts, E. B. (Ed.). 2002. *Innovation: Driving product, process, and market change.* San Francisco: Jossey-Bass; Hayes, R. & Wheelwright, S. 1985. Competing through manufacturing. *Harvard Business Review,* 63(1): 99–109; and Hayes, R. & Wheelwright, S. 1979. Dynamics of product–process life cycles. *Harvard Business Review,* 57(2): 127–136.

4. The discussion of radical and incremental innovations draws from Leifer, R., McDermott, C. M., Colarelli, G.,

O'Connor, G. C., Peters, L. S., Rice, M. P., & Veryzer, R. W. 2000. *Radical innovation: How mature companies can outsmart upstarts.* Boston: Harvard Business School Press; Damanpour, F. 1996. Organizational complexity and innovation: Developing and testing multiple contingency models. *Management Science,* 42(5): 693–716; and Hage, J. 1980. *Theories of organizations.* New York: Wiley.

5. Christensen, C. M. & Raynor, M. E. 2003. *The innovator's solution.* Boston: Harvard Business School Press.

6. Dressner, H. 2004. The Gartner Fellows interview: Clayton M. Christensen. www.gartner.com, April 26.

7. Christensen et al., op. cit.; and www.wikipedia.org.

8. Christensen, C. M., Grossman, J. H., & Hwang, J. 2008. *The innovator's prescription.* New York: McGraw-Hill; Christensen, C. M. & Raynor, M. E. 2003. *The innovator's solution.* Boston: Harvard Business School Press.

9. For another perspective on how different types of innovation affect organizational choices, see Wolter, C. & Veloso, F. M. 2008. The effects of innovation on vertical structure: Perspectives on transactions costs and competences. *Academy of Management Review,* 33(3): 586–605.

10. Drucker, P. F. 1985. *Innovation and entrepreneurship: 2000* New York: Harper & Row.

11. Birkinshaw, J., Hamel, G., & Mol, M. J. 2008. Management innovation. *Academy of Management Review,* 33(4): 825–845.

12. Steere, W. C., Jr. & Niblack, J. 1997. Pfizer, Inc. In Kanter, R. M., Kao, J., & Wiersema, F. (Eds.), *Innovation: Breakthrough thinking at 3M, DuPont, GE, Pfizer, and Rubbermaid:* 123–145. New York: HarperCollins.

13. Morrissey, C. A. 2000. Managing innovation through corporate venturing. *Graziadio Business Report,* Spring, gbr.pepperdine.edu; and Sharma, A. 1999. Central dilemmas of managing innovation in large firms. *California Management Review,* 41(3): 147–164.

14. Sharma, op. cit.

15. Canabou, C. 2003. Fast ideas for slow times. *Fast Company,* May: 52.

16. Biodegradable Products Institute. 2003. "Compostable Logo" of the Biodegradable Products Institute gains momentum with approval of DuPont™ Biomax® resin, www.bpiworld.org, June 12; Leifer et al., op. cit.

17. For more on defining the scope of innovation, see Valikangas, L. & Gibbert, M. 2005. Boundary-setting strategies for escaping innovation traps. *MIT Sloan Management Review,* 46(3): 58–65.

18. Leifer et al., op. cit.

19. Bhide, A. V. 2000. *The origin and evolution of new businesses.* New York: Oxford University Press; Brown, S. L. & Eisenhardt, K. M.

1998. *Competing on the edge: Strategy as structured chaos.* Cambridge, MA: Harvard Business School Press.

20. Caulfield, B. 2003. Why techies don't get Six Sigma. *Business 2.0,* June: 90.

21. McGrath, R. G. & Keil, T. 2007. The value captor's process: Getting the most out of your new business ventures. *Harvard Business Review,* May: 128–136.

22. For an interesting discussion of how sharing technology knowledge with different divisions in an organization can contribute to innovation processes, see Miller, D. J., Fern, M. J., & Cardinal, L. B. 2007. The use of knowledge for technological innovation within diversified firms. *Academy of Management Journal,* 50(2): 308–326.

23. Ketchen Jr., D. J., Ireland, R. D., & Snow, C. C. 2007 Strategic entrepreneurship, collaborative innovation, and wealth creation. *Strategic Entrepreneurship Journal,* 1(3–4): 371–385.

24. Chesbrough, H. 2003. *Open innovation: The new imperative for creating and profiting from technology.* Boston: Harvard Business School Press.

25. For a recent study of what makes alliance partnerships successful, see Sampson, R. C. 2007. R&D alliances and firm performance: The impact of technological diversity and alliance organization on innovation. *Academy of Management Journal,* 50(2): 364–386.

26. For an interesting perspective on the role of collaboration among multinational corporations see Hansen, M. T. & Nohria, N. 2004. How to build collaborative advantage. *MIT Sloan Management Review,* 46(1): 22–30.

27. Wells, R. M. J. 2008. The product innovation process: Are managing information flows and cross-functional collaboration key? *Academy of Management Perspectives,* 22(1): 58–60.

28. Guth, W. D. & Ginsberg, A. 1990. Guest editor's introduction: Corporate entrepreneurship. *Strategic Management Journal,* 11: 5–15.

29. Pinchot, G. 1985. *Intrapreneuring.* New York: Harper & Row.

30. For an interesting perspective on the role of context on the discovery and creation of opportunities, see Zahra, S. A. 2008. The virtuous cycle of discovery and creation of entrepreneurial opportunities. *Strategic Entrepreneurship Journal,* 2(3): 243–257.

31. Birkinshaw, J. 1997. Entrepreneurship in multinational corporations: The characteristics of subsidiary initiatives. *Strategic Management Journal,* 18(3): 207–229; and Kanter, R. M. 1985. *The change masters.* New York: Simon & Schuster.

32. Hansen, M. T., Chesbrough, H. W., Nohria, N., & Sull, D. 2000. Networked incubators: Hothouses of the new economy. *Harvard Business Review,* 78(5): 74–84.

33. Stein, T. 2002. Corporate venture investors are bailing out. *Red Herring,* December: 74–75.

34. For more on the importance of leadership in fostering a climate of entrepreneurship, see Ling, Y., Simsek, Z., Lubatkin, M. H., & Veiga, J. F. 2008. Transformational leadership's role in promoting corporate entrepreneurship: Examining the CEO-TMT interface. *Academy of Management Journal,* 51(3): 557–576.

35. Is your company up to speed? 2003. *Fast Company,* June: 86.

36. For an interesting discussion, see Davenport, T. H., Prusak, L., & Wilson, H. J. 2003. Who's bringing you hot ideas and how are you responding? *Harvard Business Review,* 80(1): 58–64.

37. Howell, J. M. 2005. The right stuff. Identifying and developing effective champions of innovation. *Academy of Management Executive,* 19(2): 108–119. See also Greene, P., Brush, C., & Hart, M. 1999. The corporate venture champion: A resource-based approach to role and process. *Entrepreneurship Theory & Practice,* 23(3): 103–122; and Markham, S. K. & Aiman-Smith, L. 2001. Product champions: Truths, myths and management. *Research Technology Management,* May–June: 44–50.

38. Burgelman, R. A. 1983. A process model of internal corporate venturing in the diversified major firm. *Administrative Science Quarterly,* 28: 223–244.

39. Hamel, G. 2000. *Leading the revolution.* Boston: Harvard Business School Press.

40. Greene, Brush, & Hart, op. cit.; and Shane, S. 1994. Are champions different from non-champions? *Journal of Business Venturing,* 9(5): 397–421.

41. Block, Z. & MacMillan, I. C. 1993. *Corporate venturing—Creating new businesses with the firm.* Cambridge, MA: Harvard Business School Press.

42. For an interesting discussion of these trade-offs, see Stringer, R. 2000. How to manage radical innovation. *California Management Review,* 42(4): 70–88; and Gompers, P. A. & Lerner, J. 1999. *The venture capital cycle.* Cambridge, MA: MIT Press.

43. Albrinck, J., Hornery, J., Kletter, D., & Neilson, G. 2001. Adventures in corporate venturing. *Strategy + Business,* 22: 119–129; and McGrath, R. G. & MacMillan, I. C. 2000. *The entrepreneurial mind-set.* Cambridge, MA: Harvard Business School Press.

44. For an interesting discussion of how different outcome goals affect organizational learning and employee motivation, see Seijts, G. H. & Latham, G. P. 2005. Learning versus performance goals: When should each be used? *Academy of Management Executive,* 19(1): 124–131.

45. Crockett, R. O. 2001. Motorola. *BusinessWeek,* July 15: 72–78.

46. The ideas in this section are drawn from Royer, I. 2003. Why bad projects are so hard to kill. *Harvard Business Review,* 80(1): 48–56.

47. For an interesting perspective on the different roles that individuals play in the entrepreneurial process, see Baron, R. A. 2008. The role of affect in the entrepreneurial process. *Academy of Management Review,* 33(2): 328–340.

48. Hoskin, R. E. 1994. *Financial accounting.* New York: Wiley.

49. We know stock options as derivative assets—that is, "an asset whose value depends on or is derived from the value of another, the underlying asset": Amram, M. & Kulatilaka, N. 1999. *Real options: Managing strategic*

investment in an uncertain world: 34. Boston: Harvard Business School Press.

50. For an interesting discussion on why it is difficult to "kill options," refer to Royer, I. 2003. Why bad projects are so hard to kill. *Harvard Business Review,* 81(2): 48–57.

51. Slywotzky, A. & Wise, R. 2003. Double-digit growth in no-growth times. *Fast Company,* April: 66–72; www.hoovers.com; and www.johnsoncontrols.com.

52. For more on the role of real options in entrepreneurial decision making, see Folta, T. B. & O'Brien, J. P. 2004. Entry in the presence of dueling options. *Strategic Management Journal,* 25: 121–138.

53. This section draws on Janney, J. J. & Dess, G. G. 2004. Can real options analysis improve decision-making? Promises and pitfalls. *Academy of Management Executive,* 18(4): 60–75. For additional insights on pitfalls of real options, consider McGrath, R. G. 1997. A real options logic for initiating technology positioning investment. *Academy of Management Review,* 22(4): 974–994; Coff, R. W. & Laverty, K. J. 2001. Real options on knowledge assets: Panacea or Pandora's box. *Business Horizons,* 73: 79, McGrath, R. G. 1999. Falling forward: Real options reasoning and entrepreneurial failure. *Academy of Management Review,* 24(1): 13–30; and, Zardkoohi, A. 2004.

54. For an understanding of the differences between how managers say they approach decisions and how they actually do, March and Shapira's discussion is perhaps the best. March, J. G. & Shapira, Z. 1987. Managerial perspectives on risk and risk-taking. *Management Science,* 33(11): 1404–1418.

55. A discussion of some factors that may lead to escalation in decision making is included in Choo, C. W. 2005. Information failures and organizational disasters. *MIT Sloan Management Review,* 46(3): 8–10.

56. For an interesting discussion of the use of real options analysis in the application of wireless communications, which helped to lower the potential for escalation, refer to McGrath, R. G., Ferrier, W. J., & Mendelow, A. L. 2004. Real options as engines of choice and heterogeneity. *Academy of Management Review,* 29(1): 86–101.

57. One very useful solution for reducing the effects of managerial conceit is to incorporate an "exit champion" into the decision process. Exit champions provide arguments for killing off the firm's commitment to a decision. For a very insightful discussion on exit champions, refer to Royer, I. 2003. Why bad projects are so hard to kill. *Harvard Business Review,* 81(2): 49–56.

58. For more on how entrepreneurial orientation influences organizational performance, see Wang, L. 2008. Entrepreneurial orientation, learning orientation, and firm performance. *Entrepreneurship Theory & Practice,* 32(4): 635–657; and Runyan, R., Droge, C., & Swinney, J. 2008. Entrepreneurial orientation versus small business orientation: What are their relationships to firm performance? *Journal of Small Business Management,* 46(4): 567–588.

59. Covin, J. G. & Slevin, D. P. 1991. A conceptual model of entrepreneurship as firm behavior. *Entrepreneurship Theory and Practice,* 16(1): 7–24; Lumpkin, G. T. & Dess, G. G. 1996. Clarifying the entrepreneurial orientation construct and linking it to performance. *Academy of Management Review,* 21(1): 135–172; and McGrath, R. G. & MacMillan, I. C. 2000. *The entrepreneurial mind-set.* Cambridge, MA: Harvard Business School Press.

60. Lumpkin, G. T. & Dess, G. G. 2001. Linking two dimensions of entrepreneurial orientation to firm performance: The moderating role of environment and life cycle. *Journal of Business Venturing,* 16: 429–451.

61. For an interesting discussion, see Day, J. D., Mang, P. Y., Richter, A., & Roberts, J. 2001. The innovative organization: Why new ventures need more than a room of their own, *McKinsey Quarterly,* 2: 21–31.

62. Crockett, R. O. 2001. Chris Galvin shakes things up—again. *BusinessWeek,* May 28: 38–39.

63. For insights into the role of information technology in innovativeness, see Dibrell, C., Davis, P. S., & Craig, J. 2008. Fueling innovation through information technology in SMEs. *Journal of Small Business Management,* 46(2): 203–218.

64. For an interesting discussion of the impact of innovativeness on organizational outcomes see Cho, H. J. & Pucik, V. 2005. Relationship between innovativeness, quality, growth, profitability, and market value. *Strategic Management Journal,* 26(6): 555–575.

65. Lieberman, M. B. & Montgomery, D. B. 1988. First mover advantages. *Strategic Management Journal,* 9 (Special Issue): 41–58.

66. The discussion of first mover advantages is based on several articles, including Lambkin, M. 1988. Order of entry and performance in new markets. *Strategic Management Journal,* 9: 127–140; Lieberman & Montgomery, op. cit.: 41–58; and Miller, A. & Camp, B. 1985. Exploring determinants of success in corporate ventures. *Journal of Business Venturing,* 1(2): 87–105.

67. Moore, G. A. 1999. *Crossing the chasm* (2nd ed.). New York: HarperBusiness.

68. Mallas, S. 2005. PepsiCo loses its Edge. *Motley Fool,* June 1, www.fool.com.

69. Lyons, D. 2006. The cheap revolution. *Forbes,* September 18: 102–111.

70. Miller, K. D. 2007. Risk and rationality in entrepreneurial processes. *Strategic Entrepreneurship Journal,* 1(1–2): 57–74.

71. Drucker, op. cit., pp. 109–110.

CHAPTER 13

Analyzing Strategic Management Cases

>learning objectives

After reading this chapter, you should have a good understanding of:

LO1 How strategic case analysis is used to simulate real-world experiences.

LO2 How analyzing strategic management cases can help develop the ability to differentiate, speculate, and integrate when evaluating complex business problems.

LO3 The steps involved in conducting a strategic management case analysis.

LO4 How to get the most out of case analysis.

LO5 How conflict-inducing discussion techniques can lead to better decisions.

LO6 How to use the strategic insights and material from each of the 12 previous chapters in the text to analyze issues posed by strategic management cases.

Case analysis is one of the most effective ways to learn strategic management. It provides a complement to other methods of instruction by asking you to use the tools and techniques of strategic management to deal with an actual business situation. Strategy cases include detailed descriptions of management challenges faced by executives and business owners. By studying the background and analyzing the strategic predicaments posed by a case, you first see that the circumstances businesses confront are often difficult and complex. Then you are asked what decisions you would make to address the situation in the case and how the actions you recommend will affect the company. Thus, the processes of analysis, formulation, and implementation that have been addressed by this textbook can be applied in a real-life situation.

In this chapter we will discuss the role of case analysis as a learning tool in both the classroom and the real world. One of the benefits of strategic case analysis is to develop the ability to differentiate, speculate, and integrate. We will also describe how to conduct a case analysis and address techniques for deriving the greatest benefit from the process, including the effective use of conflict-inducing decision techniques. Finally, we will discuss how case analysis in a classroom setting can enhance the process of analyzing, making decisions, and taking action in real-world strategic situations.

Why Analyze Strategic Management Cases?

>LO1

How strategic case analysis is used to simulate real-world experiences.

It is often said that the key to finding good answers is to ask good questions. Strategic managers and business leaders are required to evaluate options, make choices, and find solutions to the challenges they face every day. To do so, they must learn to ask the right questions. The study of strategic management poses the same challenge. The process of analyzing, decision making, and implementing strategic actions raises many good questions.

- Why do some firms succeed and others fail?
- Why are some companies higher performers than others?
- What information is needed in the strategic planning process?
- How do competing values and beliefs affect strategic decision making?
- What skills and capabilities are needed to implement a strategy effectively?

case analysis a method of learning complex strategic management concepts such as environmental analysis, the process of decision making, and implementing strategic actions through placing students in the middle of an actual situation and challenging them to figure out what to do.

How does a student of strategic management answer these questions? By strategic case analysis. **Case analysis** simulates the real-world experience that strategic managers and company leaders face as they try to determine how best to run their companies. It places students in the middle of an actual situation and challenges them to figure out what to do.[1]

Asking the right questions is just the beginning of case analysis. In the previous chapters we have discussed issues and challenges that managers face and provided analytical frameworks for understanding the situation. But once the analysis is complete, decisions have to be made. Case analysis forces you to choose among different options and set forth a plan of action based on your choices. But even then the job is not done. Strategic case analysis also requires that you address how you will implement the plan and the implications of choosing one course of action over another.

A strategic management case is a detailed description of a challenging situation faced by an organization.[2] It usually includes a chronology of events and extensive support materials, such as financial statements, product lists, and transcripts of interviews with employees. Although names or locations are sometimes changed to provide anonymity, cases usually report the facts of a situation as authentically as possible.

One of the main reasons to analyze strategic management cases is to develop an ability to evaluate business situations critically. In case analysis, memorizing key terms and conceptual frameworks is not enough. To analyze a case, it is important that you go beyond textbook prescriptions and quick answers. It requires you to look deeply into the information that is provided and root out the essential issues and causes of a company's problems.

>LO2

How analyzing strategic management cases can help develop the ability to differentiate, speculate, and integrate when evaluating complex business problems.

The types of skills that are required to prepare an effective strategic case analysis can benefit you in actual business situations. Case analysis adds to the overall learning experience by helping you acquire or improve skills that may not be taught in a typical lecture course. Three capabilities that can be learned by conducting case analysis are especially useful to strategic managers—the ability to differentiate, speculate, and integrate.[3] Here's how case analysis can enhance those skills.

1. **Differentiate.** Effective strategic management requires that many different elements of a situation be evaluated at once. This is also true in case analysis. When analyzing cases, it is important to isolate critical facts, evaluate whether assumptions are useful or faulty, and distinguish between good and bad information. Differentiating between the factors that are influencing the situation presented by a case is necessary for making a good analysis. Strategic management also involves understanding that problems are often complex and multilayered. This applies to case analysis as well. Ask whether the case deals with operational, business-level, or corporate issues. Do the problems stem from weaknesses in the internal value chain or threats in the external environment? Dig deep. Being too quick to accept the easiest or least controversial answer will usually fail to get to the heart of the problem.

2. **Speculate.** Strategic managers need to be able to use their imagination to envision an explanation or solution that might not readily be apparent. The same is true with case analysis. Being able to imagine different scenarios or contemplate the outcome of a decision can aid the analysis. Managers also have to deal with uncertainty since most decisions are made without complete knowledge of the circumstances. This is also true in case analysis. Case materials often seem to be missing data or the information provided is contradictory. The ability to speculate about details that are unknown or the consequences of an action can be helpful.

3. **Integrate.** Strategy involves looking at the big picture and having an organization-wide perspective. Strategic case analysis is no different. Even though the chapters in this textbook divide the material into various topics that may apply to different parts of an organization, all of this information must be integrated into one set of recommendations that will affect the whole company. A strategic manager needs to comprehend how all the factors that influence the organization will interact. This also applies to case analysis. Changes made in one part of the organization affect other parts. Thus, a holistic perspective that integrates the impact of various decisions and environmental influences on all parts of the organization is needed.

In business, these three activities sometimes "compete" with each other for your attention. For example, some decision makers may have a natural ability to differentiate among elements of a problem but are not able to integrate them very well. Others have enough innate creativity to imagine solutions or fill in the blanks when information is missing. But they may have a difficult time when faced with hard numbers or cold facts. Even so, each of these skills is important. The mark of a good strategic manager is the ability to simultaneously make distinctions and envision the whole, and to imagine a future scenario while staying focused on the present. Thus, another reason to conduct case analysis is to help you develop and exercise your ability to differentiate, speculate, and integrate.

Case analysis takes the student through the whole cycle of activity that a manager would face. Beyond the textbook descriptions of concepts and examples, case analysis asks you to "walk a mile in the shoes" of the strategic decision maker and learn to evaluate situations critically. Executives and owners must make decisions every day with limited information and a swirl of business activity going on around them. Consider the example of Sapient Health Networks, an Internet start-up that had to undergo some analysis and problem solving just to survive. Strategy Spotlight 13.1 describes how this company transformed itself after a serious self-examination during a time of crisis.

As you can see from the experience of Sapient Health Networks, businesses are often faced with immediate challenges that threaten their lives. The Sapient case illustrates how the strategic management process helped it survive. First, the company realistically assessed the environment, evaluated the marketplace, and analyzed its resources. Then it made tough decisions, which included shifting its market focus, hiring and firing, and redeploying its assets. Finally, it took action. The result was not only firm survival, but also a quick turnaround leading to rapid success.

How to Conduct a Case Analysis

>LO3
The steps involved in conducting a strategic management case analysis.

The process of analyzing strategic management cases involves several steps. In this section we will review the mechanics of preparing a case analysis. Before beginning, there are two things to keep in mind that will clarify your understanding of the process and make the results of the process more meaningful.

First, unless you prepare for a case discussion, there is little you can gain from the discussion and even less that you can offer. Effective strategic managers don't enter into problem-solving situations without doing some homework—investigating the situation,

Analysis, Decision Making, and Change at Sapient Health Network

Sapient Health Network (SHN) had gotten off to a good start. CEO Jim Kean and his two cofounders had raised $5 million in investor capital to launch their vision: an Internet-based health care information subscription service. The idea was to create an Internet community for people suffering from chronic diseases. It would provide members with expert information, resources, a message board, and chat rooms so that people suffering from the same ailments could provide each other with information and support. "Who would be more voracious consumers of information than people who are faced with life-changing, life-threatening illnesses?" thought Bill Kelly, one of SHN's cofounders. Initial market research and beta tests had supported that view.

During the beta tests, however, the service had been offered for free. The troubles began when SHN tried to convert its trial subscribers into paying ones. Fewer than 5 percent signed on, far less than the 15 percent the company had projected. Sapient hired a vice president of marketing who launched an aggressive promotion, but after three months of campaigning SHN still had only 500 members. SHN was now burning through $400,000 per month, with little revenue to show for it.

At that point, according to SHN board member Susan Clymer, "there was a lot of scrambling around trying to figure out how we could wring value out of what we'd

Sources: Ferguson, S. 2007. Health Care Gets a Better IT Prescription. *Baseline,* www.baselinemag.com, May 24. Brenneman, K. 2000. Healtheon/WebMD's Local Office Is Thriving. *Business Journal of Portland,* June 2; Raths, D. 1998. Reversal of Fortune. *Inc. Technology,* 2: 52–62.

already accomplished." One thing SHN had created was an expert software system which had two components: an "intelligent profile engine" (IPE) and an "intelligent query engine" (IQE). SHN used this system to collect detailed information from its subscribers.

SHN was sure that the expert system was its biggest selling point. But how could they use it? Then the founders remembered that the original business plan had suggested there might be a market for aggregate data about patient populations gathered from the website. Could they turn the business around by selling patient data? To analyze the possibility, Kean tried out the idea on the market research arm of a huge East Coast health care conglomerate. The officials were intrigued. SHN realized that its expert system could become a market research tool.

Once the analysis was completed, the founders made the decision: They would still create Internet communities for chronically ill patients, but the service would be free. And they would transform SHN from a company that processed subscriptions to one that sold market research.

Finally, they enacted the changes. Some of it was painful, including laying off 18 employees. Instead, SHN needed more health care industry expertise. It even hired an interim CEO, Craig Davenport, a 25-year veteran of the industry, to steer the company in its new direction. Finally, SHN had to communicate a new message to its members. It began by reimbursing the $10,000 of subscription fees they had paid.

All of this paid off dramatically in a matter of just two years. Revenues jumped to $1.9 million and early in the third year, SHN was purchased by WebMD. Less than a year after that, WebMD merged with Healtheon. The combined company still operates a thriving office out of SHN's original location in Portland, Oregon.

---

analyzing and researching possible solutions, and sometimes gathering the advice of others. Good problem solving often requires that decision makers be immersed in the facts, options, and implications surrounding the problem. In case analysis, this means reading and thoroughly comprehending the case materials before trying to make an analysis.

The second point is related to the first. To get the most out of a case analysis you must place yourself "inside" the case—that is, think like an actual participant in the case situation. However, there are several positions you can take. These are discussed in the following paragraphs:

- **Strategic decision maker.** This is the position of the senior executive responsible for resolving the situation described in the case. It may be the CEO, the business owner, or a strategic manager in a key executive position.
- **Board of directors.** Since the board of directors represents the owners of a corporation, it has a responsibility to step in when a management crisis threatens the company. As a board member, you may be in a unique position to solve problems.

- **Outside consultant.** Either the board or top management may decide to bring in outsiders. Consultants often have an advantage because they can look at a situation objectively. But they also may be at a disadvantage since they have no power to enforce changes.

Before beginning the analysis, it may be helpful to envision yourself assuming one of these roles. Then, as you study and analyze the case materials, you can make a diagnosis and recommend solutions in a way that is consistent with your position. Try different perspectives. You may find that your view of the situation changes depending on the role you play. As an outside consultant, for example, it may be easy for you to conclude that certain individuals should be replaced in order to solve a problem presented in the case. However, if you take the role of the CEO who knows the individuals and the challenges they have been facing, you may be reluctant to fire them and will seek another solution instead.

The idea of assuming a particular role is similar to the real world in various ways. In your career, you may work in an organization where outside accountants, bankers, lawyers, or other professionals are advising you about how to resolve business situations or improve your practices. Their perspective will be different from yours but it is useful to understand things from their point of view. Conversely, you may work as a member of the audit team of an accounting firm or the loan committee of a bank. In those situations, it would be helpful if you understood the situation from the perspective of the business leader who must weigh your views against all the other advice that he or she receives. Case analysis can help develop an ability to appreciate such multiple perspectives.

One of the most challenging roles to play in business is as a business founder or owner. For small businesses or entrepreneurial start-ups, the founder may wear all hats at once—key decision maker, primary stockholder, and CEO. Hiring an outside consultant may not be an option. However, the issues faced by young firms and established firms are often not that different, especially when it comes to formulating a plan of action. Business plans that entrepreneurial firms use to raise money or propose a business expansion typically revolve around a few key issues that must be addressed no matter what the size or age of the business. Strategy Spotlight 13.2 reviews business planning issues that are most important to consider when evaluating any case, especially from the perspective of the business founder or owner.

Next we will review five steps to follow when conducting a strategic management case analysis: becoming familiar with the material, identifying the problems, analyzing the strategic issues using the tools and insights of strategic management, proposing alternative solutions, and making recommendations.[4]

Become Familiar with the Material

Written cases often include a lot of material. They may be complex and include detailed financials or long passages. Even so, to understand a case and its implications, you must become familiar with its content. Sometimes key information is not immediately apparent. It may be contained in the footnotes to an exhibit or an interview with a lower-level employee. In other cases the important points may be difficult to grasp because the subject matter is so unfamiliar. When you approach a strategic case try the following technique to enhance comprehension:

- Read quickly through the case one time to get an overall sense of the material.
- Use the initial read-through to assess possible links to strategic concepts.
- Read through the case again, in depth. Make written notes as you read.
- Evaluate how strategic concepts might inform key decisions or suggest alternative solutions.
- After formulating an initial recommendation, thumb through the case again quickly to help assess the consequences of the actions you propose.

Using a Business Plan Framework to Analyze Strategic Cases

Established businesses often have to change what they are doing in order to improve their competitive position or sometimes simply to survive. To make the changes effectively, businesses usually need a plan. Business plans are no longer just for entrepreneurs. The kind of market analysis, decision making, and action planning that is considered standard practice among new ventures can also benefit going concerns that want to make changes, seize an opportunity, or head in a new direction.

The best business plans, however, are not those loaded with decades of month-by-month financial projections or that depend on rigid adherence to a schedule of events that is impossible to predict. The good ones are focused on four factors that are critical to new-venture success. These same factors are important in case analysis as well because they get to the heart of many of the problems found in strategic cases.

1. *The People.* "When I receive a business plan, I always read the résumé section first," says Harvard Professor William Sahlman. The people questions that are critically important to investors include: What are their skills? How much experience do they have? What is their reputation? Have they worked together as a team? These same questions also may be used in case analysis to evaluate the role of individuals in the strategic case.

2. *The Opportunity.* Business opportunities come in many forms. They are not limited to new ventures.

The chance to enter new markets, introduce new products, or merge with a competitor provides many of the challenges that are found in strategic management cases. What are the consequences of such actions? Will the proposed changes affect the firm's business concept? What factors might stand in the way of success? The same issues are also present in most strategic cases.

3. *The Context.* Things happen in contexts that cannot be controlled by a firm's managers. This is particularly true of the general environment where social trends, economic changes, or events such as the September 11, 2001, terrorist attacks can change business overnight. When evaluating strategic cases, ask: Is the company aware of the impact of context on the business? What will it do if the context changes? Can it influence the context in a way that favors the company?

4. *Risk and Reward.* With a new venture, the entrepreneurs and investors take the risks and get the rewards. In strategic cases, the risks and rewards often extend to many other stakeholders, such as employees, customers, and suppliers. When analyzing a case, ask: Are the managers making choices that will pay off in the future? Are the rewards evenly distributed? Will some stakeholders be put at risk if the situation in the case changes? What if the situation remains the same? Could that be even riskier?

Whether a business is growing or shrinking, large or small, industrial or service oriented, the issues of people, opportunities, context, and risks and rewards will have a large impact on its performance. Therefore, you should always consider these four factors when evaluating strategic management cases.

Sources: Wasserman, E. 2003. A Simple Plan. *MBA Jungle*, February: 50–55; DeKluyver, C. A. 2000. *Strategic Thinking: An Executive Perspective.* Upper Saddle River, NJ: Prentice Hall; and Sahlman, W. A. 1997. How to Write a Great Business Plan. *Harvard Business Review*, 75(4): 98–108.

Identify Problems

When conducting case analysis, one of your most important tasks is to identify the problem. Earlier we noted that one of the main reasons to conduct case analysis was to find solutions. But you cannot find a solution unless you know the problem. Another saying you may have heard is, "A good diagnosis is half the cure." In other words, once you have determined what the problem is, you are well on your way to identifying a reasonable solution.

Some cases have more than one problem. But the problems are usually related. For a hypothetical example, consider the following: Company A was losing customers to a new competitor. Upon analysis, it was determined that the competitor had a 50 percent faster delivery time even though its product was of lower quality. The managers of company A could not understand why customers would settle for an inferior product. It turns out that no one was marketing to company A's customers that its product was superior. A second problem was that falling sales resulted in cuts in company A's sales force. Thus, there were two related problems: inferior delivery technology and insufficient sales effort.

When trying to determine the problem, avoid getting hung up on symptoms. Zero in on the problem. For example, in the company A example above, the symptom was losing customers. But the problems were an underfunded, understaffed sales force combined with an outdated delivery technology. Try to see beyond the immediate symptoms to the more fundamental problems.

Another tip when preparing a case analysis is to articulate the problem.[5] Writing down a problem statement gives you a reference point to turn to as you proceed through the case analysis. This is important because the process of formulating strategies or evaluating implementation methods may lead you away from the initial problem. Make sure your recommendation actually addresses the problems you have identified.

One more thing about identifying problems: Sometimes problems are not apparent until *after* you do the analysis. In some cases the problem will be presented plainly, perhaps in the opening paragraph or on the last page of the case. But in other cases the problem does not emerge until after the issues in the case have been analyzed. We turn next to the subject of strategic case analysis.

Conduct Strategic Analyses

This textbook has presented numerous analytical tools (e.g., five-forces analysis and value-chain analysis), contingency frameworks (e.g., when to use related rather than unrelated diversification strategies), and other techniques that can be used to evaluate strategic situations. The previous 12 chapters have addressed practices that are common in strategic management, but only so much can be learned by studying the practices and concepts. The best way to understand these methods is to apply them by conducting analyses of specific cases.

The first step is to determine which strategic issues are involved. Is there a problem in the company's competitive environment? Or is it an internal problem? If it is internal, does it have to do with organizational structure? Strategic controls? Uses of technology? Or perhaps the company has overworked its employees or underutilized its intellectual capital. Has the company mishandled a merger? Chosen the wrong diversification strategy? Botched a new product introduction? Each of these issues is linked to one or more of the concepts discussed earlier in the text. Determine what strategic issues are associated with the problems you have identified. Remember also that most real-life case situations involve issues that are highly interrelated. Even in cases where there is only one major problem, the strategic processes required to solve it may involve several parts of the organization.

Once you have identified the issues that apply to the case, conduct the analysis. For example, you may need to conduct a five-forces analysis or dissect the company's competitive strategy. Perhaps you need to evaluate whether its resources are rare, valuable, difficult to imitate, or difficult to substitute. Financial analysis may be needed to assess the company's economic prospects. Perhaps the international entry mode needs to be reevaluated because of changing conditions in the host country. Employee empowerment techniques may need to be improved to enhance organizational learning. Whatever the case, all the strategic concepts introduced in the text include insights for assessing their effectiveness. Determining how well a company is doing these things is central to the case analysis process.

Financial ratio analysis is one of the primary tools used to conduct case analysis. Appendix 1 to Chapter 13 includes a discussion and examples of the financial ratios that are often used to evaluate a company's performance and financial well-being. Exhibit 13.1 provides a summary of the financial ratios presented in Appendix 1 to this chapter.

In this part of the overall strategic analysis process, it is also important to test your own assumptions about the case.[6] First, what assumptions are you making about the case

financial ratio analysis a method of evaluating a company's performance and financial well-being through ratios of accounting values, including short-term solvency, long-term solvency, asset utilization, profitability, and market value ratios.

Exhibit 13.1   Summary of Financial Ratio Analysis Techniques

Ratio	What It Measures
Short-term solvency, or liquidity, ratios:	
Current ratio	Ability to use assets to pay off liabilities.
Quick ratio	Ability to use liquid assets to pay off liabilities quickly.
Cash ratio	Ability to pay off liabilities with cash on hand.
Long-term solvency, or financial leverage, ratios:	
Total debt ratio	How much of a company's total assets are financed by debt.
Debt-equity ratio	Compares how much a company is financed by debt with how much it is financed by equity.
Equity multiplier	How much debt is being used to finance assets.
Times interest earned ratio	How well a company has its interest obligations covered.
Cash coverage ratio	A company's ability to generate cash from operations.
Asset utilization, or turnover, ratios:	
Inventory turnover	How many times each year a company sells its entire inventory.
Days' sales in inventory	How many days on average inventory is on hand before it is sold.
Receivables turnover	How frequently each year a company collects on its credit sales.
Days' sales in receivables	How many days on average it takes to collect on credit sales (average collection period).
Total asset turnover	How much of sales is generated for every dollar in assets.
Capital intensity	The dollar investment in assets needed to generate $1 in sales.
Profitability ratios:	
Profit margin	How much profit is generated by every dollar of sales.
Return on assets (ROA)	How effectively assets are being used to generate a return.
Return on equity (ROE)	How effectively amounts invested in the business by its owners are being used to generate a return.
Market value ratios:	
Price–earnings ratio	How much investors are willing to pay per dollar of current earnings.
Market-to-book ratio	Compares market value of the company's investments to the cost of those investments.

materials? It may be that you have interpreted the case content differently than your team members or classmates. Being clear about these assumptions will be important in determining how to analyze the case. Second, what assumptions have you made about the best way to resolve the problems? Ask yourself why you have chosen one type of analysis over another. This process of assumption checking can also help determine if you have gotten to the heart of the problem or are still just dealing with symptoms.

As mentioned earlier, sometimes the critical diagnosis in a case can only be made after the analysis is conducted. However, by the end of this stage in the process, you should know the problems and have completed a thorough analysis of them. You can now move to the next step: finding solutions.

Propose Alternative Solutions

It is important to remember that in strategic management case analysis, there is rarely one right answer or one best way. Even when members of a class or a team agree on what the problem is, they may not agree upon how to solve the problem. Therefore, it is helpful to consider several different solutions.

After conducting strategic analysis and identifying the problem, develop a list of options. What are the possible solutions? What are the alternatives? First, generate a list of all the options you can think of without prejudging any one of them. Remember that not all cases call for dramatic decisions or sweeping changes. Some companies just need to make small adjustments. In fact, "Do nothing" may be a reasonable alternative in some cases. Although that is rare, it might be useful to consider what will happen if the company does nothing. This point illustrates the purpose of developing alternatives: to evaluate what will happen if a company chooses one solution over another.

Thus, during this step of a case analysis, you will evaluate choices and the implications of those choices. One aspect of any business that is likely to be highlighted in this part of the analysis is strategy implementation. Ask how the choices made will be implemented. It may be that what seems like an obvious choice for solving a problem creates an even bigger problem when implemented. But remember also that no strategy or strategic "fix" is going to work if it cannot be implemented. Once a list of alternatives is generated, ask:

- Can the company afford it? How will it affect the bottom line?
- Is the solution likely to evoke a competitive response?
- Will employees throughout the company accept the changes? What impact will the solution have on morale?
- How will the decision affect other stakeholders? Will customers, suppliers, and others buy into it?
- How does this solution fit with the company's vision, mission, and objectives?
- Will the culture or values of the company be changed by the solution? Is it a positive change?

The point of this step in the case analysis process is to find a solution that both solves the problem and is realistic. A consideration of the implications of various alternative solutions will generally lead you to a final recommendation that is more thoughtful and complete.

Make Recommendations

The basic aim of case analysis is to find solutions. Your analysis is not complete until you have recommended a course of action. In this step the task is to make a set of recommendations that your analysis supports. Describe exactly what needs to be done. Explain why this course of action will solve the problem. The recommendation should also include suggestions for how best to implement the proposed solution because the recommended actions and their implications for the performance and future of the firm are interrelated.

Recall that the solution you propose must solve the problem you identified. This point cannot be overemphasized; too often students make recommendations that treat only symptoms or fail to tackle the central problems in the case. Make a logical argument that shows how the problem led to the analysis and the analysis led to the recommendations you are proposing. Remember, an analysis is not an end in itself; it is useful only if it leads to a solution.

The actions you propose should describe the very next steps that the company needs to take. Don't say, for example, "If the company does more market research, then I would recommend the following course of action. . . ." Instead, make conducting the research part of your recommendation. Taking the example a step further, if you also want to suggest subsequent actions that may be different *depending* on the outcome of the market research, that's OK. But don't make your initial recommendation conditional on actions the company may or may not take.

In summary, case analysis can be a very rewarding process but, as you might imagine, it can also be frustrating and challenging. If you will follow the steps described above, you will address the different elements of a thorough analysis. This approach can give your analysis a solid footing. Then, even if there are differences of opinion about how to interpret the facts, analyze the situation, or solve the problems, you can feel confident that you have not missed any important steps in finding the best course of action.

Students are often asked to prepare oral presentations of the information in a case and their analysis of the best remedies. This is frequently assigned as a group project. Or you may be called upon in class to present your ideas about the circumstances or solutions for a case the class is discussing. Exhibit 13.2 provides some tips for preparing an oral case presentation.

Exhibit 13.2 **Preparing an Oral Case Presentation**

Rule	Description
Organize your thoughts.	Begin by becoming familiar with the material. If you are working with a team, compare notes about the key points of the case and share insights that other team members may have gleaned from tables and exhibits. Then make an outline. This is one of the best ways to organize the flow and content of the presentation.
Emphasize strategic analysis.	The purpose of case analysis is to diagnose problems and find solutions. In the process, you may need to unravel the case material as presented and reconfigure it in a fashion that can be more effectively analyzed. Present the material in a way that lends itself to analysis—don't simply restate what is in the case. This involves three major categories with the following emphasis: Background/Problem Statement 10–20% Strategic Analysis/Options 60–75% Recommendations/Action Plan 10–20% As you can see, the emphasis of your presentation should be on analysis. This will probably require you to reorganize the material so that the tools of strategic analysis can be applied.
Be logical and consistent.	A presentation that is rambling and hard to follow may confuse the listener and fail to evoke a good discussion. Present your arguments and explanations in a logical sequence. Support your claims with facts. Include financial analysis where appropriate. Be sure that the solutions you recommend address the problems you have identified.
Defend your position.	Usually an oral presentation is followed by a class discussion. Anticipate what others might disagree with and be prepared to defend your views. This means being aware of the choices you made and the implications of your recommendations. Be clear about your assumptions. Be able to expand on your analysis.
Share presentation responsibilities.	Strategic management case analyses are often conducted by teams. Each member of the team should have a clear role in the oral presentation, preferably a speaking role. It's also important to coordinate the different parts of the presentation into a logical, smooth-flowing whole. How well a team works together is usually very apparent during an oral presentation.

How to Get the Most from Case Analysis

One of the reasons case analysis is so enriching as a learning tool is that it draws on many resources and skills besides just what is in the textbook. This is especially true in the study of strategy. Why? Because strategic management itself is a highly integrative task that draws on many areas of specialization at several levels, from the individual to the whole of society. Therefore, to get the most out of case analysis, expand your horizons beyond the concepts in this text and seek insights from your own reservoir of knowledge. Here are some tips for how to do that.[7]

>LO4

How to get the most out of case analysis.

- **Keep an open mind.** Like any good discussion, a case analysis discussion often evokes strong opinions and high emotions. But it's the variety of perspectives that makes case analysis so valuable: Many viewpoints usually lead to a more complete analysis. Therefore, avoid letting an emotional response to another person's style or opinion keep you from hearing what he or she has to say. Once you evaluate what is said, you may disagree with it or dismiss it as faulty. But unless you keep an open mind in the first place, you may miss the importance of the other person's contribution. Also, people often place a higher value on the opinions of those they consider to be good listeners.

- **Take a stand for what you believe.** Although it is vital to keep an open mind, it is also important to state your views proactively. Don't try to figure out what your friends or the instructor wants to hear. Analyze the case from the perspective of your own background and belief system. For example, perhaps you feel that a decision is unethical or that the managers in a case have misinterpreted the facts. Don't be afraid to assert that in the discussion. For one thing, when a person takes a strong stand, it often encourages others to evaluate the issues more closely. This can lead to a more thorough investigation and a more meaningful class discussion.

- **Draw on your personal experience.** You may have experiences from work or as a customer that shed light on some of the issues in a case. Even though one of the purposes of case analysis is to apply the analytical tools from this text, you may be able to add to the discussion by drawing on your outside experiences and background. Of course, you need to guard against carrying that to extremes. In other words, don't think that your perspective is the only viewpoint that matters! Simply recognize that firsthand experience usually represents a welcome contribution to the overall quality of case discussions.

- **Participate and persuade.** Have you heard the phrase, "Vote early . . . and often"? Among loyal members of certain political parties, it has become rather a joke. Why? Because a democratic system is built on the concept of one person, one vote. Even though some voters may want to vote often enough to get their candidate elected, it is against the law. Not so in a case discussion. People who are persuasive and speak their mind can often influence the views of others. But to do so, you have to be prepared and convincing. Being persuasive is more than being loud or long-winded. It involves understanding all sides of an argument and being able to overcome objections to your own point of view. These efforts can make a case discussion more lively. And they parallel what happens in the real world; in business, people frequently share their opinions and attempt to persuade others to see things their way.

- **Be concise and to the point.** In the previous point, we encouraged you to speak up and "sell" your ideas to others in a case discussion. But you must be clear about what you are selling. Make your arguments in a way that is explicit and direct. Zero in on the most important points. Be brief. Don't try to make a lot of points at once by jumping around between topics. Avoid trying to explain the whole case situation at once. Remember, other students usually resent classmates who go on and on, take up a lot of "airtime," or repeat themselves unnecessarily. The best way to avoid this is to stay focused and be specific.

- *Think out of the box.* It's OK to be a little provocative; sometimes that is the consequence of taking a stand on issues. But it may be equally important to be imaginative and creative when making a recommendation or determining how to implement a solution. Albert Einstein once stated, "Imagination is more important than knowledge." The reason is that managing strategically requires more than memorizing concepts. Strategic management insights must be applied to each case differently—just knowing the principles is not enough. Imagination and out-of-the-box thinking help to apply strategic knowledge in novel and unique ways.

- *Learn from the insights of others.* Before you make up your mind about a case, hear what other students have to say. Get a second opinion, and a third, and so forth. Of course, in a situation where you have to put your analysis in writing, you may not be able to learn from others ahead of time. But in a case discussion, observe how various students attack the issues and engage in problem solving. Such observation skills also may be a key to finding answers within the case. For example, people tend to believe authority figures, so they would place a higher value on what a company president says. In some cases, however, the statements of middle managers may represent a point of view that is even more helpful for finding a solution to the problems presented by the case.

- *Apply insights from other case analyses.* Throughout the text, we have used examples of actual businesses to illustrate strategy concepts. The aim has been to show you how firms think about and deal with business problems. During the course, you may be asked to conduct several case analyses as part of the learning experience. Once you have performed a few case analyses, you will see how the concepts from the text apply in real-life business situations. Incorporate the insights learned from the text examples and your own previous case discussions into each new case that you analyze.

- *Critically analyze your own performance.* Performance appraisals are a standard part of many workplace situations. They are used to determine promotions, raises, and work assignments. In some organizations, everyone from the top executive down is subject to such reviews. Even in situations where the owner or CEO is not evaluated by others, they often find it useful to ask themselves regularly, Am I being effective? The same can be applied to your performance in a case analysis situation. Ask yourself, Were my comments insightful? Did I make a good contribution? How might I improve next time? Use the same criteria on yourself that you use to evaluate others. What grade would you give yourself? This technique will not only make you more fair in your assessment of others but also will indicate how your own performance can improve.

- *Conduct outside research.* Many times, you can enhance your understanding of a case situation by investigating sources outside the case materials. For example, you may want to study an industry more closely or research a company's close competitors. Recent moves such as mergers and acquisitions or product introductions may be reported in the business press. The company itself may provide useful information on its website or in its annual reports. Such information can usually spur additional discussion and enrich the case analysis. (*Caution:* It is best to check with your instructor in advance to be sure this kind of additional research is encouraged. Bringing in outside research may conflict with the instructor's learning objectives.)

Several of the points suggested above for how to get the most out of case analysis apply only to an open discussion of a case, like that in a classroom setting. Exhibit 13.3 provides some additional guidelines for preparing a written case analysis.

Exhibit 13.3   Preparing a Written Case Analysis

Rule	Description
Be thorough.	Many of the ideas presented in Exhibit 13.2 about oral presentations also apply to written case analysis. However, a written analysis typically has to be more complete. This means writing out the problem statement and articulating assumptions. It is also important to provide support for your arguments and reference case materials or other facts more specifically.
Coordinate team efforts.	Written cases are often prepared by small groups. Within a group, just as in a class discussion, you may disagree about the diagnosis or the recommended plan of action. This can be healthy if it leads to a richer understanding of the case material. But before committing your ideas to writing, make sure you have coordinated your responses. Don't prepare a written analysis that appears contradictory or looks like a patchwork of disconnected thoughts.
Avoid restating the obvious.	There is no reason to restate material that everyone is familiar with already, namely, the case content. It is too easy for students to use up space in a written analysis with a recapitulation of the details of the case—this accomplishes very little. Stay focused on the key points. Only restate the information that is most central to your analysis.
Present information graphically.	Tables, graphs, and other exhibits are usually one of the best ways to present factual material that supports your arguments. For example, financial calculations such as break-even analysis, sensitivity analysis, or return on investment are best presented graphically. Even qualitative information such as product lists or rosters of employees can be summarized effectively and viewed quickly by using a table or graph.
Exercise quality control.	When presenting a case analysis in writing, it is especially important to use good grammar, avoid misspelling words, and eliminate typos and other visual distractions. Mistakes that can be glossed over in an oral presentation or class discussion are often highlighted when they appear in writing. Make your written presentation appear as professional as possible. Don't let the appearance of your written case keep the reader from recognizing the importance and quality of your analysis.

Using Conflict-Inducing Decision-Making Techniques in Case Analysis

Next we address some techniques often used to improve case analyses that involve the constructive use of conflict. In the classroom—as well as in the business world—you will frequently be analyzing cases or solving problems in groups. While the word *conflict* often has a negative connotation (e.g., rude behavior, personal affronts), it can be very helpful in arriving at better solutions to cases. It can provide an effective means for new insights as well as for rigorously questioning and analyzing assumptions and strategic alternatives. In fact, if you don't have constructive conflict, you may only get consensus. When this happens, decisions tend to be based on compromise rather than collaboration.

In your organizational behavior classes, you probably learned the concept of "group-think."[8] Groupthink, a term coined by Irving Janis after he conducted numerous studies on executive decision making, is a condition in which group members strive to reach agreement or consensus without realistically considering other viable

> **>LO5**
> How conflict-inducing discussion techniques can lead to better decisions.

Relying on "Rivals" to Stimulate Debate

When Barack Obama was elected U.S. President, he had to move quickly to select a group of reliable advisors and form a cabinet. During the presidential campaign, Obama let it be known that he was a student of Abraham Lincoln, one of his favorite former presidents. He also reported he had been reading Doris Kearns Goodwin's 2005 book *Team of Rivals,* which described Lincoln's decision to surround himself in part with politicians who were known to hold sharply different political views than his own.

Obama, who had fought a difficult primary battle with Senator Hillary Clinton of New York, created mild shock waves when he announced he would nominate her to be secretary of state. His decision, he said, was based in part on his team-of-rivals perspective—that independent and well-informed voices are needed to make the best decisions. At the press conference announcing his national security team, including Clinton, here is how Obama answered questions from the press:

> REPORTER: You've selected a number of high profile people for your national security team. How can you ensure that the staff that you are assembling is going to be a smoothly functioning team of rivals and not a clash of rivals?

Sources: Obama's National Security team announcement. Transcript published at www.nytimes.com, December 1; and Parsons, C. 2008. Obama hopes to appoint a "team of rivals." www.chicagotribune.com, November 15.

> OBAMA: I assembled this team because I'm a strong believer in strong personalities and strong opinions. I think that's how the best decisions are made. One of the dangers in the White House, based on my reading of history, is that you get wrapped up in groupthink and everybody agrees with everything and there's no discussion and there are no dissenting views. So I'm going to be welcoming vigorous debate inside the White House.

> But understand I will be setting policy as president. I will be responsible for the vision that this team carries out, and I expect them to implement the vision once decisions are made... You know, most of the people who are standing here are people who I've worked with, and on the broad core vision of where America needs to go, we are in almost complete agreement. There are going to be differences in tactics and different assessments and judgments made. That's what I expect. That's what I welcome. That's why I asked them to join the team.

Good decision making often requires dissenting voices and the expression of strong opinions. While conflict in discussion groups may be momentarily unpleasant, if it leads to high-quality decisions, everyone usually benefits in the long run.

alternatives. In effect, group norms bolster morale at the expense of critical thinking and decision making is impaired.[9] Strategy Spotlight 13.3 discusses a recent highly publicized decision to avoid groupthink by giving voice to thought leaders who were known to disagree.

Many of us have probably been "victims" of groupthink at one time or another in our life. We may be confronted with situations when social pressure, politics, or "not wanting to stand out" may prevent us from voicing our concerns about a chosen course of action. Nevertheless, decision making in groups is a common practice in the management of many businesses. Most companies, especially large ones, rely on input from various top managers to provide valuable information and experience from their specialty area as well as their unique perspectives. Chapter 11 emphasized the importance of empowering individuals at all levels to participate in decision-making processes. In terms of this course, case analysis involves a type of decision making that is often conducted in groups. Strategy Spotlight 13.4 provides guidelines for making team-based approaches to case analysis more effective.

Making Case Analysis Teams More Effective

Working in teams can be very challenging. Not all team members have the same skills, interests, or motivations. Some team members just want to get the work done. Others see teams as an opportunity to socialize. Occasionally, there are team members who think they should be in charge and make all the decisions; other teams have freeloaders—team members who don't want to do anything except get credit for the team's work.

One consequence of these various styles is that team meetings can become time wasters. Disagreements about how to proceed, how to share the work, or what to do at the next meeting tend to slow down teams and impede progress toward the goal. While the dynamics of case analysis teams are likely to always be challenging depending on the personalities involved, one thing nearly all members realize is that, ultimately, the team's work must be completed. Most team members also aim to do the highest quality work possible. The following guidelines provide some useful insights about how to get the work of a team done more effectively.

Spend More Time Together

One of the factors that prevents teams from doing a good job with case analysis is their failure to put in the necessary time. Unless teams really tackle the issues surrounding case analysis—both the issues in the case itself and organizing how the work is to be conducted—the end result will probably be lacking because decisions that are made too quickly are unlikely to get to the heart of the problem(s) in the case. "Meetings should be a precious resource, but they're treated like a necessary evil," says Kenneth Sole, a consultant who specializes in organizational behavior. As a result, teams that care more about finishing the analysis than getting the analysis right often make poor decisions.

Therefore, expect to have a few meetings that run long, especially at the beginning of the project when the work is being organized and the issues in the case are being sorted out, and again at the end when the team must coordinate the components of the case analysis that will be presented. Without spending this kind of time together, it is doubtful that the analysis will be comprehensive and the presentation is likely to be choppy and incomplete.

Make a Focused and Disciplined Agenda

To complete tasks and avoid wasting time, meetings need to have a clear purpose. To accomplish this at Roche,

the Swiss drug and diagnostic product maker, CEO Franz Humer implemented a "decision agenda." The agenda focuses only on Roche's highest value issues and discussions are limited to these major topics. In terms of case analysis, the major topics include sorting out the issues of the case, linking elements of the case to the strategic issues presented in class or the text, and assigning roles to various team members. Such objectives help keep team members on track.

Agendas also can be used to address issues such as the time line for accomplishing work. Otherwise the purpose of meetings may only be to manage the "crisis" of getting the case analysis finished on time. One solution is to assign a team member to manage the agenda. That person could make sure the team stays focused on the tasks at hand and remains mindful of time constraints. Another role could be to link the team's efforts to the steps presented in Exhibits 13.2 and Exhibit 13.3 on how to prepare a case analysis.

Pay More Attention to Strategy

Teams often waste time by focusing on unimportant aspects of a case. These may include details that are interesting but irrelevant or operational issues rather than strategic issues. It is true that useful clues to the issues in the case are sometimes embedded in the conversations of key managers or the trends evident in a financial statement. But once such insights are discovered, teams need to focus on the underlying strategic problems in the case. To solve such problems, major corporations such as Cadbury Schweppes and Boeing hold meetings just to generate strategic alternatives for solving their problems. This gives managers time to consider the implications of various courses of action. Separate meetings are held to evaluate alternatives, make strategic decisions, and approve an action plan.

Once the strategic solutions or "course corrections" are identified—as is common in most cases assigned—the operational implications and details of implementation will flow from the strategic decisions that companies make. Therefore, focusing primarily on strategic issues will provide teams with insights for making recommendations that are based on a deeper understanding of the issues in the case.

Produce Real Decisions

Too often, meetings are about discussing rather than deciding. Teams often spend a lot of time talking without reaching any conclusions. As Raymond Sanchez, *(continued)*

(continued) CEO of Florida-based Security Mortgage Group, says, meetings are often used to "rehash the hash that's already been hashed." To be efficient and productive, team meetings need to be about more than just information sharing and group input. For example, an initial meeting may result in the team realizing that it needs to study the case in greater depth and examine links to strategic issues more carefully. Once more analysis is conducted, the team needs to reach a consensus so that the decisions that are made will last once the meeting is over. Lasting decisions are more actionable because it frees team members to take the next steps.

One technique for making progress in this way is recapping each meeting with a five-minute synthesis report.

Sources: Mankins, M. C. 2004. Stop Wasting Valuable Time. *Harvard Business Review,* September: 58–65; and Sauer, P. J. 2004. Escape from Meeting Hell. *Inc. Magazine,* May, www.inc.com.

According to Pamela Schindler, director of the Center for Applied Management at Wittenberg University, it's important to think through the implications of the meeting before ending it. "The real joy of synthesis," says Schindler, "is realizing how many meetings you won't need."

Not only are these guidelines useful for helping teams finish their work, but they can also help resolve some of the difficulties that teams often face. By involving every team member, using a meeting agenda, and focusing on the strategic issues that are critical to nearly every case, the discussion is limited and the criteria for making decisions become clearer. This allows the task to dominate rather than any one personality. And if the team finishes its work faster, this frees up time to focus on other projects or put the finishing touches on a case analysis presentation.

● Effectively working in teams is a critical skill—both in the classroom and in business organizations.

Clearly, understanding how to work in groups and the potential problems associated with group decision processes can benefit the case analysis process. Therefore, let's first look at some of the symptoms of groupthink and suggest ways of preventing it. Then, we will suggest some conflict-inducing decision-making techniques—devil's advocacy and dialectical inquiry—that can help to prevent groupthink and lead to better decisions.

Symptoms of Groupthink and How to Prevent It

Irving Janis identified several symptoms of groupthink, including:

- *An illusion of invulnerability.* This reassures people about possible dangers and leads to overoptimism and failure to heed warnings of danger.
- *A belief in the inherent morality of the group.* Because individuals think that what they are doing is right, they tend to ignore ethical or moral consequences of their decisions.
- *Stereotyped views of members of opposing groups.* Members of other groups are viewed as weak or not intelligent.
- *The application of pressure to members who express doubts about the group's shared illusions or question the validity of arguments proposed.*
- *The practice of self-censorship.* Members keep silent about their opposing views and downplay to themselves the value of their perspectives.
- *An illusion of unanimity.* People assume that judgments expressed by members are shared by all.
- *The appointment of mindguards.* People sometimes appoint themselves as mindguards to protect the group from adverse information that might break the climate of consensus (or agreement).

Clearly, groupthink is an undesirable and negative phenomenon that can lead to poor decisions. Irving Janis considers it to be a key contributor to such faulty decisions as the failure to prepare for the attack on Pearl Harbor, the escalation of the Vietnam conflict, and the failure to prepare for the consequences of the Iraqi invasion. Many of the same sorts of flawed decision making occur in business organizations—as we discussed above with the EDS example. Janis has provided several suggestions for preventing groupthink that can be used as valuable guides in decision making and problem solving:

- Leaders must encourage group members to address their concerns and objectives.
- When higher-level managers assign a problem for a group to solve, they should adopt an impartial stance and not mention their preferences.
- Before a group reaches its final decision, the leader should encourage members to discuss their deliberations with trusted associates and then report the perspectives back to the group.
- The group should invite outside experts and encourage them to challenge the group's viewpoints and positions.
- The group should divide into subgroups, meet at various times under different chairpersons, and then get together to resolve differences.
- After reaching a preliminary agreement, the group should hold a "second chance" meeting which provides members a forum to express any remaining concerns and rethink the issue prior to making a final decision.

devil's advocacy
a method of introducing conflict into a decision-making process by having specific individuals or groups act as a critic to an analysis or planned solution.

Using Conflict to Improve Decision Making

In addition to the above suggestions, the effective use of conflict can be a means of improving decision making. Although conflict can have negative outcomes, such as ill will, anger, tension, and lowered motivation, both leaders and group members must strive to assure that it is managed properly and used in a constructive manner.

Two conflict-inducing decision-making approaches that have become quite popular are *devil's advocacy* and *dialectical inquiry*. Both approaches incorporate conflict into the decision-making process through formalized debate. A group charged with making a decision or solving a problem is divided into two subgroups and each will be involved in the analysis and solution.

Devil's Advocacy   With the devil's advocate approach, one of the groups (or individuals) acts as a critic to the plan. The devil's advocate tries to come up with problems with the proposed alternative and suggest reasons why it should not be adopted. The role of the devil's advocate is to create dissonance. This ensures that the group will take a hard look at its original proposal or alternative. By having a group (or individual) assigned the role of devil's advocate, it becomes clear that such an adversarial stance is legitimized. It brings out criticisms that might otherwise not be made.

Some authors have suggested that the use of a devil's advocate can be very helpful in helping boards of directors to ensure that decisions are addressed comprehensively and to avoid groupthink.[10] And Charles Elson, a director of Sunbeam Corporation, has argued that:

● Conflict-inducing decision-making techniques, such as devil's advocacy, can be very effective.

> Devil's advocates are terrific in any situation because they help you to figure a decision's numerous implications. . . . The better you think out the implications prior to making the decision, the better the decision ultimately turns out to be. That's why a devil's advocate is always a great person, irritating sometimes, but a great person.

As one might expect, there can be some potential problems with using the devil's advocate approach. If one's views are constantly criticized, one may become demoralized. Thus, that person may come up with "safe solutions" in order to minimize embarrassment or personal risk and become less subject to criticism. Additionally, even if the devil's advocate is successful with finding problems with the proposed course of action, there may be no new ideas or counterproposals to take its place. Thus, the approach sometimes may simply focus on what is wrong without suggesting other ideas.

dialectical inquiry
a method of introducing conflict into a decision-making process by devising different proposals that are feasible, politically viable, and credible, but rely on different assumptions; and debating the merits of each.

Dialectical Inquiry   Dialectical inquiry attempts to accomplish the goals of the devil's advocate in a more constructive manner. It is a technique whereby a problem is approached from two alternative points of view. The idea is that out of a critique of the opposing perspectives—a thesis and an antithesis—a creative synthesis will occur. Dialectical inquiry involves the following steps:

1. Identify a proposal and the information that was used to derive it.
2. State the underlying assumptions of the proposal.
3. Identify a counterplan (antithesis) that is believed to be feasible, politically viable, and generally credible. However, it rests on assumptions that are opposite to the original proposal.
4. Engage in a debate in which individuals favoring each plan provide their arguments and support.
5. Identify a synthesis which, hopefully, includes the best components of each alternative.

There are some potential downsides associated with dialectical inquiry. It can be quite time consuming and involve a good deal of training. Further, it may result in a series of compromises between the initial proposal and the counterplan. In cases where the original proposal was the best approach, this would be unfortunate.

Despite some possible limitations associated with these conflict-inducing decision-making techniques, they have many benefits. Both techniques force debate about underlying assumptions, data, and recommendations between subgroups. Such debate tends to prevent the uncritical acceptance of a plan that may seem to be satisfactory after a cursory analysis. The approach serves to tap the knowledge and perspectives of group members and continues until group members agree on both assumptions and recommended actions. Given that both approaches serve to use, rather than minimize or suppress, conflict, higher quality decisions should result. Exhibit 13.4 briefly summarizes these techniques.

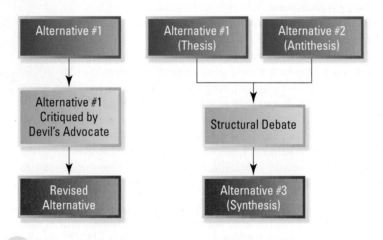

Exhibit 13.4 Two Conflict-Inducing Decision-Making Processes

Following the Analysis-Decision-Action Cycle in Case Analysis

In Chapter 1 we defined strategic management as the analysis, decisions, and actions that organizations undertake to create and sustain competitive advantages. It is no accident that we chose that sequence of words because it corresponds to the sequence of events that typically occurs in the strategic management process. In case analysis, as in the real world, this cycle of events can provide a useful framework. First, an analysis of the case in terms of the business environment and current events is needed. To make such an analysis, the case background must be considered. Next, based on that analysis, decisions must be made. This may involve formulating a strategy, choosing between difficult options, moving forward aggressively, or retreating from a bad situation. There are many possible decisions, depending on the case situation. Finally, action is required. Once decisions are made and plans are set, the action begins. The recommended action steps and the consequences of implementing these actions are the final stage.

Each of the previous 12 chapters of this book includes techniques and information that may be useful in a case analysis. However, not all of the issues presented will be important in every case. As noted earlier, one of the challenges of case analysis is to identify the most critical points and sort through material that may be ambiguous or unimportant.

In this section we draw on the material presented in each of the 12 chapters to show how it informs the case analysis process. The ideas are linked sequentially and in terms of an overarching strategic perspective. One of your jobs when conducting case analysis is to see how the parts of a case fit together and how the insights from the study of strategy can help you understand the case situation.

> **>LO6**
>
> How to use the strategic insights and material from each of the 12 previous chapters in the text to analyze issues posed by strategic management cases.

1. *Analyzing organizational goals and objectives.* A company's vision, mission, and objectives keep organization members focused on a common purpose. They also influence how an organization deploys its resources, relates to its stakeholders, and matches its short-term objectives with its long-term goals. The goals may even impact how a company formulates and implements strategies. When exploring issues of goals and objectives, you might ask:
    - Has the company developed short-term objectives that are inconsistent with its long-term mission? If so, how can management realign its vision, mission, and objectives?
    - Has the company considered all of its stakeholders equally in making critical decisions? If not, should the views of all stakeholders be treated the same or are some stakeholders more important than others?
    - Is the company being faced with an issue that conflicts with one of its long-standing policies? If so, how should it compare its existing policies to the potential new situation?

2. *Analyzing the external environment.* The business environment has two components. The general environment consists of demographic, sociocultural, political/legal, technological, economic, and global conditions. The competitive environment includes rivals, suppliers, customers, and other factors that may directly affect a company's success. Strategic managers must monitor the environment to identify opportunities and threats that may have an impact on performance. When investigating a firm's external environment, you might ask:
    - Does the company follow trends and events in the general environment? If not, how can these influences be made part of the company's strategic analysis process?
    - Is the company effectively scanning and monitoring the competitive environment? If so, how is it using the competitive intelligence it is gathering to enhance its competitive advantage?

- Has the company correctly analyzed the impact of the competitive forces in its industry on profitability? If so, how can it improve its competitive position relative to these forces?

3. *Analyzing the internal environment.* A firm's internal environment consists of its resources and other value-adding capabilities. Value-chain analysis and a resource-based approach to analysis can be used to identify a company's strengths and weaknesses and determine how they are contributing to its competitive advantages. Evaluating firm performance can also help make meaningful comparisons with competitors. When researching a company's internal analysis, you might ask:
   - Does the company know how the various components of its value chain are adding value to the firm? If not, what internal analysis is needed to determine its strengths and weakness?
   - Has the company accurately analyzed the source and vitality of its resources? If so, is it deploying its resources in a way that contributes to competitive advantages?
   - Is the company's financial performance as good as or better than that of its close competitors? If so, has it balanced its financial success with the performance criteria of other stakeholders such as customers and employees?

4. *Assessing a firm's intellectual assets.* Human capital is a major resource in today's knowledge economy. As a result, attracting, developing, and retaining talented workers is a key strategic challenge. Other assets such as patents and trademarks are also critical. How companies leverage their intellectual assets through social networks and strategic alliances, and how technology is used to manage knowledge may be a major influence on a firm's competitive advantage. When analyzing a firm's intellectual assets, you might ask:
   - Does the company have underutilized human capital? If so, what steps are needed to develop and leverage its intellectual assets?
   - Is the company missing opportunities to forge strategic alliances? If so, how can it use its social capital to network more effectively?
   - Has the company developed knowledge-management systems that capture what it learns? If not, what technologies can it employ to retain new knowledge?

5. *Formulating business-level strategies.* Firms use the competitive strategies of differentiation, focus, and overall cost leadership as a basis for overcoming the five competitive forces and developing sustainable competitive advantages. Combinations of these strategies may work best in some competitive environments. Additionally, an industry's life cycle is an important contingency that may affect a company's choice of business-level strategies. When assessing business-level strategies, you might ask:
   - Has the company chosen the correct competitive strategy given its industry environment and competitive situation? If not, how should it use its strengths and resources to improve its performance?
   - Does the company use combination strategies effectively? If so, what capabilities can it cultivate to further enhance profitability?
   - Is the company using a strategy that is appropriate for the industry life cycle in which it is competing? If not, how can it realign itself to match its efforts to the current stage of industry growth?

6. *Formulating corporate-level strategies.* Large firms often own and manage portfolios of businesses. Corporate strategies address methods for achieving synergies among these businesses. Related and unrelated diversification techniques are alternative approaches to deciding which business should be added to or removed from a portfolio. Companies can diversify by means of mergers, acquisitions, joint ventures,

strategic alliances, and internal development. When analyzing corporate-level strategies, you might ask:

- Is the company competing in the right businesses given the opportunities and threats that are present in the environment? If not, how can it realign its diversification strategy to achieve competitive advantages?
- Is the corporation managing its portfolio of businesses in a way that creates synergies among the businesses? If so, what additional business should it consider adding to its portfolio?
- Are the motives of the top corporate executives who are pushing diversification strategies appropriate? If not, what action can be taken to curb their activities or align them with the best interests of all stakeholders?

7. *Formulating international-level strategies.* Foreign markets provide both opportunities and potential dangers for companies that want to expand globally. To decide which entry strategy is most appropriate, companies have to evaluate the trade-offs between two factors that firms face when entering foreign markets: cost reduction and local adaptation. To achieve competitive advantages, firms will typically choose one of three strategies: global, multidomestic, or transnational. When evaluating international-level strategies, you might ask:

- Is the company's entry into an international marketplace threatened by the actions of local competitors? If so, how can cultural differences be minimized to give the firm a better chance of succeeding?
- Has the company made the appropriate choices between cost reduction and local adaptation to foreign markets? If not, how can it adjust its strategy to achieve competitive advantages?
- Can the company improve its effectiveness by embracing one international strategy over another? If so, how should it choose between a global, multidomestic, or transnational strategy?

8. *Formulating entrepreneurial strategies.* New ventures add jobs and create new wealth. To do so, they must identify opportunities that will be viable in the marketplace as well as gather resources and assemble an entrepreneurial team to enact the opportunity. New entrants often evoke a strong competitive response from incumbent firms in a given marketplace. When examining the role of strategic thinking on the success of entrepreneurial ventures and the role of competitive dynamics, you might ask:

- Is the company engaged in an ongoing process of opportunity recognition? If not, how can it enhance its ability to recognize opportunities?
- Do the entrepreneurs who are launching new ventures have vision, dedication and drive, and a commitment to excellence? If so, how have these affected the performance and dedication of other employees involved in the venture?
- Have strategic principles been used in the process of developing strategies to pursue the entrepreneurial opportunity? If not, how can the venture apply tools such as five-forces analysis and value-chain analysis to improve its competitive position and performance?

9. *Achieving effective strategic control.* Strategic controls enable a firm to implement strategies effectively. Informational controls involve comparing performance to stated goals and scanning, monitoring, and being responsive to the environment. Behavioral controls emerge from a company's culture, reward systems, and organizational boundaries. When assessing the impact of strategic controls on implementation, you might ask:

- Is the company employing the appropriate informational control systems? If not, how can it implement a more interactive approach to enhance learning and minimize response times?

- Does the company have a strong and effective culture? If not, what steps can it take to align its values and rewards system with its goals and objectives?
- Has the company implemented control systems that match its strategies? If so, what additional steps can be taken to improve performance?

10. *Creating effective organizational designs.* Organizational designs that align with competitive strategies can enhance performance. As companies grow and change, their structures must also evolve to meet new demands. In today's economy, firm boundaries must be flexible and permeable to facilitate smoother interactions with external parties such as customers, suppliers, and alliance partners. New forms of organizing are becoming more common. When evaluating the role of organizational structure on strategy implementation, you might ask:
   - Has the company implemented organizational structures that are suited to the type of business it is in? If not, how can it alter the design in ways that enhance its competitiveness?
   - Is the company employing boundaryless organizational designs where appropriate? If so, how are senior managers maintaining control of lower-level employees?
   - Does the company use outsourcing to achieve the best possible results? If not, what criteria should it use to decide which functions can be outsourced?

11. *Creating a learning organization and an ethical organization.* Strong leadership is essential for achieving competitive advantages. Two leadership roles are especially important. The first is creating a learning organization by harnessing talent and encouraging the development of new knowledge. Second, leaders play a vital role in motivating employees to excellence and inspiring ethical behavior. When exploring the impact of effective strategic leadership, you might ask:
   - Do company leaders promote excellence as part of the overall culture? If so, how has this influenced the performance of the firm and the individuals in it?
   - Is the company committed to being a learning organization? If not, what can it do to capitalize on the individual and collective talents of organizational members?
   - Have company leaders exhibited an ethical attitude in their own behavior? If not, how has their behavior influenced the actions of other employees?

12. *Fostering corporate entrepreneurship.* Many firms continually seek new growth opportunities and avenues for strategic renewal. In some corporations, autonomous work units such as business incubators and new-venture groups are used to focus corporate venturing activities. In other corporate settings, product champions and other firm members provide companies with the impetus to expand into new areas. When investigating the impact of entrepreneurship on strategic effectiveness, you might ask:
   - Has the company resolved the dilemmas associated with managing innovation? If so, is it effectively defining and pacing its innovation efforts?
   - Has the company developed autonomous work units that have the freedom to bring forth new product ideas? If so, has it used product champions to implement new venture initiatives?
   - Does the company have an entrepreneurial orientation? If not, what can it do to encourage entrepreneurial attitudes in the strategic behavior of its organizational members?

Summary

Strategic management case analysis provides an effective method of learning how companies analyze problems, make decisions, and resolve challenges. Strategic cases include detailed accounts of actual business situations. The purpose of analyzing such cases is to gain exposure to a wide variety of organizational and managerial situations. By putting yourself in the place of a strategic decision maker, you can gain an appreciation of the difficulty and complexity of many strategic situations. In the process you can learn how to ask good strategic questions and enhance your analytical skills. Presenting case analyses can also help develop oral and written communication skills.

In this chapter we have discussed the importance of strategic case analysis and described the five steps involved in conducting a case analysis: becoming familiar with the material, identifying problems, analyzing strategic issues, proposing alternative solutions, and making recommendations. We have also discussed how to get the most from case analysis. Finally, we have described how the case analysis process follows the analysis-decision-action cycle of strategic management and outlined issues and questions that are associated with each of the previous 12 chapters of the text.

Key Terms

case analysis, 464

financial ratio analysis, 469

devil's advocacy 479

dialectical inquiry 480

References

1. The material in this chapter is based on several sources, including Barnes, L. A., Nelson, A. J., & Christensen, C. R. 1994. *Teaching and the case method: Text, cases and readings.* Boston: Harvard Business School Press; Guth, W. D. 1985. Central concepts of business unit and corporate strategy. In W. D. Guth (Ed.). *Handbook of business strategy:* 1–9. Boston: Warren, Gorham & Lamont; Lundberg, C. C., & Enz, C. 1993. A framework for student case preparation. *Case Research Journal,* 13 (Summer): 129–140; and Ronstadt, R. 1980. *The art of case analysis: A guide to the diagnosis of business situations.* Dover, MA: Lord Publishing.

2. Edge, A. G. & Coleman, D. R. 1986. *The guide to case analysis and reporting* (3rd ed.). Honolulu, HI: System Logistics.

3. Morris, E. 1987. Vision and strategy: A focus for the future. *Journal of Business Strategy* 8: 51–58.

4. This section is based on Lundberg & Enz, op. cit., and Ronstadt, op. cit.

5. The importance of problem definition was emphasized in Mintzberg, H., Raisinghani, D. & Theoret, A. 1976. The structure of "unstructured" decision processes. *Administrative Science Quarterly,* 21(2): 246–275.

6. Drucker, P. F. 1994. The theory of the business. *Harvard Business Review,* 72(5): 95–104.

7. This section draws on Edge & Coleman, op. cit.

8. Irving Janis is credited with coining the term *groupthink,* and he applied it primarily to fiascos in government (such as the Bay of Pigs incident in 1961). Refer to Janis, I. L. 1982. *Victims of groupthink* (2nd ed.). Boston: Houghton Mifflin.

9. Much of our discussion is based upon Finkelstein, S. & Mooney, A. C. 2003. Not the usual suspects: How to use board process to make boards better. *Academy of Management Executive,* 17(2): 101–113; Schweiger, D. M., Sandberg, W. R., & Rechner, P. L. 1989. Experiential effects of dialectical inquiry, devil's advocacy, and consensus approaches to strategic decision making. *Academy of Management Journal,* 32(4): 745–772; and Aldag, R. J. & Stearns, T. M. 1987. *Management.* Cincinnati: South-Western Publishing.

10. Finkelstein and Mooney, op. cit.

Appendix 1 to Chapter 13

Financial Ratio Analysis

Standard Financial Statements

One obvious thing we might want to do with a company's financial statements is to compare them to those of other, similar companies. We would immediately have a problem, however. It's almost impossible to directly compare the financial statements for two companies because of differences in size.

For example, Oracle and IBM are obviously serious rivals in the computer software market, but IBM is much larger (in terms of assets), so it is difficult to compare them directly. For that matter, it's difficult to even compare financial statements from different points in time for the same company if the company's size has changed. The size problem is compounded if we try to compare IBM and, say, SAP (of Germany). If SAP's financial statements are denominated in German marks, then we have a size *and* a currency difference.

To start making comparisons, one obvious thing we might try to do is to somehow standardize the financial statements. One very common and useful way of doing this is to work with percentages instead of total dollars. The resulting financial statements are called *common-size statements*. We consider these next.

Common-Size Balance Sheets

For easy reference, Prufrock Corporation's 2008 and 2009 balance sheets are provided in Exhibit 13A.1. Using these, we construct common-size balance sheets by expressing each item as a percentage of total assets. Prufrock's 2008 and 2009 common-size balance sheets are shown in Exhibit 13A.2.

Exhibit 13A.1

Prufrock Corporation

Balance Sheets as of December 31, 2008 and 2009 ($ in millions)

	2008	2009
Assets		
Current assets		
Cash	$ 84	$ 98
Accounts receivable	165	188
Inventory	393	422
Total	$ 642	$ 708
Fixed assets		
Net plant and equipment	$2,731	$2,880
Total assets	$3,373	$3,588
Liabilities and Owners' Equity		
Current liabilities		
Accounts payable	$ 312	$ 344
Notes payable	231	196
Total	$ 543	$ 540
Long-term debt	$ 531	$ 457
Owners' equity		
Common stock and paid-in surplus	$ 500	$ 550
Retained earnings	1,799	2,041
Total	$2,299	$2,591
Total liabilities and owners' equity	$3,373	$3,588

Source: Adapted from Rows, S. A., Westerfield, R. W., & Jordan, B. D. 1999. *Essentials of Corporate Finance* (2nd ed.). chap. 3. New York: McGraw-Hill, 1999.

Exhibit 13A.2

Prufrock Corporation
Common-Size
Balance Sheets as
of December 31,
2008 and 2009 (%)

	2008	2009	Change
Assets			
Current assets			
Cash	2.5%	2.7%	+ .2%
Accounts receivable	4.9	5.2	+ .3
Inventory	11.7	11.8	+ .1
Total	19.1	19.7	+ .6
Fixed assets			
Net plant and equipment	80.9	80.3	− .6
Total assets	100.0%	100.0%	.0%
Liabilities and Owners' Equity			
Current liabilities			
Accounts payable	9.2%	9.6%	+ .4%
Notes payable	6.8	5.5	−1.3
Total	16.0	15.1	− .9
Long-term debt	15.7	12.7	−3.0
Owners' equity			
Common stock and paid-in surplus	14.8	15.3	+ .5
Retained earnings	53.3	56.9	+3.6
Total	68.1	72.2	+4.1
Total liabilities and owners' equities	100.0%	100.0%	.0%

Note: Numbers may not add up to 100.0% due to rounding.

Notice that some of the totals don't check exactly because of rounding errors. Also notice that the total change has to be zero since the beginning and ending numbers must add up to 100 percent.

In this form, financial statements are relatively easy to read and compare. For example, just looking at the two balance sheets for Prufrock, we see that current assets were 19.7 percent of total assets in 2009, up from 19.1 percent in 2008. Current liabilities declined from 16.0 percent to 15.1 percent of total liabilities and equity over that same time. Similarly, total equity rose from 68.1 percent of total liabilities and equity to 72.2 percent.

Overall, Prufrock's liquidity, as measured by current assets compared to current liabilities, increased over the year. Simultaneously, Prufrock's indebtedness diminished as a percentage of total assets. We might be tempted to conclude that the balance sheet has grown "stronger."

Common-Size Income Statements

A useful way of standardizing the income statement, shown in Exhibit 13A.3, is to express each item as a percentage of total sales, as illustrated for Prufrock in Exhibit 13A.4.

This income statement tells us what happens to each dollar in sales. For Prufrock, interest expense eats up $.061 out of every sales dollar and taxes take another $.081. When all is said and done, $.157 of each dollar flows through to the bottom line (net income), and that amount is split into $.105 retained in the business and $.052 paid out in dividends.

These percentages are very useful in comparisons. For example, a relevant figure is the cost percentage. For Prufrock, $.582 of each $1.00 in sales goes to pay for goods sold. It would be interesting to compute the same percentage for Prufrock's main competitors to see how Prufrock stacks up in terms of cost control.

Exhibit 13A.3

Prufrock Corporation
2009 Income
Statement
($ in millions)

Sales	$2,311
Cost of goods sold	1,344
Depreciation	276
Earnings before interest and taxes	$ 691
Interest paid	141
Taxable income	$ 550
Taxes (34%)	187
Net income	$ 363

Dividends	$121	
Addition to retained earnings	242	

Exhibit 13A.4

Prufrock Corporation
2009 Common-Size
Income Statement (%)

Sales	100.0%
Cost of goods sold	58.2
Depreciation	11.9
Earnings before interest and taxes	29.9
Interest paid	6.1
Taxable income	23.8
Taxes (34%)	8.1
Net income	15.7%

Dividends	5.2%	
Addition to retained earnings	10.5	

Ratio Analysis

Another way of avoiding the problems involved in comparing companies of different sizes is to calculate and compare *financial ratios*. Such ratios are ways of comparing and investigating the relationships between different pieces of financial information. We cover some of the more common ratios next, but there are many others that we don't touch on.

One problem with ratios is that different people and different sources frequently don't compute them in exactly the same way, and this leads to much confusion. The specific definitions we use here may or may not be the same as others you have seen or will see elsewhere. If you ever use ratios as a tool for analysis, you should be careful to document how you calculate each one, and, if you are comparing your numbers to those of another source, be sure you know how its numbers are computed.

For each of the ratios we discuss, several questions come to mind:

1. How is it computed?
2. What is it intended to measure, and why might we be interested?
3. What is the unit of measurement?
4. What might a high or low value be telling us? How might such values be misleading?
5. How could this measure be improved?

Financial ratios are traditionally grouped into the following categories:

1. Short-term solvency, or liquidity, ratios.
2. Long-term solvency, or financial leverage, ratios.
3. Asset management, or turnover, ratios.
4. Profitability ratios.
5. Market value ratios.

We will consider each of these in turn. In calculating these numbers for Prufrock, we will use the ending balance sheet (2009) figures unless we explicitly say otherwise. The numbers for the various ratios come from the income statement and the balance sheet.

Short-Term Solvency, or Liquidity, Measures

As the name suggests, short-term solvency ratios as a group are intended to provide information about a firm's liquidity, and these ratios are sometimes called *liquidity measures*. The primary concern is the firm's ability to pay its bills over the short run without undue stress. Consequently, these ratios focus on current assets and current liabilities.

For obvious reasons, liquidity ratios are particularly interesting to short-term creditors. Since financial managers are constantly working with banks and other short-term lenders, an understanding of these ratios is essential.

One advantage of looking at current assets and liabilities is that their book values and market values are likely to be similar. Often (though not always), these assets and liabilities just don't live long enough for the two to get seriously out of step. On the other hand, like any type of near cash, current assets and liabilities can and do change fairly rapidly, so today's amounts may not be a reliable guide to the future.

Current Ratio   One of the best-known and most widely used ratios is the *current ratio.* As you might guess, the current ratio is defined as:

$$\text{Current ratio} = \frac{\text{Current assets}}{\text{Current liabilities}}$$

For Prufrock, the 2009 current ratio is:

$$\text{Current ratio} = \frac{\$708}{\$540} = 1.31 \text{ times}$$

Because current assets and liabilities are, in principle, converted to cash over the following 12 months, the current ratio is a measure of short-term liquidity. The unit of measurement is either dollars or times. So, we could say Prufrock has $1.31 in current assets for every $1 in current liabilities, or we could say Prufrock has its current liabilities covered 1.31 times over.

To a creditor, particularly a short-term creditor such as a supplier, the higher the current ratio, the better. To the firm, a high current ratio indicates liquidity, but it also may indicate an inefficient use of cash and other short-term assets. Absent some extraordinary circumstances, we would expect to see a current ratio of at least 1, because a current ratio of less than 1 would mean that net working capital (current assets less current liabilities) is negative. This would be unusual in a healthy firm, at least for most types of businesses.

The current ratio, like any ratio, is affected by various types of transactions. For example, suppose the firm borrows over the long term to raise money. The short-run effect would be an increase in cash from the issue proceeds and an increase in long-term debt. Current liabilities would not be affected, so the current ratio would rise.

Finally, note that an apparently low current ratio may not be a bad sign for a company with a large reserve of untapped borrowing power.

Quick (or Acid-Test) Ratio   Inventory is often the least liquid current asset. It's also the one for which the book values are least reliable as measures of market value, since the quality of the inventory isn't considered. Some of the inventory may later turn out to be damaged, obsolete, or lost.

More to the point, relatively large inventories are often a sign of short-term trouble. The firm may have overestimated sales and overbought or overproduced as a result. In this case, the firm may have a substantial portion of its liquidity tied up in slow-moving inventory.

To further evaluate liquidity, the *quick,* or *acid-test, ratio* is computed just like the current ratio, except inventory is omitted:

$$\text{Quick ratio} = \frac{\text{Current assets} - \text{Inventory}}{\text{Current liabilities}}$$

Notice that using cash to buy inventory does not affect the current ratio, but it reduces the quick ratio. Again, the idea is that inventory is relatively illiquid compared to cash.

For Prufrock, this ratio in 2009 was:

$$\text{Quick ratio} = \frac{\$708 - 422}{\$540} = .53 \text{ times}$$

The quick ratio here tells a somewhat different story than the current ratio, because inventory accounts for more than half of Prufrock's current assets. To exaggerate the point, if this inventory consisted of, say, unsold nuclear power plants, then this would be a cause for concern.

Cash Ratio   A very short-term creditor might be interested in the *cash ratio:*

$$\text{Cash ratio} = \frac{\text{Cash}}{\text{Current liabilities}}$$

You can verify that this works out to be .18 times for Prufrock.

Long-Term Solvency Measures

Long-term solvency ratios are intended to address the firm's long-run ability to meet its obligations, or, more generally, its financial leverage. These ratios are sometimes called *financial leverage ratios* or just *leverage ratios*. We consider three commonly used measures and some variations.

Total Debt Ratio   The *total debt ratio* takes into account all debts of all maturities to all creditors. It can be defined in several ways, the easiest of which is:

$$\text{Total debt ratio} = \frac{\text{Total assets} - \text{Total equity}}{\text{Total assets}}$$

$$= \frac{\$3,588 - 2,591}{\$3,588} = .28 \text{ times}$$

In this case, an analyst might say that Prufrock uses 28 percent debt.[1] Whether this is high or low or whether it even makes any difference depends on whether or not capital structure matters.

Prufrock has $.28 in debt for every $1 in assets. Therefore, there is $.72 in equity ($1 − .28) for every $.28 in debt. With this in mind, we can define two useful variations on the total debt ratio, the *debt-equity ratio* and the *equity multiplier:*

$$\text{Debt-equity ratio} = \text{Total debt/Total equity}$$
$$= \$.28/\$.72 = .39 \text{ times}$$
$$\text{Equity multiplier} = \text{Total assets/Total equity}$$
$$= \$1/\$.72 = 1.39 \text{ times}$$

The fact that the equity multiplier is 1 plus the debt-equity ratio is not a coincidence:

$$\text{Equity multiplier} = \text{Total assets/Total equity} = \$1/\$.72 = 1.39$$
$$= (\text{Total equity} + \text{Total debt})/\text{Total equity}$$
$$= 1 + \text{Debt-equity ratio} = 1.39 \text{ times}$$

The thing to notice here is that given any one of these three ratios, you can immediately calculate the other two, so they all say exactly the same thing.

Times Interest Earned   Another common measure of long-term solvency is the *times interest earned* (TIE) *ratio.* Once again, there are several possible (and common) definitions, but we'll stick with the most traditional:

$$\text{Times interest earned ratio} = \frac{\text{EBIT}}{\text{Interest}}$$

$$= \frac{\$691}{\$141} = 4.9 \text{ times}$$

---

[1]Total equity here includes preferred stock, if there is any. An equivalent numerator in this ratio would be (Current liabilities + Long-term debt).

As the name suggests, this ratio measures how well a company has its interest obligations covered, and it is often called the interest coverage ratio. For Prufrock, the interest bill is covered 4.9 times over.

Cash Coverage   A problem with the TIE ratio is that it is based on earnings before interest and taxes (EBIT), which is not really a measure of cash available to pay interest. The reason is that depreciation, a noncash expense, has been deducted. Since interest is most definitely a cash outflow (to creditors), one way to define the *cash coverage ratio* is:

$$\text{Cash coverage ratio} = \frac{\text{EBIT} + \text{Depreciation}}{\text{Interest}}$$

$$= \frac{\$691 + 276}{\$141} = \frac{\$967}{\$141} = 6.9 \text{ times}$$

The numerator here, EBIT plus depreciation, is often abbreviated EBDIT (earnings before depreciation, interest, and taxes). It is a basic measure of the firm's ability to generate cash from operations, and it is frequently used as a measure of cash flow available to meet financial obligations.

Asset Management, or Turnover, Measures

We next turn our attention to the efficiency with which Prufrock uses its assets. The measures in this section are sometimes called *asset utilization ratios*. The specific ratios we discuss can all be interpreted as measures of turnover. What they are intended to describe is how efficiently, or intensively, a firm uses its assets to generate sales. We first look at two important current assets: inventory and receivables.

Inventory Turnover and Days' Sales in Inventory   During the year, Prufrock had a cost of goods sold of $1,344. Inventory at the end of the year was $422. With these numbers, *inventory turnover* can be calculated as:

$$\text{Inventory turnover} = \frac{\text{Cost of goods sold}}{\text{Inventory}}$$

$$= \frac{\$1,344}{\$422} = 3.2 \text{ times}$$

In a sense, we sold off, or turned over, the entire inventory 3.2 times. As long as we are not running out of stock and thereby forgoing sales, the higher this ratio is, the more efficiently we are managing inventory.

If we know that we turned our inventory over 3.2 times during the year, then we can immediately figure out how long it took us to turn it over on average. The result is the average *days' sales in inventory:*

$$\text{Days' sales in inventory} = \frac{365 \text{ days}}{\text{Inventory turnover}}$$

$$= \frac{365}{3.2} = 114 \text{ days}$$

This tells us that, on average, inventory sits 114 days before it is sold. Alternatively, assuming we used the most recent inventory and cost figures, it will take about 114 days to work off our current inventory.

For example, we frequently hear things like "Majestic Motors has a 60 days' supply of cars." This means that, at current daily sales, it would take 60 days to deplete the available inventory. We could also say that Majestic has 60 days of sales in inventory.

Receivables Turnover and Days' Sales in Receivables   Our inventory measures give some indication of how fast we can sell products. We now look at how fast we collect on those sales. The *receivables turnover* is defined in the same way as inventory turnover:

$$\text{Receivables turnover} = \frac{\text{Sales}}{\text{Accounts receivable}}$$

$$= \frac{\$2,311}{\$188} = 12.3 \text{ times}$$

Loosely speaking, we collected our outstanding credit accounts and reloaned the money 12.3 times during the year.[2]

This ratio makes more sense if we convert it to days, so the *days' sales in receivables* is:

$$\text{Days' sales in receivables} = \frac{365 \text{ days}}{\text{Receivables turnover}}$$

$$= \frac{365}{12.3} = 30 \text{ days}$$

Therefore, on average, we collect on our credit sales in 30 days. For obvious reasons, this ratio is very frequently called the *average collection period* (ACP).

Also note that if we are using the most recent figures, we can also say that we have 30 days' worth of sales currently uncollected.

Total Asset Turnover Moving away from specific accounts like inventory or receivables, we can consider an important "big picture" ratio, the *total asset turnover ratio.* As the name suggests, total asset turnover is:

$$\text{Total asset turnover} = \frac{\text{Sales}}{\text{Total assets}}$$

$$= \frac{\$2,311}{\$3,588} = .64 \text{ times}$$

In other words, for every dollar in assets, we generated $.64 in sales.

A closely related ratio, the *capital intensity ratio,* is simply the reciprocal of (i.e., 1 divided by) total asset turnover. It can be interpreted as the dollar investment in assets needed to generate $1 in sales. High values correspond to capital intensive industries (e.g., public utilities). For Prufrock, total asset turnover is.64, so, if we flip this over, we get that capital intensity is $1/.64 = $1.56. That is, it takes Prufrock $1.56 in assets to create $1 in sales.

Profitability Measures

The three measures we discuss in this section are probably the best known and most widely used of all financial ratios. In one form or another, they are intended to measure how efficiently the firm uses its assets and how efficiently the firm manages its operations. The focus in this group is on the bottom line, net income.

Profit Margin Companies pay a great deal of attention to their *profit margin:*

$$\text{Profit margin} = \frac{\text{Net income}}{\text{Sales}}$$

$$= \frac{\$363}{\$2,311} = 15.7\%$$

This tells us that Prufrock, in an accounting sense, generates a little less than 16 cents in profit for every dollar in sales.

All other things being equal, a relatively high profit margin is obviously desirable. This situation corresponds to low expense ratios relative to sales. However, we hasten to add that other things are often not equal.

For example, lowering our sales price will usually increase unit volume, but will normally cause profit margins to shrink. Total profit (or, more importantly, operating cash flow) may go up or down; so the fact that margins are smaller isn't necessarily bad. After all, isn't it possible that, as the

---

[2]Here we have implicitly assumed that all sales are credit sales. If they were not, then we would simply use total credit sales in these calculations, not total sales.

saying goes, "Our prices are so low that we lose money on everything we sell, but we make it up in volume!"[3]

Return on Assets   *Return on assets* (ROA) is a measure of profit per dollar of assets. It can be defined several ways, but the most common is:

$$\text{Return on assets} = \frac{\text{Net income}}{\text{Total assets}}$$

$$= \frac{\$363}{\$3,588} = 10.12\%$$

Return on Equity   *Return on equity* (ROE) is a measure of how the stockholders fared during the year. Since benefiting shareholders is our goal, ROE is, in an accounting sense, the true bottom-line measure of performance. ROE is usually measured as:

$$\text{Return on equity} = \frac{\text{Net income}}{\text{Total equity}}$$

$$= \frac{\$363}{\$2,591} = 14\%$$

For every dollar in equity, therefore, Prufrock generated 14 cents in profit, but, again, this is only correct in accounting terms.

Because ROA and ROE are such commonly cited numbers, we stress that it is important to remember they are accounting rates of return. For this reason, these measures should properly be called *return on book assets* and *return on book equity*. In addition, ROE is sometimes called *return on net worth*. Whatever it's called, it would be inappropriate to compare the results to, for example, an interest rate observed in the financial markets.

The fact that ROE exceeds ROA reflects Prufrock's use of financial leverage. We will examine the relationship between these two measures in more detail below.

Market Value Measures

Our final group of measures is based, in part, on information not necessarily contained in financial statements—the market price per share of the stock. Obviously, these measures can only be calculated directly for publicly traded companies.

We assume that Prufrock has 33 million shares outstanding and the stock sold for $88 per share at the end of the year. If we recall that Prufrock's net income was $363 million, then we can calculate that its earnings per share were:

$$\text{EPS} = \frac{\text{Net income}}{\text{Shares outstanding}} = \frac{\$363}{33} = \$11$$

Price-Earnings Ratio   The first of our market value measures, the *price-earnings*, or PE, *ratio* (or multiple), is defined as:

$$\text{PE ratio} = \frac{\text{Price per share}}{\text{Earnings per share}}$$

$$= \frac{\$85}{\$11} = 8 \text{ times}$$

In the vernacular, we would say that Prufrock shares sell for eight times earnings, or we might say that Prufrock shares have, or "carry," a PE multiple of 8.

Since the PE ratio measures how much investors are willing to pay per dollar of current earnings, higher PEs are often taken to mean that the firm has significant prospects for future growth. Of course, if a firm had no or almost no earnings, its PE would probably be quite large; so, as always, be careful when interpreting this ratio.

[3]No, it's not; margins can be small, but they do need to be positive!

Market-to-Book Ratio   A second commonly quoted measure is the *market-to-book ratio:*

$$\text{Market-to-book ratio} = \frac{\text{Market value per share}}{\text{Book value per share}}$$

$$= \frac{\$88}{(\$2,591/33)} = \frac{\$88}{\$78.5} = 1.12 \text{ times}$$

Notice that book value per share is total equity (not just common stock) divided by the number of shares outstanding.

Since book value per share is an accounting number, it reflects historical costs. In a loose sense, the market-to-book ratio therefore compares the market value of the firm's investments to their cost. A value less than 1 could mean that the firm has not been successful overall in creating value for its stockholders.

Conclusion

This completes our definition of some common ratios. Exhibit 13A.5 summarizes the ratios we've discussed.

I. Short-term solvency, or liquidity, ratios

$$\text{Current ratio} = \frac{\text{Current assets}}{\text{Current liabilities}}$$

$$\text{Quick ratio} = \frac{\text{Current assets} - \text{Inventory}}{\text{Current liabilities}}$$

$$\text{Cash ratio} = \frac{\text{Cash}}{\text{Current liabilities}}$$

II. Long-term solvency, or financial leverage, ratios

$$\text{Total debt ratio} = \frac{\text{Total assets} - \text{Total equity}}{\text{Total assets}}$$

$$\text{Debt-equity ratio} = \text{Total debt/Total equity}$$

$$\text{Equity multiplier} = \text{Total assets/Total equity}$$

$$\text{Times interest earned ratio} = \frac{\text{EBIT}}{\text{Interest}}$$

$$\text{Cash coverage ratio} = \frac{\text{EBIT} + \text{Depreciation}}{\text{Interest}}$$

III. Asset utilization, or turnover, ratios

$$\text{Inventory turnover} = \frac{\text{Cost of goods sold}}{\text{Inventory}}$$

$$\text{Days' sales in inventory} = \frac{365 \text{ days}}{\text{Inventory turnover}}$$

$$\text{Receivables turnover} = \frac{\text{Sales}}{\text{Accounts receivable}}$$

$$\text{Days' sales in receivables} = \frac{365 \text{ days}}{\text{Receivables turnover}}$$

$$\text{Total asset turnover} = \frac{\text{Sales}}{\text{Total assets}}$$

$$\text{Capital intensity} = \frac{\text{Total assets}}{\text{Sales}}$$

IV. Profitability ratios

$$\text{Profit margin} = \frac{\text{Net income}}{\text{Sales}}$$

$$\text{Return on assets (ROA)} = \frac{\text{Net income}}{\text{Total assets}}$$

$$\text{Return on equity (ROE)} = \frac{\text{Net income}}{\text{Total equity}}$$

$$\text{ROE} = \frac{\text{Net income}}{\text{Sales}} \times \frac{\text{Sales}}{\text{Assets}} \times \frac{\text{Assets}}{\text{Equity}}$$

V. Market value ratios

$$\text{Price-earnings ratio} = \frac{\text{Price per share}}{\text{Earnings per share}}$$

$$\text{Market-to-book ratio} = \frac{\text{Market value per share}}{\text{Book value per share}}$$

Exhibit 13A.5 **A Summary of Five Types of Financial Ratios**

Sources of Company and Industry Information*

In order for business executives to make the best decisions when developing corporate strategy, it is critical for them to be knowledgeable about their competitors and about the industries in which they compete. The process used by corporations to learn as much as possible about competitors is often called "competitive intelligence." This appendix provides an overview of important and widely available sources of information that may be useful in conducting basic competitive intelligence. Much information of this nature is available in libraries in article databases, business reference books, and on websites. This list will recommend a variety of them. Ask a librarian for assistance, because library collections and resources vary.

The information sources are organized into 10 categories:

Competitive Intelligence

Public or Private—Subsidiary or Division—U.S. or Foreign?

Annual Report Collections—Public Companies

Guides and Tutorials

SEC Filings/EDGAR—Company Disclosure Reports

Company Rankings

Business Websites

Strategic and Competitive Analysis—Information Sources

Sources for Industry Research and Analysis

Search Engines

Competitive Intelligence

Students and other researchers who want to learn more about the value and process of competitive intelligence should see four recent books on this subject.

Norton Paley. "Prioritize Competitive Intelligence: The Underpinnings of Business Strategy." In *Mastering the Rules of Competitive Strategy.* New York: Auerbach Publications, 2008.

Leonard M. Fuld. *The Secret Language of Competitive Intelligence.* New York: Crown Business, 2006.

David L. Blenkhorn and Craig S. Fleisher, eds. *Competitive Intelligence and Global Business.* Westport, CT: Praeger Publishers, 2005.

Benjamin Gilad. *Early Warning: Using Competitive Intelligence to Anticipate Market Shifts, Control Risk, and Create Powerful Strategies.* New York: American Management Association, 2004.

Public or Private—Subsidiary or Division—U.S. or Foreign?

Companies traded on stock exchanges in the United States are required to file a variety of reports that disclose information about the company. This begins the process that produces a wealth of data on public companies and at the same time distinguishes them from private companies, which often lack available data. Similarly, financial data of subsidiaries and divisions are typically filed in a consolidated financial statement by the parent company, rather than treated independently, thus limiting the kind of data available on them. On the other hand, foreign companies that trade on U.S. stock exchanges are required to file 20F reports, similar to the 10-K for U.S. companies, the most comprehensive of the required reports.

*This information was compiled by Ruthie Brock and Carol Byrne, Business Librarians at The University of Texas at Arlington. We greatly appreciate their valuable contribution.

Corporate Directory of U.S. Public Companies. San Mateo, CA: Walker's Research, LLC, 2009.

The *Corporate Directory* provides company profiles of more than 9,000 publicly traded companies in the United States, including foreign companies trading on the U.S. exchanges (ADRs). Some libraries may subscribe to an alternative online version at www.walkersresearch.com.

Corporate Affiliations. New Providence, NJ: LexisNexis, 2009.

This 8-volume directory features brief profiles of major U.S. and foreign corporations, both public and private, as well as their subsidiaries, divisions, and affiliates. The directory also indicates hierarchies of corporate relationships. An online version of the directory allows retrieval of a list of companies that meet specific criteria. Results can be downloaded to a spreadsheet. The online version requires a subscription, available in some libraries.

ReferenceUSA. Omaha, NE: infoUSA

ReferenceUSA is an online directory of more than 14 million businesses located in the United States. One of the unique features is that it includes public and private companies, both large and small. Custom and Guided search tabs are available. Also, results can be analyzed using the data summary feature, which allows for a snapshot of how the industry breaks down by size, geographic location, etc. Other subscription options are available using the ReferenceUSA interface and may be available in some libraries.

Ward's Business Directory of U.S. Private and Public Companies. Farmington Hills, MI: Gale CENGAGE Learning, 2008. 8 vols.

Ward's Business Directory lists brief profiles on more than 112,000 public and private companies and indicates whether they are public or private, a subsidiary or division. Two volumes of the set are arranged using the Standard Industrial Classifications (SIC) and the North American Industry Classification System (NAICS) and feature company rankings within industries. Some libraries may offer this business directory as part of a database called *Gale Directory Library.*

Annual Report Collections—Public Companies

Most companies have their annual report to shareholders and other financial reports available on their corporate website. Note that some companies use a variation of their company name in their Web address, such as Procter & Gamble: www.pg.com. A few "aggregators" have also conveniently provided an accumulation of links to many reports of U.S. and international corporations or include a PDF document as part of their database, although these generally do not attempt to be comprehensive.

AnnualReports.com. Weston, FL: IR Solutions
This website contains annual reports in HTML or PDF format. Reports can be retrieved by company name, ticker symbol, exchange, industry, or sector.
www.annualreports.com

Company Annual Reports Online (CAROL). London, UK: Carol Ltd.
This website is based in the United Kingdom; therefore, many reports are European. Links are also provided for companies in Asia and the United States. A pull-down menu allows selecting companies within an industry. Access is free, but registration is required.
www.carol.co.uk/

Public Register's Online Annual Report Service. Woodstock Valley, CT: Bay Tact Corp.
Visitors to this website may choose from company annual reports and 10-K filings to view online or order a paper copy. Access is free, but registration is required.
www.annualreportservice.com/

Mergent Online. New York, NY: Mergent, Inc.
Mergent Online provides company financial data for public companies headquartered in the United States, as well as those headquartered in other countries, including a large collection of corporate annual reports in PDF format. For industry ratios, Mergent Online offers an advanced search option. Industry Reports are available as one of several Mergent subscription add-ons and may not be available in all libraries.
www.mergentonline.com

Guides and Tutorials

Researching Companies Online. Debbie Flanagan. Fort Lauderdale, FL
This site provides a step-by-step process for finding free company and industry information on the Web.
www.learnwebskills.com/company/

Guide to Financial Statements and *How to Read Annual Reports.* Armonk, NY: IBM
These two educational guides, located on IBM's website, provide basic information on how to read and make sense of financial statements and other information in 10-K and shareholder annual reports for companies in general, not IBM specifically.
www.ibm.com/investor/help/guide/introduction.wss
www.ibm.com/investor/help/reports/introduction.wss

EDGAR Full-Text Search Frequently Asked Questions (FAQ). Washington DC: U.S. Securities and Exchange Commission
The capability to search full-text SEC filings (popularly known as EDGAR filings), was vastly improved when the SEC launched its new search form in late 2006. Features are explained at the FAQ page.
www.sec.gov/edgar/searchedgar/edgarfulltextfaq.htm

Locating Company Information. Tutorial. William and Joan Schreyer Business Library, Penn State University, University Park, PA
Created by librarians at Penn State, this outstanding tutorial provides suggestions for online and print resources for company information. Click on "how to" links for each item to view a brief instruction vignette.
www.libraries.psu.edu/instruction/business/information/companyi.htm

Locating Industry Information. Tutorial. William and Joan Schreyer Business Library, Penn State University, University Park, PA
Created by librarians at Penn State, this outstanding tutorial provides suggestions for online and print resources for industry information. Click on "how to" links for each item to view a brief instruction vignette.
www.libraries.psu.edu/instruction/business/information/industryi.htm

Ten Steps to Industry Intelligence. Industry Tutorial. George A. Smathers Libraries, University of Florida, Gainesville, FL
Provides a step-by-step approach for finding information about industries, with embedded links to recommended sources.
http://businesslibrary.uflib.ufl.edu/industryresearch

SEC Filings/EDGAR—Company Disclosure Reports

SEC Filings are the various reports that publicly traded companies must file with the Securities Exchange Commission to disclose information about their corporation. These are often referred to as "EDGAR" filings, an acronym for the Electronic Data Gathering, Analysis and Retrieval System. Some websites and commercial databases improve access to these reports by offering additional retrieval features not available on the official (www.sec.gov) website.

EDGAR Database Full-Text Search. U.S. Securities and Exchange Commission (SEC), Washington, DC
10-K reports and other required corporate documents are made available in the SEC'S EDGAR database within 24 hours after being filed. Annual reports, on the other hand, are typically sent directly to shareholders and are not required as part of EDGAR by the SEC, although some companies voluntarily include them. Both 10-Ks and shareholder's annual reports are considered basic sources of company research. The SEC offers a search interface for full-text searching of the content and exhibits of EDGAR SEC filings. The advanced search is recommended to locate "hard-to-find" information within documents filed by corporations and their competitors. Searches for specific types of reports or certain industries can also be performed.
http://searchwww.sec.gov/EDGARFSClient/jsp/EDGAR_MainAccess.jsp

LexisNexis Academic—SEC Filings & Reports. Bethesda, MD: LexisNexis.

Company Securities Exchange Commission filings and reports are available through the "Business" option of LexisNexis Academic. These reports and filings can be retrieved by company name, industry code, or ticker symbol for a particular time period or by a specific report. Proxy, prospectus, and registration filings are also available.

Mergent Online—EDGAR. New York, NY: Mergent, Inc.

From the "EDGAR Search" tab within *Mergent Online,* EDGAR SEC filings and reports can be searched by company name or ticker symbol, filing date range, and file type (10-K, 8-K, ARS). The reports are available in HTML, MS Word format, and PDFs. Using the "Find in Page" option from the browser provides the capability of jumping to specific sections of an SEC report.

Company Rankings

Fortune 500. New York, NY: Time Inc.

The *Fortune 500* list and other company rankings are published in the printed edition of *Fortune* magazine and are also available online.

http://money.cnn.com/magazines/fortune/fortune500/2008/full_list/index.html

Hoover's Handbook of American Business. Austin, TX: Hoover's Business Press, 2008.

This two-volume set gives a company overview, a list of competitors, and basic financial information for large American companies. A special feature is a section called "The List Lovers' Companion," which includes a variety of lists with company rankings, some that include companies listed in Hoover's Handbooks; others reprinted from *Fortune, Forbes,* and other publications. In addition to the American edition, Hoover's Handbooks are available for private companies, emerging companies, and companies headquartered outside of the United States.

Ward's Business Directory of U.S. Private and Public Companies. Farmington Hills, MI: Gale CENGAGE Learning, 2008, 8 vols.

Ward's Business Directory is one of the few directories to rank both public and private companies together by sales within an industry, using both the Standard Industrial Classification system (in vol. 5 only) and the North American Industry Classification System (in vol. 8 only). With this information, it is easy to spot who the big "players" are in a particular product or industry category. Market share within an industry group can be calculated by determining what percentage a company's sales figure is of the total given by Ward's for that industry group. Some libraries may offer this business directory as part of a database called *Gale Directory Library.*

Business Websites

Business.com. Santa Monica, CA: Business.com, Inc.

A business-focused search engine with 26 top-level industry categories and links to more than 25,000 categories and subcategories that include over 400,000 business-oriented websites that are especially useful for locating industry association information.

www.business.com/

Big Charts. San Francisco, CA: MarketWatch, Inc.

BigCharts is the world's most comprehensive and easy-to-use investment research website, providing access to professional-level research tools such as interactive charts, current and historical quotes, industry analysis, and intraday stock screeners, as well as market news and commentary.

http://bigcharts.marketwatch.com/

GlobalEdge. East Lansing, MI: Michigan State University

GlobalEdge is a Web portal providing a significant amount of information about international business, countries around the globe, the U.S. states, industries, and news.

http://globaledge.msu.edu/

Hoover's Online. Hoover's, Inc., Short Hills, NJ: Dun & Bradstreet Corp.

Hoover's includes a limited amount of free information on companies, industries, and executives. The subscribers' edition provides more in-depth information, especially for competitors and industries.

www.hoovers.com/free

Internet Intelligence Index. Cambridge, MA: Fuld & Co.

This website gathers information from a wide variety of public services. The site contains links to over 600 intelligence-related Internet sites, covering everything from macroeconomic data to individual company stock quote information. The Industry section links to a variety of industry websites, such as apparel, publishing/media, technology/telecommunications, and many more.

www.fuld.com/Tindex/I3.html

Yahoo Finance. Sunnyvale, CA: Yahoo! Inc.

This website links to information on U.S. markets, world markets, data sources, finance references, investment editorials, financial news, and other helpful websites.

http://finance.yahoo.com

Strategic and Competitive Analysis—Information Sources

Analyzing a company can take the form of examining its internal and external environment. In the process, it is useful to identify the company's strengths, weaknesses, opportunities and threats (SWOT). Sources for this kind of analysis are varied, but perhaps the best would be to locate articles from The *Wall Street Journal,* business magazines and industry trade publications. Publications such as these can be found in the following databases available at many public and academic libraries. When using a database that is structured to allow it, try searching the company name combined with one or more keywords, such as "IBM and competition" or "Microsoft and lawsuits" or "AMR and fuel costs" to retrieve articles relating to the external environment.

ABI/Inform Complete. Ann Arbor, MI: ProQuest LLC

ABI/Inform Complete provides abstracts and full-text articles covering management, law, taxation, human resources, and company and industry information from more than 4,000 business and management journals. *ABI/Inform* includes market condition reports, corporate strategies, case studies, executive profiles, and global industry conditions.

Business & Company Resource Center. Farmington Hills, MI. Gale CENGAGE Learning

Business & Company Resource Center provides company and industry intelligence for a selection of public and private companies. Company profiles include parent-subsidiary relationships, industry rankings, products and brands, investment reports, industry statistics, and financial ratios. A selection of full-text investment reports is also available.

Business Source Complete. Ipswich, MA. EBSCO Publishing

Business Source Complete is a full-text database with over 3,800 scholarly business journals covering management, economics, finance, accounting, international business, and more. The database also includes detailed company profiles for the world's 10,000 largest companies, as well as selected country economic reports provided by the Economist Intelligence Unit (EIU). The database includes case studies, investment and market research reports, SWOT analyses, and more. *Business Source Complete* contains over 1,100 peer-reviewed business journals.

Investext Research Reports. Detroit, MI: Thomson Reuters Corp.

Investext Research Reports offer full-text analytical reports on more than 30,000 companies worldwide. The research reports are excellent sources for strategic and financial profiles of a company and its competitors and of industry trends. Developed by a global roster of brokerage, investment banking, and research firms, these full-text investment reports include a wealth of current and historical information useful for evaluating a company or industry over time.

International Directory of Company Histories. Detroit, MI: St. James Press, 1988–present. 106 volumes to date.

This directory covers more than 8,500 multinational companies, and the series is still adding volumes. Each company history is approximately three to five pages in length and provides a summary of the company's mission, goals, and ideals, followed by company milestones, principal subsidiaries, and competitors. Strategic decisions made during the company's period of existence are usually noted. This series covers public and private companies and nonprofit entities. Entry information includes a company's legal name, headquarters information, URL, incorporation date, ticker symbol, stock exchange, sales figures, and the primary North American Industry Classification System (NAICS) code. Further reading selections complete the entry information. The complete collection, volume 1 to current date, is available electronically in the Gale Virtual Reference Library database from Gale CENCAGE Learning.

LexisNexis Academic. Bethesda, MD: LexisNexis

The "business" category in *LexisNexis Academic* provides access to timely business articles from newspapers, magazines, journals, wires, and broadcast transcripts. Other information available in this section includes detailed company financials, company comparisons, and industry and market information for over 25 industries. The Company Dossier research tool allows a researcher to compare up to five companies' financial statements at one time with download capabilities.

LexisNexis Statistical. Bethesda, MD: LexisNexis

LexisNexis Statistical provides access to a variety of statistical publications indexed in the American Statistics Index (ASI), Statistical Reference Index (SRI), and the Index to International Statistics (IIS). Use the PowerTables search to locate historical trends, future projections, and industry or demographic information. *LexisNexis Statistical* provides links to originating government websites when available.

The Wall Street Journal. New York: Dow Jones & Co.

This respected business newspaper is available in searchable full-text from 1984 to the present in the *Factiva* database. The "News Pages" link provides access to current articles and issues of *The Wall Street Journal.* Dow Jones, publisher of the print version of the *Wall Street Journal,* also has an online subscription available at wsj.com. Some libraries provide access to *The Wall Street Journal* through the ProQuest Newspapers database.

Sources for Industry Research and Analysis

Factiva. New York: Dow Jones & Co.

The *Factiva* database has several options for researching an industry. One would be to search the database for articles in the business magazines and industry trade publications. A second option in *Factiva* would be to search in the Companies/Markets category for company/industry comparison reports.

Mergent Online. New York: Mergent Inc.

Mergent Online is a searchable database of over 15,000 U.S. public companies and more than 20,000 international public companies. The database offers worldwide industry reports, U.S. and global competitors, and executive biographical information. *Mergent*'s Basic Search option features searching by primary industry codes (either SIC or NAICS). Once the search is executed, companies in that industry should be listed. A comparison or standard peer group analysis can be created to analyze companies in the same industry on various criteria. The Advanced Search allows the user to search a wider range of financial and textual information. Results, including ratios for a company and its competitors, can be downloaded to a spreadsheet.

North American Industry Classification System (NAICS)

The North American Industry Classification System has officially replaced the Standard Industrial Classification (SIC) as a numerical structure used to define and analyze industries, although some publications and databases offer both classification systems. The NAICS codes are used in Canada, the United States, and Mexico. In the United States, the NAICS codes are used to conduct an Economic Census every five years providing a snapshot of the U.S. economy at a given moment in time.

NAICS: www.census.gov/eos/www/naics/
Economic Census: www.census.gov/econ/census02/

NetAdvantage. New York: Standard & Poor's

The database includes company, financial, and investment information as well as the well-known publication called *Industry Surveys.* Each industry report includes information on the current environment, industry trends, key industry ratios and statistics, and comparative company financial analysis. Available in HTML, PDF, or Excel formats.

Search Engines

Google. Mountain View, CA: Google, Inc.
Recognized for its advanced technology, quality of results, and simplicity, the search engine Google is highly recommended by librarians and other expert Web surfers.
www.google.com

Clusty. Pittsburgh, PA: Vivisimo, Inc.
This search engine not only finds relevant results, but also organizes them in logical subcategories.
www.clusty.com

Cases

Case 1   Robin Hood*

It was in the spring of the second year of his insurrection against the High Sheriff of Nottingham that Robin Hood took a walk in Sherwood Forest. As he walked he pondered the progress of the campaign, the disposition of his forces, the Sheriff's recent moves, and the options that confronted him.

The revolt against the Sheriff had begun as a personal crusade, erupting out of Robin's conflict with the Sheriff and his administration. Alone, however, Robin Hood could do little. He therefore sought allies, men with grievances and a deep sense of justice. Later he welcomed all who came, asking few questions, and only demanding a willingness to serve. Strength, he believed, lay in numbers.

He spent the first year forging the group into a disciplined band, united in enmity against the Sheriff, and willing to live outside the law. The band's organization was simple. Robin ruled supreme, making all important decisions. He delegated specific tasks to his lieutenants. Will Scarlett was in charge of intelligence and scouting. His main job was to shadow the Sheriff and his men, always alert to their next move. He also collected information on the travel plans of rich merchants and tax collectors. Little John kept discipline among the men, and saw to it that their archery was at the high peak that their profession demanded. Scarlock took care of the finances, converting loot into cash, paying shares of the take, and finding suitable hiding places for the surplus. Finally, Much the Miller's son had the difficult task of provisioning the ever-increasing band of Merrymen.

The increasing size of the band was a source of satisfaction for Robin, but also a source of concern. The fame of his Merrymen was spreading, and new recruits poured in from every corner of England. As the band grew larger, their small bivouac became a major encampment. Between raids the men milled about, talking and playing games. Vigilance was in decline, and discipline was becoming harder to enforce. "Why," Robin reflected, "I don't know half the men I run into these days."

The growing band was also beginning to exceed the food capacity of the forest. Game was becoming scarce, and supplies had to be obtained from outlying villages. The cost of buying food was beginning to drain the band's financial reserves at the very moment when revenues were in decline. Travelers, especially those with the most to lose, were now giving the forest a wide berth. This was costly and inconvenient to them, but it was preferable to having all their goods confiscated.

Robin believed that the time had come for the Merrymen to change their policy of outright confiscation of goods to one of a fixed transit tax. His lieutenants strongly resisted this idea. They were proud of the Merrymen's famous motto: "Rob the rich and give to the poor." "The farmers and the townspeople," they argued, "are our most important allies. How can we tax them, and still hope for their help in our fight against the Sheriff?"

Robin wondered how long the Merrymen could keep to the ways and methods of their early days. The Sheriff was growing stronger and better organized. He now had the money and the men, and was beginning to harass the band, probing for its weaknesses.

The tide of events was beginning to turn against the Merrymen. Robin felt that the campaign must be decisively concluded before the Sheriff had a chance to deliver a mortal blow. "But how," he wondered, "could this be done?"

Robin had often entertained the possibility of killing the Sheriff, but the chances for this seemed increasingly remote. Besides, while killing the Sheriff might satisfy his personal thirst for revenge, it would not improve the situation. Robin had hoped that the perpetual state of unrest, and the Sheriff's failure to collect taxes, would lead to his removal from office. Instead, the Sheriff used his political connections to obtain reinforcement. He had powerful friends at court, and was well regarded by the regent, Prince John.

Prince John was vicious and volatile. He was consumed by his unpopularity among the people, who wanted the imprisoned King Richard back. He also lived in constant fear of the barons, who had first given him the regency, but were now beginning to dispute his claim to the throne. Several of these barons had set out to collect the ransom that would release King Richard the Lionheart from his jail in Austria. Robin was invited to join the conspiracy in return for future amnesty. It was a dangerous proposition. Provincial banditry was one thing, court intrigue another. Prince John's spies were everywhere. If the plan failed, the pursuit would be relentless and retribution swift.

The sound of the supper horn startled Robin from his thoughts. There was the smell of roasting venison in the air. Nothing was resolved or settled. Robin headed for camp promising himself that he would give these problems his utmost attention after tomorrow's raid.

* Prepared by Joseph Lampel, City University, London. Copyright Joseph Lampel © 1985, revised 1991. Reprinted with permission.

Case 2 Edward Marshall Boehm, Inc.*

Edward Marshall Boehm—a farmer, veterinarian, and nature lover living near New York City—was convinced by his wife and friends to translate some of his clay animal sculptures into pieces for possible sale to the gift and art markets. Boehm recognized that porcelain was the best medium for portraying his creations because of its translucent beauty, permanence, and fidelity of color as well as form. But the finest of the porcelains, hard paste porcelain, was largely a secret art about which little technical literature existed. Boehm studied this art relentlessly, absorbing whatever knowledge artbooks, museums, and the few U.S. ceramic factories offered. Then, after months of experimentation in a dingy Trenton, New Jersey, basement, Boehm and some chemist friends developed a porcelain clay equal to the finest in the world.

Next Boehm had to master the complex art of porcelain manufacture. Each piece of porcelain sculpture is a technical as well as artistic challenge. A 52-step process is required to convert a plasticine sculpture into a completed porcelain piece. For example, one major creation took 509 mold sections to make 151 parts, and consumed 8 tons of plaster in the molds. Sculptural detail included 60,000 individually carved feather barbs. Each creation had to be kiln-fired to 2400° where heat could change a graceful detail into a twisted mass. Then it had to be painted, often in successive layers, and perhaps fired repeatedly to anneal delicate colors. No American had excelled in hard paste porcelains. And when Boehm's creations first appeared no one understood the quality of the porcelain or even believed it was hard paste porcelain.

But Boehm began to create in porcelain what he knew and loved best—nature, particularly the more delicate forms of animals, birds, and flowers. In his art Boehm tried "to capture that special moment and setting which conveys the character, charm, and loveliness of a bird or animal in its natural habitat." After selling his early creations for several years during her lunch hours, his talented wife, Helen, left

an outstanding opthalmic marketing career to "peddle" Boehm's porcelains full time. Soon Mrs. Boehm's extraordinary merchandising skills, promotional touch, and sense for the art market began to pay off. People liked Boehm's horses and dogs, but bought his birds. And Boehm agreeably complied, striving for ever greater perfection on ever more exotic and natural bird creations.

By 1968 some Boehm porcelains (especially birds) had become recognized as collector's items. An extremely complex piece like "Fondo Marino" might sell for $28,500 at retail, and might command much more upon resale. Edward Marshall Boehm, then 55—though flattered by his products' commercial success—considered his art primarily an expression of his love for nature. He felt the ornithological importance of portraying vanishing species like U.S. prairie chickens with fidelity and traveled to remote areas to bring back live samples of rare tropical birds for study and later rendering into porcelain. A single company, Minton China, was the exclusive distributor of Boehm products to some 175 retail outlets in the United States. Boehm's line included (1) its "Fledgling" series of smaller, somewhat simpler pieces, usually selling for less than $100, (2) its profitable middle series of complex sculptures like the "Snowy Owl" selling from $800 to $5,000, and (3) its special artistic pieces (like "Fondo Marino" or "Ivory Billed Woodpeckers") which might sell initially for over $20,000.

Individual Boehm porcelains were increasingly being recognized as outstanding artistic creations and sought by some sophisticated collectors. Production of such designs might be sold out for years in advance, but it was difficult to anticipate which pieces might achieve this distinction. Many of the company's past policies no longer seemed appropriate. And the Boehms wanted to further position the company for the long run. When asked what they wanted from the company, they would respond, "to make the world aware of Mr. Boehm's artistic talent, to help world wildlife causes by creating appreciation and protection for threatened species, and to build a continuing business that could make them comfortably wealthy, perhaps millionaires." No one goal had great precedence over the others.

* Republished with permission from H. Mintzberg and J. B. Quinn, *The Strategy Process,* Prentice Hall, New York, 1996.

Case 3   The Skeleton in the Corporate Closet*

"David," Donna Cooper exclaimed. "You won't believe it, but these look like love letters! And look, they're from when he was in the service!"

David Fisher, the corporate archivist for GPC Incorporated, hastened toward the young woman sprawled on his dusty floor but cheerily holding aloft a packet of yellowed envelopes. Unaccustomed to so much commotion in this room, he was still trying to process what had just happened. A moment ago, he'd been giving Miss Cooper, the writer hired to pen GPC's 75th anniversary book, a tour of his admittedly cluttered storeroom. Following at some distance, she'd chosen another path through the debris, only to reach an impasse. He'd glanced back just in time to see her give a shove to—of all things—the founder's writing desk. The brittle wooden legs, now in their 100th year at least, could hardly have been expected to scoot across the rough cement swirls of the basement floor. One had snapped immediately, the desk had toppled, and Miss Cooper had followed the whole wreck down.

Which was when, even through the air of the old storeroom, semiopaque with suspended dust, and even despite the early-stage cataract in his left eye, David spotted something that made his historian's heart leap. The back of the desk, now splintered, had mysteriously yielded a drawer, one he had never discovered in his years of puttering around it. Visible inside were some papers. Following his wondering gaze, the infuriating, wonderful Miss Cooper had spied, and snatched out, the treasure.

A Bittersweet Discovery

She was right, of course. They were letters composed to a sweetheart by Hudson Parker after he'd shipped out with Company K, the 137th U.S. Infantry unit made up of recruits from Kansas and Missouri. The first was dated August 6, 1917—a full decade before he'd founded General Parkelite Company. David took quick note of the addressee: Mary Beatrice White. Not a name he'd heard before. Clearly this romance preceded Virginia, the woman Hud had married. David was faintly scandalized to realize that old Hud had squirreled away these letters, no doubt unbeknownst to his wife. At the same time, he was touched at the thought of an unforgotten first love. And although his first instinct would usually have been to don cotton gloves and carry the letters into better light, he instead cleared a bit of floor space near Miss Cooper and sat. There was an undeniable charm in having this young woman eagerly extract letters from envelopes and read them aloud.

Harvard Business Review's cases, which are fictional, present common managerial dilemmas and offer concrete solutions from experts.

Reprinted by permission of *Harvard Business Review.* "The Skeleton in the Corporate Closet" by Julia Kirby, June 2002. Copyright © 2002 by the Harvard Business School Publishing Corporation; all rights reserved.

"My dearest Mary," she recited. "It began raining here this morning, and it is still at it. No drill today, so I will have time to write a letter or two." Impatient to find something juicier, she scanned the rest of the letter before handing it over. "Oh, look, David, how he signs it: 'With best of love to my own little girl.'" David accepted the letter and pushed his glasses down on his nose to peer over them. As always, he took a moment to appreciate the superior penmanship of an earlier age. Then his trained eye went to work on the page, drilling for facts that could be cataloged and cross-referenced with other accounts of the founder's war years. Donna, meanwhile, merrily called out other quaint snippets.

A half-hour passed in this way before David's joints, chilled by the bare floor, started to protest, and he suggested a change of venue. "Yeah," said Donna. "It's pretty musty in here, isn't it?" But as David took a moment to prop up the damaged desk and replace its drawer, Donna pulled another paper from an envelope. "Oh, this is the kind of thing you'll like," she noted, unfolding what looked, curiously, like drafting paper. She thrust it toward him and promptly launched into the accompanying letter. "You will recall from my last letter that we expect to see action this week, Mary darling. Enclosed is a document I hardly expect you to find interesting but entreat you to keep safe till my return." Indeed, it didn't interest Donna, so she rose to her feet and briskly dusted her skirt. "Honestly, David, I don't know how you work in here. My eyes are beginning to burn." But when she turned toward him, she was dismayed to see him staring at the paper he was clutching, his own eyes filling with tears.

Our Founder, a Thief?

A day passed before David appeared at the door of Jill Pierce, the communications VP who was his boss, and asked for a meeting at her convenience. Masking her surprise (in her seven years as his superior, she couldn't recall his ever initiating contact), she invited him in on the spot. Soon she was holding the letter herself and listening to David explain its import. Shockingly, it proved that the formula for Parkelite—the miracle plastic that was the company's first patent and its bread and butter for two full decades—had been someone else's innovation, not Hud Parker's. Not to put too fine a point on it, GPC's revered founder was a thief.

David filled in the parts of the story she didn't know. Of course, she needed no reminder of what Parkelite was. Although it had long since been superseded by better materials, it had been a huge technological advance in its day. A dense synthetic polymer, it could be molded or extruded and had the advantage of not changing shape after being mixed and heated. Most important, it wasn't flammable like earlier celluloid plastics. Manufacturers had used it to make things like engine parts, radio boxes, switches—even costume jewelry and inexpensive dinnerware. At the height of its popularity, General Parkelite was producing some 200,000 tons of the stuff per year.

What Jill had never heard was that in 1938, a lawsuit had been brought against Hud Parker and General Parkelite by the father of Karl Gintz, claiming that his son had been the true, sole inventor of Parkelite. Hud and Karl had studied chemistry together at Princeton, David explained, and had been star pupils who had egged each other on. But as well as being competitors, they were close friends, even to the extent that when war broke out in Europe, they enlisted together. Both dreamed of becoming pilots in the Army's Signal Corps, and both easily made the grade. They were transferred to the 94th Pursuit Group and posted to France. But in August 1918—just a week, Jill noted with a shiver, prior to the postmark on the envelope she held—Karl had been killed in maneuvers when the wing of his French-built trainer had collapsed. David pointed out that the formulas and diagrams neatly lettered on the graph paper were clearly the genesis of Parkelite, which Hud Parker had patented in 1920. Just as clearly, they were the work of Karl Gintz. "This is the document," David concluded, "that would have allowed the Gintz family to win its case."

Unprepared for the Worst

Jill had kept her composure while David was in her office, but as soon as he left, she opened her desk drawer, fished out a bottle of liquid antacid, and took a slug. David's chief concern seemed to be who would tell Hap—that is, Hudson Parker III, GPC's longtime CEO and the grandson of the founder. But that was the least of her worries. Clearly, this was a potential PR disaster, and her mind raced through the various ways it might play out. In honor of GPC's 75th anniversary, she'd introduced a heavy dose of nostalgia into this year's advertising. Hud Parker's image was splashed everywhere, along with the tag line, "He started it all." More like he *stole* it all, Jill thought bitterly, then felt guilty that such a remark would even occur to her. What a contrast to the pride she'd felt last summer when some focus groups she'd observed had come up with words like "trusted," "straight shooting," and "dependable" to describe the GPC brand. This was a catastrophe. And with all the extra planning that the special anniversary promotions required, she was already working flat out.

On her way to the CEO's office that afternoon, she lost her nerve at least three times. The fourth time, she even had Hap's doorway in sight, only to detour to the elevator lobby instead. She had a sudden determination to go down to the archives and urge David to destroy the incriminating paper and forget about it. But the fantasy died quickly as she recalled his haggard look in her office that morning. He'd already struggled with whether he could do that, she now realized, and decided he couldn't. She stopped short of hitting the down button and turned back toward the corner office.

History in the Remaking

Three days later, it was Hap Parker who was deciding what to do with the unwelcome news and 80-year-old graph paper now in his possession.

He'd been shocked, of course, and indeed had lost an entire weekend working through the implications on a purely personal level. On Saturday morning, he'd driven the two hours to the lakeside cottage where he'd spent summer days with his grandfather half a century before. He sat cross-legged on the dock, looked across the glittering water, then put his face in his hands and wept. First for his grandfather, who regardless of this incident didn't deserve to be impugned. The Parkelite patent, after all, was only a formula. It still took a great man to build a great company—and he had. And he had hardly coasted on that initial success. Instead, he'd infused the whole organization with the importance and excitement of constant innovation. It was his continuing attention to R&D that had led to General Parkelite's next generation of products, which, along with those of competitors, had made Parkelite obsolete. He'd won the respect of business leaders—indeed, of his country. He was a World War I ace, for God's sake! And a fair-dealing businessman, philanthropist, and community leader. A compassionate employer, certainly. And a dear grandfather, revered no less by his grandchildren for his tendency to dote on them.

This line of thought led Hap directly to self-pity. For neither did he, who had always held himself to the highest standard—with his grandfather's example as his North Star—deserve to have his name smeared. What was that line from Exodus about the sins of the fathers? He struggled to retrieve a long-forgotten catechism. Something about being visited on even the third and fourth generations. And now a fresh horror occurred to him: How much would Chip suffer, and even little Teddy, if this became known?

If. Had he really allowed himself to think "if"? He meant "when."

Reputation—or Reparation?

By Monday, Hap's thoughts were back with GPC and its employees, shareholders, and customers. He was listening to Newland Lowell, GPC's legal counsel, weigh in on the matter. No doubt about it, Newland was sharp. He'd come up with angles on this thing Hap hadn't anticipated.

As soon as he'd pressed the door shut behind him, in fact, Newland had broken into an improbable grin. "I know you're upset, Hap, so I'm going to get to the bottom line first," he said. "We haven't been able to turn up an heir to Karl Gintz." When he got no reaction, he hastened to pull out his other notes. "So. Let's take this from the top."

Newland first outlined a carefully reasoned argument that the letter, had it been introduced at trial long ago, would not necessarily have changed the verdict. The jury, he managed to persuade Hap, was fundamentally sympathetic to Hud Parker and not a little suspicious of Gintz's family. "If there's one thing I've learned," Newland said, "it's that jurors vote with their hearts and then find the legal hook to hang their emotions on." Besides, there would have been no proof that Karl hadn't meant to give the intellectual property to his friend and fellow soldier. "After all, no one else in his family was a chemist. They wouldn't have been able to make heads or tails of his notes. How do we know it wasn't his intent to let your grandfather take it forward? Maybe they were collaborating on it."

"But, Newland," Hap interjected. "If that had been the case, why wouldn't Hud have simply said so?"

"We're talking about a court case," Lowell reminded him. "His legal counsel would never have let him say that."

Hap fell silent again and let Newland continue to lay out his next argument: that there was no way of knowing when the letters Hud had sent to Mary Beatrice White had come back into his possession. It could have been years after the court case. "Not to mention," Newland added, "that if he needed this paper to fudge his own documentation for the patent, then why was it still in that envelope? Isn't it conceivable that the innovation was essentially your grandfather's but that Karl had taken careful notes on it to study and perhaps improve upon?"

Believing his arguments were carrying the day, Newland finally plunged into his last set of notes. These were legal strategies for "containing the discovery"—in essence placing a gag order on the few people in the organization who knew the truth. But Hap had already begun to chafe at what were sounding increasingly like elaborate rationalizations, and this was a bridge too far. He stood up from his desk and nodded to Newland. "Thank you, that's as much as I care to hear this afternoon."

Newland Lowell had known Hap Parker long enough not to mistake his tone, courteous though it might have seemed to others. He sighed as he swept his files back into his briefcase and rose from his chair. "Look, Hap. I'll be straight with you. I know you have a strong sense of what's ethical here. But you also have an organization to take care of. Your employees will be better off, not to mention your shareholders—hell, the *world* is better off if Hud Parker remains a hero. Don't be overly fastidious about this."

Doing the Right Thing

Packing up for the day, Hap had made up his mind. It was absurd that a company whose culture was all about honesty and integrity would tolerate a lie at its core. Maybe there was no one deserving of reparations out there, but surely the company deserved to pay some. He'd find some heir, somewhere.

He wasn't 20 yards down the hall, though, before he encountered a group of three GPC managers, two of them quite new to the company and the other a veteran. As he approached, he overheard the veteran, whose back was to Hap, saying patiently to one of the others, "Well, but, of course, Kevin, that just wouldn't be right." Then, catching sight of Hap, he fell into step with him, hoping to sound out the boss on some other matter.

Just out of earshot, Hap tilted his head back toward where the three had been standing and asked, "What was that about?" The manager explained that Kevin had proposed a marketing idea that seemed a little, well, not exactly underhanded, but. . . . The kid had come to GPC from a competitor with a certain industry reputation. "You know, people there learn to work all the angles and do a lot of things with a wink," he shrugged. "Don't worry, though. He wasn't comfortable there—that's why we got him."

"So you think he's got the potential to be a GPC'er?" Hap pressed.

"Well, that's the great thing about a strong culture, isn't it, Hap? It rubs off. He'll soon pick up on how things are done around here."

The unintended irony of those words made Hap queasy. Suddenly, he couldn't imagine damaging the strong belief in GPC held by this decent man and his 8,000 coworkers. Maybe Newland was right, he thought, and he was being too narrow in his ethics—even self-indulgent.

Was it possible for the right thing to be a lie?

Case 4 The Best-Laid Incentive Plans*

Hiram Phillips finished tying his bow tie and glanced in the mirror. Frowning, he tugged on the left side, then caught sight of his watch in the mirror. Time to get going. Moments later, he was down the stairs, whistling cheerfully and heading toward the coffeemaker.

"You're in a good mood," his wife said, looking up from the newspaper and smiling. "What's that tune? 'Accentuate the Positive'?"

"Well done!" Hiram called out. "You know, I do believe you're picking up some pop culture in spite of yourself." It was a running joke with them. She was a classically trained cellist and on the board of the local symphony. He was the one with the Sinatra and Bing Crosby albums and the taste for standards. "You're getting better at naming that tune."

"Or else you're getting better at whistling." She looked over her reading glasses and met his eye. They let a beat pass before they said in unison: "Naaah." Then, with a wink, Hiram shrugged on his trench coat, grabbed his travel mug, and went out the door.

Fat and Happy

It was true. Hiram Phillips, CFO and chief administrative officer of Rainbarrel Products, a diversified consumer-durables manufacturer, was in a particularly good mood. He was heading into a breakfast meeting that would bring nothing but good news. Sally Hamilton and Frank Ormondy from Felding & Company would no doubt already be at the office when he arrived and would have with them the all-important numbers—the statistics that would demonstrate the positive results of the performance management system he'd put in place a year ago. Hiram had already seen many of the figures in bits and pieces. He'd retained the consultants to establish baselines on the metrics he wanted to watch and had seen various interim reports from them since. But today's meeting would be the impressive summation capping off a year's worth of effort. Merging into the congestion of Route 45, he thought about the upbeat presentation he would spend the rest of the morning preparing for tomorrow's meeting of the corporate executive council.

It was obvious enough what his introduction should be. He would start at the beginning—or, anyway, his own beginning at Rainbarrel Products a year ago. At the time,

Harvard Business Review's cases, which are fictional, present common managerial dilemmas and offer concrete solutions from experts.

* Steven Kerr is the chief learning officer at Goldman Sachs in New York. Prior to joining Goldman Sachs in 2001, he spent seven years as the chief learning officer and head of leadership development at General Electric. He was responsible for GE's leadership development center at Crotonville.

Reprinted by permission of *Harvard Business Review*. "The Best Laid Incentive Plans" by Steven Kerr, January 2003. Copyright © 2003 by the Harvard Business School Publishing Corporation; all rights reserved.

the company had just come off a couple of awful quarters. It wasn't alone. The sudden slowdown in consumer spending, after a decade-long boom, had taken the whole industry by surprise. But what had quickly become clear was that Rainbarrel was adjusting to the new reality far less rapidly than its biggest competitors.

Keith Randall, CEO of Rainbarrel, was known for being an inspiring leader who focused on innovation. Even outside the industry, he had a name as a marketing visionary. But over the course of the ten-year economic boom, he had allowed his organization to become a little lax.

Take corporate budgeting. Hiram still smiled when he recalled his first day of interviews with Rainbarrel's executives. It immediately became obvious that the place had no budget integrity whatsoever. One unit head had said outright, "Look, none of us fights very hard at budget time, because after three or four months, nobody looks at the budget anyway." Barely concealing his shock, Hiram asked how that could be; what did they look at, then? The answer was that they operated according to one simple rule: "If it's a good idea, we say yes to it. If it's a bad idea, we say no."

"And what happens," Hiram had pressed, "when you run out of money halfway through the year?" The fellow rubbed his chin and took a moment to think before answering. "I guess we've always run out of good ideas before we've run out of money." Unbelievable!

"Fat and happy" was how Hiram characterized Rainbarrel in a conversation with the headhunter who had recruited him. Of course, he wouldn't use those words in the CEC meeting. That would sound too disparaging. In fact, he'd quickly fallen in love with Rainbarrel and the opportunities it presented. Here was a company that had the potential for greatness but that was held back by a lack of discipline. It was like a racehorse that had the potential to be a Secretariat but lacked a structured training regimen. Or a Ferrari engine that needed the touch of an expert mechanic to get it back in trim. In other words, the only thing Rainbarrel was missing was what someone like Hiram Phillips could bring to the table. The allure was irresistible; this was the assignment that would define his career. And now, a year later, he was ready to declare a turnaround.

Lean and Mean

Sure enough, as Hiram steered toward the entrance to the parking garage, he saw Sally and Frank in a visitor parking space, pulling their bulky file bags out of the trunk of Sally's sedan. He caught up to them at the security checkpoint in the lobby and took a heavy satchel from Sally's hand.

Moments later, they were at a conference table, each of them poring over a copy of the consultants' spiral-bound report. "This is great," Hiram said. "I can hand this out just as it is. But what I want to do while you're here is to really nail down what the highlights are. I have the floor for 40 minutes, but I guess I'd better leave ten for questions. There's no way I can plow through all of this."

"If I were you," Sally advised, "I would lead off with the best numbers. I mean, none of them are bad. You hit practically every target. But some of these, where you even exceeded the stretch goal. . . ."

Hiram glanced at the line Sally was underscoring with her fingernail. It was an impressive achievement: a reduction in labor costs. This had been one of the first moves he'd made, and he'd tried to do it gently. He'd come up with the idea of identifying the bottom quartile of performers throughout the company and offering them fairly generous buyout packages. But when that hadn't attracted enough takers, he'd gone the surer route. He'd imposed an across-the-board headcount reduction of 10% on all the units. In that round, the affected people were given no financial assistance beyond the normal severance.

"It made a big difference," he nodded. "But it wasn't exactly the world's most popular move." Hiram was well aware that a certain segment of the Rainbarrel workforce currently referred to him as "Fire 'em." He pointed to another number on the spreadsheet. "Now, that one tells a happier story: lower costs as a result of higher productivity."

"And better customer service to boot," Frank chimed in. They were talking about the transformation of Rainbarrel's call center—where phone representatives took orders and handled questions and complaints from both trade and retail customers. The spreadsheet indicated a dramatic uptick in productivity: The number of calls each service rep was handling per day had gone up 50%. A year earlier, reps were spending up to six minutes per call, whereas now the average was less than four minutes. "I guess you decided to go for that new automated switching system?" Frank asked.

"No!" Hiram answered. "That's the beauty of it. We got that improvement without any capital investment. You know what we did? We just announced the new targets, let everyone know we were going to monitor them, and put the names of the worst offenders on a great big 'wall of shame' right outside the cafeteria. Never underestimate the power of peer pressure!"

Sally, meanwhile, was already circling another banner achievement: an increase in on-time shipments. "You should talk about this, given that it's something that wasn't even being watched before you came."

It was true. As much as Rainbarrel liked to emphasize customer service in its values and mission statement, no reliable metric had been in place to track it. And getting a metric in place hadn't been as straightforward as it might've seemed—people had haggled about what constituted "on time" and even what constituted "shipped." Finally, Hiram had put his foot down and insisted on the most objective of measures. On time meant when the goods were promised to ship. And nothing was counted as shipped till it left company property. Period. "And once again," Hiram

announced, "not a dollar of capital expenditure. I simply let people know that, from now on, if they made commitments and didn't keep them, we'd have their number."

"Seems to have done the trick," Sally observed. "The percentage of goods shipped by promise date has gone up steadily for the last six months. It's now at 92%."

Scanning the report, Hiram noticed another huge percentage gain, but he couldn't recall what the acronym stood for. "What's this? Looks like a good one: a 50% cost reduction?"

Sally studied the item. "Oh, that. It's a pretty small change, actually. Remember we separated out the commissions on sales to employees?" It came back to Hiram immediately. Rainbarrel had a policy that allowed current and retired employees to buy products at a substantial discount. But the salespeople who served them earned commissions based on the full retail value, not the actual price paid. So, in effect, employee purchases were jacking up the commission expenses. Hiram had created a new policy in which the commission reflected the actual purchase price. On its own, the change didn't amount to a lot, but it reminded Hiram of a larger point he wanted to make in his presentation: the importance of straightforward rules—and rewards—in driving superior performance.

"I know you guys don't have impact data for me, but I'm definitely going to talk about the changes to the commission structure and sales incentives. There's no question they must be making a difference."

"Right," Sally nodded. "A classic case of 'keep it simple,' isn't it?" She turned to Frank to explain. "The old way they calculated commissions was by using this really complicated formula that factored in, I can't remember, at least five different things."

"Including sales, I hope?" Frank smirked.

"I'm still not sure!" Hiram answered. "No, seriously, sales were the most important single variable, but they also mixed in all kinds of targets around mentoring, prospecting new clients, even keeping the account information current. It was all way too subjective, and salespeople were getting very mixed signals. I just clarified the message so they don't have to wonder what they're getting paid for. Same with the sales contests. It's simple now: If you sell the most product in a given quarter, you win."

With Sally and Frank nodding enthusiastically, Hiram again looked down at the report. Row after row of numbers attested to Rainbarrel's improved performance. It wouldn't be easy to choose the rest of the highlights, but what a problem to have! He invited the consultants to weigh in again and leaned back to bask in the superlatives. And his smile grew wider.

Cause for Concern

The next morning, a well-rested Hiram Phillips strode into the building, flashed his ID badge at Charlie, the guard, and joined the throng in the lobby. In the crowd waiting for the elevator, he recognized two young women from Rainbarrel, lattes in hand and headphones around their necks. One was grimacing melodramatically as she turned to her friend. "I'm so dreading getting to my desk," she said. "Right when I was leaving last night, an e-mail showed up from the buyer at Sullivan. I just know it's going to be some big, hairy problem to sort out. I couldn't bring myself to open it, with the day I'd had. But I'm going to be sweating it today trying to respond by five o'clock. I can't rack up any more late responses, or my bonus is seriously history."

Her friend had slung her backpack onto the floor and was rooting through it, barely listening. But she glanced up to set her friend straight in the most casual way. "No, see, all they check is whether you responded to an e-mail within 24 hours of opening it. So that's the key. Just don't open it. You know, till you've got time to deal with it."

Then a belltone announced the arrival of the elevator, and they were gone.

More Cause for Concern

An hour later, Keith Randall was calling to order the quarterly meeting of the corporate executive council. First, he said, the group would hear the results of the annual employee survey, courtesy of human resources VP Lew Hart. Next would come a demonstration by the chief marketing officer of a practice the CEO hoped to incorporate into all future meetings. It was a "quick market intelligence," or QMI, scan, engaging a few of Rainbarrel's valued customers in a prearranged—but not predigested—conference call, to collect raw data on customer service concerns and ideas. "And finally," Keith concluded, "Hiram's going to give us some very good news about cost reductions and operating efficiencies, all due to the changes he's designed and implemented this past year."

Hiram nodded to acknowledge the compliment. He heard little of the next ten minutes' proceedings, thinking instead about how he should phrase certain points for maximum effect. Lew Hart had lost him in the first moments of his presentation on the "people survey" by beginning with an overview of "purpose, methodology, and historical trends." Deadly.

It was the phrase "mindlessly counting patents" that finally turned Hiram's attention back to his colleague. Lew, it seemed, was now into the "findings" section of his remarks. Hiram pieced together that he was reporting on an unprecedented level of negativity in the responses from Rainbarrel's R&D department and was quoting the complaints people had scribbled on their surveys. "Another one put it this way," Lew said. "We're now highly focused on who's getting the most patents, who's getting the most copyrights, who's submitting the most grant proposals, etc. But are we more creative? It's not that simple."

"You know," Rainbarrel's chief counsel noted, "I have thought lately that we're filing for a lot of patents for products that will never be commercially viable."

"But the thing that's really got these guys frustrated seems to be their 'Innovation X' project," Lew continued.

"They're all saying it's the best thing since sliced bread, a generational leap on the product line, but they're getting no uptake."

Eyes in the room turned to the products division president, who promptly threw up his hands. "What can I say, gang? We never expected that breakthrough to happen in this fiscal year. It's not in the budget to bring it to market."

Lew Hart silenced the rising voices, reminding the group he had more findings to share. Unfortunately, it didn't get much better. Both current and retired employees were complaining about being treated poorly by sales personnel when they sought to place orders or obtain information about company products. There was a lot of residual unhappiness about the layoffs, and not simply because those who remained had more work to do. Some people had noted that, because the reduction was based on headcount, not costs, managers had tended to fire low-level people, crippling the company without saving much money. And because the reduction was across the board, the highest performing departments had been forced to lay off some of the company's best employees. Others had heard about inequities in the severance deals: "As far as I can tell, we gave our lowest performers a better package than our good ones," he quoted one employee as saying.

And then there was a chorus of complaints from the sales organization. "No role models." "No mentoring." "No chance to pick the veterans' brains." "No knowledge sharing about accounts." More than ever, salespeople were dissatisfied with their territories and clamoring for the more affluent, high-volume districts. "It didn't help that all the sales-contest winners this year were from places like Scarsdale, Shaker Heights, and Beverly Hills," a salesperson was quoted as saying. Lew concluded with a promise to look further into the apparent decline in morale to determine whether it was an aberration.

The Ugly Truth

But if the group thought the mood would improve in the meeting's next segment—the QMI chat with the folks at longtime customer Brenton Brothers—they soon found out otherwise. Booming out of the speakerphone in the middle of the table came the Southern-tinged voices of Billy Brenton and three of his employees representing various parts of his organization.

"What's up with your shipping department?" Billy called out. "My people are telling me it's taking forever to get the stock replenished."

Hiram sat up straight, then leaned toward the speakerphone. "Excuse me, Mr. Brenton. This is Hiram Phillips—I don't believe we've met. But are you saying we are not shipping by our promise date?"

A cough—or was it a guffaw?—came back across the wire. "Well, son. Let me tell you about that. First of all, what y'all promise is not always what we are saying we require—and what we believe we deserve. Annie, isn't that right?"

"Yes, Mr. Brenton," said the buyer. "In some cases, I've been told to take a late date or otherwise forgo the purchase. That becomes the promise date, I guess, but it's not the date I asked for."

"And second," Billy continued, "I can't figure out how you fellas define 'shipped.' We were told last Tuesday an order had been shipped, and come to find out, the stuff was sitting on a railroad siding across the street from your plant."

"That's an important order for us," another Brenton voice piped up. "I sent an e-mail to try to sort it out, but I haven't heard back about it." Hiram winced, recalling the conversation in the lobby that morning. The voice persisted: "I thought that might be the better way to contact your service people these days? They always seem in such an all-fired hurry to get off the phone when I call. Sometimes it takes two or three calls to get something squared away."

The call didn't end there—a few more shortcomings were discussed. Then Keith Randall, to his credit, pulled the conversation onto more positive ground by reaffirming the great regard Rainbarrel had for Brenton Brothers and the mutual value of that enduring relationship. Promises were made and hearty thanks extended for the frank feedback. Meanwhile, Hiram felt the eyes of his colleagues on him. Finally, the call ended and the CEO announced that he, for one, needed a break before the last agenda item.

Dazed and Confused

Hiram considered following his boss out of the room and asking him to table the whole discussion of the new metrics and incentives. The climate was suddenly bad for the news he had looked forward to sharing. But he knew that delaying the discussion would be weak and wrong. After all, he had plenty of evidence to show he was on the right track. The problems the group had just been hearing about were side effects, but surely they didn't outweigh the cure.

He moved to the side table and poured a glass of ice water, then leaned against the wall to collect his thoughts. Perhaps he should reframe his opening comments in light of the employee and customer feedback. As he considered how he might do so, Keith Randall appeared at his side.

"Looks like we have our work cut out for us, eh, Hiram?" he said quietly—and charitably enough. "Some of those metrics taking hold, um, a little too strongly?" Hiram started to object but saw the seriousness in his boss's eyes.

He lifted the stack of reports Felding & Company had prepared for him and turned to the conference table. "Well, I guess that's something for the group to talk about."

Should Rainbarrel revisit its approach to performance management?

Case 5   Growing for Broke*

Look, you've *got* to grow. It's what our economy is all about. Hey, it's what our country is all about! Certainly, it's what drives me. My father, Constantine Anaptyxi, came to America from Greece because he saw big opportunities here. He worked hard, took a few risks, and realized his dreams. I came to this company as CEO five years ago—giving up a senior VP position at a Fortune 500 manufacturer—because I saw big potential for Paragon Tool, then a small maker of machine tools. I didn't make the move so that I could oversee the company's *down*sizing! I didn't intend to create value—for our customers, for our employees, for our shareholders—by thinking small!! I didn't intend to *shrink* to greatness, for God's sake!!!

Okay, so I'm getting a little worked up over this. Maybe I'm just trying to overcome my own second thoughts about our company's growth plans. I know it isn't just about growth; it's about *profitable* growth, as my CFO, William Littlefield, is always happy to remind me. "Nicky," he'll say, "people always talk about getting to the top when they should be focusing on the bottom . . . line, that is." Quite a comedian, that Littlefield. But lame as the quip is, it tells you a lot about Littlefield and what, in my opinion, is his limited view of business. Sometimes you've got to sacrifice profits up front to make *real* profits down the line.

To me, acquiring MonitoRobotics holds just that kind of promise. The company uses sensor technology and communications software to monitor and report real-time information on the functioning of robotics equipment. By adapting this technology for use on our machine tools, we could offer customers a rapid-response troubleshooting service—what consultants these days like to call a "solutions" business. Over time, I'd hope we could apply the technology and software to other kinds of machine tools and even to other kinds of manufacturing equipment. That would make us less dependent on our slow-growing and cyclical machine-tool manufacturing operation and hopefully give us a strong position in a technology market with terrific growth potential. It would also nearly double our current annual revenue of around $400 million—and force Wall Street to pay some attention to us.

What does Littlefield say to this? Oh, he gives a thumbs-down to the acquisition, of course—too risky. But get this: He also thinks we should sell off our existing services division—a "drag on profits," he says. With the help of some outside consultants, the senior management team has spent the last few months analyzing both our services business and the pros and cons of a MonitoRobotics acquisition. Tomorrow, I need to tell Littlefield whether we should go ahead and put together a presentation on the proposed acquisition for next week's board meeting. If we do

* Reprinted by permission of *Harvard Business Review.* "Growing for Broke" by Paul Hemp, September 2002. Copyright © 2002 by the Harvard Business School Publishing Corporation; all rights reserved.

move forward on this, I have a hunch a certain CFO might start returning those headhunter calls. And I'd hate to lose him. Whatever our differences, there's no denying that he's capable and smart—in fact, a lot smarter than I am in some areas. On this issue, though, I just don't think he gets it.

Mom and Apple Pie

In 1946, when my father was 21, he left the Greek island of Tinos and came to New York City with his new bride. He worked at a cousin's dry-cleaning store in Astoria, Queens, then started his own on the other side of town. When I was seven, he took his savings and bought a commercial laundry in Brooklyn. Over the next several years, he scooped up one laundry after another, usually borrowing from the bank, sometimes taking another mortgage on the three-family home in Bensonhurst where we had moved. By the time I was a teenager, he was sitting on a million-dollar business that did the linens for all kinds of hotels and hospitals around greater New York. "Nikolas, growth is as American as Mom and apple pie," my father would say to me—he loved using all-American expressions like that. "You gotta get bigger to get better."

My mom was somewhat less expansive in her outlook. She kept my father's accounts, having studied bookkeeping in night school as soon as her English was good enough. And she had her own saying, one that deftly, if inadvertently, bolted together two other platitudes of American slang. "Keep your shirt on," she would say to my father when, arms waving, he would enthusiastically describe some new expansion plan for his business. "Or else you might lose it." My father was the genius behind his company's growth, but I have no doubt that my mother was the one responsible for its profits.

When I was 15, we moved to a nice suburb in Jersey. I never quite fit in: too small for sports, a little too ethnic for the social set, only a middling student. I worked hard, though, and went to Rutgers, where I majored in economics and then stayed on to get an MBA. Something clicked in business school. I seemed to have a knack for solving the real-world problems of the case studies. And I flourished in an environment where the emphasis was on figuring out what you *can* do instead of what you *can't,* on envisioning how things could go right instead of trying to anticipate how they could go wrong. (Thank God I didn't follow my uncle's advice and become a corporate lawyer!)

When I graduated, I got a job at WRT, the Cleveland-based industrial conglomerate where I'd interned the summer before. Over the next 15 years or so, I moved up through the ranks, mainly because of my ability to spot new market opportunities. And by the time I was 45, I was heading up the machine-tool division, a $2.3 billion business. Both revenues and profits surged in the three years I was there, it's true. But I still found my job frustrating. Every proposed acquisition or new initiative of any substance had to be approved by people at headquarters who were far removed from our business. And whenever corporate profits flagged, the response was mindless across-the-board cost cutting that took little account of individual divisions' performance.

So when I was offered the opportunity to head up a small but profitable machine-tool maker in southern Ohio, I jumped at the chance.

Sunflower Tableau

I still remember driving to work my first day at Paragon Tool five years ago. Winding through the Ohio countryside, I saw a stand of sunflowers growing in a rocky patch of soil next to a barn. "Now *there's* a symbol for us," I thought, "a commonplace but hardy plant that quickly grows above its neighbors, often in fairly tough conditions." I was confident that Paragon—a solid, unexceptional business operating in an extremely difficult industry and economic environment—had the potential to grow with similarly glorious results.

For one thing, Paragon was relatively healthy. The company was built around a line of high-end machines— used by manufacturers of aerospace engines, among others—that continued to enjoy fairly good margins, despite the battering that the machine-tool industry as a whole had taken over the previous decade and a half. Still, the market for our product was essentially stagnant. Foreign competition was beginning to take its toll. And we continued to face brutal cyclical economic swings.

I quickly launched a number of initiatives designed to spur revenue growth. With some aggressive pricing, we increased sales and gained share in our core market, driving out a number of our new foreign rivals. We expanded our product line and our customer base by modifying our flagship product for use in a number of other industries. We also made a string of acquisitions in the industrial signage and electronic-labeling field, aiming to leverage the relationships we had with our machine-tool customers. No question, these moves put real pressure on our margins. Along with the price cuts and the debt we took on to make the acquisitions, we had to invest in new manufacturing equipment and a larger sales force. But we were laying the foundation for what I hoped would be a highly profitable future. The board and the senior management team, including Littlefield, seemed to share my view.

Indeed, the CFO and I had developed a rapport, despite our differing business instincts. Early on in our working relationship, this sixth-generation Yankee started in with the kidding about my alma mater. "Is that how they taught you to think about it at Rutgers?" he'd say if I was brainstorming and came up with some crazy idea. "Because at *Wharton,* they taught us. . . ." I'd just laugh and then tell whoever else was in the room how proud we were that Littlefield had been a cheerleader for the Penn football team—like that was his biggest scholarly

accomplishment. One time he "let it slip" that in fact he was Phi Beta Kappa, and we all just groaned. I said, "Give it up, Littlefield. You may have been Phi Beta Kappa, but, despite those letters on your gold pin, you'll never out-*Greek* me." To tell the truth, our skills are complementary, and between us we manage to do a pretty good job for the company.

As Paragon grew, so did the sense of excitement and urgency among our managers—indeed, among the entire workforce. People who once had been merely content to work at Paragon now couldn't wait to tackle the next challenge. And that excitement spread throughout the small Ohio town where we are based. When I'd go with my wife to a party or speak at the local Rotary Club or even stop to buy gas, people would show a genuine interest in the company and our latest doings—it helped that we always mentioned the job-creation impact when announcing new initiatives. There's no doubt it stoked my ego to be one of the bigger fish in the local pond. But even more important for me was the sense that this was business at its best, providing people with a justified sense of well-being about the present and confidence in the future.

Anyway, my point here is that we've grown fast since I arrived, but we still have a long way to go. I've come to think that the real key to our future is in the company's services division. We currently offer our customers the option to buy a standard service contract, under which we provide periodic machine maintenance and respond to service calls. But we've been developing technology and software, similar to MonitoRobotics', that would allow us to respond immediately if a machine at a customer's site goes down. The division currently accounts for less than 10% of our revenue and, because of the cost of developing the new technology, it's struggling to turn a profit.

But I can see in the services division the seeds of a business that will ultimately transform us from a manufacturing company into a high-tech company. Such a transformation, requiring an overhaul of our culture and capabilities, won't be easy. And it will surely require significant additional investments. But the potential upside is huge, with the promise of sales and profit growth that could make our current single-digit gains seem trivial by comparison. Besides, what choice do we have? A number of our competitors have already spotted these opportunities and have begun moving ahead with them. If we don't ramp up quickly, we might well miss out on the action altogether.

A Company in Play

Just over a month ago, I was sitting at my desk preparing a presentation for the handful of analysts who cover our company. Until recently, most of them have had only good things to say about all our growth moves. But last quarter, when we again reported a year-on-year drop in earnings, a few of them started asking pointed questions about our investments and when they could be expected to bear fruit. As I was giving some thought to how I'd answer their questions in the upcoming meeting, the phone rang. It was our investment banker, Jed Nixon.

"Nicky, I think we should talk," he said. I could tell from the sound of his voice he was on to something big, and then he told me what it was: "MonitoRobotics is in play."

We both did some calendar juggling and managed to get together for lunch the very next day at Jed's office in Cincinnati. The rumor was that one of our direct competitors, Bellows & Samson, was about to launch a hostile takeover bid for MonitoRobotics. As it happened, we had just started a conversation with MonitoRobotics' management a few months before, about collaborating on remote servicing technology for machine tools. But Jed's call had had its intended effect, changing my thinking about the company: Why not acquire it ourselves?

Although MonitoRobotics' technology was designed to detect and report operating failures in robotics equipment, managers there had told us when we met that adapting it for use on other industrial machinery was feasible. Indeed, MonitoRobotics had recently licensed the technology to a company that planned to modify it for use on complex assembly lines that experienced frequent breakdowns. Our engineers had confirmed that a version could be developed for our machines—though in their initial assessment they hadn't been exactly sure how long this would take.

Still, the potential benefits of acquiring MonitoRobotics seemed numerous. It would give us a powerful presence in a fast-growing business while preempting a competitor from staking a claim there. Whatever the time lag in adapting MonitoRobotics' technology for use with our products, we would almost certainly be able to offer our customers this valuable troubleshooting service more quickly than if we continued to develop the technology ourselves. And though our products were different, MonitoRobotics and Paragon potentially served many of the same manufacturing customers. "Think of the cross-selling opportunities," Jed said, as he took a bite of his sandwich. The greatest opportunity, though, lay in the possibility that MonitoRobotics' software technology would become the standard means for machine tools—and ultimately a variety of industrial machines—to communicate their service needs to the people who serviced them and to other machines that might be affected by their shutdown.

This was a fairly speculative train of thought. But a MonitoRobotics acquisition had for me the earmarks of a breakthrough opportunity for Paragon. And our earlier conversations with its management team had been cordial, suggesting the company might welcome a friendly offer from us to counter Bellows & Samson's hostile bid. Of course, even if we were able to get MonitoRobotics at a fair price, an acquisition of this size would further delay our return to

the margins and profit growth we had known in the past. And that, I knew, wouldn't sit well with everyone.

Management Dissension

The day after my meeting with Jed, I called together members of our senior management team. There was a barely suppressed gasp when I mentioned the potential acquisition, particularly given its size. "Boy, that would be a lot to digest with everything we've got on our plate right now," said Joe McCollum, our senior VP of marketing. "It also might represent the chance of a lifetime," countered Rosemary Witkowski, head of the services division. Then Littlefield spoke up. His skepticism wasn't surprising.

"I was just running a few simple numbers on what the MonitoRobotics acquisition might mean to our bottom line," he said. "Besides the costs associated with the acquisition itself, we'd be looking at some significant expenses in the near term, including accelerated software research, hiring and training, and even brand development." He pointed out that these costs would put further pressure on our earnings, just as our profits were struggling to recover from earlier growth-related investments.

Littlefield did concede that a bold acquisition like this might be just the sort of growth move that would appeal to some of our analysts—and might even prompt a few more securities firms to cover us. But he insisted that if our earnings didn't start bouncing back soon, Wall Street was going to pillory us. Then he dropped his bombshell: "I frankly think this is an opportunity to consider getting out of the services business altogether. Eliminating the continued losses that we've been experiencing there would allow us to begin realizing the profit growth that we can expect from the investments we've made in our still-healthy machine-tool business."

Littlefield argued that, whether we acquired MonitoRobotics or not, it wasn't clear we'd be able to dominate the machine-tool services market because a number of our competitors were already flocking there. Furthermore, the market might not be worth fighting over: Many of our customers were struggling with profitability themselves and might not be willing or able to buy our add-on services. "Last one in, turn out the lights" was the phrase Littlefield used to describe the rush to dominate a profitless market.

As soon as she had a chance, Rosemary shot back in defense of her operation. "This is the one area we're in that has significant growth potential," she said. "And we've already sunk an incredible amount of money into developing this software. I can't believe you'd throw all of that investment out the window." But a number of heads nodded when Littlefield argued that we'd recoup much of that investment if we sold the money-losing business.

Several days later, I polled the members of the senior management team and found them split on the issue of the acquisition. And, to be honest, I was beginning to doubt myself on this. I respected Littlefield's financial savvy. And no one had yet raised the issue of whether Paragon, a traditional manufacturing company, had the management capabilities to run what was essentially a software start-up. We decided to hire two highly regarded consulting firms to do quick analyses of the proposed MonitoRobotics acquisition.

The Sunflowers' Successor

Today, the consultants came back to us with conflicting reports. One highlighted the market potential of Monito-Robotics' technology, noting that we might be too far behind to develop similar technology on our own. The other focused on the difficulties both of integrating the company's technology with ours and of adapting it to equipment beyond the robotics field.

So as I drove home tonight, the dilemma seemed no closer to being resolved. In many ways, I am persuaded by the cautionary message of Littlefield's number crunching. At the same time, I firmly believe the pros and cons of such a complex decision can't be precisely quantified; sometimes you just have to go with your instincts—which

in my case favor growth. As I turned the issue over in my head, I looked out the car window, half-consciously seeking inspired insight. Sure enough, there was the barn where the sunflowers had been growing five years before. But the bright yellow blossoms, highlighted by the red timbers of the barn, were gone. Instead, a carpet of green kudzu was growing up the side of the increasingly dilapidated building. This fast-growing vine, which already had ravaged much of the South, was now spreading, uncontrolled and unproductive, into southern Ohio.

My mind started to drift and the image of kudzu—a more sinister symbol of growth than the sunflower—began to merge with thoughts of my father, who had died of lung cancer two years before, and my mother, who these days spends most of her time managing her investments. Suddenly, my parents' favorite phrases came to mind. It occurred to me that kudzu was now becoming as American as Mom and apple pie. Even so, its dense foliage certainly seemed like a place where, if you weren't careful, you could easily misplace your shirt.

Should Paragon Tool further its growth ambitions by trying to acquire MonitoRobotics?

Case 6 Crown Cork & Seal in 1989*

John F. Connelly, Crown Cork & Seal's ailing octogenarian chairman, stepped down and appointed his long-time disciple, William J. Avery, chief executive officer of the Philadelphia can manufacturer in May 1989. Avery had been president of Crown Cork & Seal since 1981, but had spent the duration of his career in Connelly's shadow. As Crown's new CEO, Avery planned to review Connelly's long-followed strategy in light of the changing industry outlook.

The metal container industry had changed considerably since Connelly took over Crown's reins in 1957. American National had just been acquired by France's state-owned Pechiney International, making it the world's largest beverage can producer. Continental Can, another long-standing rival, was now owned by Peter Kiewit Sons, a privately held construction firm. In 1989, all or part of Continental's can-making operations appeared to be for sale. Reynolds Metals, a traditional supplier of aluminum to can makers, was now also a formidable competitor in cans. The moves by both suppliers and customers of can makers to integrate into can manufacturing themselves had profoundly redefined the metal can industry since John Connelly's arrival.

Reflecting on these dramatic changes, Avery wondered whether Crown, with $1.8 billion in sales, should consider bidding for all or part of Continental Can. Avery also wondered whether Crown should break with tradition and expand its product line beyond the manufacture of metal cans and closures. For 30 years Crown had stuck to its core business, metal can making, but analysts saw little growth potential for metal cans in the 1990s. Industry observers forecast plastics as the growth segment for containers. As Avery mulled over his options, he asked: Was it finally time for a change?

The Metal Container Industry

The metal container industry, representing 61% of all packaged products in the United States in 1989, produced metal cans, crowns (bottle caps), and closures (screw caps, bottle lids) to hold or seal an almost endless variety of consumer

and industrial goods. Glass and plastic containers split the balance of the container market with shares of 21% and 18%, respectively. Metal cans served the beverage, food, and general packaging industries.

Metal cans were made of aluminum, steel, or a combination of both. Three-piece cans were formed by rolling a sheet of metal, soldering it, cutting it to size, and attaching two ends, thereby creating a three-piece, seamed can. Steel was the primary raw material of three-piece cans, which were most popular in the food and general packaging industries. Two-piece cans, developed in the 1960s, were formed by pushing a flat blank of metal into a deep cup, eliminating a separate bottom, a molding process termed "drawn and ironed." While aluminum companies developed the original technology for the two-piece can, steel companies ultimately followed suit with a thin-walled steel version. By 1983, two-piece cans dominated the beverage industry where they were the can of choice for beer and soft drink makers. Of the 120 billion cans produced in 1989, 80% were two-piece cans.

Throughout the decade of the 1980s, the number of metal cans shipped grew by an annual average of 3.7%. Aluminum can growth averaged 8% annually, while steel can shipments fell by an average of 3.1% per year. The number of aluminum cans produced increased by almost 200% during the period 1980–1989, reaching a high of 85 billion, while steel can production dropped by 22% to 35 billion for the same period (see Exhibit 1).

Industry Structure Five firms dominated the $12.2 billion U.S. metal can industry in 1989, with an aggregate 61% market share. The country's largest manufacturer—American National Can—held a 25% market share. The four firms trailing American National in sales were Continental Can (18% market share), Reynolds Metals (7%), Crown Cork & Seal (7%), and Ball Corporation (4%). Approximately 100 firms served the balance of the market.

Pricing Pricing in the can industry was very competitive. To lower costs, managers sought long runs of standard items, which increased capacity utilization and reduced the need for costly changeovers. As a result, most companies offered volume discounts to encourage large orders. Despite persistent metal can demand, industry operating margins fell approximately 7% to roughly 4% between 1986 and 1989. Industry analysts attributed the drop in operating margins to (1) a 15% increase in aluminum can sheet prices at a time when most can makers had guaranteed volume prices that did not incorporate substantial cost increases; (2) a 7% increase in beverage can production capacity between 1987 and 1989; (3) an increasing number of the nation's major brewers producing containers in house; and (4) the consolidation of soft drink bottlers throughout the decade. Forced to economize following

* Professor Stephen P. Bradley and Research Associate Sheila M. Cavanaugh prepared this case. Harvard Business School cases are developed solely as the basis for class discussion. Cases are not intended to serve as endorsements, sources of primary data, or illustrations of effective or ineffective management.

9-793-035

Exhibit 1   Metal Can Shipments by Market and Product, 1981–1989 (millions of cans)

	1981	%	1983	%	1985	%	1987	%	(Est.) 1989	%
Total Metal Cans Shipped	88,810		92,394		101,899		109,214		120,795	
By Market										
For sale:	59,433	67	61,907	67	69,810	69	81,204	74	91,305	76
Beverage	42,192		45,167		52,017		62,002		69,218	
Food	13,094		12,914		13,974		15,214		18,162	
General packaging	4,147		3,826		3,819		3,988		3,925	
For own use:	29,377	33	31,039	33	32,089	31	28,010	26	29,490	24
Beverage	14,134		16,289		18,160		14,771		17,477	
Food	15,054		14,579		13,870		13,167		11,944	
General packaging	189		171		59		72		69	
By Product										
Beverage:	56,326	63	61,456	67	70,177	69	76,773	70	86,695	72
Beer	30,901		33,135		35,614		36,480		37,276	
Soft drinks	25,425		28,321		34,563		40,293		49,419	
Food:	28,148	32	26,941	29	27,844	27	28,381	26	30,106	25
Dairy products	854		927		1,246		1,188		1,304	
Juices	13,494		11,954		11,385		11,565		12,557	
Meat, poultry, seafood	2,804		3,019		3,373		3,530		3,456	
Pet food	3,663		3,571		4,069		4,543		5,130	
Other	7,333		7,470		7,771		7,555		7,659	
General packaging:	4,336	5	3,997	4	3,878	4	4,060	4	3,994	3
Aerosol	2,059		2,144		2,277		2,508		2,716	
Paint: varnish	813		817		830		842		710	
Automotive products	601		229		168		128		65	
Other nonfoods	863		807		603		582		503	
By Materials Used										
Steel	45,386	52	40,116	45	34,316	37	34,559	34	35,318	29
Aluminum	42,561	48	48,694	55	58,078	63	67,340	66	85,477	71

Source: Can Shipment Report, Can Manufacturers Institute, 1981–1989.

costly battles for market share, soft drink bottlers used their leverage to obtain packaging price discounts.[1] Overcapacity and a shrinking customer base contributed to an unprecedented squeeze on manufacturers' margins, and the can manufacturers themselves contributed to the margin deterioration by aggressively discounting to protect market share. As one manufacturer confessed, "When you look at the beverage can industry, it's no secret that we are selling at a lower price today than we were 10 years ago."

Customers   Among the industry's largest users were the Coca-Cola Company, Anheuser-Busch Companies, Inc., PepsiCo Inc., and Coca-Cola Enterprises Inc. (see Exhibit 2). Consolidation within the soft drink segment of the bottling industry reduced the number of bottlers from approximately 8,000 in 1980 to about 800 in 1989 and placed a significant amount of beverage volume in the hands of a few large companies.[2] Since the can constituted about 45% of the total cost of a packaged beverage, soft drink

Exhibit 2 Top U.S. Users of Containers, 1989

Rank	Company	Soft Drink/ Beverage Sales ($000)	Principal Product Categories
1	The Coca-Cola Company[a] (Atlanta, GA)	$8,965,800	Soft drinks, citrus juices, fruit drinks
2	Anheuser-Busch Companies, Inc.[b] (St. Louis, MO)	7,550,000	Beer, beer imports
3	PepsiCo Inc. (Purchase, NY)	5,777,000	Soft drinks, bottled water
4	The Seagram Company, Ltd. (Montreal, Quebec, Canada)	5,581,779	Distilled spirits, wine coolers, mixers, juices
5	Coca-Cola Enterprises, Inc.[a] (Atlanta, GA)	3,881,947	Soft drinks
6	Philip Morris Companies, Inc. (New York, NY)	3,435,000	Beer
7	The Molson Companies, Ltd. (Toronto, Ontario, Canada)	1,871,394	Beer, coolers, beer imports
8	John Labatt, Ltd. (London, Ontario, Canada)	1,818,100	Beer, wine
9	The Stroh Brewery Company[c] (Detroit, MI)	1,500,000	Beer, coolers, soft drinks
10	Adolph Coors Company[d] (Golden, CO)	1,366,108	Beer, bottled water

Source: Beverage World, 1990–1991 Databank.

[a]The Coca-Cola Company and Coca-Cola Enterprises purchased (versus in-house manufacture) all of its cans in 1989. Coca-Cola owned 49% of Coca-Cola Enterprises—the largest Coca-Cola bottler in the United States.

[b]In addition to in-house manufacturing at its wholly owned subsidiary (Metal Container Corporation), Anheuser-Busch Companies purchased its cans from four manufacturers. The percentage of cans manufactured by Anheuser-Busch was not publicly disclosed.

[c]Of the 4 to 5 billion cans used by The Stroh Brewery in 1989, 39% were purchased and 61% were manufactured in-house.

[d]Adolph Coors Company manufactured all of its cans, producing approximately 10 to 12 million cans per day, five days per week.

bottlers and brewers usually maintained relationships with more than one can supplier. Poor service and uncompetitive prices could be punished by cuts in order size.

Distribution   Due to the bulky nature of cans, manufacturers located their plants close to customers to minimize transportation costs. The primary cost components of the metal can included (1) raw materials at 65%; (2) direct labor at 12%; and (3) transportation at roughly 7.5%. Various estimates placed the radius of economical distribution for a plant at between 150 and 300 miles. Beverage can producers preferred aluminum to steel because of aluminum's lighter weight and lower shipping costs. In 1988, steel cans weighed more than twice as much as aluminum.[3] The costs incurred in transporting cans to overseas markets made international trade uneconomical. Foreign markets were served by joint ventures, foreign subsidiaries, affiliates of U.S. can manufacturers, and local overseas firms.

Manufacturing   Two-piece can lines cost approximately $16 million, and the investment in peripheral equipment raised the per-line cost to $20–$25 million. The minimum efficient plant size was one line and installations ranged from one to five lines. While two-piece can lines achieved quick and persistent popularity, they did not completely replace their antecedents—the three-piece can lines. The food and general packaging segment—representing 28% of the metal container industry in 1989—continued using three-piece cans throughout the 1980s. The beverage segment, however, had made a complete switch from three-piece to two-piece cans by 1983.

Exhibit 3 Comparative Performance of Major Aluminum Suppliers, 1988 (dollars in millions)

	Sales	Net Income	Net Profit Margin %	Long-Term Debt	Net Worth	Earnings Per Share
Alcan Aluminum						
1988	$8,529.0	$931.0	10.9%	$1,199.0	$4,320.0	$3.85
1987	6,797.0	445.0	6.5	1,336.0	3,970.0	1.73
1986	5,956.0	177.0	3.0	1,366.0	3,116.0	.79
1985	5,718.0	25.8	0.5	1,600.0	2,746.0	.12
1984	5,467.0	221.0	4.0	1,350.0	2,916.0	1.00
Alcoa						
1988	9,795.3	861.4	8.8	1,524.7	4,635.5	9.74
1987	7,767.0	365.8	4.7	2,457.6	3,910.7	4.14
1986	4,667.2	125.0	2.7	1,325.6	3,721.6	1.45
1985	5,162.7	107.4	2.1	1,553.5	3,307.9	1.32
1984	5,750.8	278.7	4.8	1,586.5	3,343.6	3.41
Reynolds Metals[a]						
1988	5,567.1	482.0	8.7	1,280.0	2,040.1	9.01
1987	4,283.8	200.7	4.7	1,567.7	1,599.6	3.95
1986	3,638.9	50.3	1.4	1,190.8	1,342.0	.86
1985	3,415.6	24.5	0.7	1,215.0	1,151.7	.46
1984	3,728.3	133.3	3.6	1,146.1	1,341.1	3.09

Source: *Value Line.*

[a]Reynolds Metals Company was the second-largest aluminum producer in the United States. The company was also the third-largest manufacturer of metal cans, with a 7% market share.

A typical three-piece can production line cost between $1.5 and $2 million and required expensive seaming, end-making, and finishing equipment. Since each finishing line could handle the output of three or four can-forming lines, the minimum efficient plant required at least $7 million in basic equipment. Most plants had 12 to 15 lines for the increased flexibility of handling more than one type of can at once. However, any more than 15 lines became unwieldy because of the need for duplication of set-up crews, maintenance, and supervision. The beverage industry's switch from three- to two-piece lines prompted many manufacturers to sell complete, fully operational three-piece lines "as is" for $175,000 to $200,000. Some firms shipped their old lines overseas to their foreign operations where growth potential was great, there were few entrenched firms, and canning technology was not well understood.

Suppliers Since the invention of the aluminum can in 1958, steel had fought a losing battle against aluminum. In 1970, steel accounted for 88% of metal cans, but by 1989

had dropped to 29%. In addition to being lighter, of higher, more consistent quality, and more economical to recycle, aluminum was also friendlier to the taste and offered superior lithography qualities. By 1989, aluminum accounted for 99% of the beer and 94% of the soft drink metal container businesses, respectively.

The country's three largest aluminum producers supplied the metal can industry. Alcoa, the world's largest aluminum producer, with 1988 sales of $9.8 billion, and Alcan, the world's largest marketer of primary aluminum, with 1988 sales of $8.5 billion, supplied over 65% of the domestic can sheet requirements. Reynolds Metals, the second-largest aluminum producer in the United States, with 1988 sales of $5.6 billion, supplied aluminum sheet to the industry and also produced about 11 billion cans itself.[4] Reynolds Metals was the only aluminum company in the United States that produced cans (see Exhibit 3).

Steel's consistent advantage over aluminum was price. According to The American Iron and Steel Institute in 1988, steel represented a savings of from $5 to $7 for every thousand cans produced, or an estimated savings of $500 million a year for can manufacturers. In 1988, aluminum prices increased an estimated 15%, while the lower steel prices increased by only 5% to 7%. According to a representative of Alcoa, the decision on behalf of the firm to limit aluminum price increases was attributed to the threat of possible inroads by steel.[5]

Industry Trends The major trends characterizing the metal container industry during the 1980s included (1) the continuing threat of in-house manufacture; (2) the emergence of plastics as a viable packaging material; (3) the steady competition from glass as a substitute for aluminum in the beer market; (4) the emergence of the soft drink industry as the largest end-user of packaging, with aluminum as the primary beneficiary; and (5) the diversification of, and consolidation among, packaging producers.

In-House Manufacture Production of cans at "captive" plants—those producing cans for their own company use—accounted for approximately 25% of the total can output in 1989. Much of the expansion in in-house manufactured cans, which persisted throughout the 1980s, occurred at plants owned by the nation's major food producers and brewers. Many large brewers moved to hold can costs down by developing their own manufacturing capability. Brewers found it advantageous to invest in captive manufacture because of high-volume, single-label production runs. Adolph Coors took this to the extreme by producing all their cans in-house and supplying almost all of their own aluminum requirements from their 130-million-pound sheet rolling mill in San Antonio, Texas.[6] By the end of the 1980s, the beer industry had the capacity to supply about 55% of its beverage can needs.[7]

Captive manufacturing was not widespread in the soft drink industry, where many small bottlers and franchise operations were generally more dispersed geographically compared with the brewing industry. Soft drink bottlers were also geared to low-volume, multilabel output, which was not as economically suitable for the in-house can manufacturing process.

Plastics Throughout the 1980s, plastics was the growth leader in the container industry with its share growing from 9% in 1980 to 18% in 1989. Plastic bottle sales in the United States were estimated to reach $3.5 billion in 1989, with food and beverage—buoyed by soft drinks sales—accounting for 50% of the total. Plastic bottles accounted for 11% of domestic soft drink sales, with most of its penetration coming at the expense of glass. Plastic's light weight and convenient handling contributed to widespread consumer acceptance. The greatest challenge facing plastics, however, was the need to produce a material that simultaneously retained carbonation and prevented infiltration of oxygen. The plastic bottle often allowed carbonation to escape in less than 4 months, while aluminum cans held carbonation for more than 16 months. Anheuser-Busch claimed that U.S. brewers expected beer containers to have at least a 90-day shelf-life, a requirement that had not been met by any plastic can or bottle.[8] Additionally, standard production lines that filled 2,400 beer cans per minute required containers with perfectly flat bottoms, a feature difficult to achieve using plastic.[9] Since 1987, the growth of plastics had slowed somewhat apparently due to the impact on the environment of plastic packaging. Unlike glass and aluminum, plastics recycling was not a "closed loop" system.[10]

There were many small players producing plastic containers in 1988, often specializing by end-use or geographic region. However, only seven companies had sales of over $100 million. Owens-Illinois, the largest producer of plastic containers, specialized in custom-made bottles and closures for food, health and beauty, and pharmaceutical products. It was the leading supplier of prescription containers, sold primarily to drug wholesalers, major drug chains, and the government. Constar, the second-largest domestic producer of plastic containers, acquired its plastic bottle operation from Owens-Illinois, and relied on plastic soft drink bottles for about two-thirds of its sales. Johnson Controls produced bottles for the soft drink industry from 17 U.S. plants and six non-U.S. plants, and was the largest producer of plastic bottles for water and liquor. American National and Continental Can both produced plastic bottles for food, beverages, and other products such as tennis balls (see Exhibit 4 for information on competitors).

Glass Glass bottles accounted for only 14% of domestic soft drink sales, trailing metal cans at 75%. The cost advantage that glass once had relative to plastic in the popular 16-ounce bottle size disappeared by the mid-1980s because of consistently declining resin prices. Moreover, soft drink bottlers preferred the metal can to glass because of a variety of logistical and economic benefits: faster filling speeds, lighter weight, compactness for inventory, and transportation efficiency. In 1989, the delivered cost (including closure and label) of a 12-ounce can (the most popular size) was about 15% less than that of glass or plastic 16-ounce bottles (the most popular size).[11] The area in which glass continued to outperform metal, however, was the beer category where consumers seemed to have a love affair with the "long neck" bottle that would work to its advantage in the coming years.[12]

Soft Drinks and Aluminum Cans Throughout the 1980s, the soft drink industry emerged as the largest end-user of packaging. In 1989, soft drinks captured more than 50% of the total beverage market. The soft drink industry accounted for 42% of metal cans shipped in 1989—up from 29% in 1980. The major beneficiary of this trend was the aluminum can. In addition to the industry's continued commitment to advanced technology and innovation, aluminum's penetration could be traced to several factors: (1) aluminum's weight advantage over glass and steel; (2) aluminum's ease of handling; (3) a wider variety of graphics options provided by multipack can containers; and (4) consumer preference.[13] Aluminum's growth was

Exhibit 4   Major U.S. Producers of Blow-Molded Plastic Bottles, 1989 (dollars in millions)

Company	Total Sales	Net Income	Plastic Sales	Product Code	Major Market
Owens-Illinois	$3,280	$ (57)	$754	1,3,4,6	Food, health and beauty, pharmaceutical
American National	4,336	52	566	1,2,3,6	Beverage, household, personal care, pharmaceutical
Constar	544	12	544	1,2,3,4,6	Soft drink, milk, food
Johnson Controls	3,100	104	465	2	Soft drink, beverages
Continental Can	3,332	18	353	1,2,3,4,5,6	Food, beverage, household, industrial
Silgan Plastics	415	96	100	1,2,3,4,6	Food, beverage, household, pharmaceutical, personal care
Sonoco Products Co.	1,600	96	N/A	1,3,4,6	Motor oil, industrial

Source: *The Rauch Guide to the U.S. Plastics Industry.* 1991; company annual reports.

Product code: (1) HDPE; (2) PET; (3) PP; (4) PVC; (5) PC; (6) multilayer.

also supported by the vending machine market, which was built around cans and dispensed approximately 20% of all soft drinks in 1989. An estimated 60% of Coca-Cola's and 50% of Pepsi's beverages were packaged in metal cans. Coca-Cola Enterprises and Pepsi Cola Bottling Group together accounted for 22% of all soft drink cans shipped in 1989.[14] In 1980, the industry shipped 15.9 billion aluminum soft drink cans. By 1989, that figure had increased to 49.2 billion cans. This increase, representing a 12% average annual growth rate, was achieved during a decade that experienced a 3.6% average annual increase in total gallons of soft drinks consumed.

Diversification and Consolidation   Low profit margins, excess capacity, and rising material and labor costs prompted a number of corporate diversifications and subsequent consolidations throughout the 1970s and 1980s. While many can manufacturers diversified across the spectrum of rigid containers to supply all major end-use markets (food, beverages, and general packaging), others diversified into nonpackaging businesses such as energy (oil and gas) and financial services.

Over a 20-year period, for example, American Can reduced its dependence on domestic can manufacturing, moving into totally unrelated fields, such as insurance. Between 1981 and 1986 the company invested $940 million to acquire all or part of six insurance companies. Ultimately, the packaging businesses of American Can were acquired by Triangle Industries in 1986, while the financial services businesses re-emerged as Primerica. Similarly, Continental Can broadly diversified its holdings, changing its name to Continental Group in 1976 when can sales

dropped to 38% of total sales. In the 1980s, Continental Group invested heavily in energy exploration, research, and transportation, but profits were weak and they were ultimately taken over by Peter Kiewit Sons in 1984.

While National Can stuck broadly to containers, it diversified through acquisition into glass containers, food canning, pet foods, bottle closures, and plastic containers. However, instead of generating future growth opportunities, the expansion into food products proved a drag on company earnings.

Under the leadership of John W. Fisher, Ball Corporation, a leading glass bottle and can maker, expanded into the high-technology market and by 1987 had procured $180 million in defense contracts. Fisher directed Ball into such fields as petroleum engineering equipment, and photo-engraving and plastics, and established the company as a leading manufacturer of computer components.

Major Competitors in 1989   For over 30 years, three of the current five top competitors in can manufacturing dominated the metal can industry. Since the early 1950s, American Can, Continental Can, Crown Cork & Seal, and National Can held the top four rankings in can manufacturing. A series of dramatic mergers and acquisitions among several of the country's leading manufacturers throughout the 1980s served to shift as well as consolidate power at the top. Management at fourth-ranked Crown Cork & Seal viewed the following four firms as constituting its primary competition in 1989: American National Can, Continental Can, Reynolds Metals, and Ball Corporation. Two smaller companies—Van Dorn Company and Heekin Can—were strong competitors regionally (see Exhibit 5).

Exhibit 5   Comparative Performance of Major Metal Can Manufacturers (dollars in millions)

Company[a]	Net Sales	SG&A as a % of Sales	Gross Margin	Operating Income	Net Profit	Return on Sales	Return on Average Assets	Return on Average Equity
Ball Corporation								
1988	$1,073.0	8.1%	$161.7	$113.0	$47.7	4.4%	5.7%	11.6%
1987	1,054.1	8.5	195.4	147.6	59.8	5.7	7.8	15.7
1986	1,060.1	8.2	168.0	150.5	52.8	5.0	7.6	15.2
1985	1,106.2	7.5	140.7	140.5	51.2	4.6	8.1	16.4
1984	1,050.7	7.9	174.1	123.9	46.3	4.4	7.8	16.6
1983	909.5	8.2	158.2	114.6	39.0	4.3	7.3	15.6
1982	889.1	8.4	147.4	100.5	34.5	3.9	6.9	15.8
Crown Cork & Seal								
1988	1,834.1	2.8	264.6	212.7	93.4	5.1	8.6	14.5
1987	1,717.9	2.9	261.3	223.3	88.3	5.1	8.7	14.5
1986	1,618.9	2.9	235.3	202.4	79.4	4.9	8.8	14.3
1985	1,487.1	2.9	216.4	184.4	71.7	4.8	8.6	13.9
1984	1,370.0	3.1	186.6	154.8	59.5	4.4	7.3	11.4
1983	1,298.0	3.3	182.0	138.9	51.5	4.0	6.2	9.3
1982	1,351.8	3.3	176.2	132.5	44.7	3.3	5.2	7.9
Heekin Can, Inc.								
1988	275.8	3.7	38.9	36.4	9.6	3.5	4.8	22.6
1987	230.4	4.0	33.6	30.2	8.8	3.8	5.8	26.3
1986	207.6	4.1	31.1	28.0	7.0	3.4	5.4	27.5
1985	221.8	3.2	31.8	29.0	6.8	3.1	5.2	42.5
1984	215.4	2.7	28.4	26.5	5.5	2.6	4.3	79.7
1983	181.6	3.2	24.4	22.8	3.8	2.1	3.3	102.7
1982[b]	—							
Van Dorn Company								
1988	333.5	16.5	75.3	26.7	11.7	3.5	6.6	12.2
1987	330.0	15.7	73.6	28.4	12.3	3.7	7.7	12.7
1986	305.1	16.3	70.4	26.5	11.7	3.8	7.7	12.9
1985	314.3	15.1	75.6	33.6	15.4	4.9	10.6	19.0
1984	296.4	14.7	74.9	36.5	16.8	5.7	12.9	24.9
1983	225.9	14.8	48.5	20.1	7.4	3.3	6.8	12.8
1982	184.3	16.1	37.7	12.7	3.6	2.0	3.5	6.6
American Can Company[c]								
1985	2,854.9	22.6	813.4	1670.0	149.1	5.2	5.2	10.9
1984	3,177.9	18.0	740.8	168.3	132.4	4.2	4.9	11.2
1983	$3,346.4	15.0%	$625.4	$123.6	$94.9	2.8%	3.5%	9.7%

(continued)

Exhibit 5 *(Continued)*

Company[a]	Net Sales	SG&A as a % of Sales	Gross Margin	Operating Income	Net Profit	Return on Sales	Return on Average Assets	Return on Average Equity
American Can Company[c] (cont.)								
1982	4,063.4	16.1	766.3	113.4	23.0	0.6	0.8	2.4
1981	4,836.4	15.0	949.6	223.0	76.7	1.2	2.7	7.2
1980	4,812.2	15.8	919.5	128.1	85.7	1.8	3.1	8.0
National Can Company[d]								
1983	1,647.5	5.1	215.3	93.5	22.1	1.3	2.7	6.3
1982	1,541.5	4.6	206.3	100.7	34.1	2.2	4.4	10.0
1981	1,533.9	4.6	191.7	86.3	24.7	1.6	3.1	7.5
1980	1,550.9	5.4	233.7	55.0	50.6	3.3	6.4	16.7
The Continental Group, Inc.[e]								
1983	4,942.0	6.3	568.0	157.0	173.5	3.5	4.4	9.4
1982	5,089.0	6.4	662.0	217.0	180.2	3.5	4.3	9.6
1981	5,291.0	7.2	747.0	261.0	242.2	4.6	5.9	13.6
1980	5,171.0	7.2	700.0	201.0	224.8	4.3	5.5	13.7
1979	4,544.0	6.5	573.0	171.0	189.2	4.2	5.3	13.1

Source: *Value Line* and company annual reports (for SGA, COGS, and Asset figures).

[a]Refer to Exhibit 3 for Reynolds Metals Company.

[b]Figures not disclosed for 1982.

[c]In 1985, packaging made up 60% of total sales at American Can, with the remainder in specialty retailing. In 1986 Triangle Industries purchased the U.S. packaging business of American Can. In 1987, American National Can was formed through the merger of American Can Packaging and National Can Corporation. In 1989, Triangle sold American National Can to Pechiney, SA.

[d]In 1985, Triangle Industries bought National Can.

[e]In 1984, Peter Kiewit Sons purchased The Continental Group. SG&A as a percentage of sales for Continental Can hovered around 6.5% through the late 1980s.

American National Can Representing the merger of two former, long-established competitors, American National—a wholly-owned subsidiary of the Pechiney International Group—generated sales revenues of $4.4 billion in 1988. In 1985, Triangle Industries, a New Jersey–based maker of video games, vending machines, and jukeboxes, bought National Can for $421 million. In 1986, Triangle bought the U.S. packaging businesses of American Can for $550 million. In 1988, Triangle sold American National Can (ANC) to Pechiney, SA, the French state-owned industrial concern, for $3.5 billion. Pechiney was the world's third-largest producer of aluminum and, through its Cebal Group, a major European manufacturer of packaging. A member of the Pechiney International Group, ANC was the largest beverage can maker in the world—producing more than 30 billion cans annually. With more than 100 facilities in 12 countries, ANC's product line of aluminum and steel cans, glass containers, and caps and closures served the major beverage, food, pharmaceuticals, and cosmetics markets.

Continental Can Continental Can had long been a financially stable container company; its revenues increased every year without interruption from 1923 through the mid-1980s. By the 1970s, Continental had surpassed American Can as the largest container company in the United States. The year 1984, however, represented a turning point in Continental's history when the company became an attractive takeover target. Peter Kiewit Sons Inc., a private construction firm in Omaha, Nebraska, purchased Continental Group for $2.75 billion in 1984. Under the direction of Vice Chairman Donald Strum, Kiewit dismantled Continental Group in an effort to make the operation more profitable. Within a year, Strum had sold $1.6 billion worth of insurance, gas pipelines, and oil and gas reserves. Staff at Continental's Connecticut headquarters was reduced from 500 to 40. Continental Can generated sales revenues of $3.3 billion in 1988, ranking it second behind American National. By the late 1980s, management at Kiewit considered divesting—in whole or in part—Continental Can's packaging operations, which included Continental Can USA, Europe, and Canada, as well as metal packaging operations in Latin America, Asia, and the Middle East.

Reynolds Metals Based in Richmond, Virginia, Reynolds Metals was the only domestic company integrated from aluminum ingot through aluminum cans. With 1988 sales revenues of $5.6 billion and net income of $482 million, Reynolds served the following principal markets: packaging and containers; distributors and fabricators; building and construction; aircraft and automotive; and electrical. Reynolds' packaging and container revenue amounted to $2.4 billion in 1988. As one of the industry's leading can makers, Reynolds was instrumental in establishing new uses for the aluminum can and was a world leader in can-making technology. Reynolds' developments included high-speed can-forming machinery with capabilities in excess of 400 cans per minute, faster inspection equipment (operating at speeds of up to 2,000 cans per minute), and spun aluminum tops which contained less material. The company's next generation of can end-making technology was scheduled for installation in the early 1990s.

Ball Corporation Founded in 1880 in Muncie, Indiana, Ball Corporation generated operating income of $113 million on sales revenues of $1 billion in 1988. Considered one of the industry's low-cost producers, Ball was the fifth-largest manufacturer of metal containers as well as the third-largest glass container manufacturer in the United States. Ball's packaging businesses accounted for 82.5% of total sales and 77.6% of consolidated operating earnings in 1988. Ball's can-making technology and manufacturing flexibility allowed the company to make shorter runs in the production of customized, higher-margin products designed to meet customers' specifications and needs. In 1988, beverage can sales accounted for 62% of total sales. Anheuser-Busch, Ball's largest customer, accounted for 14% of sales that year. In 1989, Ball was rumored to be planning to purchase the balance of its 50%-owned joint venture, Ball Packaging Products Canada, Inc. The acquisition would make Ball the number two producer of metal beverage and food containers in the Canadian market.

Van Dorn Company The industry's next two largest competitors, with a combined market share of 3%, were Van Dorn Company and Heekin Can, Inc. Founded in 1872 in Cleveland, Ohio, Van Dorn manufactured two product lines: containers and plastic injection molding equipment. Van Dorn was one of the world's largest producers of drawn aluminum containers for processed foods, and a major manufacturer of metal, plastic, and composite containers for the paint, petroleum, chemical, automotive, food, and pharmaceutical industries. Van Dorn was also a leading manufacturer of injection molding equipment for the plastics industry. The company's Davies Can Division, founded in 1922, was a regional manufacturer of metal and plastic containers. In 1988, Davies planned to build two new can manufacturing plants at a cost of about $20 million each. These facilities would each produce about 40 million cans annually. Van Dorn's consolidated can sales of $334 million in 1988 ranked it sixth overall among the country's leading can manufacturers.

Heekin Can James Heekin, a Cincinnati coffee merchant, founded Heekin Can in 1901 as a way to package his own products. The company experienced rapid growth and soon contained one of the country's largest metal lithography plants under one roof. Three generations of the Heekin family built Heekin into a strong regional force in the packaging industry. The family sold the business to Diamond International Corporation, a large, diversified publicly held company, in 1965. Diamond operated Heekin as a subsidiary until 1982 when it was sold to its operating management and a group of private investors. Heekin went public in 1985. With 1988 sales revenues of $275.8 million, seventh-ranked Heekin primarily manufactured steel cans for processors, packagers, and distributors of food and pet food. Heekin represented the country's largest regional can maker.

Crown Cork & Seal Company

Company History In August 1891, a foreman in a Baltimore machine shop hit upon an idea for a better bottle cap—a piece of tin-coated steel with a flanged edge and an insert of natural cork. Soon this crown-cork cap became the hit product of a new venture, Crown Cork & Seal Company. When the patents ran out, however, competition became severe and nearly bankrupted the company in the 1920s. The faltering Crown was bought in 1927 by a competitor, Charles McManus.[15]

Under the paternalistic leadership of McManus, Crown prospered in the 1930s, selling more than half of the United States and world supply of bottle caps. He then correctly anticipated the success of the beer can and diversified into can making, building one of the world's largest plants in Philadelphia. However, at one million square feet and containing as many as 52 lines, it was a nightmare of inefficiency and experienced substantial losses. Although McManus was an energetic leader, he engaged in nepotism and never developed an organization that could run without him. Following his death in 1946, the company ran on momentum, maintaining dividends at the expense of investment in new plants. Following a disastrous attempt to expand into plastics and a ludicrous diversification into metal bird cages, Crown reorganized along the lines of the much larger Continental Can, incurring additional personnel and expense that again brought the company near to bankruptcy.

At the time, John Connelly was just a fellow on the outside, looking to Crown as a prospective customer and getting nowhere. The son of a Philadelphia blacksmith, Connelly had begun in a paperbox factory at 15 and worked his way up to become eastern sales manager of the Container Corporation of America. When he founded his own company, Connelly Containers, Inc., in 1946, Crown promised him some business. That promise was forgotten by the post-McManus regime, which loftily refused to "take a chance" on a small supplier like Connelly. By 1955, when Crown's distress became evident, Connelly began buying stock and in November 1956 was asked to be an outside director—a desperate move by the ailing company.[16]

In April 1957, Crown Cork & Seal teetered on the verge of bankruptcy. Bankers Trust Company withdrew Crown's line of credit; it seemed that all that was left was to write the company's obituary when John Connelly took over the presidency. His rescue plan was simple—as he called it, "just common sense." Connelly's first move was to pare down the organization. Paternalism ended in a blizzard of pink slips. Connelly moved quickly to cut headquarters staff by half to reach a lean force of 80. The company returned to a simple functional organization. In 20 months Crown had eliminated 1,647 jobs or 24% of the payroll. As part of the company's reorganization, Connelly discarded divisional accounting practices; at the same time he eliminated the divisional line and staff concept. Except for one accountant maintained at each plant location, all accounting and cost control was performed at the corporate level; the corporate accounting staff occupied one-half the space used by the headquarters group. In addition, Connelly disbanded Crown's central research and development facility.

The second step was to institute the concept of accountability. Connelly aimed to instill a deep-rooted pride of workmanship throughout the company by establishing Crown managers as "owner-operators" of their individual businesses. Connelly gave each plant manager responsibility for plant profitability, including any allocated costs. (All company overhead, estimated at 5% of sales, was allocated to the plant level.) Previously, plant managers had been responsible only for controllable expenses at the plant level. Although the plant managers' compensation was not tied to profit performance, one senior executive pointed out that the managers were "certainly rewarded on the basis of that figure." Connelly also held plant managers responsible for quality and customer service.

The next step was to slow production to a halt and liquidate $7 million in inventory. By mid-July Crown paid off the banks. Connelly introduced sales forecasting dovetailed with new production and inventory controls. This move put pressure on the plant managers, who were no longer able to avoid layoffs by dumping excess products into inventory.

By the end of 1957, Crown had, in one observer's words, "climbed out of the coffin and was sprinting." Between 1956 and 1961, sales increased from $115 million to $176 million and profits soared. Throughout the 1960s, the company averaged an annual 15.5% increase in sales and 14% in profits. Connelly, not satisfied simply with short-term reorganizations of the existing company, developed a strategy that would become its hallmark for the next three decades.

Connelly's Strategy

According to William Avery, "From his first day on the job, Mr. Connelly structured the company to be successful. He took control of costs and did a wonderful job taking us in the direction of becoming owner-operators." But what truly separated Connelly from his counterparts, Avery explained, was that while he was continually looking for new ways of controlling costs, he was equally hellbent on improving quality. Connelly, described by *Forbes* as an individual with a "scrooge-like aversion to fanfare and overhead," emphasized cost efficiency, quality, and customer service as the essential ingredients for Crown's strategy in the decades ahead.

Products and Markets Recognizing Crown's position as a small producer in an industry dominated by American Can and Continental Can, Connelly sought to develop a product line built around Crown's traditional strengths in metal forming and fabrication. He chose to emphasize the areas Crown knew best—tin-plated cans and crowns—and to concentrate on specialized uses and international markets.

A dramatic illustration of Connelly's commitment to this strategy occurred in the early 1960s. In 1960, Crown held over 50% of the market for motor oil cans. In 1962, R. C. Can and Anaconda Aluminum jointly developed fiber-foil cans for motor oil, which were approximately 20% lighter and 15% cheaper than the metal cans then in use. Despite the loss of sales, management decided that it had other more profitable opportunities and that new materials, such as fiber-foil, provided too great a threat in the motor oil can business. Crown's management decided to exit from the oil can market.

In the early 1960s Connelly singled out two specific applications in the domestic market: beverage cans and the growing aerosol market. These applications were called "hard to hold" because cans required special characteristics to either contain the product under pressure or to avoid affecting taste. Connelly led Crown directly from a soldered can into the manufacture of two-piece steel cans in the 1960s. Recognizing the enormous potential of the soft drink business, Crown began designing its equipment specifically to meet the needs of soft drink producers, with innovations such as two printers in one line and conversion printers that allowed for rapid design changeover to accommodate just-in-time delivery.[17] After producing exclusively steel cans through the late 1970s, Connelly spearheaded Crown's conversion from steel to aluminum cans in the early 1980s.

In addition to the specialized product line, Connelly's strategy was based on two geographic thrusts: expand to national distribution in the United States and invest heavily abroad. Connelly linked domestic expansion to Crown's manufacturing reorganization; plants were spread out across the country to reduce transportation costs and to be nearer customers. Crown was unusual in that it did not set up plants to service a single customer. Instead, Crown concentrated on providing products for a number of customers near their plants. In international markets, Crown invested heavily in developing nations, first with crowns and then with cans as packaged foods became more widely accepted. Metal containers generated 65% of Crown's $1.8 billion 1988 sales, while closures generated 30% and packaging equipment 5%.

Manufacturing When Connelly took over in 1957, Crown had perhaps the most outmoded and inefficient production facilities in the industry. Dividends had taken precedence over new investment, and old machinery combined with the cumbersome Philadelphia plant had generated very high production and transportation costs. Soon after he gained control, Connelly took drastic action, closing down the Philadelphia facility and investing heavily in new and geographically dispersed plants. From 1958 to 1963, the company spent almost $82 million on relocation and new facilities. From 1976 through 1989, Crown had 26 domestic plant locations versus 9 in 1955. The plants were small (usually 2 to 3 lines for two-piece cans) and were located close to the customer rather than the raw material source. Crown operated its plants 24 hours a day with unique 12-hour shifts. Employees had two days on followed by two days off and then three days on followed by three days off.

Crown emphasized quality, flexibility, and quick response to customer needs. One officer claimed that the key to the can industry was "the fact that nobody stores cans" and when customers need them "they want them in a hurry and on time. . . . Fast answers get customers." To accommodate customer demands, some of Crown's plants kept more than a month's inventory on hand. Crown also instituted a total quality improvement process to refine its manufacturing processes and gain greater control. According to a Crown spokesperson, "The objective of this quality improvement process is to make the best possible can at the lowest possible cost. You lower the cost of doing business not by the wholesale elimination of people, but by reducing mistakes in order to improve efficiency. And you do that by making everybody in the company accountable."

Recycling In 1970, Crown formed Nationwide Recyclers, Inc., as a wholly owned subsidiary. By 1989, Crown believed Nationwide was one of the top four or five aluminum can recyclers in the country. While Nationwide was only marginally profitable, Crown had invested in the neighborhood of $10 million in its recycling arm.

Research and Development (R&D) Crown's technology strategy focused on enhancing the existing product line. As one executive noted, "We are not truly pioneers. Our philosophy is not to spend a great deal of money for basic research. However, we do have tremendous skills in die forming and metal fabrication, and we can move to adapt to the customer's needs faster than anyone else in the industry."[18] For instance, Crown worked closely with large breweries in the development of the two-piece drawn-and-ironed cans for the beverage industry. Crown also made an explicit decision to stay away from basic research. According to one executive, Crown was not interested in "all the frills of an R&D section of high-class, ivory-towered scientists. . . . There is a tremendous asset inherent in being second, especially in the face of the ever-changing state of flux you find in this industry. You try to let others take the risks and make the mistakes. . . ."

This philosophy did not mean that Crown never innovated. For instance, Crown was able to beat its competitors into two-piece can production. Approximately $120 million in new equipment was installed from 1972 through 1975, and by 1976 Crown had 22 two-piece lines in production—more than any other competitor.[19] Crown's research teams also worked closely with customers on specific customer requests. For example, a study of the most efficient plant layout for a food packer or the redesign of a dust cap for the aerosol packager were not unusual projects.

Marketing and Customer Service The cornerstone of Crown's marketing strategy was, in John Connelly's words, the philosophy that "you can't just increase efficiency to succeed; you must at the same time improve quality." In conjunction with its R&D strategy, the company's sales force maintained close ties with customers and emphasized Crown's ability to provide technical assistance and specific problem solving at the customer's plant. Crown's manufacturing emphasis on flexibility and quick response to customers' needs supported its marketing emphasis on putting the customer first. Michael J. McKenna, president of Crown's North American Division, insisted, "We have always been and always will be extremely customer driven."[20]

Competing cans were made of identical materials to identical specifications on practically identical machinery, and sold at almost identical prices in a given market. At Crown, all customers' gripes went to John Connelly, who was the company's best salesman. A visitor recalled being in his office when a complaint came through from the manager of a Florida citrus-packing plant. Connelly assured him the problem would be taken care of immediately, then casually remarked that he would be in Florida the next day. Would the plant manager join him for dinner? He would indeed. As Crown's president put the telephone down, his visitor said that he hadn't realized Connelly was planning to go to Florida. "Neither did I," confessed Connelly, "until I began talking."[21]

Financing After he took over in 1957, Connelly applied the first receipts from the sale of inventory to get out from under Crown's short-term bank obligations. He then steadily reduced the debt/equity ratio from 42% in 1956 to 18.2% in 1976 and 5% in 1986. By the end of 1988, Crown's debt represented less than 2% of total capital. Connelly discontinued cash dividends in 1956, and in 1970 repurchased the last of the preferred stock, eliminating preferred dividends as a cash drain. From 1970 forward, management applied excess cash to the repurchase of stock. Connelly set ambitious earnings goals and most years he achieved them. In the 1976 annual report he wrote, "A long time ago we made a prediction that some day our sales would exceed $1 billion and profits of $60.00 per share. Since then, the stock has been split 20-for-1 so this means $3.00 per share." Crown Cork & Seal's revenues reached $1 billion in 1977 and earnings per share reached $3.46. Earnings per share reached $10.11 in 1988 adjusted for a 3-for-1 stock split in September 1988.

International A significant dimension of Connelly's strategy focused on international growth, particularly in developing countries. Between 1955 and 1960, Crown received what were called "pioneer rights" from many foreign governments aiming to build up the industrial sectors of their countries. These "rights" gave Crown first chance at any new can or closure business introduced into these developing countries. Mark W. Hartman, president of Crown's International Division, described Connelly as "a Johnny Appleseed with respect to the international marketplace. When the new countries of Africa were emerging, for example, John was there offering crown-making capabilities to help them in their industrialization, while at the same time getting a foothold for Crown. John's true love was international business."[22] By 1988, Crown's 62 foreign plants generated 44% of sales and 54% of operating profits. John Connelly visited each of Crown's overseas plants. (See Exhibit 6 for map of plant locations.)

Crown emphasized national management wherever possible. Local people, Crown asserted, understood the local marketplace: the suppliers, the customers, and the unique conditions that drove supply and demand. Crown's overseas investment also offered opportunities to recycle equipment that was, by U.S. standards, less sophisticated. Because can manufacturing was new to many regions of the world, Crown's older equipment met the needs of what was still a developing industry overseas.

Performance Connelly's strategy met with substantial success throughout his tenure at Crown. With stock splits and price appreciation, $100 invested in Crown stock in 1957 would be worth approximately $30,000 in 1989. After restructuring the company in his first three years, revenues grew at 12.2% per year while income grew at 14.0% over the next two decades (see Exhibit 7). Return on equity averaged 15.8% for much of the 1970s, while Continental Can and American Can lagged far behind at 10.3% and 7.1%, respectively. Over the period 1968–1978 Crown's total return to shareholders ranked 114 out of the Fortune 500, well ahead of IBM (183) and Xerox (374).

In the early 1980s, flat industry sales, combined with an increasingly strong dollar overseas, unrelenting penetration by plastics, and overcapacity in can manufacturing at home, led to declining sales revenues at Crown. Crown's sales dropped from $1.46 billion in 1980 to $1.37

billion by 1984. However, by 1985 Crown had rebounded and annual sales growth averaged 7.6% from 1984 through 1988 while profit growth averaged 12% (see Exhibits 8 and 9). Over the period 1978–1988 Crown's total return to shareholders was 18.6% per year, ranking 146 out of the Fortune 500. In 1988, *Business Week* noted that Connelly—earning a total of only $663,000 in the three years ending in 1987—garnered shareholders the best returns for the least executive pay in the United States. As an industry analyst observed, "Crown's strategy is a no-nonsense, back-to-basics strategy—except they never left the basics."[23]

John Connelly's Contribution to Success
Customers, employees, competitors, and Wall Street analysts attributed Crown's sustained success to the unique leadership of John Connelly. He arrived at Crown as it headed into bankruptcy in 1957, achieved a 1,646% increase in profits on a relatively insignificant sales increase by 1961, and proceeded to outperform the industry's giants throughout the next three decades. A young employee expressed the loyalty created by Connelly: "If John told me to jump out the window, I'd jump—and be sure he'd catch me at the bottom with a stock option in his hand."

Yet Connelly was not an easy man to please. Crown's employees had to get used to Connelly's tough, straight-line management. *Fortune* credited Crown's success to Connelly, "whose genial Irish grin masks a sober salesman executive who believes in the eighty-hour week and in traveling while competitors sleep." He went to meetings uninvited, and expected the same devotion to Crown of his employees as he demanded of himself. As one observer remembered:

> The Saturday morning meeting is standard operating procedure. Crown's executives travel and confer only at night and on weekends. William D. Wallace, vice president for operations, travels 100,000 miles a year, often in the company plane. But Connelly sets the pace. An associate recalls driving to his home in the predawn blackness to pick him up for a flight to a distant plant. The Connelly house was dark, but he spotted a figure sitting on the curb under a street light, engrossed in a loose-leaf book. Connelly's greeting, as he jumped into the car: "I want to talk to you about last month's variances."[24]

Avery's Challenge in 1989
Avery thought long and hard about the options available to him in 1989. He considered the growing opportunities in plastic closures and containers, as well as glass containers. With growth slowing in metal containers, plastics was the only container segment that held much promise. However, the possibility of diversifying beyond the manufacture of containers altogether had some appeal, although the appropriate opportunity was not at hand. While Crown's competitors had aggressively expanded in a variety of directions, Connelly had been cautious, and had prospered. Avery wondered if now was the time for a change at Crown.

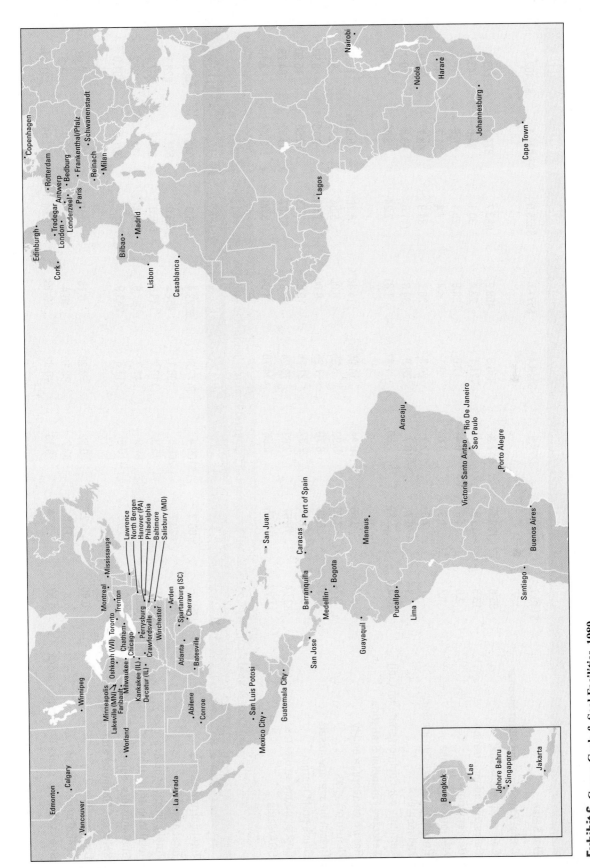

Exhibit 6 Crown Cork & Seal Facilities, 1989

Exhibit 7 Crown Cork & Seal Company Consolidated Statement of Income (dollars in millions, year-end December 31)

	1956	1961	1966	1971	1973	1975	1977	1979
Net Sales	$115.1	$177.0	$279.8	$448.4	$571.8	$825.0	$1,049.1	$1,402.4
Costs, Expenses and Other Income								
Cost of products sold	95.8	139.1	217.2	350.9	459.2	683.7	874.1	1,179.3
Sales and administration	13.5	15.8	18.4	21.1	23.4	30.1	34.8	43.9
Depreciation	2.6	4.6	9.4	17.0	20.9	25.4	5.6	16.4
Net interest expense	1.2	1.3	4.6	5.1	4.4	7.4	31.7	40.1
Provision for taxes on income	.1	7.6	12.7	24.6	26.7	34.9	48.7	51.8
Net income	.3	6.7	16.7	28.5	34.3	41.6	53.8	70.2
Earnings per common share (actual)	(6.01)	.28	.80	1.41	1.81	2.24	3.46	4.65
Selected Financial Statistics								
Return on average equity	0.55%	9.66%	16.44%	14.05%	14.46%	15.20%	15.88%	15.57%
Return on sales	0.24	3.76	5.99	6.35	6.00	5.04	5.13	5.00
Return on average assets	0.32	6.00	6.76	7.25	8.00	7.69	9.13	8.93
Gross profit margin	16.76	21.43	22.37	21.76	19.69	17.13	16.68	15.90
Cost of goods sold/sales	83.24	78.57	77.63	78.24	80.31	82.87	83.32	84.29
SGA/sales	11.73	8.65	6.56	4.70	4.09	3.65	3.32	3.13

Crown Cork & Seal Company Consolidated Statement of Financial Position (dollars in millions, year-end December 31)

	1956	1961	1966	1971	1973	1975	1977	1979
Total current assets	$50.2	$66.3	$109.4	$172.3	$223.4	$265.0	$340.7	$463.3
Total assets	86.5	129.2	269.5	398.1	457.5	539.0	631.1	828.2
Total current liabilities	15.8	24.8	75.3	110.2	139.6	170.0	210.8	287.1
Total long-term debt	20.2	17.7	57.9	41.7	37.9	29.7	12.8	12.2
Shareholders' equity	50.3	77.5	110.8	211.8	243.9	292.7	361.8	481.0
Selected Financial Statistics								
Debt/equity	0.40	0.23	0.52	0.20	0.16	0.10	0.04	0.03
Capital expenditures	1.9	11.8	32.7	33.1	40.4	49.0	58.9	55.9
Book value per share of common stock	1.57	2.74	5.19	10.62	13.13	16.64	23.54	31.84

Source: Adapted from Annual Reports.

Exhibit 8 Crown Cork & Seal Company Consolidated Statement of Income (dollars in millions except earnings per share, year-end December 31)

	1981	1982	1983	1984	1985	1986	1987	1988
Net Sales	$1,373.9	$1,351.9	$1,298.0	$1,369.6	$1,487.1	$1,618.9	$1,717.9	$1,834.1
Costs, Expenses, and Other Income:								
Cost of products sold	1,170.4	1,175.6	1,116.0	1,172.5	1,260.3	1,370.2	1,456.6	1,569.5
Sales and administrative	45.3	44.2	42.9	42.1	43.0	46.7	49.6	50.9
Depreciation	38.0	39.9	38.4	40.2	43.7	47.2	56.9	57.2
Interest expense	12.3	9.0	9.0	8.9	12.2	6.2	8.9	10.0
Interest income	—	—	—	—	—	—	(15.2)	(14.8)
Total Expenses	1,266.1	1,268.6	1,206.2	1,263.6	1,359.2	1,470.3	1,556.8	1,672.9
Income before taxes	107.8	83.2	91.8	105.9	127.9	148.6	161.1	161.2
Provision for taxes on income	43.0	38.5	40.2	46.4	56.2	69.2	72.7	67.8
Net income	64.8	44.7	51.5	59.5	71.7	79.4	88.3	93.4
Earnings per common share	1.48	1.05	1.27	1.59	2.17	2.48	2.86	3.37

Note: Earnings per common share have been restated to reflect a 3-for-1 stock split on September 12, 1988

Selected Financial Statistics

	1981	1982	1983	1984	1985	1986	1987	1988
Return on Average Equity (%):	11.72%	7.94%	9.34%	11.42%	13.94%	14.34%	14.46%	14.45%
Return on sales	4.72	3.31	3.97	4.35	4.82	4.91	5.14	5.09
Return on average assets	7.38	5.19	6.20	7.31	8.58	8.80	8.67	8.61
Gross profit margin	14.81	13.04	14.03	14.39	15.25	15.36	15.21	14.42
Cost of goods sold/sales	85.19	86.96	85.97	85.61	84.75	84.64	84.79	85.58
SGA/sales	3.30	3.27	3.30	3.07	2.89	2.88	2.89	2.78
Net Sales ($):								
United States	775.0	781.0	749.9	844.5	945.3	1,010.3	985.5	1,062.5
Europe	324.0	304.4	298.7	283.0	282.8	365.6	415.6	444.2
All others	283.6	273.1	259.1	261.3	269.3	269.0	342.5	368.6
Operating Profit ($):								
United States	62.8	58.9	55.0	67.1	88.9	92.8	95.4	70.6
Europe	20.6	19.0	24.0	17.2	17.0	21.9	22.4	33.4
All others	40.0	37.3	33.1	38.3	40.6	39.6	64.9	66.1
Operating Ratio (%):								
United States	8.1	7.5	7.3	7.9	9.4	9.7	9.6	6.6
Europe	6.3	6.2	8.0	6.0	6.0	5.9	5.4	7.5
All others	14.1	13.6	12.7	14.6	15.0	14.7	18.9	17.9

Source: Adapted from Annual Reports.

Note: The above sales figures are before the deduction of intracompany sales.

Exhibit 9 Crown Cork & Seal Company Consolidated Statement of Financial Position (dollars in millions, year-end December 31)

	1981	1982	1983	1984	1985	1986	1987	1988
Current Assets:								
Cash	$ 21.5	$ 15.8	$ 21.0	$ 7.0	$ 14.8	$ 16.5	$ 27.6	$ 18.0
Accounts receivable	262.8	257.1	240.6	237.6	279.0	270.4	280.7	248.1
Inventory	206.2	184.4	170.2	174.6	171.9	190.1	228.1	237.6
Total Current Assets	490.6	457.3	431.7	419.2	465.6	477.0	536.4	503.8
Investments	12.4	14.6	26.7	28.8	41.5	43.7	NA	NA
Goodwill	11.2	10.8	9.6	10.3	11.8	14.1	16.7	16.5
Property, plant and equipment	368.4	357.8	353.7	348.0	346.9	404.0	465.7	495.9
Other noncurrent assets	NA	NA	NA	NA	NA	NA	79.1	57.0
Total Assets	882.6	840.6	821.7	806.4	865.8	938.8	1,097.9	1,073.2
Current Liabilities:								
Short-term debt	22.7	21.6	24.4	42.0	16.3	17.2	44.0	20.2
Accounts payable	193.0	165.6	163.1	177.9	197.1	220.1	265.9	277.6
U.S. and foreign taxes	17.3	4.7	11.4	6.0	11.4	11.3	28.4	23.3
Total Current Liabilities	233.0	191.9	198.8	225.8	224.8	248.5	338.2	321.2
Long-term debt	5.8	5.6	2.8	2.7	2.2	1.4	19.7	9.4
Other	14.5	18.5	12.8	15.8	31.2	29.3	0.0	0.0
Total Long-term Debt	20.3	24.1	15.6	18.5	33.5	30.7	19.7	9.4
Deferred income taxes	55.5	57.7	57.8	60.7	71.3	79.2	89.4	93.7
Minority equity in subsidiaries	7.2	7.2	5.2	3.7	4.7	3.8	5.0	0.9
Shareholders' equity	566.7	559.8	544.3	497.8	531.5	576.6	645.6	648.0
Liability and owners' equity	882.6	840.6	821.7	806.4	865.8	938.8	1,097.9	1,073.2

Selected Financial Statistics

	1981	1982	1983	1984	1985	1986	1987	1988
Debt/equity	1.02%	0.99%	0.51%	0.54%	0.42%	0.24%	3.06%	1.45%
Debt/(debt + equity)	3.5%	4.1%	2.7%	3.5%	6.0%	5.0%	3.0%	1.4%
Shares outstanding at year end (M)	14.5	14.0	13.2	11.5	10.5	10.0	9.5	27.0
Capital expenditures ($M)	$ 63.8	$ 50.3	$ 55.5	$ 53.8	$ 50.9	$ 94.0	$ 99.5	$ 102.6
Shares repurchased (000)	75.4	528.3	863.1	1,694.5	1,006.0	677.1	638.7	2,242.9
Stock price: High[a]	$ 12.00	$ 10.00	$ 13.00	$ 15.75	$ 29.62	$ 38.25	$ 46.87	$ 46.72
Stock price: Low[a]	$ 8.00	$ 7.00	$ 10.00	$ 11.75	$ 15.12	$ 25.25	$ 28.00	$ 30.00

Source: Adapted from Annual Reports.
[a]Restated for 9/1988 stock split.

Within the traditional metal can business, Avery had to decide whether or not to get involved in the bidding for Continental Can. The acquisition of Continental Can Canada (CCC)—with sales of roughly $400 million—would make Canada Crown's largest single presence outside of the United States. Continental's USA business—with estimated revenues of $1.3 billion in 1989—would double the size of Crown's domestic operations. Continental's Latin American, Asian, and Middle Eastern operations were rumored to be priced in the range of $100 million to $150 million. Continental's European operations generated estimated sales of $1.5 billion in 1989 and included a work force of 10,000 at 30 production sites. Potential bidders for all, or part of Continental's operations, included many of Crown's U.S. rivals in addition to European competition: Pechiney International of France, Metal Box of Great Britain (which had recently acquired Carnaud SA), and VIAG AG, a German trading group, among others.

Avery knew that most mergers in this industry had not worked out well. He also thought about the challenge of taking two companies that come from completely different cultures and bringing them together. There would be inevitable emotional and attitudinal changes, particularly for Continental's salaried managers and Crown's "owner-operators." Avery also knew that the merger of American Can and National Can had its difficulties. That consolidation was taking longer than expected and, according to one observer, "American Can would be literally wiped out in the end."

Avery found himself challenging Crown's traditional strategies and thought seriously of drafting a new blueprint for the future.

Endnotes

1. Salomon Brothers. 1990. *Beverage Cans Industry Report,* March 1.
2. Davis T. 1990. Can do: A metal container update. *Beverage World,* June: 34.
3. Sheehan J. J. 1988. Nothing succeeds like success. *Beverage World,* November: 82.
4. Until 1985, aluminum cans were restricted to carbonated beverages because it was the carbonation that prevented the can from collapsing. Reynolds discovered that by adding liquid nitrogen to the can's contents, aluminum containers could hold noncarbonated beverages and still retain their shape. The liquid nitrogen made it possible for Reynolds to make cans for liquor, chocolate drinks, and fruit juices.
5. Sly, J. 1988. A "can-do crusade" by steel industry. *Chicago Tribune,* July 3: 1.
6. Merrill Lynch Capital Markets. 1991. *Containers and Packaging Industry Report.* March 21.
7. Salomon Brothers Inc. 1991. *Containers/Packaging: Beverage Cans Industry Report,* April 3.
8. Agoos, A. 1985. Aluminum girds for the plastic can bid. *Chemical Week,* January 16: 18.
9. Oman, B. 1990. A clear choice? *Beverage World,* June: 78.
10. In response to public concern, the container industry developed highly efficient "closed loop" recycling systems. Containers flowed from the manufacturer, through the wholesaler/distributor, to the retailer, to the consumer, and back to the manufacturer or material supplier for recycling. Aluminum's high recycling value permitted can manufacturers to sell cans at a lower cost to beverage producers. The reclamation of steel cans lagged that of aluminum because collection and recycling did not result in significant energy or material cost advantages.
11. Lang, N. 1990. A touch of glass. *Beverage World,* June: 36.
12. Ibid.
13. U.S. Industrial Outlook, 1984–1990.
14. The First Boston Corporation. 1990. *Packaging Industry Report,* April 4.
15. Whalen, R. J. 1962. The unoriginal ideas that rebuilt Crown Cork. *Fortune,* October.
16. Ibid.: 156.
17. In the mid-1960s, growth in demand for soft drink and beer cans was more than triple that for traditional food cans.
18. Hamermesh, R. G., Anderson, M. J. Jr., and Harris, J. E. 1978. Strategies for low market share business. *Harvard Business Review,* May–June: 99.
19. In 1976, there were 47 two-piece tinplate and 130 two-piece aluminum lines in the United States.
20. *One Hundred Years.* Crown Cork & Seal Company, Inc.
21. Whalen, The unoriginal ideas that rebuilt Crown Cork.
22. *One Hundred Years.* Crown Cork & Seal Company, Inc.
23. *BusinessWeek.* 1987. These penny-pinchers deliver a big bang for their bucks. May 4.
24. Whalen, The unoriginal ideas that rebuilt Crown Cork.

Case 7   Automation Consulting Services

As they had been doing twice a year for the past six years, the three founding partners of Automation Consulting Services (ACS) convened at Cliff Reed's summer home in Cape Cod in August 2000 to spend a weekend assessing the status of their consulting firm and planning its future. Not surprisingly, they each had come away from their recent tour of ACS' four offices with a long list of questions, concerns, and ideas for change.

Over the years, the semi-annual practice of visiting each office and holding formal meetings with its partners and principals had been an effective way for the three founding partners to identify major problems and new opportunities. This year, however, the three founders sensed that the magnitude of the issues that needed their direct attention had grown out of control. They worried that two days of brainstorming would not be an adequate response to the current challenges and those projected for the next decade.

Company Background

Clifford Reed, Jack Leland, and Angela Goldberg had founded ACS in 1993 as a technical consulting firm specializing in factory automation for industrial manufacturing firms. ACS advised clients on the development of automation strategy and long-term facilities planning and also provided guidance in the design and implementation of specific automation projects.

From its home base in Boston, ACS had expanded into three additional locations. Offices had been opened in Philadelphia and Detroit in 1995 and 1996, respectively, and ACS had acquired a local partnership in San Jose, California in 1998. By 2000, ACS had a professional staff of 83 consultants and revenues of nearly $52 million. The ACS partnership had tentative plans to open an office in Europe in the near future.

When Reed, Leland, and Goldberg had first formed their partnership in 1993, demand for automation expertise was growing steadily and their market research indicated that the trend would continue through the 2000s. From the outset, the founders had agreed that revenue growth would be a top priority. They had considered rapid growth an imperative for three main reasons. First, most of their clients and likely prospects were relatively large corporations, often with multiple manufacturing sites; these firms preferred hiring technical consulting firms that could provide the depth and breadth of expertise and geographical coverage to meet all their automation needs. Second, the founders wanted to establish as many client relationships as possible while the market was still young and fragmented in an attempt to build client exit barriers. Third, without a high growth rate, the partnership would not be able to attract, motivate, and retain ambitious junior consultants with the promise of a fast-paced promotion policy and potentially rapid career development. As of the summer of 2000, ACS management had surpassed its aggressive growth goals by doubling revenues in each year of operation, and its founders had no plans to let up the pressure for growth in the near future.

ACS' phenomenal success was attributable, in part, to the mix of talent and experience embodied in its founders. Cliff Reed was a 10-year veteran engineer from a "Big Three" auto manufacturer, where he had specialized in factory automation. Jack Leland, also an engineer, was a graduate of MIT with eight years of practical experience in manufacturing operations at a high-tech firm before founding ACS. Angela Goldberg was a Harvard MBA, with ten years of experience marketing computers and related equipment to industrial clients.

The three founders—who constituted the Executive Committee—were the only partners with firm-wide responsibilities; all other partners focused only on their own offices. Each of the four offices was headed by a managing partner who was responsible for his or her office's revenues, recruiting efforts, staffing, and client development. The offices varied substantially in size. Each office had 3 to 6 partners as well as from 8 to 31 nonpartner professionals. (See Exhibit 1 for an organizational chart.)

In keeping with the Executive Committee's emphasis on revenue growth, each office was managed as a revenue center, with the partnership as a whole treated as the sole profit center. Each partner's compensation consisted of a share of the firm's total profits in proportion to his share of total revenue generation. (The founders and other managing partners received an additional bonus tied to firm-wide and office-specific revenue growth, respectively.) Expenses were accumulated and monitored on a consolidated firm-wide basis. In addition, each ACS office monitored total

Hilary A. Weston prepared this case under the supervision of Professor Robert Simons as the basis for class discussion rather than to illustrate either effective or ineffective handling of an administrative situation.

HARVARD | BUSINESS | SCHOOL

9-190-053

	Boston	Philadelphia	Detroit	San Jose
Number of:				
– Partners (including managing partners)	6	3	3	3
– Principals	8	5	4	4
– Senior Associates and Associates	23	12	8	4
Total Professional Staff	37[a]	20[b]	15	11

[a]Boston headcount includes Cliff Reed and Angela Goldberg.

[b]Philadelphia headcount includes Jack Leland.

Exhibit 1 Automation Consulting Services Organization Chart, June 2000

hours billed and utilization[1] as proxies for office profitability. Revenues, utilization, and other performance measures for 1999 are reported, by office, in Exhibit 2.

August 2000: The Executive Committee Retreat

Cliff, Jack, and Angela had not prepared a formal agenda in advance of their two-day retreat. Instead, they began as they had in the past: by discussing their thoughts and concerns, one office at a time, based on their recent tour as well as their

[1]Utilization refers to the percentage of the professional staff's compensated working time that is charged out to clients—i.e., time that is spent on revenue-generating activities.

individual interactions with the consultants of each office. During this discussion, they kept a running list of priority problems and opportunities, which would serve as the agenda for the second day of their retreat. The following sections highlight the major issues raised on Saturday, August 19.

The San Jose Office

The Executive Committee was particularly concerned with the operations of the San Jose office, because it was the only office they had acquired rather than built and molded themselves. The acquisition had been completed less than a year ago. Consequently, the combining of management styles, practices, and personalities was still sorting itself out.

Exhibit 2   FY 1999 Summary Statistics—By Office

	Boston	Philadelphia	Detroit	San Jose
Revenues	$23,021,120	$12,481,820	$8,602,200	$7,416,000
Utilization[a] (annual average)	80%	78%	91%	82%
No. of projects completed during FY	52	24	8	15
No. of clients served during FY	29	12	5	11

[a]Utilization = (Professional hours billed to clients) ÷ (Total available professional work hours).

To date, all three partners were generally pleased with the acquired staff's skills, experience, and performance.

A recent incident, however, seemed cause for concern. Angela had discovered that one of the San Jose partners, Douglas Crowley, had employed a client billing practice of which she did not approve. Crowley had just completed a project for Powerhouse Inc., a client that needed help in expanding and automating its production capabilities. The project had involved space and equipment planning, mechanical and electrical machine design, and the development of a master plan for increasing production. As was common in ACS' work, Crowley's original proposal and the subsequent contract had stated a price range for the job with a guaranteed price ceiling, rather than a fixed price. As with all clients, Crowley billed Powerhouse monthly. Angela was outraged, however, when she learned from a principal on the project that Crowley had boosted his final bill to Powerhouse to "subsidize" another job that was running over budget.

The principal who informed Angela apparently did not consider Crowley's action a problem. In fact, before seeing Angela's reaction, he told her that "cross-subsidizing" occurred regularly, with Managing Partner Kyle Ross' approval, whenever the costs of a particular job were significantly below the contract price ceiling. "As long as a client's total bill is below the ceiling," the principal claimed, "no one was exploited by cross-subsidizing, and ACS met its revenue target." Angela saw things differently. She wanted to fire Crowley and any others who had engaged in cross-subsidizing. She was particularly angry because Powerhouse, the overcharged client, was a subsidiary of one of her oldest Boston-based clients.

Cliff and Jack agreed with Angela that Crowley's action was clearly not in line with their objective of building long-term client relationships. The founders, however, had never articulated guidelines for partners, in terms of either general business conduct or selling and billing practices. Every partner managed his clients according to his own style and strategy and that of his managing partner. The Executive Committee had never before encountered a major conflict for two reasons: first, at least one of the three founders had been on the team of most of the projects, particularly in the early years; and second, nearly all of the partners except for the three in San Jose had risen through the ACS ranks, and tended to share the same billing practices and client philosophy used by the founders.

The three realized that some type of explicit action or directive might be needed in order to prevent future departures from what they deemed acceptable billing practices. They did not, however, want to overreact and kill the entrepreneurial spirit that had allowed the firm to flourish. An aggressive managing partner like Kyle Ross was the key to ACS' revenue growth. The unwritten rule at ACS had always been local autonomy. The founders believed that this made good business sense, and their managing partners had come to expect substantial independence.

As a result of the California incident, however, Reed, Leland, and Goldberg now questioned the merit of their hands-off management style and wondered what sort of guidance they should provide for the partners and how they should communicate and enforce new policies. They worried that any action that appeared too authoritative could threaten the good working relationships they had with all of the partners. Failure to provide some guidance, however, might expose the firm to serious risks as their operations expanded both in size and geographic reach. In addition to devising appropriate preventive measures, the founders had to decide what, if any, disciplinary action to take with the San Jose consultants directly and indirectly involved in cross-subsidizing. Finally, they also had to decide whether to reveal the billing error to Powerhouse (and other mischarged clients) and whether to return to them a portion of their fees. In principle, all three partners felt they should return the fees, but they did not yet know how many dollars would be involved and they were not sure what explanation to provide to the clients.

The Detroit Office

The Detroit office was on the verge of an unforeseen crisis. Within two months, fifty percent of its current client work would be completed and almost no new projects were definitively lined up to fill the void. Nearly half of the office's professional staff would have no billable work. Meanwhile, revenues, profits, and cash flow would dwindle.

ACS had never before faced such a situation because demand for their services had always exceeded supply. The Detroit office relied on a small number of large clients and lacked the client breadth that had developed at the larger, older offices. Instead of compensating for this vulnerability with a business development plan, the Detroit partners had been focusing their attention almost exclusively on three very large existing projects. Two of the three were scheduled to end in the fall of 2000. The anticipated "Phase Two's" had not materialized on either project.

While in the Detroit office the previous week, the Executive Committee had launched a three-point crisis plan: (1) They made arrangements for several Detroit consultants to be assigned temporarily to projects based at the other three offices; (2) they designed a marketing plan to solicit work from existing and new clients; and (3) they transferred a partner with particularly strong selling skills from Boston to Detroit.

The Executive Committee realized that their crisis plan was merely a band-aid. They discussed the client prospecting system that they had tried to install two years earlier. The system, which Angela had heard about from a business school friend in a large consulting firm, was designed to monitor prospecting activity and the probable volume of upcoming work. The system worked as follows:

> Each managing partner would use a chart to keep track of the staffing requirements of all existing and prospective projects. A six-month time line, starting with the current

week, would run across the top. Down the left side the partner would list projects grouped into four categories: Ongoing, Sold-but-not-Started, Submitted Proposals, and Prospects. He would then fill in the boxes with the number of junior and senior consultants each project demanded or would demand per week and then sum each column. For bids not yet won, the managing partner would calculate expected staff utilization by applying to each contract an estimated percentage probability of winning it. He could then monitor total projected utilization for each week on the chart and use the chart to run weekly staffing meetings with the other partners. The chart would allow staff meetings to focus on how to hit a particular utilization target and where the pressure points were for new client work. The chart could also provide useful information to top management on the activity at individual offices.

In 1997, when the founders had explained the monitoring system to the rest of the partnership, most of the partners had strongly opposed its adoption. The managing partners, whose acceptance was critical, were particularly negative. They had considered the proposed system a time-consuming, bureaucratic activity that would intrude on their freedom to manage their offices autonomously. They had persuaded the founders to abandon the idea based on two arguments:

1. We have always been a decentralized partnership, in our philosophy and in our practices, and there is no evidence in our financial performance that the current arrangements are inadequate; and
2. There is no need for a detailed monitoring system to manage utilization levels since we already have the right financial incentive in place for all partners. Managing partners worry about prospecting and utilization daily—as do all partners—because the size of their paychecks depends on their annual revenue contribution.

The three founders now discussed how best to revisit the issue with the entire partnership:

Cliff: This Detroit problem has convinced me that our financial incentives alone are not a foolproof way to control utilization.

Jack: I agree. But you know that some partners will say the incentive system is just fine, as long as partners apply good judgment. Some of them will point the finger at Margolies [Detroit managing partner] and say he screwed up *despite* the incentive system.

Angela: Let's try to put aside the issue of blame for now. We need to install some preventative measures so this doesn't happen again. We have to persuade the managing partners to adopt some sort of monitoring system. We may have to agree to

let them run it on a decentralized basis to get their cooperation.

Cliff: But I think the system has to be centralized. Those staffing charts would provide extremely useful information to the three of us. We need to know what sort of prospecting activity is occurring at each office to help us with resource planning for the whole firm. Where should our next office be? What skills should we be recruiting? What sorts of bids are we losing out on? What are our competitors doing? A centralized view of the prospecting charts would also help us to better serve our large multi-site clients—the ones we work with, or could work with, out of more than one office.

Jack: You're right. But in my opinion, a more basic reason to insist that some form of the reports reaches our desks is that if we don't insist, we have no way of ensuring that everyone is adhering to the system and updating their forecasts on a regular basis.

The discussion then focused on problems of implementation. All three wondered where to begin and how to get the partners to use it. How sophisticated should the tracking system be? Should the system be maintained by partners or should new staff specialists be hired to implement and run the system? How frequently should it be updated? How often should reports be sent to the Executive Committee? Finally, the discussion returned to whether centralized monitoring would really be necessary as long as they had good managers using the data in each office.

Boston

Like the two offices discussed above, the Boston office was also confronted by a dilemma that the Executive Committee believed could become a company wide concern. Alan Shapiro, a Boston partner, had recently won a bid to oversee the automation of a university library cataloging and ordering system. ACS had never before served a client in a non-manufacturing business, and one month into the project, ACS' inexperience was revealing itself. Not only was the project running over budget and behind schedule (that had happened before), but it looked like the project team would have to bring in an outside specialist in database management to complete the work promised to the client. ACS had never before "subcontracted" work.

When the proposal for the job had initially been prepared, Angela and Cliff, who jointly managed the Boston office, had been wary about ACS' ability to meet the prospective client's needs. They had decided, however, to let Shapiro make the decision himself as to whether to bid for the job.

Angela identified two issues that the founders had to address—apart from dealing with the specific project. In her words, "First, we must figure out how to guide the firm's strategic direction and expertise so that we are not working on an ad hoc basis, relying on individual partners' decisions to bid for one-time projects. And second, if we are to articulate a strategic direction for the firm, we must determine what it should be with respect to manufacturing versus service sector clients. The service sector is growing rapidly and dramatically increasing its use of technology. But the most effective way to employ the firm's existing skill base—given the sorts of people we have already hired and developed—is to focus on manufacturing."

In addressing the strategy-setting process, Jack commented, "The three of us have always considered ACS to be a consulting firm exclusively for manufacturers, and I think that we have assumed that the partnership both understands and agrees with this focus. Maybe we've been lucky that the firm has maintained its strategic focus as long as it has. It's time we bring the whole partnership together to discuss and draft a long-term plan. The partnership should develop a set of criteria that defines our strategic focus and then each partner would be required to use the criteria as a check list in determining whether a prospective job fit within our core business. If it doesn't, he walks away from the project."

Cliff and Angela agreed with Jack that it was time to think about a longer-term strategy and put it down on paper, but they were wary about getting into formal planning and strategic checklists. Cliff also worried, "What if we cannot reach consensus, or if we do not agree with the general consensus among the rest of the partnership? A discussion among all partners could be very time-consuming, especially if we feel our strategy should be reviewed annually. I wonder if this decision as to our future strategy isn't a call we should make ourselves and then just communicate to the other partners?"

Philadelphia

Jack Leland, who managed the Philadelphia office, sensed a problem at his office that he suspected ran through the whole firm. He was concerned that the focus on revenues, at the exclusion of expenses, had allowed various expense categories at the office level to creep up and get out of control. (See Exhibit 3 for firm-wide income statement.)

Jack explained his concern:

As revenue centers, the offices are not given explicit line-by-line budgets for expenses. So, although the managing partners are given overall expense budgets, they do not really worry about the level of specific expense categories. The number of dollars being spent on recruiting events, office equipment, training, and other "supporting" activities has been creeping up, but we don't have the detailed expense information to react. The limited itemization of costs on the P&L may have been adequate a few years ago, but now there are a lot more things buried in that 15% to 20% called "Other Expenses" that we ought to be monitoring.

The founders discussed the ramifications of converting each office to a profit center so that partners would have incentives to manage costs more closely. Despite the benefits of greater control over costs and profitability, they had concerns about converting ACS offices to profit centers. First, there were the challenges of implementation. They would have to negotiate profit targets with each managing partner. Would the local partners resent this interference

Exhibit 3 Automation Consulting Services Summary Profit and Loss Statement, Fiscal Year 1999

	Boston		Philadelphia		Detroit		San Jose		Total
Revenues:	$ 23,021,120		$ 12,481,820		$ 8,602,200		$ 7,416,000		$ 51,521,140
Expenses:									
Salary and benefits[a]	7,712,076	50%	4,874,150	55%	3,078,788	57%	2,789,900	57%	18,454,914
Rent and utilities[b]	2,313,622	15%	886,210	10%	540,138	10%	636,292	13%	4,376,262
Supplies and equipment[c]	2,622,106	17%	1,417,934	16%	1,026,262	19%	783,130	16%	5,849,432
Other[d]	2,776,348	18%	1,683,798	19%	756,194	14%	685,238	14%	5,901,578
Total	15,424,152	100%	8,862,092	100%	5,401,382	100%	4,894,560	100%	34,582,186
Income (pretax)	$ 7,596,968		$ 3,619,728		$3,200,818		$2,521,440		$16,938,954
Profit Margin (pretax)	33%		29%		37%		34%		33%

[a]Includes salary, wages, and all benefits of professional and nonexempt staff; excludes distribution of profits to partners.

[b]Includes office space, heat and electricity, and telecommunications.

[c]Includes stationery, office supplies, computers and leased copiers.

[d]Includes graphics services, temp employees, travel and entertainment, subscriptions, on-line databases, library, recruiting support, training materials, and miscellaneous.

with the way they ran their practices? And how much time would the process take?

The switch to office profit centers would also require changes in their incentive plan, which currently rewarded partners based primarily on firm-wide growth and profitability rather than office-specific profits. With compensation tied solely to individual office performance, would partners still be motivated to help other offices and maintain a unified, firm-wide image?

Lastly, as Cliff noted, "It is somewhat of a Catch-22. On the one hand, we don't want to send out new signals that conflict with our basic goal of revenue growth; but on the other hand, as our growth rate inevitably slows down, cost control becomes increasingly important. It will become more difficult to absorb cost increases."

Day One Wrap-Up

On Saturday evening, the three founders spent an hour reviewing their notes and jointly summarizing the major issues raised during the day's discussions. Sunday would be spent attempting to develop solutions for these issues. Exhibit 4 reproduces the outline they developed Saturday evening.

Exhibit 4   Executive Committee Retreat

AUTOMATION CONSULTING SERVICES

AUGUST 19, 2000

DAY ONE SUMMARY — Prepared by Cliff Reed

- AS OUR FIRM'S SIZE AND EXPERIENCE BASE CONTINUE TO GROW, THE SET OF OPPORTUNITIES THAT WE CAN PURSUE GROWS EXPONENTIALLY. WE NEED MORE FORMAL MANAGEMENT SYSTEMS AND PROCEDURES THROUGHOUT THE PRACTICE IN ORDER TO:

    1) IDENTIFY AND MAINTAIN A UNIFIED COMPANY STRATEGY AND IMAGE
    2) MAINTAIN A HIGH AND PROFITABLE GROWTH RATE
    3) COMMUNICATE GOALS AND RESPONSIBILITIES TO EMPLOYEES
    4) EFFECTIVELY MOTIVATE AND MONITOR PERFORMANCE
    5) FACILITATE THE SHARING OF KNOWLEDGE AND IDEAS AMONG OFFICES

- THE EXECUTIVE COMMITTEE AND ACTIVE PARTNERS ALREADY HAVE MORE THAN ENOUGH RESPONSIBILITIES. WE MUST FIND A WAY TO LIMIT THE AMOUNT OF TIME THAT WE DEVOTE TO NEW MANAGEMENT SYSTEMS AND PROCEDURES.

- A SPIRIT OF ENTREPRENEURSHIP AND CREATIVITY IS OUR STRENGTH AND WE MUST MAINTAIN THAT SPIRIT IN THE FUTURE.

ANY NEW MANAGEMENT SYSTEMS MUST BE CONSISTENT WITH THE FIRM'S CULTURE AND OVERALL STRATEGY IN THE SIGNALS THEY SEND TO OUR EMPLOYEES.

Case 8 Enron: On the Side of the Angels*

We're on the side of angels. We're taking on the entrenched monopolies. In every business we've been in, we're the good guys.

—**Jeffrey Skilling,** President and CEO,
Enron Corporation

On the day he was elected CEO, Enron's president, Jeffrey Skilling, was pictured on the front cover of the February 12, 2001, edition of *BusinessWeek* dressed in a black turtleneck and holding an electrified orb in his right hand, appearing more sorcerer than executive. Enron was charging into the deregulated energy markets. Skilling defended Enron's activities, saying:

> We're on the side of angels. We're taking on the entrenched monopolies. In every business we're in, we're the good guys.[1]

By August 2001, the charge would be over and Skilling would resign after only six months as CEO. In September 2000, Enron's stock price was in the $85 to $90 region; by November 2001, it had declined to less than a dollar. In January 2002, John Clifford Baxter, an Enron executive, died, an apparent suicide. Timothy Belden, an Enron trader in the California markets, would later plead guilty to conspiracy to manipulate markets in the California energy market,[2] and another, John Forney, would be arrested for conspiracy and wire fraud in the same California market.[3] The angels, it seems, had come back to earth.

From Pipelines to Commodity Trader

In June 1984, the board of Houston Natural Gas (HNG), a natural gas distribution firm, hired Kenneth Lay as chair and CEO. His first task was to defend HNG from a takeover bid by refocusing HNG on its core business. In a 1990 speech, Lay characterized his leadership:

> In carrying out that assignment, between June 1984 and January 1985, $632 million of non-natural gas operations were sold and $1.2 billion of natural gas operations were purchased. As one director was heard to quip at the time, the Board gave me unlimited authority, and I exceeded it.[4]

Lay created Enron, a natural gas and oil company, in 1986, through the merger of HNG with InterNorth, a natural gas pipeline company, and other acquistions.[5] Lay, the

merger's architect and Enron's first CEO, appeared to be one of the few individuals who recognized the opportunities of deregulation in the United States and privatization abroad. By the early 1990s, Enron owned an interest in a 4,100 mile pipeline in Argentina and commenced its power marketing business worldwide.

In 1994, *Fortune* ranked Enron 1st in a new category, pipelines, and 39th overall as one of "America's Most Admired Companies." By 1996, Enron had climbed to 22nd overall. In the 1990s, Enron busily expanded its business structure into other areas, such as energy generation, broadband, and financial markets. Yet Enron maintained its dominance of the pipeline industry's ranking and was ranked in the top 20 firms overall through February 2001. In that year, *Fortune* named Enron the most innovative firm in the United States for the second consecutive year. Enron had first won the category in 1997. From 1994 to 2001, the firm steadily climbed in *Fortune*'s "America's Most Admired Company" list. Its stock price rose just as dramatically: On December 31, 1996, Enron's stock listed at 21 7/16 (adjusted for a 1999 split), and on December 31, 2000, its price was 83 1/8. In the firm's entry foyer, a huge banner was placed, reading "World's Leading Company."[6] Skilling's license plate, which had once read "WLEC" (World's Leading Energy Company) changed to "WMM" (We Make Markets).[7]

Throughout 2001, as Enron's stock declined, its rankings dropped from first to last in its industry. Enron was ranked 523 (of 530) in wise use of corporate assets and quality of management and 521 in fiscal soundness.

"Get It Done. Get It Done Now. Reap the Rewards."

Lay built a management team not of gas and energy people but primarily of MBAs. Rebecca Mark, an energy professional who rose from part-time trader to president of Enron International and Azurix Water, characterized Enron employees as ex-military, Harvard Business School, and ex-entrepreneurship types. A *Fortune* article described the employees as "aggressive, well-compensated traders."[8] Enron had developed from an oil and gas exploration and pipeline company to a derivatives trading company. In its office tower, the executive offices on the seventh floor overlooked the sixth floor, an expansive derivatives trading operation.[9]

Enron's management saw creativity and human capital as the real resource behind its future growth. In the 1999 Annual Report Letter to Shareholders, Lay wrote:

> Creativity is a fragile commodity. Put a creative person in a bureaucratic atmosphere, and the creative output will die. We support employees with the most innovative culture possible, where people are measured not by how many mistakes they make, but how often they try.[10]

* This case was prepared from published materials by Professors Donald Schepers and Naomi A. Gardberg from Baruch College, City University of New York, to provide a basis for class discussion. Copyright © 2003 by the *Journal of Business and Applied Management*. Reprinted with permission of the *Journal of Business and Applied Management*. Readers may find the two Appendixes at the end of the case helpful in reading the case. Appendix A is a timeline of major events in this case. Appendix B is a glossary of various financial terms used in the case.

Every employee received a copy of the *Code of Ethics,* and with it a memo from Lay, dated July 1, 2000, that read in part:

> As officers and employees of Enron Corp. . . . we are responsible for conducting the business affairs of the Company in accordance with all applicable laws and in a moral and honest manner. . . . An employee shall not conduct himself or herself in a manner which directly or indirectly would be detrimental to the best interests of the Company or in a manner which would bring the employee financial gain separately derived as a direct consequence of his or her employment with the Company. . . . We want to be proud of Enron and to know that it enjoys a reputation for fairness and honesty that is respected. . . . **Let's keep that reputation high.**[6]

In April 2002 Lay described Enron's culture:

> One of our greatest successes at Enron was creating a culture, an environment, where people could try to achieve their God-given potential. But certainly I wanted it to be a highly moral and highly ethical environment. I have done the best job I can of following that everywhere I have been.[11]

Skilling put his own mark on Enron's culture. Extravagance was celebrated. At one meeting, Mark rode onto the stage with another executive on a Harley. At another, an adult elephant was brought in. One executive arrived at an employee gathering with a tractor-trailer full of expensive sports cars. The floors of the parking garage were marked by words to remind employees of valued attributes: *bold, innovative, smart, united, ambitious, accomplished, resourceful, creative, confident, adventurous, adaptable,* and *undaunted.*[6]

Two realities of life existed at Enron: stock price and the Peer Review Committee (PRC).[12] Nothing else mattered. Michael J. Miller, a manager in Enron's failed high-speed Internet service venture, described the atmosphere as "Get it done. Get it done now. Reap the rewards." An acrylic paperweight from the legal department stated its mission as "To provide prompt and first-rate legal service to Enron on a proactive and cost-effective basis."[13] Below that was "Translation: We do big, complex, and risky deals without blowing up Enron." Employees were rewarded for earnings that could be quickly booked, regardless of the long-term consequences. Two of the Enron executives who closed the deal on the doomed Dabhol power project in India received bonuses in the range of $50 million just for closing the deal.[14]

Like many dot-coms in the 1990s, Enron had a high reward structure. More than 2,000 Enron employees were millionaires. Employees received free laptops and handheld devices, expensive ergonomic chairs, and lunches at Houston's finest restaurants. Enron's board of directors was also well compensated. Chosen by management, Enron directors received cash and stock worth $300,000 a year.[14]

Recruitment took place both in long, intense interviews and in visits to topless bars and strip clubs.[6] Once past an initial interview, candidates were invited to a "Super Saturday" session of eight 50-minute interviews. Offers would go out within a few days, and candidates who declined would be offered signing bonuses or other financial inducements.[12]

Central to Enron's human resource policy was Skilling's PRC, or what became known as the "rank and yank" process.[6] Every six months, each person would choose five individuals (four plus the immediate supervisor) to provide feedback on his or her performance. This feedback went to the PRC's ratings meeting, where employees were rated on a scale from 1 (excellent) to 5 (worst performing). The PRC took place behind closed doors but in plain sight, since interior walls on the trading floors were glass. The picture of the individual being discussed would appear on a slide show, visible to all on the floor, while management discussed the evaluations. The PRC was a forced ranking system, in which 15 percent of those reviewed had to receive a 5. These individuals would then be "redeployed," meaning they had to search for another job in the organization or find themselves unemployed.

On the trading floor, men rated women as potential calendar models. When one of the "candidates" would walk onto the floor, someone would yell the name of the month to alert others of her presence.[6] Gambling was also prevalent. One year, the NCAA basketball pool supposedly reached almost $90,000.[15]

This culture spilled out of the doors and into Enron's relationships with others. On one occasion, Andy Fastow, the chief financial officer (CFO), was asked by a Citigroup banker if he understood the equations on the whiteboard in the conference room next to his office. Fastow replied, "I pulled them out of a book to intimidate people."[16]

Analysts who listened to the quarterly earnings report conference calls would be derided if they had questions about the details. During the April 17, 2001, conference call, Skilling had finished presenting the numbers and was responding to questions when Richard Grubman, a managing director of Highlands Capital Management, asked about Enron's balance sheet and cash-flow statement after earnings. Enron had failed to provide either. When Grubman commented that Enron was the only financial institution that never provided such statements for these calls, Skilling shot back, "Well, thank you very much. We appreciate that, [expletive]."[6]

Enron and the Capital Markets

Prior to his employment at Enron, Skilling served as consultant to Enron for McKinsey & Co. In 1989, Enron launched GasBank at Skilling's urging for the purpose of hedging risk for natural gas producers and wholesale suppliers.[12] Both parties could arrange forward contracts (contracts to purchase or sell commodities at a future date) at set prices, and Enron would sell financial derivative contracts to convey the risk of the forward contracts to other interested investors. In 1990, Enron became a market maker, a financial clearinghouse, for natural gas, selling swaps and futures on the New York Mercantile Exchange. In the same year, Lay hired Skilling as CEO of Enron Gas Services (EGS), and Skilling hired Fastow as CFO. EGS was ultimately renamed Enron Capital and Trade Resources (ECT).

ECT provided financial and risk management services for Enron and its trading partners. The process, asset securitization, involves selling the rights to future cash-flow streams. Corporations, such as mortgage companies, would take their risky investments and sell them to another financial institution, such as an investment bank. The investment bank, in turn, would bundle a number of such investments together, separate the cash flows by level of risk, and put the result into securities it would then sell. In the case of mortgage-backed securities, investment banks might offer two securities, one based on the principal and the second on the interest payments. Each would have a different yield, based on the level of risk. Asset securitization is attractive to the originating corporation on two counts: It transfers risk of default to the investment bank and lowers cost of capital by providing immediate cash inflow.

ECT fulfilled two functions. First, it provided asset securitization services for Enron's natural gas and oil entities, making those entities much more profitable. Second, it moved Enron further toward Lay's vision of the company as a market maker for a variety of commodities. With the attainment of risk management and capital flow-through, Enron could in principle trade anything. Through the 1990s, Enron was rapidly becoming a commodities market based in Houston. Even weather risk was commoditized and traded.[6] This was supplemented with an approach Skilling would term "asset-lite": The hard assets Enron originally controlled in such deals would be sold, in many cases to special-purpose entities (SPEs) that were created by Enron.

Two Critical Elements: Mark-to-Market and the SPEs

Enron funded its growth as a financial services firm using very sophisticated financial practices, mark-to-market accounting, and SPEs. Originally termed *mark-to-model,* the *mark-to-market accounting method* was intended to assist investors in obtaining a reference point for valuing a security. A model was constructed using a number of assumptions, and the security was then valued using that model. In reality, the prices were generated by computers, not by the market process. Enron relied on this procedure to establish prices (sometimes unrealistically high) for its new commodities (e.g., weather) when there were no reference prices.[9]

The second mechanism Enron used was the creation of *special-purpose entities.* SPEs are financial devices designed to give companies greater flexibility in finance and risk management. There are two requirements for SPEs to be legitimate: First, there must be a 3 percent outside equity position; second, the outside capital must clearly be at risk.

Fastow set up a number of SPEs for Enron. Among the more famous were partnerships named Chewco, JEDI, LJM1, and LJM2 and four investments named Raptors. In 1993, Joint Energy Development Investment (JEDI), a $500 million partnership between Enron and the California Public Employees Retirement System (CalPERS), was the first SPE created. This partnership would continue until 1997, when CalPERS sold its position to Chewco, another SPE created specifically by Enron to purchase the CalPERS shares in JEDI. Enron hoped that this buyout would then encourage CalPERS to invest in JEDI II, a proposed $1 billion venture.

SPEs would be used to solve Enron's financial problems. Enron not only brokered commodities contracts but actually bought and sold natural gas. High default risk on Enron's part would ruin the swap business. SPEs provided Enron the opportunity to continually move debt from its balance sheet, keeping its high credit rating and its swap business.

As Enron expanded the use of SPEs, new investors were required to satisfy the SEC requirement of 3 percent outside equity investment. Fastow and Michael Kopper (managing director, Enron Global Finance, and a direct report to Fastow) established the "Friends of Enron." These "friends" were actually relatives or friends of Enron's executives. Fastow and Kopper funneled monies through these people to finance the "outside equity" in the SPEs.

Enron's need for a high credit rating drove the creation of over 3,000 SPEs to keep debt off the balance sheet.[9] Maturing markets meant decreasing profits, but profits were necessary to continue Enron's trading mechanism. The only way to create more profits was to open new commodity markets, exploit them quickly, and then create newer markets. The SPEs were critical to this strategy, keeping debt from the books and providing capital. Enron's stock price soared dramatically, unburdened by the debt that was accumulating in the SPEs.

The SPEs presented Enron with the opportunity to disguise debt and loss as revenue, but they did not necessarily result in cash flow.[9] Enron would establish an SPE by issuing Enron stock to collateralize the SPE, and then it would engage other entities such as banks to invest in the SPE. Enron would then "sell" the SPE that it had set up in return for either cash or a promissory note, which Enron would then book as revenue. In one case, it was a forward contract on shares of an Internet company in which Enron had invested. Another case was "dark fiber," that is, fiber optic cable that was already laid but was as yet unusable. In both cases, Enron had a "make whole" contract with the SPE, ensuring that the SPE would not lose money. However, even as the dot-com bubble burst, the shares in the Internet company declined, and the value of the dark fiber likewise dropped, Enron was able to shield its balance sheet from these losses.

Constructed on Enron stock, these SPE arrangements contained triggers, that is, valuation points at which these deals would need infusions of either more Enron stock or other collateral. For example, in an SPE named Osprey, if Enron's stock fell below $59.78, Enron was obligated to either issue new stock or provide cash sufficient to bring the value of Osprey up to cover its debt obligations.[17] In another instance, Enron's stock price decline forced restructuring of four SPEs named Raptor I, II, III, and IV in December 2000 and then required an additional infusion of stock in the first quarter of 2001 to shore up their falling credit capacity. By the end of the restructuring, Raptors II and IV owed an additional $260 million to Enron.[18]

The Investment Bank Connection   Enron's need for a high credit rating influenced its relationships with investment banks as well. In return for its business, Enron sought short-term deals that allowed it to disguise loans as sales revenue and, in turn, unload (for brief periods of time) unprofitable entities from Enron's balance sheet. Between 1992 and 2001, Enron borrowed $8 billion from Citigroup and J.P. Morgan Chase & Co. in transactions that had the appearance of gas trades rather than loans, thereby understating Enron's debt by $4 billion, and overstating its $3.2 billion cash flow from operations by 50 percent.[19] An independent bank examiner, Neal Batson, found that Enron had recorded profit of $1.4 billion through similar transactions with six investment banks.[20]

The Enron Control System

> Our philosophy is not to stand in the way of our employees, so we don't insist on hierarchical approval. We do, however, keep a keen eye on how prudent they are, and rigorously evaluate and control the risk involved in each of our activities.[10]

The Enron culture was not without its system of checks and balances, particularly in financial dealings. The board turned to those checks and balances when approving the deals with the SPEs, as well as Fastow's role in the various SPEs. It was the task of Risk Assessment and Control (RAC) to examine each deal and perform due diligence. RAC had the responsibility of overseeing and approving all deals in which Enron engaged, over 400 each year. Each deal was accompanied by a Deal Approval Sheet (DASH) assembled by the business unit responsible for the deal. Each DASH had a description of the deal, origination information, economic data, a cash-flow model, risk components, a financial approval sheet, and an authorization page.[6] Corporate policy required approval from the relevant business unit, legal department, RAC, and senior management. Many of the DASH forms for SPEs had incomplete authorizations. In particular, Skilling's signature is blank on many of the DASH forms associated with the LJM deals.[18]

As the number of deals with LJM increased, a separate LJM approval sheet was added as a control procedure. This approval sheet was printed with check marks already in the boxes. No third-party documentation was required to substantiate claims made on the document. Some conclusions were phrased as questions ("Was this transaction done strictly on an arm's-length basis?"), and some revealed low standards ("Was Enron advised by any third party that this transaction was not fair, from a financial perspective, to Enron?").[18]

Enron formed 20 deals with LJM1 and LJM2. In setting up the LJM entities, the board had waived Enron's Code of Ethics and allowed Fastow to be named general partner, with a $1 million investment in LJM1 alone. When Fastow presented the option of creating the LJM entities to the board, he portrayed them as alternative purchasers for Enron assets, providing perhaps better valuations for assets Enron was in the process of selling. In fact, there were no alternative buyers for most of what was sold to the SPEs.

The board made two critical assumptions. First, it assumed that, since the operational results of each division were at stake, each division would therefore aggressively market assets. Second, it assumed that Andersen's counsel on the LJM deals would be independent. The board relied on the reviews by Richard Causey (chief accounting officer) and Richard Buy (chief risk officer) as a first level of control. In addition, the board's audit and finance committees were assigned the task of reviewing all the previous year's transactions. The board also required that Skilling review and approve all LJM transactions, as well as review Fastow's economic interest in Enron and LJM.

Skilling, as COO and later CEO, did not sign many of the DASH forms for the LJM transactions. No evidence exists that Skilling knew how much money Fastow was making through LJM. Skilling, in one note, simply said that Fastow's first duty was to Enron because he received more compensation through salary and options than he might be making through LJM.

Neither stockholders nor analysts found it easy to monitor Enron's overall performance. Information on the financial dealings, particularly those with the SPEs, was difficult to find. The information on the SPE deals was disclosed either through proxy statements or in footnotes on the 10-Ks and 10-Qs. At one level, accounting standards required adequate information for management to assert that the related-party transactions were at least comparable with those that would have taken place with unrelated parties. However, details were often omitted. In the 2000 10-K, Enron stated, "Enron paid $123 million to purchase share-settled options from the [Raptor] entities on 21.7 million shares of Enron common stock." What Enron had actually purchased were put options, thereby betting that its stock would decline.[18]

Three International Deals

Rebecca Mark served as president of Enron Development Corporation. The power plant at Dabhol, India, was one of her achievements, though its overall value to Enron faded over time. Mark finalized the $3 billion deal in 1995, partnering Enron with General Electric and Bechtel. Enron's share was 65 percent; GE and Bechtel each owned 10 percent; and the remaining 15 percent was owned by the state of Maharashtra electric utility. In addition to the partners, four lenders (the Industrial Development Bank of India, Citibank, Bank of America, and the Overseas Private Investment Corporation, a U.S. government agency) lent $2 billion.[21]

The Dabhol plant was troubled from the beginning with local and state authorities. The Clinton administration, at Lay's request, sent Ron Brown, secretary of commerce, to India in 1995 to keep the deal afloat. During construction, there were reports of human rights violations by guards.[22] Enron distanced itself from such instances, noting that it was only leasing the property, though it also paid the guards.

There were local benefits. Roads were constructed, and the local economy benefited from increasing levels of both employment and consumption. But when the plant opened in 1999, opposition exploded as energy bills rose as much as 400 percent. Maharashtra annulled its contract, and the plant was shuttered.

Mark also negotiated the Cuiaba project in Brazil. Enron had a 65 percent share in a gas-fired power generating plant and its associated pipelines. Construction exceeded the budget by over $120 million and showed no signs of profit. In 1999, LJM1 bought a 13 percent interest in the project for $11.3 million, enabling Enron to shield the associated debts from its balance sheet. In addition, the sale allowed Enron to mark to market a related power supply contract. With the sale and recognition of this contract, Enron booked a total of $65 million profit in the last half of 1999. Enron had a secret agreement with LJM1 to buy the interest back, should it be necessary for LJM1's profit. This buyback occurred in 2001, for $13.725 million.[23]

Azurix was a 1998 spin-off from Enron. Mark was named chair and CEO, with the mandate to create deals in the water supply industry. Enron's strategy was to assert itself as an international market maker in water. With Azurix divorced from Enron, these deals could be done under Enron oversight without the debt accruing to the balance sheet.

Azurix went public in 1999, amassing $695 million in capital in the process.[12]

In 1999, Azurix acquired Wessex Water in the United Kingdom for $2.4 billion in cash and $482 million in debt.[24] Following that, Azurix bought the rights to an Argentinian water utility. These two acquisitions quickly undid Azurix, Mark, and any remaining Enron strategy involving hard assets. The Argentinian utility was plagued with contaminated water and labor union issues. The British government reduced the price Wessex could charge for its water. Mark was forced to resign in the summer of 2000, and she left Enron. Wessex Water was sold in 2002 to YTL Power International, a Malaysian firm, for $777 million in cash, with YTL also assuming $991 million in Wessex debt.[24]

It Comes Undone   Six months after taking the reins as CEO on February 12, 2001, Skilling abruptly resigned, effective August 14, 2001. His 15 years at Enron were over, but Enron would haunt him long after. Skilling cited "personal reasons" as the cause, but there was widespread speculation that more was behind it.

Exhibit 1 provides a quick glance at Enron's profit and loss from 1998 to 2000. The declining gross margin indicates that Enron's nonderivatives business was losing money. Any profitability was coming from derivatives. In fact, Enron's derivatives profits were roughly equivalent to Goldman Sachs, Inc.'s annual net revenue.[9]

In the Raptor restructurings from late 2000 to early 2001, a series of promissory notes from the Raptors had been recorded as increases in shareholders' equity, eventually totaling $1 billion. In August 2001, Andersen accountants declared that Raptors I, II, and IV were improperly accounted for and revisions were required. On November 8, 2001, Lay announced a $1.2 billion reduction to shareholders' equity, with the additional $200 million write-down resulting from a difference in contracts between the Raptors and Enron. In addition, Enron consolidated the SPEs back to 1997. Hence, the balance sheets of Chewco, JEDI, and LJM were now part of Enron's balance sheet. These adjustments reduced Enron's income by $591 million, and increased its debt

Exhibit 1   Enron Corp. and Subsidiaries Consolidated Income Statement, 2000 (in millions)

	2000	1999	1998
Nonderivatives revenues	$93,557	$34,774	$27,215
Nonderivatives expenses	94,517	34,761	26,381
Nonderivatives gross margin	(960)	13	834
Gain (loss) from derivatives	7,232	5,338	4,045
Other expenses	(4,319)	(4,549)	(3,501)
Operating income	1,953	802	1,378

Source: Testimony of Frank Partnoy in hearings before the United States Senate Committee on Governmental Affairs, January 24, 2002.

by just less than $2.6 billion. And some feared that the restatements were insufficient.

In the midst of this restructuring, Milberg Weiss Bershad Hynes & Lerach, LLP, filed a class-action suit on behalf of Enron shareholders on October 22, 2001. As part of its filing, the lawsuit disclosed the names and amounts of stock sold by Enron insiders, both senior management and directors (see Exhibit 2).[6]

During this time, Enron's one hope was a proposed merger with Dynegy, a corporation once viewed by Enron employees as an insignificant competitor. This merger also died of the same problems that had plagued Enron: fear of what was not disclosed. The merger was announced on November 9, the day after the restatements. On November 28, Standard & Poor's downgraded Enron debt to junk status, Dynegy declared the merger dead, and Enron's share price dropped from $3.69 at opening to $0.61 at close. On December 2, 2001, Enron filed for Chapter 11 bankruptcy protection. Jeff McMahon (executive vice president, finance, and treasurer, Enron Corp.) was named president and CEO following Ken Lay's resignation on January 23, 2002. McMahon would in turn resign in April 2002.

The Aftershocks

Criminal Actions In addition to engendering a number of congressional hearings, the Enron bankruptcy also brought criminal charges by the government. David Duncan, Arthur Andersen's lead auditor for Enron, pleaded guilty to obstruction of justice in April 2002 for document shredding in connection with the Enron account. Kopper pleaded guilty in August 2002 to conspiracy to commit wire fraud and money laundering, losing almost approximately $12 million that he admitted he had improperly acquired through various SPE deals. Fastow was indicted in October 2002 on 78 counts for his role at Enron and in the various SPEs, and his accounts were frozen. On January 13, 2004, Fastow pled guilty to two counts, one for covering up financial problems and one for defrauding the company, and was sentenced to 10 years in a federal prison.[25] His wife, Lea, pleaded guilty to one count of tax fraud and received a 1-year sentence. On February 21, 2004, Jeff Skilling and Rick Causey were indicted for their roles, and on July 7, 2004,[26] Ken Lay was indicted for his.[25]

The Retirement Vanishes Enron had been a significant holding in many large funds, particularly pension funds that sought to invest by industry segment. Enron employees' 401(k)s were primarily invested in Enron, and the employees were barred from selling their shares until they turned 55. Many of the 401(k)s were solely invested in Enron. As late as summer 2001, Ken Lay was predicting that Enron would regain much of its loss in stock price. His e-mail announcing the resignation of Skilling as CEO, and his own resumption of that post, ends with this:

> Our performance has never been stronger; our business model has never been more robust; our growth has never been more certain; and most importantly, we have never

had a better nor deeper pool of talent throughout the company. We have the finest organization in American business today. Together, we will make Enron the world's leading company.[12]

Exhibit 2 Senior Management and Board of Director Members Accused of Insider Trading

Senior Management and Board Members	Proceeds from Enron Stock Traded between October 1998 and November 2001
J. Clifford Baxter[a]	$ 34,734,854
Robert A. Belfer[b]	111,941,200
Norman P. Blake Jr.[b]	1,705,328
Richard B. Buy[a]	10,656,595
Richard A. Causey[a]	13,386,896
James V. Derrick Jr.[a]	12,563,928
John H. Duncan[b]	2,009,700
Andrew S. Fastow[a]	33,675,004
Mark A. Frevert[a]	54,831,220
Wendy L. Gramm[b]	278,892
Kevin P. Hannon[a]	Unknown but substantial
Ken L. Harrison[a]	75,416,636
Joseph M. Hirko[a]	35,168,721
Stanley C. Horton[a]	47,371,361
Robert K. Jaedicke[b]	841,438
Steven J. Kean[a]	5,166,414
Mark E. Koenig[a]	9,110,466
Kenneth L. Lay[a,b]	184,494,426
Rebecca P. Mark[a,b]	82,536,737
Michael S. McConnell[a]	2,506,311
Jeffrey McMahon[a]	2,739,226
Cindy K. Olson[a]	6,505,870
Lou L. Pai[a]	270,276,065
Kenneth D. Rice[a]	76,825,145
Jeffrey K. Skilling[a,b]	70,687,199
Joseph W. Sutton[a]	42,231,283
Lawrence Greg Whalley[a]	Unknown but substantial

[a]Employee, Enron Corp.
[b]Member, Enron Board of Directors

Source: Cruver, B. 2002. *Anatomy of greed: The unshredded truth from an Enron insider.* New York: Carroll and Graf Publishers: 132–133.

At the same time, however, Lay was busy selling much of his Enron stock. During 2001, Lay is reported to have sold $70 million in Enron shares. For almost an entire year, he was selling between 3,000 and 4,000 shares each workday.[27] He sold some shares back to the company to repay a loan from Enron. By doing so, he not only disposed of the stock but also circumvented disclosure laws that would have required him to report insider stock sales.

The pension funds of every state were invested, to some extent, in Enron stock. The estimated loss to these funds was $1.5 billion. Florida lost $328 million, California $142 million, and Georgia $122 million.[28]

The Accounting Profession　Fallout spread throughout the accounting profession as well, as reports of inadequate oversight continued throughout the fall of Enron. In fall 2001, the Houston office of Arthur Andersen shredded documents associated with the Enron account. Nancy Temple, a lawyer associated with Arthur Andersen's Chicago offices, e-mailed David Duncan, the lead Enron auditor for Andersen, a reminder of the corporate policy on memo retention, leading to massive document shredding efforts at Andersen's Houston offices. Duncan later pleaded guilty to criminal obstruction of justice, and Temple was named by a grand jury as one of four or five "corrupt persuaders" who encouraged the destruction of documents.[29] Andersen itself was stripped of its license to audit public corporations in the United States and ceased to do business.

A major feature of the Sarbanes-Oxley Act was aimed at the conflict that some thought brought about the Enron scandal: the mix of consulting and audit business. Andersen had both audit and consulting relationships with Enron, earning $52 million in 2001, split almost equally between consulting and audit fees. Enron was Andersen's largest client.[9] Audit firms would no longer be allowed to offer consulting services to audit clients. In addition, a number of other services were also proscribed, such as actuarial services, expert witnessing, and investment banking services, to name a few. In short, many of the services rendered by audit firms in attempts to generate extra revenue are now banned.

The Charity Fallout　Enron and its executives were very generous not only to their hometown of Houston but to educational institutions nationwide and the favorite causes of its board members. Initiatives included sponsorship of Enron Field (home to the Houston Astros), college scholarships, donations to United Way, and university endowments.

Enron also generously contributed to the causes of several of its directors.[30] For instance, when the president of M.D. Andersen Cancer Center, John Mendelsohn, became an Enron director and member of its audit committee, Enron and Lay donated $332,150 to the center. Of $60,000 donated to a think tank at George Mason University, $45,000 was contributed after Wendy Lee Gramm (wife of then-Senator Phil Gramm, R-TX, and an associate of the center) became an Enron board member. Concerned with an appearance of conflict of interest and a threat to independence, the U.S. House of Representatives passed a bill dubbed the "Enron bill" that requires disclosure of certain contributions and noncash gifts to organizations associated with board members.

Conclusion　This case is still writing its own ending. Many of the stakeholders will never recover from their losses. Criminal actions have resulted in some individuals going to jail and others being indicted and waiting for trial. Two of the investment banks, Citigroup and J.P. Morgan Chase, have settled investor lawsuits for $2.575 billion and $2.2 billion, respectively. Other investment banks still face civil actions.[31] And federal lawmakers are debating the cost of some provisions of the Sarbanes-Oxley Act. This case will evolve for years to come.

Appendix A   Enron Timeline

1984		Ken Lay becomes CEO of Houston Natural Gas (HNG).
1985		HNG merges with Internorth. Lay becomes CEO of the new company.
1986		Company changes name to Enron, and moves to Lay's hometown, Houston.
1990		Skilling leaves McKinsey & Co. to join Enron as executive officer of Enron Gas Services. Skilling hires Andrew Fastow from banking industry.
1991		Enron adopts mark-to-market accounting strategy, reporting income and value of assets at their replacement cost. Fastow forms first legitimate SPEs.
1993		Deregulation of worldwide energy markets. Enron begins marketing power and forms first SPE, JEDI, with CalPERS to invest in natural gas projects.
1994		As deregulation in the United States grows, Enron begins trading electricity.
1996		Enron commences construction of the Dabhol power plant in India. Lay promotes Skilling to Enron's president and COO.
1997		Enron buys first electric utility, Portland General Electric. Fastow promoted to head new finance department. Enron applies energy-trading model to new commodities markets such as weather derivatives, coal, pulp and paper, and bandwidth capacity. Chewco (another SPE) created to purchase CalPERS' shares of JEDI1 so that CalPERS could participate in a larger partnership, JEDI2. Chewco never meets the 3 percent outside ownership and is never a legitimate SPE.
1998		Fastow named CFO. Enron begins power trading in Argentina, becoming first power marketer, and gains control of Brazilian utility. Enron acquires U.K. utility Wessex Water and forms Azurix, a global water business. It then takes Azurix public, retaining a 69 percent stake. Enron trades most of Enron Oil & Gas for cash and its properties in India and China.
1999		New Houston Astros baseball stadium named Enron Field. Skilling and Fastow present LJM partnerships to board of directors.
2000		
	February	*Fortune* names Enron "the most innovative company in America" for the fifth consecutive year.
	April	Enron creates the first Raptor SPE.
	August	Rebecca Mark resigns due to poor results at Azurix and tension with Skilling. Stock hits all-time high of $90 and revenue surpasses $100 billion, making Enron the seventh-largest company in the Fortune 500.
2001		
	February	Lay steps down as CEO. President and COO Skilling replaces Lay as CEO.
	August	Skilling resigns, and Lay becomes CEO again. Sherron Watkins, an Enron accountant, sends anonymous memo to Lay warning of potential accounting scandal.
	September	Arthur Andersen compels Enron to change an aggressive accounting action, causing a $1.2 billion reduction in Enron's equity.
	October	SEC launches investigation of Enron's off-balance-sheet partnerships. Enron changes its 401(k) pension plan administrator, preventing employees from selling Enron stock for 30 days. Fastow is put on leave. Enron establishes special committee to investigate third-party transactions, to be known as the Powers Report. Enron's stock drops to $11.
	November	Enron strikes deal with Dynegy, its largest energy-industry rival. Dynegy backs out of the deal once more details of Enron's finances are available. Enron stock trades at less than $1 per share.
	December	Enron files for Chapter 11 bankruptcy protection and lays off 4,000 employees.

(continued)

(*continued*)

2002

January	Watkin's memo leaked to Congress. U.S. Justice Department launches a criminal investigation into Enron's fall. Enron fires Arthur Andersen LLP. Enron sells its energy trading business to UBS's investment banking unit, sells Wessex Water to a Malaysian firm, and shuts down its broadband unit. Lay resigns, and McMahon becomes CEO. Former Enron Vice Chairman Cliff Baxter is found dead as government investigation deepens.
February	Skilling testifies before Congress. Lay pleads the Fifth Amendment. Watkins testifies before Congress about her memo to Lay.
April	Andersen lays off 7,000 employees. McMahon resigns as of June 1.
August	Kopper pleads guilty to money laundering and wire-fraud conspiracy. Cooperates with authorities.
October	Fastow indicted on 78 counts of federal fraud, conspiracy, and money laundering.

2003

May	Federal prosecutors file new charges against Fastow and two others. Fastow's wife and seven other former Enron officials are indicted for fraud and other criminal charges.

2004

January	Fastow pleads guilty on two counts and receives 10 years in federal prison. Lea Fastow pleads guilty to one count of tax fraud and receives a 1-year sentence.
February	Skilling and Causey indicted on 42 counts, including securities fraud, wire fraud, and insider trading.
July	Lay indicted on 11 counts, including wire and bank fraud, as well as making false statements.

Appendix B Glossary of Terms

Adjustment	A deduction made to financial statements to charge off a loss, as with a bad debt.
Asset-lite	Enron jargon for short-term or noncapital-intensive assets.
CalPERS	California Public Employees Retirement System.
DASH	Deal Approval Sheet.
Derivative	A financial instrument whose characteristics and value depend on the characteristics and value of an underlier, typically a commodity, bond, equity, or currency.
Downgrade	A negative change in an analyst's ratings for a security.
Hedge	An investment made to reduce the risk of adverse price movements in a security, by taking an offsetting position in a related security.
Insider stock sales	The selling of a company's stock by individual directors, executives, or other employees.
JEDI	Joint Energy Development Investment—an Enron SPE.
Mark to market	An accounting method that records the price or value of a security, portfolio, or account on a daily basis to calculate profits and losses or to confirm that margin requirements are being met.
Off balance sheet	A term pertaining to financing from sources other than debt and equity offerings, such as joint ventures, R&D partnerships, and operating leases.
Option	The right, but not the obligation, to buy (for a call option) or sell (for a put option) a specific amount of a given stock, commodity, currency, index, or debt at a specified price (the strike price) during a specified period of time.
Premium	The amount by which a bond or stock sells above its par value.

Privatization	The process of moving from a government-controlled system to a privately run, for-profit system.
Put option	An option contract that gives the holder the right to sell a certain quantity of an underlying security to the writer of the option at a specified price (strike price) up to a specified date (expiration date); also called *put*.
RAC	Risk Assessment and Control, an Enron department.
Rank and yank	Employee jargon for Enron's employee review process.
Securitization	The process of aggregating similar instruments, such as loans or mortgages, into a negotiable security.
SPEs	Special-purpose entities.
Write-down	A downward adjustment in the accounting value of an asset.
Yield	The annual rate of return on an investment, expressed as a percentage.

Endnotes

1. *BusinessWeek Online*, February 12, 2001.
2. Eichenwald, K. 2002. A powerful, flawed witness against Enron. *New York Times,* October 21: C1.
3. Eichenwald, K. 2003. Ex-trader at Enron is charged in California power case. *New York Times,* June 4: C6.
4. Lay, K. 1990. The Enron story. Speech delivered on October 9 in New York to Newcomen Society of the United States.
5. A more detailed history of the origin of Enron can be found at www.hoovers.com.
6. Cruver, B. 2002. *Anatomy of greed: The unshredded truth from an Enron insider.* New York: Carroll & Graf Publishers.
7. Preston, R., & Koller, M. 2000. *Enron feels the power.* Internetweekonline: October 30.
8. O'Reilly, B. 1997. The secrets of America's most admired corporations: New ideas, new products. *Fortune,* 135(4): 60–64.
9. Testimony of Frank Partnoy in Hearings before the United States Senate Committee on Governmental Affairs, January 24, 2002.
10. 1999 Annual Report, Enron Corp.
11. Grulye, B., & Smith, R. 2002. Anatomy of a fall: Keys to success left Kenneth Lay open to disaster—From rural Missouri to helm of Enron to ignominy—Trust and willfull optimism—"The American dream is alive." *The Wall Street Journal,* April 26: A1.
12. Fusaro, P. C., & Miller, R. M. 2002. *What went wrong at Enron: Everyone's guide to the largest bankruptcy in U.S. History.* Hoboken, NJ: John Wiley & Sons.
13. Schwartz, J. 2002. As Enron purged its ranks, dissent was swept away. *New York Times,* February 4.
14. Levin, C. 2002. After Enron: Government's role and corporate cultures. *Mid-American Journal of Business,* 17(2): 7–10.
15. Banerjee, N., Berboza, D., & Warren, A. 2002. Enron's many strands: Corporate culture; at Enron, lavish excess often came before success. *New York Times,* February 26: C1.
16. Raghavan, A., Kranhold, K., & Barriounuevo, A. 2002. Full speed ahead: How Enron bosses created a culture of pushing limits—Fastow and others challenged staff, badgered bankers; Porsches, Ferraris were big—A chart to "intimidate people." *The Wall Street Journal,* August 26: A1
17. Note 8, Q3 SEC filing, 2001.
18. Report of Investigation by the Special Investigative Committee of the Board of Directors of Enron Corp. (the Powers Report).
19. Reason. CFO.com, 2002.
20. Berger, E., & Fowler, T. 2002. The fall of Enron; Enron masked loans as sales, report says; deals inflated bottom line by $1.4 billion. *Houston Chronicle,* September 22: A1.
21. Rai, S. 2002. Seeking ways to sell Enron's plant in India. *New York Times,* April 11: W1.
22. Kolker, C., & Fowler, T. 2002. The fall of Enron; roots of discontent; dead Enron power plant affecting environment, economy and livelihoods in India. *Houston Chronicle,* August 4: B1.
23. Criminal Complaint, United States Securities and Exchange Commission v. Andrew S. Fastow, October 1, 2002, #s 15–22.
24. Goldberg, L. 2002. Enron's Azurix to well Wessex Water at a loss. *Houston Chronicle,* March 26: B4.
25. Eichenwald, K. 2004. Enron ex-chief indicted by U.S. in fraud case. *New York Times,* July 8: A1.
26. Carr, R. 2004. Former Enron chief indicted. *Atlanta Constitution,* February 20: 1A.
27. Flood, M., & Fowler, T. 2002. The fall of Enron; grand jurors eye Lay; $70 million in stock sales focus of probe. *Houston Chronicle,* October 24: A1.
28. Healy, B. 2002. Shared pain: Bay State isn't alone in taking a hit from Enron. *Boston Globe,* September 10: C1.
29. Fowler, T. 2002. Andersen attorney may be next. *Houston Chronicle,* June 27: B1.
30. Weber, J., & McNamee, M. 2002. Boardroom charity: Reforms don't go far enough. *BusinessWeek,* June 10: 128.
31. Creswell, J. 2005. J.P. Morgan Chase to pay Enron investors $2.2 billion. *New York Times,* June 15: C1.

Case 9   American Red Cross*

As Marsha "Marty" Johnson Evans took the helm of the American Red Cross on August 5, 2002, she was faced with the challenge of restoring the public's faith in the organization. During the past 24 months, there had been a barrage of negative publicity regarding the American Red Cross. In June 2000 Red Cross workers went on strike. The organization was hit by a lawsuit filed by HemaCare Corporation and Coral Blood Services in January 2001. The plaintiffs alleged that the American Red Cross engaged in unfair trade practices in the pricing of blood. The Better Business Bureau made false public statements about the ability of the American Red Cross to meet its standards for charitable solicitations. Then on September 11, 2001, Americans watched in horror as terrorists flew two planes into the World Trade Center buildings and a third into the Pentagon in Washington. In the aftermath of this tragedy, donations poured into the American Red Cross, and a special fund—the Liberty Disaster Relief Fund—was established by the then-president of the Red Cross, Dr. Bernadine Healy. When it was announced that not all donations would be used for victims of the 9/11 disaster, there was a huge public outcry from donors. Healy was forced to retire, and interim president and CEO Harold Decker announced that all donations to the Liberty Disaster Relief Fund would be used in the organization's 9/11 relief efforts. Finally, on March 10, 2002, *60 Minutes,* a CBS news show, ran a misleading and inaccurate story about the American Red Cross.

On June 27, 2002, Marsha Johnson Evans was named the new CEO and president of the American Red Cross. At the time of this announcement, Evans stated:

> This is a time of great challenge for many charitable organizations including the American Red Cross. On the one hand, we need to motivate Americans to donate their time and their treasure, which is never easy, but always comes down to whether they trust an organization and believe in their work. On the other hand, we face a host of challenges including the need to better prepare this nation for disasters both natural and man-made; as well as the rigors of furnishing a safe and available blood supply with all the costs and complexity this involves.[1]

History and Operations of the American Red Cross

Henry Dunant set forth the idea of the Red Cross in 1859 when he saw wounded and dying soldiers on the battlefield in Solferino, Italy. He organized local people to bind the soldiers' wounds and to feed and care for the soldiers. Henry Dunant called for the creation of a national relief society, and this pointed the way to the future Geneva Convention. Four years later, in 1863, the International Red Cross was created in Geneva, Switzerland, with the purpose of providing nonpartisan care in time of war. The Red Cross emblem was adopted as a symbol of neutrality, although today the Red Crescent is also a recognized symbol. Today the Red Cross incorporates the International Committee of the Red Cross and the International Federation of Red Cross and Red Crescent Societies as well as national societies in 175 countries. The fundamental principles of the International Red Cross are listed in Exhibit 1. Clara Barton successfully organized the first lasting Red Cross Society in America in Washington, D.C., on May 21, 1881. The American Red Cross provided services beyond those of the International Red Cross by providing disaster relief in addition to battlefield assistance. Clara Barton served as the organization's president through 1904.[2]

As stated in its 2000–2001 Annual Report, "The American Red Cross is a humanitarian organization, led by volunteers, whose mission is to provide relief to victims of disasters and help people prevent, prepare for, and respond to emergencies." The vision of the American Red Cross is "the American Red Cross . . . always there . . . touching more lives, in new ways . . . under the same trusted symbol." Since its founding, the American Red Cross has symbolized the nobility of the human spirit by representing service and goodwill across America. Its purpose, or intent, is to "prevent and relieve human suffering." Each year March is proclaimed as American Red Cross month. To support the fundamental principles of the International Red Cross, the American Red Cross has adopted a set of values (see Exhibit 2).

The American Red Cross is governed by a board of governors that formulates policy and delegates authority to the volunteer boards of its 1,000 local chapters. Decentralization allows the Red Cross to provide immediate, effective, and efficient assistance to those in need.[3] Annually, the American Red Cross helps victims of more than 63,000 natural and man-made disasters. The worst disaster ever dealt with by the American Red Cross was the hurricane that killed an estimated 6,000 people in Galveston, Texas, in 1900.

The American Red Cross helps victims through a wide range of services:[4]

- *Armed Forces emergency services:* Help for military families—emergency communication services, financial assistance, counseling, and so forth.
- *Biomedical services:* Blood, tissue, and plasma services; research; and national testing labs. In fiscal year 2001 more than 3.8 million volunteers donated

* This case was prepared by Professors Debora J. Gilliard and Rajendra Khandekar of Metropolitan State College–Denver as a basis for class discussion rather than to illustrate either effective or ineffective handling of an administrative situation. Copyright © 2004 Deborah J. Gilliard and Rajendra Khandekar. All rights reserved.

Exhibit 1   Principles of the International Red Cross

- **Humanity:** The International Red Cross and Red Crescent Movement, born of a desire to bring assistance without discrimination to the wounded on the battlefield, endeavors, in its international and national capacity, to prevent and alleviate human suffering where it may be found. Its purpose is to protect life and health and to ensure respect for the human being. It promotes mutual understanding, friendship, cooperation, and lasting peace amongst all peoples.
- **Impartiality:** It makes no discrimination as to nationality, race, religious beliefs, class, or political opinions. It endeavors to relieve the suffering of individuals, being guided solely by their needs, and to give priority to the most urgent cases of distress.
- **Neutrality:** In order to continue to enjoy the confidence of all, the Movement may not take sides in hostilities or engage at any time in controversies of a political, racial, religious, or ideological nature.
- **Independence:** The Movement is independent. The National Societies, while auxiliaries in the humanitarian services of their governments and subject to the laws of their respective countries, must always maintain their autonomy so that they may be able at all times to act in accordance with the principles of the Movement.
- **Voluntary Service:** It is a voluntary relief movement not prompted in any manner by desire for gain.
- **Unity:** There can be only one Red Cross or one Red Crescent Society in any one country. It must be open to all. It must carry on its humanitarian work throughout its territory.
- **Universality:** The International Red Cross and Red Crescent Movement, in which all Societies have equal status and share equal responsibilities and duties in helping each other, is worldwide.

Source: American Red Cross, www.redcross.org.

Exhibit 2   Values of the International Red Cross

- **Humanitarianism:** We exist to serve others in need, independently, and without discrimination, providing relief for victims of disasters and helping people prevent, prepare for, and respond to emergencies.
- **Stewardship:** We act responsibly, effectively, and efficiently with resources entrusted to us, always seeking to improve.
- **Helping Others:** We are attentive and responsive to those we serve, always listening to their needs and looking for ways to serve through existing or new initiatives.
- **Respect:** We acknowledge, respect, and support the rights and diversity of each person in our organization and in the communities we serve.
- **Voluntary Spirit:** As a family of donors, volunteers, and staff we search for ways to provide hope to those we serve while demonstrating compassion, generosity, and appreciation.
- **Continuous Learning:** We seek, collectively and individually, to identify, obtain, and maintain competencies and the awareness required for exceptional service.
- **Integrity:** We act with honesty, demonstrate courage and accountability under pressure, and openly share ideas and information with each other.

Source: www.redcross.org.

in excess of 6 million pints of blood. The American Red Cross supplies 3,000 hospitals with about half of the blood used in the United States.

- *Community services:* Help for the homeless, seniors, and youth—food and nutrition information, transportation, and so forth.

- *Disaster services:* Educational services to prepare for disasters. Each year 83,000 volunteers help disaster victims by providing food, shelter, financial assistance, mental health counseling, and so on.
- *Health and safety services:* Swimming and lifeguard classes, HIV/AIDS education, living well

programs, and so forth. Each year more than 12 million Americans take advantage of lifesaving courses offered by the Red Cross.

- *International services:* Emergency disaster response, feeding programs, primary health care programs, Geneva Conventions, and so on. The Red Cross is able to provide long-term aid and education to those in need. Also, Red Cross delegates help local citizens rebuild infrastructure, strengthen public health, and improve response time to local disasters.
- *Nursing:* Student nurses, Jane Delano Society, and so forth.
- *Youth involvement:* Help for kids, teens, and young adults.
- *Volunteering:* Recruitment and organization of volunteers.

Financial Overview

In fiscal year 2001–2002 the American Red Cross had operating revenues of $4.117 billion. Total operating revenues for fiscal year 2000–2001 were $2.743 billion. Three main funding sources for the American Red Cross were:[5]

- *Contributions:* Fund-raising efforts by the United Way & Combined Federal Campaign, legacies, grants, and other monetary and in-kind contributions.
- *Products and services:* Fees for products, materials, and courses and fees from collecting, testing, and distributing blood and tissue.
- *Investment income and other income:* Investment income from endowments and reserve funds and income from contracts to provide various programs.

Total operating expenses for the 2000–2001 fiscal year were $2.712 billion, and major expenses included:[6]

- *Disaster costs:* Assistance to victims.
- *Funding disaster services:* Expenses of soliciting donations and administering funds, staff expenses at disaster sites, and so on.
- *Biomedical services:* Facility maintenance and expenses in blood, plasma, and tissue services.

Total operating expenses for the fiscal year 2001–2002 were $3.570 billion (see Exhibits 3, 4, and 5).[7]

Technology and Operations

Technology has helped the American Red Cross to better coordinate its efforts among its 1,400 chapters and to expand its reach across America. In 2000 it launched "iGiveLife," a service that enables blood drive sponsors to use their intranets to recruit donors and allows hospital customers to order blood products online.[8]

The Internet provides information about nonprofit organizations and can provide "click-to-donate" sites for those individuals who are willing to help out with contributions while they are online. These "click" sites appeal to a newer and often younger audience for the nonprofits. For

Cindee Archer, online media manager for the American Red Cross in Washington, D.C., the Internet serves as a vital source of information to the American public and as a new way to collect donations. Archer stated, "The Internet has definitely changed how the whole organization thinks. You feel this sense of urgency whenever there's a disaster—you want that information up as quickly as you can get it."[9] Archer worked on developing a Web site at which visitors could enter a zip code and quickly find information. The Web site helps visitors locate local Red Cross shelters, find relatives in a disaster area, keep up with breaking news, and obtain information about donating and volunteering. Cindy Archer also believed that "more and more people are coming online—this isn't going to go away, it's only going to get more pervasive."[10] However, there were costs associated with a Web site that many nonprofit groups did not realize. Russ Finkelstein, director of outreach at Action Without Borders, has stated, "Some of them think this is going to be a kind of panacea for doing fund-raising, and it's not necessarily that."[11]

About 12 million Americans enroll in Red Cross courses each year. It is now possible to make these courses available online. The Red Cross has routinely published the latest public health information, and the use of new technology will make this information available online. Wireless communication allows the American Red Cross to make faster damage assessment at the scene. The communication network allows it to locate family members during crises more efficiently. In the near future, it may be possible for the American Red Cross to offer an online shopping network to generate additional resources.[12]

Strategic Alliances

The American Red Cross has established a number of alliances with other organizations. It works with the World Health Organization to alleviate malnutrition, lack of pure water, and diarrhea in poor countries and to support primary health care. A donation of plasma product to the World Hemophilia Foundation is used to treat hemophilia. In 1999 the American Red Cross joined the Federal Emergency Management Agency for "TOPOFF," a nationwide disaster simulation that helps prepare for acts of terrorism. As a result of recent research and development, Massachusetts General Hospital and the American Red Cross jointly own a patent for a protein associated with the underlying cause of Alzheimer's disease. In addition, the American Red Cross supplies over 3,000 hospitals with blood donations.[13]

In February 2001 the American Red Cross teamed up with Coinstar, Inc., to collect Red Cross donations for disaster relief efforts. Consumers could drop loose change into the Coinstar machines located in local supermarkets. Coinstar machines were located within 2 miles of 130 million Americans. John Clizbe, vice president of Disaster Services at the American Red Cross, stated, "If every American near a Coinstar machine would donate a handful of change on their next supermarket visit, the Red

Exhibit 3 Consolidated Statement of Financial Position, June 30, 2002 (with summarized information as of June 30, 2001) (in thousands)

Assets	Unrestricted	Temporarily Restricted	Permanently Restricted	Totals 2002	2001
Current assets:					
Cash and cash equivalents	$146,247	$439,569	$ 1,386	$ 587,202	$ 177,492
Investments	309,913	11,050	12,514	333,477	355,090
Receivables, net of allowance for doubtful accounts of $19,604 in 2002 and $19,301 in 2001:					
Trade	304,543	15,258	—	319,801	317,767
Contributions, current portion	16,411	110,103	56	126,570	133,183
Other	—	—	15,825	15,825	9,302
Inventories, net of allowance for obsolescence of $7,750 in 2002 and $6,784 in 2001	197,252	6,402	—	203,654	190,272
Other assets	12,547	3,162	183	15,892	23,289
Total current assets	986,913	585,544	29,964	1,602,421	1,206,395
Investments	548,633	155,674	325,238	1,029,545	1,120,773
Contributions receivable	4,209	28,374	2,243	34,826	39,339
Prepaid pension costs	—	—	—	—	11,858
Land, buildings, and other property, net	823,541	—	—	823,541	733,177
Other assets	11,089	1,500	22,704	35,293	26,171
Total assets	2,374,385	771,092	380,149	3,525,626	3,137,713
Liabilities and Net Assets					
Current liabilities:					
Accounts payable and accrued expenses	287,209	9,453	—	296,662	293,476
Current portion of debt and capital leases	39,894	—	—	39,894	89,372
Postretirement benefits	18,924	—	—	18,924	16,807
Other current liabilities	20,653	2,840	63	23,556	18,068
Total current liabilities	366,680	12,293	63	379,036	417,723
Debt and capital leases	357,453	—	—	357,453	360,870
Pension and postretirement benefits	120,042	—	—	120,042	108,339
Other liabilities	92,623	1,180	20	93,823	86,644
Total liabilities	936,798	13,473	83	950,354	973,576
Net assets	1,437,587	757,619	380,066	2,575,272	2,164,137
Commitments and contingencies					
Total liabilities and net assets	$2,374,385	$771,092	$380,149	$3,525,626	$3,137,713

Source: American Red Cross. 2002. Annual Report.

Exhibit 4 Consolidated Statement of Activities, Year Ended June 30, 2002 (with summarized information for the year ended June 30, 2001) (in thousands)

	Unrestricted	Temporarily Restricted	Permanently Restricted	Totals 2002	Totals 2001
Operating Revenues and Gains					
Public support:					
United Way and other federated	$ 65,616	$ 122,452	$ —	$ 188,068	$ 205,549
Disaster relief	—	133,376	—	133,376	84,601
Liberty disaster relief—Sept. 11 response	—	989,060	—	989,060	—
Legacies and bequests	67,118	6,745	22,022	95,885	115,594
Services and materials	22,034	96,222	—	118,256	49,728
Grants	21,236	67,175	—	88,411	76,351
Other contributions	213,289	36,915	705	250,909	230,845
Products and services:					
Biomedical	1,924,077	—	—	1,924,077	1,686,090
Program materials	136,582	906	—	137,488	121,724
Contracts	58,171	—	—	58,171	50,175
Investment income	81,394	1,069	—	82,463	81,405
Other revenues	49,089	2,008	—	51,097	40,844
Net assets released from restrictions	1,035,410	(1,035,410)	—	—	—
Total operating revenues and gains	3,674,016	420,518	22,727	4,117,261	2,742,906
Operating Expenses					
Program services:					
Armed Forces emergency services	61,513	—	—	61,513	65,756
Disaster services	308,156	—	—	308,156	284,822
Liberty disaster relief—Sept. 11 response	617,960	—	—	617,960	—
Biomedical services	1,872,967	—	—	1,872,967	1,699,978
Health and safety services	213,614	—	—	213,614	203,058
Community services	152,902	—	—	152,902	150,108
International services	32,736	—	—	32,736	45,238
Total program services	3,259,848	—	—	3,259,848	2,448,960
Supporting services:					
Fund-raising	136,901	—	—	136,901	108,616
Management and general	174,182	—	—	174,182	154,726
Total supporting services	311,083	—	—	311,083	263,342
Total operating expenses	3,570,931	—	—	3,570,931	2,712,302
Change in net assets from operations	103,085	420,518	22,727	546,330	30,604
Nonoperating gains (losses)	(131,900)	(548)	(2,747)	(135,195)	(63,876)
Cumulative effect of accounting change	—	—	—	—	2,201
Change in net assets	(28,815)	419,970	19,980	411,135	(31,071)
Net assets, beginning of year	1,466,402	337,649	360,086	2,164,137	2,195,208
Net assets, end of year	$1,437,587	$ 757,619	$380,066	$2,575,272	$2,164,137

Source: American Red Cross. 2002. Annual Report.

Exhibit 5 Consolidated Statement of Functional Expenses, Year Ended June 30, 2002 (with summarized information for the year ended June 30, 2001)(in thousands)

Program Services

	Armed Forces Emergency Services	Disaster Services	Liberty Disaster Relief—Sept. 11 Response	Biomedical Services	Health and Safety Services	Community Services	International Services	Total Program Services
Salaries and wages	$35,329	$ 76,450	$ 4,966	$ 749,046	$100,866	$ 66,654	$ 8,340	$1,041,651
Employee benefits	6,701	16,758	773	165,697	19,894	13,698	1,706	225,227
Subtotal	42,030	93,208	5,739	914,743	120,760	80,352	10,046	1,266,878
Travel and maintenance	1,673	20,479	32,601	35,515	5,068	4,111	1,826	101,273
Equipment maintenance and rental	1,173	11,105	11,387	62,322	5,005	5,950	515	97,457
Supplies and materials	3,394	25,095	10,416	417,349	44,001	21,937	849	523,041
Contractual services	8,252	42,887	61,479	379,081	27,643	20,859	1,788	541,989
Financial and material assistance	2,803	106,406	496,338	14,132	3,528	13,811	17,236	654,254
Depreciation and amortization	2,188	8,976	—	49,825	7,609	5,882	476	74,956
Total expenses	$61,513	$308,156	$617,960	$1,872,967	$213,614	$152,902	$32,736	$3,259,848

Supporting Services

	Fund-Raising	Management and General	Total Supporting Services	2002	2001
				Total Operating Expenses	
Salaries and wages	$ 42,260	$ 81,174	$123,434	$1,165,085	$1,046,171
Employee benefits	8,436	16,145	24,581	249,808	199,204
Subtotal	50,696	97,319	148,015	1,414,893	1,245,375
Travel and maintenance	3,708	6,466	10,174	111,447	78,208
Equipment maintenance and rental	1,902	5,260	7,162	104,619	84,227
Supplies and materials	35,167	6,494	41,661	564,702	477,547
Contractual services	41,147	44,991	86,138	628,127	563,436
Financial and material assistance	1,713	4,285	5,998	660,252	175,994
Depreciation and amortization	2,568	9,367	11,935	86,891	87,515
Total expenses	$136,901	$174,182	$311,083	$3,570,931	$2,712,302

Source: American Red Cross. 2002. Annual Report.

Cross would be that much better prepared to respond to disaster immediately." Rich Stillman, COO of Coinstar, said, "You no longer need a credit card or checkbook to provide financial support to those in need. If all Americans donate the change in their wallet or pocket, those handfuls will make a huge difference in our capacity to help others this year."[14]

Masterfoods USA, a Mars Incorporated Company, created a special package of red, white, and blue M&Ms specifically to benefit the Red Cross. The national campaign theme used for this promotion was "Taking Care of America Everyday." "Through appearances on television, radio and newspapers, and creative displays in stores across the country, the new M&Ms captured the heart of America," stated Skip Seitz, senior vice president, American Red Cross Growth and Integrated Development.[15] One hundred percent of all profits from the sales of these M&Ms were donated to the American Red Cross Disaster Relief Fund. In January 2002 Masterfoods USA presented a check to the Red Cross in the amount of $3.5 million.

In August 2001 the American Red Cross and the American Society of Association Executives (ASAE) signed an agreement under which the two organizations will share data regarding disasters, declarations, and changes in legislation and will explore efforts in joint training exercises. The ASAE provides the Red Cross with demographic information about associations and assistance with identifying organizations it wishes to contact during times of need.[16]

Recent Problems

Events between 2000 and 2002 provided the American Red Cross with a number of challenges.

Worker Strike   In June 2000 Red Cross workers who collected blood donations and delivered them to hospitals went on strike after rejecting a contract offer by the American Red Cross. The workers were unhappy about long hours, frequent schedule changes, and increasing health benefit costs.[17]

Unfair Trade Practices Lawsuit   The Red Cross derived 60 percent of its revenues from the sale of blood. In providing more than half the nation's blood, the Red Cross had annual sales of more than $1.3 billion.[18] In January 2001 a California blood supplier filed an antitrust suit against the American Red Cross, claiming the organization used its clout to eliminate competitors. HemaCare Corp. and Coral Blood Services alleged that the Red Cross had cost them more than $25 million in lost business. They further alleged that the American Red Cross priced some blood products (e.g., platelets) below production costs to drive out competitors while it charged higher prices for the same products in markets where there was no competition. In the lawsuit, the plaintiffs alleged that the American Red Cross violated Section 2 of the Sherman Antitrust Act, which prohibits monopolization. The lawsuit also charged tortuous interference, unfair trade practices, and unfair competition

under the California Business and Professional Code. William Nicely, HemaCare's chief executive officer, stated, "We believe that's unfair and illegal. The Red Cross is a fine organization. We just want them to play by the rules that are reasonable and fair and compete on a level playing field."[19] Blythe Kubina, a Red Cross spokeswoman, said in a written statement, "We believe the American Red Cross has done nothing inappropriate regarding HemaCare's claims to unfair business practices and we were surprised by this lawsuit. We have been in full compliance with the law, and we will vigorously defend this lawsuit."[20]

Liberty Disaster Relief Fund   After the terrorist attacks on September 11, the American Red Cross rose to the challenge of providing the most extensive relief operation in its 120-year history. In response to the tragedy, the Red Cross set up family assistance centers to provide counseling, child care, food, financial assistance, and other services to victims' families and others affected. Respite centers were set up in New York City, Somerset County in Pennsylvania, and at the Pentagon to provide meals, sleeping quarters, and other items to relief workers and volunteers. Funds were used for travel, lodging, and meals for volunteers and staff working on-site. Financial assistance, counseling, and transportation were provided to families of missing foreign nationals.

Millions of dollars, thousands of blood donations, and help from a myriad of volunteers contributed to Red Cross efforts to provide aid to survivors, victims' families, and relief workers. Because of the large dollar amount of donations from the American people, the Red Cross created the Liberty Disaster Relief Fund to be used exclusively to meet the needs of people directly affected by the September 11 tragedy.

Within 15 days of the September 11, 2001, attack, the Red Cross had collected $202 million in donations. Deborah Goldburg, a Red Cross spokesperson, stated, "Everything is happening at such a fast pace. Right now we are just trying to keep up with responses."[21] Goldburg stated that the entire amount raised by the Red Cross since the disaster would go into the newly created Liberty Fund. She indicated that organization officials earmarked $100 million from the fund to provide short-term financial assistance to families of victims. Bernadine Healy, MD, the president and chief executive officer of the Red Cross, said in a written statement, "What has taken place is extraordinary, and we must respond in an extraordinary way. The American Red Cross has a heavy burden—to live up to the inspiration and memory of those lost. It is with great humility and pride that we carry out this noble obligation."[22]

On October 12, 2001, the American Red Cross released a spending plan for the first $300 million in the Liberty Fund. Less than 50 percent of the money raised was targeted for victims, their families, or rescue workers. The remainder was earmarked to help the Red Cross improve its own organization and expand into new aid programs that might be needed in the event of future terrorist attacks.[23] This planned distribution of funds, based on Healy's policy of using donations for a "long period of uncertainty and recovery," caused a huge uproar.[24] The donors blasted Healy because they expected their donations to be helping September 11 disaster victims now. The attorney general of New York State threatened legal action.[25] Healy finally responded with her announcement of retirement. "I had no choice," she said, claiming that the organization's board had pushed her out.[26]

On November 14, 2001, interim CEO and president of the Red Cross, Harold Decker, announced changes adopted by the American Red Cross Board of Governors to meet the immediate and long-term needs of people affected by the September 11 terrorist attacks. The Red Cross would provide increased financial support to families, participate in a database to be shared among relief agencies, hire an additional 200 caseworkers, and extend the use of toll-free telephone lines. David T. McLaughlin, chairman of the American Red Cross Board of Governors, stated, "The people of this country have given the Red Cross their hard-earned dollars, their trust, and very clear direction for our September 11 relief effort. Regrettably, it took us too long to hear their message."[27] In an article in *U.S. News & World Report,* David McLaughlin stated, "If we don't subject ourselves to public scrutiny, we will never have public trust."[28]

In addition to donating money, the American public donated blood for the disaster victims. These donations were given in response to Healy's "Together, we can save a life" public service announcement. Experts questioned the wisdom of calling for blood donations when there were very few blood recipients. By November 2001 about 10 percent of the red blood cells collected on September 11 and 12 had expired.[29] In a congressional hearing, Healy was confronted with allegations of "panicking the public into wasteful donations of blood." *The Lancet* reported, "Donors charged the organization with abuse of their good intentions."[30]

On March 7, 2002, the American Red Cross saluted the staff and volunteers who provided assistance to the more than 54,500 families affected by the attacks. David McLaughlin stated, "Today we are recognizing the work of our staff, volunteers, and donors who responded to September 11th." Harold Decker, interim president, announced that the American Red Cross received $930 million in contributions and this money was used to provide the following:[31]

BBB Wise Giving Alliance On February 16, 2002, the Better Business Bureau Wise Giving Alliance removed the American Red Cross from its "give.org" Web site, allegedly because the American Red Cross did not provide a timely report to the alliance. In addition, H. Art Taylor, president of the alliance, made some unsupported public statements regarding the Red Cross that were reported in the *Philadelphia Inquirer.* A letter from Harold Decker to the Wise Giving Alliance explained that a request by the alliance for an updated report from the Red Cross was received in January 2002. Given the recent activities of the American Red Cross, it was determined that such a report could not be provided by the due date. Jack Campbell, CFO of the Red Cross, and Bennett Weiner, COO of the alliance, agreed to a March 30 deadline for the updated report. In his letter Decker requested that there be a public retraction of Taylor's statements and that the Better Business Bureau's current report on the Red Cross be restored to the give.org Web site.[32]

60 Minutes **Program** Another onslaught of negative publicity for the American Red Cross occurred March 10, 2002, on the CBS news show *60 Minutes.* The program appears to have contained some inaccuracies concerning floods, fires, and the financial accountability of Red Cross chapters. Deborah Daley, a spokesperson for the Red Cross, sent a letter to CBS News indicating the errors and an explanation:[33]

1. In a comment about advertising practices, Mike Wallace reported, "They also decided to put a disclaimer in their ads saying that donations will be used for this and other disasters. The trouble is, it's in small print."

    In response, Deborah Daley reported, "In the West Virginia flood ad, the "this and other disasters" language appears in the same font and size as the rest of the body copy appealing for support.

2. Wallace reported, "Outside audits of local Red Cross chapters are rare. In fact, there is so little accountability that local chapters—and there are more than one thousand of them—aren't even required to submit financial reports to Red Cross headquarters in Washington."

    Deborah Daley responded that chapters are accountable in a number of ways. All chapters must have an independent annual review. Chapters that have over $100,000 in annual expenses must have an external audit conducted by an independent CPA. The largest 126 chapters must send quarterly financial reports to the national Red Cross. The Red Cross does regular audits of chapters. Chapters must meet specific national guidelines to maintain their charters. She stated that Wallace's claim that chapters "are not even required to submit financial reports" is completely false.

	$ millions
Direct assistance to 3,266 families of deceased and seriously injured	$169
Assistance to 51,000 families of displaced workers and disaster workers	270
Provision for 14 million meals, mental health services for 232,000 people, and health services for 129,000 people	94

3. As for the Alpine fire in Southern California, Wallace reported, "As of last week, 14 months after the fire, San Diego was still waiting for a full accounting of how the money donated for the fire victims has been and will be spent."

Deborah Daley responded that the chapter has provided up-to-date financial information on its response to the Alpine fire three times since November.

Looking to the Future

After a five-month search, Marsha Johnson Evans was named president and CEO of the American Red Cross on June 27, 2002. Evans had served as national executive director of the Girl Scouts of the USA for the previous four years, prior to which she had a 29-year career in the U.S. Navy, where she earned the rank of rear admiral. In his announcement, David McLaughlin, chairman of the board of governors of the American Red Cross, said, "Marty's unique style of leadership along with her experience as established administrator will bring new vigor to the American Red Cross. With great insight into our mission, she is well poised to guide our organization as we continue to provide vital services in a world faced by new challenges."[34] Evans remarked:

> In the midst of responding to the extraordinary demands of 9/11 and a lot of criticism about these efforts, my observation is that the Red Cross never lost sight of its responsibility to every community and every victim of the other disasters that occurred, some 45,000 in the months since last September. The timely and capable response day-in and day-out to these disasters speaks volumes about the character of the volunteers and staff, their talent, and most especially their dedication.[35]

As she begins to guide the organization, Marsha Johnson Evans must confront the many issues faced by the American Red Cross. How should she proceed?

Endnotes

1. American Red Cross. 2002. Press release, June 27.
2. American Red Cross. www.redcross.org.
3. American Red Cross. 2002. Press release, February 1.
4. American Red Cross. 2000–2001. Annual Reports.
5. American Red Cross. 2001–2002. Annual Reports.
6. Ibid.
7. Ibid.
8. American Red Cross. 2000. Annual Report.
9. Sanborn, Stephanie. 2000. Nonprofits reap rewards of the Web—Internet proves to be a great fund-raising tool for charities, but there are costs. *Infoworld,* 22(25): 37.
10. Ibid.
11. Ibid.
12. American Red Cross. 2000. Annual Report.
13. Ibid.
14. *US Newswire.* 2001. American Red Cross and Coinstar to launch new fundraising technology to prepare for disasters. February 12.
15. American Red Cross. 2002. Press release, February 1.
16. *Association Management.* 2001. ASAE and American Red Cross formalize partnership agreement. 53(8): 12.
17. *Fund Raising Management.* 2000. Red Cross workers on strike. 31(4): 33.
18. Greenberg, Daniel S. 2001. Blood, politics, and the American Red Cross. *Lancet,* November 24: 1789; Taylor, Mark. 2001. Red Cross faces antitrust lawsuit. *Modern Healthcare* 31, January 1: 20.
19. Taylor, Red Cross faces antitrust lawsuit.
20. Ibid.
21. Becker, Cinda. 2001. A torrent of donations; charities wrestle with how best to spend money pouring in since attacks. *Modern Healthcare* 31, October 1: 8.
22. Ibid.
23. Tyrangiel, Josh. 2001. The charity olympics: After weeks of record giving, Americans want to know: Is that money helping? *Time,* November 5: 75.
24. *PR Newswire.* 2001. Newsweek: Former Red Cross head says her fundraising message was clear . . . . December 9.
25. Greenberg, Blood, politics, and the American Red Cross.
26. Tyrangiel, Charity olympics.
27. *US Newswire.* 2001. Red Cross announces major changes in Liberty Fund: Fund solely used for people affected by September 11 tragedy. November 14.
28. Levine, Samantha. 2001. Red Crossroads. *U.S. News & World Report,* November 19.
29. Tyrangiel, Charity olympics.
30. Greenberg, Blood, politics, and the American Red Cross.
31. American Red Cross. 2002. Press release, March 7.
32. *PR Newswire.* 2002. American Red Cross letter to Better Business Bureau's Wise Giving Alliance. February 16.
33. *US Newswire,* Red Cross announces major changes in Liberty Fund.
34. American Red Cross. 2002. Press release, June 27.
35. Ibid.

Case 10   United Way of America*

United Way of America and United Way International provided support for member organizations worldwide: Over 1,300 local United Ways in the United States and 3,000 United Way organizations operating in 45 countries relied on their respective parents for resources such as leadership education, public policy advocacy, marketing support, and standards for ethical governance and financial reporting. United Ways worldwide were part of a federation of nonprofits formed by caring people to serve the needs of their communities. They raised and distributed funds to the most effective local service providers, built alliances and coordinated volunteer support among charities, businesses and other entities, and acted as best practice models of management and financial accountability—which was where problems had arisen. With three high-profile ethical scandals since 1995 at both the national and local levels, the United Way brand had to combat an erosion of trust, as well as deal with an increasingly competitive and changing environment for charitable contributors.

Even after over 120 years of solid financial performance and steady growth, since the year 2000 United Way had seemingly reached a plateau of fund-raising in the United States. Certainly there were options for growth from international members, and from the energy and direction of nationwide objectives stated by United Way of America (education about and implementation of the national 211 phone network; the early childhood educational initiatives Success by 6 and Born Learning; encouragement of nationwide voluntarism through the Lend a Hand public service announcements funded by a donation from the NFL; and the Assets for Family Success economic self-sufficiency program for working families). Yet charitable donations still had not topped the inflation-adjusted peak-year campaign of 1989.[1]

In addition, in 2007 veteran fund-raisers on all fronts were citing challenges such as competition for donations, difficulty recruiting and keeping qualified fund-raisers, difficulty raising money for general operating costs, and a growing focus on large gifts from very wealthy individuals, which, when publicized, could reduce the motivation for smaller donors to contribute (a small donor might have thought, "If someone like Bill Gates is providing funds, why do they need my dollars?").[2] From the donors' perspective, the opportunities for both individuals and businesses to engage in charitable giving had expanded, with over 40 percent of new nonprofits appearing since 2000.[3] Many of these, especially those supporting disaster relief in the wake of 9/11 and Hurricane Katrina, had a single-issue focus that had the potential of creating a close bond with the donor. This meant that some individuals might have bypassed organizations such as the United Way, believing that they had support targets that were too broad and preferring, instead, to specify exactly where donations should go (such a donor would have thought, "If I'm giving, I want to make sure my money is going where I want it to go, to the cause I want to support").

Even prior to 9/11 American donors had expressed concern about their ability to access information regarding how their donations were going to be used, what percentage of the charity's spending went toward actual current programs, how their privacy was going to be protected when giving via the Internet, and whether the charity met voluntary standards of conduct.[4] It didn't help that many nonprofits, including United Way of America, suffered widely publicized scandals over misappropriation of funds. Organizations that serve community or broader social needs must continually be perceived as legitimate, as acting in an appropriate and desirable way within "some socially constructed set of norms, values, beliefs and definitions"[5] in order to receive needed donations. It was especially difficult for nonprofits such as United Way to maintain trust since their products and services did not easily lend themselves to traditional quality assessment and performance review, and once that trust was broken it was very difficult to get it back.

United Way of America's CEO, Brian Gallagher, formally initiated a shift in strategy. Responding to the environment, Gallagher established new membership standards to enhance the level of accountability and transparency in United Way affiliates' operations, rebranded United Way as doing "what matters" in the communities it served, and updated the "standards of excellence," providing a description of benchmark standards and best practices to better reflect the organization's strategic shift from its traditional role as strictly a fund-raiser to a new mission focused on identifying and addressing the long-term needs of communities.

These initiatives required that United Way affiliates buy into the change effort, since the power of the parent organization was limited to removing the affiliate from United Way membership if it didn't comply. It was imperative for a nonprofit organization to get the necessary support at the local level in order to achieve stated organizational goals. Would Gallagher's various strategies be successfully implemented? Was the shift in strategy sufficient to ensure the continued viability of United Way, or was its very mission perhaps no longer relevant?

*By Professor Pauline Assenza of Manhattanville College, Professor Alan B. Eisner of Pace University, and graduate student Luz Barrera of Pace University. This case is based on public documents, and was developed for class discussion rather than to illustrate either effective or ineffective handling of the situation. This research was supported in part by the Wilson Center for Social Entrepreneurship, Pace University. Copyright © 2007 Pauline Assenza & Alan B. Eisner.

Overview and History of the United Way of America

United Way was founded in 1887 as the Charity Organizations Society of Denver, raising $21,700 for 22 local agencies in its second year of operation. In 1913 this model was expanded to become a "Community Chest" in Cleveland, and in 1918 a dozen fund-raising federations met in Chicago to form the American Association for Community Organizations. From 1919 to 1929, over 350 Community Chests were created, and by 1948 more than 1,000 communities had United Way Community Chests in operation. In 1973 the partnership between United Way and the National Football League began, with the goal of increasing public awareness of social service issues facing the country. Through the partnership, United Way public service announcements featured volunteer NFL players, coaches, and owners. In addition, NFL players supported their local United Ways through personal appearances, special programs, and membership on United Way governing boards.

In 1974 United Ways in America and Canada raised $1,038,995,000, marking the first time in history that an annual campaign of a single organization raised more than $1 billion. In the same year, United Way International was formed to help nations around the world create United Way–type organizations. The 1981–1985 and 1997–1998 campaigns generated the greatest percentage increase in revenues. Amounts raised since 1999 generally failed to keep up with the rate of inflation, although a $10.5 million gift from Bill and Melinda Gates and a $50 million donation by Bank of America in 1999 made that year a good one (see Exhibit 1).[6]

The United Way was essentially a financial intermediary, providing fund-raising activities, primarily through donor organizations' employee payroll deductions, and distributing the funds to agencies that could actually deliver services to clients in the target community. The parent organizations, United Way of America and United Way International, serviced the local United Way chapters, which performed the bulk of the fund-raising. Although other sources of revenue included individual donations and government grants, around 70 percent of donations came from employees in local businesses; of the employee contributions, 75 percent were considered unrestricted dollars that the local United Ways could put to use to address critical needs in their respective communities.

The parent organization United Way of America (UWA) was supported primarily by local United Way member organizations that paid annual membership fees based on an agreed-on formula, 1 percent of their communitywide campaign contributions. Trademark members, United Way member organizations raising less than $100,000, paid a fee of 0.3 percent of their total contributions. In addition to membership support, individual and corporate sponsorship, and federal grants, other sources of funds for the national umbrella organization were conferences, program service fees, promotional material sales, investment income, rental income, and service income (see Exhibits 2 and 3).

United Way was a system that operated as a federation—a network of local affiliates that shared a mission, a brand, and a program model but were legally independent from one another and from the national office. Historically, United Way had been the loosest of federations, with almost all power residing at the local level. Each United Way chapter member was not only independent but also separately incorporated and governed by a local volunteer board. Through communitywide campaigns, each local United Way, utilizing a network of local volunteers, raised funds to support a great variety of health and human services organizations.

Over the years, as United Way's local chapters grew bigger and more prosperous, they began to consider themselves as more autonomous—gatekeepers, allocators, and managers of the local public trust—and began to question whether the seal of approval bestowed by United Way affiliation was worth it in light of the declining financial rewards. Therefore, some United Way agencies considered forming their own member-oriented, self-governing federations.

Current Competition and Challenges

By 2007 the charitable-giving industry had fragmented into tiny, possibly fraudulent, single-focus agencies that could be both competitors and recipients of United Way programs. In addition, since United Way's traditional function was parceling out the contributions it received to local charities, donors began to question the need for an organization that essentially just processed money—a donor would ask, "Why not just give directly to the charity of my choice?" The perception was that the administrative function of United Way and other blanket charities just added an additional level of overhead to organizational costs, with a smaller portion of the original donation actually reaching the intended target.

In addition, donors were increasingly supporting specific causes and therefore were more attracted to alternative recipient organizations, those possibly more responsive to the idea of community based on gender, race, or sexual orientation, among other socially driven issues.[7] A spokesperson for the American Cancer Society remarked, "Today a person might have an interest in prostate cancer, because his father died of it, or breast cancer, because it is a social issue as well as a health issue. We have to remember that an organization's mission is at least as important to supporters as its integrity." This meant that "donor-advised funds, which allow people to create grant-making accounts and recommend which charities get the money" were becoming increasingly popular.[8] This did not mean that the traditional and venerable organizations, such as United Way, Red Cross, Salvation Army, and Goodwill Industries, were necessarily in trouble; it just meant that they were perhaps in need of some strategic adjustment (see Exhibits 4 and 5).

Exhibit 1 United Way Campaign History

	Amount Raised in Current $			Average Annual CPI* (1982–1984, 100)	Inflation Rate, %	Amount Raised in Constant $		
		Change					Change	
Year	$, Billions	$, Millions	%			$, Billions	$, Millions	%
1971	0.813		3.3	40.5	4.4	2.0072		−1.0
1972	0.858	45.2	5.6	41.8	3.2	2.0529	45.7	2.3
1973	0.916	58.3	6.8	44.4	6.2	2.0640	11.1	0.5
1974	0.979	62.4	6.8	49.3	11.0	1.9854	−78.6	−3.8
1975	1.023	44.1	4.5	53.8	9.1	1.9013	−84.1	−4.2
1976	1.104	81.4	8.0	56.9	5.8	1.9408	39.5	2.1
1977	1.205	100.5	9.1	60.6	6.5	1.9881	47.3	2.4
1978	1.318	112.9	9.4	65.2	7.6	2.0210	32.9	1.7
1979	1.424	105.8	8.0	72.6	11.3	1.9607	−60.3	−3.0
1980	1.526	102.5	7.2	82.4	13.5	1.8519	−108.8	−5.5
1981	1.680	154.0	10.1	90.9	10.3	1.8482	−3.8	−0.2
1982	1.780	100.0	6.0	96.5	6.2	1.8446	−3.6	−0.2
1983	1.950	170.0	9.6	99.6	3.2	1.9578	113.3	6.1
1984	2.145	195.0	10.0	103.9	4.3	2.0645	106.7	5.4
1985	2.330	185.0	8.6	107.6	3.6	2.1654	100.9	4.9
1986	2.440	110.0	4.7	109.6	1.9	2.2263	60.8	2.8
1987	2.600	160.0	6.6	113.6	3.6	2.2887	62.5	2.8
1988	2.780	180.0	6.9	118.3	4.1	2.3500	61.2	2.7
1989	2.980	200.0	7.2	124.0	4.8	2.4032	53.3	2.3
1990	3.110	130.0	4.4	130.7	5.4	2.3795	−23.7	−1.0
1991	3.170	60.0	1.9	136.2	4.2	2.3275	−52.0	−2.2
1992	3.040	−130.0	−4.1	140.3	3.0	2.1668	−160.7	−6.9
1993	3.047	7.0	0.2	144.5	3.0	2.1087	−58.1	−2.7
1994	3.078	31.0	1.0	148.2	2.6	2.0769	−31.7	−1.5
1995	3.148	70.0	2.3	152.4	2.8	2.0656	−11.3	−0.5
1996	3.248	100.0	3.2	156.9	3.0	2.0701	4.5	0.2
1997	3.402	154.0	4.7	160.5	2.3	2.1196	49.5	2.4
1998	3.577	175.0	5.1	163.0	1.6	2.1945	74.9	3.5
1999	3.769	192.0	5.4	166.6	2.2	2.2623	67.8	3.1
2000	3.912	143.0	3.8	172.2	3.4	2.2718	9.5	0.4
2001	3.949	37.0	0.9	177.1	2.8	2.2298	−42.0	−1.8
2002	3.709	−240.0	−6.1	179.9	1.6	2.0617	−168.1	−7.5
2003	3.591	−118.0	−3.2	184.0	2.3	1.9516	−110.1	−5.3
2004	3.606	15.0	0.4	188.9	2.7	1.9089	−42.7	−2.2

*CPI is annualized rate for a calendar year.

Source: United Way of America, Research Services, August 2005.

Exhibit 2 Give.org Charity Report for United Way of America, 2006

Governance:

Chief executive: Brian A. Gallagher, President and CEO

Compensation: $632,423*

Chair of the board: Rodney E. Slater

Chair's profession/business affiliation: Partner, Patton Boggs LLP

Board size: 26

Paid staff size: 180

Uses of Funds as Percentage of Total Expenses for Year Ended December 31, 2006:

Fund-raising: 0.78%

Administrative: 13.50

Programs: 85.72

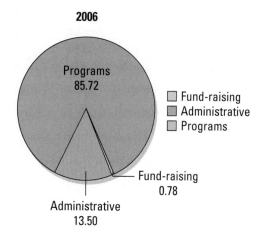

2006

Programs 85.72

Administrative 13.50

Fund-raising 0.78

□ Fund-raising
□ Administrative
□ Programs

*2005 compensation includes annual salary and, if applicable, benefit plans, expense accounts, and other allowances. UWA indicates that Gallagher's total salary represents $405,000 in salary, $52,500 in incentive pay, and $174,923 in deferred compensation.

Source: BBB Wise Giving Alliance at Give.org.

The partnership between United Way and the disaster relief organizations such as the Red Cross, the Salvation Army, Boys & Girls Clubs, and Catholic Charities was still a strong and viable one, but increasingly all these national charities needed to understand the need for a diversified revenue stream. In a video interview with UWA's Brian Gallagher, *Forbes* asked about what had changed in 2006. Gallagher noted that 55 percent of donations still came from employees in the workplace and corporate contributions from companies such as UPS, Microsoft, and IBM and that the relationship with the NFL was still a powerful one, with 50 percent of volunteers being recruited through the NFL campaign. He mentioned that online participation was growing and that individual donations averaged $200 per year per individual, with contributions coming increasingly from women and people of color, represented $75 million from all United Way chapters in 2005.[9]

Entering 2007 with the donor community becoming increasingly diverse and the societal problems increasingly challenging, charitable nonprofits needed to engage in ongoing assessment of the relevance of their respective missions. This was not a new problem. In 1999 Michael Porter and Mark Kramer considered the strategic challenges facing nonprofits. Noting that the number of charitable foundations in the United States had doubled in the two decades since the 1970s, they also believed that these philanthropic organizations were not devoting enough effort to measuring their results and to figuring out how to create the most value for society with the resources they had at their disposal. This value could have been created by selecting the appropriate grantees, signaling other donors of appropriately chosen charities, improving the performance of grant recipients, and advancing the state of knowledge and practice. However, many philanthropic organizations lacked a strategic focus; their resources were scattered across too many fields and their staffs were spread too thin, servicing too many small grants. One suggestion was that they engage in more performance assessment and unique positioning, with unique activities aimed specifically at creating value; however, this would require most nonprofits to also assess the effectiveness of their governance systems.[10]

Scandals and Governance

The year 2002 was bad for corporate scandals: Enron, ImClone, WorldCom, and Tyco all hit the headlines with examples of corporate greed and misappropriation of both funds and public trust. Given these types of wrongdoings in publicly held organizations, the tolerance of the general population for similar activities in nonprofits was increasingly eroded, especially given the nature of the relationship—one based on donor trust.

The first major scandal at United Way had occurred 10 years earlier, in 1992, when William Aramony, president and CEO of United Way of America, and two other UWA executives were convicted of fraud, conspiracy, and money laundering in a scheme that siphoned around $1 million from the organization. This event was perceived as a turning point in public perceptions of charitable organizations, and it was blamed for the first drop in United Way donations since World War II.[11]

In 2001, the United Way of the National Capital Area—the Washington, D.C., chapter and the second-largest local United Way member in the country in donations—was in the news, again because of fraud. CEO Oral Suer took more than $500,000 from the charity to pay for personal expenses, annual leave, and an early pension payout he was not entitled to. Other employees took additional money for personal use, with the total fraud amounting

Exhibit 3   United Way of America Consolidated Financial Statements

For Year Ended	Dec. 31, 2006	Dec. 31, 2005	Dec. 31, 2004
Source of Funds			
Contributions	$15,477,000	$30,439,000	$ 9,772,000
Membership support (net)	28,978,000	29,231,000	23,015.000
Campaign efforts (net)	7,717,000	—	—
Promotional material sales	6,575,000	6,514,000	7,525,000
Transaction fees	3,307,000	2,979,000	1,234,000
Conferences	2,622,000	1,892,000	1,447,000
Program service fees	942,000	1,228,000	775,000
Investment income	1,667,000	1,055,000	319,000
Rental and service income	405,000	646,000	408,000
Miscellaneous and other	425,000	241,000	147,000
Total Income	**$68,115,000**	**$74,225,000**	**$44,642,000**
Program Expenses			
Field leadership	—	—	$ 3,683,000
Brand leadership	$ 7,880,000	$ 8,872,000	6,156,000
Community impact leadership	5,031,000	6,008,000	9,051,000
Investor relations	6,639,000	5,944,000	5,446,000
Center for Community Leadership	6,519,000	5,622,000	4,972,000
Funds distribution	6,056,000	5,042,000	5,157,000
Cost of goods sold	3,266,000	3,226,000	2,940,000
Enterprise services	2,281,000	2,190,000	2,927,000
Campaign public relations	388,000	—	—
Selling expenses	325,000	1,448,000	1,123,000
Public policy	24,715,000	14,531,000	2,258,000
Total Program Expenses	**$63,100,000**	**$52,883,000**	**$43,713,000**
Total income	$68,115,000	$74,225,000	$44,642,000
Program expenses	63,100,000	52,883,000	43,713,000
Fund-raising expenses	577,000	616,000	78,000
Administrative expenses	9,934,000	6,504,000	4,489,000
Total expenses	$73,611,000	$60,003,000	$48,280,000
Income in excess of expenses	(5,496,000)	14,222,000	(3,638,000)
Beginning net assets	25,968,000	11,087,000	15,973,000
Changes in net assets	(5,076,000)	14,881,000	(4,886,000)
Ending net assets	$20,892,000	$25,968,000	$11,087,000
Total liabilities	$76,624,000	$52,626,000	$46,364,000
Total assets	$97,516,000	$78,594,000	$57,451,000

Source: United Way of America, http://national.unitedway.org/about/form990.cfm.

Exhibit 4   *Forbes* 25 Largest U.S. Charities, 2006

Name	Total Revenue ($, millions)	Total Expenses ($, millions)	Surplus/Loss ($, millions)	Net Assets ($, millions)
Mayo Clinic	6,118	5,606	512	3,546
Salvation Army	5,300	2,748	2,516	9,334
YMCAs in the United States	5,104	4,468	363	NA
United Way	4,175	4,175	0	NA
Cleveland Clinic Foundation	4,004	3,702	302	1,770
American National Red Cross	3,842	3,397	445	2,646
Catholic Charities USA	3,385	3,318	67	NA
New York Presbyterian Hospital	2,858	2,566	293	3,053
Goodwill Industries International	2,653	2,511	143	1,542
The Arc of the United States	2,211	2,149	62	714
Memorial Sloan-Kettering Cancer Center	1,973	1,605	368	3,553
Mount Sinai	1,927	1,864	63	828
Children's Hospital of Philadelphia	1,623	1,470	154	1,271
Cedars-Sinai Medical Center	1,566	1,472	94	919
Henry Ford Health System	1,535	1,440	96	321
Boys & Girls Clubs of America	1,329	1,180	149	2,436
AmeriCares	1,320	1,076	244	328
Habitat for Humanity International	1,022	801	220	1,442
Beth Israel Deaconess Medical Center	995	946	70	407
American Cancer Society	938	866	71	1,304
Nature Conservancy	936	602	334	3,852
World Vision	905	870	35	169
Planned Parenthood Federation of America	902	847	55	839
Children's Hospital	888	775	113	698
Gifts in Kind International	860	866	−6	67

Source: Forbes.com, www.forbes.com/lists/2006/14/pf_phil_06charities_The-200-Largest-U.S.-Charities_TotalRev.html.

to $1.6 million. Then, in 2002, new United Way National Capital Area CEO Norman O. Taylor was asked to resign over misstated revenues and questionable overhead and credit card charges. In 2003, the CFO of the Michigan Capital Area United Way, Jacqueline Allen-MacGregor, was imprisoned for the theft of $1.9 million from the charity, which she had used to purchase race horses for her personal farm. Also in 2003, Pipeline, Inc., which was a spin-off from the California Bay Area United Way and was created to collect contributions, was investigated for losing $18 million when the financial records did not accurately reflect the amount owed to the charity.[12] In 2006, a former CEO of the United Way of New York City was investigated for diverting organizational assets valued at $227,000 for his own personal use.[13]

To be fair, United Way was not the only high-profile charity to experience these kinds of problems since 2002. After 9/11 and Katrina, the American Red Cross had come under scrutiny for misdirection of disaster funds. In addition, the bookkeeper at Easter Seals of Iowa had stolen $230,000, the former president and seven others at Goodwill Industries of California embezzled $26 million, the financial administrator of the American Heart Association of New Jersey was convicted of a theft of $186,000, and an executive at Goodwill Industries of Michigan was found guilty of stealing $750,000 from the agency over a 23-year

Exhibit 5 *Forbes* 10 Largest Charities by Revenue, 2006

Name	Total Revenue ($, millions)	Total Expenses ($, millions)	Charitable Commitment[1] (%)	Fund-raising Efficiency[2] (%)	Donor Dependency[3] (%)
Mayo Clinic	6,118	5,606	94 —	91 ▲	−92 ▲
Salvation Army	5,300	2,748	83 —	96 ▲	30 ▼
YMCAs in the United States	5,104	4,468	81 ▼	89 ▼	64 ▲
United Way	4,175	4,716	82 ▼	91 —	100 —
Cleveland Clinic Foundation	4,004	3,702	90 ▼	93 ▼	−154 ▲
American National Red Cross	3,842	3,397	92 ▲	91 ▲	66 ▼
Catholic Charities USA	3,385	3,318	89 ▼	94 ▲	90 ▲
New York Presbyterian Hospital	2,858	2,566	77 ▼	93 ▼	−116 ▼
Goodwill Industries International	2,653	2,511	83 ▼	97 ▲	66 ▼
The Arc of the United States	2,211	2,149	89 ★	77 ★	30 ★

[1]Charitable services as percent of total expenses.

[2]Percent of private support remaining after fund-raising expenses.

[3]Percent of private support remaining after surplus.

A negative number indicates private support exceeded surplus.

▲ Ratio increase from previous reported period.

▼ Ratio decrease from previous reported period.

— Same as previously reported period.

★ No comparable data.

Source: Forbes.com, www.forbes.com/lists/2006/14/largest-american-charities-pf-philo_cz_wb_1122charities_land.html.

period.[14] What could be done to curtail this disturbing trend?

The United Way of America's board during the Aramony scandal contained many Fortune 500 CEOs who were, according to Aramony, fully informed about his compensation and perquisites.[15] Yet it appeared they still failed to exercise appropriate oversight, as did the boards at the D.C. and Michigan chapters. Finding committed and knowledgeable board members was critical to United Way's continued success. Given the federation model, each local chapter had its own board, recruited from community members who had not only fund-raising skills but also relationships with local leaders, politicians, or even regulators. Many local United Ways wanted to distance themselves from the scandals at UWA and other high-profile chapters, and therefore they tried to stress local leadership and board autonomy. Serving on such a board required a commitment to the community and to the goals of the local United Way, and, regardless of the degree of well-intentioned communication and disclosure, sometimes the goals of board members could have been in conflict.

A 2004 survey by McKinsey & Company of executives and directors at 32 of *Worth* magazine's top 100 nonprofit performers found that many nonprofit boards had recurring problems, one of which was consensus over mission and goals: "Only 46 percent of the directors we surveyed thought that other directors on their boards could both summarize the mission of the organizations they serve and present a vision of where those organizations hope to be in five years' time." In addition, for an organization such as United Way, the goals of the diverse stakeholders, both donors and recipients, may have differed widely. This lack of consensus, coupled with the difficulty of measuring and evaluating performance, meant that nonprofit boards in general needed to practice serious self-scrutiny: "The time when nonprofit boards were populated by wealthy do-gooders who just raised money, hired CEOs, and reaffirmed board policy is over."[16]

In 2006, more than 1.8 million nonprofit organizations in the United States controlled upward of $2.5 trillion in assets, received revenues of $1.25 trillion, and were increasingly relied on to help address both gaps in federal, state, and local governments' support after natural and man-made disasters and the lingering effects of society's general ills. Given the degree to which the public trust had been violated after nonprofits were found to be acting irresponsibly, the Senate Finance Committee was considering "tax-exempt reform containing provisions similar to those found in the Sarbanes-Oxley Act."[17]

This demand for greater accountability was not new. Nonprofits had sometimes been notoriously ineffective at accomplishing their social missions, been inefficient at getting maximum return on the money they raised due to high administration costs, and been willing to take on too much risk, either through inexperience or ignorance; sometimes because of lax oversight procedures, individuals in control of the nonprofits were willing to engage in outright fraud, acquiring excessive benefits for themselves. These problems were enhanced due to nonprofits' failure to provide extensive analysis, disclosure, and dissemination of relevant performance information and due to the lack of sanctions.[18] If nonprofit organizations would not police themselves, watchdog agencies would create external standards and provide public feedback, sometimes to the detriment of the organization under scrutiny (see Exhibit 6).[19]

Gallagher's Strategic Response

In 2006 United Way of America CEO Brian Gallagher was invited back by the U.S. Senate Finance Committee to participate in a roundtable discussion on needed reforms in nonprofit boards and governance. He was prepared to provide specific commentary. Since accepting the CEO position in 2001, Gallagher had been working to promote a change in the United Way strategy, including a change in mission, the creation of standards of performance excellence, and a requirement that local members certify their adherence to the membership standards.

Regarding the mission of United Way, Gallagher had worked to change the focus from fund-raising to community impact—from "How much money did we raise?" to "How much impact did we have on our community?" In his initial statement to the Senate Committee at their first meeting in 2005, Gallagher said:

> The ultimate measure of success is whether family violence rates have gone down and whether there is more affordable housing. And fundraising is [just] part of making that happen. When you are asking people to contribute, you're asking for an investment in your mission. And like a for profit business, you are then accountable to your investors, not just for keeping good books, but for creating value and offering a concrete return. For those of us in human development, that means efforts that lead to measurable improvements in people's lives. In other words, the organizations that produce the greatest results should grow and be rewarded. Those that do not should be forced to change or go out of business. The American public doesn't give us money just because our operations are clean. Why they really give us money is because they want to make a difference.[20]

As a result of the new mission, UWA required local affiliates to provide the national headquarters with annual financial reports and to embrace the revised standards of excellence developed by more than 200 United Way employees, volunteers, and consultants. Of interest is the

---

Exhibit 6   Watchdog Agencies—Information Resources for Nonprofits

- *AICPA Audit Committee Nonprofit Toolkit*
  www.aicpa.org/audcommctr/toolkitsnpo/homepage.htm
- *American Institute of Philanthropy*
  www.charitywatch.org
- *Better Business Bureau Wise Giving Alliance*
  www.give.org
- *Board Source*
  www.boardsource.org
- *Charity Navigator*
  www.charitynavigator.org
- *Governance Matters*
  www.governancematters.com
- *Guidestar*
  www.guidestar.com
- *Independent Sector*
  www.independentsector.org
- *Internet Nonprofit Center*
  www.nonprofits.org

- *IRS Exempt Organizations*
  www.irs.gov/charities
- *National Association of Attorneys General*
  www.naag.org
- *National Association of State Charity Officials*
  www.nasconet.org
- *National Council for Nonprofit Organizations*
  www.ncna.org
- *New York State Attorney General*
  www.oag.state.ny.us/charities/charities.html
- *Nonprofit Financial Center*
  www.nfconline.org
- *OMB Watch*
  www.ombwatch.org
- *Philanthropy Foundation*
  http://ephilanthropy.org
- *Standards for Excellence Institute*
  www.standardsforexcellenceinstitute.org

fact that these standards were not mandatory but were presented as guidelines, giving chapters suggestions for how they might revise their local strategies. The standards urged the affiliates to identify community problems, raise money to solve them, and demonstrate measurable progress toward their goals by adopting a code of ethics that included an annual independent financial audit. The hope was that by adopting these guidelines, the chapters would be able to provide tangible proof to donors, especially wealthy contributors, that the United Ways and the charities they support were making a difference (see Exhibit 7).[21]

Local United Ways faced a continual challenge, with inevitable tension between the diverse constituencies they served: Were their primary "customers" the donors who contribute needed funds or the agencies who were the recipients of these charitable donations? Or should the local United Way act as a networking institution, providing mechanisms for discussion of local problems and community service needs; or, going even further, should it act as an activist organization, leading the way with comprehensive community planning, advocating major public policy, and redistributing resources as needed? Kirsten Gronbjerg, of the Center on Philanthropy, Indiana University, stated, "The activist role is very difficult for United Ways to play because they need to satisfy diverse constituency groups and therefore avoid conflict. As they become more donor driven institutions, they will be less able to

take an activist approach just when such an approach is sorely needed."[22]

In addition, the local United Ways needed to maintain their internal consensus, providing a coherent and inspiring vision for their mainly volunteer workforce, while managing potential conflicts and sharing resources with other United Ways in their geographic areas. The problem of potentially scarce resources and the fact that traditional donor organizations were either consolidating their physical operations or leaving an area meant that the traditional broad base of business and industry was shrinking. This and other factors prompted the consolidation of several United Ways into more regional organizations. This movement meant potential savings and operational efficiencies from sharing marketing, financial management, and information technology functions.[23] However, it also meant a possible diffusion of mission over a larger community, with a potential loss of focus, and more challenges for communicating this mission and marketing services to a more diverse donor and recipient base.

The ongoing issues faced by United Way in its 120-year history had remained constant. Consider this: During the holiday season, "when local United Way drives take place almost everywhere, likely as not questions will arise about what United Way is up to, how well it is doing what it claims to do, and for that matter, whether United Way is the best way for you to do your charitable giving."[24] This statement was written in 1977,

Exhibit 7   United Way New Standards of Excellence

In March 2005, United Way of America unveiled new Standards of Excellence, a comprehensive description of benchmark standards and best practices. Developed in conjunction with United Way executives, staff, and volunteers throughout the country, the standards are designed to enhance the effectiveness of the 1,350 United Way affiliates.

- **Introduction to the Standards of Excellence.** Spanning more than 100 pages, the new standards provide highly detailed descriptions regarding five key areas of operation.

- **Community Engagement and Vision.** Working with formal and informal leaders to develop a shared vision and goals for a community, including the identification of priority issues affecting the overall well-being of its citizens.

- **Impact Strategies, Resources, and Results.** Creating "impact strategies" that address the root causes and barriers of a community's priority issues; mobilizing essential assets such as people, knowledge, relationships, technology, and money; effectively implementing impact strategies; and evaluating the effectiveness of impact strategies in fostering continuous improvement.

- **Relationship Building and Brand Management.** Developing, maintaining, and growing relationships with individuals and organizations in order to attract and sustain essential assets.

- **Organizational Leadership and Governance.** Garnering trust, legitimacy, and support of the United Way in local communities through leadership and overall management.

- **Operations.** Providing efficient and cost-effective systems, policies, and processes that enable the fulfillment of the United Way's mission, while ensuring the highest levels of transparency and accountability.

Source: United Way of America, http://national.unitedway.org/soe.

yet it could still apply in 2007. Concerns about United Way seemed timeless, and Brian Gallagher was only one in a long line of CEOs determined to answer the critics once and for all.

Endnotes

1. Barrett, W. P. 2006. United Way's new way. Forbes.com, January 16, retrieved from www.forbes.com/2006/01/12/united-way-philanthropy-cz_wb_0117unitedway.htr.
2. Barton, N., & Hall, H. 2006. A year of big gains. *The Chronicle of Philanthropy,* October 26, retrieved from http://philanthropy.com/free/articles/v19/i02/02000601.htm.
3. Barrett, op. cit.
4. Executive summary of the Donor Expectations Survey, conducted by Princeton Survey Research Associates in Spring 2001, as reported by Give.org BBB Wise Giving Alliance, retrieved from www.give.org/news/survey1.asp.
5. Suchman, M. 1995. Managing legitimacy: Strategic and institutional approaches. *Academy of Management Review,* 20: 571–610.
6. From the United Way Web site, http://national.unitedway.org.
7. Contesting community: The transformation of workplace charity. Report on the book by Emily Barman, published by Stanford University Press, 2006, *Philanthropy News Digest,* posted February 28, 2007, at http://foundationcenter.org/pnd/offtheshelf/ots_print.jhtml?id=171600045.
8. Barton & Hall, op. cit.
9. Charitable giving diversifies. *Forbes* Video Report, December 13, 2006, from www.forbes.com/video/?video=frn/business/ab_charity121306.
10. Porter, M. E., & Kramer, M. R. 1999. Philanthropy's new agenda; Creating value. *Harvard Business Review,* 77 (6): 121–130.
11. United Way ex-head sentenced to 7 years in prison for fraud. *The New York Times,* June 23, 1995, p. B2.
12. Gibelman, M., & Gelman, S. R. 2004. A loss of credibility: Patterns of wrongdoing among nongovernmental organizations. *International Journal of Voluntary and Nonprofit Organizations,* 15 (4): 355–381. This article provides a content analysis of worldwide NGO scandals from 2001 to 2004. Although the United States is overrepresented, it is certainly not alone in the world for incidents of wrongdoing.
13. Investigation finds former United Way of NYC CEO improperly diverted funds. *Philanthropy News Digest,* posted April 17, 2006, at http://foundationcenter.org/pnd/news/story_print.jhtml?id=140000004.
14. Gibelman & Gelman, op. cit.
15. Sinclair, M. 2002. William Aramony is back on the streets. *The NonProfit Times,* March 1.
16. Jansen, P., & Kilpatrick, A. 2004. The dynamic nonprofit board. *McKinsey Quarterly,* 2: 72–81.
17. Kelley, C., & Anderson, S. 2006. Advising nonprofit organizations. *CPA Journal,* 76 (8): 20–26.
18. Herzlinger, R. 1996. Can public trust in nonprofits and governments be restored? *Harvard Business Review,* March–April: 97–107.
19. Gibelman & Gelman, op. cit.
20. Statement of Brian A. Gallagher, president and CEO United Way of America, before United States Senate Committee on Finance, April 5, 2005, p. 1. Retrieved from http://national.unitedway.org.
21. Blum, D. E. 2005. Held to a new standard. *Chronicle of Philanthropy,* 17 (13).
22. United Way system at the crossroads: Valuable lessons from the United Way of Chicago. *Snapshots: Research Highlights from the Nonprofit Sector Research Fund,* The Aspen Institute, November–December, 2002, no. 26.
23. Gosier, C. 2007. 3 Chapters of United Way to combine. *Knight Ridder Tribune Business News,* February 23.
24. United Way: Are the criticisms fair? *Changing Times,* October 1977, p. 29.

Case 11 World Wrestling Entertainment*

For World Wrestling Entertainment (WWE), 2009 looked like it was going to be another good year. The firm had just signed a deal with WGN America, Tribune Broadcasting's national superstation, which was to run a new program called *WWE Superstars*. The hour-long action-packed weekly show would be produced by WWE and would feature superstars and divas from the entire WWE roster. "WWE programming has a tremendous track record of consistently delivering a diverse and advertiser friendly audience. We fully anticipate that *WWE Superstars* will be a ratings winner for WGN America," said Kevin Dunn, WWE executive vice president of television production.[1]

This was followed by a distribution deal with Eurosport, Europe's leading sports and entertainment group, which would distribute two weekly WWE shows. Under the terms of the two-year agreement, Eurosport would broadcast *This Week in WWE* and *WWE Vintage Collection* in all of its European territories excluding the United Kingdom, delivering WWE programming to over 200 million viewers and 58 countries across the continent. *Vintage Collection* would feature WWE legends such as Stone Cold Steve Austin, The Rock, Hulk Hogan, and Bret 'The Hitman' Hart.

These deals clearly indicate that WWE has moved out of a slump that it endured between 2001 and 2005. During the 1990's, WWE's potent mix—shaved, pierced, and pumped-up muscled hunks; buxom, scantily-clad, and sometimes cosmetically enhanced beauties; and body-bashing clashes of good versus evil—resulted in an empire that claimed over 35 million fans. Furthermore, the vast majority of these fans were males between the ages of 12 and 34, the demographic segment that makes most advertisers drool.

Just when it looked like everything was going well, WWE hit a rough patch. During 2001 the firm experienced failure with a football league, which folded after just one season, and this was followed by a drop in revenues from its core wrestling businesses. WWE was struggling with its efforts to build new wrestling stars and to introduce new characters into its shows. Some of its most valuable younger viewers were turning to new reality-based shows on television, such as *Survivor, Fear Factor* and *Jackass.*

Since 2005, however, WWE has been winning fans back around the world. It has been rebuilding its fan base through live shows, television programming, consumer products, and Internet sales (see Exhibits 1 and 2). In

fact, the firm was recently named as one of the top 200 Best Small Companies by *Forbes* magazine. WWE has been turning pro wrestling into a perpetual road show that makes millions of fans pass through turnstiles worldwide. Its three television programs, *Raw, Smackdown,* and *Extreme Championship Wrestling,* have become the leading shows among male viewers on the nights that they are broadcast. Finally, WWE has been signing pacts with dozens of licensees to sell DVDs, video games, toys, and trading cards (see Exhibits 3 to 5). "We continue to see the distribution of our creative content through various emerging channels," stated WWE's president and CEO, Linda McMahon.[2]

Developing a Wrestling Empire

Most of the success of WWE can be attributed to the persistent efforts of Vince McMahon. He was a self-described juvenile delinquent who went to military school as a teenager to avoid being sent to a reformatory institution. Around 1970, Vince joined his father's wrestling company, Capital Wrestling Corporation. He did on-air commentary, developed scripts, and otherwise promoted wrestling matches. Vince bought Capital Wrestling from his father in 1982, eventually renaming it World Wrestling Federation (WWF). At that time, wrestling was managed by regional fiefdoms, and everyone avoided encroaching on anyone else's territory. Vince began to change all that by paying local television stations around the country to broadcast his matches. His aggressive pursuit of audiences across the country gradually squeezed out most of the rivals. "I banked on the fact that they were behind the times, and they were," said McMahon.[3]

Soon after, Vince broke another taboo by admitting to the public that wrestling matches were scripted. Although he made this admission in order to avoid the scrutiny of state athletic commissions, wrestling fans appreciated the honesty. The WWF began to draw in more fans through the elaborate story lines and the captivating characters of its wrestling matches. The firm turned wrestlers such as Hulk Hogan and Andre the Giant into mainstream icons of pop culture. By the late 1980s, the WWF's *Raw is War* had become a top-rated show on cable and the firm had also begun to offer pay-per-view shows.

Vince faced his most formidable competition after 1988, when Ted Turner bought out World Championship Wrestling (WCW), one of the few major rivals that was still operating. Turner spent millions luring away WWF stars such as Hulk Hogan and Macho Man Randy Savage. He used these stars to launch a show on his own TNT channel that went up against the WWF's major show, *Raw is War*. Although Turner's new show caused a temporary dip in the ratings of the WWF's shows, Vince fought back

* This case was developed by Professor Jamal Shamsie, Michigan State University, with the assistance of Professor Alan B. Eisner, Pace University. Material has been drawn from published sources to be used for class discussion. Copyright © 2009 Jamal Shamsie and Alan B. Eisner.

Exhibit 1 Income Statements (in millions of dollars)

	2008	2007	2006	2006	2005
Period End Date:	12/31/08	12/31/07	12/31/06	04/30/06	04/30/05
Period Length:	12 Months	12 Months	8 Months	12 Months	12 Months
Revenue	526.46	485.66	262.94	400.05	366.43
Total revenue	**526.46**	**485.66**	**262.94**	**400.05**	**366.43**
Cost of revenue, total	311.78	298.77	157.09	227.17	213.29
Gross profit	**214.67**	**186.89**	**105.84**	**172.88**	**153.14**
Selling, general, administrative expenses, total	131.3	109.13	61.04	91.87	90.98
Research and development	0.0	0.0	0.0	0.0	0.0
Depreciation/amortization	13.08	9.32	5.56	10.47	11.87
Operating income	**70.29**	**68.43**	**39.24**	**70.54**	**50.29**
Other, net	−6.38	−0.52	0.88	0.55	1.35
Income before tax	**69.36**	**76.47**	**46.15**	**77.9**	**56.36**
Income tax, total	23.94	24.34	14.53	30.88	18.58
Income after tax	**45.42**	**52.14**	**31.62**	**47.01**	**37.78**
Discontinued operations	0.0	0.0	0.0	0.04	1.37
Net income	**45.42**	**52.14**	**31.62**	**47.05**	**39.15**

Source: moneycentral.msn.com and WWE.

with pumped-up scripts, mouthy muscle-men, and Lycra-clad women. "Ted Turner decided to come after me and all of my talent," growled Vince, "and now he's where he should be."[4]

In 2001, Vince was finally able to acquire WCW from Turner's parent firm, AOL Time Warner, for a bargain price of $5 million. Because of the manner in which he eliminated most of his rivals, Vince has earned a reputation for being as aggressive and ambitious as any character in the ring. Paul MacArthur, publisher of *Wrestling Perspective,* an industry newsletter, praised his accomplishments: "McMahon understands the wrestling business better than anyone else. He's considered by most in the business to be brilliant."[5]

In 2002, the WWF was hit by a British court ruling which held that the firm's *WWF* acronym belonged to the World Wildlife Fund. The firm had to undergo a major branding transition, changing its well-known name and triple logo from WWF to WWE. Although the change in name has been costly, it is not clear that this will hurt the firm in the long run. "Their product is really the entertainment. It's the stars. It's the bodies," said Larry McNaughton, managing director and principal of CoreBrand, a branding consultancy.[6] Linda McMahon stated that the new name might actually be beneficial for the firm.

"Our new name puts the emphasis on the 'E' for entertainment," she commented.[7]

Creating a Script for Success

After taking over the firm, Vince began to change the entire focus of the wrestling shows. He looked to television soap operas for ways of enhancing the entertainment value of his live events. Vince reduced the amount of actual wrestling and replaced it with wacky, yet somewhat compelling, story lines. He began to develop interesting characters and create compelling story lines by employing techniques that were quite similar to those being used by many successful television shows. There was a great deal of reliance on the "good versus evil" or the "settling the score" themes in the development of the plots for his wrestling matches. The plots and subplots ended up providing viewers with a mix of romance, sex, sports, comedy, and violence against a backdrop of pyrotechnics.

Over time, the scripts for the matches became tighter, with increasingly intricate story lines, plots, and dialogue. All the details of every match were worked out well in advance, leaving the wrestlers themselves to decide only the manner in which they would dispatch their opponents to the mat. Vince's use of characters was well thought out,

Exhibit 2   Balance Sheets (in millions of dollars, except per-share items)

Period End Date:	2008 12/31/08	2007 12/31/07	2006 12/31/06	2006 04/30/06	2005 04/30/05
Assets					
Cash and short-term investments	177.34	266.35	248.16	280.86	258.06
Cash and equivalents	119.66	135.81	86.27	175.2	56.57
Short-term investments	57.69	130.55	161.89	105.66	201.49
Total receivables, net	60.13	56.6	52.11	67.78	61.9
Accounts receivable—trade, net	60.13	56.6	52.11	67.78	61.9
Accounts receivable—trade, gross	64.85	57.96	54.2	71.48	65.2
Provision for doubtful accounts	−4.72	−1.36	−2.08	−3.7	−3.3
Total inventory	4.96	4.72	3.05	1.79	1.06
Prepaid expenses	37.6	20.05	13.33	11.14	15.19
Total current assets	**280.03**	**347.72**	**317.12**	**362.02**	**336.75**
Property, plant, equipment, total—net	92.37	77.77	67.97	67.57	66.64
Intangibles, net	1.18	2.3	3.33	1.46	2.61
Long-term investments	22.3	0.0	0.0	0.0	0.0
Other long-term assets, total	33.53	42.26	64.86	48.34	35.41
Total assets	**429.41**	**470.06**	**453.29**	**479.39**	**441.41**
Liabilities and Shareholders' Equity					
Accounts payable	18.33	21.95	14.91	19.83	15.67
Accrued expenses	27.12	30.68	25.54	28.6	21.15
Current portion of long-term debt/capital leases	1.0	0.93	0.86	0.82	0.76
Other current liabilities, total	11.88	18.01	20.47	27.59	21.1
Total current liabilities	**58.33**	**71.57**	**61.77**	**76.83**	**58.67**
Total long-term debt	3.87	4.88	5.8	6.38	7.2
Long-term debt	3.87	4.88	5.8	6.38	7.2
Deferred income tax	7.23	10.23	0.0	0.0	0.0
Total liabilities	**69.44**	**86.68**	**67.57**	**83.21**	**65.87**
Common stock	0.73	0.72	0.71	0.71	0.69
Additional paid-in capital	317.11	301.33	286.99	277.69	254.72
Retained earnings (accumulated deficit)	40.97	78.44	97.35	117.43	121.04
Other equity, total	1.17	2.89	0.67	0.36	−0.91
Total equity	**359.97**	**383.38**	**385.71**	**396.18**	**375.53**
Total liabilities and shareholders' equity	**429.41**	**470.06**	**453.29**	**479.39**	**441.41**
Total common shares outstanding	72.79	71.79	71.0	70.56	68.88

Source: moneycentral.msn.com and WWE.

Exhibit 3   Breakdown of Net Revenues (in millions of dollars)

	Dec. 31, 2008	Dec. 31, 2007	Dec. 31, 2006	Apr. 30, 2006
Live and televised entertainment	331.5	316.8	183.0	290.8
Consumer products	135.7	118.1	59.2	86.4
Digital media	34.8	34.8	20.7	22.9
WWE films	24.5	16.0	—	—
Total	526.5	485.7	262.9	400.1

Source: WWE.

Exhibit 4   Breakdown of Operating Income (in millions of dollars)

	Dec. 31, 2007	Dec. 31, 2006	Apr. 30, 2006
Live and televised entertainment	100.2	57.0	93.9
Consumer products	68.6	26.9	46.4
Digital media	6.3	3.8	2.9
WWE films	(14.8)	(1.1)	(1.3)

Source: WWE.

Exhibit 5   Percentage Breakdown of Net Revenues

	Dec. 31, 2008	Dec. 31, 2007	Dec. 31, 2006
Live and televised entertainment:			
Live events	21%	21%	20%
Venue merchandise sales	4	4	5
Television	20	19	22
Pay-per-view	18	20	20
Video on demand	1	1	1
Consumer products:			
Licensing	12	10	6
Home video	12	11	13
Magazine publishing	3	4	3
Digital media:			
WWE.com	3	4	3
WWEShop	4	4	5

Source: WWE.

and he began to refer to his wrestlers as "athletic performers" who were selected on the basis of their acting ability in addition to their physical stamina. Vince also ensured that his firm owned the rights to the characters that were played by his wrestlers. This would allow him to continue to exploit the characters that he developed for his television shows, even after the wrestler who played a particular character had left his firm.

By the late 1990s Vince had two weekly shows on television. Besides the original flagship program on the USA cable channel, WWE had added the *Smackdown* show on the UPN broadcast channel. Vince developed a continuous story line using the same characters so that his audience would be driven to both shows. But the acquisition of WCW resulted in a significant increase in the number of wrestling stars under contract. Trying to incorporate more than 150 characters into the story lines for WWE's shows proved to be a challenging task. At the same time, the move of *Raw* to the Spike TV channel resulted in a loss of viewers.

In October 2005, WWE signed a new agreement with NBC that moved *Raw* back to its USA channel and gave the firm a new show called *Extreme Championship Wrestling* on the Sci-Fi channel. Its other show, *Smackdown,* was later picked up by the new MyNetworkTV channel, which has been attracting a younger audience. All of these programs have been at the top of the ratings charts, particularly for male viewers because of the growth in popularity of a new breed of characters such as John Cena and Chris Benoit. The recently completed deal with Eurosport has provided WWE with two new shows that air throughout Europe and feature clips from the three different U.S. programs.

Managing a Road Show

A typical workweek for WWE can be grueling for the McMahons, for the talent, and for the crew. The organization is now putting on more than 300 live shows a year, requiring that everyone be on the road most days of the week. The touring crew includes over 200 members, including stagehands. All of WWE's live events, including those that are used for its two long-standing weekly shows *Raw* and *Smackdown,* as well as the newer ones, are held in different cities. Consequently, the crew is always packing up a dozen 18-wheelers and driving hundreds of miles to get from one performance to the next. Since there are no repeats of any WWE shows, the live performances must be held all year round.

In fact, the live shows form the core of all of WWE's businesses (see Exhibit 6). They give the firm a big advantage in the entertainment world. Most of the crowd shows up wearing WWE merchandise and screams throughout the show. Vince and his crew pay special attention to the response of the audience to different parts of the show. The script for each performance is not set until the day of the show, and sometimes changes are even made in the middle of a show. Vince boasted: "We're in contact with the public more than any entertainment company in the world."[8]

Although the live shows usually fill up, the attendance fee—running on average around $40—barely covers the cost of the production. But these live performances provide content for nine hours of original television programming as well as for the growing list of pay-per-view programming. Much of the footage from these live shows is also being used on the WWE Web site, which is the growth engine for the organization's new digital media business. The shows also create strong demand for WWE merchandise, ranging from video games and toys to home videos and magazines.

The whole endeavor is managed not only by Vince but by all of his family. Vince's efforts notwithstanding, the development of WWE has turned into a family affair. While the slick and highly toned Vince could be regarded as the creative muscle behind the growing sports entertainment empire, his wife, Linda, began to quietly manage its day-to-day operations. Throughout its existence, she helped to balance the books, do the deals, and handle the details that were necessary for the growth and development of the WWE franchise.

One of Vince and Linda's greatest pleasures has been to see their children move into the business. Their son, Shane, became executive vice president, Global Media and their daughter, Stephanie, moved from being a member of the creative writing team to executive vice president, Creative. "This business is my heart and soul and passion and always has been," Stephanie commented.[9] The family's devotion lies behind much of the success of WWE. "If they are out there giving 110 percent, it's a lot easer to get it from everyone else," said wrestler Steve Blackman.[10]

Pursuing New Opportunities

In 1999, shortly after going public, WWE launched an eight-team football league called XFL. Promising full competitive sport, unlike the heavily scripted wrestling matches, Vince tried to make the XFL a faster-paced, more fan-friendly form of football than the NFL's brand. Vince was able to partner with NBC, which was looking for a lower-priced alternative to the NFL televised games. The XFL kicked off with great fanfare in February 2001. Although the games drew good attendance, television ratings dropped steeply after the first week. The football venture folded after just one season, resulting in a $57 million loss for WWF. Both Vince and Linda insisted that the venture could have paid off if it had been given enough time. Vince commented: "I think our pals at the NFL went out of their way to make sure this was not a successful venture."[11]

Since then, the firm has tried to seek growth opportunities that are driven by its core wrestling business. With more characters at its disposal and different characters being used in each of its shows, WWE has been ramping up the number of live shows, including more in overseas locations. An increase in the number of shows around the globe has been helping to boost the worldwide revenues that the firm is able to generate from its merchandise.

Exhibit 6   WrestleMania's Classic Bouts

Andre the Giant vs. Hulk Hogan

WrestleMania III, March 29, 1987

- **The Lowdown:** A record crowd of 93,173 witnessed Andre the Giant, undefeated for 15 years, versus Hulk Hogan, wrestling's golden boy.
- **The Payoff:** Hogan body-slammed the 500-pound Giant, becoming the sport's biggest star and jump-starting wrestling's first big boom.

The Rock vs. Stone Cold Steve Austin

WrestleMania X-7, April 1, 2001

- **The Lowdown:** The two biggest stars of wrestling's modern era went toe-to-toe in the culmination of a two-year-long feud.
- **The Payoff:** Good-guy Austin aligned with "evil" WWE owner Vince McMahon and decimated the Rock to win the title in front of a shocked crowd.

Hulk Hogan vs. The Ultimate Warrior

WrestleMania VI, April 1, 1990

- **The Lowdown:** The most divisive feud ever—fan favorite Hulk Hogan defended his title against up-and-coming phenom the Ultimate Warrior.
- **The Payoff:** Half the crowd went into cardiac arrest (the other half were in tears) when Hogan missed his patented leg drop and the Warrior won.

Bret Hart vs. Shawn Michaels

WrestleMania XII, March 31, 1996

- **The Lowdown:** Two men who didn't like each other outside the ring locked up in a 60-minute Iron Man match for the title.
- **The Payoff:** After an hour, neither man had scored a pinfall. Finally, Michaels, aka the Heartbreak Kid, pinned Hart in overtime to win the belt.

Kurt Angle vs. Brock Lesnar

WrestleMania XIX, March 30, 2003

- **The Lowdown:** Olympic medalist Angle squared off against former NCAA wrestling champ Lesnar in a punishing bout.
- **The Payoff:** The 295-pound Lesnar landed on his head after attempting a high-flying attack. But he recovered to pin Angle and capture the championship.

Source: TV Guide.

International revenue nearly trebled from $45 million in 2002 to $120 million in 2007. The company has opened offices in six cities around the world to manage its overseas operations. "While it is based in America, the themes are worldwide: sibling rivalry, jealousy. We have had no pushback on the fact it was an American product," said Linda.[12]

There has also been considerable excitement generated by the launch of WWE 24/7, a subscriber video-on-demand service. The new service allows the firm to distribute for a fee thousands of content hours consisting of highlights from old shows as well as exclusive new programming. Within a couple of years, WWE 24/7 has shown considerable growth, generating nearly $5 million in revenue.

WWE is also pushing into a new area of digital media, building an e-commerce site that offers broadband and mobile services. The site offers a broad range of content and wide range of merchandise. In a recent tally, it was attracting more than 16 million unique users each month. But the firm has barely tapped into the online ad market, with digital media revenue accounting for less than 10 percent of its total revenue. "The real value creation and growth will come from monetizing the presence on the Internet, where the company has a fanatic and loyal fan base," said Bobby Melnick, general partner with Terrier Partners, a New York money management firm that owns WWE stock.[13]

Finally, WWE has also become involved with movie production, using its wrestling stars and releasing a few films over the last five years. Recent releases included Steve Austin's *The Condemned* and John Cena's *The Marine*. Though the films generated only a small amount of revenue in theaters, Linda believes that the movies will earn additional profit from home video markets, distribution on premium channels, and offerings on pay-per-view. In fact, *The Marine* debuted in January 2007 as the top DVD rental.

Reclaiming the Championship?

In spite of the growth of WWE in many forms, Vince and Linda have had to deal with serious challenges. In June 2007, the firm received word that Chris Benoit, one of its most popular wrestlers, had committed suicide after killing his wife and child. This was followed by news that steroids had been found in Benoit's home. Vince went on a public relations blitz to highlight WWE's steroid policy, which the company then bolstered with the suspension of at least 10 performers over the next few months. The firm's revenues dipped slightly, while the value of its stock dropped by 17 percent over the next six months.

More recently, Vince's wrestling empire has been facing a challenge from mixed martial arts (MMA), a growing form of combat sport that combines kickboxing and grappling. Because of its similarity to wrestling, this new combat sport is expected to pull away some of WWE's fans. Although MMA started in Japan and Brazil, the Ultimate Fighting Championship and the International Fight League are promoting it as a new type of spectator sport in the United States. But Dana White, president of the UFC, said: "People have been trying to count the WWE out for years. They are a powerhouse."[14]

The interest in wrestling is most evident each year with the frenzy that is created by WrestleMania, the annual pop culture extravaganza that began at New York's Madison Square Garden in 1985. Since then, it has become an almost weeklong celebration of everything wrestling. No wrestler becomes a true star until his or her performance is featured at WrestleMania, and any true fan must make the pilgrimage at least once in his or her life. Linda points to the continued popularity of this event to reject any suggestion that the fortunes of WWE may be driven by a fad that is unlikely to last. She maintains that the interest in WWE shows will survive in spite of growing competition from all other newer sources of entertainment.

Furthermore, Vince and Linda McMahon claim that their attempts to diversify were never meant to convey any loss of interest in wrestling. In fact, they believe that it was their experience with staging wrestling shows over the years that provided them with the foundation for moving into other areas of entertainment. After all, it was their ability to use wrestling to create a form of mass entertainment that made the WWE such a phenomenal success. In response to critics who question the value of wrestling matches whose outcomes are rigged, James F. Byrne, senior vice president for marketing, stated: "Wrestling is 100 percent entertainment. There's no such thing as fake entertainment."[15]

Analysts have been impressed by WWE's recent performance. Its stock has done better than most others in its particular category. They also note that the firm has little debt and considerable cash flow, making it a relatively good investment over the longer term. Six out of ten analysts who cover the stock recently rated it as a buy, while the other four said it is a hold. "For long term investors, WWE is very interesting" remarked Michael Kelman, an analyst with Susquehanna Financial Group. "We make money when we are not hot," explained Vince. "When we are hot, its off the charts."[16]

Those who understand don't need an explanation. Those who need an explanation will never understand.

—**Marty,** a 19-year-old wrestling addict, quoted in *Fortune,* October 6, 2000

Endnotes

1. Anonymous. WGN America Enters WWE Ring with WWE Superstars. PR Newswire, January 5, 2009.
2. WWE. World Wrestling Entertainment, Inc., Reports Q3 Results. Press Release, February 23, 2005.
3. Bethany McLean. Inside the World's Weirdest Family Business. *Fortune,* October 16, 2000, p. 298.
4. Diane Bradley. Wrestling's Real Grudge Match. *BusinessWeek,* January 24, 2000, p.164.
5. Don Mooradian. WWF Gets a Grip after Acquisition. *Amusement Business,* June 4, 2001, p. 20.
6. Dwight Oestricher and Brian Steinberg. WW . . . E It Is, after Fight for F Nets New Name. *Wall Street Journal,* May 7, 2002, p. B2.
7. David Finnigan. Down but Not Out, WWE Is Using a Rebranding Effort to Gain Strength. *Brandweek,* June 3, 2002, p. 12.
8. *Fortune,* October 16, 2000, p. 304.
9. Ibid., p. 302.
10. Ibid.
11. Diane Bradley. Rousing Itself Off the Mat? *BusinessWeek,* February 2, 2004, p. 73.
12. Brooke Masters. Wrestling's Bottom Line Is No Soap Opera. *Financial Times,* August 25, 2008, p. 15.
13. Paul R. La Monica. Wrestling's "Trump" Card. CNN Money.com, March 30, 2007.
14. R. M. Schneiderman. Better Days, and Even the Candidates, Are Coming to WWE. *New York Times,* April 28, 2008, p. B3.
15. Edward Wyatt. Pro Wrestling Tries to Pin Down a Share Value. *New York Times,* August 4, 1999, p. C11.
16. *BusinessWeek,* February 2, 2004, p. 74.

Case 12 Schoolhouse Lane Estates*

"The supply of grapes crushed in California's 2008 harvest was an all-time record, and it followed a record 2007 harvest. Quality was excellent—yet thousands of acres of vines are being pulled up across California with replanting of fruit trees. The *Santa Rosa Press Democrat* reported that the well-known Mondavi division of Constellation Brands was cutting 10 percent of its workforce due to a reduced demand for wines selling above $25 per bottle at retail and to a projected quarterly operating loss for the first time since the early 1990s. Several small wineries here in Sonoma County, notably DeLoach and Roshambo, have gone bankrupt in the last few years. How are things going for you on the East Coast, Jan?"

Janess (Jan) Thaw had trouble responding to the information she had just received from her cousin, Stan White, during their telephone conversation in late January 2009. She had recently prepared a business plan for the expansion of her Schoolhouse Lane Estates winery, located in Cutchogue on the North Fork of Long Island. Her plans included the purchase of grape-growing acreage as well as expansion of the winery, construction of a retail store and new tasting room, and renovation of a special events facility. The estimated cost of these initiatives was $2.4 million, and new construction would take approximately a year to complete. Her cousin Stan's information created a wave of uncertainty concerning not only these plans but also the outlook for her current business strategy. Regardless of the financing options available to her, Jan knew that she'd first have to get the strategy right.

Company History

Jan and her twin brother Nick grew up on a 35-acre potato farm adjacent to Schoolhouse Lane, located on the North Fork of Long Island. Owned by her parents, the farm barely provided for family living expenses. While her father Harry plowed the fields, her mother Suzanne taught fourth grade at a nearby public school.

The experience of growing up on a farm had a very different impact on the adult lifestyles of the children. Jan loved the land. She enjoyed walking the fields with her Dad and seeing the animals that lived on the land, especially the birds nesting in the tall oaks on the periphery of the family property.

Jan attended the agricultural school at Cornell University. She worked during the summer at small wineries in the Finger Lakes region in upstate New York. Upon graduation

*This case was prepared by Professors Raymond H. Lopez of Pace University and Armand Gilinsky, Jr., at Sonoma State University as a basis for class discussion rather than to illustrate either effective or ineffective handling of an administrative situation. All individuals and events have been disguised at the request of the host organization. Copyright © 2004, 2007, 2009 by Raymond H. Lopez and Armand Gilinsky, Jr. This case may not be reproduced without the express written permission of the authors. All rights reserved.

in 1985, she was offered an assistant winemaker position at the Glenora Winery in Hammondsport, New York. For three years she experienced all aspects of the wine-making process and saw a chance to combine her love for the land with a career path in this industry.

By contrast, her brother Nick, an avid reader and athlete, could not wait to leave the farm for college. With a full athletic scholarship to Yale, Nick thrived in what he thought was a "big city" (New Haven, Connecticut). After completing his BA in economics, he went on to Columbia University for an MBA with a concentration in finance.

A few years later Harry and Suzanne told their children that they were ready to retire and move to Sedona, Arizona. They sold their farm to Jan and Nick for one dollar in 1988 and headed west.

In January 1989 Jan and Nick each unexpectedly inherited $3 million after the death of their uncle Garry. They had very different uses for these funds. Jan paid off her student loans and immediately embarked on a long-held plan to convert the potato fields to the growing of wine grapes. Nick paid off his loans and started a financial consulting firm for private equity investors in Manhattan. Although they spoke often on the phone, Nick had not been out to the farm for more than five years. Jan would occasionally meet him for dinner in Manhattan.

During the spring of 1989 Jan planted 20 acres of grapevines on the property and named her new business Schoolhouse Lane Estates. By fall 1994 her first harvest was completed and the grapes were crushed at a local winery. Production was 60 tons of grapes, resulting in 5,000 cases of bottled wine. Within six months, the cases were all sold locally to restaurants, catering firms, and businesses for gifts and promotions. Revenues from cases sold were just over $250,000. The business seemed poised for growth.

Schoolhouse Lane Estates' wines—Cabernet Sauvignon, Merlot (red varietals), Meritage (a blend of red varietals), and Chardonnay (white wine)—were well received on their introduction to the local marketplace. Jan sold her wines at retail prices ranging from $10 per bottle for Merlot ($120 per 12-bottle case) to $36 per bottle for the Meritage ($432 per case). As demand grew, Jan decided to operate her own winery. There was a small winery on 6 acres of land just east of her vineyards. She had been speaking with the owner and sensed that he was ready to retire and move to Weaverville, North Carolina. After only three meetings, they agreed on the terms of sale, and in fall 1996 Jan was the proud owner of a winery. She invested $2.2 million, financed with a mortgage from a local Long Island bank, and was ready to oversee her first wine production in fall 1997. Having expanded its acreage, producing quality grapes, and using grape purchases from other vineyards, the renamed Schoolhouse Lane Estates generated just over $1.5 million in revenue in fiscal year 1998.

Over the next seven years, through 2004, Schoolhouse Lane Estates expanded its presence in the local wine markets. About 35 percent of sales were to off-premises accounts, such as wholesalers and retailers, and 45 percent to on-premises accounts, such as restaurants and caterers. These trade intermediaries handled Jan's products before they were resold to the final consumer, with a retail markup of 100 percent. Direct sales to consumers at retail prices by way of the tasting room accounted for the remaining 20 percent of Schoolhouse Lane's sales. Product acceptance translated into growing net revenues (Exhibit 1). Although her operating expenses for marketing and sales had grown rapidly, Jan felt that these expenditures were needed to differentiate her portfolio of fine wines from competitors' offerings and to stimulate demand from trade intermediaries.

Schoolhouse Lane's balance sheets (Exhibit 2) and statements of cash flow (Exhibit 3) reflected Jan's efforts as well as the challenges of growing her business. Most significant among these challenges was the rapid and continuing expansion of inventories, as premium red wines and red wine blends require longer aging periods in oak barrels. Growing inventories were financed with an expanding line of credit from Goose Creek Savings, a local lending bank. For a business of Schoolhouse Lane's size, however, Goose Creek Savings maintained a lending limit of $3 million, based on the replacement value of fixed assets. Goose Creek Savings was also financing a small percentage of Jan's inventories through a revolving line of credit. Either a larger bank would be needed within the year, or perhaps a more permanent source of financing would be needed. Laurel Durst, Jan's accountant and financial manager, had recently been exploring a number of working-capital financing options with the North Fork Bancorp.

Evolution of Long Island's Wine Industry

How did it all begin? A small band of hesitant artisans and amateurs pioneered the wine industry in converted barns and potato fields in the 1970s, in many cases because they sought a simpler agrarian lifestyle, or so they thought. In less than a third of a century, the profile of Long Island wine moguls had morphed to that of self-assured professionals backed by deep-pocketed investors who were also seeking a different lifestyle.

The migration to become owners of Long Island wineries was not unlike the one followed by "refugees" from the high-tech world of Silicon Valley, who bought or developed new Napa and Sonoma wineries in California in the late 1990s. Similar to what their California counterparts had accomplished in the prior decade, the showcase Long Island

Exhibit 1 Schoolhouse Lane Estates Income Statements, 2004–2008 (in thousands)

	2008	2007	2006	2005	2004
Net sales	$ 5,416.4	$ 4,924.7	$ 4,296.6	$ 3,646.5	$ 3,040.4
Cost of goods sold	3,566.2	3,152.6	2,744.5	2,318.8	1,788.6
Gross profit	1,850.2	1,772.1	1,552.1	1,327.7	1,251.8
Operating expenses:					
Marketing and advertising	145.2	130.9	116.6	101.2	89.1
Selling and administration	935.0	811.8	711.7	572.0	358.6
Total operating expenses	1,080.2	942.7	828.3	673.2	447.7
Operating income (EBIT)	770.0	829.4	723.8	654.5	804.1
Interest expense[a]	376.2	326.7	295.9	282.7	259.6
Net income before taxes	393.8	502.7	427.9	371.8	544.5
Income taxes[b]	157.3	201.3	171.6	148.5	217.8
Net income (loss)	$ 236.5	$ 301.4	$ 256.3	$ 223.3	$ 326.7
Number of cases sold	36,109	32,831	28,644	24,310	20,269
Average wholesale FOB price per 12-bottle case	$ 150.00	$ 150.00	$ 150.00	$ 150.00	$ 150.00
Average retail price per 12-bottle case	$ 300.00	$ 300.00	$ 300.00	$ 300.00	$ 300.00

[a]Prime + 2% on average balance for a line of credit.

[b]Federal and state income tax rate of 40%.

Exhibit 2 Schoolhouse Lane Estates Balance Sheets, 2004–2008 (in thousands)

	2008	2007	2006	2005	2004
Assets					
Current assets:					
Cash	$ 244.2	$ 218.9	$ 231.0	$ 216.7	$ 210.1
Accounts receivable	268.4	277.2	294.8	269.5	235.4
Inventories	3,279.1	2,839.1	2,568.5	2,183.5	1,925.0
Prepaid and other expenses	48.4	44.0	46.2	41.8	40.7
Total current assets	3,840.1	3,379.2	3,140.5	2,711.5	2,411.2
Property, plant, and equipment	3,578.3	3,440.8	3,291.2	3,254.9	3,172.4
Less: Accumulated depreciation and amortization	216.7	191.4	183.7	191.4	216.7
Net property, plant, and equipment	3,361.6	3,249.4	3,107.5	3,063.5	2,955.7
Other assets (net)	16.5	15.4	16.5	15.4	13.2
Total assets	$7,218.2	$6,644.0	$6,264.5	$5,790.4	$5,380.1
Liabilities and Capital					
Current liabilities:					
Accounts payable	$ 298.1	$ 256.3	$ 217.8	$ 194.7	$ 170.5
Accrued expenses	268.4	222.2	193.6	169.4	150.7
Line of credit (bank)[a]	1,282.6	999.9	955.9	757.9	565.4
LTD (current portion)	33.0	33.0	33.0	33.0	33.0
Total current liabilities	1,882.1	1,511.4	1,400.3	1,155.0	919.6
Long-term debt mortgage[b]	2,288.0	2,321.0	2,354.0	2,381.5	2,429.9
Equity:					
Class A common[c]	1,661.0	1,661.0	1,661.0	1,661.0	1,661.0
Class B common[d]	0.0	0.0	0.0	0.0	0.0
Retained earnings (loss)	1,387.1	1,150.6	849.2	592.9	369.6
Total equity	3,048.1	2,811.6	2,510.2	2,253.9	2,030.6
Total liabilities and equity	$7,218.2	$6,644.0	$6,264.5	$5,790.4	$5,380.1

[a]Prime + 2% on average balance for line of credit.
[b]Long-term debt (mortgage) at 7%.
[c]Class A common stock—10 votes.
[d]Class B common stock—1 vote.

wineries of the early 2000s burst on the New York culinary scene by making prize-winning and sought-after wines. While the production of world-class wines was still said to be some years away, the money, the wine-making talent, and the will to make such wines were now in place. It seemed just a matter of time before Long Island winemakers would be regarded with the same status as their California counterparts, according to the Long Island Wine Council.

The land of the North Fork, where most wineries were located, was flat to slightly rolling, planted not only with grapes but also with potatoes, sod, and fruit trees. Craggy oaks shaded the villages of Greenport, Southold, and

Exhibit 3   Schoolhouse Lane Estates Statements of Cash Flow, 2005–2008 (in thousands)

	2008	2007	2006	2005
Cash Flows from Operating Activities				
Net Income	$236.5	$301.4	$256.3	$223.3
Depreciation	25.3	7.7	34.1	24.2
Increase in receivables (net)	8.8	17.6	(25.3)	(34.1)
Increase in inventories	(440.0)	(270.6)	(385.0)	(258.5)
Increase in prepaid and other expenses	(4.4)	2.2	(4.4)	(1.1)
Increase in accounts payable	41.8	38.5	23.1	24.2
Increase in accrued expenses	46.2	28.6	24.2	18.7
Net cash provided (used) by operating activities	(85.8)	125.4	(77.0)	(3.3)
Cash Flows from Investing Activities				
Purchase of property, plant, and equipment	(137.5)	(149.6)	(78.1)	(132.0)
Other assets (net)	(1.1)	1.1	(1.1)	(2.2)
Net cash used for investing activities	(138.6)	(148.5)	(79.2)	(134.2)
Cash Flows from Financing Activities				
Increase (decrease) from bank line of credit	282.7	44.0	198.0	192.5
Increase (decrease) in long-term debt (current portion)	0.0	0.0	0.0	0.0
Increase (decrease) in mortgage	(33.0)	(33.0)	(27.5)	(48.4)
Net cash provided (used) in financing activities	249.7	11.0	170.5	144.1
Net increase in cash	25.3	(12.1)	14.3	6.6
Cash at the beginning of the year	218.9	231.0	216.7	210.1
Cash at the end of the year	244.2	218.9	231.0	216.7

Cutchogue, small and quaint with 200-year-old houses, 100-year-old churches, and plaques showing where the Pilgrims' punishment stocks used to stand on the village green. The water was never more than a few miles away, as the Long Island Sound lay to the north, and Peconic Bay and the Atlantic Ocean to the south.[1]

From its humble beginnings in 1973, the Long Island wine industry had developed steadily, with growing numbers of vineyards, wineries, and acreage, to produce quality wine products. Long Island wineries produced a broad variety of red varietals including Cabernet Sauvignon, Cabernet Franc, Merlot, Pinot Noir, and Shiraz, as well as white varietals such as Chardonnay, Gewürztraminer, Riesling, and Sauvignon Blanc. A few wineries, like Schoolhouse Lane, produced a Bordeaux-style blend of red wines called Meritage. All Long Island winery owners and their trade association, the Long Island Wine Council, anticipated continued growth and expansion well into the 21st century.

Grape growing and wine production were located primarily on the eastern end of Long Island, which jutted more than 100 miles into the Atlantic Ocean, parallel to the coastlines of Connecticut and Rhode Island. The North and South Forks of eastern Long Island were a maritime region with a unique combination of climate, soil characteristics, and growing conditions ideal for quality wine production. Bays bordering the North and South Forks insulated the vineyards and trapped moist warm air. Along with rich, sandy glacial soil, this combination created the perfect environment for growing grapes. Growing seasons were quite long (averaging approximately 200 days), and relatively mild winters encouraged the planting of Europe's noble vinifera grapes on almost all acres planted.

The Long Island wineries represented three appellations (American Viticultural Areas, or AVAs) approved by the Bureau of Alcohol, Tobacco and Firearms (BATF)—the North Fork of Long Island, the Hamptons, and, as of April

2001, the Long Island AVA. This latest designation allowed for further expansion beyond the two forks of Long Island's east end and, at the same time, protected the overall integrity of the region's wines.[2]

New York State ranked third nationally in wine production. According to the New York Farm Bureau, the state had almost 1,000 family-owned vineyards that produced 175,000 tons of grapes annually—a $40 million industry. There were 160 wineries in the four main wine-producing regions of the state: the Finger Lakes, the Lake Erie region, the Hudson River Valley, and the Long Island region. Together, these regions produced over 100 million bottles of wine each year and attracted approximately 1 million tourists.[3]

Long Island wines were sold primarily in the New York metropolitan region. Products were found at most vineyards and in local wine retail stores, as well as in a broad variety of restaurants and catering establishments. Quality had been enhanced, resulting in higher ratings by wine magazines and in national taste tests, and the market broadened up and down the East Coast. Large regional distributors had in recent years shown a growing interest in carrying these wines. Several wineries already distributed their products in Florida, California, and Texas.

Anticipating that this trend would accelerate as knowledge spread of the rising quality of Long Island wines, the Long Island wine producers hoped that recent support from a New York U.S. congressional delegation would help to overturn the ban on direct shipments outside the state.[4] New York remained the nation's largest wine-producing state that did not allow direct shipments. Current law prohibited wine producers from shipping wine directly to consumers in other states. Thirteen states already had reciprocal wine shipment laws enabling out-of-state shipments of wine, and eight had laws allowing the direct shipment of wine to customers.

Recent Developments and Industry Maturation

By 2008 Long Island boasted 60 vineyards and 42 wineries.[5] The remaining 18 vineyard owners who lacked production capacity either sold their grapes to other wineries or contracted with other wineries to produce wine.

A sure sign of the maturation of the industry on Long Island came with the announcement of a custom-crush facility to be constructed in Mattituck. This facility would cater to independent vineyard owners and grape buyers who lacked their own wine-making facilities.[6] The new custom-crush venture was led by Russell Hearn, the winemaker at Pellegrini Vineyards, along with investors Mark Lieb, a Connecticut money manager and owner of the 50-acre Lieb Vineyard, and Bernard Sussman, also a money manager and an associate of Lieb. The partners expected to fund 40 to 50 percent of the new winery with equity, borrowing the rest from a Long Island bank.

"The primary purpose of this venture is to make wines for a number of small and large producers which choose

not to, or are unable to, build their own wineries," Hearn said. "Our service would allow someone to have small amounts of wine made and bring in their own consultant [winemaker] to set the style. The number of wineries that offered custom services in the past are approaching their maximum," Hearn added. Moreover, vineyards for commercial wine production in Long Island were expected to double in the next two decades, further expanding the customer base.[7]

The Long Island wineries drew more than 640,000 visitors in 2008 for wine tours. Although traffic congestion was increasing on the two roads that fed the North Fork, some locals felt that the trade-off was worth the price. Several local residents credited the vineyards as having preserved open space that might otherwise have been developed for housing.

Wine Production in the United States

The internal structure of the U.S. wine industry similarly underwent fundamental changes after the early 1980s. In terms of product, the most significant developments were observed in table wine. After 1992, table wines represented the largest segment of production and value of shipments and accounted for more than 85 percent of total shipments annually. At the same time, table wine products responded to changes in consumers' tastes and preferences for higher-quality premium wines.

Grapes used in the production of table wines were of varying quality. Varietals were delicate, thin-skinned grapes whose vines usually took approximately four years to begin bearing fruit. As defined by the truth-in-labeling standards of the Bureau of Alcohol, Tobacco and Firearms, one varietal—the name of a single grape—had to be used if more than 75 percent of the wine was derived from grapes of that variety and if the entire 75 percent was grown in the labeled appellation of origin. Appellation denoted that "at least 75 percent of a wine's volume was derived from fruit or agricultural products and grown in the place or region indicated."[8] Developing the typical varietal characteristics that resulted in enhanced flavor, taste, and finish could take another two to three years after the four years required for newly planted vines to bear fruit. This additional growing period, in the pursuit of enhanced quality and value, increased both investment levels and operating expenses.

The wine industry was capital-intensive. In addition to having land and vineyards, a fully integrated firm needed investments in crushing facilities, fermentation tanks, barrels for aging its product, and warehouses to store the bottled and cased wine. Ownership was not essential for any of these activities. However, to control the quality and quantity of production, these investments became essential as a firm developed its brands and expanded its markets.

Since the wine industry was inherently capital-intensive, as well as seasonal and cyclical, winery owners generally experienced low profit margins and limited options for outside capital, according to Dan Aguilar of Silicon Valley Bank, a major lender to the wine industry in Napa and Sonoma counties in California. Even under the best of conditions, working capital was under some pressure. Winery owners typically sought to fund continuing operations as well as business and inventory growth from limited retained earnings and bank debt; at the same time, they had to satisfy the voracious appetites of their wineries for funds to finance some mixture of vineyards, production facilities, equipment, barrels, and tasting room and visitor facilities.[9]

Business risks were also substantial. Weather conditions could affect the quality and quantity of grape production. Insect damage and disease could affect the vines. Replanting of new vines required four to five years before commercial quantities of grapes could be expected.

In the fall of the year, usually late September to early November, depending on the weather, grapes were picked and carefully brought from the fields to the crushing facility. There was only one crop per year, and crushing took from one to two months. Consequently, the investment in this facility stood idle at least 10 months of the year. Since all the grapes in a region matured at approximately the same time, there was no way to rent out crushing capacity to other wineries at other times of the year.

After the grapes were crushed, the juice was pumped into fermentation tanks. These stainless steel vessels were temperature-controlled to balance the heat generated by the natural fermentation process. Fermentation lasted only a few weeks after the crush, so this investment was also idle more than 85 percent of the time.

From the fermentation tanks, the wine was pumped into oak barrels for aging. These barrels were expensive, costing $600 to $700 each. Due to quality concerns, they were used for only four or five years, after which their value was negligible (some were cut in half and sold as planters). A barrel-aging facility was a large open space that also had to be climate-controlled. During the aging process, some wine was lost due to evaporation through the porous oak barrels. Every two weeks each barrel was refilled up to 3 inches from its top. For premium red wines that aged in barrels for two years or longer, about 5 percent of the original wine was typically lost to evaporation.

Table wines were defined as those with 7 to 14 percent alcohol content by volume and were traditionally consumed with food. In contrast, other wine products such as sparkling wine (champagnes), wine coolers, pop wines, and fortified wines were typically consumed as stand-alone beverages. Table wines that retailed for less than $3 per 750-milliliter bottle were generally considered to be generic, or "jug," wines, while those selling for more than $3 per bottle were considered premium wines.

Premium wines generally had a vintage date on their labels. This designation signified that at least 95 percent of the grapes used in making the product had been harvested, crushed, and fermented in the calendar year shown on the label and that the grapes were from an appellation of origin (i.e., Napa Valley, Sonoma Valley, or Central Coast in California; North Fork, the Hamptons, or Long Island AVA on Long Island). Within the premium wine category, a number of market segments emerged on the basis of retail price points. "Popular premium" wines generally sold for $3 to $7 per bottle, while "super-premium" wines retailed for $7 to $14. The "ultra-premium" category sold for $14 to $20 per bottle, while any retail price above $20 per bottle was considered by the industry to be "luxury premium."

Changing Dynamics of the U.S. Wine Market

The value of alcoholic and nonalcoholic beverages consumed by Americans grew modestly from 1995 to 2007, according to figures compiled in *Adams' Wine Handbook, 2007*. For purposes of comparison, the largest beverage category was soft drinks, which in 2007 achieved almost double the dollar value of the next-largest category, coffee. The consumption of wine produced domestically, as well as imports, grew steadily over the same period, but its volume remained significantly smaller, at less than 4 percent of soft-drink volume in 2007. Wine consumption increased by 2.8 percent per year from 1996 through 2004. In the last few years, this growth has accelerated to 3.8 percent per year. This record trailed only bottled water at 10.8 percent per year and hard cider (an alcoholic beverage) at 8.8 percent per year. By contrast, overall beverage consumption grew at only 1.8 percent per year from 1996 to 2007. On a per capita basis, wine consumption rose steadily from 1.8 gallons per person per year in 1996 to just over 2.37 gallons in 2005.

Total wine consumption in the United States also reached an all-time high in 2007. At 745 million gallons, it exceeded the record consumption of 717 million gallons reached in 2006 (Exhibit 4). From the peak years in the mid-1980s, total consumption as well as per capita consumption had trended downward for more than a decade. Since the early 1990s, growth has rebounded to record consumption and sales levels for table wine (Exhibit 5). Champagne and sparkling wines are approaching the record level reached in 1999, when preparation for the new-millennium celebrations boosted sales.

Reflecting the changing tastes and preferences of the American consumer, the growth performance of table wine sales by color also underwent dramatic changes. In 1991 white wine volume accounted for almost one-half of all wine sold in supermarkets, which sold 78 percent of all wine purchased in the United States (the remaining 22 percent of wine shipments were sold through specialty wine shops, tasting rooms, the Internet, or on-premises accounts such as hotels and restaurants). Approximately one-third of total wine sales by dollars in 1991 were blush/rosé, while only 17 percent were red (Exhibit 6). By 2007 the market share of white wine and blush/rosé had declined to about 42 percent and 15 percent of total sales, respectively, but red wine had increased to 43 percent. Still, most red wines were more expensive to produce and thus sold for higher prices than either white or blush/rosé. The net result was that revenues at the wholesale and consumer levels grew more rapidly than the increase in case wine volume that was produced and then sold.

Exhibit 4 U.S. Wine Consumption, 1985–2007

	Total Wine		Total Table Wine	
Year	Millions of Gallons[1]	Gallons per Resident[2]	Millions of Gallons[3]	Gallons per Resident[2]
2007	745	247	650	2.16
2006	717	239	628	2.09
2005	692	2.33	609	2.05
2004	665	2.26	589	2.00
2003	639	2.20	570	1.96
2002	617	2.14	552	1.91
2001	574	2.01	512	1.79
2000	568	2.01	507	1.79
1999	551	2.02	482	1.76
1998	526	1.95	466	1.72
1997	520	1.94	461	1.72
1996	505	1.90	443	1.67
1995	469	1.79	408	1.56
1994	459	1.77	395	1.52
1993	449	1.74	381	1.48
1992	476	1.87	405	1.59
1991	466	1.85	394	1.56
1990	509	2.05	423	1.70
1989	524	2.11	432	1.74
1988	551	2.24	457	1.86
1987	581	2.39	481	1.98
1986	587	2.43	487	2.02
1985	580	2.43	378	1.58

[1]All wine types, including sparkling wine, dessert wine, vermouth, and other special natural and table wines.

[2]Per capita consumption in gallons is based on the resident population of the United States.

[3]Table wines include all "still" wines not over 14% alcohol content.

Source: The Wine Institute, www.wineinstitute.org; Gomberg, Fredricksen & Associates.

The forecasts from *Impact Databank* indicated that strong advances from imported wine could be expected to drive much of the growth in the U.S. wine market through 2010. Growth in consumption of domestic wines was 3.3 percent—to 193 million cases in 2003, 198 million cases in 2005, and estimated at 211 million cases by 2010. For imports, a 12 percent increase to 65 million cases was seen for 2003, and case volume was projected to reach 90 million cases by 2010. California's dominant U.S. market share of domestic table wines was forecast to slip from 67 percent in 2003 to 63 percent in 2010, due in part to strong growth from imported varietals such as Shiraz/Syrah, Chardonnay, and Pinot Grigio. *Impact Databank* also forecast that the share of red wine in the U.S. market was expected to continue to gain at a more rapid pace than white or blush wine. Late projections held that red wine consumption would grow from 98 million cases in 2003 to 128 million cases by 2010. Projected annual compound growth rates for red wines were 5.9 percent for 2000 to 2007 and 3.5 percent for 2008 to 2010. White wine consumption was forecast to grow from 90 million cases by 2003 to 100 million cases by 2010. This translated into annual compound growth rates for white wines of 4.3 percent for 2000 to 2008 and further 1 percent annual increases from 2007 to 2010.

Exhibit 5 Wine Sales in the United States (millions of gallons): Domestic Shipments and Foreign Producers Entering U.S. Distribution Channels, 1991–2007

Year	Table Wine[1]	Dessert Wine[2]	Champagne, Sparkling Wine	Total Wine	Total Retail Value ($, billions)
2007	650	62	33	745	$30.0
2006	628	57	32	717	27.8
2005	609	54	30	692	25.8
2004	589	48	30	665	24.0
2003	570	41	29	639	22.3
2002	552	38	28	617	21.8
2001	512	35	25	572	20.3
2000	499	32	28	558	19.2
1999	475	31	37	543	18.1
1998	466	31	29	526	17.0
1997	461	29	29	519	16.1
1996	439	31	29	500	14.3
1995	404	30	30	464	12.2
1994	394	33	31	458	11.5
1993	381	35	33	449	11.0
1992	405	37	33	476	11.4
1991	394	39	33	466	10.9

[1]Includes all still wines not over 14% alcohol; excludes Canadian Coolers (made from malt).
[2]Includes all still wines over 14% alcohol.
Source: The Wine Institute, www.wineinstitute.org.

Exhibit 6 Table Wine Volume Share by Color (in U.S. supermarkets)

Color	1991	1995	2002	2003	2006	2007
Red	17%	25%	39%	40%	43%	43%
White	49	41	40	40	42	42
Blush/rosé	34	34	21	20	16	15
Total	100%	100%	100%	100%	100%	100%

Source: U.S. supermarket data from ACNielsen Beverage Alcohol Team.

Competition

Since the 1960s, there has been a substantial increase in the number of firms producing wine products in the United States. From hundreds of companies in the 1970s, the number exceeded 1,800 wineries by the turn of the century. Most were relatively small; each of the 50 states already had at least one winery; and about 800 were located in California.

By 2005 the 20 largest firms produced approximately 90 percent of all American wines by volume and 85 percent by value at wholesale.[10]

The competitive structure of the industry could be classified into three types of stand-alone wineries: public conglomerates, private conglomerates, and multi-industry firms (primarily public). The largest publicly traded winery was Robert Mondavi until its sale to Constellation Brands in 2006, along with Chalone, a much smaller firm. Privately held wineries included the industry giant, E&J Gallo, as well as Kendall-Jackson, The Wine Group, and more than a thousand small- to medium-size wineries. The final group of competitors consisted of large, publicly traded multi-industry firms. These included Allied Domecq, Brown Forman (Wine Estates Division), Foster's Group (Beringer Blass), Constellation Brands (Canandaigua and Mondavi Division), Diageo (Chateau and Estates Division), Fortune Brands, Louis Vuitton Moët Hennessey (LVMH), and UST (formerly known as U.S. Tobacco).

In addition to their domestic competition, U.S. winemakers faced competition from abroad as imports gained a growing percentage share of the U.S. wine market. In addition to the traditional "Old World" supplies from France, Italy, Germany, Spain, and Portugal, a new group of countries experienced growing acceptance of their wine production. Australia, Chile, and Argentina (the "New World" suppliers) increased their market share in the last decade, offering high-quality wines at very competitive prices.

Consolidation among wineries began to accelerate in the early 1990s as larger producers purchased smaller ones to achieve greater economies of scale in marketing and economies of scope in gaining access to more varied channels of distribution. These larger wineries could then become more effective in negotiating favorable selling terms with an increasingly small number of large regional distributors.[11] The "consolidators" were generally public firms that were able to offer predominantly family-run wine businesses a means to greater liquidity of their investment in larger, more diversified firms. Concurrently, the attractiveness of wine production across the United States resulted in a growing number of entrepreneurs purchasing or starting new, small operations.

Jan Meets with Her Team

The day after her conversation with cousin Stan, Jan set up a meeting with her operations manager, Dan Henning, and her accountant, Laurel Durst. She also invited the executive director of the 16-year-old Long Island Wine Council, Nanette Hansen, to get her broader perspective of local conditions.

Jan began the meeting by presenting her plans for the expansion:

> We have an opportunity to purchase additional grape-producing acreage across Schoolhouse Lane from our vineyard, that is, to buy 28 acres for $900,000. We have been farming that land and now have the opportunity to purchase it. The winery needs expanded capacity, and I have estimates between $800,000 and $900,000 for that project. Our tasting room is overcrowded—even on weekdays—and its expansion would require $250,000. Finally, many of our neighboring competitors already have facilities for special events (weddings, birthday parties, anniversaries, business meetings, etc.), but I have a design in mind that is expected to cost $450,000. I estimate another $700,000 to $800,000 in working capital will be necessary as well, bringing the total investment up to about $2.4 million.

Dan supported Jan's plans:

> The winery is operating at 100 percent capacity, and I still had to ship some grapes over to the custom-crush facility in Mattituck. I'd like to bring all our production back here under our complete control.

The Schoolhouse Lane team was eager to hear Nanette's perspective, as she represented a broader, regional industry viewpoint. Nanette was prepared for their questions, distributing copies of the information on Long Island wineries (see Exhibits 7 and 8) to the rest of the group.

> At the Long Island Wine Council, our prime focus is the local producers and their markets. I can't tell you much about conditions in California, such as how long the "glut" of grapes will last, but we have studied the markets extensively on the East Coast.
>
> On the supply side, acreage and production have grown steadily over the last nine years, through the harvest of 2008. Grape quality has risen consistently, and yields per acre have grown slowly. A number of new owners have come to the area, bringing strong financial support to many vineyards and wineries. On the demand side, a major segment is event-driven—celebrations of either a personal or business nature. For many local wineries, this represents 40 percent or more of their revenues, and any weakness in pricing or volume will be felt quickly on cash inflows.
>
> There has been a weakening in the last four years in business spending for events. While volume has held up reasonably well, the price points have deteriorated—moderately priced premium products ($10 to $15 per bottle) have been substituted for deluxe premium wines ($25 and up per bottle). Corporate and business budgets have been tightened, and it is not likely that this trend will be reversed in the next two years. On a brighter note, on-premises sales have finally begun to rise this spring, as restaurant patrons are spending more on fine wine.
>
> Will the Long Island wine industry be adversely or positively affected by these national trends? Will the regional extent of our markets shelter us from cyclical slowdowns in demand? From conversations with our members, the next few years are still likely to be quite challenging for our industry here on the East End.

From 2004 through 2008 New York City's financial services industry experienced some of the largest declines in employment as well as reductions in salaries and bonuses. Special events sales volumes also slowed due to cost containment at parties and declining expenditures for high-end wines at restaurants. Still, overall volume and revenues were rising due to expansion of the geographic market for Long Island wines on the East Coast and growth westward through New York, Pennsylvania, Maryland, and Virginia. This geographic expansion, it was hoped by many local producers, could help offset the local trend toward lower prices to bolster sagging sales.

In response to Nanette's overview, Jan mentioned that she'd come across a *BusinessWeek* article concerning the consumption profile of wine drinkers in the United States.[12] Forecasted trends for growth in U.S. wine consumption were hardly spectacular.

Exhibit 7 Long Island Wine Industry Statistics (selected years)

Year	Number of Vineyards	Number of Wineries	Planted Acres	Acres Owned	Total Value Per Acre ($)	Wine Production (cases)
2007	60	42	3,300	4,600		570,000
2006	60	41	3,200	4,400	22,000	550,000
2005	60	38				
2004	60	30				500,000
2002	52	29	3,000	4,000		500,000
2000		21	2,200	2,800	20,000	400,000
1999		21	2,100			
1998		21				200,000
1996	40			1,800		
1995		23	1,055		15,000	200,000
1989		14				
1987		12				
1985	16	7	600			
1984	12	4	700			
1975		1				
1973	1		17		4,000	

Source: *The Wine Press, Underground Wine Journal, Wine East, Long Island Business News, Newsday,* and the Long Island Wine Council.

Exhibit 8 Estimated Values of Vineyards and Wineries on Long Island (selected years)

Year	Name	Location	Winery Capacity (cases)	Total Planted Acres	Estimated Value ($)
2001	Raphael	Peconic	10,000	70	6,000,000
2000	Gristina	Cutchogue	10,000	44	5,200,000
	Bedell Cellars	Cutchogue	8,000	50	5,000,000
	Pindar Vineyards	Peconic	80,000	42.5	
	Comtesse Thérèse	Mattituck		40	400,000
1999	Hargrave	Cutchogue	7,000	84	4,000,000
	Laurel Lake Vineyards	Laurel	5,500	23	2,000,000
	Corey Creek	Southold	4,000	30	2,500,000
	Peconic Bay Vineyards	Cutchogue		35	2,200,000
	Bidwell Vineyards	Cutchogue	15,000	34	2,900,000
1997	Laurel Lake Vineyards	Laurel		23	3,000,000
1993	Dzugas-Smith Vineyards	Cutchogue		29	245,000

Source: *The Wine Press, Underground Wine Journal, Wine East, Long Island Business News, Newsday,* and the Long Island Wine Council.

One statistic I picked up was that in many European countries, such as France, Germany, Italy, and Spain, wine is almost a necessity with meals—this is not the case here in the United States. Just over 10 percent of American adults account for 86 percent of wine consumed annually! We have not yet been successful at stimulating wine consumption to broader segments of the population. Until this occurs, perhaps our marketing strategy should be directed toward those consumers who are already drinking wine on a *regular* basis.

Ending the meeting, Jan thanked all present for sharing their ideas and expertise. She knew that she would have to prioritize each projected cost item and defend the expenditures when making a formal proposal for financing. Funding for the proposed expansion, as well as incremental working capital, might have to be sourced by some form of equity, meaning that Jan would no longer own 100 percent of Schoolhouse Lane Estates!

Jan Seeks Help

Jan decided it was time to call her brother Nick. Although he hadn't visited the North Fork in years, he had been to the Hamptons each summer, driving to his family's summer home on the beach. Jan began the call by saying, "Nick, how has your business and career been going this last year? I heard about all the reductions in financial services employment. Have you been affected?"

"My firm has maintained its competitiveness in these uncertain times," Nick assured her. "We are also diversifying our clients' portfolios from real estate and annuities into private and public equity positions. If you know of any interesting investment opportunities, we would be interested in examining the financial data."

Somewhat surprised, Jan responded, "Nick, did you know that at Schoolhouse Lane Estates, we have a financial proposal on the table? We need an equity investment of approximately $2 million. Although the equity in the business is currently low, I will not be willing to give up control."

"Send me your business plan and financial statements," Nick replied, "and I'll contact you in two weeks with a proposal. The amount you are looking for is well within the range of my clients."

"Thanks, Nick," said Jan. "I'll fax you the documents tomorrow."

Two Weeks Later

"Jan, this is your brother. I received your materials and have a proposal for an investment of $2 million. Can we meet for lunch this Wednesday, and I'll present the details? I also would like my wife to be at our meeting. As an equity strategist for a large investment banking house in Manhattan, Monica can provide some insight into the workings of the private equity market. She would also like to visit the winery."

Jan agreed and the three met for a long lunch at the Old Mill House in Peconic. After the salad, Nick presented details of his $2 million proposal to Jan.

"Although investment returns are low these days for fixed-income instruments, venture capital is still expensive. I could offer you a 10-year convertible note with interest at 6 percent," Nick began.

Sipping a glass of locally produced Gallucio Reserve Merlot, Monica added, "The note would provide the investor with potential capital gains up to his or her required return of between 20 and 25 percent per year and then be converted into common stock with a par value of $1 per share. The holder would have the option over the next five years of converting the note into company stock at today's book value. If conversion did not occur, the note would be amortized from year 6 through year 10."

"Thanks," replied Jan, "I will have to speak with my accountant concerning the number of shares that would be granted should the note be converted, so that the required rate of return will be realized by your investor. By the way, who is this investor and when can I meet her or him?"

Nick smiled as Monica said, "Jan, you have known him all your life!"

The Bank Responds

The next day, Jan's accountant Laurel took Jan's projected capital expenditures of $2.4 million for expansion of Schoolhouse Lane Estates' operations, along with the business plan for the next five years, to the North Fork Bank. The projections included two scenarios: a "best case" at a revenue growth rate of 20 percent and a "base case" at a 15 percent growth rate. Both forecasts assumed enhanced operating efficiencies and expanded profit margins with no changes in prices and no introduction of new wine products.

The bank officer was skeptical of the most optimistic case, especially after speaking with a number of other winery operators in the area. North Fork's initial proposal was for a maximum $400,000 term loan with a small increase in the revolving line of credit to $3 million. The banker's implications and position were clear—Schoolhouse Lane needed permanent equity capital to sustain its growth plans. While the longer-term outlook for the industry was quite favorable, the banker was cautious about the trading conditions for wine over the next two years (2009 and 2010).

As she walked through the parking lot at North Fork Bank, Laurel relayed this disappointing news to Jan on her mobile phone. Although Jan understood why permanent capital was needed to support her growth strategy, she was not able to add to her personal investment in the business. Her husband, Tom, a professor of history at Stony Brook University, also believed that too large a percentage of the family's assets were already tied up in the business.

Nick's Position

After receiving Jan's fax, Nick responded by e-mail with some questions concerning the timing of the expenditures outlined in Jan's proposal. He was concerned about the "grape glut" and its impact on product pricing. In addition, the economic outlook in the near term appeared to

Exhibit 9 Report of the Appraisal of Assets of the Schoolhouse Lane Estates

In response to the request of Ms. Janess Thaw, sole owner of the Schoolhouse Lane Estates, we hereby enclose our estimates of current market values for the firm's wine inventory as well as its fixed-asset position. Our personnel have carefully examined your inventories, land, winery building, and equipment and compared these assets with current market values that we have observed over the last six months. We are pleased to report to you that the quality of your inventory is excellent and your assets are in top operating condition.

With your firm's growing emphasis on the production of premium red wines (Meritage, Cabernet Sauvignon, and Merlot), our appraisal estimates that 30 percent of wine in barrels by volume has been stored for more than two years, resulting in a doubling of its book value at the time fermentation was completed in early 2008. Another 40 percent, also red wine and mostly from the 2007 harvest, has been in barrels for 14 months. Remaining wine volumes are a mixture of younger reds and white Chardonnay. We conclude that as of May 2008 the value of inventory, if sold in the local wholesale market, would result in receipts of $5.12 million.

In a separate analysis of property, plant, and equipment, our real estate expert on current market conditions estimates the value of company-owned land at $1,088,000 or $32,000 per acre on the 34 acres under cultivation by Peconic Bay. This is in contrast to $720,000, which is the current book value of this land on a historical cost basis.

The remaining $2,641,600 of depreciated book value of the winery plant and equipment has also increased in value since its original purchase. Its current replacement value is $3.35 million, according to our appraiser.

In summary, upon a sale of these three major asset categories, it is estimated that they would bring to the firm a total of $9,550,233, or $2,909,533 more than their current book value of $6,640,700. This additional value could be added to the firm's equity account of $3,048,100 at year-end 2008, bringing its total up to $5,957,633.

	Summary Data		
Asset	Book Value, Dec. 31, 2008	Adjusted Market Value, Apr. 30, 2009	Appraisal Difference
Land—34 planted acres	$ 720,000	$1,088,000	$ 368,000
Plant and equipment	2,641,600	3,347,233	705,633
Inventory	3,279,100	5,115,000	1,835,900
Total	$6,640,700	$9,550,233	$2,909,533
Less: Liabilities	4,170,100	4,170,100	—
Equity value	$2,470,600	$5,380,133	$2,909,533

It was a pleasure to provide you with the above data. If there is any additional information or clarifications that you may require, do not hesitate to contact us.

Respectfully submitted,

Sharon Brown, President

East End Associates

March 4, 2009

---

be neither clearly defined nor strong. Therefore, could Jan construct forecasts using average annual growth rates in revenues of between 5 and 10 percent (less optimistic than Jan's 15 to 20 percent)? Nick did, however, agree with his sister that enhanced efficiencies could generate faster growth in net income than the growth in revenues.

With respect to Jan's concerns over maintaining ownership control, Nick was nevertheless very understanding.

Monica had gently but firmly reminded him that the "last thing he should ever do was take over the operations of Schoolhouse Lane Estates." He thus approached this deal from a strictly financial point of view. Nick was looking for a viable and profitable investment of $2 million that would fit nicely into his portfolio. A current return of 6 percent, with a total expected annual return of 20 percent over at least a five-year holding period, was quite acceptable to him. While he might have expected a 25 percent total return on an investment with this risk profile some years ago, equity risk premiums had been trending downward in late February 2009, so a 20 percent return would meet or exceed his current portfolio needs.

Nick was aware of the lack of liquidity of an investment in Schoolhouse Lane Estates' operations. This investment would definitely have a "buy-and-hold" profile. Selling a private equity investment was traditionally accomplished through an initial public offering or an acquisition by another wine business, often years after the venture had developed into a viable, competitive, and profitable business. In evaluating his potential position in Schoolhouse Lane Estates, he was not confident that either of these scenarios would occur in the near term. His only hope for monetizing his investment in the next five years would be to sell his shares back to Jan at a reasonable value or try to sell them to another private investor.

One More Meeting

After receiving her brother's proposal, Jan again met with Dan and Laurel. She opened the meeting by saying:

> I can't believe how expensive this funding could be even under the lowest-cost presentation. Even given my most optimistic forecast of earnings growth for Schoolhouse Lane Estates and Nick's "cheapest" financing alternative, I will lose more than one-half ownership in the company. I surely do not want that to happen! Maybe we should defer our expansion plans or explore other options.

Dan countered by reiterating his desire to purchase the vineyard across the road and expand the winery's capacity:

> That property has been owned by the O'Reilly family for 55 years. We may never get an opportunity to purchase it again if it is bought by another winery. We have managed it for the last six years and know the quality of grape production.

Laurel had planned what she would recommend. An integral component of her presentation was a summary of an appraisal report that had been prepared for Schoolhouse Lane Estates by a local firm specializing in wine industry asset valuations on Long Island (Exhibit 9). The appraisal clearly showed that the current value of the firm's two largest asset categories was considerably higher than their book value (approximately $9.5 million versus book value of $6.6 million). Adding the difference of nearly $2.9 million to the firm's equity value would surely enhance Jan's bargaining position in negotiating for new funds, possibly with other investors besides her brother. Laurel then summarized and prioritized the three components of the Schoolhouse Lane Estates' expansion plans:

> I agree with Dan that our highest priority at this time is the land purchase. We can produce larger volumes of

wine, if the market so demands, at the new custom-crush facility. By postponing the other projects, Jan, you would reduce the volume of funds needed from your brother and, consequently, the dilution of your ownership position. If you really want to spend the entire $2.4 million in the next year, remember you can sell the Class B common stock that you already carry on the balance sheet.

After the meeting ended, Jan walked slowly back to her office. Almost there, she abruptly turned around, walked out of the building, and proceeded toward the vineyard. Strolling leisurely past the old oak trees with birds perching in the branches, she then ambled all the way down Schoolhouse Lane to the shore of Peconic Bay. Sitting on a large rock near the shore, she spent the next hour considering her alternatives. Should she continue the current strategy and focus on internal growth, borrow some money from the North Fork Bank, sell equity, and complete the expansion in order to sell the winery later down the road, or maybe sell all of Schoolhouse Lane Estates now? Jan knew that when she returned to the office, Dan and Laurel would be awaiting her decision.

Endnotes

1. *New York Times.* 2000. On the North Fork, dreams of Napa. July 26: F1.
2. To put this information in perspective, the California wine industry has been in business for more than 200 years and currently has 86 AVAs (www.wineinstitute.org).
3. States News Service. 2004. Washington, DC, February 5.
4. On January 29, 2004, U.S. Senators Hilary Rodham Clinton and Charles Schumer, along with U.S. Representatives Louise Slaughter, Tim Bishop, Maurice Hinchey, Sherwood Boehlert, Jack Quinn, and Arno Houghton, signed a letter calling on Governor Pataki and the New York State Legislature to overturn the direct shipping ban.
5. Canavor, N. 2003. Long Island continues to gain notoriety as wine-making region. *Long Island Business News,* April 4.
6. In contrast, nine custom-crush facilities served California's wine industry.
7. Walzer, R. 1999. Hearn pressing for $2M winery. *Long Island Business News,* October 1: 5A.
8. Bureau of Alcohol, Tobacco and Firearms, Regulatory Agency, U.S. Department of the Treasury, Title 27, Part 4, of the Code of Federal Regulations.
9. Aguilar, D. 2003. Working capital analysis for wine industry clients. Working paper, Silicon Valley Bank Wine Group, December 26.
10. The Wine Institute, www.wineinstitute.org.
11. According to Vic Motto of Motto Kryla Fisher, a Napa, California, consultant to the wine industry, there were 10,940 distributors of wine in 1990 and 5,134 in 2000 but only 2 to 3 major distributors per state. The top 10 distributors accounted for 33 percent of wine sales in 1993 and 60 percent in 2003.
12. Himelstein, L. 2002. This Merlot's for you. *BusinessWeek,* September 30: 65–68.

Case 13 QVC*

Fashion designer Chloe Dao talks casually with host Jacque Gonzales while selling her creations on a QVC show in January 2009. Models in an off-set changing room hastily switch in and out of Dao's clothing. One level above the stage, a line producer directs camera angles for product-enhancing shots, while feeding lines to Dao and Gonzales. All the time, screens are keeping a tally of the orders that are coming in against the stock that is available. Less than one minute after a mention of Dao's yellow shirt, it sells out. A blue version of the same top sells out a few minutes later. By the end of the segment, thousands of items ranging in price from $39.50 to $59.00 have been sold.

Since it was launched in 1986, QVC has rapidly grown to become the largest television shopping network. Although it entered the market a couple of years after rival Home Shopping Network, the channel managed to build a leading position. By 2008, its reach extended to over 95 million households. It shipped over 166 million packages during 2008 to customers around the world, resulting in almost $7.3 billion in sales (see Exhibits 1 and 2). It sold to customers who watched its shows across the United States, the United Kingdom, Germany, and Japan (see Exhibit 3).

The success of QVC has been largely driven by its popular television home shopping shows that feature a wide variety of eye-catching products, many of which are unique to the channel. It organizes product searches in cities all over the United States in order to continuously find new offerings that can be pitched at customers. During these events, the firm has to screen hundreds of products in order to select those that it will offer. In one of its recent searches, QVC had to evaluate the appeal of products such as nail clippers that catch clippings, bicycle seats built for bigger bottoms, and novelty items shaped like coffins.

Thousands of entrepreneurs have used QVC's product searches over the years to try to sell their products on the popular home shopping channel. A chance to display their offerings to QVC's national TV audience can transform a one-person operation into a multibillion-dollar business. "The vendors who are our success stories for this past decade have done over $1 billion in sales on QVC over the past ten years," said Marilyn Montross, the channel's director of vendor relations.[1]

But QVC is concerned about maintaining sales in an environment where consumers are spending less on the types of products that it sells. It is also trying to entice new customers by battling a perception that direct-response TV retailers sell just hokey, flimsy, or kitschy goods. Its jewelry selection features prestigious brands such as Tacori, which is worn by TV stars. It offers clothing from couture designers such as Marc Bouwer, who has made clothing for Angelina Jolie and Halle Berry. And it has provided live performances by stars such as *American Idol* alumnus Clay Aiken, whose new album it was selling. QVC's CEO Michael George claimed that his firm is trying harder to generate sales: "Consumers are being cautious with their dollar. We are by no means immune."[2]

Pursuing a Leading Position

QVC was founded by Joseph Segel in June 1986 and began broadcasting by November of the same year. In early 1986, Segel had tuned in to the Home Shopping Network, which had been launched just two years earlier. He was not particularly impressed with the crude programming and the down-market products of the firm. But Segel was convinced that another televised shopping network would have the potential to attract a large-enough client base. He also felt that such an enterprise should be able to produce significant profits because the operating expenses for a shopping network could be kept relatively low.

Over the next few months, Segel raised $30 million in start-up capital, hired several seasoned television executives, and launched his own shopping network. Operating out of headquarters that were located in West Chester, Pennsylvania, QVC offered 24-hour a day, seven-day-a-week television shopping to consumers at home. By the end of its first year of operation, QVC had managed to extend its reach to 13 million homes by satellite and cable systems; 700,000 viewers had already become customers, resulting in the shipping of 3 million orders. Its sales had already topped $100 million, and the firm was actually able to show a small profit.

Segel attributed the instant success of his company to the potential offered by television shopping. "Television's combination of sight, sound and motion is the best way to

Exhibit 1 Sales Growth

2008	$7.3 billion
2007	7.4 billion
2006	7.1 billion
2004	5.7 billion
2001	3.8 billion
1998	2.4 billion
1995	1.6 billion
1992	0.9 billion
1989	0.2 billion

Source: QVC, Liberty Media.

*This case was developed by Professor Jamal Shamsie, Michigan State University, with the assistance of Professor Alan B. Eisner, Pace University. Material has been drawn from published sources to be used for class discussion. Copyright © 2009 Jamal Shamsie and Alan B. Eisner.

Exhibit 2   Income Statement (in millions, year-end December 31)

	2008	2007	2006	2005
Net revenue	$7,303	$7,397	$7,074	$6,501
Cost of sales	(4,719)	(4,682)	(4,426)	(4,112)
Gross profit	2,584	2,715	2,648	2,389
Operating expenses*	(703)	(616)	(579)	(570)
Selling, General, and Administrative expenses	(379)	(447)	(413)	(397)
Operating cash flow	1,502	1,652	1,656	1,422
Stock compensation	(15)	(22)	(50)	(52)
Depreciation and amortization[†]	(531)	(516)	(476)	(449)
Operating income	$ 956	$1,114	$1,130	$ 921

*Operating expenses consist of commissions and license fees, order processing and customer service, credit card processing fees, and provision for doubtful accounts.

[†]Depreciation and amortization includes amortization of intangible assets recorded in connection with the purchase of QVC by Liberty Media.

Source: Liberty Media, QVC.

sell a product. It is more effective than presenting a product in print or just putting the product on a store shelf," he stated. "The cost-efficiency comes from the cable distribution system. It is far more economical than direct mail, print advertising, or traditional retail store distribution."[3]

In fall 1988, Segel acquired the manufacturing facilities, proprietary technology, and trademark rights of the Diamonique Corporation, which produced a wide range

Exhibit 3   Geographic Breakdown

	2008	2007	2006	2005
Revenue (in millions, year-end December 31)				
United States	$4,911	$5,208	4,983	4,640
United Kingdom	660	707	612	554
Germany	954	870	848	781
Japan	778	612	631	526
Homes (in millions, year-end December 31)				
United States	95	93.4	90.7	90.0
United Kingdom	23	21.8	19.4	17.8
Germany	38	37.6	37.5	37.4
Japan	22	21.1	18.7	16.7

Source: Liberty Media, QVC.

of simulated gemstones and jewelry that could be sold on QVC's shows. Over the next couple of years, Segel expanded QVC by acquiring its competitors such as the Cable Value Network Shopping channel.

By 1993, QVC had overtaken Home Shopping Network to become the leading televised shopping channel in terms of sales and profits. Its reach extended to over 80 percent of all cable homes and to 3 million satellite dishes. Segel retired during the same year, passing control of the company to Barry Diller. Since then, QVC's sales have continued to grow at a substantial rate. As a result, it has consistently widened the gap between its sales and those of Home Shopping Network, which has remained its closest competitor.

Striving for Retailing Excellence

Over the years, QVC managed to establish itself as the world's preeminent virtual shopping mall that never closes. Its televised shopping channel has become a place where customers around the world can, and do, shop at any hour at the rate of more than five customers per second. It sells a wide variety of products, using a combination of description and demonstration by live program hosts. QVC is extremely selective in choosing its hosts, screening as many as 3,000 applicants annually in order to pick three. New hosts are trained for at least six months before they are allowed to get on a show. In addition, most of the products are offered on regularly scheduled shows, each of which is focused on a particular type of product and a well-defined market. Each of these shows typically lasts for one hour and is based on a theme such as *Now You're Cooking* or *Cleaning Solutions* (see Exhibit 4).

Exhibit 4 QVC Programming Typical Weekly Schedule

Eastern Standard Time	Monday	Tuesday	Wednesday	Thursday	Friday	Saturday	Sunday
7–8 AM	The QVC MORNING SHOW	THE QVC MORNING SHOW	THE QVC MORNING SHOW	THE QVC MORNING SHOW	THE QVC MORNING SHOW FASHION FRIDAY	Select Comfort Sleep Number	AM STYLE
8–9 AM						AM STYLE	
9–10 AM	PATRICIA WEXLER, MD DERMATOLOGY	SPRING SPOTLIGHT	NutriSystem Nourish Weight-Loss Program	SUSAN GRAVER STYLE	SLEEP SOLUTIONS		
10–11 AM	CITIKNITS	BATH SHOP	FINE JEWELRY COLLECTION	ORGANIZE IT ALL	TRAVELING WITH KIDS	CREATING KEEPSAKES MAGAZINE PAPER CRAFTING	
11 AM–12 PM	HOME STYLE	DENIM & CO	ELLIOTT LUCCA HANDBAGS	WHITE MOUNTAIN FOOTWEAR	IMPERIAL GOLD		MODERN SOUL KNITWEAR
12–1 PM	BEAUTY BEAT	NOW YOU'RE COOKING	14K GOLD JEWELRY	EATING SMART		BY POPULAR DEMAND	DIALOGUES THE NEW LANGUAGE OF STYLE
1–2 PM	LINEN CLOSET	LINEA BY LOUIS DELL'OLIO	B.O.C. FOOTWEAR	BY POPULAR DEMAND	THE FAMILY ROOM	PATIO & GARDEN	LINEA BY LOUIS DELL'OLIO
2–3 PM	OUTDOOR ENTERTAINING		QON ASLETT'S CLEANING SECRETS	NINA LEONARD COLLECTION FASHION	BIRKENSTOCK COLLECTIONS	SMASHBOX COSMETICS	SUMMER FUN FASHION
3–4 PM	DENIM & CO	EPIPHANY PLATINUM CLAD SILVER & DIAMONIQUE JEWELRY	PROACTIV SOLUTION SKIN CARE		INSTANT FLOWER GARDEN	ANNA GRIFFIN ELEGANT CRAFTING	CITIKNITS
4–5 PM	QVC SAMPLER		In-Home Care	AUTO SHOP	AROUND THE HOUSE	CREATING KEEPSAKES MAGAZINE–PAPER CRAFTING	STATEMENTS ON STYLE
5–6 PM	ETIENNE AIGNER	FOCUS ON FASHION	JEWELRY SHOWCASE	PATRICIA WANG JADE STUDIO		SCRAPBOOKING DAY CELEBRATION	DENIM & CO
6–7 PM	HOME STYLE	KITCHEN IDEAS	NutriSystem Nourish Weight-Loss Program	QVC SAMPLER	KITCHEN IDEAS	Select Comfort Sleep Number	
7–8 PM	PATRICIA WEXLER, MD DERMATOLOGY	LINEA BY LOUIS DELL'OLIO	KEEP IT CLEAN	MADE FOR iPOD	ELECTRONICS TODAY	SATURDAY NIGHT BEAUTY	SUSAN GRAVER STYLE

Source: QVC.

QVC frequently entices celebrities, such as clothing designers or book authors, to appear live on special program segments in order to sell their own products. To prepare them to succeed, QVC gives celebrities training on how to best pitch their offerings. On some occasions, customers are able to call in and have on-air conversations with program hosts and visiting celebrities. Celebrities are therefore often schooled in QVC's "backyard-fence" style, which means conversing with viewers the way they would chat with a friendly neighbor.

Over the past year, QVC has been trying to capitalize on the growing success of reality-based television shows. It has begun to incorporate some of the concepts from these popular shows into its shopping programs. In one of its recently introduced shows, *Room for Improvement,* the shopping channel carried out an extensive renovation of a bedroom and a kitchen for a family. Products that were featured on the show sold well.

QVC's themed programs are telecast live 24 hours a day, seven days a week, to millions of households worldwide. The shopping channel transmits its programming live from its central production facilities in Pennsylvania through uplinks to a satellite. The representatives who staff QVC's four call centers, which handled more than 180 million calls last year, are well trained to take orders.

Of all the orders placed with QVC, more than 90 percent are shipped within 48 hours from one of the firm's distribution centers. The distribution centers have a combined floor space of 4.6 million square feet, which is equivalent to the size of 103 football fields. Finally, everyone at QVC works hard to make sure that every item works as it should before it is shipped and that its packaging will protect it during the shipping process. "Nothing ships unless it is quality-inspected first," said Paul Day, the logistics manager for QVC. "Since our product is going business-to-consumer, there's no way to fix or change a product-related problem."[4]

Searching for Profitable Products

More than 100 experienced, informed buyers comb the world on a regular basis to search for new products to launch on QVC. The shopping channel concentrates on unique products that can be demonstrated on live television. Furthermore, the price of these products must be high enough for viewers to justify the additional shipping and handling charge. Over the course of a typical year, QVC carries more than 60,000 products. As many as 2,000 items are typically offered in any given week, of which about 15 percent are new products for the network. QVC's suppliers range from some of the world's biggest companies to small entrepreneurial enterprises.

All new products must, however, pass through stringent tests that are carried out by QVC's in-house Quality Assurance Lab. In many cases, this inspection process is carried out manually by the firm's employees. Only 15 percent of the products pass the firm's rigorous quality inspection on first try, and as many as one-third are never offered to the public because they fail altogether. In addition, Jeffrey Rayport, author of a book on customer service, states that "QVC staff look for a product that is complex enough—or interesting enough—that the host can talk about it on air."[5]

About one-third of QVC's sales come from broadly available national brands. The firm has been able to build trust among its customers in large part through the offering of these well-known brands. QVC also relies on promotional campaigns with a variety of existing firms for another one-third of its sales. It has made deals with firms such as Dell, Target, and Bath & Body Works for special limited-time promotional offerings.

QVC has been most successful with products that are exclusively sold on QVC or not readily available through other distribution channels. Although such products account for another one-third of its sales, the firm has been able to earn higher margins with these proprietary products, many of which come from firms that are either start-ups or new entrants into the U.S. market.

Apart from searching for exclusive products, QVC has also been trying to move away from some product categories, such as home appliances and electronic gadgets, which offer lower margins. It has been gradually expanding into many new product categories that have higher margins, such as cosmetics, apparel, food, and toys. Several of these new categories have also displayed the strongest rates of growth in sales for the shopping channel over the past couple of years.

Expanding on the Customer Base

Since its start-up, QVC's shopping channel has managed to gradually penetrate almost all the cable television and broadcast satellite homes in the United States. But only about 10 percent of the households that it reaches have actually bought anything from the network. However, QVC has developed a large base of customers, many of whom make as many as 10 purchases in a year. QVC devotees readily call in to the live segments to offer product testimonials, are up on the personal lives of their favorite program hosts, and generally view the channel as entertaining. "As weird as it may sound, for people who love the network, it's good company," said Rayport.[6]

QVC is also hoping to attract new customers on the basis of the reasonably strong reputation that surveys indicate it has established among a large majority of its current buyers. By its initials alone, QVC promises that it will deliver *quality, value,* and *convenience* to its viewers. More than three-quarters of the shopping channel's customers have given it a score of 7 out of 7 for trustworthiness. This has led most of its customers to recommend it to their friends.

QVC has also benefited from the growing percentage of women entering the workforce, as this has resulted in a significant increase in dual-income families. Although the firm's current customer base does span several socioeconomic groups, it is led by young professional families who have above-average disposable income. They also enjoy various forms of "thrill-seeking" activities and rank shopping relatively higher as a leisure activity than does the typical consumer.

The firm is also trying to increase sales by making it easier for customers to buy its products. It is adding features such as an interactive service that enables customers to purchase any QVC product with the single click of a remote. QVC also provides a credit program to allow customers to pay for goods over a period of several months. Everything it sells is backed by a 30-day unconditional money-back guarantee. Furthermore, QVC does not impose any hidden charges, such as a restocking fee, for any returned merchandise. These policies help the home shopping channel to attract customers for products that can be viewed but cannot be touched or felt.

In 1995, QVC launched its own retail Web site to complement its television home shopping channel. The Web site has provided the firm access to more than 100 million households in the United States that have Internet connections. Initially, the site offered more detailed information about QVC offerings. Today, it hosts blogs, customer product reviews, and streaming video that shows the item currently on air. During 2007, QVC was able to generate almost $1.5 billion of sales through its Internet operations.

Positioning for Future Growth

To attract new customers, QVC has launched its first national TV, print, and outdoor ad campaign, with the theme "iQdoU?" The firm says the theme is insider lingo for "I shop QVC, do you?" Ads show a variety of products such as computers, cosmetics, and apparel. They feature celebrity vendors such as Whoopi Goldberg, who has a bedding line, and Heidi Klum, who has a jewelry line. The goal is to make QVC and QVC.com destinations for shoppers, said Doug Rose, vice president for merchandising brand development.

In 2003, John Malone purchased QVC for $14.1 billion, and from his ongoing commitment to the firm it is clear that Malone believes that the home shopping network will continue to grow in spite of the development of competing forms of home shopping. Over the years, QVC's sales have actually grown to match those of Internet giant Amazon.com. But while the Internet firm has often struggled to show strong profits, QVC has been generating tons of cash. Furthermore, QVC certainly looks like it is well positioned with its shopping channel, Web site, and streaming videos for continued growth in sales from a vast assortment of merchandise.

In fact, since the launching of its Web site, QVC has taken steps to become an innovative practitioner of electronic retailing. The Web site has moved well beyond its initial capabilities, when it simply offered supplementary information on the products that were featured on the television shopping channel. The recent introduction of the interactive service for the shopping channel represents one of the first launches of on-screen interactivity, the kind in which viewers can interact with television content simply through the remote control. Looking toward the future, QVC is already focusing on new avenues for growth, such as those that might be offered through retailing on mobile telephones.

Regular technological developments may, in fact, allow QVC to continue to offer much higher margin products to both existing and new markets. Rose claims that interactivity in all aspects of the firm's business, including its television shopping channel, will only become more pronounced in the future, making it easier for customers to act on what they see. QVC believes that it still has a lot of room to grow, since almost 90 percent of its audience has not purchased anything from the network.

In particular, Rose believes that the growing satisfaction of the shopping channel's existing customers is likely to draw in new ones. Kathy Sklar did not think much about ordering from QVC until a friend got her interested. She has since made several purchases. She now watches the channel on a regular basis to see if something catches her eye. "I've come to believe in QVC," she said. "I'll say 'What the heck, I'll try it.' "[7]

Endnotes

1. Mary Jo Feldstein. Investors, Entrepreneurs Vie for QVC Appearance. *Knight Ridder Tribune Business News,* February 11, 2005, p.1.
2. Laura Petrecca. QVC Shops for Ideas for Future Sales. *USA Today,* May 5, 2008, p. 2B.
3. QVC Annual Report, 1987–1988.
4. Eugene Gilligan. The Show Must Go On. *Journal of Commerce,* April 12, 2004, p. 1.
5. *USA Today,* May 5, 2008, p. 2B.
6. Ibid.
7. Ibid.

Case 14   McDonald's*

Even in the midst of a global economic slowdown, McDonald's reported strong results for the fourth quarter of 2008 and announced plans to add 650 more outlets by the end of 2009 (see Exhibits 1 and 2). The fast-food chain's performance was particularly impressive as rivals such as KFC and Wendy's had not managed to cope as well with the spending downturn. Same-store sales, a key indicator of the firm's health, actually rose by 7.2 percent during the last quarter from the figures reported a year earlier. Responding to McDonald's performance, CEO Jim Skinner remarked: "We continue to be recession-resistant."[1]

Analysts attribute the continued success of McDonald's to its "Plan to Win" strategy, which was first outlined by James R. Cantalupo over six years ago after overexpansion caused the chain to lose focus. The core of the plan was to increase sales at existing locations by improving the menu, refurbishing the outlets, and extending hours. The firm also added snacks and drinks, two of the few areas where restaurant sales are still growing. "We do so well because our strategies have been so well planned out," said Skinner in a recent interview.[2]

At the same time, Skinner has been monitoring pricing in order to make sure the menu stays affordable without hurting the firm's profit margins. Even as it continues to wrestle with cost increases, McDonald's has maintained the pricing on its Dollar Menu, which generates almost 15 percent of total sales. In December 2008, McDonald's did decide to replace its $1 double cheeseburger with the McDouble, a similar burger that is less expensive to make because it has less cheese. Steven Kron, an analyst with Goldman Sachs, emphasized the attractiveness of the

Exhibit 1   Income Statement (in thousands of dollars)

	2008	2007	2006
Total revenue	23,522,400	22,786,600	21,586,400
Cost of revenue	14,883,200	9,819,000	14,602,100
Gross profit	8,639,200	12,967,600	6,984,300
Operating expenses:			
Selling, general, and administrative	2,355,500	7,429,400	2,405,000
Nonrecurring	(48,500)	1,774,800	134,200
Operating income or loss	6,332,200	3,763,400	4,445,100
Income from continuing operations:			
Total other income/expenses net	237,700	103,200	123,300
Earnings before interest and taxes	6,680,600	3,982,200	4,568,400
Interest expense	522,600	410,100	402,000
Income before tax	6,158,000	3,572,100	4,166,400
Income tax expense	1,844,800	1,237,100	1,293,400
Net income from continuing ops	4,313,200	2,335,000	2,873,000
Nonrecurring events:			
Discontinued operations	—	60,100	671,200
Net income	4,313,200	2,395,100	3,544,200

Source: McDonald's.

*This case was developed by Professor Jamal Shamsie, Michigan State University, with the assistance of Professor Alan B. Eisner, Pace University. Material has been drawn from published sources to be used for class discussion. Copyright © 2009 Jamal Shamsie and Alan B. Eisner.

Exhibit 2 Balance Sheet (in thousands of dollars)

	2008	2007	2006
Assets			
Current assets:			
Cash and cash equivalents	2,063,400	1,981,300	2,136,400
Net receivables	931,200	1,053,800	904,200
Inventory	111,500	125,300	149,000
Other current assets	411,500	421,500	435,700
Total current assets	3,517,600	3,581,900	3,625,300
Long-term investments	1,222,300	1,156,400	1,036,200
Property, plant, and equipment	20,254,500	20,984,700	20,845,700
Goodwill	2,237,400	2,301,300	2,209,200
Other assets	1,229,700	1,367,400	1,307,400
Total assets	28,461,500	29,391,700	29,023,800
Liabilities and Equity			
Current liabilities:			
Accounts payable	2,506,100	3,634,000	2,739,000
Short/current long-term debt	31,800	864,500	17,700
Other current liabilities	—	—	251,400
Total current liabilities	2,537,900	4,498,500	3,008,100
Long-term debt	10,186,000	7,310,000	8,416,500
Other liabilities	1,410,100	1,342,500	1,074,900
Deferred long-term liability charges	944,900	960,900	1,066,000
Total liabilities	15,078,900	14,111,900	13,565,500
Stockholders' equity:			
Common stock	16,600	16,600	16,600
Retained earnings	28,953,900	26,461,500	25,845,600
Treasury stock	(20,289,400)	(16,762,400)	(13,552,200)
Capital surplus	4,600,200	4,226,700	3,445,000
Other stockholders' equity	101,300	1,337,400	(296,700)
Total stockholders' equity	13,382,600	15,279,800	15,458,300
Net tangible assets	$11,145,200	$12,978,500	$13,249,100

Source: McDonald's.

firm's affordable Dollar Menu: "When people are seeking value, these guys have a very powerful component."[3]

Nevertheless, there are strong concerns that McDonald's will continue to be squeezed by long-term trends that are threatening to leave it marginalized. The chain is facing a rapidly fragmenting market, where changes in the tastes of consumers have made once-exotic foods like sushi and burritos everyday options. Many of its fast-food customers continue to switch to food that is much healthier and better tasting. Furthermore, competition has been coming from quick meals of all sorts that can be found in supermarkets, convenience stores, and even vending machines.

Many analysts believe that McDonald's must continue to work on its turnaround strategy in order to meet these challenges. But they acknowledge that the firm has pushed hard to transform itself, and they are encouraged by the results that it has achieved over the last six years. Even during the past year, the chain registered growth in the number of customers served, from 56 million to 58 million a day. "They have experienced a comeback the likes of which have been pretty unprecedented," said Bob Golden, executive vice president of Technomic, a food service consultancy. "When restaurants start to slide, it really takes a lot to turn them around."[4]

Experiencing a Downward Spiral

Since it was founded, more than 50 years ago, McDonald's has been defining the fast-food business. It provided millions of Americans their first jobs even as it changed their eating habits. It rose from a single outlet in a nondescript Chicago suburb to one of the largest chain of outlets spread around the globe. But it was stumbling during the past decade (see Exhibit 3).

The decline in McDonald's once-vaunted service and quality can be traced to its expansion in the 1990s, when headquarters stopped grading franchises for cleanliness, speed, and service. By the end of the decade, the chain ran into more problems because of the tighter labor market. McDonald's began to cut back on training as it struggled hard to find new recruits, a policy that led to a dramatic falloff in the skills of its employees. According to a 2002 survey by market researcher Global Growth Group, McDonald's came in third in average service time behind Wendy's and sandwich shop Chick-fil-A Inc.

McDonald's also began to fail consistently with its new product introductions, such as the low-fat McLean Deluxe and Arch Deluxe burgers, both of which were meant to appeal to adults. It did no better with its attempts to diversify beyond burgers, often because of problems with the product development process. Consultant Michael Seid, who manages a franchise consulting firm in West Hartford, pointed out that McDonald's offered a pizza that didn't fit through the drive-through window and salad shakers that were packed so tightly that dressing couldn't flow through them.

In 1998, after McDonald's posted its first-ever decline in annual earnings, CEO Michael R. Quinlan was forced out and replaced by Jack M. Greenberg, a 16-year veteran of the firm. Greenberg did try to cut back on McDonald's expansion as he tried to deal with some of the growing problems. But his efforts to deal with the decline of McDonald's were slowed down by his acquisition of other fast-food chains such as Chipotle Mexican Grill and Boston Market.

On December 5, 2002, after watching McDonald's stock slide 60 percent in three years, the board ousted Greenberg. He had lasted little more than two years. His short tenure had been marked by the introduction of 40 new menu items, none of which caught on big, and the purchase of a handful of nonburger chains, none of which

helped the firm to sell more burgers. Indeed, his critics say that by trying so many different things and executing them poorly, Greenberg allowed the burger business to continue declining. According to Los Angeles franchisee Reggie Webb: "We would have been better off trying fewer things and making them work."[5]

Pinning Hopes on a New Leader

By the beginning of 2003, consumer surveys were indicating that McDonald's was headed for serious trouble. Measures of the service and quality of the chain were continuing to fall, dropping far behind those of its rivals. To deal with its deteriorating performance, the firm decided to bring back retired vice chairman James R. Cantalupo, 59, who had overseen McDonald's successful international expansion in the 1980s and 1990s. Cantalupo, who had retired only a year earlier, was perceived to be the only candidate with the necessary qualifications, despite shareholder sentiment for an outsider. The board felt that it needed someone who knew the company well and could move quickly to turn things around.

Cantalupo realized that McDonald's often tended to miss the mark on delivering the critical aspects of consistent, fast, friendly service and an all-around enjoyable experience for the whole family. He understood that its franchisees and employees alike needed to be inspired as well as retrained in their role of putting the smile back into the McDonald's experience. When Cantalupo and his team laid out their turnaround plan in 2003, they stressed getting the basics of service and quality right, in part by reinstituting a tough "up or out" grading system that would kick out underperforming franchisees. "We have to rebuild the foundation. It's fruitless to add growth if the foundation is weak," said Cantalupo.[6]

To begin with, Cantalupo cut back on the opening of new outlets, focusing instead on generating more sales from the chain's existing outlets. In fact, he shifted his emphasis to obtaining most of the growth in future revenues from an increase in sales in the over 30,000 outlets that were already operating around the world (see Exhibits 4 through 6). In part, McDonalds tried to draw more customers through the introduction of new products. The chain has had a positive response to its increased emphasis on healthier foods, led by a revamped line of fancier salads. The revamped menu was promoted through a new worldwide ad slogan, "I'm loving it," which was delivered by pop idol Justin Timberlake through a set of MTV-style commercials.

But the biggest success for the firm came in the form of the McGriddles breakfast sandwich, which was launched nationwide in June 2003. The popular new offering consisted of a couple of syrup-drenched pancakes, stamped with the Golden Arches, which acted as the top and bottom of a sandwich filled with eggs, cheese, sausage, and bacon in three different combinations. McDonald's estimated that the new breakfast addition has been bringing in about 1 million new customers every day.

Exhibit 3   McDonald's Milestones

1948	Brothers Richard and Maurice McDonald open the first restaurant in San Bernadino, California, that sells hamburgers, fries, and milk shakes.
1955	Ray A. Kroc, 52, opens his first McDonald's in Des Plaines, Illinois. Kroc, a distributor of milk-shake mixers, figures he can sell a bundle of them if he franchises the McDonalds' business and installs his mixers in the new stores.
1961	Six years later, Kroc buys out the McDonald brothers for $2.7 million.
1963	Ronald McDonald makes his debut as corporate spokesclown using future NBC-TV weatherman Willard Scott. During the year, the company also sells its 1 billionth burger.
1965	McDonald's stock goes public at $22.50 a share. It will split 12 times in the next 35 years.
1967	The first McDonald's restaurant outside the United States opens in Richmond, British Columbia. Today there are 31,108 McDonald's in 118 countries.
1968	The Big Mac, the first extension of McDonald's basic burger, makes its debut and is an immediate hit.
1972	McDonald's switches to the frozen variety for its successful french fries.
1974	Fred L. Turner succeeds Kroc as CEO. In the midst of a recession, the minimum wage rises to $2 per hour, a big cost increase for McDonald's, which is built around a model of young, low-wage workers.
1975	The first drive-through window is opened in Sierra Vista, Arizona.
1979	McDonald's responds to the needs of working women by introducing Happy Meals. A burger, some fries, a soda, and a toy give working moms a break.
1987	Michael R. Quinlan becomes chief executive.
1991	Responding to the public's desire for healthier foods, McDonald's introduces the low-fat McLean Deluxe burger. It flops and is withdrawn from the market. Over the next few years, the chain will stumble several times trying to spruce up its menu.
1992	The company sells its 90 billionth burger, and stops counting.
1996	In order to attract more adult customers, the company launches its Arch Deluxe, a "grown-up" burger with an idiosyncratic taste. Like the low-fat burger, it also falls flat.
1997	McDonald's launches Campaign 55, which cuts the cost of a Big Mac to $0.55. It is a response to discounting by Burger King and Taco Bell. The move, which prefigures similar price wars in 2002, is widely considered a failure.
1998	Jack M. Greenberg becomes McDonald's fourth chief executive. A 16-year company veteran, he vows to spruce up the restaurants and their menu.
1999	For the first time, sales from international operations outstrip domestic revenues. In search of other concepts, the company acquires Aroma Cafe, Chipotle, Donatos, and, later, Boston Market.
2000	McDonald's sales in the United States peak at an average of $1.6 million annually per restaurant, a figure that has not changed since. It is, however, still more than sales at any other fast-food chain.
2001	Subway surpasses McDonald's as the fast-food chain with the most U.S. outlets. At the end of the year it had 13,247 stores, 148 more than McDonald's.
2002	McDonald's posts its first-ever quarterly loss, of $343.8 million. The stock drops to around $13.50, down 40% from five years ago.
2003	James R. Cantalupo returns to McDonald's in January as CEO. He immediately pulls back from the company's 10% to 15% forecast for per-share earnings growth.
2004	Charles H. Bell takes over the firm after the sudden death of Cantalupo. He states he will continue with the strategies that have been developed by his predecessor.
2005	Jim Skinner takes over as CEO after Bell announces retirement for health reasons.
2006	McDonald's launches specialty beverages, including coffee-based drinks.

Source: McDonald's.

With his efforts largely directed at a turnaround strategy for McDonald's, Cantalupo decided to divest the nonburger chains that his predecessor had acquired. Collectively lumped under the Partner Brands, these chains were Chipotle Mexican Grill and Boston Market. The purpose of these acquisitions had been to find new growth and to offer the best franchises new expansion opportunities. But the acquired businesses had not fueled much growth and had actually posted considerable losses in recent years.

Striving for Healthier Offerings

As Skinner took over the reins of McDonald's in late 2004, he expressed his commitment to Cantalupo's plans to pursue various avenues for growth. But Skinner felt that one of his top priorities was to deal with growing concerns about the unhealthy image of McDonald's, given the rise of obesity in the United States. These concerns had recently been highlighted by the release of a popular documentary, *Super Size Me*, made by Morgan Spurlock. Spurlock vividly displayed the health risks that were posed by a steady diet of food from the fast-food chain. With a rise in awareness of the high fat content of most of the products offered by McDonald's, the firm was also beginning to face lawsuits from some of its loyal customers.

In response to the growing health concerns, one of the first steps taken by McDonald's was to phase out supersizing by the end of 2004. The supersizing option allowed customers to get a larger order of french fries and a bigger soft drink by paying a little extra. McDonald's also announced that it intends to start providing nutrition information on the packaging of its products. The information will be easy to read and will tell customers about the calories, fat, protein, carbohydrates, and sodium that are in each product. Finally, McDonald's pledged to gradually remove the artery-clogging trans-fatty acids from the oil that it uses to make its french fries.

Skinner was also trying to provide more offerings that were likely to be perceived by customers as being healthier. McDonald's continued to build on its chicken offerings, using white meat with products such as Chicken Selects. It also placed a great deal of emphasis on its new salad offerings. Although the firm had failed to attract many customers in the past with its salads, McDonald's carried

Exhibit 4 Number of Outlets

	Total	Company Owned	Franchised
2008	31,967	6,502	25,465
2007	31,377	6,906	24,471
2006	31,046	8,166	22,880
2005	30,766	8,173	22,593
2004	30,496	8,179	22,317

Source: McDonald's.

Exhibit 5 Distribution of Outlets

	2008	2007	2006	2005	2004
United States	13,918	13,862	13,774	13,727	13,673
Europe	6,628	6,480	6,403	6,352	6,287
Asia Pacific	8,255	7,938	7,822	7,692	7,567
Americas*	3,166	3,097	3,047	2,995	2,969

*Canada and Latin America.
Source: McDonald's.

Exhibit 6 Breakdown of Revenues (in millions of dollars)

	2008	2007	2006	2005	2004
United States	8,078	7,906	7,464	6,955	6,525
Europe	9,923	8,926	7,638	7,072	6,737
Asia Pacific	4,231	3,599	3,053	2,815	2,721
Americas*	1,290	2,356	2,740	2,275	1,906

*Canada and Latin America.
Source: McDonald's.

out extensive experiments and tests with its new, premium versions. It chose higher-quality ingredients, from a variety of lettuces and tasty cherry tomatoes to sharper cheeses and better cuts of meat. It offered a choice of Newman's Own dressings, a well-known higher-end brand.

McDonald's has also been trying to include more fruits and vegetables in its well-known and popular Happy Meals. In many locations, the firm is offering apple slices called Apple Dippers in place of french fries in the children's Happy Meal. The addition of fruits and vegetables has raised the firm's operating costs because the perishable nature of produce makes it more expensive to ship and store. But Skinner believes that the firm had to push more heavily on fruits and salads. "Salads have changed the way people think of our brand," said Wade Thoma, vice president for menu development in the United States. "It tells people that we are very serious about offering things people feel comfortable eating."[7]

The current rollout of new beverages, highlighted by new coffee-based drinks, represents the chain's biggest menu expansion in almost three decades. Under a plan to add a McCafe section to all of its nearly 14,000 United States outlets, McDonald's has been offering lattes, cappuccinos, ice-blended frappes, and fruit-based smoothies to its customers. "In many cases, they're now coming for the beverage, whereas before they were coming for the meal," said Lee Renz, the firm's vice president, who is responsible for the rollout.[8]

Revamping the Outlets

As part of its turnaround strategy, McDonald's has been selling off the outlets that it owned. More than 75 percent of its outlets are now in the hands of franchisees and other affiliates. Skinner is working with the franchisees to address the look and feel of many of the chain's aging stores. Without any changes to their décor, the firm is likely to be left behind by other, more savvy fast-food and drink retailers. The firm is in the midst of pushing harder to refurbish—or reimage—all of its outlets around the world. "This is all part of becoming more relevant to our consumers," said company spokesman Walt Riker. "When a customer enters our restaurant, they enter our brand."[9]

The reimaging concept was first tried in France in 1996 by Dennis Hennequin, now president of McDonald's Europe, who felt that the effort was essential to revive the firm's sagging sales. "We were hip 15 years ago, but I think we lost that," he said.[10] McDonald's is now applying the reimaging concept to its outlets around the world, with a budget of more than half of its total annual capital expenditures. In the United States, the changes cost an average of $150,000 per restaurant, a cost that is shared with the franchisees when the outlet is not company-owned.

One of the prototype interiors being tested out by McDonald's has curved counters with surfaces painted in bright colors. In one corner, a touch-activated screen allows customers to punch in orders without queuing.

The interiors can feature armchairs and sofas, modern lighting, large television screens, and even wireless Internet access. The firm is also trying to develop new features for its drive-through customers, who account for 65 percent of all transactions in the United States. The features include music aimed at queuing vehicles and a wall of windows on the drive-through side of the restaurant, allowing customers to see meals being prepared from their cars.

The chain has even been developing McCafes inside its outlets next to the usual fast-food counter. The McCafe concept originated in Australia in 1993 and has been rolled out in many restaurants around the world. McDonald's has just begun to introduce the concept in the United States as it refurbishes many of its existing outlets. In fact, part of the refurbishment has focused on the installation of a specialty beverage platform across all U.S. outlets. The cost of installing this equipment is running at about $100,000 per outlet, with McDonald's subsidizing part of the expense.

Eventually, all McCafes will offer espresso-based coffee, gourmet coffee blends, fresh baked muffins, and high-end desserts. Customers will be able to consume these products while they relax in soft leather chairs listening to jazz, big-band, or blues music. Commenting on this significant expansion of offerings, Marty Brochstein, executive editor of *The Licensing Letter,* said: "McDonald's wants to be seen as a lifestyle brand, not just a place to go to have a burger."[11]

A New and Improved McDonalds?

Even though Skinner's efforts to transform McDonald's have led to improvements in its sales and profits, there are questions about the future of the fast-food chain. The firm is trying out a variety of strategies in order to increase its appeal to different segments of the market. Through the adoption of a mix of outlet décor and menu items, McDonald's is trying to target young adults, teenagers, children, and families. In so doing, it must ensure that it does not alienate any one of these groups in its efforts to reach out to the others. Its new marketing campaign, anchored around the catchy phrase "I'm loving it," takes on different forms in order to target each of the groups that it is seeking.

Larry Light, the head of global marketing at McDonald's since 2002, insists that the firm has to exploit its brand by pushing it in many different directions. The brand can be positioned differently in different locations, at different times of the day, and for different targeted customer segments. In large urban centers, for instance, McDonald's can target young adults for breakfast with its gourmet coffee, egg sandwiches, and fat-free muffins. Light explains the adoption of this approach as multiformat strategy: "The days of mass-media marketing are over."[12]

As McDonald's expands on its concept of fast food, it is moving beyond its staple of burgers and fries to a wider variety of offerings. In particular, many analysts are questioning the decision to invest in specialty beverages during a period when consumers are cutting back on spending. In fact, there are indications that the initial sales of lattes and frappes have not met expectations. Skinner recently denied that beverage addition may not have been successful. "You have to remember that everything we do at McDonald's is for the long term," he responded.[13]

Nevertheless, the additional offerings do raise some fundamental questions. Most significantly, it is not clear just how far McDonald's can stretch its brand while keeping all of its outlets under the traditional symbol of its golden arches. Chief financial officer Paull acknowledged that burgers continued to be the main draw for McDonald's. "There is no question that we make more money from selling hamburgers and cheeseburgers," he recently stated.[14]

Above all, Skinner is convinced that McDonald's must do whatever it can to make sure that it keeps its established customer base from bolting to the growing number of competitors such as the California-based In-N-Out chain. The long-term success of the firm may well depend on its ability to compete with rival burger chains. "The burger category has great strength," added David C. Novak, chairman and CEO of Yum! Brands, parent of KFC and Taco Bell. "That's America's food. People love hamburgers."[15]

Endnotes

1. Carolyn Walkup. McD Scores Amid Downturn, but Doubts Persist about Espresso, Dollar Menu Plans. *Nation's Restaurant News,* November 3, 2008, p. 4.
2. Janet Adamy. McDonald's to Expand, Posting Strong Results. *Wall Street Journal,* January 27, 2009, p. B1.
3. *Ibid*
4. Neil Buckley. McDonald's Shares Survive Resignation. November 24, 2004, p. 18.
5. Pallavi Gogoi and Michael Arndt. Hamburger Hell. *BusinessWeek,* March 3, 2003, p. 106.
6. *Ibid.*
7. Melanie Warner. You Want Any Fruit with That Big Mac? *New York Times,* February 20, 2005, p. 8.
8. Janet Adamy. McDonald's Coffee Strategy Is Tough Sell. *Wall Street Journal,* October 27, 2008, p. B3.
9. Bruce Horovitz. You Want Ambiance with That? *USA Today,* October 30, 2003, p. 3B.
10. Jeremy Grant. McDonald's to Revamp UK Outlets. *Financial Times,* February 2, 2006, p. 14.
11. Bruce Horovitz. McDonald's Ventures beyond Burgers to Duds, Toys. *USA Today,* November 14, 2003, p. 6B.
12. Big Mac's Makeover. *Economist,* October 16, 2004, p. 65.
13. *Wall Street Journal,* January 27, 2009, p. B1.
14. *Economist,* October 16, 2004, p. 64.
15. *BusinessWeek,* March 3, 2003, p. 108.

Case 15 Procter & Gamble*

In January 2009, Procter & Gamble (P&G) announced that its revenues had declined by 3.2 percent during its previous quarter, with lower sales in nearly every business unit. Consumers were coping with the economic downturn by switching to P&G's lower-priced brands, choosing *Gain* over *Tide* detergent and *Luvs* over *Pampers* diapers. In spite of the lower revenue, CEO A. G. Lafley was pleased to report that his firm had managed to retain or gain market share in most of its product categories. At the same time, he did not expect to see much change in 2009. "We expect the environment will remain difficult and highly volatile, at least in the near term," he stated.[1]

These results suggested that the world's largest consumer products conglomerate could not maintain growth during a recession, even with million-dollar brands like Tide, Crest, Pampers, Gillette, and Right Guard. But the firm was still managing to post strong profits through the heavier use of discount coupons delivered as inserts in weekend newspapers. It also kept pushing on its premium-priced products by promoting their features. It claimed that Tide, for example, contained much less water and more cleaning agents than other, cheaper-priced detergents.

At the same time, Lafley has continued to take steps to position P&G for the longer term by focusing on speed and agility, both of which are likely to play a more significant role in the future. Since he took over the helm of P&G in June 2000, Lafley has been stripping away much of the bureaucracy in order to speed up the firm's product development and build on its well-known brands. He is trying to focus the firm on building a small number of "superbrands," each with annual sales of over $1 billion. Over the last decade, the firm has increased the number of such brands to 24 (see Exhibit 1).

During the past year, P&G has embarked on its most ambitious plan to expand into emerging markets despite the developing slowdown. "We just have a huge opportunity to service urban consumer households in developing markets who have plenty of income, even with an economic downturn," said Lafley.[2] Although emerging markets currently account for about 30 percent of P&G's annual sales, they have delivered more than 50 percent of its recent growth.

Lafley has many more ideas about how to make P&G relevant in the 21st century. He is trying to shift the focus of his firm away from its traditional reliance on household care. P&G has been making aggressive inroads into health and beauty products, making these areas account for the majority of the firm's sales and profits. Over the past year,

*This case was developed by Professor Jamal Shamsie, Michigan State University, with the assistance of Professor Alan B. Eisner, Pace University. Material has been drawn from published sources to be used for class discussion. Copyright © 2009 Jamal Shamsie and Alan B. Eisner.

the firm has even managed to establish itself as a major force in the luxury perfume business by partnering with various designer brands. In pushing for these changes, Lafley has been undertaking the most sweeping transformation of the company since it was founded by William Procter and James Gamble in 1837 as a maker of soap and candles.

An Attempted Turnaround

For most of its long history, P&G has been one of America's preeminent companies. The firm has developed several well-known brands such as Tide, one of the pioneers in laundry detergents, which was launched in 1946, and

Exhibit 1 Business Segments

Fabric Care and Home Care:
- *Key products:* Air care, batteries, dish care, fabric care, surface care
- *Billion-dollar brands:* Ariel, Dawn, Downy, Duracell, Gain, Tide

Baby Care and Family Care:
- *Key products:* Baby wipes, bath tissue, diapers, facial tissue, paper towels
- *Billion-dollar brands:* Bounty, Charmin, Pampers

Beauty:
- *Key products:* Cosmetics, deodorants, hair care, personal cleansing, prestige fragrances, skin care
- *Billion-dollar brands:* Head & Shoulders, Olay, Pantene, Wella

Grooming:
- *Key products:* Blades and razors, electric hair-removal devices, face and shave products, home appliances
- *Billion-dollar brands:* Braun, Fusion, Gillette, Mach 3

Health Care:
- *Key products:* Feminine care, oral care, personal health care, pharmaceuticals
- *Billion-dollar brands:* Actonel, Always, Crest, Oral B

Snacks, Coffee, and Pet Care:
- *Key products:* Coffee,* pet food, snacks
- *Billion-dollar brands:* Folgers,* Iams, Pringles

*Sold in 2008.

Source: P&G.

Pampers, the first disposable diaper, which was introduced in 1961. P&G built its brands through its innovative marketing techniques. In the 1880s, it was one of the first companies to advertise nationally. Later on, P&G invented the soap opera by sponsoring *Ma Perkins* when radio caught on and *Guiding Light* when television took hold. In the 1930s, P&G was the first firm to develop the idea of brand management, setting up marketing teams for each brand and urging them to compete against each other.

By the 1990s, however, P&G was in danger of becoming another Eastman Kodak or Xerox, a once-great company that might have lost its way. Sales on most of its 18 top brands were slowing as it was being outhustled by more focused rivals such as Kimberly-Clark and Colgate-Palmolive. The only way P&G kept profits growing was by cutting costs, which would hardly work as a strategy for the long term. At the same time, the dynamics of the industry were changing as power shifted from manufacturers to massive retailers. Retailers such as Wal-Mart were starting to use their size to try to get better deals from P&G, further squeezing its profits.

In 1999, P&G decided to bring in Durk I. Jaeger to try to make the big changes that were obviously needed to get P&G back on track. But the moves that he made generally misfired, sinking the firm into deeper trouble. He introduced expensive new products that never caught on while letting existing brands drift. He also put in place a companywide reorganization that left many employees perplexed and preoccupied. During the fiscal year when he was in charge, earnings per share showed an anemic rise of just 3.5 percent, much lower than in previous years. Also during that time, the share price slid 52 percent, cutting P&G's total market capitalization by $85 billion. The effects were widely felt within the firm, where employees and retirees hold about 20 percent of the stock (see Exhibits 2 to 5).

Jaeger's greatest failing was his scorn for the family. Jaeger, a Dutchman who had joined P&G overseas and worked his way to corporate headquarters, pitted himself against the P&G culture. Susan E. Arnold, president of P&G's previous beauty and feminine care division, said that Jaeger tried to make the employees turn against the prevailing culture, contending that it was burdensome and insufferable. Some go-ahead employees even wore buttons that read "Old World/New World" to express disdain for P&G's past.

A New Style of Leadership

On June 6, 2000, the day of his 30th wedding anniversary, Alan G. Lafley received a call from John Pepper, a former CEO who was now a board member. Lafley was asked to take the reins of P&G from Jaeger, a move representing a boardroom coup and unprecedented in the firm's history. In a sense, Lafley had been preparing for this job his entire adult life. He never hid the fact that he wanted to run P&G one day. Recruited as a brand assistant for Joy dish detergent in 1977, Lafley rose quickly to head P&G's soap and detergent business, where he introduced Liquid Tide

Exhibit 2   Income Statement (in thousands of dollars)

Period Ending:	2008	2007	2006
Total revenue	83,503,000	76,476,000	68,222,000
Cost of revenue	40,695,000	36,686,000	33,125,000
Gross profit	42,808,000	39,790,000	35,097,000
Operating expenses:			
Selling, general, and administrative	25,725,000	24,340,000	21,848,000
Operating income or loss	17,083,000	15,450,000	13,249,000
Income from continuing operations:			
Total other income/expenses net	462,000	564,000	283,000
Earnings before interest and taxes	17,545,000	16,014,000	13,532,000
Interest expense	1,467,000	1,304,000	1,119,000
Income before tax	16,078,000	14,710,000	12,413,000
Income tax expense	4,003,000	4,370,000	3,729,000
Net income from continuing ops	12,075,000	10,340,000	8,684,000
Net income	12,075,000	10,340,000	8,684,000

Source: P&G.

Exhibit 3   Balance Sheet (in thousands of dollars)

Period Ending:	2008	2007	2006
Assets			
Current assets:			
Cash and cash equivalents	3,313,000	5,354,000	6,693,000
Short-term investments	228,000	202,000	1,133,000
Net receivables	8,773,000	8,356,000	7,336,000
Inventory	8,416,000	6,819,000	6,291,000
Other current assets	3,785,000	3,300,000	2,876,000
Total current assets	**24,515,000**	**24,031,000**	**24,329,000**
Property, plant, and equipment	20,640,000	19,540,000	18,770,000
Goodwill	59,767,000	56,552,000	55,306,000
Intangible assets	34,233,000	33,626,000	33,721,000
Other assets	4,837,000	4,265,000	3,569,000
Total assets	**143,992,000**	**138,014,000**	**135,695,000**
Liabilities and Equity			
Current liabilities:			
Accounts payable	7,977,000	13,628,000	17,857,000
Short/current long-term debt	13,084,000	12,039,000	2,128,000
Other current liabilities	9,897,000	5,050,000	—
Total current liabilities	**30,958,000**	**30,717,000**	**19,985,000**
Long-term debt	23,581,000	23,375,000	35,976,000
Other liabilities	8,154,000	5,147,000	4,472,000
Deferred long-term liability charges	11,805,000	12,015,000	12,354,000
Total liabilities	**74,498,000**	**71,254,000**	**72,787,000**
Stockholders' equity:			
Preferred stock	1,366,000	1,406,000	1,451,000
Common stock	4,002,000	3,990,000	3,976,000
Retained earnings	48,986,000	41,797,000	35,666,000
Treasury stock	(47,588,000)	(38,772,000)	(34,235,000)
Capital surplus	60,307,000	59,030,000	57,856,000
Other stockholders' equity	2,421,000	(691,000)	(1,806,000)
Total stockholders' equity	**69,494,000**	**66,760,000**	**62,908,000**
Net tangible assets	**($24,506,000)**	**($23,418,000)**	**($26,119,000)**

Source: P&G.

Exhibit 4 Financial Breakdown (in billions of dollars)

Business Segment	Net Sales		Net Earnings	
	2008	2007	2008	2007
Fabric care and home care	23.8	21.5	3.4	3.1
Baby care and family care	13.9	12.7	1.7	1.4
Beauty	19.5	17.9	2.7	2.6
Grooming	8.3	7.4	1.7	1.4
Health care	14.6	13.4	2.5	2.2
Snacks, coffee, and pet care*	4.9	4.5	0.5	0.5

*Prior to sale of Folgers coffee in 2008.

Source: P&G.

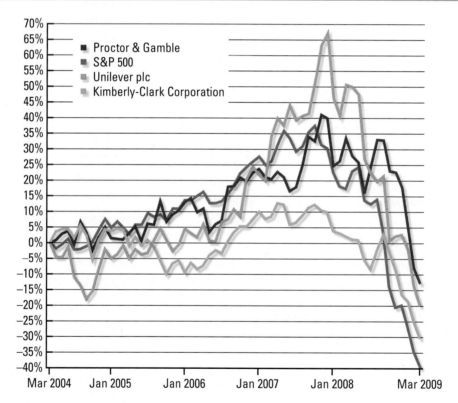

Exhibit 5 **Stock Price History, March 2004–March 2009**

Source: Data from moneycentral.msn.com.

in 1984. A decade later, he moved to Kobe, Japan, to head the Asian division. Lafley returned to Cincinnati in 1998 to run the company's entire North American operations.

By the time he had taken charge of P&G, Lafley had developed a reputation as a boss who steps back to give his staff plenty of responsibility and who helps shape decisions by asking a series of keen questions. As CEO, Lafley has refrained from making any grand pronouncements on the future of P&G. Instead, he has been spending an inordinate amount of time patiently communicating to his employees about the types of changes that he would like to see at P&G.

Lafley began his tenure by breaking down the walls between management and employees: Since the 1950s, all the senior executives at P&G had been located on the 11th floor at the firm's corporate headquarters. Lafley changed this setup, moving all five division presidents to the same floors as their staffs. Then he turned some of the emptied space into a leadership training center. On the rest of the floor, he knocked down the walls so that the remaining executives, including him, would share open offices.

Lafley chose to place his office next to the two people he talks to the most, who, in true P&G style, were officially identified by a flow study. They are the head of Human Resources, Ricard L. Antoine, and the vice chairman, Bruce Byrnes. In fact, Lafley has established a tradition of meeting with Antoine every Sunday evening to review the performance of the firm's 200 most senior executives. This reflects Lafley's determination to make sure the best people rise to the top. And Byrnes, whom Lafley refers to as "Yoda," the sagelike *Star Wars* character, gets a lot of face time because of his marketing expertise. As Lafley says, "The assets at P&G are what? Our people and our brands."[3]

Lafley's leadership style has been particularly visible in P&G's new conference room, where he and the firm's 12 other top executives meet every Monday at 8 a.m. to review results, plan strategy, and set the drumbeat for the week. The table is now round instead of rectangular. Instead of sitting where they were told, the executives now sit where they like. True to his character, Lafley maintains a low profile at most of these meetings. He occasionally joins in the discussion, but most of the time the executives talk as much to each other as to Lafley.

Indeed, Lafley's charm offensive has so disarmed most P&Gers that he has been able to make drastic changes within the company. He has replaced more than half of the company's top 30 officers (more replacements than made by any other P&G boss in memory) and trimmed its workforce by as many as 9,600 jobs. And he has moved more women into senior positions. In fact, Lafley skipped over 78 general managers with more seniority to name 42-year-old Deborah A. Henretta to head P&G's then-troubled North American baby care division. "The speed at which A. G. has gotten results is five years ahead of the time I expected," said Scott Cook, founder of software maker Intuit Incorporated, who joined P&G's board shortly after Lafley's appointment.[4]

A New Strategic Focus

Lafley has been intent on shifting the focus of P&G back to its consumers. At every opportunity that he gets, he tries to drill his managers and employees on not losing sight of the consumer. He feels that P&G has often let technology, rather than consumer needs, dictate its new products. He would like to see the firm work more closely with retail outlets, the places where consumers first see the product on the shelf. And he would like to see much more concern with the consumer's experience at home. At the end of a three-day leadership seminar, Lafley was thrilled when he heard the young marketing managers declare: "We are the voice of the consumer within P&G, and they are the heart of all we do."[5]

To better focus on serving the needs of P&G's consumers, Lafley has been putting a tremendous amount of emphasis on the firm's brands. In describing the P&G of the future, he said, "We're in the business of creating and building brands."[6] Since Lafley has taken over P&G, the firm has updated all of its 200 brands by adding innovative new products. It has begun to offer devices that build on its core brands, such as Tide StainBrush, a battery-powered brush for removing stains, and Mr. Clean AutoDry, a water-pressure-powered car cleaning system that dries without streaking.

Lafley has also pushed everyone at P&G to approach its brands more creatively (see Exhibit 6). Crest, for example, which used to be marketed as a toothpaste brand, is now defined as an oral care brand. The firm sells Crest-branded toothbrushes and tooth whiteners. There's even an electric toothbrush, SpinBrush, which was added to the Crest line after P&G acquired it in January 2001. The cheap, fun-to-use brush has created a new and positive vibe around the whole Crest brand. "People remember experiences," Lafley explained. "They don't remember attributes."[7]

A key element of Lafley's strategy, however, has been to move P&G away from basic consumer products such as laundry detergents, which can be knocked off by private labels, and shift the firm to higher-margin products. This has led him to focus more strongly on the firm's beauty and personal care business. Under Lafley, P&G made costly acquisitions of Clairol, Wella, and Gillette to complement its Cover Girl and Oil of Olay brands. His most

Exhibit 6 Significant Innovations

- Tide was the first heavy-duty laundry detergent.
- Crest was the first fluoride toothpaste clinically proved to help prevent tooth decay.
- Downy was the first ultra-concentrated rinse-add fabric softener.
- Pert Plus was the first 2-in-1 shampoo and conditioner.
- Head & Shoulders was the first pleasant-to-use shampoo effective against dandruff.
- Pampers was the first affordable, mass-marketed disposable diaper.
- Bounty was the first three-dimensional paper towel.
- Always was the first feminine protection pad with an innovative, dry-weave topsheet.
- Febreze was the first fabric and air care product that actually removes odors from fabrics and the air.
- Crest White Strips was the first patented in-home teeth-whitening technology.

Source: P&G.

dramatic innovation was that of moving his firm into prestige fragrances through licenses with Hugo Boss, Gucci, and Dolce & Gabbana. Over the past three years, prestige fragrances have become one of the fastest-growing segments of P&G's expanding beauty business.

P&G has also been considering moving out of some of its product categories. For a few years, it has been looking for potential buyers for its Pringle snacks and Iams pet foods. The firm completed a sale of its Folgers coffees late in 2008. In addition, Lafley has decided to move P&G out of the pharmaceuticals market, where it offers products such as Actonel for bone loss and Enablex for overactive bladders. He recently stated that the firm had already stopped investing in this business because of declining returns in prescription drugs. The firm would focus more on its health care products, which include Prilosec and Pepto-Bismol, which sell over the counter.

A Revolution Still in the Making

Although Lafley has given P&G a tremendous push toward rethinking its business model, it is quite clear that he has more revolutionary changes in mind. A confidential memo was circulated among P&G's top brass in late 2001 that drew a sharp response even from some of the firm's board members. The memo argued that P&G could be cut to 25,000 employees, less than one-quarter of its current size. Lafley admitted that the memo had drawn a strong reaction: "It terrified our organization."[8]

Even though Lafley did not write this infamous memo, it did reflect the central tenet of his vision: that P&G should do only what it does best and nothing more. He clearly wants a more outwardly focused, flexible company. This means that P&G does not have to do everything in-house. If no clear benefits stem from doing something within the firm, the work should be contracted out. Such a philosophy has serious implications for every facet of P&G's operations, from R&D to manufacturing.

Lafley has clearly challenged the supremacy of P&G's research and development operations. Confronting head-on the stubbornly held notion that everything must be invented within P&G, he has asserted that half of the firm's new products should come from the outside. Under his tenure, the percentage of new product ideas coming from outside the firm has increased from 10 percent, when he took over, to almost 50 percent.

A variety of other activities have also been driven out of the firm. In April 2003, Lafley turned over the manufacturing of all bar soaps, including Ivory, P&G's oldest surviving brand, to a Canadian contractor. Shortly afterward, he outsourced P&G's information-technology operation to the Hewlett-Packard Company. While Lafley shies away from saying just how much of P&G's factory and back-office operations he may eventually hand over to other firms, he does admit that facing up to the realities of the marketplace may force some hardships on its employees.

Such moves to outsource some activities may create more flexibility for the firm over the longer term. It could decide how much it wants to invest in particular brands, products, or even lines of businesses. No one would dispute that these moves are clearly revolutionary for a firm such as P&G. "He's absolutely breaking many well-set molds at P&G," said eBay's CEO, Margaret C. "Meg" Whitman, whom Lafley had recently appointed to the board.[9]

Daunting Challenges

Lafley's bold moves to remake P&G into a company that is admired, imitated, and uncommonly profitable have garnered considerable attention. Since he took over the firm, he has addressed every aspect of the firm's strategy and organization. In so doing, he has made a wide range of changes that are expected to enable his firm to respond quickly and flexibly to emerging opportunities. John Pepper, a popular former boss who returned briefly as chairman when Jaeger left, stated, "It's now clear to me that A. G. is going to be one of the great CEOs in this company's history."[10]

Lafley's push into luxury perfumes represents one of his most radical moves. Analysts have questioned whether a firm that uses a very methodological approach to making and selling mass-market goods can be successful in a business that is known to be quirky and fickle. Most firms in the prestige-fragrance business keep trying to come up with new brands, as older one lose their cachet. P&G hopes to apply its brand development methods to sustaining its fragrance brands over time. "We need to find ways to do brand building," said Hartwig Langer, the firm's president of global prestige products.[11]

The reliance on external sources for new products could be another problematic area. As any scientist will attest, decisions to purchase a new product idea often tend to be extremely hard to make. The process of picking winners from other labs is likely to be both difficult and expensive. P&G already missed a big opportunity by passing up the chance to buy water-soluble strips that contain mouthwash. Listerine managed to grab the product and has profited handsomely from the deal.

The biggest risk, though, is that Lafley will lose the people at P&G. The firm's insular culture has been famously resistant to new ideas. Employees form a tightly knit family because most of them start out and grow up together at P&G, which promotes only from within. Over the years, these people have gradually adopted the culture of the firm and come to believe in it. Lafley is well aware of his predicament. He recently admitted, "I am worried that I will ask the organization to change ahead of its understanding, capability, and commitment."[12]

Finding new avenues of growth, however, could be the only way to balance P&G's increasing reliance on Wal-Mart. Former and current P&G employees say the discounter could account for one-third of P&G's global sales by the end of the decade. Meanwhile, the pressure from consumers and competitors to keep prices low will only increase. "P&G has improved its ability to take on those challenges, but those challenges are still there," said Lehman analyst Ann Gillin.[13]

Endnotes

1. Ellen Byron. Sales Fall across P&G's Units. *Wall Street Journal,* January 31, 2009, p. B5.
2. Jonathan Birchall. P&G Set to Expand in Emerging Markets. *Financial Times,* December 12, 2008, p. 22.
3. Robert Berner. P&G: New and Improved. *BusinessWeek,* July 7, 2003, p. 62.
4. *BusinessWeek,* July 7, 2003, p. 55.
5. Ibid., p. 62.
6. Ibid., p. 63.
7. Robert Berner and William C. Symonds. Welcome to Procter & Gadget. *BusinessWeek,* February 7, 2005, p. 77.
8. *BusinessWeek,* July 7, 2003, p. 55.
9. Ibid., p. 58.
10. Ibid., p. 55.
11. Ellen Byron. P&G's Push into Perfume Tests a Stodgy Marketer. *Wall Street Journal,* November 12, 2007, p. A15.
12. *BusinessWeek,* July 7, 2003, p. 58.
13. Ibid., p. 63.

Case 16   Heineken*

In January 2009, Heineken was expecting to announce that it had achieved 5 percent growth in profits for 2008 (see Exhibits 1 and 2). Although this was considerably lower than the growth it had demonstrated over the previous five years, the firm was careful to point out that it had managed to grow in spite of a tougher economic climate. "There is certainly a chance of pace in the growth" said Jean-Francois van Boxmeer, Heineken's chief executive. "But what we'd like to underline is that we still have growth."[1]

In part, growth in 2008 resulted from the firm's high-profile acquisition of Scottish-based brewer Scottish & Newcastle, the brewer of well-known brands such as Newcastle Brown Ale and Kronenbourg 1664. Although the purchase was made in partnership with Carlsberg, Heineken was able to reap considerable gains from the deal. It acquired control of Scottish & Newcastle's operations in several crucial European markets such as the United Kingdom, Ireland, Portugal, Finland, and Belgium.

On the basis of these gains, the Scottish & Newcastle deal helped to establish Heineken as the leading brewer in

Exhibit 1   Income Statements (in millions of euros)

	2008	2007	2006	2005	2004
Revenue	14,319	12,564	11,829	10,796	10,062
EBIT	1,080	1,528	1,832	1,249	1,348
Net profit*	347	807	1,211	761	642
Dividend	210	343	294	196	173

*Includes exceptional items *before* tax in 2008 of €789m (2007: €319m).

Source: Heineken.

Exhibit 2   Balance Sheets

	2008	2007	2006
Assets	20,563	11,954	12,997
Liabilities	15,811	6,243	7,477
Equity	4,752	5,711	5,520

Source: Heineken.

*This case was developed by Professor Jamal Shamsie, Michigan State University, with the assistance of Professor Alan B. Eisner, Pace University. Material has been drawn from published sources to be used for class discussion. Copyright © 2009 Jamal Shamsie and Alan B. Eisner.

Europe. The Dutch-based firm also took over the Scottish brewer's ventures in far-flung places such as the United States and India. Van Boxmeer believed that these ventures would provide his firm with better opportunities to push its premium Heineken brand in more and more markets. Heineken would also be able to continue to add more complementary brands with international appeal and potential, such as Strongbow cider, giving it a strong presence in the United Kingdom cider market, which has been growing at a rate of almost 20 percent.

The decision to acquire a share of Scottish & Newcastle's operations was a part of a series of changes that the Dutch brewer has been making to raise its stature in the various markets and to respond to changes that are occurring in the global market for beer. Beer consumption has been declining in key markets as a result of tougher drunk-driving laws and a growing appreciation for wine. At the same time, the beer industry has become ever more competitive as the largest brewers have been expanding across the globe through acquisitions of smaller regional and national players.

The need for change was clearly reflected in the appointment in October 2005 of Jean-Francois van Boxmeer as Heineken's first non-Dutch CEO. He was brought in to replace Thorny Ruys, who had decided to resign 18 months ahead of schedule because of his failure to show much improvement in performance. Prior to the appointment of Ruys in 2002, Heineken had been run by three generations of Heineken ancestors, whose portraits still adorn the dark-paneled office of the CEO in its Amsterdam headquarters. Like Ruys, van Boxmeer faces the challenge of preserving the firm's family-driven traditions while trying to deal with threats that have never been faced before.

Confronting a Globalizing Industry

Heineken was one of the pioneers of an international strategy, using cross-border deals to expand distribution of its Heineken, Amstel, and 170 other beer brands in more than 150 countries around the globe (see Exhibits 3 and 4). For years, it has been picking up small brewers from several countries to add more brands and to get better access to new markets. From its roots on the outskirts of Amsterdam, the firm has evolved into one of the world's largest brewers, claiming a little more than 8 percent of the worldwide market for beer.

In fact, the firm's flagship Heineken brand ranked second only to Budweiser in a global brand survey jointly undertaken by *BusinessWeek* and *Interbrand* a couple of years ago. The premier brand has achieved worldwide recognition according to Kevin Baker, director of alcoholic beverages at British market researcher Canadean Ltd. A U.S. wholesaler recently asked a group of marketing

Exhibit 3 Geographic Breakdown of Revenues (in millions of euros)

	2008	2007	2006
Western Europe	7,661	5,450	5,351
Central and Eastern Europe	3,687	3,226	3,359
Americas	1,566	1,608	1,975
Africa and Middle East	1,774	1,311	1,182
Asia Pacific	279	245	560

Source: Heineken.

Exhibit 4 Heineken Brands

Market	Significant Brands
United States	Heineken, Amstel Light, Paulaner,[1] Moretti
Netherlands	Heineken, Amstel, Lingen's Blond, Murphy's Irish Red
France	Heineken, Amstel, Buckler,[2] Desperados[3]
Italy	Heineken, Amstel, Birra Moretti
Spain	Heineken, Amstel, Cruzcampo, Buckler
Poland	Heineken, Krolewskie, Kujawiak, Zywiec
China	Heineken, Tiger, Reeb*
Singapore	Heineken, Tiger, Anchor, Baron's
Kazakhstan	Heineken, Amstel, Tian Shan
Egypt	Heineken, Birell, Meister, Fayrouz[2]
Israel	Heineken, Maccabee, Gold Star*
Nigeria	Heineken, Amstel Malta, Maltina, Gulder
Panama	Heineken, Soberana, Crystal, Panama

* Minority interest.
[1] Wheat beer.
[2] Nonalcoholic beer.
[3] Tequila-flavored beer.

Exhibit 5 Leading Brewers, Ranked by 2007 Annual Sales (in millions of U.S. dollars)

1.	SAB Miller, London, U.K.	$21,410
2.	InBev,[1] Leuven, Belgium	21,253
3.	Heineken,[2] Amsterdam, Netherlands	18,505
4.	Anheuser-Busch,[1] St Louis, U.S.	16,686
5.	Kirin Holdings,[3] Tokyo, Japan	14,258
6.	Asahi, Tokyo, Japan	11,313
7.	FEMSA, Monterrey, Mexico	9,762
8.	Carlsberg,[2] Copenhagen, Denmark	8,833
9.	Group Modelo, Mexico City, Mexico	6,698
10.	Molson Coors Brewing, Denver, U.S.	6,191

[1] InBev acquired Anheuser-Busch in 2007.
[2] Does not reflect sales of Scottish & Newcastle, acquired in 2007.
[3] Includes sales of soft drinks.

Source: Beverage World

students to identify an assortment of beer bottles that had been stripped of their labels. The stubby green Heineken container was the only one that incited instant recognition among the group.

The beer industry, however, has been undergoing significant change due to a furious wave of consolidation. Most of the bigger brewers have begun to acquire or merge with their competitors in foreign markets in order to become global players (see Exhibit 5). Over the past six years, South African Breweries Plc acquired U.S.-based Miller Brewing to become a major global brewer. U.S.-based Coors linked with Canadian-based Molson in 2005, with their combined operations allowing the new firm to rise to a leading position among the world's biggest brewers. Over the past four years, Belgium's Interbrew, Brazil's AmBev, and U.S.-based Anheuser-Busch have merged to become the largest global brewer, with operations across most of the continents.

Many brewers have also expanded their operations without the use of such acquisitions. For example, Anheuser-Busch bought equity stakes in and struck partnership deals with Mexico's Grupo Modelo, China's Tsingtao, and Chile's CCU. Such cross-border deals have provided significant benefits to the brewing giants. To begin with, the deals have given them ownership of local brands, thereby propelling them into a dominant position in various markets around the world. Beyond this, acquisitions of foreign brewers can provide the firms with manufacturing and distribution capabilities that they could use to develop a few global brands. "The era of global brands is coming," said Alan Clark, Budapest-based managing director of SAB Miller Europe.[2]

Since its acquisition of Anheuser-Busch, InBev is planning to include Budweiser in its existing efforts to develop Stella Artois, Brahma, and Becks as global flagship brands. Each of these brands originated in different locations, with Budweiser coming from the United States, Stella Artois from Belgium, Brahma from Brazil, and Becks from Germany. Similarly, the newly formed SAB Miller has been attempting to develop the Czech brand Pilsner

Urquell into a global brand. Exports of this pilsner have doubled since SAB acquired it in 1999. John Brock, the CEO of InBev, commented: "Global brands sell at significantly higher prices, and the margins are much better than with local beers."[3]

Wrestling with Change

Although the management of Heineken has moved to nonfamily members for the first time, they have been well aware of the long-standing and well-established family traditions that would be difficult to change. Even with the appointment of nonfamily members to manage the firm, a little over half of the shares of Heineken are still owned by a holding company that is controlled by the family. With the death of Freddy Heineken, the last family member to head the Dutch brewer, control has passed to his only child and heir, Charlene de Carvalho, who has insisted on having a say in all the major decisions.

At the time of van Boxmeer's appointment, the family members were behind some of the changes that were announced that would support Heineken's next phase of growth as a global organization. As part of the plan, dubbed "Fit 2 Fight," the executive board was cut from five members to three, all of whom are younger than 50. Along with van Boxmeer, the board is made up of the firm's chief operating officer and chief financial officer. The change is expected to assist the firm in thinking about the steps that it needs to take to win over younger customers across different markets whose tastes are still developing.

Heineken has also created management positions that are responsible for five different operating regions and nine different functional areas. These positions were created to more clearly define different spheres of responsibility. Van Boxmeer argues that the new structure also provides incentives for people to be accountable for their performance: "There is more pressure for results, for achievement."[4] He claims that the new structure has already encouraged more risk taking and boosted the level of energy within the firm.

The management group of Heineken was cut from 36 to 13 members in order to speed up the decision-making process. Besides including the three members of the executive board, the management group consists of the managers who are responsible for the five different operating regions and five of the key functional areas. Van Boxmeer hopes that the reduction in the size of this group will allow the firm to combat the cumbersome consensus culture that has made it difficult for Heineken to respond swiftly to various challenges even as its industry has been experiencing considerable change.

Finally, Heineken has been trying to deal with its cost structure in the face of the recent increases in the prices of various commodities. The firm has always been known for its efficiencies, and over the last 10 years it considerably reduced its costs for producing beer. During the past year, it managed to pass on some of its higher costs to consumers by raising the prices of its beers as much as 4 percent in various markets.

Maintaining a Premium Position

For decades, Heineken has been able to rely on the success of its flagship Heineken brand, which has enjoyed a leading position among premium beers in many markets around the world. It was the best-selling imported beer in the United States for several decades, giving the firm a steady source of revenues and profits from the world's biggest market. But by the late 1990s, Heineken had lost its 65-year-old leadership among imported beers in the United States to Group Modelo's Corona. The Mexican beer has been able to reach out to the growing population of Hispanic Americans, who represent one of the fastest-growing segments of beer drinkers.

Furthermore, the firm was also concerned that Heineken was being perceived as an obsolete brand by many young drinkers. John A. Quelch, a professor at Harvard Business School who studied the beer industry, said of Heineken, "It's in danger of becoming a tired, reliable, but unexciting brand."[5] The firm has therefore been working hard to increase awareness of its flagship brand by spending much more on marketing the brand, particularly among younger drinkers. The average age of the Heineken drinker has been reduced from about 40 in the mid-1990s to about 30 over the past couple of years.

At the same time, Heineken has been pushing other brands to reduce its reliance on its core Heineken brand. It has already achieved considerable success with Amstel Light, which has become the leading imported light beer in the United States and has been selling well in many other countries. But many of the other brands that the firm carries are strong local brands that it has added through its string of acquisitions of smaller breweries around the world. It has managed to develop a relatively small but loyal base of consumers by promoting some of these brands as specialty brands, such as Murphy's Irish Red and Moretti.

Finally, Heineken has been stepping up its marketing to Hispanics, who account for one-quarter of U.S. sales. It concluded a deal in 2004 with a leading Mexican brewer to market and distribute that brewer's five popular brands, which include Tecate and Dos Equis, within the United States. Benj Steinman, publisher and editor of the *Beer Marketer's Insight* newsletter, claims that the deal will give a tremendous boost to Heineken. "This gives Heineken a commanding share of the U.S. import business and . . . gives them a bigger presence in the Southwest . . . and better access to Hispanic consumers," he stated.[6]

Above all, Heineken wants to maintain its leadership in the premium beer industry, which represents the most profitable segment of the beer business. In this category, the firm's brands face competition from domestic beers such as Anheuser's Budweiser Select and imported beers such as InBev's Stella Artois. Although premium brews often have slightly higher alcohol content than standard beers, they are developed through a more exclusive positioning of the brand. This allows a firm to charge a higher price for such brands. A six-pack of Heineken, for example, costs $10, versus around $7 for a six-pack of Budweiser.

Heineken's interest in the premium segment is also driven by the prospects for future growth in this category. Its success with Premium Light is significant, because even though light beers account for half of U.S. beer sales, few premium beers have been introduced in this important category. Furthermore, while Heineken expects overall global beer consumption to grow at a rate of just 2 percent over the next couple of years, the premium market is expected to grow at twice that rate. Just-drinks.com, a London-based online research service, estimates that the market for premium beer will expand by 84 percent, to $230 billion, by 2012, from $125 billion in 2004.

Building a Global Stature

Van Boxmeer is well aware of the need for Heineken to use its brands to build on its existing stature across global markets. In spite of its strong presence in markets around the world, Heineken has failed to match the recent moves of formidable competitors such as Belgium's InBev and the United Kingdom's SAB Miller, which have grown significantly through mega-acquisitions. In large part, it is assumed that the firm has been reluctant to make such acquisitions because of the dilution of family control.

For many years, Heineken had limited itself to snapping up small national brewers, such as Italy's Moretti and Spain's Cruzcampo, that have provided it with small but profitable avenues for growth. In 1996, for example, Heineken acquired Fischer, a small French brewer, whose Desperados brand has been quite successful in niche markets. Similarly, Paulaner, a wheat beer that the firm picked up in Germany a few years ago, has been making inroads into the U.S. market.

However, since other brewers started reaching out to make acquisitions all over the world, Heineken has been running the risk of falling behind its more aggressive rivals. To deal with this growing challenge, the firm has broken out of its play-it-safe corporate culture to make a few big deals. In 2003, Heineken spent $2.1 billion to acquire BBAG, a family-owned company based in Linz, Austria. Because of BBAG's extensive presence in Central Europe, Heineken has become the biggest beer maker in seven countries across Eastern Europe. The more recent acquisition of Scottish & Newcastle similarly reinforced the firm's dominance in Western Europe.

At the same time, Heineken has been making an aggressive push into Russia with the acquisition of midsize brewing concerns. Through several acquisitions since 2002, Russia has become one of Heineken's largest markets by volume. Heineken now ranks as the third-largest brewer in Russia, behind Sweden's Baltic Beverages Holding and InBev.

Rene Hooft Graafland, the company's chief financial officer, stated that Heineken will continue to participate in the consolidation of the $450 billion global retail beer industry by targeting many different markets around the world. During the past decade, the firm has added several labels to Heineken's shelf, pouncing on brewers in far-flung places such as Belarus, Panama, Egypt, and Kazakhstan. In Egypt, Ruys bought a majority stake in Al Ahram

Beverages Co. and hopes to use the Cairo-based brewer's fruit-flavored, nonalcoholic malts as an avenue into other Muslim countries.

A Break from the Past?

The acquisition of Scottish & Newcastle represented an important step in Heineken's quest to build on its existing global stature. In fact, most analysts had expected that van Boxmeer and his team would make efforts to continue to build Heineken into a powerful global competitor. Without providing any specific details, Graafland, the firm's CFO, did make it clear that the firm's management would take initiatives that would drive long-term growth. In his own words: "We are positive that the momentum in the company and trends will continue."[7]

When van Boxmeer took over the helm of Heineken, he announced that he would have to work on the company's culture in order to accelerate the speed of decision making. This led many people both inside and outside the firm to expect that the new management would try to break loose from the conservative style that resulted from the family's tight control. Instead, the affable 44-year-old Belgian has indicated that he will adhere even more closely to the firm's existing culture than did his predecessors.

Van Boxmeer's devotion to the firm is quite evident. Heineken's first non-Dutch CEO spent 20 years working his way up within the firm. Even his cufflinks are silver miniatures of a Heineken bottle top and opener. "We are in the logical flow of history" he recently explained. "Every time you have a new leader you have a new kind of vision. It is not radically different, because you are defined by what your company is and what your brands are."[8]

Furthermore, van Boxmeer seems quite comfortable working with the family-controlled structure. "Since 1952 history has proved it is the right concept," he stated about the current ownership structure. "The whole business about family restraint on us is absolutely untrue. Without its spirit and guidance, the company would not have been able to build a world leader. Your long-term strategy does not change because you have a few less successful years."[9]

Endnotes

1. Michael Steen. Heineken Forecasts 5% Growth for 2008. *Financial Times,* August 28, 2008, p. 16.
2. Jack Ewing and Gerry Khermouch. Waking Up Heineken. *BusinessWeek,* September 8, 2003, p. 68.
3. Richard Tomlinson. The New King of Beers. *Fortune,* October 18, 2004, p. 238.
4. Ian Bickerton and Jenny Wiggins. Change Is Brewing at Heineken. *Financial Times,* May 9, 2006, p. 12.
5. Ewing and Khermouch. Waking Up Heineken, p. 69.
6. Andrew Kaplan. Border Crossings. *Beverage World,* July 15, 2004, p. 6.
7. Christopher C. Williams. Heineken Seeing Green. *Barron's,* September 18, 2006, p. 19.
8. Bickerton and Wiggins. Change Is Brewing.
9. Ibid.

Case 17   Pixar*

When *Wall-E* won the Academy Award for best animated feature in February 2009, it hardly took anyone by surprise. The latest offering from Pixar Animation Studios had already been heralded by almost all the critics as soon as it was released during the prior summer. It went on to gross $533 million in theaters worldwide, landing among the top-10 animated films of all time (see Exhibit 1). *Wall-E* managed to achieve this success in spite of its challenging theme: It centered on robots and had little dialogue. Moreover, with this win, Pixar claimed its fourth feature-length animation Oscar, which represented half of the eight trophies that had been handed out since the category was added in 2001.

The recent string of successful releases—*Cars, Ratatouille,* and *Wall-E*—suggests that Pixar has continued to flourish despite its 2006 acquisition by the Walt Disney Company for the hefty sum of $7.4 billion. The deal was finalized by Steve Jobs, the Apple Computer chief executive, who also heads the computer animation firm. Jobs had developed a production and distribution pact with Disney, under which the two firms split the profits that Pixar films generated from ticket sales, video sales, and merchandising royalties. But the deal was set to expire after the release of *Cars* in summer 2006. Disney CEO Bob Iger worked hard to clinch the deal to acquire Pixar, whose track record has made it one of the world's most successful animation companies.

Both Jobs and Iger realized, however, that they must try to protect Pixar's creative culture while also trying to carry some of it over to Disney's animation efforts. Even though Pixar has continued to operate independently of Disney's own animation studios, its key talent has overseen the combined activities of both Pixar and Disney. As part of the deal, Jobs gained considerable influence over Disney by assuming the position of a nonindependent director and becoming its largest individual stockholder.

In order to ensure that Pixar manages to preserve its freewheeling entrepreneurial culture, Jobs sits on a committee that includes other top talent from the animation studio whose key task is to protect its unique approach to making movies. Pixar's lengthy process of crafting a film stands in stark contrast to the production-line approach pursued by Disney. This contrast in culture is best reflected in the Oscars which the employees at Pixar have displayed proudly but which have been painstakingly dressed in Barbie-doll clothing.

Above all, everyone at Pixar remains committed to making films that are original in concept and execution, despite the risks involved. All of the studio's films have been based on original stories, and apart from *Toy Story,* Pixar has resisted the temptation to make sequels. On behalf of Disney, Iger has reinforced the importance of maintaining the formula that was responsible for Pixar's string of successful animated films. He has pledged that he will do whatever he can to make sure "that the Pixar culture be protected and allowed to continue."[1]

Pushing for Computer Animated Films

The roots of Pixar stretch back to 1975 with the founding of a vocational school in Old Westbury, New York, called the New York Institute of Technology. It was there that Edwin E. Catmull, a straitlaced Mormon from Salt Lake City who loved animation but couldn't draw, teamed up with the people who would later form the core of Pixar. "It was artists and technologists from the very start," recalled Alvy Ray Smith, who worked with Catmull during those years. "It was like a fairy tale."[2]

By 1979, Catmull and his team decided to join forces with famous Hollywood director George W. Lucas, Jr. They were hopeful that this would allow them to pursue their dream of making animated films. As part of Lucas's filmmaking facility in San Rafael, California, Catmull's group of aspiring animators was able to make substantial progress in the art of computer animation. But the unit was not able to generate any profits, and Lucas was not willing to let it grow beyond using computer animation for special effects.

In 1985, Catmull finally turned to Jobs, who had just been ousted from Apple. Jobs was reluctant to invest in a firm that wanted to make full-length feature films using computer animation. But a year later, Jobs did decide to buy Catmull's unit for just $10 million, which was one-third of Lucas's asking price. While the newly named Pixar Animation Studios tried to push the boundaries of computer animation over the next five years, Jobs ended up having to invest an additional $50 million—more than 25 percent of his total wealth at the time. "There were times that we all despaired, but fortunately not all at the same time," said Jobs.[3]

Still, Catmull's team did continue to make substantial breakthroughs in the development of computer-generated full-length feature films (see Exhibit 2). In 1991, Disney ended up giving Pixar a three-film contract that started with *Toy Story.* When the movie was finally released in 1995, its success surprised everyone in the film industry. Rather than the nice little film Disney had expected, *Toy Story* became the sensation of 1995. It rose to the rank of third-highest-grossing animated

*This case was developed by Professor Jamal Shamsie, Michigan State University, with the assistance of Professor Alan B. Eisner, Pace University. Material has been drawn from published sources to be used for class discussion. Copyright © 2009 Jamal Shamsie and Alan B. Eisner.

Exhibit 1 Leading Animated Films (in millions of U.S. dollars)

All nine of Pixar's films released to date have ended up among the top animated films of all time, based on worldwide box office revenues.

Title		Year	Revenues	Studio
1.	Shrek 2	2004	$881	Dreamworks
2.	Finding Nemo	2003	865	Pixar
3.	Shrek 3	2007	791	Dreamworks
4.	The Lion King	1994	783	Disney
5.	Kung Fu Panda	2008	633	Dreamworks
6.	The Incredibles	2004	624	Pixar
7.	Ice Age: The Meltdown	2006	623	Fox
8.	Ratatouille	2007	616	Pixar
9.	Madagascar: Escape 2 Africa	2008	581	Dreamworks
10.	Wall-E	2008	533	Pixar
11.	Monsters, Inc.	2001	529	Pixar
12.	The Simpsons Movie	2007	526	Fox
13.	Aladdin	1992	502	Disney
14.	Toy Story 2	1999	486	Pixar
15.	Shrek	2001	455	Dreamworks
16.	Cars	2006	454	Pixar
17.	Tarzan	1999	435	Disney
18.	Madagascar	2005	407	Dreamworks
19.	Happy Feet	2006	379	Warner
20.	Beauty and the Beast	1991	378	Disney
21.	Ice Age	2002	377	Fox
22.	Toy Story	1995	359	Pixar
23.	A Bug's Life	1998	358	Pixar
24.	Dinosaur	2000	348	Disney
25.	Pocahontas	1995	347	Disney

Source: IMDB, *Variety*.

film of all time, earning $362 million in worldwide box office revenues.

Within days, Jobs decided to take Pixar public. When the shares, initially priced at $22, shot past $33, Jobs called his best friend, Oracle CEO Lawrence J. Ellison, to tell him he had company in the billionaire's club. With Pixar's sudden success, Jobs returned to strike a new deal with Disney. Early in 1996, at a lunch with Walt Disney chief Michael D. Eisner, Jobs made his demands: an equal share of the profits, equal billing on merchandise and on-screen credits, and guarantees that Disney would market Pixar films as it did its own.

Boosting the Creative Component

With the success of *Toy Story*, Jobs realized that he had hit something big. He had obviously tapped into his Silicon Valley roots and turned to computers to forge a unique style of creative moviemaking. In each of its subsequent films, Pixar continued to develop computer animation that allowed for more lifelike backgrounds, texture, and movement than ever before. For example, since real leaves are translucent, Pixar's engineers developed special software algorithms that both reflect and absorb light, creating luminous scenes among jungles of clover.

Exhibit 2   Milestones

1986	Steve Jobs buys Lucas's computer group and christens it Pixar. The firm completes a short film, *Luxo Jr.,* which is nominated for an Oscar.
1988	Pixar adds computer-animated ads to its repertoire, making spots for Listerine, Lifesavers, and Tropicana. Another short, *Tin Toy,* wins an Oscar.
1991	Pixar signs a production agreement with Disney. Disney is to invest $26 million; Pixar is to deliver at least three full-length, computer-animated feature films.
1995	Pixar releases *Toy Story,* the first fully digital feature film, which becomes the top-grossing movie of the year and wins an Oscar. A week after release, the company goes public.
1997	Pixar and Disney negotiate a new agreement: a 50-50 split of the development costs and profits of five feature-length movies. Short *Geri's Game* wins an Oscar.
1998–99	*A Bug's Life* and *Toy Story 2* are released, together pulling in $1.3 billion in box office and video revenues.
2001–04	Pixar releases a string of hits: *Monsters Inc., Finding Nemo,* and *The Incredibles.*
2006	Disney acquires Pixar and assigns responsibilities for its own animation unit to Pixar's creative brass. *Cars* is released and becomes another box office hit.
2009	*Wall-E* becomes the fourth film from Pixar to receive the Oscar for a feature-length animated film.

Source: Pixar.

In spite of the significance of these advancements in computer animation, Jobs was well aware that successful feature films would require a strong creative spark. He understood that it would be the marriage of technology and creativity that would allow Pixar to rise above most of its competition. To achieve that, Jobs fostered a campuslike environment within the newly formed outfit similar to the freewheeling, charged atmosphere in the early days of his beloved Apple, where he also returned as acting CEO. "It's not simply the technology that makes Pixar," said Dick Cook, president of Walt Disney Studios.[4]

Even though Jobs has played a crucial supportive role, it is Catmull, now elevated to the position of Pixar's president, who has been mainly responsible for ensuring that the firm's technological achievements help pump up the firm's creative efforts. He has been the keeper of the company's unique innovative culture, which blends Silicon Valley techies, Hollywood production honchos, and artsy animation experts. In the pursuit of Catmull's vision, this eclectic group has transformed office cubicles into tiki huts, circus tents, and cardboard castles with bookshelves that are stuffed with toys and desks that are adorned with colorful iMac computers.

Catmull has also been working hard to build on this pursuit of creative innovation by creating programs to develop the employees. Employees are encouraged to devote up to four hours a week, every week, to furthering their education at Pixar University. The in-house training program offers 110 different courses that cover subjects such as live improvisation, creative writing, painting, drawing, sculpting, and cinematography. The school's dean is Randall E. Nelson, a former juggler who has been known to perform his act using chain saws so that students in animation classes have something compelling to draw.

It is this emphasis on the creative use of technology that has kept Pixar on the cutting edge. The firm has turned out ever more lifelike short films, including 1998's Oscar-winning *Geri's Game,* which used a technology called *subdivision surfaces.* This makes the realistic simulation of human skin and clothing possible. "They're absolute geniuses," gushed Jules Roman, cofounder and CEO of rival Tippett Studio, when speaking of Pixar's staff. "They're the people who created computer animation really."[5]

Becoming Accomplished Storytellers

A considerable part of the creative energy at Pixar goes into story development. Jobs understands that a film works only if its story can move the hearts and minds of families around the world. His goal is to develop Pixar into an animated movie studio that is known for the quality of its storytelling above everything else. "We want to create some great stories and characters that endure with each generation," Jobs recently stated.[6]

For story development, Pixar relies heavily on 43-year-old John Lasseter, who goes by the title of vice president of the creative. Known for his Hawaiian shirts and irrepressible playfulness, Lasseter has been the key to the appeal of all of Pixar's films. Lasseter gets very passionate about developing great stories and then harnessing computers to tell those stories. Most of Pixar's employees believe that it is this passion that has enabled the studio to ensure that each of its films has been a commercial hit. In fact,

Lasseter is being regarded as the Walt Disney of the 21st century.

When it's time to start a project, Lasseter isolates a group of eight or so writers and directs them to forget about the constraints of technology. While many studios try to rush from script to production, Lasseter takes up to two years just to develop the story. Once the script has been developed, artists create storyboards and copy them onto videotapes called *reels*. Even computer-animated films must begin with pencil sketches that are viewed on tape. "You can't really shortchange the story development," Lasseter has emphasized.[7]

Only after the basic story is set does Lasseter begin to think about what he'll need from Pixar's technologists, and it's always more than the computer animators expect. Lasseter, for example, demanded that the crowds of ants in *A Bug's Life* not be a single mass of look-alike faces. To solve the problem, computer expert William T. Reeves developed software that randomly applied physical and emotional characteristics to each ant. In another instance, writers brought a model of a butterfly named Gypsy to researchers, asking them to write code so that when she rubs her antennas, viewers can see the hairs press down and pop back up.

At any stage during the process, Lasseter may go back to potential problems that he might see with the story. In *A Bug's Life,* for example, the story was totally revamped after more than a year of work had been completed. Originally, it was about a troupe of circus bugs run by P. T. Flea that tries to rescue a colony of ants from marauding grasshoppers. But because of a flaw in the story—why would the circus bugs risk their lives to save stranger ants?—codirector Andrew Stanton recast the story to be about Flik, the heroic ant who recruits Flea's troupe to fight the grasshoppers. "You have to rework and rework it," explained Lasseter. "It is not rare for a scene to be rewritten as much as 30 times."[8]

Pumping Out the Hits

In spite of its formidable string of hits, Pixar has had difficulty in stepping up its pace of production. Although they may cost 30 percent less than nonanimated films, computer-generated animated films take considerable time to develop. Furthermore, because of the emphasis on every single detail, Pixar used to complete most of the work on a film before moving on to the next one. Catmull and Lasseter have since decided to work on several projects at the same time, but the firm has not been able to release more than one movie in a year.

To push for an increase in production, Pixar has more than doubled its number of employees over the last decade. It is also turning to a stable of directors to oversee its movies. Lasseter, who directed Pixar's first three films, is supervising other directors who are taking the helm of various films that the studio chooses to develop. *Monsters Inc., Finding Nemo, The Incredibles,* and *Ratatouille* were directed by some of this new talent. But there are concerns about the number of directors that Pixar can rely on to turn out high-quality animated films. Michael Savner of Bank of America Securities commented: "You can't simply double production. There is a finite amount of talent."[9]

To meet the faster production pace, Catmull has added new divisions, including one to help with the development of new movies and one to oversee movie development shot by shot. The eight-person development team has helped generate more ideas for new films. "Once more ideas are percolating, we have more options to choose from so no one artist is feeling the weight of the world on their shoulders," said Sarah McArthur, Pixar's vice president of production.[10]

Finally, Catmull is turning to new technology to help ramp up production. His goal is to reduce the number of animators to no more than 100 per film. Toward this end, Catmull has been overseeing the development of new animation software called Luxo, which enables fewer people to do more work. While the firm's old system allowed animators to easily make a change to a specific character, Luxo adjusts the environment as well (see Exhibit 3). For example, if an animator adds a new head to a monster, the system would automatically cast the proper shadow.

Catmull is well aware of the dangers of growth for a studio whose successes came out of a lean structure that wagered everything on each film. It remains to be seen whether Pixar can keep drawing on its talent to increase production without compromising the high standards that have been set by Catmull and Lasseter. Jobs has been keen to maintain the quality of every one of Pixar's films by ensuring that each one gets the best efforts of the firm's animators, storytellers, and technologists. "Quality is more important than quantity," he recently emphasized. "One home run is better than two doubles."[11]

To preserve the studio's high standards, Catmull has been working hard to retain Pixar's commitment to quality even as the studio grows. He has been using Pixar University to encourage collaboration among all employees so that they can develop and retain the key values that are tied to their success. In addition, he has helped devise ways to avoid collective burnout. A masseuse and a doctor come to Pixar's campus each week, and animators must get permission from their supervisors if they want to work more than 50 hours a week.

Exhibit 3   Proprietary Software

Marionette: An animation software system used for modeling, animating, and lighting.

Ringmaster: A production management software system for scheduling, coordinating, and tracking a computer-animation project.

Renderman: A rendering software system for high-quality, photo-realistic image synthesis.

Source: Pixar.

To Infinity and Beyond?

The ongoing success of Pixar's films clearly indicates that the studio continued to turn out quality films even after it was acquired by Disney in 2006. This has settled some of the concerns that arose at the time of the acquisition about its possible effect on Pixar's rather unique creative culture. David Price, author of a recent book on the animation firm, stated, "Most acquisitions, particularly in media, are value-destroying as opposed to value-creating and that certainly has not turned out to be the case here."[12]

Along the same lines, Jobs recently expressed his satisfaction with the close relationship that the two animation studios have developed with each other: "Disney is the only company with animation in their DNA."[13] In fact, the acquisition of Pixar was viewed as an attempt by Disney to acquire a group in which the talent of the individuals and the quality of the finished product are valued above everything else. Disney CEO Iger has been hoping that his firm will not only be able to preserve the culture of Pixar but also be able to import parts of it into Disney's own animation unit, whose greatest successes, *The Lion King* and *Aladdin,* date back to 1994 and 1992.

To ensure this goal, Pixar president Ed Catmull was given charge of the combined animation business of both Pixar and Disney. Apart from continuing to manage Pixar, Catmull has been working hard to get Disney's animated film division back into space after a long run of lackluster movies. Disney Studios chairman Dick Cook referred to Catmull as one of the fathers of computer-generated animation, adding: "Ed sets the tone in the way he works, his accessibility and willingness to look at things."[14]

More significantly, Pixar's creative force, John Lasseter, was saddled with the role of chief creative officer of the combined company as well as the role of adviser for Disney's Imagineering division, which designs attractions for the theme parks. In an unusual arrangement within a hierarchical firm such as Disney, Lasseter reports directly to Iger. For Lasseter, his new responsibilities for Disney represent a return to his roots. He had been inspired by Disney films as a kid, and he started his career at Disney before being lured away to Pixar by Catmull. "For many of us at Pixar, it was the magic of Disney that influenced us to pursue our dreams of becoming animators, artists, storytellers and filmmakers," Lasseter recently stated.[15]

Catmull and Lasseter continue to face a challenging task. They must ensure that they keep developing hits for Pixar even as they try to turn things around at Disney. In particular, there are concerns about the ability of Pixar to hold on to the creative talent behind its recent hits. But both Catmull and Lasseter are confident that they can maintain their group while being part of Disney. "We created the studio we want to work in," Lasseter remarked recently. "We have an environment that's wacky. It's a creative brain trust: It's not a place where I make my movies—it's a place where a group of people make movies."[16]

Endnotes

1. Laura M. Holson. Disney Agrees to Acquire Pixar in a $7.4 Billion Deal. *New York Times,* January 25, 2006, p. C6.
2. Peter Burrows and Ronald Grover. Steve Jobs: Movie Mogul. *BusinessWeek,* November 23, 1998, p. 150.
3. Ibid
4. Ibid., p. 146.
5. Ibid.
6. Marc Graser. Pixar Run by Focused Group. *Variety,* December 20, 1999, p. 74.
7. *Ibid*
8. *BusinessWeek,* November 23, 1998, p. 146.
9. Andrew Bary. Coy Story. *Barron's,* October 13, 2003, p. 21.
10. Pui-Wing Tam. Will Quantity Hurt Pixar's Quality? *Wall Street Journal,* February 15, 2001, p. B4.
11. Peter Burrows and Ronald Grover. Steve Jobs' Magic Kingdom. *BusinessWeek,* February 6, 2006, p. 66.
12. Brooks Barnes. For Disney and Pixar, a Smooth (So Far) Ride. *International Herald Tribune,* June 2, 2008, p. 9.
13. *New York Times,* January 25, 2006, p. C6.
14. Nick Wingfield and Merissa Marr. A Techie's Task: Drawing Pixar's Magic to Disney. *Wall Street Journal,* January 30, 2006, p. B7.
15. Charles Solomon. Pixar Creative Chief to Seek to Restore the Disney Magic. *New York Times,* January 25, 2006.
16. Bary. Coy Story.

Case 18   Johnson & Johnson*

On January 23, 2009, health care conglomerate Johnson & Johnson announced the completion of its $1.1 billion acquisition of Mentor Corporation, a leading supplier of medical products for the global aesthetic market. J&J was the first major U.S. drug company to get into the cosmetic medicine market, doing so with the launch of its injectable wrinkle-filler Evolence during the previous year. The $4.6 billion market for such products is expected to grow to $6.7 billion by 2012. "It's a natural extension of where J&J would want to go," said Michael Weinstein, an analyst at JPMorgan Chase & Company.[1]

J&J has used such acquisitions to grow over the years. Just two years ago, the firm bought the consumer health unit of Pfizer for $16.6 billion, the biggest acquisition in its 120-year history. William C. Weldon, the firm's chief executive, is aware that it is getting much harder for J&J to spot smaller firms with promising drugs and to avoid running up against other firms that want to make the same kinds of deals. "You get to a point where finding acquisitions that fit the mold and make a contribution becomes increasingly difficult," warned UBS Warburg analyst David Lothson.[2]

Weldon recently told investors that his firm would search for other avenues for growth: "We'll come at it from a variety of different ways, to accelerate top- and bottom-line growth."[3] Given the scope of the businesses that J&J manages, he believes that the best opportunities may come from increased collaboration between its different units. The firm has the ability to develop new products by combining its strengths across pharmaceutical products, medical devices and diagnostics, and consumer products.

J&J desperately needs to find new avenues for growth. It was already alerting investors that its revenue for 2009 would show a drop from the previous year, the first decline the firm has experienced in its 120-year history (see Exhibits 1 and 2). Sales of its consumer products were slowing as a result of a decrease in the disposable income of its customers. Its pharmaceutical business was being affected by the expiration of patents on some of its best-selling drugs and by the growth of competition from generic drugs. "We are seeing some signs that consumers and patients are becoming more frugal," said Weldon. "There is downward pressure in lots of areas of health care."[4]

In fact, J&J is embarking on its biggest shake-up since Weldon took charge of the firm in 2002. It is elevating one of its rising stars, Nicholas Valeriani, to lead an office that will push for greater interaction between J&J's 250 different

*This case was developed by Professor Jamal Shamsie, Michigan State University, with the assistance of Professor Alan B. Eisner, Pace University. Material has been drawn from published sources to be used for class discussion.
Copyright © 2009 Jamal Shamsie and Alan B. Eisner.

operating companies to squeeze more value from areas where they overlap. But Weldon is also acutely aware that much of the success of J&J over the years has been based on the relative autonomy and independence that it has accorded its various business units. Any push for greater collaboration must not threaten the strong entrepreneurial spirit that has been fostered through the firm's reliance on this type of organization.

Fostering Entrepreneurship

J&J has relied heavily on acquisitions to enter into and expand into a wide range of businesses that fall broadly under the category of health care. Over the last decade alone, the firm has spent nearly $50 billion on 70 different purchases. In the last few months of 2008, J&J made two small acquisitions to move into the area of wellness and protection, which has been growing in the United States and Europe. Firms in this business focus on creating systems to foster and monitor healthy behavior among employees.

As it has grown, J&J has developed into an astonishingly complex enterprise, made up of over 250 different businesses organized into three different divisions. The most widely known of these is the division that makes consumer products such as Johnson & Johnson baby care products, Band-Aid adhesive strips, and Listerine mouthwash. The consumer products division has provided the firm with several strong brands that have generated a steady stream of revenue. "You don't have to deal with the volatility that you have in pharmaceuticals and devices," explained Weldon.[5] But pharmaceutical products and medical devices have allowed the firm to reap huge profits from blockbuster drugs such as anemia drug Procrit, schizophrenia drug Risperdal, and Cyper coronary stents. Such products generally provide operating profit margins of around 30 percent, almost double those generated by the consumer business.

To a large extent, however, J&J's success across its three divisions and many different businesses has hinged on its unique structure and culture. Most of its far-flung business units were acquired because of the potential demonstrated by some promising new products in their pipelines. Each of these units was therefore granted nearly total autonomy to develop and expand on its best-selling products (see Exhibit 3). That independence has fostered an entrepreneurial attitude that has kept J&J intensely competitive as others around it have faltered. The relative autonomy that is accorded to the business units has also provided the firm with the ability to respond swiftly to emerging opportunities.

In other words, the business units have been given considerable freedom to develop and execute their own strategies. In addition, these units have been allowed to work

Exhibit 1 Income Statement (in thousands of dollars)

Period Ending:	2008	2007	2006
Total revenue	63,747,000	61,095,000	53,324,000
Cost of revenue	18,511,000	17,751,000	15,057,000
Gross profit	45,236,000	43,344,000	38,267,000
Operating expenses:			
Research and development	7,577,000	7,680,000	7,125,000
Selling, general, and administrative	21,490,000	20,451,000	17,433,000
Nonrecurring	181,000	1,552,000	559,000
Operating income or loss	15,988,000	13,661,000	13,150,000
Income from continuing operations:			
Total other income/expenses net	1,376,000	(82,000)	1,500,000
Earnings before interest and taxes	17,364,000	13,579,000	14,650,000
Interest expense	435,000	296,000	63,000
Income before tax	16,929,000	13,283,000	14,587,000
Income tax expense	3,980,000	2,707,000	3,534,000
Net income from continuing ops	12,949,000	10,576,000	11,053,000
Net income	12,949,000	10,576,000	11,053,000

Source: J&J.

with their own resources. Many of the businesses even have their own finance and human resource departments. While this degree of decentralization entails relatively high overhead costs, none of the executives who have run J&J, Weldon included, has ever thought that this was too high a price to pay. "The company really operates more like a mutual fund than anything else," commented Pat Dorsey, director of equity research at Morningstar.[6]

In spite of the benefits that J&J has derived from giving its various enterprises considerable autonomy, there is a growing feeling that these businesses can no longer operate in near isolation. Weldon has begun to realize, as do most others in the industry, that some of the most important breakthroughs in 21st-century medicine are likely to come from the ability to apply scientific advances in one discipline to another. J&J should therefore be in a strong position to exploit new opportunities by drawing on the diverse skills of its various business units across the three divisions.

Restructuring for Synergies

Weldon strongly believes that J&J is perfectly positioned to profit from the shift toward combining drugs, devices, and diagnostics, since few companies can match its reach and strength in these basic areas. Indeed, J&J has top-notch products in each of those categories (see Exhibit 4). It has been boosting its research and development budget by more than 10 percent annually for the past few years, which puts it among the top spenders (see Exhibit 5). It now spends about 13 percent of its sales, over $7 billion, on more than 9,000 scientists working in research laboratories around the world.

Weldon believes, however, that J&J can profit from convergence by finding ways to make its fiercely independent businesses work together. In his own words, "There is a convergence that will allow us to do things we haven't done before."[7] Through pushing the various far-flung units of the firm to pool their resources, Weldon believes that the firm could become one of the few that may actually be able to attain that often-promised, rarely delivered idea of synergy.

In November 2007, J&J announced that it was breaking up its medical devices division into two groups, surgery and comprehensive care. The surgery unit will continue to work on its lucrative hip and knee replacement products, while the comprehensive unit will focus on diseases such as diabetes with a more integrated approach. For example, it will harness expertise from J&J's diagnostic tests to catch diabetes earlier and from its glucose monitoring arm to help patients living with the disease.

Although J&J is breaking up one of its divisions, Weldon views this as an opportunity to have the firm's various units working with one another to address different

Exhibit 2   Balance Sheet (in thousands of dollars)

Period Ending:	2008	2007	2006
Assets			
Current assets:			
Cash and cash equivalents	10,768,000	7,770,000	4,083,000
Short-term investments	2,041,000	1,545,000	1,000
Net receivables	13,149,000	12,053,000	10,806,000
Inventory	5,052,000	5,110,000	4,889,000
Other current assets	3,367,000	3,467,000	3,196,000
Total current assets	**34,377,000**	**29,945,000**	**22,975,000**
Long-term investments	4,000	2,000	16,000
Property, plant, and equipment	14,365,000	14,185,000	13,044,000
Goodwill	13,719,000	14,123,000	13,340,000
Intangible assets	13,976,000	14,640,000	15,348,000
Other assets	2,630,000	3,170,000	2,623,000
Deferred long-term asset charges	5,841,000	4,889,000	3,210,000
Total assets	**84,912,000**	**80,954,000**	**70,556,000**
Liabilities and Equity			
Current liabilities:			
Accounts payable	17,120,000	17,374,000	14,582,000
Short/current long-term debt	3,732,000	2,463,000	4,579,000
Other current liabilities	—	—	—
Total current liabilities	**20,852,000**	**19,837,000**	**19,161,000**
Long-term debt	8,120,000	7,074,000	2,014,000
Other liabilities	11,997,000	9,231,000	8,744,000
Deferred long-term liability charges	1,432,000	1,493,000	1,319,000
Total liabilities	**42,401,000**	**37,635,000**	**31,238,000**
Stockholders' equity:			
Common stock	3,120,000	3,120,000	3,120,000
Retained earnings	63,379,000	55,280,000	49,290,000
Treasury stock	(19,033,000)	(14,388,000)	(10,974,000)
Other stockholders' equity	(4,955,000)	(693,000)	(2,118,000)
Total stockholders' equity	**42,511,000**	**43,319,000**	**39,318,000**
Net tangible assets	**14,816,000**	**14,556,000**	**10,630,000**

Source: J&J.

Exhibit 3 Segment Information

Johnson & Johnson is made up of over 250 different companies, many of which it has acquired over the years. These individual companies have been assigned to three different divisions:

	Pharmaceuticals	Medical Devices	Consumer Products
Share of firm's sales:			
2008	39%	36%	25%
2007	41	36	24
2004	47	36	18
2001	46	35	20
Share of firm's operating profits:			
2008	43	41	15
2007	48	35	17
2004	60	31	11
2001	63	25	12

Sales by Segment (in billions of dollars)

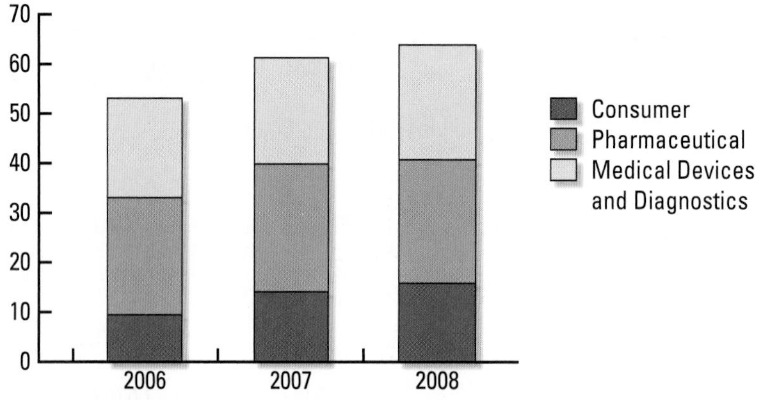

Legend: Consumer; Pharmaceutical; Medical Devices and Diagnostics

Source: J&J.

health problems. He has appointed Valeriani to head the new Office of Strategy and Growth that will attempt to get business units to work together on promising new opportunities. "It's a recognition that there's a way to treat disease that's not in silos," Weldon stated, referring to J&J's largely independent businesses.[8]

Such a push for communication and coordination will allow J&J to develop the synergy that Weldon has been seeking. But any effort to get the different business units to collaborate must not quash the entrepreneurial spirit that has spearheaded most of the growth of the firm to date. Jerry Caccott, managing director of consulting firm Strategic Decisions Group, emphasized that cultivating those alliances "would be challenging in any organization, but particularly in an organization that has been so successful because of its decentralized culture."[9]

Benefiting from Collaboration

Weldon, like every other leader in the company's history, has worked his way up through the ranks. His long tenure within the firm has turned him into a true believer in the J&J system. He certainly does not want to undermine the entrepreneurial spirit that has resulted from the autonomy that has been given to each of the businesses. Consequently, even though Weldon may talk incessantly about synergy and convergence, he has been cautious in the actual steps he has taken to push J&J's units to collaborate with each other.

For the most part, Weldon has confined himself to taking steps that foster better communication and more frequent collaboration among J&J's disparate operations. Besides appointing Valeriani, he has worked with James T. Lenehan, vice chairman and president of J&J, to set up groups that

Exhibit 4 Key Brands

Pharmaceuticals
Risperdal for schizophrenia
Procrit for anemia
Remicade for rheumatoid arthritis
Topamax for epilepsy
Duragesic for chronic pain
Doxil for ovarian cancer

Medical Devices
Depuy orthopedic joint reconstruction products
Cordis Cypher stents
Ethicon surgery products

Pharmaceutical Segment Sales
Sales by Major Product
(in billions of dollars)*
2008 Sales: $24.6 billion   Growth Rate: (1.2%)

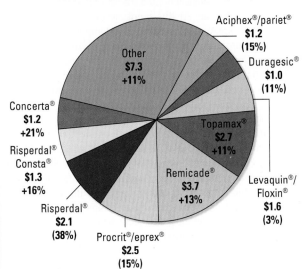

*Includes rounding.

Medical Devices & Diagnostics Segment Sales
Sales by Major Franchise
(in billions of dollars)*
2008 Sales: $23.1 billion   Growth Rate: 6.4%

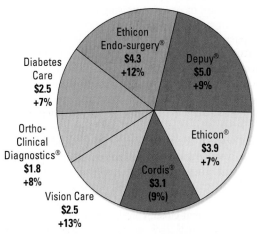

*Includes rounding.

Consumer Products
Band-Aid bandages
Johnson & Johnson baby care products
Neutrogena skin and hair care products
Listerine oral health care products
Tylenol pain killers
Rolaids antacids
Benadryl cold and cough syrups
Bengay pain relief ointments
Tuck's hemorrhoidal ointments
Visine eye drops
Rogaine hair regrowth treatments
Stayfree women's health products
Splenda sweeteners

Source: J&J.

Consumer Segment Sales
Sales by Major Franchise
(in billions of dollars)*
2008 Sales: $16.0 billion   Growth Rate: 10.8%

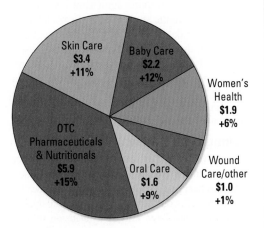

*Includes rounding.

Exhibit 5 Research Expenditures (in millions of dollars)

2008	7,577
2007	7,680
2006	7,125
2005	6,462

Source: J&J.

draw people from across the firm to focus their efforts on specific diseases. Each of the groups has been reporting every six months on potential strategies and projects.

Perhaps the most promising result of this new collaborative approach has been J&J's drug-coated stent, called Cypher. The highly successful new addition to the firm's lineup was a result of the efforts of teams that combined people from the drug business with others from the device business. They collaborated on manufacturing the stent, which props open arteries after angioplasty. Weldon claims that if J&J had not been able to bring together people with different types of expertise, it could not have developed the stent without getting assistance from outside the firm.

Even the company's fabled consumer brands have been starting to show growth as a result of increased collaboration between the consumer products and pharmaceutical divisions. Its new liquid Band-Aid is based on a material used in a wound-closing product sold by one of J&J's hospital-supply businesses, and J&J has used its prescription antifungal treatment, Nizoral, to develop a dandruff shampoo. In fact, products that have developed in large part out of such business-unit cross-fertilization have allowed the firm's consumer business to experience considerable internal growth.

Some of the projects that J&J is currently working on could produce even more significant results. Researchers working on genomic studies in the firm's labs were building a massive database using gene patterns that correlate to a certain disease or to someone's likely response to a particular drug. Weldon encouraged them to share this data with the various business units. As a result, the diagnostics team has been working on a test that the researchers in the pharmaceutical division could use to predict which patients would benefit from an experimental cancer therapy.

Dealing with Setbacks

Even as Weldon moves carefully to encourage collaboration between the business units, he has continued to push for the highest possible levels of performance. Those who know him well would say that he is compulsively competitive. Weldon has been known to state on more than one occasion that "it's no fun to be second."[10] He is such an intense athlete that he was just a sprint away from ruining his knee altogether when he finally decided to give up playing basketball.

For the most part, however, Weldon is known for letting his managers, working across J&J's units, make their own decisions on various projects. He usually likes to get briefed once a month on the progress that is being made on these projects. Beyond that, Weldon claims that he likes to trust his people. "They are the experts who know the marketplace, know the hospitals, and know the cardiologists," he once said about the team that worked on the Cypher stent. "I have the utmost confidence in them."[11] But for those executives who may fall short, Weldon does not usually have any difficulty in making it clear that he does not like to be disappointed.

Above all, Weldon is not discouraged by setbacks, such as those J&J has been facing in its pharmaceutical business, which has accounted for more than 40 percent of the firm's revenue. At this point, several of J&J's important drugs are under assault from competitors. Its well-known anemia drug Procrit has been dealing with rising competition and with growing safety concerns. Top-selling Risperdal, Duragesic, and Topamax drugs will start facing generic rivals in 2009. Furthermore, a new antipsychosis drug called Invega, recently launched to replace Risperdal, has not been able to meet sales expectations.

J&J has also been facing some challenges with sales of its medical devices. It has been losing sales on its well-selling Cypher stents because of concerns over their safety that have been raised in several studies. Additionally, these drug-coated stents have been facing growing competition from other strong rivals. To make things worse, J&J had to withdraw a promising new stent from Connor Medsystems, a recent acquisition, after it failed in trials in early summer 2007.

However, analysts believe that J&J has been working hard on developing new pharmaceutical drugs and medical devices. "We think they have a pretty good pipeline," remarked Jason Napodano, an anlayst with Zacks.[12] J&J has stated that it is on target to seek regulatory approval for up to 10 new drugs, including treatments for cancer, autoimmune diseases, and HIV. One of its promising new drugs for rheumatoid arthritis could be approved within a few months. "We're optimistic about our short and long term prospects," said Christine Poon, the head of the firm's pharmaceutical division, who has announced she will be retiring soon.[13]

Is There a Cure Ahead?

Weldon realizes that J&J may face a few challenges over the next couple of years as it tries to push out new products in a tough economic environment. But the firm's diversified portfolio of products spread across various areas of health care has helped it to weather the economic downturn with few problems. In particular, J&J has managed to offset its loss of sales in pharmaceuticals and devices with relatively stable earnings from its consumer products. "With interests spread out all over the health-care industry, J&J does not live or die by any one product," remarked Herman Saftlas, a pharmaceutical analyst for Standard & Poor's.[14]

However, Weldon is aware that he needs to keep pushing his firm to find new opportunities to expand across various areas of health care. Even as he seeks growth, Weldon is also trying to move J&J away from its pattern of heavy reliance on acquisitions. With fewer and smaller acquisitions, he will need to find ways to get the various business units to come up with sufficient new ideas to maintain his firm's growth trajectory. His decisions to break up the medical devices unit and to appoint Valeriani have been designed to generate more internal growth as a result of greater interaction between the different units.

The moves that Weldon has made may generate more collaboration between the different business units of J&J. At the same time, it is not clear that the recent changes will be enough to produce the growth that he desires. Catherine Arnold, a drug industry analyst at Credit Suisse, feels that J&J may have to push harder. "Just making these management changes is not enough," she stated. "I'd see this as a step among many to face a more challenging business environment. It's a way to eliminate some of the obstacles that their structure creates."[15]

Weldon is aware that he can maintain J&J's record growth only by finding ways to encourage its businesses to work more closely together than they ever did in the past. The firm can tap into many more opportunities when it brings together the various skills that it has developed across different divisions. At the same time, Weldon is acutely aware that much of the firm's success has resulted from the relative autonomy that it has granted to each of its business units. Even as he strives to push for more collaborative effort, Weldon does not want to threaten the entrepreneurial spirit that has served J&J so well.

Endnotes

1. Shirley S. Wang & Rhonda L. Rundle. J&J to Acquire Breast-Implant Maker. *Wall Street Journal,* December 2, 2008, p. B1.
2. Amy Barrett. Staying on Top. *Business Week,* May 5, 2003, p. 61.
3. Christopher Bowe. J&J Reveals Its Guidant Motive. *Financial Times,* January 25, 2006, p. 17.
4. Peter Loftus & Shirley S. Wang. J&J Sales Show Health Care Feels the Pinch. *Wall Street Journal,* January 21, 2009, p. B1.
5. Avery Johnson. J&J's Consumer Play Paces Growth. *Wall Street Journal,* January 24, 2007, p. A3.
6. Holly Hubbard Preston. Drug Giant Provides a Model of Consistency. *Herald Tribune,* March 12–13, 2005, p. 12.
7. Barrett. Staying on Top, p. 62.
8. Avery Johnson. J&J Realigns Managers, Revamps Units. *Wall Street Journal,* November 16, 2007, p. A10.
9. Barrett. Staying on Top, p. 62.
10. Ibid.
11. Ibid, p. 66.
12. Johanna Bennett. J&J: A Balm for Your Portfolio. *Barron's,* October 27, 2008, p. 39.
13. Jonathan D. Rockoff. J&J Profit Rises; Firm Boosts Its Forecast. *Wall Street Journal,* October 15, 2008, p. B5.
14. Bennett. J&J.
15. Johnson. J&J Realigns Managers.

Case 19 Samsung Electronics*

In January 2009, Samsung Electronics began to slim down its operations into two divisions from the five separate ones that it had a year earlier. The sets division, called digital media and communications, will focus on consumer products such as television and mobile phones. The parts unit, called device solutions, will handle electronic components such as semiconductors and LCD panels. The firm had already merged its home appliance division, which made refrigerators and air conditioners, with its digital media section over the previous year.

The reorganization followed on the heels of a major shake-up of top executives at Samsung Electronics. In the aftermath of a tax evasion scandal involving the parent firm, Yun Jong Yong, the electronic firm's long-term CEO, was replaced in May 2008 by Lee Yoon Woo. In addition, the firm has begun to appoint several younger executives to its leadership team and reassign two-thirds of its executives to different positions. "There has been a sense of crisis in the company for more than one year," said one senior manager. "Radical change is in store."[1]

The moves represented a major effort to streamline operations to better address worsening economic conditions. Four years ago, the market value of Samsung had risen above $100 billion, making it one of only four Asian companies to move above that mark. Based in Suwon, South Korea, the firm moved past well-known rivals such as Sony, Nokia, and Motorola on the basis of its revolutionary products. Its feature-jammed gadgets have racked up numerous design awards, and the company has been rapidly muscling its way to the top of consumer brand-awareness surveys.

However, in spite of these advances, Samsung has not been able to deal with the growing impact of the global economic slowdown. Although the firm has been able to boast of having a lower cost structure than most of its rivals, it was expected to announce its first-ever quarterly loss, for the last quarter of 2008. (See Exhibits 1 and 2.) Much of the downturn could be attributed to an overcapacity in the global production of memory chips and liquid crystal displays, which has forced down prices. This may ease over the next couple of years as many of Samsung's smaller rivals are dropping their plans to expand capacity.

Among all the changes that Samsung has been making, analysts have paid particular attention to the appointment of Choi Gee Sung to head the newly formed digital media and communications unit. Choi's appointment signifies a break from the firm's tradition of picking top managers

*This case was developed by Professor Jamal Shamsie, Michigan State University, with the assistance of Professor Alan B. Eisner, Pace University. Material has been drawn from published sources to be used for class discussion. Copyright © 2009 Jamal Shamsie and Alan B. Eisner.

Exhibit 1 Income Statement (in trillions of Korean won, year-end December 31)

	2008	2007	2006	2005	2004
Net sales	121,294	98,508	85,426	80,630	81,963
Gross profit	31,532	27,627	25,779	25,378	29,010
Operating profit	6,031	8,973	9,008	7,575	11,761
Net income	5,525	7,421	7,926	7,640	10,790

Source: Samsung.

Exhibit 2 Balance Sheet (in trillions of Korean won, year-end December 31)

	2008	2007	2006	2005	2004
Total assets	105,301	93,375	81,366	74,462	69,005
Total liabilities	47,186	37,404	33,426	32,854	32,604
Total shareholders' equity	58,117	55,972	47,940	41,607	36,400

Source: Samsung.

with backgrounds in engineering. In fact, Choi is likely to take over as Samsung's next CEO when Lee relinquishes this post. Referring to the shift away from its heavy focus on technology, Kang Shin Woo, chief investment officer at fund manager Korea Investment Trust Management, said, "Samsung's benchmark is shifting from Japanese companies to innovators like Apple."[2]

Discarding a Failing Strategy

The transformation of Samsung into a premier brand can be attributed to the ceaseless efforts of Yun Jong Yong, who was appointed to the position of president and CEO in 1996. When Yun took charge, Samsung was still making most of its profits from lower-priced appliances that consumers were likely to pick up if they could not afford a higher-priced brand such as Sony or Mitsubishi. The firm had also become an established low-cost supplier of various components to larger and better-known manufacturers around the world.

Although Samsung was making profits, Yun was concerned about the future prospects of a firm that was relying on a strategy of competing on price with products that were based on technologies that had been developed by other firms. The success of this strategy was tied to the ability of Samsung to continually scout for locations that would allow it to keep its manufacturing costs down. At the same time, it would need to keep generating sufficient orders to maintain a high volume of production. In particular, Yun was concerned about the growing competition that the firm was likely to face from the many low-cost producers that were springing up in other countries such as China.

Yun's concerns were well founded. Within a year of his takeover, Samsung was facing serious financial problems that threatened its very survival. The company was left with huge debt as an economic crisis engulfed most of Asia in 1997, leading to a drop in demand and a crash in the prices of many electronic goods. In the face of such a deteriorating environment, Samsung continued to push for maintaining its production and sales records even as much of its output was ending up unsold in warehouses.

By July 1998, Samsung Electronics was losing millions of dollars each month. "If we continued, we would have gone belly-up within three or four years," Yun recalled.[3] He knew that he had to make some drastic moves in order to turn things around. Yun locked himself in a hotel room for a whole day with nine other senior managers to try and find a way out. They all wrote resignation letters and pledged to resign if they failed.

After much deliberation, Yun and his management team decided to take several steps to try to push Samsung out of its precarious financial position. To begin with, they decided to lay off about 30,000 employees, representing well over one-third of the firm's entire workforce. They also closed down many of Samsung's factories for two months so that they could get rid of its large inventory. Finally, they sold off about $2 billion worth of businesses like pagers and electric coffeemakers that were perceived to be of marginal significance for the firm's future.

Developing a Premium Brand

Having managed to stem the losses, Yun decided to move Samsung away from its strategy of competition based largely on the lower price of its offerings. Consequently, he began to push the firm to develop its own products rather than copying those that other firms had developed. (See Exhibit 3.) In particular, Yun placed considerable emphasis on the development of products that would impress consumers with their attractive designs and their advanced technology. By focusing on such products, Yun hoped that he could develop Samsung into a premium brand that would allow him to charge higher prices.

To achieve this, Yun had to reorient the firm and help it to develop new capabilities. He recruited new managers and engineers, many of whom had developed considerable experience in the United States. Once they had been recruited, Yun got them into shape by putting them through a four-week boot camp that consisted of martial drills at the crack of dawn and mountain hikes that would last all day. To create incentives for this new talent, Yun discarded Samsung's rigid seniority-based system and replaced it with a merit-based system for advancement.

As a result of these efforts, Samsung began launching an array of products that were designed to make a big impression on consumers. They included the largest flat-panel televisions, cell phones with a variety of features such as cameras and PDAs, ever-thinner notebook computers. and speedier and richer semiconductors. (See Exhibit 4.) The firm calls them "wow products," and they are designed to elevate Samsung in the same way the Trinitron television and the Walkman had helped to plant Sony in the minds of consumers.

A large part of the success of Samsung's products can be tied to its efforts to focus on the specific needs of prospective customers. Mike Linton, executive vice president of Best Buy, stated that Samsung regularly gets information from retailers about the new features that customers want to see in their electronic devices. This close link with retailers helped Samsung to come up with two of its recent best-selling products: a combined DVD-VCR player and a cellular phone that also functions as a PDA. According to Graeme Bateman, head of research for Japanese investment bank Nomura Securities, "Samsung is no longer making poor equivalents of Sony products. It is making things people want."[4]

Finally, to help Samsung change its image among consumers, Yun hired a marketing whiz, Eric Kim, who has worked hard to create a more upscale image of the firm and its products. Kim moved Samsung's advertising away from 55 different advertising agencies around the world and placed it with one firm, Madison Avenue's Foote, Cone & Belding Worldwide, to create a consistent global brand image for its products. He also begun to pull Samsung out of big discount chains like Wal-Mart and Kmart and place more of its products into upscale specialty stores such as Best Buy and Circuit City.

Pushing for New Products

Yun took many steps to speed up Samsung's new product development process. He was well aware that Samsung would be able to maintain its higher margins only as long as his firm could keep introducing new products into the market well ahead of its established rivals. Samsung managers who have worked for big competitors say they have to go through far fewer layers of bureaucracy than they had to in the past to win approval for new products, budgets, and marketing plans, and this speeds up their ability to seize opportunities.

Apart from reducing the bureaucratic obstacles, Yun made heavy investments in key technologies ranging from semiconductors to LCD displays that could allow the firm to push out a wide variety of revolutionary digital products. Samsung has continuously invested more than any of its rivals in research and development, with the amount rising during the past couple of years to almost 9 percent of its revenue. It has a large force of designers and engineers working in 17 research centers located throughout the world. (See Exhibit 5.) Yun also forced the firm's own units to compete with outsiders in order to speed up the

Exhibit 3   Revenue Breakdown (in trillions of Korean won, year-end December 31)

	Year	Sales	Profits
Semiconductors Includes DRAMs, SRAMs & NAND flash chips	2007	22.3	2.3
	2006	22.8	5.1
	2005	20.3	5.4
	2004	20.2	7.8
Telecommunications Includes digital phones and handsets	2007	23.8	2.8
	2006	20.2	2.0
	2005	20.9	2.5
	2004	20.7	3.1
Digital media Includes plasma and projection displays and televisions	2007	26.5	1.1
	2006	20.7	0.7
	2005	17.7	0.2
	2004	17.6	0.4
LCD Includes panels for desktop and laptop computers	2007	17.1	2.1
	2006	13.9	0.8
	2005	8.7	0.6
	2004	7.8	1.9
Digital appliances Includes "intelligent" refrigerators, microwave ovens, air conditioners	2007	6.9	0.2
	2006	5.5	−0.1
	2005	5.6	−0.1
	2004	5.4	0.1

Source: Samsung.

process of developing innovative new products. In the liquid-crystal-display business, Samsung bought half of its color filters from Sumitomo Chemical Company of Japan and sourced the other half internally, pitting the two teams against each other. "They really press these departments to compete," said Sumitomo President Hiromasa Yonekura.[5]

As a result of these steps, Samsung claims that the time it takes to go from new product concept to rollout is now as little as five months, compared to over a year that it used to take the firm just eight years ago. In large part, this has resulted from the effort of the firm's top managers, engineers, and designers, who work relentlessly in the five-story VIP center nestled amid the firm's industrial complex in Suwon. They work day and night in the center, which includes dormitories and showers for brief rests, to work out any problems that may hold back a product launch.

The progress made by teams that pursue new product designs in the VIP center makes it possible for Samsung to reduce complexity in the early stages of the design cycle. This allows the firm to move its products quickly to manufacturing with minimal problems and at the lowest possible cost. In turn, this can lead to a faster market launch of a product that is likely to be more innovative than all others. Kyunghan Jung, a senior manager of the center, explained: "Seventy to eighty percent of quality, cost and delivery time is determined in the initial stages of product development."[6] Such an emphasis on early design issues allowed Samsung to figure out how the D600, one of its latest music-playing camera phones, could be assembled in as little as eight seconds.

The speedier development process has allowed Samsung to introduce the first voice-activated phones, handsets with MP3 players, and digital camera phones that send photos over global systems for mobile communications networks. The firm has been just as fast in digital televisions, becoming the first to market projection TVs using new chips

Exhibit 4   Global Market Ranking, 2007

Product Category	Market Rank
Memory chips	1
Computer monitors	1
LCD panels	1
LCD TVs	1
Plasma TVs	1
DVD-VCR combos	1
Projection TVs	2
DVD players	2
MP3 players	2
Laser printers	2
Mobile phones	2
Microwave ovens	3
Camcorders	4

Source: Samsung.

Exhibit 5   Designers Employed

2006	550
2004	470
2002	310
2000	210
1998	170

Source: Samsung.

from Texas Instruments that employ digital-light processing. DLP chips contain 1.3 million micromirrors that flip at high speeds to create a sharper picture. Texas Instruments had given Japanese companies the technology early in 1999, but they never figured out how to make the TV sets economically. George Danko, Best Buy's senior vice president for consumer electronics, said of Samsung, "They'll get a product to market a lot faster than their counterparts."[7]

Designing for the Digital Home

Yun was hoping that Samsung's advances in digital technologies would increase its chances of dominating the digital home. He believed that his firm was in a better position to benefit from the day that all home appliances from handheld computers to intelligent refrigerators will be linked to one another and adapted to the personal needs of consumers.

In particular, Samsung appears to be well placed to take advantage of its capabilities to design and manufacture a wide array of products that straddle traditional technology categories. "We have to combine computers, consumer electronics and communications as Koreans mix their rice with vegetables and meats," said Dae Je Chin, the head of Samsung's digital media division.[8]

Yun worked closely with Chin to summon engineers and designers from across the firm to mix wireless, semiconductor, and computer expertise in order to pursue its vision of domination of the digital home. One such product from the firm is NEXiO, a combined cell phone and handheld computer. The device has a 5-inch screen, large enough for a user to run a spreadsheet or to browse the Web. Another new offering is a refrigerator called Zipel that has a 15-inch flat-panel touch screen tucked into the door. The display can be used to surf the Internet and to send or receive e-mail.

In developing these products, Samsung has begun to place a lot of emphasis on the role of design in making its products irresistible in an increasingly competitive marketplace. Since 2000, the firm has opened or expanded design centers in San Francisco, London, Tokyo, Los Angeles, and Shanghai. (See Exhibit 6.) Inside these centers, designers observe the way that consumers actually use various products. They may watch, from behind a two-way mirror, how consumers stuff a refrigerator with bagfuls of groceries. Samsung has also begun to send its growing group of designers to various locations to spend a few months at fashion houses, furniture designers, and cosmetic specialists to stay current with trends in other industries.

Furthermore, Samsung created the post of chief design officer to make sure that designers can get their ideas to top managers. A successful rear-projection television was developed by a designer who pitched it to one of the heads of television production. Engineers are pushed to find ways to work with the designs that are presented to them. As a result of these efforts, Samsung has earned numerous citations at top design contests in the United States, Europe, and Asia. After winning 46 awards at a recent U.S. consumer electronics show, D. J. Oh, CEO of Samsung Electronics America, said, "Samsung strives to consistently lead the consumer electronics industry in product design and engineering innovation."[9]

Samsung has been relying on the attractiveness of its products to make them the centerpieces of a digital home. It has been displaying its version of a networked home in Seoul's Tower Palace apartment complex, where 2,400 families can operate appliances from washing machines to air conditioners by tapping on a wireless "Web pad" device, which doubles as a portable flat-screen TV. It may sound a bit futuristic, but when the digital home does become more realistic, Samsung will have a chance. "They've got the products, a growing reputation as the innovator, and production lines to back that up," said In-Stat/MDR consumer-electronics analyst Cindy Wolf.[10]

Exhibit 6   Samsung Milestones

1969	Samsung Electronics is established as a maker of televisions with technology borrowed from Sanyo.
1977	Samsung introduces its first color television.
1981	Samsung begins to focus on undercutting Japanese rivals with me-too products, with little emphasis on design.
1988	Samsung launches its first mobile phone.
1993	Samsung begins to reinvent the firm through design.
1994	Samsung hires design consultancy IDEO to help develop computer monitors.
1995	Samsung sets up its in-house design school, the Innovative Design Lab of Samsung.
1996	Yun Jong Yong takes over as CEO. He declares the "Year of Design Revolution," stressing that designers should lead in product planning.
1998	Asian financial crisis dents Samsung's ambitions, forcing it to cut design staff by 28%.
2000	Samsung once again focuses on design, and CEO Yun Jong Yong calls for design-led management.
2001	Yun initiates quarterly design meetings for top executives and opens design labs in Los Angeles and London.
2002	Samsung's "usability laboratory" is inaugurated in downtown Seoul.
2004	Market value of Samsung rises above $100 billion.
2008	Lee Yoon Woo takes over as CEO from Yun.
2009	Samsung is set to announce its first loss since 2000. The firm announces a major reorganization.

Source: Samsung.

Creating a Sustainable Model?

In spite of all the improvements that Samsung has made over the last decade, the firm is expected to announce its first quarterly loss since its brush with bankruptcy. With the sharp decline in demand, prices for most of the firm's products have been dropping, cutting into its profit margins. The divisional restructuring and the management changes were designed to streamline operations at Samsung to better address the worsening economic conditions. Recently, the firm stated that it hopes to eliminate bureaucracy and speed decision making at a time when flexibility is needed to deal with forces that threaten its existence.

To find new avenues for growth, Samsung recently made an unsuccessful bid to acquire SanDisk Corporation. The offer marked the first time that the firm had attempted a major acquisition. Samsung has mostly relied on organic growth to gain its status as a leading electronics firm. But the acquisition of SanDisk could have helped Samsung to expand its business into storage cards and other products that use advanced flash chips.

Given the failure to acquire SanDisk, Lee appears to be well aware of the challenges that lie ahead for Samsung. The life cycle of most electronics products can be brutally short, with prices tending to drop sharply over time. The profitability of a hardware firm rests on its ability to keep addressing new opportunities such as those offered by Microsoft's launch of the new Windows Vista operating systems. At the same time, it must keep seeking ways to reduce its costs in order to be competitive with lower-margin products.

Samsung has consistently refused to consider branching out like Sony or Apple into music, movies, and games. It has decided against such a move in spite of growing evidence that subscription-to-content can provide a firm with a more lucrative source of revenue. Instead, Yun chose to collaborate with various content and software providers such as Microsoft and Time Warner.

Lee understands that the future of Samsung lies in its ability to keep investing heavily in R&D and keep developing new factories in locations that offer lower costs. Critics point out that Samsung is still searching for a product that would be comparable to Apple's iPod or Sony's Walkman. But industry observers warn that the firm must not back off despite the current squeeze on profits. "It's critical for Samsung that the new leadership keep investing in new technologies and equipment," said Chang In Whan, chief executive at fund manager KTB Asset Management.[11]

Endnotes

1. Moon Ihlwan. Samsung Electronics: Same CEO, New Leadership Team. *BusinessWeek* online, January 19, 2009.
2. Ibid.
3. Frank Gibney, Jr. Samsung Moves Upmarket. *Time,* March 25, 2002, p. 49.

4. Cliff Edwards, Moon Ihlwan, and Pete Engardio. The Samsung Way. *BusinessWeek,* June 16, 2003, p. 60.
5. Peter Lewis. A Perpetual Crisis Machine. *Fortune,* September 19, 2005, p. 65.
6. Edwards, Ihlwan, and Engardio. The Samsung Way, p. 61.
7. Brad Stone. Samsung in Bloom. *Newsweek,* July 15, 2002, p. 34.
8. David Rocks and Moon Ihlwan. Samsung Design. *Business-Week,* December 6, 2004, p. 90.
9. Anonymous. Samsung Electronics Gets 46 CES Innovations Awards for 2009. *Wireless News,* November 24, 2008.
10. Jay Solomon. Seoul Survivors: Back from the Brink. *Wall Street Journal,* June 13, 2002, p. A1.
11. Ihlwan. Samsung Electronics.

Case 20   Lenovo's Purchase of IBM's PC Division*

In 2008, Lenovo Computer, the largest PC manufacturer in China, was still struggling to integrate IBM Corporation's PC division, which it had acquired in May 2005. The $1.25 billion takeover gave instant name recognition to the Chinese company in 160 countries and gave Lenovo an instant worldwide footprint. Until that time, most mergers involving Chinese companies had been foreign acquisitions of Chinese companies. The Lenovo-IBM deal not only went against this tradition but also was the first Chinese acquisition of a high-profile foreign brand. The breakthrough caught the attention and imagination of the world. The new company, including the newly acquired IBM division, would control over one-third of the China market, and it landed itself as the third-largest global personal computer manufacturer in the world.

Although IBM's PC division had cumulative losses of nearly $1 billion in the four years before the sale to Lenovo, the Chinese buyer planned to use its low-cost manufacturing clout to turn the ailing operations around. It also hoped to piggyback on the IBM brand's existing global distribution networks—Lenovo's dominance of the Chinese PC market had yet to be replicated overseas. Three and a half years after the acquisition, the new Lenovo Group made a $200 million profit in the third quarter of 2008. The sales of PCs in the greater China region increased 12 percent over the same period of 2007, but sales in the United States, which were largely acquired from IBM, reported a 4 percent decrease.[1] Although this decrease might be the result of the financial tsunami, it continued to fuel doubts about the wisdom of Lenovo's acquisition.

The Global PC Industry

The PC industry is in a state of rapid transition; thus innovation and the latest technology are necessary for competitiveness in this fierce and mature industry. On September 4, 2001, Hewlett-Packard (HP) announced a $19 billion acquisition of Compaq, a rival computer maker. The merger would consolidate the resources of both companies, and it was perceived as a way to free both companies from some of the cutthroat competition. The merger was partly a result of the burst of the 2001 Internet bubble and of technological changes that jeopardized the core business of both companies.[2]

Yet, despite the competition, the global PC market continued to experience strong growth, and well-established

computer companies such as Dell and HP dominated the industry. With so many choices, customers had increased bargaining power, and they showed less brand loyalty. At the time of the IBM acquisition by Lenovo in 2005, Dell had the largest share of the global PC market, with HP a close second. This situation has hardly changed even in the current PC market, although the rankings of some of the companies have switched. (See Exhibit 1 for the global market share of the PC industry in the first quarter of 2008.)

Company Background

Lenovo was a subsidiary of Legend Holdings Ltd., initially named New Technology Developer Inc. The company was founded by 11 Chinese scientists of the Chinese Academy of Sciences in 1984. Its vision was "to create a company that would bring the advantages of information technology to the Chinese people." Lenovo's product portfolio included personal computers and peripherals in electronic products.[3] By importing foreign computers from big brands such as AST, Hewlett-Packard, and IBM, the group learned how to organize sales channels and how to market PCs.

By 1990, the Legend group had begun to carry out a backward-integration strategy and developed its own PCs to suit Chinese needs. It also extended its business to IT services and integrated software services. Its continual innovation and customer-oriented products secured the brand as the market leader in China for nine consecutive years starting in 1996. (See Exhibit 2 for the PC industry share in China from 2001 to 2004, before the acquisition.)

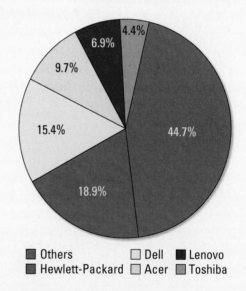

Exhibit 1 Global Market Share of PC Industry, First Quarter 2008

Source: www.enet.com.cn, June 29, 2008.

*The initial research for this case was completed by Pat C. M. Choi, S. C. Lai, Jamie Lam, Sarah S. W. Yeung, and Ada Chan as an assignment for a Current Issues in Business course at the Chinese University of Hong Kong under the direction of Professors Yuan Yi Chen and Michael Young. The purpose of the case is to serve as a basis for classroom discussion rather than to illustrate either effective or ineffective handling of an administrative situation. Copyright © 2009 Michael N. Young.

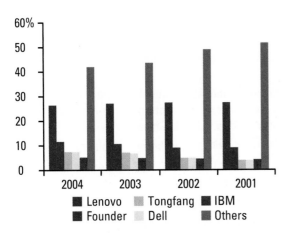

Exhibit 2 PC Industry Market Share in China up to the Acquisition—Top Five PC Companies

Source: Annual Reports of Lenovo Group Ltd., 2002–2005.

To establish a global presence, the company changed its name from Legend to Lenovo in 2001. The new name took *Le* from the old name as a nod to its heritage and added *novo,* which is Latin for "new," to represent the company's spirit of innovation. The new focus was on providing a full-solution portfolio to customers.

With support from Chinese government departments, Lenovo was the giant in the China market. After the market was opened to competition, Lenovo began to feel heat from foreign firms. Even the government bodies started to purchase computers from Dell and other foreign competitors. Small vendors served the low-end market with generic computers built from components of different brands, while big brands such as Dell and HP served the big corporations. This left Lenovo somewhat "stuck in the middle." Yet despite the intensified competition, Lenovo managed to maintain market leadership.

To further its vision of establishing a global brand name, Lenovo acquired IBM's PC division in May 2005. After the acquisition, Lenovo allied with IBM to provide a full range of solutions to customers ranging from small-medium enterprises (SMEs) to large corporations. (See Exhibit 3 for Lenovo's history.)

The Acquisition

Before acquiring IBM, Lenovo was not well known in the global market and all of its sales were from China. Shortly after the acquisition, the chairman of Lenovo, Yang Yuanqing, stated, "Lenovo of China is going to become Lenovo of the world." Lenovo intended to use the acquisition as a platform from which to expand globally. This ambition was in part fueled by the keen competition at home. As famous-brand companies set up production plants in China, they became better at competing in Lenovo's home market. To survive and thrive, Lenovo realized that it needed to establish a global-brand, leading-edge technology and highly efficient operations. It was thought that through the acquisition of IBM's PC division, these needs could be met by leveraging the two companies' core competencies. Lenovo hoped to utilize IBM's global sales capability and international management expertise to achieve more product differentiation and brand building. For IBM, the deal not only would mean shedding a big red figure from its portfolio of businesses but also would serve as a bridge for entering the China market. Without the PC division, IBM could focus on its core business of providing service, software, and server computers to its corporate clients.[4]

The acquisition of IBM's PC division also played a role in China's national plan. China was intent on moving away from being only a manufacturing hub for the rest of the world and wanted to move up the value chain by balancing investment abroad with domestic foreign investment. According to the Ministry of Commerce of the People's Republic of China (PRC), by the end of 2004, Chinese enterprise investment in foreign companies totaled $3.6 billion, a 24 percent rise from 2003. This, however, was only one-thirtieth of the amount of foreign direct investment in China.[5] To relieve pressure from revaluation of the renminbi (RMB), the PRC government was encouraging more Chinese businesses to invest abroad. (See Exhibit 4 for Chinese investment abroad.) Investing overseas, it was hoped, would alleviate some pressure from RMB revaluation.

In essence, China's government hoped to build local Chinese companies into national champions. Learning from past failures, more companies had been going out of China recently. Lenovo, a 57 percent government-owned company, was strongly supported by the Chinese Academy of Sciences, a government body.[6]

The Structure of the Deal In May 2002, John R. Joyce, senior vice president and CFO of IBM, approached Lenovo to sell IBM's underperforming PC division. Since the division had lost nearly $400 million in the previous year, Lenovo initially was not interested. Eighteen months later, as Lenovo began searching for ways to expand globally, Lenovo CFO Mary Ma visited IBM's headquarters in New York and thus began the first round of negotiation.

On December 8, 2004, Lenovo announced its intention to acquire IBM's PC division; the deal was immediately besieged with national security issues. Yet an investigation revealed that the acquisition would not compromise national security–related information. On March 9, 2005, the United States completed the review and approved the deal. The acquisition was finally completed on May 1, 2005.

As consideration for the acquisition, Lenovo paid $1.25 billion to IBM, $650 million in cash and $600 million in Lenovo Group's common stock. Upon closing the deal on May 1, 2005, 35.2 percent of Lenovo was owned by public shareholders, 45.9 percent by Legend Holdings Limited and 18.9 percent by IBM.[7] Through the acquisition, Lenovo gained IBM's PC division and management expertise. IBM was required to provide marketing support

Exhibit 3   Lenovo's Milestones

1984	Scientists establish New Technology Developer Inc., later renamed Legend Holdings Ltd., of which Lenovo was a subsidiary.
1988	Legend's Chinese-character card received the highest National Science-Technology Progress Award. Legend Hong Kong was established as a distributor of major international-brand computer products and peripherals (including those from IBM, AST, and HP) in China.
1990	Legend began to design, manufacture, and distribute its own Legend-brand computers.
1992	Legend pioneered the home PC concepts in China. Legend 1 + 1 home PCs entered the Chinese marketplace.
1995	Legend garnered second place among the top 100 Electronic Enterprises of China for the year.
1996	Legend computers became the market share leader in China for the first time.
1997	Legend signed an intellectual property agreement with Microsoft, the most valuable deal ever made in China at the time.
1999	Legend became the top PC vendor in the Asia-Pacific region.
2000	Legend ranked as one of the world's top 10 PC vendors.
2001	Legend enters a joint venture with America Online (AOL) to develop consumer interactive business in China.
2001	The new logo *Lenovo* is born.
2001	Legend, together with Intel, announced the establishment of the Intel-Lenovo Technology Advancement Center in Beijing.
2004	The English company name is formally changed from Legend Group Limited to Lenovo Group Limited.
2005	Lenovo completes the acquisition of IBM's personal computer division, making it a new international IT competitor and the third-largest personal computer company in the world.
2008	Lenovo technology flawlessly supports the 2008 Olympic Games in Beijing.

Source: Lenovo, www.lenovo.com/us/en, 2008.

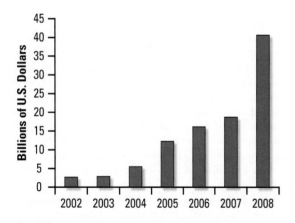

Exhibit 4 Chinese Investment Abroad

Source: Ministry of Commerce of the People's Republic of China.

and help sell Lenovo's products through its global sales force and distribution network.* Lenovo was entitled to use the IBM name for five years and the "Think" name permanently**. Chairman Yang Yuanqing said he might consider cobranding after 18 months, as cobranding would raise Lenovo's global profile.

After the deal, Lenovo became the world's third-largest PC maker, just behind Dell and HP. More than 70 percent of its sales came from overseas. Stephen M. Ward, Jr.,

*IBM had a sales force of 30,000 professionals, an extensive distribution network through IBM.com, and IBM PC specialists who would join Lenovo. IBM Global Financing and IBM Global Services, the number-one IT services organization in the world, with powerful existing enterprise channels, were to be preferred providers to Lenovo for leasing and financing services and for warranty and maintenance services, respectively.

**The Think name included IBM's Thinkpad laptops and Think desktop PCs brand.

the head of IBM's PC business, served as chief executive officer (CEO) and Yang, the former president and CEO of Lenovo, served as chairman after the acquisition. Since December 2005, William Amelio, a former executive with larger rival Dell, has been CEO of the company.

Potential Problems

Target Customer   Before the acquisition, Lenovo generally was targeting the low-end market, consisting of small and medium-size enterprises and home users in China. This cost leadership strategy was successful and resulted in tremendous growth in the domestic market over the previous two decades. In contrast, IBM targeted the higher end of the market, selling PCs primarily to augment server sales and big corporate consulting contracts. It mainly focused on large corporate and education sectors by promoting its products with unique, premium features such as IBM e-business and enhanced customer support.

Management Style   Mary Ma, Lenovo's CFO, stated that Lenovo essentially had a top-down management style.[8] For example, Lenovo had a company song that was played throughout the company's headquarters every morning and was sung by workers at the start of company-wide meetings.[9] Lenovo's management culture resembled that of many traditional Chinese state-owned firms. This heavy-handed culture was demonstrated by a massive lay-off that took place in 2004. Because of a failed strategy proposed by the management level, several hundred staff members were fired with neither beforehand notices nor negotiations.[10]

On the other hand, IBM was a typical American corporation in which speed, flexibility, and innovation were valued. A bottom-up approach to management promoted the use of "IBM ideas." An online computer application for employees to express their opinions which the company would then evaluate and implement, cash rewards for cost-saving suggestions, and open consultation and debates were vivid examples of how IBM and Lenovo differed in management style.[11]

Human Resource Management   Consistent with Lenovo's bureaucratic management style, rigorous human resource (HR) rules and regulations were implemented. Card keys kept track of when employees came to work or left; absence during working hours had to be explained or otherwise accounted for. Employees were expected to obey orders and follow detailed behavior codes. A former employee described the working environment as militaristic, which had the potential to hinder creativity.[12]

IBM adopted HR policies that focused on empowerment and self-discipline. For instance, $5,000 a year was given to individual managers, with no questions asked, for the purpose of generating business, developing client relationships, or responding to emergency needs. In essence, IBM did not strictly monitor its employees but, instead,

believed in their self-discipline. IBM adopted a value-based management system. "IBMers" believed that they could contribute to the company as well as to society as a whole. Therefore, they strived to innovate and to create products for the good of all human beings.[13]

Culture Clash   Lenovo and IBM came from two different national cultures: Chinese culture advocates humility, while American culture emphasizes confidence and outspokenness. As another example, punctuality is emphasized more in Chinese enterprises than in American ones. In Lenovo, tardiness at meetings may have resulted in the humiliation of standing behind one's chair for a minute as punishment. However, IBM employees had a high tolerance for tardiness and other discipline differences since they had to adapt to the many different cultures of their colleagues.[14]

Workforce combination also contributed to cultural clashes. Before the merger, Lenovo was a purely domestic Chinese company. Most of its employees were young graduates who had worked only at Lenovo. Few spoke English, and even fewer had international exposure or overseas training.[15] In contrast, IBM had been a global company for a long time. Being the world's largest information technology company, it comprised professionals from different ethnic groups. Its 330,000 employees were distributed in about 170 countries, and they communicated mainly in English.[16]

Synergy Realization of the New Lenovo

Top Management Team   The new Lenovo positioned itself as a global company. As a matter of fact, three years after the IBM deal, Lenovo finally morphed into a true multinational. It has spread its executives around the world, with CEO Amelio based in Singapore and the chairman, Yang Yuanqing, in Raleigh, North Carolina. Other key personnel are based in Beijing, Hong Kong, and Paris. Moreover, as Amelio puts it: "Our view is that talent is found in different parts of the world. . . . We are getting some of the best ideas from a diverse work force so that we can be more innovative."[17] Accordingly, the ranks of directors and officers comprise Chinese, U.S. and European citizens. Top management, from vice president up, consists of 10 different nationalities. Likewise, the board of directors is multinational: In addition to the four original Chinese founders, it includes directors from seven other nations.

As an American CEO with a Chinese chairman, Amelio competes head to head with Yang and is hardly the sort to take the backseat. Consequently, his relations with Yang might easily have been difficult, especially with the initial language and cultural barriers. Instead, Amelio has a "great alignment with the chairman,"[18] whom he meets every few weeks for a couple of hours. The relationship between them, as the division of labor decided, is that Yang runs the board of directors and sets the strategic direction and Amelio has operation control.

Cultural Integration Due diligence and cultural integration appraisals were undertaken before the acquisition. In January 2005, a cultural integration group, which included professionals from different departments of both Lenovo and IBM, was formed. The group was responsible for collecting and analyzing the opinions of employees from the two companies as a means of evaluating the cultural differences between the two parties. The objective was to use the findings of this analysis to define the organizational culture of the new Lenovo. Although Lenovo was the acquirer, it attempted to not impose its Chinese management style on IBM; in essence, Lenovo adjusted to the IBM style. One obvious example was that Lenovo moved its headquarters from Beijing to Purchase, New York, and later to Raleigh, North Carolina. Moreover, foreign managers were given high-profile roles, and English became the main language of executive discussion.

Nevertheless, the new Lenovo suffered clashes of the two different national cultures. For instance, the Chinese part of the firm, beset by deeply hierarchical and deferential behavior, needed to get people to talk more openly to each other. An "Executive Expressions" course was launched to help the Chinese managers learn how to put their message across and oppose their colleagues. The importance of straight talk in meetings, not afterward, was constantly emphasized to all workers. Furthermore, as it was difficult to alter deep-rooted national cultures, the only way to solve the problem was through mutual understanding and respect. Accordingly, Yang Yuanqing introduced the communication spirit into the new Lenovo: "honesty, respect, and compromise." Therefore, instead of having the cultural dominance of either party, the new Lenovo was a meet and mix of two cultures, which gave rise to a new, hybrid organizational culture.

Restructuring In August 2006, Lenovo reported its first market share increase since the acquisition. It was expected to post a second consecutive quarterly profit, despite losing money in the fourth quarter of 2005. According to analysts, much of this success stemmed from Yang Yuanqing's decision to replace former chief executive Steve Ward with William Amelio, Dell's former head in Asia.[19] Amelio had moved more quickly to slash costs in the face of slower-than-expected sales growth. Under Amelio, Lenovo had launched a $100 million program to revamp the IBM unit, including laying off about 1,000 workers, or 5 percent of the unit's workforce, and consolidating offices to stem losses in the United States. After shedding more than 1,000 jobs and cutting back-office costs, Lenovo posted a $60 million net profit in the first quarter of 2007, compared with a $116 million loss a year earlier.

While Lenovo had made strong progress during 2006, Amelio said: "It's clear we need to further accelerate that progress to be as profitable and cost-efficient as the rest of the industry." Therefore, in February 2007, Lenovo announced its plan to eliminate or relocate some 1,400 positions, or about 5 percent of its employees worldwide, in a new round of corporate restructuring. Some staff members would be redeployed, while others would be laid off. This restructuring was aimed at reducing costs, integrating global sales and back-office functions, streamlining sales and marketing operations, and producing closer links between suppliers and Lenovo's manufacturing base, particularly in emerging markets. The effort was designed to achieve annual savings of about $250 million starting in the next fiscal year, which would begin in April 2007.[20] Mr Yang promised investors that after the restructuring, the company would "grow faster than its competitors."

Sales Strategy Integration Lenovo's sales strategy in China was based on small businesses and consumers as much as on large institutions. It was looking at two business models, using what it called a relationship model and a transactional model.[21] The relationship model would cater to the upper end of its business, in the ThinkPad product set sphere, with more emphasis on direct selling to large corporations; the transactional model would generate market demand for its Lenovo 3000 range among the SME crowd and individual customers. IBM's PC division had eliminated its transactional business in 1999 and focused only on doing business with large corporations through the relationship model. However, the market for large corporations was becoming increasingly saturated in recent years, making sales more and more difficult.

To improve its U.S. sales, the new Lenovo cultivated its Chinese relationship sales model in the American market. Moreover, while exploring ways to repackage computer products sold to Chinese consumers so that they would appeal to the U.S. market, which had different design and color preferences, Lenovo sold ThinkPads through nearly 700 Circuit City stores, thus expanding on earlier deals with Best Buy and Office Depot.

Global Brand Awareness and Image Lenovo was largely an unknown entity in the United States when it bought IBM's PC division. Since Lenovo was a brand-new name to the consumer, brand recognition was very low. It was important to acquire brand recognition in the United States so that the company could apply the cost advantages from its powerful Chinese manufacturing base. Therefore, Lenovo began to raise its profile by enlisting celebrity help and by hitching its wagon to major events.

In 2006, Lenovo acquired the services of the Brazil and Barcelona footballer Ronaldinho,[22] arguably the world's most well-known face in soccer. Lenovo was hoping that some of Ronaldinho's profile would transfer to the company through a sort of branding osmosis. Sixteen Lenovo 3000 notebooks signed by Ronaldinho were auctioned on eBay, with all of the proceeds donated to charity. Between 2005 and 2007, Lenovo signed deals with the 2006 Winter Olympics in Turin, the National Basketball Association (NBA), the Carolina Hurricanes, the Washington Redskins, the Williams Formula One race-car team in Europe, and the 2008 Beijing Olympics, for which it designed the Olympic torch. It remained to be seen whether the athletic and sporting-event approach was appropriate for a company that supplied business machines to corporate clients. In the Chinese market, Lenovo also cast a huge shadow in the commercial area with some 20,000 dedicated shops in China's largest cities.[23] (See Exhibit 5 for Lenovo's balance sheet and financial statement.)

Summary

Lenovo bounded onto the international scene in May 2005 with the acquisition of IBM's personal computer division for $1.75 billion. This was viewed as an experiment to see whether Chinese companies could successfully integrate foreign acquisitions as they continued to expand internationally. With this landmark acquisition, the new Lenovo became a leader in the global PC market,

Exhibit 5 Income Statement and Balance Sheet Data for Lenovo Group Ltd., 2004–2008 (in millions of dollars)

	2004	2005	2006	2007	2008
Total revenue	2,986.4	2,906.4	13,343.5	13,978.3	16,351.5
Gross profit	436.6	375.0	1,867.9	1,886.9	2,450.0
Total operating expense	2,873.2	2,759.2	13,202.6	13,816.8	15,852.5
Operating income	113.3	147.2	140.8	161.5	499.0
Income before taxes	128.2	145.3	85.0	154.6	512.8
Net income after taxes	130.8	140.8	27.8	128.4	465.2
Net income before extraordinary items	135.7	144.3	22.3	128.4	464.3
Net income	135.7	144.3	22.3	161.1	484.3
Income available to Common excluding extraordinary items	135.7	144.3	22.3	128.4	464.3
Income available to Common including extraordinary items	135.7	144.3	22.3	161.1	484.3
Basic EPS excluding extraordinary items	0.018	0.019	0.003	0.015	0.053
Basic EPS including extraordinary items	0.018	0.019	0.003	0.019	0.055
Diluted EPS excluding extraordinary items	0.018	0.019	0.002	0.015	0.049
Diluted EPS including extraordinary items	0.018	0.019	0.002	0.018	0.051
Normalized income before taxes	122.1	154.1	157.9	163.5	515.4
Normalized income after taxes	126.8	149.3	75.2	135.8	467.5
Normalized income available to Common	126.8	149.3	75.2	135.8	467.5
Total current assets	786.0	831.6	2,749.5	3,062.4	4,705.4
Total assets	1,074.9	1,163.8	5,066.3	5,450.8	7,199.9
Total current liabilities	424.9	447.5	3,198.6	3,527.5	4,488.5
Total liabilities	496.5	493.2	4,017.0	4,617.3	5,586.8
Total equity	578.4	670.6	1,049.2	1,133.5	1,613.1
Total liabilities and shareholders' equity	1,074.9	1,163.8	5,066.3	5,450.8	7,199.9
Total common shares outstanding	7,475.59	7,474.80	8,893.20	8,893.26	9,264.07
Total preferred shares outstanding	—	0.00	2.73	2.73	1.77

Source: Annual Reports of Lenovo Group Ltd., 2004–2008.

with products serving enterprises as well as consumers throughout the world.

The restructuring costs for the newly acquired unit and severe competition in the PC sector took a heavy toll on Lenovo in the first year after the acquisition. However, in May 2007, Lenovo announced a net profit for the previous fiscal year (from April 1, 2006, to March 31, 2007), which was the first sign that the Chinese computer group had begun to turn around the PC unit. The full-year profit had increased 625 percent, to $161 million, compared with $22 million the previous year.[24] Additionally, until the first quarter of 2008, Lenovo reported profits in the American region for five successive quarters.[25] "It was a solid (final) quarter and strong fiscal year by any number of measures," said Yang Yuanqing, Lenovo chairman. "Our performance confirmed we have stabilized our business worldwide."[26]

However, the picture of new Lenovo's development in the global market as a whole showed that it was facing a tough situation. Lenovo remained the dominant player in the Chinese PC market, but even there it was losing market share to rivals, led by Acer and HP. Meanwhile, sales growth in Asia, which had propped up the company, was slowing as rivals such as Dell gained ground.

Without the Chinese market share, the picture for Lenovo looked less impressive. Europe, the United States, South America, and Russia were the new battlegrounds for the company as it sought to gain global market share and lessen its dependence on China. Industry analysts noted that Lenovo had to face tough competition in the PC market, where price wars continued to slash margins and force retrenchment. The cruel fact, according to International Data Corporation, is that Lenovo's ranking as the world's third-largest computer company, after HP and Dell, was repeatedly challenged by Taiwan's Acer.[27]

Lenovo had occupied the leading position of PC sales in China for 10 years, but this was with the help and blessings of the Chinese government. The acquisition of IBM's PC division catapulted the organization onto the international stage, and the Chinese government could do little in this newly competitive arena. Yet Lenovo's ability to turn the unit around was seen as a key test of corporate China's ability to go global and establish recognized brands outside its own borders. Would the differences between the two sides hinder Lenovo from becoming a global champion? Could new Lenovo maintain synergy from the acquisition of a radically different competitor? Simply put, was this acquisition the right choice for Lenovo? Yang Yuanqing, the CEO, remained optimistic. He stated: "We had expected most of the difficulties we are experiencing. It is unavoidable. We believe the acquisition is a better way to expand in the international market than organic growth." Time will tell whether his predictions come true.

Endnotes

1. www.lenovo.com.cn, November 10, 2008.
2. "Sheltering from the Storm," *The Economist,* September 6, 2001.
3. The peripheral products included printers and hard disks, mobile phones, digital cameras, fax machines, etc.
4. S. Lohr, "IBM Sought a China Partnership, Not Just a Sale," www.news.com, December 12, 2004.
5. Ministry of Commerce of the People's Republic of China, www.mofcom.gov.cn, 2006.
6. "The IBM/Lenovo Deal: Victory for China?" *Knowledge@ wharton,* http://knowledge.wharton.upenn.edu, January 14, 2005.
7. American Ceramic Society, "Lenovo to Acquire IBM PC Div," *American Ceramic Society Bulletin* (Columbus, OH), vol. 84, no. 2 (February 2005), p. 9.
8. "Lenovo and IBM: East Meets West, Big-Time," *Business-Week,* May 9, 2005.
9. J. Chao, "Lenovo's Corporate Culture a Key Issue as It Absorbs IBM," *Forbes,* December 14, 2004.
10. NTZJ, "蛇吞象：质量的联想," *Nantong Quality Info Net,* www.ntzj.gov.cn/wd_show.asp?id=59, 2006.
11. "Winning Innovations in HR Management," *HR Focus,* vol.71, no 6 (June 1994), p. 7.
12. Chao, "Lenovo's Corporate Culture a Key Issue."
13. P. Hemp and T. A. Stewart, "The HBR Interview: Samuel J. Palmisano: Leading Change When Business Is Good," *Harvard Business Review,* vol. 82, no 12 (2004), p. 60.
14. *IT,* May 2005.
15. Chao, "Lenovo's Corporate Culture a Key Issue.
16. IBM, www.ibm.com/us, 2006.
17. *The Business Times Singapore,* October 11, 2008.
18. *The Economist,* February 17, 2007.
19. *Financial Times,* November 9, 2006.
20. *South China Morning Post,* February 27, 2007.
21. *Irish Times,* November 10, 2006.
22. Ibid.
23. Ibid.
24. *Financial Times,* May 24, 2007.
25. www.lenovo.com.cn, November 10, 2008.
26. *Financial Times,* May 24, 2007.
27. Ibid.

Case 21   The Casino Industry*

After years of a building boom during which construction cranes shared air space with towering casino resorts, the growth of Las Vegas had been put on hold by early 2009. Ever since the mobster Bugsy Siegel opened the first of the modern-day casinos in 1946, firms had competed against each other by building more and more expensive and extravagant casino resorts. But the recent credit crunch and the economic slowdown has made it difficult for many firms to raise the required financing for their ambitious projects, forcing them to reassess their plans.

Construction has been halted on Echelon Place, which was being built on the former site of Stardust. At $4.4 billion, the 5,000-room Echelon Place was expected to be far more expensive than the previous record for a single casino, which was set when Steve Wynn built his $2.7 billion resort. MGM Mirage has struggled to find funding to continue work on the City Center, being built at an expense of more than $8 billion. Covering 67 acres, this minicity bordering the Las Vegas Strip was expected to include a luxury hotel, condominium units, a convention center, and retail space. But the drop in demand for condominium units as a result of falling real estate prices has forced the casino firm to scale down the scope of the project.

A combination of factors has suddenly taken some of the sparkle away from Las Vegas. Deteriorating economic conditions have forced potential visitors to put off their travel plans and find gambling closer to where they live. With gaming now allowed in 20 states, competition is developing all over the country, led by riverboat casinos and Native American casinos. (See Exhibit 1.) In addition, slot machines are being added at a variety of venues, such as racetracks. The need to show fiscal restraint has also led to a dramatic drop in the number of conventions being organized in Las Vegas, with several firms changing their venue.

Some concerns have been raised about the development of casinos outside the United States. In particular, Macau has emerged as a gambling resort, with the opening of Sands Macau, the city's first Las Vegas–style casino, in 2004. Other Las Vegas–based casinos have also entered this market with lavish properties such as MGM Grand Macau and Wynn Macau. But Macau does not offer much else in terms of entertainment, such as shopping, theater shows, and fine dining.

The sudden drop-off in construction activity in Las Vegas has left half-completed structures scattered among the elegant skyscrapers. Among these is the St. Regis Residences, wedged between the Venetian and Palazzo

resorts, on which construction was abruptly halted when Las Vegas Sands ran into financial difficulties. Donald Trump complained about the stalled construction on St. Regis, which is visible from his hotel-condo tower across the street. "I don't know whose idea that was. They have a concrete frame standing there; you talk about a mess," he remarked.[1]

Riding the Growth Wave

Although some form of gambling can be traced back to colonial times, the recent advent of casinos stems from the legalization of gaming in Nevada in 1931. For many years, Nevada was the only state in which casinos were allowed. As a result, Nevada still retains its status as the state with the highest revenues from casinos, with gambling revenues rising to over $12 billion by 2008. After New Jersey passed laws in 1976 to allow gambling in Atlantic City, the large population on the east coast gained easier access to casinos. However, the further growth of casinos has been possible only since 1988, as more and more states have legalized the operation of casinos because of their ability to help generate more commercial activity and create more jobs, in large part through the growth of tourism.

The greatest growth has come in the form of waterborne casinos, which operate in six states that have allowed casinos to develop at waterfronts such as rivers and lakes. As of 2008, about 80 such casinos generated about $12 billion in revenues. Several of the casinos along the Gulf Coast were destroyed or severely damaged by Hurricane Katrina. To encourage casinos to rebuild, Mississippi lawmakers passed a law in 2005 allowing casinos to operate up to 800 feet from the shore, enabling them to have a stronger foundation to withstand future hurricanes. Most of the damaged casinos in the area had reopened by early 2007.

As casinos have spread to more states, there has also been a growing tendency to regard casino gambling as an acceptable form of entertainment for a night out. Although casinos have tended to draw players from all demographic segments, a recent national survey found that their median age was 47 and their median household income was around $50,000. On the whole, casino gamblers tended to be better educated and more affluent than those who bought lottery tickets. In fact, the bigger casinos attracted a high-roller segment, which could stake millions of dollars and included players from all over the world. Many of the casinos worked hard to obtain the business of this market segment, despite the risk that the sustained winning streak of a single player could significantly weaken the earnings for a particular quarter.

The growth of casino gambling has also been driven by the significantly better payouts that casinos give players, compared with other forms of gambling. On the basis

* This case was developed by Professor Jamal Shamsie, Michigan State University, with the assistance of Professor Alan B. Eisner, Pace University. Material has been drawn from published sources to be used for class discussion. Copyright © 2009 Jamal Shamsie and Alan B. Eisner.

Exhibit 1 U.S. Casino Industry Gaming Revenues* (in millions of dollars)

	Revenues					
	2008	**2007**	**2006**	**2004**	**2002**	**2000**
Nevada, total	11,599	12,848	12,622	10,562	9,447	9,600
Las Vegas Strip	6,126	6,828	6,688	5,334	4,654	4,806
Atlantic City, total	4,641	4,921	5,218	4,807	4,382	4,301
Western towns, total	921	914	872	804	786	685
Deadwood, SD	101	98	90	78	66	53
Colorado	820	816	782	726	720	632
Other land-based, total	1,752	1,747	1,641	1,509	1,400	989
New Orleans	393	412	338	320	275	245
Detroit	1,359	1,335	1,303	1,189	1,125	744
Riverboats, total	11,241	11,785	12,065	10,626	10,156	9,038
Iowa	952	908	1,173	727	656	598
Illinois	1,569	1,984	1,924	1,717	1,832	1,658
Mississippi	2,721	2,892	2,570	2,777	2,717	2,649
Louisiana	1,794	1,785	2,229	1,562	1,610	1,447
Missouri	1,636	1,599	1,592	1,473	1,279	997
Indiana	2,569	2,625	2,577	2,370	2,062	1,689
Native American casinos	25,750	26,016	24,889	15,055	13,290	9,700
Total	55,904	58,231	57,307	43,363	39,461	34,313

*Gaming revenues include the amount of money won by casinos from various gaming activities such as slot machines, table games, and sports betting.

Source: *Casino Journal*'s National Gaming Summary, Standard & Poor's estimates, state revenue reports, author estimates.

of industry estimates, casinos typically keep less than $5 of every $100 that is wagered. This compares favorably with racetrack betting, which holds back over $20 of every $100 that is wagered, and with state-run lotteries, which usually keep about $45 of every $100 that is spent on tickets. Such comparisons can be somewhat misleading, however, because winnings are put back into play in casinos much faster than they are in other forms of gaming. This provides a casino with more opportunities to win from a customer, largely offsetting its lower retention rate.

Finally, most of the growth in casino revenues has come from the growing popularity of slot machines. Coin-operated slot machines typically account for more than 60 percent of all casino gaming revenues. A major reason for their popularity is that it is easier for prospective gamblers to feed a slot machine than to understand the nuances of various table games. Major slot-machine manufacturers, such as International Game Technology, have been making the transition to cashless or coin-free gaming by switching to the use of tickets. With the advent of new technology, server-based gaming will allow games on these machines to be changed or updated from a central system.

Betting on a Few Locations

Although casinos have spread across much of the country, two cities have dominated the casino business. Both Las Vegas and Atlantic City have seen a spectacular growth in casino gaming revenues over the years. Although Las Vegas has far more hotel casinos, each of the dozen casinos in Atlantic City typically generates much higher revenues. By 2008, these two locations accounted for almost one-third of the total revenues generated by all forms of casinos throughout the United States.

Las Vegas clearly acts a magnet for the overnight casino gamblers, offering close to 140,000 hotel rooms and many choices for fine dining, great shopping, and top-notch entertainment. This allows the casinos to generate revenues from offering a wide selection of activities apart from gambling. At MGM Mirage, for example, revenue from nongaming activities accounted for almost 60 percent of net revenue in 2008. Visitors find it easy to travel to Las Vegas as it is linked by air to many major cities both in the United States and around the world.

During the 1990s, Las Vegas tried to become more receptive to families, with attractions such as circus performances, animal reserves, and pirate battles. But the city has been very successful with its recent return to its sinful roots, with a stronger focus on topless shows, hot night clubs, and other adult offerings that are highlighted by the new advertising slogan "What happens in Vegas, stays in Vegas." Paul Cappelli, who creates advertising messages, believes that Las Vegas lost its way with the effort to become family-friendly. "People don't see Vegas as Jellystone Park. They don't want to go there with a picnic basket," he explained.[2]

For the most part, Las Vegas has continued to show a consistent pattern of growth in visitors. (See Exhibit 2.) "We still compete with Orlando and New York," said Terry Jicinsky, head of marketing for the Las Vegas Convention and Visitors Authority. "But based on overnight visitors, we're the top destination in North America."[3] In order to accommodate the growth, several of the major resorts, such as Bellagio, Venetian, and Mandalay Bay, have added new wings. Even some of the older properties, such as Caesers Palace, have undergone expensive renovations and expanded to include new features such as a coliseum and a Roman plaza.

By comparison, Atlantic City cannot compete with Las Vegas in terms of the broad range of dining, shopping, and entertainment choices. It does, however, offer a beach and a boardwalk, along which its dozen large casino hotels are lined. Atlantic City attracts gamblers from various cities in the Northeast, many of whom arrive by charter bus and stay for less than a day. City officials point out that one-quarter of the nation's population lives close enough to Atlantic City to drive there on just one tank of gas.

The opening of the much-ballyhooed Borgata Hotel Casino in 2003 has started a drive to make Atlantic City much more competitive with Las Vegas. "There's no question that this is a Las Vegas–style mega-resort," said Bob Boughner, the CEO of the Borgata.[4] As the first new casino to open in the city in 13 years, the Borgata was expected to initiate a makeover of Atlantic City that might make it a hotter destination. But changing economic conditions have led Pinnacle to postpone its plans to open another $2 billion casino.

Raising the Stakes

The gradual rise in the number of casinos, including those on riverboats, has led each of them to compete more heavily with one another to entice gamblers. Casinos have had to continuously strive to offer more in order to stand out and gain attention. This is most evident in Las Vegas and Atlantic City, the two destinations where most of the largest casinos are located next to each other. Potential gamblers have more choices when they visit either of these cities than they have anywhere else. (See Exhibit 3.)

In Las Vegas, each of the casinos has tried to deal with competition by differentiating itself in several ways. A large number of them have differentiated on the basis of a special theme that characterizes the casino, such as a medieval castle, a pirate ship, or a movie studio. Others have incorporated into the casino the look and feel of a specific foreign destination. Luxor's pyramids and columns evoke ancient Egypt, Mandalay Bay borrows looks from the Pacific Rim, and the Venetian's plazas and canals re-create the Italian resort of Venice.

Aside from ramping up the appeal of their particular properties, most casinos must also offer incentives to keep their customers from moving over to competing casinos. The incentives can be particularly helpful in retaining high rollers who come often and spend large amounts of

Exhibit 2 Las Vegas Visitors
(in millions)

2008	38.7*
2007	39.2
2006	39.0
2005	38.6
2004	37.4
2003	35.5
2002	35.1
2001	35.0
2000	35.8
1999	33.8
1998	30.6
1997	30.5
1996	29.6
1995	29.0

*Estimate.

Source: Las Vegas Convention and Visitors Authority.

Exhibit 3 Comparative Statistics

	Las Vegas	Atlantic City
Gambling legalized	1931	1976
Annual visitors	39 million	34 million
Average stay	3.4 days	1.5 days
Number of casinos	195	12
Casino revenue	$6.8 billion	$5.4 billion
Hotel rooms	140,000	16,500
Largest hotel	MGM Grand, 5,035 rooms	Borgata, 2,002 rooms

Source: Nevada Casino Control Board, Las Vegas News Bureau, New Jersey Casino Control Commission, Atlantic City Convention and Visitors Bureau.

money. Casinos try to maintain their business by providing complimentary rooms, food, beverages, shows, and other perks that are worth billions of dollars each year. Gamblers can also earn various types of rewards through the loyalty programs that are offered by the casinos, with the specific rewards being tied to the amount that the gamblers bet on the slot machines and at the tables.

Some of the larger casinos in Las Vegas are also trying to fend off competition by growing through mergers and acquisitions. In 2004, Harrah's announced that it was buying casino rival Caesars; the acquisition made Harrah's the nation's leading operator of casinos, with several properties in both Las Vegas and Atlantic City. (See Exhibit 4.) This deal came just a month after MGM Mirage stated that it was buying the Mandalay Resort Group; the purchase doubled the number of casinos Mandalay held on the Las Vegas Strip. Firms that own several casinos can pitch each of their properties to a different market and allow all of their customers to earn rewards on the firm's loyalty program by gambling at any of these properties.

The trend toward consolidation, however, does not seem to have made a serious dent on smaller firms that operate just one or two resorts that appeal to particular types of customers. Steve Wynn's success with Wynn has led him to open Encore, another glitzy casino resort next to his original property. Similarly, the recently opened 455-room Palms Hotel Casino has already become one of the hottest and most profitable properties in Las Veags. "There will always be a market for a person who doesn't feel comfortable in a big casino setting," said George Maloof, a co-owner of the Palms Resort.[5]

Responding to Growing Threats

The growth of Las Vegas and Atlantic City has been matched by the spread of casinos in many other parts of the United States. Among these casinos, the largest volume of business is generated by the riverboats that have sprung up in Iowa, Illinois, Mississippi, Louisiana, Missouri, and Indiana. However, these casinos have not had much effect on the number of visitors to Las Vegas and Atlantic City. Tom Graves, stock analyst at Standard & Poor's, has expressed his confidence in the attractiveness of Las Vegas: "There's a perception among gamblers that Las Vegas is still the foremost gaming market."[6]

All of these casinos, however, are facing increasing competition for a variety of reasons. Foremost among them is the rise in the number of Native American casinos. The Indian Gaming and Recreation Act of 1988 authorized Native Americans to offer gaming on tribal lands as a way to encourage their self-sufficiency. Of the approximately 550 Native American tribes in the United States, more than 200 have negotiated agreements with states to allow gaming on tribal land. Native American casinos are exempt from federal regulations and are not required to pay any taxes on their revenues, but they generally pay a percentage of their winnings to the state in which they are located.

Over the past decade, a large share of the growth in U.S. gaming revenues has come from Native American casinos. The impact of these casinos on the traditional casino industry is likely to increase over the next few years. Several states are reaching agreements that allow the introduction or expansion of Native American casinos because of the additional revenues that they can provide. This has created fears that the growth of Native American casinos is likely to draw gamblers away from the other types of casinos. In particular, the increase of these casinos in states such as California and New York may reduce the number of gamblers who make trips to destinations such as Las Vegas and Atlantic City.

The casino industry is also facing growing competition as a result of the move to introduce gaming machines at racetracks. Several states are passing legislation that allows racetracks to raise their revenues by providing slot machines for their visitors. Gaming machines at racetracks—sometimes referred to as "racinos"—have been growing in popularity in the six states where they are presently allowed. According to the American Gaming Association, gaming activity at racetracks has shown considerable growth over the last five years.

Finally, all casinos are closely observing the growth of gambling on the Internet. Although the United States has introduced legislation to ban Internet gambling, some 2,000 offshore Web sites generate about $15 billion in revenue. Electronic payment systems have made it possible for gamblers in the United States to make bets at these sites without cash, checks, or credit cards. Most casino operators believe that Internet gambling could represent both a threat and an opportunity for them. Placing bets through home computers offers convenience for prospective gamblers and a potentially low-cost business model for firms that already operate casinos. It is widely believed that gambling on the Internet might eventually be legalized, regulated, and taxed. "We frankly find attempts at prohibition to be very shortsighted," said Alan Feldman, senior vice president of MGM Mirage in Las Vegas.[7]

Gambling on the Future

Even as the potential for gaming revenues has remained uncertain, all the firms in the casino industry have had little choice but to keep spending in order to survive and grow. In many cases, the heavy spending has burdened casino operators with large amounts of debt that must be serviced through profits from the casino. The debt has been harder to manage when demand for casino gambling does not stay strong and even show some growth. A few casinos in Las Vegas and Atlantic City have run into financial problems, forcing some of them to close. Alladin ran into financial problems shortly after it spent heavily on renovations, and it was sold off and converted to Planet Hollywood. More recently, Tropicana Entertainment, a leading casino and riverboat operator, filed for bankruptcy.

So far, such isolated failures have not dampened the enthusiasm of most of the firms that are continuing to

Exhibit 4 Leading Casino Operators

Harrah's Entertainment

2007 Revenue: $10 billion*

2007 Income: N/A

Was purchased by a private equity firm in early 2007. Operates 38 casinos across the United States, including riverboats. Runs several upscale casinos such as Bellagio, Caesars Palace, Ballys, Paris, Flamingo, Harrahs, and Rio in Las Vegas. Also operates a casino in Canada and a casino in Uruguay.

MGM Mirage

2007 Revenue: $7.69 billion

2007 Income: $1.43 billion

Operates 17 casinos throughout the country. Most of its casinos in Las Vegas, such as MGM Grand, Bellagio, New York New York, Mirage, Treasure Island, Luxor, and Monte Carlo, cater to the high end of the market. Developing the City Center project in Las Vegas. Also operates casinos on the Gulf Coast and in Illinois and Michigan. Developed MGM Grand Macau.

Boyd Gaming

2007 Revenue: $1.98 billion

2007 Income: $121 million

Operates 16 casinos throughout the United States. Las Vegas properties that target the middle-income segment include Barbary Coast, Gold Coast, Orleans, and Sam's Town. Is developing a higher-end casino, Echelon Place, in Las Vegas. Runs the newly opened Borgata in Atlantic City.

Las Vegas Sands

2007 Revenue: $2.95 billion

2007 Income: $117 million

Operates the Venetian and Palazzo in Las Vegas. Also developing several casinos in Macau, spearheaded by the Sands Macau, and a casino in Singapore.

Penn National Gaming

2007 Revenue: $2.44 billion

2007 Income: $160 million

In 2005, merged with Argosy Gaming. Operates 15 midpriced casinos spread across the United States, including riverboats in several states. Has no properties in Las Vegas or Atlantic City. Also operates several racetracks.

Wynn Resorts

2007 Revenue: $2.69 billion

2007 Income: $258 million

Operates the higher-end Wynn Resort and Encore casino, both in Las Vegas. Also operates the Wynn Macau.

Station Casinos

2007 Revenue: $1.25 billion*

2007 Income: N/A

Operates 8 midpriced casinos in and around Las Vegas. Leading casinos are Palace Station, Sunset Station, and Boulder Station.

Pinnacle Entertainment

2007 Revenue: $924 million

2007 Income: ($2 million)

Operates 6 midpriced casinos, mostly on the Gulf Coast. Also operates casinos in the Bahamas and Argentina.

Trump Entertainment Resorts

2007 Revenue: $958 million

2007 Income: N/A

Operates Trump Taj Mahal, Trump Plaza, and Trump Marina, all in Atlantic City. Filed for bankruptcy protection in February 2009.

Ameristar Casinos

2007 Revenue: $1.10 billion

2007 Income: $69 million

Operates 8 midpriced casinos across the United States including a couple of riverboats. Has no properties in Las Vegas or Atlantic City.

Isle of Capri Casinos

2007 Revenue: $1.12 billion

2007 Income: ($97 million)

Operates 14 riverboat casinos across the United States. Also operates casinos in Grand Bahamas and the United Kingdom.

*Estimated figures.

invest heavily in casinos. Many of these gaming firms view the current economic condition as a temporary setback that has forced them to place some of their plans for growth on hold. They believe that the gaming industry has the potential to grow well into the future, a belief based in part on the growing number of aging boomers who are entering the empty-nest phase of their lives.

If the attraction of gaming continues to show the same level of growth as it has over the past decade, Las Vegas and Atlantic City should thrive even with the rise of new casinos in other locations. Some observers believe that the spread of gaming has created a bigger market for the casino resorts in these two cities. In this regard, analysts are particularly concerned about the ability of Macau to develop into a strong rival, pulling away gamblers from the United States. But it is far from clear whether this city located on the South China Sea will be able to compete with Las Vegas. Plans to develop the Cotai Strip into a "Las Vegas of Asia" will require heavy investments by many firms that must be willing to take the risks.

Nevertheless, there are questions about the possible impact of the proliferation of casinos and the availability of Internet gambling on the revenue growth of gaming centers such as Las Vegas and Atlantic City. Many industry observers believe that these gaming centers will continue to thrive, as people who gain a taste for gambling will eventually want to visit Las Vegas or Atlantic City to experience the real thing. Jan L. Jones, senior vice president for Harrah's Entertainment, remarked: "Counting Las Vegas down and out, given the entrepreneurial spirit at work here, is just foolish."[8]

Endnotes

1. Steve Friess. A Break in the Action. *New York Times,* March 6, 2009, p. D4.
2. Michael McCarthy. Vegas Goes Back to Naughty Roots; Ads Trumpet Return to Adult Playground. *USA Today,* April 11, 2005, p. B6.
3. Ibid.
4. Gene Sloan. Atlantic City Bets on Glitz: Down-at-the-Heels Resort Rolls the Dice, Wagering a Cool $2 Billion That It Will One Day Rival Las Vegas. *USA Today,* August 29, 2003, p. D1.
5. Christopher Palmeri. Little Guys with Big Plans for Vegas. *BusinessWeek,* August 2, 2004, p. 49.
6. Chris Woodyard and Matt Krantz. Latest Vegas Marriage: Harrah's, Caesars Tie Knot; $5 Billion Deal Marks Strategy to Reach More Gamblers. *USA Today,* July 16, 2004, p. B1.
7. Lorraine Woellert. Can Online Betting Change Its Luck? *BusinessWeek,* December 20, 2004, p. 67.
8. Steve Friess. Las Vegas Sags as Conventions Cancel. *New York Times,* February 15, 2009, p. 20.

Case 22   Mattel's Misfit Toys*

Several months had passed since Mattel had issued the largest toy recall in its history, but Robert (Bob) Eckert, Mattel's chairman and chief executive, knew the crisis was not over. As he prepared for the upcoming Toy Industry Association (TIA) meeting, he reflected on the past few months, the recalls, the financial fallout, Mattel's reputation, and future actions.

What a blur! Just months before, in an article written on July 19, 2007, and published on July 26, the *New York Times* had featured Mattel as a role model for manufacturing in China for the toy industry.[1] Yet in early July 2007 a European retailer had already discovered lead paint on some toys made by Mattel subsidiary Fisher-Price. In the United States, lead paint had been banned for use in toys in 1977 due to its harmful effects on child development, such as causing learning difficulties and anemia—a deficiency of hemoglobin, a molecule found inside red blood cells, which carries oxygen throughout the body. Eckert ordered Mattel's own safety lab to begin additional testing and found hazardous lead paint on toys from some vendors. On August 1, 2007, Mattel announced the largest toy recall, in units, in its history; the recalled toys included the Elmo, Big Bird, and Dora characters, licensed by Sesame Street and Nickelodeon. How did lead paint slip into Mattel's production line? How did tainted toys slip past the company's inspections?

Eckert surmised that the European retailer may have discovered the lead paint as part of a broader reaction to the April toy recall issued by RC2, a Mattel competitor and the licensor for HIT Entertainment Limited's Thomas & Friends. Swiftly, he had ordered Mattel's units and subcontractors to review inputs, processes, and inventory. The results startled Eckert, the firm, retailers, and consumers.

In addition to tracking, inspecting, and recalling toys, Eckert faced an onslaught of negative media coverage. Cartoons disparaging tainted toys appeared. Just three weeks after the recall on August 23, Dana Parker, a California mother, appeared in Eckert's lobby at Mattel's El Segundo headquarters with her two children and several garbage bags of their Fisher-Price and Mattel toys in her car. In a CNN broadcast she reportedly told Mattel personnel, "I need you guys to inspect my toys because I cannot do it."[2] Two employees from Mattel's Consumer Products Division inspected each of her toys in a company conference room and found that all were safe. Eckert worried to what degree this mother's frustration represented Mattel's consumers.

Meanwhile, Mattel's executives rerouted toys from China to its Mexico factory for additional testing. On August 13 the CEO of a long-time vendor responsible for the first Mattel toy recall committed suicide in the factory. Two days later, Eckert issued additional recalls of 9.5 million toys in the United States and 11 million in foreign countries for lead paint and for product design, for example, toys with strong magnets that are a hazard if swallowed. In fact, most of the toys were recalled due to the magnets. The recall of the Sarge character from *Cars* for lead paint raised the ire of Pixar and its corporate parent, Disney.

In a move that shocked the industry, on September 21 Thomas Debrowski, Mattel's executive vice president for worldwide operations, met with the Chinese product safety chief, Li Changjiang, and apologized for Mattel's weak safety controls. "Our reputation has been damaged lately by these recalls," Debrowski told Li. "And Mattel takes full responsibility for these recalls and apologizes personally to you, the Chinese people, and all of our customers who received the toys."[3]

Eckert gazed at the Sarge sitting next to his daughter's photo. What could Mattel have done differently? Did it need to do more than it was already doing to avoid a repeat? Could Mattel avoid developing the reputation of producing misfit toys? How could he balance competitive pressures and restore consumer confidence in his company, which was founded on creativity, fun, safety, and, above all, trust? Looking further out, was there an opportunity to further differentiate Mattel from the other companies, like RC2, that were also in the midst of this recall?

Mattel Becomes a Role Model

Ruth and Elliott Handler and Harold (Matt) Matson founded Mattel in a southern California garage workshop in 1945. Mattel became a major player in the toy industry with the 1959 launch of the Barbie doll. By 2006 Mattel owned such brands as Barbie, Hot Wheels, American Girl, and even Fisher Price, and it licensed products from Disney and the *Harry Potter* movies. Mattel was the world's largest toy maker, with 2006 revenue of $5.65 billion.

Mattel's use of offshoring and outsourcing predated the recent globalization and labor arbitrage trend. In fact, the first Barbie dolls were made in Japan in 1959. According to an industry expert quoted in the July 2007 *New York Times* article, "Mattel was in China before China was cool, and they learned to do business there in a good way. They understood the importance of protecting their brand, and they invested."[4]

During the 1980s Mattel decided to take more control of its toy production. In particular, Mattel executives were

* This case was developed by Professors Naomi A. Gardberg and Donald H. Schepers, Baruch College–CUNY. Material has been drawn from published sources to be used for class discussion. The authors gratefully acknowledge the efforts of Jenny Rea, an outstanding research assistant, and Zicklin MBA students Edward Acevedo, Mike Gambale, Isaac Hefez, Audrey Pouvreau, and Monique Sampson. Copyright © 2009 Naomi A. Gardberg and Donald H. Schepers.

concerned about a flood of imitation Barbie dolls if the icon was outsourced. They also thought that they could produce toys more efficiently by building large plants with greater economies of scale. Thus, Mattel's outsourcing strategy took shape. The company would produce and protect its core brands rather than use less costly outsourcing to the lowest-cost local manufacturer. However, short-term products featuring characters from movies and television shows other than Mattel's own brands would be outsourced.[5]

According to SEC filings, Mattel found that its bargaining power with retailers was eroding during the 2000s. Mattel sold nearly half of its toys through only three mass merchandisers, Target, Toys "R" Us, and Wal-Mart. To reduce dependence on these retailers, Mattel created a direct-mail catalog and Web site for selling directly to consumers.

Worker Safety   In 1996, during the holiday shopping season, a *Dateline* broadcast ran an exposé on Mattel's alleged use of sweatshop labor in Indonesia. The story alleged that Mattel hired underage workers and overworked them.[6] *U.S. News & World Report* published a cover story with the headline "Sweatshop Christmas" the same month. The company called the allegations unfounded.

Yet, in response, Mattel hired Dr. Prakash Sethi, a professor at Baruch College–CUNY, and created the International Center for Corporate Accountability (ICCA), a not-for-profit, independently incorporated organization, to monitor working conditions at Mattel facilities. Sethi, who had a reputation as a critic of worker mistreatment, agreed to monitor Mattel only if the firm allowed him to post his reports "publicly and uncensored."[7] As a result, Mattel was considered one of the most successful companies manufacturing in China.

> In 1997, Mattel created an extensive independent monitoring program, which provides objective checks and balances to evaluate compliance to our GMP [Global Manufacturing Principles] standards. The system is overseen by an independent monitoring organization that proactively and thoroughly inspects the company's owned-and-operated facilities around the world, as well as those of our suppliers, on aspects of day-to-day operations. Independent and internal auditors are continuously assessing our performance with GMP. (Mattel Web site)

In 2007 Sethi told the *New York Times* that "Mattel is the gold standard" for worker conditions. Sean McGowan, managing director and toy analyst at Wedbush Morgan Securities, told the *New York Times,* "Mattel talks about this with a passion, and it is not just lip service."[8]

Mattel gradually shifted production from the United States to lower-wage countries. In 2002 Mattel closed its last U.S. manufacturing facility and offshored its production to Mexico.[9]

The company generated about 50 percent of revenues from core products in 12 company-owned and -operated factories, including five in China, by 2006. This was among the highest proportions in the industry and reflected Mattel's emphasis on its core brands. Mattel made or sourced about 65 percent of its toys in China. The 35 percent of toys produced outside China included Barbie dolls made in Indonesia and large Fisher-Price Little People toys made at Mattel's plant in Tijuana, Mexico.

Toy Safety   Despite its care in factory conditions, Mattel was not immune to toy safety recalls. The firm, including Fisher-Price and American Girls, issued 25 recalls between 1982 and July 2007 due primarily to consumer misuse or design flaws. For example, its 1998 recall of 10 million Fisher-Price Power Wheels electronic cars stemmed from consumer misuse rather than a design flaw. The cars, made in the United States, were subject to teenagers and young adults purposely overriding the safety features.

Elisha Chan, Mattel's director of product integrity and corporate responsibility, was responsible for dangerous product defects such as lead-based paint in 2007. He told the *New York Times* that suppliers were monitored closely and that Mattel had canceled contracts with firms that submitted fake or tainted supplies. In its own factories Mattel produced small batches of new toys (up to 5,000) before ramping up production. Mattel tested up to 5,000 new toys in this way each year. After full-scale production commenced, supplies were tested as they arrived at the factory and toys were periodically removed from the assembly line for testing. The company safety lab in Shenzhen, China, tested toys made by outside companies.

In contrast, many Western companies operating in China did not test their raw materials, although suppliers were known to use cheaper materials to increase their profit. Dane Chamorro, regional director of Control Risks, a global consulting firm, concurred: "This is very common. . . . The samples you get are always fantastic; but once they rope you in they can cut back. And a lot of Chinese companies will do anything to cut costs."[10] During July 2007 Jim Walter, a senior vice president at Mattel, stated, "We are not perfect; we have holes. But we're doing more than anyone else."[11] McGowan, the Wedbush Morgan Securities analyst, told the *New York Times,* "All the toy testing and safety measures cost money. But the Mattel brand can command a premium price."[12]

Misfit Toys

Several of Mattel's Chinese subcontractors bought less expensive lead paint from suppliers not on Mattel's list of eight approved suppliers.[13] The U.S. government had begun regulating the use of lead in consumer products such as paint, furniture, and toys in the 1970s.[14] Lead paint on children's toys was completely banned in the United States in 1977.[15]

Long-time Mattel supplier Lee Der produced 937,000 of the toys recalled due to excessive amounts of lead. Typically, Chinese firms had long supply chains that hindered tracing the exact origin of components, chemicals, and food additives.[16] However, in this instance the paint was sold to the firm by the best friend of Lee Der's CEO, Zhang

Shuhong. On August 13, 2007, Zhang Shuhong hung himself in the toy factory.

Two days later Mattel recalled another 19 million toys from China, citing excessive lead paint on 436,000 die-cast toy cars and too-easily removed small, powerful magnets on the remaining 18.2 million toys. The two recalls involved different manufacturers. Eckert stated, "We have had recalls every year since I've been here," but "the second recall was different; it was going to receive a different level of scrutiny."[17] He told CNN, "I'm disappointed, I'm upset, but I can ensure your viewers that we are doing everything we can about the situation. . . . Every production batch of toys is being tested, and we'll continue to enforce the highest quality standards in the industry."[18] Mattel's stock price dropped on news of the recall, but it recovered in after-hours trading.

In a full-page ad published in the *New York Times,* the *Wall Street Journal,* and *USA Today,* Eckert, a father of four, said that "nothing is more important than the safety of our children." "Our long record of safety at Mattel is why we're one of the most trusted names with parents," Eckert wrote. "And I am confident that the actions we are taking now will maintain that trust."

With each recall, Eckert attributed the flaws to Chinese subcontractors. But on September 21, 2007, Mattel took responsibility for the recalls, blaming a design flaw rather than a manufacturing mishap. The "vast majority of those products that were recalled were the result of a design flaw in Mattel's design, not through a manufacturing flaw in China's manufacturers," Debrowski said. "We understand and appreciate deeply the issues that this has caused for the reputation of Chinese manufacturers."[19]

In October 2007 Mattel announced a sales decline of $30 to $50 million and a charge of $40 million due to product scares, delayed shipments, and revoked import licenses.[20]

The U.S. Toy Industry

In 2007, the U.S. toy market was valued at $40.3 billion (Exhibit 1). However, Euromonitor International estimated that the traditional toys and games segment, which represented 67.42 percent of the market, was expected to increase by only 1.4 percent from 2008 to 2013 (Exhibit 2). The toy industry was segmented into two main categories: traditional toys and games (such as cars and trains, dolls and accessories, and board games) and video games. It segmented ages into four groups: 7 and under, 8 to 12, 13 to 17 and 18 and over (Exhibit 3).[21] During the first eight months of 2006, the 7-and-under age group accounted for 62 percent of toy sales.

In line with other industries, the toy industry was using less domestic production. In 2004, 73 percent of U.S. toys were imported, with over 72 percent of imports coming from the People's Republic of China (PRC). By 2007, over 88 percent of U.S. toy imports were from China. Exhibit 4 contains data on toy manufacturing and imports from 2000 to 2007. The shift in manufacturing raised little attention until 2007, when a series of recalls due mainly to lead paint attracted the attention of consumers, retailers, and regulators.

Industry Regulation The toy industry was governed by both U.S. federal government monitoring and regulation and industry self-regulation. The Federal Hazardous Substances Act and its amendments, such as the 1969 Child Protection and Toy Safety Act, were the basic laws covering toy safety. In 1973 the Consumer Product Safety Act created the Consumer Product Safety Commission (CPSC). The CPSC, headquartered in Bethesda, Maryland, maintained teams of field inspectors to monitor both domestic and foreign-made toys for (1) paint and other similar surface-coating materials, (2) pacifiers and rattles, (3) toy-cap noise levels, (4) electrical-thermal toys, (5) chemistry sets, (6) sharp edges and points, (7) small parts, which could be swallowed or inhaled, (8) use and abuse testing, (9) hazardous substances, (10) flammability, and (11) art materials.

In recent years, the CPSC had received diminishing budgets. The number of personnel involved in the Children's and Other Hazards Division dropped from 228 in 2003 to 168 in 2006. Likewise, its budget dropped from $27.7 million to $25.6 million.[22] During the 1997–2006 timeframe, however, the pace of imports accelerated, with a 200 percent increase from 1997 to 2006. Over 85 percent of all recalls came from the imported products.[23]

The role of the CPSC is both proactive and reactive. The five parts to its powers are (1) develop voluntary industry standards, working with industry; (2) issue and enforce mandatory standards or ban products if no standards would protect the public; (3) force recalls or product repairs;

Exhibit 1   Retail Sales of Toys and Games by Sector: Value 2001–2007 (in millions of dollars)

	2001	2002	2003	2004	2005	2006	2007
Traditional toys and games	23,295.7	23,558.1	23,470.2	22,946.6	22,282.6	22,508.2	22,191.8
Video games	9,447.0	10,212.5	10,316.9	10,220.9	10,812.3	12,748.5	18,143.7
Toys and games	32,742.7	33,770.6	33,787.1	33,167.5	33,094.9	35,256.7	40,335.5

Source: Official statistics, trade associations, trade press, company research, store checks, trade interviews, Euromonitor estimates.

Exhibit 2 Sales of Toys and Games by Sector, 2008–2013

Forecast Sales of Toys and Games: Value (in millions of dollars)						
	2008	2009	2010	2011	2012	2013
Traditional toys and games	22,348.3	22,458.9	22,724.0	23,052.8	23,476.2	23,952.7
Video games	23,759.5	26,750.1	28,210.6	29,860.3	32,197.8	35,389.0
Toys and games	46,104.8	49,209.0	50,934.6	52,913.1	55,674.0	59,341.8

Forecast Retail Sales of Toys and Games: Value Growth (in percent)		
	2008–2013 CAGR	2008–2013 Total
Traditional toys and games	1.4	7.2
Video games	8.3	49.0
Toys and games	5.2	28.7

Source: Official statistics, trade associations, trade press, company research, store checks, trade interviews, Euromonitor estimates.

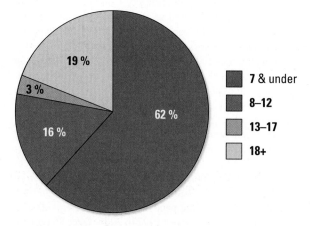

Exhibit 3 Dollar Share of Toy Industry Sales by Age Group (first 8 months of 2006)

Source: C. Annicelli, "Darkest before the Dawn," *Playthings,* November 2006, p. 30.

(4) conduct research on potential product hazards; and (5) inform and educate consumers through media, state and local governments, and private organizations, as well as by responding to consumer inquiries.[24] For known hazards, the CPSC works with the industry to establish voluntary standards to protect the public. The CPSC then expects the industry to abide by those standards, and it could force a recall if a company distributed a product in violation of the voluntary standards. The CPSC can ban a product before it is marketed only when no standard would protect the public from the harm.

With regard to the toy recalls, the CPSC's jurisdiction covered paint, hazardous materials, and small magnets that could be swallowed. Warren noted, "With lead poisoning known to be a danger to all children, the United States undertook a remarkable, if still far from complete, purging of environmental lead, resulting in a reduction in average blood-lead levels to less than two micrograms per deciliter at century's end, from almost 15 in the mid-1970s.[25] Yet, as Warren noted, other countries had not acted as vigorously to ban lead and other toxic substances or to enforce legislation regarding these substances. The lax product safety and environmental regulations lowered manufacturing costs in these countries but also prolonged the risk to U.S. children, as well as the workers and children in those countries.

In addition to complying with federal regulations, the U.S. toy industry had established voluntary safety standards. The Toy Industry Association, Inc. (TIA), a not-for-profit trade association for producers and importers of toys and youth entertainment products sold in North America, represented over 500 companies who accounted for approximately 85 percent of domestic toy sales. Appendix A contains TIA's mission statement. TIA members included licensors, designers, inventors, safety consultants, testing laboratories, communications professionals, and the media. According to its Web site, "Our long history of leadership in toy safety includes the development of the first comprehensive toy safety standard. We continue to work with government officials, consumer groups and industry leaders on ongoing programs to ensure safe play."[26] The TIA posted a separate Web site with safety tips for parents (www.toyinfo.org).

The TIA was itself a member of the International Council of Toy Industries (ICTI), which consisted of toy trade associations from Australia, Austria, Brazil, Canada, China, Chinese Taipei, Denmark, France, Germany, Hong Kong, Hungary, Italy, Japan, Mexico, Netherlands, Russia, Spain, Sweden, the United Kingdom, and the United States. ICTI's Web site stated, "The health and safety of children

Exhibit 4   U.S. Toy Imports (in millions of dollars)

	2000	2001	2002	2003	2004	2005	2006	2007
Total U.S. Toy Imports								
Wheeled toys	486	256	331	367	407	420	449	na
Dolls and accessories	1,475	1,219	1,258	1,226	1,005	1,038	1,053	na
Toys	7,631	7,267	7,654	7,769	7,937	8,272	8,295	10,512
Games	3,475	5,124	5,479	4,985	5,199	6,746	7,460	11,494
Festive articles	2,083	2,215	2,329	2,402	2,654	2,766	2,793	2,958
Total	15,150	16,081	17,051	16,749	17,202	19,242	20,050	24,964
U.S. Toy Imports from China								
Wheeled toys	292	109	124	171	219	220	251	na
Dolls and accessories	1,295	1,073	1,160	1,119	925	962	966	na
Toys	6,300	5,948	6,424	7,769	7,937	7,300	7,326	9,253
Games	1,129	1,406	2,517	4,985	5,199	4,857	5,981	10,118
Festive articles	1,685	1,856	2,005	2,402	2,654	2,487	2,540	2,674
Total	10,700	10,392	12,227	16,446	16,934	15,826	17,064	22,045

Sources: M. Lauzon, 2005. "China: The World's *Toy* Makers, *Plastics News,* vol. 17, no. 42 (2005), pp. 16–18 and USA Trade Online.

throughout the world is the driving force behind ICTI, which promotes international toy safety standards and a responsible attitude to advertising and marketing to children."

ICTI developed its CARE (Caring, Awareness, Responsible, Ethical) Process "to promote ethical manufacturing, in the form of fair labor treatment, as well as employee health and safety, in the toy industry supply chain worldwide. Its initial focus is in China, where 70 percent of the world's toy volume was manufactured. Its intent was to provide a single, fair, thorough and consistent program to monitor toy factories' compliance with ICTI's Code of Business Practices (the 'Code')."[27] The ICTI CARE Process engaged toy companies and individual factories producing toys. To be considered an ICTI CARE member, a company must have committed to purchasing products only from factories enrolled in the CARE Process. Factories were audited by independent auditing firms that were specially trained with regard to ICTI's code.

Toy Industry Trends   Over the next five years the numbers of children under 5 years old and of those ages 5 to 9 were predicted to increase nearly 5 percent and about 4 percent, respectively, in the United States (Exhibit 5). In 2006 American grandparents spent more than $30 billion, or $500 per child, each year on their grandchildren, a twofold increase over the amount spent a decade earlier.[28] Grandparents represented 25 percent of the annual toy

Exhibit 5   U.S. Population Projections (in millions)

Age	2007	2010	2015	2020
Under 5	20,724	21,100	22,076	22,846
5–9	19,849	20,886	21,707	22,732
10–14	20,309	20,395	21,658	22,571

Source: Data for 2007 from "Table 1: Annual Estimates of the Population by Sex and Five-Year Age Groups for the United States: April 1, 2000, to July 1, 2007" (NC-EST2007-01), Population Division, U.S. Census Bureau; data for 2010-2020 from "Table 12: Projections of the Population by Age and Sex for the United States: 2010 to 2050" (NP2008-T12), Population Division, U.S. Census Bureau.

dollars spent. The number of U.S. grandparents was predicted to swell from 70 million to well over 115 million by 2010 due to baby boomers entering the grandparent cohort. As a result, manufacturers have targeted baby-boomer grandparents with nostalgic toys such as Fisher-Price's Snoopy Sniffer pull toy and with promotions such as KB Toys' Grandparents' Rewards Club.[29]

To be profitable, toy makers have had to keep pace with the rapidly changing world, stay on the edge of technology, provide youngsters with appropriate toys for their enjoyment,

Exhibit 6   Top 5 Ways Kids Spend Their Free Time*

Watching TV/movies	16%
Playing with toys	9
Being with friends	6
Using computer for recreation	6
Video games	6

*Represents the percentage of their free time spent participating in these activities.

Source: NPD Group, 2006.

and challenge their creativity and imagination. According to the NPD Group's Kids Leisure Time Study, over 81 percent of children ages 5 to 12 played with toys each week. Yet playing with toys was second to watching TV and movies, which accounted for 16 percent of their free time (Exhibit 6). Children were also being exposed to technology at an earlier age. The average age that children begin using consumer electronic (CE) devices declined from 8.1 years in 2005 to 6.7 years in 2007. This age compression challenged traditional toy manufacturers to maintain interest in their products and/ or incorporate technology in toys at an earlier age.

Innovative toys incorporated voice recognition and animatronics as well as infrared vision and artificial intelligence. Some video game system used patented motion-capture technology to place the child on-screen and literally "in" the game. Concerns over childhood obesity increasingly have pressured parents to provide toys that promote a more active lifestyle (such as Dance, Dance Revolution) and aid in their children's creative and intellectual growth.

The Competition

The U.S. toy industry consisted of manufacturers and retailers. *Manufacturers* is a loose term as the majority of the products in certain segments are outsourced to offshore subcontractors. Three manufacturers, Mattel, Hasbro, and JAKKS Pacific, dominated the U.S. toy industry. In addition, some smaller manufacturers such as RC2 produced a smaller range of toys for specific niches. A large number of smaller players that competed in new product development existed. When these companies stumbled onto a unique idea and enjoyed temporary success, they were usually acquired by a market leader.

Major foreign manufacturers, including such brands as Danish Lego and Canadian MEGA Brands, also sold toys in the United States. The growth of big-box retailer Toys "R" Us and discounter Wal-Mart changed the balance of power in the industry, as each could demand concessions on price and other product features. The buyer power of the big-box retailers had driven smaller manufacturers, as well as retailers, nearly out of business. Appendix B provides a list of the major manufacturers and summarizes their financial results for 2007.

Hasbro   Hasbro was founded by two brothers, Henry and Helal Hassenfield, in Providence, Rhode Island, in 1923. In 2006 Hasbro was the second-largest toy maker, behind Mattel, with revenue exceeding $3.15 billion. Its toys and brands included G.I. Joe, Tonka Toys, Nerf Balls, and Weebles, as well as board games such as Scrabble, Candy Land, and Monopoly. The firm also produced Marvel, Star Wars, Spider-Man, and Transformer toys under license from the filmmakers. These toys sold for higher prices than Hasbro's other products but also incurred higher costs due to the licensing fees. Hasbro's Playskool line included both toys and baby care items. The company viewed its core-brand products as a more consistent revenue stream than its licensed products. Similar to the case with Mattel, in 2006 almost 50 percent of Hasbro's sales came from three customers: Wal-Mart (24 percent), Toys "R" Us (11 percent) and Target (13 percent).

Hasbro owned just two manufacturing facilities, in the United States and in Waterford, Ireland. It outsourced most production to Chinese makers and a small amount of production to suppliers in Europe, other Asian countries, and the Americas. Its U.S. plant in Massachusetts produced games. The company first began manufacturing action figures in Hong Kong in the 1960s. In 2006 Hasbro reduced its manufacturing in Ireland while transferring production to Chinese suppliers. In addition, the company has begun product development and engineering in China. Hasbro partnered with Li & Fung to manage its Chinese supply chain and to act as its exclusive distributor in China. With Li & Fung, Hasbro has begun to sell toys in Chinese department stores (Isetan and New World) and hypermarkets as well. Hasbro required that its suppliers met international standards. Both Hasbro employees and approved ICTI auditors inspected vendors. During 2007 Hasbro had no product recalls due to lead paint. It did, however, have three recalls related to burn dangers with its Easy-bake Oven.

JAKKS Pacific   Although only 12 years old, JAKKS Pacific was one of the United States' top toy companies, making and selling action figures under exclusive license for the World Wrestling Federation, die-cast and plastic cars (Road Champs, Remco), preschool toys (Child Guidance), pens and markers (Pentech), fashion dolls, and even pet products. In 2007 JAKKS Pacific had revenue of $756.4 million. It employed 419 full-time employees in the United States, 154 in Hong Kong, and 25 in China. Target, Toys "R" Us, and Wal-Mart accounted for nearly 60 percent of company sales.

JAKKS's growth strategy included expanding product lines through licensing agreements and acquisitions. The company partnered with Jelly Belly Candy Co. to create a line of art activities and stationery based on Jelly Belly jelly beans and with HIT Entertainment to license Bob the Builder, Thomas & Friends, and Barney characters for a variety of arts and crafts products. JAKKS acquired Play Along, maker of plush toys, action figures, dolls, and preschool toys, in 2004. Play Along licenses included Care Bears, Teletubbies, and Cabbage Patch Kids. JAKKS Pacific, Ltd., its Hong Kong division, oversaw overseas vendors' operations. In 2007 JAKKS Pacific avoided lead-paint-based recalls but did issue a recall for 245,000 battery packs for toy vehicles manufactured in China.

Lego Lego was the world's fifth-largest toy maker, with 2005 sales of $1.1 billion. The company was still owned by grandchildren of its founder, Ole Kirk Christiansen. Since its founding in 1934, it made over 200 billion building blocks. Lego licensed and created products to complement television and movie releases such as HIT Entertainment's *Bob the Builder, Star Wars,* and *Indiana Jones.* Until recently, Lego manufactured toys in Denmark, the United States, and Switzerland. It shifted production from the United States and Switzerland to the Czech Republic and Mexico and began outsourcing electronic components of certain toys primarily to electronics manufacturers, such as Flextronics (headquartered in Singapore), to reduce costs.

In an interview with *Plastics News,* Lego spokeswoman Charlotte Simonsen explained that Lego utilized centralized, highly automated production to produce its standardized plastic building blocks.[30] Plants in Eastern Europe, including the Czech Republic, were close to its headquarters in Billund, Denmark, allowing for oversight and rapid response. These highly automated plants made Lego less sensitive to labor costs than were other makers.

As a result, Lego made only 3 percent of its products in China. Analysts believed that Lego could benefit from the recalls, as parents searched for alternatives to products made in China. In 2006 Lego recalled about 358,000 plastic trucks containing Lego Duplo bricks. A wheel on the truck could come off, exposing a metal axle that could injure a toddler; the bricks were not recalled.

RC2 Founded in 1989 as Racing Champions Corporation, RC2 grew to be one of the larger toy companies in the United States by 2006. Although RC2's revenue of $518.8 million was a fraction of Mattel's, the firm's recall of 1.5 million Chinese-made Thomas & Friends wooden trains, popular with preschoolers, set off the wave of recalls and a near panic among parents of preschoolers. In contrast to Mattel and Hasbro, RC2 earned much of its revenue from production of licensed products such as Thomas & Friends, Bob the Builder, and NASCAR vehicles. In addition, RC2 owned the Learning Curve family of brands (Eden and Lamaze) and First Years, and it produced various replicas of cars and trucks. Of the affected U.S. toy makers, RC2 was least dependent on the major retailers. Wal-Mart accounted for only 16 percent of sales.

Unlike the typical toys from China that were recalled, Thomas & Friends toys were usually "purchased in upscale toy stores for $10 to $70 apiece, often by politically empowered parents who are extremely averse to exposing their children to contaminants of any kind."[31] More than two-thirds of RC2's products targeted young children.

RC2 primarily served as a middleman linking content and characters to manufacturers. It told analysts that it would prefer not to own its own plants. In 2006, 91.8 percent of RC2's products were manufactured in China. According to its financial filings, RC2 had long-term relationships with seven Chinese companies that produced about half its products. The recalled products were made in Dongguan, where half of China's toys originate. Paradoxically, the second recall in 2007 included green trees.

Retailers

Toy retailing in the United States radically changed with the birth of Toys "R" Us and the growth of Wal-Mart. Wal-Mart, with over 33 percent of the industry's sales, dominated the industry, followed by Target, Toys "R" Us, and Kmart, in 2006. Few independent toy retailers remained, as many lifelong specialty stores had been forced out when retailers, especially Wal-Mart, demanded discounted prices. Exhibits 7 and 8 contain data on sales by distribution channel. Discount department stores accounted for 53 percent of 2006 toy and games sales,[32] while toy stores accounted for 20 percent. Retail-channel performance showed continued share growth in the mass/discount channel. Online toy sales continued to increase, generating over $1.3 billion in 2007, a 2.6 percent increase over the prior year. These sales come from traditional retailers' sites, such as Target; e-retailers, such as Amazon.com; and manufacturers, such as Mattel. Appendix C provides a list of the major retailers and summarizes their financial results for 2007.

Wal-Mart Wal-Mart had been the world's largest toy retailer since 2000. Its estimated 2006 toy sales reached $10,750 million in the United States.[33] However, toys and sporting goods accounted for just 5 percent of the company's sales. Wal-Mart's market share provided it with the ability to negotiate with suppliers for discount prices. If a manufacturer's product lines were not offered at Wal-Mart store locations, the company's sales often fell below expectations due to Wal-Mart's growing market share. Wal-Mart's low wholesale prices forced competitors to outsource production overseas to reduce their overhead costs. In addition, Wal-Mart's deep discounting of toys in October acted as a preemptive strike to undercut its competitors.

Toys "R" Us Once the largest toy retailer in the United States, Toys "R" Us reported the second-highest 2006 toy sales, $5.7 billion. Sales had declined from $6.2 billion in 2005 due to its reorganization and severing of its relationship with Amazon.com. In 2005, two private investment firms (KKR and Bain Capital) and a real estate company (Vornado Realty Trust) bought Toys "R" Us for $6.6 billion. The combined firm owned, operated, or leased 587 Toys "R" Us stores and 230 Babies "R" Us stores by the end of 2006.

Target In 2006 Target's $3.45 billion in toy and game sales and 23 percent market share placed it in fourth place when games-only retailer GameStop was excluded.

	Percent of Retail Value					
	2003	2004	2005	2006	2007	2008
Store-based retailing	94.8	92.6	91.7	91.4	90.9	90.8
Grocery retailers	3.0	3.6	4.1	4.6	4.8	4.9
Nongrocery retailers	82.8	80.4	79.3	78.4	76.3	75.5
Mixed retailers	48.0	50.3	52.7	53.4	50.7	48.7
Leisure and personal-goods retailers	34.8	30.1	26.5	25.0	25.6	26.8
Other store-based retailing	9.0	8.6	8.3	8.4	9.7	10.4
Nonstore retailing	5.2	7.4	8.3	8.6	9.1	9.2
Vending	0.2	0.2	0.2	0.2	0.2	0.3
Home shopping	1.8	2.0	2.1	2.1	2.1	2.0
Internet retailing	3.2	5.1	5.8	6.1	6.7	6.8
Direct selling	0.1	0.1	0.1	0.1	0.1	0.1
Total	100.0	100.0	100.0	100.0	100.0	100.0

Source: Official statistics, trade associations, trade press, company research, store checks, trade interviews, Euromonitor estimates.

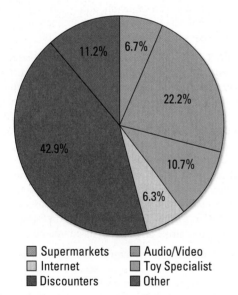

- ▪ Supermarkets   ▪ Audio/Video
- ▪ Internet   ▪ Toy Specialist
- ▪ Discounters   ▪ Other

Exhibit 8 Retail Sales of Toys and Games by Distribution Format, 2006

Source: Euromonitor International (2007).

Target's online store ranked third behind eBay and Amazon.com in terms of visits. In 2006, Target launched "Time to Play!" toy boutiques inside the toy departments of each of its stores and introduced its own line of toys called Play-Wonder for children ages 2 to 5 years. In addition, Target stocked a larger assortment of high-margin specialty toys than Wal-Mart stocked. In 2006 electronics, entertainment, sporting goods, and toys accounted for 23 percent of sales.

China Supplies the World's Toys

China was the world's largest toy-producing and -exporting nation, with more than 8,000 companies employing more than 3.5 million people in 2006. More than 30,000 different toys were made in China and exported to 100 countries and territories.[34] Exports to the United States grew consistently to over $22 billion in 2007 (see Exhibit 4).

Toy manufacturing in China was shaped by two competing pressures: quality enhancement and cost reduction. On one hand, many export-oriented manufacturers had worked to increase product quality and quality control and had been certified by major international business standards groups. Over 300 toy makers had applied for Code of Business Practices certification developed by the ICTI.[35]

On the other hand, foreign firms had forced Chinese toy makers to reduce costs. As noted above, in the United States toys were increasingly sold through mass merchandisers. "Retailers force prices down. It's relentless. It forces toy companies to manufacture as inexpensively as they can," said Frank Clarke, a spokesman for the Toy Industry Association, in an interview in *Plastics News*.[36] As costs for plastics and energy soared, manufacturers perceived labor as a potential source of cost savings.

Several factors made China an attractive toy supplier. First, the average wage in China was $200 per month. The Chinese government believed that China would stay competitive on the world market as long as wages remained below $600 per month. Second, China's currency, the yuan, was considered undervalued relative to the dollar. The yuan floated in a narrow band near 8.1 to the U.S. dollar. The Chinese government was under increasing pressure from the U.S. and European governments to increase the yuan's value to stem the flood of Chinese exports across product categories. Either inflation in China or a revaluation of the yuan could decrease China's attractiveness as a manufacturer.

Another trend in China was a transition from companies' merely serving as outsourcing partners in a foreign manufacturer's value chain to their creating domestic research and design activities. With the support of the Chinese Ministry of Labor and Social Security, the China Toy Association created a certification for trained toy designers to improve the nation's product design capability.[37] Some Chinese firms began registering their own intellectual property with regard to toy design at home and abroad.

Surprisingly, some toy manufacturing left China, much as it had shifted from Taiwan to China in the 1990s. Labor shortages in some parts of China drove up wages to the point that some Chinese manufacturers invested in even lower-wage countries, such as Vietnam. In addition, threats by the U.S. government made makers wary. Still, in 2005 toy exports to the United States from the rest of Asia were only about 7 percent of those from China.[38]

Interestingly, the Chinese domestic toy market remained virtually untapped. The nation has 300 million children under the age of 14.

Recalls and Aftermath

In 2007 a safety and public relations crisis gripped the United States toy industry. Through mid-November 2007 toy manufacturers and the U.S. Consumer Product Safety Commission recalled over 25 million units through 60 recalls. Most of these recalls were due to lead paint found on products manufactured in China. From Thomas, the cheeky tank engine, to Diego and Barbie, some of the most loved toy brands were affected.

The tipping point for the recall crisis seemed to be RC2's June 2007 recall of 1.5 million Chinese-made wooden railroad toys and set parts due to lead paint. The maker, Hansheng Wood Products Factory, was later included in an August 2007 export ban announced by the General Administration for Quality Supervision, Inspection and Quarantine, a China quality watchdog.[39] Toy recalls were not, however, a new problem for the industry and consumers. Exhibit 9 contains recall data for 1988 to 2007.[40] The number of recalls involving toys made in China had increased along with the percentage of toys manufactured there. Most of the 2007 toy recalls were for traditional toys targeted to the most vulnerable age group: toddlers.

In a recent editorial the *Wall Street Journal* described the Chinese environment that spawned the product safety recalls and left Chinese consumers vulnerable to unsafe products.[41] Possible explanations included an ideological vacuum in postcommunist China due to Mao's destruction of traditional Chinese values and beliefs and the absence of any values other than wealth or the current business environment in which fierce competition and thin margins make every dollar count. A more comprehensive explanation was "a political system without popular elections or an effective system of checks and balances has helped create a culture in which the Chinese are not accountable to *each other*" (italics in original).[42] As a result, no codified set of ethics to guide national behavior existed.

In a *New York Times* interview, Sean McGowan, managing director and toy analyst at Wedbush Morgan Securities, contended that toy recalls were not over: "If I went

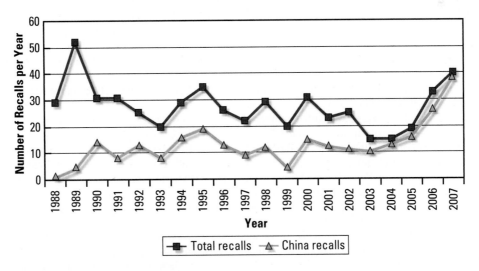

Exhibit 9 Toy Recalls, 1988–2007

Source: H. Bapuji and P. W. Beamish, "Toy Recalls—Is China Really the Problem?" *Canada-Asia Commentary,* 45 (2007), pp. 1–8.

down to the shelves of Wal-Mart and tested everything, I'm going to find serious problems. The idea that Mattel—with its high standards—has a bigger problem than everybody else is laughable. If we don't see an increase of recalls in this industry, then it's a case of denial."[43] Prakash Sethi, who has served as an independent monitor of working conditions in Mattel's factories through ICCA, agreed: "If Mattel, with all of its emphasis on quality and testing, found such a widespread problem, what do you think is happening in the rest of the toy industry, in the apparel industry and even in the low-end electronics industry?" However, Sethi added, "there is something to be said about the pressure that American and European and multinational companies put on Chinese companies to supply cheap products. The operating margins are razor thin, so you really should not be surprised that there is pressure to cut corners."[44]

Several companies, who license characters to toy makers, announced additional inspection protocols. For example, Nickelodeon, which owns Dora the Explorer and Diego, hired a third-party monitor to check on all the companies that licensed its characters, including Mattel[45] and RC2.[46] Sesame Workshop and Disney both announced additional testing programs.[47] Disney's tests of its character toys for lead paint included random testing of toys on retail shelves. Wal-Mart revealed that one of the biggest concerns of its shoppers was the safety of toys manufactured in China.[48]

In addition, Toys "R" Us hired engineers to randomly choose toys on its shelves for testing by an independent lab. In a *New York Times* interview, Ron Boire, president of Toys "R" Us, stated: "Trust but verify. We have to be confident. I have to be able to put my head on the pillow and say 'I've done everything I can.'"[49]

The Chinese government initiated a crackdown on product safety for numerous industries. It revoked the export licenses of about 300 toy makers, closed approximately 2,000 unlicensed factories, and banned lead paint completely for use in U.S. toy exports.[50]

Nonetheless, the toy recalls threatened sales of Chinese products during the 2007 holiday season.[51] A Harris poll found that over 90 percent of Americans were aware of the recalls. Yet only 6 percent were confident that they had a recalled toy in their home, and even fewer reported taking action. Most respondents overestimated the number of recalls on lead paint rather than design flaws. Almost 50 percent of respondents reported that they would avoid products or toys from China in the 2007 holiday season. Only about 10 percent of respondents stated that they would not avoid Chinese products or toys. Interestingly, the CPSC was the public's most trusted source of product safety information.

The U.S. toy recalls affected the industry elsewhere.[52] The EU threatened a ban on Chinese goods, including toys, if China failed to comply with EU health and safety measures. In 2008, Brazil's government banned Mattel toy imports until it verified that Mattel's toys met local safety regulations.

On September 19, 2008. toy industry representatives testified before the U.S. Senate Subcommittee and the U.S. House Subcommittee on the question of the safety of toys sold in the United States and the possibility of tighter government control. In addition, critics called for the U.S. government to restore the CPSC's budget to pre-Bush levels. In 2007 and 2008, the Bush administration cut the commission's budget by 10 percent, forcing a reduction in the number of investigators and agents.[53]

Thomas H. Moore, commissioner of the CPSC, told Congress that a number of parties—including the Bush administration, the U.S. Congress, regulators, manufacturers, importers, retailers, and "anyone else who may have been active or inactive participants in enabling the policy decisions and priorities that have led us to this point"—shared blame for the recent wave of toy recalls. At a hearing of the U.S. House of Representatives Subcommittee on Commerce, Trade and Consumer Protection, Moore said that those who stood by and "quietly acquiesced while the [CPSC] was reduced to a weakened regulator, largely relying on the regulated to regulate themselves, must examine and correct the role that they played in putting the commission in its current state."[54]

Moore also said that Congress had been right in rejecting the Bush administration's staffing and budget proposal for fiscal year 2008, which would have reduced the CPSC staff by 19 full-time employees. However, Moore added that simply throwing resources at the CPSC in response to public alarm over the recent recalls would not resolve the situation. Instead, Moore endorsed an incremental approach to increasing the CPSC's budget and staff. "It has taken years for the commission to get to its present position and it will take years to correct," said Moore.[55]

On November 19, 2007, California attorney general Jerry Brown sued 20 toy makers and retailers, including Mattel and Toys "R" Us, due to "unlawful quantities of lead." The state accused the companies of knowingly exposing children to lead and failing "to provide warning of the risk, which is required under the Safe Drinking Water and Toxic Enforcement Act of 1986, known as Proposition 65."[56]

Eckert caught himself staring at Sarge. The next weeks would be challenging as Mattel and its competitors developed a new strategy for dealing with the challenges in their competitive environment and the loss of consumer confidence. He felt fairly comfortable about the manner in which Mattel had dealt with the crisis as it unfolded. Not everything had been perfect, but it was a crisis, after all, and he thought Mattel's reputation would survive. He knew that was not a given, and so he and his team still needed to work on the problems. He thought it was important to review how they had come to this crisis, review all strategic elements, and revise their strategy going forward. And with all the dynamics in the industry and consumer base changing as rapidly as they were, he thought there might be the possibility that a stronger Mattel would emerge from the experience.

Appendix A   Toy Industry Association Mission Statement

Our Mission

Our mission is to lead the growth and health of the toy industry. We are committed to addressing the needs of our diverse membership, building on our history of leadership in safety standards, advocacy on legislative and trade issues, visibility in the media, and philanthropy to children.

Developing the highest universal standards

We have a dedicated team leading the industry's safety initiatives, and we fulfill the role of chair in the ongoing review process for ASTM F963, the comprehensive toy safety standard.

Ensuring safe play for children

We educate manufacturers on safety and quality standards, and we lead public initiatives to educate consumers on safe play.

Protecting the rights of factory workers

We educate members on compliance with ethical manufacturing standards to ensure compliance with the ICTI CARE Program.

Enhancing the image and growth of the toy industry

We generate major feature stories and broadcast segments on the latest toys and trends, and we serve as industry spokesperson on vital issues in the news.

Supporting free trade and fair representation on regulatory issues

We voice issues with regulators in the U.S. and internationally. Our advocacy helps prevent unwarranted legislative or regulatory actions and ensure fair representation.

Appendix B   Toy and Games Manufacturers' Key Numbers, 2007

Key Numbers	Mattel	Hasbro	JAKKS Pacific	Lego	RC2	Industry Median	Market Median
Annual sales ($ millions)	**5,970.1**	3,837.6	857.1	1,584.5	518.8		
Employees	**31,000**	5,900	598	4,199	821 (2006)		
Market cap ($ millions)	**5,374.2**	4,054.9	549.1	—			
Profitability:							
Gross profit margin	46.10%	**58.9%**	36.70%	65.0	45.70%	35.20%	52.60%
Pretax profit margin	9.80%	12.20%	**12.90%**	18.1	2.9%	2.10%	4.70%
Net profit margin	8.60%	8.50%	**10.10%**	12.8	1.6%	2.20%	2.50%
Return on equity	**22.2%**	25.6%	13.4%	17.9	1.8%	9.1%	6.8%
Return on assets	**10.0%**	10.4%	9.3%	—	1.1%	1.2%	0.7%
Return on invested capital	**13.2%**	13.9%	11.5%	60.7	1.3%	5.6%	3.4%
Valuation:							
Price/earnings ratio	10.47	12.19	**5.81**	—	21.57	7.93	10.38
Per-share data ($):							
Revenue per share	17.20	29.37	**33.40**	—	26.32	8.07	5.58
Dividends per share	**0.75**	0.76	—	—	—	0.54	0.68
Cash flow per share	1.41	**4.16**	2.60	—	1.11	0.05	0.33
Long-term debt per share	**2.12**	5.10	3.56	—	5.44	0.69	2.94
Book value per share	6.76	9.74	**26.43**	—	21.85	3.07	5.02
Total assets per share	15.41	24.47	**37.52**	—	37.80	5.41	10.65

Source: Hoover's, by license from EDGAR Online.

Appendix C Toy and Games Retailers' Key Numbers, 2007

Key Numbers	Wal-Mart	Target	Toys "R" Us
Annual sales ($ millions)	348,650.0	63,367.0	13,050
Employees	1,900,000	352,000	59,000
Market cap ($ millions)	193,151.9	50,294.4	Private
Profitability:			
Gross profit margin	24.50%	33.70%	—
Pretax profit margin	5.30%	6.50%	—
Net profit margin	3.40%	4.00%	1.10%
Return on equity	21.3%	17.7%	—
Return on assets	8.2%	5.8%	—
Return on invested capital	11.5%	7.6%	—
Valuation:			
Price/earnings ratio	16.02	10.43	—
Operations	—	—	—
Inventory turnover	7.6	4.9	—
Days cost of goods sold in inventory	48	75	—
Net receivables turnover flow	127.8	8.6	—
Per-share data ($):			
Revenue per share	102.97	86.69	—
Dividends per share	0.95	0.60	—
Cash flow per share	5.38	5.74	—
Working capital per share	(1.97)	8.96	—
Long-term debt per share	8.69	23.17	—
Book value per share	16.71	18.04	—
Total assets per share	42.79	62.49	—

Sources: Public companies trading on the New York Stock Exchange, the American Stock Exchange, and the NASDAQ National Market.
Hoover's, by license from EDGAR Online.

Endnotes

1. D. Barboza and L. Story, Toymaking in China, Mattel's way, *New York Times,* July 26, 2007.
2. Mom confronts Mattel at corporate HQ over toy recall, *abc7.com,* August 23, 2007, http://abclocal.go.com/kabc/story?section=local&id=5599290. (accessed December 17, 2007).
3. J. Thottam, Why Mattel apologized to China, *Time,* September 21, 2007.
4. Barboza and Story, Toymaking in China.
5. L. Story, Lead paint prompts Mattel to recall 967,000 toys, *New York Times,* August 2, 2007, p. C1.
6. Barboza and Story, Toymaking in China.
7. Ibid.
8. Ibid.
9. M. Lauzon, Mattel Inc. ending U.S. production, *Plastics News,* vol. 13, no. 6 (2001), pp. 1–2.
10. Barboza and Story, Toymaking in China.
11. Ibid.
12. Ibid.
13. Story, Lead paint prompts Mattel to recall 967,000 toys.
14. C. Warren, The little engine that could poison, *New York Times,* June 22, 2007, p. A21.
15. CPSC, CPSC announces final ban on lead-containing paint (press release).
16. Associated Press, Toy company CEO kills self, August 13, 2007, www.cnn.com/2007/WORLD/asiapcf/08/13/china.toymaker.ap/index.htnl (accessed August 13, 2007).
17. L. Story, After stumbling, Mattel cracks down in China, *New York Times,* August 29, 2007.
18. CNN, Mattel CEO: 'Rigorous standards' after massive toy recall, 2007, www.cnn.com/2007/US/08/14/recall/index.html?iref=newssearch
19. Thottam, Why Mattel apologized to China.
20. D. Pimlott, Mattel earnings dented by recall of 21m toys, *Financial Times,* October 16, 2007, p. 28.
21. C. Annicelli, Darkest before the dawn, *Playthings,* November 2006, p. 30.
22. CPSC, 2007 Performance and accountability report, www.cpsc.gov/cpscpub/pubs/reports/2007par.pdf.
23. CPSC, 2009 Performance budget request, www.cpsc.gov/cpscpub/pubs/reports/2009plan.pdf.
24. www.cpsc.gov/about/faq.html.
25. Warren, The little engine that could poison.
26. Toy Industry Association, *2001–2002 Toy Industry Fact Book* www.toyassociation.org/AM/Template.cfm?Section=About_TIA&Template=/TaggedPage/TaggedPageDisplay.cfm&TPLID=3&ContentID=2546.
27. ICTI, www.toy-icti.org, 2007 (accessed December 12, 2007).
28. D. Kaplan, Grand-scale grandparents, *Houston Chronicle,* November 5, 2006, www.chron.com/disp/story.mpl/front/4310259.html (accessed 12-13-07).
29. Ibid.
30. M. Lauzon, China: The world's *toy* makers, *Plastics News,* vol. 17, no. 42 (2005), pp. 16–18.
31. Warren, The little engine that could poison.
32. D. French, Top 25 retailers. *Playthings,* November 11, 2007, www.playthings.com/index.asp?layout=articlePrint&articleID=CA6500235 (accessed December 12, 2007).
33. Ibid.
34. M. Liang, Bigger and better: The continued growth of China's toy industry, *Playthings,* October 2006, p. 14.
35. Ibid.
36. Lauzon, China: The world's *toy* makers.
37. Liang, Bigger and better.
38. Lauzon, China: The world's *toy* makers.
39. Associated Press, Toy company CEO kills self.
40. H. Bapuji and P. W. Beamish, Toy recalls—Is China really the problem? *Canada-Asia Commentary,* 45 (2007), pp. 1–8.
41. E. Parker, Made in China, *Wall Street Journal,* July 12, 2007, p. A15.
42. Ibid.
43. L. Story and D. Barboza, Mattel recalls 19 million toys sent from China, *New York Times.* August 15, 2007, p. A1.
44. Ibid.
45. L. Story, Lead paint prompts Mattel to recall 967,000 toys, *New York Times,* August 2, 2007, p. C1.
46. D. Barboza and L. Story, RC2's train wreck, *New York Times,* June 20, 2007.
47. L. Story, Disney to test character toys for lead paint, *New York Times,* September 10, 2007, p. C1.
48. Story, After stumbling, Mattel cracks down in China.
49. Story, Disney to test character toys for lead paint.
50. Recall news briefs, *Playthings,* 2007, http://playthings.com/index.asp?layout=articlePrint&articleID=CA6478002) (accessed December 7, 2007).
51. HarrisInteractive, Recent toy recalls threaten sales of Chinese products this holiday season, *The Harris Poll,* no.114, November 14, 2007.
52. Recall news briefs, *Playthings.*
53. Warren, The little engine that could poison.
54. Anonymous, Blame for toy recall problems shared by many, *Business and the Environment,* vol. 18, no. 10 (2007). p. 11.
55. Ibid.
56. Associated Press, California sues Mattel over tainted toys, 2007, www.msnbc.com/id/21886363 (accessed November 19, 2007).

Case 23 Apple Inc.: Taking a Bite Out of the Competition*

In September 2008, after announcing record year-end results, Steve Jobs, Apple Inc.'s CEO, commented, "We don't yet know how this economic downturn will affect Apple. But we're armed with the strongest product line in our history, the most talented employees and the best customers in our industry. And $25 billion of cash safely in the bank with zero debt."[1] Then, in January 2009, in the midst of the economic downturn that had seen most of its competitors reporting reduced results, Apple reported one of its best quarters, surpassing $10 billion in quarterly revenue for the first time in its history[2] (see Exhibits 1 and 2).

Also in January came the news that Apple's visionary leader and CEO, Steve Jobs, would be taking a medical leave of absence until the end of June. Although Jobs, then 53 years old, had appeared to be completely cured of the pancreatic cancer that sidelined him in 2004, he had lost considerable weight during 2008, causing speculation that his cancer had returned. Jobs's physicians found that a hormone imbalance, a side effect of the cancer treatment, was creating a nutritional problem that needed monitoring and treatment.[3] Stating that his "health-related issues are more complex than I originally thought," Jobs asked COO Tim Cook to be responsible for Apple's day-to-day operations, while Jobs remained "involved in major strategic decisions."[4] This news caused Apple shares to drop 7.56 percent on that day and prompted the Securities and Exchange Commission to wonder whether the Apple board of directors (which included former vice president Al Gore and Google's CEO, Dr. Eric Schmidt, among others) "was as forthcoming about [Jobs's] illness as it should have been."[5]

For market watchers, Apple investors, and the sometimes cultlike Apple users, the possibility that CEO Steve Jobs might finally depart from the company he helped found in 1976 was unsettling news. One analyst said that an Apple without Jobs "would still be a remarkable company, but with less of the competitive edge that Jobs helped create. . . . If he isn't able to return, I think you'd see a high-functioning company, but one without the lightning strike of genius. [Apple would] have a human batting average."[6]

Apple, at the top of *BusinessWeek*'s Most Innovative Companies list since 2004,[7] had distinguished itself by excelling over the years not only in product innovation but also in revenue and margins (since 2006 Apple had consistently reported gross margins of around 30 percent). Founded as a computer company in 1976, and known

initially for its intuitive adaptation of the "graphical user interface" or GUI (via the first mouse and the first onscreen "windows"),[8] Apple had dropped the word *computer* from its corporate name in 2007. Apple, Inc., in 2009 was known for having top-selling products not only in desktop (iMac) and notebook (MacBook) personal computers but also in portable digital music players (iPod), online music services (iTunes), mobile communication devices (iPhone), digital consumer entertainment (Apple TV), and handheld devices able to download third-party applications, including games (iPod Touch via the App Store). (See Exhibit 3.)

Although most of those innovations occurred after 1998, when Apple was under Steve Jobs's leadership, there was a 12-year period in which Jobs was not in charge. The company's ongoing stated strategy had been to leverage "its unique ability to design and develop its own operations system, hardware, application software, and services to provide its customers new products and solutions with superior ease-of-use, seamless integration and innovative industrial design."[9] This strategy required not only product design and marketing expertise but also scrupulous attention to operational details. Given Apple's global growth in multiple product categories, and the associated complexity in strategic execution, would the potential loss of one man be sufficient to prevent the company from sustaining its competitive advantage? Was Steve Jobs essential to Apple's success?

Company Background

Founder Steve Jobs Apple Computer was founded in Mountain View, California, on April 1, 1976, by Steve Jobs and Steve Wozniak. Jobs was the visionary and marketer, Wozniak was the technical genius, and A. C. "Mike" Markkula, Jr., who had joined the team several months earlier, was the businessman. Jobs set the mission of empowering individuals, one person–one computer, and doing so with elegance of design and fierce attention to detail. In 1977 the first version of the Apple II became the first computer ordinary people could use right out of the box, and its instant success in the home market caused a computing revolution, essentially creating the personal computer industry. By 1980 Apple was the industry leader and went public in December of that year.

In 1983, Wozniak left the firm and Jobs hired John Sculley away from PepsiCo to take the role of CEO at Apple, citing the need for someone to spearhead marketing and operations while Jobs worked on technology. The result of Jobs's creative focus on personal computing was the Macintosh. Introduced in 1984, with the now-famous Super Bowl television ad based on George Orwell's novel,[10] the Macintosh was a breakthrough in terms of elegant design and ease of use. Its ability to handle large graphic

*This case was prepared by Professor Alan B. Eisner of Pace University and Professor Pauline Assenza of Manhattanville College. This case was solely based on library research and was developed for class discussion rather than to illustrate either effective or ineffective handling of an administrative situation. Copyright © 2009 Alan B. Eisner and Pauline Assenza.

Exhibit 1 Apple Sales

	2008 (in millions)	Change	2007 (in millions)	Change	2006 (in millions)
Product Net Sales					
Desktops	$ 5,603	39%	$ 4,020	21%	$ 3,319
Portables	8,673	38	6,294	55	4,056
iPod	9,153	10	8,305	8	7,676
Music	3,340	34	2,496	32	1,885
iPhone*	1,844	N/A	123	N/A	—
Peripherals	1,659	32	1,260	15	1,100
Software, services	2,207	46	1,508	18	1,279
Total net sales	**$32,479**	**35%**	**$24,006**	**24%**	**$19,315**
Cost of sales	21,334		15,852		13,717
Gross margin	**$11,145**		**$ 8,154**		**$ 5,598**
Gross margin %	34.4%		34%		29%
Research and development	$ 1,109		$ 782		$ 712
Percent of net sales	3.4%		3.3%		3.7%
Selling, general, and administrative	$ 3,761		$ 2,963		$ 2,433
Percent of net sales	11.6%		12.3%		12.6%
Total operating expenses	**$ 4,870**		**$ 3,745**		**$ 3,145**
Net income†	**$ 4,834**		**$ 3,496**		**$ 1,989**
Region Net Sales					
Americas	$14,573	26%	$11,596	23%	$ 9,415
Europe	7,622	40	5,460	33	4,096
Japan	1,509	39	1,082	(11)	1,211
Retail	6,315	53	4,115	27	3,246
Other	2,460	40	1,753	30	1,347

*iPhone sales derived from handset sales, carrier agreements, and Apple-branded and third-party iPhone accessories. Total revenue reported for iPhone in 2007 represented only one fiscal quarter.

†Net income reflects other income and expense, plus provision for income taxes.

Source: Apple 10K SEC filing.

files quickly made it a favorite with graphic designers, but it had slow performance and limited compatible software was available, so the product was unable to significantly help Apple's failing bottom line. In addition, Jobs had given Bill Gates at Microsoft some Macintosh prototypes to use to develop software, and in 1985 Microsoft subsequently came out with the Windows operating system, a version of GUI for use on IBM PCs.

Steve Jobs's famous volatility led to his resignation from Apple in 1985. Jobs then founded NeXT Computer; the NeXT Cube computer proved too costly for the business to become commercially profitable, but its technological contributions could not be ignored. In 1997, then Apple CEO Gilbert Amelio bought out NeXT, hoping to use its Rhapsody, a version of the NeXTStep operating system, to jump-start the Mac OS development, and Jobs was brought back as a part-time adviser.

Under CEOs Sculley, Spindler, and Amelio
John Sculley tried to take advantage of Apple's unique capabilities. Because of this, Macintosh computers were easy to use, with seamless integration (the original plug-and-play) and reliable performance. This premium performance meant Apple could charge a premium price.

Exhibit 2   Apple First Quarter 2009 Sales

	1st Quarter 2009 (in millions)	1st Quarter 2008 (in millions)	Percent Change
Product Net Sales			
Desktops	$ 1,043	$1,515	(31%)
Portables	2,511	2,037	23
iPod	3,371	3,997	(16)
Music	1,011	808	25
iPhone*	1,247	241	417
Peripherals	378	382	(1)
Software, services	606	628	(4)
Total net sales	**$10,167**	**$9,608**	**6%**
Region Net Sales			
Americas	$ 4,501	$4,298	5%
Europe	2,771	2,471	12
Japan	481	400	20
Retail	1,740	1,701	2
Other	674	738	(9)

*iPhone sales derived from handset sales, carrier agreements, and Apple-branded and third-party iPhone accessories. Total revenue reported for iPhone in 2007 represented only one fiscal quarter.

Source: Apple 10Q SEC filing.

However, with the price of IBM compatibles dropping, and Apple's costs, especially R&D, way above industry averages (in 1990 Apple spent 9 percent of sales on R&D, compared to 5 percent at Compaq and 1 percent at many manufacturers of IBM clones),[11] this was not a sustainable scenario.

All Sculley's innovative efforts were not enough to substantially improve Apple's bottom line, and he was replaced as CEO in 1993 by company president Michael Spindler. Spindler continued the focus on innovation, producing the PowerMac, based on the PowerPC microprocessor, in 1994. Even though this combination produced a significant price-performance edge over both previous Macs and Intel-based machines, the IBM clones continued to undercut Apple's prices. Spindler's response was to allow other companies to manufacture Mac clones, a strategy that ultimately led to clones' stealing 20 percent of Macintosh unit sales.

Gilbert Amelio, an Apple director and former semiconductor turnaround expert, was asked to reverse the company's financial direction. Amelio intended to reposition Apple as a premium brand, but his extensive reorganizations and cost-cutting strategies couldn't prevent Apple's stock price from slipping to a new low. However, Amelio's decision to stop work on a brand-new operating system and try to jump-start development by using NeXTStep brought Steve Jobs back to Apple in 1997.

Steve Jobs's Return   One of Jobs's first strategies on his return was to strengthen Apple's relationships with third-party software developers, including Microsoft. In 1997, Jobs announced an alliance with Microsoft that would allow for the creation of a Mac version of the popular Microsoft Office software. He also made a concerted effort to woo other developers, such as Adobe, to continue to produce Mac-compatible programs.

In late October 2001, Apple released its first major noncomputer product, the iPod. This device was an MP3 music player that packed up to 1,000 CD-quality songs into an ultraportable, 6.5-ounce design: "With iPod, Apple has invented a whole new category of digital music player that lets you put your entire music collection in your pocket and listen to it wherever you go," said Steve Jobs. "With iPod, listening to music will never be the same again."[12]

This prediction became even truer in 2002 when Apple introduced an iPod that would download from Windows—its first product that didn't require a Macintosh computer and thus opened up the Apple "magic" to everyone. In 2003 all iPod products were sold with a Windows version of iTunes, making it even easier to use the device regardless of computer platform.

Exhibit 3   Apple Innovation Time Line

Date	Product	Events
1976	Apple I	Steve Jobs, Steve Wozniak, and Ronald Wayne found Apple Computer.
1977	Apple II	Apple logo first used.
1979	Apple II +	Apple employs 250 people; the first personal computer spreadsheet software, VisiCalc, is written by Dan Bricklin on an Apple II.
1980	Apple III	Apple goes public with 4.6 million shares; IBM personal computer announced.
1983	Lisa	John Sculley becomes CEO.
1984	Mac 128K, Apple IIc	Super Bowl ad introduces the Mac desktop computer.
1985		**Jobs resigns** and forms NeXT Software; Windows 1.01 released.
1986	Mac Plus	Jobs establishes Pixar.
1987	Mac II, Mac SE	Apple sues Microsoft over GUI.
1989	Mac Portable	Apple sued by Xerox over GUI.
1990	Mac LC	Apple listed on Tokyo Stock Exchange.
1991	Powerbook 100, System 7	System 7 operating-system upgrade released, the first Mac OS to support PowerPC-based computers.
1993	Newton Message Pad (one of the first PDAs)	Sculley resigns; Spindler becomes CEO; PowerBook sales reach 1 million units.
1996		Spindler is out; Amelio becomes CEO; Apple acquires NeXT Software, with Jobs as adviser.
1997		Amelio is out; **Jobs returns** as interim CEO; online retail Apple Store opened.
1998	iMac	iMac colorful design introduced, including USB interface; Newton scrapped.
1999	iMovie, Final Cut Pro video editing software	iBook (part of Powerbook line) becomes best-selling retail notebook in October; Apple has 11% share of notebook market.
2000	G4Cube	**Jobs becomes permanent CEO.**
2001	iPod, OS X	First retail store opens, in Virginia.
2002	iMac G4	Apple releases iLife software suite.
2003	iTunes	Apple reaches 25 million iTunes downloads.
2004	iMac G5	**Jobs undergoes successful surgery for pancreatic cancer.**
2005	iPod Nano, iPod Shuffle, Mac Mini	First video iPod released; video downloads available from iTunes.
2006	MacBook Pro	Apple computers use Intel's Core Duo CPU and can run Windows software; iWork software competes with Microsoft Office.
2007	iPhone, Apple TV, iPod Touch	Apple Computer changes name to Apple Inc.; Microsoft Vista released.
2008	iPhone 3G, MacBook Air	App Store launched for third-party applications for iPhone and iPod Touch and brings in $1 million in one day.
2009	17-inch MacBook Pro, iLife, iWork '09	iTunes Plus provides DRM-free music, with variable pricing; **Jobs takes medical leave.**

Source: Apple.com; CNET News, "Apple Turns 30," http://news.cnet.com/2009-1041-6053869.html?tag=txt: *Wikipedia*, "Apple Inc." entry.

In April 2003, Apple opened the online iTunes Music Store to everyone. This software, downloadable on any computer platform, sold individual songs through the iTunes application for 99 cents each. When announced, the iTunes Music Store already had the backing of five major record labels and a catalog of 200,000 songs. Later that year, the iTunes Music Store was selling roughly 500,000 songs a day. In 2003, the iPod was the only portable digital player that could play music purchased from iTunes, and this intended exclusivity helped both products become dominant.

After 30 years of carving a niche for itself as the premier provider of technology solutions for graphic artists, Web designers, and educators, Apple appeared to be reinventing itself as a digital entertainment company, moving beyond the personal computer industry. The announcement in 2007 of the iPhone, a product incorporating a wireless phone, a music and video player, and a mobile Internet browsing device, meant Apple was also competing in the cell phone/smartphone industry. Steve Jobs subsequently announced on January 9, 2007, that Apple Computer would become Apple Inc. This name change confirmed for many commentators that Apple had made the shift from being a computer company to being an integrated digital consumer electronics company. Jobs said, "Apple's name change doesn't have any direct impact on the business, but it does accomplish the following—it signals to employees the company's long-term strategy, it clarifies the marketing message and it prods investors to compare Apple to consumer electronics firms rather than just computer makers." It also meant that Apple was now "much more diversified, so you don't compare it by peer group as much as by product line."[13]

In 2008, Apple expanded the iPhone to operate on AT&T's 3G network, and it introduced the iPod Touch, a portable media player and Wi-Fi Internet device that allowed users to purchase and download music directly from iTunes without a computer. Then, in July 2008, Apple opened the App Store. Users could now purchase applications written by third-party developers specifically for the iPhone and iPod Touch. These applications included games, prompting analysts to wonder whether Apple was now becoming a competitor in the gaming market.

Apple was becoming a diversified digital entertainment corporation (see Exhibit 4). Apple also had not abandoned its computing roots. Even with the growth of the iPod/iTunes and iPhone categories, computer sales, especially the portable category, continued to see substantial growth (see Exhibit 5).

Analysts had already believed Apple had "changed the rules of the game for three industries—PCs, consumer electronics, and music . . . and appears to have nothing to fear from major rivals."[14] Apple was now taking bites out of the competition on all fronts (see Exhibit 6).

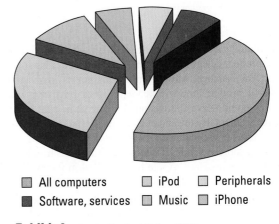

☐ All computers ☐ iPod ☐ Peripherals
■ Software, services ☐ Music ☐ iPhone

Exhibit 4 Apple Product Sales, 2008

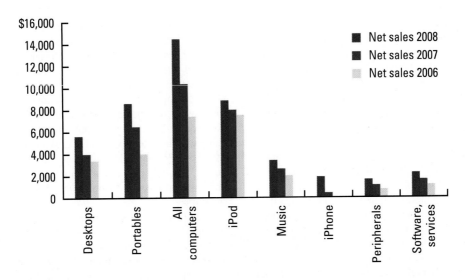

Exhibit 5 Apple Product Sales, 2006–2008

Exhibit 6 Apple's Product Lines and Major Competitors

Product Category	Apple Products	Major Competitors
Computers	iMac, Mac Pro, Mac mini, MacBook, MacBook Pro, MacBook Air	HP, Dell, Toshiba in the laptop, Acer in the netbook form factor
Portable music/media players	iPod Shuffle, iPod Nano, iPod Classic, iPod Touch	Creative Zen, SanDisk Sansa, Archos, Microsoft Zune
Smartphones	iPhone	Nokia, RIM, Samsung, LG, Sony Ericsson, HTC
Music/media downloads	iTunes, the App Store	Amazon, MySpace
Handheld gaming devices	iPod Touch, iPhone	Nintendo, Sony
Software*	Safari Web browser, QuickTime	Microsoft IE, Mozilla Firefox, Google Chrome, Windows Media Player, RealNetworks
Home theater downloads	Apple TV	Possibly Tivo

*Includes only the software that is sold separately to use on either Windows or Mac computers.

Apple's Operations

Maintaining a competitive edge required more than innovative product design. Operational execution was also important. For instance, while trying to market its increasingly diverse product line, Apple believed that its own retail stores could serve the customer better than could third-party retailers. By the end of 2008, Apple had an average of 247 stores open, including 19 international locations, with average store revenue of about $29.9 million. In addition to the "Genius Bars" Apple had installed in its own retail stores, Apple had also invested in programs to enhance reseller sales, including the placement of Apple employees and knowledgeable contractors at selected third-party reseller locations, explaining that it "believes providing direct contact with its targeted customers is an efficient way to demonstrate the advantages of its . . . products over those of its competitors."[15]

In further operational matters, regarding a head-to-head competition against Dell in the computer market, for instance, Steve Jobs was quick to point out that market share wasn't everything. While Dell's perceived dominance might have been partly the result of its efficient supply chain management, Apple had outperformed Dell in inventory and other metrics since 2001.[16] In addition, Apple had the best margins, partly because of its simpler product line, leading to cheaper manufacturing costs.[17] In 2008, Apple beat Dell and HP (as well as Nokia, IBM, Samsung, and Sony Ericsson) and took the number-one spot on AMR Research's Supply Chain Top 25.[18]

Regarding suppliers of components for Apple's diverse products, Apple had entered into certain multiyear agreements with suppliers of key components, including microprocessors, NAND flash memory, dynamic random access memory (DRAM), and LCD displays. Some of these long-term supplier-agreement partners included Hynix Semiconductor, Intel Corporation, Micron Technology, Samsung Electronics, and Toshiba Corporation. Also, in addition to using its own manufacturing facilities in Ireland, Apple had been outsourcing manufacturing and final assembly of iMacs, iPods, and iPhones to partners in Asia, paying close attention to scheduling and quality issues.

Supply chain and product design and manufacturing efficiencies were not the only measures of potential competitive superiority. Apple had also historically paid attention to research and development, increasing its R&D investment year after year. In 2008, Apple spent $1.1 billion on R&D, a 42 percent increase from the previous year and more than twice what was spent in 2005.[19] On the basis of 2007 numbers, among its current rivals, Apple's R&D investment was beaten only by Microsoft, Hewlett-Packard, and Google.[20]

Status of Apple's Business Units in 2008

The Apple Computer Business In the computer market, Apple had always refused to compete on price, relying instead on its reliability, design elegance, ease of use, and integrated features to win customers. Some analysts believed Apple had the opportunity to steal PC market share as long as its system was compatible, and no longer exclusively proprietary, and offered upgrades at a reasonable cost.[21] But the real opportunity for increased market share was the Intel-based iMac desktop and the MacBook/MacBook Pro portable, both using the Intel Core Duo processor. The only part of the computer system not designed and manufactured by Apple was this processor and the memory.

In 2008, Apple introduced its newest computer product, the MacBook Air, the "world's thinnest notebook."[22] Although the design was considered "revolutionary," the stripped-down product did not have an optical drive except as a separate external purchase, had limited connectivity with only one USB port, and had a battery that was not

Exhibit 7   Domestic PC Market Share, Fourth Quarter 2008

Company	4Q08 Shipments (thousands of units)	4Q08 Market Share (%)	4Q07 Shipments (thousands of units)	4Q07 Market Share (%)	4Q08–4Q07 Growth (%)
Dell	4,465.8	28.6	5,344.6	30.8	−16.4
Hewlett-Packard	4,288.3	27.5	4,439.5	25.6	−3.4
Acer	2,373.9	15.2	1,527.3	8.8	55.4
Apple	1,255.0	8.0	1,159.3	6.7	8.3
Toshiba	1,002.7	6.5	900.0	5.2	12.0
Others	2,219.2	14.2	3,992.6	23.0	−44.0
Total	**15,609.8**	**100.0**	**17,363.3**	**100.0**	**−10.1**

Note: Data include desk-based PCs, mobile PCs (notebooks and netbooks), and X86 servers.

Source: Gartner, January 2009, as reported at http://apple20.blogs.fortune.cnn.com/2009/01/16/despite-everything-mac-sales-grew-year-to-year.

user-replaceable. Even so, with its aluminum construction, it was perceived to be sturdy and much easier to carry than other full-size notebooks and therefore most appropriate for travelers in Wi-Fi hotspot areas.[23]

The continuing push to convert customers to the Macintosh computing products saw Apple sell 2,524,000 Mac computers, both desktops and laptops, worldwide during the first quarter of 2009, an increase of almost 9 percent over the same quarter in the previous year, in spite of the worldwide economic decline.[24] Sales of Apple computers in the United States did see a decline over the previous quarter, but not as much as the yearly domestic shipments of Dell (down 16.4 percent) and HP (down 3.4 percent).[25] According to market analysis done by Gartner, the Mac's domestic market share slipped from 9.5 to 8 percent in October, moving Apple from third to fourth place in Gartner's survey of PC vendor units shipped in 4Q08 (see Exhibit 7).

The Personal Digital Entertainment Devices:
iPod   Although many analysts felt the MP3 player market was oversaturated, Apple introduced the iPod Touch in 2007, intending it to be "an iPhone without the phone," a portable media player and Wi-Fi Internet device without the AT&T phone bill.[26] The iPod Touch borrowed most of its features from the iPhone, including the finger-touch interface, but it remained mainly an iPod, with a larger viewing area for videos. Apple released the second-generation iPod Touch in 2008, with upgraded features that turned it into "more pocket PC than MP3 player"[27] and allowed it to download programs such as games from Apple's new App Store. Both the iPhone and the iPod Touch were positioned as "viable devices in the mobile games market" during fall 2008, subsequently producing a significant jump in application downloads on Christmas Day 2008.

Apple reported selling a record 22,727,000 iPod units during the first quarter of 2009, a growth of 3 percent over

Exhibit 8   Portable Music Player (MP3) Worldwide Market Share, 2008 (in percent)

Company	July 2008	1Q08	1Q07	2Q06
Apple (iPod)*	73.4	71	70	75
SanDisk (Sansa)	8.6	11	10	10
Microsoft (Zune)	2.6	4	3	—[†]
Other	15.4	—	—	Samsung: 2.5 Sony: 2
Creative (Zen)	—[‡]	2	4	5

*As of September 2008, Apple reported over 160 million iPods sold; iTunes as the number-one distributor of music in any format in the U.S., with a catalog of 8.5 million songs, over 30,000 TV episodes, and over 2,500 films including 600 in high-definition video; and over 100 million applications downloaded from the App Store since its launch in July 2008.

[†]Released in 2006.

[‡]Included in other.

Source: NPD data, as reported at www.manifest-tech.com/ce_gallery/portable_gallery_players.htm.

the same period in the previous year.[28] This contributed to Apple's extending its lead over rivals (see Exhibit 8).

Mobile Communication Devices: iPhone   In 2007, further competition came from the blurring of lines between the digital music player and other consumer electronic devices: The telecom players wanted to join the digital music market. While others may have seen the computer as central to the future of digital music, the telecom companies thought the mobile phone could become a center of this emerging world. Apple's entry, the new iPhone device, combined an Internet-enabled smartphone and video iPod.

The iPhone allowed users to access all iPod content and play music and video content purchased from iTunes. Apple made an exclusive arrangement with AT&T's Cingular Wireless network to provide cellular service.

The iPhone debuted with a 4-GB model for $499 and an 8-GB model for $599, and estimates from component manufacturers suggested it would cost between $230 and $265 to make, yielding Apple's preferred gross margin of about 50 percent.[29] This would allow room for price adjustments based on component or customer demand. The smartphone market in 2007 was estimated at 10 percent of all mobile phone sales, or 100 million devices a year. Steve Jobs said he "would like to see the iPhone represent 1 percent of all mobile phone sales by the end of 2008."[30] This proved to be a conservative estimate.

In July 2008, Apple began selling iPhone 3G, the second-generation of the iPhone product. The 3G service upgrade accompanied expanded worldwide distribution, through carrier relationships in over 70 countries. Either because of the increased access or because of Apple's marketing push, 6.9 million iPhone 3Gs were sold in the first quarter of its availability, compared to "6.1 first-generation iPhone units sold in the prior five quarters combined."[31] As one analyst commented, "When Steve Jobs first introduced the iPhone in 2007, he pointed out that the market for cell phones worldwide was far greater than the market for any other type of consumer electronic device."[32] Worldwide appeal for the iPhone was growing: The iPhone was launched in Saudi Arabia and the UAE in February 2009, through Mobily and Etisalat, and got 25,000 subscribers

in the first few hours of its availability.[33] Now it appeared that Jobs was correct: He had forecast a 1 percent market share of the cell phone market in 2008 and had achieved 1.1 percent (see Exhibit 9).

Going into 2009, it appeared that the cell phone landscape was changing yet again, with smartphones becoming the device of choice for most manufacturers—smartphones with multiple features, including cameras. New cell phones with megapixel cameras debuted at Barcelona's 2009 Mobile World Congress from Sony Ericsson and Samsung: "What's behind the megapixel marathon? It's no secret that the iPhone's camera is one of its weakest points. Seems to me the competition is looking for vulnerabilities and has identified imaging capability as something they can deliver that the iPhone so far hasn't."[34] Along with Sony Ericcson and Samsung, other cell phone makers, LG and Taiwanese manufacturer High Tech Computers (HTC), offered new phones with touch screens in an attempt to compete with the iPhone.[35]

Part of the popularity of the iPhone during the 2008 holiday season was explained by analysts as being the result of the highly prolific output of third-party software developers, whose applications were available via Apple's App Store, where they could be downloaded to the iPhone, either increasing its capability or allowing users to play games and otherwise entertain themselves. This prompted these analysts to wonder whether gaming companies such as Nintendo and Sony would have to pay attention to Apple as a competitor in the gaming market. The analysts quoted one iPhone customer who said he had sold

Exhibit 9   Worldwide Market Share—Cell Phones, 2008

Manufacturer	Percent Market Share	Percent Increase over 2007	Comments
Nokia	38.6	1.8	2008 4th-quarter growth stalled.
Samsung	16.2	2.7	Strong 4th quarter; new products 1Q09.
LG	8.3	1.5	North America grew; new products 1Q09.
Sony Ericsson	8.0	(0.7)	2008 3d-quarter stalled; new products 1Q09.
Motorola	8.3	(5.1)	Nothing new in the pipeline.
Research in Motion	1.9	0.9	New products; good growth potential.
Kyocera	1.4	—	
Apple iPhone	1.1	0.8	First released in mid-2007; strong 4Q08.
HTC	1.1	—	New to market; new products 1Q09.
Sharp	1.0	—	
Other	14.1	—	Expect handset shipment contraction in 2009 to be down 5%–10%, due to worldwide economic conditions; smartphones may prosper.

Source: From ABIresearch, January 29, 2009, www.abiresearch.com/press/1357-Enter+the+Year+of+the+Smartphone%3A+171+Million+and+Rising.

his Sony PSP and might get rid of his Nintendo DS, since "the short amount of time I've had the iPhone, I've played more games on that than on my PSP and DS combined."[36] Regarding additional upgrades to the iPhone, or to other products in the smartphone group, CEO Steve Jobs agreed that Apple's iPhone business "had become too big to ignore" and that the iPhone had accounted for 39 percent of Apple's business in 2008.

However, analysts believed that the idea of Apple transforming the smartphone industry as it had the MP3 player market might require that Apple broaden its market even more. New offerings might include cell phone products that could compete with the new netbook PCs: a portable book reader to compete with Amazon's new Kindle reader, a portable movie player, and even a low-cost, entry-level phone—and all should provide services and add-ons through the App Store so that "average users can clearly see that there are enough high-quality services on offer to justify spending $30 per month [for a] mobile broadband subscription."[37]

Responding to a rumor of the possible release of a low-end $99 iPhone by summer 2009, Apple's acting-CEO Tim Cook said, "We're not going to play in the low-end voice phone business. That's not who we are, that's not why we're here. [Our] goal is not to lead unit sales, but to build the world's best phone."[38]

Digital Entertainment Solutions: Apple TV

In 2007, CEO Steve Jobs had considered the Apple TV product to be a "hobby" device, rather than a core business such as computers, music, or phones, saying, "A lot of people have tried and failed to make it a business."[39] In 2009, analysts were wondering whether the product was "at a crossroads," particularly since Apple sold more than three times the number of units it had sold in 2007.[40] Apple had not made any major changes to the hardware, but it had updated the software in 2008, allowing movie fans to rent DVD-quality or HD movies from the iTunes Store directly via their widescreen TV for $2.99 to $3.99 depending on the movie release dates. All audio or video purchases from iTunes downloaded to Apple TV could also be synced back to the user's computer, iPod, or iPhone.[41]

In 2009, Apple announced it had signed a $500 million five-year contract with South Korean LCD panel maker LG Display Co. Since Apple uses the LCD flat-panel display in the MacBook Pro laptop, this was likely a move to ensure manufacturing capacity to meet Apple's demand.[42] However, analysts wondered whether this deal, plus Apple's recent patent filings, also might help Apple develop DVR (digital video recorder) as well as iTunes functionality into a networked HDTV; they pointed out that such a device could "replace most, if not all, of the other living room set top boxes."[43]

The Software Market

Although Apple had always created innovative hardware, software development was also an important goal, with implications for long-term sales growth. Software was increasingly becoming Apple's core strength.[44] The premier piece of Apple software was the operating system. OS X allowed Apple to develop software applications such as Final Cut Pro, a video-editing program for professionals' digital camcorders, and the simplified version for regular consumers, called iMovie. The iLife software provided five integrated applications allowing the computer to become a home studio: iMovie; iDVD, for recording photos, movies, and music onto DVDs; iPhoto, for touching up digital photos; GarageBand, for making and mixing personally created music; and the iTunes digital music jukebox. Also available was iWork, containing a PowerPoint-type program called Keynote and a word-processor/page-layout program called Pages. Both iLife and iWork underwent major upgrades in 2009, further increasing their respective abilities to compete with Microsoft applications.

Apple's Web browser Safari was upgraded in 2009 to further compete with Windows Internet Explorer, Mozilla Firefox and the new entrant Chrome from Google. Apple announced, "Safari 4 was the world's fastest and most innovative browser,"[45] but analysts were quick to point out that Google's Chrome, which debuted six months earlier, was perhaps the first to take the browser interface in a new direction. One commentator called Chrome "a wake-up call for the Safari UI guys. . . . It's not that any particular feature of Chrome is so wonderful, or even that the sum of those features puts Safari back on its heels in the browser wars. It's the idea that someone other than Apple has taken such clear leadership in this area. Google Chrome makes Safari's user interface look conservative; it makes Apple look timid. And when it comes to innovation, overall daring counts for a lot more than individual successes or failures on the long-term graph."[46] Reviews of Apple's Safari upgrade noted, "Whether or not the individual features of Chrome inspired Apple, it's clear that Apple isn't going to let Google have the lead in browser innovation without a fight. And the more innovation that happens, the better it will be for users of Web browsers—which at this point is pretty much everybody with a computer!"[47]

Operating Systems

Further opportunity for software development came from the Mac's new ability to run Windows. This meant that software such as iWorks could now convert Microsoft Office files to run on a Mac. In the past, third-party software developers such as Adobe always had to make a sometimes risky decision to create Mac OS versions of their popular products. Now that the Macs were using Intel Core Duo chips, much more versatility and cross-platform compatibility made it more profitable to design and develop for the Mac market.

An additional opportunity for operating-system competition opened up in 2007 with the introduction of the "netbook" category of portable computers. Smaller and cheaper than a regular laptop or notebook, these machines didn't have the computing power to run the full version of either Windows XP or Mac OS X, so most manufacturers used the Linux operating system.[48] Microsoft announced in late 2008 that its new operating system, Windows 7, the replacement for Vista, would be capable of running on a netbook. However, according to CEO Steve Jobs, Apple did not have any plans for producing a netbook product.[49] Since the Apple operating system, designed to run only on Apple computers, was not available for independent sale, the new Windows operating system might gain traction in another computing category once again.

iTunes Arguably, Apple's most innovative software product was iTunes, a free downloadable software program for consumers running either newer Mac or Windows operating systems. It was bundled with all Mac computers and iPods and connected with the iTunes Music Store for purchase of digital music and movie files that could be played by iPods and the iPhone and by iTunes on PCs.

Although the volume was there, iTunes had not necessarily been a profitable venture. Out of the 99 cents Apple charged for a song, about 65 cents went to the music label; 25 cents went for distribution costs, including credit card charges, servers, and bandwidth; and the balance went to marketing, promotion, and the amortized cost of developing the iTunes software.[50]

Several competitors had tried to compete with the iTunes service. RealNetworks' Rhapsody subscription service, Yahoo MusicMatch, and AOL music downloads all had competed for the remaining market share, using the potentially buggy Microsoft Windows Media format.[51] Even though one commentator had said in 2004 that "ultimately someone will build a piece of software that matches iTunes,"[52] as of 2008 the only serious competition was from Amazon and My Space.

Making it potentially worse for Apple's competitors, music artists were overwhelmingly supportive of Apple, since, as Jobs reported, "almost every song and CD is made on a Mac, it's recorded on a Mac, it's mixed on a Mac. The artwork's done on a Mac. Almost every artist I've met has an iPod, and most of the music execs now have iPods. And one of the reasons Apple was able to do what we did was because we are perceived by the music industry as the most creative technology company."[53]

Steve Jobs had negotiated a deal with the Big Five record companies (Sony Music Entertainment, BMG, EMI, Universal, and Warner) to sell songs on iTunes. In 2007 Jobs asked the music labels to stop requiring that digital music distributors such as iTunes use copyright protection. By taking the lead in this, Apple could potentially come out ahead of the game again: If copyright protection was not required, iTunes songs could be played on non-iPod music players, and music purchased on other services could be played on the iPod. In what might have been perceived as a PR ploy, Jobs said that allowing music to be sold online without digital rights management (DRM) technology would "create a truly interoperable music marketplace— one that Apple would embrace 'wholeheartedly.'"[54]

In January 2009, Apple subsequently announced that "all four major music labels—Universal Music Group, Sony

BMG, Warner Music Group, and EMI, along with thousands of independent labels, are now offering their music in iTunes Plus, Apple's DRM (digital rights management)-free format with higher-quality 256 kbps ACC encoding for audio quality virtually indistinguishable from the original recordings."[55] This made iTunes, with its 10 million DRM-free tracks, "the largest music store library on Earth."[56] In addition, iPhone 3G customers could download music directly onto their phone for the same price as downloading to their computer, the price having changed to include three price points, $0.69, $0.99, or $1.29, depending on what the music labels charged Apple. This tiered pricing was supposedly adopted in response to potential competition from other download sites such as Amazon and MySpace, although analysts pointed out that the music labels had previously demanded variable pricing and that Apple needed this cooperation from the content providers.[57] As of 2009, the iTunes Store had sold over 6 billion songs, and analysts projected that by 2012 it could "well account for a staggering 28 percent of *all* music sold worldwide."[58]

The App Store In March 2008, Apple announced that it was releasing the iPhone software development kit (SDK), allowing developers to create applications for the iPhone and iPod Touch and sell these third-party applications via the Apple App Store. The App Store was made available on version 7.7 of iTunes, and it was directly available from the iPhone and iPod Touch products. This opened the window for another group of Apple customers, the application developers, to collaborate with Apple. Developers could purchase the iPhone Developer Program from Apple for $99, create either free or commercial applications for the iPhone and iPod Touch, and then submit these applications to be sold in the App Store. Developers would be paid 70 percent of the download fee iPhone or iPod Touch customers paid to the App Store, and Apple would get 30 percent of the revenue. The applications ranged from simple audio files that were available for free (e.g., ringtones), to straightforward programs that sold for 99 cents (e.g., a program that turned the iPhone into a simple voice recorder), to full-featured applications that retailed for up to $69.99 (e.g., ForeFlight Mobile, which allowed pilots to get weather and airport information).

The App Store opened in July 2008, at the same time as the introduction of the iPhone 3G, and as of February 2009, over 15,000 programs had been offered for sale, creating 500 million downloads, and millions of dollars in revenue, collectively, for developers.[59] The success of this distribution channel for smartphone add-ons had Microsoft and other manufacturers, such as Nokia and Blackberry maker Research in Motion, rushing to open their own mobile software stores, hoping to follow Apple's "runaway success"[60] in yet another category.

The Future of Apple Although Steve Jobs was credited with Apple's ability to innovate and to appeal especially to a certain type of consumer (Jobs estimated Apple's market share in the creative-professional marketplace as over 50 percent),[61] Jobs himself credited his people:

> We hire people who want to make the best things in the world . . . our primary goal is to make the world's best PCs—not to be the biggest or the richest. We have a second goal, which is to always make a profit—both to make some money but also so we can keep making those great products. . . . [regarding the systemization of innovation] the system is that there is no system. That doesn't mean we don't have process. Apple is a very disciplined company, and we have great processes. But that's not what it's about. Process makes you more efficient . . . but innovation . . . comes from saying no to 1,000 things to make sure we don't get on the wrong track or try to do too much. We're always thinking about new markets we could enter, but it's only by saying no that you can concentrate on the things that are really important.[62]

Given Steve Jobs's announced medical leave, the media was particularly interested in the rest of Apple's management team. In late 2008, Tony Fadell, Apple's senior vice president of the iPod Division, and his wife Danielle Lambert, vice president of Human Resources, had announced that they were reducing their roles within the company to devote more time to their young family.[63] Sometimes credited as the "father of the iPod" and part of the team involved in the development of the iPhone,[64] Fadell would remain with the company as an adviser to the CEO. Fadell would be replaced by Mark Papermaster, in the position of senior vice president of Devices Hardware Engineering. Papermaster would lead Apple's iPod and iPhone hardware engineering teams and would report directly to Steve Jobs. Papermaster was previously a vice president at IBM and had played a major role in IBM's PowerPC chip design. This role led IBM to hold up Papermaster's move to Apple for several months while it worked out a noncompete agreement.[65]

With the exception of Fadell's reduced role, Apple's upper management had been stable since 1999. This stability among the nine executive officers had relieved some analysts as they contemplated what might happen to Apple if Steve Jobs did not return from his medical leave of absence.[66] In fact, COO Tim Cook, designated to take over Apple operations during Jobs's absence, had run Apple operations in 2004 while Jobs recovered from his pancreatic cancer. Since his arrival in 1998, Cook had been called the "genius behind Steve" because of his handling of the day-to-day business at Apple.[67]

Most analysts had no doubt that Apple had many top-notch executives, but there was no evidence of a clear succession plan, nor was there a history of nurturing top performers to "broaden their skills and groom them for bigger jobs."[68] This was a problem, as Apple had gotten larger over time, with multiple product lines, critical supplier alliances, diverse distribution outlets, and an increasingly global market. However, while agreeing that it would be very difficult to replace Steve Jobs's visionary product design and marketing skills, analysts pointed out that Jobs had been "on a creative tear" since the introduction of the iPod in 2001—and since Apple had traditionally maintained a "top-secret pipeline of products" ready to roll out in "the next few years," it was possible that "were Jobs no longer around, Apple could live off those products for some time."[69]

During the 2009 first-quarter conference call, Apple presenter and COO Tim Cook was asked whether he felt he was a "de facto successor" in the event Steve Jobs did not return from his medical leave in July. Cook responded, "There is an extraordinary breadth and depth and tenure to Apple's executive team . . . they manage 35,000 employees, all of whom are wicked smart. . . . I strongly believe that Apple is doing the best work in its history."[70] The rest of the executive management team agreed. However, at the time, Steve Jobs was still CEO of the company.

Endnotes

1. "Apple reports fourth quarter results," October 21, 2008, from www.apple.com/pr/library/2008/10/21 results.html.
2. "Apple reports first quarter results," January 21, 2009, from www.apple.com/pr/library/2009/01/21results.html.
3. "Letter from Apple CEO Steve Jobs," January 5, 2009, from www.apple.com/pr/library/2009/01/05sjletter.html
4. "Apple Media Advisory," January 14, 2009, from www.apple.com/pr/library/2009/01/14advisory.html
5. A. Hesseldahl, "Apple's impressive quarterly numbers," *BusinessWeek,* January 22, 2009, from www.businessweek.com/technology/content/jan2009/tc20090121_101972.htm?link_position=link5.
6. G. Keizer, "Apple can still thrive, sans Job," *Computerworld,* January 15, 2009, from www.pcworld.com/article/157735/jobs.html?loomia_ow=t0:a16:g12:r2:c0.240847:b21196707.
7. See www.businessweek.com/magazine/content/08_17/b4081062882948.htm.
8. Apple was the first firm to have commercial success selling GUI systems, but Xerox developed the first systems in 1973. Xerox PARC researchers built a single-user computer called the Alto that featured a bit-mapped display and a mouse and the world's first what-you-see-is-what-you-get (WYSIWYG) editor. From www.parc.xerox.com/about/history/default.html.
9. From the Apple, Inc., 2008 Annual Report, 10-K filing, available at www.apple.com/investor.
10. Note: January 24, 2009, is the 25th anniversary of the Macintosh, unveiled by Apple in the "Big Brother" Super Bowl ad in 1984. Watch via YouTube: www.youtube.com/watch?v=OYecfV3ubP8. See also the 1983 Apple keynote speech by a young Steve Jobs, introducing this ad: www.youtube.com/watch?v=lSiQA6KKyJo.
11. See D. A. Mank and H. E. Nystrom, "The relationship between R&D spending and shareholder returns in the computer industry," *Engineering Management Society, Proceedings of the 2000 IEEE,* 2000, pp. 501–504.
12. "Ultra-portable MP3 music player puts 1,000 songs in your pocket," October 23, 2001, from www.apple.com/pr/library/2001/oct/23ipod.html.

13. "What's in a name? For Apple, a focus on the digital living room," *Knowledge@Wharton,* January 24, 2007, from http://knowledge.wharton.upenn.edu/article.cfm?articleid=1641.

14. B. Schlender, "How big can Apple get?" *Fortune,* February 21, 2005, from http://money.cnn.com/magazines/fortune/-fortune_archive/2005/02/21/8251769/index.htm.

15. From the Apple, Inc., 2008 Annual Report, 10-K filing, available at /www.apple.com/investor.

16. P. Burrows, "The seed of Apple's innovation," *Business-Week Online,* October 12, 2004, from www.businessweek.com/bwdaily/dnflash/oct2004/nf20041012_4018_db083.htm?chan=search.

17. F. Fox, "Mac Pro beats HP and Dell at their own game: Price," *lowendmac.com,* May 16, 2008, from http://lowendmac.com/ed/fox/08ff/mac-pro-vs-dell-hp.html.

18. "AMR Research Supply Chain Top 25, 2008," from www.amrresearch.com/supplychaintop25.

19. P. McLean, "Apple outlines shift in strategy, rise in R&D spending, more," *AppleInsider,* November 5, 2008, from www.appleinsider.com/articles/08/11/05/apple_outlines_shift_in_strategy_rise_in_rd_spending_more.

20. R. Hertzberg, "Top 50 technology R&D spenders," *CIO Zone,*2008, from www.ciozone.com/index.php/Editorial-Research/Top-50-Technology-R&D-Spenders/50-Biggest-R.html.

21. "Growing market share—branding in the computer industry 2006," www.stealingshare.com/content/1137644625875.htm.

22. "Apple introduces MacBook Air—the world's thinnest notebook," January 15, 2008, from www.apple.com/pr/library/2008/01/15mbair.html.

23. "Apple MacBook Air (80GB)," *CNET Review,* January 25, 2008, from http://reviews.cnet.com/laptops/apple-macbook-air-80gb/4505-3121_7-32818756.html.

24. "Apple reports first-quarter results," January 21, 2009, from www.apple.com/pr/library/2009/01/21results.html.

25. P. Elmer-DeWitt, "Despite everything, Mac sales grew year-to-year," *Apple 2.0—Blogs,* January 16, 2009, from http://apple20.blogs.fortune.cnn.com/2009/01/16/despite-everything-mac-sales-grew-year-to-year.

26. P. Elmer- DeWitt, "Apple challenges Sony and Nintendo," *Apple 2.0—Blogs,* December 13, 2008, from http://apple20.blogs.fortune.cnn.com/2008/12/13/apple-challenges-sony-and-nintendo.

27. D. Bell, "Apple iPod Touch (second generation, 16GB)," *CNET Review,* September 11, 2008, from http://reviews.cnet.com/portable-video-players-pvps/apple-ipod-touch-second/4505-6499_7-33248627.html?tag=mncol;txt.

28. "Apple reports first-quarter results," January 21, 2009, from www.apple.com/pr/library/2009/01/21results.html.

29. A. Hesseldahl, "What the iPhone will cost to make," *BusinessWeek Online,* January 18, 2007, from www.businessweek.com/technology/content/jan2007/tc20070118_961148.htm.

30. E. Zemen, "Ballmer says iPhone won't succeed. Has Windows mobile?" *Information Week,* May 1, 2007, from www.informationweek.com/blog/main/archives/2007/05/ballmer_says_ip.html.

31. "Apple reports fourth-quarter results," October 21, 2008, from www.apple.com/pr/library/2008/10/21results.html.

32. "Phone reaches 1% market share in worldwide cellphone market," *Edible Apple,* February 1, 2009, from www.edibleapple.com/iphone-reaches-1-market-share-in-worldwide-cellphone-market.

33. A. Sambridge, "25,000 Saudi iPhone subscribers within hours of launch," *ArabianBusiness.com,* February 23, 2009, from www.arabianbusiness.com/547625-25000-saudi-iphone-subscribers-within-hours-of-launch.

34. Y. Arar, "Sony Ericsson, Samsung duke it out for megapixel supremacy," *PC World,* February 15, 2009, from www.pcworld.com/article/159579/article.html?tk=nl_cxanws.

35. Y. Arar, "Next-gen cell phone stars shine in Barcelona," *PC World,* February 17, 2009, from www.pcworld.com/article/159659-6/nextgen_cell_phone_stars_shine_in_barcelona.html.

36. N. Wingfield and C. Lawton, "Apple's iPhone faces off with the game champs," *Wall Street Journal: Personal Technology,* November 12, 2008, from http://online.wsj.com/article/SB122644912858819085.html.

37. Ibid.

38. A. Kim, "Analyst speculation on $99 iPhone and higher resolution iPhone 3G," *MacRumors.com,* February 11, 2009, from www.macrumors.com/2009/02/11/analyst-speculation-on-99-iphone-and-higher-resolution-iphone-3g.

39. R. Block, "Steve Jobs live from D 2007," *engadget,* May 30, 2007, from www.engadget.com/2007/05/30/steve-jobs-live-from-d-2007.

40. M. G. Siegler, "Hobby turning serious? Apple TV gets a survey, Valentine's promotion," *VentureBeat DigitalMedia,* February 9, 2009, from http://venturebeat.com/2009/02/09/hobby-turning-serious-apple-tv-gets-a-survey-valentines-promotion.

41. "Apple introduces new Apple TV software & lowers price to $229," January 15, 2008, from www.apple.com/pr/library/2008/01/15appletv.html

42. C. Foresman, "LG Display deal could mean impending Cinema Display refresh," *ars technical,* January 12, 2009, from http://arstechnica.com/apple/news/2009/01/lg-display-deal-could-mean-impending-cinema-display-refresh.ars.

43. D. Chartier, "Rumors return of Apple's living room device to rule them all," *ars technical,* February 5, 2009, from http://arstechnica.com/apple/news/2009/02/rumors-return-of-apples-living-room-device-to-rule-them-all.ars.

44. Schlender, "How big can Apple get?"

45. "Apple Announces Safari 4—the world's fastest and most innovative browser," February 24, 2009, from www.apple.com/pr/library/2009/02/24safari.html.

46. J. Siracusa, "Straight out of Compton: Google Chrome as a paragon of ambition, if not necessarily execution," *ars technica,* September 2, 2008, from http://arstechnica.com/staff/fatbits/2008/09/straight-out-of-compton.ars.

47. J. Snell, "Google Chrome: A wake-up call for Safari," *PC World,* February 24, 2009, from www.pcworld.com/businesscenter/article/160129/google_chrome_a_wakeup_call_for_safari.html?loomia_ow=t0:a16:g12:r4:c0.334067:b22235984.

48. M. Horowitz, "What is a netbook computer?" *CNET News,* October 12, 2008, from http://news.cnet.com/ what-is-a-netbook-computer.

49. E. Ogg, "Three things Apple won't do," *CNET News,* October 15, 2008, from http://news.cnet.com/8301-13579_ 3-10066317-37.html.

50. S. Cherry, "Selling music for a song," *Spectrum Online,* December 2004, from www.spectrum.ieee.org/dec04/3857.

51. D. Leonard, "The player," *Fortune,* March 8, 2006, from http://money.cnn.com/magazines/fortune/fortune_archive/ 2006/03/20/8371750/index.htm.

52. A. Salkever, "It's time for an iPod IPO," *BusinessWeek,* May 5, 2004, from www.businessweek.com/technology/content/ may2004/tc2004055_8689_tc056.htm.

53. J. Goodell, "Steve Jobs: The *Rolling Stone* interview," *Rolling Stone,* December 3, 2003, from www.rollingstone .com/news/story/5939600/steve_jobs_the_rolling_stone_ interview.

54. A. Hesseldahl, "Steve Jobs' music manifesto," *Business-Week Online,* February 7, 2007, from www.businessweek .com/technology/content/feb2007/tc20070206_576721 .htm?chan=search,

55. "Changes coming to the iTunes Store," January 6, 2009, from www.apple.com/pr/library/2009/01/06itunes.html.

56. Ibid.

57. C. Breen, "Variable iTunes pricing and the future," *Macworld,* January 13, 2009, from www.macworld.com/article/138173/ itunesvariablepricing.html?loomia_ow=t0:a16:g2:r6: c0.0465853:b20601077.

58. E. Van Buskirk, "iTunes Store may capture one-quarter of worldwide music by 2012," *Wired.com,* April 27, 2008, from www.wired.com/entertainment/music/news/2008/04/ itunes_birthday.

59. R. Kim, "Apple App Store developers look to next level," *SFGate.com,* February 9, 2009, from /www.sfgate.com/ cgi-bin/article.cgi?f=/c/a/2009/02/08/BU8U15ADEB.DTL.

60. Reuters, 2009. "Microsoft, Nokia gun for Apple's App Store," *internetnews.com,* February 17, 2009, from www. internetnews.com/breakingnews/article.php/3803411.

61. Goodell, "Steve Jobs: The *Rolling Stone* interview."

62. Burrows, "The seed of Apple's innovation."

63. "Mark Papermaster joins Apple as senior vice president of Devices Hardware Engineering," November 4, 2008, in "Apple reports first quarter results," January 21, 2009, from www.apple.com/pr/library/2009/01/21results.html.

64. A. Kim, "Tony Fadell ('father of the iPod') leaves Apple," *MacRumors.com,* November 4, 2008, from www.macrumors .com/2008/11/04/tony-fadell-father-of-ipod-leaves-apple.

65. S. Weintraub, "Why did Apple hire away IBM's Mark Papermaster?" *Computerworld Blogs,* November 1, 2008, from http://blogs.computerworld.com/why_did_apple_hire_ away_ibms_mark_papermaster.

66. G. Keizer, "Apple can still thrive, sans Jobs," *PCWorld,* January 15, 2009, from www.pcworld.com/article/157735/ jobs.html?loomia_ow=t0:a16:g12:r2:c0.240847: b21196707.

67. A. Lashinsky, "The genius behind Steve," *Fortune,* November 10, 2008, from http://money.cnn.com/ 2008/11/09/technology/cook_apple.fortune/index.htm? postversion=2008111010.

68. P. Burrows, "What Fadell's departure means for Apple," *Busi-nessWeek,* November 5, 2008, from www.businessweek .com/technology/content/nov2008/tc2008115_625046.htm? chan=technology_technology+index+page_computers.

69. Lashinsky, "The genius behind Steve."

70. Hesseldahl, "Apple's impressive quarterly numbers."

Case 24   Jamba Juice*

How would you like to enjoy a Berry Topper smoothie with organic granola for breakfast, a high-protein Sourdough Parmesan Pretzel and Razzmatazz raspberry smoothie for a quick lunch, or an Omega-3 Oatmeal Cookie rich in fatty acids for a midafternoon snack? Or how about a Cold-buster smoothie packed with antioxidants when you get the sniffles, a Protein Berry Workout smoothie when you get back from the gym, and a Peanut Butter Moo'd chocolaty treat when your sweet tooth starts to ache?

Jamba Juice had something to satisfy your every taste and nutritional desire. The Jamba Juice Company gradually expanded its product line over the past several years to offer Jamba products that pleased a broader palate, but was it biting off more than it could chew? In light of mounting same-store sales declines and financial losses, newly appointed CEO James White (December 1, 2008) had his work cut out for him.

Background

Juice Club was founded by Kirk Perron and opened its first store in San Luis Obispo, California, in April 1990.[1] While many small health food stores had juice bars offering fresh carrot juice, wheat germ, and protein powder, dedicated juice and smoothie bars were sparse in 1990 and didn't gain widespread popularity until the mid- to late 1990s.

Juice Club began with a franchise strategy and opened its second and third stores in northern and southern California in 1993. In 1994, management decided that an expansion strategy focusing on company stores would provide a greater degree of quality and operating control. In 1995, the company changed its name to Jamba Juice Company to provide a point of differentiation as competitors began offering similar healthy juices and smoothies in the marketplace.

In March 1999, Jamba Juice Company merged with Zuka Juice Inc., a smoothie retail chain with 98 smoothie retail units in the western United States. On March 13, 2006, Jamba Juice Company agreed to be acquired by Services Acquisition Corp. International (headed by Steven Berrard, former CEO of Blockbuster Inc.) for $265 million.[2] The company went public in November 2006. In August 2008, Jamba Juice faced significant leadership changes. Steven Berrard agreed to assume the responsibilities of interim CEO, replacing Paul E. Clayton.[3] In December 2008, James White was named CEO and president, while Berrard remained chairman of the board of directors. Prior to joining Jamba Juice, White had been senior vice president of Consumer Brands at Safeway, a publicly traded Fortune 100 food and drug retailer.

Jamba Juice stores were owned and franchised by Jamba Juice Company, which was a wholly owned subsidiary of Jamba, Inc. As of 2008, there were 729 Jamba Juice stores (511 company-owned and -operated and 218 franchised) located in 23 states.[4] During fiscal year 2008, Jamba, Inc., had over $342 million in revenue, a huge increase compared to the just over $23 million in revenue during fiscal year 2006 (see Exhibits 1 to 3).[5]

Company Culture

Jamba attempted to provide a unique company culture in which team members could execute at high levels while expressing their passion for the brand. Jamba believed its vision and values were more than bulletin-board postings; they were embodied in the store teams, the support staff, and the leadership team. Jamba's ability to execute its growth strategy was highly dependent on the maintenance and enhancement of its unique culture. To ensure that the culture continued to drive business execution, Jamba's leadership team attempted to focus on the following:

Leadership capability: Jamba focused on attracting and retaining quality individuals who executed the business strategy while building the platform for future growth.

Store-level capability: Jamba stores were the foundation of the business and had to execute flawlessly; leadership ensured that stores were fully staffed and trained in order to provide the energetic and memorable Jamba store experience.

Community: An employee-shared appreciation of community involvement was a key to developing and sustaining emotional connections with customers; commitment to the communities where Jamba operated was vital to maintaining customer loyalty and sustaining the passion of Jamba team members.

Store Management and Personnel

Jamba Juice Company's operations team was the foundation for its performance and vital to long-term growth. Jamba recruited and retained leaders with broad experience in management and industry. The company also supported its store operations with a combination of regional directors of operations, district managers, and store general managers.

Jamba's team of regional directors of operations (RDOs) averaged more than 15 years of industry experience. Their backgrounds included experience in full-service restaurants and high-growth retailers, with several RDOs

* This case was developed by Professor Alan B. Eisner, Pace University; Jerome C. Kuperman, Minnesota State University–Moorhead; and Professor James Gould, Pace University. Material has been drawn from published sources to be used for class discussion. Copyright © 2009 Alan B. Eisner.

Exhibit 1 Income Statements

	Fiscal Year Ended		
	Dec. 30, 2008	Jan. 1, 2008	Jan. 9, 2007
Revenue:			
Company stores	$ 333,784	$ 306,035	$ 22,064
Franchise and other revenue	9.106	11.174	1.051
Total revenue	342,890	317,209	23,115
Costs and operating expenses:			
Cost of sales	89,163	84,226	6,039
Labor	120,251	102,661	8,524
Occupancy	44,868	37,458	3,590
Store operating	43,714	39,942	4,222
Depreciation and amortization	24,717	19,168	1,878
General and administrative	48,057	48,384	6,195
Store pre-opening	2,044	5,863	285
Impairment of long-lived assets	27,802	1,550	—
Store lease termination and closure	10,029	718	—
Trademark and goodwill impairment	84,061	200,624	—
Other operating	3,817	4,806	675
Formation and operating	—	—	—
Total costs and operating expenses	498,523	545,400	31,408
Loss from operations	(155,633)	(228,191)	(8,293)
Other income (expense):			
Gain (loss) on derivative liabilities	7,895	59,424	(57,383)
Interest income	365	3,517	4,177
Interest expense	(2,064)	(181)	(71)
Total other income (expense)	6,196	62,760	(53,277)
Income (loss) before income taxes	(149,437)	(165,431)	(61,570)
Income tax benefit (expense)	274	52,135	2,544
Net income (loss)	$(149,163)	$(113,296)	$(59,026)

Source: Jamba 10-K report.

having previously held vice president of operations titles. RDOs managed teams of district managers and reported directly to two experienced retail zone vice presidents, who in turn reported to the vice president of operations. In addition to drawing on individuals with vast outside experience, Jamba recognized the potential of those within the company: 40 percent of its district managers had been internally developed and promoted to their management positions.

Attracting and developing team members who provided superior service was paramount to producing the positive customer experience that Jamba strived for. Jamba sought to hire customer-service-oriented people and provided team members with financial incentives and opportunities for advancement when they fulfilled service expectations.

To aid team members in performing well, Jamba provided training programs for all team members and

Exhibit 2 Balance Sheets (in thousands of dollars)

	2008	2007	2006
Assets			
Current assets:			
Cash and cash equivalents	25,881	27,882	87,379
Net receivables	4,594	14,504	9,590
Inventory	3,435	3,582	2,356
Other current assets	7,183	10,682	5,443
Total current assets	**41,093**	**56,650**	**104,768**
Long-term investments	520	2,028	2,142
Property, plant, and equipment	95,154	128,861	85,305
Goodwill	—	—	94,162
Intangible assets	2,998	87,599	177,580
Other assets	4,520	1,038	3,596
Deferred long-term asset charges	1,435	—	—
Total assets	**145,720**	**276,176**	**467,553**
Liabilities and Stockholders' Equity			
Current liabilities:			
Accounts payable	58,594	57,830	42,233
Short/current long-term debt	2,344	9,290	71,197
Other current liabilities	1,922	4,746	3,917
Total current liabilities	**62,860**	**71,866**	**117,347**
Long-term debt	23,110	—	—
Other liabilities	2,659	—	64,331
Deferred long-term liability charges	16,670	20,802	—
Total liabilities	**105,299**	**92,668**	**181,678**
Stockholders' equity:			
Common stock	55	53	52
Retained earnings	(317,892)	(168,729)	(55,433)
Capital surplus	358,258	352,184	341,256
Total stockholders' equity	**40,421**	**183,508**	**285,875**
Net tangible assets	**$37,423**	**$95,909**	**$14,133**

Source: finance.yahoo.com.

supported center staff and its leadership team. Training and support included formal programs, such as manager-in-training for new managers, and informal one-on-one discussions held between general managers, district managers, and regional directors of operations. The goals of all the programs were to shorten the learning curve and create greater confidence in order to achieve success through strong performance and results as rapidly as possible.

Maintaining the Jamba Juice Company corporate culture was essential as the company continued to expand. Strong culture was also critical to developing the Jamba

Exhibit 3   Store Locations

Store Count as of December 30, 2008			
	Company Stores	Franchise Stores	Total
Arizona	12	22	34
California	338	50	388
Colorado	17	6	23
Florida	22	1	23
Illinois	34	—	34
Indiana	1	—	1
Minnesota	8	1	9
New Jersey	2	2	4
Nevada	11	2	13
New York	20	1	21
Oregon	9	15	24
Utah	10	7	17
Washington	26	11	37
Wisconsin	1	—	1
Bahamas	—	1	1
Hawaii	—	34	34
Idaho	—	5	5
Massachusetts	—	1	1
North Carolina	—	3	3
Oklahoma	—	8	8
Pennsylvania	—	2	2
Texas	—	46	46
Total	**511**	**218**	**729**

brand and ensuring its continued success. Jamba believed that team members were the key to its success and that its culture fostered personal interaction, mutual respect, trust, empowerment, enthusiasm and commitment. Jamba Juice Company carefully screened potential team members to ensure they held many of its core values and fit into the culture. By placing an emphasis on its mission statement and values and encouraging responsibility and accountability at every level, Jamba believed that it had created a sense of team member loyalty and an open and interactive work environment, resulting in a highly passionate workforce.

Store Design

The color scheme employed by Jamba Juice stores was consistent among stores, providing a bright and cheerful theme with colors that embody Jamba's commitment to fresh and healthy juices, smoothies, and other energizing products. The highly interactive Jamba experience was designed to attract customers with the enticing aroma of fresh fruit, vegetables, and wheatgrass and the high-energy sounds of whirring blenders and team members calling out greetings.

To highlight Jamba's commitment to providing a memorable and pleasant customer experience, and to facilitate high foot traffic through its stores, Jamba worked with a retail design consultant to formulate a model plan for its stores that would showcase natural materials used in construction, highlight the high-quality natural ingredients used in Jamba's products, and provide for efficient customer flow. Additional focus was placed on the "theater" aspect of smoothie making by providing an environment in which all food preparation could be conducted behind glass and in the open so that customers could watch as their order was freshly made with all-natural ingredients. The layout offered a casual bar-type atmosphere featuring interior stools and exterior tables and chairs, glass cases displaying baked goods, and shelving in front of cash registers. Supported by the theater of the fully displayed production process, Jamba Juice Company believed that the Jamba experience was a competitive advantage.

Advertising and Marketing

According to Jamba Juice Company's top management, the Jamba brand communicated the passion and positive energy of the Jamba experience. The company's focus on its brand was designed to ensure that customers were aware of the positive product attributes and the vision and values of the Jamba team. Jamba Juice Company believed that the branding efforts were instrumental to generating strong same-store sales growth and laying the foundation for new-unit growth. The brand initiatives encompassed the following:

Brand communications: Generating awareness and loyalty through the communication of the product benefits and the eventual development of an emotional connection with the customer.

Product: Optimizing and innovating—devoting additional resources to optimizing the current menu and developing new, appealing menu items.

Store environment: Presenting a store environment that was an energizing and memorable experience for customers.

Jamba Juice Company's marketing focused on communicating the benefits of the products and the brand's values through many creative and nontraditional avenues. Marketing efforts were concentrated on store locations to build unique and pleasant experiences that would generate positive word of mouth. As Jamba Juice Company entered new markets, it had to communicate the Jamba story, the benefits of its products, and their usage occasions. Jamba augmented its in-store communications with small promotional events, community involvement, and opportunistic grassroots marketing.

Jamba Juice Company believed that it benefited from national media attention, which provided it with a significant competitive advantage. Historically, Jamba had not engaged in any mass-media promotional programs, relying instead on word of mouth, trade-area marketing, and in-store promotions to increase customer awareness. However, Jamba was featured in stories appearing in the *Wall Street Journal,* the *New York Times, USA Today,* and a host of local newspapers and magazines.

Jamba also capitalized on the openings of new sites as opportunities to reach out to the media and secure live local television coverage, radio broadcasts, and articles in local print media. Openings were also frequently associated with a charitable event, thus serving to reinforce Jamba Juice Company's strong commitment to its communities.

Products

Jamba Juice stores offered customers a range of blended beverages, nutritional supplements, and healthy snacks. Jamba smoothie and juice options were made with real fruit and 100 percent fruit juices, were blended to order, and provided four to six servings of fruits and vegetables. Jamba smoothies and baked goods were rich in vitamins, minerals, proteins, and fiber and were available in a variety of sizes: Sixteen (16 fl oz—475 mL), Original (24 fl oz—710 mL), or Power (30 fl oz—890 mL). Jamba Juice offered several different categories of smoothies and juices, including Smoothies with Organic Granola (three flavors, 360–450 calories/12 fl oz); Fresh Squeezed Juices (three flavors, 90–220 calories/16 fl oz); Jucies (two flavors, 170–180 calories/16 fl oz); Yogurt and Fruit Blends (two flavors, 220–240 calories/16 fl oz); All Fruit (four flavors, 200–220 calories/16 fl oz); Jamba Light (three flavors, 150–160 calories/16 fl oz); Blended with a Purpose (six flavors, 240–280 calories/16 fl oz); Jamba Classics (ten flavors, 260–320 calories/16 fl oz); and Creamy Indulgences (three flavors, 340–530 calories/16 fl oz). Matcha Green Tea, a substitute for coffee, was offered in a form of smoothie or as a 4-ounce "Shot." In addition to the natural nutrients in Jamba smoothies, Jamba offered supplements in the form of Boosts and Shots. Boosts included 10 combinations of vitamins, minerals, proteins, and extracts designed to give the mind and body a nutritious boost. A complimentary Boost was offered with each Jamba smoothie. Shots included three combinations of wheatgrass, green tea, orange juice, and soymilk designed to give customers a natural concentrate of vitamins, minerals, and antioxidants.

As a complement to its drink offerings, Jamba also offered a small selection of baked goods. Each of these items was made with natural ingredients and was high in protein and/or fiber. The baked-goods segment included eight varieties of sweet or savory breads, pretzels, and cookies.

Supplies

Smoothie and juice products depended heavily on supplies of fresh and fresh-frozen fruit and vegetables. The quality of each smoothie depended to a large degree on the quality of the basic produce ingredients from which it was made. It was therefore essential that the supply of produce was of the highest quality and was consistent throughout the year. To achieve these dual goals, and realize the lowest possible purchase costs, Jamba Juice Company purchased all of its projected requirements for the coming year from suppliers at the height of the season for that particular type of produce.

Jamba Juice Company conducted quality assurance testing at the time of packing to ensure that the produce met its high standards, which matched or exceeded USDA grade-A standards. The produce was then flash-frozen and stored by the suppliers for shipment to distributors throughout the year. Jamba Juice Company contracted with independent distribution companies to distribute produce to the stores. Jamba believed that by clustering future store development it could begin to lower distribution costs and therefore reduce the cost of goods sold.

All of Jamba's nutritional supplements (e.g., boosts) and baked goods were created to very exacting specifications. After quality control checks at the support center, all products were shipped directly to stores by outside distributors. Jamba Juice Company did not maintain central warehousing facilities.

Smoothie Competitors

In 2007, Jamba was the smoothie industry leader and had several fairly strong competitors with similar health and fitness focuses (see Exhibit 4).

Juice It Up!   Juice It Up! was founded in 1995 and advertised itself as an innovator in the smoothie and fresh-juice industry, with signature blends setting new standards for taste and nutrition. Juice It Up! aspired to spread perpetual summer across America and serve up its own amped-up take on fitness culture. It specialized in the "southern California style" juice bar and offered blended-to-order fresh-fruit smoothies, fresh squeezed juices, and other beverages.

Planet Smoothie   Since 1995, Planet Smoothie had been serving a variety of fresh-fruit smoothies in numerous locations across the country. Planet Smoothie advertising claims included "fast fuel" on the go, for any diet or none at all; low fat, low carb, low cal; and high protein, high energy, high in vitamins and supplements. Planet Smoothie juice bars offered fresh smoothies, and Planet Smoothie Cafés offered smoothies, sandwiches, and salads.

Smoothie King Franchises   Smoothie King Franchises, Inc., founded in 1989, offered blended fruit and juice drinks in more than 50 flavors that could be fortified with dietary supplements. The stores also carried sports drinks, energy bars, supplements, and sports nutrition

Exhibit 4 Smoothie Industry Competitors

	Jamba Juice	Juice It Up!	Planet Smoothie	Smoothie King
Smoothies/ drinks	12 oz. drink	16 oz. drinks	22 oz. drinks	20 oz. drinks
	Smoothies with Granola 3 flavors 360–450 calories	*Smoothies* 22 flavors 210–380 calories	*Energy Smoothies* 6 flavors 265–525 calories	*Stay Healthy* 9 flavors 325–560 calories
	16 oz. drinks	*Brazilian Blends* 2 flavors 250–685 calories	*Weight-Loss Smoothies* 6 flavors 265–380 calories	*Trim Down* 26 flavors 215–400 calories
	Fresh Squeezed Juices 3 flavors 90–220 calories	*Power Shakes* 3 flavors 360–470 calories	*Multivitamin Smoothies* 6 flavors 225–365 calories	*Get Energy* 15 flavors 165–520 calories
	Jucies 2 flavors 170–180 calories	8 oz. drink		*Build Up* 13 flavors 300–1,065 calories
	Yogurt and Fruit Blends 2 flavors 220–240 calories	*Healthy Way Juices* 6 flavors 70–140 calories	*Cool-Blend Smoothies* 6 flavors 300–560 calories	*Snack Right* 13 flavors 360–550 calories
	All Fruit 4 flavors 200–220 calories	20 oz. drinks	*Protein Smoothies* 3 flavors 350–515 calories	*Indulge* 10 flavors 430–780 calories
	Jamba Light 3 flavors 150–160 calories	*Nondairy Coolers* 8 flavors 270–360 calories	*Merlin's Planet Living* 2 flavors 340–415 calories	
	Blended with a Purpose 7 flavors 240–280 calories	*Cocoa Shakes* 2 flavors 350 calories		
	Jamba Classics 10 flavors 260–320 calories	Other drinks		
	Creamy Indulgences 3 flavors 340–530 calories	*Hot Teas and Cocoas* *Organic Coffee*		
Food	High-protein/high-fiber pretzels, bread, cookies		(Food is available at Planet Smoothie Cafés, but not at juice bars.)	Energy and protein bars, granola, soy chips, veggie chips, high-protein cookies
Supplements	*Boosts:* 12 combinations of vitamins, minerals, proteins, and extracts *Shots:* 3 combinations of wheatgrass, green tea, soymilk, orange juice	*Boosts:* 7 combinations of vitamins, minerals, proteins, and extracts *Shots:* wheatgrass	*Blasts:* 9 combinations of vitamins, minerals, proteins, and extracts	*Supplements:* 7 combinations of vitamins, minerals, proteins, and extracts

Source: nutritional information for Jamba Juice from www.jambajuice.com/#/smoothies; for Juice It Up! from www.juiceitup.com/products_nutrition.html; for Planet Smoothie from www.planetsmoothie.com/nutrition.aspx; for Smoothie King from www.smoothieking.com/smoothies/nutritional-chart.php.

items. Smoothie King outlets could be found in about 35 states and South Korea. It advertised itself as the premier smoothie bar and nutritional lifestyle center in the industry.

In addition to being a leader in the smoothie industry, Jamba was also a formidable competitor within the broader quick-service restaurant (QSR) arena. On *QSR Magazine*'s 2007 Top 50 Quick-Service and Fast-Casual Chains list, Jamba Juice ranked 47 overall (compared against all burger, sandwich, Mexican, chicken, pizza/pasta, Asian, seafood, and snack segments).[6] Cold Stone Creamery (number 41), Baskin-Robbins (32), Dunkin' Doughnuts (9), and Starbucks (6) were the only companies in the "Snack" QSR market segment that ranked higher on the list than Jamba Juice.

Customers

The Jamba Juice Company's increasingly broad product selection made it a competitor against a variety of "snack" providers (coffee houses, doughnut shops, ice cream parlors), as well as fast-food meal establishments (burgers, pizza, tacos, fried chicken). Jamba's core customers were health-conscious consumers who led, or aspired to lead, a healthy lifestyle. Therefore, Jamba positioned its products as healthy alternatives to conventional fast-food fare. Due to vast options in size, calorie content, and relative sweetness, Jamba smoothies and baked goods could serve as a light snack, a sweet treat, or even a meal replacement for on-the-go customers who wanted to avoid highly processed or sugar-rich convenience foods. The company's commitment to fresh produce and natural products bolstered its image as a leading provider of premium natural food and beverages and positioned it well to benefit from the healthy alternatives trend.

Fast-Food Alternative Smoothies had been called the fast food of the new millennium. Consumers who once grabbed a hot dog or hamburger for lunch were now choosing a fresh-fruit smoothie as a healthy alternative. For example, a Jamba Juice 30-ounce Protein Berry Workout with Whey smoothie provided 21 grams of protein and 7 grams of fiber for only 480 calories and 1.5 grams of fat. In contrast, a McDonald's Quarter Pounder and small french fries provided 26 grams of protein and 6 grams of fiber but also had 660 calories and 32 grams of fat. In addition to being easier on the waistline and arteries, the Jamba smoothie also provided 110 percent of the USRDA for calcium, 120 percent of vitamin C, and 80 percent of vitamin D, while the McDonald's meal offered only nominal mineral value and a host of artificial preservatives. This type of comparison by educated consumers was what helped Jamba draw in new customers as they looked to "clean up" their diets.

Treat Alternative The growing number of consumers focused on living a healthy lifestyle had a major impact on the grocery, restaurant, and health care industries. Consumers increasingly demanded products that supported their interests in fitness and nutrition while also providing high-quality taste and a "treat" they could feel good about. Jamba's Creamy Indulgences line provided customers with a treat they could perceive as being as decadent as ice cream but one they could enjoy while consuming fewer calories and less sugar.

Functional Foods Functional foods included ingredients that provided extra benefits beyond basic nutrition—such as antioxidants to fight free radicals or plant sterols to block cholesterol. Jamba believed that consumers increasingly looked for products that offered specific health benefits in addition to great taste. In order to cater to these multidimensional desires, Jamba Juice introduced the Blended with a Purpose line of smoothies, including Coldbuster, Protein Berry Workout[M], Acai Super-Antioxidant, and Fit n' Fruitful.

Energy Beverages With consumers increasingly living highly active and on-the-go lifestyles, demand for a convenient source of energy and refreshment had grown dramatically. The energy beverage market captured a significant amount of this growth because the beverages were more convenient and portable than traditional hot coffee and tea drinks. But most retail ready-to-drink energy beverages were high in both sugar and caffeine. For consumers seeking a healthy source of energy, Jamba Juice introduced beverages and Boosts that combined natural caffeine sources, such as Matcha Green Tea and Guarana, with the nutritional benefits of fruit to provide a healthy and flavorful source of sustained energy.

Jamba's Growth Strategy

The Jamba Juice Company's growth strategy was to expand its existing markets and develop new markets, while leveraging its support infrastructure. Understanding that it required strong unit-level economics across regions and platforms to continue growth, Jamba Juice Company strived to achieve three things: unit economics (i.e., continue to improve on store profitability), new-unit growth (i.e., continue to expand in existing markets as well as emerging and new markets), and leveraged infrastructure (i.e., continue to build on and leverage existing infrastructure to improve profitability).

Jamba Juice Company had a multidirectional strategy that included increasing company-owned stores, developing new stores, increasing same-store sales, increasing customer frequency, and developing alternative product channels.

Increasing the Number of Company-Owned Stores During 2007, Jamba began acquiring the assets of Jamba Juice franchised stores as a means of further enhancing its position in the healthy blended-beverage market. Over 30 franchise stores were acquired during the first three quarters of 2007, and Jamba expected to continue making additional franchise acquisitions as part of its ongoing growth strategy. In 2006, approximately

33 percent of Jamba's stores were franchised, but franchises accounted for only about 4 percent of its revenue. By April 2008, 71 percent of Jamba stores were company-owned.

Developing New Stores Jamba generally characterized its stores as either traditional or nontraditional locations. Traditional locations included strip malls and various retail locations, while nontraditional locations included alternative distribution channels such as colleges and universities, airports, and store-within-a-store locations.

Traditional stores averaged approximately 1,400 square feet in size and were designed to be fun, friendly, energetic, and colorful to represent the active, healthy lifestyle that Jamba Juice Company promoted. These stores were located either in major urban centers or in suburban strip malls.

Nontraditional stores were located in areas that allowed Jamba to generate awareness and try out new products to fuel the core business. Jamba's nontraditional opportunities included store-within-a-store locations, airports, shopping malls, colleges, and universities:

Store-within-a-store: Jamba Juice Company was developing franchise partner relationships with major grocers and retailers to develop store-within-a-store concepts. The franchise partnerships provided it with the opportunity to reach new customers and enhance the brand without making significant capital investments. Jamba's premium brand appealed to major retailers that focused on enhancing their customers' in-store experience. The company was confident that the flexibility of the Jamba concept to fit into many formats enabled Jamba to build awareness outside its traditional locations.

Airports: Jamba operated several airport locations and had the opportunity to develop stores in numerous additional airports. Jamba Juice Company's highly portable product appealed to travelers on the go and provided an energizing boost to tiring air travel.

Shopping malls: Jamba had opportunistically established stores in shopping malls that presented attractive expansion opportunities. In addition, as with the airport locations, the indoor setting helped to alleviate weather and seasonal vulnerabilities that challenge traditional locations.

Colleges and universities: The Jamba brand was believed to be extremely appealing to the average college student's active, on-the-go lifestyle, and Jamba expected to continue to develop on-campus locations.

Other potential nontraditional store locations: Additional high-traffic, nontraditional locations existed for Jamba to explore. Many large health clubs included a juice and smoothie bar within their

buildings, and new gyms were popping up every day as the American culture became more health- and fitness-conscious. There was an opportunity for Jamba to partner with a major gym chain or individual private gyms with high memberships rates. Another possibility was to partner with a large school district. Schools across the country were under increasing scrutiny to offer healthy alternatives to the traditional fat, carbohydrate, and preservative-rich foods served in cafeterias. Many schools had other fast-food kiosks within the school (which attracted additional criticism); therefore, offering a Jamba kiosk might have been a viable option that was economically profitable for Jamba and politically profitable for the schools.

Jamba Juice Company had followed a strategy of expanding its store locations in existing markets and opening stores in select new markets. In mid-2007, Jamba had approximately 640 stores, with plans to expand store count to as many as 1,095 by 2010.[7] However, by the end of fiscal year 2007, Jamba's store expansion plans had changed. In early 2008, a financial analyst predicted that Jamba's widely recognized brand poised it to "expand in an under-penetrated and growing health food market."[8] However, the same analyst recognized that Jamba was experiencing declines in store traffic and store-level margins due to the subprime crisis and that Jamba therefore planned to slow its expansion until the economy had a chance to recover.[9] In May 2008, Jamba announced its plans to close 10 underperforming company-owned stores by the end of the year and terminate signed leases for seven unbuilt locations.[10]

Increasing Same-Store Sales Jamba Juice Company was passionate about creating fresh new products that met a variety of customer needs, and it listened carefully to customer feedback. An example was the introduction of the Sixteen, a 16-ounce size offering, introduced to satisfy customers' demands for smaller smoothies. As energy drinks continued to gain momentum, Jamba introduced its Match Green Tea Shots and 3G Energizer smoothie to provide a healthy, inventive, and high-energy option for its customers.[11] Jamba anticipated devoting additional resources to its research and development team in an effort to build on recent new product successes and take its product innovation abilities to the next level.

Expanding the menu to include other products such as coffee, espresso, salads, soups, and hot pockets seemed to be the wave of the future as the juice bar industry continued to evolve. Planet Smoothie had taken this approach by creating Planet Smoothie Cafés, which offered breakfast, sandwiches, salads, and soft drinks in addition to juices and smoothies. Planet Smoothie advertised these cafés as "one-stop shops for your fast food abatement program."

In 2008, Jamba officially launched its on-the-go, healthy breakfast alternatives for the rapidly growing breakfast market in quick-service restaurants. "We're encouraging

America to make breakfast a priority, and feel the difference a healthy breakfast can make in their day," commented Paul Coletta, senior vice president, Marketing and Brand Development.[12] New breakfast products, including Granola Toppers and Chunky Smoothies, were designed to be denser and more filling products that could still be served in a cup (12 oz or 16 oz) but would be eaten with a spoon. The Jamba breakfast menu also listed yogurt-blend smoothies, juices, and baked goods. In late 2007 Jamba also began adding fast-cook ovens to its stores cache of equipment. Initially tested hot menu items were to include whole-wheat hot-pocket sandwiches in three flavors.

Increasing Customer Frequency   One of the key objectives of Jamba's growth strategy was to increase the frequency of customer visits, which averaged less than two per month for 80 percent of Jamba customers.[13] Jamba viewed the conversion of "light users" (two or less times per month) to "heavy users" (eight or more times per month) as a significant opportunity to increase sales year-round and significantly decrease weather and seasonal vulnerabilities.

The main driver of Jamba's revenue and profit was the sale of smoothies during hot weather. In southern states (e.g., California), where the weather remained warm year-round, Jamba experienced fairly steady sales. However, in the northern states (e.g., New York), where there was a cold and fairly lengthy winter season, Jamba experienced severe seasonal variability. Jamba Juice Company intended to continue developing fresh concepts that appealed to customers at any time of day and in any weather or season. One way Jamba was doing this was by planning tests for the use of the fast-cook ovens (installed to heat hot-pocket sandwiches) to make soup, hot tea, and coffee products.

Another potential avenue for Jamba to overcome seasonal variation was to continue developing the functional-foods concept for additional product offerings. The functional-foods industry realized $15.4 billion worth of sales in 2006 and was expected to experience rapid growth over the next decade.[14]

Developing Alternative Product Channels   Jamba Juice Company's strong association with premium, flavorful beverages translated well into ready-to-drink beverages available in a variety of retail locations. According to a Frost and Sullivan 2005 report on the U.S. beverage market, sales of energy drinks experienced a four-year compound average growth rate of nearly 90 percent and in 2004 were a $1.3 billion market.

In late 2007, Jamba Juice Company reached a licensing agreement with Nestlé under which Nestlé would manufacture six of Jamba's juice and smoothie ready-to-drink products for distribution in eight western states in mid-2008.[15] Nestlé planned to gradually expand distribution of the Jamba drinks into other U.S. markets and possibly even into overseas markets. The products would contain nonfat milk, which would differentiate them from other juice-drink competitors, including Naked Juice (owned by Pepsi) and Odwalla (owned by Coca-Cola). Kraft had a similar deal with Starbucks to distribute its Frappuccino drinks. The launch of ready-to-drink beverages in May 2008 enjoyed an early success and exceeded initial expectations as it captured a significant share of the premium juice segment.[16]

Can Jamba Grow without Losing Its "Healthy Alternatives" Brand Identity?

Jamba Juice Company's desire to grow by expanding its selection of nonjuice menu items seemed to follow the Starbucks model. Once only coffee houses, most Starbucks stores now offered a variety of muffins, fruit plates, sandwiches, quiches, and desserts. This menu expansion helped Starbucks attract customers who were looking for a light meal or dessert to go with their coffee and also attracted noncoffee drinkers who just came in for the food. Offering iced coffees and teas helped Starbucks overcome some of its seasonal variability, giving customers a cool-drink offering during hot-weather months. Offering ready-to-go-drinks in grocery and convenience stores also enabled Starbucks to get its products to a wider customer base.

Likewise, Jamba set out to strengthen its customer reach by offering ready-to-drink products, hot food and drink items to attract customers during the cold-weather months, and a range of breakfast and lunch food items to complement its juice-based offerings and satisfy customer desires all day and all year-round. Could Jamba attract the Dunkin' Doughnuts breakfast business, the McDonald's lunch crowd, the Baskin-Robbins dessert seekers, and perhaps even the Starbucks afternoon energy fixers? By expanding its menu very broadly, would Jamba run the risk of being categorized as a fast-food restaurant, rather than being viewed as a fast-food alternative? Or could Jamba follow Starbucks' path of broadening its menu base but still maintaining its stature as a higher-end establishment? CEO James White has some tough decisions to make, particularly given Jamba's declining same-store sales.

Endnotes

1. Jamba Juice Company—Company History. Retrieved September 19, 2008, from Fundinguniverse.com.
2. Jamba Juice Company and Services Acquisition Corp. International Announce Merger. Retrieved September 20, 2008, from www.sec.gov/Archives/edgar/data/1316898/000110465906015960/a06-6826_1ex99d1.htm.
3. Jamba, Inc. Announces Changes to Its Senior Management Team. Retrieved September 20, 2008, from http://ir.jambajuice.com/releasedetail.cfm?releaseid=326728.
4. Jamba, Inc. Reports Financial Results for Second Quarter Fiscal Year 2008. Retrieved September 18, 2008, from http://ir.jambajuice.com/releasedetail.cfm?releaseid=331140.
5. Jamba, Inc. Form 10-K (Annual Report). Retrieved April 10, 2008, from http://ir.jambajuice.com/sec.cfm.

6. The QSR 50. Retrieved November 16, 2007, from www.qsrmagazine.com/reports/qsr50/2007/charts/qsr50-2.phtml.

7. L. Lee. A smoothie you can chew on: To appeal to diners as well as drinkers, Jamba Juice is adding heft to its concoctions. *BusinessWeek,* June 11, 2007, p. 64.

8. Zacks Analyst Blog Highlights: Jamba Juice, Krispy Kreme, Starbucks and PeopleSupport. Retrieved April 10, 2008, from http://news.money-central.msn.com/ticker/article.aspx?symbol=US:JMBA&feed=BW&date=20080110&id=8018383.

9. Ibid.

10. Jamba Announces Organizational Changes and Store Development Reductions. Retrieved September 20, 2008, from http://ir.jambajuice.com/releasedetail.cfm?releaseid=310697.

11. 2007 Jamba Juice Press Release, as reprinted in Jamba Report Blog. Retrieved September 19, 2008, from www.jambajuice.com.

12. Jamba Launches Breakfast Nationwide. Retrieved September 21, 2008, from http://ir.jambajuice.com/releasedetail.cfm?releaseid=298765.

13. Lee. A smoothie you can chew on.

14. M. Rogers. Beverages: Where form meets function. *Chain Leader,* 2007. Retrieved November 20, 2007, from www.chainleader.com/archives/2007/10/liquid.asp.

15. W. Swarts. Jamba's juice deal with Nestle froths up shares. *SmartMoney,* 2007. Retrieved April 10, 2008, from www.smartmoney.com/onedaywonder/index.cfm?story=20071204.

16. Nestlé USA and Jamba Announce Early Success with Ready-to-Drink Beverages. Retrieved on September 17, 2008, from http://ir.jambajuice.com/releasedetail.cfm?releaseid=331141.

Case 25   China's Geely Automotive Holdings, Ltd.: Targeting the U.S. Market*

Geely Automotive Holdings, Ltd., is an automobile manufacturer based in China's historically important city of Hangzhou, the capital city of Zhejiang Province. In 2008, Geely's founder, Shufu Li, was taking stock of the company's recent successes and considering the next move. Two years earlier, in 2006, at the North American Auto Show in Detroit, Geely had captured the global auto industry's imagination by unveiling its latest, top-of-the-line sedan, the 7151 CK (see Appendix A). This was the first time a Chinese automaker had participated in this premier, global event. Furthermore, Geely, which is China's largest privately owned automaker, announced that it planned to enter the U.S. market with a future, upscale version of the 7151 CK. Geely planned to sell this sedan for less than $10,000 and to have it in showrooms by 2008. The company hoped to sell 25,000 vehicles in the United States in the first year and to reach 100,000 vehicles by 2013.

Historically, Chinese vehicle exports had primarily been limited to buses and trucks and other heavy equipment. But Chinese manufacturers had steadily been upgrading their technology and production efficiency in an attempt to compete overseas. Many manufacturers, Geely included, felt that Chinese manufacturers were ready to compete in the large, potentially lucrative U.S. market with low-priced vehicles.

By 2008, however, the company realized that it needed to reevaluate this strategy. The U.S. auto industry was facing a historic slowdown, while the growth of the China market had been much greater than expected. Should Geely forge ahead with plans to tackle the U.S. market, or should it further postpone its U.S. ambitions and focus on the growing upscale segment of the Chinese market much closer to home?

China's Automobile Industry

There are two types of automobile manufacturers in China: joint ventures and domestic independent manufacturers. The majority of the major automakers in China assembled foreign models that were developed by their joint-venture partners, such as Volkswagen from Germany, General Motors and Chrysler from the United States, Citroen from France, and Toyota and Honda from Japan. Foreign manufacturers and their Chinese partners controlled more than 80 percent of China's auto market in 2007. These joint ventures were so prevalent that they left little market share for the independent manufacturers. Even so, Geely

was already one of the top-10 producers in China and had dreams of becoming a major global player.

In 2007, China's automotive industry expanded at a rate of 22 percent, and profit rose to ¥100 billion ($12.8 billion). The profit growth in the auto industry was driven by the increases in demand for cars in both the domestic and overseas markets. This growth helped China to overtake Germany and become the world's third-largest carmaker, after Japan and the United States.[1] The Paris-based International Organization of Motor Vehicle Manufacturers, organizer of the Detroit Auto Show and other large car shows around the world, estimated that China could be the world's largest producer of automobiles by 2010.

Chinese carmakers do not break down overseas sales by country, but, in general, exports paled in comparison to production for the domestic Chinese market. Besides Geely, a few other Chinese automakers were also considering expanding to overseas markets, including Chang'an Automobile Group Co., Ltd., Beijing Automotive Industry Holding Co., Ltd., and Chery Automobile Co., Ltd.[2] According to the China Association of Automobile Manufacturers, the mainland exported 610,000 vehicles in 2007, which was an increase of approximately 80 percent over 2006.

Geely's Background

Geely, whose name denotes fortune and luck (吉利) in Chinese, was founded in 1986 in Zhejiang Province. The company initially began by manufacturing refrigerators and related accessories. In 1994 Geely began to manufacture motorcycles, and in 1997 the company entered the automotive industry as the first private company approved by the central government to produce automobiles in China.

With the company motto of "passion in professional dedication, innovation, communication and hard work,"[3] Geely began to attract attention and the company experienced rapid growth. The company established a broad distribution network consisting of 18 sales agents in 108 locations all over China. In 2007, Geely sold 184,176 units, which was a 7 percent increase over 2006. It also exported 29,063 units in 2007, which was a 93.8 percent increase over 2006. According to Geely spokesperson Lawrence Ang, the export business was expected to pick up in 2007 on strong sales in the Middle East and North American markets, while new orders also had been received from Russia and Ukraine.[4] Geely aimed to sell 1 million vehicles annually by 2010; two-thirds were to be sold in overseas markets.[5]

Competition continued to increase in China's automotive industry, particularly from the joint ventures. On several occasions Geely was nearly driven out of business, but Li remained resilient in the face of these challenges. Unlike many of his competitors, he did not attempt to obtain a foreign

*The initial research for this case was completed by Richard Lin, Royal Chan, Annie Wong, and Kimmy Ho as an assignment for a Current Issues in Business course at the Chinese University of Hong Kong under the direction of Professors Yuan Yi Chen and Michael Young. The purpose of the case is to serve as a basis for classroom discussion rather than to illustrate either effective or ineffective handling of an administrative situation. Copyright © 2009 Michael N. Young.

Exhibit 1 Geely's New Corporate Logo

partner. He believed that partnering with a foreign firm was a losing proposition in the long run because Chinese partners had little bargaining power over their larger, more established foreign partners. Thus they were forced to take a back seat in decision making. Furthermore, the alliances often did not bring about the advanced technology that was promised by the foreign partner. Instead, foreign partners often maintained tight control with the goal of maximizing their return. Li liked the independence of financial and operational decisions that came from remaining free of a foreign partner.

Moving to the Higher End of the Market Geely was known as a price leader in China, providing a series of models ranging in price from ¥30,000 ($3,950) to ¥80,000 ($10,500). These prices put the dream of owning an automobile within reach of consumers in China's rural areas, where incomes were lower. Geely had developed an effective cost control system. First, each product had its own specialized manufacturing base to enhance efficiency. For instance, the plant in Shanghai focused primarily on midlevel automobiles, whereas the operations at Ningbo in Zhejiang Province manufactured the lower-end models, with prices ranging between ¥50,000 ($6,580) and ¥70,000 ($9,200). The models manufactured at Taizhou in Zhejiang Province were at the lowest end, with prices around ¥30,000 ($3,950). In addition, cost saving was achieved through vertical integration; by producing many components in-house, Geely was able to further reduce costs and keep other information regarding its manufacturing processes proprietary.

Although Geely primarily assumed a price-leader position when it first entered the market, management began to realize that this strategy may not have been effective in the long term because the profit margins for low-end products were razor-thin. Thus, in 2004, having cemented its leading position in the low-end segment, Geely ventured into the middle to high-end market. Prior to this, Geely had only four different models in China, targeted at the low end of the market: Gale Wind, Maple, Uliou, and Merrie, all priced from ¥30,000 ($3,950) to ¥80,000 ($10,500). By the end of 2004, Geely introduced its first midlevel model,

Beauty Leopard, which ranged from ¥80,000 ($10,500) to ¥88,000 ($11,580).

Then Geely began targeting the sporty segment and midlevel portions of the market with models that it hoped to put into production in the near future. For instance, 23 new models were introduced at China's automotive exposition in April 2008. Moreover, in order to present a new image, Geely paid ¥3.6 million ($0.47 million) for the design of a new logo, which was put into use at the end of 2007 (see Exhibit 1).

Research and Development From 1997 to 2005, Geely invested over ¥6.47 billion ($0.83 billion) in R&D to help in its pursuit of an independent development path. Geely had been investing more than 10 percent of annual sales revenue in R&D and had established the Geely Automobile Research School and the Geely Engine Research School. Geely had mastered most of the key technologies that were crucial to making automobiles, including knowledge of engines, drive trains, ancillary power systems, interior equipment, and exterior equipment. Moreover, the company claimed to be the first Chinese automaker that independently undertook research in transmissions. Li believed that by mastering technology, Geely would be able to maintain its competitive advantage when facing foreign rivals. Independent development of technology also increased Geely's procurement systems, compared to other local carmakers.

To improve product design and quality, Geely began cooperating with several foreign automakers from such countries as South Korea, Germany, and Italy. Experts from foreign companies and institutes were invited to Geely to share their experience and provide training. Meanwhile, Geely's employees were sent abroad to receive further professional training. This knowledge exchange gave Geely's employees opportunities to develop their capabilities. The R&D initiatives enabled Geely to gain a more advantageous position in the local market and to enhance its international profile. These factors increased Geely's confidence in its ability to successfully compete in the U.S. market. Geely's financial information from 2003 to 2007 is presented in Exhibit 2.

Exhibit 2   Income Statement and Balance Sheet Geely Automobile Holdings Ltd (2004–2008)

In Millions of Hong Kong Dollars (except for per share items)	2008	2007	2006	2005	2004
Total revenue	4,289.00	120.7	111.7	89.2	28.1
Gross profit	651.3	14	14.9	9.5	1.3
Total operating expense	3,542.70	123	103.2	95.6	41.3
Operating income	746.3	−2.3	8.5	−6.4	−13.2
Net income before taxes	917.9	281.3	189.8	101.5	69
Net income after taxes	866.1	279.8	188.4	101.5	69
Net income before extra. items	879.1	276.8	183.6	97.5	69.4
Net income	879.1	276.8	183.6	97.5	71.5
Income available to com excl extraord	879.1	276.8	183.6	97.5	69.4
Income available to com incl extraord	879.1	276.8	183.6	97.5	71.5
Basic EPS excluding extraordinary items	0.15	0.056	0.044	0.024	0.017
Basic EPS including extraordinary items	0.15	0.056	0.044	0.024	0.017
Diluted EPS excluding extraord items	0.143	0.055	0.044	0.024	0.017
Diluted EPS including extraord items	0.143	0.055	0.044	0.024	0.017
Normalized income before taxes	682.2	281.3	189.8	101.5	69
Normalized income after taxes	643.6	279.8	188.4	101.5	69
Normalized inc. avail to com.	656.6	276.8	183.6	97.5	69.4
Total current assets	5,110.60	777.8	144.9	59.1	20.4
Total assets	10,151.00	2,675.70	1,622.00	757.9	598.8
Total current liabilities	5,273.50	70	97.9	48	17.5
Total liabilities	5,953.10	528.3	715.9	55.9	24
Total equity	4,197.90	2,147.40	906.1	702	574.8
Total liabilities & shareholders' equity	10,151.00	2,675.70	1,622.00	757.9	598.8
Total common shares outstanding	6,489.76	5,201.08	4,151.39	4,120.27	4,120.27
Total preferred shares outstanding	—	—	—	—	—

Source: Annual Reports of Geely Automobile Holdings Ltd 2004-2008.

Expansion in China and Overseas   Geely was on the fast track for expansion. In addition to operating its original manufacturing facilities in Ningbo, Linhai, Taizhou, and Shanghai, after 2005 Geely had government approval to establish three more bases: at Xiangtan in Hunan Province in central China, Lanzhou in Gansu Province in northern China, and Jinan in Shandong Province in eastern China. Geely was also planning to set up a complete vehicle production base in Harbin, capital of Heilongjiang Province in northeastern China. Its talks with the Heilongjiang provincial government were nearing conclusion, and the first phase of the project would have a capacity of 100,000 to 150,000 vehicles annually. This would be the automaker's eighth manufacturing facility in China. In addition, Geely had signed an agreement with the Cixi city government of Zhejiang Province to build a

¥18.8 billion ($2.47 billion) auto industrial city with an annual production capacity of 1 million units in the Cixi economic development zone.[6]

Moreover, after the exhibition of its four car models at the 2005 Internationale Automobil-Ausstellung (IAA) in Frankfurt, Germany, Geely began to design and build a car model just for export to Western countries. It began working with Magna Steyr of Austria, but the start date for exporting vehicles to Europe was not confirmed.[7] The company had set up production plants in Indonesia and Russia, each with the capacity to produce 50,000 cars. It was reported that Geely was in talks with four or five countries about future cooperation, with discussions to set up assembly plants in Africa, Europe, and the United States. In addition, in October 2006 Geely signed an agreement with Manganese Bronze Holdings, the leading manufacturer of the distinctive London black taxi. Under the agreement, Geely became the largest shareholder of the British automaker. At the same time, Geely and Manganese also set up a joint venture to produce the black taxis in Shanghai, which would be sold in Britain and other overseas markets. This venture came into production in mid-2008.

Obstacle to Entering the U.S. Market

Geely's engineers had determined what they needed to do to bring the company into compliance with U.S. regulatory standards, and they planned to make the necessary changes within 18 months. Geely's primary selling point, as with many Chinese products, was low price. But low price alone was not enough; the company still had to convince American auto consumers—arguably the most sophisticated in the world—that China could produce a quality car.

The entry of a new competitor was not good news for Detroit's "Big Three" automakers—General Motors (GM), Ford, and Chrysler. In late 2008, the Big Three were beset by bad news resulting from the recession that had begun in August of that year partly because of defaults on subprime mortgages. In October 2008, the CEOs of the Big Three jointly traveled to testify before the U.S. Congress to ask for an unprecedented $25 billion rescue package that would include, among other things, loan guarantees to help them retool and avoid drastic layoffs. Auto sales in the United States were at a historic low, and the Big Three automakers continued to face unrelenting competition from Japanese and Korean automakers. The last thing they wanted was increased competition from Chinese competitors. Rick Wagoner, the CEO of General Motors, stated after the 2006 Detroit auto show: "It's not an issue in short term. The product won't be competitive. But in long term you'd be crazy about having not looked at what the Chinese could do given what others have done."[8]

The market share of the Big Three American automakers had eroded significantly during the previous few years, with sharp declines in sales of their most profitable models. GM, which lost $4 billion in North America in the third quarter of 2008, had been struggling with high labor and commodities costs, loss of market share, and sluggish sales of sport utility vehicles (SUVs). As part of a broader restructuring effort, GM slashed 30,000 jobs and closed 12 facilities in 2008. Ford, which suffered a loss of $3 billion over the third quarter of 2008, was also aiming to stem erosion of its market share in the United States. Chrysler had been the exception in the U.S. car market in recent years, mainly because of its earlier extensive restructuring and the popularity of its newly launched models. But even Chrysler was threatened by possible loss of sales because of intensive use of incentives in previous years.

While the Big Three struggled to maintain profits (or minimize losses) and keep up market share, Japanese automakers such as Toyota, Nissan, and Honda had, until the 2008 recession, increased market share while offering relatively few incentives. In short, American consumers had acquired a taste for Japanese cars and were willing to pay relatively more for them. The ranking of automobile sales in

the U.S. market in 2007 was as follows: GM, Toyota, Ford, Chrysler Group, Honda, and Nissan. Ford slid to the number-three position in the U.S. auto market, outmaneuvered by Toyota's surging sales of small cars and gas-electric hybrids.[9]

Many factors were acting to suppress demand for automobiles in the United States in 2008, such as high gasoline prices, rising interest rates, and weakening consumer confidence. In short, U.S. automakers were facing one of the toughest situations that they had ever encountered. This had the potential to create political and other unexpected threats and obstacles for Geely as protectionist sentiment tends to increase in recessions.

Combating the Perception of Poor Quality of Chinese Products On top of the problems caused by the recession, Americans were very picky about their cars. In 2008, China was world-renowned as the world's workshop, dominating industries from shoes and toys to tools and basic electronics. But were Americans ready to purchase a Chinese-made car? People still remembered the Yugo, which was imported into the United States from the former Yugoslavia from 1985 to 1991. The car was billed as the lowest-priced new car in America and retailed for about $4,000. Only 141,511 Yugos were sold, but the car quickly became infamous for poor quality.[10] Geely did not want to be the next Yugo.

Although Geely received encouragement and support from the Chinese government, there were numerous challenges that had to be overcome for the company to succeed. Other things equal, low price was associated with low quality, and products from China had a reputation for shoddy workmanship. For example, the Landwind SUV,[11] made by Chinese automaker Jiangling Motors, had gained the reputation of being of extremely poor quality, and this had tarnished the image of Chinese automobiles. On the German Allgemeiner Deutscher Automobil-Club (ADAC) test, which was comparable to the European New Car Assessment Programme (NCAP) safety standards in passenger-cabin protection, the Landwind scored 0 out of 5. The passenger cabin completely collapsed on collision (see the YouTube video "Landwind crash test"). Since safety was an important factor in consumers' decision to buy, the test result seriously eroded Western consumers' confidence in the safety of Chinese cars.

Some analysts predicted that American consumers would not be willing to buy a Chinese car until 2010. An auto professional with IRN in Grand Rapids put it this way: "There are many good products out there right now, so it's not like when the Japanese came to the U.S. in the 70s and the Big Three were building some real crap."[12]

Lack of Innovation and Pirating of Designs Lack of innovative design was also seen as a problem for Chinese automobiles. Market observers of the Detroit Auto Show in 2006 were unimpressed by the simple curves of mainland cars. They also commented on the shoddy finish and the tinny sounds of the doors.[13] Although Geely engineers were trying to modify car designs and engineering, Li knew that Chinese engineers still had a long way to go before they could satisfy the sophisticated tastes of American buyers. Cars were a relatively new phenomenon in China and still beyond the reach of average Chinese consumers. In contrast, the United States was a car-based society, and Americans' association with cars began at birth—nearly every living American came home from the hospital in the family car.

Furthermore, Chinese products had a reputation for infringing on others' intellectual property rights. For instance, Chery and Geely were both accused of copying technology from GM and Toyota, respectively. GM said that Chery's popular small QQ model was a rip-off of its Chevrolet Spark. Although neither GM nor Toyota prevailed in court, the lawsuits inevitably tarnished the image of Chinese carmakers.

Meeting Environmental Protection Agency Standards

With the increasing concern about global warming and environmental protection, meeting the U.S. auto emission requirements was also a challenge for Geely.[14] In 2006, Geely failed to pass its first emission test held by the U.S. Environmental Protection Agency (EPA). Despite the failure, Qu Wei, the project manager of Geely International, remained confident. He stated: "The failure is acceptable as our original plan is to start selling in 2008. Before then we will conduct a series of tests on both safety and emissions through which we will know better about the U.S. emission standards and improve our products to bring them fully into compliance with the local regulations." However, Geely later announced that it would not export its CK sedan into the United States as originally forecast. Instead, the company planned to develop a new sedan for delivery in 2009.[15]

Distribution Problems

Distribution channels are critical in the automobile industry. On the one hand, the relationship between manufacturers and their intermediaries often involves long-term commitments that are difficult to change.[16] On the other hand, an organization must be ready to adjust its distribution practices— sometimes under conditions of considerable uncertainty about market developments. The U.S. automakers had experimented with various methods of distribution through the years.[17] In addition to selling through distributorships, manufacturers often got their cars to the public through rentals. The mature automobile market in the United States complicated Geely's distribution strategy; Geely would have to struggle for years on its own to set up a dealer network.

Trade Friction between China and the United States

The United States had been experiencing a trade deficit since the 1970s, and the problem was getting worse in recent years. A major factor in the imbalance was trade with China. In 2006, the trade deficit of the United States with China reached $232.5 billion. In an attempt to pacify local industries and alleviate the trade deficit, the U.S. government imposed quotas and import duties on some goods imported from China, such as textiles and televisions. Being a Chinese brand name, Geely had to face this potential crisis.

Renminbi Revaluation Some economists and members of Congress charged that China enjoyed an unfair advantage because it kept the value of its currency, the renminbi (RMB), artificially low. Even after several RMB revaluations upward by 2008, the United States was still urging China to revaluate the exchange rate of the RMB against other currencies. However, the possibility of RMB revaluation posed uncertainty over Geely's entry into the U.S. market. Any increase in the value of the RMB would be passed along in terms of higher prices for Geely's automobiles. Although the price of Geely cars would remain relatively low even if the RMB appreciated, any increase in price would marginally decrease Geely's competitive edge.

Summary

In April 2008, Geely Automotive Holdings, Ltd., admitted that it would not be able to enter the North American market in that year. Although the company had predicted at the 2006 Detroit Auto Show that 2008 was a feasible date, Geely now realized that it would take more time to build a dealer network and meet regulatory hurdles.[18] Geely also was taking into consideration that demand for automobiles had grown much more rapidly than expected in China and other emerging markets while auto sales had stagnated and were even falling in the United States. Car sales increased by 21 percent in China in the first quarter of 2008, and were showing no signs of slowing after five years of 20 to 30 percent annual growth.[19]

Geely seemed to be taking a more cautious stance. Vice president Frank Zhao commented: "It takes time to prepare the right product, the right sales network, and even the supplier systems. . . . Without all those things being ready, I don't think you can do a good job. . . . The U.S. is the largest and most difficult market in the world, and the customers are quite picky. Our brand recognition is low, so we'll have to promote it. It has to be a long-term strategy." He declined to provide a definite timetable for tackling the U.S. market. He wanted to make sure that when Geely entered the market, it would do so professionally and successfully and not end up as the butt of jokes like the infamous Yugo.

Thus Geely's managers faced numerous challenges. Should they rapidly pursue the U.S. market? How could they gain acceptance among sophisticated American car buyers? How could they build up a distribution network? Should they forget about the American market and concentrate on the fast-growing markets at home? Should they shift the business-level strategy from price-leader to differentiator, where there are higher margins? Whatever route Geely decided to take, it was certain the coming Chinese year of the ox would provide both challenges and opportunities.

Appendix A   Some of Geely's Models

The 7151 CK on display at the Detroit Auto Show

The Beauty Leopard

Endnotes

1. *South China Morning Post,* May 10, 2007.
2. SinoCast China Transportation Watch, January 24, 2007.
3. www.geely.com.
4. *South China Morning Post,* January 5, 2007.
5. *South China Morning Post,* May 15, 2007.
6. "Geely on Fast Lane for Expansion," *Financial Times Information,* October 18, 2006.
7. "Despite Obstacles, Chinese Carmakers Are Keen to Come to Europe; Players to Watch in the Race to Export from East to West," *Crain Communications,* December 11, 2006.
8. "China Sets Sights on U.S. Car Market," *CBS News,* January 10, 2006, www.cbsnews.com/stories/2006/01/10/business/main1198519_page2.shtml.
9. *The Washington Post,* January 4, 2008.
10. http://en.wikipedia.org/wiki/Yugo.
11. "Can Chinese products survive a crash test?" (WTO column), *China Business Infocentre,* 2005 www.cbiz.cn/news/showarticle.asp?id=2354.
12. "Geely, Chery Hold Off on U.S. Entry until 2010, or So," *VNU Business Media, Inc.,* December 4, 2006.
13. *Financial Times,* January 4, 2007.
14. "No Gear Shift in Geely US plan," *shanghaidaily,* 2006.
15. *VNU Business Media, Inc.,* August 21, 2006.
16. "The Economic Impact of Rising Gasoline Prices in Ohio," *Marketing Channels,* July 2004, www.house.gov/strickland/2005GasReportFinal.htm.
17. Dual Distribution Channels: The Competition between Rental Agencies and Dealers," *Marketing Science at the University of Florida,* 1997, http://bear.cba.ufl.edu/centers/MKS/abstracts/vol16/no3/purohit.html.
18. *The Dominion Post,* January 27, 2007.
19. *The Globe and Mail,* April 21, 2008.

JetBlue sold approximately 42.6 million shares of common stock to Deutsche Lufthansa, the German carrier, in January 2008. Lufthansa paid $300 million, net of transaction costs, for this stake in JetBlue, whose stock had lost about two-thirds of its value since an operational meltdown on February 14, 2007 (Exhibits 1 and 2). The stock purchase could be a precursor to an eventual takeover of JetBlue by Lufthansa if the U.S. laws restricting foreign ownership of domestic airlines to 25 percent change at a later point in time. JetBlue's CEO, David Barger, said, "There was never really any dialogue about 'what if,'" and added that the deal doesn't change JetBlue's strategy of avoiding takeover and growing alone.[1]

However, whether JetBlue sticks seriously to its growing-alone strategy remains to be observed. This is because, of late, JetBlue appears to be moving away from its core strategy, in quite interesting ways, of being a low-cost player providing the distinctive "JetBlue experience." In its efforts to boost revenues, the airline began charging $10 to $20 for seats with extra legroom, doubled its ticket-change fee to $100, and introduced refundable tickets that cost more than nonrefundable ones. Further, the airline

*This case study was prepared by Naga Lakshmi Damaraju of The Indian School of Business, Alan B. Eisner of Pace University, and Gregory G. Dess of the University of Texas at Dallas. This case study has been developed purely from secondary sources. The purpose of the case is to stimulate class discussion rather than illustrate effective or ineffective handling of a business situation. Copyright © 2009 Damaraju, Eisner, and Dess.

began charging $7 for a pillow-and-blanket kit, an amenity usually provided free of charge by other airlines.[2] Breaking another low-cost rule, JetBlue moved away from ticket sales through its own Web site and signed up with travel agencies and the Galileo and Sabre global distribution systems in August 2006 and with online travel agencies such as Orbitz in January 2008, These moves raise the question: Will JetBlue be what it was envisaged to be?

The U.S. Airline Industry[3]

Deregulation of the U.S. airline industry in 1978 ushered in competition in the previously protected industry. Several low-cost, low-fare operators entered the competitive landscape that Southwest had pioneered. In 1971 Southwest initiated service as a regional carrier, but by 1990 it became a major airline when its revenues crossed the $1 billion mark.[4] The Southwest model was based on operating a single-type aircraft fleet with high utilization, having a simplified fare structure with single-class seating, and achieving high productivity from its human and physical assets. In contrast, the "hub-and-spoke" system, increased labor costs, and increases in multitype aircraft fleets bloated the cost structure of the major airlines. There are three primary segments in the airline industry: major airlines, regional airlines, and low-fare airlines. Major U.S. airlines, as defined by the Department of Transportation, are those with annual revenues of over $1 billion. Eighteen passenger airlines belong to this category, the largest of which are American Airlines,

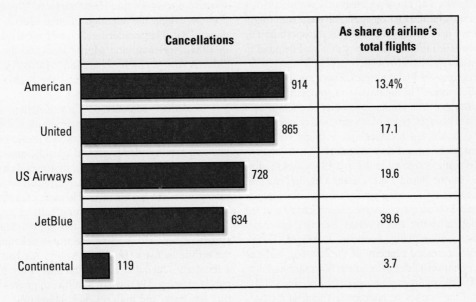

	Cancellations	As share of airline's total flights
American	914	13.4%
United	865	17.1
US Airways	728	19.6
JetBlue	634	39.6
Continental	119	3.7

Exhibit 1 **Flight Cancellations Feb. 13–15, 2007, due to Severe Weather**
Source: FlightStats.

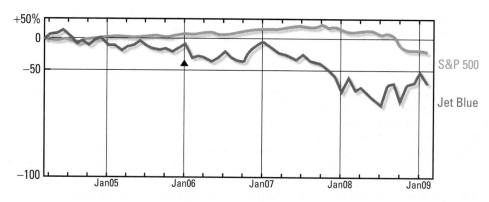

Exhibit 2 JetBlue's Stock Performance vs. S&P 500

Source: http://finance.yahoo.com. Copyright © 2009 Yahoo! Inc.

Continental Airlines, Delta Air Lines, Northwest Airlines, and United Airlines. These airlines offer scheduled flights to most large cities within the United States and abroad and also serve numerous smaller cities. Most major airlines adopted the hub-and-spoke route system. In this system, the operations are concentrated in a limited number of hub cities, while other destinations are served by providing one-stop or connecting service through the hub.

As of the end of 2008, there were 18 major airlines. Regional airlines typically operate smaller aircraft on lower-volume routes than do major airlines. Unlike the low-fare airlines, the regional airlines do not have an independent route system. They typically enter into relationships with major airlines and carry their passengers on the "spoke"—that is, between a hub or larger city and a smaller city. There were six regional major U.S. airlines at the end of 2008. The low-fare airlines operate from "point to point" and have their own route system. The target segment of low-fare airlines is fare-conscious leisure and business travelers who might otherwise have used alternative forms of transportation or not traveled at all. Low-fare airlines stimulated demand in this segment and also have been successful in weaning business travelers from the major airlines. There are four major low-cost U.S. airlines. The main bases of competition in the airline industry are fare pricing, customer service, routes served, flight schedules, types of aircraft, safety record and reputation, code-sharing relationships, in-flight entertainment systems, and frequent-flier programs.

The economic downturn in the late 1990s and the terrorist attacks on the World Trade Center and the Pentagon on September 11, 2001, severely affected the airline industry. The demand for air travel dropped significantly and led to a reduction in traffic and revenue. Security concerns, security costs, and liquidity concerns increased. Lower fares and also increased capacity of the low-cost airlines created a very unprofitable environment for traditional networks. Most of the traditional network airlines, since 2001, have filed for bankruptcy or undergone financial restructuring, mergers, and/or consolidations. With these restructurings, many of them have been able to significantly

reduce labor costs, restructure debt, and generally gain a more competitive cost structure. The major airlines are able to provide innovative offerings similar to those of low-cost airlines while still maintaining their alliances, frequent-flier programs, and expansive route networks. The gap between low-cost airlines and traditional network airlines has been diminishing quite drastically.

Neeleman and JetBlue[5]

Born in São Paulo, Brazil, and brought up in Salt Lake City, David Neeleman dropped out of the University of Utah after his freshman year to move back to Brazil and become a missionary. After two years of missionary work, he made his modest beginning in establishing his own business by renting out condominiums in Hawaii. He then established his own travel agency and began chartering flights from Salt Lake City to the islands to bring in prospective clients for his rental services. Neeleman's sales prowess caught the attention of June Morris, who owned one of Utah's largest corporate travel agencies. Soon after, in 1984, Neeleman and Morris launched the Utah-based "Morris Air," a charter operation. Morris Air was closely modeled after Southwest Airlines, the legendary discount airline in the United States.

Neeleman considered Herb Kelleher, Southwest's founder, his idol. He studied everything Kelleher accomplished and tried to do it better, which meant keeping costs low and turning planes around quickly, among a host of other operational and strategic activities and choices. While following the Southwest model, Neeleman brought his own innovations into the business. He pioneered the use of "at-home reservation agents," routing calls to agents' homes to save money on office rent and infrastructure expense. He also developed the first electronic ticketing system in the airline industry. By 1992, Morris Air had grown into a regularly scheduled airline and was ready for an initial public offering (IPO) when Southwest, impressed by Morris's low costs and high revenue, bought the company for $129 million. Neeleman became the executive vice president of Southwest. However, Neeleman could not adjust to

Southwest's pace of doing things. By 1994, he was at odds with the top executives and left after signing a five-year noncompete agreement. In the interim between leaving Southwest and establishing JetBlue, Neeleman developed the electronic ticketing system he had initiated at Morris Air into one of the world's simplest airline reservation systems: Open Skies. He sold Open Skies to Hewlett-Packard in 1999. During the same period, he was also a consultant to a low-fare Canadian start-up airline, WestJet Airlines.[6] In 1999, after the noncompete agreement with Southwest Airlines ended, Neeleman launched his own airline. He raised about $130 million of capital in two weeks, an unprecedented amount for a start-up airline.[7] Weston Presidio Capital and Chase Capital, venture capital firms that had backed Neeleman's prior ventures, were return investors, and financier George Soros was also brought into the deal. "David's a winner; I knew anything David touched would turn to gold," said Michael Lazarus of Weston Presidio Capital, which had earlier funded Morris Air. "We were intrigued with his ideas about a low-cost airline."[8] With such strong support from venture capitalists, JetBlue began as the highest-funded start-up airline in U.S. aviation history.

JetBlue commenced operations in August 2000, with John F. Kennedy International Airport (JFK) as its primary base of operations. In 2001 JetBlue extended its operations to the West Coast with its base at Long Beach Municipal Airport, which served the Los Angeles area. In 2002 the company went public and was listed on Nasdaq as JBLU. JetBlue had expected to sell 5.5 million shares at about $24 to $26 in its initial public offering. Instead, it sold 5.87 million shares at $27 per share through its lead underwriters Morgan Stanley and Merrill Lynch. The shares closed at $47, up by $20, on the first day of trading. JetBlue's stock offering was one of the hottest IPOs of the year.[9] JetBlue had been established with the goal of being a leading low-fare passenger airline that offered customers a differentiated product and high-quality customer service. It was positioned as a low-cost, low-fare airline providing quality customer service on point-to-point routes. JetBlue had a geographically diversified flight schedule that included both short-haul and long-haul routes. The mission of the company, according to David Neeleman, was "to bring humanity back to air travel." To stimulate demand, the airline focused on underserved markets and large metropolitan areas that had high average fares. The "JetBlue effect" aspired to bring about fares going down, traffic going up, and JetBlue ending up with a big chunk of business (Exhibit 3).

JetBlue was committed to keeping its costs low. To achieve this objective, the company originally operated a single-type aircraft fleet comprising Airbus A320 planes as opposed to the more popular but costly Boeing 737. The A320s had 162 seats compared to 132 seats in the Boeing 737. According to JetBlue, the A320 was thus cheaper to maintain and also was more fuel-efficient. Since all of JetBlue's planes were new, the costs of maintenance were also lower. In addition, the single type of aircraft kept training costs low and increased manpower utilization. JetBlue was the first to introduce the "paperless cockpit," in which pilots, equipped with laptops, had ready access to flight manuals that were constantly updated at headquarters. As a result, pilots could quickly calculate the weight, balance, and takeoff performance of the aircraft instead of having to download and print the manuals to make the calculations. The paperless cockpit thus ensured faster takeoffs by reducing paperwork and helped in achieving quicker turnarounds and higher aircraft utilization.[10] No meals were served on the planes, and pilots even had to be ready, if need be, to do the cleanup work on the plane to minimize the time the aircraft was on the ground. Turnaround time was also reduced by the airline's choice of less congested airports.[11] Innovation was everywhere; for example, there were no paper tickets to lose and no mileage statements to mail to frequent fliers. With friendly, customer service–oriented employees; new aircraft; roomy leather seats with 36 channels of free LiveTV, 100 channels of free XM satellite radio, and movie channel offerings from FOXInflight; and wider legroom (one row of seats was removed from its A320 aircraft to create additional space), JetBlue promised its customers a distinctive flying experience, the "JetBlue experience." With virtually no incidences of passengers being denied boarding; high completion factors

Exhibit 3 The JetBlue Effect*

Route	Increase in Daily Passengers, %	Decrease in Average Fare, %	JetBlue's Share of Local Traffic, %
New York to Miami/Ft. Lauderdale	14	17 (to $121.50)	23.1
New York to Los Angeles Basin	2	26 (to $219.31)	18.0
New York to Buffalo	94	40 (to $86.09)	61.2

*Figures as of second quarter, 2003.

Source: Data from BACK Aviation Solutions, adapted from W. Zellner, "Is JetBlue's Flight Plan Flawed?" *BusinessWeek,* February 16, 2004.

(99.6 percent as compared to 98.3 percent at other major airlines); the lowest incidence of delayed, mishandled, or lost bags; and the third-lowest number of customer complaints, the company was indeed setting standards for low-cost operations in the industry. The company was voted the best domestic airline in the Conde Nast Traveler's Readers' Choice Awards for five consecutive years. It was also rated the World's Best Domestic Airline by readers of *Travel + Leisure Magazine* in 2006. In addition, it earned the Passenger Service Award from *Air Transport World*.[12]

Expansion and Growth

JetBlue grew over the years to serve more than 52 destinations in 21 states, Puerto Rico, Colombia, Mexico, and the Caribbean (Exhibit 4). In 2008, JetBlue added services to Puerto Plata (Dominican Republic) and St. Marteen (Netherlands Antilles). In January 2009, it started services to Bogota, Colombia. Services to San Jose and Costa Rica were expected to commence in March 2009 and to Montego Bay, Jamaica, in May 2009.[13]

However, divergence from JetBlue's original model was evident. From operating a single aircraft type, which was the basis of having low training costs, flexibility in manpower management, and so on, the airline moved to include a second type of aircraft, the Embraer 190, which it was not comfortable operating. Also, JetBlue acquired LiveTV, LLC, in 2002 for $41 million in cash and the retirement of $39 million of LiveTV debt.[14] Further, the company was embarking on other paths where it did not necessarily have prior experience. On February 6, 2007, *USA Today* announced that JetBlue planned to enter into an alliance with Aer Lingus, an Irish flag carrier. The alliance was expected to facilitate easy transfers for both airlines' customers, but unlike traditional code-share

alliances, it would not allow either airline to sell seats on the other airline, meaning customers would have to make individual reservations with both carriers.[15] On February 14, 2007, JetBlue's first code-share agreement with Cape Air was announced. Under this agreement, JetBlue passengers from Boston's Logan Airport would be carried to Cape Air's destinations throughout Cape Cod and the surrounding islands, and customers would be able to purchase seats on both airlines under one reservation. While Lufthansa's January 2008 acquisition of a minority equity stake in JetBlue did not automatically lead to any code-share agreements, Lufthansa expects to have "operational cooperation" with JetBlue.

Nevertheless, high fuel prices, the competitive pricing environment, and other cost increases have been making it increasingly difficult to fund JetBlue's growth profitability. The airline suffered its first-ever losses after its IPO in 2005. It posted net losses of $1 million and $20 million for 2006 and 2005, respectively, and an unprecedented $76 million loss for 2007, with the primary reason being rising fuel costs (see Exhibits 5 and 6). In July 2008, the company modified its growth plans by deferring a total of 21 aircraft deliveries from between 2009 and 2011 to between 2014 and 2015 and sold several of its Airbus A320s from 2006.[16]

Despite the airline's much touted unique culture, in 2006 the International Association of Machinists (IAM) attempted to unionize JetBlue's ramp service workers. Though the union organizing petition was dismissed by the National Mediation Board because fewer than 35 percent of eligible employees supported an election, unionization is a possibility going forward.[17] What this means to JetBlue's cultural fabric remains to be seen.

Exhibit 4   JetBlue's Growth

| Year | Destinations | Employees | Operating Aircraft | | |
			Owned	Leased	Total
2000	12	1,174	4	6	10
2001	18	2,361	9	12	21
2002	20	4,011	21	16	37
2003	21	5,433	29	24	53
2004	30	7,211	44	25	69
2005	33	9,021	61	31	92
2006	49	10,377	70	49	119
2007	**53**	11,632	**77**	**57**	134
2008	52	11,852	83	59	142

Source: JetBlue SEC filings.

Exhibit 5   Statements of Operations Data (in millions of dollars, except per-share data; year-end December 31)

	2008	2007	2006	2005	2004
Operating revenues	3,388	2,842	2,363	1,701	1,265
Operating expenses:					
Salaries, wages, and benefits	694	648	553	428	337
Aircraft fuel	1352	929	752	488	255
Landing fees and other rents	199	180	158	112	92
Depreciation and amortization	205	176	151	115	77
Aircraft rent	129	124	103	74	70
Sales and marketing	151	121	104	81	63
Maintenance materials and repairs	127	106	87	64	45
Other operating expenses	422	389	328	291	215
Total operating expenses	3,279	2,673	2,236	1,653	1,154
Operating income	109	169	127	48	111
Government compensation	—	—	—	—	—
Other income (expense)	−185	−128	−118	−72	−36
Income (loss) before income taxes	−76	41	9	−24	75
Income tax expense (benefit)	—	23	10	−4	29
Net income (loss)	−76	18	−1	−20	46
Earnings (loss) per common share					
Basic	−0.34	0.10	—	−0.13	0.3
Diluted	−0.34	0.10	—	−0.13	0.28

Source: JetBlue SEC filings.

The Operations Meltdown and Beyond[18]

Valentine's Day 2007 is perhaps the nightmare in JetBlue's hitherto glorious history for more than one reason. Not only did the event destroy JetBlue's reputation for customer friendliness and cost Neeleman his job, but it also exposed the critical weaknesses in the systems that had kept the airline's operations going.

There was trouble in the Midwest for several days before the Valentine's Day storm reached the East Coast. Unlike the blowing snow and frigid temperatures in cities such as Chicago, the storm turned into freezing rain and sleet as it slammed the mid-Atlantic region, causing havoc on major highways, and virtually shutting down airports. Most other airlines canceled dozens of flights in preparation for the storm. However, JetBlue management opted to wait it out. With its policy of doing whatever it can to ensure a flight is completed, even if this means waiting for several hours, the airline sent outbound flights to the runway at John F. Kennedy airport in New York at about 8 a.m. This was done to ensure that the planes would be ready to take off as soon as the weather let up. However, instead of letting up, the weather deteriorated further. The federal aviation guidelines do not allow planes to take off in ice-pellet conditions, and so the JetBlue planes and equipment were soon literally freezing to the tarmac. By about 3 p.m., with no hope of getting the planes off the ground, the airline began calling in buses to bring the passengers back to the terminal. By then, however, the damage had been done. Airport terminals, more so in the JFK hub, were filled with passengers still expecting to get on flights, and compounding the problem, they were now being joined by hundreds of infuriated passengers returning from the JetBlue planes. "Things spiraled out of control. We did a horrible job," said Neeleman in a conference call early the next week. "We got ourselves into a situation where we were doing rolling cancellations instead of a massive cancellation. Communications broke down, we weren't able to reach out to passengers and they continued to arrive at the airports . . . it had a cascading effect." The chaotic situation could not be brought under control for another week.

Exhibit 6   Operating Statistics (year-end December 31)*

	2008	2007	2006	2005	2004
Revenue passengers ($ thousands)	21,920	21,387	18,565	14,729	11,783
Revenue passenger-miles ($ millions)	26,071	25,737	23,320	20,200	15,730
Available seat-miles (ASMs) ($ millions)	32,442	31,904	28,594	23,703	18,911
Load factor (%)	80.4	80.7	81.6	85.2	83.2
Break-even load factor (%)[†]	84.2	80.7	81.4	86.1	77.9
Aircraft utilization (hours per day)	12.1	12.8	12.7	13.4	13.4
Average fare ($)	139.40	123.23	119.73	110.03	103.49
Yield per passenger-mile (cents)	11.72	10.24	9.53	8.02	7.75
Passenger revenue per ASM (cents)	9.42	8.26	7.77	6.84	6.45
Operating revenue per ASM (cents)	10.44	8.91	8.26	7.18	6.69
Operating expense per ASM (cents)	10.11	8.38	7.82	6.98	6.1
Operating expense per ASM, excluding fuel (cents)	5.94	5.47	5.19	4.92	4.75
Airline operating expense per ASM (cents)[†]	9.87	8.27	7.76	6.91	6.04
Departures	205,389	196,594	159,152	112,009	90,532
Average stage length (miles)	1,120	1,129	1,186	1,358	1,339
Average number of operating aircraft during period	139.5	127.8	106.5	77.5	60.6
Average fuel cost per gallon ($)	2.98	2.09	1.99	1.61	1.06
Fuel gallons consumed (millions)	453	444	377	303	241
Percent of sales through jetblue.com during period	76.7	75.7	79.1	77.5	75.4
Full-time equivalent employees at period end[†]	9,895	9,909	9,265	8,326	6,413

*See the appendix at the end of this case for a glossary of the terms used in this table.

[†]Excludes results of employees and operations of LiveTV, LLC, that are unrelated to the airline operations.

Source: JetBlue SEC filings.

A number of shortcomings in the company's information systems were responsible for this debacle, according to Charles Mees, the new CIO who had joined the company a few months before the event. The reservation system, for example, was not expanded enough to meet the extreme customer call volume. As the seriousness of the Valentine's Day situation became apparent, managers with JetBlue's Salt Lake City–based reservation office began calling in off-duty agents to assist with the expected high volume of calls. These agents normally work primarily from their homes, using an Internet-based communications system to tap into the company's Navitaire Open Skies reservation system. (Headquartered in Minneapolis, Navitaire hosts the reservation system for JetBlue and about another dozen discount airlines.) The passengers who were bumped off the planes or arrived at JFK and other East Coast airports to find their JetBlue flights had been canceled had only one option for rebooking their flights: Call the JetBlue reservation office. JetBlue customers did not have the option of using airport kiosks to rebook their flights via its Web site. The company had been working on the online rebooking issue since December 2006, but the new feature was not yet ready to be rolled out in February 2007. As a result, the Salt Lake City reservation agents were suddenly flooded with calls from irate passengers trying to get on another flight or to find out about compensation possibilities. With Mees's emergency call to Navitaire, the system could be boosted to accommodate up to 950 agents at one time (up 300 from the original 650), but then it hit a wall. Even with the boosted capacity, there was difficulty finding enough bodies to staff the phones. Off-duty crews and airport personnel volunteered for the task, but they were not trained in how to use the system.

Also in a mess was the baggage-handling mechanism. As passengers struggled through terminals to make new reservations, their bags piled up in huge mounds at airports. Very interestingly, JetBlue did not have a computerized system in place for recording and tracking lost bags. Since the airline hardly ever canceled flights, if there were bags left over at the end of a flight, airport personnel figured out ownership by looking up a passenger's record. However, such a process became totally unmanageable with massive cancellations happening. The airline had entered into an agreement earlier with Lufthansa in 2003 to purchase a system called BagScan, but the system was never implemented. Mees admits, "We didn't prioritize it—probably because it is so focused on the [Enterprise Resource Planning] project." JetBlue was growing fast and needed increased capabilities in the Enterprise Resource Planning system to handle its human resource functions.

There were also other system headaches to deal with. JetBlue uses several applications from Sabre Airline Solutions of Southlake, Texas, as part of its core operations infrastructure. This is in addition to the Navitaire reservation system. The application, Sabre Flight Control Suite, provides the airline with utilities to manage, schedule, and track its planes and crews, while Sabre's Dispatch Manager is used to develop actual flight plans. Another application, Flite Trac, within the Flight Control Suite, interfaces with the Navitaire reservation system. This application provides real-time information to managers on factors such as flight status, fuel information, passenger lists, and the original, revised, estimated, and actual arrival times. Sabre CrewTrac is another application that tracks crew assignments, ensures legal requirements are met, and provides pilots and flight attendants with access to their schedules via a secure Web portal. During the disastrous Valentine's Day event, there was a glitch between these Sabre applications and Navitaire's

SkySolver, which JetBlue uses to figure out the best way to emerge from flight disruptions.

Neeleman said, "We had so many people in the company who wanted to help who weren't trained to help. We had an emergency control center full of people who didn't know what to do. I had flight attendants sitting in hotel rooms for three days who couldn't get a hold of us. I had pilots e-mailing me saying, 'I'm available, what do I do?'" Mees said he did not have any idea why the information could not be transferred or why the system incompatibility could not be discovered beforehand. He, of course, added that there were other day-to-day priorities to manage. "In the heat of battle at any rapidly growing company, you're always trying to address your most immediate needs," Mees said. "But you've got to continually remind yourself that you have to take a step back and look at the things that aren't right in front of you—find out what the tipping points are—before they can impact you." Southwest, by contrast, handled the Valentine's Day weather disaster with ease by simply canceling most services during the disrupted period. It looked as if JetBlue had completely missed out on this obvious solution (see Exhibit 7 for a direct-competitor comparison).

The airline's reputation was hitting rock-bottom. Apart from announcing huge compensations to customers—refunds and future flights, which were to cost the airline about $30 million—Neeleman quickly announced the new Customer Bill of Rights. The Customer Bill of Rights basically outlined self-imposed penalties for JetBlue and major rewards for its passengers if the airline experienced

Exhibit 7 Direct-Competitor Comparison

Performance Indicators	JetBlue	AMR Corp.	Southwest Airlines	UAL Corp.	Industry
Market cap	1.89B	3.18B	6.37B	1.54B	529.88
Employees	9,398	85,500	34,545	55,000	5.55K
Quarterly revenue growth (YOY)	17.90%	8.00%	11.70%	1.50%	13.10%
Revenue (TTM)	3.32B	23.98B	10.78B	20.68B	1.59B
Gross margin (TTM)	25.45%	19.64%	24.65%	7.88%	19.66%
EBITDA (TTM)	287.00M	724.00M	1.40B	−239.00M	54.78M
Operating margins (TTM)	2.74%	−2.12%	7.50%	−5.51%	4.67%
Net income (TTM)	−23.00M	−1.80B	346.00M	−4.10B	N/A
EPS (TTM)	−0.109	−7.126	0.468	−33.205	0.3
P/E (TTM)	N/A	N/A	18.4	N/A	8.98
PEG (5-yr expected)	N/A	N/A	2.33	N/A	0.63
P/S (TTM)	0.55	0.13	0.57	0.07	0.29

Note: YOY = year over year; TTM = trailing 12 months.

Source: http://finance.yahoo.com, as of January 2009.

operational problems and could not adjust to weather-related cancellations within a "reasonable" amount of time. For example, the bill contained provisions for notifying customers, prior to scheduled departure, of delays, cancellations, and diversions and their causes. It also promised that the airline would take necessary action to deplane customers if an aircraft is ground-delayed for five hours. Further, if a flight landed and was unable to taxi in to a gate right away, customers were to receive compensation ranging from $25 to the full amount of their one-way fare (in vouchers redeemable toward a future JetBlue flight), depending on the extent of delay. All these announcements and even a public apology could, of course, not restore things to normalcy. Neeleman was pushed out as CEO on May 10, 2007. Dave Barger, the president, assumed the position of chief executive officer.

JetBlue's move to sell a 19 percent stake to Lufthansa, along with smaller moves such as selling pillows and blankets and increasing various fees, came in the wake of a weaker balance sheet and immediate debt that had to be taken care of. Amid these difficulties, JetBlue did manage to build a new, state-of-the-art terminal at JFK in the fall of 2008. However, with rising fuel costs, increasing competition from other low-cost airlines such as Virgin America, a global recession that would seemingly loom for the next couple of years, and, to top it all, a leadership change from charismatic Neeleman to nuts-and-bolts airline operator Barger, JetBlue seems to be headed for some interesting times.

Endnotes

1. Associated Press. December 2007, www.msnbc.msn.com/id/22248073.
2. M. Maynard. JetBlue starts selling blankets and pillows. *New York Times,* August 5, 2008, www.nytimes.com/2008/08/05/business/05pillow.html.
3. This section draws heavily on the SEC filings of JetBlue for the years 2008 and 2009. Other sources include W. Zellner.

Look who's buzzing the discounters. *BusinessWeek,* November 24, 2003; W. Zellner. Folks are finally packing their bags. *BusinessWeek,* January 12, 2004; and a joint study by A. T. Kearney and the Society of British Aerospace Companies, The emerging airline industry, www.atkearney .com/shared_res/pdf/Emerging_Airline_Industry_S.pdf.
4. www.southwest.com/about_swa/airborne.html.
5. This section draws heavily on A. T. Gajilan. The amazing JetBlue. *Fortune Small Business,* 2004, www.fortune/smallbusiness/articles/0.15114,444298-2,00.html.
6. Brazilian-American Chamber of Commerce of Florida. 2004 Excellence Award. *Chamber News,* 2004, www.brazilchamber .org/news/chambernews/ExcellenceAward2004.htm.
7. JetBlue Airways Corporation, *International directory of company histories,* http://galenet.galegroup.com.
8. Gajilan. The amazing JetBlue; L. DiCarlo. Management and trends, Jet Blue skies. *Forbes.com,* January 31, 2001, www.forbes.com/2001/01/31/0131jetblue.html.
9. JetBlue IPO soars. *CNNmoney,* April 12, 2002, http://money.cnn.com/2002/04/12/markets/ipo/jetblue.
10. WEBSMART50. *BusinessWeek,* November 24, 2003, p. 92.
11. Interview with David Neeleman by Willow Bay of CNN Business Unusual. Aired June 23, 2002, www.cnn.com/TRANSCRIPTS/0206/23/bun.00.html.
12. JetBlue SEC filings, 2006.
13. JetBlue SEC filings, 2007.
14. From the company's press releases, www.jetblue.com.
15. JetBlue, Aer Lingus to forge world's first international discount alliance. www.usatoday.com, February 6, 2007.
16. D. Field. AirTran and JetBlue scale back growth. *Airline Business,* 2008, www.flightglobal.com/articles/2008/06/17/224704/airtran-and-jetblue-scale-back-growth.html.
17. M. Schlangenstein. No union vote for JetBlue. *Bloomberg News,* July 19, 2006, http://findarticles.com/p/articles/mi_qn4188/is_20060719/ai_n16541848.
18. This section draws heavily on the following sources: D. Bartholomew and M. Duvall. What really happened at JetBlue? www.baselinemag.com,; J. Bailey. Long delays hurt image of JetBlue. *New York Times,* 2007, p. 1.

Appendix A   Glossary of Key Terms Used*

aircraft utilization The average number of block hours operated per day per aircraft for the total fleet of aircraft.

available seat-miles The number of seats available for passengers multiplied by the number of miles the seats are flown.

average fare The average one-way fare paid per flight segment by a revenue passenger.

average stage length Average number of miles flown per flight.

break-even load factor The passenger load factor that will result in operating revenues being equal to operating expenses, assuming constant revenue per passenger mile and expenses.

load factor The percentage of aircraft seating capacity that is actually utilized (revenue passenger-miles divided by available seat miles).

operating expense per available seat-mile Operating expenses divided by available seat-miles.

operating revenue per available seat-mile Operating revenues divided by available seat-miles.

passenger revenue per available seat-mile Passenger revenue divided by available seat-miles.

revenue passenger-miles The number of miles flown by revenue passengers.

revenue passengers The total number of paying passengers flown on all flight segments.

yield per passenger-mile The average amount one passenger pays to fly 1 mile.

*From JetBlue SEC filings, 2008.

Case 27   Southwest Airlines: Does "LUV" Last?*

For the first time in its history, Southwest Airlines had its "LUV" for customers questioned. The Federal Aviation Administration (FAA) levied a record $10.2 million fine on the airline, accusing it of flying 117 planes on nearly 60,000 flights between June 18, 2006, and March 14, 2007, after missing mandatory safety checks.[1] In the confusion that followed, Southwest swiftly grounded 44 aircraft as part of an internal investigation into claims that it had failed to properly inspect its aircraft. The grounding was the largest since 1998 when the government ordered emergency wiring inspections of 179 Boeing 737s in Southwest's fleet.[2]

Both the FAA and Southwest testified. FAA officials were blamed for being "too close" to the airline and being lax in their regulatory duties. Southwest's chairman Herb Kelleher and chief executive Gary Kelly said that safety was not compromised by the missed inspections. According to them, only a tiny section of the plane's skin had missed being inspected and the cracks in that section would not have led to any catastrophic accident. Both of them said that the planes should have been taken out of service when it was known that they missed inspection. This was a "black eye" on the airline's safety record, according to Kelly.[3]

Background and Growth

The inconvenience and expense of ground travel by bus or automobile between the cities of Houston, Dallas, and San Antonio—the Golden Triangle that was experiencing rapid economic and population growth during the late 1960s—offered an opportunity for an intrastate airline. The idea was suggested by Rollin King, a San Antonio entrepreneur who owned a small commuter air service, when his banker, John Parker, complained about the issue. King then talked to Herb Kelleher—a New Jersey–born, New York University Law School graduate who moved to San Antonio in 1967 to practice law. They soon pooled the seed money to start Southwest Airlines. The infant Southwest Airlines (SWA) fought long-drawn legal battles, primarily engineered by the major airline carriers, for over four years before it got its first flight off the ground in 1971. Later on, the company had to work around a regulation intended to penalize SWA's decision to operate out of Dallas Love Field instead of moving to the new Dallas–Fort Worth (DFW) airport. With Kelleher's brilliant legal expertise and extensive lobbying of the House of Representatives, the issue was settled and SWA was allowed to operate out of Love Field in 1979. The struggle for existence in the initial years worked to the advantage of the company, as the struggle created the esprit de corps for which the airline became so well known. The employees were caught up in fighting for the "SWA cause" that created "the warrior mentality, the very fight to survive," according to Colleen Barrett, who became the president and chief operating officer of SWA in 2001. (She now is the president emeritus.)[4]

Kelleher, however, was not the first chief executive officer of Southwest. Lamar Muse, an airline veteran who worked earlier with Trans Texas, Central, and Universal Airlines, was brought in to get the company off to a good start. That was followed by the brief tenure of Howard Putnam, another airline veteran, who was hired from United Airlines, where he worked from 1978 to 1982. Herb Kelleher served as the chairman of the board during that period; then he took the CEO position in 1982 and championed Southwest's expansion (at that time the company had only 27 planes and $270 million in revenues, and it flew to only 14 cities).[5] SWA was one of a kind right from its beginning. It was the pioneer of the "low-cost strategy." It flew planes point-to-point—short-haul flights bypassing the expensive hub-and-spoke operations. It chose less popular, less congested airports to achieve quicker turnarounds.

SWA offered airfares so low that it gave the bus and car travel companies a run for their money. It served no meals on its airlines and provided only a snack of peanuts. That saved plenty of money and manpower. There was no assigned seating, which reduced boarding times and helped planes turn around faster. The average turnaround time for planes was around 25 minutes. The faster turnaround times and higher aircraft utilization enabled the airline to operate with fewer planes and gate facilities than would otherwise have been necessary. SWA's attractive flight attendants in hot pants were a source of live entertainment on flights (e.g., the flight attendants made funny presentations of the otherwise routine and boring safety instructions or performed preflight tricks such as popping out of overhead bins).[6] Southwest was the first major airline to introduce ticketless travel and one of the first to put up a Web site and offer online booking.[7] It operated a single aircraft type, the Boeing 737, that kept its training costs low and manpower utilization high as **having only one type of plane** offered great flexibility in manpower deployment. Starting with three Boeing 737s in 1971, the company fleet grew to 537 Boeing 737 aircraft providing service to 64 cities in 32 states throughout the United States, with 397 city pairs being served nonstop, by the end of 2008 (see Exhibits 1, 2, and 3).[8]

* This case study was prepared by Professor Naga Lakshmi Damaraju of The Indian School of Business, Professor Alan B. Eisner at Pace University, and Professor Gregory G. Dess at the University of Texas at Dallas. The purpose of the case is to stimulate class discussion rather than to illustrate effective or ineffective handling of a business situation. The authors thank Professor Michael Oliff at the University of Texas at Dallas for his valuable comments on an earlier version of this case. Several parts of the case are from an earlier version. Copyright © 2009 Damaraju, Eisner, and Dess.

	2008	2007	2006	2005	2004
Financial Data (in millions, except per-share amounts)					
Operating revenues	11,023	9,861	9,086	7,584	6,530
Operating expenses	10,574	9,070	8,152	6,859	6,126
Operating income	449	791	934	725	404
Other expenses (income) net	171	−267	144	−54	65
Income before taxes	278	1,058	790	779	339
Provision for income taxes	100	413	291	295	124
Net income	178	645	499	484	215
Net income per share, basic	0.24	0.85	0.63	0.61	0.27
Net income per share, diluted	0.24	0.84	0.61	0.6	0.27
Cash dividends per common share	0.018	0.018	0.018	0.018	0.018
Total assets at period-end	14,308	16,772	13,460	14,003	11,137
Long-term obligations at period-end	3,498	2,050	1,567	1,394	1,700
Stockholders' equity at period-end	4,953	6,941	6,449	6,675	5,527
Operating Data					
Revenue passengers carried	88,529,234	88,713,472	83,814,823	77,693,875	70,902,773
Enplaned passengers	101,920,598	101,910,809	96,276,907	88,379,900	81,066,038
Revenue passenger-miles (RPMs) (000s)	73,491,687	72,318,812	67,691,289	60,223,100	53,418,353
Available seat-miles (ASMs) (000s)	103,271,343	99,635,967	92,663,023	85,172,795	76,861,296
Load factor	71.20%	72.60%	73.10%	70.70%	69.50%
Average length of passenger haul (miles)	830	815	808	775	753
Average aircraft stage length (miles)	636	629	622	607	576
Trips flown	1,191,151	1,160,699	1,092,331	1,028,639	981,591
Average passenger fare	119.16	106.6	104.4	93.68	88.57
Passenger revenue yield per RPM	14.35¢	13.08¢	12.93¢	12.09¢	11.76¢
Operating revenue yield per ASM	10.67¢	9.9¢	9.81¢	8.9¢	8.5¢
Operating expenses per ASM	10.24¢	9.1¢	8.8¢	8.05¢	7.97¢
Fuel costs per gallon (average)	2.44	1.7	1.53	1.03	0.83
Fuel consumed, in gallons (millions)	1,511	1,489	1,389	1,287	1,201
Full-time equivalent employees at period-end	35,499	34,378	32,664	31,729	31,011
Size of fleet at period-end	537	520	481	445	417

*Refer to the appendix at the end of this case for a glossary of the terms used in this table.

Source: Southwest Airlines, SEC filings, Form 10-K, www.sec.gov.

The SWA Leadership and Culture

There are many stories about Herb Kelleher's flamboyant style as CEO. He smoked cigars, loved Wild Turkey whiskey, was often seen dressed up as Elvis Presley, and publicly arm-wrestled and won over a rival company CEO to settle a dispute over an advertisement slogan.[9] Kelleher truly believed that business could and should be fun—at too many companies, people put on masks when they came into the office. At work, people were not themselves and would be overly serious, which explained why most

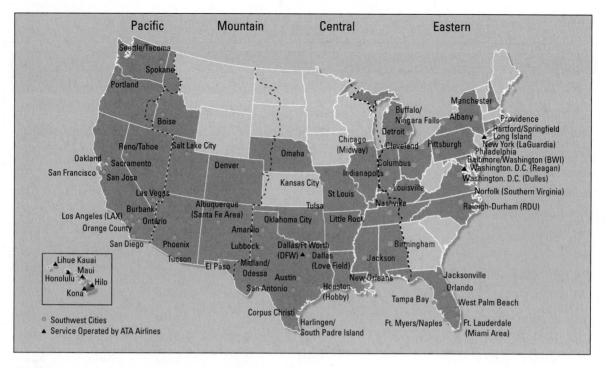

Exhibit 2 Cities Served by Southwest Airlines

Source: Printed with permission from Southwest Airlines, www.southwest.com/about_swa/routemap.html.

Exhibit 3 Growth in the Number of Cities Served by Southwest Airlines, 1994–2008

Year	Number of Cities Served
1994	44
1995	45
1996	49
1997	51
1998	52
1999	56
2000	57
2001	58
2002	58
2003	58
2004	58
2005	61
2006	63
2007	64
2008	64

Source: Southwest Airlines, Forms 10-K filed with SEC.

business encounters were bland and impersonal. Therefore, SWA tried not to hire people who were humorless, self-centered, or complacent. Not surprisingly, there was no human resource department but, rather, a People Department at Southwest. The guiding principle for recruitment at SWA was "Hire for attitude and train for skills," which Kelleher believed was the most important principle. When an employee from the People Department said to him, "Herb, I'm getting a little embarrassed because I've interviewed 34 people for a ramp agent position in Amarillo," Kelleher replied, "If you have to interview 134 people to find the appropriate person to be a ramp agent in Amarillo, do it. Because the most important thing is to get the right people and if you get the wrong ones they start poisoning everybody else."[10]

Kelleher's penchant for laughter and fun became a part of Southwest's culture. Prospective employees were asked how humor helped them out of a difficult situation. Prospective pilots were sometimes asked to pull on shorts, and the ones who saw fun in it passed the interview. All people at the company were to be treated with dignity and respect, and Kelleher did not believe in hierarchical barriers. When a vice president complained to the CEO that customers, gate agents, pilots, and baggage handlers had more access to the CEO than he did, Kelleher said to him, "Let me explain this: They're more important than you are." Kelleher recognized that the key to satisfied customers was having satisfied employees. So employees came

Exhibit 4   Mission Statement of Southwest Airlines

The mission of Southwest Airlines is dedication to the highest quality of Customer Service delivered with a sense of warmth, friendliness, individual pride, and Company Spirit.

To Our Employees

We are committed to provide our Employees a stable work environment with equal opportunity for learning and personal growth. Creativity and innovation are encouraged for improving the effectiveness of Southwest Airlines. Above all, Employees will be provided the same concern, respect, and caring attitude within the organization that they are expected to share externally with every Southwest Customer.

Source: Southwest Airlines, www.southwest.com/about_swa/mission.html.

first, and that orientation was embodied in the airline's mission statement (Exhibit 4).

The culture was put into operation through a number of policies and programs. The casual-dress policy reinforced the company's desire that people be themselves on the job. Celebrations such as spirit parties, culture parties, and weekly deck parties were organized at headquarters regularly to bring employees together. Activities at the events included gong shows, talent shows, dance contests, limbo contests, and famous-person look-alike themes. The culture committee at SWA welcomed new employees with a "New Hire Welcome Kit" that included a bag, T-shirt, badge holder, pen, and welcome letter. To build solidarity across all departments, there was an employee recognition program in which employees recognized each other's achievements. This practice helped community building within and across departments. For example, one work group committee recognized flight attendants 10 times a year with "Hokey Days," named for the broom apparatus used by flight attendants to sweep the cabin after the flights. Committee members chose two locations at which to honor flight attendants, greeted each arriving plane, waited until passengers got off, and then boarded with goodies. Flight attendants were asked to relax while the committee members cleaned the plane for them. There were similar programs to honor other departments as well.[11] There was also the "Walk a Mile Program," designed to foster problem solving and cooperation, in which an employee could do somebody else's job for a day (while operations people obviously could not fly the airplanes, pilots could do the work of operations agents).[12] Further, the company had the "Star of the Month," a program that recognized the distinct contributions of employees toward excellence in customer service—outstanding employees were featured in *Spirit,* Southwest's in-flight magazine.[13]

The company also expressed warmth toward its employees in other ways. At Southwest's headquarters in Dallas, the walls were covered with more than 10,000 picture frames that contained photos of employees' pets, of stewardesses in miniskirts, of Southwest planes gnawing on competitor's aircraft. Also there were teddy bears, jars of pickled hot peppers, and pink flamingos. There was cigarette smoking and lots of chuckling. "To me, it's comfortable," said Colleen Barrett, who was most responsible for nurturing the Southwest culture from its early days. "This is an open scrapbook. We aren't uptight. We celebrate everything. It's like a fraternity, a sorority, a reunion. We are having a party!" she said. Barrett also regularly traveled to meet the employees and personally sent them birthday cards, not so much to win their loyalty as to communicate the true spirit of a family. The company celebrated with its employees when good things happened and grieved with them when they had devastating experiences.[14] Barrett said, "What we do is very simple, but it's not simplistic. We really do everything with passion. We scream at each other and we hug each other."[15]

Cost consciousness was another important part of the culture. "Yes, our culture is almost like a religion," said Gary Kelly, the erstwhile CFO and the present CEO of Southwest. "But it's a dichotomy. In many ways we are conservative. Financially, for instance," he added.[16] According to Herb Kelleher, close attention to costs had produced the kind of financial success Southwest had seen. He said, "Even in the best of times, we kept our costs low and questioned every expenditure. For years, I used to approve every expenditure over $1,000. Why? To encourage a cost-conscious culture. I couldn't look at all of them, of course. But I would question them selectively, and that kept people paying attention."[17]

Treating employees well at Southwest did not mean that they were paid high salaries. By creating value through intangibles, the company kept wages lower than those of competitors. Officers at Southwest were paid about 30 percent less, on average, than their counterparts at other airlines. But the airline made stock options widely available, so all employees—not just executives—could share in the company's financial success. Southwest even had a policy that its officers received pay increases that were no larger, proportionally, than what other employees received. But employees were also expected to take pay reductions when times were not good. Job security was ensured, however, with a "no-furlough policy," and Southwest did not lay off a single employee during the economic downturn after the terrorist attacks on September 11, 2001, while many of its competitors did.[18] Caring for employee happiness showed positive results. Southwest had less employee turnover than its competitors. For years, Southwest enjoyed the loyalty of its employees despite the high level of employee unionization. "Once labor leaders realize that you're trying to take care of your people, most of the edge [in contract negotiations] is gone," said Kelleher.[19]

Southwest's employees worked more hours than their counterparts at other airlines. Southwest pilots flew nearly 80 hours a month compared to United's 50 hours. Southwest pilots were paid by trip, not per hour, which created a strong interest in keeping flights on schedule. Also, the pilots tended to be cost-conscious because a big part of their compensation came from stock options. On some occasions, pilots even pitched in to help ground crews move luggage to ensure on-time flights—something virtually unheard of at Southwest's bigger rivals. Flight attendants at Southwest worked about 150 hours a month, compared with 80 hours at many other airlines, according to union president Thom McDaniel. Southwest attendants were required by contract to make a reasonable effort to tidy the airplane between flights, a job performed by maintenance personnel at rival airlines. According to an airline labor expert, senior flight attendants at United got as many as 52 vacation days a year (compared with 35 days for veterans at Southwest) and they never had to clean up after the passengers.[20]

Maintaining focus on the core business was another element for both controlling costs and pursuing a niche strategy. Kelleher consciously ensured that the company did not diverge into allied businesses such as car rentals or reservations. Most of Southwest's growth had been organic; that is, it occurred by adding more flights on its existing routes and by connecting more dots (adding cities). The airline started complementing its short-haul flights with long-haul flights and began transcontinental services. According to Kelleher, the airline did not plan to have international flights as they would require a total change in the way it operated and would involve training its 35,000 employees to handle that change.[21]

The cost consciousness and employee commitment translated into operational excellence and increased profitability (Exhibit 5). Southwest's planes flew about 10.9 hours per day, much more than any other airline except JetBlue, which flew close to 13.0 hours per day. Southwest could offer lower fares—as much as 50 percent lower than its major rivals—and still remain profitable. With such low costs, it created what was called the "Southwest effect," an explosion in **the numbers of people traveling by plane, including many who would have gone by car before.**[22] The term *Southwest effect* was coined by the U.S. Department of Transportation to refer to the consistent phenomenon of a decrease in average fares and a stimulation of demand that occurred when Southwest Airlines entered any market.[23]

In May 1988 Southwest became the first airline to win the coveted Triple Crown for a month: Best On-Time Record, Best Baggage Handling, and Fewest Customer Complaints. Since then, Southwest has won it more than 30 times, as well as five annual Triple Crowns for 1992, 1993, 1994, 1995, and 1996. Southwest crossed its $1 billion revenue mark in 1990, thereby becoming a major airline, and topped the monthly domestic originating-passenger rankings for the first time in May 2003. It was also the largest carrier on the basis of scheduled domestic departures. Stories of Southwest employees providing excellent customer service abound, and Southwest even set up an internal TV system to show how its employees treated customers.[24]

Exhibit 5 Comparison with Key Competitors and Industry

Measures of Comparison	Southwest	AMR Corp.	Continental	JetBlue	Industry (Regional Airlines)
Market cap	6.64B	3.10B	2.12B	1.96B	528.70M
Employees	34,545	85,500	40,100	9,398	5.55K
Quarterly revenue growth (YOY)	11.70%	8.00%	8.80%	17.90%	13.10%
Revenue (TTM)	10.78B	23.98B	15.29B	3.32B	1.59B
Gross margin (TTM)	24.65%	19.64%	14.80%	25.45%	19.66%
EBITDA (TTM)	1.40B	724.00M	350.00M	287.00M	54.78M
Operating margins (TTM)	7.50%	−2.12%	−0.55%	2.74%	4.67%
Net income (TTM)	346.00M	−1.80B	−351.00M	−23.00M	N/A
EPS (TTM)	0.468	−7.126	−3.419	−0.109	0.3
P/E (TTM)	19.17	N/A	N/A	N/A	8.84
P/S (TTM)	0.59	0.12	0.13	0.58	0.29

Note: YOY = year over year; TTM = trailing 12 months.

Source: yahoofinance.com, January 4, 2009.

The Changing Times and Challenges

Southwest Airlines had a change in leadership in August 2001 when Herb Kelleher relinquished power to two of his close aides. Colleen C. Barrett, vice president for customers, became the president and chief operating officer; and James F. Parker, general counsel, became the chief executive officer. Barrett and Parker had worked together for over 22 years, and both had worked with Kelleher for much longer—from the time he was a lawyer. In contrast to Kelleher's obtrusive personality, Parker was a quiet diplomat. He had been the company's lead labor negotiator for years, and his opponents said he pursued the company line quite forcefully, if politely, in talks. "He will surprise you because he doesn't look like he's tough, but he doesn't give anything away," said a former vice president of the airline's pilot association.[25] Unlike Kelleher, Parker was not as fond of celebrations because he didn't see them as contributing to productivity. But he came to realize that the party preparations were a model of teamwork and employee bonding, and he started participating in the celebrations in 2002.[26]

Barrett had been the culture keeper of Southwest since the earliest days of the company. However, she was a reluctant public speaker. Thus, she let Parker take the lead with Wall Street and the media. It was too early to guess whether the lieutenants could replace the "rock star" personality of Kelleher, who had exuded warmth to his employees. Kelleher remained chairman of the board and focused on long-range strategy and government affairs. He maintained control of schedule planning and aircraft acquisitions, the backbone of Southwest's strategy during the period of transition.[27]

The growth of the company and the consequent increase in the number of employees also posed challenges to keeping the culture intact. The distance between the rank and file and top management was growing. While Colleen Barrett could reach all the employees through personally signed birthday cards when the company was small, the task was becoming increasingly unrealistic. Even though she continued to sign cards, she could reach only a fraction of Southwest's 35,000 employees dispersed in different cities. Keeping in close touch with employees was becoming an increasingly challenging task. In earlier times of difficulty, Herb Kelleher personally addressed and rallied his troops, but such an exercise was no longer easy.

In addition, the warm employee relations at Southwest seemed to chill over time. Unions were becoming more aggressive in expressing their frustration, in contrast to earlier days when disputes were resolved more amicably and peacefully. In the summer of 2001, ramp workers picketed near company headquarters with signs that read "Record Profits Empty Pockets." They complained that staff shortages, combined with Southwest's record passenger loads and its drive to improve on-time performance, meant that they had to lift more bags and had to do so more quickly, which put them at risk of injury.[28] And, for the first time in company history, in July 2002 Southwest's mechanics union asked federal mediators to intervene to break a contract deadlock over pay. While the company was nowhere near a strike, the incident clearly signaled the strains appearing in employee relations.[29]

In 2002 the company was also engaged without much success in a contract renegotiation with flight attendants. In July 2003 a group of flight attendants staged a demonstration at the headquarters, carrying signs stating "Spread the LUV" and handing out cards to travelers that read "Give our flight attendants a break." The move was an expression of frustration over management's idea of increasing the flight attendants' work hours. Also, workers who had been working hard to boost the productivity of the company were not seeing much return from profit sharing and a stock value that was falling. After years of hard work, some long-time employees felt that they had no more to give. Karen Amos, a 26-year Southwest veteran, said, "We have been there for them. There comes a time when it becomes too much."[30] The company had to drop the move to increase work hours, but still could not get a deal made with the flight attendants. Some workers perceived that the company had been fairer in its negotiations in past years.

In November 2003, after 11 rounds of talks without success, the flight attendants threw a Thanksgiving party at Salt Lake City International Airport, primarily as a means of putting pressure on management to accept their demands for holiday pay and better working conditions. Kevin Onstead, a Southwest negotiator and flight attendant, said, "We are concerned about the culture of the airline. We are fighting for the recognition of our contribution to that culture. We've been key in Southwest Airlines' success. Flight attendants are prepared to strike as a last resort. We are willing to do whatever it takes to get a fair contract."[31] The negotiations had not borne fruit by early 2004. Thom McDaniel, president of the TWU, said that the flight attendants were willing to return to the negotiating table. However, he made the point that the latest management offer fell short of their expectations. "We feel that our culture is at risk because of the actions taken by Southwest's management during these negotiations."[32] Many of the employee groups started feeling that Southwest Airlines was no longer the underdog and that their pay should match the profitability of the company. Love (LUV) alone no longer seemed to be enough. That meant a twin challenge in terms of culture and costs.

In July 2004 James Parker abruptly resigned as CEO of Southwest amid strained labor negotiations with the flight attendants. Some people said that Parker had spent too much time in the back offices of Southwest and was never really cut out for a job in the limelight.[33] Herb Kelleher stepped into the negotiations, and the flight attendants walked away smiling with a 31 percent pay raise.[34]

Gary C. Kelly, former chief financial officer of Southwest, took the helm. Kelly was certainly energetic, showing up at the office Halloween party in 2004 dressed as Gene Simmons, leader of the rock group Kiss.[35] He, of course, decided later that he was better off being Kelly than someone else. Kelly audaciously acquired six gates at Chicago's Midway Airport from bankrupt carrier ATA and signed Southwest's first ever code-share agreement with ATA, primarily in response to AirTran eyeing a move into Chicago. In December 2008, the airline agreed to provide an online link to WestJet's booking portal that helps its customers book flights to Canada. Later, Southwest formally filed an application with the DoT for rights to fly its own planes to Canada.[36] Southwest was already experiencing cost increases per average seat-mile (ASM), a key metric used to measure performance in the industry, primarily due to increases in fuel costs and wages. The cost per ASM went up from 7.07 cents in 1995 to 9.10 cents in 2007, with fuel costs, wages, and benefits as the major contributors (Exhibit 6). Southwest's cost per average seat-mile, however, remained below that of the big carriers. The company was already working hard on controlling costs. With more of its customers making reservations online and the labor cost advantage narrowing between major airlines after restructuring, further cost squeezing appeared to be a difficult proposition. Though Kelly did not concede it openly, he understood that further cost reductions would be hard to come by without modest fare increases and possible employee layoffs—something that was totally against Southwest's culture.[37] In 2007, a new fare structure was introduced that included Business Select, which gave customers priority in boarding.[38]

Intensifying competition in the low-fare segment was another factor that had become difficult to ignore. While competitors such as JetBlue and AirTran were not direct threats to Southwest on its existing routes, further expansion of those carriers could bring them head-on with Southwest. These new airlines offered far more attractive services, such as leather seats and in-flight entertainment systems, for almost the same fare. Therefore, these rivals could make the no-frills approach of Southwest pale before them. Whether Southwest's loyal customers would still stick with the airline when they could get more value for their money elsewhere was another significant question. Southwest's investments to automate and significantly streamline the ticketing and boarding process with computer-generated bag tags, automated boarding passes, and self-service boarding pass kiosks, and its investments to increase the functionality of its Web site, along with its moves to enhance aircraft interiors with leather seats, can hardly be described as *not* being motivated by competition.[39] That JetBlue caught Southwest's attention was clear by the comment that Southwest was studying the possibility of introducing an in-flight entertainment system, although at the time it was too costly to adopt. Thus, matching amenities with those of the emerging competition could pose additional challenges to SWA's low-cost strategy. Kelleher's reaction to the emerging competition was simple—he had seen that movie before.

Meanwhile, Southwest entered the Philadelphia market, a stronghold of US Air, in May 2004. The Philadelphia market was one of the most overpriced and underserved. Southwest aimed at capturing the market with its tried and tested low-cost, no-frills formula, albeit with leather seats on some of its newer planes. US Air responded, "We will be a vigorous competitor to Southwest in Philadelphia on every route they fly."[40]

In addition to establishing the ATA code share for Chicago's Midway,[41] Kelly added Phoenix to the code share in April 2005.[42] Then Kelly directed Southwest's entry into Pittsburgh in May 2005, announcing, "The Pittsburgh International Airport will be a great addition to our system."[43] In October 2005 Southwest began service out of Southwest Florida International Airport in Fort Myers, making it the 61st Southwest city.[44] Robert M. Ball, executive director of Florida's Lee County Port Authority, said

Exhibit 6   Southwest Airline's Operating Expenses per Average Seat Mile, 2000–2008 (in cents)

Category	2008	2007	2006	2005	2004	2003	2002	2001	2000
Salaries, wages, and benefits	3.23	3.22	3.29	3.27	3.18	3.10	2.89	2.84	2.81
Fuel and oil	3.60	2.55	2.31	1.58	1.30	1.16	1.11	1.18	1.34
Maintenance materials and repairs	0.70	0.62	0.51	0.52	0.60	0.60	0.57	0.61	0.63
Aircraft rentals	0.15	0.16	0.17	0.19	0.23	0.25	0.27	0.29	0.33
Landing fees and other rentals	0.64	0.56	0.53	0.53	0.53	0.52	0.50	0.48	0.44
Depreciation and amortization	0.58	0.56	0.56	0.55	0.56	0.53	0.52	0.49	0.47
Other	1.34	1.43	1.43	1.41	1.37	1.37	1.47	1.49	1.44
Total	10.24	9.10	8.80	8.05	7.77	7.53	7.33	7.38	7.46

Source: Southwest Airlines, Form 10-K filed with SEC, 2000–2008.

after courting Southwest for nearly a decade, "We have been working closely with Southwest for many years and are pleased they have selected Southwest Florida as their newest destination."[45] Kelly was on hand to wave the banner, and he said, "Now, our Southwest Florida customers have to look no further than their own backyard for Southwest's legendary low fares and great customer service." Denver, Colorado, and Washington Dulles International Airport were added to the list in 2006. Service to San Francisco commenced in 2007, raising the number of cities served to 64.[46]

Wright Amendment and Beyond With legacy carriers achieving significant labor restructuring agreements and thus eroding SWA's once considerable wage-rate advantage, overcapacity in the East pushing down passenger yields lower than SWA would prefer, and other low-cost carriers such as JetBlue and AirTran carving their niches and reducing the "underserved and overpriced markets" that form the heart of Southwest's commercial strategy, further growth and even cost reductions have been difficult to come by.[47] Kelly pushed for the repeal of the Wright amendment.[48] Southwest entered into an agreement with the City of Dallas, the City of Forth Worth, American Airlines Inc. (which has its hub at Dallas–Fort Worth airport), and the DFW International Airport Board, following which these five parties sought enactment of legislation that would amend the original Wright amendment. Congress responded with a reform act that substantially reduced earlier restrictions. This has worked to Southwest's advantage because it can fly to many more destinations from Love Field than earlier, provided the flights stop first in a state within the Wright perimeter. This includes New Mexico, Oklahoma, Missouri, Arkansas, Louisiana, Mississippi, Kansas, and Alabama, along with Texas.[49] Southwest controls about 90 percent of the Love Field market. Southwest's passenger traffic at Love Field has risen by about 18 percent since the Wright restrictions were loosened in October 2006. This, of course, has a price war brewing between American and Southwest.[50]

None of the members of senior management would concede that Southwest is becoming a different creature. This is primarily because of the huge psychic investment the airline has in being the "underdog." "We're bigger, let's put it that way," says Kelleher. "I think the airline business is fundamentally an opportunistic business. . . . We suddenly have some opportunities materializing that are new to us."[51]

After the much troubled negotiations with flight attendants a couple of years ago, the recent row with the FAA about safety issues and laxity in flight inspections also raises brows about Southwest in action. While Southwest continued its march ahead with its 36th consecutive year of profitability, a pertinent question to ask would be, Is Southwest above cost-cutting pressures when it comes to its business practices?

Endnotes

1. J. Donvan and D. Morris. Southwest CEO on airline's safety. 2008, http://abcnews.go.com/Business/CEOProfiles/story?id=4432181&page=1.
2. A. Levin. Southwest grounds planes due to failed inspections. 2008, www.usatoday.com/money/industries/travel/2008-03-12-swa-grounds-planes_N.htm.
3. D. Q. Wilber. Airline safety alarms unheeded. Washington Post, 2008, www.washingtonpost.com.
4. K. Freiberg and J. Freiberg. Nuts! Southwest Airlines' crazy recipe for personal and business success. Austin, TX: Bard Press, 1996, pp. 20–27, http://archives.californiaaviation.org/airport/msg15249.html.
5. Ibid.
6. Ibid., p. 6.
7. Greylock Associates. Herb Kelleher, chairman, CEO and president, Southwest Airlines. 2003.
8. Southwest Airlines. 10-K filings, 2003, 2006.
9. B. McConnell. The wild, flying turkey with wings: Creating customer evangelists—A profile of Herb Kelleher. 2001, www.creatingcustomerevangelists.com/resources/evangelists/herb_kelleher.asp.
10. Herb Kelleher. Interview with Mark Morrison of *Business-Week* at Texas McComb's School of Business. December 23, 2003, www.businessweek.com.
11. Southwest Airlines. Great Place to Work Institute—Innovation Awards. 2003, www.greatplacetowork.com/education/innovate/honoree-2003-southwest.htm.
12. Herb Kelleher. *Leader to Leader,* 1997, no. 4, www.pfdf.org/leaderbooks/L2L/spring97/kelleher.html.
13. Southwest Airlines. www.southwest.com/careers/stars/stars.html.
14. S. Shinn. LUV, Colleen. *BizEd.,* March–April 2003.
15. Serwer. Southwest Airlines: The hottest thing in the sky. *Fortune,* March 8, 2004, pp. 88–106.
16. Ibid.
17. What makes Southwest Airlines fly? http://knowledge.wharton.upenn.edu/articles.cfm?catid=2&articleid=753.
18. Ibid.; Kelleher. *Leader to Leader;* M.. Freedman. Non-stop growth? *ABCNews.com,* July 2, 2002.
19. What makes Southwest Airlines fly?
20. S. B. Donnelly. One airline's magic. *Time.* October 28, 2002, pp. 45–47.
21. Kelleher. Interview with Mark Morrison; McConnell. The wild, flying turkey with wings.
22. W. Zellner. Southwest: After Kelleher, more blue skies. *BusinessWeek,* April 2, 2001, p. 45.
23. Southwest Airlines. www.southwest.com/swatakeoff/-southwest_effect.html.
24. www.southwest.com; Serwer. Southwest Airlines: The hottest thing in the sky, pp. 88–106.
25. Freedman. Non-stop growth?
26. M. Trotman. Inside Southwest Airlines, storied culture feels strains. *Wall Street Journal Online,* July 11, 2003, http://online.wsj.com.
27. Zellner. Southwest: After Kelleher, more blue skies; W. Zellner and M. Arndt. Holding steady. *BusinessWeek,* February 3, 2003, pp. 66–68.

28. Trotman. Inside Southwest Airlines.
29. Roman. Southwest Air's family feud. 2002, p. 48.
30. Trotman. Inside Southwest Airlines.
31. G. Warchol. Southwest crews rally for their cause. *Salt Lake Tribune,* November 26, 2003, www.sltrib.com/2003/Nov/11262003/Business/Business.asp.
32. Southwest flight attendants may resume contract talks. *AIRwise News,* February 18, 2004, www.airwise.com/news/airlines/southwest.html.
33. Global agenda. Economist.com,. July 16, 2004, p. 1, www.economist.com.
34. Barney Gimbel. Southwest's new flight plan. *Fortune,* May 16, 2005, pp. 93–97.
35. From SEC filings.
36. Wendy Zellner. Dressed to kill . . . competitors. *BusinessWeek,* February 21, 2005, p. 60.
37. From company press releases.
38. Gimbel. Southwest's new flight plan.
39. Southwest Airlines. SEC Form 10-K filings.
40. Serwer. Southwest Airlines: The hottest thing in the sky.
41. Zellner. Dressed to kill . . . competitors.
42. Southwest Airlines. Press releases, March 7, 2005, and June 28, 2005.
43. Southwest Airlines. Press release, May 4, 2005.
44. Southwest Airlines. Press release, July 14, 2005
45. Southwest Airlines. Press release, June 27, 2005.
46. Southwest Airlines. Press release, May 11, 2007.
47. P. Flint. Southwest keeps it simple. *Air Transport World,* April 2005, p. 26.
48. The federal law that limited airlines operating at Dallas Love Field to serving destinations in Texas and seven nearby states primarily with an intention to protect the then new Dallas–Fort Worth International Airport. Southwest was not initially a part of the agreement and therefore its original quest for existence led to its "underdog" mentality.
49. SEC filing, 2006.
50. B. Mutzabaugh. Southwest soars at Dallas Love following relaxed Wright rules. *USAToday,* March 23, 2007, http://blogs.usatoday.com/sky/wright_amendment/index.html.
51. Gimbel. Southwest's new flight plan.

Appendix A   Key Terms Used

Aircraft utilization. The average number of block hours operated per day per aircraft for the total fleet of aircraft.

Available seat-miles. The number of seats available for passengers multiplied by the number of miles the seats are flown.

Average fare. The average one-way fare paid per flight segment by a revenue passenger.

Average stage length. The average number of miles flown per flight.

Break-even load factor. The passenger load factor that will result in operating revenues being equal to operating expenses, assuming constant revenue per passenger-mile and expenses.

Load factor. The percentage of aircraft seating capacity actually utilized (revenue passenger-miles divided by available seat-miles).

Operating expense per available seat-mile. Operating expenses divided by available seat-miles.

Operating revenue per available seat-mile. Operating revenues divided by available seat-miles.

Revenue passenger-miles. The number of miles flown by revenue passengers.

Revenue passengers. The total number of paying passengers flown on all flight segments.

Yield per passenger mile. The average amount one passenger pays to fly 1 mile.

Case 28 Dippin' Dots Ice Cream*

By 2009 Dippin' Dots had billed itself as the ice cream of the future for almost 20 years. However, Dippin' Dots was close to a meltdown. Founder Curt Jones said, "[Dippin' Dots] just got hit by a perfect storm" of soaring operating costs and plummeting sales. Jones has resumed daily control over financially troubled Dippin' Dots after a three-year break from operations. Jones let go of President Tom Leonard, who had run Samsonite before joining Dippin' Dots in August 2006, and Operations Vice President Dominic Fontana, who had spent about 17 years with Häagen-Dazs. Jones described the separations as amicable and regrettable.[1]

Founded by Curt Jones and incorporated in 1988, Dippin' Dots, Inc., headquartered in Paducah, Kentucky, was the company that made the "ice cream of the future."[2] The company's chief operation was the sale of BB-size pellets of flash-frozen ice cream in some two-dozen flavors to franchisees and national accounts throughout the world. As a Six Flags customer commented, "I gotta say, man, they're pretty darn good. . . . Starts off like a rock candy but ends up like ice cream."[3]

Dippin' Dots was the marriage between old-fashioned handmade ice cream and space-age technology. Dippin' Dots were tiny round beads of ice cream that were made at super-cold temperatures, served at subzero temperatures in a soufflé cup, and eaten with a spoon. The super-cold freezing of Dippin' Dots ice cream, done by liquid nitrogen, cryogenically locked in both flavor and freshness in a way that no other manufactured ice cream could offer, since the process virtually eliminated the presence of trapped ice and air, giving the ice cream a fresh flavor and a hard texture. Not only had Jones discovered a new way of making ice cream, but many felt his product proved to be much more flavorful and richer than regular ice cream. According to Jones, "I created a way . . . [to] get a quicker freeze so the ice cream wouldn't get large ice crystals. . . . About six months later, I decided to quit my job and go into business."

Jones was a microbiologist by trade, with an area of expertise in cryogenics. His first job was researching and engineering as a microbiologist for ALLtech Inc., a bioengineering company based in Lexington, Kentucky. During his days at ALLtech, Jones worked with different types of bacteria to find new ways of preserving them so that they could be transported throughout the world. He applied a method of freezing using super-cold temperatures with

substances such as liquid CO_2 and liquid nitrogen—the same method used to create Dippin' Dots.

One process Jones developed was "microencapsulating" the bacteria by freezing their medium with liquid nitrogen. Other scientists thought he was crazy because nothing like that had ever been done before. Jones, however, was convinced his idea would work. He spent months trying to perfect the process and continued to make progress. While Jones was working over 80 hours a week in ALLtech's labs to perfect the microencapsulating process, he made the most influential decision of his life. He took a weekend off and attended a family barbeque at his parents' house. It just so happened that his mother was making ice cream the day of the barbeque. Jones began to reminisce about homemade ice cream prepared the slow, old-fashioned way. Then Jones wondered if it was possible to flash-freeze ice cream. Instead of using a bacteria medium, was it possible to microencapsulate ice cream?

The answer was yes. After virtually reinventing a frozen dessert that had been around since the second century BC,[4] Jones patented his idea to flash-freeze liquid cream, and he opened the first Dippin' Dots store.[5] Once franchising was offered in 2000, the "Ice Cream of the Future" could be found at thousands of shopping malls, amusement parks, water parks, fairs, and festivals worldwide. Dippin' Dots ice cream was transported coast to coast and around the world by truck, train, plane, and ship. In addition to being transported in specially designed cryogenic transport containers, the product was transported in refrigerated boxes known as *pallet reefers*. Both types of containers ensured the fastest and most efficient method of delivery to franchisees around the world. The product was served in 4-, 5-, and 8-ounce cups and in 5-ounce vending prepacks.

Product Specifics

Dippin' Dots were flash-frozen beads of ice cream typically served in a cup or vending package. The ice cream averaged 190 calories per serving, depending on the flavor, and had 9 grams of fat. The ice cream was produced by a patented process that introduced flavored liquid cream into a vat of –325-degree liquid nitrogen, where it was flash-frozen to produce the bead or dot shape. Once frozen, the dots were collected and either mixed with other flavors or packaged separately for delivery to retail locations. The product had to be stored at subzero temperatures to maintain the consistency of the dots. Subzero storage temperatures were achieved by utilizing special equipment and freezers supplemented with dry ice. Although storage was a challenge for international shipping, the beads could maintain their shape for up to 15 days in their special containers. To maintain product integrity and consistency, the

* This case was prepared by Professor Alan B. Eisner of Pace University, Professor Pauline Assenza of Manhattanville College, and graduate student Brian R. Callahan of Pace University as a basis for class discussion rather than to illustrate either effective or ineffective handling of an administrative situation.

ice cream had to be served at 10 to 20 degrees below zero. A retail location had to have special storage and serving freezers. Because the product had to be stored and served at such low temperatures, it was unavailable in regular frozen-food cases and could not be stored in a typical household freezer. Therefore, it could be consumed only at or near a retail location, unless stored with dry ice to maintain the necessary storage temperature.

Industry Overview

The frozen dairy industry has traditionally been occupied by family-owned businesses such as Dippin' Dots, full-line dairies, and a couple of large international companies that focused on only a single sales region. The year 2008 was a relatively flat year for the production and sale of ice cream, as volume in traditional varieties remained flat and new types of ice cream emerged. Despite higher ingredient costs, manufacturers were continually churning out new products, though at a slower rate than in the previous year. These ranged from super-premium selections to good-for-you varieties to cobranded packages and novelties. Most novelty ice creams could be found together in supermarket freezer cases, in small freezers in convenience stores, and in carts, kiosks, or trucks at popular summertime events. Ice-cream makers had been touched by consolidation trends affecting the overall food and beverage industry that extended beyond their products, as even the big names were folded into global conglomerates.

The ice-cream segment in the United States had become a battleground for two huge international consumer product companies seeking to corner the ice-cream market. Those two industry giants were Nestlé SA of Switzerland, the world's largest food company, with more than $90 billion in annual sales, and Unilever PLC of London and Rotterdam, with over $52 billion in annual revenues. Both had been buying into U.S. firms for quite a while, but Nestlé, which already owned the Häagen-Dazs product line, upped the ante with its June 2003 merger with Dreyer's Grand/Edy's Ice Cream, Inc., of Oakland, California. But even as the two giants dominated the U.S. ice-cream industry, about 500 small businesses continued to produce and distribute frozen treats. As one commentator said, "Like microbrewers and small-scale chocolate makers, entrepreneurs are drawn to ice cream as a labor of love."[6] Some of the better-known brands were regional ones, such as Blue Bell, based in Brenham, Texas (see Exhibit 1).

A total of $24 billion was spent on ice cream in 2008, and ice cream and related frozen desserts were consumed by more than 90 percent of households in the United States.[7] Consumers spent $8.9 billion on products for at-home consumption, while $13.9 billion went toward away-from-home purchases. Harry Balzar, of the market research firm NPD Group, said about ice cream in general, "It's not a small category, but one that has remained flat for more than a decade, and is not likely to grow."[8]

The challenge for producers was to woo customers away from competitors and sustain a loyal fan base by continuing to innovate. The trend toward more healthy treats had spurred the major players, Nestlé and Unilever, to develop reduced-fat product lines that still had the taste and texture of full-fat ice cream. Edy's/Dreyer's, Breyers, and Häagen-Dazs had all continued to experiment, and the "slow-churned," "double-churned," and "light" products were seeing increased sales since their introduction in 2004.[9]

In October 2002, it was announced that Good Humor–Breyers Ice Cream of Green Bay, Wisconsin, and Ben & Jerry's of Vermont had formed a unified retail sales division named Unilever Ice Cream. The new organization brought together both companies and represented the five Unilever North American ice-cream brands, which include Ben & Jerry's, Breyers, Good Humor, Popsicle, and Klondike. Good Humor–Breyers had created several new cobranded novelties specifically for convenience-store and vending locations. The company had also set out to expand the availability of single-serve novelties by placing freezers of its products in Blockbuster video stores and Breyers-branded kiosks in 30 Chicago-area Loews theaters. In addition to prepackaged products, freshly scooped ice cream was served at the kiosks. The new sales team would focus solely on the out-of-home ice-cream business and, therefore, exclude grocery channels.

Another novelty product delivery system in the independent scoop shop was the "slab" concept. Employees at franchises such as Marble Slab Creamery, Cold Stone Creamery, and Maggie Moo's worked ingredients on a cold granite or marble slab to blend premium ice cream with the customer's choice of tasty additives, such as crumbled cookies, fruits, and nuts, before serving in a cup or cone. The novelty was the entertainment of watching the preparation. All three chains ranked in *Entrepreneur*'s list of the top-500 franchise opportunities in 2006, but commentators were skeptical of sustainability once the novelty wore off, especially since the average price was $5 for a medium serving.[10] As of 2008, only Cold Stone Creamery was able to maintain its spot in the list of the top-500 franchises. Cold Stone Creamery ranked in the 90th position.[11]

Industry Segmentation

Frozen desserts come in many forms. Each of the following foods has its own definition, and many are standardized by federal regulations:[12]

- **Ice cream** consists of a mixture of dairy ingredients, such as milk and nonfat milk, and ingredients for sweetening and flavoring, such as fruits, nuts, and chocolate chips. Functional ingredients, such as stabilizers and emulsifiers, are often included in the product to promote proper texture and enhance the eating experience. By federal law, ice cream must contain at least 10 percent butterfat before the addition of bulky ingredients, and it must weigh a minimum of 4.5 pounds to the gallon.
- **Novelties** are separately packaged single servings of a frozen dessert, such as ice-cream sandwiches,

Exhibit 1 Top Brands*

Top-10 Ice Cream/Sherbet Brands*				
	Sales ($ millions)	Percent Change vs. Year Ago	Unit Sales (millions)	Percent Change vs. Year Ago
Total category	$4,403.0	−0.3%	1,370.0	−0.4%
Private label (ice cream)	812.8	−2.7	285.9	−0.4
Breyers	638.8	7.5	196.7	10.0
Dreyer's/Edy's Grand	445.1	−1.0	130.9	−4.7
Häagen-Dazs	287.3	12.1	83.4	7.2
Dreyer's/Edy's SlowChurned	284.0	100.8	76.8	93.3
Blue Bell	253.2	2.0	75.0	1.0
Ben & Jerry's	207.6	8.7	67.8	10.1
Wells' Blue Bunny	122.0	14.0	34.6	17.1
Turkey Hill	116.9	13.8	41.8	14.1
Private label (sherbet/sorbet/ices)	59.8	−4.0	27.3	−2.7

Top-10 Frozen Novelty Brands[†]						
	Sales ($ millions)	Percent Change vs. Year Ago	Dollar Share	Unit Sales (millions)	Percent Change vs. Year Ago	Unit Share
Total category	$2,470.7	2.3%	100.0	819.4	−0.1%	100.0
Private label	317.9	−4.0	12.9	134.5	−3.2	16.4
Nestlé Drumstick	131.3	−0.6	5.3	38.0	−3.8	4.6
Weight Watchers	127.4	57.3	5.2	28.9	54.1	3.5
Klondike	126.2	−5.0	5.1	42.7	−7.5	5.2
Popsicle	113.3	10.4	4.6	41.5	5.0	5.1
Dreyer's/Edy's Whole Fruit	103.4	−1.3	4.2	31.6	−9.9	3.9
Carvel	93.2	6.0	3.8	5.9	2.4	0.7
The Skinny Cow	84.3	16.2	3.4	19.5	12.8	2.4
Dreyer's/Edy's Dibs	83.6	97.8	3.4	25.2	91.6	3.1
Häagen-Dazs	57.4	7.6	2.3	19.0	8.1	2.3

*Total sales of all forms of ice cream/sherbet brands in supermarkets, drug stores, and mass merchandisers (excluding Wal-Mart).

[†]Total sales of all forms of frozen novelty brands in supermarkets, drug stores, and mass merchandisers (excluding Wal-Mart).

Source: Information Resources Inc.

fudge sticks, and juice bars, which may or may not contain dairy ingredients.

- **Frozen custard** or **french ice cream** must also contain a minimum of 10 percent butterfat as well as at least 1.4 percent egg yolk solids.
- **Sherbets** have a butterfat content of between 1 and 2 percent and have a slightly higher sweetener

content than ice cream. Sherbet weighs a minimum of 6 pounds to the gallon and is flavored either with fruit or other characterizing ingredients.

- **Gelato** is characterized by an intense flavor and is served in a semifrozen state. Gelato contains sweeteners, milk, cream, egg yolks, and flavoring.

- **Sorbet** and **water ices** are similar to sherbets, but they contain no dairy ingredients.
- A **quiescently frozen confection** is a frozen novelty such as a water-ice novelty on a stick.
- **Frozen yogurt** consists of a mixture of dairy ingredients, such as milk and nonfat milk, which have been cultured, as well as ingredients for sweetening and flavoring.

Dippin' Dots Growth[13]

The growth of Dippin' Dots, Inc., had been recognized in the United States and the world by industry watchdogs such as *Inc.* magazine, which ranked Dippin' Dots as one of the 500 fastest-growing companies two years in a row, 1996 and 1997. Dippin' Dots Franchising, Inc., ranked number four on *Entrepreneur* magazine's 2004 list of the top-50 new franchise companies, and it achieved the 101st spot on *Entrepreneur*'s Franchise 500 for 2004. In 2005, Dippin' Dots ranked number two as a top new franchise opportunity and climbed to number 93 on the Franchise 500 list. By the end of 2009, Dippin' Dots had slid to 175th position on *Entrepreneur*'s Franchise 500 list.[14] Exhibit 2 shows the growth of franchises for Dippin' Dots.

Despite the company's apparent success, the achievements of Curt Jones and Dippin' Dots have not been without obstacles. Once Jones had perfected his idea, he needed to start a company for the new process of flash-freezing ice cream. Like many new entrepreneurs, Jones enlisted the help of his family to support his endeavor. It was essential to start selling his product, but he had no protection for his idea from competitors.

The first obstacle confronting Jones was the need to locate funding to accomplish his goals. He needed money for the patent to protect his intellectual property and needed

Exhibit 2 Dippin' Dots Franchise Growth

Year	U.S. Franchises	Canadian Franchises	Foreign Franchises	Company Owned
2008	420	0	0	2
2007	441	0	0	3
2006	448	1	0	2
2005	635	1	0	2
2004	618	1	0	2
2003	598	0	0	2
2002	580	0	0	2
2001	569	0	0	3
2000	525	0	0	1

Source: www.entrepreneur.com/franchises/dippindotsfranchisinginc/289468-1.html.

seed money to start manufacturing the ice cream once the patent was granted. At the same time that Jones was perfecting the flash-freezing process for his ice cream, he was also working on a Small Business Association (SBA) loan to convert the family farm into one that would manufacture ethanol. However, instead of using the farm to produce the alternative fuel, Jones's parents took out a first, and then a second, mortgage to help fund Jones's endeavor. Thus, Jones initiated the entire venture by self-funding his company with personal and family assets.

Unfortunately, the money from Jones's parents was only enough to pay for the patent and some crude manufacturing facilities (a liquid nitrogen tank in his parent's garage). He next had to open a store, and doing so required even more money—money that Jones and his family did not have. They were unable to get the SBA loan because, while the product was novel and looked promising, there was no proof that it would sell. So Jones and his newly appointed CFO (his sister) went to an alternative lender who lent them cash at an exorbitant interest rate that was tacked onto the principal weekly if unpaid.

Now in possession of the seed money they needed, Curt Jones and his family opened their first store. Its summertime opening created a buzz in the community. The store was mobbed every night, and Dippin' Dots was legitimized by public demand. With the influx of cash, Jones was able to move his manufacturing operation from his family's garage into a vacant warehouse. There he set up shop and personally made flash-frozen ice cream for 12 hours every day to supply the store.

After the store had been operating for a few months, the Joneses were able to secure small business loans from local banks to cover the expenses of a modest manufacturing plant and office. At the same time, Jones's sister made calls to fairs and other events to learn whether Dippin' Dots products could be sold at them. Luckily for the Joneses, the amusement park at Opryland in Nashville, Tennessee, was willing to have them as a vendor. Unfortunately, the first Dippin' Dots stand was placed in front of a roller coaster, and people generally did not want ice cream before they went on a ride. After a few unsuccessful weeks, Jones moved the stand and business picked up considerably. Eventually, the Joneses were able to move to an inline location, which was similar to a store, where Dippin' Dots had its own personnel and sitting area to serve customers.

Through word of mouth, interest in Curt Jones and Dippin' Dots spread. Soon other entrepreneurs contacted Jones about opening up stores to sell Dippin' Dots. In 1991 a dealership network was developed to sell ice cream to authorized vendors and provide support with equipment and marketing. During that time, Jones employed friends in corporate jobs. Dippin' Dots grew into a multimillion-dollar company with authorized dealers operating in all 50 states and internationally (see Exhibit 3).

By the end of the 1990s, Jones was happy with his company, but he felt as if Dippin' Dots had hit a plateau and needed to reach the "next level" to continue to prosper.

Exhibit 3   Milestones

1988	Dippin' Dots is established as a company in Grand Chain, Illinois.
1989	First amusement park account debuts at Opryland USA in Nashville.
1990	Production facility moves to Paducah, Kentucky.
1991	Dealer network is established for fair, festival, and commercial retail locations.
1994	First international licensee is set up (Japan).
1995	New 32,000-square-foot production facility opens in Paducah.
1997	Production facility expands by 20,000 square feet; earns spot on *Inc.* 500 list of fastest-growing private companies in the United States.
2000	Dippin' Dots Franchising, Inc., is established, and first franchise is offered; litigation against competitors is initiated to protect patent.
2001	Dippin' Dots enlists 30 new franchisees. *Franchise Times* magazine lists Dippin' Dots third nationally, behind Baskin-Robbins and Dairy Queen, in number of franchises.
2002	Dippin' Dots Franchising, Inc., achieves 112th spot on *Entrepreneur* magazine's Franchise 500 list. Dippin' Dots Franchising, Inc., ranks 69th on *Entrepreneur* magazine's list of the fastest-growing franchise companies. Dippin' Dots Franchising, Inc., is ranked as the number-one new franchise company by *Entrepreneur.* Dippin' Dots becomes a regular menu offering on menus at McDonald's restaurants in the San Francisco Bay area.
2003	Dippin' Dots Franchising, Inc., achieves 144th spot on *Entrepreneur* magazine's Franchise 500 list. Dippin' Dots Franchising, Inc., ranks number four on *Entrepreneur*'s list of the top-50 new franchise companies. Dippin' Dots' opens the Ansong manufacturing plant, 80 miles south of Seoul, South Korea.
2004	Dippin' Dots Franchising, Inc., ranks number four on *Entrepreneur*'s Top-50 New Franchise Companies list. Dippin' Dots Franchising, Inc., achieves 101st spot on *Entrepreneur* magazine's Franchise 500 list. Curt Jones and Dippin' Dots are featured on a segment of the *Oprah Winfrey Show,* appearing in 110 countries. Dippin' Dots is featured among the top-10 ice-cream palaces on the Travel Channel. Curt Jones is quoted in Donald Trump's best-selling *The Way to the Top* (p. 131).
2005	International Dairy Foods Association names Dippin' Dots Best in Show for Dot Delicacies. Dippin' Dots also wins three awards for package design. Dippin' Dots Franchising, Inc., ranks number one on *Franchise Times* magazine's Fast 55 list of the fastest-growing young franchises in the nation. Ice-cream cake and ice-cream sandwiches (Dotwiches) are introduced to launch the Dot Delicacies program.
2006	Company leadership is restructured. Curt Jones becomes chairman of the board. Tom Leonard becomes president of Dippin' Dots, Inc. Dots 'n Cream, conventional ice cream enhanced by beads of Dippin' Dots, is introduced for market testing in Kroger stores in the Midwest. The 200th franchisee begins operations.
2007	Dippin' Dots is available in Colombia, and www.dippindots.com V.5 is launched.
2008	Dippin' Dots Franchising, Inc., ranks 112th on *Entrepreneur*'s Franchise 500 list.
2009	Curt Jones returns to running the day-to-day operations of the firm. Dippin' Dots slides to 175th on *Entrepreneur*'s Franchise 500 list.

Source: Company Web site, www.dippindots.com/company/history.

He began working with his friend and now controller and director of franchising, Chad Wilson, to develop the franchise system. By January 2000, all existing Dippin' Dots dealers were required to sign a franchise agreement and pay the associated franchise fees for any location they operated or planned to operate.

A franchise location was any mall, fair, national account, or large family entertainment center. According to the franchising information in 2008, the initial franchise fee was $12,500, with an estimated initial investment range from $80,428 to $235,250.[15] The result was a cash inflow for Dippin' Dots franchising. Franchisees were required to pay a 4 percent royalty fee and contribute one-half percent of their gross incomes to an advertising fund, which Jones said had greatly enhanced marketing.

The Future

Dippin' Dots was counting on youthful exuberance to expand growth. "Our core demographic was pretty much 8- to 18-year-olds," said Terry Reeves, corporate communications director. "On top of that, we're starting to see a generation of parents who grew up on Dippin' Dots and are starting to introduce the products to their kids." Although Dippin' Dots seems to appeal more to youngsters, the product still has to have staying power as customers grow older. As one individual commented, "How can this stuff keep continuing to call itself the 'ice cream of the future'? Well the future is now folks and they have been pushing this sorry excuse for ice cream off on me at amusement parks and zoos since I was a little kid."[16]

In 2002 McDonald's reportedly spent $1.2 million on advertising to roll out Dippin' Dots in about 250 restaurants in the San Francisco area. Jones called the deal "open-ended" if it worked favorably for both firms. "I think both companies are proceeding with the impression that nothing was going to be overcommitted," he said. "We're growing at a 10 to 15 percent annual rate and we're excited about the potential of McDonald's, but it's too early to tell." By mid-2007 Dippin' Dots was available only at a few McDonald's franchises in southern California. Storage and transportation issues were problematic, and the price of the product, 5 ounces for $5, was too steep for all but the die-hard Dippin' Dots fans.

In other marketing efforts, Dippin' Dots ads had been running in issues of *Seventeen* and *Nickelodeon* magazines. Reeves said the company had been "inundated with e-mails" once the June 2002 issue of *Seventeen* hit the newsstands. Additionally, Dippin' Dots had hired a Hollywood firm to place its ice cream in the background of television and movie scenes, including the 2003 *Cheaper by the Dozen*. In 2002 the Food Network's "Summer Foods: Unwrapped" showcased Dippin' Dots as one of the most unique and coolest ice-cream treats. 'N Sync member Joey Fatone ordered a Dippin' Dots freezer for his home after seeing a Dots vending machine at a theater the band rented in Orlando. Caterers also sought Dippin' Dots for their star clients. A recent birthday party at the home of NBA star Shaquille O'Neal featured Dippin' Dots ice cream. Dippin' Dots continued to pursue the celebrity word-of-mouth route by serving Dippin' Dots products at events such as the MTV awards and celebrity charity functions.

According to Jones, in 2006 almost half of Dippin' Dots sales came from national accounts such as stadiums, theaters, and theme parks like Six Flags; the rest of the estimated $50 million income came from approximately 150 franchisees, many with multiple locations.[17]

Dippin' Dots had met increased competition in the out-of-home ice-cream market. The major threats to Dippin' Dots were other franchise operations such as Ben & Jerry's, Häagen-Dazs, Baskin-Robbins, Carvel, Dairy Queen, and newcomers such as Cold Stone Creamery, Maggie Moo's, and Marble Slab Creamery (see Exhibit 4). In addition, a very similar type of flash-frozen ice cream called Frosty Bites was introduced in the spring of 2000 by eight disenfranchised former dealers of Dippin' Dots. Another company, Mini Melts, was also manufacturing a similar product, and two brothers who were formerly part of the Dippin' Dots dealer network brought this flash-frozen ice cream into the competitive mix.

In 2002 Jones had thought that introducing a formal franchising agreement would provide protection against copycats and unify the company's public image, since Dippin' Dots was often unrecognizable under its unstructured dealership network of locations.

> Terry Reeves, corporate communication director, said: [T]he stronger and more unified Dippin' Dots retail offering became through franchising, the more [franchisees] were able to be considered for better retail properties (high-end malls, better locations, and so on). This obviously strengthened our system and bolstered overall sales for the company and for our franchisees. While franchise fees and royalties were a new income source, much of the profit was put back into the business to promote future growth.

Although one dealer commented that Dippin' Dots used incoming franchise fees from royalties on sales for its own corporate means rather than to improve franchise support, most dealers did convert to the new franchise system. Dippin' Dots Franchising, Inc., grandfathered existing dealers' locations by issuing a franchise and waiving the franchise fee for the first contract period of five years. Many dealers had to renew their contracts in 2004; while many were initially apprehensive of converting to a franchised system, less than 2 percent left the system, and the firm showed franchise growth.

In an attempt to counteract the copycat threats from Frosty Bites and Mini Melts, Dippin' Dots brought a patent infringement lawsuit against them in 2005. However during the jury trial, Dippin' Dots testimony in support of the original patent revealed that Jones had made sales of the beaded ice-cream product to over 800 customers more than a year before submitting the patent application. Even though Jones argued that these sales were for the purpose of market testing and that the production method may have subsequently been further refined, therefore deserving of a patented process, the court rendered the patent nonenforceable since these sales were not disclosed to the Patent Office. An appeal by Dippin' Dots was denied in 2007, and the patent was declared invalid.[18]

Mini Melts, released from the lawsuit, continued to expand manufacturing facilities throughout the world; it had plants in South Korea, the Philippines, the United Arab Emirates, Hong Kong, and China as well as the United Kingdom and the United States. Instead of having franchises, Mini Melts sold dealerships for vending machines

Exhibit 4   Ice-Cream Franchises, 2008

Franchise Name and Description	Start-Up Costs ($ thousands)	Number of Franchises
2 Scoops Cafe Ice cream parlor/cafe	99–175	1
Abbott's Frozen Custard Frozen custard	120–126.8	20
All American Specialty Restaurants Inc. Ice cream, frozen yogurt, deli sandwiches, espresso	171–485	30
Applegate Inc. Ice cream	137.7–322	7
Baskin-Robbins USA Co. Ice cream, frozen yogurt, frozen beverages	121.3–419.6	2,699
Ben & Jerry's Ice cream parlor	173.3–438.9	417
Blue Sky Creamery Ice cream, gourmet coffees, desserts	98.8–564.4	9
Bruster's Real Ice Cream Homemade ice cream	179–1,200	253
California Quivers Carts and kiosks serving fresh-fruit ices	45–149.3	3
Carvel Ice cream, ice-cream cakes	46.9–388.7	501
Cefiore Frozen yogurt	196.5–425	27
Cold Stone Creamery Ice cream, Italian sorbet	292.4–438.98	1,394
Culver Franchising System Inc. Frozen custard, specialty burgers	1.6M–3,200	376
Dairy Queen Soft-serve dairy products, sandwiches	700–1,300	4,551
Dippin' Dots Franchising Specialty ice cream, frozen yogurt, ices, sherbet	80.4–235.3	420
Freddy's Frozen Custard LLC Frozen custard, steakburgers, hot dogs	332–788	15
FreshBerry Natural Frozen Yogurt Natural frozen yogurt, smoothies, yogurt popsicles	78–273	0
Häagen-Dazs Shoppe Co. Inc., The Ice cream, frozen yogurt	143.9–427.1	259
Happy Joe's Pizza, pasta, ice cream	98.2–1,100	56
La Paletera Franchise Systems Inc. Fruit bars and cups, smoothies, ice cream	94.5–185.7	35

(continued)

Exhibit 4   Ice-Cream Franchises, 2008

Franchise Name and Description	Start-Up Costs ($ thousands)	Number of Franchises
<u>Little Scoops</u> Retro 50s-style ice-cream party place for children	100–168.5	6
<u>MaggieMoo's Int'l, LLC</u> Ice cream, smoothies, cakes	219.6–335.7	185
<u>Marble Slab Creamery Inc.</u> Ice cream, frozen yogurt, baked goods	220.5–381	280
<u>Melt Inc.</u> Gelato, Italian coffees, crepes	200–400	8
<u>Paciugo Italian Gelato</u> Gelato	178.7–434.1	31
<u>Repicci's Italian Ice</u> Italian ice	30–391.7	30
<u>Ricky's Candy, Cones & Chaos</u> Candy, ice cream, parties	378.5–563.8	8
<u>Rita's Italian Ice</u> Italian ices, frozen custard, gelati	198.2–445.9	521
<u>Ritter's Frozen Custard</u> Frozen custard	249–818	62
<u>Shake's Frozen Custard</u> Frozen custard	168–800	30
<u>Strickland's</u> Homemade ice cream, related products	224.5–337	14
<u>Tasti D-Lite</u> Frozen desserts	240.5–439.6	36
<u>Ziiing Frozen Yogurt</u> Frozen yogurt	165.6–506.6	9

Source: www.entrepreneur.com/franchises/categories/ffqicecr.html.

and kiosks carrying its products. Mini Melts CEO Tom Mosey was nominated by Ernst and Young as Entrepreneur of the Year and has been listed in the *Inc.* 500 for two separate ventures over the years.[19]

In spite of these challenges, Jones, always the inventor, was investing in R&D to create a conventional ice-cream product that had super-frozen dots embedded in it. He was developing a new product that could withstand conventional freezers while preserving the super-frozen dots in the ice cream. Called Dots 'n Cream and available in vanilla, chocolate, mint chocolate chip, and banana split, this product was introduced for market testing in Kroger stores in the Midwest in 2006. Thus, Dippin' Dots could finally have a take-home ice-cream option. As of February 2009, the Dots 'n Cream product was available only in St. Louis at Shop 'n Save.[20] Such a long time after introduction, Dots 'n Cream was still in limbo, or St. Louis anyway.

The other new product introduced by Dippin' Dots was Dot Delicacies. The first product to be introduced in this category was named Dotwiches. As of February 2009, there were seven different Dot Delicacies: Add a Topping, Solar Freeze, Sundaes, floats, milkshakes, Dot Cakes, and Dotwiches. These products are available at most of the retail locations where Dippin' Dots ice cream is sold.

Despite the development of new products, the company's experience and resource base are clearly in the ice-cream manufacturing and scoop-shop retailing businesses. Dealing with supermarket chains, packaging, and distribution is a challenge for this relatively small firm. However, opportunities might still be pursued by enlarging the franchise and national-account businesses for scoop shops and vending machines. Jones has continued to assess his company's situation, identifying and choosing among the best strategic options for Dippin' Dots' growth.

Endnotes

1. Joe Walker. Dippin' Dots founder takes control of company after management layoffs. *Paducah Sun* (Kentucky), 2009, *Newspaper Source,* EBSCO*host,* accessed April 6, 2009.

2. Information, unless otherwise stated, is derived from the Dippin' Dots Web site (www.DippinDots.com), the Dippin' Dots 10-year anniversary video, and the self-published Dippin' Dots Corporate Profile.

3. Associated Press. Business blazing for supercold Dippin' Dots. July 23, 2006, www.msnbc.msn.com/id/14001806.

4. Ice cream's origins are known to reach back as far as the second century BC, although no specific date of origin is known and no inventor has been indisputably credited with its discovery. We know that Alexander the Great enjoyed snow and ice flavored with honey and nectar. Biblical references also show that King Solomon was fond of iced drinks during harvesting. During the Roman Empire, Nero (AD 54–86) frequently sent runners into the mountains for snow, which was then flavored with fruits and juices. Information from Ice Cream Media Kit, International Dairy Foods Association.

5. The idea of using liquid nitrogen to make ice cream had been around in scientific circles for some time. To learn how to make ice cream this way at home, see www.polsci.wvu.edu/-henry/icecream/icecream.html, from an article in *Scientific American,* April 1994, pp. 66–71. See also www.subzeroicecream.com/press/coldfacts2006.pdf.

6. G. Anderson. America's favorite ice cream. *CNN/Money.com,* July 29, 2005, http://money.cnn.com/2005/07/25/pf/goodlife/summer_ice_cream.

7. Author estimates; and Dairy Facts/International Ice Cream Association, www.idfa.org.

8. K. Murphy. Slabs are joining scoops in ice cream retailing. *New York Times,* October 26, 2006, www.nytimes.com/2006/10/26/-business/26sbiz.html?ex=1319515200&en=5f77555844021708&ei=5088&partner=rssnyt&emc=rss.

9. J. Moskin. Creamy, healthier ice cream? What's the catch? *New York Times,* July 26, 2006, www.nytimes.com/2006/07/26/dining/-26cream.html?ex=1182916800&en=501180740dd57a44&ei=5070. Note: *Slow-churned* and *double-churned* refer to a process called low-temperature extrusion, which significantly reduces the size of the fat globules and ice crystals in ice cream.

10. Murphy. Slabs are joining scoops in ice cream retailing.

11. www.entrepreneur.com/franchises/rankings/franchise500-115608/2008,-2.html.

12. All definitions are taken from the IDFA Web site, www.idfa.org/facts/icmonth/page4.cfm.

13. Dippin' Dots 10th anniversary promotional video.

14. www.entrepreneur.com/franchises/rankings/franchise500-115608/2009,-4.html.

15. www.dippindots.com/franchise/information.

16. S. Michelle. *Yelp Reviews–Chicago,* November 17, 2006, www.yelp.com/biz/qnA4ml7Lu-9W4SDJOF1YPA.

17. Associated Press, op. cit.

18. Undisclosed prior sales doom Dippin' Dots patent. *IP Law Observer,* May 1, 2007, re Dippin'Dots, Inc. v. Mosey (Fed. Cir. 02/09/07—No. 2005-1330, 2005-1582, http://www.iplawobserver.com/-2007/05/undisclosed-prior-sales-doom-dippin.html.

19. See www.minimelts.com.

20. See www.dippindots.com/dots-n-cream/locations.

Case 29   Keurig Coffee*

On November 3, 2008, Michelle Stacey was appointed president of Keurig, Inc., a wholly owned subsidiary of Green Mountain Coffee Roasters, following the resignation of Nicholas Lazaris. Stacey joined Keurig with more than 20 years of experience as a senior executive in marketing and global business management with the Gillette Company and then as the vice president and general manager of Global Professional Oral Care with Procter & Gamble. Speaking of Stacey's appointment, Lawrence J. Blanford, Green Mountain Coffee Roasters (GMCR) president and CEO, said, "I am extremely pleased that Michelle will be joining the team at Keurig and GMCR. Michelle has an impressive track record of success in organizational leadership, strategic planning, global marketing and supply chain management at major Fortune 500 companies and leading consumer brands. Her depth of experience with and understanding of, consumer package goods and technology-oriented products with a razor/razorblade business model are perfectly suited to our strong platform for growth at GMCR and Keurig."[1] Michelle Stacey faced several potential challenges at Keurig including transitioning Keurig from a technology-driven to a marketing-driven company, maintaining the entrepreneurial and innovative culture at Keurig, Inc., expanding the distribution network for Keurig, and dealing with potential elasticity-of-demand concerns given the retail prices of Keurig's at-home products and decreased consumer spending.

Coffee Consumption in the United States

The U.S. annual per capita consumption of coffee was estimated to be 424 servings, which included in-home and out-of-home roast and ground, instant, and ready-to-drink (bottled/canned) coffee.[2] The total coffee market in 2008 was estimated to be 1.8 billion pounds, or $19.3 billion.[3] Although coffee consumption had remained relatively flat over the past few years, a consumer survey by the National Coffee Association revealed that the percentage of people drinking gourmet coffee on a daily basis increased from 14 percent in 2007 to 17 percent in early 2008.[4]

While specialty coffee was only about 17 percent of total domestic coffee consumption by volume, the sector had grown to over half the value of the U.S. coffee industry.[5] The specialty coffee market was estimated to be worth $11 billion annually.[6] Specialty coffee consumption had increased over 48 percent in the United States from 2001 to 2006.[7]

*This case was prepared by graduate student Keith F. Moody and Professor Alan B. Eisner of Pace University as a basis for class discussion rather than to illustrate either effective or ineffective handling of an administrative situation. Material has been drawn from published sources. Copyright © 2009 Keith F. Moody and Alan B. Eisner.

"Pod" Brewing Market

While the entire category of coffee-maker sales posted a 3 percent drop in 2008 as compared to 2007, sales of single-serve (pod) units increased 50 percent. Although machines that make single-cup brews accounted for just 6 percent of the 90 million brewers in U.S. homes, the trend was gaining momentum as consumers were trading old-school coffee pots for machines that made gourmet coffee at home. Approximately 18.5 million coffee brewers were sold each year in the United States, and Keurig's goal was to convert half of the 90 million American homes with coffee brewers to Keurig brand pod brewers.[8] As recently as 2007, research by the NPD Group indicated that the single-serve proposition wasn't compelling enough for consumers to replace their existing coffee makers with pod machines. NPD's research indicated that a significant proportion of purchasers were unsatisfied and cited unreliable machines as a problem as well as the coffee itself. The pods available, consumers complained, were pricey, often hard to find, and limited in terms of flavor and blends. In its survey, the NPD Group found that some consumers were dissatisfied with the performance of pod machines, with 17 percent of machines returned, thrown out, or given away. John Block, director of the NPD Group, said, "Manufacturers and retailers have a great opportunity to improve their position in the marketplace by listening to consumer feedback, and integrating all three attributes that customers want most into their product offering: a reliable pod machine, easy-to-find refills and a variety of coffee flavors."[9] According to NPD, Keurig was the leading single-cup brewing system in the at-home market, with 82 percent of the market in terms of dollar sales and 81 percent in terms of unit share as of December 31, 2008 (see Exhibit 1).

A MultiChannel Strategy for the Away-From-Home Market

Keurig initially focused on the away-from-home (AFH) commercial segment of office users. Increasing demand and brand awareness enabled Keurig to pursue a multi-channel strategy, providing widespread exposure through consumer trial. Starbucks and other specialty coffee purveyors had laid the groundwork for launching into the AFH office coffee service (OCS) market by educating consumers about gourmet coffee and moving coffee beyond the commodity category. Starbucks may be responsible for a paradigm shift regarding the price elasticity of coffee. The price elasticity impacting consumer purchases of Robusta coffee by the can shifted with the proliferation of fresh-ground Arabica beans served in a coffeehouse, often for $2 or more per cup. This paradigm shift enabled Keurig to offer a single-cup brewing system to offices, capitalizing

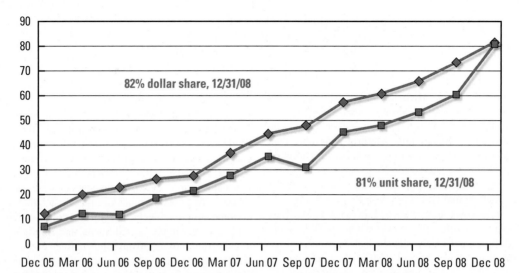

Exhibit 1 **Keurig: Number One in Single-Serve at-Home Market**

Source: NPD data. Keurig Inc.

on consumer demand to replicate coffeehouse-quality java in the office.

There were approximately 2.6 million coffee brewers in offices nationwide, serviced by a network of approximately 1,700 distributors. Of those offices, GMCR estimated that 12 percent had single-cup brewers and that about half of them were Keurig brewers.[10] While Keurig brewers were estimated to be in 30 percent of offices in New England, national penetration in the office channel was only about 6 percent.

Keurig continued working with its network of Keurig authorized distributors (KADs) to execute office acquisition plans and conduct lead generation, demonstrations, and sampling programs to build Keurig's office coffee business. In addition to Keurig's traditional distributor network, customers such as Office Depot and Staples were helping Keurig grow through their business-to-business solutions for both large- and small-office applications.

Another AFH single-serve opportunity Keurig identified was the hotel market. There were approximately 5 million coffee makers in hotel rooms across North America. Keurig believed that 40 percent of those rooms catered to travelers who would appreciate the benefits of single-serve brewing. The Keurig team went through a rigorous process to develop new brewer concepts for the market. The development of a new "hotel in-room" brewer was one example (see Exhibit 2).

Single-Cup Brewer System Competition

Consumers had many single-cup brewing systems to choose from in North America and throughout the world. Competition in the single-cup brewing system market was increasing as relatively low barriers to entry encouraged new competitors to enter the market, particularly with lower-cost brewers that brewed coffee packaged in

nonpatented pods. Many current and potential competitors had substantially greater financial, marketing, and operating resources than did Keurig. According to Keurig, its primary competitors were Flavia Beverage Systems (manufactured by Mars), the Tassimo beverage system (manufactured and marketed by Kraft), the Senso brewing system (manufactured and marketed by Philips and Sara Lee), and a number of additional single-cup brewing systems and brands. Kraft's Tassimo system was made primarily for at-home use, while the Mars's Flavia system targeted offices.

In a January 2009 *Consumer Reports* article on coffeemakers, pod machines were covered. The article stated, "With pod machines you simply drop in a sealed packet of coffee—no grinding, no scooping, and no mess. But many lock you into the company's coffee, which tends to be pricey, and the results have been unimpressive." According to *Consumer Reports,* "Cuisinart's Cup-O-Matic SS-1, $200, did best among the pod models tested. It took standard pods or your own grind and lets you pick regular or bold in five cup sizes. It was reasonably quick: about three minutes for the first cup, one minute thereafter. But the model occasionally leaked extra water into the cup, diluting the coffee." *Consumer Reports* also tested the Keurig Breville BKC600XL, $300. The article commented that the Keurig machine "accepts any K-cup as well as loose coffee grounds. It was fairly quiet but that first cup takes almost four minutes." *Consumer Reports* recommended, "If you want coffee for one in a hurry and you insist on the neatness and convenience of a pod machine, consider the Cuisinart for its flexibility and speed. Otherwise, we recommend our top-scoring to-go model, the Melitta Take2 ME2TM. It's quick, brewed superbly, and costs just $25." (See Appendix A for a review of the 10 top-selling single-serve coffee makers, as of December 2008.)

Exhibit 2 Keurig Hotel in-Room Brewer

The History of Keurig

Taking its name from the Dutch word for "excellence," Keurig was launched in 1990 by Peter Dragone and John Sylvan with the belief that coffee should always be served fresh, whether at home or at the office, just as in a gourmet coffeehouse. Dragone and Sylvan noticed that people were leaving the office in search of a fresh cup of coffee and asked themselves, "Why do we brew coffee by the pot when we drink it by the cup?" From this question, the revolutionary concept of Keurig K-Cup portion-pack brewing was born. In 1994, Keurig secured a patent and came up with a prototype. Two venture-capital firms kicked in $1 million and gave Dragone and Sylvan one year to prepare a model for mass production. When they missed the deadline, the venture capitalists offered more money but demanded that Nick Lazaris, a veteran executive who once served as chief of staff to West Virginia governor (now senator) Jay Rockefeller, be brought on. In 1998, after eight years of development, Keurig released an industrial-strength, single-serve machine that delivered a perfect cup of coffee or tea every time.

Keurig was a technology company in the coffee industry. Keurig brewers represented a fusion of technology and design. To maintain and enhance its position as a leader in the gourmet single-cup market, Keurig invested significant resources and capital in engineering and research and development. This led to a strong and growing portfolio of market-leading, proprietary technology. Keurig's integrated engineering team drove fast and innovative product development in all three areas that supported Keurig's single-cup system: brewers, portion packs, and high-speed packaging lines that manufactured the portion packs. Keurig's integrated approach to new product development has resulted in accelerated new product launches since 2004. Keurig employed over 30 degreed engineers from varied disciplines. The engineering team at Keurig included mechanical, software, and nutritional science, as well as quality assurance and industrial engineering. As of 2009,

Keurig held 26 U.S. and 65 international patents covering its portion packs, packaging line, and brewer technology (72 were utility patents and 19 were design patents), and Keurig had additional patent applications in process. The Keurig system was based on three fundamental elements:

1. A patented and proprietary portion-pack system (K-Cup) that used a specially designed filter and was sealed in a low-oxygen environment to ensure freshness (see Exhibit 3).
2. Specially designed, proprietary high-speed packaging lines that manufactured K-Cups at the coffee roaster's facilities using fresh-roasted and ground coffee (or tea).
3. Brewers that precisely controlled the amount, temperature, and pressure of water to provide a consistently superior cup of coffee or tea in less than a minute when used with K-Cups.

Keurig's patented system eliminated the need to measure coffee or water—the two primary culprits for suboptimal java. With the Keurig system, pressurized hot water was filtered through a small plastic pod, called a K-Cup, that combined both filter and coffee (see Exhibit 4).

Keurig maintained a sizable quality control team to assist engineering in establishing quality standards; to communicate standards to all manufacturing partners, roasters, and suppliers; and to audit compliance with Keurig's established standards. The company's emphasis on quality products, easy-to-use features, and innovative technologies earned Keurig high marks in customer satisfaction, with 94 percent customer satisfaction from tracked brewer purchasers.

A licensing agreement enabled Green Mountain Coffee Roasters to package its high-quality Arabica beans in Keurig's patented container, the K-Cup. GMCR started distributing the new single-cup Keurig premium coffee system to office coffee service and food service providers in 1998. GMCR and Keurig sold the system through select distribution channels. The system featured the single-cup Keurig brewer and eight varieties of Green Mountain coffee, including blends, flavored, decafs, and estate coffees. Keurig's K-Cup packaging guaranteed that each cup of coffee was as fresh as "the first cup of every pot." Keurig's strategy to gain market share in the office market was to sell machines to distributors and encourage them to give the machines away or lease them for a small fee. The economics of the strategy worked for distributors because the real profit was in selling K-Cups. If an office went through 30 or 40 K-Cups per day, a distributor recouped the cost of the machine in less than six months of K-Cup sales.

When Keurig launched its first single-cup brewer for the office market in 1998, it partnered with Green Mountain Coffee to manufacture and sell Keurig's patented K-Cups. Although Green Mountain Coffee was the first roaster to sell its coffee in Keurig's single-cup brewing system, by 2003 GMCR was competing for Keurig's sales with three other North American roasters: Diedrich Coffee, Timothy's, and Van Houtte, a vertically integrated roaster and office coffee distributor in Canada and the United States. Since 2003, Keurig has licensed several additional coffee roasters to package gourmet coffee and teas into K-Cups, all of which paid royalties to Keurig based on the number of K-Cups shipped. For each K-Cup shipped, roasters paid

The magic behind Keurig Brewed® freshness and taste

Air-tight Foil Lid

Pressurized Hot Water Flows Through for Precise Brewing
Freshly Ground 100% Gourmet Arabica Beans
Self Contained Paper Filter

Oxygen, Light and Humidity Barrier

RESULT: Coffee House Taste By The Cup®

Exhibit 3 **The Keurig K-Cup**

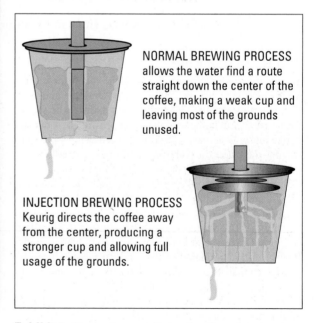

NORMAL BREWING PROCESS allows the water find a route straight down the center of the coffee, making a weak cup and leaving most of the grounds unused.

INJECTION BREWING PROCESS Keurig directs the coffee away from the center, producing a stronger cup and allowing full usage of the grounds.

Exhibit 4 **Normal versus Injection Brewing Process**

Keurig a royalty of approximately $.04. This unique licensing-agreement system enabled Keurig to offer the industry's widest selection of gourmet-brand coffees and teas in a proprietary single-cup format. The wide coffee selection proved to be a key differentiator for Keurig's brewing system. Consumers could choose from 11 gourmet brands and over 130 varieties of coffees and teas in K-Cups. As of 2006, more than 1 billion cups of Keurig Brewed coffee and tea had been consumed since Keurig launched in 1998.[11] Green Mountain Coffee continued to be the leading K-Cup roaster, accounting for 57 percent of K-Cups shipped in fiscal 2008.[12] As of 2008, more than 2 billion K-Cups had been shipped since 1998 (see Exhibit 5).[13]

In 1998, GMCR held a minority investment of less than 5 percent in Keurig, Inc. This partnership with Keurig developed into an important growth driver in fiscal 2000, as the unique Keurig one-cup brewing system gained momentum in the marketplace. K-Cup sales made up 15.7 percent of total sales at GMCR in fiscal 2000. GMCR's partnership with Keurig continued to be an important growth driver in fiscal 2001, with K-Cup sales accounting for 20.4 percent of total revenue for GMCR. Keurig's ownership structure changed in 2002 as a result of agreements with GMCR and Van Houtte. Keurig sold stock to Van Houtte, raising $10 million to seed Keurig's at-home business launch. The investment secured Van Houtte a 28 percent ownership position in Keurig. Simultaneously, GMCR invested $15 million, by acquiring and executing stock options, to purchase 42 percent of Keurig. As a result of these strategic moves, GMCR and Van Houtte joined Memorial Drive Trust (MDT) as the top-three shareholders of Keurig. MDT, an investment advisory firm, had been the primary venture investor in Keurig since 1995 and led Keurig's board of directors. Separate shareholder agreements with MDT, however, restricted both GMCR and Van Houtte from holding a seat on Keurig's board of directors. In a 2002 article, Nick Lazaris was quoted as saying: "Keurig has not had, nor does it expect to have, any single shareholder owning a majority of Keurig's stock. GMCR will be joining Van Houtte and Memorial Drive Trust, as one of Keurig's largest shareholders. Led by Memorial Drive Trust, a U.S. based profit-sharing plan

Exhibit 5   Keurig K-Cup Shipments, All Roasters

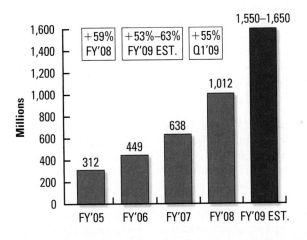

Company-wide Keurig brewer and K-Cup portion pack shipments (Unaudited data in thousands)					
	52 wks. Ended Sept. 27, 2008	52 wks. Ended Sept. 29, 2007	53 wks. Ended Sept. 30, 2006	Percent Growth 2008	Percent Growth 2007
At Home Brewers (Consumer)	883	422	219	109	93
Away from Home Brewers (Commercial)	100	57	28	75	104
Total Keurig brewers shipped	983	479	247	105	94
Total K-Cups shipped (system-wide)	1,012,356	637,823	448,880	59	42
Total K-Cups sold by GMC	578,939	359,056	255,412	61	41

Source: Keurig Inc.

that has served as the lead venture investor in Keurig since 1995, Keurig's Board of Directors remains fully in control of Keurig's business strategy, and no roaster or other commercial business partner will have a seat on Keurig's Board of Directors."[14] Nick Lazaris defended Keurig's independence from roasters in a letter to Keurig's distributors and other roasters:

> Our core strategy remains unchanged: we are committed to a multi-roaster strategy that relies on strong relationships with selected gourmet coffee roasters who take a great deal of pride in the coffee consumption experience that supports the meaning of their brand to consumers.[15]

As of 2005, Keurig remained effectively controlled by MD Co. (controlled by MDT), which owned approximately 23 percent of Keurig's capital stock. As a result of contractual limitations and restrictions agreed to by GMCR and certain other stockholders of Keurig, MD Co. retained the ability to elect a majority of Keurig's board of directors, make certain types of amendments to Keurig's certificate of incorporation, and approve or reject a sale of Keurig's business. In June 2006, GMCR completed its acquisition of Keurig for $104.3 million.

Expanding Keurig's Family of Brands

In addition to offering Green Mountain Coffee and GMCR's affiliated Newman's Own Organics and Celestial Seasonings Tea brands, which were packaged and sold by Green Mountain Coffee, Keurig offered several other North American K-Cup brands as of year-end 2006: Diedrich, Gloria Jean's, Coffee People, Timothy's, Emeril's, Van Houtte, Bigelow, Tully's, and Twinings.

In January 2007, Keurig, Inc., and Caribou Coffee, the second-largest publicly traded gourmet coffee company in the United States in terms of number of retail stores, announced a partnership to market Caribou's gourmet coffees in Keurig K-Cups. "We are proud to welcome Caribou to the Keurig family," stated Nick Lazaris, former president of Keurig. "Caribou is an exceptionally strong brand with a loyal following among gourmet coffee lovers. Our office and home Keurig users will be delighted with Caribou in K-Cups.[16] . Under license from Caribou Coffee, Keurig served as the wholesale distributor and a direct retailer for Caribou Coffee K-Cups. In addition, many Keurig premium retail partners added Caribou Coffee K-Cups to the selection of K-Cups already carried in 6,700 stores coast to coast. For the office coffee channel, Caribou Coffee K-Cups were offered through Keurig's authorized distributors for marketing to offices at which Keurig brewers were installed. Caribou marketed both Caribou Coffee K-Cups and Keurig brewers in many of its coffeehouses.

As Keurig gained momentum across the United States, the diversity of the K-Cup brand portfolio increased in importance because regional preferences could not be underestimated as national penetration progressed.

The addition of Caribou Coffee, a strong Midwest brand, helped build K-Cup sales and introduce Green Mountain Coffee to areas beyond its core market.

In September 2008, GMCR announced an asset purchase agreement to acquire the Tully's coffee brand and wholesale business. Tully's was a well-respected specialty coffee roaster, with Pacific Northwest roots and heritage. The Tully's wholesale business division distributed coffee to over 5,000 supermarkets, located primarily in the western states, and also sold coffee in K-Cup portion packs. The Tully's acquisition was designed to provide GMCR with a complementary West Coast brand and business platform to facilitate future geographic growth and brand expansion.

Keurig's Management Information System

Calli Prendergast, vice president of Information Systems at Keurig, stated, "By having e-Commerce (third party) manage our applications (accounting, e-Commerce, and Customer Relationship Management), we can focus on serving our customers better and growing our business." Before Keurig evolved from its traditional away-from-home, business-to-business (B2B) product offering, served through KADs, to a new line of at-home, business-to-consumer (B2C) products, it was evident that a new system was needed to process the large number of transactions Keurig handled each day and incorporate sufficient reserve capacity for the large amount of projected sales growth. It was determined that Keurig could reap significant cost and efficiency benefits by integrating the new system with its existing back-end ERP and front-end CRM system. Keurig contracted ePartners, a Microsoft-based software and services consultancy, to design and implement a system consisting of an integrated suite of products. The complete solution included a system based on Microsoft Dynamics GP (formerly Great Plains), Microsoft Commerce Server, Great Plains Siebel Front Office, and Microsoft SQL Server. The system included a highly customized, easy-to-use, and professional B2B and B2C e-commerce site with full integration to Great Plains and Great Plains Siebel Front Office. The solution was deployed in an application outsourcing (hosted) model for high availability and access throughout the world through ePartners and Data Return. At the outset of Keurig's at-home product line, the e-commerce system served as the only means of order entry for the consumer marketplace. The system increased the efficiency of Keurig's customer service agents (CSAs) by enabling them to gain direct access to the customer's order without having to wait for a report from the accounting department. Issue resolution times decreased significantly, resulting in higher levels of customer satisfaction. The accounting staff also improved their efficiency because the system eliminated the need to retrieve order information for CSAs. The hosted nature of the system allowed Keurig to keep IT costs low, maintain high availability, and focus on selling

Keurig systems. The IT system served as the foundation for Keurig's ongoing business and allowed Keurig to keep pace with the tremendous growth it continued to experience.

Keurig's Organizational Culture under the Leadership of Nick Lazaris

In March 2008, Lazaris resigned to pursue other career opportunities, including teaching entrepreneurial management in a turnaround environment at Harvard Business School. Lawrence J. Blanford, president and CEO of GMCR, said, "On behalf of the entire Board and everyone at GMCR, I would like to thank Nick Lazaris for his outstanding leadership, passion and guidance. I have great admiration for Nick's intelligence, integrity and entrepreneurial skills culminating in creating such an outstanding, fast-growth business. Under his strong leadership, Keurig is now the #1 single-cup office and home coffee brewing system in North America. Nick was appropriately recognized when he received the 2006 Entrepreneur of the Year Award from Ernst & Young."

Robert Stiller, chairman and founder of GMCR, said, "Nick Lazaris truly is a great American entrepreneur. The Keurig brewer was under development for several years prior to Nick joining Keurig, but I credit his great leadership with transforming a promising opportunity into a thriving business by introducing a successful single-cup system to the market. He assembled a talented, creative and deep leadership team at Keurig as well as an extensive and strong supply chain to support its rapid growth."

Lazaris said, "I am very proud of my partners on the Keurig team. . . . Together, we not only developed high quality, innovative single-cup brewing technologies, but we developed innovative 'go to market' strategies to create the single-cup market category and built a defensible position against competitors many times our size."[17]

Lazaris received a BS from MIT in 1972 and an MBA from Harvard in 1975. Serving as chief of staff to West Virginia governor Jay Rockefeller in the late 1970s and early 1980s, Lazaris had a learning experience that he carried over to Keurig. Following his stint in the public sector, Lazaris worked for the Barry Wright Corporation, a manufacturer of products that handled and protected data records. In 1989, Lazaris started Carr Picture Frames, where he was the vice president of sales and marketing. He left in 1995 and moved on to Office Specialists, where he was the general manager of the Tech Specialists Division. In 1997 Lazaris was recruited to become president of Keurig, Inc.

At Keurig, Lazaris set clear objectives and regularly measured his progress toward them. His management style placed emphasis on regular communication among the management team by holding weekly meetings. He believed that being able to respond to objectives required effective communication. Lazaris said that he "listens, thinks, analyzes, and acts before making decisions in business and follows the Keurig mantra: hard work, smart work, and teamwork."[18] Lazaris held over 10 U.S. patents in addition to several international patents. In a September 2004 interview with *Appliance Magazine,* Lazaris stated, "I liken myself to a composer writing a symphony, where each of the senior managers has a role to play, much like a person in an orchestra has an instrument to play."

An entrepreneurial environment was fostered at Keurig that encouraged innovation and independent thinking. The entrepreneurial spirit was defined as a can-do attitude, a determination to succeed in extremely challenging times, and the ability to motivate others to look for solutions during those dark moments. Lazaris said, "An entrepreneur is fundamentally someone who's able to take an idea or a product or service and create an organization that is self-sustaining in the marketplace, generating both sales and profits."

Corporate Social Responsibility Shaped the Organizational Culture at GMCR

Green Mountain was committed to conducting its business in a socially responsible manner. The company believed that doing well financially could go hand in hand with giving back to the community and protecting the environment. In its 2008 annual report, GMCR stated that its success was supported by its long-standing commitment to social and environmental responsibility. That commitment, combined with GMCR's entrepreneurial spirit and highly engaged workforce, enhanced GMCR's competitive advantage and provided the company an "opportunity to create better coffee, and brew a better world." GMCR allocated at least 5 percent of its pretax profits to social and environmental projects every year. GMCR posted its Corporate Social Responsibility Report at www.BrewingABetterWorld.com.

GMCR worked to protect the environment. Waste reduction and responsible energy use were two of its top priorities, and had been since 1983, when GMCR began composting in its retail coffee shops. In 1989, GMCR developed Earth-Friendly coffee filters. More recent examples of GMCR's commitment to protecting the environment included working with International Paper to bring to market the world's first to-go cup made with renewable materials, installing an on-site biodiesel fueling station, and embracing carbon offsets.

As the single-cup coffee market and Keurig brewing systems grew in popularity, GMCR understood that the environmental impact of the system was one of its most significant challenges. Finding a more environmentally friendly approach to the packaging challenge posed by the K-Cup portion-pack waste stream was a big priority for GMCR. The company was actively researching alternatives to the petroleum-based materials that made up the majority of Keurig K-Cup packaging. GMCR commissioned Life-Cycle Analysis in 2008 to help quantitatively understand the environmental impact of the K-Cup portion pack, as compared to using a typical drip brewer, and identify the best opportunities to reduce its impact. GMCR worked to identify the right definition of *environmentally friendly* for the Keurig system and all its packaging. Since the term *environmentally friendly* can mean many things (carbon-neutral, biodegradable, compostable, petroleum-free, etc.), GMCR was researching what was possible today and tomorrow, taking into account the current state of packaging technology, consumer preferences, community infrastructure, performance requirements, and the demands of the marketplace. GMCR continued to offer the My K-Cup product, a reusable filter assembly that could be refilled by the consumer, could be easily cleaned, and was compatible with all Keurig home brewers presently sold. On the brewer side, all Keurig engineers had been trained in the European RoHS directive, which restricted the use of certain hazardous substances in electrical and electronic

equipment, and GMCR intended that all Keurig brewers be RoHS-compliant by the end of 2008.

Keurig Fueled Sales Growth at GMCR

In fiscal 2008, GMCR net sales increased by $158.6 million, or 46 percent, as compared to fiscal 2007 (see Exhibit 6). Net sales for the Keurig segment were $253.6 million in fiscal 2008 (including $39.2 million of intercompany brewer sales and royalty revenue), an increase of over 188 percent (see Exhibit 7) compared to fiscal 2007. As a reseller, Keurig placed K-Cups and brewers side by side in outlets such as Bed Bath & Beyond, Macy's, and Target, as well as many more. Keurig merchandised brewers and K-Cups in over 16,000 retail outlets in fiscal 2008 (see Exhibit 8). When sold through resellers, Green Mountain coffee is typically one of several roasters represented. Showcasing the entire family of K-Cup roasters accelerated brewer penetration by increasing consumer acceptance outside GMCR's core

Exhibit 6   Summary Financial Data (in thousands except per-share data)

	52 wks. Ended Sept. 27, 2008	52 wks. Ended Sept. 29, 2007	53 wks. Ended Sept. 30, 2006	52 wks. Ended Sept. 24, 2005	52 wks. Ended Sept. 25, 2004
Select Statement of Operations Data:					
Coffee pounds shipped	32,000	26,818	24,613	19,879	17,734
Net sales	$500,277	$341,651	$225,323	$161,536	$137,444
Gross profit	$176,905	$131,121	$ 82,034	$ 56,975	$ 54,084
Income before equity in earnings of Keurig Inc., net of tax benefit	$ 22,299	$ 12,843	$ 9,406	$ 9,448	$ 8,901
Equity in earnings of Keurig, Inc. net of tax benefit	N/A	N/A	($936)	($492)	($1,076)
Net income	$ 22,299	$ 12,843	$ 8,443	$ 8,956	$ 7,825
Net income per diluted share	$ 0.87	$ 0.52	$ 0.36	$ 0.39	$ 0.35
Weighted average shares outstanding	25,565	24,773	23,727	23,000	22,227
Select Balance Sheet Data: (at end of period)					
Working capital	$ 79,170	$ 30,775	$ 29,150	$ 17,172	$ 11,723
Total assets	$357,648	$264,527	$234,006	$ 91,147	$ 78,332
Long-term debt	$123,517	$ 90,050	$102,968	$ 8,748	$ 17,298
Stockholders' equity	$139,520	$ 90,099	$ 74,940	$ 60,392	$ 44,415
Long-term debt/equity	88.50%	90.90%	137.40%	14.50%	38.90%
Return on equity	18.60%	14.80%	12.50%	17.10%	19.70%

Source: Green Mountain Coffee, Inc. 2008, 2007 and 2004 Annual Report

Exhibit 7   Green Mountain Coffee and Keurig: Net Sales (before taxes, in millions)

				Percent Sales Growth	
	2008	2007	2006	2008	2007
Green Mountain Coffee	$246.7	$242.0	$207.6	1.9%	16.6%
Keurig	$253.6	$134.8	$ 24.1	88.1%	4.6%
Inter-company eliminations	$ 0.0	−$ 35.1	−$ 6.4	—	4.5%
Total Company	$500.3	$341.7	$225.3	46.4%	51.7%

Source: Green Mountain Coffee, Inc. 2008 and 2007 Annual Report

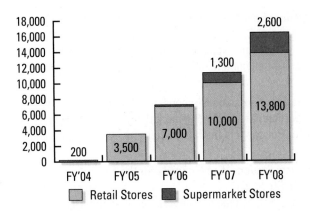

Exhibit 8 Retail Stores and Supermarkets Selling Keurig at-Home Brewers

Exhibit 9 Keurig Brewer Shipments (all channels)

market and underscored the variety available through the Keurig system. In fiscal 2008, GMCR shipped 983,000 Keurig at-home and away-from-home brewers, an increase of 105 percent over the previous year's shipments (see Exhibit 9). The number of K-Cups shipped by all licensed roasters increased 59 percent over the previous year.

Challenges Brewing at Keurig

Nick Lazaris led Keurig as a technology-driven company during a time when purchasers of single-serve coffee machines were "innovators" and "early adopters." These were the customers purchasing new technology, before it had been perfected and before the price came down. In transitioning Keurig from a technology- to a marketing-driven company, Michelle Stacey's challenge was to develop a strategy for transforming an idea that made sense to early adopters—"Why do we brew coffee by the pot when we drink it by the cup?"—into one that made sense to the early majority. The marketing plan refinement and execution would become increasingly

more critical if single-cup brewers approached the tipping point. Keeping in mind that brewers sold today impact pod sales for the life of the brewer, what strategic approach should Keurig adopt under the leadership of Michelle Stacey?

During her career, Stacey had managed the integration of several acquisitions, a relevant experience given the formerly independent Keurig's ongoing integration as a wholly owned subsidiary of GMCR. But the entrepreneurial and innovative culture at Keurig, Inc., that Nick Lazaris had fostered was reminiscent of the old "Bell Labs," resulting in innovative technology. Was this core competence still relevant as Keurig transitioned from a technology- to a marketing-driven company?

Could elasticity of demand be incorporated into Keurig's strategy given the retail prices of Keurig's at-home brewers and K-Cups, consumer spending trends during the recession, and the value proposition of the K-Cup and My K-Cup versus competitive single-cup brewers and the retail prices at Starbucks?

Exhibit 10   Keurig Senior Management Team

- **Michelle Stacy—President:** Stacey brought more than 20 years of experience to Keurig, including marketing and global business management at the senior executive level with the Gillette Company and then Procter & Gamble (P&G). At P&G, Stacy was vice president and general manager of Global Professional Oral Care, where she managed the Global Professional activities for the Crest and Oral-B brands. Stacy has experience as a vice president of marketing in Blades and Razors and Personal Care. Stacy holds a BA in liberal arts from Dartmouth College and an MBA from Kellogg School at Northwestern University.

- **Dick Sweeney—Cofounder, Vice President of Manufacturing and Operations:** Sweeney cofounded Keurig in 1993 and joined the company full-time as one of its first employees in 1996. He brought to Keurig more than 25 years of experience in manufacturing, product development, and consulting in the area of industrial and consumer appliances. Sweeney has developed several U.S. and international Keurig brewer and packaging patents. Sweeney received his BS from New Jersey Institute of Technology and his MBA from Fairleigh Dickinson University.

- **Kevin Sullivan—Vice President of Engineering and Product Development:** Sullivan is responsible for all engineering at Keurig, including brewer development and K-Cup packaging. He joined Keurig in 2003, bringing more than 20 years of engineering experience in consumer appliances and high-volume consumer disposables. Sullivan earned an MBA from New Hampshire College and a BA in mechanical engineering from the University of Massachusetts–Amherst.

- **Basil Karanikos—Vice President of Packaging Engineering:** Karanikos is responsible for all engineering and product development surrounding Keurig's K-Cup portion pack, including packaging manufacturing equipment. Karanikos received his BSEE from Worcester Polytechnic Institute, where he also continued his graduate studies.

- **Chris Stevens—Vice President of Sales, At-Work Division:** Stevens is responsible for the North America Sales Organization in Keurig's Away-from-Home Division. Stevens joined Keurig in 1996, bringing more than 20 years of experience in consumer goods sales and marketing as well as general management. His sales team recruits, trains, and manages all of Keurig's authorized distributors in the United States and Canada. Stevens received his BS from Notre Dame and completed the Executive Education program at Columbia Business School.

- **Dave Manley—Vice President of At-Work Division and Consumer Direct:** Manley is responsible for Keurig marketing in the channels of away-from-home, Keurig Consumer Direct on www.keurig.com, and hotels. Manley joined Keurig in 2002 after more than 20 years of executive experience in consumer goods sales and marketing. Manley received his BA from DePauw University and his MBA from Purdue University.

- **John Whoriskey—Vice President, General Manager of At-Home Division:** Whoriskey is responsible for Keurig's At-Home Division, including the retail business. Whoriskey joined Keurig in 2002, bringing over 20 years of experience that included president and VP-level experience in marketing and sales in the home furnishing, gift, and consumer products industries. Whoriskey received his BS and MBA from Boston College.

- **Mark Wood—Vice President of New Business:** Wood is responsible for new business development at Keurig, including managing the relationships with K-Cup licensed roaster partners, and international opportunities. Wood received his BA from the University of Rochester and his MBA from Harvard.

- **Mike Degnan—Vice President, General Counsel:** Degnan manages legal affairs for Keurig, including leadership of outside counsel in the areas of contracts and patents. Degnan received both his BS and JD from Boston College.

- **Ian Tinkler—Vice President of Brewer Engineering:** Tinkler leads Keurig's brewer engineering effort. Tinkler joined Keurig in 2005, bringing more than 25 years of engineering experience. He holds an MBA from Rockford College and a mechanical engineering degree from Hatfield Polytechnic in England.

- **John Heller—Vice President of Finance:** Heller is responsible for the accounting, finance, and procurement functions at Keurig. Heller joined Keurig in 2007. He received his BS from USMA and his MBA from Duke University and is a licensed CPA.

Appendix A   The 10 Top-Selling Single-Serve Coffee Makers*

1. **Keurig Special Edition B60 ($149):** "The B60 features a 5.25, 7.25, and 9.25 oz setting for different cup sizes, a programmable clock, blue back lighting and has the ability to adjust the temperature down 5 degrees from 192 F. This is the most pimped out coffee maker we've ever owned. The handle on the K-Cup jaws is also tricked out with chrome. The only big difference in the LED features is the ability to adjust the brew temperature. We did adjust it up and down and it works."

2. **Keurig Elite B40 ($99):** "The Keurig Elite B40 features a 7.25 oz Brew, a removable reservoir tank, and auto turn off after 2 hours which you can set on or off. For a single purpose, make me a great cup of coffee machine the B40 at $99.95 couldn't be better. The coffee it produces is of the same quality as the B60. Unlike the B60 where you can adjust the temperature, the B40 comes out at 192 F and brews a great cup of coffee.

   We think that the Keurig B40 and B60 models are a good buy. We really like the Keurig B60 because of the blue lights and travel mug settings the most. Keurig K-Cups cost $13.95 for a box of 24 or about $0.58/K-Cup."

3. **Aeropress Single-Serve Coffee Maker ($30):** "You will need espresso ground coffee from either your grinder or by purchasing some pre-ground coffee, but making a cup of Aeropress coffee is very easy and intended to make one cup of perfect coffee or espresso. To start, you'll need a decent coffee grinder to get the nice fine grind the Aeropress likes. Once you've ground up your coffee to a nice fine grind, the Aeropress comes with a measuring spoon to make sure you put the right amount in the chamber. The Aeropress is an entirely new way to make coffee. You could compare it to a French press but you would be wrong. Because of an almost giant syringe like coffee gadget, you build air pressure by pushing espresso ground coffee through the chamber with a filter paper on the bottom of the Aeropress."

4. **Keurig Mini B30 ($79):** "Keurig recently introduced the Keurig B30 commercial hotel and office coffee brewer followed by the Keurig Mini B30 designed for home and commercial use. The Keurig B30 is very similar to the Keurig B130, but it comes in red, black, and white colored casings, and is also My K Cup compatible. Simply getting a fresh cup of water to use in the Keurig B30 each time was not time consuming, and waiting for the brewer to heat up for the 3 minutes was also not that long of a time. On the larger Keurig models, coffee is more immediate than on the Keurig B30."

5. **Braun TA1400 Tassimo ($169):** "The *Tassimo* utilizes a new hot beverage brewing system in the form of T-Discs. Each T-Disc has a bar code on it to tell the machine how the hot beverage needs to be prepared, and the brewing of the coffee happens inside each T-Disc as water is pushed through it. Tassimo makes: single serve coffee, crema coffee, espresso, lattes, cappuccinos, tea and hot chocolate. Tassimo was the first single-serve coffee system to have liquid milk instead of powdered milk to make cappuccinos and lattes. You don't have to keep the milk T-Discs cold because they are shelf stable and ultra-pasteurized. By using milk T-Discs to make a latte or cappuccino, the Tassimo eliminates the need for a steam wand or frothing attachment."

6. **Hamilton Beach BrewStation Deluxe 12-Cup Coffee Maker:** "The Hamilton Beach (HB) Coffeemaker may make 12 cups total like a typical drip coffee maker, but it dispenses them one cup at a time. The HB has all the bells and whistles you'd expect for a drip coffee maker with the convenience of single serve coffee, however the cleanup and brewing of the coffee takes longer than what you get using a single serve coffee maker like the Senseo or Keurig systems."

7. **Keurig Platinum B70 K-Cup Single-Cup Brewer ($199):** "The difference from the Keurig B70 compared with the B40 and B60 is a smaller footprint, larger reservoir and reduced noise during brewing. There is a new look and design for the Keurig B70. It's thinner and sleeker than the B60. We liked the new closing mechanism for inserting the K Cup into the Keurig B70, and found it closes easier. We were disappointed that for $199.95 you didn't get a charcoal water filter in the B70. Though we use filtered water at SingleServeCoffee.com, many people don't have this option and it makes a big difference. We hope in the future Keurig offers a water filter option so you get the best cup possible if you don't have filtered water. We tried coffee from all 3 different models—the B40, B60, and B70—and found the coffee all to be the same when brewed at the standard 7.25 oz setting. We also used the K Cup re-useable coffee filter in all the models and found the coffee to be nearly the same."

8. **Bosch Tassimo Suprema Single-Serve Brewer/Hot-Beverage System ($139):** "The Tassimo hot beverage system has been out in the U.S. for the past two years, and when it launched was made by Braun. In 2007 Tassimo decided they needed to update the system, and went with a new partner—Bosch. The new Bosch Tassimo is completely redesigned. Gone is the loud brewing, the spill back of water after brewing a cup, and the unit heats and brews much faster. We tested the Tassimo TAS4511UC model; there is also a $99.99 Bosch Tassimo available in select grocery and mass merchandise stores. The main difference in the two models is the water reservoir filtration, and aesthetics. One question that will come up with any single-serve coffee system, "Can I use my own coffee?" Not with the Tassimo hot beverage system, but the *Tassimo* does offer single serve coffee from Starbucks and Seattle's Best. There are over 30 other coffee blends and flavors available in T Disc format."

9. **Bosch Tassimo Suprema:** See review for number 8.

10. **Breville BKC600XL Gourmet K-Cup Brewer ($299):** "*Breville* is widely known for making exceptional small kitchen appliances, and for producing very attractive small appliances. Keurig and Breville teamed up to introduce a high end Keurig brewer designed by Breville. The results were exceptional—a very polished interesting stainless steel design, with Keurig K Cup brewing technology, and all the features you can get in any Keurig machine—including the re-useable My K Cup integrated into the machine, allowing you to use your own ground coffee instead of K Cups, and a charcoal water filter in the tank reservoir. If you want a super attractive K-Cup single serve coffee maker, and are willing to pay $100 more and get all the features of any Keurig brewer, then the Breville Brewer is for you.. We think the design alone is worth the premium—this brewer screams high end."

*From SingleServeCoffee.com, December 8, 2008.

Endnotes

1. "Green Mountain Coffee Roasters Announces Appointment of Michelle V. Stacey as Keurig, Inc. President," *Business and Finance Week* (Atlanta), November 1, 2008, p. 215.
2. Nestlé S.A.
3. *Datamonitor.*
4. Katy Marquardt, "Brewing Profits, a Cup at a Time: Green Mountain Heats Up the Single-Serve Coffee Market," *U.S. News & World Report,* November 17, 2008, p. 55.
5. Specialty Coffee Association of America and National Coffee Association, personal interviews, 2005.
6. *Business 2.0,* October 2006, p. 62.
7. Specialty Coffee Association of America and the National Coffee Association.
8. Marquardt, "Brewing Profits, a Cup at a Time."
9. Mike Duff, "Latest Brewers May Serve Up Sales, Good Coffee," *Retailing Today,* April 23, 2007, p. 46.
10. Green Mountain Coffee Roasters, Annual Report, 2007.
11. www.cariboucoffee.com, press releases, April 14, 2007.
12. Green Mountain Coffee Roasters, Annual Report, 2008.
13. Ibid.
14. *Canadian Corporate News,* February 2, 2002.
15. Internal memo, February 5, 2002.
16. *Business Wire,* January 8, 2007.
17. *Business Wire,* March 31, 2008.
18. *Appliance Magazine,* 2004.

Case 30   Weight Watchers International Inc.*

Weight Watchers, while the undeniable industry standard, had lost some of its luster by 2009 as many potential consumers considered it the prior generation's answer to weight loss or simply not the right weight loss choice for them. Originally started in 1963 by Jean Nidetch as a support group for women in her home, Weight Watchers International Inc. had grown into a multibillion-dollar weight-loss goliath in a matter of four decades' time. Aware of this stigma, Weight Watchers had set out that year to reinvent itself.

The market for weight-loss products was growing and obesity levels were on the rise in more and more parts of the world, which made weight management an attractive industry for firms, especially deeply entrenched firms such as Weight Watchers. However, faced with increased competition from other firms, most notably NutriSystem Inc., Weight Watchers had to increase customer value and seek new target segments to preempt the competition and stay on top of its promising industry. In the highly competitive weight management industry, Weight Watchers International Inc. was in a position where it had to remain cognizant of the major trends that, at the time, had the potential to adversely affect industry and firm profitability and revenues. Those trends, as they related to Weight Watchers and the weight-loss industry, included the temporary emergence of fad diets, decreased effectiveness of marketing and advertising programs, the need for the development of new and innovative products and services, the development of more favorably perceived or more effective weight management methods (such as pharmaceuticals), and the threat of impairment of the Weight Watchers brand and other intellectual property.[1]

The challenge for Weight Watchers was repositioning itself and creating a forward-focused diet plan for the 21st century while staying true to the mission initially established by Jean Nidetch, Weight Watcher's founder. The brand needed to remain relevant and, at the same time, pursue additional medium- to long-term initiatives, such as reaching out to new market segments.[2] How could Weight Watchers retain market leadership while staying hip, relevant, and preemptive? While Weight Watchers had made the effort to introduce new products for several years and had been in the process of shifting its strategic focus from narrow- to broad-based differentiation, the question still remained whether the company could stay true to its core

values, mission, and models and, at the same time, embrace effective expansion.

In 2007, Weight Watchers attempted to reinvent itself through the introduction of marketing and product innovations both in the United States and abroad. It began to look beyond its core market of women, expanded its business model, launched new programs, and rejuvenated its brand. However, the continued expansion and innovation initiatives raised several concerns. Will this expansion in scope move Weight Watchers too far from its original mission and core philosophy? Will the extensions of the Weight Watchers brand succeed at attracting new members without losing the existing ones?

History and Expansion

Jean Nidetch began Weight Watchers in an unlikely, and unintended, way. The origins of Weight Watchers started when Jean invited six women into her home to help both herself and her neighbors and friends lose weight by communally discussing their weight-loss issues. Nidetch's belief, which became the core of the Weight Watchers philosophy, was that anyone could be given a "diet" but the group and social setting of "talk therapy" was the true component not only to losing weight but also *to keeping it off*. She believed in the fostering of success through group support, and she created a simple reward system that included pins and tie bars to reward increments of weight loss. The idea was so simple, yet so effective![3]

The basic concept of the Weight Watchers plan, as it existed in 2009, consisted of two components. First, there was the Weight Watchers program, and second, there was the group support. The program was essentially a food plan and an activity plan. The food plan was intended to provide people with the educational tools they needed for weight loss as well as to provide control mechanisms so that individuals could find their way to healthier food choices.[4] The company radically simplified the food selection process involved in dieting by assigning each food a corresponding Point value, which eliminated the need to tally calories.[5] In the past, Weight Watchers had been recognized more for its food plan, but by 2009 it was getting noticed for its activity plan as well.[6]

Nidetch accomplished what she set out to do and so much more. Weight Watchers, targeting primarily women, ages 25 to 55, experienced a rapid expansion. Of the behemoth that Weight Watchers came to be, Nidetch said, "My little group became an industry. I really didn't mean it to—it was really just a club for me and my fat friends." She continued by commenting on something a lecturer once said, "It's a place where you walk in fat and hope nobody notices you, and four or five months later you walk out thin and hope that everyone sees you." Nidetch believed that

*This case was developed by Professor Alan B. Eisner, Pace University; Professor Helaine J. Korn, Baruch College–City University of New York; and graduate student Jennifer M. DiChiara, Pace University. Material has been drawn from published sources to be used for class discussion. Copyright © 2009 Alan B. Eisner.

the love, information, companionship, and commiseration of fellow overweight individuals were the key components needed for the effective formula many people needed to succeed at weight loss. This idea has been perpetuated at Weight Watchers and has been translated into meeting leadership—all employees who now lead meetings are formerly overweight individuals who were successful on the plan.[7]

What Weight Watchers evolved into was a global branded consumer company providing weight management services in nearly 30 countries. By 2009, Weight Watchers was selling a wide range of branded products and services, including meetings conducted by Weight Watchers International and its franchisees (and the products sold at the meetings), Internet subscriptions to WeightWatchers.com (the company's Internet answer to weight management), licensed products sold by retailers, magazine subscriptions, and other publications.[8] In addition, the company had put its name and Point values on a variety of food products sold in supermarkets, such as Progresso soups,[9] and it had created a separate Weight Watchers menu for Applebee's restaurants.[10] Gradual expansion and the onset of the dot-com era inevitably led to the creation of WeightWatchers.com, an Internet-based version of the Weight Watchers plan designed to increase brand awareness.

WeightWatchers.com

WeightWatchers.com, as it existed in 2009, offered two subscription options: Weight Watchers Online and Weight Watchers eTools.[11] At the time, WeightWatchers.com was the leading Internet-based weight management provider in the world.[12] It held the position of market leader in the Internet category, with a growing business that still had relatively low awareness in the mind of the average weight-loss consumer.[13] However, the company also initiated TV advertising for Weight Watchers Online, as well as launching Weight Watchers Online for Men.[14]

In 2009, WeightWatchers.com was not only the leading subscription-based weight-loss site on the Internet but also the official Web site for Weight Watchers International Inc. It offered information on the Weight Watchers plan, provided several paid and free weight-loss tools, and housed an online messaging board, a series of fitness videos, and so on. Weight Watchers eTools, which could be accessed through the site, offered an integrated, multifeature food diary with a database of over 29,000 foods, along with their corresponding Point values, a recipe database, a restaurant guide, and a personal weight tracker. All of these tools helped Weight Watchers to foster its primary mission: helping people lose weight.[15] WeightWatchers.com allowed the company, for the first time, to bring in an entirely new group of customers who might not have considered the program otherwise.[16]

Industry and Competitive Environment

While Weight Watchers International Inc. had experienced stock price volatility in the past, as had the majority of its competitors, because of rival weight management options such as the over-the-counter weight-loss drug *Alli,*

launched by GlaxoSmithKline in June 2006, there had been no widely supported "magic pill" option to weight management to date. In the absence of a safe and effective pharmaceutical alternative for weight loss, Weight Watchers and its competitors had faced a weight management industry characterized by not only competition but great opportunity as well. Along with expanding waistlines had come an expanding market for weight management companies, and the time had come for such companies to be creative and innovative in sustaining and increasing market positions. At that time, no firm had been able to fare so well for so long in an industry plagued with fad diets and "the next best thing," as Weight Watchers had been.

Obesity was on the rise in the developed countries, especially in North America, and Weight Watchers was well positioned to help consumers as they began their weight-loss battles.[17] In 2009, weight loss constituted a $30 billion–a-year industry in the United States alone.[18] Nearly one-third of Americans were reported to be on a diet, according to a *Restaurants & Institutions* New American Diner Study.[19] Further, the American Heart Association had estimated that 65 percent of the population was overweight.[20] Particularly noteworthy was the rise of U.S. baby boomers as a significant proportion of the dieting population as they came to be more health conscious and proactive in their weight management than prior generations had been and they were looking for new ways to gain control of their weight.[21] The obesity problem was not confined to the United States, however, and this made geographic expansion a possibility for weight-loss firms. For example, obesity was becoming an epidemic in Asia, a market that, at the time, was largely untapped in terms of weight loss.[22] In Europe too, nearly half of the continent's population was overweight.[23] Overall, the statistics proved there were tremendous opportunities in the weight-loss industry, and it became much harder to compete for the market share.

Weight Watchers was attempting to reinvent itself while still paying close attention to the moves of its weight-loss rivals. Competition for Weight Watchers International Inc. had included both price competition and competition from self-help, pharmaceutical, surgical, dietary supplement, and meal replacement products, as well as other weight management brands, diets, programs, and products.[24] The main competitors for Weight Watchers included Jenny Craig and Slim Fast as well as NutriSystem (Nasdaq: NTRI), Town Sports (Nasdaq: CLUB), eDiets (Nasdaq: DIET), and Life Time Fitness Inc. (NYSE: LTM).[25]

CEO Kirchhoff believed that most competitors were essentially in a different business than Weight Watchers was. He said, "Most of the companies that are out there aggressively marketing are in the business of providing and delivering meals. Weight Watchers is in the business of helping people change behavior. So in that sense, we're teaching people how to fish, and they are selling people fish."[26]

According to an article in *Consumer Reports,* it was determined that Weight Watchers offered dieters the best staying power. Weight Watchers earned the highest overall rating, on account of its nutritionally based diet, weekly meetings, and weigh-ins for behavioral support. *Consumer Reports* liked the facts that the plan did not exclude any food group and that its Point system encouraged low-fat, high-fiber meals. Slim Fast came in second and was recommended for dieters who did not like to spend time in the kitchen. The Zone was recommended for those who wanted a short-term, high-protein diet plan, while the Ornish plan was found to provide fairly large portions for low calories. Atkins' nutritional difficulties dropped its rating below those of the other diets. Exhibit 1 outlines the company's main competitors, their specialties, and their competitive advantages as presented by *Consumer Reports.* Jenny Craig, eDiets, South Beach Diet, and Volumetrics were also studied, but they were not ranked in the follow-up article, which cited a "lack of long-term, published clinical trials" on which to base the rankings.[27]

Business Model

Weight Watchers' business model yielded high profit margins and strong cash flow as a result of the company's low variable expenses and low capital expenditure requirements.[28] Revenues for Weight Watchers International Inc., as shown in Exhibit 2, were principally gained from meeting fees (members paid to attend weekly meetings), product sales (bars, cookbooks, and the like, sold as complements to weight management plans), online revenues (from Internet subscription products), and revenues gained from licensing (the placement of the Weight Watchers logo on certain foods and other products) and franchising (franchisees typically paid a royalty fee of 10 percent of their meeting fee).[29] The costs of running meetings were low, with part-time class instructors paid on a commission basis, and many meeting locations were rented hourly[30] in inexpensive local facilities such as churches. This lean organizational structure allowed wide profit margins.[31] Meeting fees were paid up front or at the time of the meeting by attendees, resulting in net negative working capital for Weight Watchers—an indication of cash-flow efficiency.[32]

What was perhaps most important about Weight Watchers' business model was its flexibility. The number of meetings could be adjusted according to demand and seasonal fluctuations. The business model's reliance on a variable cost structure had enabled the company to maintain high margins even as the number of meetings over the same time period was expanded. When attendance growth outpaced meeting growth, the gross margins of Weight Watchers typically improved. Since fiscal year 2001, Weight Watchers International has maintained an annual gross margin in the operating segment of 50 percent or more.[33]

UBS analyst Andrew McQuilling commented on Weight Watchers' achievement of a near-perfect business model. McQuilling said: "There are three things we can always count on: death, taxes, and people's tendency to overeat. Since 1977, sales [for Weight Watchers] have compounded at a 13 percent rate. It's a profitable business that satisfies a growing market, so to speak. Weight Watchers is not just a fad. It's a perfect business. It's as if it sells air. The company has a 40 percent return on invested capital. People pay a fee to join and then pay to attend meetings."[34]

Unlike the privately owned Jenny Craig and Curves, which maintained their own centers with food inventories, Weight Watchers kept its capital costs low by allowing its meetings to be held anywhere. This model has allowed Weight Watchers to gain entry into the workplace at wellness-minded companies via its Weight Watchers at Work Program.[35]

Performance

Despite the high leverage, Weight Watchers' financial health was considered "decent" at the time, according to a statement by Morningstar analyst Kristan Rowland. Bank of America analyst Scott Mushkin agreed, touting Weight Watchers' classroom-based approach as the only one with empirical evidence of success. The strong brand and doctor-recommended methods, it was expected, would help increase business for Weight Watchers as the fad diets faded out of fashion.[36] Exhibits 3 to 5 show financial statements of the firm.

Innovation

Domestically and abroad, Weight Watchers was fortunate enough to build on a foundation of four decades of weight management expertise that had allowed the company to become one of the most recognized and trusted brand names among weight-conscious consumers worldwide.[37]

The innovation initiatives at Weight Watchers were focused on the three main objectives: (1) rejuvenating the brand through use of more effective marketing, (2) providing more customer value through introduction of new products, and (3) broadening the customer mix by targeting new customer segments.

The Brand With regard to its brand, Weight Watchers had been fortunate to have consumers consider its brand credible and effective. The company needed to more adequately differentiate its lifestyle-based approach from the strictly dieting orientation utilized by many of its competitors. In a focus group for Weight Watchers, a woman who had considered joining expressed concern that her weight would be called out in public and that she would have to tell her whole weight-loss struggle as if she were at an Alcoholics Anonymous meeting. Thus, one of the primary challenges for Weight Watchers was to correct these types of misperceptions as to what Weight Watchers actually was.[38] Weight Watchers had the challenge of dispelling concerns that the meeting experience would be something akin to a "Biggest Loser" weigh-in and competition.

The second thing that Weight Watchers was trying to do was to reenergize the brand with more effective and differentiated marketing. In order to sustain Weight Watchers' brand image and combat some of the misconceptions in the consumer market, Weight Watchers International Inc. hired McCann Erickson, the U.S. advertising agency that reignited the MasterCard brand, to bring the same vitality to the

Exhibit 1 Competitors for Weight Watchers

Diet Name	Weight Watchers	Jenny Craig	Slim Fast	eDiets	Zone Diet (men's menu)	Atkins Diet	Ornish Diet	Volumetrics
				Competitors				
What it is	Venerable program that uses weekly meetings and weigh-ins for motivation and behavioral support for diet and exercise changes, or you can sign up for similar support online. Dieters either earn or spend "points" with food and exercise or consume specified foods on a "Core" plan. A vegetarian menu is available.	Dieters sign up for individual counseling and meal plans at company outlets, by phone, or online. Centerpiece of the diet is eating Jenny Craig–prepared foods of single-serving entrees and snacks, supplemented by dairy, salads, and other vegetables you prepare yourself. Vegetarian menu is also available.	Brand line of controlled-calorie shakes and bars, widely available in drugstores and supermarkets. Company Web site provides weekly menus. On standard meal plan, a bar or shake for breakfast and lunch with additional food. For dinner, a low-calorie meal you fix yourself.	Well-established online subscription diet site offers 24 meal plans customized for various eating preferences and desired weight loss. Membership includes access to support groups, experts, menu plans, and recipes. The standard eDiets.com weekly menu we analyzed met dietary guidelines and delivered the number of calories promised.	The "Zone" was created to be the ideal balance of food to keep blood sugar and hormones ready to fight obesity and diseases. To stay in the Zone, every meal must consist of 30% fat calories, 30% protein, and 40% carbs. Diet allows many fruits but practically no grains.	One of the more widely known low-carb diets starts with a two-week induction period that bans practically all carbs. The longer "ongoing weight loss" phase is only slightly less restrictive, gradually adding more fruits, vegetables, and wines.	Ultra low-fat vegetarian regimen bans all meat, fish, oils, alcohol, sugar, and white flour. Ornish's clinical studies have shown that strictly following the diet can prevent or reverse disease. He believes it is easier to make drastic changes in the diet than small ones.	Based on research at Penn State, diet aims to maximize the amount of food available per calorie, mainly by use of reduced-fat products, liberal addition of vegetables, and low-fat cooking techniques. Encourages first course of broth-based soup or low-calorie salad to take the edge off appetite.

Diet Name	Competitors							
	Weight Watchers	Jenny Craig	Slim Fast	eDiets	Zone Diet (men's menu)	Atkins Diet	Ornish Diet	Volumetrics
Pros and cons	Behavioral support is proved to increase adherence to any diet. Scored average on weight loss in this group but first in long-term adherence. Recipes judged to be appetizing and fairly easy to prepare.	Diet requires minimal food preparation and meets dietary guidelines. Published study of actual client histories revealed high dropout rate, though those who stuck with the plan lost considerable weight. Clinical trial had better adherence.	Menu we analyzed meets dietary guidelines. Convenient for people with little time or desire to cook. Clinical studies show above-average long-term weight loss but high long-term dropout rate.	Customizable plans are appealing, especially for those with wheat or lactose intolerances, but clinical studies find average adherence and below-average weight loss.	The recipes were judged simple to prepare. The meal plan had a good nutritional profile, but figuring out the diet without a meal plan involved a lot of math. Weight loss below average.	There's growing evidence that dieters on Atkins aren't as hungry as on some other diets. Many find it too restrictive, so long-term adherence is below average. Long-term weight loss is average. Its nutritional profile is far outside dietary guidelines.	Provides the most food per calorie of any diet evaluated. Lower in fat than guidelines recommend. Studies show average long-term weight loss and below-average long-term adherence.	Recent clinical trials show best overall weight loss of any diet evaluated. The recipes were judged to be appetizing but somewhat time-consuming to prepare.

Source: "Diet Plans," *Consumer Reports*, June 2007, pp. 16–17.

Exhibit 2 Weight Watchers' Revenue Sources (in millions)

	2008	2007	2006	2005
Meeting fees	$ 908.0	$ 880.7	$ 723.1	$ 681.1
Product sales	339.8	337.7	293.3	285.5
Online revenues	185.8	151.6	129.4	109.7
Licensing, franchise royalties and others	102.2	97.1	87.5	75
Total	$1,535.8	$1,467.2	$1,233.3	$1,151.3

Source: Weight Watchers International.

Exhibit 3 Income Statements (in thousands)

	2008	2007	2006
Total revenue	1,535,812	1,467,167	1,233,325
Cost of revenue	700,835	653,231	557,165
Gross profit	834,977	813,936	676,160
Operating expenses:			
Selling, general, and administrative	409,930	378,329	296,112
Operating income or loss	425,047	435,607	380,048
Income from continuing operations:			
Other income/expenses net	1,969	161	126
Earnings before interest and taxes	427,016	435,768	380,174
Interest expense	92,667	109,277	49,532
Income before tax	334,349	326,491	330,642
Income tax expense	132,002	125,311	120,817
Minority interest	1,984	—	—
Net income from continuing ops	204,331	201,180	209,825
Net income	204,331	201,180	209,825

Source: Yahoo! Finance.

Weight Watchers brand. It was hoped that by taking a fresh perspective on the way that Weight Watchers advertises and markets, McCann Erickson could differentiate Weight Watchers from the other, mostly unsuccessful, weight-loss and diet aids in order to position the company as more empathetic and contemporary to the consumer.[39] Of marketing, David Kirchhoff said: "I think we do a very good job of marketing to people who have been with us before, so-called rejoins, but I think we could do a much better job of marketing to people who have never been with us before."[40]

Weight Watchers believed that its advertising must accomplish three basic tasks. First, it had to be noticed when it was seen. Second, on noticing it, people had to associate the advertising with the Weight Watchers brand. Third, it had to accomplish both the first and the second aims while communicating something new about Weight Watchers that would cause consumers to reconsider Weight Watchers as their *solution*—a plan at which they could be successful.[41] Weight Watchers realized that it had not been doing a very good job of communicating any newness or innovation coming from within the company. Only by creating marketing activities that did a better job of relaying the meaningful benefits of Weight Watchers to consumers could the company convince people to join up. Consumers already had a perception of

Exhibit 4 Balance Sheets (in thousands)

	2008	2007	2006
Assets			
Current assets:			
Cash and cash equivalents	47,322	39,823	37,504
Net receivables	70,181	62,472	43,767
Inventory	40,121	44,607	38,548
Other current assets	67,417	39,434	34,927
Total current assets	**225,041**	**186,336**	**154,746**
Property plant and equipment	37,508	37,649	31,033
Goodwill	51,296	51,364	51,329
Intangible assets	777,103	751,730	712,930
Other assets	3,120	3,229	3,127
Deferred long-term asset charges	12,684	15,913	49,227
Total assets	**1,106,752**	**1,046,221**	**1,002,392**
Liabilities and Stockholders' Equity			
Current liabilities:			
Accounts payable	168,141	209,920	138,262
Short/current long-term debt	224,032	45,625	18,922
Other current liabilities	102,951	102,886	79,348
Total current liabilities	**495,124**	**358,431**	**236,532**
Long-term debt	1,485,000	1,602,500	830,237
Other liabilities	11,459	9,834	3,990
Deferred long-term liability charges	2,685	1,786	—
Total liabilities	**1,994,268**	**1,972,551**	**1,070,759**
Stockholders' equity:			
Retained earnings	1,131,080	950,213	770,539
Treasury stock	(1,684,828)	(1,570,054)	(540,318)
Other stockholders' equity	(333,768)	(306,489)	(298,588)
Total stockholders' equity	**(887,516)**	**(926,330)**	**(68,367)**
Net tangible assets	**(1,715,915)**	**(1,729,424)**	**(832,626)**

Source: Yahoo! Finance.

what Weight Watchers was. Accordingly, Weight Watchers had to actively emphasize the innovative things that it was doing in order to overcome consumers' preconceived notions.[42] The company needed to show its consumers that it was different from the other diets out there to unleash the power that Weight Watchers believed had become a little dormant in its brand.[43] Weight Watchers also had to consider the potential of marketing to relay relevant information that would appeal to a wider net of demographic groups.

The Program To increase customer value, Weight Watchers introduced two new programs that provided members with more flexibility and satisfaction. One innovation was the implementation of a Monthly Pass payment option. When a member became a Monthly Pass subscriber, he or she participated in an eight-month recurring billing commitment in exchange for complete access to the full range of product offerings, including meetings and eTools. So the underlying benefit was customization—members

Exhibit 5   Cash Flow Statements (in thousands)

	2008	2007	2006
Net income	204,331	201,180	209,825
Operating activities, cash flows provided by or used In:			
Depreciation	25,959	20,746	14,880
Adjustments to net income	29,769	39,744	47,335
Changes in accounts receivables	(343)	(2,099)	(10,656)
Changes in liabilities	7,408	70,728	22,936
Changes in inventories	(7,469)	(12,220)	(9,250)
Changes in other operating activities	(18,489)	466	(9,292)
Total cash flow from operating activities	**241,166**	**318,545**	**265,778**
Investing activities, cash flows provided by or used in:			
Capital expenditures	(16,281)	(18,030)	(14,329)
Investments	—	—	—
Other cash flows from investing activities	(55,905)	(30,799)	(157,042)
Total cash flows from investing activities	**(72,186)**	**(48,829)**	**(171,371)**
Financing activities, cash flows provided by or used in:			
Dividends paid	(55,045)	(58,524)	(51,792)
Sale/purchase of stock	(107,898)	(1,015,081)	(146,354)
Net borrowings	(625)	793,549	101,054
Other cash flows from financing activities	3,507	10,879	6,234
Total cash flows from financing activities	**(160,061)**	**(269,177)**	**(90,858)**
Effect of exchange rate changes	(1,420)	1,780	2,479
Change in cash and cash equivalents	**7,499**	**2,319**	**6,028**

Source: Yahoo! Finance.

could utilize the different options as they saw fit in meeting their weight-loss needs. And it seemed to work! People on the Monthly Pass were losing 30 percent more weight since the pass's implementation.[44] Further, there was a higher attendance intensity for Monthly Passers than for those that used pay-as-you-go.[45] If a member canceled his Monthly Pass because he had reached his goal weight, and then later regained weight, he knew that he could always return to Weight Watchers because the plan had worked in the past. Accordingly, Weight Watchers International Inc. attempted to offer a better weight-loss proposition, which was hoped to drive more referrals and better return rates.

The Monthly Pass commitment plan not only was important to innovativeness but also represented an overall better and more effective way for members to approach weight loss. Monthly Pass allowed members to move away from a week-to-week focus in favor of a more holistic approach to incorporating Weight Watchers into their lives, complemented by the free inclusion of Weight Watchers eTools, a hallmark feature of the Weight Watchers Online program.[46]

Weight Watchers CEO David Kirchhoff touted the implementation of the Monthly Pass as a sign of the company's commitment to continually offering better value to its consumers. Aside from the plan's financial benefits, Kirchhoff said that the most important thing about Monthly Pass was that it provided a better weight-loss proposition and created a completely new way for customers to interact with Weight Watchers in a couple of different areas—first, in meetings, and second, through the Internet.[47] Kirchhoff believed that Monthly Pass had become the "new gold standard in weight loss."[48]

In addition, Monthly Pass was also beneficial to the company in that it gave Weight Watchers a salable proposition. Before the development of Monthly Pass, when potential customers called to make an inquiry, there was no way to sell them something at that moment to get them committed.

With the development of Monthly Pass, the call center could now sell the product over the phone to consumers, in addition to the pass's availability on the Weight Watchers Web site.[49] However, Weight Watchers also wanted to continue to offer its conventional pay-as-you-go plan because the company aimed to appeal to the widest variety of consumers with the most payment options available.[50]

Another creative program that Weight Watchers implemented was the new and improved TurnAround Program, which allowed members to personalize their daily target Points by gender, age, weight, height, and daily activity, while leaving no food off-limits. Following results of a consumer survey on dieting, Weight Watchers also added new foods to the Core Food List, snack options, information about knowing your hunger signals, more recipe and meal ideas, tips for eating out, success stories, and the like.[51] The lower-carbohydrate-focused Core Plan, of which the Core Food List was a part, was Weight Watchers answer to the ease of use that low-carb diets provided—it eliminated the need to count Points and did not restrict portion sizes.[52] The Core Plan offered an alternative to the Flex Points Plan under the umbrella of the TurnAround Program.

The Customers Innovation at Weight Watchers also involved broadening the customer mix and targeting new customer segments. Weight Watchers began to actively consider expanding beyond its target consumer market of women, ages 25 to 55.[53] In the company's attempt to appeal to other demographic groups, such as men and the Hispanic community in the United States, Weight Watchers needed to retool its offering and approach to appear more relevant to weight-loss consumers who sought different methods of weight management.

In terms of the Hispanic community, the company was working to better serve the growing Hispanic population in California—for example, by offering improved Spanish-language meeting materials as well as by increasing the number of Spanish meetings offered.[54] Concurrently, Weight Watchers undertook a comprehensive market segmentation study aimed at yielding valuable insights intended to drive its new strategy.[55]

Men, another attractive market segment, appeared to be more the self-help type and were not as much in favor of a group-support experience.[56] Weight Watchers meetings were attended mostly by women, with men making up only 5 percent of members. Morgan Stanley analyst Catherine Lewis said, "Weight Watchers has a pipeline of unpenetrated and underpenetrated markets" and, thus, was testing home weight-loss services for men.[57]

Atkins, the low-carbohydrate-focused diet plan, held great appeal for men in the beginning of the new millennium.[58] By 2009, Atkins was much less popular in the weight-conscious community, and there existed a void in weight management services for men that Weight Watchers International was hoping to fill.

To do so, Weight Watchers Online, the step-by-step online guide to following the Weight Watchers plan, and

Weight Watchers eTools, the Internet weight-loss companion to conventional meetings, were being intentionally customized for men and their unique set of weight-loss challenges.[59] The WeightWatchers.com for Men customization was born of the realization that Weight Watchers should appear to be more culturally relevant to more groups of people who want different things.[60] Launched in late March 2007,[61] the customized products were targeted to attract men, who were estimated in 2003 to represent only 5 percent of Weight Watchers' members.[62]

A research study showed that about 70 percent of men are overweight and about 30 percent of men are obese. Yet, according to the study, only 28 percent of men were actively engaged in weight loss. Weight Watchers sought to provide the weight-loss answer for men by applying its 40 years of experience to its newly customized Internet offerings for men. While the fundamental concepts of weight loss—eat less and exercise more—were the same for both genders, the approach to weight loss for each gender was different. The chief scientific officer for Weight Watchers International, Karen Miller-Kovach, noted, "Men and women are biologically and emotionally different, and multiple variables factor into how each loses weight." However, the same underlying motivators for weight loss were shared between the genders: "appearance and health."[63] So, while the preferred means may have been different, the desired end was the same.

In regard to WeightWatchers.com for Men, Alexandra Aleskovsky, general manager of WeightWatchers.com, said: "Men have been losing weight with Weight Watchers for over 40 years, and hundreds of thousands are on [the] plan right now. Weight Watchers can help so many more men get in shape by offering our Internet products in ways that are more directly relevant to them, which is why we customized our offerings for men." As such, Weight Watchers Online for Men allowed men to follow the Weight Watchers plan and get food and fitness ideas and other content and resources tailored specifically to them.[64] The new products afforded Weight Watchers a new opportunity to appeal to a large market segment that might not have otherwise considered giving the program a try.[65]

Weight Watchers also aimed at appealing to men by enlisting a male celebrity spokesman to join the ranks. Greg Grunberg, of the television show *Heroes,* had been successful at Weight Watchers and signed on to promote the diet in the company's ad campaigns. His conversion to the diet had not been easy, however. Grunberg admitted that initially he considered Weight Watchers as an "old lady's diet, a soccer mom diet." However, Weight Watchers helped Grunberg lose over 30 pounds,[66] and he decided to pass that weight-loss message on to others.

The launch of Weight Watchers Online for Men was considered by the executives to be a "new product for a new market," and the company focused on getting the product experience right, delivering on consumer expectations, and doing a good job. Once the company felt that it was delivering the product correctly; it planned to be more aggressive in marketing it. However, even before the active targeting to men, the percentage of men as an increase of the Weight Watcher's total market had been on the rise. For example, if the overall online business was up 22 percent, the growth in men's business was up quite a bit more than that. Weight Watchers was pleased with the early results of the male-focused products and was working toward identifying the proper levers for building that part of the business.[67]

Questions Remain

Following the onslaught of fad diets such as the low-carbohydrate-focused Atkins Challenge and South Beach Diet, Weight Watchers attempted to reinvent itself in several ways. It began to look beyond its core market of women, to include men, as well as to branch out to characteristically underserved weight-loss markets. Weight Watchers expanded its business model to include not only in-person meetings but also online weight management tools. Building off a solid foundational business model, Weight Watchers hoped not only to expand its core consumer base but also to appeal to a wider range of consumers from both genders and to a larger span of age and demographic groups. Weight Watchers had been successful in introducing several innovations, including Monthly Pass, TurnAround, and Weight Watchers for Men. Through those and other means, Weight Watchers attempted to achieve broad differentiation that had "something for everyone."

David Kirchhoff, the president and CEO of Weight Watchers, expressed his delight with the results, and noted that the company "benefited from the continued positive impact of [Weight Watchers'] Monthly Pass commitment plan in North America, robust product sales around the world and the expanding awareness of [the] Weight Watchers Online internet product. . . . [Weight Watchers is] focused on. . .[bringing] new energy to the brand with more effective and differentiated marketing."[68] Kirchhoff continued, "The Company is taking meaningful steps to achieve its long-term growth aspirations by focusing on improving member success and increasing [Weight Watchers'] overall relevance."[69] Of Weight Watchers' plans for the future, Kirchhoff said: "We will succeed in our efforts because our mission is too important for us not to succeed. All of us believe we can make a fundamental difference in the world by making a difference in our members' lives. We all recognize that we can only do this if we operate at the very highest level in the most consistent way."[70]

The question remains, then: Will Weight Watchers be effective in staying true to the core of Jean Nidetch's goals while still expanding to different target groups, different dieting platforms, and different means of offering them? Will this expansion in scope move Weight Watchers too far from its original mission and core philosophy? Can Weight Watchers attract new customers without losing the existing ones? How should Weight Watchers remain innovative but still stay true to the goals it originally set out to accomplish and the methods it eventually set out to use? Only time will tell, but one thing is for sure: The weight-loss industry is not going away, and members of Weight Watchers' senior management have many tough and exciting decisions to make.

Endnotes

1. Weight Watchers International Inc. Form 10-K, Annual Report.
2. Ibid.
3. J. T. Nidetch and J. Rattner. *The Story of Weight Watchers.* Penguin Group, 1979.
4. Weight Watchers International Inc. at CIBC World Markets 7th Annual Consumer Growth Conference—Final. *Fair Disclosure Wire* (Quarterly Earnings Reports), July 10, 2007.
5. M. Schrange. The Weight of Innovation. *Technology Review,* February 2003, p. 21.
6. Weight Watchers International Inc. at CIBC World Markets.
7. Ibid.
8. MSN Money. Weight Watchers International Inc.: Company Report. Moneycentral.msn.com, 2009.
9. Let the Countdown to Soup Begin! *Business Wire,* August 14, 2007.
10. G. Perrenot and K. Durnan. Lunch Ladies: Applebee's Weight Watchers Menu. *Dallas Morning News,* April 11, 2005.
11. MSN Money. Weight Watchers International Inc.
12. Weight Watchers International Inc. Company Overview—Press Release: Weight Watchers Declares Quarterly Dividend. *PRNewswire* (FirstCall), September 4, 2007, accessed from www.weightwatchersinternationalinc.com, September 23, 2007.
13. Event Brief of Q1 2007 Weight Watchers International, Inc. Earnings Conference Call—Final. *Fair Disclosure Wire,* May 3, 2007.
14. Ibid.
15. New Fitness Videos on WeightWatchers.com Go Live; Comprehensive Fitness Offerings Round Out Online Weight-Loss Plan from Weight Watchers. *PR Newswire,* December 11, 2006.
16. Weight Watchers International Inc. at CIBC World Markets.
17. H. Choe. Weight Watchers' Attractive Figures. *BusinessWeek Online,* November 30, 2004.
18. Schrange. The Weight of Innovation.
19. Healthcare Weighs In. *Restaurants & Institutions,* April 15, 2007, p. 17.
20. T. Serafin. The Fat of the Land. *Forbes,* April 10, 2006, p. 104.
21. Weight Watchers: Booming Revenues. *MarketWatch: Food,* April 2003, pp. 12–13.
22. E. Wahlgreen. The Skinny on Weight Watchers. *BusinessWeek Online,* November 17, 2003.
23. C. McGrath and J. Rossi. Dieter's Delight (cover story). *Kiplinger's Personal Finance,* January 2003, p. 1.
24. Weight Watchers International Inc. Form 10-Q.
25. BullMarket.com Offers Investment Opinions on Companies in the Weight Loss and Fitness Industries. *Business Wire,* June 13, 2007.

26. Event Brief of Q4 2006 Weight Watchers International, Inc. Earnings Conference Call—Final. *Fair Disclosure Wire,* February 15, 2007.

27. J. Shaver. Weight Watchers Tops List. *Fitness Business Pro,* June 2005, p. 8.

28. Choe. Weight Watchers' Attractive Figures.

29. Weight Watchers International Inc. Form 10-K, Annual Reports.

30. Choe. Weight Watchers' Attractive Figures.

31. E. Florian. When It Comes to Fat, They're Huge. *Fortune,* October 14, 2002, p. 54.

32. Choe. Weight Watchers' Attractive Figures.

33. Weight Watchers International Inc. Form 10-K, Annual Reports.

34. D. Rynecki and A. McQuilling. Keep an Eye on Weight Watchers Inc. *Fortune,* February 9, 2004, p. 138.

35. Serafin. The Fat of the Land.

36. M. Hogan. Heavy Debt, Big Worries? *BusinessWeek Online,* July 27, 2006, p. 13.

37. Weight Watchers International Inc. Form 10-K, Annual Reports.

38. Event Brief of Q2 2007 Weight Watchers International, Inc. Earnings Conference Call—Final. *Fair Disclosure Wire* (Quarterly Earnings Reports), August 1, 2007.

39. Event Brief of Q1 2007 Weight Watchers International, Inc. Earnings Conference Call—Final. *Fair Disclosure Wire,* May 3, 2007.

40. Event Brief of Q4 2006 Weight Watchers International, Inc. Earnings Conference Call—Final. *Fair Disclosure Wire,* February 15, 2007.

41. Event Brief of Q1 2007 Weight Watchers International, Inc. Earnings Conference Call.

42. Ibid.

43. Ibid.

44. Ibid.

45. Ibid.

46. Ibid.

47. Ibid.

48. Ibid.

49. Ibid.

50. Ibid.

51. Americans Resolve to Focus on Health in 2007: New Weight Watchers Survey Reveals 92 Percent Have a Health-Related Resolution. *Business Wire,* December 26, 2006.

52. Choe. Weight Watchers' Attractive Figures.

53. B. P. Sunoo. Changing Behavior at Weight Watchers. *Workforce,* July 1997, pp. 27–29.

54. Event Brief of Q4 2006 Weight Watchers International, Inc. Earnings Conference Call.

55. Event Brief of Q2 2007 Weight Watchers International, Inc. Earnings Conference Call.

56. Ibid.

57. G. G. Marcial. Hefty Gains for Weight Watchers? *Business-Week,* October 21, 2002, p. 168.

58. T. Gower. Medicine: Healthy Man: Exercise without Dieting—It's a Losing Battle; Guys Tend to Hit the Gym to Lose Excess Pounds, Even though Cutting Calories May Be the More Efficient Way. *Los Angeles Times* [Home Edition], April 12, 2004, p. F3.

59. Weight Loss: Announcing the Laugh of Weight Watchers Online for Men and Weight Watchers eTools for Men. *Women's Health Law Weekly,* April 22, 2007, p. 251.

60. Weight Watchers International Inc. at CIBC World Markets.

61. Event Brief of Q2 2007 Weight Watchers International, Inc. Earnings Conference Call.

62. Wahlgreen. The Skinny on Weight Watchers.

63. Weight Loss: Announcing the Laugh of Weight Watchers Online for Men.

64. Ibid.

65. Event Brief of Q1 2007 Weight Watchers International, Inc. Earnings Conference Call.

66. B. Lye et al. A Dad Tries a "Soccer Mom Diet." *People,* May 28, 2007, p. 103.

67. Event Brief of Q2 2007 Weight Watchers International, Inc. Earnings Conference Call.

68. Ibid.

69. Weight Watchers Announces First Quarter 2007 Results. *PRNewswire* (First Call), May 3, 2007, accessed from www.weightwatchersinternational.com, September 23, 2007.

70. Event Brief of Q1 2007 Weight Watchers International, Inc. Earnings Conference Call.

Case 31 A Horror Show at the Cinemaplex?*

If the motion picture industry's performance in 2007 were a feature presentation, the marquee would read "Massive Box Office: Smashing Records—the Sequel!" At $9.63 billion, box office revenue set another record in 2007, a full 5 percent above the record set in 2006.[1] An astonishing 1.4 billion tickets were sold in 2007. But beyond the headlines, the industry is a study in contradictions:

- The number of theaters is declining, but the number of screens is at an all-time high.
- Revenues are up, but attendance is largely flat. The 1.4 billion tickets sold in 2007 is little improved from 1997, when 1.35 billion tickets were sold, and is a fraction of the 4 billion sold in 1946, when the average person attended 28 films a year, compared to 6[2] today (Exhibits 1 and 2).
- The U.S. population is increasing, but the size of the market in the core demographic group is growing more slowly (Exhibit 3).
- The average American spends more time than ever on entertainment each year—3,500 hours —but only 12 hours at the movies.[3] The average person spends as much time watching TV every three days.

Movies remain as popular as ever, but opportunities for viewing outside the theater have greatly increased. While motion picture studios have increased revenues through product licensing, DVD sales, and international expansion, the exhibitors—movie theaters—have seen their business decline. Movies are more available than ever, but fewer people are venturing to the theater to see them. Many theaters have ceased operation, driven from the market by consolidation and the loss of patrons.

Will the marquee at the local theater exhibitor soon change to "A Horror Show at the Cinemaplex?" How has this come to be? What can exhibitors do to respond?

The Motion Picture Industry

The motion picture industry consists of three stages: studio production, distribution, and exhibition (the theaters that show the films). All stages of the industry are undergoing consolidation.

Studio Production The studios produce the lifeblood of the industry: They create content. Films from the top-10 studios produce over 90 percent of domestic box office receipts (Exhibit 4). Studios are increasingly part of larger corporations, managed as any other profit center. Management is a challenge, as investments are large and a success formula is elusive. Profitability swings wildly. The cost of bringing a typical feature to market exceeds $100 million, up 25 percent in five years.[4] Typically one-third of production costs are marketing expenses.

Studios know their core audience: 12- to 24-year-olds. This group purchases nearly 40 percent of theater tickets. Half are "frequent moviegoers," attending at least one movie per month. Profits are driven by the studio's ability to satisfy this fickle audience. In 2008, films based on two successful comic book characters meet with widely different fates.[5] Paramount's successful *Iron Man* was produced

*This case study was prepared by Professor Steve Gove of Virginia Tech and Professor Brett P. Matherne of Loyola University of New Orleans. The purpose of the case is to stimulate class discussion rather than to illustrate effective or ineffective handling of a business situation. Copyright © 2009 Steve Gove and Brett P. Matherne.

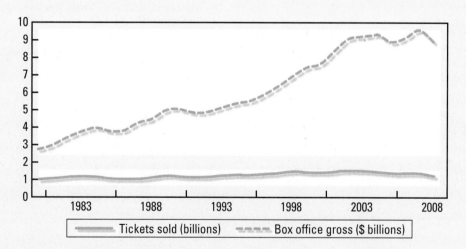

Exhibit 1 Domestic Tickets Sold and Box Office Gross
Source: Boxofficemojo.com and U.S. Census.

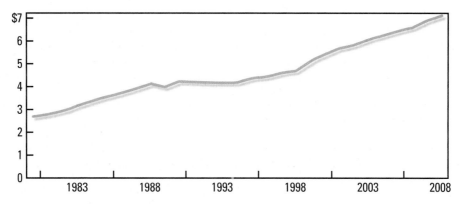

Exhibit 2 **Average Movie Ticket Price**

Source: Boxofficemojo.com.

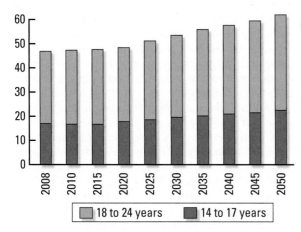

Exhibit 3 **Population Trend among 14–17 and 18–24 Age Groups (in millions)**

Source: U.S. Census.

Exhibit 4   Market Share of Film Production, 2007

Studio Parent and Label	Combined Share (%)
Time Warner (Warner Brothers and New Line)	19.8
Sony (Sony and MGM)	16.7
Viacom (Viacom and Paramount)	15.5
Disney (Disney, Buena Vista Pictures, and Miramax)	15.4
Universal Studios	11.4
News Corp (20th Century Fox)	10.5
Lion's Gate	3.6
DreamWorks SKG*	0.0
	92.9

*Dreamworks share in 2005 was 5.7 percent.

Source: Adapted from Mintel Report, "Movie Theaters—U.S.—February 2008."

for $140 million and grossed $318 million at the domestic box office. Warner Bros. *Speed Racer*, produced for $20 million less and released the following weekend, was a flop, grossing just $44 million.

Demographic trends are unfavorable. The U.S. population will increase 17 percent by 2025, an increase of 54 million people. But the number of 12- to 24-year olds is expected to increase only 9 percent, just 4 million more potential viewers. In terms of current theaters and screens, this increase amounts to fewer than 700 additional viewers per theater, roughly 100 per screen.

Distribution   Distributors are the broker intermediaries between the studios and the exhibitors. Distribution entails all steps following a film's artistic completion, including marketing, logistics, and administration. Exhibitors negotiate a percentage of the studio's gross or purchase rights to films and profit from the box office receipts. Distributors

select films and market them to exhibitors, seeking to maximize potential attendees. Distributors coordinate the manufacture and distribution of the film to exhibitors. They also handle collections, audits of attendees, and other administrative tasks. There are over 300 active distributors, but much is done by a few major firms, including divisions of studios. Pixar, for example, coproduced *Finding Nemo* with Disney, and distribution was done by Disney's Buena Vista.

Exhibition   Studios have historically sought full vertical integration through theater ownership, allowing greater control over audiences and capturing exhibition profits. A common practice was for the studio to use its theater ownership to reduce competition by not showing pictures produced by rivals. This ended in 1948 with the Supreme Court's ruling against the studios in *United States v. Paramount Pictures.* Theaters were soon divested, leaving it to studios and theaters to negotiate film access and rental.

Theaters are classified according to the number of screens at one location (Exhibit 5). Single-screen theaters were the standard from the introduction of film through the 1980s. They have since rapidly declined in number, having been replaced by theater complexes. These include miniplexes (2 to 7 screens), multiplexes (8 to 15 screens), and megaplexes (16 or more screens). The number of theaters decreased more than 15 percent between 2000 and 2007, but the number of screens increased due to growth in megaplexes. Nearly 10 percent of the theaters are now megaplexes, and the number of screens is at a historical high of 40,077 (Exhibit 6).[6] Many analysts argue that the industry has overbuilt and too many theaters and screens exist to make the business profitable.

The economy affects attendance, which tends to increase as the economy declines. In 2008, the economy was marked by rapid increases in gas prices, a decline in the stock market, and significant layoffs. One summer movie patron commented, "There's not a whole lot you can do for $10 anymore."[7] Movies do remain a bargain in the entertainment business. Four tickets to a movie cost under $27, compared to $141 for an amusement park or $261 for a pro football game.[8] For many, the air-conditioned comfort of a dark theater and the latest Hollywood release offers a break not just from the summer heat but from reality. "It's escapism, absolutely. It's probably a subconscious thing, and people don't realize it. But there's just so much going on, with people trying to pay their mortgages and get by. It's an escape for a couple of hours."[9]

Declining ticket sales and the increased costs associated with developing megaplexes began a wave of consolidation among exhibitors. Four companies now dominate: Regal, AMC, Cinemark, and Carmike. Operating 1,405 theaters in the country (just 19 percent), these companies control 42 percent of the screens. This market share provides these exhibitors with negotiating power for access to films, prices for films and concessions, and greater access to revenues from national advertisers.

There is little differentiation in the offerings of the major theater exhibitors—prices within markets differ little, the same movies are shown at the same times, and the food and services are nearly identical. Competition between theaters often comes down to distance from home, convenience of parking, and proximity to restaurants. Innovations by one theater chain are quickly adopted by others. However, the chains serve different geographic markets and do so in different ways.[10] Regal focuses on midsize markets, using multiplexes and megaplexes. Regal's average ticket price of $7.43 is the highest among the leaders. AMC concentrates on urban areas with megaplexes and on large population centers such as those in California, Florida, and Texas. Cinemark serves smaller markets, operating as the sole theater chain in over 80 percent of its markets. Cinemark's average ticket price in 2008 of $5.11 was the lowest of the majors. Carmike concentrates on small to midsized markets, targeting populations of less than 100,000 that have few other entertainment options. Carmike's average ticket price in 2008 was $5.89, but its average concession revenue, $3.05 per patron, is the highest among the majors.

The different approaches of the companies is reflected in the cost of fixed assets per screens. These costs result from decisions made on how to serve customers, such as the level of technology and the finish of the theater—digital projectors and marble floors cost more than traditional projectors and a carpeted lobby.[11] Despite multiplex and megaplex facilities, Regal's cost per screen is the highest, $430,000. Carmike, the rural operator, has the lowest, at just $206,000. Cinemark is in the middle, at $367,000. Data are not available for AMC, but its cost pre screen is expected to be near or exceed that of Regal.

The Business of Exhibition

There are three primary sources of revenue for exhibitors: box office receipts, concessions, and advertising. Managers have low discretion; their ability to influence revenues and expenses is limited. Operating margins among exhibitors

Exhibit 5 Number of Theaters by Complex Size

	2000	2007	% Change
Single screens	2,368	1,748	−26.18%
Miniplexes (2–7 screens)	3,170	2,296	−27.57%
Multiplexes (8–15 screens)	1,478	1,617	9.40%
Megaplexes (16+ screens)	405	616	52.10%
Total	7,421	6,277	−15.42%

Source: Developed by author from Entertainment Industry, 2007 Report, "Motion Picture Association of America"; and Mintel Report, "Movie Theaters—U.S.—February 2008."

average a slim 10 percent. This is before significant expenses such as facility and labor costs. The result is marginal or negative net income. Overall, the business of exhibitors is best described as loss leadership on movies: The firms make money selling concessions and showing ads to patrons who are drawn by the movie.

Box Office Revenues Ticket sales constitute two-thirds of exhibition business revenues. The return on these receipts, however, is quite small. A power imbalance results in contracts that return the vast majority of box office receipts to the studios. The record-setting revenues at the box office have been the result of increases in ticket prices and have flowed back to the studios.

Concessions Moviegoers frequently lament the high prices of concessions. Concessions average 25 to 30 percent of revenues. Direct costs are less than 15 percent of the sales prices, making concessions the largest source of exhibitor profit. Concession profits are influenced by three factors: attendance, pricing, and material costs. The most important is attendance: More attendees = more concession sales. Per-patron sales are influenced by prices—a common moviegoer complaint is high concession prices. The $3.75 price for a large soda is not set by whim but is the result of market research and profit maximization calculation. Costs are influenced by purchase volume, with larger chains able to negotiate better prices on everything from popcorn and soda pop to cups and napkins.

Advertising Exhibitors also generate revenue through preshow advertising. Although it constitutes just 5 percent of revenues, advertising is highly profitable. Mintel reports that advertising revenues among exhibitors are expected to increase at a rate of approximately 10 percent over the coming decade.[12] Audiences signal consistent dislike for advertising at the theater. Balancing the revenues from ads with audience tolerance is an ongoing struggle for exhibitors.

Overall, the exhibitor has limited control over both revenues and profits. Box office receipts are the bulk of revenues, but they yield few profits. Attendance allows profitable sales of concessions and advertisements, but there are significant caps on the volume of concession sales per person and sales prices seem to have reached maximum. Advertising remains an attractive avenue for revenues and profits, but audiences loathe it.

The Process of Exhibition

The fundamentals of film exhibition have changed little since the early 1940s. To show a picture, each theater receives a shipment of physical canisters containing a "release print" from the distributor. Making release prints requires $20,000 to $30,000 in up-front costs and $1,000 to $1,500 for each print. Thus a modern major motion picture opening on 2,500 screens simultaneously entails $2.50 million to $3.75 million in print costs. This is borne by the studios but paid for by movie attendees.

Each release print is actually several reels of 35-millimeter film that are manually loaded onto projector reels, sequenced, and queued for display by a projector operator. The film passes through the projector, which shines intense light through the film, projecting the image through a lens that focuses the image on the screen. A typical projection system costs $50,000, and one is needed for each screen.

Digital cinema is becoming economically viable. Digital cinema involves a high-resolution (4,096-by-2,160) digitized image projected onto the screen. Basic digital systems cost $150,000 to $250,000 per screen. Conversion of an existing eight-screen theater to digital thus involves an investment of $1.2 million to $2.0 million. The costs for digital release prints are far lower than those for traditional film, but the cost savings most directly benefit the studio, whereas the costs of converting the theaters are borne by the exhibitors. The number of digital theaters is expanding rapidly. In 2004, there were under 100; by 2009, there were approximately 4,600, accounting for 12 percent of screens.

Exhibit 6 Exhibition Market Leaders

Company	Theater Brands	Number of U.S. Theater Locations	Number of U.S. Screens	Average Screens per Theater
Regal	Regal, United Artists, Edwards	526	6,355	12
AMC	AMC, Loews	315	4,585	14
Cinemark	Cinemark, Century	284	3,606	12
Carmike	Carmike	280	2,412	8
Total for leading four exhibitors		1,405	16,958	
Industry total		7,421	40,077	

Source: Mintel Report, "Movie Theaters—U.S.—February 2008," SEC filings, and author estimates.

Due to the costs of digital systems, most theaters use a mixture of technologies, with a minority of digital-projection screens in any one facility.

The Theater Experience

For a significant number of moviegoers, the draw of the theater is far more than the film that is showing. Moviegoers describe attending the theater as an experience, with the appeal based on:

- The giant theater screen.
- The opportunity to be out of the house.
- The advantage of not having to wait to see a particular movie on home video.
- The experience of watching the movie with a theatrical sound system.
- The theater as a location option for a date.[13]

The ability of theaters to provide audiences with more than what they can have at home appears to be diminishing. Of the reasons why people go to the movies, only the place aspects—the theater as a place to be out of the house and as a place to go on dates—seem immune from substitution. Few teenagers want at-home movies and popcorn, and mom and dad, with their dates.

The overall experience currently offered by theaters falls short for many people. Marketing research firm Mintel reports that the reasons for not attending the theater more frequently are largely the result of the declining experience. Specific factors include the overall cost, at-home viewing options, interruptions such as cell phones in the theater, rude patrons, the overall hassle, and ads prior to the show.[14] Patrons report general dismay with the theater experience. A recent *Wall Street Journal* article reported on interruptions ranging from the intrusion of soundtracks in adjacent theaters to cell phones. "The interruptions capped a night of movie going already marred by out-of-order ticketing kiosks and a parade of preshow ads so long that, upon seeing the Coca-Cola polar bears on screen, one customer grumbled: 'This is obscene.'"[15] Recounting bad experiences is a lively topic for bloggers. Here is a typical comment: "I say it has gotten worse. I hate paying $9.00 for a ticket and the movie is 90–100 minutes long, people talking on the cell phone, the people who work at the theaters look like they are bored, and when you ask them a question, the answer is very rude. I worked as an usher in the late 60's and we had to wear uniforms and white gloves on Friday and Saturday nights, those days are long gone."[16]

A trip to the local cinemaplex can be eye-opening even for industry insiders. In 2005, Toby Emmerich, New Line Cinema's head of production, faced a not-so-common choice: attending *War of the Worlds* in a theater or in a screening room at actor Jim Carrey's house. Said Emmerich in an *LA Times* article: "I love seeing a movie with a big crowd, but I had no idea how many obnoxious ads I'd have to endure—it really drove me crazy. After sitting through about 15 minutes of ads, I turned to my wife and said, 'Maybe we should've gone to Jim Carrey's house after all.'"[17]

The unique value proposition offered by movie theaters' large screens, the long wait for DVD releases, and the advantages of theatrical sound systems also appear increasingly to be fading. Ever-larger television sets, better DVD content, and the adoption of high-definition technology in the home are all eroding the value of theaters. One blogger posts, "Whereas the electronics industry has been innovating to create immersive experiences from the comfort of our own home, the U.S. theater industry has been dragging their feet."[18]

Home Viewing Technology Home television sets are increasingly large, high-definition sets coupled with inexpensive yet impressive audio systems. In 1997, the screen size of the average television was just 23 inches. Currently, almost all LCD televisions sold have screens 36 inches or larger.[19] Because set size is measured as the diagonal screen size, increases in viewable area are greater than the measurement suggests. The viewing area of sets doubled from 250 square inches to 550 square inches.

The FCC requirement that all broadcasters convert to digital broadcasts by June 2009 is widely credited with starting a consumer movement to upgrade televisions. Since the 1950s, television transmissions were formatted as 480 interlaced vertical lines (480i) of resolution. The new, digital format is high-definition (HD), providing up to 1,080 vertical lines of resolution (1,080p).[20] Three-quarters of all televisions sold since 2006 are HD-capable.

As LCD technology became the standard for both computer and television screens, manufacturing costs declined. Wholesale prices for televisions fell 65 percent from the late 1990s to 2007.[21] In 2006, the average television retailed for $29 per diagonal inch of set size. The price is expected to decrease to $22 within five years.[22] Consumers, however, are actually spending more on televisions, consistently electing to purchase larger sets to achieve a better viewing experience. Sharp, a leading manufacturer of televisions, predicts that by 2015 the average screen will reach 60 inches.[23]

Large-screen televisions, DVD players, and audio and speaker components are commonly packaged as low-cost home theaters. The average DVD player now costs just $72,[24] and high-definition DVD players are beginning to penetrate the market. Retail price wars during the 2008 Christmas season led to HD Blu-Ray players dropping below $200. These home-theater systems offer a movie experience that rivals many theaters, all for $1,000 to $2,000. Says Mike Gabriel, Sharp's head of marketing and communications, "People can now expect a home cinema experience from their TV. Technology that was once associated with the rich and famous is now accessible to homes across the country."[25]

Content Availability and Timing Even the best hardware offers little value without content to display. Rental firm Netflix advertises a selection of more than 100,000 titles extending well beyond new and classic films and including television shows, sports events, and music performances. HD content is increasingly available to maximize the experience offered by HD televisions. Satellite and cable television providers have engaged in a game of one-upmanship to provide the greatest percentage of HD content available to subscribers. By the end of 2009, for example, 2,000 movies will be available on Blu-Ray DVD.[26]

Movie fans no longer have to wait long for the summer's blockbuster to appear on DVD. The time period between theatrical and DVD releases has declined 40 percent since 2000. The top-five films in 2000 were released on DVD an average of 37 weeks after their box office opening. In 2007, the lag was just 23 weeks. Studios have experimented with simultaneous releases to theaters, pay-per-view, and DVD.

Overall, the visual and audio experience available in the home is rapidly converging with that available at the movie theater. As a blogger on the movie fan site Big Picture posted:

> I used to go to the movies all the time—even my blog is called the Big Picture. Then I started going less—and then less still and now hardly at all. My screen at home is better, the sound system is better, the picture is in focus, the floors aren't sticky and the movies start on time. My seat is clean. And there's no idiot chattering away 2 rows behind me, and (this is my favorite) *there's no cell phones ringing. Ever.*[27]

Is this a horror show at the cinemaplex?

Endnotes

1. Motion Picture Association of America (MPAA), "2007 entertainment industry market statistics."
2. A. Serwer, "Extreme makeover: With big screens and high-def in more and more living rooms, movie theaters are taking radical new measures to woo filmgoers," *Fortune,* vol. 153 (2006), pp. 108–116.
3. Mintel Report, "Movie theaters—U.S.—February 2008."
4. Motion Picture Association of America (MPAA), "2007 entertainment industry market statistics."
5. All data on these two films are from www.BoxOfficeMojo.com.
6. Developed by author from Entertainment Industry, 2007 Report, "Motion Picture Association of America."
7. John Woestendiek and Chris Kaltenbach, "$10 is small price for a big escape: Movie box office figures are flourishing despite, or because of, economic worries," *Baltimore Sun,* July 8, 2008, accessed on Factival, December 5, 2008.
8. Motion Picture Association of America (MPAA), "2007 entertainment industry market statistics."
9. Woestendiek and Kaltenbach, "$10 is small price for a big escape."
10. Data on the firms, screen sizes, and location are from Web sites and SEC filings.
11. All data are from SEC filings, based on net property and plant and equipment reported in 2007 balance sheet and on the number of screens.
12. Mintel Report, "Movie theaters—U.S.—February 2008—Segment performance—Cinema advertising."
13. Mintel Report, "Movie theaters—U.S.—February 2008—Reasons to go to movies over watching a DVD."
14. Mintel Report, "Movie theaters—U.S.—February 2008—Reasons why attendance is not higher."
15. Kate Kelly, Bruce Orwall, and Peter Sanders, "The multiplex under siege," *Wall Street Journal,* December 24, 2005, p. P1.
16. Blog comment on Cinema Treasures, "Over the past ten years, the movie theater experience has . . .," http://cinematreasures.org/polls/22, accessed December 11, 2008.
17. Incident reported in Patrick Goldstein, "Now playing: A glut of ads," *Los Angeles Times,* July 12, 2005, p. E-1 (print ed.), http://articles.latimes.com/2005/jul/12/entertainment/et-goldstein12, accessed December 5, 2008.
18. Designs of the Week, "The movie theater experience," November 23, 2008, www.sramanamitra.com/2008/11/23/designs-of-the-week-the-movie-theater-experience, accessed December 11, 2008.
19. DuBravac, 2007.
20. Ibid.
21. Ibid.
22. Bob Keefe, "Prices on flat-screen TVs expected to keep falling," *Atlanta Journal-Constitution,* March 15, 2008.
23. "Average TV size up to 60-inch by 2015 says Sharp," *TechDigest,* www.techdigest.tv/2008/01/average_tv_size.html, accessed December 11, 2008.
24. Motion Picture Association of America (MPAA), "2007 entertainment industry market statistics."
25. "Average TV size up to 60-inch by 2015 says Sharp."
26. www.movieweb.com.
27. The Big Picture, "Why is movie theatre revenue attendance declining?" http://bigpicture.typepad.com/comments/2005/07/declining_movie.htm, accessed December 11, 2008.

Case 32 Build-A-Bear Workshop*

Selling brand experience was not something new in the retail industry, but combining it with the teddy bear was a unique concept from Build-A-Bear Workshop Inc. When founder and CEO Maxine Clark opened the first company store during the dot-com era of the late 1990s, many critics were skeptical about the future of her brick-and-mortar business. Nobody expected the small start-up selling customizable teddy bears and other stuffed animals to make any profits, let alone become one of the country's fastest-growing retailers. Maxine Clark managed to build a successful nationwide organization, focused on personalization and customer involvement, with a simple motto: "Where Best Friends Are Made." In 2005, her efforts were praised with Fast Company's Customer-Centered Leader Award,[1] and the future held great potential for Build-A-Bear.

However, while Build-a-Bear celebrated its 10th anniversary with the making of its 50-millionth furry friend in 2007, the company's future prospects began to fade. Following a huge success in the early years of operations, Build-A-Bear Workshop was faced with a decline in sales figures as of 2008. The comparable store sales for fiscal 2008 declined by 14.0 percent, following a 9.9 percent decline in 2007, a 6.5 percent decline in 2006, a 0.2 percent decline in 2005, and an 18.0 percent decline in 2004. While a different reason or issue was blamed for each decline, these declines were a significant issue for the firm. The 2007 decline was primarily blamed on changing customer preferences, competition from other children's activities, and weaker mall traffic, and the 2008 decline was blamed on a decrease in consumer spending and a recession. Consequently, gross margin decreased to $190.5 million for fiscal 2008 from $209.1 million for fiscal 2007, a decrease of $18.6 million, or 8.9 percent. As a percentage of net retail sales, gross margin decreased to 41.3 percent for fiscal 2008 from 44.7 percent for fiscal 2007 (See Exhibits 1 and 2).[2]

Although Build-A-Bear had performed impressively in the past, experts in the toy industry now questioned whether it could further innovate its products and bring more value to the customers. Had Build-A-Bear reached its potential? What new products could Build-A-Bear offer to maintain its market share and step up its financial performance? The company's recent differentiation strategies focused on opening new Build-A-Bear Workshops in areas other than the traditional mall-based locations to compensate for the slowdown in mall traffic. Build-A-Bear was also excited about launching a new Build-A-Bearville Web site during the winter of 2008 at which customers could bring their furry friends to life online and experience new adventures in a virtual world. Build-A-Bearville was designed to compete directly with popular Webkinz World, an online world of plush animals where kids could play games and care for their virtual pets. The Webkinz World Web site was launched in 2005 and since then had experienced enormous success among children and their parents around the world.[3] Could Build-A-Bearville help break the Webkinz obsession and get the kids to return to Build-A-Bear?

Build-A-Bear Background

It all started on a simple idea that Maxine Clark heard over 30 years ago from Stanley Goodman, former CEO of May Department Store, "Retailing is entertainment and the store is a stage—and when the customers are happy, they spend more money." On the basis of this idea, Build-A-Bear Workshop brought the teddy bear alive and was the only global company that offered an interactive make-your-own-stuffed-animal retail-entertainment experience. Inspired by Goodman's statement, Clark brought the brand experience to the toy industry in 1996 and established Build-A-Bear headquarters in St. Louis, Missouri.[4] Clark created a custom-teddy-bear empire built with "heart" and was personally involved in setting the strategic agenda, building the organization, and maintaining the strategic leadership. As the former president of Payless Shoe Source, Clark based the Build-A-Bear concept on two of the hottest trends in retailing—entertainment and customization. Her years of retailing experience paid off and gave Clark unique insights into creating her own successful concept for mall-based retailing.[5] Having no children of her own, Clark took every opportunity to interact with her customers, employing both low- and high-tech methods to communicate with Build-A-Bear fans.[6] Weekly store visits and numerous e-mails provided Clark with valuable customer feedback that she put into practice to build a truly customer-centered organization.

Since the opening of the first store in 1996, Build-A-Bear Workshop capitalized on its unique experience and attracted a strong base of loyal customers. The company's target market consisted mainly of families with children, primarily ages 3 to 12. Build-A-Bear stores also appealed to grandparents, aunts, and uncles of children and to teen girls who occasionally brought along their boyfriends as well. The Build-A-Bear experience was also sought by child-centric organizations, such as scouting organizations and schools, that were looking for interactive entertainment options of the type Build-A-Bear Workshop could provide. Overall, it was the company's belief that its stores, which were primarily located inside malls, were "destination locations and drew guests from a large geographic reach."[7]

Exhibit 1 Income Statements

	Fiscal Year		
	2008	**2007**	**2006**
Revenues:			
Net retail sales	$460,963	$468,168	$432,572
Franchise fees	4,157	3,577	3,521
Licensing revenue	2,741	2,616	979
Total revenues	467,861	474,361	437,072
Costs and expenses:			
Cost of merchandise sold	270,463	259,078	227,509
Selling, general, and administrative	185,608	177,375	158,712
Store preopening	2,410	4,416	3,958
Store closing	2,952	—	—
Interest expense (income), net	(799)	(1,531)	(1,530)
Total costs and expenses	460,634	439,338	388,649
Income before income taxes	7,227	35,023	48,423
Income tax expense	2,663	12,514	18,933
Net income	$ 4,564	$ 22,509	$ 29,490
Earnings per common share:			
Basic	$ 0.24	$ 1.11	$ 1.46
Diluted	$ 0.24	$ 1.10	$ 1.44
Shares used in computing common per share amounts:			
Basic	19,153,123	20,256,847	20,169,814
Diluted	19,224,273	20,448,793	20,468,256

Source: Build-A-Bear Workshop, 10-K report.

The theme-park-environment stores operated as specialty retailers of plush animals and related products, including approximately 30 styles of teddy bears as well as various clothing, shoes, and accessories for the stuffed animals. Build-A-Bear Workshop stores generated very strong sales wherever they opened. The company differentiated itself from the competition with marketing initiatives that facilitated stronger connections with its customers.[8] Approximately 3,000 square feet in size, every Build-A-Bear store stood out thanks to a highly visual and colorful appearance, with custom-designed fixtures featuring teddy bears and other themes relating to the Build-A-Bear Workshop experience.

Build-A-Bear Experience

Build-A-Bear Workshop provided a unique and exceptional approach to the entertainment retail industry. The company's core concept was based on allowing its customers, uniquely termed "guests," to make, personalize, and customize stuffed animals of their choosing. The customization feature provided customers with more value than they would receive from mass-produced products. In addition, personalizing the product stimulated customers' creativity and gave them a feeling of empowerment. This concept "capitalized on what was believed to be the relatively untapped demand for experience-based shopping as well as the widespread appeal of stuffed animals."[9] As Maxine Clark pointed out, "We [at Build-A-Bear] don't think about ourselves as a toy store—we think of ourselves as an experience. Unlike the rest of the industry, Build-A-Bear Workshop sales don't peak around holidays; they are evenly distributed."[10]

The Build-A-Bear Workshop atmosphere was based on a highly visual environment, with the teddy bear theme carried throughout the store creating a fantasy land where stuffed animals came to life. "Shopping at one of the Build-A-Bear's colorful, [brightly] lit stores [was] one part consumption, ten parts entertainment,"[11] and this entertainment

Exhibit 2   Balance Sheets (in thousands of dollars, except share and per-share data)

	January 3, 2009	December 29, 2007
Assets		
Current assets:		
Cash and cash equivalents	$ 47,000	$ 66,261
Inventories	50,586	48,638
Receivables	8,288	7,068
Prepaid expenses and other current assets	16,151	14,624
Deferred tax assets	3,839	3,606
Total current assets	125,864	140,197
Property and equipment, net	123,193	139,841
Goodwill	30,480	42,840
Other intangible assets, net	3,903	4,016
Investment in affiliate	7,721	4,307
Other assets, net	8,991	8,330
Total Assets	$300,152	$339,531
Liabilities and stockholders' equity		
Current liabilities:		
Accounts payable	$ 37,547	$ 45,044
Accrued expenses	12,593	11,788
Gift cards and customer deposits	29,210	34,567
Deferred revenue	7,634	8,708
Total current liabilities	86,984	100,107
Deferred franchise revenue	2,033	2,511
Deferred rent	41,714	41,697
Other liabilities	1,696	1,608
Commitments and contingencies		
Stockholders' equity:		
Preferred stock, par value $0.01, Shares authorized: 15,000,000: No shares issued or outstanding at January 3, 2009 and December 29, 2007	—	—
Common stock, par value $0.01, Shares authorized: 50,000,000:		
Issued and outstanding: 19,478,750 and 20,676,357 shares, respectively	195	207
Additional paid-in capital	76,852	88,388
Accumulated other comprehensive (loss) income	(12,585)	6,314
Retained earnings	103,263	98,699
Total stockholders' equity	167,725	193,608
Total Liabilities and Stockholders' Equity	$300,152	$339,531

Source: Build-A-Bear Workshop, 10-K report.

factor provided Build-A-Bear Workshop with a competitive edge in the toy industry.

The culture at Build-A-Bear Workshop encouraged employee contribution and collaboration, and the resulting above-average employee retention rates at Build-A-Bear contributed to the quality of the guest experience, the building stone of the company's differentiation.[12] Maxine Clark recognized that Build-A-Bear's success was largely dependent on the support of her employees, also known as "associates."[13] Therefore, Build-A-Bear was highly selective in the hiring process and ensured that the chosen associates stayed actively involved in what was happening with the company. For instance, fewer than 4 percent of the applicants for store manager were hired in 2008.[14] Build-A-Bear's excellent customer service largely contributed to the chain's overall customer satisfaction, which was close to 90 percent.[15]

The primary role of the associates, also referred to as the "Master Bear Builders," was to share the experience with the guests and guide them at each phase of the bear-making process. The process itself consisted of eight steps carried out on the Build-A-Bear "assembly line," which comprised different bear-making stations.

At the *Choose Me* stage, customers were introduced to all the furry characters in the store and would select one, which soon became their new friend. Each store usually carried over 30 different stuffed animals, which varied with the season. The prices of the Build-A-Bear furry friends ranged from $10 to $25. At the *Hear Me* station, customers could personalize their new friend with a sound selected from several choices, including giggling, barking, meowing, or growling, which would be placed inside their stuffed animal during the stuffing process. Guests could even record their own 10-second Build-A-Sound message for an additional $8. The *Stuff Me* station allowed customers to stuff their new friend with the help of one of the Master Bear Builders. At this stage, customers would bring their stuffed animal to life by selecting a small satin heart and placing it inside their new furry friend. Each animal was also given a special bar code that would allow it to be reunited with its owner if ever lost. The furry friend would then be neatly pulled shut at the *Stitch Me* station. Next, customers could brush their animal at the *Fluff Me* station to make sure their new friend was well groomed. At *Dress Me,* customers were able to express the true personality and style of their new best friend by choosing from hundreds of outfits and accessories. Build-A-Bear provided the "beary" latest furry fashions thanks to partnering with fashion leaders such as Limited Too, Skechers, Hello Kitty, Disney, and Harley-Davidson. Build-A-Bear Workshop also licensed a variety of college and university logos that were placed on Tiny Tees shirts, and it sold bear-sized MLB, NBA and WNBA, NFL, NHL, and NASCAR sports stuff. At the *Name Me* stage, customers registered their new friend on one of the in-store computers. This information was used to create their personalized birth certificate and enter their friend in the Find-A-Bear ID program. Finally, customers concluded their bear-making process at the *Take Me Home* station, where they received their customized birth certificate and each new furry friend was then placed in its own Cub Condo carrying case.[16]

Build-A-Bear Workshop provided a unique shopping experience, as customers created an emotional bond with the toy through the interactive process of bringing it to life. As CEO Maxine Clark commented, "The store offers a total experience from start to finish. It's about so much more than just coming in and buying an off-the-shelf bear, although you can do that too if you want. But most people prefer to make their own—even if they have to stand in line to do it. Shoppers are, and typically desire to be, involved in the entire bear-making process."[17]

To emphasize the strength of its brand, Build-A-Bear Workshop instituted the Fur Stuff Club (a loyalty rewards program),[18] as well as a bear identification system that aimed to unite children with their lost BBW teddy bears.[19] The company's CIO, Dave Finnegan, believed that the "experience starts with the [stuffed animal's] barcode." As customers registered their furry friends at a designated kiosk, each consumer would be prompted to scan the bar code and add his or her name, mailing address, and e-mail address—information that would later be stored in the corporate database. Build-A-Bear also launched an automated Stuff Fur Stuff Club, which served as an electronic history of the guests' preferences and purchases. The program tracked the purchased products, the frequency of the customers' visits, as well as their response to certain offers. The Stuff Fur Stuff Club encouraged loyalty and attracted shoppers by awarding them 1 point for every $1 they spent. After earning 100 points, customers would receive a $10 reward. Thanks to the automated program, the company could analyze purchase patterns and history trends and learn who was redeeming their points and what they were using the points for.[20] Both the bear identification system and Stuff Fur Stuff were differentiating features that allowed Build-A-Bear to recognize and communicate important information to its guests, as well as stay ahead of the changing customer preferences.[21]

Expansion and Innovation

In November 2004, the company expanded the make-your-own concept from stuffed animals to dolls with the opening of its first Friends 2B Made stores, where guests could make their own doll friends. By the end of 2006, Build-A-Bear Workshop operated one stand-alone Friends 2B Made store and eight other Friends 2B Made stores adjacent to, or within, Build-A-Bear Workshop stores in the United States.[22] The company also expanded its merchandise assortments by establishing licensing agreements with professional baseball, basketball, hockey, and football teams and with NASCAR.

In 2005, Build-A-Bear Workshop partnered with Ridemakerz, allowing fathers and sons to customize their own toy cars.[23] In the same year, the company introduced Build-A-Bear Workshop On Tour, with a bear-covered mobile trailer that opened up into a complete 800-square-foot Build-A-Bear Workshop store. The On Tour idea was part of the company's integrated marketing strategy to bring the Build-A-Bear Workshop brand and experience to places other than malls where families go and have fun, such as various sporting and entertainment venues across the country.[24]

Build-A-Bear Workshop teamed up with major-league baseball to provide fans across the country with opportunities to support their favorite teams in unique ways. Build-A-Bear opened five Build-A-Bear Workshop ballpark stores across the country. The ballpark stores were open during the teams' home games and included the same experience and interaction as the mall-based stores, with exclusive animals, outfits, and accessories. Clark also believed that the promotion of Scott Seay in 2006 to president and chief operating "bear" would allow Build-A-Bear to gain efficiencies throughout the organization.[25]

In March 2009, John Haugh joined Build-A-Bear Workshop as president and chief marketing and merchandising bear. Prior to joining Build-A-Bear Workshop, Haugh served as president of It's Sugar, LLC, a candy and confectionary retailer. Haugh stepped in at a difficult time to be a retailer, amid the economic recession of 2008–2009. Meanwhile, Tina Klocke was named chief operations and financial bear. Klocke assumed formal responsibility for store operations in addition to her continuing role as chief financial bear.

Changing Industry

Although Build-A-Bear Workshop's interactive experience was unique in the toy retail industry, this didn't make the competition any less intense. Kids changed their preference at a rate so fast that a phenomenon one year could be gone the next year. To compete with others in catching children's new preferences and activity time, a specialty retail store such as Build-A-Bear Workshop had to face competition from all different directions, including toy manufacturers like Hasbro and Mattel, which sell their products through giant retail chain stores—Wal-Mart, Toys "R" Us, Target, Kmart, Sears, and other discounted chains. Other competitors included, but were not limited to, American Girl, Vermont Teddy Bear, Russ Berrie, Ty, Fisher-Price, Mattel, Ganz, Applause, Boyd's, Commonwealth, and Gant. Maxine Clark considered her competition to be every company that tried to attract the customer's time and entertainment money.[26] As products in the toy industry became more commoditized, many companies searched for new ways to differentiate their offerings beyond simply manufacturing and delivering the toys to the customers. Following the Build-A-Bear example, some of the company's main competitors, including Vermont Teddy Bear and American Girl, took initiatives to recast their traditional products and services in ways that would create experiences for their customers.

Vermont Teddy Bear, established in Burlington in 1981, marketed its product as the "only bear made in America and guaranteed for life." Struggling to find customers in the local area, the company developed the unique "Bear-Gram" concept of mailing customized teddy bears to visiting tourists. The new concept had huge success, and the company experienced tremendous growth. In 1993, the Vermont Teddy Bear Company hit number 58 on the *Inc. Magazine* list of the fastest-growing private companies in the United States. Since the customers received their furry friends through the mail, Vermont Teddy Bear needed to find innovative ways to create experience for the bear owners. To involve customers in the bear-making process, the company invited all of its fans to regularly scheduled Vermont Teddy Bear plant tours. Each tour featured many fun activities for the young visitors and their friends and families, including a lunch at the Hungry Bear Café or a visit to the Bear Shop, the Bear Museum, and the Vermont Teddy Bear Hospital. The company also created a "wow!" experience for the recipients of its teddy bears thanks to its unique packaging. The gift box included an airhole for the bear and a warning not to turn the box upside down lest the bear get a headache, as well as a sweet treat and a personalized card with a colorful drawing of the headquarters and all the employees' first names. In the Vermont Teddy Bear locations, bear counselors assisted customers with the selection and personalization of their bears. The company also let its customers be creative by customizing a teddy bear look-a-like that captured the personality and appearance of someone special to them.

Another Build-a-Bear competitor, American Girl Inc., also decided to move to a new level in providing value for its customers. Founded in 1986, American Girl specialized in manufacturing high-end dolls, books, and magazines for young girls. Since it was acquired by Mattel Inc. in 1998, American Girl started a rapid retail expansion and concentrated on further product development. To create additional customer value, American Girl took steps to develop new engaging experiences between the dolls, the girls, and their families. In 2005, the company opened its first American Girl (AG) Places, in New York, Los Angeles, and Chicago, providing visitors with a unique retail experience through which they could engage in many exciting activities and bond with their new doll friends. Every AG Place included a theater showing a live play concentrated on the doll collection, a café for grown-up dining experiences or birthday parties, and a doll hair salon or a photo studio. Encouraged by the success of the AG Places, in 2007 American Girl opened two American Girl Boutique and Bistros, in Dallas and Atlanta. These new locations were the company's latest way to connect with girls by allowing them to celebrate special times with their families and friends in a fun and casual environment. According to Ellen L. Brothers, the president of American Girl and the executive vice president of Mattel, the company became much more than a place that sells dolls. "It's the place where imaginations soar—from boutiques to special events, from the café to the theater and beyond."[27]

Changing Market

While providing unique experiences for the customers became an important competitive advantage in the toy industry, there were also other factors shaping the competitive environment that required attention. While the Internet had helped bolster the retail toy industry, it had also intensified competition dramatically. According to the Toy Industry Association's 2007 report, increasingly popular electronic gadgets, video, and online games like the Nintendo Wii game console and the www.webkinz.com online community could easily attract children's attention and thus reduce the time kids spent with their plush animals. This shift has changed the focus of some companies, such as Hasbro, which turned to the Web to bring attention to new editions of its board games Monopoly and Trivial Pursuit.[28] Furthermore, according to the technology-loving experts, electronic toys had the potential to provide the best educational applications thanks to interactive displays of pictures, lights, and sounds. Electronic toys were deemed to be very helpful when teaching young children about cause and effect and hand-eye coordination—two important behavioral learning skills.[29]

NPD Group statistics indicated that in 2007 the sales of online/Internet games increased by 9 percent, bringing that segment's share of the $22.2 billion market to 7 percent, while the sales of plush toys were flat, at $1.3 billion.[30] Build-A-Bear Workshop recognized the need to infuse more technology into its product line offerings to stay ahead of its competitors. One way in which Build-A-Bear attempted to expand on technology was by offering a technology-based platform for its customization experience through the introduction of a Build-A-Bear video game for Nintendo DS. The Nintendo DS simulation, a game in which players could customize a digitized bear (or character) on screen, attempted to re-create the in-store experience by reproducing the process of shopping and creating a bear in a Build-A-Bear Workshop as a video. Through the use of a touch screen, wireless technology, enhanced graphics, and innovative control mechanisms, the game simulated the same bear-building process as the one in the stores. The game featured eight different characters to be played with and cared for, as well as a kitchen and a dining room to prepare meals for the online characters. The users could also design the room of their favorite character.[31]

Maxine Clark stated that 80 percent of the customers were repeat guests who planned their visit in advance, which meant people who had visited the stores loved them.[32] Build-A-Bear Workshop's special mix in products and highly interactive, theme- park-like environment inside the malls were what kept customers coming back and were the key components in the franchises' rapid success. But the declining comparable same-store sales meant that sales based on the repeat customers were not enough. To attract more people to its stores, the company organized Build-A-Party events for kids' birthday parties and scout outings.

The company stayed true to its differentiation strategy by not following the example of its competition, which often used markdowns to sell products. Instead, Build-A-Bear Workshop tried to increase its brand awareness as an experienced retailer by allocating large portions of its budget to national television advertising, direct mail, and other types of publicity (7 to 7.5 percent of total revenues in 2009).[33]

At the same time, there was only so much the company could do when most of its stores were inside malls, where traffic was declining partly because of the rising gas price and weak economy. To cope with this issue, Build-A-Bear Workshop had already tried to explore other options such as opening new stores outside the malls and relying more on the online storefront and licensing.

Besides its dependency on mall traffic, Build-A-Bear Workshop also faced constraints that were related to children's ages and preferences. Even as management was strategically trying to lure more customers to the stores, the company was facing a generation of kids that got older younger. The "kids getting old younger (KGOY)" phenomenon was noted on the Toy Industry Association's Web site: "Kids are seeking more sophisticated entertainment . . . and doing so at younger and younger ages." Tastes were maturing and becoming more sophisticated at a younger age, reducing the available time slot for products designed for children. The KGOY generation was very familiar with what technology could offer. Given that children ages 1 to 14 were the recipients of approximately 80 percent of Build-A-Bear's stuffed animals, the Wellbeing study of kids ages 8 to 15 revealed valuable information for the company. According to the findings of the study, announced on Nickelodeon and MTV in November 2006, children throughout the world were growing up younger and appeared to be experiencing higher levels of stress in their daily lives. Despite their young age, kids already felt pressure to succeed. Thus, getting a good grade in school was their top priority. Those who were growing up in an environment with more news media outlets generally felt less safe regardless of where they came from in the world.[34] All the findings related to age compression were based on the current generation of children and therefore could be valuable to the toy industry if translated into business-specific strategies. In other words, with the kids' concerns and priorities on the table, what could Build-A-Bear do to make its brand more appealing to them?

The Toy Industry Association's 2007 report contained another interesting finding related to the age factor: The heart of the toy industry belonged to kids seven and under. This segment accounted for over 60 percent of total industry dollar volume, and the reason was simple: These children had more time to spend with toys because they faced fewer school hours, had less homework, and were not as diverted by youth electronics and video games.[35] Considering the new trends in children's preferences, should Build-A-Bear Workshop look into having multiple strategies targeting different age groups?

Financials and the Future

The early years of Build-A-Bear Workshop were marked with great success. The company's physical locations grew from 150 stores at fiscal year-end 2003 to 292 company-owned stores in the United States, Canada, the United Kingdom, Ireland, and France in 2008. Due to this rapid expansion, Build-A-Bear Workshop saw an increase in its revenues from $301.7 million in fiscal year 2004 to $437.1 million in 2006. Its compound annual revenue growth rate reached 20.4 percent, and its net income jumped from $18.5 million in fiscal year 2004 to $29.5 million in 2006, ultimately resulting in a compound annual net income growth rate of 26.5 percent.[36]

Since new stores generated much higher sales per square foot, part of the company's growth came from opening up more stores. New stores typically paid for themselves in their first year of operation, and comparable same-store sales began to decline in the second and third years. Before 2009, Build-A-Bear Workshop had planned to open 25 to 30 new stores per year so that 75 percent of the U.S. population would be within 30 miles of a Build-A-Bear Workshop. In addition, the company signed licensed product agreements with leading manufacturers to use the Build-A-Bear Workshop brand to develop products for retailers. Internationally, the company's expansion plan was to have well-capitalized franchisees with retail or real estate expertise. Build-a-Bear Workshop operated 292 stores primarily in major malls throughout the United States and Canada, 54 stores in the United Kingdom and Ireland, and an Internet store (see Exhibit 3).[37]

Unfortunately, the initial successful performance did not last forever. Build-A-Bear Workshop's comparable store sales declined steadily from 2004 to 2008.[38] As of 2009, new store development was placed on hold while the economy had a chance to recover from the recession.

Since Build-A-Bear Workshop could not efficiently capitalize in the market, the word on Wall Street was speculation that the firm's current cash flow could support a buyout price much higher than its present value. One of the potential buyers might have been Disney, which already had a partnership with the company and could leverage the Build-A-Bear brand to promote Disney movies and TV shows. To evaluate alternative strategies that could increase its share value, possibly the buyout option as well, Build-A-Bear Workshop hired the investment bank Lehman Brothers, but the findings of the analysis have yet to be released.[39]

Clark, who was aware of the strategic challenges that Build-A-Bear was facing, was optimistic about the future and stated, "We [at Build-A-Bear] believe that through our highly profitable business model and unique retail-entertainment concept, we will continue to grow total revenues, increase net income, and generate excess cash flow."[40] Had Build-A-Bear Workshop reached a mature stage in the domestic market, as indicated by its slower comparable store sales and increases in profit? To sustain its domestic market position in such a dynamic competitive industry, Build-A-Bear Workshop will have to continue building on its creativity and boost innovation in its offerings. As Maxine Clark said, "Ray Kroc didn't invent hamburgers.

Exhibit 3 Store Data

Store Data	Fiscal Year				
	2008	2007	2006	2005	2004
Number of stores at end of period					
North America	292	272	233	200	170
Europe	54	49	38	—	—
Total Stores	346	321	271	200	170
Square footage at end of period					
North America	856,504	810,208	712,299	615,194	514,341
Europe	77,520	70,577	56,701	—	—
Total square footage	934,024	880,785	769,000	615,194	514,341
Average net retail sales per store	$ 1,329	$ 1,576	$ 1,761	$ 1,864	$ 1,857
Net retail sales per gross square foot - North America	$ 445	$ 516	$ 573	$ 615	$ 602
Consolidated comparable store sales change (%)	(14.0)%	(9.9)%	(6.5)%	(0.2)%	18.1%

Source: Build-A-Bear Workshop, 10-K report.

Howard Schultz didn't invent coffee. And Oprah didn't invent talk shows. They just invented how to do it and how to do it better." Clark would have to invent a way to turn the Build-A-Bear experience into a lasting legend.

Endnotes

1. Lucas Conley. "Customer-Centered Leader: Maxine Clark." *Fast Company,* 2005.
2. Build-A-Bear Workshop Inc. Annual Reports, 2006, 2007, 2008.
3. Warren Buckleitner. "Plush Animals with a Key to Enter Their Web World." *New York Times,* January 25, 2007.
4. Maxine Clark. "Build-*A*-Bear's Founder Shares Her Story," *BusinessWeek Online,* September 18, 2007.
5. "Leading Entrepreneur Shares Secrets of Success in Innovative New Book." *PR Newswire,* April 20, 2006.
6. B. Tsiantar. "Not Your Average Bear." *Time,* July 2005.
7. Build-A-Bear Workshop Inc. Form 10-Q, 2007.
8. Ibid.
9. Ibid.
10. L. Conley. "Customer-Centered Leader: Maxine Clark." *Fast Company,* 2005.
11. Carol Lynn Mithers. "A Bear of a Business." Ladies Home Journal, November 2003.
12. Build-A-Bear Workshop Inc. Annual Report, Form 10-K, 2006, p. 7.
13. Build-A-Bear Workshop Inc. Annual Report, 2006, p. 14.
14. Build-A-Bear Workshop Inc. 10-K report, 2008.
15. D. Howell. "Retailers Attribute Success to Out-of-Box Innovations." *DSN Retailing Today,* October 2, 2000, pp. 4–58.
16. Build-A-Bear Workshop Inc. Annual Report, 2006.
17. M. Wilson. "This Bear Market Toys with Success." *Chain Store Age,* January 1998, pp. 50–53.
18. Build-A-Bear Workshop Inc. Annual Report, 2006.
19. C. Imbs. "Maxine Clark: A Beary Good Idea." *St. Louis Commerce,* July 2004.
20. D. M. Amato-McCoy. "Levels of Loyalty." *Chain Store Age,* April 2007, pp. 51–53.
21. Build-A-Bear Workshop Inc. Annual Report, 2006, p. 9.
22. Build-A-Bear Workshop Inc. 10-K reports.
23. Joanne Kaufman. "After Build-A-Bear, Build-A-Toy-Car." *New York Times,* May 29, 2007.
24. Build-A-Bear Workshop Inc. Press release, January 10, 2005.
25. Build-A-Bear Workshop Inc. Annual Report, 2006.
26. Ann C. Logue. 2005. "Warm, Fuzzy and Business Savvy." *NYSE Magazine,* October–November 2005.
27. www.americangirl.com.
28. *New Media Age* (London), October 20, 2005, p. 18.
29. http://toy-tma.com.
30. Toy Industry Association. Annual Report, 2007.
31. www.estarland.com/index.asp?page=NintendoDS& product=29856&q=.
32. Maxine Clark. "Build-A-Bear Chief Maxine Clark Discusses Changing the Retail Industry." *Webster University's School of Business & Technology Newsletter,* Summer 2006.
33. Build-A-Bear Workshop Inc. Form 10-K, 2008.
34. Patrick Feely. "The Toy Industry and Youth Marketing Today: Going beyond 'KGOY.'" *Toy Industry Association,* April 10, 2005.
35. Ibid.
36. Build-A-Bear Workshop Inc., Form 10-K, Annual Report, 2006, p. 4
37. Build-A-Bear Workshop Inc. 10-K report, 2008.
38. Ibid.
39. "Build-A-Bear Brings Out the Bulls." *BusinessWeek Online,* June 29, 2007.
40. "Build-A-Bear Workshop, Inc. Announces It Is Evaluating Strategic Alternatives for Enhancing Long-Term Shareholder Value." *M2PressWIRE,* June 28, 2007.

Case 33 Reader's Digest: For Whom and for How Much Longer?*

In March 2009, after the company posted an operating loss of $337 million for fiscal 2008, there were rumors that The Reader's Digest Association (RDA) was "exploring" financial restructuring, including bankruptcy.[1] Standard and Poor's had downgraded the RDA corporate rating, and Moody's Investors Service had put RDA on the list of companies most likely to default on debt, citing "broadening global decline in consumer spending and the erosion in RDA's mature print-based publishing products."[2] Although RDA's then 88-year-old *Reader's Digest* magazine was still the number-one consumer magazine in the United States, with over 8 million subscribers, plus 40 million subscribers in 70 countries overseas, its circulation numbers were falling compared to those of its top competitors. (See Exhibit 1.)

RDA's flagship *Reader's Digest* magazine had long had the reputation of being a "hinterlands magazine read by kindly grandparents." RDA had admitted its apparent inability to attract and retain new and younger magazine subscribers and product customers in view of the maturing of an important portion of its customer base.[3] Extensive restructuring, reduction in staffing levels, acquisitions, and development of international ventures initiated by CEO Thomas O. Ryder starting in 1998 had produced some improvements, but the subsequent years did not sustain earnings.

Thomas Ryder retired in 2006, and on March 2, 2007, the stockholders of The Reader's Digest Association, Inc., decided to accept a $2.4 billion buyout offer from private equity firm Ripplewood Holdings LLC. This transaction would finally return RDA to private status after a 17-year run as a public company. Ripplewood acquired RDA in a buyout of RDA's outstanding common shares and assumption of RDA's debt. The deal was worth $17 per share to RDA shareholders. Included in the transaction was the integration of two of Ripplewood's portfolio companies: WRC Media, Inc., publisher of *Weekly Reader* magazine and the *World Almanac;* and Direct Holdings U.S. Corp., the exclusive worldwide marketer of TimeLife music, videos, DVDs, and books.

Ripplewood installed well-respected publishing executive Mary Berner as the new CEO and commented, "One of the big advantages of being private is that you can tolerate failure and make experiments . . . [without having to worry] about next quarter's earnings."[4] Berner's stated focus was on how to build on the platform that was already there. "The company has done an excellent job of diversifying both products and geography . . . with a depth and breadth of content that is one of its biggest strengths.

How to leverage that digitally is one of our first initiatives," she said.[5] Berner also believed that the addition of the Weekly Reader and TimeLife product lines would provide more opportunities for growth, since now RDA would have "one of the largest music collections in the world."[6]

One of Berner's first acts was to restructure the company, reorganizing how the brands were marketed to consumers and advertisers by breaking them out of their corporate silos and grouping them by subject matter, such as food and entertaining and health and wellness. To aid in this, Berner recruited many of her former executives at Conde Nast/Fairchild Publications. Media observers commented that perhaps the new team was needed in order to market the brands more aggressively.[7] Commentators on publishing industry mergers and acquisitions noted, "Companies that are valued the highest in the market are brands that are surrounded by multiple forms of media in good market positions that provide their readers and their advertisers with a comprehensive environment to interact."[8] Ripplewood's stated strategic approach was "to enhance the value of the businesses it acquires through a combination of strategic, operational, and financial actions."[9] However, at the time, analysts once again had cause to question RDA's long-term viability: "It's a fabulous brand, but its equity is eroding daily. . . . Reader's Digest could fade into history if they don't make drastic changes."[10]

The return to private status in 2007 was intended to give RDA breathing room out of the public eye, but the economic climate going into 2009 was not favorable for many industries, publishing included. RDA's situation was not helped by the circumstances of its leveraged buyout: the Ripplewood deal had included the assumption of RDA's $776.3 million debt loan with a $1.31 billion term loan and $300 million of revolving credit, of which $206 million was still outstanding at the end of 2008.[11] (See Exhibit 2.)

Since 2007 CEO Berner had instituted several changes to the RDA lineup, including divesting businesses, reconfiguring the RDA Web presence, redesigning the flagship magazine, continuing global expansion, and launching new magazines. However, her program to "launch growth initiatives, reduce costs and transform the company culture" was not working in the face of reduced consumer spending and a drop in magazine advertising worldwide.[12] In January 2009, Berner announced a plan to cut 280 employees worldwide, about 8 percent of the company's global workforce, leaving RDA with about 3,220 full-time employees. RDA also asked U.S. workers to take unpaid leave in 2009 and 2010, and it suspended its matching contributions to 401(k) retirement plans.[13] The hope was that this "recession plan" would allow RDA to meet the coming debt obligations, but it owed creditors $2.1 billion and its interest payments alone in 2008 were over $160 million.[14]

*This case was prepared by Professor Pauline Assenza of Manhattanville College and Professor Alan B. Eisner of Pace University. This case was solely based on library research and was developed for class discussion rather than to illustrate either effective or ineffective handling of an administrative situation. Copyright © 2009 Pauline Assenza and Alan B. Eisner.

Exhibit 1 Reader's Digest Magazine—Selected Top-Ranked Competitors (ranked by circulation)

Magazine*	2008 Circulation, Copies	Change from 2007 (%)	2008 Circulation, Revenue ($ millions)	Publisher	Comments
Reader's Digest	8,307,292	−14.2	204.9	RDA	Private
Better Homes and Gardens	7,655,501	−0.3	169.2	Meredith Corporation	Public—85 million customer database, book publisher, owns TV stations, largest U.S. Hispanic publisher
National Geographic	5,060,712	0.2	172.6	National Geographic Society	Private
Good Housekeeping	5,060,712	0.2	104.3	Hearst Corporation	Private—diversified media, TV, radio, real estate, also publishes *Cosmopolitan, O Oprah Magazine*
Family Circle	3,906,135	−1.5	83.4	Meredith Corporation	See above
Woman's Day	3,897,370	−0.7	72.6	Hachette Filipacchi	Private—owned by France's Lagardere Group, publishes *Elle*
Ladies Home Journal	3,842,434	−1.9	66.2	Meredith Corporation	See above
People	3,746,426	1.9	559.1	Time, Inc.	Private
Time	3,374,366	0.0	184.4	Time, Inc.	Private
Prevention	3,335,348	−1.6	74.9	Rodale	Private—26 million customer database
TV Guide	3,266,323	−0.3	192.5	Open Gate Capital	Private—purchased from Macrovision in 2008
Sports Illustrated	3,239,968	0.2	284.4	Time, Inc.	Private
Taste of Home	3,200,261	0.4	62.8	RDA	Private
Newsweek	2,720,034	−12.9	126.6	Washington Post Co.	Public—*Washington Post* newspaper, TV stations, Kaplan, Inc.
Glamour	2,322,713	0.6	59.1	Conde Nast Publications	Private—also publishes *Vogue, GQ, The New Yorker*
Parenting	2,076,347	9.2	29.9	Bonnier Corp.	Private, Swedish owned, also publishes *Field & Stream, Popular Science*
US Weekly	1,903,989	−0.1	269.3	Wenner Media	Private—also publishes *Rolling Stone*
Every Day with Rachel Ray	1,776,692	19.1	47.8	RDA	Private
Birds & Blooms	1,520,638	NA	30.3	RDA	Private
Women's Health	1,168,483	37.9	29.0	Rodale	See above
Family Handyman	1,162,252	−9.7	28.3	RDA	Private

*In the list, *Reader's Digest* through *Taste of Home* were the 14 top-ranked U.S. magazines in 2008.

Source: 2008 circulation data reported by Audit Bureau of Circulation (ABC), at www.magazine.org/consumer_marketing/circ_trends/index.aspx.

Exhibit 2 Adjusted EBITDA and Debt/Leverage Trends, Fiscal Year 2008 (in millions of dollars)*

FY2008 Adjusted EBITDA		
	FY2007	**FY2008**
Revenue[1]	$2,873	$2,899
Net Loss	$ (262)	$ (502)
Income Tax Provision/(Benefit)	(45)	(5)
Interest Expense, Net	160	167
Depreciation & Amortization	100	86
Non-Cash/ One-Time / Other Items	274	475
EBITDA	$ 227	$ 222
Adjustments		
Supply Chain & Other Savings	$ —	$ 73
Global Head count Reductions	26	18
Impact of WRC/TL Integration	25	10
Public-to-Private Savings	7	—
Total Adjustments	$ 58	$ 101
Adjusted EBITDA	$ 285	$ 323

[1] Excludes purchase accounting-related adjustments.

Debt/Leverage Trends					
	6/30/2007	12/31/2007	6/30/2008	9/30/2008	12/31/2008
Revolver / Overdraft Facility	$ (85)	$ (173)	$ (205)	$ (182)	$ (229)
Term Loan B (L + 200)	(1,309)	(1,311)	(1,313)	(1,297)	(1,292)
Senior Subordinated Notes (9%)	(600)	(600)	(600)	(600)	(600)
Gross Debt	$(1,994)	$(2,084)	$(2,117)	$ (2,079)	$ (2,121)
Cash	50	120	79	36	70
Net Debt	$(1,944)	$(1,964)	$(2,038)	$ (2,044)	$ (2,051)
Pro Forma LTM Metrics:					
Adjusted EBITDA	$ 285	$ 330	$ 323	$ 291	$ 258
Interest Expense	156	169	167	163	156
Capex	28	27	26	24	17
Credit Statistics:					
Gross Debt/EBITDA	7.0×	6.3×	6.6×	7.20×	8.12×
Bank Covenant (Gross Debt/EBITDA)	—	—	—	8.75×	8.75×
Net Debt/EBITDA	6.8×	6.0×	6.3×	7.03×	7.95×
EBITDA / Interest Expense	1.8×	2.0×	1.9×	1.8×	1.7×
(EBITDA - Capex) / Interest Expense	1.6×	1.8×	1.8×	1.6×	1.5×

*Due to the acquisition by Ripplewood Holdings, for purposes of financial restatement, the original Reader's Digest Association results were excluded for the period July 1, 2005 to March 1, 2007. Therefore, financial statements for 2007 reflect the activities of Ripplewood businesses WRC Media and Direct Holdings plus only four months of the original Reader's Digest Association activities. This makes comparability of financial statements for the original Reader's Digest Association prior to 2008 very difficult.

Source: RDA company reports.

Would the future be able to report that *Reader's Digest,* once named one of the most successful magazines in the Western world,[15] had recovered enough financial stability to redefine its product line, expand its global physical and digital presence, and find a new generation of customers to inspire? Would the nonpublishing revenue streams, like the online weight-loss program *Change-One* and the social networking community of *allrecipes.com,* help? Now that almost any type of information was available online for free, what would that mean to a company whose flagship product was a 5- by 7-inch pocket-size compendium of human interest stories, educational material, humor, and practical advice? Was the overall strategy still sound, or would The Reader's Digest Association finally cease to exist?

Reader's Digest Association Business Mix As of 2009, The Reader's Digest Association, Inc., was a global multibrand media and marketing company that educated, entertained, and connected audiences around the world. The company used its editorial and content-delivery skills to serve communities. With offices in 45 countries, it marketed books, magazines, music, video, and educational products reaching 130 million households in 79 countries. It published 92 magazines, including 50 editions of *Reader's Digest,* the world's largest-circulation magazine; operated 65 branded Web sites generating 18 million unique visitors and 250 million page views per month; and sold approximately 68 million books, music, and video products across the world yearly. In 2006 the Young & Rubicam Brand Asset Valuator study named Reader's Digest as one of the strongest publishing brands in the United States.[16] As of June 30, 2008, total global circulation for RDA's magazines was approximately 39 million, with estimated global readership of over 100 million. Its global headquarters were in Pleasantville, New York.

In 2009, the company was organized around three primary business segments: *Reader's Digest United States* (formerly Reader's Digest North America), which included RD Community, Food & Entertaining, Home & Garden, and Health & Wellness; *Reader's Digest International,* comprising RD Europe, RD Asia Pacific, and RD Canada and Latin America; and *School & Educational Services* (see Exhibit 3). Although the *Reader's Digest* magazine was the oldest and most recognizable product, many of the newer ventures maintained the vision and mission first articulated by founders DeWitt and Lila Wallace in 1922. There were total revenues of $2.9 billion in 2008 produced from these "affinity"-based segments (see Exhibit 4).

The History of Reader's Digest DeWitt and Lila Wallace founded The Reader's Digest Association in 1921 to publish *Reader's Digest,* a magazine with condensed articles, which were intended to provide lasting interest and enduring significance, to "inform, enrich, entertain, and inspire" its readers.[17] The first 5,000 copies were printed, and 1,559 were delivered to subscribers by mail. In 1929, *Reader's Digest* began selling at newsstands, and the circulation grew to 62,000. By 1935 circulation had passed the 1 million mark. By 1945 the magazine had editions circulated in 16 counties and by 1970 had expanded into 13 more.

As of 1955, RDA had expanded into the worldwide publishing of condensed books, recorded music, and direct-mail sweepstakes and accepted its first advertising, but it did not carry liquor ads until 1978 and never carried cigarette ads. In 1963, RDA founded QSP, Inc., a school and youth-group fund-raising organization. In 1985, RDA pioneered the use of computers in direct-mail marketing with the opening of a $15 million data center at its global headquarters in Pleasantville, and in 1990 The Reader's Digest Association, Inc., became a public company trading on the New York Stock Exchange. In 1996, the *Reader's Digest* Web site was launched, and by 2000 the magazine was available in 13 countries in Eastern Europe.

Regarding the company's strategic direction, in 1997 the magazine was redesigned by moving the table of contents inside, and new CEO Thomas Ryder reorganized the corporate structure to focus on five basic, growing consumer interests: home, health, family, finance, and faith. He sold some assets, including part of RDA's art collection and real estate holdings. Some warehouse jobs were also moved outside the company, and several hundred employees were laid off. Ryder also acquired Books Are Fun (BAF), Ltd., in 1999 to increase distribution channels for existing products and add new nonpublishing products.

In 2000 Ryder purchased Reiman Publications, LLC, for $760 million. Reiman's publications were almost wholly consumer-content-driven and included *Taste of Home,* one of the best-selling food magazines in North America. This acquisition helped RDA reduce reliance on sweepstakes magazine sales. In 2003 RDA launched ChangeOne, a Web-based weight-loss program. RDA also reorganized once again into the three divisions of Reader's Digest North America, Reader's Digest International, and Consumer Business Services. In November 2004, RDA sold the original Reader's Digest Chappaqua property, including the Georgian mansion built by the Wallaces in 1939.

In 2005 RDA launched *Everyday with Rachel Ray,* featuring that popular author and TV personality, and RDA continued to expand its reach beyond publishing by acquiring allrecipes.com, a food Web site intended to connect cooks across the United States, and by creating *Taste of Home Entertaining,* an entertaining and party-planning business meant to extend the Taste of Home brand, which included the food magazine, cooking schools, and a best-selling cookbook. However, even with all the restructuring and expansion activity, RDA financials had not seen any appreciable change in revenue since 2002, and profits, especially from the Consumer Business Services (QSP and BAF) had continued to decline. (See Exhibits 5, 6, and 7.)

In March 2007 RDA became a private company again after its acquisition by Ripplewood Holdings.

Exhibit 3 Business Segments

Reader's Digest United States					
RD Community	**Health & Wellness**	**Home & Garden**	**Food & Entertaining**	**School & Educational Services**	**International**
Reader's Digest magazine	*Best Health*—Canadian magazine	*The Family Handyman*—largest do-it-yourself U.S. magazine	*Allrecipes.com*—for people to share recipes, leading social networking food Web site in U.S., versions in U.K. and Ireland, Australia and New Zealand, Germany, and France.	Originally called Consumer Business Services, this segment included Books Are Fun (BAF), a direct marketer of books and gifts in North America, and QSP, a school and youth group fund-raising organization, both divested during 2008; now included the following, acquired from Ripplewood Holdings during the 2007 buyout:	*Our Canada*
Selecciones—the Spanish Language version	*Best You*—rework of *Best Health* for the U.S. market, launched in 2009	*Fresh Home*—launched in 2009			*DaHeim*—Germany
RD Large Print edition	*Health Smart*—Australian magazine	Reiman Media Publications—acquired by RDA in 2000	*Every Day with Rachel Ray*—one of the fastest-growing magazines in 2008		*Meidan* *Suomi*—Finland
Select Editions—condensed book volumes	Change One—Web site, book, weight-loss program	*Backyard Living*—ceased production in 2009	*Taste of Home*—largest food magazine in U.S.	Weekly Reader—educational products for students in grades pre-K to 12	*Nasza Piekna Polska*—Poland
RD Store—online shopping for books, music, and videos	Family Health—Web site with health info	*Birds & Blooms*—largest U.S. bird-lover magazine	*Taste of Home Healthy Cooking*—launched in 2008 as rework of *Light & Tasty*		*Joy*—Mexico
Reader's Digest Trade Publishing—included the books *Taste of Home Cookbook, Extraordinary Uses for Ordinary Things, 1,801 Home Remedies, Atlas of the World*	*Purpose Driven Connection*—magazine, website, multimedia community around the ministry of pastor Rick Warren, launched in 2009	*Country* *Country Woman* *Farm & Ranch Living* *Reminisce*	*Taste of Home Cooking for 2* *Taste of Home Simple & Delicious*	Compass Learning—digitally based curriculum materials	*Receptar*—do-it-yourself magazine, Czech Republic *Handyman*—do-it-yourself magazine, Australia
		Country Store—Reiman Publications online catalog	Taste of Home Entertaining—home-party-planning business, created in 2006, sold 2009		*Discovery Channel Magazine*—collaboration between Discovery Networks Asia and RD Asia, launched in 2008
					TimeLife—books, music, videos, DVDs (brand name licensed from Time Warner, Inc., up for renewal in 2013), acquired from Ripplewood

Product Diversity

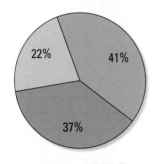

% of Revenue

- 40%
- 27%
- 19%
- 7%
- 7%

☐ Books
☐ Music and Videos
☐ Magazine Subscriptions
☐ Magazine Advertising
☐ Food and Gift / Other

Divisional Overview

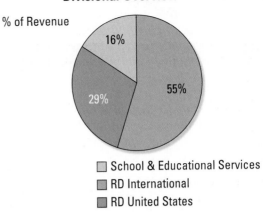

% of Revenue

- 55%
- 29%
- 16%

☐ School & Educational Services
☐ RD International
☐ RD United States

RD U.S. Revenue by Affinity

- 41%
- 37%
- 22%

☐ Home & Garden / Health & Wellness
☐ RD Community
☐ Food & Entertaining

2008 RD U.S. Revenue: $0.8 billion

RD International Revenue by Territory

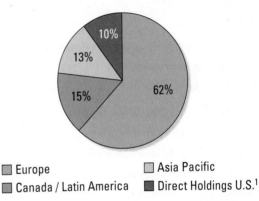

- 62%
- 15%
- 13%
- 10%

☐ Europe
☐ Asia Pacific
☐ Canada / Latin America
☐ Direct Holdings U.S.[1]

2008 RD International Revenue: $1.6 billion

School & Educational Services Revenue by Segment

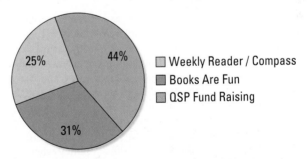

- 44%
- 31%
- 25%

☐ Weekly Reader / Compass
☐ Books Are Fun
☐ QSP Fund Raising

2008 School & Educational Services Revenue: $0.5 billion

Exhibit 4 2008 Revenue Picture (total revenue = $2.9 billion)

[1] Direct Holdings U.S. reports to Europe.

Source: Reader's Digest.

Where to Go from Here? In 2007, new RDA CEO Mary Berner began her reign by restructuring RDA once again, changing to the affinity-based focus in the United States (RD Community, Food & Entertaining, Home & Garden, and Health & Wellness) and clearly separating the International business segment from the U.S. activities. Berner also continued RDA's international expansion with the launch of *Health Smart* magazine in Australia and *Our Beautiful Poland (Nasza Piekna Polska)* in Poland. In 2008, this expansion was continued: *Reader's Digest* magazine

Exhibit 5   The Reader's Digest Association, Inc., Income Statement, Prior to Acquisition, 2004 to 2006 (in millions of dollars, year-end June 30)

	2006	2005	2004
Revenues	$2,386.2	$2,389.7	$2,388.5
Product, distribution, and editorial expenses	(997.1)	(970.9)	(972.9)
Promotion, marketing, and administrative expenses	(1,240.0)	(1,337.5)	(1,294.5)
Goodwill charge	(187.8)	(129.0)	—
Other operating items, net	(6.8)	14.1	(8.8)
Operating (loss) profit	**(45.5)**	**(33.6)**	**112.3**
Other (expense) income, net	(41.1)	(45.8)	(46.2)
(Loss) income before provision for income taxes	**(86.6)**	**(79.4)**	**66.1**
Income tax provision	(30.8)	(11.5)	(16.6)
Net (loss) income	**$ (117.4)**	**$ (90.9)**	**$ 49.5**
Basic and diluted (loss) earnings per share			
Basic (loss) earnings per share			
Weighted average common shares outstanding	95.9	97.4	97.1
Basic (loss) earnings per share	**$ (1.24)**	**$ (0.95)**	**$ 0.50**
Diluted (loss) earnings per share			
Adjusted weighted average common shares outstanding	95.9	97.4	99.2
Diluted (loss) earnings per share	**$ (1.24)**	**$ (0.95)**	**$ 0.49**
Dividends per common share	**$ 0.40**	**$ 0.30**	**$ 0.20**

Source: From RDA 2006 Annual Report, http://www.rd.com/corporate/2006/content.html.

was launched in Turkey, People's Republic of China, and Serbia. *Discovery Channel Magazine* was launched in Asia Pacific, and *Best Health* was launched in Canada.

In 2008, in an attempt to reduce costs and streamline the product line, Berner sold the fund-raising business QSP, Inc., to subsidiaries of Time, Inc., for a purchase price of $110 million, sold the home-party-planning business Taste of Home Entertaining, and sold the principal operating assets of display merchandiser Books Are Fun to Imagine Nation Books for $16.8 billion. Then, in 2009, from the Weekly Reader Publishing Group, RDA sold off Gareth Stevens, the library publishing division, and World Almanac Education Library, the library wholesaling division. This ended Thomas Ryder's experiment in diversifying out of the publishing business, and it left the School & Educational Services business segment with only the WRC Media product lines Weekly Reader and Compass Learning.

The editorial philosophy of the Reiman publications, making extensive use of reader-generated content, was pushed to all the affinities, resulting in 85 percent of the Home & Entertaining and 50 percent of the Home & Garden content being contributed by readers. RDA believed that, in addition to reducing editorial costs, utilizing a significant amount of reader-generated, community-oriented content created a bond with its customers, generating strong renewal rates, and was a unique differentiator in the print world as well as a popular trend in the online world.

Supporting the customer-centered approach, since RDA sold magazine subscriptions, books, and music and video products principally through direct mail, RDA had a policy whereby customers could return any book or home entertainment product for a full refund of the amount paid. RDA believed that this policy was essential to RDA's reputation and therefore generated a greater number of orders. Also appealing to readers, although most magazine publishers traditionally generated more than 50 percent of revenue from advertising, RDA advertising had historically represented a significantly smaller percentage of its total magazine revenue. Approximately 83 percent of total international fiscal 2008 revenue for *Reader's Digest* was generated by circulation revenue (subscription, newsstand, and other retail sales) and only 17 percent by advertising revenue. This reduced the "clutter" in the magazine.

Exhibit 6 The Reader's Digest Association, Inc., Reportable Segment Results, Prior to Acquisition, 2002 to 2006 (in millions of dollars, year-end June 30)

	2006	2005	2004[1]	2003[1]	2002
Revenues					
Reader's Digest North America	$ 939	$ 917	$ 919	$ 932	$ 649
Reader's Digest International	1,031	1,012	970	1,008	1,078
Consumer Business Services	446	485	525	563	668
Intercompany eliminations	(30)	(24)	(26)	(28)	(26)
Total revenues	**$2,386**	**$2,390**	**$2,388**	**$2,475**	**$2,369**
Operating profit (loss)					
Reader's Digest North America	$ 115	$91	$ 71	$ 61	$ (2)
Reader's Digest International	78	76	57	49	106
Consumer Business Services	(3)	29	59	91	88
Magazine previously deferred promotion expense[2]	—	(77)	(27)	—	—
Goodwill charge[3]	(188)	(129)	—	—	—
Corporate unallocated	(40)	(38)	(44)	(22)	(7)
Other operating items, net[4]	(7)	14	(9)	(40)	(27)
Operating profit (loss)	**$ (45)**	**$ (34)**	**$ 112**	**$ 139**	**$ 158**
Intercompany eliminations					
Reader's Digest North America	$ (11)	$ (9)	$ (1)	$ (1)	$ (4)
Reader's Digest International	(6)	(4)	(4)	(4)	(6)
Consumer Business Services	(13)	(11)	(11)	(11)	(16)
Total intercompany eliminations	**$ (30)**	**$ (24)**	**$ (26)**	**$ (28)**	**$ (26)**

[1] In the first half of 2005, we made minor modifications to the composition of two of our reportable segments to reflect a change in the manner in which senior management and our chief operating decision maker internally manage certain smaller business units. Reader's Digest Young Families and Trade Publishing which were included in Consumer Business Services, are now included in Reader's Digest North America.

[2] In connection with our change to expensing magazine deferred promotion costs when the promotion is mailed to prospective customers, our reportable segment operating (loss) profit in 2005 includes such expense as incurred. Amortization of previously deferred promotion costs in 2005 and our deferred promotion charge recorded in the fourth quarter of 2004 are not included in segment results reviewed by our chief operating decision maker. For the year ended June 30, 2005, amortization of previously capitalized magazine promotion costs related to: 81% to Reader's Digest North America and 19% to Reader's Digest International. For the year ended June 30, 2004, our magazine deferred promotion charge related to: 45% to Reader's Digest North America and 55% to Reader's Digest International.

[3] The goodwill charge related to Books Are Fun, part of the Consumer Business Services reportable segment, is not included in segment results.

[4] Other operating items, net in 2004, principally comprising severance and contract terminations, were attributable to: 12% to Reader's Digest North America, 22% to Consumer Business Services, 61% to Reader's Digest International and 5% to corporate departments that benefit the entire organization. In 2003, these items, principally severance, were attributable to: 13% to Reader's Digest North America, 6% to Consumer Business Services, 64% to Reader's Digest International and 17% to corporate departments that benefit the entire organization.

Source: From SEC 10K filing June 30, 2006.

However, in a move to increase revenue, Berner decided to begin promoting and accepting advertising in Reiman magazines.

In 2008, Berner redesigned the *Reader's Digest* magazine logo, layout, and Web site and initiated a redefinition of RDA's mission. The logo redesign was met by conflicting response from long-time readers: "old cover—comforting and familiar; new cover—cold and cluttered."[18] The original mission statement that had guided the company since its founding in 1921 was "we create products that inform, entertain and inspire people of all ages and cultures around the world." Berner's new mission was meant to focus the company around a "new RDA" that created "communities around branded content that can be consumed by customers

Exhibit 7 The Reader's Digest Association, Inc., Revenue by Product and Geographic Area, Prior to Acquisition, 2002 to 2006 (in millions of dollars, year-end June 30)

Net Revenues by Product	2006	2005	2004	2003	2002
Books	$ 955.1	$ 971.6	$ 968.5	$ 982.9	$ 963.8
Magazines—subscription & other	$ 683.7	$ 689.8	$ 702.7	$ 750.1	$ 610.1
Magazines—advertising	$ 158.9	$ 153.2	$ 150.0	$ 151.0	$ 151.4
Music & videos	$ 264.1	$ 262.7	$ 240.3	$ 257.4	$ 328.8
Food & gift	$ 215.1	$ 215.0	$ 228.7	$ 244.9	$ 256.7
Fees from financial services marketing alliances	—	—	$ 16.9	$ 13.2	$ 20.8
Other	$ 109.3	$ 97.4	$ 81.4	$ 75.4	$ 37.0
Totals	**$2,386.2**	**$2,389.7**	**$2,388.5**	**$2,474.9**	**$2,368.6**

Revenues by Area	2006	2005	2004	2003	2002
United States	$1,202.6	$1,232.6	$1,291.3	$1,351.8	$1,176.7
International	$1,189.2	$1,162.6	$1,102.1	$1,124.6	$1,196.3
Inter-area	($5.6)	($5.5)	($4.9)	($1.5)	($4.4)
Totals	**$2,386.2**	**$2,389.7**	**$2,388.5**	**$2,474.9**	**$2,368.6**

Source: All data are from the RDA 10K filing of 2006.

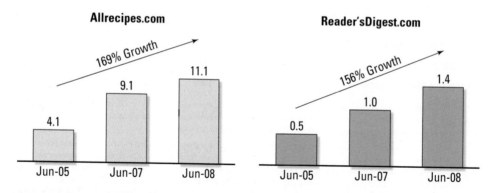

Allrecipes.com

169% Growth

Jun-05	Jun-07	Jun-08
4.1	9.1	11.1

Reader'sDigest.com

156% Growth

Jun-05	Jun-07	Jun-08
0.5	1.0	1.4

Exhibit 8 Average Monthly Unique Visitors (in millions):
Sources: WebTrends and Omniture.

when, where and how they want it." The mission read: "We are a global multi-brand and marketing company that educates, entertains and connects audiences around the world. We are dedicated to providing our customers with the inspiration, ideas and tools that *simplify* and *enrich* their lives." The new vision was to "create the world's largest multiplatform communities based on branded content." [19]

Berner also began developing a "global digital repository of all content, which will facilitate and expedite access to content and permit use of it across multiple platforms and channels." [20] In fiscal 2008 RDA saw "double digit growth in digital revenue driven by advertising and consumer transactions." [21] This underscored the necessity for continuing to increase Web traffic to all RDA Internet locations. (See Exhibit 8.)

The commitment to interactive media was underscored by the creation of a position in early 2009—president, Global RDA Interactive—with responsibility for all of RDA's digital activities. This position was charged with leading RDA's "efforts to expand digital media and marketing globally including e-commerce and other revenue-generating initiatives." [22]

Also in 2009, RDA Launched *Fresh Home* and *Best You* magazines, both reworked from RDA international

Exhibit 9 The Reader's Digest Association, Inc., Consolidated Balance Sheet, Historical Data after Acquisition, 2007 to 2008 (in millions of dollars, except share data, year-end June 30)*

	2008	2007
Assets		
Current assets		
Cash and cash equivalents	$ 79.40	$ 50.20
Accounts receivable, net	304.20	326.00
Inventories	190.70	188.10
Prepaid and deferred promotion costs	61.50	61.40
Prepaid expenses and other current assets	169.80	164.90
Total current assets	805.60	790.60
Property, plant and equipment, net	108.30	117.70
Goodwill	1,664.00	1,844.30
Other intangible assets, net	977.80	1,090.70
Prepaid pension assets	290.90	336.50
Other noncurrent assets	119.50	218.80
Total assets	$3,966.10	$4,398.60
Liabilities and stockholders' equity		
Current liabilities		
Short-term debt	$ 25.60	$ 13.10
Accounts payable	242.10	238.20
Accrued expenses	284.60	320.60
Income taxes payable	29.20	22.70
Unearned revenues	378.80	311.90
Other current liabilities	11.90	11.30
Total current liabilities	972.20	917.80
Long-term debt	2,091.90	1,981.40
Unearned revenues	137.60	102.20
Accrued pension	84.00	112.90
Postretirement and post employment benefits other than pensions	25.50	61.10
Other noncurrent liabilities	399.90	536.70
Total liabilities	$3,711.10	$3,712.10
Commitments and contingencies		
Stockholders' equity		
Preferred stock		20.70
Paid-in capital	1,008.80	1,001.80
Accumulated deficit	(907.20)	(405.10)
Accumulated other comprehensive gain	153.40	69.10
Total stockholders' equity	255.00	686.50
Total liabilities and stockholders' equity	$3,966.10	$4,398.60

*For purposes of financial restatement, the historical original Reader's Digest Association results were excluded for the period July 1, 2005, to March 1, 2007. Therefore, all historical financial statements for 2006 and 2007 reflect only the businesses of WRC Media and Direct Holdings. This makes comparability of financial statements for the original RDA prior to 2008 very difficult.

Source: RDA company reports.

Exhibit 10 The Reader's Digest Association, Inc., Income Statement, after Acquisition, Pro Forma, Unaudited, 2006 to 2008 (in millions of dollars, year-end June 30)[*]

	2008	2007	2006
Revenues	$2,786.40	$2,691.10	$2,622.90
Product, distribution and editorial expenses	(1,223.40)	(1,245.10)	(1,177.40)
Promotion, marketing and administrative expenses	(1,568.20)	(1,544.00)	(1,528.80)
Goodwill and intangible asset impairment	(307.20)		(187.80)
Other operating items, net	(25.00)	(49.00)	(7.20)
Operating loss	($337.40)	($147.00)	($278.30)
Other income (expense), net	($169.10)	($160.10)	($161.00)
Loss before benefit (provision) for income taxes, discontinued operations, extraordinary item	(506.50)	(307.10)	(439.30)
Income tax benefit (provision)	4.50	45.00	43.50
Loss from continuing operations	(502.00)	(262.10)	(395.80)
Income from discontinued operations, extraordinary gain			62.40
Net (loss) income	($502.00)	($262.10)	($333.40)

[*]The pro forma information represents WRC Media, Direct Holdings, and Reader's Digest Association for the 12 months ending 2007 as if the acquisition occurred as of July 1, 2006. This makes comparability of financial statements for the original RDA prior to 2008 very difficult.

Source: RDA company reports.

magazines. RDA also embarked on an alliance with pastor Rick Warren, launching *Purpose Driven Connection*. These new ventures prompted one analyst to comment that instead of launching new magazines into an uncertain economic environment, could RDA have "plowed these resources into paying its own debt"?[23] But others were cautiously positive, especially about the global appeal of Rick Warren's *Purpose Driven Connection* message. The product was conceived as a magazine plus a DVD and companion guide, a multimedia curriculum for the members of Evangelical small groups that could facilitate spiritual discussion. Alyce Alston, RDA president of the Health & Wellness affinity, which had responsibility for this launch, pointed out that "if we touched just 1 percent of Evangelicals in America, that's 900,000 members."[24]

As its long history indicated, RDA had had its ups and downs. It appeared once again that this fixture of the American newsstand might be facing an inevitable decline (see Exhibits 9 and 10).

The unfortunate timing of the private equity leveraged buyout might have finally created the ultimate risk factor. In its 2008 Annual Report, RDA noted that "there can be no assurances that our businesses will generate sufficient cash flows from operations to fund our day-to-day operations, and, more importantly, our debt service obligations . . . a decline in our operating results or available cash could cause us to experience difficulties in complying with covenants contained in our financing agreements,

which could result in our bankruptcy or liquidation."[25] Was there, indeed, anything Mary Berner could do to prevent this?

Endnotes

1. J. Horwitz. "Reader's indigestion." March 23, 2009, from http://tbm.thebigmoney.com/articles/impressions/2009/03/20/readers-indigestion.
2. Standard & Poor's. 2009. "Reader's Digest Assn. Inc. rating cut to 'CCC' from 'B− '; Outlook negative." February 19, 2009; Moody's Investors Service. "Moody's downgrades Reader's Digest's CFR and PDR to Caa3; Approximately $2.1 billion of debt affected." February 20, 2009, from the Reader's Digest 8K SEC filing of March 23, 2009.
3. RDA. Annual Report, 2006.
4. R. Ali. "Reader's Digest to be sold for $1.6 billion to private equity; online still small but growing part." November 16, 2006, from www.paidcontent.org/entry/readers-digest-sold-16-billion-to-private-equity-online-still-small-but-gro.
5. "So what do you do, Mary Berner?" *Mediabistro.com*, March 7, 2007, www.mediabistro.com/articles/cache/a9542.asp.
6. K. J. Kelly. "Berner to help Digest." *New York Post*, March 3, 2007, www.nypost.com/seven/03032007/business/berner_to_help_digest_business_keith_j__kelly.htm.
7. M. Flamm. "New chief lures Conde Nast allies as she plots overhaul of old-line publisher." *Crain's New York Business*, May 14, 2007, p. 3.

8. M. Steinmetz. "M&A boomtown: How long will it last?" *Publishing Executive,* February 1, 2007, www.pubexec.com/story/story.bsp?sid=47357&var=story.

9. "Ripplewood Holdings announces." 2007.

10. Flamm. "New chief lures Conde Nast allies."

11. E. Savitz. "Reader's Digest: Bankruptcy candidate du jour." March 4, 2009, http://blogs.barrons.com/techtraderdaily/2009/03/04/readers-digest-bankruptcy-candidate-du-jour.

12. "RDA economic 'recession plan' to include job eliminations." January 28, 2009.

13. Ibid.

14. Horwitz. "Reader's indigestion."

15. N. Angeletti and A. Oliva. *Magazines That Make History.* University Press of Florida, 2004.

16. Reader's Digest, 10K Annual Report, June 30, 2008, p. 27.

17. Information in this section is from Reader's Digest. "Timeline." http://www.rd.com; and from Peter Canning. *American Dreamers: The Wallaces and Reader's Digest.* Simon & Schuster, NY, 1996, http://syracuseuniversitypress.syr.edu/encyclopedia/entries/readers-digest.html.

18. "Reading that's hard to digest." *Brand New* (blog), December 12, 2007, www.underconsideration.com/brandnew/archives/reading_thats_hard_to_digest.php.

19. Reader's Digest Association. PowerPoint presentation, Q2 Fiscal 2009 update, February 26, 2009.

20. Reader's Digest. 10K Annual Report, June 30, 2008, p. 27.

21. Ibid.

22. "Lara Bashkoff Named President, Global RDA Interactive for the Reader's Digest Association, Inc." February 2, 2009, http://phx.corporate-ir.net/phoenix.zhtml?c=71092&p=irol-newsArticle&ID=1254738&highlight=.

23. Z. Bissonnette. "Reader's Digest launches three new magazines." *Blogging Stocks,* March 3, 2009, www.bloggingstocks.com/2009/03/03/readers-digest-launches-three-new-magazines.

24. A. Sullivan. "Rick Warren's magazine: A publishing leap of faith." *Time.* March 10, 2009, www.time.com/time/nation/article/0,8599,1884038,00.html.

25. Reader's Digest. 10K Annual Report, June 30, 2008, p. 27.

Case 34   General Motors*

On March 5, 2009, auditors for General Motors, in one of the bleakest assessments yet of the automaker's prospects, said that the firm's survival was in substantial doubt even if it received the additional $30 billion it was hoping to borrow from the federal government. The announcement by Deloitte & Touche underscores how difficult it will be for GM to successfully complete the restructuring plan that it filed with the Treasury Department a month earlier. Although GM had already received $13.4 billion in government loans, it recently announced a loss of $30.9 billion during 2008 (see Exhibits 1 to 3).

The lack of progress must be frustrating for Wagoner. Since he took over the struggling firm in 2000, he has tried to deal with GM's problems through a series of restructurings. The most serious efforts have been

*This case was developed by Professor Jamal Shamsie, Michigan State University, with the assistance of Professor Alan B. Eisner, Pace University. Material has been drawn from published sources to be used for class discussion. Copyright © 2009 Jamal Shamsie and Alan B. Eisner.

made since 2005, when the firm announced a $10.6 billion loss, its first loss in 12 years. Wagoner has since cut back on the firm's production capacity, offered buyouts to hourly workers, and made pivotal agreements with the union to reduce health care costs for active and retired workers. He has also pushed GM to offer more attractive cars that would generate better reviews and improve profit margins.

In the latest attempt to turn GM around, Wagoner has come up with yet another restructuring plan. He plans to shrink the brands down to four: Chevrolet, Cadillac, Buick, and GMC (see Exhibit 4). GM announced plans to sell or phase out Hummer and Saab. GM hopes to spin off Saturn, which it once hoped would build small cars to counter the best of the Japanese rivals. Pontiac, the brand that it had hoped to recast with a sporty image, will be reduced to just one or two models and essentially cease to exist as a separate line. It also intends to lay off another 47,000 of its 244,000 workers worldwide and to close five more plants

Exhibit 1   Income Statement (in thousands of dollars)

Period Ending	31-Dec-08	31-Dec-07	31-Dec-06
Total revenue	148,979,000	181,122,000	207,349,000
Cost of revenue	149,311,000	169,001,000	164,682,000
Gross profit	(332,000)	12,121,000	42,667,000
Operating expenses:			
Selling, general, and administrative	20,952,000	16,511,000	29,319,000
Others	—	—	4,071,000
Operating income or loss	(21,284,000)	(4,390,000)	9,277,000
Income from continuing operations:			
Total other income/expenses net	(1,921,000)	2,284,000	2,721,000
Earnings before interest and taxes	(29,388,000)	(3,351,000)	11,998,000
Interest expense	—	2,902,000	16,945,000
Income before tax	(29,388,000)	(6,253,000)	(4,947,000)
Income tax expense	1,766,000	37,162,000	(2,785,000)
Minority interest	108,000	(406,000)	—
Net income from continuing ops	(30,860,000)	(43,297,000)	(1,978,000)
Discontinued operations	—	4,565,000	—
Net income	(30,860,000)	(38,732,000)	(1,978,000)

Source: Yahoo! Finance.

Exhibit 2 Balance Sheet (in thousands of dollars)

Period Ending	31-Dec-08	31-Dec-07	31-Dec-06
Assets			
Current assets:			
Cash and cash equivalents	14,053,000	24,817,000	24,123,000
Short-term investments	13,000	2,139,000	138,000
Net receivables	7,711,000	9,659,000	20,173,000
Inventory	16,405,000	20,222,000	20,046,000
Other current assets	3,142,000	3,566,000	—
Total current assets	**41,324,000**	**60,403,000**	**64,480,000**
Long-term investments	2,903,000	10,854,000	11,760,000
Property, plant, and equipment	42,030,000	49,983,000	53,728,000
Goodwill	—	736,000	799,000
Intangible assets	265,000	330,000	319,000
Other assets	4,427,000	24,461,000	22,139,000
Deferred long-term asset charges	98,000	2,116,000	32,967,000
Total assets	**91,047,000**	**148,883,000**	**186,192,000**
Liabilities and Stockholders' Equity			
Current liabilities:			
Accounts payable	58,180,000	64,291,000	63,370,000
short/current long-term debt	15,754,000	6,047,000	5,666,000
Total current liabilities	**73,934,000**	**70,338,000**	**69,036,000**
Long-term debt	31,603,000	38,556,000	42,505,000
Other liabilities	69,027,000	75,502,000	78,902,000
Deferred long-term liability changes	1,823,000	2,967,000	—
Minority interest	814,000	1,614,000	1,190,000
Total liabilities	**177,201,000**	**185,977,000**	**191,633,000**
Stockholders' equity:			
Common stock	1,017,000	943,000	943,000
Retained earnings	(70,610,000)	(39,392,000)	406,000
Capital surplus	15,755,000	15,319,000	15,336,000
Other stockholders' equtiy	(32,316,000)	(13,964,000)	(22,126,000)
Total stockholders' equity	**(86,154,000)**	**(37,094,000)**	**(5,441,000)**
Net tangible assets	**(86,419,000)**	**(38,160,000)**	**(6,559,000)**

Source: GM.

Exhibit 3 Market Shares

	United States	Global
2008	21.0*	13.0*
2007	23.5	13.3
2006	24.2	13.5
2004	27.2	14.3
2002	28.3	15.0
2000	29.0	15.2
1990	35.0	16.5

*Estimated.

Source: GM.

Exhibit 4 U.S. Sales by Division, 2008

Division	Sales	Top-Selling Models
Chevrolet	1,790,519	Silverado Pickup, Cobalt, Malibu, Impala
GMC	361,739	Sierra Pickup, Acadia
Pontiac	267,348	G, Vibe
Cadillac	161,159	CTS, DTS
Buick	137,197	Lucerne, Enclave
Saturn	188,004	Vue, Aura
Hummer	27,485	H2, H3
Saab	21,368	9-3, 9-5

Source: GM, Motorintelligence.com.

in North America on top of the nine it had already decided to shut a few months earlier.

But Wagoner's biggest challenge lies in striking deals with GM's bondholders and its workers. He is trying to work out a deal to swap debt for equity with bondholders in order to reduce GM's debt from $27 billion to $9 billion. Wagoner is also engaged in intense negotiations with the United Automobile Workers on reducing costs to bring them more in line with those of foreign automakers. In particular, GM is searching for new terms for funding a trust fund for health care costs of retired workers that had been hailed as a successful move to reign in costs when it was painstakingly negotiated in 2007.

Wagoner insists that it takes time to deal with problems that have grown as a result of mistakes that were made by GM's management over the last 30 years. He has complained that former heads from Frederic Donner to Roger Smith had built up a bloated bureaucracy that cranked out boring, low-quality cars for many years. Wagoner is confident, however, that the latest series of moves was "comprehensive, responsive and achievable."[1] But it is becoming clear that even if he is successful, GM is likely to also lose leadership of the U.S. market, having already been replaced in 2008 by Toyota as the world's largest automaker.

Seeking Greater Integration

When Wagoner took over in 2000, he possessed considerable knowledge of GM as a long-time insider. He knew which brutal facts needed to be confronted, and he was aware of the specific veterans who could handle key jobs. He moved rather quickly to assemble a new management team to help him turn around GM's performance. In order to start turning out more cars that consumers would buy, he brought Robert A. Lutz out of retirement and appointed him to head the firm's crucial product development. Lutz had sparked Chrysler's resurgence during the 1990s with cars such as the Dodge Viper and PT Cruiser.

Under Lutz, GM has been trying to get all of the functional areas to work together more closely throughout the product development process. In the past, even if a bold design made it off the drawing board, it had little chance of surviving as it was handed over to marketing, then passed to engineering, and finally sent to manufacturing. Analysts recall the rollout of the much anticipated Pontiac Aztec, which would eventually be regarded as a vehicle whose design appealed to few consumers. Since then, there has been a concentrated effort to wean the GM culture away from a focus on engineering processes. Lutz has pushed designers to get more involved with the development process and engineers to find ways to stick with the original car design.

Against all odds, Wagoner has also made real progress in tearing down the boundaries between the firm's free-wheeling fiefdoms operating around the world. For most of its history, GM has been run as a collaboration of relatively autonomous geographic divisions that rarely worked with one another. In 1994, there were 27 different units within the firm that were purchasing parts, making it difficult to achieve economies of scale. Consequently, GM's overseas operations have failed to generate sufficient profits, as the company has had to respond to stronger competitors that have competed on a more global basis. The various geographic divisions have therefore failed to show profitability on a consistent basis, moving back and forth between profits and losses (see Exhibits 5 and 6).

Wagoner has been working with Lutz to restructure GM's four different geographic units in order to get them to collaborate with one another on designing, manufacturing, and marketing cars. Gradually, key decisions about the firm's product development are being made at GM's headquarters rather than at various far-flung subsidiaries. A global council in Detroit now decides how to allocate GM's funds for new model development and serves as a check on units whose plans veer off course. The efficiencies that

Exhibit 5 Breakdown by Region (in billions of dollars)

Region	Revenues	Net Profit or Loss
North America:		
2007	112.4	−3.3
2006	116.7	−4.6
2005	111.4	−8.2
2004	115.3	1.4
Europe:		
2007	37.4	−0.5
2006	33.3	−0.3
2005	31.9	−1.0
2004	31.2	−0.8
Latin America and Africa:		
2007	18.9	1.3
2006	14.6	0.5
2005	11.8	−0.6
2004	8.9	0.1
Asia Pacific:		
2007	21.0	0.7
2006	15.5	1.2
2005	10.8	−0.1
2004	7.0	0.7

Source: GM.

Exhibit 6 Capacity Utilization

	Year	Production as % of North American Capacity
GM	2008	69.5
	2004	79.9
Ford	2008	68.2
	2005	79.1
Chrysler	2008	59.4
	2005	93.1
Toyota	2008	78.6
	2005	98.5

Source: Autodata, Edmunds.com.

have been created by these changes are likely to reduce the firm's overall cost structure over the next few years.

Through such efforts at greater integration between different parts of the organization, GM has been able to reorganize the product development process to make it speedier, cheaper, and more effective. The firm has also been trying to improve this process by adopting practices that the Japanese have perfected over many years. In past decades, only a small percentage of parts were reused from one generation of cars to the next. Lutz has managed to raise that to 40 to 60 percent, about on par with the Japanese. GM has also been trying to develop several models that share frame parts or a similar chassis. "GM is managing its product development more efficiently than ever," Lutz recently declared.[2]

Coping with Multiple Brands

For years, GM built its position of dominance by offering cars that were designed for different customers by separate divisions. Each of these divisions came to represent a distinct nameplate or brand. GM's extensive brand lineup has long been it's primary weapon in beating back both domestic and foreign rivals. But as the firm's market share began to decline, it became difficult to design and market cars under several brands. To cut costs, GM began to share designs and parts across divisions, leading to some loss of distinctiveness between the different brands.

Analysts have been questioning GM's decision to build as many as eight divisions, with the recent addition of Hummer. In particular, Saab, Pontiac, Hummer, and Saturn have been struggling to attract customers for many years. The firm has been forced to dump large numbers of these cars at discount rates to car-rental firms, corporate-fleet buyers, and GM's own employees. As a result of these practices, Saturn, Saab, and Hummer generated an average pretax loss of $1.1 billion a year between 2003 and 2007. Wagoner did wind down the Oldsmobile division soon after he took over. But the estimated $1 billion that GM had to spend to settle with its dealers made him reluctant to close other divisions.

The decision to carry so many brands required that GM offer over 60 different models of cars and trucks. With so many vehicles to support, the firm could offer new models on only a small percentage of them in any given year. This made several of its cars look considerably older, tarnishing the image of the firm. The current model of the best-selling Chevy Impala, for example, will be a decade old before it will be replaced. A. Andrew Shapiro, an analyst, explained that carrying several brands made it difficult for GM to make sufficient investments to build up any of them. He stated that this has had serious consequences for the firm: "No particular brand or brands can achieve the share of voice that they need."[3]

Of the four brands that GM finally decided to close down or spin off, Saturn had once held the most promise. The division was started in 1985 as a completely separate car company that would attract customers away from

Toyota and Honda. Saturns featured dent-resistant plastic bodies, its dealers promised friendly, no-haggling sales, and customers were invited to an annual "homecoming" cookout at the Saturn plant in Spring Hill, Tennessee. But GM executives decided in the mid-1990s to divert funds away from Saturn in order to support the firm's other sagging brands. The firm did not add any new vehicles to the Saturn lineup for five years, despite pleas from dealers. Recently, GM decided to start selling vehicles from its European Opel division, with some design changes, as Saturns in the United States.

Shapiro believes that GM should have started to think seriously about cutting back on its car divisions during the 1980s. By then, a number of new brands had been successfully introduced into the U.S. market, including Japanese luxury brands such as Lexus, Acura, and Infiniti and Korean mass-market brands such as Hyundai and Kia. But GM had actually added more brands until Wagoner finally decided to phase out Oldsmobile by 2004. "There are always short-term reasons for not doing something," explained Shapiro.[4]

Struggling with Inflated Costs

GM has been burdened with a high cost structure as a result of the generous contracts that it signed to end a prolonged strike by the United Automobile Workers (UAW) during 1970. The firm's management claimed that it made sense to cave in to the union's demands as the strike was proving to be very costly. In spite of the favorable terms, relations with labor have been far from peaceful. The continuing problems with labor eventually led Roger Smith to spend billions of dollars to automate GM's factories with robots. The system was abandoned because it did not work well and it created new inefficiencies.

Wagoner faced his biggest challenge in dealing with the lavish health and retirement benefits that GM had accorded to its workers. Those huge legacy costs made it difficult for Wagoner to cut back on GM's production, even as he had to rely heavily on incentives to get these cars off the dealers' lots. Wagoner explained the pressures that he faced to generate revenues in order to meet the firm's cost obligations: "We have a huge fixed-cost base. It's 30 years of downsizing and 30 years of increased health-care costs. It puts a premium on us running this business to generate cash."[5]

Over the past couple of years, Wagoner managed to negotiate with the United Auto Workers for some relief from the escalating health care costs. He was able to persuade employees and retirees to pay for part of their health care–related costs for the first time. In 2007, Wagoner was able to turn the corner by making an agreement with the UAW to push responsibility for retiree health care benefits off GM's books. GM negotiated with the union to create a health care trust, called a *voluntary employees' beneficiary association,* which would take over responsibility for these costs. The firm agreed to provide funding for this trust to be set up.

At the same time, Wagoner has also been trying to push down costs through a series of downsizings, closing plants and laying off employees. Since 2005, GM claims that it has cut as much as $9 billion in its annual operating costs through such moves. Wagoner's latest effort includes plans to cut 10,000 white-collar jobs worldwide, including 3,400 in the United States. Salaries for employees who remain will be cut by 10 percent, at least through the end of 2009. Under the terms of GM's recent contract with the UAW, the firm can hire up to 16,000 new workers at wages of $16 an hour or less, which represents a substantial savings over the $29 hourly wage for older union members (see Exhibit 7).

However, Wagoner is under considerable pressure to further decrease GM's cost structure in order to qualify for the loans that it requires from the government. He has had to resume intense negotiations with the UAW to extract some cuts in the amount that it must pay to laid-off workers to supplement their unemployment benefits. GM is also pressing the union to accept company stock for as much as 50 percent of its next scheduled contribution to the health

Exhibit 7   Cost Structure

	Hourly Wages for 2008	
	GM	**Foreign Automakers**
Automakers	U.S. Plants	U.S. Plants
Wages	$29	$26
Wage-related (includes vacation, overtime)	14	9
Retiree benefits	3	3
Other (mostly health insurance for current employees)	12	11

Source: Autodata, Edmunds.com.

care trust it set up for retired workers. But the constant demand for concessions has led Mike Green, president of one of UAW's local units, to question: "Where does it all stop? Our typical person works between 30 and 40 years. They did their part. Why should they have it taken away with the sweep of a pen?"[6]

Restoring the Product Balance

As GM began to struggle with sales of its lineup of passenger cars in the late 1980s, it started to shift its emphasis to bigger sports utility vehicles. This allowed the firm to deal with the loss of smaller-car customers to more nimble and inventive Japanese competitors. The bigger SUVs provided GM with ample profits in spite of its inflated cost structure. It is estimated that the firm was able to earn between $10,000 and $15,000 on every big SUV that it sold. In contrast, GM admittedly lost money on most of its passenger cars. "In the 1990's, G.M.'s North American operations were very profitable only because of these big vehicles," said John Cesesa, an auto analyst. "That was how they stayed alive."[7]

Within a short time, GM became the biggest producer of full-size sports utilities. By 1995, the firm was cranking out 200,000 of these seven-passenger vehicles at one of its largest plants. Such a strong focus on bigger vehicles for many years diverted GM's attention from the development of a stronger lineup of smaller cars. Even when sales of the big SUVs began to taper off in 2005 because of higher gas prices in the aftermath of Hurricane Katrina, GM was still pushing for the development of the next generation of big SUVs and pickups. "We made so much money on these vehicles for so long, I guess we just didn't see it coming," said Clifford J. Vaughn, a senior truck executive who retired from GM in 1996.[8]

Wagoner defends the decision of GM to stick with full-size SUVs because they were still generating sufficient revenues for the firm. The profits from these vehicles were considered to be crucial to carry GM through the overhaul of its North American operations and to offset its eroding market share. Wagoner explained that the firm was incurring heavy expenses as a result of its plant closings and employee layoffs. Furthermore, GM needed funds to invest in the development of smaller cars.

In part, however, GM's preference for SUVs had been driven by its relative lack of success with smaller cars. Going back to the late 1980s, the firm introduced a family of midsize cars that it had spent six years developing. But the Chevrolet Lumina, Pontiac Grand Prix, Oldsmobile Cutlass, and Buick Regal were plagued with high manufacturing costs, quality problems, and safety concerns and did not attract many buyers. Now GM has been trying to catch up with established competitors, pouring resources into new cars like the Chevrolet Malibu and pushing into the crossover market with entries like the Buick Enclave and the GMAC Arcadia.

GM has also been struggling with its response to emerging alternate technologies. It was the first to introduce an electric car, EV1 in 1998. After spending over $1 billion to develop the car, it made only about 1,500 EV1s before scrapping the model a year later. It gradually shifted its efforts to developing a new fuel-cell car to be called the Sequel, which a GM executive referred to as a "game changer."[9] By 2008, GM had decided to bank on electric cars again, with the Chevrolet Volt, a four-passenger car that will be powered by lithium-ion batteries. It is designed to run on those batteries for 40 miles, but is capable of being charged overnight when plugged into a household electrical socket. The firm expects to introduce the new car in 2010, although several observers are not sure that GM will be able to launch it by then.

Firing on All Cylinders?

With the loss that GM announced for 2008, the firm has accumulated a total net loss of almost $85 billion over the last four years. Until now, GM had been able to offset its sharp losses in North America with some success in its overseas operations, notably in China, Russia, and Brazil. But the firm incurred significant losses in all geographic areas, with losses in Europe alone rising to $1.9 billion. Chief Financial Officer Ray Young attributed the worldwide losses to the developing economic crisis: "The impact of the credit crisis has started to spread to emerging markets."[10]

In spite of these dire signs, Wagoner remains convinced that GM should finally be able to turn things around by 2012 as a result of the drastic changes that he has just announced. He believes that additional loans from the Treasury Department and the Energy Department will allow the firm to return to profitability. But many industry analysts remain unconvinced about GM's ability to return to profitability in such a short span of time. Rob Kleinbaum, who worked at GM for a decade and consulted for it for 15 more years, said, "They face extremely hard choices about the future of the company, and they have historically chosen not to make a choice."[11]

Although Wagoner admits that GM faces significant challenges, he has argued that seeking bankruptcy will pose considerable risks and place a heavier burden on the government. He remains convinced that bankruptcy would make consumers think twice about buying cars from GM. Wagoner also claims that much more government funds would be needed as debtor-in-possession financing should the company seek bankruptcy because such money is not likely to be available from private sources.

Based on GM's recently announced decisions to undertake the biggest reorganization in its history, it appears that the firm is finally willing to accept the seriousness of the situation that it is facing. For years, managers had shrugged off various possible threats, staying wedded to the status quo. There is considerable doubt among industry observers that GM will now be able to move fast enough to become competitive again. "Unless they totally restructure from top to bottom, I mean throw out everything, GM will fail," said Dan Gode, an accountant at New York University who has studied the carmaker's business model.[12]

Endnotes

1. Bill Vlasic and Nick Bunkley. Automakers Seek $14 Billion More, Vowing Deep Cuts. *New York Times,* February 18, 2009, p. A18.
2. David Welch and Kathleen Kerwin. Rick Wagoner's Game Plan. *BusinessWeek,* February 10, 2003 p. 54.
3. Micheline Maynard. A Painful Departure for Some GM Brands. *New York Times,* February 18, 2009, p. B4.
4. Ibid.
5. Alex Taylor III. Finally GM Is Looking Good. *Fortune,* April 1, 2002, pp. 51–52.
6. Bill Vlasic and Nick Bunkley. G.M. Is Pressing Union for Cuts in Health Care. *New York Times,* February 17, 2009, p. A18.
7. Bill Vlasic and Nick Bunkley. General Motors, Driven to the Brink. *New York Times,* October 26, 2008, p. BU5.
8. Ibid.
9. Alex Taylor III. GM and Me. *Fortune,* December 8, 2008, p. 94.
10. Sharon Terlep, John D. Stroll, and Neil King, Jr. Slump Sends GM to $30.9 Billion Annual Loss. *Wall Street Journal,* February 27, 2009, p. B1.
11. Ken Bensinger. Sibling Rivalry Reflects GM's Woes. *Los Angeles Times,* February 16, 2009, p. A12.
12. Ibid.

Case 35   Nintendo's Wii*

Not only did Nintendo sit behind Sony and Microsoft in terms of overall sales, but it also derived most of its revenue from the video game business. Sony had more than 180,500 employees, and its 2008 revenues were over $88 billion.[1] Microsoft had more than 81,000 employees, and its 2008 revenues were $60 billion.[2] Nintendo was founded in 1889 but had roughly only 3,000 employees and 2008 revenues of $16.4 billion.[3] Thus, Nintendo sat in the middle of two potentially dominating firms. Yet Nintendo was in the lead in video console sales growth and second, to Microsoft, in overall units sold (Microsoft had shipped its product a year ahead of Nintendo and Sony). Sales continued to soar, and within two years of its release, Nintendo Wii became the market leader of the generation. However, some observers questioned whether Nintendo's CEO Iwata would manage to keep the Wii momentum rolling into the next generation of gaming systems.

Nintendo's all-conquering Wii game console is showing its first signs of weakness, with Japanese sales falling below those of Sony's PlayStation 3 during March 2009.[4] However, Nintendo was less than frightened, since the Wii outsold the PS3 by almost three to one in the larger U.S. market in February 2009, selling 750,000 units.

Background

Although Nintendo dates back to 1889 as a playing-card maker, Nintendo's first video game systems were developed in 1979 and were known as TV Game 15 and TV Game 6.[5] In 1980 Nintendo developed the first portable LCD video game with a microprocessor. In 1985 Nintendo created the Nintendo Entertainment System (NES), an 8-bit video game console. The original NES was very successful, as its graphics were superior to any home-based console that was available at the time, and as a result more than 60 million units were sold worldwide.[6] The NES set the bar for subsequent consoles in platform design, as well as for accepting games that were manufactured by third-party developers. As competitors began developing 16-bit devices, such as Sega's Genesis system or NEC's PC Engine, Nintendo knew that it had to respond and develop its own 16-bit system.

The Super Nintendo Entertainment System (SNES) was developed to stay current with the competitors. The Super Nintendo was released in 1991 and, when purchased, came with one game, Super Mario World. This was the successor to the previous Mario Brothers games that

were played on the original 8-bit NES. In 1996 Nintendo released Nintendo 64, which caused the popularity of the Super Nintendo to decline. The Nintendo 64 is Nintendo's third-generation video game console and was named after the 64-bit processor. During its product lifetime, more than 30 million Nintendo 64 units were sold worldwide.[7]

The Nintendo 64, like its predecessors, used cartridges to play its games, but at the time, the competing systems of Sony and Sega were using CDs for game storage. Cartridges could store 64 megabytes of data, while CDs could store around 700 megabytes of data. Also, CDs were much cheaper to manufacture, distribute, and create; thus many game developers that traditionally supported Nintendo platforms began creating games that would support the other platforms to increase profits.[8] At the time, the average cost of producing a Nintendo 64 cartridge was cited as $25, compared to 10 cents to produce a CD. Therefore, game producers passed the higher expense to the consumer, which explains why Nintendo 64 games tended to sell for higher prices than Sony PlayStation games. While most Sony PlayStation games rarely exceeded $50, Nintendo 64 titles could reach $70.[9] Third-party developers naturally switched to the systems that used a less expensive CD platform (such as the PlayStation).

In 2001 Nintendo released its GameCube, which was part of the sixth-generation era of video game systems. These systems included Sony's PlayStation 2, Microsoft's Xbox, and Sega's Dreamcast. Although the GameCube did not use cartridges, Nintendo began producing its games using a proprietary optical-disk technology. This technology, while similar in appearance to CDs, was actually several inches smaller in diameter and was unable to be played using a standard CD player.

Genyo Takeda, general manager of Integrated Research and Development for Nintendo, explained that innovation and creativity were fostered by giving several different development teams "free rein to couple a dedicated controller or peripheral with a GameCube title, and then see whether or not the end result was marketable. This project gave rise not only to the Donkey Kong Bongos and the Dancing Stage Mario Mix Action Pad, but also to a number of ideas and designs that would find their way into the Wii Remote."[10]

When Nintendo released the Wii video game console in 2006, it was already in the midst of a very competitive market. The previous generation of video game consoles consisted of the Sega Dreamcast, Sony PlayStation 2, Nintendo GameCube, and Microsoft Xbox. These systems were all released between 1999 and 2001 in the United States, and although the GameCube sold more systems than the Sega Dreamcast, it fell into third place behind the PlayStation 2

*This case was prepared by graduate student Eshai J. Gorshein and Professor Alan B. Eisner of Pace University. This case was based solely on library research and was developed for class discussion rather than to illustrate either effective or ineffective handling of an administrative situation. Copyright © 2007, 2009 Alan B. Eisner.

and the Xbox. The PlayStation 2 sold more than 115 million units worldwide, more than twice the combined unit sales of the GameCube and Xbox (21 million and 24 million, respectively). The next generation of video game consoles was about to become even more competitors.

As of 2008, Nintendo's revenues and income were on attractive upward trajectories (see Exhibits 1 and 2). Exhibit 3 shows that Nintendo's stock price was soaring, despite the recession, relative to that of its larger competitions.

The Launch of the Wii

In 2006 Nintendo released its direct successor to the GameCube, the Wii (pronounced "we"). There were many reasons cited as to why the name *Wii* was chosen, but perhaps the most compelling reason was that "'Wii' sounded like 'we,' which emphasized that the console was for everyone. Wii could be remembered easily by people around the world, no matter what language they spoke. No confusion."[11] Initially the system was known by its code name, Revolution, but later the name was changed to Wii.

Nintendo stated that it wanted to make the Wii a system that would make anyone who tried it talk to his or her friends and neighbors about it.[12]

The Wii was created to establish a new standard in game control, using an innovative and unprecedented interface, the Wii Remote.[13] The Wii Remote was what made the Wii a unique home console. The remote acted as the primary controller for the Wii. Its motion-sensor capabilities allowed the user to interact and manipulate objects on the screen by moving and pointing the remote in various directions.[14] The Wii Remote was the size of a traditional remote control, and it was "limited only by the game designer's imagination."[15] For example, in a game of tennis it served as the racket when the user swung his or her arm, or in a shooting game it served as the user's gun. Not only did the remote serve as a controller, but it also had a built-in speaker and a rumble feature for even greater tactile feedback and game involvement.

The Wii remote came with an arm strap that could be tied to the user's wrist so that the remote couldn't fly away

Exhibit 1 Income Statements (in millions of yen, except per-share items; year-end March 31)

	2008	2007	2006	2005	2004
Revenue	1,672,420	966,534	509,249	515,292	514,805
Cost of revenue, total	972,362	568,722	294,133	298,115	307,233
Gross profit	700,061	397,812	215,116	217,177	207,572
Selling, general, and administrative expenses, total	172,433	131,414	92,410	83,524	82,218
Research and development	37,000	37,706	30,588	20,505	15,820
Depreciation/amortization	3,405	2,664	1,764	1,621	1,846
Unusual expense (income)	10,740	(3)	(2,227)	(123)	(2,065)
Total operating expense	1,195,940	740,503	416,668	403,642	405,052
Operating income	476,483	226,031	92,581	111,650	109,753
Interest/investment income, nonoperating	(48,151)	60,619	71,514	31,846	(58,877)
Interest income(expense), net nonoperating	(48,151)	60,619	71,513	31,846	(58,877)
Gain (loss) on sale of assets	3,671	(132)	(20)	(13)	761
Other, net	1,777	3,087	2,398	1,924	1,335
Net income before taxes	433,780	289,605	166,472	145,407	52,972
Provision for income taxes	176,532	115,348	68,138	57,962	19,692
Net income after taxes	257,248	174,257	98,334	87,445	33,280
Minority interest	99	37	46	(24)	(79)
Net income	**257,347**	**174,294**	**98,380**	**87,421**	**33,201**

Source: reuters.com.

Exhibit 2   Balance Sheets (in millions of yen, except for per-share items; year-end March 31)

	2008	2007	2006	2005	2004
Cash and equivalents	899,251	962,197	812,064	826,653	767,270
Short-term investments	353,070	115,971	64,287	20,485	17,375
Cash and short-term investments	1,252,320	1,078,170	876,351	847,138	784,645
Accounts receivable—trade, net	145,611	87,780	42,312	49,263	25,465
Total receivables, net	145,611	87,780	42,312	49,263	25,465
Total inventory	104,842	88,609	30,835	49,758	30,955
Other current assets, total	144,060	140,114	69,231	47,730	49,695
Total current assets	1,646,830	1,394,670	1,018,730	993,889	890,760
Property, plant, and equipment, total—gross	30,559	32,812	32,645	32,479	31,925
Property, plant, and equipment, total—net	55,149	57,597	55,968	54,417	55,083
Intangibles, net	2,009	505	319	354	245
Long-term investments	73,756	92,412	60,213	73,393	53,866
Other long-term assets, total	24,737	30,405	25,470	10,432	10,072
Total assets	1,802,480	1,575,590	1,160,700	1,132,480	1,010,030
Accounts payable	335,820	301,080	83,817	111,045	57,945
Accrued expenses	1,848	1,779	1,732	1,650	1,712
Other current liabilities, total	229,553	165,576	96,724	92,752	53,588
Total current liabilities	567,221	468,435	182,273	205,447	113,245
Minority interest	98	138	176	222	232
Other liabilities, total	5,292	5,141	4,160	5,351	6,303
Total liabilities	572,611	473,714	186,609	211,020	119,780
Common stock, total	10,065	10,065	10,065	10,065	10,065
Additional paid-in capital	11,640	11,586	11,585	11,584	11,584
Retained earnings (accumulated deficit)	1,380,430	1,220,290	1,096,070	1,032,830	964,524
Treasury stock—common	(156,184)	(155,396)	(155,112)	(129,896)	(86,898)
Unrealized gain (loss)	5,418	8,898	10,717	7,194	6,650
Other equity, total	(21,495)	6,432	762	(10,315)	(15,677)
Total equity	1,229,870	1,101,880	974,090	921,466	890,248
Total liabilities and shareholders' equity	1,802,480	1,575,590	1,160,700	1,132,490	1,010,030

Source: reuters.com.

when being used. The remote was powered by two AA batteries, which could power it for approximately 30 to 60 hours.[16] Exhibit 4 shows the Wii and Wii Remote.

The second part of the Wii remote innovation was the Wii Nunchuk. The Nunchuk was designed to perfectly fit the user's hand, and it connected to the remote at its expansion port. The Nunchuk had the same motion-sensing capabilities that the remote had, but it also had an analog stick to help the user move his or her characters. In addition to the analog stick, the Nunchuk had two buttons that gave the user quick access to other game functions. Thus the Nunchuk offered some of the benefits of a standard game controller coupled with the high-technology motion sensors of the remote. Users could hold a Nunchuk in one

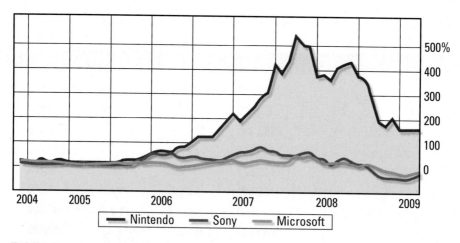

Exhibit 3 Five-Year Stock Chart of Nintendo, Sony, and Microsoft, 2004–2009

Source: reuters.com.

Exhibit 4 Wii Game Console and Remote

hand and the Wii remote in the other while playing the Wii Sports Boxing game and be transformed into the boxing ring with on-screen opponents. The game controls were intuitive for jabs and punches; however, a missed block did not hurt as much as if one were really in the boxing ring.

The ambidextrous nature of the Wii controllers was something seldom seen in other game controllers; the Wii controllers permitted the user to hold the remote and Nunchuk whichever way felt most comfortable.[17]

Features

In addition to the Wii Remote, there were other features unique to the Wii. One was the Wii Menu, which was the first screen that appeared on the television when the Wii was turned on. According to Nintendo, the Wii Menu easily integrated itself into the everyday lives of its users.[18]

The menu displayed several different icons; one of them was the Mii Channel (pronounced "me"). This channel gave the users the ability to create and personalize a 3-D caricature of themselves. Another icon was the Everybody Votes Channel, which permitted individuals to vote in national and worldwide polls on a variety of topics. There was also the New Channel, which gave the individual up-to-date breaking news from around the world, organized into a variety of topics. The Forecast Channel was another icon displayed on the Wii Menu. This allowed the individual to view weather reports from anywhere around the world. Users had the ability to download older Nintendo games from the Wii Shopping Channel. A Wii Message Board allowed users to leave messages on the Wii for other users of the same console or leave reminders for themselves. The Internet Channel allowed individuals to surf the Internet from their Wii. The Photo Channel allowed the user to view photos stored on a standard SD memory card. And lastly there was the Disc Channel, which gave the user the ability to play Wii games or Nintendo GameCube disks.[19] The Wii was backward-compatible with the Nintendo GameCube's games, memory cards, and controllers.

Online Capabilities

Nintendo's Wii was the first Nintendo console that had online capabilities. The Wii could connect to the Internet in several different ways. One way was via a standard wireless protocol—a consumer's home high-speed Internet hookup (usually from a cable TV service or telephone company DSL). Another way the Wii could connect to the Internet was via the Nintendo DS, which had wireless capability built in. The Wii could also be connected to the Internet via an optional wired USB–Ethernet adapter.

According to Nintendo of America's president and COO, Reggie Fils-Aime, the Wii would "offer online-enabled games that consumers will not have to pay a subscription fee for. They'll be able to play right out of the box. . . . It will not have any hidden fees or costs."[20] However as of mid-2007, no such games existed. So far, the only consoles to allow an individual to play games interactively with other users online were the competing products: Microsoft Xbox 360 and Sony PlayStation 3.

The Wii was released in North America on November 19, 2006, and worldwide cumulative sales as of September 30, 2008, were in excess of 34 million units (see Exhibit 5).[21] In 2006, Wii units were simultaneously released in Japan, the Americas, Oceania, Asia, and Europe. Two years later, Nintendo expanded the Wii market to South Korea and Taiwan.[22]

However, although the sales numbers were quite large, Nintendo had been experiencing production problems with the Wii. Nintendo was unable to meet demand during 2007 and also struggled throughout 2008. In an interview on the Web site Game Theory, Perrin Kaplin, Nintendo vice president of marketing and corporate affairs, suggested that shortages were expected for some time. "We are at absolute maximum production and doing everything we can . . . but demand continues to be really high."[23]

Demographics

According to Nintendo, one of the key differences between the Wii and the competitors' systems was the broad audience that the Wii targeted.[24] Many of the Wii games were able to be played by people of all ages, and they were easier to control than the complicated controllers of the Sony PlayStation 3 or Microsoft Xbox 360. Nintendo's TV commercials of the Wii showed people of different ages and social classes playing the Wii. According to Nintendo, the Wii remote allowed people of all ages to enjoy its use. Nintendo wanted to create a controller that was "as inviting as it was sophisticated."[25] Nintendo's goal was to create games that everyone could play and a system that would appeal to women and people who had never played video games in the past. Shigeru Miyamoto, a senior director at Nintendo, explained, "Most of the game business is going down a similar path toward hyperrealistic graphics which re-create sports or movies. . . . We want to put a little more art into it in a way that casual consumers can enjoy the game."[26] The Wii offered something for both the advanced gamer and the person who had never played a video game before. The advanced gamer would enjoy the remote's unique features, whereas the novice gamer could use the remote as his or her hand and wouldn't need elaborate instructions on how to play a new game straight out of the box. Although the Nintendo games were easily played by a greater range of ages, the graphics were undoubtedly a relative weakness of the product.

Although Nintendo had been able to target a large range of age groups, it seemed to lack the lineup of games offered by other systems. Nintendo had focused on its proprietary Mario Brothers series games, as well as low-graphic, low-complexity games that could be played by people in a wide range of age levels. PlayStation 3's top-selling game was Resistance: Fall of Man, which had won many awards; but more important, it had a rating of Mature (a rating given by the Entertainment Software Rating Board), which meant that it was suitable for audiences of 17 and older only. Xbox's best-selling game was Gears of War, which also had a rating of Mature. The Wii's best-selling games were The Legend of Zelda: Twilight Princess, which had a rating of *Teen,* which meant it was suitable for ages 13 and up, and Wii Sports, which was rated *Everyone,* suitable for all audiences. One of the Wii's shortcomings was obviously its graphics.[27] It was widely believed that the Wii had 2.5 times the power of the GameCube but hardly enough to compete with the Xbox 360 or PlayStation 3.

Although Nintendo hoped to target people of all ages, it had long been seen as a system that made video games for children, as evident from its Mario, Zelda, and Donkey Kong series. It was going to be difficult for Nintendo to position itself as a console for gamers of all ages and tastes.

Gaining the Interest of Game Developers

As evident from the history of game consoles, game developers have tried to make games more and more complex with each new generation of systems. This meant that more money was invested in the production of each subsequent generation of games. Because game developers were spending more money on developing games, they were at great financial risk if games did not succeed. Thus, many developers felt more secure in simply creating sequels to existing games, which in turn restricted innovation. The Wii's innovative controller, the Wii remote, required a rethinking and reengineering of the human interface for game developers and programmers. Another issue with developing games for the Wii was that its graphics were not quite as good as those of the PlayStation 3 and Xbox 360, and therefore game developers were required to be

Exhibit 5 Wii Cumulative Unit Sales

Region	Units Sold	First Available
The Americas	15,190,000	11/19/06
Japan	6,100,000	12/2/06
Other Regions	12,450,000	12/8/06
Total	**34,550,000**	

Source: Nintendo.

more creative and develop special Wii editions of their games.

Many game developers used virtual-machine software in developing new games. It was believed that game developers could develop games for the Wii and then make them for other platforms on the basis of the same programming, thereby reducing production costs. However, while the Wii remote distinguished itself from its competitors, it created a hurdle for developers. When a developer created a game for the PlayStation 3, she could create the same game for the Xbox 360 and vice versa, whereas when a developer created a game for the Wii, it required significant rework to deploy the title for the other platforms. Converting a title from the Xbox 360 or PlayStation 3 also required significant work to modify the game to incorporate code for the Wii Remote's special features.

The Competition

The launches of the Wii and the PlayStation 3 in November 2006 were the beginning of the battle for market share in the fierce competition of the seventh generation of video game consoles (see Exhibit 6). Although the Xbox 360 was released a year earlier, Microsoft intended to relaunch the Xbox 360 after some minor enhancements.

The price of $249 for the Wii included the Wii Remote, the Nunchuk attachment, the sensor bar, and the Wii Sports software title. The Wii sports title included tennis, baseball, golf, bowling, and boxing games. This retail price was much less than the prices of the PlayStation 3 and Xbox 360, possibly due to the fact that the Wii did not have as advanced a central processor unit or a high-definition video player.

Xbox 360

The Xbox 360 by Microsoft was released in November 2005, giving it a year lead over Nintendo's and Sony's new systems. While the configurations were changed several times, the Xbox 360 came in three different versions: Elite ($399 retail), Premium System ($299 retail), and Core System ($199 retail) as of 2009.

Although the prices were quite expensive to the retail consumer, in reality Microsoft was losing money on each sale. Take, for example, Microsoft's cost of producing the Premium System. It cost Microsoft $470 before assembly and an additional $55 for the cost of the cables, power cord, and controllers, bringing Microsoft's cost to $526. Thus, Microsoft was losing $227 on the sale of each system. This was the case not only with the Xbox 360 but also with its predecessor, the Xbox. There, too, Microsoft was selling a system for $299 that cost Microsoft $323 to produce.

One of the important features of the Xbox 360 was Xbox Live. According to Microsoft, Xbox Live was the "premier online gaming and entertainment service that enables you to connect your Xbox to the Internet and play games online."[28] This feature allowed individuals to play online against other users from around the world. Thus

Exhibit 6 Game Systems Comparison, 2009

	Nintendo	Sony	Microsoft
Console name	Wii	PlayStation 3	Xbox 360
Game format	12-cm Wii optical disk	Blu-Ray disc, DVD-Rom, CD-Rom	HD DVD, DVD, DVD-DL
Hard drive	None	80 GB or 160 GB	60 GB, or 120 GB
Price	$249	$399 (80 GB) or $499 (160 GB)	$199, $299, $399
Ethernet	Wi-fi standard	Wi-fi optional	Wi-fi optional
Online services	WiiConnect24, Wii Channels, no online game play	PlayStation Network, has online game play	Xbox live, has online game play
Controller	Wii remote (wireless, motion sensing)	Max 7 SixAxis (wireless)	Wired or wireless
Backward compatibility	Yes (Nintendo GameCube)	Yes (PlayStation 2)	Yes (certain Xbox games)
Game count	532	354	470*

*As of April 2009, there were 470 games specifically designed for the Xbox360. However, there were an additional 500+ games from the previous version of the Xbox that function on the Xbox360.

Source: Company reports, gamestop.com, and author estimates.

Microsoft had created a community of individuals who were able to communicate with one another by voice chats and/or play against each other in a video game. It even allowed users to "see what their friends are up to at any time" and to look not only at their friends' lists but also their friends' friends lists.[29] Another service offered by Xbox Live was the Xbox Live Marketplace, which enabled users to download movies, game trailers, game demos, and arcade games. It was estimated that more than 70 percent of connected Xbox users were downloading content from the Xbox Live Marketplace, totaling more than 8 million members.[30] According to Microsoft, there were more than 12 million downloads in less than a year and, due to this popularity, major publishers and other independent gamers had submitted more than 1,000 Xbox Live games.[31] Similar to the Wii, the Xbox 360 had a dashboard that showed up when the system was powered up. This gave the user the ability to play either DVDs or games.

The Xbox 360 had the capability to play high-definition DVDs.[32] The CPU of the Xbox 360 was a custom triple-core PowerPC-based design manufactured by IBM and known as the Xenon. The Xbox 360 played all its games in 5.1-channel Dolby Digital surround sound, and along with the HD display, the Xbox 360 could truly display excellent picture and sound quality. However, a consumer who did not have a high-definition-enabled television set was not able to enjoy the high-definition features of the system. The Xbox 360 played all its games on dual-layer DVDs, which could store up to 8.5 GB per disc but also had the ability to play many other formats.[33] The system had an Ethernet port and three USB ports but could also connect to the Internet via a wireless network.

Microsoft began production of the Xbox 360 only 69 days before the launch date.[34] As a result, Microsoft was unable to supply enough systems to meet the initial demand, and therefore many potential customers were not able to purchase a console at launch.[35] However, according to Bill Gates, Microsoft had over 10 million units out in the market by the time Sony and Nintendo launched their systems.[36]

Sony PlayStation 3

The PlayStation 3 was Sony's seventh-generation video game console. The PlayStation 3 had many advanced features, including a Cell Broadband Engine 64-bit processor that features a main power-processing element and up to eight parallel-processing elements. This was a multiprocessing unit that provided advanced support for graphics-intense games. Another notable feature of the PlayStation 3 was its ability to play Blu-Ray discs. Blu-Ray was a form of high-definition video, which enabled game developers to create games of higher sophistication.[37] Another key feature of the PlayStation 3 was the SixAxis wireless controller. This controller had sensors that could determine when a player maneuvered or angled his or her controller to allow game play to become a "natural extension of the player's body."[38] Although this was a more advanced remote than a standard wired remote, it lacked the true motion-sensing capabilities of the Wii Remote in its first version.[39]

The PlayStation 3 could play music CDs, connect to the Internet, copy CDs directly to its hard drive, play Blu-Ray discs and DVDs, connect to a digital camera, view photos, and more. However, a consumer who did not have a high-definition-enabled television set was not able to enjoy the high-definition features of the system.

Sales in North America were initially strong but tapered off rapidly, with 1.3 million units sold during the first six months of sales.[40] The United Kingdom also saw record-breaking sales of PlayStation 3, with more than 165,000 units (through heavy preordering) in its first two days on the shelves,[41] although the total European sales for the first six months of availability were only 920,000 units.[42] Sony CEO Howard Stringer attributed the slowing sales to a lack of software titles and said that Sony expected at least 380 new PlayStation 3 games to hit the market by 2008.[43] However, halfway into 2009, there were only 354 titles available for the PlayStation 3. Sony introduced new 40GB and 80 GB versions of PlayStation 3, and thanks to new features cumulative sales rose to 9.2 million units by March 2008.[44]

Part of the PlayStation Network's success was the ability to play games online. This allowed individuals to play with other players who were located in other parts of the world. The PlayStation Network allowed users to download games, view movie and game trailers, and text-message and chat with friends. Users were also able to browse the Internet and open up to six windows at once.[45]

Since the launch of the PlayStation 3, there have been mixed reports about it. On the positive note, MSN stated that the PlayStation 3 was a "versatile and impressive piece of home-entertainment equipment that lives up to the hype . . . the PS3 is well worth its hefty price tag."[46] However, *PC World* magazine ranked the PlayStation 3 eighth out of the Top-21 Tech Screw-Ups of 2006.[47]

While Sony and Microsoft envisioned long-term profits on software sales of PlayStation 3 and Xbox 360, both companies experienced losses producing their seventh-generation consoles. Among the three rivals, Nintendo was the only one earning a significant profit margin on each Wii unit sold. According to David Gibson at Macquarie Securities, sales of Nintendo Wii bring $6 of operating profit per console. [48]

Supply and Demand

When the Xbox 360 hit stores in November 2005, thousands of video game fans waited outside stores (some even in freezing weather) to be the first to purchase the console. And although the console quickly sold out, it became available several months later and there have not been problems purchasing one since. The same held true with the release of the PlayStation 3. Although it quickly sold out in stores, it was available thereafter, and anyone willing to spend the money is able to purchase it. However, Nintendo fans have had problems finding a Wii to purchase since its launch in

November 2006. Lucky customers might have walked into a retailer at the moment the latest Wii shipment arrived or might have waited in lines for hours for the privilege of paying the retail price of only $249. The unlucky customers had to search various auction Web sites such as eBay and pay premiums of double to triple the retail price.

There had been a great deal of speculation regarding the production problems with the Wii. Several analysts had argued that lack of availability of the Wii was a marketing ploy to create hype and increase demand. However, others have hypothesized that Nintendo was having production problems and was unable to meet the huge demand for the Wii. The predictions of Billy Pidgeon, program manager for IDC's Consumers Markets, that consumers would have a difficult time purchasing the Wii through late 2008 proved right. Pidgeon stated that he believed that the Wii would continue to be a successful force in the gaming industry and that Nintendo needed to start shipping out more consoles. Furthermore, he said that he didn't believe "supply will meet demand for the Wii until 2009."[49]

The supply problem was confirmed by Nintendo CEO Satoru Iwata during a company financial briefing and later on a Web site question–and-answer session in May 2007. Iwata said, "We are currently facing product shortages . . . we have been running short of inventories, and [the retailers] are getting after us."[50] Iwata said further, "Making a significant volume of the high-tech hardware, and making an additional volume, is not an easy task at all. In fact, when we clear one bottleneck for a production increase, we will face another one."[51] The supply shortage first hit the United Kingdom in 2006 and quickly spread to North America by the end of 2007. Demand for Wii units outpaced supply in the U.S. market, and as of July 2008, Nintendo was still having a hard time restocking its retail shelves on time.[52]

There were 235 games for the Nintendo Wii by the end of its release year. By 2009, however, the total number of games for the Wii (532 games) exceeded the total number of games available for its main competitor, Xbox 360 (470 games), depending on whether one counted backward compatibility with previous-generation games. The number of games indicates that the Wii was obviously a successful system—one that had drawn a good amount of interest from game developers and gamers around the world. The production problem, then, was augmented because there was great interest in the Wii. However, if Nintendo did not meet the hardware demand, game developers could simply begin developing software for systems that were available to consumers.

CEO Iwata claimed that "shipments will increase and that we are trying to increase the shipments in order to comply with the needs of patiently waiting customers," as well as increase the number of software titles available for the system from Nintendo and third-party software developers.[53] Iwata's plan and strategic management helped to achieve record sales for Nintendo Wii within 2 years of its launch. With more than 40 million (including software) units sold worldwide by January 2009,[54] Nintendo Wii claimed first place in the game industry; its main competitor, Xbox 360, was far behind, with only 28 million units.[55] However, the question remained as to whether Nintendo's Iwata could manage to keep the Wii momentum rolling into the next generation of gaming systems.

Endnotes

1. Sony. Annual Report, March 31, 2008.
2. Microsoft. Annual Report, June 30, 2008.
3. Nintendo. Annual Report, March 31, 2008.
4. Robin Harding and Chris Nuttall. Nintendo plays it cool as Sony's PS3 dents Wii's Japanese sales. *Financial Times,* April 7, 2009..
5. Nintendo. Annual Report, March 31, 2008.
6. www.nintendo.com/systemsclassic?type=nes.
7. Nintendo. Annual Report, March 31, 2008.
8. C. Bacani and M. Mutsuko. Nintendo's new 64-bit platform sets off a scramble for market share. *AsiaWeek,* April 18, 1997, www.asiaweek.com/asiaweek/97/0418/cs1.html.
9. Biggest blunders. *GamePro,* May 2005, p. 45.
10. http://wii.nintendo.com/iwata_asks_vol2_p1.jsp.
11. Chris Moriss. "Nintendo goes Wii . . ." April 2006, http://money.cnn.com/2006/04/27/commentary/game_over/nintendo/index.htm.
12. T. Surette. Nintendo exec talks Wii Online marketing. *GameSpot.com.* August 17, 2006,. www.cnet.com.au/games/wii/0,239036428,240091920,00.htm.
13. Nintendo. Annual Report, 2006.
14. See http://wii.nintendo.com.
15. http://wii.nintendo.com/controller.jsp.
16. http://wii.ign.com/articles/718/718946p1.html.
17. http://wii.nintendo.com/controller.jsp.
18. See http://wii.Nintendo.com.
19. See http://wii.nintendo.com
20. Surette. Nintendo exec talks Wii online.
21. Nintendo. Consolidated Financial Statements, October 30, 2008.
22. See http://wii.Nintendo.com.
23. http://livenintendo.com/2007/04/12/more-supply-problems-for-the-wii.
24. Nintendo. Annual Report, March 31, 2007.
25. http://wii.nintendo.com/controller.jsp.
26. En garde! Fight foes using a controller like a sword. *New York Times,* October 30, 2006, www.nytimes.com/2006/10/30/technology/30nintendo.html?ex=1319864400&en=135a11a72ad4a4f7&ei=5088&partner=rssnyt&emc=rss.
27. www.pcmag.com/article2/0,1895,2058406,00.asp.
28. www.Xbox.com/en-US.
29. www.xbox.com/en-US/live/globalcommunity/fosteringcommunity.htm.
30. www.microsoft.com/Presspass/press/2007/nov07/11-13XboxLIVEFivePR.mspx.
31. Ibid.
32. www.microsoft.com/Presspass/press/2007/jul07/07-26ComicConXboxHDDVDPR.mspx.

33. www.xbox.com/en-AU/support/xbox360/manuals/xbox360specs.htm.

34. money.cnn.com/2006/07/05/commentary/-column_gaming/index.htm?section=money_latest.

35. news.bbc.co.uk/2/hi/technology/4491804.stm.

36. www.microsoft.com/presspass/press/2006/may06/05-09E32006BriefingPR.mspx.

37. www.us.playstation.com/PS3/About/BluRay.

38. www.us.playstation.com/PS3/About/WirelessController.

39. www.scei.co.jp/corporate/release/pdf/060509be.pdf.

40. www.cbsnews.com/stories/2007/01/07/ap/business/-mainD-8MGN9J80.shtml.

41. news.bbc.co.uk/1/hi/technology/6499841.stm.

42. news.bbc.co.uk/2/hi/technology/6499841.stm.

43. N. Layne and K. Hamada. Sony promises more games to boost PS3 demand. *reuters.com,* June 21, 2007, http://www.reuters.com/article/-technologyNews/idUST28081120070621?sp=true.

44. Sony. Annual Report, March 31, 2008.

45. www.us.playstation.com/PS3/Network.

46. tech.uk.msn.com/features/article.aspx?cp-documentid=4370234.

47. www.pcworld.com/article/id,128265-page,4-c,industrynews/article.html.

48. Chana R.Schoenberger. "Wii's future in motion." *Forbes,* December 12, 2008, www.forbes.com/2008/11/28/nintendo-wii-wii2-tech-personal-cz-cs-1201wii.html.

49. http://news.teamxbox.com/xbox/13335/Analyst-Supply-Wont-Meet-Demand-for-the-Wii-Until-2009.

50. *Nintendo Investor Relations,* www.nintendo.co.jp/ir/en/library/events/070427qa/02.html.

51. E. Boyes. Nintendo: Wii have a supply problem. *CNET .News.com,*2007, http://news.com.com/Nintendo+Wii+have+a+supply+problem/2100-1043_3-6181842.html.

52. www.npd.com.

53. *Nintendo Investor Relations,* www.nintendo.co.jp/ir/en/library/events/070427qa/02.html.

54. Ibid.

55. www.microsoft.com. Press release, January 6, 2009.

Case 36   One Ford: The Shape of Ford Motor Company to Come?*

Despite joining GM and Chrysler in a request for emergency loans from Washington to avoid filing for bankruptcy, Ford had so far been determined not to actually seek use of its portion. Instead, Ford would tap credit lines it had the foresight to establish before credit markets dried up in order to bolster its cash position.[1] Ford might be facing the most challenging times of its history. Low sales had been hurting the company for years, and now macroeconomic issues such as a weak economy, volatile financial markets, and lack of liquidity in the market were adding complications for the already troubled firm. Jim Farley, Ford group vice president for marketing and communications, talking about low sales, said that "consumers and businesses are in a very fragile place. An already weak economy compounded by very tight credit conditions has created an atmosphere of caution."[2]

In January 2009, the struggling automaker posted a full-year net loss of $14.6 billion for 2008, the largest single-year loss in the company's history.[3] Attempts at restructuring Ford had been under way for years. Former CEO Jacques Nasser emphasized acquisitions to reshape Ford, but day-to-day business activities were ignored in the process. When he left in October 2001, Bill Ford took over and emphasized innovation as a core strategy to reshape Ford. Although "morale improved, still U.S. market share continued its decade-long-slide from 25 percent in 1997 to 13.7 percent in January 2009."[4] In an attempt to stem the downward slide at Ford, and perhaps to jump-start a turnaround, Alan Mulally was elected as president and chief executive officer of Ford on September 5, 2006. Mulally, former head of commercial airplanes at Boeing, was expected to steer the struggling automaker out of the problems of falling market share and serious financial losses (see Exhibit 1). Mulally was emphasizing his vision of "One Ford" to reshape the company, which claimed "to remain on track for both its overall and North American Automotive pre-tax results to be breakeven or profitable in 2011."[5] But could Mulally do it?

Why Would Ford Invite In an Outsider?

The Ford empire had been around for over a century, and the company had not gone outside its ranks for a top executive since hiring Ernest Breech away from General Motors Corporation in 1946 (see Exhibit 2).[6] Since taking the CEO position in 2001, Bill Ford had tried several times to find a qualified successor, "going after such industry luminaries

as Renault-Nissan CEO Carlos Ghosn and DaimlerChrysler chairman Dieter Zetsche."[7] Now Mulally had been selected and was expected to accomplish "nothing less than undoing a strongly entrenched management system put into place by Henry Ford II almost 40 years ago"—a system of regional fiefdoms around the world that had sapped the company's ability to compete in today's global industry and one that Chairman Bill Ford couldn't or wouldn't unwind.[8]

It had become more common to hire a CEO from outside the family or board. According to Joseph Bower from Harvard Business School, around one-third of the time at S&P 500 firms, and around 40 percent of the time at companies that were struggling with problems in operations or financial distress, an outsider was appointed as CEO. The reason might be to get a fresh point of view or to get the support of the board. "Results suggest that forced turnover followed by outsider succession, on average, improves firm performance."[9] Bill Ford claimed that to undertake major changes in Ford's dysfunctional culture, an outsider was more qualified than even the most proficient auto industry insider.[10]

An outsider CEO might also help restore faith in Ford management among investors, who had been discontented with the Ford family's high dividends and extravagant lifestyle. The Ford family controlled about 40 percent of the company's voting shares through their ownership of all its class B stock and holdings of common stock. The class B family shares had almost the same market value as that of common stock, but the voting rights of the family shares were exceptionally high by industry standards (see Exhibits 3 and 4). The dividend stream had been an annuity, which over the years had enabled various family members to own a football team, fund museums and philanthropic causes, and even promote the Hare Krishna movement. Given that the company was experiencing serious financial problems, these activities had raised stockholder dissent, as the annual retained earnings in the past had been dissipated as dividends instead of reinvested in firm operations or acquisitions to increase the net value of the firm.

Mulally—The New Savior

Alan Mulally came from a metal-bending business that, like automaking, was influenced by global competition, had a unionized workforce, and was subject to complex regulations and rapidly changing technologies.[11] Although he was not an auto guy, he had a proven record in an industry that faced issues similar to those faced by the automobile industry, and a lot of his expertise and management techniques were highly transferable. In his own words, "Everybody says, well, I'm not a car guy, so you couldn't make a contribution here. But I'm a product (guy) and I'm a designer."[12]

*This case study was prepared by Professor Helaine J. Korn of Baruch College, City University of New York; Professor Naga Lakshmi Damaraju of the Indian School of Business; and Professor Alan B. Eisner of Pace University. The purpose of the case is to stimulate class discussion rather than to illustrate effective or ineffective handling of a business situation. Copyright © 2009 Helaine Korn, Naga Damaraju, and Alan Eisner.

Exhibit 1 Ford Motor Company and Subsidiaries: Income Statements (in millions, except per-share amounts; year-end December 31)

	2008	2007	2006
Sales and revenues			
Automotive sales	$ 129,166	$154,379	$143,249
Financial Services revenues	17,111	18,076	16,816
Total sales and revenues	146,277	172,455	160,065
Costs and expenses			
Automotive cost of sales	127,103	142,587	148,866
Selling, administrative and other expenses	21,430	21,169	19,148
Goodwill impairment	—	2,400	—
Interest expense	9,682	10,927	8,783
Financial Services provision for credit and insurance losses	1,874	668	241
Total costs and expenses	160,089	177,751	177,038
Automotive interest income and other non-operating income/(expense), net	(755)	1,161	1,478
Automotive equity in net income/(loss) of affiliated companies	163	389	421
Income/(Loss) before income taxes	(14,404)	(3,746)	(15,074)
Provision for/(Benefit from) income taxes	63	(1,294)	(2,655)
Income/(Loss) before minority interests	(14,467)	(2,452)	(12,419)
Minority interests in net income/(loss) of subsidiaries	214	312	210
Income/(Loss) from continuing operations	(14,681)	(2,764)	(12,629)
Income/(Loss) from discontinued operations	9	41	16
Net Income/(loss)	$ (14,672)	$ (2,723)	$ (12,613)
Average number of shares of Common and Class B Stock outstanding	2,273	1,979	1,879
Amounts per share of common and class B stock			
Basic income/(loss)			
Income/(Loss) from continuing operations	$ (6.46)	$ (1.40)	$ (6.73)
Income/(Loss) from discontinued operations	—	0.02	0.01
Net income/(loss)	$ (6.46)	$ (1.38)	$ (6.72)
Diluted Income/(loss)			
Income/(Loss) from continuing operations	$ (6.46)	$ (1.40)	$ (6.73)
Income/(Loss) from discontinued operations	—	0.02	0.01
Net income/(loss)	$ (6.46)	$ (1.38)	$ (6.72)
Cash dividends	$ —	$ —	$ 0.25

Source: Ford Motor Company.

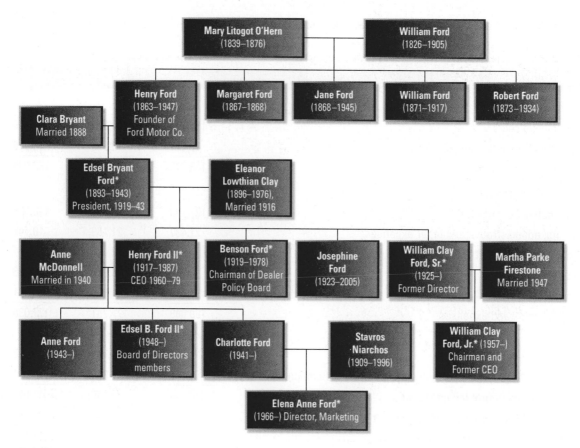

Exhibit 2 Ford Family Tree

Note: Family tree includes descendants of Henry Ford who worked at Ford Motor Co. and their children.

*Ford Family members who have worked at Ford Motor Co.

Source: Benson Ford Research Center, WSJ research.

Prior to joining Ford, Mulally served as executive vice president of the Boeing Company and as president and chief executive officer of Boeing Commercial Airplanes. In those roles, he was responsible for all the Boeing Company's commercial airplane programs and related services.[13] The advanced 777 aircraft, which Mulally led the development of in the early 1990s, became the most popular twin-engine jet in its class and was a testimony of Mulally's product and technology ingenuity. Under his leadership, Boeing regained its market leadership from Airbus. The appointment of Mulally at Ford was seen by the market as a move to utilize his experience and success in managing manufacturing and assembly lines to help shape the future of Ford.

Bill Ford praised Mulally as "an outstanding leader and a man of great character."[14] He noted that Mulally had applied many of the lessons from Ford's success in developing the Taurus to Boeing's creation of the revolutionary Boeing 777 airliner. "Clearly, the challenges Boeing faced in recent years have many parallels to our own," said Bill Ford about Mulally's appropriateness for the top position at Ford.[15] In his e-mail to Ford employees announcing

the appointment of Mulally, Bill Ford wrote, "Alan has deep experience in customer satisfaction, manufacturing, supplier relations and labor relations, all of which have applications to the challenges of Ford. He also has the personality and team-building skills that will help guide our Company in the right direction."[16]

Nonetheless, when Mulally took over the steering wheel, Ford was already poised to make significant structural changes as the company announced details of its accelerated "Way Forward" plan. Moreover, the company seemed to indicate that Mulally's appointment would not change the timelines and decisions associated with the restructuring actions, according to analyst Himanshu Patel of J. P. Morgan. This indicated that in spite of the appointment of Mulally as CEO, much of the decision making still remained with Bill Ford, who said he would remain "extremely active" in the business.

What Changes Did the New CEO Bring In?

In his effort to point Ford in the right direction, Mulally flew to Japan in January 2007 to meet with top executives of Ford's toughest competitor, Toyota, to seek their advice.[17]

Exhibit 3 Ford Motor Company and Subsidiaries: Sector Balance Sheets (in millions)

	December 31, 2008	December 31, 2007
Assets		
Automotive		
Cash and cash equivalents	$ 6,377	$ 20,678
Marketable securities	9,296	2,092
Loaned securities	—	10,267
Total cash, marketable and loaned securities	15,673	33,037
Receivables, less allowances of $221 and $197	3,464	4,530
Inventories	8,618	10,121
Deferred income taxes	302	532
Other current assets	4,032	5,514
Current receivable from Financial Services	2,035	509
Total current assets	34,124	54,243
Equity in net assets of affiliated companies	1,069	2,283
Net property	28,352	35,979
Deferred income taxes	7,204	9,268
Goodwill and other net intangible assets	1,584	2,051
Assets of discontinued/held-for-sale operations	—	7,537
Other assets	1,512	5,614
Non-current receivable from Financial Services	—	1,514
Total Automotive assets	73,845	118,489
Financial Services		
Cash and cash equivalents	15,672	14,605
Marketable securities	8,607	3,156
Finance receivables, net	96,101	112,733
Net investment in operating leases	23,120	30,309
Retained interest in sold receivables	92	653
Equity in net assets of affiliated companies	523	570
Goodwill and other net intangible assets	9	18
Assets of discontinued/held-for-sale operations	198	—
Other assets	7,345	7,217
Total Financial Services assets	151,667	169,261
Intersector elimination	(2,535)	(2,023)
Total assets	$222,977	$285,727

(*continued*)

Exhibit 3   Ford Motor Company and Subsidiaries: Sector Balance Sheets (in millions) *(continued)*

	December 31, 2008	December 31, 2007
Liabilities and stockholders' equity		
Automotive		
Trade payables	$ 10,635	$ 15,718
Other payables	2,167	3,237
Accrued liabilites and deferred revenue	32,395	27,672
Deferred income taxes	2,790	2,671
Debt payable within one year	1,191	1,175
Total current liabilities	49,178	50,473
Long-term debt	24,655	25,779
Other liabilities	24,815	41,676
Deferred income taxes	614	783
Liabilities of discontinued/held-for-sale operations	—	4,824
Total Automotive liabilities	99,262	123,535
Financial Services		
Payables	1,970	1,877
Debt	128,842	141,833
Deferred income taxes	3,280	6,043
Other liabilities and deferred income	6,184	5,390
Liabilities of discontinued/held-for-sale operations	55	—
Payable to Automotive	2,035	2,023
Total Financial Services liabilities	142,366	157,166
Minority interests	1,195	1,421
Stockholders' equity		
Capital stock		
Common Stock, par value $0.01 per share (2,341 million shares issued of 6 billion authorized)	23	21
Class B Stock, par value $0.01 per share (71 million shares issued of 530 million authorized)	1	1
Capital in excess of par value of stock	9,076	7,834
Accumulated other comprehensive income/(loss)	(10,085)	(558)
Treasury stock	(181)	(185)
Retained earnings/(Accumulated deficit)	(16,145)	(1,485)
Total stockholders' equity	(17,311)	5,628
Intersector elimination	(2,535)	(2,023)
Total liabilities and stockholders' equity	**$ 222,977**	**$285,727**

Source: Ford Motor Company.

Exhibit 4 Ford Motor Company and Subsidiaries: Sector Statements of Cash Flows (in millions, year-end December 31)

	2008		2007		2006	
	Automotive	Financial Services	Automotive	Financial Services	Automotive	Financial Services
Cash flows from operating activities of continuing operations						
Net cash flows from operating activities	$(12,440)	$ 9,107	$ 8,725	$ 6,402	$(4,172)	$ 7,316
Cash flows from investing activities of continuing operations						
Capital expenditures	(6,620)	(76)	(5,971)	(51)	(6,809)	(39)
Acquisitions of retail and other finance receivables and operating leases	—	(44,562)	—	(55,681)	—	(59,793)
Collections of retail and other finance receivables and operating leases	—	42,479	—	45,518	—	41,867
Net (increase)/decrease in wholesale receivables	—	2,736	—	1,927	—	6,113
Purchases of securities	(41,347)	(23,831)	(2,628)	(8,795)	(4,068)	(19,610)
Sales and maturities of securities	43,617	18,429	2,686	15,974	4,865	13,591
Settlements of derivatives	1,157	1,376	1,051	(190)	308	178
Proceeds from sales of retail and other finance receivables and operating leases	—	—	—	708	—	5,120
Proceeds from sale of businesses	3,156	3,698	1,079	157	56	—
Cash paid for acquisitions	(13)	—	—	—	—	—
Transfer of cash balances upon disposition of discontinued/held-for-sale operations	(928)	—	(83)	—	(4)	—
Investing activity from Financial Services	9	—	—	—	1,185	—
Investing activity to Financial Services	—	—	(18)	—	(1,400)	—
Other	40	276	19	(230)	(290)	129
Net cash (used in)/Provided by investing activities	(929)	525	(3,865)	(663)	(6,157)	(12,444)
Cash flows from financing activities of continuing operations						
Cash dividends	—	—	—	—	(468)	—
Sales of Common Stock	756	—	250	—	431	—
Purchases of Common Stock	—	—	(31)	—	(183)	—

(continued)

	2008		2007		2006	
	Automotive	Financial Services	Automotive	Financial Services	Automotive	Financial Services
Changes in short-term debt	104	(5,224)	(90)	1,009	414	(6,239)
Proceeds from issuance of other debt	203	41,960	240	32,873	12,254	46,004
Principal payments on other debt	(594)	(45,281)	(837)	(38,594)	(758)	(35,843)
Financing activity from Automotive	—	(9)	—	18	—	1,400
Financing activity to Automotive	—	—	—	—	—	—
Other	(252)	(352)	35	(123)	(147)	(192)
Net cash (used in)/provided by financing activities	217	(8,906)	(433)	(4,817)	11,543	3,945
Effect of exchange rate changes on cash	(309)	(499)	506	508	104	360
Net change in intersector receivables/payables and other liabilities	(840)	840	(291)	291	1,321	(1,321)
Net increase/(decrease) in cash and cash equivalents from continuing operations	(14,301)	1,067	4,642	1,721	2,639	(2,144)
Cash flows from discontinued operations						
Cash flows from operating activities of discontinued operations	—	—	16	10	(11)	—
Cash flows from investing activities of discontinued operations	—	—	—	—	—	—
Cash flows from financing activities of discontinued operations	—	—	—	—	—	—
Net increase/(decrease) in cash and cash equivalents	$(14,301)	$ 1,067	$ 4,658	$ 1,731	$ 2,628	$ (2,144)
Cash and cash equivalents at January 1	$ 20,678	$ 14,605	$16,022	$ 12,874	$13,373	$ 15,018
Cash and cash equivalents of discontinued/held-for-sale operations at January 1	—	—	(2)	—	19	—
Net increase/(decrease) in cash and cash equivalents	(14,301)	1,067	4,658	1,731	2,628	(2,144)
Less: Cash and cash equivalents of discontinued/held-for-sale operations at December 31	—	—	2	—	2	—
Cash and cash equivalents at December 31	$ 6,377	$ 15,672	$20,678	$ 14,605	$16,022	$ 12,874

Source: Ford Motor Company.

This was a huge break from the Ford tradition, and only an outsider CEO would have the courage and imagination to openly try to learn from foreign competitors.

Mulally had set his own priorities for fixing Ford: "At the top of the list, I would put dealing with reality."[18] The newly elected CEO signaled that "the bigger-is-better worldview that has defined Ford for decades was being replaced with a new approach: Less is More."[19] Ford needed to pay more attention to cutting costs and transforming the way it did business than to traditional measurements such as market share.[20] The vision was to have a smaller and more profitable Ford. There were echoes in Detroit of Mulally's smaller-is-better thinking. GM was in the middle of its own revamping plan, and Chrysler was also preparing a plan of cutbacks.[21] "Less is More" could be a new trend in the auto industry.

Mulally's cutback plan built on the 14 plant closures and 30,000-plus job cuts announced by Ford in January 2007. Ford's new plan added two more North American plants to the closure list and exceeded the targeted $5 billion in cost cuts by the end of 2008,[22] but it pushed back a target for North American profitability by one year to 2009 and then again to 2011.[23] The company targeted seven vehicle manufacturing sites for closure and planned to have optimum capacity at that point. At the same time, it also planned to increase the plant utilization and production levels in each production unit, while focusing more on larger, more fuel-efficient vehicles. The overall strategy seemed to be toward restructuring as a tool to obtain operating profitability at lower volume and with a changing mix of products that better appealed to the market.

Mulally also refocused the company on the Ford brand when he announced a formal review of Volvo in July 2007 as the first step to putting the division up for sale. Volvo had been acquired eight years earlier to be part of the Premier Automotive Group of Ford, among Jaguar, Aston Martin, and Land Rover.[24] However, Volvo's primary selling point of superior safety had been challenged as other manufacturers made advances in safety technologies in their own brands. Ford was also reviewing bids for Jaguar and Land Rover, both of which had lost money in four out of the five previous years. Mulally said that the "real opportunity going forward is to integrate and leverage our Ford assets around the world" and decide on the best mix of brands in the company's portfolio.[25]

Since his appointment, Mulally had made some structural and procedural changes in the company. For instance, instead of discussing business plans monthly or semiannually as they used to do at Ford, executives now met with Mulally weekly. The in-depth sessions were a contrast to executives' previous efforts to explain away bad news, said Donat R. Leclair, Ford's chief financial officer. "The difference I see now is that we're actually committed to hitting the numbers. Before, it was a culture of trying to explain why we were off the plan. The more eloquently you could explain why you were off the plan, the more easy it was to change the plan."[26]

Mulally also did some senior executive reorganization at Ford, and many of the newly appointed executives reported to him directly, including a global head of product development. In addition, the head of worldwide purchasing, the chief of quality and advanced manufacturing, the head of information technology, the chief technical officer, and the leaders of Ford's European division, its Asia, Pacific, and Africa units, and its Americas unit all reported directly to him.[27]

A Shift toward Smaller and More Fuel-Efficient Cars

The global economic downturn and financial crisis had a significant impact on the global sales volumes in the auto industry, which were likely to decline over 10 percent in 2009.[28] See Exhibit 5 for weakening vehicle sales figures in the U.S. market. Mulally clearly understood that the once profitable business of manufacturing and selling trucks and SUVs was history. Oil prices had been persistently increasing over the last few years. This caused a dramatic change in consumer's car buying habits, reducing the demand for large vehicles. And that was not all: The diminished demand for SUVs resulted in a situation in which leased cars returned at the end of the lease period were being sold for much less than their residual values.

Exhibit 5 Vehicle Sales by Segment, January 2009

	January 2009	% Change from January 2008
Cars	315,863	−36.3
Midsize	143,726	−39.7
Small	112,073	−30.7
Luxury	54,934	−35.1
Large	5,130	−54.3
Light-duty trucks	341,113	−37.8
Pickup	100,500	−38.3
Crossover	129,820	−27.5
Minivan	34,102	−48.1
Midsize SUV	36,423	−52.6
Large SUV	15,935	−46.8
Small SUV	16,004	−12.5
Luxury SUV	8,329	−47.4
Total SUV/Crossover	206,511	−35.4
Total SUV	76,691	−45.6
Total Crossover	129,820	−27.5

Source: www.motorintelligence.com.

Adjusting these residual values to their fair values contributed to the losses.[29] Brenda Hines, spokewoman for Ford Credit, said that "about 85 percent of the impaired vehicles were trucks and SUVs".[30]

The core strategy at Ford centered around a change in products, shifting to smaller and more fuel-efficient cars. Ford would import European-made small vehicles, the European Focus and Fiesta, into North America. It also planned to convert three truck-manufacturing plants to small-car production.[31] The Ford, Lincoln, and Mercury lines would all be upgraded, emphasizing fuel-economy improvement and the introduction of hybrid cars. By the end of 2010, two-thirds of spending would be on cars and crossovers–up from one-half in 2009.[32]

In 2009, the first applications of Ford's EcoBoost engines were introduced. EcoBoost used direct-injection technology for up to 20 percent better fuel economy, up to 15 percent fewer CO_2 emissions, and superior driving performance. The goal was to offer this engine on more than 80 percent of the North American–manufactured cars by the end of 2012.[33]

Globalizing the Ford Brand

In the auto industry it was common practice that different regions cooperated and companies basically sold the same cars around the world. This was not the case at Ford. Since it had set up its European operations, Ford Europe and Ford North America had gone separate ways. Moreover, due to Ford Europe's relative success while Ford North America was faltering, Ford Europe was reluctant to cooperate with changes that would bring the two into greater alignment. Nonetheless, Mulally was committed to making this happen.[34]

Under the One Ford vision, Mulally intended to globalize the Ford brand, meaning that all Ford vehicles competing in global segments would be the same in North America, Europe, and Asia within the next five years.[35] The company was looking for a reduction of complexity, and thus costs, in the purchasing and manufacturing processes. The idea

was to deliver more vehicles worldwide from fewer platforms and to maximize the use of common parts and systems. Ford was uniquely positioned to take advantage of its scale, global products, and brand to respond to the changing marketplace.[36] "We grew up regionally, Toyota grew up globally, essentially, and so we are going to try to use the best of those worlds going forward,"[37] said Mulally.

About the Ford Motor Company

Ford Motor had been sinking since 1999, when profits reached a remarkable $7.2 billion ($5.86 per share) and pre-tax income was $11 billion. At that time people even speculated that Ford would soon overtake General Motors as the world's number-one automobile manufacturer.[38] But soon Toyota, through its innovative technology, management philosophy of continuous improvement, and cost arbitrage due to its presence in multiple geographic locations, overtook the giants—GM and Ford. Compounding this were Ford's internal organizational problems and a failed diversification strategy led by Jacques Nasser, the CEO at that time. Ford's market share began to drop—from 25 percent in 1999 to 13.7 percent in 2009 (see Exhibits 6 and 7),[39] with major blows to market share in the light-vehicle segment. Moreover, Ford's stock prices decreased significantly over the last decade. While stocks traded at close to $60 in February 1999, prices in February 2009 were as low as $1.58.[40] See Exhibit 8 for Ford's stock performance compared to that of General Motors and the Standard & Poor's (S&P) 500.

In 2006, Chevrolet outsold Ford for the first time since 1986 in the sport utility vehicle market. Despite an extensive mechanical update, the much-improved Ford Explorer, which had been the world's best-selling sport utility vehicle, fell behind the dated Chevy TrailBlazer in sales. It did not help that the new Explorer looked just like the model it replaced. The long-neglected Ford Ranger, which had been the top-selling small pickup, fell behind competing models from both Toyota Motor and Chevrolet, and despite 20 years of trying, Ford had never been able to build a competitive minivan. Ford's most successful

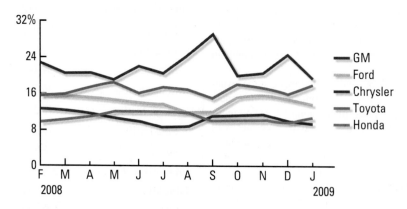

Exhibit 6 U.S. Market Share, 2008–2009
Source: www.motorintelligence.com.

Exhibit 7 Sales and Share of Total Market, by Manufacturer

	Sales			Market Share	
	Jan. 2009	Jan. 2008	% Chg	Jan. 2009	Jan. 2008
General Motors Corp.	127,243	249,154	−48.9	19.4	23.9
Total Cars	43,319	103,006	−57.9	6.6	9.9
Domestic Car	41,724	97,686	−57.3	6.4	9.4
Import Car	1,595	5,320	−70.0	0.2	0.5
Total Light Trucks	83,924	146,148	−42.6	12.8	14.0
Domestic Truck	83,924	146,148	−42.6	12.8	14.0
Import Truck	. . .	. . .	n.a.	. . .	. . .
Ford Motor Company	90,131	147,717	−39.0	13.7	14.1
Total Cars	28,707	44,259	−35.1	4.4	4.2
Domestic Car	28,707	44,259	−35.1	4.4	4.2
Import Car	. . .	. . .	n.a.	. . .	. . .
Total Light Trucks	61,424	103,458	−40.6	9.3	9.9
Domestic Truck	61,424	103,458	−40.6	9.3	9.9
Import Truck	. . .	. . .	n.a.	. . .	. . .
Chrysler LLC	62,157	137,392	−54.8	9.5	13.2
Total Cars	15,719	43,167	−63.6	2.4	4.1
Domestic Car	15,676	43,043	−63.6	2.4	4.1
Import Car	43	124	−65.3	. . .	. . .
Total Light Trucks	46,438	94,225	−50.7	7.1	9.0
Domestic Truck	46,438	94,225	−50.7	7.1	9.0
Import Truck	. . .	. . .	n.a.	. . .	. . .
Toyota Motor Sales USA Inc.	117,287	171,849	−31.7	17.9	16.5
Total Cars	67,263	94,586	−28.9	10.2	9.1
Domestic Car	38,277	55,438	−31.0	5.8	5.3
Import Car	28,986	39,148	−26.0	4.4	3.7
Total Light Trucks	50,024	77,263	−35.3	7.6	7.4
Domestic Truck	27,985	40,607	−31.1	4.3	3.9
Import Truck	22,039	36,656	−39.9	3.4	3.5
American Honda Motor Co Inc.	71,031	98,511	−27.9	10.8	9.4
Total Cars	40,532	55,345	−26.8	6.2	5.3
Domestic Car	30,562	40,632	−24.8	4.7	3.9
Import Car	9,970	14,713	−32.2	1.5	1.4
Total Light Trucks	30,499	43,166	−29.3	4.6	4.1
Domestic Truck	26,089	30,817	−15.3	4.0	2.9
Import Truck	4,410	12,349	−64.3	0.7	1.2
Totals:					
Total Car	315,863	496,067	−36.3	48.1	47.5
Domestic Car	87,745	190,432	−53.9	13.4	18.2
Import Car	228,118	305,635	−25.4	34.7	29.3
Total Truck	341,113	548,587	−37.8	51.9	52.5
Domestic Truck	191,786	343,831	−44.2	29.2	32.9
Import Truck	149,327	204,756	−27.1	22.7	19.6
Total Light Vehicle Sales	656,976	1,044,654	−37.1	100.0	100.0

Source: www.motorintelligence.com

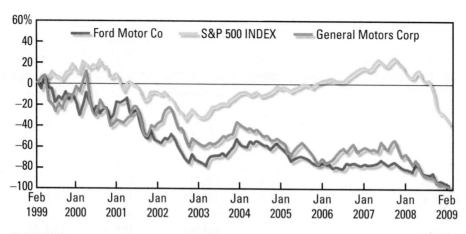

Exhibit 8 Ford 10-Year Stock Price History

Source: MSN Money.

vehicles were the F-series pickup trucks (see Exhibits 9 and 10). In 2008, for the 27th consecutive year, Ford F-series was ranked as America's top-selling vehicle.[41]

The company also experienced serious financial problems. Ford's turnaround plan aimed to cut $5 billion in costs by the end of 2008 by slashing 10,000 white-collar workers and offering buyouts to all of its 75,000 unionized employees. The loss, including restructuring costs, was Ford's largest quarterly loss since the first quarter of 1992, when the company lost $6.7 billion due mainly to accounting changes. "Ford and the entire auto industry faced an extraordinary slowdown in all major global markets in the fourth quarter that clearly had an impact on our results," [42] commented Mulally.

Automobile Industry in the United States

The automotive industry in the United States was a highly competitive, cyclical business. The number of cars and trucks sold to retail buyers, or "industry demand," varied substantially from year to year depending on "general economic situations, the cost of purchasing and operating cars and trucks, the availability of credit and fuel." Because cars and trucks were durable items, consumers could wait to replace them; industry demand reflected this factor (see Exhibit 11).

Competition in the United States intensified in the last few decades with Japanese carmakers gaining a foothold in the market. To counter the problem of being viewed as foreign, Japanese companies had set up production facilities in the United States and thus gained acceptance from American consumers. Production quality and lean production were judged to be the major weapons that Japanese carmakers used to gain an advantage over American carmakers. "The Toyota Motor Company of Japan issued a 2007 forecast that would make it first in global sales, ahead of General Motors, which has been the world's biggest auto company since 1931."[43] For American consumers, Toyota vehicles have been "a better value proposition"

than Detroit's products, said Mulally, who was the first Detroit leader who readily said he was an avid student of Toyota.[44] However, even Toyota's sales were hurt by the weakened economy, and the Japanese carmaker cut its annual profit forecast by half in November 2008. [45]

While there was a glut in the U.S. automobile market, the markets of Asia, Central and South America, and central and Eastern Europe all showed increasing promise for automobiles, and the automobile industry entered into an era of "global motorization."

Challenges Mulally and Ford Continue to Face

Mulally was faced with a lot of challenges. He had considerable experience dealing with manufacturing and labor relations issues, but he did not have much background in finance. Given the cash drain at Ford due to restructuring costs and product development, and the B + junk credit rating of Ford stock, cash was crucial to keep the company afloat, and Mulally's abilities would be tested.[46]

Mulally's fearlessness was well suited to pushing through projects at Boeing, but its suitability to Ford's culture remained to be seen. Like every new leader, he had to move with confidence in his early days, but as an industry outsider, he would have to take care to avoid violating the long-standing industry norms.[47]

"Mulally's approach to management and communication hasn't been seen before in the halls of Ford, which have historically been the atmosphere of a kingdom with competing dukes."[48] Mulally was still in the honeymoon period, but already clashes had surfaced between his management style and the "Ford way."

Mulally busied himself breaking down a global structure in which Ford Europe, Ford Asia, Ford North America, Ford Australia, and Ford South America had long created redundancies of efforts, products, engineering platforms, engines, and the like as a way of perpetuating each

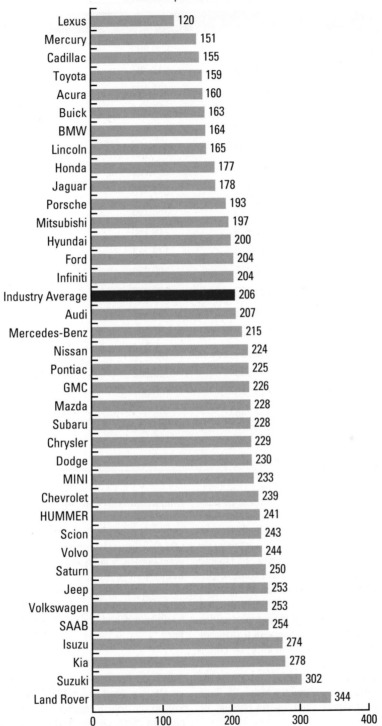

2008 Nameplate Ranking
Problems per 100 Vehicles

Lexus	120
Mercury	151
Cadillac	155
Toyota	159
Acura	160
Buick	163
BMW	164
Lincoln	165
Honda	177
Jaguar	178
Porsche	193
Mitsubishi	197
Hyundai	200
Ford	204
Infiniti	204
Industry Average	206
Audi	207
Mercedes-Benz	215
Nissan	224
Pontiac	225
GMC	226
Mazda	228
Subaru	228
Chrysler	229
Dodge	230
MINI	233
Chevrolet	239
HUMMER	241
Scion	243
Volvo	244
Saturn	250
Jeep	253
Volkswagen	253
SAAB	254
Isuzu	274
Kia	278
Suzuki	302
Land Rover	344

Exhibit 9 Vehicle Dependability Rankings, 2008

Source: J.D. Power and Associates, 2008 Vehicle Dependability Study.

Exhibit 10   Top-Selling Vehicles in the United States, 2008 (ranked by total units)

Rank	Vehicle	2008	2007	2007 RANK	%Change
1	Ford F-Series P/U	515,513	690,589	1	−25.4
2	Chevy Silverado-C/K P/U	465,065	618,257	2	−24.8
3	Toyota Camry	436,617	473,108	3	−7.7
4	Honda Accord	372,789	392,231	6	−5.0
5	Toyota Corolla	351,007	371,390	4	−5.5
6	Honda Civic	339,289	331,095	8	+2.5
7	Nissan Altima	269,668	284,762	9	−5.3
8	Chevrolet Impala	265,840	311,128	7	−14.6
9	Dodge Ram P/U	245,840	358,295	5	−31.4
10	Honda CR-V	197,279	219,160	11	−10.0
11	Ford Focus	195,823	173,213	15	+13.1
12	Chevrolet Cobalt	188,045	200,620	14	−6.3
13	Chevrolet Malibu	178,253	128,312	26	+38.9
14	GMC Sierra P/U	168,544	208,243	12	−19.1
15	Toyota Prius	158,884	181,221	16	−12.3
16	Ford Escape	156,544	165,596	17	−5.5
17	Ford Fusion	147,569	149,552	20	−1.3
18	GM Pontiac G6	140,240	150,001	28	−6.5
19	Toyota Tundra	137,249	196,555	23	−30.2
20	Toyota RAV4	137,020	172,752	18	−20.7

Source: www.reuters.com.

division's independence.[49] Since the initial purpose of having an outsider CEO was to break the dysfunctional Ford culture, the clashes were expected and generally viewed as constructive.

However, the clashes also had their drawbacks. Unable to accept the Mulally management approach, some senior executives left Ford. The international chief of the company, Mark A. Schulz, was one of them. "He had decided to retire this year after working for more than three decades at the company. Mr. Schulz is just the latest in a string of senior executives to leave since Mulally took over. Ford's second-ranking North American executive, its North American manufacturing chief and its chief of staff also all announced their departures after Mulally's hiring."[50] Ford had lost some of its most experienced leaders because of the outsider CEO.

Despite his rich experience and proven success in turning around the manufacturing operations at Boeing, Mulally was still not completely qualified or accepted as an auto guy. "He recently had to ask what the name of the auto industry's lobby group is (Alliance of Automobile Manufacturers) and what NADA stands for (National Automobile Dealers Assn.)."[51] He had to learn the business and its unique terms on the fly. Speaking the auto language was still critical for an outsider CEO to be accepted in a giant company such as Ford, which had a long and distinct tradition of promoting insider leaders.

Nonetheless, Mulally was confident that his years of experience running a big manufacturer and his technical background had prepared him for the challenges facing Ford.[52]

Looking Ahead

The 2008 year-end earnings report was not without some good news. Ford had reduced automotive costs by $1.4 billion in the fourth quarter and $4.4 billion in 2008 versus costs in 2007. Global dealer stocks were reduced by more than 50,000 vehicles, compared with the third quarter, and Ford now had among the lowest days' supply in the industry. According to Mulally, "The progress we continued to make in the fourth quarter gives us great confidence that we have the right plan, the right people and the right

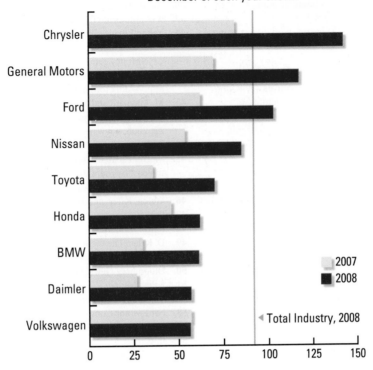

Average number of days a vehicle sits on the lot before being sold,
December of each year shown

Exhibit 11 Dealer Turnover

Note: Includes data from all brands sold by that manufacturer in the U.S.

Source: J.D. Power.

products to create a viable, profitably growing Ford for all of our stakeholders."[53] He added, "Our market share growth in the fourth quarter in the U.S. and Europe is a positive sign that customers recognize the value of our new products and understand that a new and different Ford is emerging."[54] However, Ford continued to face tough times and a treacherous business environment: A deeper economic and industry slowdown was projected, industry volumes were expected to decline even more in 2009, and market share was expected to remain low. Only time would tell whether the smaller-is-better strategy was the lifesaver for Ford and whether it was the right time to apply it or was too late.

Endnotes

1. B. Vlasic. After record loss, Ford will tap lines of credit to bolster cash. *New York Times,* January 30, 2009, p. B3.
2. M. Dolan, J. D. Stoll, and S. Terlep. Auto sales succumb as credit grows tight. *Wall Street Journal,* October 2, 2008, p. B1.
3. Vlasic. After record loss, Ford will tap lines of credit.
4. Autodata Corp.
5. Ford Motor Company. http://media.ford.com/article_display.cfm?article_id=29746.
6. F. Knowles. Boeing exec flies the coop: Ford hires Mulally to turn things. *Chicago Sun-Times,* September 6, 2006.
7. D. Welch, D. Kiley, and S. Holmes. Alan Mulally: A plan to make Ford fly. *BusinessWeek,* 2006.
8. D. Kiley. Mulally: Ford's most important new model. *BusinessWeek Online,* January 9, 2007, www.businessweek.com.
9. K. Rakesh. The changing of the guard: Causes, process and consequences of CEO turnover. 1998.
10. S. Berfield. The best leaders. *BusinessWeek Online,* December 18, 2006, www.businessweek.com.
11. D. Levin. Mulally's hire by Ford may be too late. Bloomberg.com, 2006.
12. K. Crain. Mulally wants fewer platforms, fewer dealers. *New York Times,* November 20, 2006.
13. Ford Motor Company. http://media.ford.com/article_display.cfm?article_id=24203.
14. Ibid.
15. Ibid.
16. Ibid.
17. M. Maynard. Ford chief sees small as virtue and necessity. *New York Times,* January 25, 2007, www.nytimes.com.
18. Ibid.
19. Ibid.
20. M. Maynard. Ford expects to fall soon to no. 3 spot. *New York Times,* December 21, 2006, www.nytimes.com.
21. Maynard. Ford chief sees small as virtue and necessity.
22. Ford Motor Company. Press release, January 29, 2009, http://media.ford.com/images/10031/4Qfinancials.pdf.

23. John Stoll. Ford looks to reshape business model, executive says. *Dow Jones Newswires,* September 18, 2006.
24. Micheline Maynard. Ford seeks a future by going backward. *New York Times,* July 17, 2007, p. C1.
25. Nick Bunkley and Micheline Maynard. Ford breaks string of losing quarters, but says respite will be brief. *New York Times,* July 27, 2007, p. C3.
26. Maynard. Ford chief sees small as virtue and necessity.
27. Bloomberg News. Ford reorganizes executives. *New York Times,* December 15, 2006, www.nytimes.com.
28. Ford Motor Company. Press release, January 29, 2009, http://media.ford.com/images/10031/4Qfinancials.pdf.
29. P. Ingrassia. Can America's auto makers survive? *Wall Street Journal Europe.* August 8, 2008, p. 13.
30. B. Vlasik and N. Bunkley. At Ford, end of era takes a toll. *New York Times,* July 27, 2008, p. C1.
31. N. Van Praet. US$8.7B loss turns Ford. *Financial Post,* July 25, 2008.
32. Ford Motor Company. http://media.ford.com/article_display.cfm?article_id=28660.
33. Ibid.
34. A. Taylor III. Can this car save Ford? *Fortune,* May 5, 2008.
35. Ford Motor Company. http://media.ford.com/article_display.cfm?article_id=29746.
36. Ford Motor Company. http://media.ford.com/article_display.cfm?article_id=28660.
37. B. Pope. That's why they call it earnings. *WARD'S Dealer-Business,* January 2008.
38. Autodata Corp.
39. www.motorintelligence.com.
40. Yahoo Finance. Ford Historical Prices.
41. P. Valdes-Dapena. "Autos: 2008 Winners and Losers." CNNMoney.com, January 2008.
42. Ford Motor Company. Press release, January 29, 2009, http://media.ford.com/images/10031/4Qfinancials.pdf.
43. M. Maynard and M. Fackler. Toyota is poised to supplant GM as world's largest carmaker. *New York Times,* December 22, 2006, www.nytimes.com.
44. Ibid.
45. Martin Fackler. Wary of global downturn, Toyota cuts profit forecast by more than half. *New York Times,* November 4, 2008, www.nytimes.com.
46. Welch, Kiley, and Holmes. Alan Mulally.
47. Ibid.
48. Kiley. Mulally.
49. D. Kiley. The record year Ford hopes to shake off. *Business-Week Online,* January 26, 2007, www.businessweek.com.
50. Bloomberg News. Ford reorganizes executives.
51. Kiley. Mulally.
52. Maynard. Ford chief sees small as virtue and necessity.
53. Ford Motor Company. http://media.ford.com/article_display.cfm?article_id=29746.
54. Ibid.

Case 37 American International Group and the Bonus Fiasco*

After two decades of rapid growth and expansion in an environment of very little regulatory oversight and unbounded optimism about the power of the markets to create limitless wealth, the U.S. financial system came crashing down in the second half of 2008. What started as a sudden decline in housing prices after years of speculative growth very soon snowballed into a full-fledged financial crisis. Major banking companies such as Citicorp and Bank of America found their equity base wiped out by loan losses. Investment banking firms such as Merrill Lynch and Bear Stearns, which operate largely outside the regulatory framework of the Federal Reserve, were in even bigger trouble because they were highly leveraged. Fearing a complete financial meltdown, Henry Paulson, secretary of the Treasury in the Bush administration, announced a bailout package of $750 billion on September 16, 2008, to restore confidence in the banks and to jump-start the credit markets.

What exactly does the government do in a bailout? A bailout can take many forms. For example, the government can buy stock in a troubled institution, thus shoring up its equity base.

The very fact that the government has an equity stake may be taken as an implicit government guarantee by creditors, suppliers, and clients because concerns about solvency and ability to stay in business are assuaged. Alternatively, the government can extend a loan to the institution, to be paid back when the company becomes profitable again. Another approach is for the government to buy preferred stock in the company. In this case the government is entitled to a fair return on the investment. Finally, the government can buy distressed assets of the institution, thereby helping it to clean up its balance sheet. Irrespective of the form of the bailout, all bailouts represent a temporary or, in some cases, long-term commitment of public money to private companies.

As the economic crisis gathered momentum and the credit markets came to a standstill in the fall of 2008, it became clear that banks were not the only institutions in trouble. American International Group (AIG), one of the largest and most respected insurance companies in the world, found itself in even bigger financial distress in September 2008 when the rating agencies suddenly lowered its credit rating. Not only did this cause the cost of borrowing to go up for AIG, but it also triggered the requirement that the company post collateral with its counterparties. Unable to do so, AIG approached the government for a bailout. In the next few months, the government pumped an astounding $85 billion into AIG alone to prevent it from going bankrupt. Insurance companies are generally supposed to be risk-averse and prudent. How did AIG get into such a big mess?

The primary culprit for the problems of AIG was a somewhat exotic financial product called credit default swaps (CDSs). In simple terms, these swaps represented an insurance cover to holders of mortgage-backed securities: If the value of the securities went down, AIG would make good the losses suffered by the owners. In good times, when real estate prices were climbing steadily each year, the CDSs were pure profits for AIG. Emboldened by what it perceived as negligible risk and motivated by the prospect of ever-increasing profits, AIG sold hundreds of billions of dollars' worth of these instruments. Although insurance is a business regulated by the states, these products were outside the range of regulation.

Right from the beginning, there was considerable controversy about whether the government should try to bail out any failing firm in a market economy. Even those who were not ideologically opposed to the bailout were skeptical whether the government efforts would be enough to save the company. There were also concerns about how the company would spend the bailout money.

Immediately after the first bailout was announced, AIG attracted considerable negative press when it was reported that AIG executives attended a lavish retreat in California that featured spa treatments, banquets, and golf outings. Total tab: $444,000. Immediately thereafter, AP reported that AIG executives spent $86,000 on a luxurious English hunting trip.[1] This was only days after the Fed had extended a $37.8 billion loan on top of the $85 billion mentioned earlier. The company's response: "We regret that this event was not canceled."[2]

In March 2009, it was disclosed that AIG had paid $218 million in bonus payments to employees of the financial services division, the very division that was responsible for issuing the credit default swaps that got the firm into trouble. Overall, 418 managers were the beneficiaries of these "retention" bonuses, although 53 of them were no longer with the company! The highest bonus was $6.4 million. Six managers received more than $4 million each, and 51 people received between $1 million and $2 million.

The announcement of these bonuses sparked instant outrage among the public. President Barack Obama accused the company of "recklessness and greed." Noting that AIG had "received substantial sums" of federal aid, the president announced that he was asking Treasury Secretary Timothy Geithner "to use that leverage and pursue every legal avenue to block these bonuses and make the American taxpayers

*This case was prepared by Professor Abdul A. Rasheed of the University of Texas at Arlington, Graduate Student Brian Pinkham, and Professor Gregory G. Dess of the University of Texas at Dallas. This case was based solely on library research and was developed for class discussion rather than to illustrate either effective or ineffective handling of an administrative situation. Copyright © 2009 Abdul A. Rasheed and Gregory G. Dess.

whole."[3] Andrew Cuomo, New York State's attorney general, threatened to subpoena the executives and engage in a "name and shame" campaign by making the list of bonus recipients public.[4] The House even passed a bill that effectively imposed a punitive 90 percent tax on the bonuses.[5]

At the same time, there were others who felt that the payments represented contractual obligations and therefore populist sentiments should not be allowed to violate the sanctity of contracts. Many of the employees felt that they had every right to receive the payments they were promised and worked for. Their feelings were best expressed in the following resignation letter sent by Jake DeSantis, an executive vice president of the American International Group's financial products unit, to Edward M. Liddy, the chief executive of AIG.

Dear Mr. Liddy:

It is with deep regret that I submit my notice of resignation from A.I.G. Financial Products. I hope you take the time to read this entire letter. Before describing the details of my decision, I want to offer some context:

I am proud of everything I have done for the commodity and equity divisions of A.I.G.-F.P. I was in no way involved in—or responsible for—the credit default swap transactions that have hamstrung A.I.G. Nor were more than a handful of the 400 current employees of A.I.G.-F.P. Most of those responsible have left the company and have conspicuously escaped the public outrage.

After 12 months of hard work dismantling the company—during which A.I.G. reassured us many times we would be rewarded in March 2009—we in the financial products unit have been betrayed by A.I.G. and are being unfairly persecuted by elected officials. In response to this, I will now leave the company and donate my entire post-tax retention payment to those suffering from the global economic downturn. My intent is to keep none of the money myself.

I take this action after 11 years of dedicated, honorable service to A.I.G. I can no longer effectively perform my duties in this dysfunctional environment, nor am I being paid to do so. Like you, I was asked to work for an annual salary of $1, and I agreed out of a sense of duty to the company and to the public officials who have come to its aid. Having now been let down by both, I can no longer justify spending 10, 12, 14 hours a day away from my family for the benefit of those who have let me down.

You and I have never met or spoken to each other, so I'd like to tell you about myself. I was raised by schoolteachers working multiple jobs in a world of closing steel mills. My hard work earned me acceptance to M.I.T., and the institute's generous financial aid enabled me to attend. I had fulfilled my American dream.

I started at this company in 1998 as an equity trader, became the head of equity and commodity trading and, a couple of years before A.I.G.'s meltdown last September, was named the head of business development for commodities. Over this period the equity and commodity units were consistently profitable—in most years generating net profits of well over $100 million. Most recently, during the dismantling of A.I.G.-F.P., I was an integral player in the pending sale of its well-regarded commodity index business to UBS. As you know, business unit sales like this are crucial to A.I.G.'s effort to repay the American taxpayer.

The profitability of the businesses with which I was associated clearly supported my compensation. I never received any pay resulting from the credit default swaps that are now losing so much money. I did, however, like many others here, lose a significant portion of my life savings in the form of deferred compensation invested in the capital of A.I.G.-F.P. because of those losses. In this way I have personally suffered from this controversial activity—directly as well as indirectly with the rest of the taxpayers.

I have the utmost respect for the civic duty that you are now performing at A.I.G. You are as blameless for these credit default swap losses as I am. You answered your country's call and you are taking a tremendous beating for it.

But you also are aware that most of the employees of your financial products unit had nothing to do with the large losses. And I am disappointed and frustrated over your lack of support for us. I and many others in the unit feel betrayed that you failed to stand up for us in the face of untrue and unfair accusations from certain members of Congress last Wednesday and from the press over our retention payments, and that you didn't defend us against the baseless and reckless comments made by the attorneys general of New York and Connecticut.

My guess is that in October, when you learned of these retention contracts, you realized that the employees of the financial products unit needed some incentive to stay and that the contracts, being both ethical and useful, should be left to stand. That's probably why A.I.G. management assured us on three occasions during that month that the company would "live up to its commitment" to honor the contract guarantees.

That may be why you decided to accelerate by three months more than a quarter of the amounts due under the contracts. That action signified to us your support, and was hardly something that one would do if he truly found the contracts "distasteful."

That may also be why you authorized the balance of the payments on March 13.

At no time during the past six months that you have been leading A.I.G. did you ask us to revise, renegotiate or break these contracts—until several hours before your appearance last week before Congress.

I think your initial decision to honor the contracts was both ethical and financially astute, but it seems to have been politically unwise. It's now apparent that you either misunderstood the agreements that you had made—tacit or otherwise—with the Federal Reserve, the Treasury, various members of Congress and Attorney General Andrew Cuomo of New York, or were not strong enough to withstand the shifting political winds.

You've now asked the current employees of A.I.G.-F.P. to repay these earnings. As you can imagine, there has been a tremendous amount of serious thought and heated discussion about how we should respond to this breach of trust.

As most of us have done nothing wrong, guilt is not a motivation to surrender our earnings. We have worked 12 long months under these contracts and now deserve to be paid as promised. None of us should be cheated of our payments any more than a plumber should be cheated after he has fixed the pipes but a careless electrician causes a fire that burns down the house.

Many of the employees have, in the past six months, turned down job offers from more stable employers, based on A.I.G.'s assurances that the contracts would be honored. They are now angry about having been misled by A.I.G.'s promises and are not inclined to return the money as a favor to you.

The only real motivation that anyone at A.I.G.-F.P. now has is fear. Mr. Cuomo has threatened to "name and shame," and his counterpart in Connecticut, Richard Blumenthal, has made similar threats—even though attorneys general are supposed to stand for due process, to conduct trials in courts and not the press.

So what am I to do? There's no easy answer. I know that because of hard work I have benefited more than most during the economic boom and have saved enough that my family is unlikely to suffer devastating losses during the current bust. Some might argue that members of my profession have been overpaid, and I wouldn't disagree.

That is why I have decided to donate 100 percent of the effective after-tax proceeds of my retention payment directly to organizations that are helping people who are suffering from the global downturn. This is not a tax-deduction gimmick; I simply believe that I at least deserve to dictate how my earnings are spent, and do not want to see them disappear back into the obscurity of A.I.G.'s or the federal government's budget. Our earnings have caused such a distraction for so many from the more pressing issues our country faces, and I would like to see my share of it benefit those truly in need.

On March 16 I received a payment from A.I.G. amounting to $742,006.40, after taxes. In light of the uncertainty over the ultimate taxation and legal status of this payment, the actual amount I donate may be less—in fact, it may end up being far less if the recent House bill raising the tax on the retention payments to 90 percent stands. Once all the money is donated, you will immediately receive a list of all recipients.

This choice is right for me. I wish others at A.I.G.-F.P. luck finding peace with their difficult decision, and only hope their judgment is not clouded by fear.

Mr. Liddy, I wish you success in your commitment to return the money extended by the American government, and luck with the continued unwinding of the company's diverse businesses—especially those remaining credit default swaps. I'll continue over the short term to help make sure no balls are dropped, but after what's happened this past week I can't remain much longer—there is too much bad blood. I'm not sure how you will greet my resignation, but at least Attorney General Blumenthal should be relieved that I'll leave under my own power and will not need to be "shoved out the door."

Sincerely,

Jake DeSantis

Liddy was clearly in an unwinnable situation. On the one hand, the politicians and the press were pillorying him for authorizing lavish bonuses while the company was essentially on welfare payments from the taxpayer. On the other hand, his own employees were upset at him that he was pandering to the politicians by describing these contractual payments as "distasteful."

Endnotes

1. AIG executives spent thousands during hunting trip. Associated Press, October 17, 2008, http://ap.google.com/article/ALeqM5g3InVeHoYnmXZnM2ACXSgjG0-nIQD93R68VO0.
2. A. Taylor. AIG execs' retreat after bailout angers lawmakers. Associated Press, October 11, 2008, http://thecoffeedesk.com/news/index.php/archives/76kers.
3. T. Raum. Obama: AIG can't justify "outrage" of exec bonuses with taxpayer money keeping company afloat. Associated Press, March 16, 2009, http://finance.yahoo.com/news/Frank-assails-bonuses-paid-to-apf-14646988.html.
4. Cuomo issues subpoena to AIG on credit derivatives data. March 27, 2009, www.rttnews.com/Content/BreakingNews.aspx?Node=B1&Id=895234%20&Category=Breaking%20News.
5. J. D. McKinnon and A. Jones. Laws may not hinder effort to tax AIG bonuses. *Wall Street Journal,* March 18, 2009, http://online.wsj.com/article/SB123742691757579925.html.

Case 38 eBay: Expanding into Asia*

On March 31, 2008, eBay welcomed a new president and CEO, John Donahoe. Donahoe joined the company in 2005 as president of eBay Marketplaces and within three years managed to double the revenues and profits for that division. The new CEO replaced Meg Whitman, who had served as the president of the company for a decade and led eBay to become one of the fastest-growing companies in history. "eBay and its millions of users are in great hands as they head into the future," said Whitman, confident in Donahoe's capabilities.[1] Donahoe was set on improving overall customer satisfaction and protection, and shortly after his election he introduced significant changes to fee structure, seller standards, and feedback at eBay.[2] However, despite Donahoe's strategic management, eBay still faced challenges in its Asia Pacific market.

On August 14, 2008, eBay was granted approval by the South Korea's Fair Trade Commission to buy a combined 36.6 percent stake in Gmarket from the company's largest shareholder, Interpark Corp., and Interpark's chairman Ki Hyung Lee. Partly owned by Yahoo, Gmarket was one of the leading online auctioneers and shopping malls in South Korea.[3] The news suggested that eBay was once again struggling to compete in the Asian market. eBay followed the same strategy in December 2006 when it shut down its existing site in China and bought 49 percent of a joint venture with Beijing-based Tom Online. The move was expected to give eBay some of the local expertise it desperately needed to compete with China's top auction site, Taobao. Despite Meg Whitman calling the deal an evolution of the company's China strategy and not a failure, analysts viewed it as an indication that U.S. Web players were still lacking success with their strategy in Asia.[4] With Asia's population exceeding 3.7 billion, more than half the world's population, and Internet usage in the region skyrocketing at 406 percent, eBay needed to develop a strategy that would successfully adapt to Asian local markets and compete with Taobao and other major local competitors.

eBay

Since its inception in 1995, eBay enjoyed strong revenue growth and was a dominant player in the online auction industry. The company posted net income of $1.78 billion and revenue of $8.54 billion for 2008, up dramatically from 2007's net income of $0.35 billion and revenue of $7.62 billion. (See Exhibit 1.) "Despite the extremely challenging economic environment in 2008—including a slowdown

in global e-commerce, a strengthening dollar, and declining interest rates—we delivered . . . an 11 percent increase from the prior year, and . . . a solid operating margin of 24 percent," commented CEO John Donahoe.[5]

eBay's founder, Pierre Omidyar, envisioned a community built on commerce, sustained by trust, and inspired by opportunity. The company's mission was to "enable individual self-empowerment on a global scale" and employ "business as a tool for social good." Omidyar cited "trust between strangers" as the social impact tied to eBay's ability to remain profitable. The company's unique business model, which united buyers and sellers in an online marketplace, had attracted over 221 million registered users. eBay enabled e-commerce at multiple levels (local, national, and international) through an array of Web sites, including eBay Marketplaces, PayPal, Skype, Rent.com, and Shopping.com. The company's range of products and services had evolved from collectibles to household products, customer services, automobiles, and so on. The variety of products attracted a range of users that included students, small businesses, independent sellers, major corporations, and government agencies.

Despite eBay's outstanding growth performance, the company still faced a number of challenges in both domestic and international markets. The low entry barriers in the online marketplace attracted a number of large dot-com competitors, including Amazon, Yahoo, uBid, and Overstock. Historically, the company had acquired other online competitors, such as Stubhub (tickets), but established players such as Yahoo and Amazon posed a major threat to eBay's market share and ability to sustain profitability. Still, eBay's top management felt that the company would end up as a specialty business, an idea suggesting that it would face little threat from these major competitors:

> We have specialized in e-commerce, payment and voice communication. Google stands for search, Yahoo largely stands for content—so I think we may on the fringe compete, but I suspect that over time the businesses will become more specialized. (*Meg Whitman, February 8, 2006*)

The company had no plans for further big acquisitions but intended to expand and identify synergies within existing business lines.

eBay acknowledged its inability to grow and compete in certain international markets. The company localized sites in 24 countries and a presence in Latin America through its investment in MercadoLibre.com. However, eBay's numerous attempts to penetrate the Asia Pacific market, specifically China and Japan, ended in failure, with the company pulling out of Japan and buying out Chinese start-up Eachnet, essentially canceling years of

*This case was prepared by Professor Alan B. Eisner and graduate student David J. Morates of Pace University. This case was solely based on library research and was developed for class discussion rather than to illustrate either effective or ineffective handling of an administrative situation. Copyright © 2007, 2009 Alan B. Eisner.

Exhibit 1   Income Statements (in thousands, except per-share amounts; year-end December 31)

	2004	2005	2006	2007	2008
Net revenues	$3,271,309	$4,552,401	$5,969,741	$7,672,329	$8,541,261
Cost of net revenues	614,415	818,104	1,256,792	1,762,972	2,228,069
Gross profit	2,656,894	3,734,297	4,712,949	5,909,357	6,313,192
Operating expenses:					
Sales and marketing	798,555	1,143,580	1,587,133	1,882,810	1,881,551
Product development	240,647	328,191	494,695	619,727	725,600
General and administrative	335,076	479,418	744,363	904,681	998,871
Provision for transaction and loan losses	157,447	212,460	266,724	293,917	347,453
Amortization of acquired intangible assets	65,927	128,941	197,078	204,104	234,916
Restructuring	—	—	—	—	49,119
Impairment of goodwill	—	—	—	1,390,938	—
Total operating expenses	1,597,652	2,292,590	3,289,993	5,296,177	4,237,510
Income from operations	1,059,242	1,441,707	1,422,956	613,180	2,075,682
Interest and other income, net	71,745	111,099	130,017	154,271	115,919
Interest expense	(8,879)	(3,478)	(5,916)	(16,600)	(8,037)
Income before income taxes	1,122,108	1,549,328	1,547,057	750,851	2,183,564
Provision for income taxes	(343,885)	(467,285)	(421,418)	(402,600)	(404,090)
Net income	$ 778,223	$1,082,043	$1,125,639	$ 348,251	$1,779,474
Net income per share:					
Basic	$ 0.59	$ 0.79	$ 0.80	$ 0.26	$ 1.37
Diluted	$ 0.57	$ 0.78	$ 0.79	$ 0.25	$ 1.36
Weighted average shares:					
Basic	1,319,458	1,361,708	1,399,251	1,358,797	1,303,454
Diluted	1,367,720	1,393,875	1,425,472	1,376,174	1,312,608

Source: eBay.

invested work. According to many analysts, the company's recent interest in its South Korean rival Gmarket Inc. and joint venture with Beijing-based Tom Online were further indications that eBay couldn't compete in these countries. To remain successful and enjoy the same financial performance as it had in the past, eBay needed to develop an effective strategy to compete in major Asian markets and mitigate the risk of existing local competitors.

Evolution of Auctions

Traditional Auctions   According to Greek scribes, the first known auctions occurred in Babylon in 500 BC. At that time, women were sold on the condition of marriage, and it was considered illegal for daughters to be sold outside auctions. Auctions evolved during the French Revolution and throughout the American Civil War, where colonels auctioned goods that were seized by armies.[6] Although there were various types of auctions, they all provided a forum where sellers could find buyers or hobbyists who were looking to purchase rare items and collectibles. Auctions were considered one of the purest markets, since buyers paid what they were willing to spend for an item, thereby determining the true market value of the item. Over time, auction formats continued to evolve, and through technological advances and improved communication they found a new home—the Internet.

Online Auctions The primary difference between traditional and online auctions was that the online auction process occurred over the Internet as opposed to at a specific location where both buyers and sellers were present. Online auctions offered strategic advantages to both parties that were not typically available in traditional auctions. Buyers could select from millions of products and engage in multiple auctions simultaneously. Given the massive inventory of an online auction market, items were usually available in multiple auctions, allowing buyers to compare starting bid prices and search for better prices. Sellers were exposed to millions of buyers, since more buyers had access to the Internet and felt comfortable making purchases online. The net impact was increased price competition, since there were more buyers who were willing to purchase items at a higher price. Thus, the Internet gave buyers and sellers access to a marketplace that spanned the world.

Online auctions also offered the following strategic advantages:

1. *No time constraints.* A bid could be placed at any time.
2. *No geographic constraints.* Sellers and buyers could participate from any location with Internet access.
3. *Network economies.* The large number of bidders attracted more sellers, which attracted more bidders, and so on. This created a large system that had more value for both parties. Online auctions also allowed businesses to easily sell off excess inventory or discontinued items. This was done through either business-to-business (B2B) or business-to-consumer (B2C) auctions. Offering products and services in an online auction helped small businesses build their brand and reputation by establishing a devoted customer base. Finally, some businesses used the online marketplace as an inexpensive yet effective way to test-market for upcoming products.

E-Commerce

Although Vannevar Bush originally conceived the idea of the Internet in 1945, it wasn't until the 1990s that the Internet became overwhelmingly popular. According to Internet World Stats, in December 2008 there were over 1.5 billion Internet users in over 150 countries. Exhibit 2 shows Internet usage growth between 1995 and 2010.

As of December 19, 2008, North America was considered the region most penetrated by the Internet, with approximately 73.6 percent of the population already online. However, Internet usage growth between 2000 and 2008 was considerably less in North America than in other regions. The regions with the highest Internet usage growth were developing countries where penetration was low, such as Africa, Asia, Latin America, and the Middle East. Considering close to 80 percent of the world's population resides in these areas, it is inevitable that Internet usage growth will continue to increase dramatically in these regions. Exhibit 3 shows the world Internet usage and population as of December 2008.

Although Asia constituted approximately 57 percent of the world's population, its penetration rate was only 15.3 percent. Compared to other regions with high usage growth rates such as Africa and the Middle East, Asia invested more in its technology infrastructure and contained by far the most current Internet users, making it a more attractive market. Exhibit 4 provides more detail on how Asia stacks against the rest of the world in terms of Internet usage.

As the usage growth of the Internet increased, so did the popularity of e-commerce. E-commerce, or electronic commerce, was the concept of conducting business transactions over the Internet. As in the case with online auctions, e-commerce eliminated boundaries such as time and geography, allowing businesses and customers to interact with one another constantly. As more users were exposed to the Internet, they became comfortable with the idea of conducting transactions online. In correlation with Internet growth usage, revenue generated through e-commerce increased dramatically since the 1990s. Exhibit 5 shows U.S. online retail revenues generated through e-commerce over the 2003–2008 period.

E-commerce grew rapidly in other regions as well, especially in Asia since China's admission into the World Trade Organization (WTO) on December 11, 2001. Induction in the WTO allowed China to conduct business with other nations more freely by reducing tariffs and eliminating market and government impediments.

Company Background

Computer programmer Pierre Omidyar founded the online auction Web site in San Jose, California, on September 3, 1995. Omidyar was born in Paris, France, and moved to Maryland with his family when his father took on a residency at Johns Hopkins University Medical Center. Omidyar became fascinated with computers and later graduated from Tufts University with a degree in computer science. While living and working in the San Francisco Bay area, he met his current wife, Pamela Wesley, a management consultant, who later became a driving force in launching the auction Web site. The couple's vision was to establish an online marketplace where people could share the same passion and interest as Pamela had for her hobby of collecting and trading Pez candy dispensers.[7] Omidyar also envisioned an online auction format that would create a fair and open marketplace, where the market truly determined an item's value. To ensure trust in the open forum, Omidyar based the site on five main values:

1. People are basically good.
2. Everyone has something to contribute.
3. An honest, open environment can bring out the best in people.
4. Everyone deserves recognition and respect as a unique individual.
5. You should treat others the way you want to be treated.

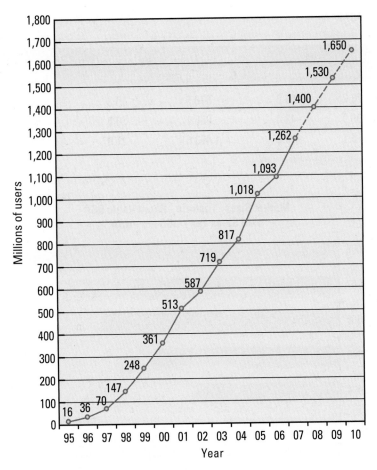

Exhibit 2 **Internet Usage Growth, 1995–2010**

Source: Internet World Stats—Global Village Online, 2008.

Exhibit 3 World Internet Usage and Population Statistics, 2008

World Regions	Population (millions)	Population (%)	Internet Usage (millions)	Percent Penetrated	Usage as % of World	Usage Growth, 2000–2008 (%)
Africa	955.2	14.3	51.1	5.3	3.5	1,031.2
Asia	3,776.2	56.6	578.5	15.3	39.5	406.1
Europe	800.4	12.0	384.6	48.1	26.3	266.0
Middle East	197.1	2.9	41.9	21.3	2.9	1,176.8
North America	337.2	5.1	248.2	73.6	17.0	129.6
Latin America	576.1	8.6	139.1	24.1	9.5	669.3
Australia	33.9	0.5	20.2	59.5	1.4	165.1
Total	**6,676.1**	**100.0**	**1,463.6**	**21.9**	**100.0**	**305.5**

Source: Internet World Stats—Usage and Population Statistics, 2008.

Exhibit 4 Internet Usage in Asia

Regions	Population (millions)	Internet %	Internet Users (millions)	Usage % Penetrated	Usage as % of World	Usage Growth, 2000–2008 (%)
Asia	3,776.2	56.6	578.5	15.3	39.5	406.1
Rest of world	2,899.9	43.4	885.1	30.5	60.5	258.8
Total	**6,676.1**	**100.0**	**1,463.6**	**21.9**	**100.0**	**305.5**

Source: Internet World Stats—Usage and Population Statistics, 2008.

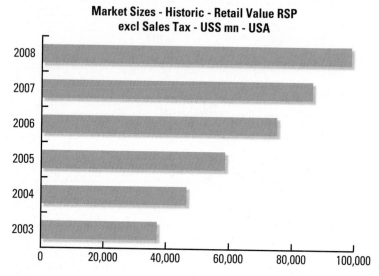

Market Sizes - Historic - Retail Value RSP excl Sales Tax - USS mn - USA

Exhibit 5 **U.S. Online Retail Revenues**

Source: Internet World Stats—E-Commerce Market Size and Trends, 2006.

On Labor Day weekend in 1995, Omidyar launched Auction Web, an online trading platform. After the business exploded, Omidyar decided to dedicate more attention to his new enterprise and work as a consultant under the name Echo Bay Technology Group. When he tried to register a Web site for his company, Omidyar discovered Echo Bay was unavailable, so he decided to use the abbreviated version *eBay*, which also stood for "electronic bay area." The company's name was also selected to attract San Francisco residents to the site and prompt them to buy and sell items.

Initially, the company did not charge fees to either buyers or sellers, but as traffic grew rapidly Omidyar was forced to charge buyers a listing fee to cover Internet service provider costs. When Omidyar noticed that the fees had no impact on the level of bids, he realized the potential for profitability of his business. To handle and manage the company's day-to-day operations, Omidyar hired Jeffrey Skoll (B.A.Sc. University of Toronto, MBA Stanford University). Skoll was hired as the company's first president, and he wrote the business plan that eBay later followed from its emergence as a start-up to its maturity as a financial success. The two worked out of Skoll's living room and various Silicon Valley facilities until they eventually settled in the company's current location in San Jose, California.

By the middle of 1997, less than a year under the name eBay, the company was hosting nearly 800,000 auctions a day.[8] Although the rapid expansion of eBay's traffic caused the company to suffer a number of service interruptions, the site remained successful and continued to gain the confidence of its strong customer base. Skoll remained president until early 1998, when the company hired Meg Whitman as president and CEO. At the time, the company had only 30 employees and was solely located in the United States; in a decade the number of employees went up to over 15,000. In September 1998, eBay launched a successful public offering, making both Omidyar and Skoll instant billionaires. By the time eBay went public, less than three years after Omidyar had created the company, the site had more than a million registered users. The company grew exponentially in the late 1990s and, based on its 2008 performance, indicated no sign of stopping. Exhibit 6 highlights the company's recent growth performance by segments.

Exhibit 6   eBay Growth (in millions, year-end December 31)

	2006	2007	2008
Supplemental Operating Data:			
Marketplace Segment:			
Gross merchandise volume[1]	$52,474	$59,353	$59,650
Payments Segment:			
Net total payment volume[2]	$35,800	$47,470	$60,146
Communications Segment:			
Registered users[3]	171.2	276.3	405.3
SkypeOut minutes[4]	4,095	5,650	8,374

[1] Total value of all successfully closed items between users on eBay Marketplaces trading platforms during the period, regardless of whether the buyer and seller actually consummated the transaction.

[2] Total dollar volume of payments, net of payment reversals, successfully completed through our payments network or on Bill Me Later accounts during the period, excluding the payment gateway business.

[3] Cumulative number of unique user accounts, which includes users who may have registered via non-Skype based websites, as of the end of the period. Users may register more than once and, as a result, may have more than one account.

[4] Cumulative number of minutes that Skype users were connected with Skype's VoIP product to traditional fixed-line and mobile telephones.

Source: eBay.

Whitman stepped down as the president and CEO of the company on March 31, 2008. Through a decade of her successful leadership, Whitman had managed to build an increasingly diversified portfolio of businesses and transformed a company with just 30 employees and $4.7 million in revenue into one of the fastest-growing companies in history, with revenues of $8.5 billion. "With humor, smarts and unflappable determination, Meg took a small, barely known online auction site and helped it become an integral part of our lives," said Omidyar, chairman of the board, about Whitman, who remained on the board of directors.[9] Both Omidyar and Whitman were confident that the new CEO, John Donahoe, was a good choice to lead eBay. Donahoe joined the company in 2005 as president of eBay's largest division, Marketplaces, and within three years managed to double the revenues and profits for this business unit. Before joining eBay, Donahoe served as the CEO of Bain & Company, an international consulting firm based in Boston.[10] "I'm extremely confident in John's skills and the abilities of John's veteran management team," Meg Whitman commented on the transition.[11]

Shortly after his election, Donahoe announced fundamental changes targeted at improving the overall buying experience and protection for eBay users. The changes included lowering fees for listing items and raising minimum standards for the sellers, as well as offering incentives and discounts to reward sellers with the best buyer satisfaction ratings.[12] In addition, in June 2008, the company improved buyer and seller protection on eBay. First-time buyers were protected for 100 percent of an item's purchase price, while sellers would receive improved protection when items were paid for with PayPal.[13] Donahoe was confident that these changes would significantly reinforce healthy and frequent trading at eBay.

Year 2008 was also marked by eBay's increased commitment to social responsibility. On April 28, 2008, the eBay Foundation, the charitable division of eBay Inc., introduced an online fund-raising campaign, Community Gives. The new campaign aimed at generating funds for providing low-income families with children's books, caring for mistreated animals, and supplying water in poverty-stricken regions. "The mission of the initiative is to build on the positive impact of our businesses and make the most of our opportunity to be a force for good in the world," said Bill Barmeier, eBay's vice president of Global Citizenship.[14] By June 2008, eBay's Community raised $150 million for global causes through charity listings on eBay, an increase of $50 million since 2007.[15] In September 2008, eBay launched a new online marketplace, WorldofGood.com, offering products that had positive impact on people and the environment. "We created the WorldofGood.com marketplace to enable shoppers to purchase socially responsible products with confidence," commented Robert Chatwani, general manager of WorldofGood.com.[16]

eBay Platforms

eBay's overall strategy comprised three primary components: products, sense of community, and aggressive expansion. All three components evolved around the various geographic and specialty platforms the company introduced.

Product Categories eBay had an array of product categories and trading platforms that offered a range of pricing formats, such as fixed pricing. Relatively new for the company, establishing a fixed-price format allowed eBay to compete directly with major competitors such as Amazon.com and penetrate new market space. Before fixed pricing, selling prices were solely determined by the highest auction bid, and this took days or weeks depending on the length of the auction. eBay's different trading platforms also offered distinct services and target-specific market niches, which allowed eBay to broaden its customer base. The platforms included:

- *PayPal:* Founded in 1998 and acquired by eBay in 2002, PayPal enabled individuals to securely send payments quickly and easily online. PayPal was considered the global leader in online payments, with tens of millions of registered users.
- *Rent.com:* Acquired by eBay in February 2005, Rent. com was the most visited online apartment listing service in the United States, with more than 20,000 properties listed.
- *Skype:* Acquired by eBay in October 2005, Skype was the world's fastest-growing online communication solution, allowing free video and audio communication between users of Skype software. By 2008, Skype connected more than 405 million registered users.[17]

eBay's acquisition of Skype was expected to enhance the customer experience by improving communication between buyers and sellers. According to former CEO Meg Whitman, "Communications is at the heart of e-commerce and community. By combining the two leading e-commerce franchises, eBay and PayPal, with the leader in Internet voice communications, we will create an extraordinary powerful environment for business on the Net." However, some analysts were confused by the hefty $2.6 billion acquisition and cited the move as being defensive and trying to acquire as much online traffic as possible. Still, eBay felt Skype would increase trade velocity in the marketplace, which was critical for categories that required more involved communications.

- *Shopping.com:* With thousands of merchants and millions of products and reviews, Shopping.com empowered consumers to make informed choices, which drove value for merchants. The company was acquired by eBay in August 2005.
- *Stubhub.com:* Acquired by eBay in January 2007, StubHub was an online marketplace for selling and purchasing tickets for sports events, concerts, and other live entertainment events.
- *Online classifieds:* By January 2009, eBay had the world-leading portfolio of online classifieds sites, including Intoko, Gumtree, LoQUo.com, and mobile.de, as well as Netherlands-based

Marktplaats.nl.[18] In 2007, eBay expanded its classifieds business through its acquisition of Kijiji.[19] In October 2008, eBay further diversified its classifieds portfolio by acquiring Den Bla Avis and BilBasen, providers of successful classifieds businesses in Denmark, for $390 million. "We are the global leader in classifieds with top positions in Canada, Australia, Germany, Japan and the United Kingdom, and sites in more than 1,000 cities across 20 countries," said CEO John Donahoe after the latest acquisition.[20]

- *eBay Express:* Introduced in April 2006, eBay Express behaved like a standard Internet shopping site but gave sellers access to over 200 million buyers worldwide. Sellers could design product categories within minutes and buyers could purchase from multiple sellers by using a single shopping cart.
- *eBay Motors:* This specialty site was considered the largest marketplace for automobile buyers and sellers. Buyers could purchase anything from automobile parts to new or antique vehicles.

The use of product categories such as eBay Express and eBay Motors provided further depth in eBay's product offerings and enabled the company to target a broader market.

Sense of Community The underlying key to all eBay sites and trading platforms was creating trust between sellers and buyers. The company created "community values," and this was why eBay users were willing to send money to strangers across the country. The Feedback Forum was created in February 1996 and encouraged users to post comments about trading partners. Originally, Omidyar handled disputes between buyers and sellers via e-mail by putting the disputing parties in touch with each other to resolve the issue themselves. He soon realized that an open forum where users could post opinions and feedback about one another would create the trust and sense of community the site required. Buyers and sellers were encouraged to post comments (positive, negative, or neutral) about each other at the completion of each transaction. The individual feedback was recorded and amended to a user profile, which ultimately established a rating and reputation for each buyer and seller. eBay users could view this information before engaging in a transaction. The company believed that the feedback forum was critical for creating initial user acceptance for purchasing and selling over the Internet and that it contributed more than anything else to eBay's success.

Aggressive Expansion To compete effectively and create a global trading platform, the company continued to develop in U.S. and international markets that utilized the Internet. With intense competition in the online auction industry, eBay aimed to increase market share and revenue through acquisitions and partnerships in related and unrelated businesses. For example:

- In June 2000, eBay acquired Half.com for $318 million.
- In August 2001, eBay acquired MercadoLibre, Lokau, and iBazar, Latin American auction sites.
- On August 13, 2004, eBay took a 25 percent stake in Craigslist, an online central network of urban communities.
- In September 2005, eBay invested $2 million in the Meetup social networking site.
- In August 2006, eBay announced international cooperation with Google.
- In January 2007, eBay acquired online ticket marketplace Stubhub for $310 million.

During this period, eBay also made a number of acquisitions and investments in international markets. In addition, in mid-2006, eBay announced an agreement to share services, such as advertising and online payments, with Yahoo in an attempt to minimize the intense competition of rival search-engine giant Google.[21]

Company Business Model

eBay's business model was based on a person-to-person marketplace on the Internet where sellers conveniently listed items for sale and interested buyers bid on these items. The objective was to create a forum that allowed buyers and sellers to come together in an efficient and effective manner. The business model overcame the inefficiencies of traditional fragmented marketplaces, which tended to offer a limited variety of goods. According to former CEO Meg Whitman, the company started with commerce and what grew out of that was a community, essentially creating a community-commerce model.[22] The company's success relied primarily on establishing a trustworthy environment that attracted a large number of buyers and sellers. As eBay's reputation grew, so did the number of buyers and sellers, keeping the company in line with Omidyar's original vision. However, as new competitors entered the online auction business and the popularity of the Internet increased, eBay tweaked its business model to accommodate the changes in the fast-paced environment.

The company was aggressively expanding globally and looking for new products and services to offer to customers. It was also looking closely at the kind of merchants who sold on eBay. In the beginning, eBay focused on a consumer-to-consumer business model, but since some of the individuals became small dealers, the model changed to a mix of consumer-to-consumer and business-to-consumer. The sellers wanted to maintain their business on eBay, since it was their most profitable distribution channel. eBay wanted new ways to generate revenue as a result of more small dealers and businesses selling their products through the company's Web site.

eBay generated revenue through three main channels: marketplaces, payments, and, most recently, communications. Marketplaces, which generated revenue by charging sellers a fee for every item they sold, accounted for over 65 percent of the company's revenue. As of December 2008, marketplace revenue was approximately $5.6 billion of the company's $8.5 billion total revenue. Another $2.4 billion of the company's revenue came from fees charged through electronic payments made through the company Web site, primarily via PayPal. The newest source of revenue for eBay was communications (Skype), which produced $551 million of the company's revenue. Although free, eBay's communication software generated revenue through its premium offerings such as making and receiving calls to and from landline and mobile phones, as well as voice mail, ring tones, and call forwarding. Despite its small percentage of eBay's total revenue, the product was new and experienced the strongest growth between 2007 and 2008, when its revenue almost doubled. Exhibit 7 shows the company's recent revenue performance by type.

In addition to the primary revenue sources, there were specific elements of eBay's business model that made the company a success. eBay's dominance of the online auction market and the large number of buyers, sellers, and listed items were primary reasons for eBay's tremendous growth. The trust and safety programs, such as the Feedback Forum, continued to attract and retain new and current eBay users. The cost-effective and convenient trading, coupled with the strong sense of community, added further value to the company's business model. However, as the company continued to grow and new trends evolved, eBay had to continue to adjust its model to remain competitive. Exhibit 1 presents the company's consolidated income statement.

International Expansion

As competition intensified in the online auction industry, eBay expanded its international presence in an effort to create an online global marketplace. Gradually, eBay localized sites in the following countries:

- *Asia Pacific:* Australia, China, Hong Kong, India, Malaysia, New Zealand, Philippines, Singapore, South Korea, and Taiwan.
- *Europe:* Austria, Belgium, Denmark, France, Germany, Ireland, Italy, Netherlands, Poland, Spain, Sweden, Switzerland, and the United Kingdom.
- *North America:* Canada and the United States.

In many of the international Web sites, eBay provided local-language and -currency options to gain popularity and ensure the sense-of-community feeling. In most cases, eBay expanded its business by either acquiring or forming a partnership with a local company. This strategy helped eBay better understand local cultures and ensure that the company was meeting specific local needs. This approach proved successful with the company's equity investment in MercadoLibre.com, which targeted Argentina, Brazil, Chile, Colombia, Costa Rica, Dominican Republic, Ecuador, Mexico, Panama,

Exhibit 7   Net Revenues by Type (in thousands, except percent changes)

	Year Ended December 31, 2006	Percent Change from 2006 to 2007	Year Ended December 31, 2007	Percent Change from 2007 to 2008	Year Ended December 31, 2008
Net Revenues by Type					
Net transaction revenues					
Marketplaces	$3,864,502	21%	$4,680,835	1%	$4,711,057
Payments	1,401,824	31%	1,838,539	26%	2,320,495
Communications	189,110	93%	364,564	44%	525,803
Total net transaction revenues	5,455,436	26%	6,883,938	10%	7,557,355
Marketing services and other revenues					
Marketplaces	469,788	45%	683,056	28%	875,694
Payments	38,706	128%	88,077	(6)%	83,174
Communications	5,811	197%	17,258	45%	25,038
Total marketing services and other revenues	514,305	53%	788,391	25%	983,906
Total net revenues	$5,969,741	29%	$7,672,329	11%	$8,541,261
Net Revenues by Segment:					
Marketplaces	$4,334,290	24%	$5,363,891	4%	$5,586,751
Payments	1,440,530	34%	1,926,616	25%	2,403,669
Communications	194,921	96%	381,822	44%	550,841
Total net revenues	$5,969,741	29%	$7,672,329	11%	$8,541,261
Net Revenues by Geography:					
U.S	$3,108,986	20%	$3,742,670	6%	$3,969,482
International	2,860,755	37%	3,929,659	16%	4,571,779
Total net revenues	$5,969,741	29%	$7,672,329	11%	$8,541,261

Source: eBay.

Peru, Uruguay, and Venezuela. At the end of 2006, MercadoLibre.com reported 18 million registered users who performed 15.8 million transactions worth $1.1 billion.[23] Other notable international growth acquisitions are listed below.

Asia Pacific

- *July 2003:* Acquired China-based Eachnet for approximately $150 million. eBay's failure to manage the company resulted in its recent partnership with communications company Tom Online.
- *June 2004:* Acquired all outstanding shares of India's Baazee.com, which later became eBay India.
- *September 2004:* Acquired Korean rival Internet Auction Co. by purchasing nearly 3 million shares.

Acquisition was not proved successful due to intense competition from top Korean auction site GMarket.

Europe

- *1999:* Acquired Alando auction house for $43 million, a company that later became eBay Germany. Alando was previously considered Germany's leading online trading company. Germany became eBay's second-largest market, accounting for 21 percent of the company's total listings.
- *November 2004:* Acquired Dutch competitor Marktplaats.nl, which had 80 percent of the Netherlands market share.

- *April 2006:* Acquired Sweden's leading online auction company, Tradera.com, for $48 million.
- *October 2008:* Acquired Denmark's leading online classifieds businesses, Den Bla Avis and BilBasen, for $390 million.[24]

For the most part, eBay was successful in expanding in Europe and Latin America, where it was able to quickly adapt to local needs through its partners. The company was also successful in countries it expanded to from the ground up, such as Canada and the United Kingdom. In 2007, the United Kingdom accounted for 15.5 percent of eBay's total listings. By engaging the local community in these countries, eBay customized its sites to meet specific local needs while providing access to the online global community.

eBay was considered the leader in each of its markets with the exception of Japan and China, in which it struggled repeatedly to gain market share. In 2002, eBay was forced to pull out of Japan due to rising costs and intense competition by rival Yahoo Japan. eBay also faced fierce competition in Korea, where GMarket, another investment of Yahoo, dominated the market.

Despite its lack of success in local Asian markets, eBay continued its attempts to expand into the region, recognizing the tremendous growth potential that was available. In June 2006, eBay formed a joint venture with PChome Online in Taiwan. PChome Online was an Internet service provider in Taiwan, with more than 10 million members.[25] The company offered services such as Internet portal, e-commerce platform, and telecommunications. The move was expected to provide eBay with the local e-commerce expertise it needed to launch a new trading Web site that catered to the needs of Taiwan's Internet users.

In 2006, eBay emphasized its commitment to the Chinese e-commerce market by announcing a new joint venture with Beijing-based Internet Company Tom Online Inc. Tom Online, which primarily sold cell phone add-on services, such as ring tones and avatars, put in $20 million for a 51 percent share and management control of eBay's online China site, Eachnet.[26] In 2002, eBay purchased a 30 percent stake in Eachnet and within a year bought out local investors. Central management control of Eachnet was maintained in eBay's San Jose, California, location. Many believed the move was a result of eBay's failure to adapt to local needs and successfully compete with China's online auction market leader Taobao, which controlled approximately 70 percent of the market. Jack Ma, the chief executive of Alibaba.com, Taobao's parent company, believed eBay's failure in China was due to an inability to build a community effect in the country, which according to Ma begins with customer satisfaction. Ma also felt that since eBay had to adhere to a global platform, meeting specific local needs was difficult because changes at a global level had to be approved in the United States, which further limited the company's ability to produce a Web site tailored to

the Chinese market.[27] In an Interview with *Internetnews* in 2005, Ma stated eBay's lack of success in China was predominantly due to the company's quickness to replace local management with foreigners and the mind-set to control the market through spending rather than building it from the ground up.[28] In 2008, eBay sought approval from South Korea's Fair Trade Commission to secure a stake in its successful competitor, Gmarket. This news suggested that eBay was once again struggling to compete in the Asian market.

Competitors

As eBay's product offerings and pricing formats evolved, so did its range of competitors. Originally, the company faced competition from alternative auctions or other venues for collectors, such as flea markets and garage sales. However, as the company grew and introduced fixed pricing, the range of competitors included large companies like Wal-Mart and Kmart that also had retail Web sites. eBay's product platforms, like eBay Motors, put the company in direct competition with auto dealers and other online auto sites such as Autobytes. Still, eBay faced the harshest competition from major online companies that included Yahoo and Amazon, which also had online auctions that rivaled eBay's.

Yahoo! eBay's larger online competitor was Yahoo, which also had a strong global presence, particularly in Asian markets. Yahoo originally started as a search engine and quickly evolved to include additional products and services such as Yahoo! Mail, Yahoo! Maps, and Yahoo! Messenger. The company also offered e-commerce services through Yahoo! Shopping, Yahoo! Autos, Yahoo! Auctions, and Yahoo! Travel. Like eBay, Yahoo's e-commerce sites allowed users to obtain relevant information and make transactions and purchases online. However, Yahoo's business model primarily focused on generating revenue through search advertising. In the United States, in response to potential threats from Web giant Google, Yahoo and eBay formed an alliance in which Yahoo utilized eBay's payment system, PayPal, and eBay gained additional advertising through Yahoo searches. Still, Yahoo posed a major competitive threat in foreign markets, particularly Asia Pacific, through its partnerships with GMarket and Taobao.

GMarket Yahoo's stake in Korean auction site GMarket proved successful, with more than 17.2 million unique visitors. Founded in 2000, GMarket was a Korean online auction and shopping-mall Web site that generated its revenue by charging a fee based on selling price.[29] Like Taobao, GMarket offered fixed prices and provided an option to negotiate prices with sellers on an exclusive basis. This allowed buyers to conduct deals instantly instead of waiting until bids were completed. GMarket also offered cheaper listings. These options along with constant new features allowed GMarket to dominate the Korean online auction industry.[30] GMarket frequently introduced new marketing initiatives to provide sellers with various options to attract new customers. GMarket grew financially powerful in 2006 when it launched its IPO and Yahoo purchased a 9 percent stake in the company. In 2008, eBay decided to secure an interest in its rival and was granted approval to purchase a combined 36.6 percent stake in Gmarket from Interpark Corp. and its chairman.[31]

Taobao   In 2005, Yahoo entered a strategic partnership with Alibaba.com, Taobao's parent company, which created an instant threat in the Chinese market. The move created one of the largest Internet companies in China, one with a leading position in business-to-business e-commerce, consumer e-commerce, and online payments. Like GMarket, Taobao offered buyers and sellers quick and convenient ways to conduct business. Its instant messaging and fixed price arrangements allowed transactions to be conducted quickly. In 2006, the company partnered with Intel to offer customers a wireless platform. This further improved communication and convenience when customers were conducting transactions. In 2009, Taobao was eBay's largest competitor in China, controlling over 70 percent of the Chinese online auction market.

Amazon   Despite not having a huge presence in the online auction industry, Amazon was still considered a fierce online global competitor. Amazon started as Earth's biggest bookstore and rapidly evolved to selling everything, including toys, electronics, home furnishings, apparel, health and beauty aids, groceries, and so on. Still, books, CDs, and DVDs accounted for more than 65 percent of the firm's sales. Although Amazon had a large international presence, the company's linkage to brick-and-mortar shops in the United States made it a greater threat locally than in foreign markets. Amazon's international local sites were in Canada, the United Kingdom, Germany, Japan, France, and China. Despite its large online presence, Amazon scaled back its online auction business, cutting staff and shutting down Livebid, as part of an overall corporate restructuring.

The Future of eBay

eBay had a number of opportunities in which it had already taken action. By 2009, eBay had made a number of strategic acquisitions that included Rent.com, international classified Web sites, Stubhub.com, Shopping.com, and Skype. These acquisitions added and complemented eBay's product offerings and further diversified the company's targeted market. With increased competition from Google and other major online companies, eBay had to continue to diversify and provide depth in its product offerings to remain competitive. Creating options and targeting distinct market niches would enable eBay to distinguish itself from competitors. This was particularly important because as e-commerce and Internet usage rates continued to grow, so would the market opportunity for eBay. Because of its market-leading brand, eBay was in a unique position to capture a significant share of the market at an early stage.

eBay could also expand its existing products and services, such as PayPal and Skype. Both products were relatively new and had the potential to grow and attract new customers, especially in international markets. Expanding PayPal into international markets would enable eBay to provide a simple way to conduct transactions across market borders. Considering the growth potential in developing markets such as those in Africa, Asia, and the Middle East, expanding PayPal would attract many new customers, thus increasing eBay's revenue base. In line with e-commerce growth, as more customers felt comfortable with conducting transactions online, PayPal had the potential to be the preferred form of payment over the Internet.

However, for eBay to capitalize on these opportunities, the company would have to overcome the challenges of expanding into large foreign markets such as China and Japan. With almost 70 percent of the North American population using the Internet and only a 15.3 percent usage rate in Asia Pacific, eBay had a tremendous opportunity to expand and gain new customers. Considering that the Asia Pacific region had more than 50 percent of the world's population and was experiencing some of the largest online usage growth percentages in the world, tapping into this market was critical for eBay to expand.

Endnotes

1. eBay. Meg Whitman to Step Down as President and CEO of eBay (press release). http://news.ebay.com/releasedetail.cfm?ReleaseID=289314.
2. eBay. eBay Announces Bold Changes Aimed at Improving Overall Customer Experience (press release). http://news.ebay.com/releasedetail.cfm?ReleaseID=290446.
3. South Korea OKs eBay's Purchase of Gmarket. August 15, 2008, http://www.marketwatch.com/news/story/south-korea-oks-ebays-purchase/story.aspx?guid=%7BBBF3F40DB-7BD5-4E21-9715-3074575DC155%7D.
4. F. Balfour. Tom Online: eBay's Last China Card. *Business-Week Online,* December 19, 2006.
5. eBay. Annual Report, 2008.
6. The History of Auction Method of Marketing. National Auctions Association, 2005, www.onlyatauction.com.
7. Pierre Omidyar—The Man behind eBay. Internet Based Moms, April 2007.
8. Biography—Pierre Omidyar. Academy of Achievement, www.achievement.org, November 9, 2005.
9. eBay. Meg Whitman to Step Down.
10. eBay corporate Web site.
11. eBay. Meg Whitman to Step Down.
12. eBay. eBay Announces Bold Changes.
13. eBay. eBay and PayPal Increase Protections for Buyers and Sellers to Shop with Confidence (press Release). http://news.ebay.com/releasedetail.cfm?ReleaseID=317542.
14. eBay. eBay Inc. and eBay Foundation Join Forces to Launch *Community Gives* (press release). http://news.ebay.com/releasedetail.cfm?ReleaseID=306929.

15. eBay. eBay Giving Works Celebrates Milestone of $150 Million Raised and Unveils New Program Enhancements (press release).http://news.ebay.com/releasedetail.cfm?ReleaseID=317520.

16. eBay. eBay Launches New Online Marketplace for Ethically Sourced and Eco-Friendly Products (press release). http://news.ebay.com/releasedetail .cfm?ReleaseID=331792.

17. eBay. Annual Report, 2008.

18. eBay. eBay Acquires Leading Classifieds Sites in Denmark (press release). http://news.ebay.com/releasedetail.cfm?ReleaseID=338504.

19. eBay corporate Web site.

20. eBay. eBay Inc. Buys Leading Payments and Classifieds Businesses, Streamlines Existing Organization to Improve Growth (press release). http://news.ebay.com/releasedetail.cfm?ReleaseID=338505.

21. Hoover's Company Records. In-Depth Records: eBay, Inc. February 13, 2007.

22. Q&A with eBay's Meg Whitman. *BusinessWeek Online,* May 31, 1999.

23. Argentina: MercadoLibre Has 18mil Registered Users. *IT Digest,* January 25, 2007, www.infobae.com.

24. eBay. eBay Acquires Leading Classifieds Sites in Denmark.

25. eBay. eBay and PChome Online to Form Joint Venture in Taiwan (press release). www.ebay.com.

26. Market Spotlight: Asia Internet strategy. LexisNexis, December 21, 2006.

27. Alibaba CEO Says Taobao Will Dominate China Online Auctions. *Forbes.com,* May 2005.

28. S. Kuchinskas. *Internetnews,* October 22, 2004, www.internetnews.com.

29. M. Ihlwan. Gmarket Eclipses eBay in Asia. *BusinessWeek Online,* June 28, 2006.

30. Out-eBaying eBay in Korea. *BusinessWeek Online,* July 17, 2006.

31. South Korea OKs eBay's Purchase of Gmarket. August 15, 2008, http://www.marketwatch.com/news/story/south-korea-oks-ebays-purchase/story.aspx?guid=%7BBF3F40DB-7BD5-4E21-9715-3074575DC155%7D.

Case 39   Ann Taylor: Survival in Specialty Retail*

Going into 2009, after the "worst holiday season in four decades," headlines announced that the declining economy was generating a "wave of retail closures" among many well-known companies, including Home Depot, Sears, Zales, Gap, Talbots, Lane Bryant, and Ann Taylor.[1] The chief executive of JCPenney's had called the 2008 situation "the most unpredictable environment in his 39-year retail career."[2] One industry group estimated that over 6,000 retail stores had closed in 2008, a 25 percent increase from the previous year, and that up to 12,000 might close in 2009.[3] A representative from the National Retail Federation (NRF) suggested that these businesses should "look at where they're underperforming and how they can change their operations so that they have a little bit more power in another area, or a little bit more growth potential."[4] Kay Krill, president and CEO of Ann Taylor Stores Corporation (ANN), was already considering this advice.

Krill had been appointed president of ANN in late 2004, and she succeeded to president/CEO in late 2005 when J. Patrick Spainhour retired after eight years as CEO. At that time, there was concern among commentators and customers that the Ann Taylor look was getting "stodgy," and the question was how to "reestablish Ann Taylor as the preeminent brand for beautiful, elegant, and sophisticated occasion dressing."[5] To reestablish the brand, Kay Krill acknowledged the importance of the consumer, since for Ann Taylor to succeed long term, "enough women still need to dress up for work."[6]

Krill's challenge was based on the ANN legacy as a women's specialty clothing retailer. Since 1954, Ann Taylor had been the wardrobe source for busy, socially upscale women, and the classic basic black dress and woman's power suit with pearls were Ann Taylor staples. The Ann Taylor client base consisted of fashion-conscious women from the age of 25 to 55. The overall Ann Taylor concept was designed to appeal to professional women who had limited time to shop and who were attracted to Ann Taylor stores by their total wardrobing strategy, personalized client service, efficient store layouts, and continual flow of new merchandise.

ANN had two divisions focused on different segments of this customer base:

- Ann Taylor (AT), the company's original brand, provided sophisticated, versatile and high-quality updated classics.

- Ann Taylor LOFT (LOFT) was a newer concept that appealed to women who had a more relaxed lifestyle and work environment and who appreciated the more casual LOFT style and compelling value. Certain clients of Ann Taylor and Ann Taylor LOFT cross-shopped both brands.

Ann Taylor Factory was the company's newest division. The merchandise in this division's stores was specifically designed to carry the Ann Taylor Factory label. The stores were located in outlet malls, where customers expected to find Ann Taylor and other major-label bargains.

ANN had regularly appeared in the *Women's Wear Daily* "Top-10" list of firms selling dresses, suits, and evening wear and the "Top-20" list of publicly traded women's specialty retailers. These listings recognized the total company, that is, the result of the impact of all three divisions. Since 2005, the LOFT division, with more square footage per store, had outsold the flagship Ann Taylor (AT) division stores.[7] Since its emergence as a distinctly competitive division, LOFT had been such a success for the company that some analysts credited the division for "keeping the entire ANN corporation afloat."[8] Financial data from 2004 to 2009 show the performance of LOFT compared to AT. (See Exhibit 1.)

Krill acknowledged the ongoing challenge:

> To be successful in meeting the changing needs of our clients, we must continually evolve and elevate our brands to ensure they remain compelling—from our product, to our marketing, to our in-store environment.[9]

Although Krill believed that the overall Ann Taylor brand still had its historic appeal, the question remained whether that appeal could be sustained indefinitely in such a risky and uncertain specialty retail environment where success was so dependent on the "ability to predict accurately client fashion preferences."[10]

Krill was evaluating the company and its growth prospects. Macroeconomic conditions had worsened, and the retailing environment was being threatened by slowing consumer demand. As one analyst put it:

> More mature female shoppers are probably more likely to be very careful how they spend their money in this economy. They are not your footloose-and-fancy-free teen shoppers. These consumers are far more likely to open their pocketbooks only if the merchandise is right (and now, probably only if the price is right, too).[11]

Within the company, Krill was contemplating how to revitalize the flagship AT store brand and what effect that would have on the growth of LOFT. In addition, ANN had recently launched a beauty business as a department

Exhibit 1 AT versus LOFT Financial Performance, 2004–2009

	Jan 31, 2009	Feb 2, 2008	Feb 3, 2007	Jan 28, 2006	Jan 29, 2005	Jan 31, 2004
Net Sales (in millions)						
Total company	$2,194.6	$2,396.5	$2,343.0	$2,073.1	$1,853.6	$1,587.7
Ann Taylor	689.2	866.6	912.8	873.9	854.9	867.9
Ann Taylor LOFT	1,088.4	1,174.4	1,146.5	991.9	826.6	588.8
Other*	417.0	355.6	283.7	207.3	172.2	131.1
Comparable-Store Sales Percentage [increase or (decrease)]						
Total company	(14.8%)	(3.3%)	2.8%	0.1%	3.6%	5.3%
Ann Taylor	(19.9)	(3.7)	3.1	0.6	(2.7)	3.2
Ann Taylor LOFT	(11.4)	(5.4)	1.9	(0.3)	12.8	9.4

Consolidated Income Statement (as percentage of net sales)[†]					
	Jan 31, 2009	Feb 2, 2008	Feb 3, 2007	Jan 28, 2006	Jan 29, 2005
Net sales	100%	100%	100%	100%	
Cost of sales	51.9	47.8	46.3	49.1	
Gross margin	48.1	52.2	53.7	50.9	
Selling, general, and administrative expenses	47.8	44.4	44.1	44.6	
Restructuring and asset/goodwill impairment	17.2	1.4	—	—	
Operating income (loss)	(16.9)	6.5	9.6	6.3	
Interest income	0.1	0.3	0.7	0.4	
Interest expense	0.1	0.1	0.1	0.1	
Income before income taxes	(16.9)	6.7	10.2	6.6	
Income tax provision	(1.7)	2.6	4.1	2.7	
Net income	(15.2%)	4.1%	6.1%	3.9%	
Percent change from prior period:					
Net sales	(8.4%)	2.3%	13.0%	11.8%	16.7%
Operating income	(339.2)	(30.6)	70.8	24.8	(38.7)
Net income	(443.3)	(32.0)	74.6	29.4	(37.2)

*Includes Ann Taylor Factory stores and Internet business.

[†]All fiscal years presented contain 52 weeks, except for the fiscal year ended February 3, 2007, which contains 53 weeks.

Source: Company financials, http://investor.anntaylor.com.

within the AT and LOFT stores, had expanded the high-end fashion offerings in AT as a separate Collections line, had announced the opening of LOFT Outlet stores to complement Ann Taylor Factory, and was considering a new concept store specifically targeting the "older" segment of women, ages 55 to 64. Krill was firmly committed to long-term growth and felt that she could pursue that growth agenda even as the economy worsened. However, she was confronted with significant questions. For example, was her agenda too aggressive? Were the actions she had undertaken the kinds of moves needed to unleash what she believed was the firm's "significant untapped potential"?[12]

Ann Taylor Background

Ann Taylor was founded in 1954 as a wardrobe source for busy, socially upscale women. Starting out in New Haven, Connecticut, Ann Taylor founder Robert Liebeskind established a stand-alone clothing store. When Liebeskind's father, Richard Liebeskind, Sr., a designer himself, as a good luck gesture gave his son exclusive rights to one of his best-selling dresses, "Ann Taylor," the company name was established. Ann Taylor was never a real person, but her persona lived on in the profile of the consumer.

Ann Taylor went public on the New York Stock Exchange in 1991 under the symbol ANN. In 1994 the company added a mail-order catalog business, a fragrance line, and free-standing shoe stores positioned to supplement the Ann Taylor (AT) stores. The mail-order catalog attempt ended in 1995, and the lower-priced apparel concept, Ann Taylor LOFT, was launched. LOFT was meant to appeal to a younger, more casual and cost-conscious, but still professional, consumer. CEO Sally Kasaks incorporated more casual clothing, petite sizes, and accessories in an attempt to create a one-stop shopping environment, to "widen market appeal and fuel growth."[13] Following losses in fiscal 1996 that could be attributed to a fashion misstep—cropped T-shirts didn't fit in with the workplace attire—Kasaks left the company. New ANN CEO Patrick Spainhour, who had been chief financial officer at Donna Karan and also had previous experience at Gap, shelved the fragrance line and closed the shoe stores in 1997.

Originally, the LOFT stores were found only in outlet centers, but in 1998 the LOFT stores in the discount outlet malls were moved to a third division, Ann Taylor Factory (Factory). The Factory carried clothes from the Ann Taylor (AT) line. The concept offered customers direct access to the AT designer items "off the rack" without elaborate promotion and with prices regularly 25 to 30 percent less than at the high-end Ann Taylor stores. The LOFT concept was revamped, and stores were opened in more prestigious regional malls and shopping centers. By 1999 LOFT clothes were a distinct line of "more casual, yet business tailored, fun, and feminine" attire, and they were about 30 percent less expensive than the merchandise at the flagship Ann Taylor division's stores.[14] At that time, the LOFT was under the direction of Kay Krill, who had been promoted to the position of executive vice president of the LOFT division.

Ann Taylor attempted a cosmetic line in 2000, which it discontinued in 2001. In 2000, the Online Store at www.anntaylor.com was launched, only to be cut back in late 2001 when projected cash-flow goals were not met. In early 2001 Spainhour restructured management reporting relationships, creating new president positions for both the AT and LOFT divisions. Kay Krill was promoted from executive vice president to president of LOFT. Spainhour commented:

> Kay has been instrumental in developing the strategy for the Ann Taylor Loft concept since its inception. Her in-depth understanding of the Ann Taylor Loft client, and strong grounding in the Ann Taylor brand, combined with her proven ability in driving the development of this division, make her an ideal choice for the new President position.[15]

Kay Krill was made president of the entire ANN corporation in 2004, bringing both Ann Taylor and LOFT under her control. In February 2005 Kay Krill announced that LOFT had reached $1 billion in sales; she stated:

> This is an important milestone for our Company. In an intensely competitive and fragmented apparel market, Ann Taylor LOFT has been one of the industry's most successful and fastest-growing apparel retail concepts since its launch in 1998. . . . LOFT's success reaffirms the importance of maintaining a strong connection with our client and evolving with her wardrobe needs over time.[16]

In June 2005 ANN completed a move to new corporate headquarters in Times Square Tower in New York City.[17] In the fall of 2005, Chairman and CEO J. Patrick Spainhour retired and President Kay Krill was elevated to the CEO position. In a conference call following her promotion, Krill stated her goals as "improving profitability while enhancing both brands . . . restoring performance at the Ann Taylor division and restoring the momentum at LOFT."[18]

Krill felt that the outlook for fiscal year 2006 was cautiously positive, and she announced continued plans for expansion and related capital expenditure. The stock responded with new highs, moving to a peak of over $40 in late 2006. At that time, analysts were mainly supportive, citing "confidence in the retailer's strong management team, improving store products, and conservative inventory management."[19] ANN's stock price subsequently retreated in 2007 and 2008, along with the rest of the retailing sector.

Challenges in the macroeconomic climate prompted Krill to announce a restructuring plan in 2008. Krill said:

> We understand that the economy invariably goes through cycles. We firmly believe that the manner in which we approach growth and manage our business through these cycles will differentiate us and determine our success in the market over the long term. In this regard, we have planned . . . cautiously and realistically, focusing on three key areas—the evolution of our brands and channels, the reduction of our overall cost structure, and the continued pursuit of growth.[20]

However, after a posted loss of $333.9 million in 2008 and the continuing economic uncertainty going into 2009, ANN was reluctant to give any profit forecast for the coming quarters (see Exhibits 2, 3, and 4).

The Apparel Retail Industry

Industry Sectors Practically speaking, industry watchers tended to recognize three separate categories of clothing retailers. Industry publications such as the *Daily News Record* (DNR—reporting on men's fashion news and business strategies) and *Women's Wear Daily*

Exhibit 2 Income Statements (in thousands of dollars)

	Jan 31, 2009	Feb 2, 2008	Feb 3, 2007	Jan 28, 2006	Jan 29, 2005
Net sales	2,194,559	2,396,510	2,342,907	2,073,146	1,853,583
Cost of sales	1,139,753	1,145,246	1,085,897	1,017,122	906,035
Gross margin	1,054,806	1,251,264	1,257,010	1,056,024	947,548
Selling, general, and administrative expenses	1,050,560	1,061,869	1,031,341	924,998	842,590
Restructuring charges	59,714	32,255	—	—	—
Asset impairment charges	29,590	1,754	1,832	—	—
Goodwill impairment charge	286,579	—	—	—	—
Operating (loss)/income	(371,637)	155,386	223,837	131,026	104,958
Interest income	1,677	7,826	17,174	9,318	5,037
Interest expense	1,462	2,172	2,230	2,083	3,641
(Loss)/income before income taxes	(371,422)	161,040	238,781	138,261	106,354
Income tax (benefit)/provision	(37,516)	63,805	95,799	56,389	43,078
Net (loss)/income	(333,906)	97,235	142,982	81,872	63,276

Source: Ann Taylor Stores Corporation.

(WWD—reporting on women's fashions and the apparel business), as well as industry associations such as the National Retail Federation (NRF), reported data within the clothing sector, which was divided into three categories:

- Discount mass merchandisers: Chains such as Target, Wal-Mart, TJX (TJ Maxx, Marshall's, A.J. Wright, Bob's Stores), and Costco.
- Multitier department stores: Those offering a large variety of goods, including clothing (e.g., Macy's and JCPenney's) and the more luxury-goods-focused stores (e.g., Nordstrom's and Neiman Marcus).
- Specialty store chains: Those catering to a certain type of customer or carrying a certain type of goods, for example, Abercrombie & Fitch for casual apparel.

More specifically in the case of specialty retail, many broadly recognized primary categories existed such as women's, men's, and children's clothing stores (e.g., Victoria's Secret for women's undergarments,[21] Men's Wearhouse for men's suits, Abercrombie Kids for children ages 7 to 14[22]). Women's specialty stores were "establishments primarily engaged in retailing a specialized line of women's, juniors' and misses' clothing."[23]

Specialty Retailer Growth: Branding Challenges

Unlike department stores that sold many different types of products for many types of customers, specialty retailers focused on one type of product item and offered many varieties of that item. However, this single-product focus increased risk, as lost sales in one area could not be recouped by a shift of interest to another, entirely different product area. Therefore, many specialty retailers constantly sought new market segments (i.e., niches) that they could serve. However, this strategy created potential problems for branding.[24] A participant at the NRF convention commented:

> Brand building, acquisition, and tiering is hotter than ever in retail and consumer products—so much so they may be contributing to shorter life spans for some brands and perhaps diluting the value of all. In any event, the massive proliferation of brands in recent years—some out of thin air, others even reborn from the grave—brings with it a minefield of potential dangers.[25]

Gap, Inc., was an example of a specialty retailer that had added several brand extensions to appeal to different customer segments. In addition to the original Gap line of casual clothing, the company offered the following: Old Navy with casual fashions at low prices, Banana Republic for more high-end casual items, and Piperlime as an online shoe store. However, in 2005 Gap had also spent $40 million to open a chain for upscale women's clothing called Forth & Towne, which closed after only 18 months. The store was supposed to appeal to upscale women over 35—the baby-boomer segment—but, instead, the designers seemed "too focused on reproducing youthful fashions with a more generous cut" instead of finding an "interesting, affordable way" for middle-aged women to "dress like themselves."[26]

Chico's FAS, Inc., was another specialty retailer that tried brand expansions. Chico's focused on private-label,

Exhibit 3 Balance Sheets (in thousands of dollars)

	Jan 31, 2009	Feb 2, 2008	Feb 3, 2007	Jan 28, 2006	Jan 29, 2005
Assets					
Current assets:					
Cash and cash equivalents	112,320	134,025	360,560	380,654	62,412
Short-term investments	—	9,110	—	—	192,400
Accounts receivable	14,081	16,944	16,489	17,091	12,573
Merchandise inventories	173,447	250,697	233,606	204,503	229,218
Deferred income taxes	25,422	29,161	—	—	—
Refundable income taxes	35,270	—	—	—	—
Prepaid expenses and other current assets	63,056	67,954	79,950	73,964	90,711
Total current assets	423,596	507,891	690,605	676,212	587,314
Property and equipment, net	469,687	561,270	564,108	512,765	434,328
Goodwill	—	286,579	286,579	286,579	286,579
Deferred financing costs, net	1,275	288	652	1,017	1,382
Deferred income taxes	53,253	23,314	—	—	—
Other assets	12,628	14,413	26,559	16,333	17,735
Total assets	960,439	1,393,755	1,568,503	1,492,906	1,327,338
Liabilities and Stockholders' Equity					
Current liabilities:					
Trade notes and accounts payable	109,205	125,388	106,519	97,398	88,340
Accrued salaries and bonus	23,883	13,000	28,304	8,633	21,617
Accrued tenancy	42,710	44,945	45,024	44,036	32,264
Gift certificates and merchandise credits redeemable	45,605	54,564	52,989	45,916	38,892
Accrued expenses and other current liabilities	84,180	74,979	66,582	61,603	62,633
Total current liabilities	305,583	312,876	299,418	257,586	243,746
Deferred lease costs	217,614	230,052	214,466	198,714	—
Deferred income taxes	1,898	1,960	—	—	—
Other liabilities	18,832	9,383	4,708	2,124	—
Stockholders' equity:					
Common stock, $.0068 par value; 200,000,000 shares authorized; 82,476,328 and 82,288,607 shares issued, respectively	561	560	559	558	545
Additional paid-in capital	791,852	781,048	753,030	723,230	669,128
Retained earnings	432,502	766,408	670,307	527,325	445,410
Accumulated other comprehensive loss	(7,702)	(3,460)	(5,373)	—	—
	1,217,213	1,544,556	1,418,523	1,239,107	1,103,337
Total stockholders' equity	416,512	839,484	1,049,911	1,034,482	926,744
Total liabilities and stockholders' equity	960,439	1,393,755	1,568,503	1,492,906	1,327,338

Source: Ann Taylor Stores Corporation.

Exhibit 4   Statement of Annual Cash Flows

	Jan 31, 2009	Feb 2, 2008	Feb 3, 2007	Jan 28, 2006	Jan 29, 2005
Operating activities:					
Net (loss)/income	(333,906)	97,235	142,982	81,872	63,276
Adjustments to reconcile net (loss)/income to net cash provided by operating activities:					
Goodwill impairment charge	286,579	—	—	—	—
Deferred income taxes	(23,690)	(9,361)	(10,809)	(15,421)	(5,022)
Depreciation and amortization	122,222	116,804	105,890	93,786	78,657
Loss on disposal and write-down of property and equipment	29,581	6,736	7,896	3,497	1,301
Noncash compensation expense	12,829	19,019	24,722	770	5,350
Noncash interest and other non-cash items	2,506	1,039	483	789	1,858
Noncash restructuring and asset impairment charges	39,775	29,876	—	—	—
Tax (deficiency)/benefit from exercise/vesting of stock awards	(580)	2,180	8,189	12,566	7,262
Amortization of stock awards	—	—	—	—	10,400
Changes in assets and liabilities:					
Accounts receivable	2,863	(455)	602	(5,024)	56
Merchandise inventories	77,250	(17,091)	(29,103)	24,715	(57,159)
Prepaid expenses and other current assets	4,899	(13,599)	(13,543)	24,678	(28,621)
Refundable income taxes	(35,270)	—	—	—	—
Other noncurrent assets and liabilities, net	(12,610)	24,264	21,042	50,510	32,713
Accounts payable and accrued expenses	370	550	37,580	28,185	62,196
Net cash provided by operating activities	172,818	257,197	295,931	311,323	169,259
Investing activities:					
Purchases of marketable securities	(1,180)	(70,947)	—	—	—
Sales of marketable securities	9,407	54,525	—	—	—
Purchases of available-for-sale securities	—	—	—	(20,600)	(414,150)
Sales of available-for-sale securities	—	—	—	213,000	532,125
Purchases of property and equipment	(110,342)	(139,998)	(165,926)	(187,613)	(152,483)
Net cash used for investing activities	(102,115)	(156,420)	(165,926)	4,787	(34,508)
Financing activities:					
Proceeds from the issuance of common stock pursuant to Associate Discount Stock Purchase Plan	2,544	3,526	3,295	3,006	2,950
Proceeds from exercise of stock options	3,864	14,409	26,743	47,279	19,872
Excess tax benefits from stock-based compensation	366	2,328	4,992	—	—
Repurchases of common and restricted stock	(103,281)	(347,575)	(185,129)	(48,153)	(121,698)

(*continued*)

Exhibit 4   Statement of Annual Cash Flows (*continued*)

	Jan 31, 2009	Feb 2, 2008	Feb 3, 2007	Jan 28, 2006	Jan 29, 2005
Proceeds from financing of fixed assets	7,578	—	—	—	—
Repayments of fixed assets financing and capital lease obligations	(2,176)	—	—	—	—
Payments of deferred financing cost	(1,303)	—	—	—	(22)
Net cash used for financing activities	(92,408)	(327,312)	(150,099)	2,132	(98,898)
Net decrease in cash	(21,705)	(226,535)	(20,094)	318,242	35,853
Cash and cash equivalents, beginning of year	134,025	360,560	380,654	62,412	26,559
Cash and cash equivalents, end of year	112,320	134,025	360,560	380,654	62,412
Supplemental disclosures of cash flow information:					
Cash paid during the year for:					
Interest	1,063	1,723	1,769	1,293	1,770
Income taxes	20,370	77,355	94,723	47,030	58,226
Accrual for purchases of property and equipment	12,066	22,213	16,359	—	—

Source: Ann Taylor Stores Corporation.

casual-to-dressy clothing for women age 35 and older, with relaxed, figure-flattering styles constructed out of easy-care fabrics. An outgrowth of a Mexican folk art boutique, Chico's was originally a stand-alone brand. Starting in late 2003, Chico's FAS decided to promote two new brands: White House/Black Market (WH/BM) and Soma by Chico's (Soma).

Chico's WH/BM brand was based on the acquisition of an existing store chain, and it focused on women age 25 and older, offering fashion and merchandise in black-and-white and related shades. Soma was a newly developed brand offering intimate apparel, sleepwear, and active wear. Each brand had its own storefront, mainly in shopping malls, and was augmented by both mail-order catalog and Internet sales. The idea was that the loyal Chico's customer would be drawn to shop at these other concept stores, expecting the same level of quality, service, and targeted offerings that had pleased her in the past.

Although Chico's had been a solid performer during the decade, surpassing most other women's clothing retailers in sales growth, a downturn in 2006 caused Chico's shares to fall more than 50 percent when the company reported sales and earnings below analysts' expectations. Chico's had seen increasing competition for its baby-boomer customers, and it said it had lost momentum, partly because of "fashion missteps" and lack of sufficiently new product designs. The company's response was to create brand presidents for the three divisions to hopefully create more "excitement and differentiation."[27]

In an attempt to better manage the proliferation of brands, many firms, similar to Chico's, created an organizational structure in which brands had their own dedicated managers, with titles such as executive vice president (EVP)/general merchandise manager, chief merchandising officer, or outright "brand president."[28] Since each brand was supposedly unique, companies felt the person responsible for a brand's creative vision should be unique as well.

An alternative to brand extension was the divestiture of brands. In 1988 Limited Brands[29] acquired Abercrombie and Fitch (A&F) and rebuilt A&F to represent the "preppy" lifestyle of teenagers and college students ages 18 to 22. In 1996 Limited Brands spun A&F off as a separate public company. Limited Brands continued divesting brands: teenage clothing and accessories brand The Limited TOO in 1999, plus-size women's clothing brand Lane Bryant in 2001, professional women's clothing brand Lerner New York in 2002, and in 2007 the casual women's clothing brands Express and The Limited. Paring down in order to focus mostly on its key brands Victoria's Secret and Bath & Body Works, the corporation made it clear that it was still not done reconfiguring itself.[30]

Women's Specialty Retail: Competitors and the "Older-Women" Segment

The National Retail Federation, a trade group based in Washington, D.C., reported that the retail niches showing the greatest growth were department stores, stores catering to the teenage children of baby boomers, and apparel chains aimed at women over 35.[31] The four major women's specialty retailers that were trying to target older upscale shoppers were Ann Taylor, Chicos FAS, Coldwater Creek, and Talbots. Ann Taylor was the only one of these with a significant brand extension for the younger professional, but all four were pursuing a shopping environment and merchandise that were clearly focused on women over 35. As Talbot's CEO Trudy Sullivan noted, "Nobody is clearly winning in the 35+ consumer space right now . . . we need to absolutely wow her with this irresistible product and none of us have done that."[32] (See Exhibit 5.)

This "older" group of women was part of the baby-boomer demographic, born between 1946 and 1964, and the purchasing power of these women had not gone unnoticed.[33] Accounting for nearly half of the $102.7 billion in women's clothing purchases in 2007, these women were very diverse, ranging from "traditional types who prefer flat shoes and ankle-length skirts to women who resemble characters from *Desperate Housewives*."[34]

To respond to this diversity in the marketplace, women's specialty retailer Talbot's, Inc., acquired catalog and mail-order company J.Jill Group in 2006. J.Jill was a women's clothing specialty retailer offering casual fashion through multichannel mail-order, Internet, and in-store venues. J.Jill targeted women ages 35 to 55, while Talbot's focused on the 45 to 65 age group. Although the acquisition had supposedly positioned Talbot's as a "leading apparel retailer for the highly coveted age 35+ female population,"[35] Talbot's subsequently decided to sell off this division in 2009, in the wake of retailing's "abysmal holiday season." Analysts were not surprised, since Talbot's had never made an acquisition before and had encountered problems integrating the two businesses.[36]

Coldwater Creek, with its large jewelry, accessory, and gift assortment in addition to apparel, targeted women over 35 with incomes in excess of $75,000 by appealing with a Northwest/Southwest lifestyle approach that included a group of spa locations. Coldwater's customer was not considered "trendy" by any means: "She's never going to be a fashion leader . . . but she wants to look modern."[37] Coldwater Creek had created a common brand identity for its three distribution channels: catalog, Internet, and in-store shopping, but it was having trouble finding the "proper merchandise approach to reclaim some of the baby boomer women's market" as this sector's consumers tightened discretionary spending in 2008.[38]

Chico's FAS was one of the first to introduce the concept of apparel designed for the lifestyle of dynamic mature women who were at the higher-age end of the boomer demographic.[39] Chico's, along with Coldwater Creek, was one of the recipients of the 50+ Fabulous Company Award, an award that promoted positive images of women who were in their 50s or older. The founder of 50+ Fabulous had established this award to promote "the value of 50+ women in the workplace and beyond," noting that "companies have been slow to recognize the vast potential" of this demographic.[40] Chico's had always been aware of the need to focus its branding on the older women's segment. As a result of this focus, Chico's ended the difficult 2008 year with "strong brand equity," one of the few specialty retailers with "staying power."[41]

In August 2007 Kay Krill announced that ANN would be creating a new chain of stores, expected to launch sometime in 2008 or 2009, targeting this "older-women" segment. Krill stated:

> While there are a number of companies that currently play in the broader boomer market, we believe that this particular segment has been the most significantly underserved and is a huge opportunity for us.[42]

Some analysts wondered about this move into an overlooked but risky market that had "tripped up several competitors." They pointed out that although ANN's clothes were expected to be more fashionable, the company still faced stiff competition, made even tougher given the uneven performance of AT and LOFT.[43] In 2008, as a result of the overall economic conditions, Krill announced that this new concept offering would have to be delayed at least until 2009.[44]

ANN Operational Information[45]

At the end of fiscal year 2008, ANN had 935 stores in 46 states, the District of Columbia, and Puerto Rico, with flagship locations in New York, San Francisco, and Chicago. (See Exhibit 5.) The company had also had an online presence since 2000, transacting sales at www. anntaylor.com and www.anntaylorLOFT.com. This "very profitable" Internet channel was considered "a meaningful and effective marketing vehicle for both brands," representing 10 percent of AT sales, less than that for LOFT, and was a way for ANN to reach out to the international market.[46]

Substantially, all merchandise offered in ANN's stores was exclusively developed for the company by its in-house product design and development teams. ANN sourced merchandise from approximately 220 manufacturers and vendors, none of whom accounted for more than 3 percent of the company's merchandise purchases in fiscal 2008. Merchandise was manufactured in over 19 countries, including China, the Philippines, Indonesia, India, Hong Kong, and Thailand.

ANN's planning departments analyzed each store's size, location, demographics, sales, and inventory history to determine the quantity of merchandise to be purchased for, and then allocated to, the stores. The company used a centralized distribution system with a single warehouse in Louisville, Kentucky. At the store level, merchandise was typically sold at its original marked price for several weeks. After that, markdowns were used if inventory did not sell. Store planners recognized that the lack of inventory turnover could have been the result of poor merchandise design, seasonal adaptations or changes in client preference, or incorrectly set original prices.

Recent ANN initiatives focused on improving supply chain speed, flexibility, and efficiency. Reduced floor inventory levels, combined with the use of new "quick-sourcing" software, were meant to help create quicker inventory turns. Faster turns would lead to continual updating of floor

Exhibit 5 Selected Retail Performers

Company/ Ticker Symbol	2008 Revenue (millions)	Percent of Comparable-Store Sales Increase (Decrease) 2007/2006/2005	Number of Stores	Locations Served	Merchandise Market Served	Comments
Ann Taylor/ ANN	$2,194.6	(14.8)/(3.3)/2.8	935	46 states plus Puerto Rico	Specialty women's— private-label "total wardrobing strategy" to achieve the "Ann Taylor look" in suits, separates, footwear, and accessories	Brands are Ann Taylor for updated professional classics; Ann Taylor LOFT for lower-priced, more casual wear; and Ann Taylor Factory for outlet-priced items.
Talbots/ TLB	$2,289.3*	(14.2)/(5.7)/1.3	878	47 states plus Canada and the United Kingdom	Specialty— women's apparel, shoes, and accessories via store, catalog, and Internet	Brands are Talbots and Modern Classics for women. Brands target high-income, college-educated professionals over 35 years old.
Chico's FAS/CHS	$1,582.4	(15.1)/(8.1)/2.1	1,074	47 states plus U.S. Virgin Islands and Puerto Rico	Specialty women's— privately branded clothing, intimate garments, and gifts for fashion-conscious women with moderate to high income	Brands are Chico's for women over 35, White House/Black Market for women over 25, and Soma intimates.
Coldwater Creek, Inc./CWTR	$1,024.2	(18.7)/(7.9)/8.5 averages	348	48 states	Specialty women's— apparel, accessories, jewelry, and gifts via store, catalog, Internet, and spa locations	Offers Coldwater Creek brand of clothing and jewelry, cosmetics and personal care products to women over 35 with income in excess of $75,000; socially responsible.

*2007 year-end data.

Source: 10K filings, plus data from "Top 100 Retailers," *Stores: A Magazine of the National Retail Federation* July 2008, www.nrf.com/modules .php?name=News&op=viewlive&sp_id=543.

(*continued*)

Exhibit 5 Selected Retail Performers (*continued*)

Company Name*	Total Revenue (millions)	Net Income (millions)	Inventory Turnover	Revenue $ per Employee
Abercrombie & Fit	3,540.30	272.30	10.06	42,771
AnnTaylor Stores Corp.	2,194.60	−333.90	10.38	119,597
Charming Shoppes, Inc.	2,474.90	−224.20	7.52	86,470
Chico's FAS Inc.	1,582.40	−19.10	11.47	109,734
Coldwater Creek Inc.	1,024.20	−25.90	7.46	91,700
Limited Brands Inc.	9,043.00	220.00	7.45	99,756
Talbots, Inc. (2007 data)	2,289.30	−188.80	6.73	138,288
The Gap, Inc.	14,526.00	967.00	9.46	108,701

Company Name*	Selling, General, & Admin., % Total Revenue	Gross Margin (%)	Operating Margin (%)	Net Profit Margin (%)
Abercrombie & Fit	54.55	66.71	12.41	7.69
AnnTaylor Stores Corp.	47.87	48.06	−16.93	−15.22
Charming Shoppes, Inc.	27.97	25.37	−7.22	−9.87
Chico's FAS Inc.	52.79	51.79	−2.5	−1.21
Coldwater Creek Inc.	38.6	34.23	−4.51	−2.53
Limited Brands Inc.	25.56	33.24	6.51	2.43
Talbots, Inc. (2007 data)	33.1	32.12	−8.14	−8.25
The Gap, Inc.	NA	37.5	10.66	6.66

*All results are stated in U.S. dollars, using the latest filings as of April 2009.

Source: Mergent Online.

merchandise and a greater emphasis on full-price selling.[47] As a result, ANN was hoping to see fewer markdowns and higher margins. The new quick-sourcing software was just one example of continued efforts to improve the company's information systems.

ANN used a real estate expansion program designed to reach new clients either by opening new stores, relocating stores, or expanding the size of existing stores. Store locations were determined on the basis of various factors, including:

- Geographic location.
- Demographic studies.
- Anchor tenants in a mall location.
- Other specialty stores in a mall or in the vicinity of a village location.
- The proximity to professional offices in a downtown or village location.

Two potential concerns were emerging for ANN as a result of its recent investments in store expansion and

remodeling. First, the increasing sales volume threatened to put stress on the company's internal distribution system. The distribution center in Louisville had been investing in incremental improvements through automation and software integration. However, the distribution center had only sufficient capacity to supply 1,050 stores. After that, ANN's logistical experts cautioned that the building footprint would have to be expanded.[48] A second concern was whether projected earnings, given economic weakness, would actually be able to cover the projected long-term lease obligations[49] (see Exhibit 6).

Ann Taylor's Brand Identity

When ANN went public in 1991, the Ann Taylor brand, with its historically loyal following, was a candidate for brand extension. At one point in its history, the company had five separate store concepts: Ann Taylor (AT), Ann Taylor's Studio Shoes, Ann Taylor LOFT, Ann Taylor Petites (clothing for women 5 feet 4 inches and under), and Ann Taylor Factory. In addition, ANN's management had

Exhibit 6 Stores' Operational Data

	FY2008	FY2007	FY2006	FY2005	FY2004	FY2003
Employees, total	18,400	18,400	17,700	16,900	14,900	13,000
Inventory turns*	5.4	4.7	5.0	4.7	4.5	4.1
Net sales per sq ft	$ 402	$ 457	$ 474	$ 461	$ 471	$ 456
Net sales (revenue) per employee	$119,597	$130,603	$130,227	$123,008	$124,743	$122,467
Average sq ft per store:						
Ann Taylor	5,300	5,300				
Ann Taylor LOFT	5,900	5,700				
Ann Taylor Factory	7,300	6,700				

*Inventory turns can be calculated differently, depending on whether yearly average or year-end inventory values are used. These numbers are from ANN's 10K filing.

Specific Store Detail (in number of stores)

	Total Open at Beginning of Fiscal Year	Opened during Fiscal Year*				Closed during Fiscal Year	Open at End of Fiscal Year*					Expanded during Fiscal Year
		ATS	ATL	ATF	LOS		ATS	ATL	ATF	LOS	Total	
2003	584	8	61	1		6	354	268	26		648	8
2004	648	10	77	8		5	359	343	36		738	6
2005	738	9	73	15		11	357	416	51		824	12
2006	824	11	52	7		25	348	464	57		869	16
2007	869	14	52	11		17	349	512	68		929	14
2008	929	4	25	23	14	60	320	510	91	14	935	8

*ATS = Ann Taylor; ATL = Ann Taylor LOFT; ATF = Ann Taylor Factory; LOS = LOFT Outlet Stores.

Source: Company reports, http://investor.anntaylor.com.

experimented with a makeup line and children's clothes. By 2005, the company had closed the shoe stores, reduced the accessories inventory that stores carried, and eliminated the makeup line. However, ANN was still offering petites, as a separate section in the AT and LOFT stores, and was experimenting with children's clothes and sleepwear through the LOFT division. A separate maternity section in selected LOFT stores was also undergoing a trial period.

Since 1999 analysts had warned that ANN needed to be wary of cannibalization within the brands. The analysts speculated that customers might turn away from AT in order to buy at LOFT. ANN had always tried to respond to the customer with "wardrobing," a philosophy of "outfitting from head to toe," combining relaxed everyday wear with more dressy pieces.[50] Since LOFT sold more relaxed but still tailored items at a lower price than AT, it was possible that some of AT's customers shopped at LOFT for things that they previously would have bought at AT.

The industry was used to brand extensions such as Gap's Old Navy chain. In contrast to Gap, LOFT used "Ann Taylor" in its name, reinforcing the perception of customers that they could get the same brand for less. As one analyst put it:

> It's not clear that the Ann Taylor customer will continue paying $88 for a silk cardigan sweater when she knows she can pick up a similar cardigan for $39 . . . a few blocks away at LOFT.[51]

In the fall of 2005, one of Krill's first actions as ANN's new CEO was to recruit Laura Weil to the new position of corporate operations officer (COO). Weil came from American Eagle Outfitters, where she had focused on financial issues involving real estate, pricing, sourcing, and logistics. In addition, Weil handled the divestiture of underperforming assets. In her role as COO at ANN, she would be expected to "focus on inventory management and merchandise planning, information systems and supply chain operations."[52]

The appointment of Weil and four other staff changes reconfigured ANN's top management structure. Krill created three positions that reported directly to her—COO, executive vice president (EVP) of planning and allocation, and EVP/chief marketing officer. These three additional positions provided specific expertise while still allowing Krill to "lead both divisions [AT and LOFT] in a more hands-on-way." Krill then focused on merchandising and marketing, especially brand differentiation.[53] AT and LOFT continued to have separate EVPs for merchandising and design and separate senior vice presidents for divisional marketing, design, sourcing, and store direction.

Krill asked her staff to spend time with ANN customers and develop "brand books," or profiles, of the typical Ann Taylor (AT) and LOFT clients.[54] The "Ann" (AT) marketing profile was of a married 36-year-old working mother with two children and a household income of $150,000. She would lead a busy, sophisticated life. When giving a presentation to a client, she'd wear a formal suit with a blouse, not a camisole, underneath, and her idea of dressing down at work might be a velvet jacket with jeans.

In contrast, the typical LOFT client was in her 30s and married, with children, worked in a laid-back less corporate environment, and had a household income between $75,000 and $100,000. She would call her style "casual chic" and might wear pants and a floral top with ruffled sleeves to work, while on the weekend she would wear a printed shoulder-baring halter top with cropped jeans. Krill had always felt that both AT and LOFT were recognizably different from one another. In 2005, Krill stated that there was "a pretty clear differentiation," with "special occasion and work primarily being the focus" at AT and "more relaxed, separates and fashion" at LOFT.[55]

In support of the AT brand, the company expanded its focus on special events with the introduction of its Celebrations collection. The company introduced Celebrations in the AT stores as a line of classic, elegant dresses and coordinating accessories for special occasions, such as weddings and engagement parties. Of particular interest to long-term ANN customers was the introduction of dye-to-match sashes and accessories for bridesmaids, with fully coordinated jewelry and shoe styles, offered in petites as well as regular sizes (petites being women shorter than 5 feet 4 inches). The expansion of the selection in petite sizes, especially online, was seen as a "great opportunity," since some department stores had reduced their petite offerings.[56]

Top Management Team Turnover

As Krill was working to resolve branding issues between divisions, improve efficiencies, and find ways to expand the company, she also had to deal with a variety of top management team resignations. In the spring of 2006, COO Laura Weil left abruptly after only a few months on the job. Weil's many responsibilities at ANN had included merchandise planning; information systems; all supply chain operations including sourcing, logistics, and distribution; real estate; construction and facilities; and purchasing; as well as finance, accounting, and investor relations.[57] Krill decided not to replace Weil and eliminated the position on the organizational chart. Krill assumed leadership of LOFT again, playing a dual role while searching for a new divisional president.

Krill commented, "I believe that building a winning team is critical to fully realizing our company's full potential."[58] However, it appeared that creating that "winning team" was taking longer than anticipated. One source wondered about the pressure on Krill, especially since she didn't have a strong operating partner to help with merchandising and other creative decisions.[59]

Even though Krill had made differentiation between AT and LOFT a top priority, analysts continued to challenge Krill's efforts, noting that it had been hard to get both divisions moving forward simultaneously. As one analyst said, "It just seems like it's a struggle to get both of these divisions firing on all cylinders at the same time."[60] Krill responded to the comment that consistency had been a problem:

> The notion that Ann Taylor got soft because I was supporting the LOFT team is really a completely inaccurate comment. As CEO of the company I have to spend my time on many things, and if one of our businesses is softening in any way I will focus extra time on it.[61]

In August 2007, long-time CFO James Smith and Chief Marketing Officer Elaine Boltz both resigned, and then in July 2008 long-time Chief Supply Chain Officer Anthony Romano also left to "pursue other interests."[62] Although she had hired a new CFO and chief marketing officer in late 2007, these departures left Krill once again without a lot of depth at the top.[63] However, Krill had experience with management turnover as she had dealt with seven resignations, seven new hires, and two promotions in her upper-management team over two years' time. As of the end of 2008, she had finally filled the AT and LOFT divisional president positions.

Future Plans and Initiatives

As part of a multiyear restructuring program begun in 2008, ANN was focused on reducing excess costs, and it planned to do so by closing underperforming stores, downsizing ANN's corporate and divisional staff by eliminating approximately 260 positions, reducing executive compensation bonus payouts as a result of higher performance goals, eliminating merit pay increases, and consolidating "all purchasing activities under a centralized strategic procurement organization to leverage scale."[64] The restructuring program included a suspension of the share repurchase plan and a scale back of capital spending and was expected to result in ongoing annualized savings of approximately $80 million to $90 million.[65] The pretax costs of this restructuring were forecast to be $65 million to $70 million over the period from 2008 to 2010, but Krill felt that the company was "well positioned to support our brands and focus on strengthening our underlying business" due to the "debt-free balance sheet and approximately $295 million in available liquidity."[66]

The company also planned to close underperforming stores and open fewer stores than it had in previous years. A shift of emphasis was planned to "aggressively invest in factory channel expansion" for both the existing Ann Taylor Factory stores and a new Ann Taylor LOFT factory outlet concept.[67] These stores offered merchandise for 25 to 30 percent less than the cost at the AT or LOFT regular stores. The outlet or factory business had delivered "strong gross margin" previously and was considered "an important growth driver" even though "the general economic softness" was "having some impact on this price sensitive consumer."[68]

Krill also announced that the Collections line, an augmentation of the Celebrations bridal and special-occasion apparel line introduced in late 2006, would have its own department within the Ann Taylor (AT) stores. With offerings 40 percent more expensive than regular AT merchandise, the Collections line would be an attempt to "grab more affluent working women who weren't feeling pinched in the pocketbook" and would be built around the suits and dresses that created Ann Taylor's reputation. The plan was to introduce this upscale, expensive product in some of the top-selling Ann Taylor locations around the country, where AT was already "sitting next to Neiman's, Prada, Gucci," since "we know there's a client there who has an appetite for more upscale, expensive product."[69]

In addition, Krill announced that ANN would be developing an exclusive beauty business. The company introduced Ann Taylor label fragrance and bath and body products as a separate department within AT stores for the 2007 holiday season, and it launched beauty products in the LOFT division during 2008. Krill believed that specialty stores, with only a 10 percent share of the overall beauty products market, were in a position to increase that share. Responding to comments about ANN's previous foray into the cosmetic business, Krill said, "In the past, we've dipped our baby toes in, and have not done it justice. Now we are trying to find meaningful ways to grow the business."[70] Results in 2008 showed that although the fragrance line had done well, the body care component had not. The line of maternity clothes in selected LOFT stores was also still undergoing a test of its viability.[71]

Regarding ANN's new initiatives, one brand consultant commented:

> Tweaking a few elements of a product line doesn't work. Branding is far more than just product. It is about the entire entity and the perception that entity (in all of its components) has created in the consumer's mind. . . . The most successful brands in any category never fail to cater to and reward their core customers all the time. [And, responding specifically to the announcement of the upscale Collections line,] . . . trying to be too many things to a diverse audience under one roof is a losing business strategy for an established brand.[72]

Krill responded:

> The Company remains firmly committed to long-term growth, and we believe we have significant untapped potential ahead of us . . . we are relentlessly focused on strengthening our business, improving our gross margins with tight inventory management, executing our restructuring program with excellence, and pursuing growth in a measured and prudent manner. Beyond 2008, we are confident that we have positioned the Company for long-term growth and success.[73]

Krill appeared to be confident in her strategies for the future, and ANN's board was apparently pleased with her overall performance, granting her a total compensation of $7.84 million in 2008, a 14 percent pay increase.[74] However, the retail environment was increasingly unpredictable. Had Krill's new strategies been well considered, given the ongoing challenges of AT and LOFT and the difficult retail environment going into 2009? What else could Krill have done to create growth? Should ANN have focused on improving its current businesses or on developing new initiatives?

Endnotes

1. C. Hill, "Retailers such as Ann Taylor, Sears and Talbots face clogins, bankruptcies, takeovers in 2009," *New York Daily News,* December 29, 2008, www.nydailynews.com/money/2008/12/29/2008-12-29_retailers_such_as_ann_taylor_sears_and_t.html.

2. N. Maestri, "Retailers try to thrive in tumultuous climate," *Reuters.com,* June 16, 2008, www.reuters.com/article/email/idUKN1332245620080616.

3. Hill. "Retailers such as Ann Taylor."

4. T. Adams, "Economy generating 'wave' of retail closures," *Columbus Ledger-Enquirer, McClatchy Tribune Business News,* June 14, 2008.

5. K. Krill, as quoted in "Q3 2005 Ann Taylor stores earnings conference call—Final," *Fair Disclosure Wire,* December 2, 2005.

6. A. Merrick, "Parent trap: Once a bellwether, Ann Taylor fights its stodgy image," *Wall Street Journal* (Eastern edition), July 12, 2005, p. A.1.

7. ANN representatives noted that there was no apparent cause-and-effect relationship between AT sales decline and the growth of LOFT. Personal communication, Beth Warner, Director, Corporate Communications, Ann Taylor Stores Corporation, July 2007.

8. R. Tucker, "LOFT continues to pace Ann Taylor," *Women's Wear Daily,* August 12, 2004, p. 12.

9. "Letter to Shareholders," ANN 2007 Annual Report, http://investor.anntaylor.com/phoenix.zhtml?c=78167&p=irol-reportsAnnual.

10. "Q1 2008 Ann Taylor stores earnings conference call," May 22, 2008, http://seekingalpha.com/article/78473-ann-taylor-stores-corp-q1-2008-earnings-call-transcript.

11. A. Lomax, "More fickle fashion," Motley Fool, May 23, 2008, www.fool.com/investing/general/2008/05/23/more-fickle-fashion.aspx?terms=ann&vstest=search_042607_linkdefault.

12. "Letter to Shareholders."

13. M. Wilson, "Reinventing Ann Taylor," *Chain Store Age Executive with Shopping Center Age,* January 1995, p. 26.

14. M. Summers "New Outfit," Forbes, December 27, 1999, p. 88.

15. "Krill promoted to president of the Ann Taylor Loft division of Ann Taylor, Inc.," May 3, 2001, http://investor.anntaylor.com/news/20010503-40453.cfm?t=n.

16. "Ann Taylor announces LOFT division reaches $1 billion in sales," February 12, 2005, http://investor.anntaylor.com/news/20060213-187405.cfm?t=n.

17. C. Curan, "Ann Taylor LOFTs expansion plans right into a storm," *Crain's New York Business,* April 30, 2001, p. 4.

18. Krill, as quoted in "Q3 2005 Ann Taylor stores earnings conference call."

19. "Ann Taylor stores jumps on strong earnings," *Associated Press,* March 10, 2006, http://news.moneycentral.msn.com/ticker/article.asp?Feed=AP&Date=20060310&ID=5570346&Symbol=US:ANN.

20. "Letter to Shareholders."

21. Victoria's Secret is a division of Limited Brands, which also operates Pink (a subbrand of Victoria's Secret focused on sleepwear and intimate apparel for high school and college students), Bath & Body Works and C.O. Bigelow (personal beauty, body, and hair products), The White Barn Candle Co. (candles and home fragrances), Henri Bendel (high-fashion women's clothing), and La Senza (lingerie sold in Canada and worldwide).

22. Abercrombie & Fitch, as of 2008, had four brand divisions in addition to the flagship Abercrombie & Fitch stores: abercrombie (the brand name is purposely lowercase) for kids ages 7 to 14; Hollister Co. for southern California surf-lifestyle teens; RUEHL No. 925 for ages 22 to 35; and Gilly Hicks: Sydney, launched in 2008, specializing in women's intimate apparel.

23. www.census.gov/svsd/www/artsnaics.html.

24. According to the American Marketing Association (AMA), a brand is a "name, term, sign, symbol or design, or a combination of them intended to identify the goods and services of one seller or group of sellers and to differentiate them from those of other sellers. . . . Branding is not about getting your target market to choose you over the competition, but it is about getting your prospects to see you as the only one that provides a solution to their problem." A good brand will communicate this message clearly and with credibility, motivating the buyer by eliciting some emotion that inspires future loyalty. From http://marketing.about.com/cs/brandmktg/a/whatisbranding.htm.

25. B. Felgner, "New challenges in branding," *Home Textiles Today,* February 5, 2007, p. 1.

26. J. Turner, "Go forth and go out of business," *Slate,* February 26, 2007, www.slate.com/id/2160668.

27. G. Lee, "Chico's outlines plan to improve on results," *Women's Wear Daily,* March 8, 2007, p. 5.

28. The responsibilities of these positions include "creative vision" for the brand: marketing materials, store design, and overall merchandising (developing product, ensuring production efficiency, monitoring store inventory turnover, and adjusting price points as needed).

29. In 2007, Limited Brands owned the brands Victoria's Secret (including Pink, a Victoria's Secret subbrand) and Bath & Body Works—its two major brands—and C.O. Bigelow, Henri Bendel, White Barn Candle, and La Senza.

30. "Limited Brands cutting 530 jobs," *Columbus Business First,* June 22, 2007, http://columbus.bizjournals.com/columbus/stories/2007/06/18/daily26.html.

31. Sandra M. Jones, "Sweetest spots in retail," *Knight Ridder Tribune Business News,* July 31, 2007, p. 1.

32. Pia Sarkar, "Talbots still can't find its way," October 24, 2007, www.thestreet.com/newsanalysis/retail/10386340.html.

33. See, for instance, the web site www.aginghipsters.com, a "source for trends, research, comment and discussion" about this group.

34. Teri Agins, "The boomer balancing act: Retailers say new looks for middle-age women are both youthful and mature," *Wall Street Journal* (Eastern edition), November 3, 2007, p. W3.

35. "Talbots completes the acquisition of the J.Jill Group; combined company creates leading brand portfolio for the age 35+ female market; key executives promoted to maximize growth," *Business Wire,* May 3, 2006, from Talbot's Inc., http://phx.corporate-ir.net/phoenix.zhtml?c=65681&p=irol-newsArticle&ID=851481&highlight=.

36. J. Abelson, "Talbots is seeking a buyer for J.Jill," *Boston Globe,* November 7, 2008, www.boston.com/business/articles/2008/11/07/talbots_is_seeking_a_buyer_for_j_jill.

37. Sharon Edelson, "Coldwater Creek brings natural vibe to Manhattan," *Women's Wear Daily,* August 13, 2007, p. 4.

38. Associated Press. "Curbed spending to weigh on Coldwater Creek," *Motley Fool,* February 17, 2009, www.fool.com/news/associated-press/2009/02/17/curbed-spending-to-weigh-on-coldwater-creek.aspx.

39. Some marketers believe that the boomers are a bifurcated demographic: Although the boomer market encompasses those born between 1946 and 1964, boomers born between 1946 and 1954 have slightly different life experiences than those born between 1955 and 1964.

40. "50+ Fabulous awards companies that promote positive images of 50+ women," *Business Wire,* January 30, 2007.

41. "Investor interest in specialty apparel companies examined in Wall Street transcript specialty retail report," *Wall Street Transcript Online,* March 25, 2009, http://finance.yahoo.com/news/Investor-Interest-in-twst-14741666.html.

42. Kevin Kingsbury and Angela Moore, "Ann Taylor tries for a better fit," *Wall Street Journal* (Eastern edition), August 25, 2007, p. B6.

43. Michael Barbaro, "Ann Taylor said to plan boomer unit," *New York Times,* August 13, 2007, p. C3.

44. ANN 2007 Annual Report, http://investor.anntaylor.com/phoenix.zhtml?c=78167&p=irol-reportsAnnual.

45. Information in this section comes from ANN 10K filing as of FY2007.

46. "Q1 2008 Ann Taylor stores earnings conference call."

47. J. O'Donnell, "Retailers try to train shoppers to buy now; Limited supplies, fewer sales could get consumers to stop waiting for discounts," *USA Today,* September 26, 2006, p. B3.

48. "Ann Taylor: Upgrade with style," *Modern Material Handling* (Warehousing Management edition), March 2006, p. 38.

49. S. D. Jones, "Moving the Market—Tracking the numbers/outside audit: Ann Taylor's data draw a big critic; research firm questions retailer's earnings quality amid high costs of capital," *Wall Street Journal* (Eastern edition), July 17, 2006, p. C3.

50. K. Kennedy, "This is not your momma's clothing store—not by a longshot," *Apparel Industry Magazine* (Altanta), December 2000, pp. 22–25.

51. C. Curan, "Ann Taylor aims for LOFT-y goal with new stores," *Crain's New York Business,* March 29, 1999, p. 1.

52. M. Derby, "Wall Street bullish on Ann Taylor's Weil," *Women's Wear Daily,* October 3, 2005, p. 20.

53. D. Moin, "Ann Taylor stores taps two to fill out executive ranks," *Women's Wear Daily,* March 3, 2005,.

54. A. Merrick, "Boss talk: Asking 'what would Ann do?' In turning around Ann Taylor, CEO Kay Krill got to know her customers, 'Ann' and 'Loft,'" *Wall Street Journal* (Eastern edition), September 15, 2006, p. B1.

55. "Q3 2005 Ann Taylor stores earnings conference call—final," *Fair Disclosure Wire,* December 2, 2005.

56. "Ann Taylor and Ann Taylor Loft—The specialty resource for petites," August 23, 2006, http://investor.anntaylor.com/news/20060823-208165.cfm?t=n.

57. D. Moin, "Laura Weil exits Ann Taylor," *Women's Wear Daily,* May 5, 2006, p. 2.

58. ANN 2005 Annual Report, http://investor.anntaylor.com/annual.cfm.

59. D. Moin, "Rebound at Ann Taylor: CEO Kay Krill fashions retailer's new career," *Women's Wear Daily,* June 26, 2006, p. 1.

60. "Q4 2007 Ann Taylor stores earnings conference call," March 14, 2008, http://seekingalpha.com/article/68606-ann-taylor-stores-corporation-q4-2007-earnings-call-transcript?page=8.

61. "Q1 2008 Ann Taylor stores earnings conference call."

62. "Ann Taylor announces executive management changes," July 15, 2008, http://investor.anntaylor.com/phoenix.zhtml?c=78167&p=irol-newsArticle&ID=1174968&highlight=.

63. Jeanine Poggi, "Specialty retailers see high exec turnover," *Women's Wear Daily,* August 20, 2007, p. 2-2.

64. "Ann Taylor launches strategic restructuring program to enhance profitability; Multiyear program expected to generate $50 million in ongoing annualized pretax savings; Company takes a conservative approach to new store growth for fiscal 2008", *PR Newswire,* January 30, 2008.

65. "Ann Taylor expands strategic restructuring program," November 6, 2008, http://investor.anntaylor.com/phoenix.zhtml?c=78167&p=irol-newsArticle&ID=1223638&highlight=.

66. Ibid.

67. "Ann Taylor launches strategic restructuring program."

68. "Q1 2008 Ann Taylor stores earnings conference call."

69. Amy Merrick, "Ann Taylor's loftier goal: A more upscale shopper," *Wall Street Journal,* September 14, 2007, http://online.wsj.com/public/article/SB118972474680527004.html.

70. David Moin, "New in beauty: Ann Taylor taps Robin Burns to develop collection," *Women's Wear Daily,* March 16, 2007, p. 1.

71. "Q1 2008 Ann Taylor stores earnings conference call."

72. Eli Portnoy, "Another mid-priced retail brand, Ann Taylor, trying to go upscale," September 14, 2007, http://theportnoygroup.typepad.com/my_weblog/2007/09/another-mid-pri.html.

73. "Letter to Shareholders."

74. A. Pasquarelli, "Fashion chief got pay raise amid falling sales, layoffs," *Crain's New York,* April 3, 2009, www.crainsnewyork.com/article/20090403/FREE/904039971.

Case 40 FreshDirect: Delivering the Goods?*

People are traveling less and eating out less . . . they are turning to us for things to eat at home."[1]

—Steve Druckman,
Chief Marketing Officer, FreshDirect

Turnover at the top of FreshDirect placed Priceline.com veteran and investor Richard Braddock in the CEO seat. He was the fifth CEO in eight years. Just as he took over the job, employee morale was at an all-time low, a union vote was in the planning, and gasoline prices were fluctuating wildly, affecting delivery costs greatly. The economic downturn of late 2008 was having a negative impact on many facets of consumer spending. However, with consumers cutting down on spending and eating at home more often, FreshDirect was in a position to directly benefit. The question was how Braddock was going to navigate the waters of uncertain times.

With a bold promise on its Web site entry page, FreshDirect claimed, "Our food is fresh, our customers are spoiled. . . . Order on the web today and get next-day delivery of the best food at the best price, exactly the way you want it, with 100 percent satisfaction guaranteed."[2] Operating out of its production center in Long Island City, Queens, FreshDirect offered online grocery shopping and delivery service to about 150 zip codes in Manhattan, Queens, Brooklyn, Nassau County, Riverdale, Westchester, and New Jersey. FreshDirect also offered pickup service at its Long Island City facility, as well as corporate service to selected delivery zones in Manhattan and summer delivery service to the Hamptons on Long Island. When it was launched in July 2001 by Joseph Fedele and Jason Ackerman, FreshDirect pronounced to the New York area that it was "the new way to shop for food." This was a bold statement given that the previous decade had witnessed the demise of numerous other online grocery ventures. However, the creators of FreshDirect were confident in the success of their business because their entire operation had been designed to deliver one simple promise to grocery shoppers: "higher quality at lower prices."

While this promise was an extremely common tagline used within and outside the grocery business, FreshDirect had integrated numerous components into its system to give real meaning to these words. Without a retail location, FreshDirect didn't have to pay expensive rent for a retail space. To offer the highest-quality products to its customers, FreshDirect had created a state-of-the-art production center and staffed it with expert personnel. The 300,000-square-foot production facility located in Long Island City

was composed of 12 separate temperature zones, ensuring that each piece of food was kept at its optimal temperature for ripening or preservation—kept colder and cleaner than in any retail environment.

Further quality management was achieved by a SAP manufacturing software system that controlled every detail of the facility's operations. All of the thermometers, scales, and conveyor belts within the facility were connected to a central command center. Each specific setting was programmed into the system by an expert from the corresponding department, including everything from the ideal temperature for ripening a cantaloupe to the amount of flour that went into French bread. The system was also equipped with a monitoring alarm that alerted staff to any deviation from the programmed settings.

Another quality control element that had been made an integral part of the FreshDirect facility was an extremely high standard for cleanliness, health, and safety. The facility itself was kept immaculately clean, and all food-preparation areas and equipment were bathed in antiseptic foam at the end of each day. Incoming and outgoing food was tested in FreshDirect's in-house laboratory, which ensured that the facility adhered to USDA guidelines and the Hazard Analysis and Critical Control Point food safety system and that all food passing through FreshDirect met the company's high safety standards.[3]

System efficiency had been the key to FreshDirect's ability to offer its high-quality products at such low prices. FreshDirect's biggest operational design component for reducing costs had been the complete elimination of the middleman. Instead of going through an intermediary, both fresh and dry products were ordered from individual growers and producers and shipped directly to FreshDirect's production center, where FreshDirect's expert staff prepared them for purchase. In addition, FreshDirect did not accept any slotting allowances.[4] This unique relationship with growers and producers allowed FreshDirect to enjoy reduced purchase prices from its suppliers, enabling it to pass even greater savings on to its customers.

Each department of the facility, including the coffee roaster, butcher, and bakery, was staffed by carefully selected experts, enabling FreshDirect to offer premium fresh coffees (roasted on site), pastries and breads (baked on site), deli, cheese, meats (roast beef dry-aged on site), and seafood. Perishable produce was FreshDirect's specialty—by buying locally as much as possible and using the best sources of the season, it was able to bring food the shortest distance from farms, dairies, and fisheries to the customer's table.

FreshDirect catered to the tastes of its Manhattan clientele by offering a full line of heat-and-serve meals prepared in the FreshDirect kitchen by New York executive chef

*This case was prepared by Professor Alan B. Eisner of Pace University as a basis for class discussion rather than to illustrate either effective or ineffective handling of an administrative situation. Thanks to graduate student Rohit R. Phadtare for research assistance. Copyright © 2009 Alan B. Eisner.

Michael Stark (formerly of Tribeca Grill) and his team. Partnering with chef Terrance Brennan of New York's French-Mediterranean restaurant Picholine, FreshDirect also sold "restaurant-worthy" four-minute meals. Made from raw ingredients delivered in a "steam valve system" package, these complete meals were not frozen but were delivered ready to finish cooking in a microwave.

The proximity of FreshDirect's processing facility to its Manhattan customer base was also a critical factor in its cost-effective operational design. The processing center's location in Long Island City put approximately 4 million people within a 10-mile radius of the FreshDirect facility, allowing the firm to deliver a large number of orders in a short amount of time.[5] Further cost controls had been implemented through FreshDirect's order and delivery protocols. Products in each individual order were packed in boxes, separated by type of item (meat, seafood, and produce packed together; dairy, deli, cheese, coffee, and tea packed together; grocery, specialty and nonrefrigerated product packed together), and placed on a computerized conveyor system to be sorted, assembled, and packed into a refrigerated truck for delivery.

As of 2008, orders had to be a minimum of $30, with a delivery charge between $5.79 and $6.79 per order, depending on the order dollar amount and delivery location. Delivery was made by one of FreshDirect's trucks and was available only during a prearranged two-hour window on weekdays from 2 p.m. to 11:30 p.m. and all day, starting at 7:30 a.m., on the weekends.

Competing with other online grocers, specialty gourmet/gourmand stores in Manhattan, and high-end chain supermarkets like Whole Foods, Trader Joe's, and Fairway, FreshDirect was trying to woo the sophisticated New Yorker with an offer of quality, delivered door-to-door, at a price more attractive than others in the neighborhood. Operating in the black for the first time in 2005[6] by choosing to remain a private company and expanding gradually, FreshDirect's owners hoped to turn a daily profit, steadily recovering the estimated $60 million start-up costs, silencing critics, and winning converts.[7]

Founding Partners

FreshDirect was launched in July 2001. Cofounder and former chief executive officer Joseph Fedele was able to bring a wealth of experience in New York City's food industry to FreshDirect. In 1993 he cofounded Fairway Uptown, a 35,000-foot supermarket located on West 133 Street in Harlem. Many critics originally questioned the success of a store in that location, but Fairway's low prices and quality selection of produce and meats made it a hit with neighborhood residents, as well as many downtown and suburban commuters.

Vice Chairman and Chief Financial Officer Jason Ackerman had gained exposure to the grocery industry as an investment banker with Donaldson Lufkin & Jenrette, where he specialized in supermarket mergers and acquisitions. Fedele and Ackerman first explored the idea of starting a large chain of fresh-food stores, but they realized maintaining a high degree of quality would be impossible with a large enterprise. As an alternative, they elected to pursue a business that incorporated online shopping with central distribution. Using the failure of Webvan, the dot-com delivery service that ran through $830 million in five years of rapid expansion, as their example of what not to do, Fedele and Ackerman planned to start slow, use off-the-shelf software and an automated delivery system, and pay attention to details such as forming relationships with key suppliers and micromanaging quality control.[8]

FreshDirect acquired the bulk of its $100 million investment from several private sources, with a small contribution coming from the State of New York. By locating FreshDirect's distribution center within the state border and promising to create at least 300 new permanent, full-time, private-sector jobs in the state, FreshDirect became eligible for a $500,000 training grant from the Empire State Development Jobs Now Program. As its name implied, the purpose of the Jobs Now program was to create new, immediate job opportunities for New Yorkers.

CEO Successions

Although the press was mostly positive about FreshDirect's opportunities, growth and operational challenges remained. In the words of an ex-senior executive of FreshDirect, "The major problem seems to be constant change in Senior Management. I think they are now on their 4th CEO."[9] Actually, the company is currently on its fifth CEO in eight years of operation. FreshDirect cofounder Joseph Fedele had remained CEO until January 2004, when cofounder Jason Ackerman succeeded him in that position. Since then, FreshDirect had experienced multiple CEO changes. Jason Ackerman stayed as CEO of FreshDirect for a little over seven months, until Dean Furbush succeeded him in that position in September 2004. Ackerman remained vice chairman and chief financial officer. The tenure of Dean Furbush lasted a little over two years. Steve Michaelson, president since 2004, replaced Furbush as the CEO of FreshDirect in early 2007.[10] In 2008, Michaelson left for another firm, and FreshDirect's chairman of the board, Richard Braddock, expanded his role in the firm and took over as CEO. Braddock said, "I chose to increase my involvement with the company because I love the business and I think it has great growth potential." Braddock previously worked at private equity firm MidOcean Partners and travel services retailer Priceline.com, where he also served as chairman and CEO.[11]

Business Plan

While business started out relatively slow, Fedele had hoped to capture around 5 percent of the New York grocery market, with projected revenues of about $100 million in the first year and $225 million by 2004. As of March 2003, FreshDirect had reached the milestone of 2,000 orders a day and was attracting around 3,000 new customers a day, for a total customer base of around 40,000.[12] FreshDirect service was originally slated for availability citywide by the end of 2002. However, to maintain its superior service and product quality, FreshDirect had chosen to slowly expand its service area. By the spring of 2009, FreshDirect had delivery available to selected zip codes and neighborhoods throughout Manhattan and as far away as Westchester and the Hamptons on Long Island (in the summer only).

The company had employed a relatively low-cost marketing approach, which originally consisted mainly of billboards, public relations, and word of mouth to promote its products and services. In 2003 FreshDirect hired Trumpet, an ad agency that promoted FreshDirect as a better way to shop by emphasizing the problems associated with traditional grocery shopping. For example, one commercial stressed the unsanitary conditions in a supermarket by showing a grocery shopper bending over a barrel of olives as she sneezed, getting an olive stuck in her nose, and then blowing it back into the barrel. The advertisement ended with the question "Where's your food been?" Another ad showed a checkout clerk morph into an armed robber, demand money from the customer, and then morph back into a friendly checkout clerk once the money was received. The ad urged viewers to "stop getting robbed at the grocery store."[13] As of 2009, FreshDirect enlisted celebrity endorsements from New York City personalities such as film director Spike Lee, actress Cynthia Nixon, former mayor Ed Koch, supermodel Paulina Porizkova, and chef Bobby Flay.[14] FreshDirect was number 58 in the Internet Retailer Top 500 Guide, with posted sales of $240 million in 2007, up 20 percent from $200 million in 2006.

Operating Strategy

FreshDirect's operating strategy had employed a make-to-order philosophy, eliminating the middleman in order to create an efficient supply chain.[15] By focusing its energy on providing produce, meat, seafood, baked goods, and coffees that were made to the customer's specific order, FreshDirect offered its customers an alternative to the standardized cuts and choices available at most brick-and-mortar grocery stores. This strategy had created a business model that was unique within the grocery business community. A typical grocery store carried about 25,000 packaged goods, which accounted for around 50 percent of its sales, and about 2,200 perishable products, which accounted for the other 50 percent of sales. In contrast, FreshDirect offered around 5,000 perishable products, accounting for about 75 percent of its sales, but only around 3,000 packaged goods, which comprised the remaining 25 percent of sales.[16]

While this stocking pattern enabled a greater array of fresh foods, it limited the number of brands and available sizes of packaged goods, such as cereal, crackers, and laundry detergent. However, FreshDirect believed customers would accept a more limited packaged-good selection in order to get lower prices, as evidenced in the success of wholesale grocery stores, which offered bulk sales of limited items. Jason Ackerman identified the ideal FreshDirect customers as those who bought their bulk staples from Costco on a monthly basis and bought everything else from FreshDirect on a weekly basis.[17]

FreshDirect's Web Site

FreshDirect's Web site not only offered an abundance of products to choose from but also provided a broad spectrum of information on the food that was sold and the manner in which it was sold (see Exhibit 1). Web surfers could take a pictorial tour of the FreshDirect facility; get background information on the experts who managed each department; get nutritional information on food items; compare produce or cheese based on taste, price, and usage; specify the thickness of meat orders and opt for one of several marinades or rubs (see Exhibit 2); search for the right kind of coffee based on taste preferences; and read nutritional information for a variety of fully prepared meals. A large selection of recipes was available depending on the items chosen.

For example, if you wanted to purchase chicken, you were first asked to choose from breasts & cutlets, cubes & strips, ground, legs & thighs, specialty parts, split & quartered, whole, or wings. Once your selection was made—let's says you chose breasts & cutlets—you were given further options based on your preference for skin, bone, and thickness. The final selection step offered you a choice of rubs and marinades, including teriyaki, sweet & sour, garlic rosemary, poultry seasoning, lemon herb rub, and salt & pepper rub. Throughout, the pages offered nutritional profiles of each cut of meat as well as tips for preparation and storage.

FreshDirect employed several different delivery models. Customers within the city were attracted to the FreshDirect service because it eliminated the need to carry groceries for possibly a substantial distance from the closest grocery store or to deal with trying to park a car near their apartment to unload their purchases. Orders made by customers within the city were delivered directly to their homes by a FreshDirect truck during a prearranged two-hour delivery window.

Suburban customers were served in a slightly different manner. Many suburban customers worked at corporations in the tri-state area that could arrange for depot drop-off in the office parking lot, creating a central delivery station. FreshDirect would send a refrigerated truck, large enough to hold 500 orders, to these key spots during designated periods of time. Suburbanites could then exit their office building, go to their cars, swing by the FreshDirect truck, pick up their order, and head home. FreshDirect could also provide delivery to the parking lot of football or concert events to provide for tailgate or picnic needs. In addition to providing delivery, FreshDirect allowed customers to pick up their orders directly from the processing center. Orders were ready at the pickup desk five to ten minutes after they were called in.

Business customers in Manhattan could also order for delivery at the office. Chef-prepared breakfast and luncheon

Exhibit 1 FreshDirect Web Site

catering platters and restaurant-quality individual meals were available for business meetings and upscale events. FreshDirect provided dedicated corporate account managers and customer service representatives for corporate clients; however, FreshDirect only provided delivery, not set-up and platter arrangement services. The corporate delivery minimum order was $50, and delivery costs were $14.99 (see Exhibit 3).

The Retail Grocery Industry

In the United States in 2008, according to the U.S. Department of Commerce, supermarket chains made almost $500 billion in sales. The typical supermarket store carried an average of 45,000 items, averaged just under 49,000 square feet in size, and averaged just over $18 million in sales annually.[18] The top-10 supermarket chains in the United States commanded a large amount of the total grocery industry business (see Exhibit 4).

The supermarket business had traditionally been a low-margin business with net profits of only 1 to 2 percent of revenues. Store profits depended heavily on creating a high volume of customer traffic and rapid inventory turnover, especially for perishables such as produce and fresh meat. Competitors had to operate efficiently to make money, so tight control of labor costs and product spoilage was essential. Online grocery retailers, like FreshDirect—because of the flexibility of information control, automated order fulfillment, and reduced real estate costs—could potentially

Exhibit 2 Example of FreshDirect Meat Selection

have operating margins of up to 10 percent, rather than the 3 to 4 percent of traditional supermarkets.[19] Because capital investment costs were modest—involving mainly the construction of distribution centers and stores—it was not unusual for supermarket chains to realize 15 to 20 percent returns on invested capital.

The Online Grocery Segment

The online grocery shopping business was still in the early stages of development in 2004, with this segment accounting for less than 1 percent of total grocery sales. Total online sales were about $2.4 billion in 2004, over $4.2 billion in 2006, and $6.5 billion in 2008 and were estimated to reach $8.4 billion by 2010.[20] However, the 5 million people who shopped online for groceries still represented only 2 percent of the online population.[21]

Online grocery shopping had been slow to catch on, and industry newcomers had encountered high start-up and operating costs. Sales volumes and profit margins remained too small to cover the high costs. The problem,

according to industry analysts, was that consumers had been largely disappointed in the service, selection, and prices they had gotten from industry members. This, coupled with the extensive investment needed in warehousing, fulfillment, and inventory control, meant that the "pure play" e-grocery business models were risky. There was a belief that better success would come from traditional grocery retailers that chose to venture online.[22]

However, some analysts expected online grocery sales to grow at a rapid pace as companies improved their service and selection, personal computer penetration of households rose, and consumers became more accustomed to making purchases online.[23] An article in *Computer Bits* examined the customer base for online grocers, looking specifically at the types of consumers who would be likely to shop online and the kinds of home computer systems that were required for online shopping. An Andersen Consulting report identified six major types of online shoppers (see Exhibit 5) and estimated that by the end of 2010, 15 to 20 million households would order their groceries online.[24]

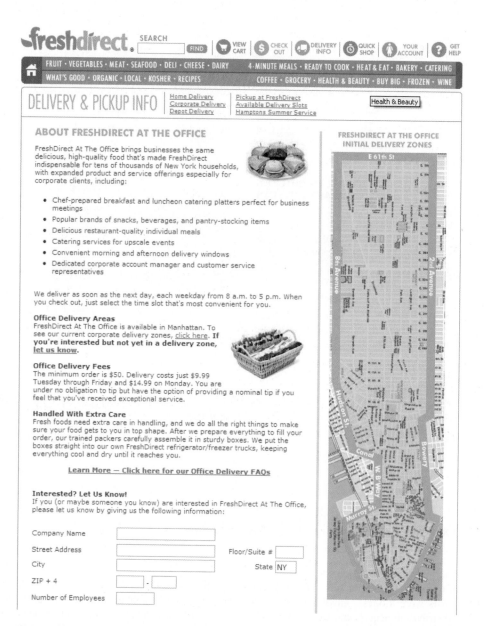

Exhibit 3 FreshDirect at the Office

A MARC Group study concluded, "Consumers who buy groceries online are likely to be more loyal to their electronic supermarkets, spend more per store 'visit,' and take greater advantage of coupons and premiums than traditional customers."[25]

One of the problems with online grocery shopping was that consumers were extremely price-sensitive when it came to buying groceries and the prices of many online grocers were above those at supermarkets. Shoppers, in many cases, were unwilling to pay extra to online grocers for the convenience of home delivery. Consumer price sensitivity meant that online grocers had to achieve a cost structure that would allow them to (1) price competitively, (2) cover the cost of selecting items in the store and delivering individual grocery orders, and (3) have sufficient margins to earn attractive returns on their investment. Some analysts estimated that to be successful, online grocers had to do 10 times the volume of a traditional grocer.[26]

Potential Competitors in the Online Grocery Segment

When online grocers started appearing within the industry, many established brick-and-mortar grocers began offering online shopping in an attempt to maintain and expand their customer base. Two basic models were used for online order fulfillment: (1) to pick items from the shelves of

Exhibit 4 Top-10 North American Food Retailers

Supermarket Chain	Stores	2008 Sales ($ billions)	Comments
Wal-Mart Super Centers	3,153	$ 240.8	Includes Sam's Clubs
Kroger	3,662	70.24	Includes jewelry, 5% of TTL $
Costco Wholesale Corp.	518	63.1	Groceries were $36.6B
Safeway	1,738	42.3	Based in California
Supervalu	2,504	34.34	1,124 Albertson's stores
Loblaw Cos.	1,435	27.35	Stop & Shop, Giant Foods
Publix Super Markets	925	23.0	Based in Florida
Ahold USA	706	20.9	Based in the Netherlands
C&S Wholesale Grocers	0	19.4	Supplies products to above
Delhaize America	1,586	18.2	Food Lion, Hannaford Bros.

Source: *Supermarket News,* http://supermarketnews.com/top75/.

Exhibit 5 Types of Online Shoppers and Their Propensity to Be Attracted to Online Grocery Shopping

Types of Online Shoppers	Comments
Traditional shoppers	Might be older technology-avoiders or simply shoppers who like to sniff-test their own produce and eyeball the meat selection.
Responsible shoppers	Feed off the satisfaction of accomplishing this persistent to-do item.
Time Starved	Find the extra costs associated with delivery fees or other markups a small price to pay for saving time.
New technologists	Use the latest technology for any and every activity they can, because they can.
Necessity users	Have physical or circumstantial challenges that make grocery shopping difficult; likely to be the most loyal group of shoppers.
Avoiders	Dislike the grocery shopping experience for a variety of reasons.

Source: Andersen Consulting.

existing stores within the grocer's chain, and (2) to build special warehouses dedicated to online orders. The demand for home delivery of groceries had been increasing, but in many market areas the demand had not yet reached a level that would justify the high cost of warehouses dedicated to the fulfillment of online orders.[27]

Safeway began an ambitious online grocery venture by establishing GroceryWorks, an online shopping system that included a series of warehouses dedicated to filling online orders. Unfavorable returns forced Safeway to reevaluate its system, and it eventually chose to form a partnership with Tesco, a U.K.-based grocer. Tesco filled its online orders from the shelves of local stores in close proximity to

the customer's home. Safeway and Tesco worked together on GroceryWorks in Portland, Oregon, where they received a positive initial response from customers.[28]

The craze over health food had created room in the grocery industry for organic food suppliers to enter as an attractive substitute to traditional groceries. When asked what kept him up at night, FreshDirect's former CEO Dean Furbush said that Whole Foods or Trader Joe's moving into a FreshDirect neighborhood was his biggest threat as that hurt FreshDirect the most.

Whole Foods, the Austin, Texas–based supermarket chain with the organic health food focus, had already threatened FreshDirect's sales in Manhattan. Trader Joe's, another specialty food retailer, was also opening a store in downtown Union Square, prime territory for Fresh-Direct.[29] Although commentators believed there was enough room for all, including the street farm markets, FreshDirect focused on organic foods to respond to the threats of Whole Foods and other specialty food stores.[30] With the shift among some customers to paying attention to local, sometimes organic suppliers, FreshDirect highlighted its support of and partnership with the local companies that provided produce, poultry, fish, cheese, milk, eggs, and specialties such as wine (Exhibit 6). However, its efforts have been inconsistent in that area. For example, in order to facilitate shoppers and check-out operators to distinguish between organic and non-organic produce, FreshDirect wraps organics in plastic, which in itself is not organic. FreshDirect chairman Jeff Turner recognized that such an approach seemed incongruous.[31]

Exhibit 6 FreshDirect Local Market Offerings

Rivals in the NYC Online Grocery Segment—YourGrocer.com

FreshDirect's most geographically significant competitor in the online grocery industry was YourGrocer.com (see Exhibits 7 and 8). YourGrocer was launched in New York City in 1998 with the goal of being the leading online grocery service for the New York metropolitan area. By November 2001 the company ran out of money and was forced to shut down. In the spring of 2002 new capital resources were found, and the company reopened for business. However, the second time around, YourGrocer's approach was a little different.

YourGrocer was created with a bulk-buying strategy, believing that customers would order large, economical quantities of goods from the Web site and the company would make home deliveries in company trucks. During YourGrocer's first life, the ambitious business plan covered a large service area and included the acquisition of another online grocery company, NYCGrocery.com.[32] But the business plan was modified in the second life. The company reduced the size of its staff, got rid of warehouses, decided to rent instead of owning its delivery vans, and scaled down its delivery routes.[33] Nassau County and New Jersey were eliminated from the service area, leaving only Manhattan, the Bronx, Brooklyn, Queens, Rockland, Westchester County, and Fairfield County (Connecticut).

YourGrocer offered a limited selection of items that could be purchased only in bulk. Deliveries were made in varied time slots, depending on the customer's location in the New York area. There was a $75 minimum order with a $9.95 delivery charge (see Exhibits 9 and 10).

Peapod

Founded in 1989 by brothers Andrew and Thomas Parkinson, Peapod (see Exhibits 11 and 12) was an early pioneer in e-commerce, inventing an online home-shopping service for grocery items years ahead of the commercial emergence of the Internet. With its tagline "Smart Shopping for Busy People," the company began providing consumers with a home-shopping experience in the early 1990s, going so far as to install modems in customer homes to provide an online connection.

From its founding in 1989 until 1998, the company's business model involved filling customer orders by forming alliances with traditional grocery retailers. The company

Exhibit 7 Profiles of Selected Online Grocers, 2009

Name	Minimum Area Covered	Delivery Order	Delivery Charge	Method	Specialization
FreshDirect	Manhattan, Queens, Brooklyn, Nassau County, Riverdale, Westchester, New Jersey	$50	$4.99–$9.99 depending on order size and destination; tipping optional	Trucks; available weekdays 2 p.m.–11:30 p.m. and all day on weekends	• Mostly perishables: fresh produce, meats, baked goods • Low prices because there is no middleman
YourGrocer	Manhattan, Bronx, Westchester, Greenwich, Brooklyn, Queens, Rockland	$75	$9.95 for orders > $75; $14.95 for orders < $75	Rented vans; available select days and times, depending on location	• Bulk orders of packaged goods
Peapod	Chicago, Boston, D.C., Long Island, Connecticut, New Jersey, Rhode Island	$50	$6.95 for orders < $100; $9.95 for orders > $100; tipping optional	Truck; available 7 a.m.–1 p.m. and 3:30 p.m.–10 p.m. weekdays, 7 a.m.–1 p.m. weekends	• Partner with Giant Foods and Stop & Shop; items picked from shelves of local warehouses near customer's home
NetGrocer	Lower 48 states, D.C., special service to Alaska, Hawaii, APO/FPO	None	$5.99–$624.99, depending on order size and destination	FedEx; order delivered within 3–7 business days	• Only nonperishables; no fresh produce

Source: Company Web sites.

Exhibit 8   Comparison of Prices for Selected Online Grocers

Grocery Item	Prices			
	FreshDirect	**YourGrocer**	**Peapod**	**NetGrocer**
Tide laundry detergent	$9.99/100 oz.	$24.88/340 oz ($7.31/100 oz.)	$7.69/100 oz.	$11.19/100 oz.
Wish-Bone Italian dressing	$1.89/8 oz.	$5.98/48 oz. ($0.99/8 oz.)	$1.89/8 oz.	$1.95/8 oz.
Cheerios	$4.69/15 oz. ($6.25/20 oz.)	$7.39/37 oz. ($3.99/20 oz.)	$4.19/20 oz.	$5.89/20 oz.
Ragu spaghetti sauce	$2.29/26 oz.	$7.99/135 oz. ($1.54/26 oz.)	$1.67/26 oz.	$2.69/26 oz.
Granny Smith apples	$4.99/4 pack (no per-lb. price)	$7.69/5 lb.bag ($1.54/lb.)	$3.99/3-lb.bag ($1.33/lb.)	Fresh produce not available

Source: Company Web sites.

chose a retail partner in each geographic area where it operated and used the partner's local network of retail stores to pick and pack orders for delivery to customers. Peapod personnel would cruise the aisles of a partner's stores, selecting the items each customer ordered, pack and load them into Peapod vehicles, and then deliver them to customers at prearranged times. Peapod charged customers a fee for its service and collected fees from its retail supply partners for using their products in its online service. Over the next several years, Peapod built delivery capabilities in eight market areas: Chicago; Columbus, Ohio; Boston; San Francisco/ San Jose; Houston, Dallas, and Austin, Texas; and Long Island, New York.

In 1997, faced with mounting losses despite growing revenues, Peapod management shifted to a new order fulfillment business model utilizing a local company-owned and -operated central distribution warehouse to store, pick, and pack customer orders for delivery. By mid-1999 the company had opened new distribution centers in three of the eight markets it served—Chicago, Long Island, and Boston—and a fourth distribution center was under construction in San Francisco.

In the late spring of 2000, Peapod created a partnership with Royal Ahold, an international food provider based in the Netherlands. At the time, Ahold operated five supermarket companies in the United States: Stop & Shop, Tops Market, Giant-Landover, Giant-Carlisle, and BI-LO. In September 2000 Peapod acquired Streamline.com, Inc.'s operations in Chicago and the Washington, D.C., markets and announced that it planned to exit its markets in Columbus, Ohio, and Houston, Dallas, and Austin, Texas. All of these moves were made as a part of Peapod's strategic plan for growth and future profitability. Under Peapod's initial partnership agreement with Ahold, Peapod was to continue as a stand-alone company, with Ahold supplying

Peapod's goods, services, and fast-pick fulfillment centers. However, in July 2001 Ahold acquired all the outstanding shares of Peapod and merged Peapod into one of Ahold's subsidiaries.

In 2009 Peapod provided online shopping and delivery service in many metropolitan areas, including Chicago, Boston, Rhode Island, Connecticut, New Jersey, Long Island, and Washington, D.C. Peapod employed a centralized distribution model in every market. In large markets, orders were picked, packed, loaded, and delivered from a freestanding centralized fulfillment center; in smaller markets, Peapod established fast-pick centralized fulfillment centers adjacent to the facilities of retail partners.[34] Peapod's proprietary transportation routing system ensured on-time delivery and efficient truck and driver utilization.

NetGrocer

NetGrocer.com was founded in 1996 and advertised itself as the first online grocer to sell nonperishable items nationwide (see Exhibits 13 and 14). NetGrocer served all 48 continental U.S. states and the District of Columbia and had special service to Alaska, Hawaii, APO, and FPO destinations. All customer orders were filled in its single 120,000-square-foot warehouse in North Brunswick, New Jersey. Orders were shipped by Federal Express and were guaranteed to reach any part of NetGrocer's service area within three to seven days.

NetGrocer offered its customers a large selection of brand-name and specialty nonperishable items that were difficult to find in a local supermarket. The key customer segment for NetGrocer's services were busy families, urban dwellers, special-needs groups (e.g., dieters, diabetics), and senior citizens. Customers purportedly enjoyed the benefits of convenient online shopping from home 24 hours a day, access to thousands of products, and delivery

Exhibit 9 Yourgrocer.com Web Site

Exhibit 10 Yourgrocer's Service Focus

New YourGrocer focuses on providing **three benefits** that families in the area most value:

1. **Easy ordering** over the Internet or on the phone to save hours of thankless shopping. You can use your last order as a starting point to save even more time.

2. **Delivery** right to the home or office, which eliminates the burden of lifting and transporting heavy and bulky items each month.

3. **Significant savings** with everyday low prices—not short-duration specials—which reduce what you pay for stock-up groceries and household supplies on average by 25% to 30% below local supermarkets.

Source: www.yourgrocer.com.

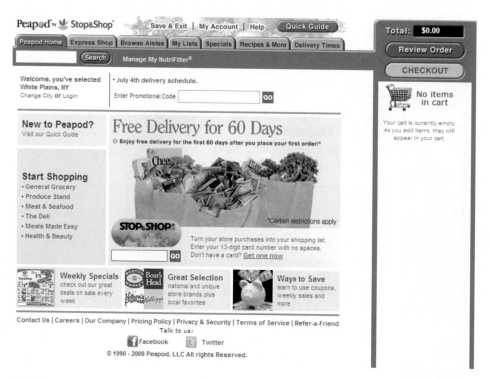

Exhibit 11 Peapod Web Site

of their orders directly to their homes. Manufacturers also benefited from NetGrocer, as they were able to distribute their products nationwide, rapidly and easily.

Most Recent Challenges

As the online grocery retailing business continued to mature, all players needed to pay attention to customer perception. Online retailing giant amazon.com had entered the dry-goods grocery delivery business, posing a threat to other online retailers because of its existing loyal customer base and legendary customer service. Creating a grocery section in 2006, Amazon offered over 10,000 nonperishable items, including "long-time staples, from Kellogg's to Jiffy Pop."[35] The selection of dry goods rather than perishables meant Amazon, unlike FreshDirect and Peapod, didn't have to worry about delivery costs on time- and climate-sensitive items. However, even Amazon suffered grocery delivery failures, from out-of-stock problems to delivery glitches and Web site technical outages. Online grocery retailers needed to "serve their online customers just like they would serve the customers who come into their physical stores."[36]

Even though FreshDirect had been able to woo local New Yorkers, gaining a Fast Company "Local Hero" award, the company had to absorb "hundreds of thousands of dollars in parking tickets to get its customers its orders within the delivery window."[37] And, in 2007, New York City government proposed a congestion charge for traffic entering Manhattan, adding to FreshDirect's delivery expenses. The rising cost of fuel was also a potential threat, even though FreshDirect included a fuel surcharge on orders, based on the average retail price of gasoline.[38] These expenses, coupled with penalties accrued from parking violations, might have put significant pressure on FreshDirect's ability to achieve its target profit levels.

Environmental concerns also started to creep in as a major issue for FreshDirect. First, because of the conveyor packing system at the processing facility, FreshDirect was forced to use lots of cardboard boxes to deliver the groceries: Produce came in one box, dry goods in another, and a single tube of toothpaste in its separate cardboard delivery container. Although FreshDirect had transitioned to the use of 100 percent postconsumer recycled paper,[39] the reusability of the cardboard boxes was very limited and the general public was increasingly becoming aware that their tax dollars were used to "collect and dispose of the huge stacks of cardboards that FreshDirect's customers leave in the trash."[40] As one environmentally conscious consumer observed, "I was baffled by the number of boxes they used to pack things. Groceries worth $40 came in five boxes. And after I unpacked, I had to discard the boxes. There was no system of returning them to FreshDirect to be recycled."[41]

A second issue that environmentally conscious consumers became concerned about was the additional exhaust fumes that FreshDirect trucks contributed to the urban atmosphere.[42] Third, FreshDirect trucks double-parked in busy city streets had only made the traffic congestion problems worse. "It's probably no exaggeration to say that FreshDirect has built its financial success on its ability

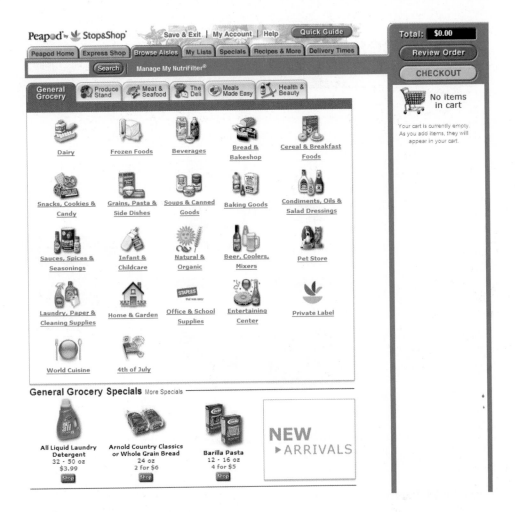

Exhibit 12 Peapod Product Selection

to fob off its social and environmental costs on the city as a whole."[43] Lastly, some city dwellers even expressed concern about FreshDirect's adverse effect on the overall makeup of their neighborhoods: "It is not just the impact they have on congestion, pollution, space, etc., but their very adverse impact on the best of businesses in neighborhoods that they can undersell because of their externalized costs. It is these small businesses, farmers markets and local grocery stores, that FreshDirect undercuts, that are some of the best businesses for supporting and preserving our walkable, diverse and safe neighborhoods."[44]

FreshDirect served only selected neighborhoods within New York City. As the neighborhood selection process was highly arbitrary, many people who lived in neighborhoods that FreshDirect did not serve had started to accuse the company of discrimination. As one customer put it, "FreshDirect is the most convenient way to shop for groceries in NYC . . . unless you live in a Public Housing building—they won't deliver to you!"[45] Others echoed similar concerns in terms of FreshDirect's decision to not serve specific neighborhoods: "These are neighborhoods

that FreshDirect deems underserved, or in plain terms . . . not worth the bother."[46]

Some of the recent challenges FreshDirect faced were union-related. FreshDirect's 500 truck drivers recently joined Local 348 of the United Food and Commercial Workers Union. Some of the reasons cited by the workers for this move were that "they made us work 12 and 14 hours a day, then . . . when some of us refused we were suspended for three days without pay." Also, the workers complained that the wages were pretty low as compared to wages at other grocery chains in New York. According to the workers, the initial beginning salaries at FreshDirect were just higher than $7, with the average per-hour pay being around $8.50. Workers also claimed that the health benefit premiums were high and not easily affordable. A firm spokesman replied to these complaints that "we have incredibly generous benefits that are more than competitive."[47]

Just a few days before Christmas in December 2007, FreshDirect asked its 900 plant workers to provide legal papers proving their immigration status.[48] As a result, many workers left immediately, some of whom had been

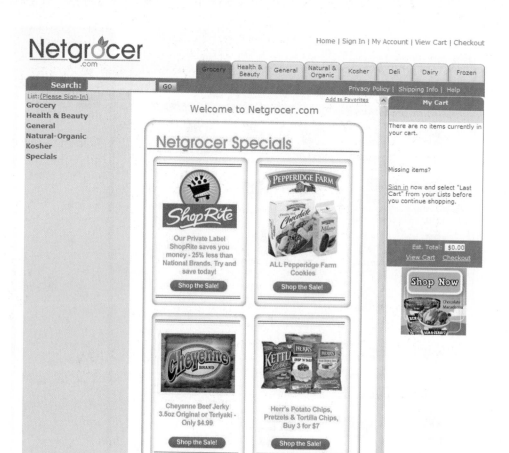

Exhibit 13 Netgrocer.com Web Site

associated with FreshDirect for 5 to 6 years.[49] Surprisingly, the majority of the workforce rejected the proposal of unionizing (around 80 percent voting against unionization). However, the number of workers voting was only 530, not 900, because so many employees had left the company after the immigration-status audit was announced.[50] FreshDirect was successful in suppressing the union revolt, but remaining workers were demoralized and the company's image was tainted among its customers.[51]

Aside from the labor challenges, FreshDirect was working hard to woo its customers. FreshDirect started a line of four-minute meals. These fresh meals were packed in microwavable containers, and as the name implies, they could be ready to eat after four minutes in a microwave oven.

FreshDirect had teamed up with some well-know Manhattan restaurants and chefs to introduce the four-minute meal concept. The lineup included Rosa Mexicano for Mexican cuisine,[52] chef Floyd Cardoz's Tabla for Indian cuisine,[53] chef Tina Bourbeau's Presto Italiano line of Italian cuisine, and several others. Another promotion was FreshDirect's "Valentine's Dinner for Two," which allowed customers to "prepare an easy and romantic restaurant-quality meal for a special someone in the comfort of their own homes." The menu had a variety of options, including appetizers, desserts, entrées, wines, champagnes, and so on. This menu came in the price range of $69 to $99, and the meal needed less than 20 minutes of cooking time.[54]

FreshDirect expanded its delivery options with a fixed-price unlimited-delivery program in addition to the standard per-delivery fee program, which cost $5.49 to $6.79 depending on location. The unlimited-delivery program gave customers an unlimited number of deliveries for a set fee of $59 for six months or $99 per year.[55] FreshDirect also reduced its minimum order to $30 from $50 in late 2008. Another innovation was the company's online customer-created shopping list. Customers could create and save their own shopping lists, such as a weekly list, mother-in-law list, and party list. In addition, the company offered its own tailored lists, such as Simple Suppers, Pantry Basics, Top 20 Most Popular FreshDirect Items, Healthy Snacks, and Entertaining Essentials, to help customers create lists of their own.[56]

Neither labor strife nor economic downturn had stopped FreshDirect's growth. Looking into the future,

Exhibit 14   Netgrocer Shipping Charges (in dollars)

Shipping region 2

Shipping region 3

Shipping region 1

Order Total	Shipping Region 3	Shipping Region 2	Shipping Region 1
Brackets	**Rates**	**Rates**	**Rates**
0–24.99	9.99	9.99	6.99
25–49.99	15.99	14.99	9.99
50–74.99	23.99	20.99	14.99
75–99.99	29.99	27.99	16.99
100–124.99	35.99	31.99	20.99
125–149.99	41.99	39.99	26.99
150–199.99	63.99	59.99	31.99
200–299.99	92.99	83.99	49.99
300–499.99	116.99	110.99	59.99
500–749.99	218.99	211.99	119.99
750–999.99	319.99	312.99	179.99
1,000–	624.99	613.99	401.99

there was speculation that FreshDirect might want to "seek public funding to underwrite growth possibilities."[57] Since Whole Foods Market's acquisition of Wild Oats Markets, analysts felt that some private players in the New York market, such as FreshDirect, might consider pursuing investment capital through an initial public offering.

Endnotes

1. Aili McConnon. *BusinessWeek,* September 15, 2008, p. 16.
2. www.freshdirect.com/site_access/site_access.jsp.
3. D. Dubbs. Catch of the day. *Multichannel Merchant,* July 1, 2003, http://multichannelmerchant.com/opsandfulfillment/ orders/fulfillment_catch_day.
4. A "slotting allowance" is defined by the American Marketing Association as "1. (retailing definition) A fee paid by a vendor for space in a retail store. 2. (sales promotion definition) The fee a manufacturer pays to a retailer in order to get distribution for a new product. It covers the costs of making room for the product in the warehouse and on the store shelf, reprogramming the computer system to recognize the product's UPC code, and including the product in the retailer's inventory system." www.marketingpower.com/mg-dictionary-view2910.php.
5. T. Laseter et al. What FreshDirect learned from Dell. *Strategy Business,* Spring (30), 2003, www.strategy-business .com/press/16635507/8202.

6. C. R. Schoenberger. Will work with food. *Forbes,* September 18, 2006, http://members.forbes.com/global/2006/0918/041 .html.

7. C. Smith. Splat: The supermarket battle between Fairway, FreshDirect and Whole Foods. *New York: The Magazine,* May 24, 2004, http://nymag.com/nymetro/food/industry/n_10421.

8. L. Dignan. FreshDirect: Ready to deliver. *Baseline: The Project Management Center,* February 17, 2004, www.baselinemag.com/print_article2/0,1217,a=119342,00.asp.

9. *Chelsea-Wide Blogs,* 2006, http://chelsea.clickyourblock .com/bb/-archive/index.php?t-128.html.

10. Michaelson named CEO at FreshDirect; Furbush resigns. *Supermarket News,* January 9, 2007, http://supermarket-news.com/retail_financial/-michaelson_named_ceo_at_ freshdirect_furbush_resigns_337/index.html.

11. FreshDirect's chairman hopes to deliver the goods in bigger role." InternetRetailer.com, July 14, 2008.

12. Five months in Manhattan and FreshDirect passes the 2,000-order-a-day mark and has over 40,000 customers. *Business Wire,* February 12, 2003.

13. S. Elliot. A "fresh" and "direct" approach. *New York Times,* February 11, 2003.

14. J. Bosman. FreshDirect emphasizes its New York flavor. *New York Times,* January 31, 2006, www.nytimes.com/ 2006/01/31/business/-media/31adco.html?ex= 1182657600&en=14d9c9f5d468064f&ei=5070.

15. Laseter et al. What FreshDirect learned from Dell..

16. Ibid.

17. Ibid.

18. Food Market Institute. *Supermarket Facts: Industry Over-view 2006,* www.fmi.org/facts_figs/superfact.htm.

19. D. Leonhardt. Filling pantries without a middleman. *New York Times,* November 22, 2006, www.nytimes.com/2006/11/22/ -business/22leonhardt.html?pagewanted=1&ei=5070&en= 102ea06150518b7a&ex=1182657600.

20. J. McTaggart. Fresh direction. *Progressive Grocer,* vol. 83, no. 4 (2004), pp. 58–60.

21. S. Koeppen. Online shopping: Way to go? *CBS News,* July 28, 2006, www.cbsnews.com/stories/2006/07/28/earlyshow/ living/ConsumerWatch/main1844539.shtml.

22. M. Kempiak and M. A. Fox. Online grocery shopping: Consumer motives, concerns and business models. *First Monday,* vol. 7, no. 9 (2002), www.firstmonday.org/issues/ issue7_9/kempiak.

23. S. Machlis. Filling up grocery carts online. *Computerworld,* July 27, 1998, p. 4.

24. S. Anderson. Is online grocery shopping for you? *Computer Bits,* April 11, 2001.

25. B. Woods. America Online goes grocery shopping for e-commerce bargains. *Computer News,* August 10, 1998, p. 42.

26. L. M. Fisher. Online grocer is setting up delivery system for $1 billion. *New York Times,* July 10, 1999, p. 1.

27. Online supermarkets keep it simple. *Frontline Solutions,* vol. 3, no. 2 (2002), pp. 46–49.

28. Ibid.

29. J. Smerd. Specialty foods stores will go head-to-head at Union Square. *New York Sun,* March 4, 2005, www.nysun .com/article/10058?page_no=1.

30. NYC's FreshDirect launches street fight against Whole Foods. *Progressive Grocer,* March 3, 2005, www.allbusiness .com/retail-trade/food-stores/4258105-1.html.

31. We don't have time to waste. *New Zealand Herald,* February 3, 2007.

32. E. Joyce. YourGrocer.com wants to come back. *ECommerce,* May 15, 2002, http://ecommerce.internet.com/news/news/ -article/0,,10375_1122671,00.html.

33. L. Fickenscher. Bouncing back from cyber limbo: Resurgence of failed dot coms after downsizing. *Crain's New York Business,* June 24, 2002.

34. Peapod, Inc.. Corporate fact sheet, www.peapod.com/ corpinfo/peapodFacts.pdf.

35. K. Regan. Amazon dips toe into online grocery business. *E-Commerce Times,* June 15, 2006, www.ecommercetimes .com/-story/51136.html.

36. M. Hamstra. Online stores may need to bone up on their execution. *Supermarket News,* January 29, 2007, http:// supermarketnews.com/viewpoints/-online-stores-bone-up-execution/index.html.

37. A. Danigelis. Customers' first local hero: FreshDirect. *Fast Company,* September 2006, www.fastcompany.com/ customer/-2006/articles/local-fresh-direct.html.

38. See www.freshdirect.com/about/index.jsp, and click on FAQs.

39. FreshDirect transitions to eco-friendly boxes. *Supermarket News,* May 11, 2007, http://supermarketnews.com/fresh_ market/-freshdirect_eco_friendly/index.html.

40. FreshDirect builds a grocery empire on free street space. *StreetsBlog,* November 22, 2006, www.streetsblog. org/2006/11/22/fresh-direct-builds-a-grocery-empire-on-free-street-space.

41. A. S. Wadia. Is FreshDirect good for you? *Metroblogging NYC,* January 30, 2007, http://nyc.metblogs.com/archives/ -2007/01/is_freshdirect.html.

42. FreshDirect builds a grocery empire on free street space.

43. Ibid.

44. Ibid.

45. N. Rodriguez. FreshDirect.com discriminates! *Metroblog-ging NYC,* February 7, 2007, http://nyc.metblogs.com/ archives/-2007/01/is_freshdirect.phtml.

46. Wadia. Is FreshDirect good for you?

47. *Daily News* (New York), September 28, 2007.

48. *Daily News* (New York), December 21, 2007.

49. *Daily News* (New York), December 12, 2007.

50. *New York Times,* December 24, 2007.

51. Lisa Fickenscher. *Crain's New York Business,* January 14, 2008.

52. www.progressivegrocer.com, April 18, 2007.

53. www.progressivegrocer.com, February 28, 2008.

54. www.progressivegrocer.com, February 7, 2007, and February 5, 2008.

55. *Supermarket News,* October 20, 2008.

56. www.progressivegrocer.com, October 19, 2007.

57. D. Merrefield. How different companies approach the growth challenge. *Supermarket News,* February 5, 2007, http://supermarketnews.com/viewpoints/how-different-companies-approach-growth-challenge/index.html.

photo credits

Chapter 1: page 20, The McGraw-Hill Companies, Inc./John Flournoy, photographer; page 23, The McGraw-Hill Companies, Inc./Doug Sherman, photographer

Chapter 2: page 53, Royalty-Free/CORBIS; page 70, The McGraw-Hill Companies, Inc./John Flournoy, photographer

Chapter 3: page 86, The McGraw-Hill Companies, Inc./John Flournoy, photographer; page 99, Keith Eng 2007

Chapter 4: page 133, Corbis; page 148, The McGraw-Hill Companies, Inc./L.Niki

Chapter 5: page 171, Royalty-Free/CORBIS; page 184, The McGraw-Hill Companies, Inc./Andrew Resek, photographer

Chapter 6: page 201, The McGraw-Hill Companies, Inc./Christopher Kerrigan, photographer; page 219, The McGraw-Hill Companies, Inc./Andrew Resek, photographer

Chapter 7: page 252, Getty Images; page 260, Digital Vision/Getty Images

Chapter 8: page 278, The McGraw-Hill Companies, Inc./John Flournoy, photographer; page 288, JupiterImages

Chapter 9: page 318, Janis Christie/Getty Images; page 321, The McGraw-Hill Companies, Inc./John Flournoy, photographer

Chapter 10: page 366, Digital Vision/Getty Images; page 368, The McGraw-Hill Companies, Inc./Jill Braaten, photographer

Chapter 11: page 404, The McGraw-Hill Companies, Inc./Lars A. Niki, photographer; page 412, The McGraw-Hill Companies, Inc./Rick Brady, photographer

Chapter 12: page 441, The McGraw-Hill Companies, Inc./Andrew Resek, photographer; page 453, The McGraw-Hill Companies, Inc./Andrew Resek, photographer

Chapter 13: page 478, Digital Vision/Getty Images; page 479, PhotoDisc Imaging/Getty Images

Case 35: page C272, Product courtesy of Brian, Willy, Taylor, and Carly. The McGraw-Hill Companies, Inc./Jill Braaten, photographer

company index

name index

subject index

Page numbers followed by n refer to footnotes.